MARKETING
Real People, Real Choices

MARKETING
Real People, Real Choices

Michael R. Solomon
Auburn University

Elnora W. Stuart
Winthrop University

Prentice Hall, Upper Saddle River, New Jersey 07458

Acquisitions Editor: Donald J. Hull
Development Editor: Sylvia Dovner
Assistant Editor: John Larkin
Editorial Assistant: Jim Campbell
Editor-in-Chief: James Boyd
Director of Development: Steve Deitmer
Marketing Manager: John Chillingworth
Production Editor: Aileen Mason
Production Coordinator: Renee Pelletier
Managing Editor: Valerie Q. Lentz
Manufacturing Supervisor: Arnold Vila
Manufacturing Manager: Vincent Scelta
Senior Designer: Ann France
Design Director: Patricia Wosczyk
Interior Design: Ginidir Marshall/Lorraine Castellano
Cover Design: Maureen Eide
Illustrator (Interior):   Electra Graphics, Inc.
Composition: Progressive Information Technologies
Cover Illustration: Diana Ong

Credits and acknowledgments for materials borrowed from other sources and reproduced, with permission, in this textbook appear on pages 743–745.

Library of Congress Cataloging-in-Publication Data

Solomon, Michael R.
    Marketing: real people, real choices/Michael R. Solomon, Elnora W. Stuart.
      p.   cm.
    Includes bibliographical references and index.
    ISBN 0-205-15206-6
    1. Marketing--Vocational guidance.   I. Stuart, Elnora W.
II. Title.
HF5415.35.S65   1997
658.8′0023′73--dc20

                       96-41884
                       CIP

ISBN: 0-205-15206-6

Prentice-Hall International (UK) Limited, London
Prentice-Hall of Australia Pty. Limited, Sydney
Prentice-Hall Canada, Inc., Toronto
Prentice-Hall Hispanoamericana, S.A., Mexico
Prentice-Hall of India Private Limited, New Delhi
Prentice-Hall of Japan, Inc., Tokyo
Simon & Schuster Asia Pte. Ltd., Singapore
Editora Prentice-Hall do Brasil, Ltda., Rio de Janeiro

Printed in the United States of America

10 9 8 7 6 5 4 3 2 1

To Gail, Amanda, Zachary, and Alexandra—
my favorite market segment

M.S.

To Sonny, Patrick, and Marge

E.S.

Brief Contents

Contents

Part 5 Delivering the Product 467

Chapter 14 Channel Management, Physical Distribution, and Wholesaling 467

REAL PEOPLE, REAL CHOICES:
MEET CECELIA GARDNER, A DECISION MAKER AT FIRST UNION NATIONAL BANK 468

SPOTLIGHT on Relationship Marketing:
The Japanese Keiretsu 480

REAL PEOPLE, REAL CHOICES:
DECISION TIME AT FIRST UNION NATIONAL BANK 485

SPOTLIGHT on Ethics:
Multilevel Marketing 489

REAL PEOPLE, REAL CHOICES:
HOW IT WORKED OUT AT FIRST UNION NATIONAL BANK 503

Chapter 15 Retailing and Direct Marketing 511

REAL PEOPLE, REAL CHOICES:
MEET GÖRAN CARSTEDT, A DECISION MAKER AT IKEA 512

SPOTLIGHT on Relationship Marketing:
Excellence at Dollar General Stores 532

REAL PEOPLE, REAL CHOICES:
DECISION TIME AT IKEA 533

SPOTLIGHT on Global Marketing:
Excellence at Patagonia and Lands' End 536

Part 6 Communicating About the Product   551

Chapter 16   Connecting with the Consumer: Strategy, Marketing, and Marketing Communications   551

REAL PEOPLE, REAL CHOICES:
MEET TOM EPPES, PRESIDENT, PRICE/MCNABB FOCUSED COMMUNICATIONS   552

SPOTLIGHT on Ethics:
Blurring the Boundaries between Editorial and Commercial Messages   558

REAL PEOPLE, REAL CHOICES:
DECISION TIME AT PRICE/MCNABB   580

SPOTLIGHT on Relationship Marketing:
Excellence at Microsoft   585

REAL PEOPLE, REAL CHOICES:
HOW IT WORKED OUT AT PRICE/MCNABB   590

$\mathcal{P}$reface

So, you're starting your first marketing course and trying to figure out what's in store for you this term. Welcome to our book! Let us take this opportunity to help you get out of vacation mode and get serious (well, not too serious—we hope you'll have a little fun in this course). Here's why this course is one of the most important you are going to take.

More than ever, people in business must work hard to satisfy the needs of individual customers and the needs of society as a whole. That's what marketing is about—creating long-term satisfaction with an organization's goods or services while profiting the firm *and* providing benefits to the community. The goal of this book is to show you how to do just that.

As you are reading this book, the world stands on the edge of the twenty-first century. While some may predict doom and gloom, we believe that you are beginning your careers at the most exciting time in history. We have started taking our first baby steps on the information superhighway. Science and technology are improving the quality of life at an unprecedented rate. Many people in the industrialized world are turning from desires based on materialism and wealth to a focus on the environment, social responsibility, and the preservation of human dignity. As political and technical barriers fall, we increasingly live and work in a global marketplace.

A marketing textbook that will accurately portray the excitement and challenge of the marketing profession has to be dynamic, realistic, and even-handed about the consequences of marketing decisions. It also has to give students an inside view of life "in the trenches" of the marketing world. Instead of simply painting a rosy picture of how great marketing strategies turned out, it should provide readers with a sense of how these decisions were made in the first place—and emphasize that the "correct" choice is not always so obvious beforehand as it is after the fact!

We'd like to take a minute to tell you about this book and to show you how we've gone about crafting a brand new text to lead a new generation of marketing students into the twenty-first century.

WHY SHOULD YOU WANT TO READ THIS BOOK?

Well, that's easy—the professor assigned it and you want to get a good grade! We hope, though, you will want to learn about marketing for other reasons, and we want to make this as enjoyable and useful an experience as possible. There's nothing worse than slogging through a boring textbook and memorizing long lists of terms you'll forget after spring break anyway.

Hey, we've been there! That's why we've worked hard to show you how much of what you'll learn in this course is related to the rest of your life. After all, the actions of marketers affect us everywhere we turn—from the clothes we buy to the music we enjoy to the food we order, and even to the politicians we vote for, the college we choose, and the church or synagogue we attend.

This course is a chance for you to learn about how all sorts of goods and services are developed and "magically" appear in stores, and about the techniques used to convince you to choose one option over many others competing for your attention and your hard-earned cash.

CAREERS IN MARKETING— OR NOT

Throughout the book we provide information to help you get started on a career in marketing (we even include an appendix, "Careers in Marketing," to give you a bit of a head start). But what if you're an accounting student or majoring in some other aspect of business? Why is it important to understand marketing? Quite obviously, we believe everyone should study marketing because it is the single most important function of every organization (of course, we're somewhat biased!). But even if you disagree, you must realize that the changing nature of organizations is leading to greater integration across departments and functional areas of business. For an accountant to do his or her job, he or she must understand all the areas of the firm, just as a marketer should know something about accounting, finance, management, and so on.

What if you're "just visiting" the business disciplines, and your real interest is in the arts, engineering, education, or some other field? We'll try to show you how a knowledge of marketing concepts applies to many other activities as well. But whatever your major, you're also a consumer. This means marketing activities affect you throughout your life. As a person who buys or receives shelter, food, clothing, utilities, and perhaps Nine Inch Nails CDs, you are a *customer,* the target of a multitude of marketing strategies. If nothing else, then, an understanding of how marketing works can make you a more intelligent consumer. Perhaps you will be better able to manage your resources, understand how marketing communications attempt to encourage your purchase of a variety of goods and services, and appreciate the huge impact marketers have on fashion, music, sports, and other aspects of popular culture.

UNIQUE FEATURES OF THIS BOOK

Several aspects of this book make it unique and—we hope—will make the process of learning about marketing enjoyable and effective. These features have been developed with the help of many marketing professors (maybe even your own) who were selected because they love to teach the principles of marketing course and wanted a book that would enhance their efforts. From the very beginning, this book took shape based on their suggestions and comments. We also showed numerous drafts to our own students to be sure that they liked what we were up to. So, we'd like to think that we practice what we preach by starting the development process from "day one" with a focus on the needs of *our* customers—you!

DECISION-MAKING FOCUS: REAL PEOPLE, REAL CHOICES

One of the most important features of this text is an emphasis on decision making. Rather than simply listing a bunch of terms that you must memorize, we've tried to put you in the driver's seat wherever possible. One way we've done this is to introduce you in each chapter to a marketing executive who had to make a decision. As the title of the book suggests, we're focusing on *real people* who had to make *real choices*. This strategy serves as an important reminder that *decisions are not made by companies,* they are made by flesh-and-blood people. The companies and people we worked with to bring you this exciting feature are:

Chapter, Company/Organization, Person

1. Levi Strauss & Co., Steve Goldstein
2. Harley-Davidson, Inc., Frank Cimermancic
3. The Sierra Club, Rhonda Lieberman
4. MTV Europe, Peter Einstein
5. Mercedes-Benz of North America, Inc., Bob Baxter
6. Sebago, Inc., Dan Wellehan
7. Unitog, Bob Wilhelm
8. Burrell Communications Group, Sarah Burroughs
9. Nabisco, Bob Masone
10. Intel Corporation, Dennis Carter
11. Lutheran Health Systems, Rich Mackesy
12. Bojangles' Restaurants, Inc., Randall Poindexter
13. MCI Communications, Lisa Adelman
14. First Union National Bank, Cecelia Gardner
15. IKEA, Göran Carstedt
16. Price/McNabb Focused Communications, Tom Eppes
17. Dentsu, Inc., Hiroshi Tanaka
18. Karen Weiner Escalera Associates, Inc., Victoria Feldman
19. General Electric, Kathleen Carroll-Mullen

We've benefited from the cooperation of a variety of dedicated businesspeople from around the globe who have had to "talk the talk and walk the walk" by making difficult choices. These men and women represent organizations as diverse as a global giant that supplies denim products and other apparel to millions of consumers at play (Levi Strauss & Co.) to a company that profits by supplying uniforms to consumers at work (Unitog). From "hogs" (Harley-Davidson motorcycles) to hospitals (Lutheran Health Systems), from a Swedish retailer (IKEA) to a Japanese advertising agency (Dentsu), we've enlisted people who are on marketing's front lines to share their experiences with you.

Whether the businessperson makes Topsider shoes (Sebago) or broadcasts Top 40 videos (MTV Europe), the choices they face on a daily basis will help to bring marketing issues to life for you. In each chapter, we describe the problem our decision maker was facing and lay out some of his or her options. Then we ask *you* to choose from among these options. But, just in case you're the type of person who likes to read a mystery novel starting with the last page to find out "whodunit," we end the chapter by telling you what choice the person made and what happened as a result. In some cases we've also captured the executive on videotape to give you an even more complete picture of how marketing decisions are made.

RELATIONSHIP FOCUS

Another aspect of marketing that we emphasize is the importance of building long-term relationships with customers and business partners rather than selling them something and disappearing into the night. This seems like common sense, but you'd be surprised how many "traditional" marketers are only slowly coming around to the realization that satisfying people the first time and every time makes good business sense. One way we've focused on this dimension is by presenting a box in each chapter called "Spotlight on Relationship Marketing," where we illustrate an organization that practices what it preaches about building bonds with people.

NEW ERA OF MARKETING FOCUS

These bonds, however, can't be built in a vacuum. Good business is responsible business. Marketing decisions that benefit only the firm and its customers aren't such good decisions after all. Contrary to what some people believe, it *is* possible to make money and still do good works. That's why we emphasize what we call the "New Era of Marketing" and single out firms for praise that conduct business ethically and that return value to society and to the environment. We believe in this so strongly that we've devoted one of our first chapters to "The New Era" (Chapter 3), and many chapters also feature a "Spotlight on Ethics" that highlights the issues faced by companies and individuals as they go about their business.

GLOBAL MARKETING FOCUS

Another feature that we're proud of is our emphasis on global marketing. Talk to businesspeople and consumers around the world, and you'll find that all too often the stereotype of the "ugly American" is true. For a long time, American companies prospered by simply "doing their thing" and not worrying too much about adapting their outlook to the needs and preferences of people in other countries.

Now, the party's over: From advertising on the World Wide Web to negotiating a complicated merger with a foreign firm, marketing decisions are often global decisions. Where possible we've tried to emphasize the importance of a trans-national perspective. Our featured executives include marketers from Sweden, Japan, and the United Kingdom. Many of our corporate examples are non-American, as are a large number of the advertisements we have chosen to illustrate key points. And, of course, we also offer an entire chapter on global marketing for your traveling pleasure. So, it's time for the journey to begin: relax, sit back, and enjoy the flight!

TO THE INSTRUCTOR

Learning Aids

This text includes many tools that will enable students to learn about the world of marketing. These include:

- *Real People, Real Choices Boxes:* Each chapter begins with a profile of an executive who has to make a marketing decision. In the middle of the chapter we describe the choices available to that executive, including the pros and cons of each option. Students are asked to make a decision and to justify their choice. The option chosen and the results are presented at the end of the chapter.

- *Colorful Exhibits with Extended Captions:* Each chapter contains numerous advertisements and photos from around the world that illustrate key concepts. However, unlike many texts' presentations, these exhibits are more

than "fluff"—most feature important textual material so that students will be motivated to spend time with each exhibit and understand why it was chosen.

- *Chapter Summary:* At the end of each chapter, a summary of the key points, based on the chapter objectives, provides a means of strengthening students' understanding of the chapter topic.

- *Review Questions:* Each chapter features a review, which presents four different types of assignments. The first section, "Marketing Concepts: Testing Your Knowledge," asks students to identify and explain the main ideas expressed in the chapter.

  In the second section, "Marketing Concepts: Discussing Choices and Issues," students are encouraged to expand their thinking on the chapter's ideas. Here students are often asked to look into the future and to determine whether certain marketing practices are ethical or in the best interests of the customer, the marketer, and/or society as a whole.

  In the third section of the review, "Marketing Practice: Applying What You've Learned," students take the role of the marketing professional and apply the chapter concepts to making marketing decisions.

  Because we believe the best way to learn is by experience, we have designed the feature "Marketing Mini-Project: Learning by Doing." In these mini-projects, students are directed to go outside their classroom and learn more about the subject.

  The four sections of the "Review Questions" combine to provide students with assignments that require

  decision making
  problem solving
  communication
  writing
  role playing
  group activities
  research

- *Key Terms:* Key terms are shown in bold in the chapter and are defined in the margins of the chapter as well as in the glossary in the back of the book.

- *Cases:* Each chapter presents two cases to reinforce concepts. The first case is titled *Marketing in Action: Real People at . . .* Each of these scenarios, based on a real situation, was chosen to illustrate how marketing executives implemented some of the key ideas presented in the chapter. Discussion questions following the case guide students through the decision-making process and ask them to identify the key issues that faced the company and what the organization learned as a result. The second case in each chapter has a decision-making focus and is called *Marketing in Action: Real Choices at . . .* In each of these cases, a real marketing decision must be made. Students must analyze the facts and make a recommendation for the firm's best course of action.

■ *Appendixes:* There are three brief appendixes that provide supplemental information for students. First, a career appendix shows students how to go about the task of planning a career (or at the minimum, finding the first job) using the marketing planning process. The second appendix is a condensed version of a marketing plan. This appendix was adapted from an actual student project with a real firm. Finally, the marketing math appendix shows students the "how to" of a variety of important quantitative financial analyses and calculations.

Supplements for the Instructor

V.I.P. Supplements Program (Video/Internet/Presentation)

In addition to the traditional supplements package, we are proud to bring you the Prentice Hall V.I.P. Supplements Program. VIDEO: Custom Case Videos, ABC News/Wall Street Journal videos, EFFIE Awards, and New York Festivals Vol. 1–3. Covering the gamut of marketing topics, these videos are free when you adopt the text. INTERNET: Prentice Hall Learning Internet Partnership (PHLIP) will be supporting the text with weekly updates and faculty support among other features (http://www.prenhall.com/phbusiness). PRESENTATION: Prentice Hall presents the CD ROM *Multimedia Presentations for Marketing and Advertising,* which organizes hundreds of media for easy use. The CD, available to adopting instructors, includes:

■ Approximately 300 illustrations taken from the text and other sources.
■ Many EFFIE award-winning television and print advertisements.
■ Key concept video taken from the *On Location!* custom video series.
■ Lecture notes tying the media to each chapter in the book.

The media resources are built into *Presentation Manager 2.0,* a "point and click" lecture-management software program that allows the instructor to create superb state-of-the-art presentations on his or her own, or use premade presentations with notes tied to the book.

Instructor's Resource Manual

This comprehensive guide includes a chapter summary for a quick review, a list of key teaching objectives, and answers to all end-of-chapter discussions and case questions. Also included are teaching notes and exercises for the "Real People, Real Choices" segments. In addition, the manual includes a comprehensive video guide that summarizes each video and provides answers to the video case discussion questions. The *Manual* was prepared by David Moore of LeMoyne University with input and information provided by the text authors.

Test Item File

Prepared by Thomas Quirk of Webster University, the Test Item File contains over 1,400 multiple choice, true/false, and essay questions.

Prentice Hall Custom Test

Based on the #1 best-selling, state-of-the-art test generation software program developed by Engineering Software Associates (ESA), *Prentice Hall Custom Test* is not only suitable for your course, but customizable to your personal needs. With *Prentice Hall Custom Test's* user-friendly test creation and powerful algorithmic generation, you can produce tailor-made, error-free tests quickly and easily. You can create an exam, administer it traditionally or on-line, evaluate and track students' results, and analyze the success of the exam—all with a simple click of the mouse.

Color Transparencies

Prepared by Jimidene Murphey of South Plains College, one hundred full-color transparencies highlight key concepts for presentation. Each transparency is accompanied by a full page of teaching notes that includes relevant key terms and discussion points from the chapters.

PowerPoint Transparencies

All acetates are available on *PowerPoint 4.0.* The disk is designed to allow you to present the transparency to your class electronically.

"Real People, Real Choices" Videos

Based on the "Real People, Real Choices" segments in the text, these videos take a closer look at the real-life decisions made by executives in a wide range of businesses. Shot on location from London, England, to Charlotte, North Carolina, these videos are designed to give students insight into the decisions made by marketing executives in a variety of businesses. The whole concept of Real People, Real Choices comes to life in these videos, available to adopters of the text free from Prentice Hall. The six segments are:

1. Peter Einstein—MTV Europe
2. Robert Baxter—Mercedes-Benz of North America
3. Daniel Wellehan—Sebago, Inc.
4. Dennis Carter—Intel
5. Randall Poindexter—Bojangles' Restaurants
6. Kathleen Carroll-Mullen—General Electric

Supplements for the Student

Study Guide

Prepared by Charles W. Beem of Bucks County Community College, this study guide includes chapter overviews, learning objectives, key terms and definitions, and detailed outlines for note-taking and review. A case analysis exercise is also included for each chapter. To reinforce students' understanding of the chapter material, the guide includes a section of multiple-choice questions.

Career Paths in Marketing Version 2.0

This multimedia CD-ROM lets students have fun while they explore the world of marketing careers. The CD, which won the 1995 New Media Magazine Gold Invision Award for best new educational software program, assesses students' career desires and aptitudes and provides tips for résumé writing and interviewing, background information on many different career paths, and interactive video interviews with the actual marketing managers who appear in the *On Location!* video series available with the book. Available in 1997, the software provides further value by acting as a computerized study guide directly linked to the book.

ACKNOWLEDGMENTS

Many people contributed to this project, and we are deeply indebted to them. Numerous colleagues in academia and business provided their support and helpful suggestions on chapter content and structure, including Basil Englis, Tina Lowery, Henry Solomon, Annalise Roberts, Brian Kurtz, Paul Schurr, Pam Ellen, Paula Bone, Sidney Bennett, Bobbi Fuller, Angela Letourneau, Darrell Parker, Barbara Price, Emma Jane Riddle, John Robbins, Jane Thomas, and Terry Shimp. Carol Warfield, Department Head of Consumer Affairs, and Dean June Henton of the School of Human Sciences provided invaluable support and encouragement on behalf of Auburn University. A special thanks to Deans Jerry Padgett and Roger Weikle of the School of Business Administration at Winthrop University, as well as to a host of other friends in the faculty and administration of Winthrop for their help and understanding. A special note of thanks to Gail Solomon for her unflagging devotion and assistance throughout this project.

We are grateful to the helpful input provided by members of our Electronic Advisory Panel, who participated in our Internet bulletin board over a period of several years while the book was being developed. Many thanks go to

Christie Amato, *University of North Carolina, Charlotte*
Xenia Balabkins, *Middlesex County College*
Gary Brunswick, *Northern Michigan University*
Daniel D. Butler, *Auburn University*
Joe Cote, *Washington State University*
Bernice N. Dandridge, *Diablo Valley College*
Mary K. Ericksen, *Bloomsburg University*
Peter Gillett, *University of Central Florida*
James I. Gray, *Florida Atlantic University*
Audrey Guskey-Federouch, *Duquesne University*
Barbara Howard, *Northern Virginia Community College*
Eva Hyatt, *Appalachian State University*
Michael Hyman, *New Mexico State University*
Craig Kelley, *California State University, Sacramento*
Frederic Kropp, *University of Oregon*
Russell Laczniak, *Iowa State University*
Dana Lascu, *University of Richmond*
Kenneth R. Lord, *State University of New York at Buffalo*
H. Lee Meadow, *Northern Illinois University*
Vernon Q. Murray, *Marist College*
Harold Perl, *County College of Morris*
Robert Pitts, *DePaul University*

Stephen Ramocki, *Rhode Island College*
Tom Rossi, *Broome Community College*
Lois Smith, *University of Wisconsin, Whitewater*
Debbie M. Thorne, *University of Tampa*
Rajhiv Vaidyanathan, *University of Minnesota, Duluth*
Robert W. Veryzer, Jr., *Rensselaer Polytechnic Institute*

We would also like to thank the 19 busy executives who gave generously of their time as we worked with them to write the "Real People, Real Choices" feature. We certainly learned a lot from their experiences "in the trenches," and we hope our readers will, too:

Steve Goldstein, *Levi Strauss & Co.*
Frank Cimermancic, *Harley-Davidson, Inc.*
Rhonda Lieberman, *The Sierra Club*
Peter Einstein, *MTV Europe*
Bob Baxter, *Mercedes-Benz of North America, Inc.*
Dan Wellehan, *Sebago, Inc.*
Bob Wilhelm, *Unitog*
Sarah Burroughs, *Burrell Communications Group*
Bob Masone, *Nabisco*
Dennis Carter, *Intel Corporation*
Rich Mackesy, *Lutheran Health Systems*
Randall Poindexter, *Bojangles' Restaurants, Inc.*
Lisa Adelman, *MCI Communications*
Cecelia Gardner, *First Union National Bank*
Göran Carstedt, *IKEA*
Tom Eppes, *Price/McNabb Focused Communications*
Hiroshi Tanaka, *Dentsu, Inc.*
Victoria Feldman, *Karen Weiner Escalera Associates, Inc.*
Kathleen Carroll-Mullen, *General Electric*

The book also benefited from the many constructive suggestions offered by reviewers at other colleges:

David Andrus, *Kansas State University*
Allen Appell, *San Francisco State University*
Maryann Bohlinger, *Community College of Philadelphia*
Sally Boyes-Hyslop, *California State Polytechnic University*
William Carner, *University of Texas at Austin*
Joseph Chapman
Ruth Clottery, *Barry University*
Wayne Coleman, *Texas A&M University — Corpus Christi*
Elizabeth Cooper-Martin, *Georgetown University*
Jane Cromartie, *University of New Orleans*
Katherine Dobie, *University of Wisconsin — Eau Claire*
Nermin Eyuboglu, *CUNY — Bernard M. Baruch College*
Lisa Flynn, *Florida State University*
Wanda Fujimoto, *Central Washington University*
S. J. Garner, *Eastern Kentucky University*
Kenneth Lord, *SUNY Buffalo*
Michael Mayo, *Kent State University*
H. Lee Meadow, *Northern Illinois University*
Robert Moore, *University of Connecticut*

Ken Olson, *County College of Morris*

Ben Soo Ong, *California State University — Fresno*

Charles Patti, *University of Hartford*

Akshay Rao, *University of Minnesota*

Lynn Richardson, *University of Alabama — Birmingham*

Robert Ross, *Wichita State University*

Eddie Sanders, Jr., *Chicago State University*

T. N. Somasundaram, *University of San Diego*

Robert Stevens, *Northeast Louisiana University*

Jeffrey Strieter, *SUNY Brockport*

Donna Tillman, *California State Polytechnic University*

Jerry Wilson, *Georgia Southern University*

Mark Young, *Winona State University*

George Zinkhan, *University of Georgia*

We owe a lot to the many people at Prentice Hall and at Allyn & Bacon who turned an idea into a reality. Our special thanks go to Suzy Spivey, Judy Fifer, and Bill Barke at Allyn & Bacon, and to Jim Boyd, Jim Campbell, John Chillingworth, Steve Deitmer, Ann France, Don Hull, Joanne Jay, Laura Kelley, John Larkin, Valerie Q. Lentz, Aileen Mason, Bill Oldsey, Vincent Scelta, Melissa Steffens, Arnold Vila, and Patricia Wosczyk at Prentice Hall.

Special thanks to our team of sales managers and representatives known as the Prentice Hall Principles of Marketing Task Force. The insights and guidance provided by this team of field personnel at a two-day meeting in New Jersey has helped us shape a book that better meets requirements of professors and students. We thank

Melissa Bruner, *Sales Representative, Texas*

Tim Kent, *District Sales Manager, Wisconsin*

Tom Nixon, *National Sales Specialist*

Leslie Oliver, *Sales Representative, Michigan*

William "Butch" Porter, *District Sales Manager, North Carolina*

Jim Ruppel, *Sales Representative, Colorado*

Above all, we would like to express our profound gratitude and admiration to Sylvia Dovner, who patiently worked with us through thick and thin, in stormy weather and in calm. She personifies what a "heroic" editor should be and is an inspiration to us.

Writing this book was a profound learning experience for both of us. We have endured first-hand the ups and downs of the new product development process and the importance of teamwork and cooperation in crafting an innovative new market offering that will satisfy the needs of our readers. We hope instructors and students will enjoy the final product.

Michael R. Solomon
Auburn, Alabama

Elnora W. Stuart
Rock Hill, South Carolina

CHAPTER

1

The World of Marketing

When you have completed your study of this chapter,
you should be able to:

CHAPTER OBJECTIVES

1. Explain what marketing is all about and describe the marketing mix.

2. Describe how marketers develop strategies for finding and reaching a market.

3. Explain the evolution of the marketing concept.

4. Explain why the marketing system is important to both individual and business customers in the marketplace, in our daily lives, and in society.

5. Explain marketing's role within an organization.

REAL PEOPLE, REAL CHOICES:

Meet Steve Goldstein, Levi Strauss

Steve Goldstein is keenly aware of the power of marketing to create value. As vice president of research and development for the Levi's® brand at Levi Strauss & Co., he knows that all aspects of marketing are vital to the long-term success of a product like Levi's jeans. Each of the Levi's brands has a specific marketing program, and Goldstein oversees numerous marketing initiatives for all the Levi's® brand product lines, including 501 jeans (the world's original jeans), Red Tab® jeans, Westernwear, and denim jackets and shirts. Goldstein also manages the overall creative direction and strategic focus of the brands' advertising done by Foote, Cone, Belding of San Francisco, which has been the Levi's ad agency for sixty-five years. He works with a team of advertising and retail marketing managers, research directors, and public relations managers at Levi Strauss, which employs approximately 30,000 people in many countries and whose familiar red "batwing" symbol is one of the ten best-known trademarks in the world.

Mr. Goldstein has been in charge of Levi's Menswear Division since 1980. Prior to that he was manager of menswear marketing services at Levi Strauss. He held a variety of positions with SmithKline Corporation prior to joining the company. He holds a bachelor's and a master's degree from Yale University, and he earned a management certificate from the Wharton School at the University of Pennsylvania. He has been a guest lecturer on marketing topics at Yale, Stanford, and Berkeley.

MARKETERS AND CUSTOMERS: A PERFECT FIT

Marketing is about people—marketers and customers—and about the ways marketers try to create a perfect fit between themselves and the customers. Finding and keeping the right customers is no simple task in today's business environment where the competition is tougher than ever. Sharp marketers must first identify prospective customers and then go about the business of providing goods and services that suit their needs better than competitors' offerings.

Levi's jeans are a great example of a product that has succeeded for many years because they are carefully designed, made, and marketed to make millions of people around the world feel both comfortable and stylish. Steve Goldstein, who is responsible for the overall image and management of Levi's brands, knows the value of finding out just how to appeal to the firm's customers. On any given day his tasks might include attending a consumer discussion group to determine the members' preferences in jeans, their shopping habits, and even the magazines they read or TV shows they watch, or he might meet with the ad agency to brainstorm creative ideas for promotions that will speak to these and similar consumers. He might also attend a presentation of sample Levi's jeans to discuss their quality, comfort, and fashionableness, or he could be meeting with retail partners to discuss which jeans to stock and how to display them.

Levi Strauss & Co. has prospered by satisfying its customers in many ways, but the company is also sensitive to the needs and concerns of its employees and the general public. All of these efforts have helped to make it the world's largest apparel manufacturer and are part of what marketing's all about.

This book is about marketing. In later chapters we'll look at the issues that make a firm stand out from all the others in the marketplace. We'll also consider the decisions marketers must make when planning marketing activities and strategies. Before we can get into these issues, though, we need to take a look at the big picture of marketers and consumers. In this chapter, we'll tackle the job of providing a capsule view of the marketing process by answering these questions about the world of marketing: What? How? When? Why? Where? and Who?

WHAT IS MARKETING?

Marketing. Lots of people talk about it, but what is it? When you ask people to define marketing, you get many answers. Some say, "That's what you do when you push your cart down the grocery aisles." Others respond, "That's what happens when a pushy salesman tries to sell me something I don't want." Still others might say, "Oh, that's simple. TV commercials." Some students might answer, "That's some course I have to take before I can get my business degree!" Finally, the student in the front row chimes in, "Marketing is the process of planning and executing the conception, pricing, promotion, and distribution of ideas, goods, and services to create exchanges that satisfy individual and organizational objectives."[1] Guess which one of these definitions is correct?

Each of these explanations actually has a grain of truth to it. Part of marketing does involve the actual act of obtaining goods and services. Unfortunately, some obnoxious arm twisting may occur when a salesperson tries to persuade a customer to make a purchase. Yes, advertising is an important part of marketing. And, marketing is a very important business function, so anyone who plans a business career needs to know about it.

As you've probably guessed, though, the final definition is the most accurate. This response is the official definition provided by the American Marketing Association in 1985. Let's take another look at this rather long sentence: "**Marketing** is the process of planning and executing the conception, pricing, promotion, and distribution of ideas, goods, and services to create exchanges that satisfy individual and organizational objectives." That's a real mouthful. In this section, we'll break down this definition to see what it means. Let's start at the end and work backward.

MARKETING SATISFIES NEEDS

". . . Satisfy individual and organizational objectives" is the most important part of the definition. It tells us about the central aspect of marketing: *satisfying needs.* Marketing involves at least two parties—a seller and a buyer—each of whom have needs. Products are *bought* to satisfy consumers' needs. A **consumer** is the ultimate user of a purchased good or service, although the consumer doesn't necessarily have to be the one who actually does the buying. Consumers can be individuals or organizations, whether a company, a government, a rap group, or a charity, and they all have very different needs. But the seller, or marketer, also has needs: to make a profit and to remain in business. So products are *sold* to satisfy marketers' objectives. This satisfaction, in turn, begins with the marketer's ability to identify consumers' needs and to develop goods and services that satisfy those needs. When you strip away the big words, marketing is all about satisfying needs.

The Marketing Concept

The basic notion that identifying consumers' needs and providing products that satisfy those needs ensure the organization's long-term profitability has been termed the **marketing concept.** The essence of the marketing concept is simple, yet it has enormous implications for the way products—whether goods, services, or ideas—are developed, communicated, and sold. This concept can be boiled down to a few words: "*MARKETING SATISFIES NEEDS!*"

A **need** refers to any difference between a consumer's actual state and some ideal or desired state. When the difference is big enough, the consumer is motivated to take some action to satisfy the need. When you're hungry, you take action by buying a snack. If you're not happy with the way your hair looks, you may invest in a new haircut. Needs can

marketing: the process of planning and executing the conception, pricing, promotion, and distribution of ideas, goods, and services to create exchanges that satisfy individual and organizational objectives

consumer: the ultimate user of a purchased good or service

marketing concept: a management orientation that focuses on identifying and satisfying consumer needs to ensure the organization's long-term profitability objectives

need: recognition of any difference between a consumer's actual state and some ideal or desired state

Exhibit 1.1
The Swiss firm Ste. Suisse Microelectronique et d'Horlogerie S.A. (S.M.H. for short) changed the face of the low-priced watch market when it introduced the Swatch watch. These inexpensive pieces of "time-keeping jewelry," known for their high quality and colorful, trendy designs, have been snapped up by more than 100 million consumers since the early 1980s. The watches satisfy consumers' need for a reliable timepiece at a reasonable price, and the consumers also get the benefit of wearing a colorful and trendy fashion accessory. Another benefit is that these watches can be bought at drugstores, department stores, and fashion boutiques rather than at high-end jewelry stores, which many people find intimidating.

be related to physical functions (like eating) or to psychological ones (like wanting to look good). And the same product can potentially satisfy a number of different needs. For example, an Armani sweater can address the basic physical need for warmth, an individual need for self-expression, and/or a social need to be regarded by others as a fashion plate.

The forces that drive people to buy and use products are generally straightforward, as when a person purchases a pair of blue jeans for everyday wear. But even the use of an everyday product like blue jeans may be related to deeper needs: Research has shown that Levi's jeans are used by wearers to say important things about the type of person they would like to be. Some pairs of jeans have been handed down over several generations, and from time to time the company even receives a beat-up pair in the mail, with a letter from the owner requesting that they be given a proper burial![2]

The specific way a need is satisfied depends on the individual's unique history, learning experiences, and cultural environment. The particular form of product used to satisfy a need is termed a **want,** which is the desire to satisfy needs in specific ways that are culturally and socially influenced. For example, two classmates may feel their stomachs rumbling during a lunchtime lecture and feel an intense need for food. However, the way each person goes about satisfying this need might be quite different. The first person may be a health nut who fantasizes about gulping down a big handful of trail mix, while the second person may be equally aroused by the prospect of a greasy cheeseburger and fries. Needless to say, marketers often go to great lengths to encourage consumers that their wants will be best satisfied with the products their company happens to make.

When a product satisfies a need or want, it delivers a **benefit.** Marketers try to develop

want: the desire to satisfy needs in specific ways that are culturally and socially influenced

benefit: the outcome that occurs when a product satisfies a need

products that provide some benefit, whether functional (for example, selling a garment that covers the body and provides warmth) or experiential (for example, selling a clothing item that makes the wearer feel sexy, natural, or sophisticated). A big part of the game is to identify what benefits people are looking for, develop a product that delivers those benefits, and convince people that the product can do this better than a competitor's product. As the renowned management expert Peter Drucker once wrote, "The aim of marketing is to make selling superfluous."[3] In other words, if marketers succeed in creating a product that truly meets the customer's needs, he or she will buy it without any additional "persuasion" from a salesperson.

Of course, all the people in the world can want your product, but this popularity won't do much good unless they have the means to obtain it. When desire is coupled with the buying power or resources to satisfy a want, the result is **demand.** So, the potential number of customers for, say, a snappy red BMW convertible is the number of people who want the car—*minus* those who can't afford to buy or lease one.

demand: customers' desire for products coupled with the resources to obtain them

Satisfying Society's Needs, Too

In recent times the focus on customer need satisfaction has been expanded by those who believe in the **societal marketing concept,** which emphasizes that customer needs must be satisfied in ways that are *also* beneficial to society as a whole. This philosophy is being practiced by large firms, such as Levi Strauss, and also by many small businesses who see their mission as turning a profit while also providing benefits to their communities. These efforts include satisfying society's needs for a cleaner, safer environment, which can be met by developing recyclable packaging, adding extra safety features like car air bags, or voluntarily modifying a manufacturing process to reduce pollution. For example, Working Assets, a long-distance phone service, includes announcements about political issues with its monthly bill. These announcements list phone numbers of key decision makers and give customers a free three-minute call to phone them. Working Assets also encourages subscribers to round their payment up to the nearest $5, and it passes the difference on to cause-related organizations. The company expects to donate about $1 million a year to nonprofit groups.[4]

societal marketing concept: an orientation that focuses on satisfying consumer needs while also addressing the needs of the larger society

The societal marketing movement even has a trade association, called Businesses for Social Responsibility, that helps its more than 700 company members to work for better environmental responsibility and lobby for such quality-of-life issues as job training, family leave, and day care. Many members donate a portion of their profits to nonprofit organizations. This trend is affectionately termed the "Ben & Jerry's movement," because it was inspired by two men who built a small ice cream company into a profitable and socially responsible marketing organization. We'll meet them again in Chapter 3, where we discuss the issues involved in socially responsible marketing in more detail.[5]

MARKETING IS AN EXCHANGE OF VALUE

". . . To create exchanges . . ." in the definition of marketing identifies the heart of every marketing act. An **exchange,** which occurs when something is obtained by providing something else in return, means that some transfer of value occurs between a buyer and a seller. The buyer receives an object, service, or idea that satisfies a need, for which the seller receives something he or she feels is of equivalent value.

exchange: the process by which some transfer of value occurs between a buyer and a seller

For an exchange to occur, at least two people or organizations must be willing to make a trade, and each must have something that is valued by the other. Both parties must also agree on the value of the exchange and how it will be carried out. And each party must be free to accept or reject the other's offer or terms for the exchange. Under these conditions, a gun-wielding robber's offer to "exchange" your money for your life does not constitute a valid exchange! More commonly, people complain that they were "robbed" by a store or other business, which implies that the exchange was not satisfactory.

A trade of equal value must actually occur for an exchange to take place. In modern society most exchanges occur in the form of a *monetary transaction,* where currency (in the form of cash, check, or a credit card) is surrendered in return for a good or service. Even the nature of this basic act is evolving, as so-called e-money systems are being developed that permit many transactions to be made without coins and paper money ever changing hands.

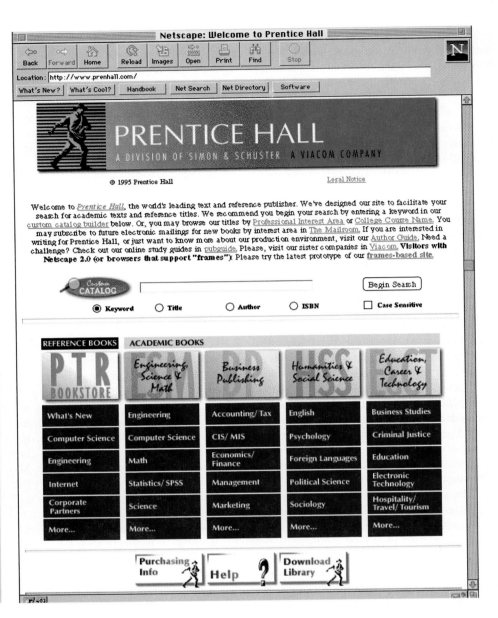

Transactions can also be nonmonetary, and the value that is exchanged doesn't have to be a physical product that you can hold or even see: A politician can agree to work toward certain goals in exchange for your vote, or a clergyman can offer you salvation in return for your faith.

In some instances a *barter transaction* occurs, where two parties agree to exchange goods or services that they both agree have approximately equal value. For example, you may agree to help a friend study for an accounting exam in return for being allowed to borrow his or her new car to impress a date next Saturday. While barter goes on between individuals all the time, many people don't realize that it's also a very frequent form of exchange, called *countertrade,* in international trading. Economic and political conditions have forced many countries, especially in Eastern Europe and the Third World, to rely on barter to a great extent. For example, PepsiCo arranged a deal with Russia where it provided Pepsi and other products in exchange for such Russian products as Stolichnaya vodka.[6]

CUSTOMERS COME IN MANY FORMS

customer: any person or organization that receives a product of value in the marketing exchange process, whether or not the person or organization will be the actual user of the product

A **customer** is any person or organization that receives something of value in the exchange process. While we often think of a customer as an individual adult, in reality there are many kinds of customers, including children, corporations, and the government. In addition, the person or organization who purchases a product may not necessarily be the one who winds up using it. A parent may send a "care package" of delicacies to a student away at school. A corporate buyer may purchase steel that will be used by others to manufacture a car. A government official may hire a consulting firm to evaluate how well a service is being delivered to taxpayers. Your professor (very wisely, we might add!) selected a marketing textbook for you to use in this course.

For a marketing effort to succeed, the organization must know who its customers are, what appeals to them, and how they go about deciding what to buy. Sega of America introduces about sixty-five new video games a year to keep up with the changing tastes of its core market of teens. To find out what appeals to them, the company conducts *focus groups* with teens two to three times weekly, where small groups of video users are gathered together to talk about their likes and dislikes. Researchers also visit kids at home to see how they're using the games and even go shopping with them at malls. By getting close to their customers, Sega found that kids shop for video games like adults shop for cars: They read guidebooks, ask friends for their advice, and often rent new titles before buying them. Clearly, this market takes its games seriously.[7]

A **market** consists of all the customers, and potential customers, who share a common need that can be satisfied by a specific product, who have the resources to exchange for it, who are willing to make the exchange, and who have the authority to make the exchange. You can invent a wonderful product and put together a sizzling ad campaign, but all your efforts will be wasted if you haven't directed your efforts to people who want your product. In addition, these customers have to have the means to obtain the product: Many students in your class might buy that BMW convertible today if they could, but most of them will probably have to put those plans on hold for at least a few years. In addition, they would have to be willing to (possibly) go into debt to get the car, and they would have to have the approval of other concerned parties, such as a spouse or fiancée who might have other ideas about how to spend that money.

market: all of the customers and potential customers who share a common need that can be satisfied by a specific product, who have the resources to exchange for it, who are willing to make the exchange, and who have the authority to make the exchange

(ALMOST) ANYTHING CAN BE MARKETED

". . . Ideas, goods, and services . . ." is the part of the marketing definition that tells us that just about everything can be marketed. Although marketing is most often associated with products such as jeans or breakfast cereals, in reality many other aspects of society can and do benefit from practicing the principles of marketing. Indeed, some of the best marketers come from the ranks of services (for example, American Express), nonprofit organizations (for example, Greenpeace), politicians (for example, Bill Clinton), athletes (for example, Michael Jordan), performers (for example, Rod Stewart), and even places (for example, Graceland). Ideas, such as democracy, religion, and art, also compete for acceptance in a "marketplace." In this book we'll refer to any good, service, or idea that can be marketed as a **product,** even though what is being sold may not have a physical form.

Consumer Goods and Services

Popular products like Levi's jeans are all around us. **Consumer goods** are the products purchased by individual consumers for personal or family use. We use up some consumer goods in relatively short periods, such as when we buy pizza, toothpaste, perfume, and running shoes. Other consumer goods—like a new car, a computer, or a digital television set—are more lasting. And when we buy a product, we are responding to a specific marketing attempt to satisfy a need.

A lot of people don't realize that many products can't be seen, tasted, or worn. Whether we're in need of air travel or zipper repair, these intangible products are *services* that we pay for and use, but never own. These transactions contribute an average of more than 60 percent to the Gross National Product of all industrialized nations, and service organizations from banks to bistros are working hard to develop their products to meet consumers' needs (as we'll see in Chapter 11).[8]

For example, the Marriott Corporation is working on improving aspects of its service so that guests will have a more positive experience. Many people complain about the time spent checking in at a hotel, so Marriott launched a new program called "1st 10" that eliminates a trip to the front desk. Pertinent information, such as the guest's time of ar-

product: a good, service, idea, place, or person offered in the exchange process to satisfy consumer or business customer needs and wants

consumer goods: the goods purchased by individual consumers for personal or family use

In advertising, they say one of the surest ways to get your message across is to put celebrities in your ad.

Jim Morrison 1943-1971

Janis Joplin 1943-1970

John Belushi 1949-1982

River Phoenix 1970-1993

Partnership for a Drug-Free America®

Exhibit 1.3
Idea marketing encourages people to endorse such ideas as equal rights or to buy into beneficial behaviors such as using seat belts, family planning and safe sex, or quitting smoking. Often called *social marketing,* it applies marketing principles to the promotion of social ideas and issues. A major campaign to combat drug use was undertaken by the Partnership for a Drug-Free America, a group organized by the American Association of Advertising Agencies. This campaign was the largest *pro bono* effort (meaning the ad agencies involved donated their services) in history. As one involved executive noted, "We are approaching the problem posed by the $110 billion illegal drug industry from a marketing point of view. What we're doing is competing with drug pushers for market share of nonusers."

rival and credit card number, is collected when the reservation is made. The program reduces average check-in time to $1\frac{1}{2}$ minutes, which is considerably less than the typical experience of the weary traveler.[9]

Business-to-Business Marketing

Business-to-business marketing, as we'll see in Chapter 7, refers to the marketing of goods and services by one business to another. Although consumer goods are more visible, in reality more goods are sold to businesses and other organizations than to individual consumers. **Industrial goods** are bought by businesses and organizations for further processing or for use in doing business. For example, automakers buy tons of steel to use in the manufacturing process and computer systems to track manufacturing costs, parts inventories, new-car shipments, and other information essential to operations. Business-to-business services—from cleaning to consulting—also exceed consumer services in extent of activity.

Although the same basic principles hold, there are some important differences between marketing consumer and industrial goods and services. Marketing an industrial product tends to be more complex, and the role of a competent salesperson who

industrial goods: goods bought by individuals or organizations for further processing or for use in doing business

understands how the product really works is essential. Also, industrial products are purchased by trained professional buyers, and often more than one person is involved in the decision.

Not-for-Profit Marketing

You don't have to be a businessperson to use marketing principles. As we'll see in Chapters 7 and 11, many not-for-profit organizations, from museums to churches, charities, and hospitals, are now practicing the marketing concept. Even governments, from the local level on up, are getting into the act as they adopt marketing techniques to create more effective taxpayer services and to attract new businesses and industries to their locations. The intense competition raging for support of civic and charitable activities means that only those not-for-profits that meet the needs of their constituents and donors will survive.

You've probably seen evidence of the "marketing revolution" among nonprofits at your own school. Colleges used to take only some of the many students who wanted to come. No more. Demand is slackening; between 1988 and 1991, freshman enrollment dropped by 8 percent. Many schools are increasingly aggressive about finding students—especially those who can pay their own way. As one educational consultant observed, "The expression 'a student of value' used to mean a valedictorian, student-body president, or varsity athlete. Now the phrase more and more means a student who can pay." Many schools are now doing sophisticated market research to determine who their best prospects are, and they are bombarding these potential students with flashy videotapes and brochures. Some schools are even offering scholarships to those enrolled elsewhere or discounts on books or tuition in exchange for names of likely applicants from their former high schools![10]

People Marketing

You may have heard the expression, "Stars are made, not born." It means that many of the famous people that you pay to see in concerts, stadiums, movies, and so on got to be that way with the help of some shrewd marketing:[11] They (and their handlers) developed a "product" that they hoped would appeal to some segment of the population. For example, a dance called the "achy breaky" was invented to promote a song called "Achy Breaky

Exhibit 1.4
Basketball player Shaquille O'Neal's marketing strategy is to be sure he is the biggest fish in any pond where he swims. He and his agent developed a marketing concept they called "Team Shaq," in which they contract with a small group of companies (including Spalding basketballs, Kenner action figures, and a hand-held electronic game by Tiger Electronics) who are willing to work together to develop the player's image; designed a Shaq logo; and copyrighted the name "Shaq" and the phrase "Shaq Attaq." Shaq lined up endorsements before he played his first professional game, and in fact he was signed by Reebok as a twenty-year-old just out of college. To further define his image, Shaq cut a rap album that sold 700,000 copies. His 1993 income: $15.2 million, of which "only" $3.3 million came from his basketball salary!

Heart," by country singer Billy Ray Cyrus. The singer's record company produced an instructional video targeted to dance teachers and began promoting dance contests at country bars. This strategy worked as the previously unknown Cyrus' album went to the top of the charts in 1992.[12]

The celebrity manufacturing process is most apparent in the Hollywood star system that operated in the earlier part of the century. In studio's "celebrity factories," unknowns were systematically discovered, developed, and packaged to emerge as "stars."[13] Many celebrities even adopt catchy "brand names," following some of the same rules that product marketers use to name soap or cars. These rules include memorability (for example, Evel Knievel), suitability (for example, fashion designer Oscar Renta reverted to his old family name of de la Renta, which sounds more aristocratic and sophisticated), and distinctiveness (for example, Steveland Morris Hardaway was given the name Stevie Wonder when he began his recording career).

Although it may seem strange to think about marketing people, in reality we often talk about ourselves and others in marketing terms. It's common for people to speak of "positioning" themselves for job interviews, to admonish others not to "sell themselves short," or to emphasize the importance of clothing and other parts of our "package" for success on the job or in getting a date. In addition, many consumers retain personal image consultants to devise a "marketing strategy" for them, while others undergo plastic surgery, physical conditioning, cosmetic makeovers, and so on to improve their "product images." Consumers' desire to package and promote themselves thus affects marketers of goods and services ranging from cosmetics and exercise equipment to résumé specialists and dating agencies.[14]

Marketing Sports, Entertainment, and Places

Sports and entertainment activities do not just happen; they must be carefully planned. Whether the organization be a sports team or a ballet company, sound marketing principles help to ensure that fans or audience members will continue to support the activity by buying tickets. Movies and TV shows along with concerts and other entertainment events are all results of marketing efforts. Many critics have gone so far as to observe that the Super Bowl is more of a marketing event than a sports happening. As we'll see in Chapter 11, both sports and the arts are hotbeds of activity for marketing in the 1990s.

Places can also be marketed. We are all familiar with the Disney organization's marketing efforts to promote its theme parks. Tourism marketing, whether for resorts like Club Med or even states—"Virginia is for Lovers," and "I ♥ New York"—is also a rapidly growing source of marketing activity. Indeed, tourism is New York State's second largest industry, accounting for 10 percent of private sector jobs.[15]

MARKETING HAS MANY TOOLS: THE MARKETING MIX

". . . Conception, pricing, promotion, and distribution . . ." in the definition of marketing means that whether it's a box of detergent, a sports medicine clinic, a rap CD, or a pair of Levi's, a product must be invented or developed, assigned value and meaning, and made available to interested consumers.

As marketers determine the best way to present a good or service for consumers' consideration, they have a number of decisions to make. The marketer's strategic toolbox is called the *marketing mix,* which consists of the factors that can be manipulated and used together to create a desired response in the marketplace. These factors are the product itself, the price of the product, the place where it is made available, and the promotion that makes it known to consumers. Just as a radio DJ puts together a collection of separate songs (a musical mix) to create a certain mood, the idea of a *mix* in this context reminds us that no *single* marketing activity is sufficient to accomplish the organization's objectives.

As shown in Figure 1.1, each is a piece of the puzzle that must be combined with other pieces to accomplish marketing objectives. By carefully crafting a marketing mix, the organization gives the consumer a reason to be its customer. The name of the game is to be better than the competition in the minds of consumers.

The success of the computer retailer CompUSA illustrates how a carefully planned marketing strategy can make one merchant stand out in a crowded market. The Dallas-based chain posted sales of $1.3 billion in 1993 by offering buyers more than needed hard-

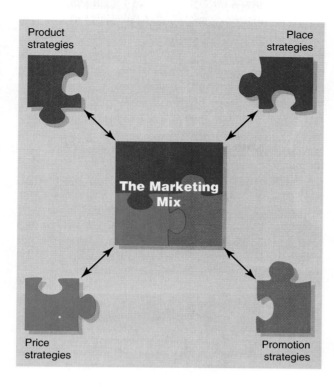

Product
strategies

Place
strategies

The Marketing Mix

Price
strategies

Promotion
strategies

**Figure 1.1
The Marketing Mix**

ware. The chain's spacious "superstores" carry software and a wide array of computer-related products, making it possible to do one-stop computer shopping. The company also offers next-day delivery on phone and mail orders and has a thirty-day replace or refund policy. CompUSA stores hold classes that teach customers how to buy a computer and use different kinds of software, and kids are welcomed to the stores on Saturdays to try out new computer games and play with karaoke machines. What pleases customers most, though, is CompUSA's promise to match or beat competitors' prices for every product it sells.

CompUSA carefully blends different elements of the marketing mix to create an effective strategy. The elements in the marketing mix are commonly known as the *Four P's* for Product, Price, Promotion, and Place. We'll examine these components of the marketing mix in detail later in this book. For now, let's briefly look at each "P" to gain some insight into its meaning and role in the marketing mix.

Product

The *product* is a good, service, idea, place, person—whatever is being offered for sale in the marketing exchange process. But more than a good or service, a product is the quality and character of the offering. This aspect of the marketing mix includes the design and packaging of a good, as well as its physical features (whether standard or optional) and any associated services, such as free delivery, installation, maintenance, or repair for some specified length of time.

Levi Strauss's success is largely due to the high level of customer satisfaction with the product element of its marketing mix. Levi's jeans, which require thirty-three complicated steps to produce, have double inner seams for durability and come with five pockets. The product has existed for almost 150 years, and its distinctive leather label with a tiny red tab is a sign of authenticity and a guarantee that the jeans will last for a long time. A consumer can buy a pair of Levi's 501 blue jeans, or perhaps choose another style that fits differently (for example, boot cut), or that comes in another color. Any version that is chosen will be accompanied by a guarantee of satisfaction from a widely known and highly regarded major company, so that's part of the product as well.

Price

Price refers to the assignment of value, or the amount the consumer must exchange in order to receive the offering. The decision about how much to charge for something is not as simple as it sounds. The price of an offering is an important determinant of whether the product will be available to a market the company aims to serve, as well as how it will

Exhibit 1.5
In today's world of marketing, where consumers' dollars are scarce and their time is at a premium, many not-for-profit organizations have learned the lessons taught by private enterprises. They are adopting marketing practices and developing marketing mix strategies designed to satisfy the customer. The Hogle Zoo in Utah has adapted a well-known airline slogan to use in this clever ad, which displays one of the zoo's more colorful "products."

be viewed by that market (for example, jeans that cost $30 are viewed differently than those that cost $80). Procter & Gamble, which used to determine its prices based on what a product cost to develop plus a profit, now does research on what consumers in different countries can afford and develops products that it can offer at lower prices when necessary. For example, in Brazil P&G launched Pampers Uni, a less expensive version of its Pampers brand of diapers.[16]

Place

Place refers to the availability of the product to the customer at the time and location where it is desired. This P is also known as *channels of distribution,* which refers to the series of firms that work together to get a product from a producer to a consumer. For consumer goods like Levi's jeans, these intermediary firms include wholesale firms that work together with the manufacturer and with retail firms like JCPenney and The Gap to have the right amount of jeans in the right styles at the right time, say, for back-to-school shopping.

The Taco Bell fast-food chain has a long-term plan to move into nontraditional outlets. Its distribution strategy is a key part of its overall marketing plan, as the company steadily expands to make its Super Burritos available in such places as kiosks in malls, movie theaters, airports, stadiums, and convenience stores. The chain also offers nontraditional meal hours, staying open very late to provide late night "munchies." Its recent ads, run on MTV, advise viewers to "Get Late at the Bell."

Distribution decisions go beyond simple convenience; they also affect the product's meaning. An item that is purchased in a swanky department store often has a different image than one bought in a discount store. And items that are hard to locate add to their value. Over the years a thriving black market has been created for Levi's jeans in other countries where they are hard to find. People in parts of Europe and Asia have been known to pay huge sums for a pair of Levi's. We'll cover issues related to distribution and purchasing in Chapters 14 and 15.

Promotion

Promotion refers to a marketer's efforts to inform or persuade consumers or organizations about goods, services, or ideas. It includes all of the marketing activities that are designed to encourage potential customers to buy the product and can take many forms, including personal selling, television advertising, store coupons, billboards, and publicity releases. Levi's is famous for its innovative and offbeat television commercials that reinforce its image as a product that allows you to "be yourself." The company also promotes itself in other ways, such as when the company's French office organized a public exhibition about the firm that used paintings, posters, videos, and other materials to trace the development of the company from 1850 onward.[17]

MARKETING IS A PROCESS

"Marketing is a process of planning and executing . . ." in the definition of marketing means that marketing is not a one-shot operation. It involves a series of steps that entail both careful thought (planning) and action (executing). One of the purposes of this book is to show you how the marketing process meshes with other business functions to create a product, communicate its meaning, and make it available to satisfy the needs of interested consumers.

The idea of marketing being a *process* has also taken on a new meaning in the 1990s: It reminds us that really successful marketing exchanges occur continually over time. For many marketers the view that doing business is a one-time deal in which a company tries to "put one over" on its customers by delivering a minimal product at a maximum price no longer holds. The concept of **relationship marketing,** which is becoming increasingly popular in the marketing community, sees marketing as a process of building long-term relationships with customers to keep them satisfied and to keep them coming back.

The centerpiece of this philosophy is simple, yet very important: Forging a long-term relationship with a customer is more important than making a killing on each individual transaction. Practitioners of relationship marketing believe that in the long run, making the effort to provide quality products, good service, and fair prices will pay off. As we'll see in Chapter 3, these bonds mean that the organization's marketing practices take into account consumers' long-term interest in broader issues, such as product safety and protection of the natural environment.

relationship marketing: a marketing philosophy that focuses on building long-term relationships with customers to satisfy mutual needs

HOW IS MARKETING DONE?

When it's done right, marketing is a strategic decision process, in which marketing managers determine what marketing strategies will be used to help the organization meet its long-term objectives. A marketing plan is then developed and implemented. Of course, if we told you here exactly how marketing is done, we'd "give away the ending" and you wouldn't have any reason to read the rest of this book. So we'll keep you in suspense. For now, though, we can very briefly summarize how marketers go about the business of making decisions and planning their actions. In this section, we'll also take a brief look at several key marketing strategies—the strategies marketers use to identify customers and offer goods and services they believe will satisfy the customers' needs and wants.

MARKETING PLANNING

The first phase of the marketing planning process involves analyzing the organization's current situation. Managers take a hard look at the organization's strengths and weaknesses, which even includes an assessment of internal politics that might help or hinder the development and marketing of products. The analysis must also take into account the threats and opportunities the organization will encounter in the marketplace, such as the actions of competitors, cultural and technological changes, the economy, and so on. These issues will be the focus of Chapters 2 and 3, but to see how far-reaching these concerns can be, consider some of the many factors that a firm like Levi Strauss has to think about when planning and developing its marketing strategy:

- What jean styles will its core customers of young people be looking for in three to five years?
- Which (if any) customer groups that don't currently buy Levi's products might the company go after?
- Will a new product line help the firm reach some new group of consumers, as was the case when it introduced its Dockers line to hold on to maturing customers who needed a "bit" more room in their casual slacks?
- How will new developments in computerized production technologies affect the denim manufacturing process?
- What changes in domestic and global politics might affect the company's ability to buy raw materials?
- Will the current trend for many companies to institute "Casual Fridays," where employees can wear jeans to work, affect long-term demand for Levi's products?
- How will consumers' growing awareness about the use of child labor in Third World countries that produce jeans affect their attitudes toward the company, even though it makes a concerted effort to monitor the exploitation of children by vendor companies?
- How are marketing and other business majors now in school being prepared to work in companies like Levi Strauss?

Answers to these and a host of other questions provide the foundation for developing an organization's marketing plan. They support management's decisions for setting specific marketing objectives and determining what strategies and actions will be taken to meet these objectives. These decisions are also related to the organization's overall objectives and rely on knowing who the organization's customers are and what they want.

Some firms choose to focus on reaching as many customers as possible by offering its products to a **mass market,** which consists of all possible customers in a market, regardless of the differences in their specific needs and wants. Marketing planning becomes a simple matter of developing a basic product and a single strategy for reaching everyone. While this approach can be cost effective, the organization risks losing potential customers to competitors whose marketing plans are directed at meeting the needs of different groups within the market. Because today's world is so complex and it's easier to tailor pieces of the marketing mix to reach specific groups, mass marketing isn't as common a strategy as it once was.

FINDING AND REACHING A TARGET MARKET

Today, the driving force in the success of an organization's marketing plan is its ability to find and reach a market consisting of the group(s) of customers having specific needs and wants that the organization can satisfy. For example, fashion designer Donna Karan

mass market: all possible customers in a market, regardless of the differences in their specific needs and wants

and her company, Donna Karan New York, don't make clothes for everyone. First, Karan only designs clothing for women. She further narrows down her market by focusing on the needs of working women. To get even more specific, her products are intended to appeal to working women who want practical clothes. These clothes will not be the favorites of trendy "clothes horses" who want to go to work looking like they just came off the cover of *Vogue*. Recognizing that many women are not skinny fashion models, Karan has successfully defined a segment of the clothing market for women—specifically, those working women who are willing to pay good money for generously cut work clothes that wear well and last.[18]

A *market segment* is a distinct group of customers within a larger market who are similar to one another in some way and whose needs differ from those of other customers in the larger market. Depending on its goals and resources, a company may choose to focus on only one segment or on several. The chosen segment(s) become the organization's **target market** toward which it directs its efforts.

Target marketing is a strategic decision process that determines both the market and the tactics used to reach it. By first slicing up the "marketing pie" and targeting specific pieces of it, marketers can develop products that meet the segment's specific needs and also design tactics based on the similarities of the segment to stimulate the desired response in the marketplace. As we'll see in much more detail in Chapter 8, the process of identifying and appealing to a specific group of customers involves three steps.

Segmenting the Market

The first step in the target-marketing process is to divide the overall market into *segments*, where the consumers in each segment have one or more important characteristics in common, characteristics that set them apart from others. Consumers can be segmented along many dimensions, such as sex, age, income, place of residence, or even hobbies and leisure activities. The business-to-business market can be segmented by such characteristics as line of business, size, level of sales, and so on. Modern market research techniques, which we'll discuss in Chapter 5, allow marketers to collect detailed information on these

target market: the market segment(s) on which an organization focuses its marketing plan and toward which it directs its marketing efforts

REAL PEOPLE, REAL CHOICES:

DECISION TIME AT LEVI STRAUSS

Steve Goldstein had a problem. As he examined the sales figures for men's jeans, he saw that business was flat and even starting to decline. Part of the problem, of course, was that he and his colleagues had been a little *too* successful at meeting the needs of this market. As the traditional Levi's jeans customer got older, he wanted to buy pants other than jeans and pants that weren't quite so tight-fitting. Jeans sales dropped dramatically in the 1980s as baby boomers (aged eighteen to thirty-four) graduated to more conservative clothes. In response, Levi Strauss did its homework. The company's research showed that consumers would be receptive to buying other, nonjeans styles bearing the Levi's name. When Levi Strauss noticed that a line of slacks sold by their Japanese subsidiary were catching on, they introduced them in the United States under the Dockers name. By the early 1990s the Dockers line was pulling in almost a half-billion dollars in sales.[19]

So, although sales of Dockers were booming, these men wanted more. They needed to add variety to their wardrobes, especially since dress codes in many workplaces and social situations were evolving to make the wearing of more casual clothes acceptable—even for grown-up baby boomers. Mr. Goldstein knew that the members of this market were more sophisticated about fashion and that, unlike their fathers before them, they tended to own a "wardrobe of jeans" rather than just one or two pairs of traditional models. Since many of them had already accumulated enough of Levi's more traditional tight-fitting styles (the 501 and 505 models), they saw no need to continue to buy still more of the same, especially if they were as comfortable as they used to be. How to sell more jeans to this large consumer segment? Mr. Goldstein mulled over his options:

Option 1. Make looser-fitting jeans under the Dockers label. These men already like the Dockers brand, so why not offer them blue denim jeans, with a more comfortable fit, and call them Dockers, too? This strategy would earn the new model instant recognition and acceptance by the target group. On the other hand, Dockers have been positioned as the cotton casual *alternative* to jeans and dress slacks, so making denim Dockers jeans would be a contradiction in terms. It might confuse consumers and erode the value of the Levi's brand, which has become synonymous with jeans for many people around the world.

Option 2. Forget it. The core of Levi's business is the 501 and 505 tighter-fitting jeans. Concentrate on selling more of these. Bigger-fitting jeans will never catch on with the eighteen- to thirty-four-year-olds anyway. Sure, we'll make those "big" jeans, but we'll market them only to the younger kids. We'll keep things simple and focus our resources on just one style of jeans. Of course, this strategy leaves a huge opportunity for our competition to outflank us; they might try to eat into our lead in the market by depicting us as the "old-fashioned, tight jeans company."

Option 3. Market a line of modified looser-fitting jeans to the eighteen- to thirty-four-year-olds. Keep the Levi's brand on it but give it its own number to distinguish it from 501 and 505. Position the new jeans in such a way that they don't conflict with the strong image of the 501 brand. This alternative would allow Levi's to cover its flank with a fashion fit. It would broaden the appeal of the Levi's brand by keeping the company current with new developments in the fashion world. On the other hand, if this strategy was not handled correctly it would make the 501s and 505s, which are tighter fits, look out-of-date. The preeminent position of these brands in the marketplace *must* be protected as they represent the heart and soul of the Levi's business.

Now, join the Levi Strauss decision team: Which option would you choose and why?

or any other consumer characteristics of interest and to group consumers in precisely defined market segments.

Choosing a Targeting Strategy

The second step in target marketing is to evaluate the segments identified in the segmentation process. Here, the marketer weighs each of the segments in terms of relative attractiveness and profitability potential against the organization's resources and ability to satisfy the segments' needs. On the basis of this analysis the organization decides on a targeting strategy that determines whether it will focus on a single segment or a broader market that encompasses several segments.

Positioning the Product

In the third step the marketer plans the product's *market position,* which refers to the way consumers in the target market perceive competitive brands or types of products. The aim of a positioning strategy is to obtain a *competitive advantage* over competing products in the minds of consumers. To achieve this positioning objective, the marketer carefully blends the elements—the Four P's—in the marketing mix. That is, a product is developed to meet the needs of the target market, as are price, place, and promotion strategies that specifically appeal to these consumers. These specific strategies may vary from one country to another or be injected with fresh ideas over time to maintain or change the product's position if necessary.

Many familiar products have well-established positions in the minds of consumers, often as the result of long-running, carefully crafted promotional campaigns. So, Coke is "the real thing," while Pepsi strives to be the drink of the younger generation. A BMW is viewed by many as a high-status, serious driving machine, while a Civic del Sol is carefree and a little funky. Here is how Levi Strauss envisions its ideal market position in the minds of jean wearers the world over:

> Levi Strauss would like to be seen as the maker of products for straightforward, honest, independent, adventurous, perhaps even a little rebellious, men and women between 15 and 25 years of age. Levi's wearers care for what is genuine, enjoy one another's company, feel attracted to the opposite sex, and will express their sense of freedom and enjoyment in a manner acceptable to all, irrespective of age.[20]

When did marketing begin? The evolution of a concept

Some of the most successful companies in the 1990s are those that have defined their marketing activities more broadly than merely providing goods and services to satisfy the needs of a select group of customers. While it's true that products have always been paramount in the minds of marketers, the notion that businesses and other organizations succeed when they satisfy customers' needs is actually a pretty recent idea. Until about forty-five years ago, marketing was basically viewed as a way to produce goods for consumers more efficiently. In this section we'll take a quick historical look at how marketing practice has developed since then, and we'll see how modern marketers are doing more than just satisfying customers. Table 1.1 (page 18) lists some of the milestones in the world of marketing during this period.

THE PRODUCTION ORIENTATION

Organizations that emphasize the most efficient ways to produce and distribute products, without really worrying about whether these products best satisfy consumers' needs, have a **production orientation.** This focus works best in a *seller's market,* when demand is greater than supply. Essentially consumers don't have a choice and have to take whatever is available. Under these conditions marketing plays a relatively insignificant role in the

production orientation: management philosophy that emphasizes the most efficient ways to produce and distribute products

Table 1.1
Marketing Milestones

Year	Marketing Event
1955	Ray Kroc opens his first McDonald's.
	Marlboro Man makes his debut.
1956	Lever Brothers launches Wisk, America's first liquid laundry detergent.
1957	Ford rolls out Edsel, loses more than $250 million in two years.
1959	Mattel introduces Barbie.
1960	The FDA approves Searle's Enovid as the first oral contraceptive.
1961	Procter & Gamble launches Pampers.
1962	Wal-Mart, Kmart, Target, and Woolco open their doors.
1963	The Pepsi Generation kicks off the cola wars.
1964	Blue Ribbon Sports (now known as Nike) ships its first shoes.
	Ford launches the Mustang.
1965	Donald Fisher opens The Gap, a jeans-only store in San Francisco.
1971	Cigarette advertising is banned on radio and television.
1973	Federal Express begins overnight delivery services.
1976	Sol Prices opens first warehouse club store in San Diego.
1979	Bernard Marcus and Arthur Blank start Home Depot in Atlanta.
1980	Ted Turner creates CNN.
1981	MTV begins.
1982	Gannett launches USA Today.
1983	Chrysler introduces minivan.
1984	AT&T long-distance monopoly ends.
	Apple Computer introduces Macintosh.
1985	New Coke is launched; Old Coke is brought back seventy-nine days later.
1990	Saturn, GM's first new car division since 1919, rolls out its first car.
1993	Phillip Morris reduces price of Marlboros by forty cents a pack, loses $13.4 billion in stock market value in one day.
1994	In largest switch in ad history, IBM yanks its business from scores of agencies worldwide and hands its entire account to Ogilvy & Mather.

Source: Patricia Sellers, "To Avoid Trampling, Get Ahead of the Mass," *Fortune* (1994) 201–202.

firm's efforts as management concentrates on finding more efficient ways to produce and distribute more and more goods.

Prior to 1925 this attitude was common among U.S. companies. The best example is the automobile industry, where the invention of the assembly line allowed companies to make large numbers of a complex product available to the masses. Faced with production shortages and intense consumer demand, the emerging car business was driven by production needs, and Henry Ford's marketing slogan promising that people could have any color car they wanted—as long as it was black—captured the prevailing philosophy of the day.

Firms that focus on a production orientation tend to develop a narrow view of the market, called *marketing myopia*, which sees consumers as a homogeneous group that will be satisfied with the basic function of a product. Ivory Soap, long a flagship product of Procter & Gamble, has been in decline for some time, because P&G viewed the brand as a basic soap, not as a cleansing product that could provide other benefits as well. Ivory Soap lost much of its share of the soap market to newer soaps, such as deodorant soaps and "beauty" soaps containing cold cream, that offered innovative features consumers desired.

Some firms today still manage to get by with a production orientation that reduces manufacturing costs—for example, firms that manufacture inexpensive kitchen items, "generic" paperware products, and other goods where price may be more important than quality or variety to a large number of consumers. Similarly, in Eastern European countries such as Romania that are just now experiencing a free-market economy, consumers are eager to buy any product on the market, regardless of quality. As a result, products such as a cola type drink, mass-produced in the Middle East and bearing a label similar to Coca-Cola's, finds ready buyers no matter how bad it tastes.

THE SALES ORIENTATION

When more products are being produced than customers are willing and eager to buy, businesses feel more pressure to engage in the "hard sell," where salespeople aggressively push their wares. For example, during the Great Depression in the 1930s the competition for consumers' thin pocketbooks was intense and firms were forced to shift their focus from producing goods to selling their goods in any way they could. This **sales orientation** means that management emphasizes aggressive sales practices and that marketing is seen strictly as a sales function. But it doesn't mean that consumers get what they want; rather, they are being pushed into buying what is available.

Many firms turned to a sales orientation in the years after World War II. During the war the United States dramatically increased industrial capacity to manufacture tanks, combat boots, parachutes, and countless other wartime goods. After the war ended, the peacetime economy boomed; Americans had plenty of money, and manufacturers used the capacity they had built up to turn out an abundance of civilian favorites.

Consumers eagerly bought all the things they couldn't get during the war years, but once these initial needs and wants were satisfied, they began to get more selective about where they put their money. As the economy moved from a seller's market to a *buyer's market,* in which the supply is greater than the demand, the race for consumers' hearts (and pocketbooks) was on.

Thus, the sales orientation became standard marketing practice into the 1950s. But consumers, as a rule, don't like to be pushed, and the hard sell did a lot to give marketing a bad image. Again, the automobile industry provides a good example of the sales orientation: Unscrupulous car salesmen probably had the worst reputation of any industry, and for many years automakers continued the tendency to produce what came to be called "anniversary cars"—cars that sat on the lot for more than a year before a salesperson could convince someone to buy them.

Companies that still follow a sales orientation tend to be more successful at making one-time sales than at building repeat business. This focus is most likely to be found among companies that sell *unsought goods,* or products that people are unwilling to seek out on their own, such as insurance or cemetery plots. As we'll see in Chapter 19, successful marketing managers today emphasize salesperson competency in meeting a customer's needs, rather than ability to ram a product down someone's throat whether they need it or not. They've learned that "selling ice to Eskimos" only works for so long.

sales orientation: a management philosophy that emphasizes aggressive sales practices and sees marketing strictly as a sales function

THE CONSUMER ORIENTATION

At Direct Tire Sales, a company in Watertown, Massachusetts, customers find an unusual sight: The customer lounge is clean, there is free coffee with fresh cream and croissants, employees wear ties, and the company will even pay your cab fare home if your car isn't ready on time. People don't mind paying 10 to 15 percent more for this extra service.[21] Direct Tire Sales has found that it pays to have a **consumer orientation** that zeroes in on ways to satisfy customers' needs and wants.

In the 1950s firms found that a selling orientation would work for a short time, but then customers began to balk at hard-sell techniques. Thus, the consumer orientation began to take hold. The adoption of a consumer orientation made sense: It showed management a way to stay afloat and even slip ahead of competitors in the changing economy, and it elevated marketing's role in the organization. Marketers were encouraged to do consumer research and segment markets, to assist in tailoring products to the needs of different consumer groups, and to do a better job of designing marketing messages that

consumer orientation: a management philosophy that focuses on ways to satisfy customers' needs and wants

communicated the product's benefits to picky consumers. In essence, the marketing concept, the idea that an organization can ensure its future by identifying and satisfying consumer needs, was born.

Automakers of the 1950s began to focus more on customers, but not all of their efforts had a happy ending. Ford Motor Company's misguided attempt to introduce the "ultimate car" for consumers—the Edsel—was a dismal failure that cost the company millions. General Motors, on the other hand, successfully developed cars for different lifestyles and incomes. By catering to the needs of young, returning veterans with the economical Chevrolet ("See the U.S.A. in a Chevrolet!"), to wealthier older people with the Cadillac, and to other groups with the Buick, Pontiac, and Oldsmobile, GM was able to claim a 52 percent share of the U.S. car market by 1962.[22]

The 1960s were prosperous years. The economy was stable, the population was growing, and there was very little overseas competition. But by the 1970s the trickle of low-priced, high-quality foreign goods into U.S. markets, particularly from Japan, grew to a steady stream and virtually flooded markets like home electronics by the 1980s. The U.S. auto industry was caught napping during this period. Honda introduced its Civic to the U.S. market in 1973, immediately making friends with American drivers who needed and wanted a high-quality but economical car. Despite the gasoline shortages in the 1970s and the increasing popularity of small Japanese cars, U.S. automakers continued to pump out huge gas guzzlers with uneconomical V-8 engines.

Economic forces were also at work in the 1970s and 1980s. Inflation in the 1970s and recession in the 1980s took their toll on company profits. Many businesses responded to the need to sustain profits by cutting production costs or by acquiring other firms doing business in markets with greater growth potential. Other companies looked for less dramatic ways to secure their long-term profitability and survival. Many began to see that, by itself, the marketing concept of identifying and satisfying consumer needs was insuffi-

Exhibit 1.7
The Xerox Corporation, a producer of photocopying machines for businesses, once dominated the market, to the point that some people still refer to a photocopy as a "Xerox copy." But in the early 1980s, high-quality Japanese photocopiers that cost less and broke down less often threatened to put the company out of business. Forced to rethink its position, the company recognized that it had lost sight of its customers' need for a quality product and had let its costs go up, driving up the price of inferior quality products. With a new emphasis on total quality, which includes superior products that are more reasonably priced and extensive customer services that satisfy its customers, Xerox has regained much of its competitive position.

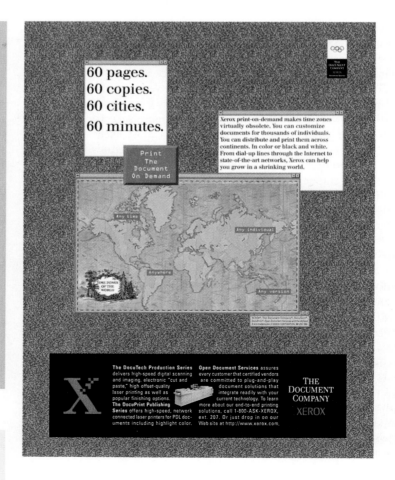

cient; they had to do it *better* than the competition, just as the Japanese were doing. Firms increasingly concentrated on improving the quality of their products, and by the early 1990s a commitment to *total quality*—a management effort to involve all employees in continuous quality improvement to satisfy consumers—was well entrenched in the U.S. marketing community.

This change in thinking is evident in the auto industry, formerly famous for a zealous sales orientation. Automakers are focusing on turning out cars and trucks that are easy to sell because they come equipped the way people want them. One company is even introducing a computer network to allow car dealers to track what options are selling where (including competitors' models), so local dealers can anticipate the tastes of their own customers and avoid getting stuck with "anniversary cars" that they have to push.[23]

All of the major automakers have adopted this philosophy (as Ford's motto reminds us, "Quality is Job One!"). When Chrysler acquired the Jeep division from American Motors, the company took this rough-and-ready vehicle to new heights by focusing on quality, installing technologically advanced systems, and providing luxury-car features like tilt steering wheels, sun roofs, and plush interiors that were missing in competing 4 × 4 sports vehicles. General Motors started its Saturn division, which designed new cars from scratch based on total quality principles. Ford has also adopted this orientation and is hard at work designing "world cars" like the Mondeo that will meet the high standards of consumers in many countries.

THE NEW ERA ORIENTATION

Yet another fundamental change in marketing is occurring in the 1990s as the search for long-term growth continues. While the customer is still king, many of today's forward-thinking organizations are seeing their commitment to quality as more than simply satisfying consumers' needs. A **New Era orientation** to marketing decision making means a devotion to excellence in designing and producing products, as well as creating products that benefit the customer *plus* the firm's employees, shareholders, and fellow citizens. One outgrowth of this new way of thinking is the focus on relationship marketing that was discussed earlier in the chapter; another is the emphasis on social marketing that, as we saw earlier, includes efforts to promote consumers' health, safety, and social well-being.

Environmental stewardship is yet another facet of the New Era orientation that fosters the idea that consumers' current needs can be satisfied in ways that benefit society's long-term interests. The Body Shop, a U.K. firm, for example, satisfies consumers' basic cosmetics need with products from shampoo to foot powder, all made from natural ingredients, and appeals to consumers who like to pamper themselves with more exotic offerings like raspberry bubble bath and orchid oil cleansers. The Body Shop uses biodegradable or recyclable packaging, and consumers can return its recyclable plastic containers to the store. None of its products are tested on animals, and the firm donates part of its profits each year to such causes as saving the rain forests.

As we will see in Chapter 3, New Era firms embrace marketing practices that seek both *economic profit* and *social profit*. Citibank, for example, gained both by developing technology that permits the blind and visually impaired to use its ATM machines.[24] Planning in New Era firms no longer solely revolves around developing strategies that use the firm's strengths to capture opportunities; it also considers how the firm's actions will affect the welfare of its community and of the world at large. New Era managers support such efforts as encouraging cultural diversity, ethical business practices, and helping the environment in their quest for profitability.[25]

The critical issue in a firm's decision to adopt a New Era orientation is the cost of putting its principles into practice. Many managers argue that it cuts too heavily into profits, while others wisely realize that profit goals and social responsibility are not mutually exclusive. Consider, for example, Levi Strauss's decision to develop its Naturals line of jeans. No chemical dyes were used to color the jeans; consumers found that the natural color actually improved with repeated washing, and demand for the jeans during the line's first year was overwhelming. Clearly, the marketing strategies underlying Naturals resulted in benefits for the environment, the consumer, and the company.

New Era orientation: a management philosophy in which marketing decision making means a devotion to excellence in designing and producing products and creating products that benefit the customer plus the firm's employees, shareholders, and fellow citizens

WHY IS MARKETING IMPORTANT?

Marketing principles are important to everyone from small businesses to major corporations, from homemakers to high-powered executives. The basic principles of marketing apply to the sale of canned peas, to the delivery of food and clothing to needy people, to the fortunes of a symphony orchestra. Because meeting the needs of consumers and society in an efficient way touches on so many aspects of our daily experience, it's helpful to sit back and think about the role that marketing plays in our lives.

MARKETING CREATES UTILITY

utility: the usefulness or benefit received by consumers from a product

Marketing activities play a major role in the creation of **utility,** which means that some benefit is received from a product. By working to ensure that people have the type of product they want, where and when they want it, the marketing system makes our lives easier when it works the way it's supposed to and harder when it does not. A shopper in the United States, Canada, or Western Europe may take for granted that he or she can pick and choose from thousands of items in the local grocery store. His or her counterpart in parts of Eastern Europe, where lines form at dawn to buy soup bones, would happily change places.

Form utility: the consumer benefit provided by organizations when they change raw materials into finished products desired by consumers

The marketing system provides different kinds of utility. That is, it adds to the value of an exchange in several ways. **Form utility** refers to an organization's ability to alter raw materials into finished products desired by consumers. A firm's buying and distribution system allows it to accumulate the large numbers of items often required to construct a product. A dress manufacturer that combines cotton, thread, buttons, zippers, and so on into an elegant evening gown is providing form utility, as is a restaurant that assembles many fresh fruits and vegetables to create a salad bar.

Form utility applies to intangible services as well. For example, Working Assets, a long-distance phone service, buys telephone time in bulk from a major carrier, then resells this time to subscribers.[26] By acting as an intermediary between the phone company and the customer, Working Assets creates utility by making the "raw materials" (in this case, phone service) more economical to the end buyer.

place utility: the consumer benefit provided when organizations make products available where customers want them

Place utility means making products available where customers want them. The most sophisticated evening gown sewn in New York's garment district is of little use to the woman in Kansas City who needs it for a ball next Saturday night, unless the dress is delivered to a local store where she can select it. Providing place utility is beneficial for more than just dress buyers, though: The efficient distribution of needed products is central to the success of relief efforts and charities. For example, a Belgium organization called Terre (Earth) recycles twenty-five tons per day of used clothing that has been discarded throughout Belgium. Terre collects these items, sorts them, and then distributes them to Africa, Eastern Europe, India, and Afghanistan.[27]

time utility: the consumer benefit provided by storing products until they are needed by buyers

possession utility: the consumer benefits provided by an organization by allowing the consumer to own, use, and/or enjoy the product

Time utility is created by storing products until they are needed by buyers. Think about what would happen if, say, birthday cakes were available only once a year—unless your birthday happened to fall around that time, you would be stuck with a hard (and moldy) surprise on your big day! Fortunately, marketers provide time utility by keeping items in inventory and producing new ones to meet our demands when we're ready to make an exchange. Time utility is increasingly prized in a society where people always seem to be short on time. Products like bank machines that give you cash any time of the day or night, or e-mail that lets you retrieve your messages at a time you choose, provide continuous time utility.[28]

Finally, **possession utility** provides benefits by allowing the consumer to own, use, and/or enjoy the product. A mortgage company allows a young couple to buy a home they could never afford otherwise. Levi Strauss makes a product that becomes an important part of people's wardrobes; for many wearers, their worn-in jeans are a central part of their identities.

SPOTLIGHT ON RELATIONSHIP MARKETING

Holding on to Customers

Companies in the 1990s have realized that to survive and be successful, they have to hang on to the customers they already have. Home Depot, which has been called the best retail organization in America, knows that customer service is the key to return shoppers. Typical shoppers may spend up to $25,000 in a lifetime even though they spend only an average of $38.00 per visit. The success of Home Depot is obviously related to its philosophy: "Every customer has to be treated like your mother, your father, your sister, or your brother." Employees are encouraged to build long-term relationships with customers, to spend as much time as it takes to educate customers in the "how to" of home repairs.

Other forward-thinking retailers are devising different routes to customer loyalty. Pizza Hut spent $20 million in 1993 to create electronic profiles of 9 million customers who have received deliveries since 1984. With this database Pizza Hut can send out coupons matched to the tastes of the addressees.

Spiegel has used information about the purchases of customers to develop twenty small boutique-like catalogs within the larger Spiegel catalog. Women who like romantic apparel receive a small catalog within a catalog, while those who prefer low price receive a different selection from which to choose. Banc One surveys 35,000 customers every quarter to provide superior banking service. Nearly 60 percent of its branches are open on Saturdays, 20 percent are open on Sundays, and sales representatives are available through a customer hotline twenty-four hours a day.

Hertz, still the top choice for car rental customers, has created the Club Gold Program. For $50 a year, members simply board the airport courtesy bus, tell the driver their last name, and get dropped off in front of their auto—the one with their last name in glowing lights above it. Since the bus driver has radioed ahead, Hertz starts the car and turns on the air conditioning or heat so you will be ready to go.

Sources: Christopher Power, "How to Get Closer to Your Customers," *Business Week/Enterprise* (1993) 42–45; Patricia Sellers, "Companies That Serve You Best," *Fortune* (May 31, 1993) 74–88.

MARKETING FACILITATES EXCHANGE

One of the advantages of modern marketing is that it makes it easier for buyers and sellers to come together—whether physically, through the mail, or electronically—to exchange items of value. Clever marketers seem to have just the right product ready and waiting whenever and wherever we need or want it, usually at a price we are willing to pay. Of course, you now know that this happy circumstance is the result of target-marketing strategies and a skillful blend of the Four P's (product, price, place, and promotion) in the marketing mix. But it also relies on another type of exchange—the exchange of information that lets marketers know what we need and information in the form of marketing communications that lets us know what marketers are offering. Let's take a quick look at these information and communications systems that are key to facilitating the exchange process.

The Information System

Although some people believe in lucky guesses and "seat of the pants" decision making, smart marketers know that information is power. Managers need to know as much as they can about conditions in the outside world, the desires of customers, and even about their own company's capabilities and weaknesses, so that they can make intelligent choices. A firm's *information system* includes the procedures and technology it uses to collect and analyze information. This system is fed by many sources, ranging from the manager's day-to-day observations and experiences to elaborate studies (perhaps by an outside firm hired for this purpose) that evaluate the perceived quality of the company's products vis-à-vis competitors, consumers' attitudes and priorities, sales trends in different markets, and so on.

Marketers collect information *about* and *from* consumers to know how good a job they are doing in meeting needs. As we saw earlier in this chapter, to segment the market and develop targeting strategies the firm needs to know where its best potential lies and what will turn on these consumers. It also needs feedback from consumers to know how they are reacting to its products and to assess what new products are likely to be well received. Firms that have adopted a quality perspective understand that consumers not only keep them in business, they also play an important role as participants in the design and evaluation process.

For example, Fidelity Investments, the largest mutual fund firm with $113 billion in assets and 8 million customer accounts, holds "service labs," meetings in which groups of customers test prototypes of forms, pamphlets, and so on. Feedback prompted Fidelity to simplify its automated phone service and expand its toll-free numbers, so customers can reach the individual they need faster. Fidelity also conducted a client survey where customers rated seventy different "service attributes." It found that customers value polite treatment even ahead of investment performance and statement accuracy! Phone workers now get a three-day course on phone etiquette.[29]

The organization also needs to collect information from the other firms with which they do business. Marketers rely on feedback from trade groups, the government, market research companies, distributors, their own salespeople, and their retailers. Many companies such as the makers of Lee Jeans[30] are aggressively developing sophisticated technology that allows them to know almost immediately what is selling and what is sitting. Procter & Gamble, one of the largest marketing organizations, is now using a system called *continuous product replenishment*. When a box of detergent is scanned at checkout, the information is transferred directly to P&G's computers, which figure out where and when to replenish the product. Improvements in the efficiency of distribution allowed the company to lower its prices and eliminate the need to rely on constant price changes to lure consumers to the aisles.[31] As P&G's experience illustrates, an information system is vital for tracking sales, shipments, inventories, and so on. It enables the firm to know what's hot and what's not and how it can improve its procedures for getting its products into consumers' eager hands more efficiently. We'll learn more about how information systems work in Chapter 5.

The Communications System

Even the perfect product won't sell if no one knows about it. Firms also need a *communications system,* consisting of the different methods used to inform and persuade consumers by the company and outside firms such as advertising and public relations agencies. The communications system is responsible for letting customers know what a product will do, why it's better than the competition, and what its position in the marketplace will be. This system may be fairly simple, especially for smaller firms like local retailers who designate someone to be sure that an ad runs in the local paper each week and that the mannequins in the window are wearing the latest inventory. In larger firms the communications system is typically a huge operation, often composed of specialists who work in-house plus several outside firms. For example, the Coca-Cola Company owes much of its success to its mastery of communications. Coke hires numerous advertising and promotion agencies to create ways to communicate about its different product lines. Over the years the company has crafted an image for Coke that is known the world over. The familiar Coke logo can be found almost anywhere you look around the globe. It is pasted on rooftops and beamed into homes via clever TV commercials; Coke memorabilia such as coasters, trays, and glasses have become collector's items.[32] The company even operates a Coca-Cola Museum in Atlanta that has become a major tourist attraction. All of these techniques represent different facets of Coke's communications system. They facilitate exchange by helping to create value for the brand and also make it very easy for Coke drinkers to locate the product when the urge for a cold one strikes. We'll focus on the central role played by marketing communications in Chapters 16 through 19.

Companies often use other marketing firms, including advertising agencies, sales promotion firms, public relations firms, and direct marketing specialists, to help spread the word. Communications can occur via many media vehicles, such as television, store displays, sweepstakes, magazines, and billboards. These methods of communications are increasingly being coordinated to allow the marketer to present a clear and consistent image of the product wherever the consumer runs into it. This movement toward the use of *integrated marketing communications* will be highlighted in Chapter 16.

Some of the most exciting developments in marketing communications revolve around efforts to cultivate long-term relationships with customers. The automaker Lexus sent hundreds of its owners and potential owners to a dinner, followed by a performance of the play "Phantom of the Opera." At the dinner there was a low-key display of the cars. Each nonowner who attends the festivities is eventually sent a personalized "thank you" note. At the bottom of each note, in small print, is a query that offers more information about the cars—and the opportunity to request a test drive.

MARKETING'S ROLE IN OUR DAILY LIVES: OPERA TO OPRAH

For better or for worse, we all live in a world that is significantly influenced by the actions of marketers. We are surrounded by marketing stimuli in the form of advertisements, stores, and products competing for our attention and our dollars. Much of what we learn about the world is filtered by marketers, such as when we see images of rich or beautiful people in TV commercials or magazines. Ads show us how we should act with regard to recycling, alcohol consumption, and even the types of houses and cars we wish to own. This influence extends from "serious" goods and services like health care, classical music, and university enrollments to "fun" things like sports, hip-hop music, and talk shows (though many people take these products pretty seriously too!).

Popular Culture

Popular culture consists of the music, movies, sports, books, celebrities, and other forms of entertainment consumed by the mass market. Marketer-influenced events like the Super Bowl, Christmas shopping, presidential elections, the Teenage Mutant Ninja Turtles, newspaper recycling, and cigarette smoking are all examples of products and activities that touch many of our lives. For example, consider the *product icons* that marketers use to create an identity for their products. Various mythical creatures and personalities—from the Pillsbury Doughboy to the Jolly Green Giant—have been at one time or another central figures in popular culture. In fact, it is likely that more consumers could recognize such characters than could identify past presidents, business leaders, or artists!

The relationship between marketing and culture is a two-way street. The goods and services that are popular at any point in time often provide a valuable mirror of important developments and changes in the larger society. Consider, for example, some American products that reflected underlying cultural processes at the time they were introduced:

- The TV dinner, which hinted at changes in family structure.
- Cosmetics made of natural materials and not animal-tested, which reflected consumers' apprehensions about pollution, waste, and animal rights.

popular culture: the music, movies, sports, books, celebrities, and other forms of entertainment consumed by the mass market

Marketing and Myths

Marketing messages often communicate **myths,** stories that contain symbolic elements and express the shared emotions and ideals of a culture.[33] Consider, for example, the way that a company like McDonald's takes on "mythical" qualities. The "golden arches" are a universally recognized symbol, one that is virtually synonymous with American culture. They offer sanctuary to Americans around the world, who know exactly what to expect once they enter. Basic struggles involving good versus evil are played out in the fantasy world created by McDonald's advertising, as when Ronald McDonald confounds the Hamburglar. McDonald's even has a "seminary" (Hamburger University) where inductees go to learn appropriate behaviors. Other companies have given us mythical characters that reflect such cultural messages as the "great mother" image (for example, Betty Crocker and Aunt Jemima), the innocent maiden (for example, the Ivory Snow Girl), and "the good old days" (for example, Pepperidge Farm).[34]

myths: stories that contain symbolic elements and express the shared emotions and ideals of a culture

MARKETING'S ROLE IN SOCIETY

In many ways we are "at the mercy" of marketers, because we rely on them to sell us products that are safe and perform as promised, to tell us the truth about what they are selling, and to price and distribute these products fairly. Conflicts often arise in business between the goal to succeed in the marketplace and the desire to conduct business honestly and maximize consumers' well-being by providing them with safe and effective goods and services. Although many would argue that by the time people reach college, graduate school, or actually are employed by companies it is a little late to start teaching ethics, many universities and corporations are focusing very intently on teaching and reinforcing ethical behavior.

Exhibit 1.8
Just where is Margaritaville? It's not a place, it's a state of mind created by singer/songwriter Jimmy Buffett. The 1977 song "Margaritaville" immortalized a mythical tropical paradise ("wasting away in Margaritaville") that is still beloved by "parrotheads"—Buffett fans sporting gaudy, bird-filled Hawaiian shirts who are a Caribbean answer to Dead Heads (Grateful Dead fans). Jimmy Buffett is turning the Margaritaville myth into a marketing empire. In the mid 1980s Buffett opened a bar, restaurant, and souvenir shop, called Jimmy Buffett's Margaritaville, in Key West, Florida. A second Margaritaville opened more recently in New Orleans.

Ethical Behavior Is Good Business

Companies usually find that stressing ethics and social responsibility is also good business, at least in the long run. In 1987 the Chrysler Corporation was involved in a scandal when the company was accused of resetting the odometers of supposedly new cars that had actually been driven by managers prior to sale. The company only admitted the practice after some managers tried to get out of paying speeding tickets by claiming that their speedometers didn't work because the cable was disconnected![35] These actions caused the company great embarrassment and years of hard work to restore the public's trust.

In contrast, Procter & Gamble voluntarily withdrew its Rely tampons from the market following reports of women who had suffered toxic shock syndrome (TSS). Although scientists did not claim a causal link between the usage of Rely and the onset of TSS, the company agreed with the Food & Drug Administration to undertake extensive advertising notifying women of the symptoms of TSS and asking them to return their boxes of Rely for a refund. The company took a $75 million loss and sacrificed an unusually successful new product that had already captured about one-quarter of the billion-dollar sanitary product market.[36]

Social and Ethical Criticisms of Marketing

Whether intentionally or not, some marketers do violate their bond of trust with consumers. In some cases these actions are actually illegal, as when a manufacturer deliberately mislabels the contents of a package or a retailer adopts a "bait and switch" selling strategy, whereby consumers are lured into the store with promises of inexpensive products with the sole intent of getting them to switch to higher-priced goods.

In other cases marketing practices have detrimental effects on society even though they are not explicitly illegal. Some companies erect billboards for alcohol and tobacco products in low-income neighborhoods where abuse of these products is a big problem, while others sponsor commercials depicting groups of people in an unfavorable light to get the attention of a target market (for example, many people have complained that Coors' "Swedish bikini team" campaign demeans women in an attempt to appeal to young male beer drinkers). Throughout this book we will highlight ethical issues, providing examples of companies that have acted responsibly as well as irresponsibly. For now, let's consider three of the most common criticisms of marketing.

1. *Marketers create artificial needs.* The marketing system has come under fire from both ends of the political spectrum. On the one hand, some members of the religious right believe that advertising contributes to the moral breakdown of society by presenting sinful images of materialistic pleasures. On the other hand, some leftists argue that the same deceitful promises of material pleasure function to buy off people who would otherwise be revolutionaries working

Exhibit 1.9
One of the most common and stinging criticisms of marketing is that marketing techniques (especially advertising) are responsible for convincing consumers to buy things that they don't really need or want and for making them believe they will be unhappy or somehow inferior and unsuccessful if they don't have these things. The American Association of Advertising Agencies, an industry group, sponsored this ad to combat these criticisms and to remind people that a need is a basic motive for taking some action, while a want represents one way that society has taught us that the need can be satisfied.

to change the system.[37] They argue that the system creates demand that only its products can satisfy.

A Response: People's needs already exist; marketers simply recommend ways to satisfy them. For example, while thirst is a biologically based need, we are taught to want Coca-Cola to satisfy that thirst rather than, say, goat's milk. A basic objective of advertising is to create awareness that these needs exist, rather than to create them. In some circumstances, however, the marketer can engineer an environment to make it more *probable* that a need will be activated, as, for example, when movie theaters sell popcorn and bars supply free peanuts to patrons to stimulate thirst.

2. *Marketing teaches us to value people for what they own rather than who they are.* Goods are arbitrarily linked to desirable social attributes, so we learn that we can be popular, happy, and so on only if we buy these products. One critic even argued that the problem is that we are not materialistic enough in the true sense of the word—we do not sufficiently value goods for the utilitarian functions they deliver, but instead focus on the irrational value of goods for what they symbolize. According to this view, for example, "Beer would be enough for us, without the additional promise that in drinking it we show ourselves to be manly, young at heart, or neighborly. A washing machine would be a useful machine to wash clothes, rather than an indication that we are forward-looking or an object of envy to our neighbors."[38]

A Response: Products are designed to meet existing needs, and advertising helps only to communicate their availability. Advertising is an important source of consumer information.[39] It is a service that reduces the time a consumer spends searching for a needed product that suits his or her self-image.

3. *Marketers promise miracles.* Consumers are led to believe that products have magical properties; they will do special and mysterious things for them that will transform their lives. They will be beautiful, have power over others' feel-

ings, be successful, be relieved of all ills, and so on. Marketers provide simple, anxiety-reducing answers to complex problems.

A Response: Marketers simply do not know enough about people to manipulate them. Consider that the failure rate for new products ranges from 40 percent to 80 percent. In testimony before the Federal Trade Commission, one executive observed that while people think that advertisers have an endless source of magical tricks and/or scientific techniques to manipulate people, in reality, the industry is successful when it tries to sell good products and unsuccessful when selling poor ones.[40]

WHERE DOES MARKETING FIT IN THE ORGANIZATION?

The role that the marketing function plays in an organization varies widely. To a large extent, the importance accorded to marketing—and to the people who are supposed to do it—depends on whether the organization has adopted the marketing concept. Thus, top management in some firms is very marketing-oriented (and often the CEO came from the marketing ranks), while in others marketing is almost an afterthought. Sometimes the term "marketing" is used when what the company really means is sales or advertising. In the case of organizations, particularly not-for-profit ones, that are just waking up to the idea of marketing, there may not be anyone in the company that is specifically designated as "the marketing person." In contrast, some firms that focus on total quality are realizing that the basic marketing concept in fact applies to all aspects of a firm's activities. The result of this thinking has been a trend toward integrating marketing with other business functions instead of setting it apart as a separate function.

MARKETING'S ROLE IN THE FIRM

A firm's marketing-related decisions must affect and be affected by its other operations. Marketing managers must work with financial and accounting officers to figure out whether products are profitable, to set marketing budgets, and to help determine prices. They must work with people involved in manufacturing to be sure that products are produced on time and in the right quantities. Anticipating demand is very important, especially when marketers do *too* good a job at creating desire for a product and production is unable to keep up. For example, about ten years ago Coleco underestimated the demand for its Cabbage Patch dolls, which had become the rage among American children. Faced with a limited supply of the product, some retailers reported near-riots among parents as they tried desperately to buy the dolls for their children.[41]

THE BIG PICTURE: PRODUCT AND CORPORATE MARKETING

Marketing strategies must be formed at several layers in an organization, especially in large corporations that have many brands or product lines. Kellogg's, for example, has many brands of cereal, such as Special K, Rice Krispies, Raisin Bran, Frosted Flakes, and so on. Procter & Gamble has many product lines from cleaning products to cosmetics, many of which feature more than one brand; its line of laundry detergents, for instance, has eight brands, including Tide, Cheer, and Ivory Snow. When a firm has many brands of similar products, its goal is to satisfy different customer segments in a market with brands that offer different product benefits. And to be effective in reaching its targeted customers, each line or brand must have its own set of marketing plans and strategies. Large corporations manage this task by assigning overall responsibility to division managers who develop their particular marketing plans and strategies. Managers at the very top of the organization coordinate these plans, while managers at lower levels carry them out.

Exhibit 1.10
In the 1990s more and more successful firms know they must look beyond their own borders for potential customers if they are to continue to grow and remain profitable. The desirability of expanding to foreign markets is certainly obvious to the Mattel Corporation, which has made much of its profits over the years by supplying Barbie dolls to millions of American girls, making it the best-selling toy ever. In a way Barbie has been *too* successful—the average American girl owns eight Barbies—so the U.S. market is getting saturated, and Mattel is now looking to global markets to offset the company's reliance on American Barbie sales. Europe has nearly twice as many children as the United States, and numbers in Mexico, South America, Japan, and Southeast Asia are even greater.

Similarly, many large corporations organize themselves by establishing separate business units that have very different product lines. The goals are similar—to satisfy customers in different markets by providing a variety of products—and marketing planning and responsibility is layered in a similar way. For example, Paramount Communications, which owns Prentice Hall (the company that publishes this book), also owns other publishing companies and several diverse businesses including a movie studio and the New York Knicks basketball team. So, at the top layer of the organization, Paramount is concerned with how the marketing activities of its different businesses are contributing to company profitability. Prentice Hall top management is concerned with how its marketing decisions and plans are fitting into the big picture of Paramount's overall business goals, while lower-level managers are concerned with producing, pricing, promoting, and distributing the textbooks to accomplish the plans.

In Chapter 2 we'll look more closely at the role marketing managers play in a corporation's strategic planning process and at how successful marketers develop, implement, and evaluate marketing plans. Chapter 4 will show how marketers develop and plan their activities when they decide to enter global markets. Multinational companies not only market their products around the world but also set up shop to produce their goods in many different countries. Mattell Corporation, for example, now makes 75 percent of its toys in plants around the world in such countries as Indonesia, Malaysia, China, Mexico, and Italy.[42]

WHO ARE MARKETERS?

Marketers are drawn from many fields of study and backgrounds. While (not surprisingly) many marketers majored in the subject in college and/or went on for an M.B.A., many others are drawn from diverse areas. Business-to-business salespeople who sell technically complex products often have backgrounds in science and engineering. Retailers and fashion marketers may have been trained in merchandising or design. Advertising copywriters often have degrees in English.

While many students assume that the "typical" marketing job is in a large, consumer-oriented company like Procter & Gamble, in fact marketing specialists are found in many types of organizations. In smaller organizations one person (perhaps the owner) may handle all of the marketing responsibilities. In larger organizations specialized managers work on different aspects of the marketing strategy. An extended discussion of career paths in marketing can be found in Appendix A.

One goal of this book is to show you how marketing fits into the activities of many kinds of organizations. The best way to do that is to introduce you to *Real People* who are involved with different aspects of marketing every working day. These marketing professionals

are found in consumer goods companies like Levi Strauss and financial services companies like First Union Bank. You'll see them helping to develop quality "big-ticket items" like Mercedes automobiles and also in organizations like the Sierra Club, working to advance the cause of environmental responsibility. They are in the United States, in Sweden, and in Japan.

You'll meet the people in our diverse group of marketers in every chapter of this book. At the beginning of each chapter we'll introduce you to one of these professionals in a special box called "Real People, Real Choices." In the middle of the chapter we'll tell you about a specific marketing-related decision he or she had to make and share with you the possible alternatives. That way, you'll be able to form your *own* opinion about which choice might be the best. Finally, we'll let you in on what alternative was actually selected—and whether or not the decision was a good one. As you get to know each person and something about what they do, we hope you'll come to understand that all of these very different and talented people have something important in common—they are all doing it to satisfy needs!

ℛEAL PEOPLE, REAL CHOICES:

HOW IT WORKED OUT AT LEVI STRAUSS

Mr. Goldstein chose option 3. Levi's introduced "Loose Fitting Jeans" and gave them the numbers 550 and 560. The advertising created to support the new models featured slightly older people than those shown in the typical 501 spots and carefully positioned the line as a "loose interpretation of the original" so that it did not erode or conflict with the 501 image.

Levi Strauss is now the number one marketer of loose-fitting jeans in the United States, and Mr. Goldstein's strategy illustrates how a marketer can create pants (or any other product) that "fit" the needs of several different customer groups—even when their waistlines bulge a little too much for traditional 501s! The positive imagery backing up the Levi's name is strong enough to support a whole wardrobe of clothes, and by continuing to modify its strategy and listen to its customers the company is able to hold on to them, by the seat of the pants, for life.

Chapter 1 Summary

Objective 1. Explain what marketing is all about and describe the marketing mix.

Marketing is the process of planning and executing the conception, pricing, promotion, and distribution of ideas, goods, and services to create exchanges that satisfy individual and organizational objectives. Organizations that seek to ensure their long-term profitability by identifying and satisfying customers' needs and wants have adopted the marketing concept. Today the societal marketing concept is being adopted by many firms that try to satisfy customers in a way that is also beneficial to society as a whole. Marketing activities are important to firms that provide goods and services to individual and business consumers, as well as not-for-profit organizations and those involved in the marketing of sports, entertainment, places, people, and ideas.

The marketing mix includes four tools used to create the desired response from consumer and business markets. First, the product is what is being offered to satisfy customer needs. The price is the assigned value or amount to be exchanged for the offering. The place or channel of distribution gets the product to the customer. Promotion involves efforts to inform and persuade customers to choose the offering. Marketers design the marketing mix so that consumers and business customers will seek to exchange or trade money or something else of value for the product.

Objective 2. Describe how marketers develop strategies for finding and reaching a market.

The strategic process of marketing planning begins with an assessment of factors within the organization and in the external environment that will help or hinder the development and marketing of products. Based on this analysis, marketing objectives are set and strategies are developed. Many firms use a target marketing strategy in which the overall market is divided into segments and the most attractive is targeted. Then the marketing mix is strategically designed to gain a competitive position in the target market.

Objective 3. Explain the evolution of the marketing concept.

Early in this century, companies followed a production orientation in which they focused on the most efficient ways to produce and distribute products. Beginning in the 1930s some firms adopted a sales orientation that encouraged salespeople to push products aggressively on customers. In the 1950s organizations began to adopt a consumer orientation that focused on customer satisfaction and that led to the widespread adoption of the marketing concept. Today many firms are moving toward a New Era orientation that includes not only a commitment to quality but also concern for both economic and social profit. Outgrowths of this orientation are relationship marketing, which focuses on building long-term relationships with customers, social marketing, which advocates social changes and promotes worthy causes, and environmental stewardship, which emphasizes marketing practices that benefit society's long-term interests.

Objective 4. Explain why the marketing system is important to individual and business customers in the marketplace, in our daily lives, and in society.

Marketing creates several kinds of utility—that is, the usefulness or benefit provided by a product. By transforming raw materials into desirable products, marketing provides form utility. Place and time utility mean that products are available when and where customers want them. Possession utility means that customers are able to own, use, and enjoy products obtained in the exchange process. Marketing systems facilitate this process by making it easier for buyers and sellers to come together. Information systems are used to collect and analyze data that help the firm find, reach, and satisfy customers, while communication systems provide the means for informing, persuading, and influencing consumers.

Marketing also influences the popular culture—movies, sports, music, and so on—that people in a society want and like, while the products in the marketplace are expressions of that culture and people's ideals. Marketing messages from companies like McDonald's, Betty Crocker, and Ivory Snow either create or provide images of cultural myths. Despite the fact that many companies are stressing ethics and social responsibility, the acts of a few have caused marketing to be criticized as untrustworthy and harmful to society. In particular, marketing is accused of creating artificial needs, teaching people to value things too much, and promising miracles.

Objective 5. Explain marketing's role within an organization.

The importance of the role of marketing within an organization depends on whether the organization has adopted the marketing concept. Some firms may see marketing as a sales or advertising function, while firms that focus on total quality are likely to integrate the marketing concept into all business functions. Marketing decisions cannot be made in isolation from an organization's other operations, so that marketing, finance, manufacturing, research and development, and other functional areas must work together to achieve the organization's goals. A firm's brands, product lines, and corporate structure affect the way in which it does marketing planning.

Review Questions

Marketing Concepts: Testing Your Knowledge

1. Briefly, tell what marketing is.
2. What is the marketing concept? How is it different from the societal marketing concept?
3. What are the elements of the marketing mix?
4. What are target markets? How do marketers select and reach target markets?
5. Trace the evolution of the marketing concept.
6. What is utility? How does marketing create different forms of utility?
7. How does marketing facilitate exchange?
8. How is marketing related to popular culture?
9. What are some of the criticisms of marketing?
10. What is the role of marketing within the organization?

Marketing Concepts: Discussing Choices and Issues

1. The marketing concept focuses on the ability of marketing to satisfy customer needs. As a typical college student, how does marketing satisfy your needs? What areas of your life are affected by marketing? What areas of your life (if any) are not affected by marketing?
2. Do you think students should study marketing even if they are not planning a career in marketing or business? Explain your reasoning.
3. In this chapter a number of criticisms of marketing were discussed. Have you heard these criticisms? What other criticisms of marketing have you heard? Do you agree or disagree with these criticisms and why?

Marketing Practice: Applying What You've Learned

1. An old friend of yours has been making and selling leather handbags and book bags to acquaintances and friends of friends for some time and is now thinking about opening a shop in your small college town. But he is worried about whether he'll have enough customers who want hand-crafted bags to keep a business going. Knowing that you are a marketing student, he's asked you for some advice. What can you tell him about product, price, promotion, and distribution strategies that will help him get his business off the ground?
2. Assume you are employed by your city's Chamber of Commerce. One major focus of the chamber is to get industries to move to your city. As a former marketing student, you know that marketing cities to attract businesses involves the same kind of planning and strategies used to market any other product to potential customers. Next week you have an opportunity to speak to the members of the chamber, and your topic will be "Marketing a City." Develop an outline for that presentation.
3. As a marketing professional, you have been asked to write a short piece for a local business newsletter about the state of

marketing today. You think the best way to address this topic is to review how the marketing concept has evolved and to discuss the New Era orientation of marketing. Write the short article you will submit to the editor of the newsletter.

4. As college students, you and your friends sometimes discuss the various courses you are taking. One of your friends says to you, "Marketing's nothing but selling stuff. Anybody can do that without taking a course." Another friend says, "Yeah, all marketers do is write stupid ads." As a role-playing exercise, present your arguments against these statements to your class.

Marketing Mini-Project: Learning by Doing

The purpose of this mini-project is to develop an understanding of the importance of marketing to different organizations.

1. Working as a team with two or three other students in your class, select an organization in your community that practices marketing. It may be a manufacturer, a service provider, a retailer, a not-for-profit organization—almost any organization will do. Then schedule a visit with someone in the organization who is involved in the marketing activities. Ask for an amount of time in which the person can give your group a tour of the facilities and explain the organization's marketing activities.
2. Divide the following list of topics among your team, and ask each person to be responsible for developing a set of questions to ask during the interview to learn about the company's marketing program:
   - What customer segments the company targets
   - How it determines customer needs and wants
   - What products it offers, including features, benefits, and goals for customer satisfaction
   - What its pricing strategies are, including any discounting policies it has
   - What promotional strategies it uses and what these emphasize to position the product(s)
   - How it distributes products and whether it has encountered any problems
   - How marketing planning is done and who does it
   - Whether social responsibility is part of the marketing program and if so, in what ways
3. Develop a team report on your findings. In each section of the report, share what you learned that is new or surprising to you compared to what you expected.
4. Develop a team presentation for your class that summarizes your findings. Conclude your presentation with comments on what your team believes the company was doing that was particularly good and what was not quite so good.

Key Terms

Endnotes

1. "AMA Board Approves New Definition," *Marketing News* (March 1, 1985): 1.

2. Michael R. Solomon, "Deep-Seated Materialism: The Case of Levi's 501 Jeans," *Advances in Consumer Research* (1986): 619–622.

3. Peter F. Drucker, *Management: Tasks, Responsibilities, Practices* (New York: Harper & Row, 1972).

4. Mark D. Fefer, "Calling All Liberals," *Fortune* (Autumn/Winter 1993): 28.

5. Marian Courtney, "A Company with a Social Conscience," *The New York Times* (March 6, 1994): 1.

6. M. Luqmani, G. Habib, and S. Kassem, "Marketing to LDC Governments," *International Business Review* (Spring 1988): 56–67.

7. Patricia Sellers, "They Understand Your Kids," *Fortune* (Autumn/Winter 1993): 29–30.

8. Lee D. Dahringer, "Marketing Services Internationally: Barriers and Management Strategies," *J. Serv. Marketing* (Summer 1991): 5–17.

9. Faye Rice, "The New Rules of Superlative Service," *Fortune* (Autumn/Winter 1993): 50.

10. Sarah Lubman, "A 'Student of Value' Means a Student Who Can Pay the Rising Cost of College," *The Wall Street Journal* (Jan. 5, 1994): B1.

11. Randall Lane, "Prepackaged Celebrity," *Forbes* (Dec. 20, 1993): 86.

12. John Leland, "The Big Hunk of Country," *Newsweek* (June 22, 1992): 53.

13. Irving J. Rein, Philip Kotler, and Martin R. Stoller, *High Visibility.* (New York: Dodd Mead & Company, 1987).

14. John W. Schouten, "Selves in Transition: Symbolic Consumption in Personal Rites of Passage and Identity Reconstruction," *Journal of Consumer Research* (March 1991): 412–425; Michael R. Solomon, "The Wardrobe Consultant: Exploring the Role of a New Retailing Partner," *Journal of Retailing* (Summer 1987): 110–128; Michael R. Solomon and Susan P. Douglas, "Diversity in Product Symbolism: The Case of Female Executive Clothing," *Psychology & Marketing* (Fall 1987): 189–212; Joseph Z. Wisenblit, "Person Positioning: Empirical Evidence and a New Paradigm," *Journal of Professional Services Marketing* (1989): 51–82.

15. Edwin McDowell, "States Turn Entrepreneurial to Augment Tourism Funds," *The New York Times* (May 18, 1993): D1.

16. Bill Saporito, "Behind the Tumult at P&G," *Fortune* (March 7, 1994): 74.

17. Rein Rijkens, *European Advertising Strategies* (London: Cassell, 1992).

18. Susan Caminiti, "Her Own Best Customer," *Fortune* (Autumn/Winter 1993): 22.

19. Rein Rijkens, *European Advertising Strategies* (London: Cassell, 1992).

20. Fred Pfaff, "Levi's Dockers Weigh Into Casuals," *Adweek's Marketing Week* (Sept. 24, 1990): 26.

21. Rahul Jacob, "How to Retread Customers," *Fortune* (Autumn/Winter 1993): 23–24.

22. Stephen Phillips and Amy Dunkin, "King Customer," *Business Week* (March 12, 1990): 88–94.

23. James Bennet, "A Way for Car Dealers to Squeeze Out the Lemons," *The New York Times* (March 6, 1994): F11.

24. Wilma Randle, "ATMs Open to Blind at Citibank," *Chicago Tribune* (Oct. 19, 1992): 1.

25. Rockwell International, *Annual Report* (1992).

26. Mark D. Fefer, "Calling All Liberals," *Fortune* (Autumn/Winter 1993): 28.

27. Marlise Simons, "Gold in Streets (Some Call It Trash)," *The New York Times* (Jan. 4, 1994): A4.

28. Richard Normann and Rafael Ramirez, "From Value Chain to Value Constellation: Designing Interactive Strategy," *Harvard Business Review* (July–Aug. 1993): 65–70.

29. Gilbert Fuchsberg, "Gurus of Quality are Gaining Clout," *WSJ* (1990).

30. Janet Bamford, "After Careful Re-Tailoring, VF Is Looking Smart," *Business Week* (June 22, 1992): 66, 68.

31. Bill Saporito, "Behind the Tumult at P&G," *Fortune* (March 7, 1994): 74.

32. "Images," *Ad Age* (Feb. 14, 1994): 5.

33. Conrad Philip Kottak, "Anthropological Analysis of Mass Enculturation," *Researching American Culture* (Ann Arbor, MI: University of Michigan Press 1982); Joseph Campbell, *Myths, Dreams, and Religion* (New York: EP Dutton, 1970).

34. Sal Randazzo, "Advertising as Myth-Maker; Brands as Gods and Heroes," *Ad Age* (Nov. 8, 1993): 32.

35. "Dear Chrysler: Outsiders' Advice on Handling the Odometer Charge," *The Wall Street Journal* (June 26, 1987): 19.

36. Larry Edwards, "The Decision Was Easy," *Advertising Age* (Aug. 26, 1987): 106. For research and discussion related to public policy issues, see Paul N. Bloom and Stephen A. Greyser, "The Maturing of Consumerism," *Harvard Business Review* (Nov.–Dec. 1981): 130–139; George S. Day, "Assessing the Effect of Information Disclosure Requirements," *Journal of Marketing* (April 1976): 42–52; Dennis E. Garrett,

"The Effectiveness of Marketing Policy Boycotts: Environmental Opposition to Marketing," *Journal of Marketing* (Jan. 1987): 44–53; Michael Houston and Michael Rothschild, "Policy-Related Experiments on Information Provision: A Normative Model and Explication," *Journal of Marketing Research* (Nov. 1980): 432–449; Jacob Jacoby, Wayne D. Hoyer, and David A. Sheluga, *Misperception of Televised Communications* (New York: American Association of Advertising Agencies, 1980); Gene R. Lacznizk and Patrick E. Murphy, *Marketing Ethics: Guidelines for Managers* (Lexington, MA: Lexington Books, 1985): Lynn Phillips and Bobby Calder, "Evaluating Consumer Protection Laws: Promising Methods," *Journal of Consumer Affairs* (Summer 1980): 9–36; Donald P. Robin and Eric Reidenbach, "Social Responsibility, Ethics, and Marketing Strategy: Closing the Gap Between Concept and Application," *Journal of Marketing* (Jan. 1987): 44–58; Howard Schutz and Marianne Casey, "Consumer Perceptions of Advertising as Misleading," *Journal of Consumer Affairs* (Winter 1981): 340–357; Darlene Brannigan Smith and Paul N. Bloom, "Is Consumerism Dead or Alive? Some New Evidence," *Advances in Consumer Research* (1984): 369–373.

37. William Leiss, Stephen Kline, and Sut Jhally, *Social Communication in Advertising: Persons, Products, & Images of Well-Being* (Toronto: Methuen, 1986); Jerry Mander, *Four Arguments for the Elimination of Television* (New York: William Morrow, 1977).

38. Raymond Williams, "Advertising: The Magic System," *Problems in Materialism and Culture* (London: New Left Books, 1962).

39. George Stigler, "The Economics of Information," *Journal of Political Economy* (1961): 69.

40. Quoted in William Leiss, Stephen Kline and Sut Jhally, *Social Communication in Advertising: Persons, Products, & Images of Well-Being* (Toronto: Methuen, 1986).

41. "Cabbage-Hatched Plot Sucks in 24 Doll Fans," *The New York Daily News* (Dec. 1, 1983).

42. Linda Grant, "Mattel Gets All Dolled Up," *U.S. News & World Report* (Dec. 13, 1993): 72.

MARKETING IN ACTION: REAL PEOPLE AT SAM & LIBBY'S

Sam & Libby Inc. is a $100 million shoe and apparel company located in San Carlos, California, owned by Sam and Libby Edelman. When the couple met in 1978, Libby was fashion editor of *Seventeen* magazine, and Sam was vice president of sales for Lighthouse Footwear. When asked how they went on to build their business from scratch, Sam responded, "It began with a vision, followed by a quality product made with integrity, and finally the establishment of an efficient distribution system." In other words, the million-dollar word that would turn their idea into a successful business was "marketing."

Success for the Edelmans is not a fairy tale—it's the result of careful planning combined with lots of marketing savvy and hard work. In 1987 the Edelmans began planning their company, including devising a business strategy that outlined their objectives. As Sam said, "Our goal was to build a diversified fashion product marketing company." Their vision was "to be world leaders in translating social trends into lifestyle products." More importantly, the Edelmans believed in their plan, and today Sam and Libby look like the perfect American couple in a 1990s-style TV sitcom: young, attractive, trendy, and owners of an incredibly successful business.

The Edelmans believed in their vision and set about creating an image for their company and its products that they knew customers would strive for—the "thirty-something ideal." They thought about busy cosmopolitan professionals who want it all: wealth, satisfaction, happiness, and fun—and guess whom they based that image on? Libby recalls, "First, we defined our customer, then we decided *we* would be the image of the company." The foundation of Sam and Libby's marketing plan was "to package themselves as real, involved people who care about what's important in life."

Next came the product decision. The Edelmans know that a great marketing plan is nothing without a great product. As Libby says, "If the product doesn't work, everything else fails." So they created products that symbolized themselves, products with a personality. Sam & Libby's flagship product is an inexpensive ballet-slipper-style women's shoe. As Libby explains, "The shoes are designed for real people, women who are on the run from sunup to sundown and beyond." Women's shoes were followed up by the introduction of children's shoes in 1990, men's shoes in 1991, and junior casual and weekend apparel in 1992. Sam and Libby now have 140 employees, including more than ten designers who work with them to create about thirty new shoe styles each season.

Combining a great product with a clever marketing plan has been successful for Sam and Libby in "billboard-size letters." But pricing has also played a big role in their success. The average retail price for a pair of Sam & Libby's shoes is $40, and the apparel lines sell for an average price of $38 per item. To keep prices down, their shoes are produced in Brazil, Taiwan, and China. Clothing is manufactured in Hong Kong, Turkey, India, and the United States. As Frank Doroff, Bloomingdale's department stores' executive vice president observes, "They offer great fashion at incredible prices. That's an ideal combination."

Sam handles the company's marketing, financial, and business strategies. The fashion, advertising, and public relations end of the business is Libby's responsibility. She travels the country making personal appearances and meeting with retailers and customers, showing them there really is a Libby behind the Sam & Libby brand.

Sam and Libby's products are distributed in over 2,000 department stores nationwide. In addition, in 1992 Sam and Libby decided to deal directly with their customers by opening their first retail shoe store in Beverly Hills, California. The retail venture was planned very carefully. As Sam said, "We watched Banana Republic and The Gap very closely. We reasoned that nobody was doing in footwear what they were doing in apparel."

What is next for Sam and Libby? They are contemplating fashions for a new generation of buyers. As Libby says, "We intend to market our product to the whole family—teenagers to fifty-plus buyers." Never content to rest on their laurels, the Edelmans are looking at getting into children's clothing plus several licensing opportunities where manufacturers would buy the right to put their names on what they make and sell. And to think it all started from a simple ballet shoe.

Source: Adapted from "A Perfect Pair," *Entrepreneur* (Oct. 1992) 144–149.

Things to Talk About

1. What consumer needs and wants are satisfied by Sam & Libby products?

2. What are Sam & Libby's targeting and positioning strategies?

3. How have Sam & Libby developed the elements of the marketing mix?

4. Do the Edelmans have a customer orientation in their business?

5. What secrets to success have Sam and Libby discovered?

MARKETING IN ACTION:
REAL CHOICES AT THE U.S. POSTAL SERVICE

For years, the U.S. Post Office had been criticized for its bloated and inefficient bureaucracy. Stories abound about letters that were mailed years ago finally showing up in someone's box. Although mail carriers pride themselves on their ability to deliver on time in rain, sleet, or snow, a lot of customers have trouble believing this claim. Indeed, surfers on the Internet commonly refer to letters routed through the Post Office as "snail mail!"

The recognition that changes are needed to stay afloat is hardly new. As far back as 1971, the Postal Service was reorganized in an attempt to improve its service quality. The organization was removed from government control and began operating more like a business. But even with these changes, postal officials were hampered by a lack of resources to compete with Federal Express, UPS, and other private mail and package carriers that often meet people's needs faster, cheaper, and more conveniently.

The Postal Service still operates under government price regulations, and rate changes must be requested and approved by the Postal Rate Commission, a process that involves public hearings and can take up to fourteen months. By that time, let alone the time required to generate revenues from a rate hike, the Postal Service has lost another batch of customers to the competitors. And, as its customer base shrinks, so do the overall revenues needed to support the sprawling, still-bureaucratic structure of the organization.

Clearly, the Postal Service has been caught between a rock and a hard place and faced with limited choices to solve its dilemma. Postal officials could continue to seek small rate hikes just to keep the "business" operating, or it could look for alternative ways to increase revenues—say, by giving the Service a healthy dose of marketing.

Today, the Post Office is fighting back with a variety of marketing activities intended to keep its doors open and plenty of mail flowing through them. One new marketing program is a service for medium and small commercial clients. These smaller customers had, in the past, been ignored in favor of the big corporations that account for a lot of postal activity. In 1993 the Post Office introduced fifty business centers where small- and medium-volume mailers could learn how to improve the cost and efficiency of delivering their outgoing and incoming mail through the Post Office. Encouraged by the initial success of these business centers, the Post Office has plans to add eighty to 100 more of these facilities.

The Postal Service is taking a different approach in its attempts to persuade consumers to send more letters: Instead of designing and selling stodgy stamps featuring the faces of largely unknown dead people that interest only the most hard-core stamp collectors, stamps are now featuring people and subjects that appeal to large numbers of consumers. In 1994, for example, the Postal Service parted with tradition and introduced an Elvis Presley stamp. In developing the stamp, the Postal Service even asked citizens to vote for which Elvis—a young or an older Elvis—should be depicted. Over 800,000 consumers voted (the younger version won) and in the process supplied the Postal Service with their names and addresses so they could receive brochures offering collector stamp packages priced from $5.95 to $19.95. And before the stamp was introduced for sale on January 8 (Martin Luther King's birthday), the Post Office had already taken over 100,000 phone and mail orders for the stamps. Working jointly with the Presley estate, the Postal Service has also licensed more than 100 products, everything from T-shirts to blankets with the Elvis stamp on them, that are being sold at retail outlets.

Revenue from the Presley program, which is expected to reach $20 million, is impressive, but is only a small fraction of the Postal Service's total revenue needs of $43 billion. However, there's a fringe benefit for the Postal Service: If the Elvis fans don't want to part with their Elvis stamps by actually licking them and sticking them on envelopes, the Postal Service gets to keep $20 million even though it doesn't actually have to deliver these letters!

Inspired by this success, the Postal Service plans to develop other "music series" stamps featuring country artists such as Hank Williams and Patsy Cline, rock stars like Buddy Holly and Bill Haley, and the Broadway musicals *Show Boat, Porgy and Bess, Oklahoma,* and *My Fair Lady.* In addition, the Postal Service is aggressively advertising on TV and radio, focusing on priority mail and express mail for special occasions and holiday periods. Other ads promote the Postal Service's toll-free number for ordering stamps by mail, and many Post Office branches are beginning to look like retail outlets for labels, packaging supplies, specialized mailing containers, and even printed gift boxes that are billed as "prewrapped" and ready for easy mailing.

Not everyone is thrilled by these promotional activities. Critics have raised questions about whether the Postal Service is spending its money in the best way possible. In response to such criticism, Marty Roberts of the Postal

Service's marketing communications department has said, "If advertising or marketing helps a person make a decision on how to mail better, it's a good thing."

Source: Adapted from "U.S. Postal Service Discovers the Merits of Marketing," *Marketing News* (Feb. 1, 1993) 9, 18.

Things to Think About

1. Why did the Postal Service decide to develop a marketing program?

2. How has the Postal Service applied the marketing concept to its operations?

3. What consumer markets are being targeted by the Postal Service's marketing activities?

4. How is the Postal Service trying to attract and satisfy these consumers?

5. What are some ways the Postal Service might respond to the criticisms about its marketing activities?

2

Strategic Planning: Making Choices in a Dynamic Environment

When you have completed your study of this chapter, you should be able to:

1. Describe the strategic planning process and explain how strategic decisions are made.

2. Tell how firms gain a competitive advantage and describe the factors that influence marketing objectives.

3. Discuss the role of marketing strategies in planning and development of the marketing plan.

4. Explain the factors involved in the implementation and control of the marketing plan.

REAL PEOPLE, REAL CHOICES:

MEET FRANK CIMERMANCIC, HARLEY-DAVIDSON, INC.

Other motorcycle marketers scatter when Frank Cimermancic roars into town. As director of business planning for Harley-Davidson, Mr. Cimermancic's job is to understand the desires of hard-core bikers, weekend bikers, and biker wannabees. At first blush his job seems easy. The company is the industry leader in the big-bike product category, and every day more "regular" people join the ranks of the hard-core riders who pride themselves on living on the edge. New riders, some known as "RUBs" (rich urban bikers), join HOGs (Harley Owners' Groups) in droves, and numerous magazines sell belt buckles, leather jackets, and other Harley-Davidson paraphernalia to the adoring masses. In 1994 the company reported record attendance at HOG rallies in the United States, as well as at events in the Czech Republic, Germany, England, France, Norway, Canada, New Zealand, and Australia.[1]

How did Mr. Cimermancic wind up in a marketing leadership position at America's largest and most famous motorcycle company? On graduation from Marquette University in 1973, he decided against an accounting career after discovering that he preferred to work in a field like marketing that permitted a bit more creativity. He found that his earlier studies in biology gave him the statistical skills needed for marketing research, which is where he began his career. Mr. Cimermancic went to work for Harley in 1979, beginning as a business planning analyst and becoming a business planning manager. In 1989 he became director of business planning. In this capacity he must constantly peer down the highway, trying to determine what the road will look like in the future, and tailor Harley's strategy to stay in the lead in the race for market success.

PLAN WELL AND PROSPER

All firms operate in a dynamic environment where, among other factors, consumer interests, new technologies, the competition, and the economy are continuously changing. Whether a firm is a major motorcycle manufacturer or a tiny, family-run motorcycle repair shop, planning for the future is the key to prosperity. While it's true that some "seat-of-the-pants" businesses, where no planning is ever done, are very successful, most don't do as well as they could. Others get left out of the race altogether because they failed to plan ways to take advantage of opportunities and ward off threats.

Planning helps a firm control its destiny. For example, in the early 1980s Harley-Davidson was about to ride off into the sunset, close to bankruptcy. Declining interest in motorcycles had shrunk industry sales, the economy was entering a period of recession, and Harley's reputation for poor quality and sluggish service didn't help attract the few customers still willing and able to buy. Through strategic planning, however, Harley lived to see another day—and to see its bikes rev up and take off.

Of course, strategic planning isn't limited to helping a firm find ways to overcome crises; it's an ongoing process that keeps the company ahead of the pack. By 1993 Harley had overcome its quality and service problems and had made a dramatic comeback. The previous year it had $1.2 billion in sales and $74 million in profits. Over 250,000 customers were proud to belong to the Harley Owners' Group. Overseas sales were growing, and United States sales were so brisk that keeping up with demand seemed to be Harley's greatest challenge. But Harley's management knew the real challenge in its now-friendly business environment was strategically planning how to *keep on* growing and prospering.

Strategic planning starts at the very top of the organization, where the firm's executive officers define what the organization is all about and what it wants to achieve. The planning process is then carried forward by lower-level managers in all functional areas of the firm, who develop specific strategies and action plans that will fulfill top management's vision. In this chapter we'll look at the planning tools that help top managers make the decisions that guide the business. We'll also examine the stages in the marketing planning process that lead to the development and implementation of a marketing plan.

STRATEGIC PLANNING: GUIDING THE BUSINESS

In successful firms, *planning* is an ongoing process of anticipating the future and making decisions that guide the business in both the short and long runs. A firm's planning decisions take into account its current situation and its future destination. Planning identifies and builds on a firm's strength, and it helps managers at all levels make informed decisions in the face of changes in the marketing environment. In large firms like IBM, Sony, and Kodak that operate in many markets, planning is a complex process involving many people, each of whom plays a specific role in keeping the business going. At a small business like Mac's Diner, however, planning is quite different; Mac himself is chief cook, occasional dishwasher, and sole company planner.

This section focuses on mid- to large-size firms where planning occurs at three levels within the organization. The process begins with top managers who develop plans that map the big picture of the firm's future. At lower levels in the organization, middle managers and supervisors animate this image by focusing on the strategies and plans that will turn it into reality. These three planning levels are depicted in Figure 2.1 (page 42).

Strategic planning is the managerial decision process that matches the organization's resources and capabilities to its market opportunities for long-term growth and survival. It involves decisions that focus on the firm's ability to respond to changes, and on the resources the firm has or is willing to acquire to take advantage of anticipated opportunities. In developing a strategic plan, top management defines the firm's purpose (its business mission) and what it hopes to achieve (its primary goals and objectives). In large firms planning at this level also determines how the business will be organized (its business and product portfolio) and what major marketing strategies will be used (its marketing direction).

As illustrated in Figure 2.1, the planning decisions made at each level in the firm are interrelated. Top management's strategic decisions influence the choices made by lower-level managers who, in turn, take steps to support the strategic plan. **Tactical planning,** done by middle managers, concentrates on the specific strategies and tactics for the short term that support the firm's long-term strategic plan. Typically, tactical planning includes a five-year plan and a detailed annual plan for the coming year. Still further down the organizational ladder, supervisory managers are responsible for **operational planning,** which focuses on the details of day-to-day activities that execute the tactical plans. Planning at this level outlines the coming year's activities and includes detailed quarterly or semiannual plans.

For example, if a corporate goal for growth is to reach customers the company does not currently serve, the marketing director, a middle manager, is responsible for setting marketing objectives and developing tactical plans to target and reach this market segment. Supervisory managers, such as sales, advertising, and distribution managers, are responsible for planning the specific activities that turn the tactical marketing plan into reality.

The firm's overall strategic plan unifies the planning decisions made at each level of the marketing function and coordinates the planning efforts of managers in other functional areas in the firm, such as finance, manufacturing, R&D (research and development), and human development. Managers in these functional areas develop their own

strategic planning: a managerial decision process that matches an organization's resources and capabilities to its market opportunities for long-term growth and survival

tactical planning: a decision process that concentrates on developing detailed plans for strategies and tactics for the short term that support an organization's long-term strategic plan

operational planning: a decision process that focuses on developing detailed plans for day-to-day activities that carry out an organization's tactical plans

tactical and operational plans that are also consistent with the overall plan, so that (ideally) all employees in the firm are involved in a cooperative effort to achieve the firm's strategic goals and objectives. In large corporations that have separate brand, product line, or business divisions, individual strategic plans that guide the division in fulfilling its role in the overall corporate plan are developed by the managers of each. The divisional plans are coordinated at the corporate level by the organization's executive officers, so that the entire organization is moving in the same direction.

The strategic plan developed by top management usually focuses on the long-term horizon—ten years or so into the future—but the process also includes annual planning to review the long-term strategic plan and to set the firm's total budget and profitability goals for the year. In this section we'll take a closer look at the four key stages in top-level strategic planning and at the planning tools management uses to decide how to organize the business and set its marketing direction.

DEFINING THE FIRM'S BUSINESS MISSION

In the first stage of strategic planning, a firm's top executives define its *business mission.* Top management's vision of why the firm exists and how it will differ from other firms is a strategic decision that influences all other planning efforts in the organization. It identifies the firm's long-term commitment to the type of business it is in and the place in the market it wants to take.

Decision making in this strategic planning stage revolves around such questions as: What business are we in? What customers should we serve? What kinds of products and benefits can we create for them? How should we develop the firm's capabilities and focus its efforts? In many firms the answers to questions like these become the lead items in the organization's strategic plan. They become part of a **mission statement** that describes the organization's overall purpose and what it hopes to achieve in terms of its customers, products, and resources. This "big picture" perspective is catching on—more than 50 percent of all big companies were reported to have mission statements in 1994, double the number five years earlier.[2]

The mission statement defines the scope of the firm's activities and identifies its strategic focus. For example, AT&T sees itself as being in the *communications business*—a mission based on satisfying customer needs in various ways—not in the *telephone business,* which is a narrowly defined product-oriented mission that limits the goods and services it offers to customers. Product-oriented missions tend to be based on existing products and technologies that restrict a firm's opportunities as they become outdated, while a consumer-oriented mission allows a firm to seek new ways to satisfy needs.

mission statement: a formal statement in an organization's strategic plan that describes the overall purpose of the organization and what it intends to achieve in terms of its customers, products, and resources

A well-conceived mission statement spells out the organization's scope and focus and sets the direction for everyone's efforts. If the mission statement emphasizes the firm's intention to provide the highest quality possible, for example, everyone in the organization, from the chief production officer to the newest shipping clerk, shares this focus. Employees in all areas of the firm work independently at specific tasks and activities, but the collective emphasis of their individual efforts is established by the firm's business mission.

A statement of business mission usually covers four basic areas:[3]

- The group of individuals or firms—the *customer segment*—the firm will serve
- The nature of the *benefits* the firm will attempt to supply
- The *stage in the value-adding process* in which the firm will compete
- The *competencies* the firm will develop

The *customer segment* identified in the mission statement provides both focus and boundaries, or scope, for the organization insofar as the organization will devote itself to reaching and satisfying this carefully chosen group. Management's decision on how broadly or narrowly to define the segment depends on the organization's resources and management's belief in the likelihood that the organization will be successful in satisfying the segment's needs.

As we saw in Chapter 1, consumers can be grouped into specific market segments according to such characteristics as age, income, occupation, interests, and so on, but typically a customer segment identified in the mission statement may include one or more of these consumer groups who desire the same or similar product benefits despite other differences they may have. For example, Harley-Davidson's customer segment of big-bike riders includes both white- and blue-collar consumers in various age and income groups who happen to share a love for riding a "hog" on the open road.

The *benefits* the firm will attempt to supply, as described in the mission statement, also provide a focus and scope for the firm's activities. Consumers don't buy just products; they buy product benefits that satisfy needs. Specifying these benefits in the mission statement reminds everyone in the firm of what (they hope) the customer actually takes away from the purchase. For example, while many firms market toothpaste—a product that provides the basic function of cleaning teeth—Crest offers its customers the underlying benefit of cavity prevention. Aquafresh provides a breath freshener, and Rembrandt focuses on whitening teeth.

The *stage in the value-added process* in the mission statement refers to the chain of activities involved in designing, producing, marketing, delivering, and servicing of products. Value of some kind is added to a product in each of these stages, and management's decision is to identify the stages in which the firm can provide the greatest added value for its customers. Some firms determine that they are able to handle all or many stages in the total process, while others decide that they will be most successful if they specialize in only one stage. For example, Harley-Davidson knows that its strength lies in designing and manufacturing quality bikes, so it leaves the selling and merchandising to other firms who contract with it for the right to use the Harley name on clothing, belts, and even on trendy restaurants.

Manufacturing firms like Harley-Davidson tend to concentrate on the early stages in the value-added process as they convert raw materials and other inputs into finished consumer goods. Wholesale firms emphasize the value added by the delivery system, while retailers may focus on adding value in the form of pre- and postsale services, such as helping the customer to select the perfect pair of pants to go with that leather Harley jacket and altering them after they've been purchased. Business-to-business firms may emphasize their superior ability to process information or implement state-of-the-art technology, as when a consulting firm like Arthur Andersen, Price-Waterhouse, or Kurt Salmon handles such diverse functions as flowcharting production, accounting and payroll, or pensions and benefits for corporate clients.

The final element of a firm's mission statement, the *competencies* the firm will develop, refers to the skills or capabilities the organization will focus on. This management decision determines which technologies the firm will invest in and which skills or competencies it will seek to develop and employ. McDonald's, for example, owes much of its success (with billions of burgers sold around the world) to its competency in providing tasty low-cost food and fast service in clean facilities to large numbers of McCustomers at a time. Firms choose to develop different skills from those of their competitors to create better benefits for customers or to create greater value at lower costs. Large firms typically gain access to new technologies, as when Sony bought a game development firm called Psygnosis to help it develop more appealing, diverse products.[4]

Many organizations spend a year or more developing their first mission statement, only to evaluate and change it every year or two. The ideal mission statement has a long time horizon, and it cannot be too broad, too narrow, or too shortsighted. A mission that is too broad will not provide adequate focus for the organization (for example, it doesn't do much good simply to claim that "we are in the business of making high-quality products"), whereas one that is too narrow may inhibit managers' ability to visualize possible growth opportunities. The railroad industry provides a classic example of the plight of firms who narrowly define their business: The giant railroad companies might be prospering still if they had seen their mission as the transportation business instead of the railroad business and turned their interest to bus lines, trucking companies, or airlines.[5]

If an organization's mission is too shortsighted and inflexible the firm may not be able to adapt to environmental changes. For example, in the 1980s Kodak faced numerous life-threatening problems, including intense competition from Japanese film and camera companies. With the development of electronic cameras capable of storing images on CDs, a future of filmless photography came a giant step closer—an exciting possibility, but not the greatest news for a company that views itself as being in the film business! Abandoning its product-oriented mission of producing film for amateur photographers, the Kodak of the 1990s now says that it is in the imaging business—a consumer-oriented mission—with a focus on products that process and convert images on film or in the form of electronic data.[6] This broader view led to the development of successful new products for its core business and has allowed Kodak to venture beyond the photography business to related businesses such as electronic publishing, medical and graphics arts imaging, printing, and digital scanning.

SETTING CORPORATE GOALS AND OBJECTIVES

corporate goals: broadly defined outcomes an organization hopes to achieve within the time frame of its long-term strategic plan

In the second stage of the strategic planning process, top management translates the firm's business mission into the goals and objectives of the organization. **Corporate goals,** which are a direct outgrowth of the mission statement, broadly identify desired outcomes within the general time frame of the firm's long-range strategic business plan. For example, to turn around the hard times in the 1980s and ensure its future for the 1990s and beyond, Harley-Davidson's managers set goals calling for a new emphasis on quality, the redesign of its touring bikes, and investing in marketing to soften Harley's "Hell's Angel's" image and attract new customers.

Corporate goals include both business and marketing objectives that relate to such issues as earnings, cash flow, and use of the firm's resources, as well as its products, consumer markets, and customer satisfaction. *Corporate objectives* state the specific levels of business and marketing accomplishments that are to be achieved by the organization as a whole, usually stated in terms of profits and growth. For example, a firm might seek a 10 percent increase in profitability by increasing productivity, reducing costs, or divesting itself of an unprofitable division whose operations cost more than the division brings in. Similarly, a firm's specific growth objectives could be linked to developing new products, investing in new technologies, or entering new markets.

In 1990, for example, Campbell Soup was near the bottom of the food industry when David W. Johnson became president and CEO of the company. Johnson saw Campbell as a firm that had lost its direction and focus, and his first act was to develop a set of measurable business objectives that focused on growth. Measures undertaken included jettisoning business divisions that didn't fit in with Campbell's core products and large-scale restructuring of the company into divisions that unified and coordinated business activities. As a result, Campbell exceeded its growth goals in both 1991 and 1992 while launching 122 new products.[7] That's a lot of chicken soup.

If the corporate goals are long-term, the strategic plan will include objectives for interim time periods, such as one, three, or five years, to guide the firm as it moves toward its long-range vision. The firm's mission statement, the resources it has available, and top management's view of the marketing environment all are factors that influence the firm's goals and objectives as well as the time frame for achieving them. The strategic plan, however, does not specify *how* the desired outcomes will be reached. This task falls to lower-level managers who develop the tactical and operational plans—the "nuts and bolts" of the plan—for achieving corporate goals and objectives.

The short-term tactical plans developed by general and middle managers in all functional areas of the firm contain specific and measurable objectives that support the corporate goals and objectives. These objectives become the yardsticks of performance that measure how well the company is doing. Elyria Foundry, a small company that makes metal castings, involves everyone in the firm in the process of setting goals and objectives.[8] Employees suggest objectives to the manager, who suggests objectives to the CEO, who combines all of the objectives into a single list. To make the list, the objectives suggested by employees must be tied to one of the firm's overall goals, such as a commitment to customer service. The objectives must also be specific (for example, all calls answered on the second ring) and measurable (for example, 99 percent on-time delivery). At the end of the year the CEO convenes a meeting of the firm's employees, presents the results of last year's objectives, and summarizes the next year's list. This simple system has earned the CEO awards for his company's performance.

PLANNING FOR GROWTH: THE BUSINESS PORTFOLIO

Once management has defined a firm's business mission and determined its goals and objectives, the planning focus turns to how the business is organized. In this stage of the strategic planning process, top managers analyze the current organizational structure and evaluate strategies and opportunities for growth that are consistent with its mission and objectives. Management's decisions also are influenced by the firm's resources as well as by its short- and long-term profitability goals.

Portfolio Analysis: Strategic Business Units

In small companies that offer a single good or service, the firm's organization is simple. But many mid- to large-size firms, realizing that relying on only one product can be risky, have become multiproduct firms with self-contained divisions organized around products or brands. These **strategic business units** (SBUs) are individual units within the firm that operate like separate businesses, each having its own mission, business and marketing objectives, resources, managers, and competitors. As illustrated in Figure 2.2 (page 46), each SBU has its own strategic focus within the firm's overall strategic plan, and each has its own target market and strategies for reaching its goals. SBUs are usually formed around goods and services that share a similar production technology or customer base.

For example, Arthur Andersen & Co., a large accounting firm, has two operating units that are like separate businesses. The Arthur Andersen unit offers auditing, business advisory and corporate specialty services, and tax services. Andersen Consulting offers accounting software products, systems integration services, and related product lines to business customers who are also likely to be clients of the Arthur Andersen unit.

Harley-Davidson, Inc., is another example. Most people don't realize that motorcycles are not its only business; the company also owns the Holiday Rambler Corporation (which makes motor homes) and the Utilimaster Corporation (a subsidiary of Holiday Rambler that manufactures parcel delivery vans, truck bodies, and specialty vehicles). It's hard to confuse a "hog" with a squat delivery van, so naturally each division has to develop its own priorities and procedures.

Large corporations like Procter & Gamble have many divisions or SBUs that are organized by product lines or brands, including many that compete in the same markets. A firm like General Electric, a $60-billion giant, is in many different businesses: light bulbs, aircraft engines, medical equipment, financial services, high-performance plastics and ceramics, and more. These firms know that if one product or line of business fails or per-

strategic business units (SBUs): individual units within the firm that operate like separate businesses, each having its own mission, business and marketing objectives, resources, managers, and competitors

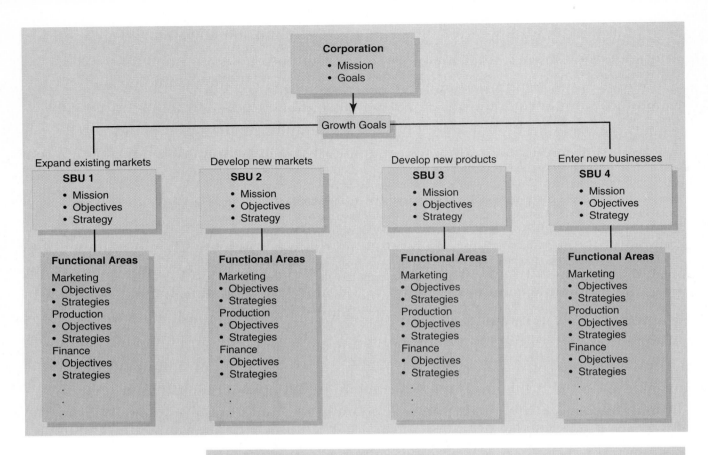

Figure 2.2
The Role of Strategic Business Units

forms poorly, another business unit can sustain the firm's economic health, and many of them hedge their bets even further by establishing international divisions to compete around the world.

Clearly, the task of planning and managing these diverse businesses by a small group of executives at corporate headquarters would be a complex and nearly impossible task. By establishing strategic business units, firms improve the planning process and make each piece of their business more manageable. Each SBU, responsible for its own costs and revenues, acts as a separate profit center within the larger organization. In other words, an SBU operates as a business within a business. It has a single general manager, who works like the larger firm's president or chief executive officer (CEO).

Developing several SBUs provides some important advantages to larger firms. First, SBUs place planners *closer to customers.* SBU managers can often better understand and respond to the needs of their particular customer segment(s) than can top corporate managers. SBUs tend to create a sense of *entrepreneurial spirit,* much like you find at a small business. Managers are more likely to feel a sense of ownership, to respond to opportunities more creatively, and to be willing to take risks. In addition, SBUs generally promote a *strong market focus* for strategic plans. This focus allows the business unit to be more responsive to its ever-changing marketing environment. Finally, SBUs *limit the scope* of managers' responsibilities by channeling their efforts to their units' specific products and markets. When managers focus on one customer segment or one product, chances for success are greater.

Just as the collection of different stocks an investor owns is called a portfolio, the different businesses or products owned by a larger firm is called its **business portfolio.** Having a diversified portfolio of businesses or products with different revenue-generating and revenue-using characteristics reduces the firm's dependence on one product or one group of customers. For example, giant petroleum firms once engaged in one line of business:

business portfolio: the group of different businesses, products, or brands owned by an organization and characterized by different income-generating and growth capabilities

finding, extracting, refining, and selling oil. When they were no longer willing to depend solely on the ups and downs of the petroleum market to determine their viability in the energy business, top managers decided to protect themselves from declines in petroleum sales by investing in a *portfolio* of energy-producing technologies, including those relying on coal, uranium, solar power, and wind.

Portfolio analysis, the process of evaluating a firm's business mix, is a management tool for assessing the potential of a firm's strategic business units. It helps management decide which of its current SBUs should receive more—or less—of the firm's resources and which new businesses or products are consistent with the firm's mission and overall goals and objectives. Four models that have been devised to assist management in this process are the growth-market share matrix developed by the Boston Consulting Group, the General Electric/McKinsey business grid, the product/market growth matrix, and Porter's Generic Strategy Model. These tools use criteria based on a business unit's marketing opportunity and business position relative to competing firms to suggest a strategy for portfolio development.

The Boston Consulting Group Matrix

The Boston Consulting Group (BCG) matrix provides a portfolio management strategy in which mature, market-leading products generate cash that is used for investment in new products. New products are chosen for their potential to become future cash generators.

In the BCG matrix, shown in Figure 2.3, the vertical axis represents the *market growth rate,* a measure of the market's attractiveness. The horizontal axis shows the firm's *relative market share*—that is, its sales relative to the nearest competitor's—which is an indicator of the company's current strength in the market. When both axes are combined, four quadrants representing four different types of SBUs are formed. Each quadrant of the BCG grid has a special meaning, indicated by a symbol.

- *Stars:* Like Hollywood celebrities, stars get all the firm's attention and huge investments. Stars are business units with a dominant market share in *high-growth* markets—a win-win situation. Because the SBU has a dominant share of the market, stars generate large revenues, but they also require large amounts of funding for increases in production capacity and for promotion. Because the market has large growth potential, competition is increasing, and marketing strategies are designed to maximize market share in the face of competition. The firm aims to get the largest share of loyal customers so that when market growth slows, the product will become a "cash cow" (read on).

- *Cash cows:* Cash cows are business units having a dominant market share in a *low-growth* potential market. Because the growth potential is low, new competitors are not encouraged to enter the market. At the same time, the SBU

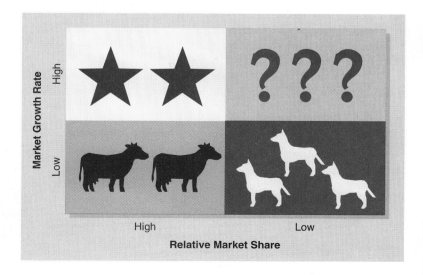

**Figure 2.3
BCG Growth–Market Share Matrix**

has a well-established product and a high market share that can be sustained with minimal funding. Firms usually "milk" cash cows of their profits to fund the growth of other products in a portfolio.

- *Question marks:* Question marks are business units with low market shares in *fast-growth* markets. When an SBU is a question mark, it suggests that the firm has failed to compete successfully. Something is wrong: Perhaps the product offers fewer benefits than competing products. Possibly the price is too high, the distributors are ineffective, or the advertising is too weak. One option the firm has is to pump in even more money and hope that market share will improve. But this decision can be risky, because the firm may find itself "throwing good money after bad," gaining nothing but a negative cash flow and disappointment.

- *Dogs:* By dog, BCG really means a mongrel, a business unit nobody wants. Dogs are business units with a small share of a *slow-growth* market. These SBUs are typically characterized by highly specialized products for very limited markets that are not likely to grow quickly, if at all, and the firm is sure to have difficulty making them profitable. Sometimes large firms sell off their dogs to smaller firms that may be able to nurture them.

Procter & Gamble (P&G), an American marketing giant, provides an interesting tale of a product portfolio strategy involving three brands of toilet paper: a cash cow and two dogs that went by the names of Charmin, White Cloud, and Banner. In 1993 the toilet paper market had become extremely competitive and as more and more new brands were introduced, customers became confused about which to choose. Additionally, consumers were beginning to lose interest in highly advertised premium-priced brands, preferring instead everyday low prices offered by generic store brands.

Both Charmin and White Cloud were quality-oriented brands, and both sold at a premium price. In the past P&G had spent $8.1 million to advertise Charmin, resulting in over $312 million in sales. Nearly $8 million was devoted to White Cloud, but this investment yielded sales of only $66 million. Unlike these two P&G offerings, Banner, at $3.6 million in sales, was a low-priced *value brand*—and not supported by much advertising. In the BCG grid Charmin was a cash cow—a "power brand" in industry parlance. White Cloud and Banner were dogs. Which one of the dogs should be sent to the dog pound? Despite its limited promotion and low-price position, Banner did make a profit, so P&G decided to keep it. White Cloud was renamed Charmin Ultra, which further strengthened the Charmin power brand while reducing P&G's overall use of resources.[9]

The GE/McKinsey Business Grid

The General Electric/McKinsey (GE/M) business-planning grid, shown in Figure 2.4, is another portfolio management strategy used by many firms. The GE/M grid provides a detailed assessment of the SBU based on industry attractiveness and company business strengths. This analytical tool measures a brand according to an *industry attractiveness index* that includes such factors as market size, market growth, economies of scale, competitors, and the stability of sales. A similar index of *business strength* is calculated using evaluations of the firm's image, market share, distribution effectiveness, promotion effectiveness, and innovativeness.[10]

The grid allows a firm to place its strategic business units into nine different categories based on high, medium, and low industry attractiveness and business strengths.

Figure 2.4
GE/McKinsey Business Grid

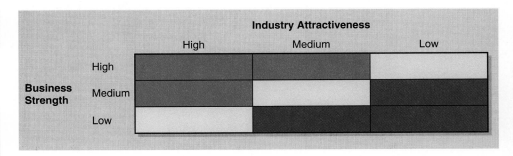

These categories are then analyzed like the colors used in traffic lights: SBUs in the green zone are strong units and provide attractive opportunities for firms to invest and grow. SBUs winding up in the yellow areas are medium in overall attractiveness, suggesting that the firm should maintain its current levels of investment. Strategic business units falling in the red areas of the grid are low in overall attractiveness. The firm might consider *harvesting* (taking profits until the business finally dies) or divesting these weak SBUs.

This portfolio strategy is illustrated by Coors, a major brewery. A few years ago managers decided that the Coors Light brand was highly attractive—a "green" on the grid—and worthy of further investment. The firm launched a new promotional scheme for Coors Light that involved the Colorado Silver Bullets, an all-female professional baseball team that drew large crowds playing against all-male, minor-league, and semipro opponents. By comparison, shrinking sales of original Coors made it only minimally attractive—a hanger-on loitering in the red zone—and the recipient of little promotional support, perhaps indicating a trial harvesting strategy.

At about this time Coors launched Zima, a clear drink termed "a sexy new product" by Coors' managers, but viewed as nothing more than a fad by Coors' competitors. Zima, a yellow, represents a middle-level industry-business opportunity, mostly because of its uncertain long-term prospects once the novelty of a clear beer beverage wears off.[11] Coors continued its efforts to expand this new product category it created. In 1995 the company launched Zima Gold, a stronger version of the original Zima brand.[12]

Product-Market Growth Matrix

Planning a firm's business portfolio also involves developing growth strategies for each of its business units that support the firm's overall growth objectives. Top management must decide which fundamental marketing direction(s) will provide the best growth opportunities for each SBU given its current marketing environment. This process focuses on the firm's product mix and determines whether the firm would be better off putting its resources into existing products or trying to grow by developing or acquiring new products. It also relies on an assessment of the growth potential of existing markets and new markets. Combining these options provide four different fundamental marketing strategies, as shown in the product-market growth matrix in Figure 2.5.

■ **Market penetration:** These strategies are designed to increase sales of existing products to current customers, nonusers, and users of competing brands in served markets. For example, a soup company can advertise new uses for soup in lunches and dinners, causing current customers to use and buy a larger quantity of soup and nonusers to see more reasons to begin buying. To capture a larger share of purchases in a served market, a company can cut prices, improve distribution convenience, and conduct promotions aimed at increasing consumption at the expense of competitors. Orange juice manufacturers

market penetration: growth strategies designed to increase sales of existing products to current customers, nonusers, and users of competitive brands in served markets

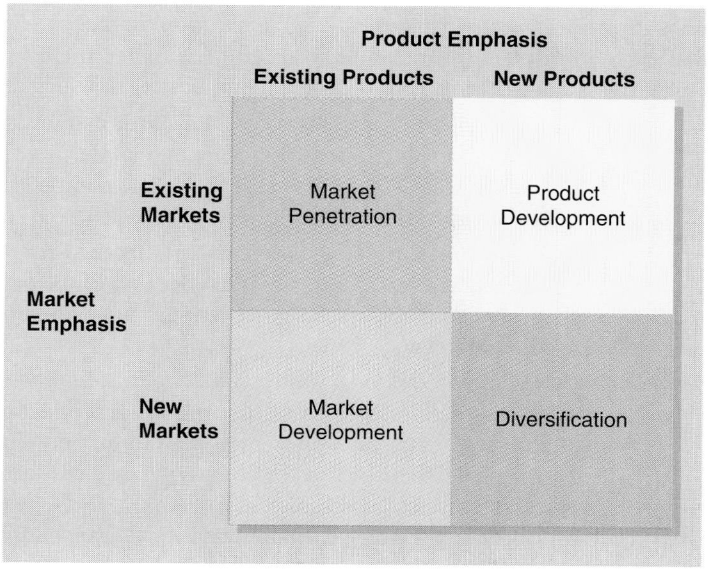

Figure 2.5
Product–Market Growth Matrix

Source: Adapted from Igor H. Ansoff, "Strategies for Diversification," *Harvard Business Review* (Sept.–Oct.) 113–124; Roger A. Kerin, Vijay Mahajan, P. Rajan Varadaarajan, *Strategic Market Planning* (Allyn and Bacon: Boston, 1990) 230.

have long sought to get users to increase their consumption by drinking OJ all day long. As the long-running ads proclaim, "It's not just for breakfast anymore!"

■ **Market development:** These strategies introduce existing products to new markets. This approach can mean reaching new customer segments within an existing geographic market, or it may mean expanding into new geographic areas. KFC, Pizza Hut, and Burger King (all owned by PepsiCo) have achieved growth through global expansion—by opening fast-food restaurants in many markets outside the United States. Business hotels see new markets when they advertise "weekend getaways" to nonbusiness travelers.

■ **Product development:** These strategies create growth by selling new products in existing markets. Product development may mean that the firm improves a product's performance, or it may mean extending the firm's product line. In recent years quality improvements have boosted sales at U.S. automakers Chrysler, Ford, and General Motors. McDonald's has begun a new chain of restaurants called Hearth Express serving home-style food—rotisserie chicken, twice-baked squash, baked beans, and fresh-baked bread.[13]

■ **Diversification:** These strategies emphasize both new products and new markets to achieve growth. The Mattel Corporation diversified its operations when it recently acquired the Fisher-Price toy company for $1.1 billion.[14] This move gives Mattel a new product line with distinct features and benefits for babies and very young children and opens a new market of baby brothers and sisters of Barbie owners. The Disney organization believes in diversification as it has moved over the years from cartoons and comics to theme parks and is now getting into cruises and movies for adults.

Many firms ultimately choose to rely on more than one fundamental marketing strategy to achieve growth. Harley, for example, was able to grow with a market development strategy that successfully targeted rich urban bikers, and with a product development strategy that called for redesigning and improving the quality of its bikes to generate sales among existing HOGs. Coca-Cola has also grown over the years by focusing on market penetration strategies in the United States and Canada, market development strategies in international markets, and product development strategies for creating new soft drinks and licensing its name to apparel and other companies.

Porter's Generic Strategy Model

The *Porter generic strategy model* helps managers to make decisions about which marketing direction a firm should choose, depending on the competitive position it seeks. The model allows managers to consider two different sets of marketing alternatives: (1) competing in a broad target market versus a narrow target market, and (2) competing on the basis of product cost versus *product differentiation,* or the product features and benefits that make it different from competitors' products. When these two perspectives are combined, this framework yields four distinct competitive strategies:

■ A *cost leadership* strategy occurs when a firm markets a single lower-cost product to a broad target market. Having the standardized product allows the firm to take advantage of economies of scale and compete on price. Short-haul airlines such as Aloha Airlines in Hawaii have achieved success with this strategy.

■ A *product differentiation strategy* means that the firm produces a unique product, aimed at a broad target market. Because of the product's unique benefits, the company is able to charge a premium price. Pricey cosmetics like Clinique use this strategy.

■ Using either a *cost focus strategy* or a *differentiation focus strategy,* a business unit or a small independent firm produces a product for a small segment of an industry that is not appealing to the competition. In some cases the firm believes it can best succeed by competing on a cost basis—a cost-focus strategy. For example, HealthLine, Eckerd Drug Stores' own brand of incontinence products, is priced lower than the national brands such as Depends. In other instances a business may compete based on product differences—that is, a

market development: growth strategies that introduce existing products to new markets

product development: growth strategies that focus on selling new products in served markets

diversification: growth strategies that emphasize both new products and new markets

differentiation focus strategy. Coors' Zima, with its odd taste and clear color, illustrates this strategy in the beer industry.

The Porter model relates these strategies to the firm's market share and its return on investment or profitability. If a firm has a small market share it can still be successful and profitable by developing a focused strategy. If the firm has a high market share it can achieve high levels of profitability either by developing a cost leadership approach or by providing a well-differentiated product. SONY differentiates its products, so it must continually invest in its capability to invent new products and unique product features. Wal-Mart succeeds on cost leadership, so it must continually find ways to drive costs down. If, however, the firm cannot offer either a unique product or lower cost, its chances for high levels of return are poor.

THE MARKETING PLANNING PROCESS

In our discussion of a firm's strategic planning in the previous section, we often talked about customers and products and markets and even marketing strategies. It is, in fact, difficult if not impossible to separate organizational strategic planning from marketing planning, because marketing is such an integral part of any organization. Some people even refer to such top-level planning as *strategic market planning,* meaning planning for success in one or more markets.

Of course, it is important for an organization to plan ways to gain a return on its investment or to set goals aimed at increasing its value to stockholders. But without marketing plans, the firm would not have a viable product at a price consumers are willing to pay, the means to get that product to the place consumers want it, or a way to promote the product to the right consumers. Without these elements of the marketing mix that were introduced in Chapter 1, most firms would not even be able to exist—at least for long. Marketing is not just one of the various functional areas of a business—it is the most essential area (you heard it here first).

The marketing concept pervades (or at least it should) other parts of the organization. R&D (research and development) aims to design products that have more of whatever the customer wants or needs in the way of product benefits and features. Accounting looks for ways to make it easy and convenient for customers to pay for goods and services, whereas human resources focuses on finding and training employees who can deliver high levels of customer satisfaction along with the goods and services. The firm's financial gurus try to balance the cost of all the firm's activities against the returns they bring in the marketplace.

As we saw in Chapter 1, Henry Ford taught American businesses that marketing success comes with a production orientation of making more goods faster and cheaper, but today's consumer-oriented firms have added a quality focus to this "any color they want, as long as it's black" perspective. A quality focus helps to ensure that the planning and activities of the different functions are directed toward the same goal and that the overall performance of the firm will not be marred by conflicting objectives on the part of each. In fact, many firms practice **cross-functional planning,** which means that managers work together in developing tactical plans that specifically consider the objectives of other functional areas to collectively carry out the firm's strategic plan.

Some organizations have encouraged cross-functional communications by physically merging people who work in various areas of the organization so that there is no office area specified as "marketing" or as "data processing." The Chiat/Day advertising agency has gone one step further. In their new corporate offices there are no areas designated for use by any single person. People come to work in the morning, pick up a notebook computer or whatever equipment they need, and find a desk or a conference table or some other place to work—all based on what they will be doing that one day.

The marketing planning process plays an important role in the development of the strategic plan itself. It includes monitoring changes in the marketing environment and assessing the firm's capability to take advantage of opportunities it identifies. The steps in

cross-functional planning: an approach to planning in which managers work together in developing tactical plans for each functional area in the firm, so that each plan considers the objectives of the other areas

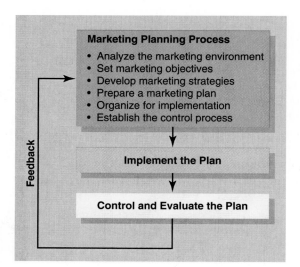

Figure 2.6
The Marketing Management Planning Process

Marketing Planning Process
- Analyze the marketing environment
- Set marketing objectives
- Develop marketing strategies
- Prepare a marketing plan
- Organize for implementation
- Establish the control process

Feedback

Implement the Plan

Control and Evaluate the Plan

the marketing planning process, as outlined in Figure 2.6, involve analyzing the marketing environment, setting marketing objectives, developing marketing strategies, preparing a marketing plan, organizing for implementation, and establishing the control process.

In this section we'll first look at the foundation for marketing planning—determining the strategic focus of the marketing effort—which influences the development of all marketing plans and activities. Then we'll examine the steps in the market planning process that lay the groundwork for the rest of the plan. We'll see how marketers assess the marketing environment and set marketing goals and objectives. Although we only touch on the factors in a firm's environments that can make or break the firm, we'll return to them in much greater detail in the next chapter, and in later sections of this chapter we'll look at the remaining steps in the marketing planning process.

CREATING A COMPETITIVE ADVANTAGE: MARKETING'S STRATEGIC FOCUS

competitive advantage: an advantage over competitors that an organization gains through its superior capabilities and unique product benefits that provide greater value in the minds of consumers

The underlying goal of all marketing strategies and plans is to create a **competitive advantage** for the firm—that is, to develop some reason why consumers will perceive its products to be of greater value than competing products. It focuses the marketing effort on the reasons why a customer—whether a housewife comparing canned vegetables, a teen deciding among CD players, or a company purchasing agent selecting a new computer system—will choose the firm's products over all others.

Decision makers throughout the firm are guided by this strategic focus, which has two interdependent elements: *distinctive competencies* and *differential benefits*. These elements guide management's decisions about deploying the firm's resources and developing a product with a difference.

Identifying Distinctive Competencies

distinctive competency: a superior capability of a firm in comparison to its direct competitors

A **distinctive competency** is a capability that is superior to the competition's, is not easily imitated, and can be used to create unique goods and services. This capability helps the firm create what customers want. Because competing firms can't do as well, they can't create similarly attractive goods and services. Intel, a firm that leads the industry in making the brains of today's computers, spends huge sums on R&D, which gives the company a distinctive competency.[15]

A firm's edge over the competition may take the form of an ability to create more reliable products, to develop novel product features, to replace a customer's stock more efficiently, or to create more effective advertising. Cost leadership, which means keeping costs (and the ultimate selling prices) below those of the competition, is another way to gain advantages. Wal-Mart has distinctive competencies in inventory control, distribution, and buying power. These competencies keep Wal-Mart's costs low and keep customers flocking to the stores.

Being alert to changes in technology can influence the development of a distinctive competency for a firm. Cone Mills Corporation, for example, developed its distinctive competency by investing heavily in the expensive high-tech machinery necessary for dying denim threads before they are woven into denim fabric. This investment makes it difficult for other mills to catch up, and as a result Cone is a major supplier to Levi Strauss & Co. and other apparel manufacturers around the world with sales of over $705 million annually.[16]

Providing Differential Benefits

Differential benefits are the reasons customers are willing to pay a premium for a firm's product or to exhibit a strong brand preference when choosing among competing offerings. Differential benefits result from the firm's distinctive competencies and help to build customer loyalty. Marketing seeks to identify the unique benefits the firm can provide and what benefits make a difference to customers.

Note that a differential benefit does not necessarily mean simply offering something *different*. For example, some years ago Mennen marketed a deodorant with a distinctive feature: The new product included vitamin D. Unfortunately, consumers did not see any reason to pay for the privilege of spraying vitamin D under their arms. Despite advertising claims, they saw no benefit from the purchase and the product failed. The moral: Effective product benefits must be both *different* from what the competition offers and *wanted* by potential customers.

differential benefits: values customers obtain from using, experiencing, or possessing a firm's product that are superior to those of competing products

EVALUATING THE MARKETING ENVIRONMENT

The first step in developing a strategic marketing direction and a specific marketing plan is to identify marketing opportunities by evaluating the internal and external environments of the organization. By **internal environment,** we mean all of the controllable elements inside an organization that influence in what way and how well the organization operates. The **external environment** includes uncontrollable elements outside of the organization that may affect its performance either positively or negatively. The external en-

internal environment: the controllable elements inside an organization including its people, its facilities, and how it does things that influence the operations of the organization

external environment: the uncontrollable elements outside of an organization that may affect its performance either positively or negatively

SPOTLIGHT ON GLOBAL MARKETING

"I'd Like to Buy the World a Coke"

When the actors in one advertising campaign for Coca-Cola sang, "I'd like to buy the world a Coke . . ." they weren't kidding. Coke has 46 percent of the *world's* soft drink business. To sell so much of its product, the Coca-Cola Company must have bottles full of distinctive competency.

Customers around the globe, whether in places like exotic Shanghai or the rough-and-tumble Aussie outback, have easy access to Coke. The familiar red cans and classic bottles are available almost anywhere a delivery truck can travel, but the competition's cans are not. While Coke sales in the 1970s were slipping at home, the company was mapping out the global market, and by the mid to late 1980s, 60 percent of its sales were coming from outside the United States.

One source of Coke's distinctive competency in the global marketplace is its highly successful franchise system for distribution. This system got a head start way back in 1929, when Robert

Woodruff took over the firm and began to sell the soda overseas. Later on, in World War II, Woodruff decreed that every soldier would have access to a 5-cent Coke. The U.S. government liked this morale-building effort, and assisted Coke in building sixty-four overseas bottling plants.

The Coke company's skill in creative advertising is another competency that helped open up global markets for Coke. It has been able to project its long-standing positive image – "The Pause That Refreshes" (1929) and "It's the Real Thing" (1941) – around the world by adapting its ads to local cultures. Coke allows local agencies to edit its largely standardized commercials, so the final versions highlight close-ups of local faces and places. By continuing to do what it does best, this marketing giant keeps on buying the world a Coke – one bottle at a time.

Sources: Robert F. Hartley, *Marketing Mistakes,* 5 ed. (New York: Wiley, 1992); Gary Hoover, Alta Campbell, and Patrick J. Spain, eds., *Hoover's Handbook of American Business 1993* (Austin, TX: The Reference Press, 1992); Milton Moskowitz, Robert Levering, and Michael Katz, *Everybody's Business* (New York: Doubleday, 1990).

vironment includes everything from consumers to government regulations to competitors to the overall economy. The evaluation of these business environments is often referred to as a *SWOT analysis* because it seeks to identify meaningful strengths (S) and weaknesses (W) inside the organization and opportunities (O) and threats (T) coming from outside. Strengths and weaknesses may be found in the firm's employees and their skills, technologies used, access to resources, and the firm's organizational culture. Opportunities and threats are found in the external environment, including the economy, competition, technology, laws and regulations, social and cultural trends, and global trends.

The unlikely story of Packard Bell's victory over IBM illustrates how a firm's strengths plus a market opportunity can yield success. In 1994 Packard Bell actually surpassed IBM in sales of its IBM-compatible personal computers (PCs). Packard Bell used its consumer marketing know-how and presence in numerous retail stores to prosper from the strongest opportunity for growth in the computer industry, the PC consumer market.[17] IBM's marketing strength had long been its personal selling skills that effectively reached Fortune 500 companies, the largest of U.S. business customers, but it lacked the know-how Packard Bell had acquired in consumer goods marketing: effective market segmentation, retail distribution, brand management, advertising, pricing, sales promotion, and product development.[18]

On the other hand, a firm also has to be cautious about taking advantage of short-term opportunities that can ultimately turn into threats. For example, Marlon Brando's performance as the leader of an unsavory Harley-riding motorcycle gang in the 1959 movie *The Wild One* inspired many would-be bikers to buy Harleys and form similar gangs of tattooed hellions that went by such names as The Wild Ones and Hell's Angels. For Harley-Davidson, the popularity of these motorcycle gangs at the time created an opportunity for increased sales, expanded market share, and enhancement of Harley's "power" mystique, but over the long haul this opportunity limited Harley's long-term growth possibilities as the gangs' (and Harley's) image became increasingly negative.

Information about a firm's external and internal environments helps managers keep their balance in a constantly shifting marketplace. Firms that regularly or continuously monitor what is going on both inside and outside their own four walls are able to capitalize on opportunities and minimize threats because they are able to develop strategies that successfully match business strengths to market opportunities.

Assessing the Internal Environment: Strengths and Weaknesses

Marketing management uses a variety of methods to identify internal strengths and weaknesses. Analyses such as *operations and resource audits* help marketers identify skills and resources that give the firm a competitive advantage, and might be used to determine marketing strategy, say, by creating new customer benefits for existing and new products.

An *operations audit* compares planned outcomes to actual marketing results by examining the activities of the firm's functional areas. When reasons for a particular outcome are unclear, managers look in detail at the underlying processes. For example, a favorable sales trend for Jaguars may not in itself reveal much about which aspect of the marketing mix was responsible for this good fortune. Did the product offer unusually strong benefits, such as improved reliability? Was expanded distribution reaching untapped markets? Was recent advertising especially effective? By looking into possible causes of a favorable sales trend, marketing strengths are discovered.

A *resource* is something a firm uses to create its product or to execute its strategic plans. Resources may be either tangible or intangible. They include money, people, company reputation, brand image, and physical possessions—anything that provides a firm with competitive advantages. A *resource audit* complements an operations audit by uncovering strengths not currently utilized in the firm's operations and provides managers answers to these questions.[19]

- How are resources used today?
- How could resources be used to sustain, renew, or create differential benefits?
- Do we have the right people in the right jobs?[20]
- What steps are needed to shift resources from where they are now to where they ought to be?
- What additional resources are needed?

By answering questions like these, Dow Chemical shifted enormous financial resources to developing capital equipment for chemical refining to gain the ability to keep costs low and product quality high.[21] Dow saw an opportunity and made the decision to invest what was necessary to take advantage of it.

The skills of a firm's employees are such a critical resource that workers are sometimes referred to as *human capital* and their know-how as *intellectual capital.*[22] Firms develop know-how, the foundation of their distinctive competency, when they train workers. Motorola, for example, sustains its key differential benefit, product reliability, partly by investing thirty-six hours of training per year in each employee.[23] The same goes for Federal Express, which invests twenty-seven hours, and Andersen Consulting, which invests an average of 109 hours in its employees.[24]

A resource audit also examines that most intangible of resources, *organizational culture,* especially as it affects the organization's willingness to take risks. A firm's culture—the collective attitudes, shared beliefs, and practices of its managers—may be an organization's most important resource. High-performance organizational cultures are adaptive, able to absorb information about the changing external environment, and take actions that exploit opportunities. Low-performance organizational cultures are far less adaptive, gradually causing the firm to become outmoded.[25]

Scanning the External Environment: Opportunities and Threats

The external environment includes the influences beyond a firm's direct control that affect the firm's situation. Some of these influences provide opportunities for growth, whereas others signal possible danger down the road. Marketing managers scan the firm's external environment not only to find new opportunities, but to ward off threats: As the old saying goes, "Forewarned is forearmed."

For example, from 1976 to 1979 Coke's growth in the United States dropped from 13 percent annually to 2 percent. Pepsi launched the "Pepsi Generation" campaign that delivered a good-feeling differential benefit and swept up baby boomers with its message of idealism and youth. Then Pepsi launched the "Pepsi Challenge," a vivid message declaring that people preferred the taste of Pepsi in blind taste tests. By 1984 Coke's market share lead had slipped by 2.9 percent. It was trailing in the grocery store market by 1.7 percent. Best customers of Coke, those that drank Coke exclusively, went from 18 percent to 11 percent. All of this happened as Coke *outspent* Pepsi on advertising by $100 million! Coke also had more vending machines, more fountains, more shelf space, and was competitively priced! Despite these efforts, Pepsi loomed as a threatening influence, forcing Coke to look for new ways to regain its strength and further motivating the firm to develop its overseas markets.

Environmental scanning can also identify possible opportunities for expansion, though sometimes what seems like a tempting possibility may not be in the organization's best interests. As the song goes, sometimes an organization has to know when to hold 'em and know when to fold 'em: Opportunities are only promising if the firm is capable of exploiting them. For example, the retail giant Kmart devoted money and people to acquiring and growing the PACE warehouse chain. Then Kmart's core discount store business declined. It did not have the resources to support the additional business and was forced to sell its PACE Warehouse operations to rival Wal-Mart. This move allowed Kmart to shift people and money—its basic resources—back to the task of restoring the differential benefits of its core business.

Evaluating the firm's environment involves a careful analysis of the potential fit between an organization's capabilities and the many intriguing possibilities that present themselves. The question is whether or not the firm has the specific strengths, expertise, and/or resources to take full advantage of the opportunity. For example, General Electric has acquired the skills and technologies to produce high-quality electrical appliances. Developing a product to satisfy a need in the marketplace for a new type of camera or computer might be a good move for GE, but branching into a chain of fast-food restaurants is not likely to be a successful venture. This opportunity simply does not fit with GE's strengths or business mission. Exxon, another industrial giant, learned this lesson the hard way a few years ago. A brief foray into the office products business proved to be a disaster, because the company was unable to transfer its expertise in marketing automotive products to this new environment.

SETTING MARKETING OBJECTIVES

Once marketing management has identified the firm's strengths and weaknesses, the next step in the planning process is to develop objectives. The SWOT analysis—that is, the strengths of the organization and the opportunities it faces—determine the firm's overall objectives as well as the specific objectives of the functional areas.

Marketing objectives state what is to be accomplished by the marketing function to achieve the firm's overall goals and objectives. For example, when Sam's Clubs, the Wal-Mart warehouse club, experienced flat sales in 1994, the company launched a new business strategy that emphasized market development by getting small businesses in already-served geographical markets to become regular customers. Marketing objectives included targets for hiring and training salespeople to sell memberships to small businesses, as well as targets for the number of new memberships the salespeople would secure.

Most marketing objectives are expressed in some quantified form, such as the specific amount of market share or sales volume desired. Because numbers don't (usually) lie, quantitative objectives allow managers to decide later how effective the marketing strategies and plans actually were. In some situations, however, qualitative objectives may be more relevant, such as improving a brand's image, gaining industry leadership, or improving customer loyalty. Like strictly quantitative objectives, qualitative objectives are measurable. For example, an improvement in brand image can be assessed by polling customers over time to determine whether their feelings about a brand have changed or stayed the same. Measurable marketing objectives provide useful (although sometimes sobering) feedback about the firm's capabilities and how realistic its expectations for growth should be.

Sales Objectives

In almost all cases, no matter what the overall organizational strategies are, marketing objectives include one or more quantitative goals relating to sales. Whether these sales objectives are stated in terms of dollar sales or unit sales, they are based on *forecasts* of demand in the total market and the level of sales the firm can be expected to make in that market during a specific time period. The specific volume of sales stated in a firm's objectives relies on its assessment of opportunities in the SWOT analysis.

Reliable sales predictions are critical to achieving the firm's profit goals, which also rely on an assessment of costs associated with the firm's internal resources. The projected revenues from predicted sales determine marketing budgets and affect planning for the marketing mix. Sales forecasts also affect all of the firm's planning efforts, and errors can often lead to disaster, as when Coleco underestimated demand for its Cabbage Patch dolls, causing desperate parents to line up for long hours at retail stores trying to buy one of the few available.

Marketing managers use a variety of techniques to forecast sales. Some firms use the simplest method available—*executive opinion,* which means just what the name implies: Top-level executives use intuition or "gut feelings" based on past experiences to predict demand and forecast sales. Other firms rely on *sales force opinions* by soliciting individual sales projections from each of the firm's sales representatives. Firms that use these methods generally back up their forecasts with an analysis of *historical sales.* Historical sales data are most useful when conditions in the external environment are stable, so that last year's sales growth rate can safely be used to obtain next year's projections. But market conditions and people's preferences do change, and even Cabbage Patch dolls lose some of their appeal over time.

Marketing management also uses quantitative sales data to measure performance in achieving profit goals and to evaluate the marketing plan's overall success. We'll look at the sales analysis techniques marketers use to evaluate the marketing plan later in this chapter, and in Chapter 5 we'll examine other methods firms use to gather marketing information to help managers predict demand and set sales objectives.

Product-Oriented Objectives

If a firm has decided that its growth strategy is to focus on product development (new or improved products for existing customers), its objectives will be product-oriented. Because it is more profitable to retain customers than it is to replace them after they become dissatisfied, firms often set objectives for improvements in quality or service to develop customer loyalty. In the breakfast cereal market, where consumers are more likely to be fickle than loyal, firms like Kellogg and General Mills might set objectives for developing brands to suit the tastes of everyone—children, teens, adults, and even grandparents—in the family, or they may set goals for a new product to retain customers who are being lured away by a competitor's new honey-coated fruit-and-fiber cereal. In other cases a firm may decide to modify a product by taking advantage of trends, as when Frito-Lay developed its line of "lite" snacks.

Other objectives related to product development may have to do with identifying consumer preferences and the percentage of growth the firm will gain when the product is introduced. For example, when General Motors (GM) developed a new model of its mid-size sport-utility vehicle, the Blazer, it sought a sales increase from 226,000 to 300,000 units annually.[26] To achieve this growth, marketing objectives during the early stages of product development were to identify ways to make the Blazer more attractive to customers by finding out what its existing customers wanted in a mid-size utility vehicle; later, other objectives were developed for the number of customers to be reached by advertising and sales promotions.

Market-Oriented Objectives

Firms often determine that their best path to new customer growth is using either market development strategies (existing products sold to new customers) or diversification strategies (new products for new customers). When a firm's goal is to penetrate existing markets, it might set performance objectives for particular segments of its market. For example, if a firm's market share varies by geographic area, it may set high market share objectives for areas where its share is currently low to focus its activities in the areas where it needs to grow. Coca-Cola, for example, has long held a substantially larger market share position in the Southeast area of the United States, so in the war with Pepsi it makes sense for Coke to focus on areas where its sales are weak.

A firm might also set goals for reaching new customers by changing its image or redesigning advertising and promotions to attract underserved segments within its existing markets. Other market-oriented objectives may be related to the share of consumer purchases, frequency of purchase, number of different products purchased, and so on.

Firms that seek growth by developing new products for new markets often do so by acquiring other firms. In other cases a firm may have the technology and resources to successfully develop and market new products on its own. In either case, marketing objectives will focus on issues related to developing both the market and the product. Rubbermaid, for example, which was named the most admired corporation in the world by *Fortune* magazine in 1994, had sales of $1.8 billion in 1993 with earnings of $184.2 million.[27] Rubbermaid's marketing strategy is to enter a new product category every twelve to eighteen months. The company initially built its success on rubber kitchen tools and containers and in the past has expanded its product lines to include mailboxes, toys, snap-together furniture, and other household products. Most recently it entered the hardware, cabinet, and garden shed markets. Thirty-three percent of Rubbermaid's sales are from products introduced in the past five years. In 1994 alone it turned out over 300 new products. Nine out of ten of these new items are successful, a very high hit rate by most standards. To keep these new products coming, 14 percent of profits get plowed right back into research and development.

DEVELOPING STRATEGIES: ELEMENTS OF A MARKET PLAN

A firm's SWOT analysis and its sales and marketing objectives lay the groundwork for the development of specific strategies and plans. This stage of the marketing planning process determines how the firm will address issues in its marketing environment and achieve its goals and objectives. The firm must decide which markets to target and how to develop marketing mix strategies to reach that market. In this section we'll briefly review the elements that influence planning and the development of a marketing plan. Throughout the rest of this book we'll look closely at many of the elements involved in developing marketing strategies and action plans.

SELECTING A TARGET MARKET

A critical component of the planning process is selecting the group(s) of customers the organization will go after—its *target market.* A market is all the people or organizations that are or could become buyers of a firm's products. Sometimes the target market is a total market, and sometimes it is only part of the market. For example, to a grocer in the tiny village of Silver Creek, New York, the market includes the whole village and the nearby farmland. A grocer in urban New York City may target residents within just a few blocks—merely a small fraction of the vast number of people who live in Manhattan, but still more than enough to create an attractive market for the store.

The target market is a market segment selected because of its relative attractiveness compared to other markets, as well as the firm's belief that its offerings are most suited to winning customers in that market. That is, the firm assesses the potential demand—the number of consumers it believes are willing and able to pay for its products—and decides it has distinctive competencies that will create a competitive advantage in the minds of these consumers. The selection of a target market is also dependent on the firm's growth goals, which determine whether the firm will target its existing customers with new strategies or will seek new target markets.

In addition to making sure the organization has the ability to be successful in meeting the needs of a target market, the marketing strategies must be customized to address the unique characteristics of targeted customers and their buying preferences and practices. The more precisely a firm defines its target market, the more likely it will be able to develop strategies for the elements in the marketing mix that closely match the target consumers. Thus, organizations typically gather large amounts of data about consumers to identify target markets, as we'll see in Chapter 6, and we'll look at the process of selecting a target market in more depth in Chapter 8.

DEVELOPING MARKETING MIX STRATEGIES

Marketing mix strategies identify how marketing will accomplish its objectives in the firm's target markets. Typically, strategies are developed for tailoring the marketing mix—product, price, promotion, and place—to meet the target market's needs. In addition, depending on the firm's growth goals, these strategies may be designed to gain market share by emphasizing the development of new products or expansion of target markets.

In developing marketing mix strategies, marketing managers also take into account that the strategy for any one element of the mix affects the strategies for other elements in the mix. Marketing mix strategies are interrelated and interdependent. That is, plans developed for one element of the mix both influence and are influenced by the strategies developed for the other elements of the mix.

Product Strategy

In developing a *product strategy,* marketers decide which product(s) to market to each segment they have targeted and what characteristics of the product will provide the unique benefits targeted customers want. Product strategies determine what design is best for the product, what features it will have, how it will be packaged, and what warranty it will carry. Product strategy decisions also determine what is needed to satisfy the target market, what other services the firm might offer along with the product, how the product will be positioned relative to the competition, and whether or not variations of the product will be offered. These and other product decisions must all be evaluated in terms of how they will affect the price and distribution of the product, as well as the type of promotions that will be required. The various aspects of product strategy will be addressed in detail in Chapters 9 through 11.

REAL PEOPLE, REAL CHOICES:

DECISION TIME AT HARLEY-DAVIDSON, INC.

In 1903, intrigued by the recent invention that was "taking the work out of bicycling," William Harley and Arthur Davidson set to work in a backyard shed to perfect their own ideas for a better motorcycle. Milwaukee became home to a legend. By 1979 Harley sold 52,000 of the 132,000 motorcycles available industry-wide at that time. Soon, though, decline set in: Only 27,000 units were sold in 1983, and the total market had fallen to 117,000 units. A marketer's worst nightmare is a declining share in a declining market. By 1985 unit sales were up to 30,000 units, but still the company flirted with bankruptcy.

By 1986, even though the market was dwindling, the company's share improved drastically as it initiated plans for a dramatic turnaround. Harley's manufacturing people greatly improved the reliability and quality of the product, while its marketers changed the brand's image to appeal to a new target market of white-collar riders.

These strategies worked: Soon, celebrities like Kurt Russell, Elizabeth Taylor, Arnold Schwarzenegger, and Sylvester Stallone were featured in the media atop their Harleys. The "hog" had become a fashion statement and in the process caused the whole industry to experience a renaissance—it became hip to buy a bike. In fact, Harley's strategy in a sense worked *too* well: Demand for the bikes outstripped Harley's capacity to make them. Suddenly, Frank Cimermancic and Harley-Davidson's marketing team faced a problem.

The company calculated that it needed to spend $300 million to build manufacturing capacity to meet the current demand for new "hogs." But if the firm committed to this expensive course of action, would the customers still be there down the road? Was the popularity of buying, riding, and even collecting Harley-Davidson motorcycles merely a fad, or was it here to stay? Harley's traditional blue-collar customers weren't caught up in the frenzy, and some of these riders were even a bit turned off by all the hoopla as they saw their chosen lifestyle get "yuppified." Mr. Cimermancic worried that the newer white-collar customers would leave the market as soon as celebrities moved on to the next fad. Motorcycle clubs for upscale riders, such as the "Rolex Rangers," might disappear overnight! With his team's assistance, Frank Cimermancic supplied senior management with a view of the external environment Harley would most likely face in a few years. The Harley team also identified three alternative courses of action:

Option 1. Invest $300 million in new manufacturing capacity. If demand continued to grow, Harley would be positioned to reap the benefits. If demand dropped or stabilized, however, disaster waited on the side of the road.

Option 2. Do nothing and see if demand continues to grow. On the one hand, if demand petered out the company could harvest profits from the fad and avoid making an additional investment. On the other hand, if the biking lifestyle continued to flourish and Harley could not meet the demand, it would find itself cheated out of the market it had created by other companies that were ready and eager to supply bikes to new waves of riders.

Option 3. Contract out manufacturing to other producers who would actually make the bikes and put the Harley name on them. This strategy would allow the company to "have its cake and eat it too" by letting it adjust its production capacity to meet market demands without actually investing any more money in the process. On the other hand, Harley would have to face the consequences of potentially lower product quality and erosion of customer loyalty: Would you want to explain inferior workmanship to a dissatisfied customer who has the Harley-Davidson logo tattooed on his arm?

Now, join Harley-Davidson's decision team: If you were the director of business planning for Harley-Davidson, which option would you recommend, and why?

Exhibit 2.1
Chrysler's minivan, introduced in the early 1980s, not only brought in much-needed profits for the ailing car company, but caught on so well that what was then a new type of vehicle has become an established auto category. This blockbusting success didn't just happen — it came about because Chrysler developed powerful and tightly focused marketing mix strategies. The product was designed to deliver just what the family target market wanted in the way of safety features, van-like roominess, and carlike comfort. The pricing strategy called for a price that was consistent with what families paid for the average station wagon, and the place strategy relied on distributing the minivan through Chrysler's well-established dealer network. The promotion strategy included nationwide advertising that focused on family needs and product benefits, sales promotions in the form of rebates, and personal selling at Chrysler dealerships that focused on test drives and high-quality service when needed.

Pricing Strategy

A *pricing strategy* includes pricing objectives and states the specific prices to be charged for a product. Pricing helps to determine how customers perceive a product's value and whether or not customers will accept the product. If targeted consumers are not willing to pay the price charged, all of the other marketing efforts are worthless. A firm's pricing strategies are influenced by the pricing of competing products, because a product's price is often the determining factor in how well it fares compared to other products in a target market.

Firms commonly rethink a product's pricing strategy in response to changes in a competitor's pricing strategy. For example, during a period where personal computer (PC) manufacturers had allowed inventory to build up, Compaq Computer Corporation announced a 22 percent price cut on its product line. Because shoppers so often compare IBM's PCs to Compaq's, within a week of Compaq's announcement IBM stated in a press release that it would drop its prices by up to 27 percent.[28]

Pricing strategies must go hand in hand with product strategies. If the product has many features and an extensive warranty, pricing must reflect these extra costs. It must also take into account the cost of promoting the product as well as getting it to the place where consumers can buy it. These and other issues involved in the price aspect of the marketing mix will be addressed in Chapters 12 and 13.

Promotion Strategy

A *promotion strategy* includes plans for advertising, consumer sales promotion, trade promotions, the sales function, publicity, and point-of-purchase materials. That is, it includes all other marketing activities that communicate product benefits and features to the target market. Promotion strategies must also be integrated with the other marketing mix strategies. For example, if the product will have multiple features, then advertising plans must be designed to deliver a more complex message. If the product is going to sell at a high price, promotion must communicate a high-quality, luxury image.

A product's image can be communicated in many ways; even the appearance of employees speaks volumes about the company they represent. To dispel its black-clad image, for example, Harley-Davidson officials began to wear red or white shirts at motorcycle rallies to send a more wholesome, less threatening message to participants. The company's 1988 ad slogan was, "Life should be so simple," which tapped a yearning for freedom among many "mainstream" consumers who perhaps had only fantasized about actually owning a bike.

Promotion strategies address such issues as the message or theme to be developed, how the message will be delivered, and the mix of advertising, sales promotion, and personal selling that will be used. Today's marketers realize that their plans for different promotional elements also must be *integrated* with each other so that they work together to form a single coherent message for customers. This need for consistency has led some cutting-edge marketers to think in terms of an *integrated communications strategy,* which means that marketers consciously blend all of the promotion elements together to communicate with their target markets. The elements of the promotional mix will be covered in Chapters 17 through 19, and we'll discuss specifically this emerging approach to marketing communications in Chapter 16.

Distribution Strategy

The *place or distribution strategy* describes how the product will be made available to targeted customers when and where they want it. In developing a distribution strategy marketers must decide whether the product will be sold directly to the final customers or whether the distribution channel will include retailers and wholesalers. Which retailers will be selected depends on the product, pricing, and promotion strategies. If the firm is producing a high-quality, top-of-the-line product, it should be distributed through specialty stores rather than through discount merchandisers.

SPOTLIGHT ON RELATIONSHIP MARKETING

Locking Up Customers at Diebold, Inc.

Diebold, Inc., began in 1859 as a safe manufacturer. Today it sells over a half-billion dollars per year of ATMs, security products, and equipment for banks. Despite competitive pressures, a recession in worldwide markets, and rapid technological changes that demand ever-increasing capital investments, Diebold continues to grow by keeping its customers satisfied. Let's see how they do it.

Diebold's marketing strategies aim to build long-term relationships with customers and to reinforce the firm's commitment to total quality. The marketing program at Diebold involves customers, suppliers, and the entire work force including top management. The planning process at Diebold begins with studies of customers' operations and includes surveys, market studies, and industry studies that provide further insights to help the company satisfy customers' needs. Senior managers routinely meet with customers to hear what concerns them, what their expecta-

tions are, and what they may want in the future. Ideas also come from sales consultants and service technicians. And Diebold involves selected best customers in a customer advisory council, where they play a key role in shaping the company's policies.

Quality teams create a partnership with the customer to develop products and systems that work better for everyone. When one of Diebold's clients is opening a new branch to serve its financial customers, Diebold sales consultants offer computer-aided branch-design equipment. For bank customers who want to equip their branches with computers that work efficiently with ATMs, Diebold has created InterBold, a joint venture with IBM to combine ATMs with related computer systems. Service is provided by 2,300 trained technicians linked by hand-held computers to a centralized command and information system. Customers can link into the same system to check on the status of service calls. By anticipating customers' needs during its planning process, Diebold is plotting a secure future.

Source: Diebold, "Corporate Profile" (1993): 2.

Distribution plans must also include how the product will be physically carried to the members of the firm's distribution channel, where distribution centers should be located, and even how the product will be displayed once it gets to the point of sale. For example, with help from Harley-Davidson, many motorcycle dealerships were transformed from dark and menacing caverns to bright and friendly retail environments complete with neon lights, mirrored dressing rooms, and stylish clothing. The distribution aspect of the marketing mix will be addressed in Chapters 14 and 15.

PREPARING A MARKETING PLAN

The final part of the marketing planning process is to prepare a formal **marketing plan,** a document that identifies where the organization is now, where it wants to go, how it plans to get there, and who will be responsible for carrying out each part of the marketing strategy. In large firms top management often requires a written plan because it encourages managers to formulate concrete objectives and strategies and often forces them to make difficult decisions. In small entrepreneurial firms a well-thought-out marketing plan is often a key factor in attracting investors who will help turn the firm's dreams into reality.

Typically a marketing plan outlines the activities included in the planning process. The first part of the plan is a thorough description of the firm's current situation, often called the "Business Review," which includes the results of the SWOT analysis. On the basis of this analysis and review of the current situation, marketing problems and opportunities are outlined and the selected target markets are identified and explained. Next, marketing objectives are stated and justified.

The next part of the plan includes a presentation of the planned positioning strategy. Specific strategies and action plans, or *tactics* for the elements of the marketing mix, are detailed. Finally, information about how the plan is to be implemented and controlled, including budgets and timing, is included. Sometimes organizations require that marketing plans include alternative or contingency plans, a predetermined change in direction should monitoring of marketing activities show that the objectives are not being met by the initial strategies. An example of a brief marketing plan is found in Appendix B.

IMPLEMENTATION AND CONTROL OF THE MARKETING PLAN

Sometimes firms develop excellent marketing plans but fail when it comes to carrying them out. The reasons for this failure are not always clear. One problem may be that planning has been limited to top managers, and managers may not have a clear understanding of the day-to-day operations of the marketing function. Because they are out of touch with what *really* happens on the factory floor or in the store, the objectives they set up are easier said than done (and this is one reason why the practice of "management by walking around," where key executives spend more time in typical working situations, has become so popular). Another problem may be related to long- versus short-term objectives. Because management rewards are often tied to short-term profit objectives, implementation of the marketing plan may focus too heavily on short-term results to the detriment of the firm's long-term goals.

In this section we'll look at two key factors in the successful implementation of marketing plans: the marketing budget and the organization of the marketing function. These management decisions determine what the marketing function can afford to spend on each of its strategies and how they will be carried out. We'll also look at the ways in which marketing plans can be controlled and evaluated. These activities not only measure the performance of the marketing function, but provide valuable feedback for the development of future marketing plans.

IMPLEMENTING THE MARKETING PLAN

Implementation means putting plans into action—bringing the strategies to life on an everyday basis. The implementation sections of a marketing plan contain a marketing budget, development of specific action plans, and the assignment of major areas of responsibility to individuals or teams.

The Marketing Budget

The **marketing budget** is a statement of the total amount to be spent on the marketing function and the allocation of money or the spending limit for each activity under the marketer's control. Often a budget also projects revenues and profits.

Firms use different methods to determine total marketing spending. The simplest and most frequently used technique is the *percentage-of-sales method,* where the amount to be spent on marketing activities is calculated as a percentage of past sales or projected future sales. The percentage of sales method of budgeting is simple to implement, but the method has an important weakness: It tends to result in *increasing* spending on marketing activities when sales are up and *decreasing* spending when sales are down. If marketing activities do indeed lead to increased sales, the percentage of sales method is philosophically wrong, because it fails to fund marketing activities when they are most needed.

A more logical method for budgeting is the *objective-and-task method.* Managers develop marketing objectives, then list the activities they feel will allow the organization to reach those objectives, and finally add up the costs of completing those activities. This method is philosophically sound, but the downside is that it requires marketers to specify the activities that will enable the organization to reach its objectives. Because most marketers don't have a reliable crystal ball they can use to predict the future, their abilities to make these connections are never perfect. Still, an educated guess is usually better than none at all.

Organizing the Marketing Function

Another important element of successful marketing plan implementation is the organization of the marketing function. When we speak of marketing organization, we are talking about how a firm breaks up the work into different jobs and assigns people to departments or geographic territories or functional units. Organization relates to "who reports to whom." Different firms find that different types of organizations meet their needs best.

A *functional* structure separates marketing into distinct components, such as advertising, sales promotion, sales force management, marketing research, and so on. Some firms feel that customer needs or usage differ by geographic region, and they structure the marketing function with a *geographic* type of organization, perhaps setting up one marketing function for, say, Eastern Europe and another for Western Europe. Firms that have a *product* or *brand* type of organization may have a number of different brand mangers and product group or product line managers. Procter & Gamble pioneered the brand management system where managers of different brands in the same product category actively compete against each other. In recent years P & G has added product line managers to ensure that the firm's long-term interests are not lost in the fight for short-term brand success. More recently General Motors radically restructured its marketing activities by appointing brand managers, each of whom is responsible for developing pricing and promotion strategies for a designated model.[29]

CONTROLLING THE MARKETING PLAN

Control means measuring actual performance, comparing it to planned performance, and making necessary changes in plans and implementation. This process requires that marketing managers develop the means to gain feedback on whether activities are being performed, and whether they are being performed well and in a timely manner. Gathering such feedback allows managers to determine whether they should continue with the marketing plan, activate the contingency plan, or go back to the drawing board. It also provides feedback for the next year's planning activities. For now we'll briefly review some

---

implementation: the stage of the strategic management process in which strategies are put into action on a day-to-day basis

marketing budget: a statement of the total amount to be spent on the marketing function and the allocation of money or the spending limit for each activity under a marketer's control

control: measuring actual performance, comparing it to planned performance, and making necessary changes in plans and implementation

DE NIEUWE
MULTI-ZONE VAATWASSER

Whirlpool

BRENGT KWALITEIT TOT LEVEN!

Exhibit 2.2
Firms that operate in the fast-changing global marketplace often need to change or adapt their organizational structure to succeed. Whirlpool, the third leading appliance company in Europe, found that it needed to simplify its organization as Europe moved toward a single, common market. Whirlpool replaced its separate sales organizations in seventeen countries with four regional sales offices, which, along with changes in marketing strategy, helped Whirlpool to increase its European sales while the overall appliance market remained flat.

of the tools and techniques that help managers control the marketing plan, and then we'll take a closer look at some of these approaches in later chapters.

Trend Analysis

Sometimes firms develop *trend analyses* to provide feedback for setting sales goals, developing strategies, and measuring company performance. An example of how trend analysis can help a firm develop new strategies comes from Lotus Development Corp. Lotus saw its spreadsheet market share plummet from 80 percent to 55 percent in the late 1980s. Though the firm had shown an ability to constantly reinvent its short-life-cycle software, such as the spreadsheet application Lotus 123, some industry experts thought Lotus had finally lost its touch. But by analyzing sales data, Lotus identified a sales trend for groupware and unified software packages that gave Lotus hints of future success that affected subsequent marketing budgets and activities.[30] Lotus was thus able to develop new applications and make its software applications work together as a unified package.

Sales and market-share trends show whether the overall marketing program is on track when the marketing activity relates directly to sales. Firms often look at sales trends by territory, by geographic region, and by customer type to determine weaknesses in the marketing plan. In direct-mail selling, the response rate and average sales per order provide feedback on the quality of the mailing list and the drawing power of a particular catalog or offer. The analysis of sales may also include measures of costs and profitability, as a firm may have to limit operations if some are not profitable.

Marketing Research

Sometimes firms use traditional marketing research to obtain feedback on marketing activities, an activity we will explore in detail in Chapter 5. Since Abbott Laboratories, a supplier of blood screening and testing equipment to the medical field, began in 1989 to conduct annual surveys of its customers, the company's sales have doubled![31] The following tools may be used to get feedback on a firm's services:[32]

- *Customer complaint feedback:* Feedback comes from assessment of customer complaints received through 800-numbers.
- *Posttransaction surveys:* Surveys ask customers about the purchase experience while it is fresh in their minds.
- *Customer focus group interviews:* Small discussion groups are conducted to provide a forum for customers' ideas and reactions to products.
- *Mystery shoppers:* Mystery shoppers are experts who masquerade as "regular people" and then report back on how they were treated by a manufacturer or retailer. Hotels, stores, banks, and ski resorts often use mystery-shopper feedback to keep themselves on their toes.
- *Market surveys:* Systematically gathered market information is used to compare a company's product to those of competitors and to identify areas for improvement.
- *Employee surveys:* Measures of employee morale and attitudes tell managers whether there may be obstacles to improved service.

When it comes to techniques for doing market research, a firm's choices are almost limitless, and many firms are devising unique ways to learn about consumer needs and wants. Honda, maker of the highly successful Accord, for example, had its factory workers call over 47,000 Accord owners to see if they were happy with their purchases and to get ideas for possible improvements.[33] Though it is unusual to use factory workers in market research, today's firms are recognizing the importance of getting the entire organization involved in obtaining customer feedback.

The Marketing Audit

The *marketing audit* is a comprehensive review of a business unit's marketing system. The purpose of the audit is to determine whether there are ways that the marketing programs can be improved. Because a marketing audit should be objective and unbiased, it is best completed by an independent consulting organization rather than by the firm itself. Alternatively, marketing audits can be conducted by employee teams drawn from outside the marketing function.

In either case, the people who conduct the audit engage in a systematic examination of the internal and external marketing environment, as well as the objectives, strategies,

REAL PEOPLE, REAL CHOICES:

How It Worked Out at Harley-Davidson, Inc.

Mr. Cimermancic and his colleagues at Harley Davidson chose option 1: They have put $300 million into the business since 1989 to build capacity, which now has been increased by 60%. In 1994 the company shipped 95,800 motorcycles, up 17 percent from the previous year. In 1995 Harley-Davidson reached its production objective a year early by attaining the capacity to produce 100,000 units a year. The plan now is to further increase production capacity to 115,000 units by 1997 by investing an additional $30 million in capital expenditures. About 30 percent of this production is exported to more than thirty countries.

Harley-Davidson is now in the process of developing the next set of strategic plans for growth beyond even that level in subsequent years.[34] Company research indicates that riders want a technologically advanced machine that still retains a classic 1940s look. Harley is going back to the basics to reach out to the twentysomething generation, where its market share is not as high. By anticipating the needs of this next generation of riders, Frank Cimermancic and the marketing team at Harley-Davidson are betting on a long-term growth strategy that will keep the company profitable down the road.

Table 2.1
Information Gathered in a Marketing Audit

1. Marketing Philosophy

Support organizational objectives

Focus on customer needs

Social responsibility included in decision making

Different offerings for different segments

A total system perspective

2. Marketing Organization

Integration of different marketing functions

Integration of marketing with other functional areas of the organization

Organization for new-product development

Qualifications and effectiveness of marketing management personnel

3. Marketing Information Systems

Effective use of marketing research

Current study data available

Timely communication of relevant information to marketing planners

Knowledge of sales potential and profitability for various market segments, territories, products, channels, and order sizes

Monitoring effectiveness of marketing strategies and tactics

Cost effectiveness studies

4. Strategic Orientation

Formal marketing planning

   Objectives

   Environmental scanning

   Sales forecasting

   Contingency planning

Quality of current marketing strategy

   Product strategies

   Distribution strategies

   Promotion strategies

   Pricing strategies

Contingency planning

5. Operations

Communications and implementation of planning

Effective use of resources

Ability to adapt to changes

Source: Adapted from Philip Kotler, "From Sales Obsession to Marketing Effectiveness," *Harvard Business Review* (Nov.–Dec. 1977) 70–71.

and activities of the marketing plan and even the people involved. Auditors interview managers, customers, dealers, salespeople, and so on. Table 2.1 shows the areas of the firm's marketing function that are evaluated by specific types of information gathered in a marketing audit.

Chapter 2 Summary

Objective 1. Describe the strategic planning process and explain how strategic decisions are made.

Strategic planning by top-level managers involves defining the firm's business mission, setting corporate goals and objectives, establishing a business portfolio, and determining its strategic marketing direction. A firm's mission is its commitment to a type of business and a position in the marketplace and is influenced by management's vision of the firm's future. Broad corporate goals that identify what the firm hopes to achieve are derived directly from the firm's mission statement, while decisions for specific, measurable objectives are influenced by the analysis of a firm's internal strengths and weaknesses as well as external opportunities and threats.

Decisions about the firm's portfolio of strategic business units are often made with the help of such planning tools as the Boston Consulting Group matrix, which assesses SBUs on market growth potential and the firm's relative market share, and the General Electric/McKinsey business planning grid, which measures industry attractiveness and the firm's business strengths. Managers may determine the firm's marketing direction with the help of such tools as the product-market growth matrix, which identifies four strategies for market penetration, market development, product development, and diversification, and Porter's generic strategy model, which weighs broad market versus narrow market strategies and product cost versus product development strategies.

Objective 2. Tell how firms gain a competitive advantage and describe the factors that influence marketing objectives.

A competitive advantage means that a firm has developed reasons for customers to select its product over all others in the market. A firm gains a competitive advantage when it has distinctive competencies—or capabilities that are stronger than those of the competition—and is able to provide differential benefits, product benefits that are uniquely different from the competition. Creating a competitive advantage is the strategic focus of an organization's marketing planning process.

Marketing planning begins with an evaluation of the internal and external environments to identify the firm's strengths and weaknesses, opportunities and threats. Based on this SWOT analysis, marketing managers then set quantitative and qualitative market objectives that are linked to the firm's overall goals and objectives. Marketing attempts to satisfy the firm's product goals by developing reliable sales objectives based on demand predicted by the assessment of the external marketing environment and the costs associated with the firm's internal resources. Product-oriented and market-oriented objectives are set depending on the firm's goals for growth—that is, whether it will seek to grow by developing new products or by expanding its markets.

Objective 3. Discuss the role of marketing strategies in planning and development of the marketing plan.

The marketing planning process determines what strategies and action plans the firm will use to achieve its marketing objectives and overall strategic goals. Marketing selects the target market(s) the organization will go after and decides what marketing mix strategies will be used to meet the needs of that market. Product strategies include decisions about products and product characteristics that will appeal to the target market. Pricing strategies state the specific prices to be charged and are influenced both by the cost of the marketing mix elements and targeted customers' willingness to pay. Promotion strategies include plans for advertising, consumer and trade sales promotion, the sales function, publicity, point-of-purchase materials, and other marketing communications activities to reach the target market. Distribution strategies outline how the product will be made available to targeted customers when and where they want it.

The final step in the marketing planning process is the development of a written marketing plan that describes the firm's current situation, states the marketing objectives, identifies the specific strategies and action plans that will be used, and outlines how the plan will be implemented and controlled. It may include contingency plans that are to be used if objectives are not being met by the initial strategies.

Objective 4. Explain the factors involved in the implementation and control of the marketing plan.

Implementation or putting the plan into action includes development of the marketing budget, often using a percentage-of-sales or an objective-and-task method. Also essential to successful implementation is effective organization of the marketing function—that is, breaking the work up into different jobs assigned to different people. Control is the measurement of actual performance and comparison with planned performance. Planners may use trend analyses or other forms of marketing research to obtain performance feedback. A comprehensive review of the marketing system is sometimes conducted using a marketing audit.

Review Questions

Marketing Concepts: Testing Your Knowledge

1. How are strategic, tactical, and operational planning alike? How are they different?
2. What is a mission statement? Why is a mission statement important to an organization? What should a mission statement include?
3. What is a business portfolio? Why do firms develop SBUs? What planning tools can a firm use to plan and assess its portfolio of SBUs and its strategic marketing direction?
4. Why is marketing planning important to a firm? What is cross-functional planning? How does it help a firm achieve its marketing objectives?
5. What does it mean for a firm to have a competitive advantage? What gives a firm a competitive advantage?
6. What is a SWOT analysis? What role does it play in the planning process?
7. What role do a firm's sales objectives play in the marketing planning process? How do growth goals affect decisions to set product-oriented strategies versus market-oriented strategies?
8. What factors influence the selection of a target market? What is the relationship between the target market and the development of marketing mix strategies?
9. What are some of the factors that firms consider when developing product strategies? What are some of the influences on pricing strategies? What are some issues involved in developing promotion strategies? What do firms consider when developing distribution strategies?
10. Why do firms develop formal marketing plans? What are the elements of a formal marketing plan?
11. What are the important elements of the implementation and control of marketing plans?

Marketing Concepts: Discussing Choices and Issues

1. The Boston Consulting Group matrix identifies products as stars, cash cows, question marks, and dogs. Do you think this is a useful way for organizations to examine their businesses? What are some examples of products that fit in each category?
2. Do you agree with the idea that marketing is a firm's most essential functional area, or do you think a firm's success depends equally on all of its functional areas? Explain your reasoning.
3. Do you think firms should concentrate on developing products that are better in some way than competitor's products, or should each firm focus on making the best product it can without regard to competing products? As a consumer, which approach is more likely to produce products that satisfy you most?
4. Which do you think is more important to the development of successful marketing plans—the assessment of the firm's internal environment or its assessment of the external environment—and why?

Marketing Practice: Applying What You've Learned

1. Assume that you are the marketing director for a local microbrewery and that your boss, the company president, has decided to develop a mission statement. He's asked you to outline the points that you think should be included in the statement. Develop that outline and present it to your class.
2. As the director of marketing for a small manufacturer of specialty jams and jellies, you are currently developing the marketing budget and trying to decide whether to use a percentage-of-sales method or an objective-and-task budgeting plan. Outline the pros and cons of each for your firm. In a role-playing format, use this information to convince a classmate why you have chosen one of the methods as opposed to the other.
3. Working in a small group with four to six classmates, select a product that you all use, such as toothpaste or shampoo. Identify the different brands of the product used by each person in the group, and find out what product features and benefits caused each person to choose the particular brand. Then combine your responses to create a list of all possible product attributes a manufacturer might consider in developing a new brand for that product.
4. Assume you are the new marketing assistant in a small metropolitan hospital whose market consists of the residents in the city district and the students and faculty of a large nearby university. You have been asked for ideas that the organization might use in promotional activities to draw clients who might otherwise choose a larger facility across town. Develop a list of the consumer segments in the hospital's market (for example, elderly, children, college athletes, international students) and identify possible features and benefits the hospital might emphasize in its promotions to attract each segment.

Marketing Mini-Project: Learning by Doing

The purpose of this mini-project is to gain an understanding of marketing planning through actual experience.

1. Select one of the following for your marketing planning project:
   - Yourself (in your search for a career)
   - Your university
   - A specific department in your university

2. Next, develop the following elements of the marketing planning process:
   - A mission statement
   - A SWOT analysis
   - Objectives
   - A description of the target market(s)
   - A brief outline of the marketing mix strategies—the product, pricing, distribution, and promotion strategies—that satisfy the objectives and address the target market

3. Prepare a formal, but brief, marketing plan using Appendix B as a guide.

Key Terms

Endnotes

1. "1994 Annual Report," Harley-Davidson Inc.
2. Gilbert Fuchsbert, "'Visioning' Missions Becomes Its Own Mission," *The Wall Street Journal* (Jan. 7, 1994): B1–B2.
3. George S. Day, *Strategic Market Planning: The Pursuit of Competitive Advantage* (New York: West, 1984).
4. Mark Landler, "If at First You Don't Succeed . . . Why Big Multimedia Strategies Have Such a Short Shelf Life," (*The New York Times* (May 8, 1995): D1.
5. Theodore Levitt, "Marketing Myopia," *Harvard Business Review* (July–Aug. 1960): 45–56.
6. Seth Lubove, "Aim, Focus and Shoot," *Forbes* (Nov. 26, 1990): 67, 68, 70.
7. Jeffrey Zygmont, "In Command at Campbell," *Sky* (March 1993): 52–62.
8. Leslie Brokaw, "The Annual One-Page Company Game Plan," *Inc.* (June 1993): 111–113.
9. Stuart Elliott, "P. & G.'s White Cloud a Casualty of Brand Wars," *The New York Times* (May 6, 1993): D2, D20.
10. Roger A. Kerin, Vijay Mahajan, and P. Rajan Varadarajan, *Strategic Market Planning* (Boston: Allyn and Bacon, 1990).
11. Patricia Sellers, "A Whole New Ball Game in Beer," *Fortune* (Sept. 19, 1994): 79–86.
12. Bob Ortega, "Coors, Breaking New Ground, to Unveil a Stronger Zima 'Clear Malt' Beverage," *The Wall Street Journal* (May 1, 1995): B12.
13. Jeanne Whalen, "Places in the Hearth," *Advertising Age* (Oct. 31, 1994): 6.
14. Linda Grant, "Mattel Gets All Dolled Up," *U.S. News & World Report* (Dec. 13, 1993): 72.
15. James B. Treece, "Sometimes, You Still Gotta Have Size," *Business Week/Enterprise* (Fall 1993): 200–201.
16. Amy Feldman, "'Oh, the Places You'll Go,'" *Forbes* (Nov. 22, 1993): 160–161.
17. David Kirkpatrick, "What's Driving the New PC Shakeout," *Fortune* (Sept. 19, 1994): 109–122.
18. Ibid.
19. Peter F. Drucker, "Managing for Business Effectiveness," *Harvard Business Review* (May/June 1963): 53-60.
20. Tim Smart and Judith H. Dobrzynski, "Jack Welch on the Art of Thinking Small," *Business Week/Enterprise* (Fall 1993): 212–216.
21. Christopher Power, "How to Get Closer to Your Customers," *Business Week/Enterprise* (Fall 1993): 42–45.
22. Thomas A. Stewart, "Your Company's Most Valuable Asset: Intellectual Capital," *Fortune* (Oct. 3, 1994): 68–74.
23. Ronald Henkof, "Companies that Train Best," *Fortune* (March 22, 1993): 62–75.
24. Ibid.
25. John P. Kotter and James L. Heskett, *Corporate Culture and Performance* (New York: Free Press, Shawn Tully, "The Modular Corporation," *Fortune* (Feb. 8, 1993): 106.
26. Mike McKesson, "Blazer Aims for High Sales," *Times Union* (Sept. 8, 1994): C-12.
27. Allan Farnham, "America's Most Admired Companies," *Fortune* (Feb. 7, 1994): 50–52.
28. Laurie Hays, "IBM to Slash Prices Up to 27% On Business PCs," *The Wall Street Journal* (Aug. 24, 1994): A3, A5.
29. Raymond Serafin, "Why GM Opted for Brand Management," *Advertising Age* (Oct. 23, 1995): 3.
30. Gary McWilliams, "Software's Comeback Kid," *Business Week* (Aug. 16, 1993): 101–102.
31. Tim Triplett, "Abbott Labs Exec Tells Benefits of Satisfaction Measurement," *Marketing News* (April 11, 1994): 6.
32. Leonard L. Berry, A. Parasuraman, and Valarie A. Zeithaml "Improving Service Quality in America: Lessons Learned," *Academy of Management Executive,* (May 1994): 34.
33. Terence P. Paré, "How to Find Out What They Want," *Fortune* (Autumn/Winter Supplement 1993): 39–41.
34. "1994 Annual Report," Harley-Davidson Inc.

CASE 2-1

MARKETING IN ACTION:
REAL PEOPLE AT COLGATE-PALMOLIVE

The Colgate-Palmolive Company is fast becoming a world leader in developing successful international brands. The global marketing of new products is the key to Colgate's 15 percent annual earnings growth over the past eight years. Since 1989, Colgate and its seventy-seven worldwide subsidiaries have managed 1,462 new product introductions around the globe. Almost a fourth of all current sales come from products that have been introduced during the past five years. Colgate is working to create products that can be sold by most if not all of its worldwide subsidiaries. That takes a lot of strategic planning.

The complex job of managing such worldwide activity is the responsibility of people like John Steele. Steele is senior vice president of Colgate-Palmolive and head of its global business development group. He is responsible for managing the twelve Colgate megabrands. These twelve brands are of "megaimportance" to the corporation because they are responsible for about 80 percent of Colgate's sales. Many of these products are sold under different names in different countries, but the basic concepts are the same, right down to the packaging.

In marketing these megabrands around the world, Steele says, "We have to really make sure that those equities [the brands] are tightly controlled." Many products such as Coca-Cola intentionally change formulas from country to country in order to satisfy local tastes. But with increasing travel and with U.S. cable television going into homes around the globe, consumers in Tokyo and Jerusalem want the same personal-care product—like Colgate toothpaste—as they do in Boston and Los Angeles.

Colgate controls the marketing consistency of its product with its unique system of "Bundle Books." Each Bundle Book is a marketing plan blueprint and a guide for marketing a particular Colgate product almost anywhere around the globe. These invaluable resources come in the form of looseleaf binders containing everything the company knows about a category or product, the conclusions it has drawn from this information, and the marketing direction it is taking. Each book outlines the steps that need to be taken in a particular country to successfully launch a new product.

Each 150- to 200-page book is prepared in New York by a team of four or five members of Colgate's global marketing group with special knowledge of a product category.

The team gathers input from research and development, sales, marketing, advertising, and public relations and from Colgate's advertising agencies and prepares a Bundle Book that includes a product overview, its formula, additives, fragrance, color, stability, and so on; information on the product family; consumer research; and a definition of the marketing opportunity in a particular country. The books also provide details on packaging and graphics, pricing, advertising plans, and specific advertising executions, and it lists key contacts for answers to questions.

Colgate's experience with its Total toothpaste brand illustrates the value of its Bundle Book. In introducing this new product, the marketing plan was first tested in six countries simultaneously: Australia, Colombia, Greece, the Philippines, Portugal, and Britain. These test countries represented markets with and without widespread television coverage and a range of economic and social characteristics that influence consumer buying patterns. From testing in these six countries Colgate was able to develop its Bundle Book for Total. Since then Total has been introduced into sixty-six countries in the fastest global launch in Colgate's history. (Total is not sold in the United States because it contains the drug Triclosan, which is not yet approved by the Food and Drug Administration.) In all sixty-six countries the introductions used the advertising, packaging, pricing, and positioning outlined by the Bundle Book. Results were better than expected. Market share ranges from 6 to 13 percent in each of the six lead countries.

Source: Adapted from Sharon Kindel, "Selling by the Book," *Sales and Marketing Management*, (Oct. 1994) 101–109.

Things to Talk About

1. What type of growth strategy has Colgate-Palmolive adopted? Explain how the firm is implementing that strategy.

2. What environmental factors have supported Colgate-Palmolive's belief in global marketing consistency?

3. How does Colgate use its system of Bundle Books to launch products in global markets?

4. What do you see as Colgate-Palmolive's distinctive competencies?

5. What secrets to success has Colgate-Palmolive discovered?

MARKETING IN ACTION:
REAL CHOICES AT JACK IN THE BOX

The Jack in the Box fast food restaurant chain began in 1941 as a carhop restaurant called Topsy's Drive-In. From one restaurant, the chain grew first to four restaurants under the name Oscar's and then in 1950 was renamed Jack in the Box, when the first drive-through hamburger stand using the Jack in the Box name was opened in San Diego. Then in 1953 the company opened four new Jack in the Boxes. By 1968 approximately 300 outlets were in operation, and in 1990 the Yorba Linda, California, outlet became the home of the thousandth Jack in the Box restaurant. Today the company operates and franchises approximately 1,200 Jack in the Box restaurants in the United States, Mexico, and Hong Kong.

Over the years the Jack in the Box organization created a competitive advantage by trying hard to live up to its motto, "When you want something better . . ." Jack in the Box has focused on offering fast-food patrons more than just hamburgers and fries. In 1969 Jack in the Box was the first fast-food restaurant chain to offer a breakfast menu. The chain was also the first to offer a prepackaged salad. Overall, Jack in the Box tries to introduce three to four new menu items per year. In 1993 these products were the Beef Gyro, the Smoked Chicken, Cheddar and Bacon Sandwich, and Teriyaki Bowls. In 1994 the new products were the Colossus, the Sourdough Ranch Chicken Sandwich, The Monterey Roast Beef Sandwich, and the Chicken Caesar Sandwich. Jack in the Box's menu usually contains between forty-five and fifty individual items.

In January of 1993 disaster struck, and the Jack in the Box restaurants faced a fast-food nightmare. Outlets in Washington State, Idaho, and Nevada experienced outbreaks of food poisoning that left two children dead and 400 other people ill. After nearly a week, Jack in the Box admitted its responsibility in the food poisoning incidents, set up a toll-free number to handle customer complaints, and changed its meat supplier. As a member of the Industry Council on Food Safety, Jack in the Box had a long-standing concern about food safety, which made the situation especially disheartening to management.

As a result of national media coverage, consumers everywhere avoided Jack in the Box restaurants and sales plummeted. By early February chain-wide sales had declined by 40 percent. Some industry experts questioned whether Jack in the Box would ever fully recover from the disaster. Company management had some important choices to make if the chain were to survive.

In emergency planning sessions, harried managers considered several strategies to help overcome the company's devastated sales and get the restaurant chain back on track. The priority, of course, was to address the food poisoning issue. It could increase food safety by taking a number of measures, such as instituting an intense food training program for all employees in the chain or investing in state-of-the-art equipment for all of its restaurants.

Managers also weighed several strategies that might overcome negative perceptions of the company and draw its customers back. It could attempt to increase the perceived value of the chain by adding even more new products to its already full menu. It could also make changes in promotion strategies by stepping up advertising with messages giving consumers positive information about the company, or it could try discount pricing promotions for special menu items. The company could also try to enhance the chain's image by redoing the exteriors of stores using brighter colors, larger signs, and improved lighting and by renovating the interiors to take on a fresh, clean look.

In the struggle to redirect the company's existing marketing plan in a hurry, the most important choice Jack in the Box market managers faced was which one of the strategies would work best and bring about the desired results as quickly as possible.

Sources: Andrea Adelson, "Jack in the Box Franchisees Cite Parent Concern in Suit," *The New York Times* (July 8, 1993); Ronald Grover, Dori Jones Yang, and Lura Holson, "Boxes in at Jack in the Box," *Business Week* (Feb. 15, 1993); Calvin Sims, "After the Food Poisoning, Foodmaker Is Still Struggling," *The New York Times* (April 26, 1994); Calvin Sims, "How Jack in the Box Is Confronting Its Nightmare," *The New York Times* (July 10, 1993) p. B1, 51.

Things to Think About

1. What is the problem facing Jack in the Box?
2. What factors are important in understanding this problem?
3. What other actions might Jack in the Box consider to address the problem?
4. What are your recommendations for solving Jack in the Box's problem?
5. What are some ways to implement your recommendations?

3

Decision Making in the New Era of Marketing: Enriching the Marketing Environment

When you have completed your study of this chapter, you should be able to:

1. Explain why New Era organizations focus on ethics and social responsibility.

2. Describe the New Era emphasis on quality.

3. Discuss some of the important aspects of an organization's internal environment.

4. Explain why marketers scan the components of an organization's external business environment.

REAL PEOPLE, REAL CHOICES:

MEET RHONDA LIEBERMAN, THE SIERRA CLUB

Rhonda Lieberman is on the lookout for polluters, from big companies to neighborhood litterbugs. She works hard to make the earth a more livable place by making sure the public knows who is helping this cause and who is hurting it. Ms. Lieberman is media director for the Washington office of the Sierra Club, the largest grass-roots environmental organization in America. She works closely with the organization's lobbying and conservation team and with the 600,000 Sierra Club volunteers around the country. Her mission is to promote Sierra Club issues and activities to print and broadcast media, develop messages for the club, and act as a clearinghouse for information the club provides to the media and to the public.

Ms. Lieberman has nearly twenty years of experience as a journalist. She has focused her career in broadcast journalism and has worked at the local and network levels, including stints at CBS and Mutual Broadcasting as well as the Washington, D.C., affiliates of ABC TV and CBS Radio. Ms. Lieberman also worked for Hill and Knowlton, Inc., the world's largest public relations firm, where she produced national broadcast material for business, health care, international, and government clients.

BUYING AND SELLING THE FUTURE

Oil spills. Deforestation. Acid rain. Global warming. Pesticides. Herbicides. Air pollution. Water pollution. Noise pollution. Toxic waste. The list goes on and on. Much of the damage that threatens the future of our planet has been attributed to the actions of businesses that have used up, worn out, or contaminated the world's resources in their quest for profits. But businesses aren't solely to blame—they've been partners in crime with customers who want it all: air conditioners, electric blankets, wrinkle-free pajamas, disposable diapers, curly hair, perfect pears, seaside condos, faster cars, the greenest lawn.

Assigning blame won't save the best and the most beautiful our world has to offer, but the Sierra Club is dedicated to making things better by creating public awareness and lobbying for the enactment of government regulations that curb environmental abuses. Although this organization relies heavily on volunteers to fulfill its mission, these activities are costly.

Just as the Sierra Club scans the natural environment looking for threats to the future, it must continually look to its business environment for opportunities that will bring in much-needed funding and support for the causes it champions while using its *own* limited resources more effectively. Today, organizations ranging from the nonprofit Sierra Club to business powerhouses like 3M are finding that it's possible, and profitable, to take actions that benefit both the marketer and society at large.

Through the efforts of the Sierra Club and other public interest groups over the last twenty-five years, many industrial environmental offenders have been forced to change their ways. These marketers are voluntarily taking responsibility for their actions that may harm the natural environment, and that's not all. They are balancing the need for short-term profits against long-term survival for themselves and the people and places around them. This new marketing orientation also means taking on moral and social responsibilities that will make the world a better place now and in the future.

In this chapter we'll look closely at the *New Era of Marketing* by focusing on its key components: ethics and quality. Then we'll see how this evolving marketing orientation influences the marketing decisions a firm makes when its scans its internal and external business environments for strengths and weaknesses, opportunities and threats.

THE NEW ERA: A FOCUS ON ETHICS AND SOCIAL RESPONSIBILITY

As we head toward the end of this century, forward-looking businesses are moving to what we can think of as a *New Era of Marketing.* As we saw in Chapter 1, this New Era orientation is bringing about basic changes in how firms turn the fundamental marketing concept into modern marketing practice. New Era marketers have come to realize that decisions and strategies designed to satisfy consumer needs and wants must not only be economically sound, they must also have a strong ethical foundation and be socially responsible. The new challenge for marketing is to achieve economic success through actions that also benefit society and our natural environment.

Many believe there are some fundamental changes taking place in the business community. It's not simply a matter of lots of firms jumping on the social responsibility bandwagon and staying there only until something else comes along. Business is actually taking the leadership position on social issues. Of course, a lot of companies have been giving back to their communities for decades, just because it is the right thing to do. For example, during the early part of this century, the owners of large textile firms in small towns across the South built hospitals so that their workers would be able to get good medical care and YMCAs to provide recreation facilities.[1]

What's different today is that firms are seeing a connection between a healthy society and a healthy business, between the well-being of the community and the well-being of the firm. The old objective of marketing is helping the organization to prosper economically. Aspiring tycoons, don't panic: Marketing is still concerned with the firm's "bottom line." But now marketing management also considers **social profit,** which is the net benefit both the firm and society realize from a firm's ethical practices and socially responsible behavior. Marketing's new role is to assist in creating social profit by adhering to ethical business practices and making strategic decisions to help the environment, promote diversity, and serve the community.[2]

Creating social profit is so important to Ben and Jerry's, the Vermont superpremium ice cream firm, that it is one of the principle missions of the company — that is, "To . . . improve the quality of life of our employees and a broad community: local, national, and international."[3] The firm gives 7.5 percent of pretax profits to a foundation that, among other things, creates opportunities for minority populations. Waste from ice cream manufacturing is recycled by feeding it to some happy Vermont pigs who think they died and went to heaven.

In this section we'll take a look at the big picture of ethical behavior and the marketplace. We'll then consider how ethical decision making influences marketing mix strategies and what consumers are doing to ensure that marketers behave ethically. Finally, we'll see what New Era firms are doing to achieve social profit.

social profit: the benefit an organization and society receive from its ethical practices, community service, efforts to promote cultural diversity, and concern for the natural environment

ETHICAL BEHAVIOR IN THE MARKETPLACE

In the New Era of marketing, we are witnessing greater concern about the consequences of business decisions based on short-term profits instead of long-term benefits. As John Shad, the former chairman of the U.S. Securities and Exchange Commission, has suggested, the "greed decade" of the 1980s is being replaced by an "ethics era" — a period where both executives and consumers are becoming concerned about the downside of "business as usual."[4]

Ethics essentially are rules of conduct, the standards against which most people in a culture judge what is right and what is wrong, good or bad. **Business ethics** mean that firms behave according to basic values that are universal and endorsed by most people in its environments. These universal values include honesty, trustworthiness, fairness, respect, justice, integrity, concern for others, accountability, and loyalty.

This renewed emphasis on ethical business practices requires that firms make decisions and engage in activities that are both morally defensible and beneficial to the com-

business ethics: rules of conduct for an organization that are standards against which most people in its environments judge what is right and what is wrong

Figure 3.1
Marketing Ethics Continuum

Source: Adapted from N. Craig Smith and John A. Quelch, *Ethics in Marketing* (Homewood, IL: Richard D. Irwin, 1993).

munity in which the firm operates. Sometimes these decisions can be costly in the short term when they result in lost business. For example, despite robust sales of a video game called Night Trap made by Sega, executives at Toys "Я" Us decided to pull the product from store shelves. This costly action came after receiving complaints from parents about the game, where players defend a group of barely dressed sorority sisters against zombies, who suck out the students' blood with a giant syringe if they win.[5]

Notions of right and wrong do differ among people, organizations, and cultures. Some businesses, for example, believe it is all right for salespeople to persuade customers to buy, even if it means giving them false information, while other firms feel that anything less than total honesty with customers is terribly wrong. Because each culture has its own set of values, beliefs, and customs, ethical business behaviors are defined quite differently in different parts of the world. Giving "gifts" in exchange for getting business from suppliers or customers is a way of life in many countries, even though this may be considered bribery or extortion in the United States. In some parts of the globe, business deals are commonly signed, sealed, and delivered with a handshake, and written contracts are seen as an insult (and are even forbidden in Muslim countries). As we'll see in Chapter 4, these differences can make or break a firm's ability to do business in the global marketplace.

The Ethical Continuum: Who Is Responsible for Behavior in the Marketplace?

While most discussions of business ethics focus on the proper way for companies to behave, in fact ethical decision making in the marketplace is a two-way street: Both businesspeople and consumers must take responsibility for ensuring that marketing exchanges are fair and beneficial to both parties. The *marketing ethics continuum* in Figure 3.1 illustrates the roles each party can choose to play in the exchange process. These roles range from *caveat emptor* ("let the buyer beware") to *caveat venditor* ("let the seller beware").

At the *caveat emptor* end of the continuum, the marketers' interests are in the forefront. Earlier in this century this role was taken by traveling "doctors" selling "snake oil" that miraculously "cured" every ailment known to humankind. Today some people (though obviously not the thousands who call in regularly) consider the telephone "psychic readings" advertised on TV infomercials to be examples of a *caveat emptor* situation.

At the *caveat venditor* end, consumer interests are most important.[6] Here the emphasis is on providing high quality, fair prices, and timely service, among other things. In their desire to satisfy customers, for example, many retailers have instituted very liberal return policies in which they are willing to give refunds for any item a customer chooses to return. (A few courageous stores, such as Nordstrom's, have even been known to give refunds on items they don't even sell.)

These retailers know that some unscrupulous consumers will take advantage of such policies, and many have been burnt by what has come to be called *retail borrowing*, where the consumer purchases an item of clothing such as a party dress or an expensive business suit, wears it for a special occasion, and returns it the next day as if it had not been worn. Still, these stores have made the calculated decision to overlook the selfish actions of a few people to provide better value to the majority of their customers who don't abuse their exemplary service.

The *consumer sovereignty* area of the continuum—probably the *ideal* position—is where customer interests are still on center stage, but consumers are not relieved of all responsibility for ensuring that marketing exchanges are conducted ethically. For example, marketers must be responsible for designing products that are safe and for providing adequate safety information on labels and packaging. Consumers, in turn, are expected to

Turning Rebating into a Consumer Sport

Many marketing promotions designed to get consumers to try a new cereal or to buy a certain brand of toaster rely on cash-back rebates—one per customer—for making the purchase. But greedy customers are managing to get not one but hundreds of rebates. *Rebate scamming,* the practice of obtaining undeserved rebates from firms, is gaining in popularity even as grandmothers are being sent to jail for participating in this new "hobby."

It is estimated that over 100,000 consumers are involved in the rebate scam and are costing businesses more than half a billion dollars a year. Rebating newsletters, rebating clubs, and rebating magazines—including one called *Refunding Makes Cents* that has over 20,000 subscribers—are helping rebaters learn how to make thousands of dollars a year with rebate coupons. And who ends up paying the bill? As with other forms of consumer theft, the costs are passed along to the consumer.

Serious rebate scammers start with hundreds of rebate coupons and UPC proof-of-purchase seals, ingeniously obtained in a variety of ways, and then buy their own cash registers to create sales receipts for their "purchases." Many rebaters simply pick up lots of rebate coupons at the store and collect proof-of-purchase seals by salvaging empty packages from trash dumpsters. But the big-timers attend rebate swap meets, no matter how far away, to build up a treasure trove of coupons and build their fortunes.

Some rebaters regard the practice as an innocent (although addictive) hobby, and they are astonished to learn that mailing in ten or twenty or thirty rebate coupons with different names and addresses on each is actually illegal. So, to those would-be rebate scammers who think they've discovered the road to riches, *caveat emptor!*

Source: "The Rebating Game," *Dateline NBC* (May 5, 1995).

---

read product warnings and directions, to evaluate alternatives before they buy, and to avoid using a product in ways it was not intended to be used once the purchase has been made.

The High Costs of Unethical Marketing Behavior

In the New Era of marketing, managers understand that ethical behavior is not only the right way to act, it also serves the organization's best interests. Unethical practices can wind up costing dearly in the long run, both financially and in damage to a firm's reputation. Many consumers already have a negative attitude toward business in general and toward marketing practices in particular, and any business practice that is less than honest and fair only reinforces this view.

In 1993 DuPont discovered the *financial cost* of an ethically shaky decision to avoid responsibility for a situation—a cost that ultimately added up to over $350 million! The nation's farmers learned that their crops were being damaged by one of DuPont's agricultural products that had become contaminated during the manufacturing process. At first DuPont was a responsible supplier and paid claims for the crop losses. Later on DuPont shifted gears, trying to avoid the cost of responsibility, and major lawsuits ensued that may very well have cost the company more than its original amount of liability for the problem.[7]

Honda experienced the *reputational cost* of unethical practices when a recent lawsuit spotlighted alleged bribes received by former executives of the car company from dealers in exchange for preferential treatment. Sixteen former employees pleaded guilty in a federal investigation to receiving "gifts" including such goodies as a helicopter tour of Hawaii and a $25,000 shopping spree in Hong Kong. In an attempt to ensure that this type of activity does not occur again, Honda set up a financial disclosure policy for its senior executives and established a corporate ethics committee. In addition, employees must sign Honda's revised Business Ethics and Conflict of Interest Policy every year to certify that their conduct is appropriate.[8]

As we have seen, businesses are not the only sources of wrongdoing that have long-run costs: Consumers ultimately pay the price for such practices as "retail borrowing" and "rebating" when retailers and manufacturers are forced to raise prices to cover their losses. Most unethical consumer behavior comes from a feeling that the producer of a product or the retailer who sells it is a large, wealthy organization that makes millions of dollars in profits—"Because the company is so rich, it's okay to rip it off"—but in truth most firms must pass along the costs of unethical consumer behavior if they are to stay in business.

Crimes committed by consumers against businesses have been estimated at more than $40 billion per year. These include shoplifting, employee pilferage, arson, and insurance fraud. In fact, a retail theft is committed every five seconds. It has been estimated that a family of four spends about $300 extra per year because of markups taken by stores to compensate for losses. This problem is not unique to the United States, either: Inventory losses in Great Britain, for example, are estimated at more than 1 million pounds per day.[9]

Unethical practices also can be costly for both marketers and consumers in business-to-business marketing. For example, a supplier of materials or parts who fails to meet delivery dates or who skimps on quality materials can force a manufacturer to stop production altogether or to take time to find alternate suppliers. These actions end up affecting consumers, whether through job layoffs, higher prices, or defective products.

Policing Ethical Behavior

Ethical business practices have become so important in the New Era of marketing that 20 percent of Fortune 500 companies now employ ethics officers. These managers develop training programs and carry out reviews of the firm's ethical conduct as it seeks to achieve its goals and objectives.

Like Honda, many firms have also developed their own *codes of ethics,* or written standards of behavior to which everyone in the organization must subscribe. These documents eliminate any confusion about what the firm considers to be ethically acceptable behavior for employees in the workplace and in their dealings with the public. To help member firms avoid the pitfalls of unethical behavior in their marketing efforts, the American Marketing Association (AMA) has developed a written Code of Ethics that outlines the responsibilities of marketers. The Code, shown in Figure 3.2, also covers the rights and duties of the parties in the marketing exchange process and the issues pertaining to customer relationships.[10]

THE ROLE OF ETHICS IN THE MARKETING MIX

As we've seen in previous chapters, marketing mix strategies are crucial to a firm's success in achieving its marketing objectives. Marketing managers are responsible for determining the best way to price, package, promote, and distribute their offerings to reach profit and market share objectives. New Era managers also take into account the ethical side of each of the 4Ps in the marketing mix.

Making a Product Safe

In developing product strategies, marketing management relates key ethical decisions to product safety. A firm may decide to skimp on design, safety testing, and production to cut costs or rush a new product to market ahead of the competition. One infamous example is the case of the Ford Pinto. Ford Motor Company designed the car with an unprotected gas tank that could explode in rear-end crashes. Consumer watchdog Ralph Nader claimed that Ford had tested a safe fuel system as early as 1970 but had not installed it because it was not mandated by federal regulations. In 1978, in one of over fifty civil cases filed against Ford for injuries sustained due to exploding gas tanks, a California jury awarded $128.5 million dollars in compensatory and punitive damages—the biggest award of its type ever at that time. Later the amount was cut in an appeal and Ford ended up paying $7 million. In June of 1978 Ford recalled 1.5 million Pintos made between 1971 and 1976 to install two plastic shields to protect Pinto gas tanks in rear-end collisions.[11]

New Era firms that emphasize ethical and social responsibility have even been known to voluntarily remove best-selling products from retailers' shelves when product safety is in question. For example, as mentioned in Chapter 1, Procter & Gamble voluntarily withdrew its Rely tampons from the market following reports that some women had suffered toxic shock syndrome (TSS) after using the product. Although scientists did not claim a

Members of the American Marketing Association are committed to ethical, professional conduct. They have joined together in subscribing to this Code of Ethics embracing the following topics:

Responsibilities of the Marketer

Marketers must accept responsibility for the consequences of their activities and make every effort to ensure that their decisions, recommendations, and actions function to identify, serve, and satisfy all relevant publics: customers, organizations and society.

Marketers' professional conduct must be guided by:
1. The basic rule of professional ethics: not knowingly to do harm;
2. The adherence to all applicable laws and regulations;
3. The accurate representation of their education, training and experience; and
4. The active support, practice, and promotion of this Code of Ethics.

Honesty and Fairness

Marketers shall uphold and advance the integrity, honor, and dignity of the marketing profession by:
1. Being honest in serving consumers, clients, employees, suppliers, distributors, and the public;
2. Not knowingly participating in conflict of interest without prior notice to all parties involved; and
3. Establishing equitable fee schedules including the payment or receipt of usual, customary, and/or legal compensation for marketing exchanges.

Rights and Duties of Parties in the Marketing Exchange Process

Participants in the marketing exchange process should be able to expect that:
1. Products and services offered are safe and fit for their intended uses;
2. Communications about offered products and services are not deceptive;
3. All parties intend to discharge their obligations, financial and otherwise, in good faith; and
4. Appropriate internal methods exist for equitable adjustment and/or redress of grievances concerning purchases.

It is understood that the above would include, but is not limited to, the following responsibilities of the marketer:
In the area of product development and management,
- disclosure of all substantial risks associated with product or service usage;
- identification of any product component substitution that might materially change the product of impact on the buyer's purchase decision;

- identification of extra cost-added features.

In the area of promotions,
- avoidance of false and misleading advertising;
- rejection of high pressure manipulations, or misleading sales tactics;
- avoidance of sales promotions that use deception or manipulation.

In the area of distribution,
- not manipulating the availability of a product for purpose of exploitation;
- not using coercion in the marketing channel;
- not exerting undue influence over the reseller's choice to handle a product.

In the area of pricing,
- not engaging in price fixing;
- not practicing predatory pricing;
- disclosing the full price associated with any purchase.

In the area of marketing research,
- prohibiting selling or fundraising under the guise of conducting research;
- maintaining research integrity by avoiding misrepresentation and omission of pertinent research data;
- treating outside clients and suppliers fairly.

Organizational Relationships

Marketers should be aware of how their behavior may influence or impact on the behavior of others in organizational relationships. They should not demand, encourage, or apply coercion to obtain unethical behavior in their relationships with others, such as employees, suppliers, or customers.
1. Apply confidentiality and anonymity in professional relationships with regard to privileged information;
2. Meet their obligations and responsibilities in contracts and mutual agreements in a timely manner;
3. Avoid taking the work of others, in whole, or in part, and represent this work as their own or directly benefit from it without compensation or consent of the originator or owner;
4. Avoid manipulation to take advantage of situations to maximize personal welfare in a way that unfairly deprives or damages the organization of others.

Any AMA member found to be in violation of any provision of this Code of Ethics may have his or her Association membership suspended or revoked.

Figure 3.2
AMA Code of Ethics

Source: American Marketing Association.

causal link between the usage of Rely and the onset of TSS, the company agreed with the Food & Drug Administration to undertake extensive advertising notifying women of the symptoms of TSS and asking them to return their boxes of Rely for a refund. The company took a $75 million loss and sacrificed an unusually successful new product that had already captured about one-quarter of the billion-dollar sanitary product market.[12]

Exhibit 3.1
Sometimes a company's efforts to please its customers can backfire and cause lawsuits that many believe are frivolous or that result in harsh financial judgments against the firm. A recent example is the multimillion-dollar lawsuit against McDonald's filed by a woman who claimed that the coffee she bought in a drive-through line was too hot, causing her to burn herself. Although the dollar amount of the award was eventually reduced, customers are not likely to find their McCoffee quite so hot any longer, and other fast-food chains are working on ways to make dining and driving safer.

Pricing the Product Fairly

The potential for unethical decision making when developing pricing strategies is so great that many pricing practices are now illegal. For example, a firm that competes in a market where there are only a few other firms cannot decide to collude with these other firms to develop a *price-fixing strategy* to sell their products for the same price, thus eliminating any price competition in the marketplace. Because price fixing hurts the consumer, it is a violation of federal law.

A *price discrimination strategy*—charging lower prices to larger customers—is acceptable only if it reflects real savings due to differences in manufacturing costs or if it is necessary to meet competitors' pricing. In general, the legality of a discriminatory pricing decision is based on the effect of the strategy on the competition: If pricing restricts free competition, then it is likely to be ruled illegal.

A pricing strategy that is unethical but not illegal is *price gouging*—that is, deciding to raise a product's price to take advantage of its popularity. Popular toys such as Ninja turtles and Power Rangers have been subject to price-gouging strategies during the Christmas shopping season. In 1995, because of the expected scarcity of space for the Olympic Games in Atlanta, many landlords increased the rent on apartments near the downtown area, driving existing tenants out of their homes.

New Era firms, on the other hand, believe in treating the customer fairly. When Hurricane Andrew hit south Florida in 1993, many local building materials firms raised the prices of plywood and other building materials, knowing that residents would pay anything to protect what was left of their possessions. Home Depot, on the other hand, didn't just keep its prices at their previous level; outlets in the hurricane area sold materials for restoring walls and roofs at cost. In the process, Home Depot gained the loyalty of many Floridians and others around the country who heard the story.[13]

Describing the Product Accurately

Marketing management's decisions on how to promote the firm's products are likely to draw the most criticism about unethical practices. In developing advertising strategies, one questionable practice relates to the use of celebrity endorsements or consumer testimonials in advertising. According to the Federal Trade Commission, a company must disclose whether celebrities are paid for endorsing a product. In addition, the endorser's claims about the product must be substantiated and honestly reflect his or her opinion or experience.

Despite these rules, many consumers, already generally disillusioned by advertising claims, are losing trust in celebrity messages. In a recent one-year period, for example, 52 percent of consumers said they find celebrity advertising "less than credible."[14] Other advertising decisions that are subject to criticism relate to the use of deceptive advertising, offensive advertising, and the stereotyping of women and ethnic minorities in ads. New Era firms, on the other hand, know that providing honest and respectful communications is the best way to go. When all advertisers behave in an ethical manner, it "keeps the playing field level," and everyone, advertisers and customers alike, benefit.

In personal selling, as we saw earlier, the decision to give potential customers gifts or other bribes to secure business is not only unethical but is also illegal in the United States. Managers who encourage salespeople to make the sale by any means promote such unethical practices as deception and manipulation of unwary consumers. For example, one life insurance company has its agents scan newspapers for stories of drive-by shootings and other crimes in Los Angeles. Then the agents call on households in the affected neighborhoods, showing clippings of the shootings. These agents are not only relying on scare tactics, but playing on people's emotional concerns for families and loved ones to sell life insurance.[15]

New Era marketers, on the other hand, feel that they serve their markets best when advertising is honest and respectful of consumers. The Body Shop, for example, instead of using elaborate store displays to sell personal care products in their stores, simply places cards next to items giving customers information about the ingredients and uses of each.[16]

Getting the Product Where It Belongs

The way a firm chooses to get its products to the place where consumers want them at the time they want them can also involve ethical decisions. Many of these are less obvious to consumers because they pop up primarily in dealings between the firm and the other organizations with which it does business. For example, because of their size, many large retailers are forcing manufacturers to pay large *slotting allowances,* fees in exchange for agreeing to stock the company's products on valuable shelf space. While the retailers claim that such fees merely pay the cost of adding another product to their inventory, many manufacturers feel that slotting fees are more akin to highway robbery. Certainly the practice prevents smaller manufacturers who cannot afford the slotting allowances from getting their products to consumers. Other ethical problems between firms will be discussed in Chapter 14.

CONSUMERISM: FIGHTING BACK

Organized activities that bring about social and political change are not new to the American scene. Women's right to vote, child labor laws, minimum wages, equal employment opportunity, and the ban on nuclear weapons testing have all been the result of *social movements,* in which citizens, public and private organizations, and businesses work to procure changes that benefit some segment of society. **Consumerism** refers to the social movement directed toward protecting consumers from harmful business practices. Like other social movements, consumerism activities include the use of economic, moral, and legal pressure to force businesses to make ethical decisions and treat their customers fairly.

The American consumerism movement was born in the early 1900s. The public outcry over Upton Sinclair's book *The Jungle*, which portrayed the horrors of the meat-packing industry, was a driving force in the establishment of federal agencies like the Food and

consumerism: a social movement directed toward protecting consumers from harmful business practices

Drug Administration (1906) and the Federal Trade Commission (1914), as well as numerous other acts to protect consumers' interests.

Consumerism as we now know it evolved in the 1960s, when along with numerous other protest movements, consumer activism emerged as a powerful social force. Consumers organized to demand better-quality products, safer products, and honest product information—and to boycott companies that did not comply. Such books as Rachel Carson's *Silent Spring* in 1962, which attacked the irresponsible use of pesticides, and Ralph Nader's *Unsafe at Any Speed* in 1965, which exposed safety defects in General Motors' Corvair automobile, fueled the fire to force businesses to mend their ways. Among the results were the establishment of government oversight and regulatory agencies and legislation— including the Cigarette Labeling Act of 1966 and the Child Protection and Safety Act of 1969—to address some of these issues.

In 1962 President John F. Kennedy, in his inaugural speech, outlined the rights of consumers to be protected by the federal government. These rights, which have come to be called the **"Consumer Bill of Rights,"** include the following:

- *The right to be safe:* Consumers should be assured that products are not dangerous when used as intended.
- *The right to be informed:* Consumers should be provided with adequate information to make intelligent product choices. This right means that product information provided by advertising, packaging, and salespeople should be honest and complete.
- *The right to be heard:* Consumers should have the means to complain or express their displeasure to obtain redress or retribution. Both government agencies and industry self-regulatory groups should make sure that customer complaints can be independently heard and evaluated.
- *The right to choose freely:* Consumers should be able to choose from a variety of products. No one manufacturer or business should be allowed to control the price, quality, or availability of goods and services. This right, which is, of course, energetically supported by business, counters the criticism that marketing activities create an unnecessary proliferation of products that cause scarce economic resources to be used inefficiently.

Consumers continue to have a vigorous interest in consumer-related issues, and New Era marketers are responding by voluntarily making changes to prevent both consumer anger and government intervention. New Era managers have learned that the best way to avoid the potentially negative effects of consumerism activities is to be proactive and proconsumer—to have their best interests in mind when making marketing decisions. By providing safe products and by voluntarily taking products that have been found to be unsafe off the market, New Era marketers are slowly chipping away at some of the consumer distrust of business. Even manufacturers of products that many consider to be intrinsically hazardous are sensitive to selling defective or unsafe products. In 1995, for example, Philip Morris took the unprecedented step of recalling 8 billion of its cigarette products due to the possibility that filters were contaminated during manufacturing. This precautionary move cost the tobacco giant $100 million.[17]

SOCIAL RESPONSIBILITY: SERVING THE ENVIRONMENT

A firm gains both economic and social profit when it places a high value on **social responsibility** by engaging in activities that promote society's welfare and the public good. But social responsibility is even more than that. It is really a mindset or value system that causes an organization to evaluate all its business decisions in terms of their likely short- and long-term effects on the company, its employees, consumers, its community, and the world at large.

Although a firm benefits from making socially responsible decisions, these actions often come at a cost. Socially responsible decisions may mean higher production and operating costs for the firm, especially as they relate to eliminating practices that abuse or overuse the natural environment. When New Era firms make socially responsible deci-

Consumer Bill of Rights: the rights of consumers to be protected by the federal government, as outlined by President John F. Kennedy, including the right to safety, the right to be informed, the right to be heard, and the right to choose

social responsibility: a management practice in which organizations seek to engage in activities that have a positive effect on society and promote the public good

sions about the use of natural resources, reduction of waste, and protection of air, water, and land, they assume a position of **environmental stewardship.** Nonprofit groups can play an important role in nudging other marketers down the New Era path. The Sierra Club, in concert with other pro-environment citizen's groups, developed an Environmental Bill of Rights that includes goals for citizens, government, and businesses:

■ Prevent pollution so that air, water, food, and communities are free from toxic chemicals.

■ Expand citizens' right to know about toxins, particularly as they affect infants, children, pregnant women, and the elderly.

■ Preserve America's wild and beautiful national heritage for our children and future generations.

■ Conserve America's natural resources by controlling waste, increasing energy efficiency, and protecting against overuse and abuse.

■ Encourage sustainable technologies that meet human needs without destroying the environment.

More and more firms in the New Era are making the choice to protect or enhance the natural environment as they go about their business activities. Texaco, for example, implemented an oil and lubricant collection and recycling program for Texaco service stations. For large industrial customers, Texaco is developing "total fluid management" programs in which Texaco manages lubrication within an entire plant: making sure equipment is lubricated properly, maintaining an inventory of lubricants, and reclaiming products to prevent waste and protect the environment.[18]

Other New Era marketers have focused their efforts on reducing wasteful packaging. Gillette has eliminated the outer boxes on some deodorants, Kodak's Ektar films are no longer packaged in cardboard boxes,[19] and Procter & Gamble introduced refillable containers for Downy fabric softener,[20] along with friendlier refill packaging. In total, about 55 percent of all packaging was environmentally friendly by 1996.[21]

The decisions to emphasize environmentally friendly resources must be made at the very top of the firm by managers who develop the firm's mission statement and set the firm's overall goals and objectives. For example, Knight-Ridder, which publishes over two dozen newspapers, proclaims in its *Annual Report,* "We will be good stewards of our environment and will employ the human and financial resources to support these principles."[22] Knight-Ridder preserves resources, reduces wastes and emissions, and practices energy conservation.

Green Marketing

As we saw in Chapter 2, a firm's business mission identifies its long-term commitments and focuses the activities of everyone in the firm in the same direction. When a firm focuses on environmental stewardship, marketing managers support that focus in developing strategic marketing plans and marketing mix strategies. As a result, New Era marketers design packaging, distribution, promotions, and other communications such as direct mail offers, billing, and sales promotion materials so as to avoid waste and to eliminate material and visual pollution. This strategy is commonly called **green marketing,** especially when it creates a differential benefit in the eyes of customers. Consider these recent green marketing efforts:

■ Melitta U.S.A. introduced unbleached coffee filters that remove damaging chlorine bleach. The company also donates two trees for every one tree used in the production of filter paper "to preserve this resource for future generations."

■ Procter & Gamble has developed many different "ultra" versions of products. The resulting reduction in package sizes not only cuts the amount of packaging that goes to landfills but also increases the company's profits. Even retailers save, because such packages cut retailers' costs by 10 percent and increase dollar sales per cubic foot by 17 percent.[23] Mentadent, the Chesebrough-Pond's toothpaste containing baking soda and peroxide, by offering a refill package selling for less than the product with a plastic pump, saves 50 percent on packaging costs.[24]

environmental stewardship: a position taken by an organization to protect or enhance the natural environment as it conducts its business activities

green marketing: a marketing strategy that supports environmental stewardship by creating an environmentally founded differential benefit in the minds of consumers

■ Green marketing is also important in industrial settings. Nucor and U.S. Steel have recently developed a joint venture to develop a process for manufacturing steel from iron carbide. Because iron carbide is both a source of iron and contains carbon, it could produce an energy-efficient method for making steel. And the process could provide a cost savings to the firm of 20 percent, or $50 per ton. Furthermore, because the steel-making process would be confined within closed furnaces, it would be a much cleaner process.[25]

Does Green Marketing Pay?

Does green marketing lead to red ink for a marketer, or do these efforts pay off? According to a Roper Starch study of "green" ads, consumers only respond to ads that make a connection between what the firm is doing for the environment and a positive result for the individual consumer. For example, an ad by Ford Motor Company discussing how Ford vehicles meet California's emission standards and mentioning electric cars failed to convince consumers that there was anything in Ford's "green" programs for them personally. On the other hand, ads like the one for Revlon's New Age Naturals creams that uses the slogan "Because we believe what is good for the earth is good for all of us" and promises users healthier skin—a real benefit—can be very successful. The lesson for marketers is that saving the planet isn't enough; you have to save people too.[26]

Green marketing programs generally get good marks from consumers. A Roper Poll in 1994 showed that between 1990 and 1993, the number of "green consumers," people who are active in their environmental efforts, increased from 48 percent to 55 percent of the U.S. population.[27] In another recent marketing research effort, 77 percent of consumers said they were more environmentally conscious.[28] On the other hand, these same customers are leery of empty or downright false green marketing claims by companies that try to win their loyalty by claiming to be "green" when they're not.

Despite some abuses, many consumers still are likely to see green marketing as an important product benefit and to pay attention to green marketing advertising claims. In all, about 11 percent of new product introductions are accompanied by environmental promotions.[29] Research suggests that these claims are more likely to make an impact on consumers in developed countries such as the United States, Canada, the Netherlands, and Norway, while consumers in such less-developed countries as India, Brazil, Chile, and Nigeria are least likely to be aware of environmental problems and more likely to blame their governments for such problems.[30]

SERVING SOCIETY: CAUSE MARKETING

An important part of a firm's social responsibility is service to the community. Many organizations feel that the best way to serve their communities is through **cause marketing.** In the past this practice usually involved running a short-term promotion and then donating profits to a charitable organization. Cause-related marketing in its promotion-only form is widely thought to have begun with the American Express campaign to raise money for the renovation of the Statue of Liberty in 1983.[31] Such programs, however, faced a major problem: Many consumers saw them as gimmicky and insincere, especially in cases where there was no apparent connection between the company and the cause. The result was that product sales increased during the two- or three-month duration of the promotion, but there were no long-term benefits to either the sponsoring firm or the cause it was trying to help.

cause marketing: a marketing strategy in which an organization seeks to serve its community by promoting and supporting a worthy cause or by allying itself with nonprofit organizations to tackle a social problem

From One-Night Stands to Commitments

Today, New Era firms are abandoning this one-shot approach by instead allying themselves with one or more nonprofit groups to seriously tackle a social problem, such as illiteracy or child abuse.[32] Avon's Breast Cancer Awareness Crusade is a well-known example of cause marketing. In its first year the program educated an estimated 40 million women and raised nearly $7 million through the sale of its breast-cancer awareness pin, a pink enameled ribbon similar to the red ribbons worn for AIDS awareness.[33] Avon's five-year program began with educating its 415,000 U.S. sales representatives about breast cancer and the importance of early detection. Through the sales reps, Avon distributed 16 million of its brochures titled "10 facts every woman should know about breast cancer" in one month alone. Avon also helped to produce a public television special, "The Breast Care Test," cosponsored an ABC program, "The Other Epidemic," and produced a Spanish-language television program for the Telemundo network.

Does Cause Marketing Pay?

Besides being expensive in terms of dollars, developing alliances between a brand and a cause carries the same risks as associations with a celebrity: If the reputation of the cause is damaged in some way, the fallout may affect the brand image. For that reason, most firms realize they are better off making alliances with general causes than with specific groups or charities.

These firms believe that sales of their products do benefit from cause-marketing activities. According to a Cone/Roper survey of 2,000 American adults, 84 percent believe that cause marketing creates a positive image of a company, and 78 percent say they would be more likely to buy a product associated with an important cause. In addition, 66 percent say they would switch brands, 62 percent would switch retailers, and 54 percent would pay more for the product.[34]

SERVING THE COMMUNITY: PROMOTING CULTURAL DIVERSITY

In 1993 two groups of hungry Secret Service agents walked into a Denny's restaurant. One group got served right away. The other group, composed of six African-Americans, waited . . . and waited . . . and waited. These agents filed a lawsuit, charging unequal treatment of minorities at Denny's.[35] Although Denny's has written policies concerning equal and fair treatment of customers and employees, the lawsuit suggests the policies were not being practiced. Negative press had a substantial effect not only on Denny's sales, but also on employee morale.[36] Failure to promote *diversity* at Denny's caused a marketing failure.

As the Denny's Restaurant organization discovered, another important area of social responsibility is the promotion of **cultural diversity.** This practice involves the inclusion of people of different sexes, races, ethnic groups, and religions in a firm's mixture of customers, suppliers, employees, and distribution channel partners. To create diversity, New Era firms make sure that marketing policies and hiring practices give people an equal chance to work for the firm and buy the firm's products.

As with environmental stewardship, concern for cultural diversity starts at the top in New Era firms. Managers in the organization, from the CEO on down, feel a personal commitment to recruit and hire members of minority groups; they also support training programs for minority employees who may otherwise not have equal opportunities to achieve management positions. The Prudential Insurance Company's "Managing Diversity Program" is a good example of a program aimed at attracting and cultivating minority and female employees. One factor that led to this program was an internal company assessment that determined that minorities and women felt that there was a lack of opportunity for them. Other marketing research showed that the lack of internal company diversity would hinder the success of marketing efforts aimed at other cultures.[37]

> **cultural diversity:** a management practice that emphasizes people of different sexes, races, ethnic groups, and religions in activities involving an organization's employees, customers, suppliers, and distribution channel partners

Supporting Diversity Through Business Partnerships

In New Era firms, the same sense of responsibility that fosters diversity in the workplace also causes firms to encourage the development of minority entrepreneurs as suppliers, distributors, dealers, and franchisees. General Motors, for example, cultivates minority supplier partnerships through its Equal Partners Program, which was begun in 1994.[38] The program does more than just award contracts to minority suppliers. GM actually acts as mentors to the minority firms, working with them to develop five-year plans as well as continuous improvement programs for improving the suppliers' quality, service, and price. All in all GM makes more than $1 billion a year in purchases from minority vendors. Recently GM has introduced a second program whereby it asks its major suppliers to help expand the minority supplier business opportunities by developing programs of their own with a minority purchasing goal of 5 percent of their total sales to GM.[39]

Nordstrom, which operates seventy-seven stores in fourteen states, also has a model minority supplier program. For two years prior to the opening of any new store, Nordstrom holds "Project Previews," fairs aimed at introducing Nordstrom to minority and nonminority suppliers in the area and answering the vendors' questions. Nordstrom's Minority- and Women-Owned Business Development Program, begun in 1989, has generated over $700 million in purchases from minority businesses.[40]

New Era firms that are serious about the needs of minorities are making a big impact on communities through policies that attract minority operators of franchised outlets. Indeed, to understand how firms' cultural diversity programs can contribute to their communities, one need look no farther than the next fast-food outlet. Especially in inner cities or other areas where poverty is high and chances for legitimate employment are slim to none, franchised fast-food restaurants can be an avenue of opportunity for young people looking for a chance to begin a career.

As one McDonald's franchise owner, an African American who operates four restaurants in Los Angeles, observes, "We're teaching kids American values—the work ethic, showing up on time, how to dress, the importance of working as a team." Another franchise owner in Houston offers classes on financial planning to his workers, pays for books for employees who go to college, and visits high schools to put students through mock interviews.[41]

Does Diversity Pay?

While there are costs associated with cultural diversity programs, in the long run they provide important benefits for individual firms and for business in general. As firms like Prudential know, promoting cultural diversity is in the firm's self-interest. Approximately 30 million blacks, 22 million Hispanics, and 7 million Asian Americans live in the United States and together spend over $500 billion a year, which adds up to one of the fastest-growing and most profitable markets around.[42] When firms engage in programs that help minorities in the workplace and in the community, they receive the respect and loyalty of many consumers. And, by improving the standard of living of these groups, everyone benefits.

Within the organization, an emphasis on diversity allows a firm to maximize its chances of hiring capable employees. In addition, having diversity within the marketing and sales groups increases the firm's ability to respond to customers' expectations. Diversity in a sales or marketing group is not easy to attain. One study showed that of the youngest workers, the ones you might think would be most likely to accept diversity, over half said they prefer working with people of the *same* race, sex, gender, and education. In addition, the failure of diversity in many companies is all too clear. Minority workers feel discrimination, which reduces their motivation. And women are more than twice as likely as men to feel their career advancement opportunities are not good.[43]

THE SOCIAL PROFIT AUDIT

We have discussed many kinds of social profit: firms' ethical practices and socially responsible decisions to emphasize green marketing, cause marketing, and cultural diversity. When a firm takes social profit seriously, it conducts a *social profit audit* that looks at its efforts to achieve social profit in much the same way the firm evaluates its success in achieving dollar profit.

Ben & Jerry's Ice Cream practices this concept by establishing what it calls a "two-part bottom line." Its managers test the success of their business decisions by tracking the outcomes of its objectives for creating both dollar profit and social profit. The firm's financial auditors create an income statement that shows its economic bottom line, while independent social auditors review and report on the other part of the company's bottom line, its social profit. Further, Ben & Jerry's makes this information public, even when the results are not as flattering as the company would like.

To measure social profit, firms first decide what they hope to achieve in the areas of ethical practices, green marketing, community service, and diversity. The firm's top managers determine the broad principles and goals that guide the planning of lower-level managers throughout the firm. Just as short-term planning at lower levels in a firm should support the firm's long-term business goals, planning in every functional area in New Era firms includes specific and measurable objectives as well as detailed plans related to top management's vision of how the firm should contribute to the public good.

Plans developed by the human resource function, for example, can include an objective like "improve employee awareness and knowledge of what sexual harassment is and how it should be dealt with in the workplace." A production objective might call for the "reduction of particulate emissions from our factory by 20 percent in each of the next five years." In the marketing plan, an objective might be to "improve product safety features" or to "increase customer awareness and knowledge of the safe use of the product" or to "increase the amount of recycled materials used in product packaging."

THE NEW ERA: A FOCUS ON QUALITY

To borrow a phrase from Ford Motor Company, "Quality is Job 1" in the New Era of marketing. **Quality** refers to the level of performance, dependability, and cost that consumers expect when they buy a product to satisfy wants and needs. In today's highly competitive marketing environment, New Era firms are dedicated to delivering quality that goes *beyond* customers' expectations. New Era managers see quality as more than a differential benefit. By adopting a *total quality focus,* New Era firms create a distinctive competency that is the result of involving everyone in the organization in the quality effort.

quality: the level of performance, dependability, and cost that customers expect in products that satisfy their needs and wants

The New Era focus on quality is what influences the actions and business practices of the world's most admired, successful companies. Firms like Merck (pharmaceuticals), Rubbermaid (rubber and plastics products), Wal-Mart Stores (retailing), 3M (scientific, photo, and control equipment), and Coca-Cola (beverages), according to one study, share five common characteristics:[44]

1. Long-term profits
2. High-quality management
3. High-quality products or services
4. Ability to attract and keep talented people
5. Responsibility to the community and environment.

We've already looked at how New Era thinking influences a firm's sense of responsibility to its community and the natural environment. In this section we'll see how a quality focus affects a firm's profitability, its management practices, and its employees. We'll also look at marketing's role in defining quality in the marketplace.

QUALITY AND THE BOTTOM LINE

Not too long ago many U.S. firms shunned the idea of a quality focus on the grounds that it would cost too much. New Era firms, however, have discovered that a quality focus pays off, both today and down the road. As quality gets higher, costs get lower.[45] Profits rise as quality production methods reduce the costs of rework, redesign, salvage, inspection, and testing associated with defective goods.[46] In fact, Motorola claims that its quality focus *saved* the company $700 million in manufacturing costs over a five-year period.[47]

Delivering on quality reduces the costs of handling returns of defective goods and honoring warranties. It also eliminates the expense of hiring, training, and assigning employees to the unpleasant chore of dealing with customer complaints, a task that often falls to the marketing function. Quality practices also avoid the problems and costs of misplaced orders and billing mistakes that anger customers. A quality focus preserves the firm's reputation and keeps customers satisfied.

Of course, quality is not exactly a concept that was just discovered. The fundamental relationship between quality and customer satisfaction has long been recognized by U.S. marketers. As far back as 1875, Montgomery Ward & Co. was the first American company to offer a money-back guarantee if customers weren't satisfied with the quality of their purchases.[48] What is new, though, is the attempt to integrate a quality perspective into every aspect of marketing and manufacturing to create and deliver a product that's right the first time, rather than simply making good if it isn't. A quality focus helps marketing achieve this goal several ways:

- By creating *customer value* that builds customer loyalty.
- By creating *job satisfaction* so salespeople, marketing staff, and others in the firm are motivated to create customer value.
- By creating *profit* so shareholders will invest in employees and programs to create customer value.

TOTAL QUALITY MANAGEMENT

Most firms have learned that staying in the race today means providing the measure of quality customers expect to get for the price they pay. Today's New Era marketers are trying hard to listen to customers gauge how satisfied they are, to learn what they consider the firm's successes and failures, and to determine customer expectations for new products.[49] That's why the Federal Express Corporation has embarked on what it calls a Powership program involving a panel of 20,000 companies that it services. FedEx surveys 1,000 of its Powership customers monthly for information on ways to improve its quality and its buyer-seller relationships.[50]

The extent to which a firm commits itself to quality and strives to deliver quality beyond expectations relies on its management practices. New Era firms that have adopted a total quality focus have also adopted the principles and practices of **total quality management (TQM),** a company-wide system for quality development, quality maintenance, and quality improvement. TQM seeks to ensure customer satisfaction with product quality by involving *all* employees, regardless of their function, in efforts to continually improve quality in all of the operations of the organization. Many top-level managers see TQM as the key to winning in today's global marketplace, while some marketing managers suggest that TQM is really just the marketing concept put into practice.

In the 1970s the power of the TQM approach surfaced in world markets and jolted many American and European companies out of the complacency of doing business as usual. The Japanese, acting on the advice of W. Edwards Deming, an American statistician and consultant to the postwar reconstruction of Japanese business, were using quality management practices and flooding world markets with lower-cost but far superior-quality products that consumers were only too eager to buy. Since then American businesses have been working on their own versions of TQM to catch up.

Today successful production-oriented business and service-oriented firms have developed TQM approaches for creating quality and value. With the Marriott Hotel chain, for example, the TQM approach starts with a statement of business principles: "The mission of Marriott Hotels is to provide lodging and related services in a manner that builds strong, lasting, and satisfying relationships with customers, employees, owners, shareholders, and the communities in which it operates."[51] By religiously following TQM principles, the Marriott Rivercenter in San Antonio has increased on-time check-ins from 79 percent to 93 percent. Overall guest satisfaction has risen to 99 percent. Teams of employees came up with over fifty improvements that work. Employee morale is up. As the manager says, "Today, we have one product: Every guest leaves satisfied. That's all we do."[52]

Kaizen: Creating and Maintaining Quality

The Japanese concept of *kaizen*—continuous improvement of everything by everyone—stems from the belief that quality can always be created and, once created, can always be improved. *Kaizen* is the very heart of a firm's commitment to total quality. No matter how well a firm's goods and services satisfy customers, there will always be more demanding customers waiting for that product that's just a bit better. More important, there will always be competitors who are trying to steal these customers away.

QUALITY COMES HOME

A few years ago, we set a goal: improve product and service quality ten-fold.

It wasn't enough. So, two years ago, we committed ourselves to a hundred-fold improvement focused on one superordinate goal: total customer satisfaction.

And it's transformed the way we do business.

It means we approach perfection in everything we do, every day. Its principles extend to the way we handle our jobs, the way we feel about ourselves, the way we treat our suppliers and associates and—most important—you, our customer.

The effects of this pervasive culture have won for Motorola, Inc., the Department of Commerce' first Malcolm Baldrige National Quality Award, the American equivalent of the Nobel Prize for quality.

And, just recently, the first annual "Semiconductor Supplier of the Year" award from Dataquest. As the industry's leading, high-technology market research and consulting firm, Dataquest honored Motorola Semiconductor Products Sector after surveying more than 800 procurement sites of 168 electronics sources chosen from Electronic Business' top 200 companies.

But quality is a moving target and a leader who rests on his laurels doesn't remain a leader. So absolute perfection, or Six Sigma as we call it, remains our foremost operational initiative in all products we produce, all services we perform, all things that we do.

Our driving thrust is continuous renewal. Our focus on quality and service is crucial to our survival and success. And the rewards are enormous.

A culture dedicated to total customer satisfaction will result in more profitable companies and industries, a stronger nation and a better world.

Our home.

Motorola wins Dataquest 1988 Supplier-of-the-Year Award

Winner 1988

MOTOROLA

Exhibit 3.2
Motorola Inc. was one of the first companies to win the prestigious *Malcolm Baldrige National Quality Award,* named for Secretary of Commerce Malcolm Baldrige and established by Congress in 1987 to recognize standards of quality excellence in U.S. firms. Two awards are given in each year in each of three categories: manufacturing, service, and small business. Motorola, known for its manufacturing goal of "Six Sigma" (meaning fewer than four defects per million parts), proudly displays the award symbol in its advertising, as do other winners, including companies like AT&T, Xerox, Federal Express, IBM, the Cadillac division of General Motors, and the Granite Rock Company of Watsonville, California. In Japan, businesses compete for a similar award—the Deming prize—named for the American business consultant who taught the importance of quality to postwar Japan.

In its infancy, implementing total quality management meant that firms implemented various quality control processes to detect and correct product defects. Many firms broadened the scope of TQM by focusing on *continuous improvement programs* in which product and process improvement are seen as a never-ending circle in which old processes may be replaced and existing product standards are challenged and upgraded. *Total quality assurance programs* aggressively seek to continuously improve quality—as defined by the customer—not just in products, but in all of a firm's business activities.

For example, when Motorola first adopted a TQM approach, its quality improvement efforts were directed at improving production methods to reduce product defects. Now the company has developed a broader understanding of quality and incorporated TQM into its marketing processes.[53] Instead of focusing just on reducing product defects, Motorola is now focusing on customer satisfaction and value to the customer. Motorola executives make ten or twenty visits a year to customers, talking not just with managers but with the people who use their products. Motorola believes that products should be designed for customer-defined quality: If the customer does not like a product, then Motorola considers the product to have a design defect.

Many firms use an important quality improvement tool known as *benchmarking.* Instead of just looking inwardly to make improvements in a process, benchmarking goes outside the firm so that performance is measured against the "best of class," or leading performer in its industry. Once a benchmark firm has been identified and studied, a firm can evaluate its own successes and failures and set goals to do as well or better than the benchmark firm.

Some New Era business-to-business marketers set benchmarks for themselves by measuring their ability to satisfy key customers. For example, Xerox has used L.L. Bean as a benchmark in evaluating its order entry system. In Great Britain, ICL, a computer manufacturer, has used a large clothing manufacturer as a benchmark for its distribution system. Johnson Controls, a leading provider of building management services and products, first identified "best in class" service practices and then focused on customer needs to create its own service vision, and increased customer satisfaction in the process.[54]

Employee Empowerment: Improving Quality from the Bottom Up

Because total quality relies on employees to succeed, it requires the full support of managers throughout the firm. Continuous quality improvement relies on people management and the ability of managers to create a work environment that is "without fear and finger pointing."[55] In TQM programs every employee is encouraged (even expected) to use his or her knowledge to improve quality.[56] Thus all personnel take responsibility for maintaining quality rather than leaving it to someone else in the quality control department.

Firms that involve all employees in developing, maintaining, and improving quality generally rely on an important principle of the TQM approach. *Employee empowerment* is the TQM practice that gives all employees the authority to make decisions about their work without supervisory approval. Empowered employees can stop an assembly line if they see a problem—without asking anyone's permission or approval. At Ritz-Carlton, an award-winning hotel chain, employees are trained and encouraged to drop what they are doing to help a customer, even if it's something that is not in their job descriptions.[57] In New Era firms employees who are allowed to manage themselves and have control over the tasks assigned to them are more motivated, more productive, and more satisfied with their jobs.

Many firms also develop *participatory management programs* that involve employees in the firm's planning and decision making. Springfield Remanufacturing Company (SRC), an engine rebuilding plant, knows the importance of participatory management. When SRC was bought by new owners in 1983, an employee stock-ownership plan was put into place so that the 720 employees now own 33 percent of the company, and all are trained and encouraged to read the accounting records. When SRC lost a big General Motors contract, employees voted to keep everyone on the payroll but also challenged teams of employees to work together to develop 100 new products. As a result, instead of suffering the expected loss, SRC sales increased 30 percent.[58]

Employee training is an important strength of an employee empowerment program in a quality-focused firm. In addition to specific job skills training, quality-focused firms help employees learn about the company's business mission, its competitive situation, target markets, customer needs, and so on. Many employee empowerment programs go even further and provide employees with opportunities to gain high school or college degrees through on-site educational programs.

Quality-focused firms are willing to sacrifice short-term profits by investing in training programs to improve quality today and ensure profits tomorrow. For example, 120 employees a week pass through the classrooms of General Electric's highly respected training center that offers entry-level studies in manufacturing, sales, personnel relations, marketing strategy, engineering, and finance.[59] Wal-Mart has also invested heavily in training its employees to be friendly and knowledgeable and in warehouse technology, allowing it to surpass Kmart, Sears, and other competitors in marketing productivity and customer satisfaction.[60] When Fuji Industries took control of Subaru, it sent all of its over 700 dealers to special seminars on customer service.[61]

The Team Approach: Creating Customer Value

Teams, working together with the goal of improvement, are a key component of quality improvement programs.[62] *Functional teams* include members from the same functional area of the organization, while *cross-functional* teams may include members from finance, accounting, engineering, and marketing, all working together to solve a problem.

Many of today's successful quality-focused firms have assigned responsibility for quality improvement to *quality circles,* or teams of four to ten self-managed workers who

Creating World-Class Quality at Chrysler Corporation

In 1987 it appeared that Chrysler was on the ropes, like a staggering boxer about to lose the fight of his life. The company would eventually lose hundreds of millions of dollars and over 25 percent of its work force, and, of course, many of its customers, mainly to Japanese competition.

What to do? Chrysler CEO Lee Iacocca and his senior managers decided that nothing short of a quality revolution would do the trick. The company had no choice but to go back to basics and build cars that would lure customers to Chrysler showrooms and keep them coming back for more.

Chrysler's Neon, a subcompact car, is perhaps the greatest symbol of Chrysler's rebirth. The goal in 1990 was to build America's first small car that could compete with Toyota's and Honda's quality *and* sell at a profit, which was no small challenge. Chrysler needed to develop the Neon quickly, so the company was forced to develop processes that resulted in project completion in record time and eventually saved 40 percent of typical new-car development costs. It had to be made cheaply, and it was: It cost $500 less to build than any competing subcompact. It needed world-class quality, and it's rated equal to the Toyota Corolla in reliability. Here's how teams at Chrysler achieved these goals.

New product development began with persistent, even relentless, attention to what customers wanted, rather than designing what the company assumed people would buy. Chrysler's researchers found that Ford's new Escort was failing because of lackluster styling and a rough-running engine, and they found out what subcompact owners really wanted: the feel of a large car, the reliability of a Japanese car, the fun of a sports car, and the safety of a Volvo. And, make sure the engine has *zip,* add airbags and reinforced doors for safety, give it jazzy oval headlights, but skip power windows – they add cost and people don't need them. Drive prototypes hundreds of thousands of miles to diagnose reliability.

Teamwork was the key. *Concurrent engineering,* simultaneous work by teams of marketers, purchasing agents, design engineers, and manufacturing engineers, created the car. Chrysler's team partnered with twenty-five suppliers, who would furnish 70 percent of the car's value. The company also involved its production employees at the Neon plant in Belvidere, Illinois, who identified over 4,000 changes in the car and production process. Chrysler's new focus on long-term customer satisfaction has allowed the company to come roaring back from the verge of bankruptcy as it builds relationships with a whole new generation of drivers.

Source: David Woodruff and Karen Lowry Miller, "Chrysler's Neon: Is This the Small Car Detroit Couldn't Build?" *Business Week* (May 3, 1993): 116–126.

meet regularly to plan and discuss quality.[63] In the auto industry, where defects and potential product recalls are a marketer's worst nightmare, Ford has established quality circles for assembly line workers. Each group regards itself as the customer of the preceding group and a supplier for the next group on the line, so that quality circle employees are accountable to co-workers in another circle.

In cross-functional quality circles, marketing staff and salespeople learn to work effectively with production employees, distribution personnel, accountants, and others in the organization through training in the skills of teamwork, running meetings, and problem solving. Allied Signal, maker of aerospace and automotive products and engineering materials, had each of its 88,000 employees attend a four-day training course. Workers formed teams and learned to assess their business units, address problems, and set goals for creating customer value.[64]

DEFINING QUALITY IN THE MARKETPLACE

Everyone wants quality, but people seem to have different ideas of what it is. Like beauty, quality is in the eyes of the beholder. This notion forms a basic tenet of a total quality focus: Quality is what the customer perceives it to be. An auto isn't comfortable, or powerful, or even good looking unless the customer thinks it is. Food isn't delicious, a dishwasher isn't quiet, and a toy isn't easy to assemble unless the customer says it is.

In quality-focused New Era firms, the first task of marketing is to find out what the customer wants, and because customer needs change, successful New Era marketers continually monitor customers to keep ahead of changing perceptions of quality. But keeping on top of what customers want is just the beginning. The more important task in quality marketing programs is to deliver a perceived quality product at the right place and at the right price.

Adding a Dose of Quality to the Marketing Mix

In addition to developing marketing mix strategies that deliver the level of quality customers want, New Era firms continuously seek ways to improve product, place, price, and promotion.

- *Product:* One way New Era firms are improving quality for their customers is by improving the support they offer for the products they sell. For example, Entergy Corporation, a public utility holding company, needed to improve its ability to help clients having problems with their electric service. Solving these problems isn't exactly like replacing a defective shirt or computer chip: If some technical problems are not solved quickly, they can result in the shutdown of a nuclear plant costing $1 million a day in lost revenue.[65] Entergy had previously provided customer support by supplying thirteen help desks in a four-state area. It found that consolidating its help desks, which serve 2.3 million external customers and over 10,000 internal company customers, greatly improved its service.

- *Place:* Clark-Reliance Corporation produces a number of industrial products such as high-tech electronic sensors used by utility companies and refineries. Clark-Reliance used teamwork to improve its delivery. Sales and production departments, brought together to review how customers obtained the company's products, came up with ways to increase its on-time delivery rate from 30 to a whopping 90 percent.[66]

- *Price:* Sometimes technology can improve quality by allowing a company to give customers what they want while keeping prices low. Taco Bell Corp., a subsidiary of PepsiCo Inc., is the largest quick-service Mexican restaurant in the world. In Taco Bell restaurants, making a burrito is "a high tech happening" that uses the TACO (Total Automation of Company Operations) system. When a customer places an order, the cashier enters it into a register. The order is immediately displayed on several screens so that workers can begin preparing the food. As a fringe benefit of the system, Taco Bell can monitor each day exactly what is sold in each of its 4,000 restaurants, information that is essential for the type of management and inventory control that makes a specific store profitable, even though each taco sells for only fifty-nine cents.[67]

- *Promotion:* Some quality-focused firms are re-engineering the communications function, doing away with the traditional functional groups, departments, and specialties, and are redesigning the way communications are organized. In the traditional communications model, firms send messages to the outside when they want to, to the people they want to, when there is money available. New Era firms realize that customers need and want communications when it is right for them, not right for the company.[68] Hanes Companies invested heavily in developing its novel egg-shaped packaging and creating in-store displays that enabled the firm to show women how its L'Eggs line of stockings was superior to the competition. As a result Hanes is the dominant player in that industry.[69]

Ensuring the Meaning of Quality

One way that quality-focused marketers define and ensure quality for themselves and their customers is through independent organizations that approve or test products. When a firm's products meet an organization's standards for quality and safety, marketers proudly display the bestowed "seal of approval" on the products and in advertising. For example, most electrical products carry the seal of Underwriters Laboratories, an organization that tests and approves the design and manufacturing processes to ensure the safety of these products. Other products may carry the Good Housekeeping Seal of Approval, or they may be recommended by the American Dental Association, the Consumers Union, or even "Doctor Mom."

Many firms look to the uniform standards of the International Standards Organization. This Geneva-based organization initially developed a set of criteria in 1987 to regulate product quality in Europe. The broad set of guidelines, known as *ISO 9000,* covers issues related to the manufacture and installation of products, as well as postsale servicing, and any firms wishing to sell their products in Europe are at a great disadvantage if they do not comply.[70] A version of ISO 9000 has also been developed for American companies, which includes an on-site audit that determines whether quality assurance procedures are in place and whether the employees understand the procedures. DuPont, General Electric, Eastman Kodak, British Telecom, and Phillips Electronics are among the companies demanding ISO 9000-certified products from suppliers.[71]

THE INTERNAL BUSINESS ENVIRONMENT IN THE NEW ERA OF MARKETING

Examining the organization's internal environment is an important step in planning. When developing long- and short-term marketing plans, managers rely on the SWOT analysis to assess the strengths and weaknesses of the organization and its ability to take advantage of opportunities and ward off threats. In Chapter 2 we saw how firms use operations audits and resource audits to evaluate past successes and failures and to judge whether or not resources are fully and effectively utilized. Managers typically use such techniques to assess whether the firm's plans and decisions have accomplished its profit and growth goals.

Firms that have a New Era orientation, as we've seen, are also attempting to achieve social profit by creating an internal environment that fosters ethical behavior and social responsibility, and they are emphasizing quality practices in all aspects of the firm's internal operations to achieve customer satisfaction. The SWOT analysis in New Era firms also includes an assessment of the firm's strengths and weaknesses related to quality, ethics, and social responsibility.

In this section we'll look at how these issues influence a firm's internal environment as well as its goals and decisions. We'll also see that the organization's relationships with other groups—its publics—affects its ability to deliver both economic and social profit.

CORPORATE CULTURE

Just as people who live in different countries share beliefs and values that set them apart from others, members of a business organization also live in their own "world"—at least from nine to five—complete with its own values, traditions, even superstitions. A firm's **corporate culture** is the set of shared management attitudes, values, and beliefs that influences the practices and norms of behavior for everyone in the organization. Successful firms maintain their cultures over time by hiring managers who will be good team players in the firm's established culture; failing firms have been known to replace their entire management teams to create a culture that's more conducive to winning. For example, Lexmark International, a former division of IBM, fired 60 percent of its manufacturing and support managers to institute a team-based quality culture.[72]

In much the same way that the firm's mission statement identifies the scope of the firm's business activities, a firm's corporate culture defines the *way* these activities are carried out. Cultures that value quality constantly strive to improve and ensure the quality of the firm's goods and services. At IBM, for example, service to the customer has been a core value for many years. One way of delivering extra value, according to IBM's annual report, is by "understanding quality as our customers see it. Our aim is to make every offering and every contact perfect in the eyes of our customers."[73]

corporate culture: the set of values, norms, beliefs, and practices held by an organization's managers

Corporate attitudes and beliefs also influence how employees interact with others in the organization. Some corporate cultures are characterized as being very formal and procedurally oriented. But the norm in more and more New Era firms is a culture that thrives on interpersonal contact, encourages informal communications, and promotes the development of relationships among employees in different functional areas *and* between employees and managers. For example, Intel prides itself on what the company calls an "open door" management philosophy: All employees, including the president, work in open cubicles that are accessible to everyone else. No closed doors means that everyone can feel free to get involved in all aspects of the firm's operations.

Risk-Taking Cultures

Some corporate cultures are more inclined to take risks than others. These firms also value innovativeness, individuality, and creativity. Firms with more conservative corporate cultures discourage nontraditional actions and go out of their way to avoid risks. In these firms getting managers to buy into a new way of doing things is like inviting the board of directors to go on a sky-diving mission.

The overall tendency to tolerate or encourage risk affects the firm's critical business decisions as well as the plans and strategies of individual managers within the organizational structure. For example, the marketers of Arm & Hammer baking soda took a risk as they tried to salvage a troubled product. With more women in the work force, less baking at home was occurring, and sales of baking soda fell accordingly. Instead of simply tinkering with Arm & Hammer's marketing mix, the firm responded creatively by coming up with radically different ways to use the product. Arm & Hammer successfully promoted its humble baking soda as a refrigerator deodorizer, swimming pool disinfectant, and even as a toothpaste supplement.[74]

Increasingly, large firms have found themselves at a disadvantage trying to compete with smaller, more innovative companies, especially small start-up businesses. In some cases it's like trying to turn a battleship versus maneuvering a small boat. In contrast to the battleship captains, **entrepreneurs** are creative business people with high-risk dispositions who run these small firms and who are willing to follow through with new ideas. Like sailboat skippers, they are better able to make decisions on the spot to respond quickly to changes in the wind and thus take advantage of emerging opportunities in the external business environment.

More and more large New Era firms are seeking to hire managers with an entrepreneurial spirit who will foster a corporate culture that allows the company to act as if it were a small one in terms of its willingness to go out on a limb and take risks. General Electric, for example, has transformed its corporate culture and revamped its organizational structure, according to its CEO, to "create a small-company soul in a big-company body."[75]

To gain the agility of a small company, many New Era firms have developed what they call *intrapreneur programs* that encourage managers to "live dangerously" by seeking new solutions to old problems, even if this means taking a bit of a risk. Others reorganize the firm's structure to establish or acquire strategic business units that, as we saw in Chapter 2, are essentially separate, small companies under the corporate roof.

In New Era firms, where the corporate culture values entrepreneurship and risk taking, planning and decision making is decentralized, taking a "bottom up approach." SBU managers and others are responsible for their own plans and decisions. In fact, innovative ideas and successful risk-taking ventures on the part of these managers often influence the strategic direction of the entire firm as determined by managers at the top of the corporate ladder.

Profit-Centered versus People-Centered Cultures

An organization's basic business orientation is often the determining factor in its corporate culture. If the firm's business mission limits the firm's focus to economic profit and its chief objectives are increasing revenues and decreasing costs, management attitudes will be profit-centered, often at the expense of employee satisfaction. Employees may be asked to do more for less or risk losing their jobs. This pressure-cooker orientation can result in low wages, lack of incentives in the form of pay raises or job promotions, stringent

entrepreneur: a creative business person with a high-risk disposition who is willing to start up or manage a risky business venture

Exhibit 3.3
Perhaps the most innovative entry in the auto industry is the "Swatchmobile" being produced by Mercedes-Benz in association with the inventor of the Swatch watch. This "micro-compact car," as it's being called, is just over eight feet long but is capable of holding two people and one overnight bag. A car this small is risky business in an industry where consumers are still in love with minivans and rugged 4×4's, but the Swatchmobile developers are banking on congested city streets, rising gas prices, and concerns about air pollution to woo drivers away from their gas guzzlers. The Swatchmobile's prospects will also rise as more governments impose energy-consumption taxes on automobiles and take other measures to preserve the environment. In Japan, tax benefits to midget car owners have already created a very big market for very small cars.

codes of conduct, rigid job descriptions, inflexible hours, and emphasis on the time clock when managers are forced to produce quantity rather than quality. Customers also feel the effects in terms of flimsy products, slipshod services, and high-pressure sales tactics.

In New Era firms, where the business mission includes a concern for employees, customers, and society as well as shareholder profits, the internal atmosphere is quite different. Managers build employee satisfaction through training and incentive programs, creativity workshops, and policies for fair and equal treatment, including the prevention of sexual harassment and discrimination. Employees are allowed to dress casually all or part of the time and to work flexible hours. Many New Era firms have established day-care centers and split-shift programs in which mothers of very young children can share one job with each working only half a day. Other firms are encouraging "telecommuting," where employees work at home and communicate with the office via computer modem.

The corporate culture in many New Era firms fosters employee loyalty. Some firms, for example, keep employees on the payroll during economic downturns when production is dramatically reduced, feeling a sense of responsibility to employees and their families. And some allow leaves of absences in times of family illness or other crises that require employees to be at home. These organizations have found that when they regard their employees as valuable resources and partners rather than as a necessary evil, their workers will more likely help them to find new ways to create better products and services that build customer loyalty as well.

RELATIONSHIPS WITH BUSINESS PARTNERS AND PUBLICS

A very important measure of a firm's internal strengths relates to the relationships it develops outside the organization. No firm operates in a vacuum. Doing business means interacting with others outside the corporate walls. The quality of these relationships can mean the difference between winning and losing the marketing game. **Publics** are groups that have either a current or potential interest in an organization and its objectives.

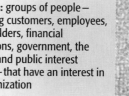

publics: groups of people — including customers, employees, shareholders, financial institutions, government, the media, and public interest groups — that have an interest in an organization

These groups include stockholders, business partners, public agencies, the media, and even competitors.

Relationships with Suppliers

Good relations with suppliers, or *vendors*, that provide the raw materials, parts, equipment, and other resources that allow a firm to produce goods and services are essential. Suppliers can have a profound impact on a firm's marketing strategy. The best product in the world can't be sold if the resources and parts aren't available to manufacture it. Failure to deliver on time, high prices, and availability of needed materials affect both the quantity and the timely delivery of the firm's product and have a direct bearing on the product's price tag. For example, in recent years the cost of paper has risen dramatically, which in turn has affected the cost of such products as college textbooks like this one.

New Era firms also know that they can't make quality products if they can't get quality parts from their suppliers. Motorola, for example, spends $600 million a year to give each of its employees at least forty hours of training a year and has extended that training to its suppliers. Motorola found that some suppliers pretended they knew how to use quality methods and agreed to parts specifications that they couldn't meet. As a manager at one of Motorola's plants observed, "We used to usually end up hating each other." The remedy was to develop a class for suppliers on statistical process control.[76]

Relationships with Intermediaries

Intermediaries are firms that work with the organization to promote and distribute its goods and services to customers. Some of these intermediaries are involved in the physical distribution of goods and services; these include transportation companies and warehouses that are involved in stocking and moving goods after they have been manufactured. When Xerox decided to pursue the low-end desktop printer market, it planned to sell its printer through major distributors who would buy the product and then sell to affiliated resellers who would in turn sell to end users. Xerox knew that building good relationships with resellers would be vital to the product's success, and the company developed a strong support network for these intermediaries. The company trains resellers on the unique selling points of the Xerox printer so they can explain these to customers, and it also provides the technical backup support so that resellers can make the printers work in the user's unique computer environment.[77]

Other marketing intermediaries may be service agencies such as marketing research firms, advertising and public relations agencies, and consulting firms that the firm retains to help plan and execute marketing strategy. Most firms also rely on financial intermediaries, such as banks and insurance companies, that help to finance the company's operations by providing credit or insurance. And many firms develop relationships with government intermediaries in the form of federal and state government agencies that, as we'll see later in this chapter, affect the way firms go about their business.

Relationships with Competitors

It goes without saying that most firms don't get excited about the quality of their relationships with competitors. The marketing concept, the Consumer Bill of Rights, and numerous government policies all focus on the need for a competitive marketplace. But *competitive* does not mean *adversarial* to the point that one or both companies get severely injured in the marketing wars. For instance, over the past couple of decades there have been several "hamburger wars" in which the giants of the fast-food industry tried to steal market share by attacking their competitors. The result was that many consumers became disgusted with the "attack" advertising and everyone lost.

When a firm sets out to destroy a competitor, everyone gets hurt: Reputations are destroyed, resources are wasted, and consumers lose confidence in the competitive market system. Indeed, firms often find it is to their advantage to cooperate with others in the same business, and many are active in trade organizations such as the Cosmetics, Toiletries, and Fragrances Association that engages in lobbying and public relations activities benefiting everyone in the industry.

Relationships with the Public

Companies need to be sensitive to the concerns of various citizens' groups, including organizations focused on the environment, product safety, protection of minorities, and so on. Building good relationships with these and other activist groups benefits an organization in two ways. First, by understanding the concerns of these groups, the firm is able to develop socially responsible programs and practices that will gain the favor of the groups and others in the community. Second, when a firm develops communications with groups, they will most likely be more willing to work with the firm to make changes than to organize some form of public protest when problems arise.

Adolph Coors, a beer manufacturer, developed a good relationship with several publics in a unique way. In 1993 Coors promoted a romance novel as part of a $40 million, five-year cause-marketing campaign against illiteracy. The book, titled *Perfect*, reached *The New York Times'* bestseller list. The campaign stimulated thousands of inquiries concerning the reading program. This doing-good activity improved Coors' reputation in the community and favorably influenced Coors' all-important relationship partners: customers, employees, and shareholders.

SCANNING THE EXTERNAL BUSINESS ENVIRONMENT IN THE NEW ERA

Firms scan the external business environment searching for factors beyond their direct control that create opportunities and pose threats. This phase of marketing's SWOT analysis helps a firm "manage" its dynamic business environment. The idea that marketers should continually scan their external business environment and develop marketing programs that keep pace with changes is not a new one by any means. Traditionally firms have looked to the external environment for signs of economic, competitive, technological, legal, social, demographic, and other trends that will affect the firm itself or its industry.

For example, consumer trends toward fitness and good health ultimately led to reduced amounts of red meat in the average American diet that drastically affected the fortunes of the beef industry. Similarly, the rising average age in the United States has meant more opportunities for the marketing of luxury goods and services to maturing adults with larger disposable incomes, while the increasing elderly population has brought about opportunities for home health-care services and assisted-living facilities.

As the world moves toward the twenty-first century, marketers will face ever-greater challenges in the race to stay one step ahead of the competition. Technological advances make existing products obsolete almost overnight—last year's electronic products, for example, are rarely up to speed today and will seem like dinosaurs tomorrow! And the information superhighway has just begun to influence how marketers compete for consumers' attention and attract their loyalty. In addition, New Era marketers know that winning in today's competitive environment also means taking actions that reap social profit and benefit the natural environment and the public good.

What is different for New Era firms is that decision making considers more than these environmental trends. Marketing decision making for New Era firms means that firms consider each of these trends in terms of its overall focus on quality and ethical and social responsibility. Instead of simply asking how the firm can respond to these trends to create new profitable opportunities, New Era firms seek to find quality-focused, socially responsible ways to respond to create both economic and social profit. The decision model in Figure 3.3 (page 98) illustrates the elements in the internal and external environment that influence goals and decisions made by New Era firms.

In this section we'll consider some of the complex issues that will spell the difference between success and failure for an organization in the twenty-first century. We'll look at the factors in the business environment that firms must take into account as they chart a

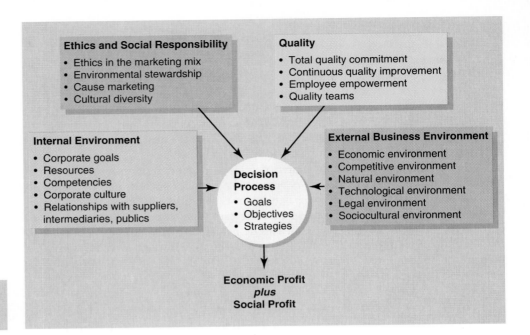

**Figure 3.3
Decision Model for Firms in
the New Era of Marketing**

Ethics and Social Responsibility
- Ethics in the marketing mix
- Environmental stewardship
- Cause marketing
- Cultural diversity

Quality
- Total quality commitment
- Continuous quality improvement
- Employee empowerment
- Quality teams

Internal Environment
- Corporate goals
- Resources
- Competencies
- Corporate culture
- Relationships with suppliers,
  intermediaries, publics

External Business Environment
- Economic environment
- Competitive environment
- Natural environment
- Technological environment
- Legal environment
- Sociocultural environment

Decision
Process
- Goals
- Objectives
- Strategies

Economic Profit
plus
Social Profit

course for the rest of the 1990s. Specifically, we'll examine how New Era firms examine the major elements of the external business environment: the economy, the competition, the natural environment, technology, laws and regulations, and social forces.

THE ECONOMIC ENVIRONMENT

Assessing the economic environment means evaluating factors that influence buying patterns. Studying economic indicators allows marketers to project trends and adjust their plans. Even the best-run company may find it hard to turn a profit when there are no customers around who can afford to buy its products or services.

In the 1950s U.S. marketing managers had the luxury of planning in a friendly economic environment, unfettered by global ties that today link national economic systems. Today's economic links make economic forecasting especially complex. For instance, when Germany maintained high interest rates to curb inflation resulting from borrowing to rebuild East Germany, all of Europe experienced slow growth, and U.S. businesses saw fewer exports to the region. But whether a firm's customers are in Europe, Asia, Latin America, or all at home in the United States, understanding economic linkages is essential.

The Business Cycle: What Goes Around, Comes Around

The state of the economy in the country where a firm does business is vital to the success of its marketing plans. As we saw in Chapter 1, a firm's market(s) consist of people who need and want its products *and* who are able to buy them. The overall pattern of changes or fluctuations of an economy is called the **business cycle.** All economies go through cycles of *prosperity* (high levels of demand, high employment, and incomes), *recession* (falling demand, employment, and incomes), and *recovery* (gradual improvement in production, lowering unemployment, and increasing income). A severe recession is called a *depression;* prices actually fall, but there is still little demand because few people have disposable income. This is accompanied by high unemployment. *Inflation* is another economic indicator of concern to marketers. Earnings adjusted for inflation, referred to as *real income,* measure whether inflation is increasing or decreasing. During inflationary periods, dollar incomes increase, but real income—what the dollar will buy—decreases because goods and services cost more.

The *Gross Domestic Product (GDP)* is both a measure of the current state of the economy and a predictor of future economic trends. The GDP represents the total value of

business cycle: the overall patterns of change in the economy—including periods of prosperity, recession, depression, and recovery—that affect consumer and business purchasing power

Exhibit 3.4
Activity in many industries rises and falls depending on the time of day or time of year. *Seasonal consumption patterns* are especially important to retailers who see the Christmas season as their make-or-break time, because 50% or more of their annual sales take place in the fourth quarter of the year. In other businesses, consumption patterns may vary by the day of the week or the time of day, as most restaurant owners know. Ski resorts depend on seasonal weather patterns—except in Japan, where entrepreneurs have put a ski slope indoors!

goods and services produced in a country regardless of whether the firms are U.S.- or foreign-owned. Typically the U.S. GDP grows at about 3 percent per year. Growth below this level indicates that the economy is slowing down and that a recessionary period might be just around the corner. Growth above this level may signal unacceptable levels of inflation in the economy.

Today businesses operate in a global marketplace where the business cycle of one country affects the ability of firms in another country to sell their products. Part of this is due to fluctuating prices in the currency of different countries in the world money markets. For example, if there is a period of inflation in the United States but no inflation in other countries, one of the ultimate results is that U.S. dollars will buy fewer Japanese yen. For example, one dollar may buy only 190 yen instead of 200 yen. As a result, the price of Japanese products sold in the United States goes up (in U.S. dollars). In turn, however, U.S. products sold in Japan cost fewer yen, increasing sales for U.S. manufacturers. For example, a camera made in Japan might cost $300 at one point in time but would sell for over $350 six months later.

The Power of Expectations

Many economists suggest that changes in the economy are primarily a "self-fulfilling prophecy": When consumers feel that the economy is going to get better, they spend money to buy goods and services, industry flourishes, and, lo and behold, the economy improves! Similarly, if consumers fear a recession will occur in the next year or so, they may begin saving their money and stop making purchases; inventories of goods grow, industries slow production, and the recession begins—simply because people expected it to! Consumer beliefs about what the future holds determine **consumer confidence,** or the extent to which people are optimistic or pessimistic about the future health of the economy and how they personally will fare down the road.

Government and private research firms periodically conduct surveys of consumer confidence and make forecasts that wise marketers heed. One such ongoing study is conducted by a business organization called The Conference Board. This survey attempts to "take the pulse" of the consumer to let companies know what people will be in the mood to buy, if, in fact, they're planning to buy at all. When consumer expectations about the economy are riding high, new products, fad products, and luxury items will be on their minds. When their confidence in the economy is low, they'll think twice about replacing that old sofa or taking a trip.

Business-to-business marketers also try to stay on top of whether consumers plan to be in the market for new houses, cars, and other big-ticket items like refrigerators, televisions, and furniture. Firms that rely on selling materials, parts, and services to the producers of big-ticket items know that consumer confidence indirectly affects their own business demand. Many business-to-business managers also rely on *The Wall Street Journal*'s report on the National Association of Purchasing Management's survey of more than 300 purchasing managers, which signals growth or decline in the manufacturing sector of the economy.[78]

consumer confidence: an indicator of future spending patterns as measured by the extent to which people are optimistic or pessimistic about the state of the economy

The Search for Value

In the 1980s, when consumer confidence was high, consumers expected that they could have whatever they wanted. They were willing and able, with the help of more than a few credit card companies, to indulge in new, bigger, better, more. For many products, the right color was a more important product attribute than its price or durability. But in the early 1990s many Americans began to redefine this view of the relationship between price and value. Shopping habits changed: no shopping 'til you drop. Trips to the high-fashion stores in the mall turned into trips to discount outlets to look for bargains. And so the search for value began. Consumers who could easily afford any car they wanted began to see a $35,000 Lexus as a better-value luxury car than an $80,000 Mercedes. Clothes bearing top designer brand names were passed over for more "value-priced" brands.

The shift in buying patterns has forced many marketers who capitalized on the 1980s craze to acquire high-tech gadgetry and status symbols to reposition themselves for today's more cautious and conservative consumers. For example, Sharper Image, regarded as the yuppie toy store of the 1980s due to inventory like a $649 model of a Ferrari Testarossa, has doubled the number of items it sells at what the company terms a "popular price"—that is, at a price affordable to the average consumer.[79] By continually scanning the economic environment, marketers can keep an eye on consumers' expectations to determine if the pendulum will start to swing back to the "He who dies with the most toys, wins" attitude of the last decade.

THE COMPETITIVE ENVIRONMENT

In the race for consumer dollars, successful firms take home the gold by taking the lead and keeping ahead of the competition. For example, when one airline realizes it is suddenly losing business to a competitor that has begun to offer lower fares for flights to the same destination, it can quickly develop competitive strategies that offer an even lower fare or that offer the same low fare, plus some other benefit such as hotel discounts or half-price fares for family members.

Competition in the Micro Environment

Firms face different forms of competition in their target markets. The most obvious form of competition a firm faces is **brand competition,** where competitors offering similar products or services vie for consumer dollars based on the brand's reputation or perceived benefits. Nike, Reebok, and Adidas are three brands that compete for the same shoe purchase with similar products, and the consumers' choice often comes down to a preference for one athlete endorser versus another or perhaps a product feature like an inflatable heel.

A second form of competition is **product competition,** where competitors offering very different products attempt to satisfy the same consumer needs and wants. For example, a consumer interested in "working out" may join the YMCA or Gold's Gym, or he or she may choose to purchase a Soloflex machine.

A third type of competition is a broader type competition for the consumer's limited discretionary income. *Discretionary income* is the amount of money people have left over after paying for such necessities as housing, utilities, food, and clothing. Few consumers are wealthy enough to buy anything and everything, so each is constantly faced with choices: whether to spend "leftover" money on a shiny new red convertible, to go on a fantastic vacation at a ski resort in Japan next summer, or perhaps even to donate it to the Sierra Club.

Competition in the Macro Environment

The competitive structure of the industry in which the firm operates defines the total market for that industry and allows marketers to identify the number of competitors it's likely to find in its target markets. And it's important to remember that this analysis will yield different results in domestic and foreign markets. For example, Pepsi and Coca-Cola compete ferociously to claim the greater market share in the United States, though (for now anyway) Coca-Cola dominates most overseas markets by a wide margin.

brand competition: a marketing situation in which firms offering similar products or services compete for consumers based on their brand's reputation or perceived benefits

product competition: a marketing situation in which competitors offering very different products compete to satisfy the same consumer needs and wants

Some firms, such as utility companies, are classified as *monopolies*. A **monopoly** exists when only one seller controls the market with no competitors offering alternative products to satisfy a particular need. Because the firm is "the only game in town," firms face little pressure to keep prices low or to produce quality goods or services. Typically this problem is brought under control by the government, which regulates the organization's activities. In such cases marketing efforts often are relatively insignificant and likely to be directed toward *reducing* demand, as when the local power company mounts an advertising campaign urging people to curb their use of air conditioners and other appliances during times of peak demand.

With the exception of utilities that ensure a basic level of service for most citizens, monopolies are quite rare in the United States because regulations generally encourage competition and a free marketplace. The Postal Service had a monopoly on mail delivery and long-distance communications until the Bell System stepped in and created its own monopoly. But those days are long gone for both organizations. The post office is now battling fax machines and on-line communications, the Bell companies are plagued by those persistent ads and discount strategies offered by Sprint and MCI, and both are worrying about UPS and FedEx. Monopolies are more common in socialistic or communist countries like Cuba, where the government is responsible for providing for a population's needs, but even these situations are getting harder to find since the downfall of communism in Europe.

At the other extreme is a state of **perfect competition** in which many small sellers, all of whom offer similar products, are unable to have an impact on quality, price, or supply. Each firm in a market sells basically the same goods or services, and consumers simply buy from the next guy if they don't like what is being offered. In some cases the product itself determines its quality and availability. While true conditions of perfect competition are rare, agricultural markets come the closest. Gasoline and home heating oil are two nonagricultural products that are also close to being examples of this type of market structure.

In the United States a more common market structure is an **oligopoly,** where a relatively small number of sellers, each holding substantial market share, compete in a market with many buyers. Typically these firms focus on differentiating their products on the basis of quality and price. A few large firms in an industry, such as General Motors, Ford, Toyota, and Honda in the auto industry, tend to dominate the market.

Although these companies compete fiercely with one another for market share, at the same time they often find it to their advantage to cooperate in order to create a selling environment that benefits them all. For example, a lobbying group called The Daylight Savings Time Coalition, composed of representatives from such industries as convenience store chains, fast-food companies, and manufacturers of barbecue-related products, played a big role in convincing Congress to move the start of Daylight Savings Time up by a month. These businesses argued that the extra evening daylight would allow customers to shop later (and presumably, put whatever they'd bought on the barbecue grill once they got it home)—and in the process generate added sales for them.[80]

An oligopoly is most likely to be found in industries requiring substantial investment in equipment or technology to produce a product, so there are high "barriers to entry" facing others who wish to get in the game. For example, entering the auto industry to make and sell cars to hundreds of thousands of people is not likely to be a successful venture for an entrepreneur, but finding a small niche where a modified product can be offered to a smaller market may be. This is the case for specialized companies that take an existing car like a Mercedes, a Lincoln, or even a Volkswagen on occasion and turn it into a stretch limousine complete with built-in bar, TV set, and hot tub.

The macro environment in which a firm operates is rarely a pure oligopoly or monopoly or state of perfect competition. Most U.S. firms operate in an "imperfect" market that is characterized by elements of each of these structures. In **monopolistic competition** many sellers, each having slightly different products, compete for the many buyers in a market. In this type of market structure competing firms, such as Nike, Reebok, Adidas, and others, have slightly different products and offer consumers some unique benefit that could allow the firm to monopolize the market. For example, while every major athletic shoe manufacturer sells many types of basketball shoes, an NBA wannabe can only obtain Air Jordans from Nike.

monopoly: a market situation in which one firm, the only supplier of a particular product, is able to control the price, quality, and supply of that product

perfect competition: a market structure in which many small sellers, all of whom offer similar products, are unable to control the quality, price, or supply of a product

oligopoly: a market structure in which a relatively small number of sellers, each holding a substantial share of the market, compete in a market with many buyers

monopolistic competition: a market structure in which many firms, each having slightly different products, compete in a market with many buyers by offering the consumer unique benefits that could allow one firm to monopolize the market

Analyzing the Competition

Before a firm can begin to develop strategies that will create a competitive advantage in the marketplace, it has to know who its competitors are and what they're doing. Lessons learned from marketing's analysis of the successes and failures of competing firms play a significant role in the firm's ability to compete. Marketing management sizes up the competition according to its strengths and weaknesses, monitors the marketing strategies of other firms, and tries to predict their next moves.

New Era firms know that effectively responding to competitors helps a firm prosper. Often competition forces a firm to drive costs down and push quality higher. General Motors, Xerox, and IBM, for example, didn't reduce costs and increase quality until Japanese competitors lured their customers away with cheaper, better products. This loss required dramatic changes to win back customers they had taken for granted.[81] In recent years trade agreements between countries have created more opportunities for international marketing activities and spurred competition in many markets. U.S. firms are facing rougher and tougher competition as consumers at home and abroad happily find clothing, household accessories, and other goods in greater variety at lower prices each year.

New Era marketers continually monitor the competitive environment to detect unanticipated moves by competitors that may require an immediate change in marketing strategy. The desirability of being flexible enough to respond quickly to changes was demonstrated by First Interstate, the third-largest bank in California. Two competitors were merging, which meant they were about to close duplicated branches at many locations. First Interstate saw this interruption in customer service as a market opportunity. Its employees went to these locations, set up billboards, and handed out coupons for free checking. By giving customers a reason to switch banks at a time when they had to change their buying habits anyway, First Interstate attracted new customers. By responding to a sudden opportunity, the bank picked up 110,000 new accounts and over $750 million in deposits.[82]

THE NATURAL ENVIRONMENT

Earlier in this chapter we looked at the cost of doing business—the price the world is paying for the production and exchange of goods and services—as measured by the damage a firm inflicts on the natural environment. We also saw that New Era organizations like the Sierra Club are actively seeking ways to preserve and protect our air, water, and land. Over and above these good-intentioned concerns, firms scan the natural environment in search of changes that threaten its ability to compete in a marketplace with limited natural resources.

Conserving Natural Resources

Alarming changes are taking place in the natural environment as resources become depleted or even extinct, and firms today are paying increasing attention to how the availability and usage of natural resources influences marketing strategy. A key issue for many firms is the declining supply of fossil fuels. As the costs of energy produced by fossil fuels continues to rise, manufacturers are being forced to seek ways to reduce energy consumption in the production process and to produce goods that use less energy. Further, the future holds even more drastic changes for firms and consumers alike in a world without oil that is also without plastic goods.

Another important issue in the 1990s is the destruction of the South American rain forests, as huge swaths of densely wooded lands are being stripped bare to supply the raw materials necessary to make mahogany furniture, rubber, and other products. Many firms are supporting the efforts to save the rain forests in order to conserve this source of supply and to preserve the genetic pool of plants and animals for medical research and development of disease-curing drugs.

Curbing Environmental Abuses

Today's marketers also scan the environment for threats and opportunities posed by public concern about environmental abuses. In the late 1980s, for example, the crowds of

REAL PEOPLE, REAL CHOICES:

DECISION TIME AT THE SIERRA CLUB

It was spring of 1995, and Rhonda Lieberman and her colleagues at the Sierra Club were preparing for the fight of their lives. Changes in the American political landscape were ushering in a new era of conservativism and support for big business. Many of the regulations that had been established to protect the environment were in imminent danger of being weakened or eliminated by the 104th Congress, which was seeking to fight what many of its members perceived to be overly burdensome and unfair constraints on the free marketplace.

Although virtually every public opinion poll showed that most Americans wanted more, not less, protection of environmental resources, legislators and industry lobbyists intent on streamlining the federal bureaucracy were proposing such actions as lifting the moratorium on offshore oil leasing, doubling the level of clearcut logging in national forests, cutting funding for national parks, and prohibiting the Administration from forcing car and truck manufacturers to improve fuel economy. To make matters worse, the public's attention was starting to drift to other important social issues, such as homelessness and crime. Membership in environmental groups, including the Sierra Club, the Wilderness Society, and Greenpeace, had plunged dramatically in the first half of the 1990s as supporters started writing checks for other causes instead.[83]

The Sierra Club needed to find ways to mobilize public support for environmental causes, and particularly to develop a campaign to urge elected officials at the local, state, and federal levels to oppose measures that threatened to reverse progress the organization felt it had made over a twenty-five-year period. The Club joined a coalition of national environmental organizations to create an Environmental Bill of Rights, which proclaimed among other things that Americans were entitled to clean air, water, and food, uncontaminated public spaces, and the promotion of energy-efficient technologies.

Efforts were begun to collect signatures on a petition affirming these rights. This effort would then be used in a public relations campaign to attract media attention, solicit new donors, and galvanize activists around the country. Now the Sierra Club was faced with a critical decision: How should signatures be collected to achieve the goal of a million signers while getting the most publicity mileage out of this campaign? Rhonda Lieberman considered three possibilities:

Option 1. Focus solely on door-to-door canvassing to obtain the signatures, relying on local community activists. This approach has the advantage of providing face-to-face contact, which is more persuasive. In addition, the names and addresses gathered locally can be used for future lobbying and fund-raising efforts. On the other hand, this strategy might not provide a wide enough reach for the campaign. Also, there is always the possibility that the canvassers will not be able to accurately deliver the message; a lot depends on the competence and motivation of each volunteer.

Option 2. Recognize that in the current political climate this goal would not easily be achievable, and instead channel the organization's efforts toward more realistic goals, such as combatting efforts to dismantle the Clean Water Act. An advantage to this approach is that narrowing the efforts to one issue will focus more concentrated attention on it, and also a single issue is easier to understand and explain to the public. In addition, requesting action on one issue is more feasible. Asking for too much and criticizing too much might make the Sierra Club look like "Chicken Little." That is, if the group's message is too catastrophic, no one will take it seriously. On the other hand, though, the organization does have a large agenda that must be addressed, and it might be irresponsible to focus on only one or two issues.

Option 3. Develop media opportunities to create attention for the issue and stage "events" where a large number of signatures might be collected at once. This approach would create greater impact and a lot of publicity whenever an event occurred. On the other hand, the group runs the danger of being seen as a "flash in the pan"; attention would be riveted to the cause only until the next day, when it would be replaced by some other "hot" topic on the evening news.

Now, join the Sierra Club decision-making team: Which option would you choose, and why?

burger-crazed customers at McDonald's showed signs of thinning out: Consumers were beginning to worry less about getting a fast meal and more about the plastic packaging that clogged their landfills and littered their streets and yards. Before long McDonald's was under full attack by the Environmental Defense Fund, and even the mighty Hamburglar couldn't fight the battle that was turning "McProfit" into "McStruggle." Sales dropped off as environmentally conscious consumers fled the Golden Arches, and luring them back meant expensive changes in packaging and costly recycling programs. It also meant joining the Environmental Defense Fund, establishing an environmental affairs unit to monitor and reshape public opinion, and adding ecological education to the curriculum at Hamburger University.[84] These efforts helped McDonald's public image considerably, as the firm discovered that many people are more concerned about clogged landfills than they are about clogged arteries.

Like McDonald's, many companies are acting to curb these abuses. Even the U.S. government decided to use its buying power by setting environmentally sound goals for purchases by U.S. agencies. These goals included buying computers that use 60 percent less electricity when idling, stationery made from 50 percent recycled material, buying thousands of alternative-fuel vehicles, and phasing out air conditioners and refrigerators that use ozone-depleting compounds.[85]

THE TECHNOLOGICAL ENVIRONMENT

In today's world of marketing, technology, like no other force in a firm's external business environment, has the potential to revolutionize or destroy an industry. In many businesses a firm's ability to monitor its technological environment and stay on top of the latest developments can mean life or death; for other firms, it's the difference between profits and losses. From Silicon Valley in California to Silicon Alley in Massachusetts, marketers who manage to stay in the game find that the competition gets tougher every day, as more and more bright, young entrepreneurs turn garage workshops into powerful industry-leading firms. This image of Apple Computers' founders laboring in their garage has inspired thousands of aspiring Steve Jobs's to innovate with a dollar and a dream.

In the past fifty years marketing applications of technology have spurred the race for product development, bringing about countless "new and innovative" goods and services, many of which have since become commonplace necessities: the television set (around 1950), commercial jet airline service (1958), the microwave oven (1967), hand-held calculators (1973), the personal computer (1974), compact disks (1983), fax machines (1988), and the World Wide Web (1996). Many of the scientific discoveries that led to the development of such products were the result of government research efforts during World War II and the Space Race.

Some of the most exciting technological developments that affect marketers today involve the improved abilities of organizations to communicate with customers, complete transactions more effectively, and deliver goods and services more efficiently. Customer service has been greatly enhanced by the use of toll-free telephone numbers and easy computer access to customer databases. Technological advances have made it possible for people to buy virtually anything they want (and even some things they don't want) without ever leaving their homes, simply by typing their orders into their computers, or by placing a call to the Home Shopping Network. And firms are only beginning to experiment with

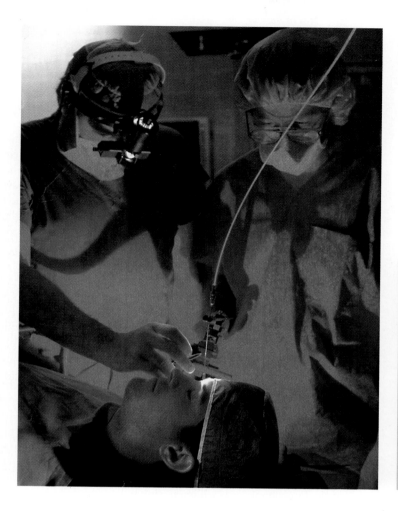

Exhibit 3.5
Scientific research has a major impact on firms that produce technology-based goods and services, and it creates opportunities for firms in many other industries. In recent years research in many fields has influenced such diverse goods as suntan lotion and sodium-free canned peas. In medicine, research and technology have brought about dramatic changes in products from pills to prostheses and have lead to state-of-the-art services like laser surgery.

the powerful marketing opportunities available on the Internet. Physical distribution has improved due to automated inventory control afforded by such advancements as bar codes and computer light pens. Some of these developments will be discussed in later chapters on distribution and communications.

Staying on Top of Change

Changes in technology can dramatically transform an industry, just as transistors revolutionized data processing and consumer electronics, and today's firms must quickly respond to technological developments or risk losing their competitive edge. Successful marketers continuously monitor ongoing research projects in government and private research organizations, and they scan the external business environment in search of ideas and trends to spark their own research efforts. Firms that develop their own unique technologies are also on the watch for competitors who have the resources or capabilities to catch up quickly. R&D is a big-budget item for firms like 3M, Kodak, and Sony.

Keeping on top of research and technological developments gives marketers the edge in developing products and strategies that make a difference. Even marketers who don't put technological innovations directly into their products can find profitable product opportunities by monitoring the research published in industry publications and scientific journals. For example, the *New England Journal of Medicine* and the *Journal of the American Medical Association* publish the latest in medical research, and, as we'll see in Chapter 5, the American Marketing Association and other industry groups provide research reports that can be invaluable to marketers.

When individual inventors feel they have come across something exciting they usually want to protect their exclusive right to produce and sell the invention by applying for a *patent.* Thus, by monitoring government patent applications, marketers may discover innovative products they can purchase from the inventor. And there are other ways marketers keep in touch with research and technology. Many of the most important inventions are part of government-funded research grants. Clever marketers keep track of what government grant goes to whom for what research, hoping to identify potentially profitable projects.

Innovation versus Technophobia

The risk-taking aspect of a corporate culture is closely tied to the organization's willingness to adapt to new technology and to invest in state-of-the-art equipment. For many firms technology and equipment that open doors of opportunity represent a major investment. Unfortunately, shortsighted managers in these firms often have a case of technophobia, where they are leery of adopting new procedures. They argue that the technology itself eats away the firm's profit base, let alone the costs of training and lost production time for installing and debugging new systems. Why risk the investment today, they ask, when the technology will change tomorrow?

Consider, for example, the plight of Encyclopedia Britannica, Inc., the prestigious book collection that has been the last word in referencing the world's knowledge for over 200 years. Despite its clear superiority to other encyclopedias in terms of content, the company fell on hard times because it failed to adapt to changes in how knowledge is being stored and retrieved. While competitors such as Grolier and Funk & Wagnalls moved quickly to offer CD-ROM versions of their encyclopedias that sell for less than $100, Britannica only recently offered its collection on CD-ROM—and with a price tag of $995.[86]

The corporate cultures in forward-looking New Era firms see technology as an investment the firm can't afford *not* to make. This view holds that when technology is on the roll, a firm can choose to be the steamroller or part of the road. Firms that choose the steamroller option lead the way in today's competitive environment. Technology is the means for improving quality and increasing efficiency; it encourages employees' creativity and fosters ideas for innovation. New Era managers also see technology as the key to the future, even if it means a risky investment at the expense of short-term profits. General Electric, for example, was willing to sink billions of dollars into technology for its factory automation division and its newly established medical imaging business.

THE LEGAL ENVIRONMENT

Legal and regulatory controls are prime motivators for many business decisions. The legal environment, which includes the activities of legislative and regulatory bodies at the global, national, state, and local levels, affects every aspect of a firm's marketing endeavors. For example, Louisiana-Pacific Corp. invested $100 million to change its technology after being fined $3 million by the Environmental Protection Agency for toxic emissions.[87]

Only by careful and continuous monitoring of the legal environment can marketers be sure that the firm's production, product development, pricing, distribution, and advertising decisions are not in violation of the many laws and regulations that are intended to ensure competition, protect consumers, and protect businesses from each other and, in some cases, from consumers. Table 3.1 lists some of the major federal laws that seek to protect and preserve the rights of American consumers and businesses.

While some businesspeople argue that excessive legislation only ties the hands of firms that are trying to compete in the open marketplace, others recognize that many laws ultimately help firms by maintaining fair competition, protecting businesses, and supporting troubled industries. The U.S. government helps small businesses by providing management counseling and small business loans. It has also responded to many firms that lobby for legislation that creates demand for products they "happen" to make, such as smoke detectors, infant car seats, and lead-free gasoline.[88]

The Watchdogs of Business: Regulatory Agencies

Federal and state governments have also created a host of *regulatory agencies,* governmental bodies that monitor business activities and enforce laws. The major watchdogs regulate different industries or different types of marketing activities.

- The Food and Drug Administration (FDA) enforces laws and regulations relating to foods, drugs, cosmetics, and veterinary products.
- The Federal Trade Commission (FTC) enforces laws relating to several areas of business practice. It is responsible for enforcing laws against deceptive advertising, and for product labeling regulations.
- The Federal Communications Commission (FCC) regulates communications by telephone, radio, and TV.
- The Interstate Commerce Commission (ICC) regulates interstate bus, truck, rail, and water operations.
- The Consumer Product Safety Commission (CPSC), established under the Consumer Product Safety Act, protects the public from potentially hazardous products.
- The Environmental Protection Agency (EPA) develops and enforces regulations aimed at protecting the environment.

Table 3.1
Overview of the Legal Environment

Law	Purpose
Sherman Antitrust Act (1890)	Developed to eliminate monopolies and to guarantee free competition. Prohibited exclusive territories (if they restrict competition), price fixing, and predatory pricing.
Food and Drug Act (1906)	Prohibited harmful practices in the production of food and drugs. Created the Food and Drug Administration (FDA).
Clayton Act (1914)	Prohibited tying contracts, which require a dealer to take other products in the seller's line. Prohibited exclusive dealing if it restricts competition.
Federal Trade Commission Act (1914)	Created the Federal Trade Commission to monitor unfair practices.
Robinson-Patman Act (1936)	Prohibited price discrimination (offering different prices to competing wholesalers or retailers) unless cost-justified.
Wheeler-Lea Amendment to FTC Act (1938)	Revised the FTC Act. Made deceptive and misleading advertising illegal.
Lanham Trademark Act (1946)	Protected and regulated brand names and trademarks.
Fair Packaging and Labeling Act (1966)	Ensured that product packages were labeled honestly, and reduced undue number of different package sizes.
National Traffic and Motor Vehicle Safety Act (1966)	Set automobile and tire safety standards.
Cigarette Labeling Act (1966)	Required health warnings on cigarettes.
Child Protection Act (1966) and Child Protection and Toy Safety Act (1969)	Banned dangerous products used by children. Set standards for child-resistant packaging.
Consumer Credit Protection Act (1968) and Fair Credit Reporting Act (1970)	Protected consumers by requiring full disclosure of credit and loan terms and rates. Regulated the use of consumer credit reporting.
Consumer Products Safety Commission Act (1972)	Created the Consumer Product Safety Commission to monitor and recall unsafe products. Set product safety standards.
Magnuson-Moss Consumer Product Warranty Act (1975)	Regulated warranties.
Children's Television Act (1990)	Limited the amount of television commercials aired on children's programs.
Nutrition Labeling and Education Act (1990)	Required that new food labeling requirements be set by the FDA.

Adapting to a Regulatory Environment

Sometimes (in fact, many times) firms object to a government's watchdog activities when they put a stop to its marketing plans. Lysol is an example of one firm that coped a bit more creatively with government regulation. Way back in 1966, the FTC objected to Lysol's claim that it helped to prevent the spread of colds. By 1974 the company no longer made this claim in its advertising. Instead, the firm funded research at a leading medical school on the topic, and used the resulting data to convince the FTC that Lysol does in fact inhibit the spread of colds. Commercials making this claim began to appear again in 1983.[89]

New Era firms know that the best of all worlds is when no government regulation is needed because firms work together to make sure everyone plays fair. In fact there are a number of organizations that serve as self-imposed watchdogs on marketing activities. The most active of these is the National Advertising Division (NAD) of the Better Business Bureau. The NAD receives and investigates complaints about advertising. If the NAD investigation supports a complaint, it is turned over to a National Advertising Review Board (NARB) panel that may make a recommendation to the offending advertiser to change or cease the advertising. As a voluntary, independent entity, the NARB has no power to enforce its recommendations to advertisers. Most advertisers, however, comply because they believe it is in the best interest of all advertisers to clean their own house rather than forcing the government to step in and do it for them.

Navigating the Global Legal Environment

Although some feel the United States has far too many laws regulating business conduct, America actually has relatively few legal controls compared to many other countries. Operating in global markets is difficult because of the variety of regulations that govern business activities in different countries. In some cases, for example, advertising content is regulated by the local government. Comparative advertising is illegal in France, and advertising birth control products is illegal in Italy. Pricing in Germany is controlled, and special sales can be held only for a particular reason, such as going out of business or the end of the season. Advertising also focuses more on the provision of factual information rather than on the aggressive hard sell. Indeed, it is illegal to mention the names of competitors.[90]

As we will see in Chapter 4, often understanding the basic philosophy and attitudes toward business of the ruling political party in another country is important to marketers. One particular political party may be more pro-business and supportive of open competition in the marketplace, while the opposing party can be characterized as significantly anti-business and interested in increasing regulations to control business activities.

THE SOCIOCULTURAL ENVIRONMENT

In both consumer and business-to-business markets, an understanding of social and cultural factors is a must. Quite obviously, awareness of demographic or lifestyle trends is important in developing marketing strategy for General Motors, Procter & Gamble, or Nike. It is equally important to firms that sell goods and services to hospitals, building contractors, airports, or universities because it is the consumer market that drives the business-to-business market. If consumers didn't want college educations, universities would not be in business.

In evaluating the consumer environment, marketers need to understand how consumers' attitudes, beliefs, and ways of doing things in different parts of the country or the world might affect the firm's strategies. The consequences of ignoring these issues became evident during the 1994 Soccer World Cup, when both McDonald's and Coca-Cola made the mistake of reprinting the Saudi Arabian flag, which includes sacred words from the Koran, on disposable packaging used in promotions. Despite their delight at having a Saudi team in contention for the Cup, Muslims worldwide protested this borrowing of sacred imagery, and both companies had to scramble to rectify the situation.[91]

Demographics

Demographics are statistics that measure observable aspects of a population, such as birth rate, age distribution, and income. The changes and trends revealed in demographic studies are of great interest to marketers, because the data can be used to locate and predict the size of markets for many products, ranging from home mortgages to brooms and can openers. Imagine trying to sell baby food to a single male or an around-the-world vacation to a couple making $15,000 a year! We'll consider these issues in detail in Chapters 6 and 8 and look briefly at some of the important demographic variables here.

- *Age:* Consumers of different age groups obviously have very different needs and wants. While people who belong to the same age group differ in many other ways, they do tend to share a set of values and common cultural experiences that they carry throughout life.[92] Levi Strauss, for example, has been successful in developing the idea that it is a "brand for life" by introducing products such as Dockers to meet the needs of their consumers as they age. As a Levi's marketing executive explained, "In the 1960s, growth [in the jeans market] was due to adoption of jeans by fifteen- to eighteen-year-olds. . . . Now these people are twenty-five to forty-nine and Dockers meshes perfectly with what the Levi brand image is about for them."[93]

- *Gender:* Many products, from fragrances to footwear, are targeted to either men or women. Differentiating by sex starts at a very early age—even diapers are sold in pink versions for girls and blue for boys. As proof that consumers take these differences seriously, consider that market research has revealed that most parents refuse to put male infants in pink diapers![94]

- *Family structure:* A person's family and marital status is yet another important demographic variable, since it has such a big effect on consumers' spending priorities. Young bachelors and newlyweds are the most likely to exercise, go to bars, concerts, and movies, and to consume alcohol. Families with young children are big purchasers of health foods and fruit juices, while single-parent households and those with older children buy more junk food. Home maintenance services are most likely to be used by older couples and bachelors.

- *Social class and income:* People who are grouped within the same social class are approximately equal in terms of their incomes and social standing in the community. They work in roughly similar occupations, and they tend to have similar tastes in music, clothing, art, and so on. They also tend to socialize with one another, and share many ideas and values regarding the way one's life should be lived.[95] The distribution of wealth is of great interest to marketers, because it determines what groups have the greatest buying power and market potential.

- *Race and ethnicity:* African Americans, Hispanic Americans, and Asian Americans are the three fastest-growing ethnic groups in the United States. As our society becomes increasingly multicultural, new opportunities develop to deliver specialized products to racial and ethnic groups, and to introduce other groups to these offerings.

    Sometimes this adaptation is just a matter of putting an existing product into a different context. An African American product manager at Pillsbury realized that the company had overlooked the importance of baking as a cultural activity for many African American and Hispanic American consumers. At her urging, small changes were made to appeal to these groups. For example, the company's cornbread twists had been promoted as going with chili, but in packages delivered to African American areas a recipe for corn muffins—the perfect "go with" for greens—was included instead. The company also added Spanish advertising, and detailed preparation instructions for Hispanics who were not used to baking with mixes. Even the "white bread" Pillsbury Dough Boy now appears in some commercials as a blues singer or a rap star.[96]

- *Geography:* Many national marketers tailor their offerings to appeal to consumers who live in different geographic areas. Heileman Distilleries is now fifth in sales in the United States, largely because of its regional marketing efforts. The company operates ten breweries across the country, and its position in each of its markets is backed up with sponsorship of major local events and other regional promotions. As the company's marketing vice president explained, "The primary objective of being a regional brand is to make the consumer think that 'this product is mine'. . . . People tend to think positively about their hometowns, and a product strongly identified with this aura is likely to strike a responsive chord."[97] Some of Heileman's successful regional brands include Old Style, Colt 45, Lone Star, Rainier, and Samuel Adams.

Values and Lifestyles

Lifestyle refers to the patterns of living that reflect how people choose to spend their time and money. These choices express a person's values, attitudes, interests, and opinions that make a statement about who one is in society and who one is not. A person's lifestyle is influenced by factors that are shared by others in similar social and economic circumstances. Still, each person also provides a unique "twist" that allows him or her to inject some individuality into a chosen lifestyle. For example, a "typical" college student (if there is such a thing) may dress much like his or her friends, hang out in the same places, and like the same foods, yet may nevertheless indulge a passion for running marathons, stamp collecting, or community activism that makes him or her a unique person.

Lifestyles are not set in stone. People's tastes and preferences evolve over time, so that consumption patterns that were viewed favorably at one point in time may be laughed at (or sneered at) later. Bell-bottomed trousers, for example, were viewed as high style in the 1970s and as being totally ridiculous in the 1980s, but wide-legged pants are now starting to look good again to some consumers.

We'll take a closer look at demographics and lifestyles in Chapter 6 and how they affect consumers' buying patterns and influence the marketing mix. For now, though, let's review a few of the major consumer trends that are shaping New Era marketing strategies today.

■ *Voluntary simplicity and environmentalism:* Consumers are forsaking their pursuit of status symbols for a life that is "outwardly simple and inwardly rich."[98] Interest has grown in wilderness products, camping activities, coffeehouses that encourage customers to linger and talk with friends, and all-natural prod-

> **lifestyle:** the patterns of living that express people's values, attitudes, interests, and opinions and that reflect how they choose to spend their time and money

ℛEAL PEOPLE, REAL CHOICES:

HOW IT WORKED OUT AT THE SIERRA CLUB

The Sierra Club chose option 3. Through a coordinated media planning effort with other organizations, the Save Our Summer (SOS) Campaign was created. The idea behind the campaign was to reach people at the times and places where they were most likely to be aware of the need to preserve natural resources: while they were enjoying outdoor summertime activities.

The coalition held a kickoff press conference on the steps of the Capitol in Washington, D.C., to announce the Bill of Rights campaign and followed up with a series of press events around the country to reach Americans at play, at the beach, in the parks, and on rivers and lakes. The Sierra Club also bought radio ads to criticize key national legislators who voted in Congress to dismantle environmental laws such as the Clean Water Act. By carefully orchestrating events designed to take advantage of the power of free publicity to influence consumers' attitudes and behaviors, the Sierra Club was able to harness contemporary promotional techniques to win "market share" for pro-environmental causes.

ucts. With the introduction of its Origins line of cosmetics, the Esteé Lauder Company was the first major U.S. beauty company to bring natural, non-animal-tested products in recyclable containers into department stores.[99]

■ *A return to value:* Many consumers are no longer interested in the niceties of fancy stores, especially when the products for sale there are marked up too high. They are becoming what the Grey Advertising agency calls "precision shoppers." Picking and choosing carefully, they no longer shy away from lesser-known house brands and are flocking in droves to warehouse stores offering self-serve products by the case in drab surroundings.

■ *Decreased materialism and emphasis on self-fulfillment:* In the last decade products like Godiva chocolate, Filofax binders, and BMW cars watched their sales soar as consumers strove to acquire tokens of success. Today, though, things are a bit different. Disenchantment with the accumulation of status goods has led many consumers to focus on the acquisition of experiences, whether from travel, high-quality music reproduction, or virtual reality games.

Chapter 3 Summary

Objective 1. Explain why New Era organizations focus on ethics and social responsibility.

Firms in the New Era of marketing emphasize social profit as well as economic profit. Companies behave ethically because it is morally right and because it allows them to earn goodwill that helps them achieve economic goals. Different firms operate along an ethics continuum that places business interests at one end, where unethical business practices are likely to occur. At the other end of the continuum consumer interests are paramount, and businesses may face unethical behavior by consumers in such forms as shoplifting and employee pilferage. New Era marketers consider ethical issues in developing marketing strategies and are often influenced by consumerism, a social movement aimed at protecting consumers from harmful business practices.

Social responsibility means that New Era firms act in ways that benefit the public, the community, and the natural environment. New Era marketers assume social responsibility through environmental stewardship, in which the firm's actions either improve or do not harm the natural environment, and cause marketing, which focuses on marketing strategies that promote the public good. New Era firms also practice social responsibility by promoting cultural diversity—that is, by including people of different sexes, races, ethnic groups, and religions as customers, suppliers, employees, and distribution channel members.

Objective 2. Describe the New Era emphasis on quality.

Quality-focused firms in the New Era of marketing strive to provide goods and services that go beyond customer expectations about the relationship between cost and value. Total quality management (TQM) is a management philosophy that focuses on satisfying customers and reducing production costs through such programs as continuous quality improvement, employee empowerment, and a team approach that involves employees in all levels of the organization in cross-functional planning and task-related activities. Marketing activities in quality-focused firms center around defining consumer perceptions of quality and developing marketing mix strategies that promote quality.

Objective 3. Discuss some of the important aspects of an organization's internal environment.

Success in the New Era of marketing rests heavily on an organization's corporate culture, the set of shared values, attitudes, and beliefs that influences its decisions and practices. New Era firms are more people-centered and concerned with the welfare of employees. Another aspect of the internal environment in New Era firms is the value placed on the firm's relationships with its suppliers, intermediaries, competitors, and various publics. Important publics include employees, shareholders, government, media, financial institutions, and consumers.

Objective 4. Explain why marketers scan the components of an organization's external business environment.

Understanding the economic environment is essential to marketing planning. The business cycle of prosperity, recession, recovery, and depression affect all business activities. A cause-and-effect relationship exists between the stages in the business cycle and consumer expectations about the general economy, their income, and their search for value.

In a firm's competitive environment, brand competition, product competition, and the more general competition for consumers' limited discretionary income affect the development of marketing strategies that give the firm a competitive advantage. The amount of competition within a specific industry is determined by whether that industry is a monopoly, an oligopoly, or an example of perfect competition or "imperfect" monopolistic competition.

The natural environment has major effects on business. Raw materials and energy sources are becoming depleted, forcing companies to revise production methods and to develop energy conservation strategies and technologies for themselves and the consumer goods they produce. Activist groups and consumers concerned about abuses to the natural environment influence many of the activities and business practices of many firms.

In the technological environment, marketing applications of public and private research revolutionize many industries, creating opportunities for some and making others obsolete. R&D funding is essential in forward-looking firms, and innovative, risk-taking firms tend to be more willing to adapt to new technology.

The legal environment affects production, product development, pricing, distribution, and advertising activities. Many businesspeople see laws and regulations as hindrances to business, but others look to the benefits of laws that protect competition in a free market and help businesses.

The sociocultural environment helps marketers identify consumer groups and predict their purchasing preferences. Consumer demographics segment a population according to such characteristics as age, gender, family structure, social class, race, and geography, while consumer values and lifestyles indicate the way people conduct their lives.

Review Questions

Marketing Concepts: Testing Your Knowledge

1. What is meant by the New Era of marketing? Why do marketers in the New Era think ethics are important?
2. What is social responsibility? How does social responsibility affect marketing decision making?
3. Explain consumerism. What is the Consumer Bill of Rights?
4. What is a total quality focus? What are some of the components of a Total Quality Management approach?
5. What is "corporate culture"? What are some ways that the corporate culture of one organization might differ from that of another? How does corporate culture affect decision making?
6. Describe the business cycle. What is consumer confidence? How do consumer expectations affect the business cycle?
7. What different types of competition do marketers face?
8. What factors in the natural environment have a direct effect on businesses?
9. How do technological advances affect marketing?
10. What purposes do laws and government regulations serve in the marketplace? How do they help marketers?
11. What is the sociocultural environment? What are some examples of sociocultural trends currently affecting marketing decision making?

Marketing Concepts: Discussing Choices and Issues

1. This chapter states that some current consumer trends include concern for the environment and a return to value. What are some examples of current products that would be negatively affected by these trends? What are some products that have a good chance of being positively affected? What are some ideas for new products that would be in tune with these trends?
2. Taking a firm's perspective, what do you think are the positive and negative aspects of social profit?
3. The U.S. government has been both criticized and praised for its efforts to regulate and control business practices. What is your stand on this issue as a consumer?

4. Do you believe that marketers have the right to use any or all public spaces to deliver advertising messages? Where would you draw the line in terms of places and products that should be restricted?
5. Consumer privacy has become an important ethical issue as hundreds of firms from home mortgage companies to L.L. Bean maintain large databases that record numerous details about people's personal lives. Do you think the sharing of this information violates consumers' right to privacy? Why or why not?

Marketing Practice: Applying What You've Learned

1. As a college graduate, one of the first things you will need to do when you are hired by a business firm or nonprofit organization is to learn about the organization's corporate culture. Make a list of the typical elements of a corporate culture. Make suggestions for how you might develop a better knowledge and understanding of each of these elements of the corporate culture once you accept your next position.
2. You have recently been employed by the marketing department of a firm that disposes of hazardous waste. Your new boss is a believer in the New Era of marketing and feels that building relationships with not only customers but all of the organization's publics is important. She has asked that you prepare a report listing the various publics you see as important to the organization. She has also asked that you make suggestions for ways to develop better relationships with each of these groups. Develop that report.
3. As an employee of a business consulting firm that specializes in helping people who want to start small businesses, you have been assigned a client who is interested in starting a video delivery service, in which customers call in their video orders for home delivery. As you begin thinking about this client's potential for success, you realize that understanding the external environment for this business is essential. First, decide which environmental factors are most important to this client. Then choose one of these factors and use your library to identify the current and future trends in this area.

Finally, in a role-playing situation, present all of your recommendations to the client.

4. Assume you are employed in the marketing department of a medium-sized firm in the furniture industry, a manufacturer of "case goods," such as end tables, cocktail tables, wall units, dining room chairs, and so on. Your firm has recently been purchased, and the new owner is terribly concerned about social responsibility. Every member of the marketing department has been asked to put together a report on how this firm can become a more socially responsible organization. Develop your report for the new owner of the firm.

Marketing Mini-Project: Learning by Doing

This mini-project is designed to help you find out more about the New Era of marketing focus on ethics and social responsibility.

1. With one or several other students in your class, select a demographic group of consumers to study. You may wish to study college females, college males, young professionals, retail employees, young mothers, older citizens, or a specific ethnic group.
   a. Develop a brief questionnaire that will allow you to obtain information from members of this group about their experiences with businesses. You might want to ask about some or all of the following:

■ Their best experience with a business

■ Their worst experience with a business

■ Opinions about the ethical behavior of business in general

■ How businesses ought to behave

■ The responsibility of businesses to the environment

■ The responsibilities of businesses to promote cultural diversity

■ Such consumer behaviors as shoplifting, returning used merchandise, and so on

■ The ethical behavior of retail employees.

   b. Obtain responses to your questionnaire from members of your selected demographic group.
2. Analyze the responses to your survey and prepare a report for your class on what you have learned. In what ways might the unique perspectives or characteristics of the group you selected have influenced their responses?
3. What recommendations would you make to marketers on ways to improve their dealings with this group? To government? To consumers? To retail stores? To your marketing instructors? Include these recommendations in your report.

Key Terms

Endnotes

1. J.W. Cash, *The Mind of the South* (New York: Vintage Books, 1941).
2. "1992 Annual Report," Rockwell International.
3. Ben & Jerry's, hand-out available at the factory store (1993).
4. N. Craig Smith and John A. Quelch, *Ethics in Marketing* (Homewood, IL: Richard D. Irwin, 1993).
5. Joseph Pereira, "Toys 'R' Us Says It Decided to Pull Sega's Night Trap From Store Shelves," *The Wall Street Journal* (Dec. 17, 1993): B5F.
6. Thomas Donaldson and Patricia Werhand, *Ethical Issues in Business: A Philosophical Approach* (Upper Saddle River, N.J.: Prentice Hall, 1988).
7. Joseph Weber, Gail DeGeorge, and Beth Regan, "So Much For Making Nice, *Business Week* (June 28, 1993): 28–30.
8. "When Gift Giving Goes Too Far," *Sales & Marketing Management* (June 1995): 15.
9. Catherine A. Cole, "Deterrence and Consumer Fraud," *Journal of Retailing* (Spring 1989): 107–120; Roy Carter, "Whispering Sweet Nothings to the Shop Thief," *Retail & Distribution Management* (Jan./Feb. 1986): 36.
10. Rajendra S. Sisodia, "We Need Zero Tolerance Toward Ethics Violations," *Marketing News,* (March 1990): 4, 14.
11. *Facts on File* (March 17, 1978): 185; *Facts on File* (April 14, 1978): 264; *Facts on File* (May 19, 1978): 366; *Facts on File* (July 28, 1978): 569; *Facts on File* (Sept. 22, 1978): 718–719.
12. Larry Edwards, "The Decision Was Easy," *Advertising Age* (Aug. 26, 1987) 2: 106.
13. Joan C. Szabo, "Business Pitches in after Andrew," *Nation's Business* (Oct. 1992): 37–39.
14. Thomas R. King, "Credibility Gap: More Consumers Find Celebrity Ads Unpersuasive," *The Wall Street Journal* (July 5, 1989): B5, 31.
15. Alfred G. Haggerty, "Bang! Bang! Selling Life Insurance: When Bullets Fly," *National Underwriter* (Oct. 1990): 14.
16. Allan J. Magrath, "Contrarian Marketing," *Across the Board* (Oct. 1990): 46–50.
17. Ronald Smothers, "Recall of Contaminated Cigarettes Leaves Many Smokers Unfazed." *The New York Times* (June 2, 1995): A18.

18. "Seeing 'Green': Marketing, Environment Can Mix," *Texaco Marketer* (April 1993): 18–20.

19. "Big Trend: Smaller Packaging," *U.S.A. Today* (April 1): B1 [cited in *Marketing Executive Report* (April 1993) Chicago: American Marketing Association] 7.

20. Jacquelyn Ottman, "The Power of Green Lies in Marketers' Hands," *Marketing News* (March 1): 10.

21. "Concerned Consumers Push for Environmentally Friendly Packaging," *Boxboard Containers* (April 1993): 4.

22. "1992 Annual Report," (Knight-Ridder, Inc.) 66.

23. Pam Weisz, "Ultra-Clean: Retail Cheers Still More P&G Concentrates," *Brandweek* (Aug. 22, 1994): 1, 6.

24. Pam Weisz, "Mentadent Gets Buyer-Eco-Friendly," *Brandweek* (Feb. 21, 1994): 10.

25. Stephen Baker, "The Odd Couple of Steel," *Business Week* (Nov. 7, 1994): 106–107.

26. Kevin Goldman, "'Green' Campaigns Don't Always Pay Off, Survey Finds," *The Wall Street Journal* (April 11, 1994): 38.

27. Jacquelyn Ottman, "Ignore Environmental Issues at Your Own Marketing Peril," *Brandweek* (May 9, 1994): 17.

28. Howard Schlossberg, "Report Says Environmental Marketing Claims Level Off," *Marketing News* (May 24, 1993): 12.

29. Ibid.

30. Gary Levin, "Too Green for Their Own Good," *Advertising Age* (April 12, 1993): 29.

31. Nancy Arnott, "Marketing With a Passion." *Sales & Marketing Management* (Jan. 1994): 64–71.

32. Ibid.

33. Fiona Gibb. "Avon: Pinning Down an Issue," *Sales & Marketing Management* (Sept. 1994): 85.

34. Nancy Arnott. "Marketing With a Passion." *Sales & Marketing Management* (Jan. 1994): 64–71.

35. Laura Bird, "Denny's TV Ad Seeks to Mend Bias Image," *The Wall Street Journal* (June 21, 1993): B3.

36. Chuck Hawkins, "Denny's: the Stain That Isn't Coming Out," *Business Week* (June 28, 1993): 98–99.

37. Robert J. Kelly, "Toward a More Diverse Sales Force," *Sales & Marketing Management* (March 1994): 33–34.

38. Jerry Bowles, "Minority Business Enterprises," *Fortune* (May 15, 1995): 150.

39. Jerry Bowles, "Profit Through Partnership," *Fortune* (May 15, 1995): 147–162.

40. Ibid.

41. Jonathan Kaufman, "A Break Today: McDonald's Owner Phil Hagans Becomes a Role Model for Inner-City Teenagers," *The Wall Street Journal* (Aug. 23, 1995): A1.

42. Brian Silverman, "Don't Ignore the Obvious," *Sales & Marketing Management* (April 1994): 112–113.

43. Sue Shellenbarger, "Work-Force Study Finds Loyalty Is Weak. Diversions of Race and Gender Are Deep," *The Wall Street Journal* (Sept. 3, 1993): B1–B2.

44. Jennifer Reese, "America's Most Admired Corporation," *Fortune* (Feb. 8, 1993): 44–72.

45. Charles H. Fine. "Quality Improvement and Learning in Productive Systems," *Management Science* (Oct. 1986): 686–705; Ray R. Gehani, "Quality Value-Chain: A Meta-Synthesis of Frontiers of Quality Movement." *Academy of Management Executive* (May, 1993): 29–42; David A. Garvin, *Managing Quality* (NY: Free Press, 1988); L.W. Phillips, D.R. Chang, and R.D. Buzzell, "Product Quality, Cost Position and Business Performance," *Journal of Marketing* (1983): 26–43.

46. Philip B. Crosby, *Quality is Free: The Art of Making Quality Certain* (New York: The New American Library, 1979).

47. Lois Therrien, "Motorola and NEC: Going for Glory," *Business Week* (Special Issue on Quality, 1991): 60–61.

48. Bernard F. Brennan, "Remarks on Marketing Ethics," *Journal of Business Ethics* (April 4, 1991): 255–257.

49. Brian Oliver, "A Most Satisfying Form of Research," *Marketing* (April 30, 1992): 24–27.

50. Aimee L. Stern, "Courting Consumer Loyalty With the Feel-Good Bond," *The New York Times* (Jan. 17, 1993): 10.

51. Linda Silverman Goldzimer and Gregory L. Beckmann, *I'm First, Your Customer's Message to You* (New York: Berkley Books, 1989): 59.

52. "Making Guests Happy at Marriott." *Fortune* (May 31, 1993).

53. B.G. Yovovich, "Motorola's Quest for Quality," *Business Marketing* (Sept. 1991): 14–16.

54. William Bentley, "A Case for Change: Redefining the Service Organization," *Fortune* (July 10, 1995): S4.

55. Byron J. Finch and Richard L. Luebbe, *Operations Management* (New York: The Dryden Press, 1995): 104.

56. Mary Walton, *Deming Management at Work* (New York: Perigee Books, 1990).

57. Howard Schlossberg, "Measuring Customer Satisfaction is Easy To Do—Until You Try It," *Marketing News* (April 26, 1993): 5.

58. Tom Rusk, M.D. and Patrick Miller, "Doing the Right Thing," *Sky* (Aug. 1993): 18–22.

59. Thomas A. Stewart, "GE Keeps Those Ideas Coming," *Fortune* (Aug. 12, 1991): 43.

60. Allan J. Magrath, "Marching to a Different Drummer," *Across the Board* (June 1992): 53–54.

61. Ibid.

62. Ibid.

63. Peter W. Moir, *Profit by Quality* (NY: Wiley, 1988): 29.

64. Amal Kumar Naj, "Allied Signal's Chairman Outlines Strategy for Growth," *The Wall Street Journal* (Aug. 17, 1993): B2.

65. Patrice Rhoades-Baum. "Consolidating Support Functions: This Strategic Move Helps Companies Meet Business Needs," *Fortune* (July 10, 1995): S9.

66. Stanley Brown, "Now It Can Be Told," *Sales & Marketing Management* (Nov. 1994): 34, 38.

67. Patrick Bultema, "From Cost Center to Profit Center: The Changing Bent of Support Operations," *Fortune* (July 10, 1995): S2–S3.

68. Don E. Schultz, "Maybe We Should Start All Over With an IMC Organization," *Marketing News* (Oct. 25, 1993): 8.

69. Ibid.

70. John Holusha, "Global Yardsticks are Set to Measure 'Quality,'" *The New York Times* (Dec. 23, 1992): D6.

71. Ronald Henkoff, "The Hot New Seal of Quality," *Fortune* (June 28, 1993): 116–120.

72. John A. Byrne, "The Horizontal Corporation," *Business Week* (Dec. 20, 1993): 79.

73. "IBM Stockholders' Report," First quarter (1990).

74. P. Rajan Varadarajan, Terry Clark, and William M. Pride, "Controlling the Uncontrollable: Managing Your Market Environment," *Sloan Management Review* (Winter 1992): 39–47.

75. Jack Welch, "Welch on Welch," *Financial World* (April 3, 1990): 62–65.

76. Kevin Kelly and Peter Burrows. "Motorola Training for the Millennium," *Business Week* (March 28, 1994): 158–163.

77. Lorien Golaski, "Xerox Turns Channels Over to Boehner," *Business Marketing* (Aug. 1994): 34.

78. Melissa Levy, "Manufacturing Showed Growth During October," *The Wall Street Journal* (Nov. 2): A2.
79. Cyndee Miller, "Sharper Image Revamps Product Line, Sells Items Consumers Can Actually Buy," *Marketing News* (May 11, 1992): 2.
80. P. Rajan Varadarajan, Terry Clark, and William M. Pride. "Controlling the Uncontrollable: Managing Your Market Environment," *Sloan Management Review* (Winter 1992): 39–47.
81. Peter Nulty, "Why Not to Kill Your Competitor," *Fortune* (May 3, 1993): 71–72.
82. Nancy J. Perry, "Even Bankers Can Learn to Sell," *Fortune* (July 12, 1993): 96.
83. Timothy Aeppel, "Green Groups Enter a Dry Season as Movement Matures," *The Wall Street Journal* (Oct. 21, 1994): B1.
84. "The Green Revolution: McDonald's," *Advertising Age* (Jan. 29, 1991): 32.
85. Mary Beth Regan, "Uncle Sam Goes on an Eco-Trip," *Business Week* (June 28, 1993): 76.
86. Mark Landler, "Slow-to-Adapt Encyclopedia Britannica is for Sale," *The New York Times* (May 16, 1995): D1.
87. Mary Beth Regan, "How Much Green in 'Green' Paper?" *Business Week* (Nov. 1, 1993): 60–61.
88. P. Rajan Varadarajan, Terry Clark, and William M. Pride, "Controlling the Uncontrollable: Managing Your Market Environment," *Sloan Management Review* (Winter 1992): 39–47.
89. Ibid.
90. Matthias D. Kindler, Ellen Day, and Mary R. Zimmer, "A Cross-Cultural Comparison of Magazine Advertising in West Germany and the U.S.," unpublished manuscript (Athens, GA: The University of Georgia, 1990).
91. "Packaging Draws Protest," *Marketing News* (July 4, 1994): 1.
92. Natalie Perkins, "Zeroing in on Consumer Values," *Ad Age* (March 22, 23, 1993).
93. "Levi's Broadens Appeal," Quoted in *Magiera* (March, 1989), *Ad Age* (July 17, 1989): 1.
94. Jennifer Lawrence, "Gender-Specific Works for Diapers—Almost Too Well," *Ad Age* (Feb. 8, 1993): S-10.
95. Richard P. Coleman, "The Continuing Significance of Social Class to Marketing," *Journal of Consumer Research* (Dec. 1983): 265–280.
96. Linda Keene, "Making a Stale Business Poppin' Fresh," *Sales and Marketing Management* (April 1992): 38–39.
97. Quoted in George Rathwaite, "Heileman's National Impact with Local Brews," *Marketing Insights* (Premier Issue): 108.
98. Ronald D. Michman, "New Directions for Life-Style Behavior Patterns," *Business Horizons* (July–Aug. 1984): 60.
99. Pat Sloan, "Cosmetics: Color it Green," *Advertising Age* (July 23, 1990): 1.

CASE 3-1

MARKETING IN ACTION: REAL PEOPLE AT THE BODY SHOP

In recent years the cosmetics industry has discovered it needs a makeover. Total industry growth has come to a halt. Also, the market itself has changed: No longer are revered brand names a guarantee of customer loyalty. And consumers have become increasingly concerned about the need to sacrifice animals for the sake of developing a better blush. The window of opportunity has been opened for new competitors to enter the market and build their brands.

One successful challenger is CEO Anita Roddick, founder of the United Kingdom's Body Shop International. A maverick in the cosmetics industry, Roddick doesn't spend her time in a big-city, high-rise office; instead, she travels Africa, Asia, and Latin America foraging for secret ingredients she can incorporate into such unique Body Shop products as White Musk Shower Gel. Roddick also spends her time trying to assist developing nations through business partnerships with suppliers of her exotic "raw materials."

Roddick opened the first Body Shop in 1976 on a narrow side street in Brighton, England. The store's neighbor, an undertaker, was not pleased with the cosmetics store's name, the "Body Shop," and sent Roddick a letter of complaint. Roddick leaked the story of the letter to the press, saying that the "undertaker was ganging up on a woman shopkeeper." This free publicity gave the Body Shop a big boost once the story hit the papers. Roddick learned from this incident, as she came to realize the value of talking (for free) about her business and her sense of responsibility for doing good.

MARKETING IN ACTION: REAL PEOPLE AT THE BODY SHOP (CONTINUED)

The Body Shop now operates over 1,100 stores in forty-five countries worldwide. The Shops sell hair and skin care products made with naturally based, biodegradable ingredients. The scents—orange blossoms, mint, jasmine, and more—are all natural, too. The company requires pesticide tests on all of the natural ingredients used in its products, but none of the products are animal tested. The stores carry soap bars shaped like endangered species and feature such imaginative items as kits of soothing scents and creams for expectant mothers that also include a flannel cloth for mopping their brows.

The staff wears T-shirts promoting environmental causes, and leaflets about the company's social concerns are available for customers to take away. Packaging is kept to a minimum, and recycled materials are used as often as possible. Only biodegradable plastic bags are used, and customers are encouraged to return empty bottles and have them refilled for a discount. And, there are no alluring product displays in Body Shop store windows. Rather, windows contain posters supporting important causes.

Some Body Shops have no manager. Instead, the staff works together to collectively handle accounting, staffing, and administrative responsibilities. Despite this loose organizational structure, all Body Shops have a well-trained staff. Employees receive extensive training on a range of topics including products, sources of product ingredients, dealing with a multicultural customer base, employee law, time management, and employee relations.

Body Shop sales in 1994 were over $600 million. Typical Body Shop customers are twenty-nine-year-old females who appreciate the company's business practices and love its world-class quality products. Like many consumers these days, Body Shop customers tend to be skeptical and distrustful of the advertising and sales hype used by traditional cosmetics marketers, and they've responded well to the Body Shop's messages regarding social responsibility and environmental activism. Says Roddick, "It is not simply a question of buying a bubble bath."

The Body Shop spends absolutely no money on advertising. Instead, the company tells its customers where their products come from, what they are made of, how they are tested, and how to use them in straightforward window displays, catalogs, and point-of-purchase product descriptions. Inside the store, customers find cards beside every product telling what's in it and describing its function. Roddick explains, "It would be wrong for people to think we have some kind of moral problem with using advertising. But using glamorous images or miracle cure claims—those kinds of things you won't see us doing."

Anita Roddick says she is trying to put idealism back into business, that business can and must be a force for positive social change. Meanwhile, companies like Procter & Gamble and L'Oréal are trying to cash in on the Body Shop's success by moving into natural-style products. As one industry analyst observed, "The Body Shop came up with a brilliant concept. The difficulty is, you can't patent natural products." Still, the Body Shop is banking on the idea that honesty, idealism, and social responsibility won't go out of style.

Sources: Allan J. Magrath, "Contrarian Marketing," *Across the Board* (Oct. 1990): 46–50; Jacob Rahul, "Body Shop International: What Selling Will Be Like in the 1990s," *Fortune*, (Jan. 13, 1992): 63–64; Charles Siler, "Body Shop Marches to Its Own Drummer," *Advertising Age*, (Oct. 10, 1994): 4; Lonnit Wallace, "Lessons in Marketing—From a Maverick," *Working Woman* (Oct. 1990): pp. 81–84.

Things to Talk About

1. What principles of the New Era marketing orientation has the Body Shop adopted?
2. What value does the Body Shop offer customers?
3. How would you describe the corporate culture of the Body Shop?
4. How has the Body Shop responded to trends in its business environment?
5. What secrets to success has the Body Shop discovered?

MARKETING IN ACTION: REAL CHOICES AT NICKELODEON

Nickelodeon is a cable network developed just for kids that doesn't kid around. It offers many types of children's programming including animation, comedy, adventure, live action, music, and magazine shows for kids two to fifteen. Its weekly schedule includes syndicated reruns of older shows during "Nick at Nite," plus the usual kid-fare of cartoon shows such as Bullwinkle and Gumby. According to Nickelodeon's president, Geraldine Layborne, "The major role we can play in kids' lives is to give them back their childhood in an era when there are lots of pressures on kids to grow up fast. If we can provide them with an environment that's filled with humor that's appropriate to their age and to their lives and can help raise self-esteem, then that's a major accomplishment."

As a result of this philosophy, programming isn't limited to cartoons and other fun shows. It also includes many innovative programming ideas focusing on what's good for kids, such as just-for-kids specials on Magic Johnson's campaign for AIDS education, the Los Angeles riots, and the presidential election. The award-winning Nick News, a program that provides children-focused world news, has been syndicated nationally. The network's "Big Help" program encourages kids to perform volunteer services in their communities.

Nickelodeon's biggest competitive advantage is its ability to make kids feel respected, listened to, appreciated, and important. To help ensure that programming is "kid tested and kid approved," Nick sponsors an on-line panel of seventy kids that sign on via CompuServe three times a week to talk with each other and with Nickelodeon staff. In fact, just about everything the company does is based on the belief that kids' TV should put kids first and that what's good for kids is good for business.

Nickelodeon has adopted the New Era marketing orientation in its business practices. The corporate culture supports the focus on customers and encourages the creation of "customer" loyalty by satisfying kids (and their parents). Network executives believe that their long-term success has been closely tied to the company's emphasis on ethical behavior and social responsibility toward kids. Nickelodeon supports cultural diversity in its hiring practices and has focused many of its programs on dispelling the kind of sex-role stereotyping that prevents little girls from dreaming about being firefighters and little boys from realizing that men do become nurses. At times, though, it has had difficulty finding producers who can develop quality programs for kids of different colors.

Like any other New Era firm, Nickelodeon has to keep its eye on the bottom line as well as its kids. Because the network's biggest source of revenue is its advertisers, management knows that keeping these "customers" happy and keeping their business means television programming that is in line with the advertisers' target markets and marketing strategies. Today's marketers of children's products are well aware of the dramatic shifts underway in the U.S. population and are gearing up for the tide to change. Especially in the lucrative toy market, product development and promotional strategies will be increasingly aimed at Latino, African American, and Asian children, and far less emphasis will be put on the play habits, learning patterns, and family lifestyles of white suburban children.

To balance the high costs of original programming, Nickelodeon must continue to rely on reruns and cartoons for a healthy part of its air time. But that's hard to do if Nick wants to keep up with the needs of sponsors, one of its important publics. Most of the old shows don't include people of color, let alone children, and even when they do, the children are rarely cast as heroes and heroines. Nickelodeon's progress toward committing itself to minority programming has also been slowed by a number of other hurdles.

The question of how much of its resources to put into developing original programs that meet the needs of minority kids is clearly tied to Nickelodeon's basic business philosophy. Is it ethically and socially responsible, for instance, to keep these costs down by force-fitting minority children into existing program formats designed for white children? This question obviously raises others about the direction and focus for the programs and the best way for Nick to maintain its standards for meaningful, quality programs that kids want to see. Then there's the question of how much air time should be given over to minority programming and when—without the risk of losing its current primarily white audience of older kids. For Nickelodeon, there's a lot more to speaking to kids of color than learning a language.

Sources: Tibbett Speer, "Nickelodeon Puts Kids Online," *American Demographics/The 1994 Directory*, 16–17; "'Addicted' to Research, Nick Shows Strong Kids' Lure," *Advertising Age* (Feb. 10, 1992): S2, S22; "Netting the Numbers," *Advertising Age*, (Feb. 10, 1992): S2, S22; "Viacom's Nickelodeon Sets Venture to Make Children's Products," *The Wall Street Journal* (May 11, 1995): B2.

Things to Think About

1. What is the problem facing Nickelodeon?

2. What factors are important in understanding this problem?

3. What alternatives might Nickelodeon consider?

4. What are your recommendations for solving the problem?

5. What are some ways to implement your recommendations?

4

Think Globally and Act Locally:
The International
Marketing Environment

When you have completed your study of this chapter,
you should be able to:

1. Explain why firms decide to seek global marketing opportunities.

2. Explain how less-developed, developing, and developed countries provide different global marketing opportunities.

3. Understand how elements of the political, legal, and cultural environments influence a firm's decision to enter global markets.

4. Explain the different strategies a firm can choose to enter global markets.

5. Understand the arguments for standardization versus localization of marketing strategies in global markets.

Real People, Real Choices:

Meet Peter Einstein, a Decision Maker at MTV Europe

Peter Einstein is the general in charge of MTV's invasion of Europe. As director of marketing and network development for MTV Europe, he is a key decision maker in the battle to shape the musical tastes of Europe's youth. Founded in 1987, MTV Europe is a pan-European cable and satellite channel that transmits music-based programs for young adults across the continent. The network has a single feed across Europe and broadcasts in English. Based in London, MTV Europe was the first attempt by American-based MTV Networks to bring its music programming to another continent.

Peter Einstein has overall responsibility for all business areas affecting the growth and development of MTV Networks throughout Europe. He must decide what markets to enter and help to design the most appealing way for MTV Europe to win the loyalty of viewers in each country, from Switzerland to Spain. He is also responsible for VH-1, which was introduced over the last year to Great Britain and Germany as a local musical channel targeted at an older audience. Mr. Einstein began his fourteen-year career with MTV Networks in the United States, where he helped catapult MTV, Nickelodeon, Nick at Nite, and VH-1 into nearly every cable home in America before joining MTV Europe in 1990. Mr. Einstein holds a B.Sc. in business administration from Ithaca College and an M.B.A. in marketing from Babson College.

"It's a small world after all"

Marketers and their customers indeed live in a small world. We are as likely to buy a product made on the other side of the globe as one made in our own town, state, or country. Although people have valued exotic delicacies from around the globe since ancient times, in the 1990s products from other places are no longer novelties or only for the very rich—they are an accepted part of our lives.

Fans of MTV Europe would agree that the world is becoming a smaller place. Young adults in Berlin can park themselves in front of the TV and check out the same new "buzz clips" as their counterparts are watching in Paris, Rome, or Zurich. MTV Europe's basic programming concept is the same as the American version, but over 80 percent of the programs originate in Europe. Today's marketing environment creates both opportunities and challenges for companies like MTV that are willing to go global.

The development of sophisticated transportation and communications networks that make it easy for countries to import and export products and the changing political climate (particularly in Eastern Europe and Asia) have created vast markets that in many cases are still growing. MTV Asia, for example, began broadcasting in 1991.[1] Many major firms consider virtually any market around the world fair game. However, this game is not always so easy to play: Competition in these markets comes from both local and other foreign firms, and there are many differences in other countries' laws, customs, and consumer preferences to take into account.

In this chapter we'll take a look at the "big picture" of international marketing by focusing on the opportunities and pitfalls of doing business in what is becoming an increasingly small world. After reviewing some of the different opportunities in specific regions of the globe, we'll consider some of the factors that make it more or less desirable to try to expand to foreign markets. We'll also look at different ways to enter these markets. Finally, we'll examine the issue of how much, if at all, a marketing strategy must be adapted to suit the specific tastes of people who live in other parts of our small world.

IN SEARCH OF OPPORTUNITY: GOING GLOBAL

More and more successful firms in today's intensely competitive marketing environment are finding out that "going global" is the only way to go. A firm's management decision to enter the international marketplace to keep profits up and expand its market share is often influenced by a number of factors. Unfavorable home market conditions that limit the growth of businesses in a particular industry often force many firms to look at foreign markets. The demand for a firm's products in a foreign country tempts many marketers, while lower costs of manufacturing, materials, and labor in some countries attract others.

That's why the world's largest companies today choose to set up operations in an assortment of countries. In 1995 the biggest of all global marketers was NTT, a Japanese firm with a market value of $129 billion. This communications giant was followed by the British firm Royal Dutch/Shell, worth almost $108 billion.[2] In this section we'll first take a look at some of the reasons why firms like NTT and Royal Dutch/Shell decide to go global; then we'll consider the factors that influence why firms choose one country over another to set up international operations. That is, we'll see what affects the level of demand for certain types of products in foreign markets.

DECIDING WHETHER TO EXPAND GLOBALLY

The decision on whether to expand to global markets to sell the firm's products or to manufacture them in another country typically depends on the company's goals for growth and management's assessment of the business environment at home. When a firm finds limited opportunities for growth in its home market, its looks to foreign countries, where its chances for success may be greater.

Leveling of Domestic Demand

One factor in a firm's home market that influences its decision to go global is the **leveling of domestic demand,** which can reduce a firm's profitability and prohibit its growth. In the United States, Western Europe, and Japan, where population growth is basically stable, many markets are saturated; people simply no longer need as much of a firm's products. In other cases products like digital television sets that make use of advanced technology limit the demand for older products. As a result of factors like these, U.S. exports to Western Europe and Japan have dropped dramatically over the last decade, but sales to developing nations located in Latin America and Asia have increased by over 150 percent since 1985![3]

In addition, people at home can become less enthusiastic about certain products. For example, a conservative climate in the United States has dimmed the appeal of the Playboy bunny. The company has seen the U.S. circulation of *Playboy* magazine slide by 50 percent since 1972, but there seems to be no shortage of centerfold fans overseas. Playboy Enterprises, which recently launched its seventeenth foreign edition in South Africa, sells its bunny logo merchandise in numerous shops in China and, with a Malaysian partner, has even introduced branded condoms in Asia.[4]

Comparative Advantage

Another country can look attractive to a firm seeking to expand because it has resources that can create a **comparative advantage** for the firm. In the global marketplace this principle supersedes the interests of individual firms and holds that each country should ideally produce its specialty, so in the long run all countries—and the firms operating within them—will have an advantage over other countries and their firms competing in that particular kind of business.

Areas of the world that are long on people but short on sophisticated technology can more economically produce low-tech goods, whereas more advanced areas should concentrate on more expensive, high-tech products and services that require more spe-

leveling of domestic demand: a market condition in which such factors as market saturation, changing tastes, and improved technology reduce domestic demand and prohibit business growth

comparative advantage: the superiority of one country in producing certain products due to its resources, technology, or some other factor that gives it an advantage over other countries

cialized training and manufacturing resources. General Electric, an American firm that is the world's third largest company, made the decision to take its operations to global markets in the 1990s. GE's strategy for shifting operations from the industrialized world of the United States to Asia and Latin America meant becoming an assembler of low-tech goods in some countries and a manufacturer of appliances and other products for export in others.

Comparative Market Potential

Perhaps the most tempting reason to look at foreign markets comes down to what seems to be limitless opportunities for growth in some countries around the world. A country's population growth rate, its economic condition, and other factors determine its comparative **market potential**—that is, whether demand for products is high and opportunities for sales abound relative to other markets.

To get a sense of a staggering market potential, imagine a captive market of well over a billion people—the current population of China alone—all waiting eagerly to buy your product! By the year 2000, the world population is projected to be over 6.1 billion people. Over 60 percent of these people will live in areas that are just beginning to have the income and desire for Western products.[5] It's no wonder that global marketing is one of the key trends of the 1990s!

CHOOSING WHERE TO EXPAND

A country's economic environment is the number one consideration when a firm assesses opportunities in the global business environment. A country's *stage of economic development,* which is determined by its GDP (Gross Domestic Product), is the driving force in global opportunity, but a firm's decision may also be influenced by the products the firm has to offer as well as characteristics of the market. These characteristics include a country's standing on the *Human Development Index,* which is based on measures of health, education, and purchasing power. Countries ranking high on this index include Japan, Switzerland, and the United States. Some of the lowest-scoring countries are Nigeria, Egypt, and Indonesia.[6]

Less-Developed Countries

A country at the lowest stage of economic development is categorized as a **less-developed country (LDC).** In LDCs the economy is based primarily on agriculture and other land uses. A number of nations in Africa and South Asia are characterized as less-developed countries. In these countries the standard of living is low, as is the citizenry's level of literacy. These countries tend to offer limited opportunities for many product categories, especially luxury items. Many less-developed countries depend on a *subsistence economy,* where most people grow what they need and barter for the rest.

Although most consumers in these lands may not be the best prospects for luxury cars or diamond jewelry, their sheer volume may make them attractive markets for staples and relatively inexpensive discretionary items (including, unfortunately, such products as cigarettes). These countries may export raw materials, such as minerals or rubber, to industrial nations. Indeed, some of these countries are witnessing a marketing boom as their economies begin to get a bit healthier. For example, the amount of advertising activity in Zimbabwe has doubled over the last four years, while such major firms as Unilever, Nestlé, Eveready, and Coca-Cola are aggressively undertaking marketing efforts in Kenya.[7]

Developing Countries

When a country begins to move from an agricultural to an industrial-based economy, it is categorized as a **developing country.** In developing countries standards of living, education, and the use of technology are on the rise. There may be a visible middle class, to a large degree created by the success of small entrepreneurs.

Because 77 percent of the world's population lives in developing areas, the sheer number of potential customers, many of whom also can provide a valuable source of skilled labor, attracts many firms to these markets. Further, the economy of the developing

market potential: a market condition in which a country's (or market's) population growth rate, economic condition, and other characteristics create high levels of demand and potential opportunities for businesses

less-developed country: a country at the lowest stage of economic development, characterized by low standards of living, little or no technology, extremely low per capita GDP, and limited market potential

developing country: a country at the middle stage of economic development, characterized by rising standards of living, some use of technology, a relatively low GDP, a high market potential for many goods, and a potentially attractive labor supply

world is expanding at a rate of 5 to 6 percent annually.[8] Throughout Latin America, Eastern Europe, and the countries of the Pacific Rim (generally, Asia excluding Japan), a new crop of consumers is panting for its share of Western-style products, from Coca-Cola to Levi's jeans.[9]

- *Eastern Europe:* Eastern Europe, with its 300 million consumers, "needs it all," according to the general manager of an IKEA furniture store in Budapest, who claims that "basic needs satisfied in the West are not yet fulfilled here."[10] With low incomes for now, Eastern Europeans are limited in what they can purchase. But their transition to a free-market economy has brought with it a hunger for Western goods that is expected to keep increasing. Even now consumers in Warsaw frequent posh boutiques that carry upscale merchandise such as Christian Dior perfume and Valentino shoes. French wines and cheeses are sold at gourmet counters in simple grocery stores.[11]

  Still, doing business in a developing country is no picnic. Companies seeking to market their products in Eastern Europe must grapple with the remains of inefficient business practices left over after the fall of communism. Kmart, which is being squeezed by fierce competition from other mega-retailers in the United States, is hoping to expand to Europe, using former Eastern bloc countries as a beachhead for its invasion. The company is encountering some rough going as it tries to impose Western-style operations on a centralized system. Under the old system, items that didn't sell were sent back to a warehouse—only to be brought back to stores a few years later and put on sale again. Managers are unfamiliar with the concept of markdowns and sales, and distribution is difficult. While Kmart spent about $120 million to buy stores in Czechoslovakia, the company decided to delay putting its name on many of them until its problems were resolved.[12]

- *Latin America:* The countries of Latin America are just emerging from decades of state control, thus opening their economies to foreign business.[13] Many government-controlled industries have recently been *privatized* (sold to private investors), and a building boom is expected to improve decayed roads, bridges, and other parts of the *infrastructure* required to move goods through these countries efficiently.

  A number of trade agreements already in existence allow goods to flow easily across borders: Mercosur (Argentina, Paraguay, Brazil), Ancom (Peru, Bolivia, Ecuador, Colombia, Venezuela), and Caricom (the Caribbean nations). These may prove to be the foundation on which will be built a unified Latin American market.[14] Already, global firms are moving rapidly into Latin America. Pepsico, for example, has declared the area its highest strategic priority, and the company is opening KFC, Pizza Hut, and even Taco Bell franchises throughout the region.[15] This interest is quite understandable, especially because as of now Latin America leads the entire European community, Africa, the Middle East, and Asia in consumption of Pepsi's arch rival, Coca-Cola![16]

- *Pacific Rim Countries:* With the world's highest economic growth rates, the Pacific Rim countries are entering an age of prosperity. The economies of Southeast Asia and China are predicted to grow two to three times faster than most other regions.[17] By the year 2000 economic activity in East Asia, from Japan to Indonesia, will equal that of the United States and will be about $\frac{4}{5}$ of the European Union.[18] It has been estimated that Asian consumers between now and the year 2000 will buy an additional 58 million cars and 87 million televisions alone!

  Taiwan, China, South Korea, Malaysia, Indonesia, Thailand, Singapore, and Hong Kong have been nicknamed "the Dragons of Asia" because of their tremendous economic growth: The economies of Singapore, Malaysia, and Indonesia are expanding at an average of more than 6 percent a year. The number of non-Japanese Asian multimillionaires is expected to double to 800,000 by 1996, and the percentage of people living below the poverty line has decreased from 33 percent to 10 percent, even though the population has grown by 40 percent since 1970. In Hong Kong alone 1,200 people drive Rolls-Royces.[19]

The People's Republic of China, with its population of 1.2 billion, is the biggest sleeping dragon: It will most assuredly become Asia's largest consumer market after Japan by the year 2000. China's gross national product increased from $100 billion in 1983 to $400 billion in 1992. According to one expert, "In the Seventies the most sought after items in China were a sewing machine, a bicycle, and an electric fan. In the Eighties Chinese were looking for a TV, a refrigerator, and a washing machine. In the Nineties they want a VCR, a motorcycle, and a telephone."[20] While trade is booming, China's treatment of human rights abuses continues to hinder its relationships with developed countries.

Western companies are busy finding opportunities in Asia, as evidenced by the recent success of United States and European record companies there. Tower Records, the American music store chain, has opened outlets in Taiwan, Hong Kong, and Singapore. While Western musicians such as Michael Jackson, Elton John, and Eric Clapton sell well, they are outsold ten to one by local stars. The Chinese like sentimental love ballads and snap up songs based on Western or Japanese tunes (for example, Bee Gees hits sung with Chinese lyrics have gone over well). Said one MTV Asian programming executive, "It's decaffeinated Western pop."[21]

Developed Countries

A **developed country** is characterized by highly sophisticated marketing systems, strong private enterprise, and a high market potential for limitless types of goods and services. Such countries are economically advanced and offer a wide range of opportunities for international marketers. The United States, the United Kingdom, Canada, France, Italy, Germany, and Japan are some of the most economically developed countries.

Some of the most interesting and challenging marketing issues for American companies arise when they vie with Japanese firms for dominance in global markets. With an affluent population of 124.5 million, Japan has accomplished an economic miracle. Rising from the ashes of World War II, it has transformed itself into a marketing powerhouse. While it has come under intense criticism for its policies that make it difficult for other countries to sell their products at a competitive price within the country, Japan imports close to $50 billion per year in products and services from America alone.[22] This track record puts Japan second behind Canada as the United States' largest trading partner.

Many European and American firms are trying to capitalize on Japanese consumers' desires for Western products by competing head-to-head against Japanese companies on their own "turf." The Japanese have an ever-increasing desire for higher living standards. They demand impeccable service. To succeed in Japan, a company must offer quality at a competitive price. Knowledge of the local markets and culture is a necessity for global marketers who want to succeed in Japan.

Still, many European and American companies have had mixed success. One problem is that Western businesspeople are often frustrated by the business practices of the Japanese, because there are such vast cultural differences between East and West. In contrast to the Western style of aggressive decision making, for example, *nemawashi,* the Japanese decision-making process, is strictly from the bottom up and by consensus.[23] Another problem is that when the Japanese say "yes," they only mean that they will politely consider doing or buying something, which is not the action-oriented response impatient Westerners expect to hear. Despite these differences, the Japanese do love American products, and companies from Mrs. Fields and The Gap to Disney and Kentucky Fried Chicken are patiently learning how to provide them, Japanese-style.

Economic Communities

Many countries in specific regions of the world are entering into agreements that facilitate trade among themselves and regulate trade with international firms outside the group. The goal of these multicountry agreements is to create an **economic community** in

developed country: a country at the highest level of economic development, characterized by high standards of living, extensive use of modern technology, a high per-capita GDP, and a high market potential for limitless goods and services

economic community: a group of countries that have agreed to work together in the regulation of international trade for the good of all member nations

which trade policies of member countries are coordinated. Economic communities are an important and growing economic force. For example, The Association of Southeast Asian Nations (ASEAN) includes six nations—Malaysia, Indonesia, the Philippines, Thailand, Singapore, and Brunei—that together are now a larger market for Japanese goods than is the United States.[24] For global marketers, economic communities have the positive effect of eliminating the need for a firm to adapt its actions to the specific policies of each country. On the other hand, this advantage can be offset because these same agreements tend to favor the home industries of member countries.

■ *European Union:* Perhaps the most familiar economic community is the European Union (EU). Begun in 1957 as an agreement among six countries, it now includes most of Western Europe and is comprised of twelve member nations—the United Kingdom, France, Italy, Germany, Spain, Portugal, Ireland, Denmark, Belgium, the Netherlands, Luxembourg, and Greece. In 1960, before the EU gained momentum, more than 60 percent of European countries' foreign trade occurred with non-European countries, while more than 60 percent of this activity now stays within the community.[25]

Presently many of the laws called for by the European Union still have not been implemented in all twelve member countries, and unity is drifting as unemployment rises and countries try to protect their own industries.[26] While the population represented by the EU is more than 300 million strong, it is not growing, and competition for "Euroconsumers" is intensifying.[27] Recently the EU rejected a proposed unified monetary system, and pressure is building internally to close its markets to Eastern European countries as economies shrink.[28]

Although the unification of the European Union has not happened as smoothly as many predicted, the prospect of many separate economies eventually being combined into one market of 325 million consumers has led some marketers to begin to standardize their prices and brand names. Many companies are consolidating the different brands sold in individual countries into common "Eurobrands" and modifying their promotional strategies. For example, although orange is a popular packaging color in the Netherlands, when Lever Brothers adopted a pan-European packaging for its Cif liquid cleaner, the bottle was switched to white. The company tried to build enthusiasm in Holland for this change by creating a TV ad showing an orange bottle doing a striptease. They then sold the white bottle in an orange wrapper, urging housewives to strip it at home.[29]

The Sara Lee Company is a good example of an American firm that is making serious efforts to conquer the European market. Europe now accounts for 60 percent of the company's household and personal-care products, such as Kiwi shoe polish, Zwitsal baby products, Sanex skin care, Hanes hosiery and shirts, Champion sportswear, and Playtex and Bali intimate apparel. Its European hosiery brands include Pretty Polly in Britain, Dim in France, and Belinda in Germany.[30] In 1993, $\frac{1}{3}$ of the company's profits came from Europe.

■ *NAFTA:* The world's largest economic community is now comprised of the United States, Canada, and Mexico. Representing a market of 370 million consumers and a total $6.5 trillion in output, it has become a unified trading bloc under the provisions of the *North America Free Trade Agreement* (NAFTA) passed by the U.S. government in 1993.[31] The United States and Canada have traded freely under the Canada-U.S. Free Trade Agreement, passed in 1989.

The newest member of the trading bloc, Mexico, is already the United States' third-largest trading partner, behind Canada and Japan. Exports to Mexico from the United States have tripled since 1986 to $40.6 billion.[32] Many U.S. marketers are taking a fresh look at possibilities in Mexico, particularly because the country's demographics paint a positive outlook for the future. Its population is young and growing, with many people moving into the middle-income range. Fifty percent of its 92.5 million people are under twenty, and another 30 percent are between twenty and forty, making them prime candidates for American products such as blue jeans.[33] Although Mexico continues to suffer from high labor turnover, a poor transportation system, and a weak currency, major opportunities for growth abound. Procter & Gamble alone exports $100 million worth of consumer products to Mexico each year, a figure the company expects to double in the next five years.[34]

Real People, Real Choices:

Decision Time at MTV Europe

MTV Europe's initial marketing objectives were to raise awareness and build viewership for the channel. Because it had a limited budget, the network focused on creating high-profile promotions. Although these were sometimes translated into different languages, the basic approach was pan-European, reflecting MTV's slogan of "One World, One Music."

Although MTV Europe's efforts were highly visible, marketing research revealed some problems. One was that the network's European target audience was less homogeneous than had been assumed. Another problem was that local competition was beginning to emerge. Several alternative local music channels were launching, backed by large media groups and even by record labels. Competitors included Viva in Germany, Videomusic in Italy, MCM/Euromusique in France, and ZTV in Sweden, all of which were trying to chip away at MTV's monopoly on the loyalty of young music fans.

These competitors had several advantages. They could tailor their programming to suit their individual markets, rather than trying to please an entire continent. They could also broadcast in their native language, which was particularly important in such countries as France and Italy, where relatively few young people speak English well enough to understand MTV. Finally, local channels were able to establish closer bonds with local advertisers and cable markets. MTV, which had to service over thirty-seven territories with a marketing department of only six people, could not match this coverage.

Overall, the research revealed that many viewers felt MTV to be "foreign," with more of an American than European identity. The network found a lot of variability across territories in terms of awareness of MTV and loyalty to the channel and that viewers had trouble forming the type of bond with MTV that many American viewers have forged.

With these findings, Peter Einstein faced a critical decision: Should MTV maintain its pan-European strategy or instead try to develop regional programming that would better fit the needs of viewers in different countries? If it did adopt a regional approach, to what extent should its programming vary by country? Mr. Einstein had to decide among three options:

Option 1. Stay with the existing pan-European strategy, transmitting the same programming across Europe.

Option 2. Largely maintain the pan-European entity and regionalize a few parts of the channel. For example, broadcast Italian programming to the Italian audience for a few hours per day or produce local programming in English.

Option 3. Create different regional channels to compete head to head with local alternatives. For example, create an MTV France to compete with MCM/Euromusique.

Now, join the MTV Europe decision team: Which option would you choose, and why?

THE GLOBAL MARKETING ENVIRONMENT

While some major companies from Coca-Cola to Unilever have been marketing globally for a long time, many others are only beginning to adjust their thinking. It is one thing to export some surplus goods now and then to foreign distributors and quite another to establish a more permanent presence in a foreign country.

A careful assessment of the global marketing environment is essential to a firm looking to expand internationally. A firm that enters foreign markets faces political and legal policies that can hamper its ability to set up shop, while the economy and characteristics of the local population, including its customs, its language, and even products that are taboo (forbidden), can inhibit the success of a firm's efforts to market its products. These environmental issues are summarized in Figure 4.1.

In this section we'll first consider some of the political and legal hurdles global marketers must overcome and then move on to some of the cultural differences that make life difficult for international marketers. As we'll see, it's a small world, but still not *that* small.

THE POLITICAL AND LEGAL ENVIRONMENT

When entering a foreign market, a firm must carefully weigh the risks and costs against the potential to succeed. A company's fortunes often are affected by political and legal issues that may be beyond its control. Japan, for example, is notorious for its government policies that favor domestic industries, although of late it is feeling a lot of political pressure to ease up on these restrictions. Roadblocks such as huge delays in processing necessary paperwork, high import taxes, and a network of close business linkages (called *keiratsu*) make it very hard for foreigners to penetrate this closed system.[35]

Political Risk Assessment

Because political conditions around the world can be so unpredictable and have such huge consequences, companies seeking to expand to other countries must engage in some form of **political risk assessment,** in which they try to identify countries where the political and legal environment is favorable for expansion.

In the broadest case, a country may impose **economic sanctions** that exert political and economic pressure on another country by restricting trade. The most stringent of

political risk assessment: a process in which international marketers weigh a foreign country's market potential against political conditions that may hinder marketing success

economic sanctions: government actions that prohibit or restrict trade with a particular country for political reasons

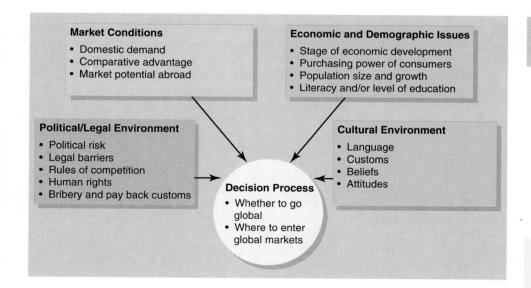

Market Conditions
- Domestic demand
- Comparative advantage
- Market potential abroad

Economic and Demographic Issues
- Stage of economic development
- Purchasing power of consumers
- Population size and growth
- Literacy and/or level of education

Political/Legal Environment
- Political risk
- Legal barriers
- Rules of competition
- Human rights
- Bribery and pay back customs

Decision Process
- Whether to go global
- Where to enter global markets

Cultural Environment
- Language
- Customs
- Beliefs
- Attitudes

Figure 4.1
Decision Model for Entering Global Markets

these is a *boycott* that prohibits all trade with that particular country. The U.S. prohibition of trade with Cuba affected the fortunes of many companies, much to the distress of hard-core cigar smokers in America, for example, whose fondness for lighting up an aromatic Cuban cigar became nothing more than a dream. In other cases a government may impose economic sanctions that apply only to certain types of goods.

Within some countries war or political upheaval can cause the government to take over the operations of all foreign companies doing business within its borders. **Expropriation** occurs when the company is reimbursed (often not for the full value) for its assets, but in the extreme the government may resort to **nationalization,** which allows government takeover of a company's assets without giving anything in return.

On the home front, economic sanctions can also restrict business activities with foreign countries. For example, in the early 1980s the U.S. government revoked an export license for International Harvester, blocking the sale of a $300 million combine manufacturing plant to Russia to show displeasure with Russia's involvement with Poland.[36] In other cases a company trying to do business with a country whose political activities are not popular may damage its domestic market. In 1994, for example, when the U.S. government lifted the boycott on Vietnam—Asia's last untapped market—word got out that the Mobil Corporation was beginning negotiations in Vietnam through a foreign subsidiary, and the company found itself being picketed by POW/MIA groups.[37]

In some formerly high-risk countries, changes in economic or political conditions are now creating a more hospitable business environment. In the 1990s, for example, Peru appears to be one such shining star; terrorism is no longer a big threat, and the government is working hard to encourage foreign investment.[38] But many developing countries that are attractive to global marketers remain politically unsettled, and even though the political conditions are less volatile, the government in power may choose to closely control the operations of foreign firms.

In other situations the government may demand that the companies comply with a long list of conditions before setting up shop. For example, Coca-Cola left India when the government demanded that it turn over its secret formula. Arch rival PepsiCo later agreed in 1988 to tough conditions to gain entry to this growing market.[39]

Legal Barriers to Global Markets

Virtually every country in the world sells something to other countries. Each country maintains its own regulations and agreements with its international trading partners. Depending on their stringency or leniency, trade regulations may be either an incentive or a barrier to a firm seeking entry in foreign markets. In some cases a government can adopt a policy of **protectionism,** which is the erection of trade barriers to protect domestic industries from foreign competition. These barriers impose various restrictions on foreign businesses.

To protect their home industries, many governments set an import **quota** that limits the amount of a certain type of good that can be brought in from other countries. An extreme form of quota is an *embargo* that prohibits any amount of a certain type of good from being imported into the country.

Another widely used trade barrier is a **tariff,** a tax on imported goods that is designed to make them more expensive, thus giving domestic competitors an advantage in the marketplace. Tariffs can take one of three forms. A *specific tariff* is a tax based on the number of items imported. An *ad valorem tariff* is a tax based on the value of the product. Finally, a *mixed tariff* combines the two types, where the payment might be $20 on each item plus 20 percent of its value.[40] These measures usually have the effect of adding to the price of imported goods, making them less desirable to domestic consumers.

The **General Agreement on Tariffs and Trade (GATT)** accords are an important component of the legal environment in the global marketplace. This series of agreements, established in 1948 under the United Nations, reduced import tax levels and trade restrictions among its 122 member nations from all around the globe. Today the pact involves more than 130 member nations, and the *Uruguay Round,* a series of nego-

expropriation: the official seizure of foreign-owned property in a country, frequently without full-value payment to the foreign owners

nationalization: the official seizure of foreign-owned property in a country, without any payment to the foreign owners

protectionism: government policies that erect trade barriers to protect a country's domestic industries

quota: a government trade regulation limiting the quantity of certain goods that is allowed entry into a country

tariff: a tax on goods entering a country that makes them more expensive than domestic goods and gives domestic industries a price advantage

General Agreement on Tariffs and Trade (GATT): a series of agreements that promotes international trade among participating countries by reducing taxes and restrictions

tiations begun in 1986, further opens the global market for international trade. As a result of this latest round of negotiations, Japan and Korea will begin to open their rice markets, and India will permit entry of some foreign textiles. The revised GATT cuts import taxes on manufactured goods by an average of 37 percent. It also bars its member countries from restricting competition in most services, such as software and advertising.[41]

Rules of Competition

Rules vary from country to country regarding such issues as *collusion* (where competing firms agree to coordinate pricing strategies), product quality, warranties, patents, trademarks, and copyright laws. Governments can regulate a foreign firm's ability to price its products, which has a big impact on how competitive it will be in that country. Some countries outlaw a practice called *dumping,* in which a company tries to get a toehold in a foreign market by pricing its products lower than they are offered at home. In a recent case Eastman Kodak accused rival Fuji Photo Film of selling color photographic paper in the United States for as little as $\frac{1}{4}$ of what it charges in Japan.

Local content rules stipulate that a certain portion of a product must be made with components supplied by industries in the country. For example, under the guidelines of NAFTA, cars built by Mercedes-Benz in Alabama will eventually need to have 62.5 percent of their components made in North America to be able to enter Mexico and Canada duty-free.[42]

local content rules: government regulations on the production of goods by foreign manufacturers that control the portion of domestic components used in the manufacturing process

These regulations can cause headaches for marketers, especially when a product's country of origin is part of its sales appeal. For example, New Balance Athletic Shoe, Inc., ran into problems because its advertising claimed the shoes are "Made in the USA." The Federal Trade Commission cracked down on the company: While it is true that its shoes are sewn and glued in America, most of the soles and some of the presewn "uppers" are imported from China. Legal issues like these can have a wide impact, because many American companies, from automakers to computer manufacturers, import parts from other countries and then assemble the finished product at home.[43]

Human Rights

Some governments and individual companies are especially vigilant about denying business opportunities to countries that mistreat their citizens or that allow firms doing business there to exploit their workers. The *Generalized System of Preferences* is a set of regulations that allows developing countries to export goods duty-free to the United States: The catch is that each country must constantly demonstrate it is making progress toward improving the rights of its workers. In 1993, for example, the United States imported toys, textiles, and furniture worth $580 million from Indonesia under this system.[44]

Spreading the Grease

In Japan, it's *kuroi kiri* (black mist), in Germany, it's *schmiergeld* (grease money), while Mexicans refer to *la mordida* (the bite), the French say *pot-de-vin* (jug of wine), and the Italians speak of the *bustarella* (little envelope). They're all talking about *baksheesh,* the Middle Eastern term for tip or gratuity. In many cultures business success depends as much on "baksheesh" as on luck or ability. *Bribery* occurs when someone voluntarily offers payment to get an illegal advantage. *Extortion* occurs when payment is extracted under duress by someone in authority from a person seeking what they are lawfully entitled to.[45]

Bribery is a way of life in many countries. The *Foreign Corrupt Practices Act* of 1977 puts U.S. businesses at a disadvantage, because it bars them from paying bribes to sell products overseas.[46] In some countries, including Italy and Germany, bribery is not considered a big deal; bribes can even be deducted as a business expense.[47] In other countries local regulations or access to executives may be governed by a system of bribery or connections. In China the giving of gifts to establish *guanxi* (connections) averages 3 to 5 percent of a firm's operating costs. In Russia organized criminals set prices and threaten un-

Concern for Exploited Workers at Levi Strauss

United States firms looking to expand their operations overseas often are enticed by the very low wages they can pay to local workers. Although they provide needed jobs, some companies have been criticized for exploiting workers by paying wages that fall below even local poverty levels, for damaging the environment, and for selling poorly made or unsafe items to foreign consumers.

Levi Strauss & Co. is a notable exception to this pattern of abuse. The world's largest brand-name apparel manufacturer operates in more than sixty countries worldwide, and it has been singled out for its dedication to what CEO Robert Haas calls "responsible commercial success." This philosophy emphasizes the adoption of ethical business practices that encourage work force diversity, honesty, and a concern for human rights. A company task force developed guidelines for doing business abroad, taking into account working conditions, the environment, and human rights.

In Bangladesh Levi Strauss grew concerned about child-labor violations when two contractors admitted they hired girls as young as age eleven to work full time sewing Dockers pants, but said the children were the sole support of their families. Instead of just requiring the contractors to fire the girls, Levis agreed to pay for the girls' school tuition, books, and uniforms, and the contractors agreed to hire them back when they reached the age of fourteen.

And, while more than 40 percent of its annual revenues now come from international sales, the company passed on the opportunity to put more than a billion people in its jeans when it decided not to establish operations in China due to concerns about abuses there. Levi's vice president for corporate marketing explained the company's decision: "There are wonderful commercial opportunities in China. But when ethical issues collide with commercial appeal, we try to ensure ethics as the trump card. For us, ethical issues precede all others."

Sources: Michael Janofsky, "Levi Strauss: American Symbol with a Cause," *The New York Times* (Jan. 4, 1994): C4; Russell Mitchell, "Managing by Values," *Business Week* (Aug. 1, 1994): 46(7); and Mitchell Zuckoff, "Taking a Profit, and Inflicting a Cost," *Boston Globe* (July 10, 1994): 1.

---

dersellers, and in Italy an elaborate web of relationships among the Mafia, politicians, and prominent businessmen was recently exposed.

Restrictions on Advertising

Every country regulates some aspects of advertising, including what can be shown, where it can be shown, and who can show it. The problem for global marketers is that these rules vary widely from place to place. Many countries put limits on foreign TV production, and in some cases television networks are state controlled and may not even accept advertising. Consider these examples:

- In Russia the scary-sounding Inspectorate for the Control of the Condition of Advertising and Artistic Decorations attempted to clamp down on the invasion of Western marketing messages by requiring all stores to display their signs in the Russian language. Retailers are fighting back; they are concerned that the Western brand names so avidly sought by Russian shoppers will not have the same cachet when translated.[48]

- In Kenya posters and other outdoor boards are illegal, so advertisers rely on the "mobile cinema," a free traveling show set up in an open field on a collapsible screen that shows vintage films and paid advertising to villagers.[49]

- In Germany the type of product information that can be communicated is regulated. Even Coca-Cola, one of the world's most widely advertised products, must adapt: Diet Coke is known as Coca-Light in Germany because the use of the word *diet* is regulated. Pricing is controlled by the government, and special sales can be held only for a particular reason, such as going out of business or the end of the season. Advertising focuses more on the provision of factual information than on the aggressive hard sell because it is illegal to mention the names of competitors.[50]

PAS DE PANIQUE, ON VOUS EXPLIQUE.

MUSIC TELEVISION®

THE CULTURAL ENVIRONMENT

Even when a firm makes its way through the maze of political and legal issues that can hamper entry into foreign markets, it still needs to understand and adapt to the characteristics and practices of the people who live there. The cultural environment embraces all of the factors that make people unique, including their language, beliefs, and customs

A country's demographic characteristics, for example, play an extremely important role in determining the products and services that are likely to succeed in that environment. Birthrates and age distributions are particularly important for forecasting future market potential and the demand for different types of products. While the U.S. population is steadily growing older (it has been estimated that the U.S. population aged fifty-five and older will grow by over 60 percent between now and the year 2015), about $\frac{1}{3}$ of all Latin Americans and 40 percent of Africa's population are now less than fourteen years old.[51] These people will obviously have very different needs than will their "aging" North American counterparts.

Language

The language barrier often is a huge problem confronting marketers who wish to break into foreign markets. It affects everything from product labeling and usage instructions to advertising and personal selling. These issues range from the provision of safety warnings on product labels to differences in regional weights and measures to indicate contents.

In addition, the meaning of a brand name can get mangled as it travels around the world. Some specific translation obstacles that have been encountered around the world include the following:[52]

- Fresca (a soft drink) is Mexican slang for lesbian.
- When spelled phonetically, Esso (now known as Exxon in the United States) means "stalled car" in Japan.
- Ford had several problems in Spanish markets. The company discovered that a truck model it called "Fiera" means ugly old woman in Spanish. Its Caliente model, sold in Mexico, is slang for a streetwalker. In Brazil Pinto is a slang term meaning "small male appendage."
- When Rolls-Royce introduced its "Silver Mist" model in Germany, it found that the word "mist" is translated as excrement. Similarly, Sunbeam's hair curling iron, called the "Mist-Stick," translated as manure wand.

- Vicks is German slang for sexual intercourse, so the company name had to be changed to Wicks in this market.

Customs and Beliefs

A global marketer must learn about the characteristics of people in different countries and be ready to adapt to local practices (the pivotal relationship between marketing and culture will be discussed in more detail in Chapter 6). A willingness to be open to unfamiliar customs was certainly demonstrated by a vice president at Caterpillar, Inc., a company that exports farm and industrial products worth over 3 billion per year. When toasting a new relationship with a Saudi *sheik,* he was expected to eat the choicest part of a lamb: its eyes. His reaction sums up what sometimes must be done to succeed in foreign cultures: "You just swallow hard and do it."[53]

Recognizing that Anglo-Saxon business practices dominant in many multinational corporations are not appropriate outside of the United States and Britain, Motorola Inc. has even opened a special center for cultural training at its Illinois headquarters to teach its employees how to act with foreign colleagues. The company tries to combat the problems associated with violating a local custom after the fact—often when it's too late. To illustrate, a Motorola trainer summarized this difference among three European countries: "In Germany, everything is forbidden unless it's allowed. In Britain, everything is allowed unless it's forbidden. And in France, everything is allowed even if it's forbidden."[54]

Basic beliefs about such cultural priorities as the role of family, proper relations between the sexes, and the importance of a career affect people's responses to products and promotional messages. When companies do not take these differences into account, trouble can result. In the late 1970s Procter & Gamble introduced Pampers diapers in Japan. This product, which was very successful in the United States, did not sell well because P&G had neglected to consider some important cultural differences between American and Japanese parents. One was that the typical Japanese mom changes her baby's diaper about fourteen times a day, twice as often as her American counterpart. The company also learned to promote a white unisex diaper in Asia despite the popularity of color-coded ones in the United States. When women chose a pink package, they admitted they had a daughter—but male children are much more desirable in many Asian cultures.[55]

This association between pink diapers and femininity illustrates how deep-seated (and often unconscious) cultural beliefs can be. Consumers around the world have different values, religious beliefs, and aesthetic preferences that strongly affect what products and advertisements appeal to them, turn them off, or even make them angry. Colors and symbols take on very different meanings around the globe. Pepsodent toothpaste found this out when it promised white teeth to people in Southeast Asia, where black or yellow teeth are status symbols. In Arab countries alcohol and pork are forbidden to Islamic consumers (even stuffed pig toys are taboo), and advertisers don't dare to show nudity or even the faces of women in photos.[56] Even local superstitions can affect marketing practices: For example, the Japanese are superstitious about the number four. *Shi,* the word for four, is also the word for death, so Tiffany sells glassware and china in sets of five in Japan.

I'd Like to Buy the World a Coke: Exporting American Culture

One factor that makes it easy for some U.S. firms to decide to go global is the special appeal that American products hold for consumers around the world. The American appeal is so strong that some non-U.S. companies go out of their way to create an American image. A British ad for Blistex, lip cream, for example, includes a fictional woman named "Miss Idaho Lovely Lips" who claims Blistex is "America's best-selling lip cream."[57] Whether or not that's true, what we do know is that some venerable products owe at least some of their worldwide success to their strong association with an American lifestyle. Harley-Davidson, for example, has had spectacular results by capitalizing on its classic American image. Bike sales abroad now account for almost a quarter of total company sales.[58]

However, not everyone is happy about the creeping "Americanization" of their cultures. The French have been the most outspoken opponents of this contaminating influence. The government banned the use of such English terms as *le drugstore, le fast food,* and even *le marketing.*[59] The French debate over Americanization was brought to a head by the 1992 opening of EuroDisney in a Paris suburb. In addition to the usual attractions, hotels with names like The Hotel New York, The Newport Bay Club, and The Hotel Cheyenne attempt to recreate portions of America. One critic described the theme park as "a horror made of cardboard, plastic, and appalling colors—a construction of hardened chewing gum and idiotic folklore taken straight out of a comic book written for obese Americans."[60]

The conflict created by exporting American culture was evident in recent trade negotiations on GATT, which deadlocked over the export of American movies to Europe. As one French official put it, "French films are the cinema of creation. American films are products of marketing." The United States share of the European cinema market is about 75 percent; U.S. audiovisual exports to the European Union were about $3.7 billion in 1993, while European Union exports to the United States were only $288 million. The European Union is fighting to allow national governments to continue subsidizing films and retain quotas on TV programs produced outside Europe.[61]

MARKET ENTRY STRATEGIES: HOW BIG A GLOBAL COMMITMENT?

While not all marketing organizations have the resources or desire to market their products in other countries, many find it to their advantage to do so. In some cases different aspects of their operations may be well suited to a foreign country. Just like a romantic relationship, a firm deciding to go global must determine the level of commitment it will make to operating in another country. This commitment can range from a casual involvement to a full-scale "marriage."

The successful expansion of the Quintiles Transnational Corporation, a drug-testing company based in North Carolina, illustrates how a firm can steadily inch its way toward ever-greater global involvement. Even though it had only thirty-five employees in one U.S. location, Quintiles opened its first overseas location in 1987 and now has offices in five countries. In each case the firm started small by hiring a native of the host country to manage its branch office. Later it standardized its software and communications procedures to permit each of its offices around the world to work together. By working with local people and tailoring its activities to the capabilities of each country, Quintiles saw its revenues increase from $1.9 million in 1986 to $60 million in less than a decade.[62]

Generally, the more a firm becomes involved in a global relationship, the more control it will have over how its products are treated there. On the other hand, this control comes at a price: The firm has more to lose if the arrangement doesn't work out or if political or economic instability develops. As shown in Figure 4.2 (pages 134 and 135), a firm's strategy and level of commitment can lead to outright ownership of a foreign business or co-ownership with a domestic firm in a particular country. In this section we'll review the different strategies for entering the global marketplace, beginning with simple exporting deals that require the least commitment and ending with a discussion of marketing firms that truly consider the entire world as their focus.

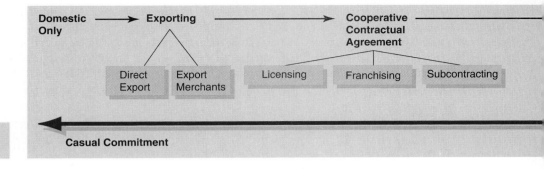

Figure 4.2
Market Entry Strategies

EXPORTING STRATEGIES

An *exporting strategy* allows a firm to sell its products in global markets and cushions the firm against downturns in its domestic market. Because the goods that will be exported are produced at home, the firm is able to maintain control over design and production decisions.[63] Sometimes, however, these advantages may be offset by foreign barriers to entry, such as tariffs and quotas, or negated by local content laws requiring that the products have a high proportion of components made in the host country. In addition, the added expense of shipping may prevent the firm from being able to compete with products produced in the host country.

If a firm chooses to export, it must decide whether it will attempt to sell its products on its own or rely on some type of intermediary or "middleman" to represent it in the host country. Direct export is more likely to be considered if the firm views the foreign market as a long-term opportunity and is willing to pay the price necessary to establish a presence in that country. If it is not, it is usually easier to use a representative who already has established connections in the country.

Export Merchants

Representatives of global firms in a host country are specialists known as **export merchants,** who understand the local market and are better able to find buyers, negotiate terms, adapt to local government regulations, and so on.[64] These home country intermediaries take several forms. A *manufacturer's export agent* is an intermediary (usually one person) who works with the firm in a short-term capacity for a straight commission, negotiating the sale of products to another country on a one-time basis. This arrangement is satisfactory for a very casual exporting strategy, but firms seeking to export on a more regular basis may find it preferable to establish a more long-term relationship with foreign agents.

An *export management company* makes contact with foreign customers and negotiates with them, does research on foreign markets, exhibits the firm's products at international trade shows, and makes sure the goods are suitable for local conditions. Minimum investment is required to get into international markets through an export management company, especially because there is no need to commit any company personnel. On the other hand, management companies seldom have the resources to market the firm's products intensively in any one place, so it's hard to get deep distribution in the host countries.

A *trading company* accumulates and distributes goods from many countries. These companies often sell manufactured goods to developing countries and, in turn, buy their raw materials and unprocessed goods. Big trading companies, such as the Hudson's Bay Company and the East India Company, once played a very important role in the development of international trade as well as the colonization of the British Empire. The United Africa Company (now a subsidiary of Unilever) is still active; it operates department stores, grocery stores, and auto agencies throughout Africa.[65]

CONTRACTUAL STRATEGIES FOR FOREIGN OPERATIONS

Contractual strategies help a firm gain entry to a foreign market by arranging for goods and services to be produced in the host country. A firm that chooses this strategy

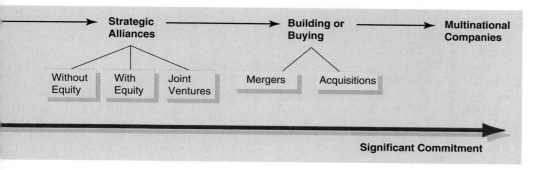

assigns production rights to a foreign enterprise and provides the enterprise with resources and technology to fulfill its contractual obligations. In a service- or consumer-oriented industry the firm also lends its corporate image and trade names to the foreign firm.

Licensing

A **licensing** agreement is a global market-entry strategy in which a firm sells a limited right to produce and market its product in return for *royalties,* an agreed-upon percentage of sales. Because the products are actually produced by a domestic firm, the global marketer bypasses many of the pitfalls and barriers to market entry in a foreign country. Licensing contracts usually cover a specified region where the original firm does not already sell the product. For example, McDonnell Douglas's F-15 fighter plane is produced in Japan by Mitsubishi Heavy Industries and Kawasaki Heavy Industries. United States firms had about 32,000 licensing arrangements between 1952 and 1980 in Japan alone. Currently U.S. licensers earn over $12 billion a year worldwide from licensing.

A licensing contract allows a firm to earn profits on existing products with no significant new investment. It is especially helpful for small firms that lack the resources to expand into foreign markets on their own. On the other hand, the firm is in danger of losing control over how the product is produced and marketed. Another problem is that after the arrangement ends, the company that bought the license now has the ability to make a similar product on its own: In effect, the firm risks creating a future competitor.

licensing: a contractual arrangement that assigns the limited right to produce and market a firm's goods to another in exchange for a fee or royalties on sales

Franchising

Franchising is a special type of licensing agreement: Instead of selling the rights to make its products, a firm sells its entire business system to foreign companies. Franchising is best suited to service- and consumer-oriented businesses. More than 400 U.S. franchising companies, including such well-known firms as Coca-Cola, 7-Eleven, Mrs. Fields, Century 21, and Tiffany's, operate about 40,000 outlets internationally. McDonald's, a major franchiser, is believed to be opening a new international franchise outlet every eighteen minutes.[66] Successful franchises such as KFC and Pizza Hut are household names in many countries.

Franchising is an attractive way to gain quick access to foreign markets. Successful foreign franchises also pave the way for additional international expansion as more and more people around the world come to recognize the corporate image. However, the parent company faces the difficult job of policing its franchises to be sure they are run according to company standards, although most agreements allow franchises to adapt the company's offerings to suit local tastes. McDonald's, for example, serves beer in Germany, wine in France, and sugarcane juice in Malaysia.[67]

franchising: a contractual arrangement that assigns limited rights to an entire business to another in exchange for a fee or royalties on sales

Subcontracting

Another type of contractual arrangement is **subcontracting,** which is also known as *outsourcing.* Under this arrangement a company contracts with a foreign firm to produce custom components or perform production tasks on either a temporary or permanent basis. For example, Ford subcontracts axles for its passenger cars to Mazda and has

subcontracting: a contractual arrangement in which a firm purchases custom components or production services from another firm on a permanent or temporary basis

agreements with Yamaha in Japan, Cosworth in the United Kingdom, and Porsche in Germany for the design and development of some car engines for Ford models produced in Europe.

Subcontracting is ideal if the firm practices the principle of comparative advantage by letting others produce what they are best at. Sun Microsystems Inc. became one of the fastest-growing makers of workstations for engineers by contracting with Toshiba and Tokyo Electron Laboratories in Japan to manufacture finished computers, allowing Sun to focus on design and marketing tasks. Subcontracting also offers cost reductions, because foreign suppliers may operate with less expensive and restrictive work rules. New York-based clothing manufacturer Gitano outsources its products in many underdeveloped countries. When labor costs begin to rise in one, Gitano simply looks elsewhere for a better buy.

On the downside, by allowing other companies to take the lead in developing parts of its product, a firm may lose a competitive edge in creating necessary technology. For example, the slow start by American companies in the development of high-definition TV (HDTV) is partly due to outsourcing agreements for Japanese-made VCRs, in which Japanese manufacturers got the edge in developing the next generation of television sets.

GAINING ENTRY THROUGH STRATEGIC ALLIANCES

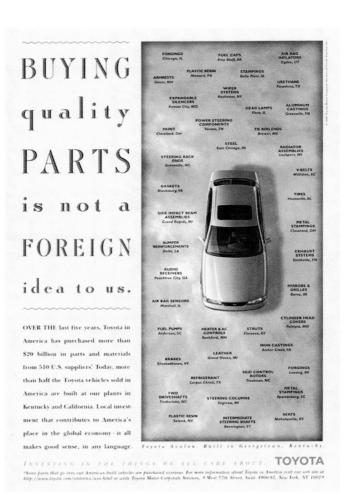

Firms that seek a deeper commitment to a foreign market develop **strategic alliances** in the form of partnership agreements with one or more domestic firms in the country. Strategic alliances allow companies easier access to new markets, especially because these partnerships often bring with them preferential treatment in one of the partner's home

strategic alliance: a formal partnership agreement between two firms to pool their resources in order to achieve common goals

Exhibit 4.2
Many global marketers are expanding their production operations to foreign countries, and many find it an advantage to use locally made parts and materials, even though local content rules do not require that they do so. Some global firms even incorporate an emphasis on local content in their promotional strategies. Although Toyota is closely associated with Japan in the minds of American consumers, this Camry ad emphasizes that the car is actually built in the United States with American parts.

countries. Relationships can be struck on a selective project basis, so only those that clearly benefit both partners will be undertaken. These "marriages of convenience" allow firms to pool their resources to achieve common goals.

One downside of a strategic alliance is the difficulty two companies, especially rivals, can have in developing cooperative agreements based on trust. The merger of different corporate cultures can also cause problems in terms of one or the other's willingness to reveal company secrets, share technology, take risks, and adopt standards for treating employees. A firm can choose a strategy that minimizes some of these problems through agreements that involve some form of loose cooperation only. It can also strike a deal that requires each firm to invest some of its own resources, or equity, in a new operation, thereby raising the stakes for cooperation.

Strategic Alliances without Equity Investment

In some cases firms create partnerships to allow each to focus on those aspects of the business it does best. These arrangements often take the form of a *joint production and marketing agreement.* For example, AT&T entered a reciprocal agreement with Compagnie Generale d'Electricite that would allow AT&T to help the French company sell digital telephone switches in the United States.

The idea is to create *synergy* between two companies, where cooperation results in added benefits for each contributor. *Vertical synergy* (also known as *complementary* or *x-type synergy*) results when two firms agree to cooperate in complementary activities involving different tasks, as when one designs and develops a product that the other actually manufactures, or when each produces a separate component.

Parts for Boeing's new 777 commercial jet, for example, are produced by companies in *six* different countries and are then put together in the United States.

- Alenia (formerly Aeritalia) of Italy is making the outboard wing flaps
- Aerospace Technologies of Australia is making the rudder
- Mitsubishi, Kawasaki, and Fuji of Japan provide the plane's fuselage panels, doors, and wing ribs
- Korean Air provides the flap covers
- Menasco Aerospace of Canada produces the landing gear
- GE of Britain contributes the primary flight computers[68]

Horizontal synergy (also known as *joint* or *y-type synergy*) involves cooperation between two firms who work together on the same task, as when they cooperate to market a new product or to make their product or service more appealing to customers in a country. Continental Airlines and Air France, for example, signed a pact to blend their schedules and share passenger check-ins to provide greater convenience to both airlines' customers.[69]

Strategic Alliances with Equity Investment

A firm can strengthen its hold in a foreign market by entering a **strategic equity alliance** with a foreign firm, in which each firm has an equity or financial stake in the partnership. Because each partner is economically invested in an equity alliance, this strategy motivates companies to work harder to make the partnership a success. On the other hand, these alliances tend to be complex and require very detailed contracts specifying the responsibilities of each party, making them difficult to manage. One common type of equity alliance is a **joint venture,** which usually results in the formation of a separate, jointly run corporate entity.

In the international auto industry, which we tend to think of as fiercely competitive, many companies actually own pieces of each other. For example, General Motors owns 40 percent of Isuzu and 5 percent of Suzuki, as well as $\frac{2}{3}$ of Raba, which produces cars in Hungary. Ford and Nissan are jointly developing a minivan, and Ford operates a joint venture with Volkswagen in Brazil and owns 25 percent of Mazda. Figure 4.3 (page 138) shows some of the complex strategic alliances that exist among major automakers.

strategic equity alliance: agreement between firms that requires an equity investment on the part of each

joint venture: a strategic equity alliance that usually results in a jointly run corporate entity

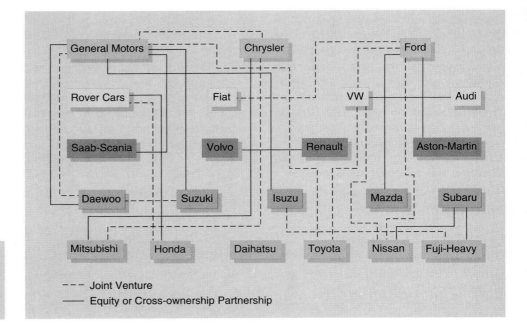

Figure 4.3
Equity Alliances in the Auto Industry

Source: Center for the Study of American Business, Washington University.

MULTINATIONAL OPERATIONS

The most common way to expand foreign operations is to become a business owner in the host country. Ownership gives a firm maximum freedom, control, and profit, and it is also an effective way to overcome import restrictions. Instead of starting from scratch in their quest to become multinational organizations, most firms rely on growth strategies that take advantage of an existing firm's political savvy and market position in the host country. In a *merger,* two firms combine all or part of their organizations to form a new firm with strategic advantages for both, while an *acquisition* involves the purchase of one company by another to gain strategic benefits for itself.

On the downside, mergers and acquisitions often require a very large investment to complete the deal. In developing countries a multinational firm also faces the high costs of training employees, updating equipment, and so on. While most overseas operations of U.S. firms in developing countries are wholly owned, many find that strings attached by the host government complicate the transition. In Mexico, for example, IBM had to agree to purchase high-tech components from Mexican companies and to manufacture software destined for other Latin American markets.[70]

In addition, local sentiment about an acquisition may be negative. The Japanese, for instance, still consider mergers and acquisitions to be antisocial activities. Of course, Americans are not wild about U.S. companies being bought by foreigners either; consider the major uproars that ensued when Japanese firms bought such American mainstays as the Seattle Mariners baseball team and Rockefeller Center in Manhattan!

In fact, the Ford Motor Company is going a step further as it invests $6 billion to build a "world car," the midsize Mondeo. The car was designed in Detroit, the United Kingdom, and Germany. Ford created worldwide engineering standards for the Mondeo so that it would be adaptable to any market. The company is reorganizing its global structure in an ambitious plan called Ford 2000. While its units currently focus on developing different cars and trucks for different markets, Ford is now creating centers dedicated to developing vehicles that will be sold worldwide. Ford estimates that it could save up to $3 billion a year by globalizing its product development process. On the other hand, if the company develops a bad product, it could stumble in many markets rather than in only one. While the Ford project is more complex, expensive, and risky than the global strategies of most companies, this undertaking recognizes the view of many marketers that sees the entire world as a single marketplace.[71]

Excellence at Citibank

Citibank has taken aggressive steps to build relationships with customers around the globe. Its foreign operations account for about 10 percent of the almost $11 billion the bank earns each year. In the Asia-Pacific region (composed of sixteen nations), Citibank has customer deposits of $12.5 billion, and it continues to expand in Vietnam as well.* It has more than 500 branches in Europe, many of which were the result of Citibank's acquisition of local banks that grew more profitable under the Citibank corporate roof.

Travelers can walk into a Citibank branch anywhere around the world to cash a check, but the company also works hard at offering other services that make it the bank of choice for people from New York to New Delhi. In Europe, its branches were the first to offer interest-bearing checking accounts and twenty-four-hour banking services. The company flew Asian bankers to its credit-card service center in Sioux Falls, South Dakota, for lessons on customer service and marketing.† The company has even trained drugstore clerks in Australia to accept deposits in partnership with a local branch.

Part of the bank's unique service are its efforts to satisfy the needs of customers with dual residences and those in interna-tional businesses. Branches provide statements that show accounts held in any country, and the customer can tap services from 1,322 branches in forty countries, including access to 170,000 global ATMs. Citibank works especially hard to cultivate the loyalty of its wealthier customers in many countries. Its target audience is relatively small: international-minded people who demand superior services and who tend to live in large cities. In Europe, Citigold branches promise people with at least $100,000 on deposit separate tellers, swanky premises, and personal attention within three minutes of entering a branch. Customers are greeted by a representative, who steers them to an appropriate bank officer.

Citibank's worldwide growth has occurred even though some countries, such as India and Singapore, impose restrictions on the number of branches that can be opened. Citicorp, Citibank's parent company, is still expanding its reach overseas by buying European insurance companies that it plans to revitalize by providing the same quality service it gives its banking customers around the globe.‡

---

* "Hanoi to Admit Companies," *The New York Times,* (May 24, 1993): D2.
† Rahul Jacob, "Capturing the Global Consumer," *Fortune,* (Dec. 13, 1993): 166(2).
‡ Patrick Oster, "Citibank Combs a Continent," *Washington Post,* (June 13, 1993): H1(2).

HOW "GLOBAL" SHOULD A GLOBAL MARKETING STRATEGY BE?

Developing marketing strategies can be a complex process for firms that choose to do business in global markets. Success in nondomestic markets often depends on the ability of marketing managers to apply the marketing mix in an effective, efficient, and insightful way in each and every country where the firm operates. Each market presents its own set of conditions that affect a firm's strategic marketing decisions, and global firms face the crucial issue of whether to adapt to each country's unique marketing environment.

The debate over choosing a standardized strategy, where essentially the same approach is used in every market, versus a localized strategy, where a lot of fine-tuning is done to adapt to the unique needs of each country, has been raging for some time in marketing circles. On the one hand, advocates of standardized strategies argue that the world has become so small and tastes so homogenized that basic needs and wants are the same everywhere.[72] Coca-Cola uses the same formula worldwide, as does Häagen-Dazs ice cream.[73] Those in favor of localized strategies feel that the world is not *that* small, after all. Products and promotional messages must be tailored to local cultural environments. Kraft adds such "extras" as lemon, egg, or mustard to its mayonnaise to please European palettes.[74]

As corporations have increasingly found themselves competing in many markets around the world, this debate has intensified. In this section we'll first examine some of the factors that influence a firm's choice, and then we'll look at both sides of the coin in

	Standardized Strategy	Localized Strategy
Product Issues		
Market appeal	Narrow	Broad
Technical complexity	Simple	Complex
Visual component	High	Low
Promoted via universal image (e.g., sex or wealth)	High	Low
Strong identification with one country (e.g., Italian leather, French wine)	High	Low
Financial Issues		
Cost of R&D	High	Low
Importance of price	High	Low
Investment capital availability	High	Low
Environmental Issues		
Unique cultural factors influencing consumption	Absent	Present
Legal environment	Similar	Different
Geographic factors	Similar	Different
Government involvement in operations	Low	High
Market Issues		
Degree of urbanization	Urban	Rural
Population size	Large	Small
Sophistication of marketing institutions	Sophisticated	Primitive

Source: Adapted from George E. Belch and Michael A. Belch, *Introduction to Advertising and Promotion: An Integrated Communications Perspective,* 2 ed. (Homewood, IL: Irwin, 1993); Alexander Hiam and Charles D. Schewe, *The Portable MBA in Marketing* (New York: Wiley, 1992).

the debate. Table 4.1 summarizes a number of conditions that favor choosing one perspective over the other.

GLOBAL IMPLICATIONS FOR THE MARKETING MIX

In global markets as in domestic markets, creating a competitive advantage for the firm is the chief goal of marketing mix strategies. The trick is identifying and developing an area of expertise that makes the firm stand out from others in a global market. The principle of comparative advantage means that when a firm enters a country, it is likely to find a group of domestic firms in a particular industry that have developed unique competencies that it must exceed. Decision making is also complicated by local regulations and other issues that affect the quality, pricing, promotion, and distribution of the firm's products.

Product Decisions

When a firm enters a global market, it may have to modify its existing product strategies to satisfy local safety standards, legal regulations, and consumer quality expectations. It may also need to modify its products to suit local customs, preferences, and perceptions about how products should be used, but in many countries a firm's ability to conduct marketing research to decide how to adapt its products is often limited, as we'll see in Chapter 5.

A country's level of development determines what products the firm offers. Sony, for example, is not likely to be successful marketing VCRs in a country where there are few television sets, but it may find a big market for Walkman radios or tape players. In some

おいしいピザは、
ドミノ・ピザ。

D OMINO'S PIZZA is the largest home-delivery pizza chain in the world with over 5,500 stores in 33 different countries. DOMINO'S PIZZA is also the pioneer of the 30-minutes Guarantee and the Quality Guarantee, and our mission is : To safely deliver a hot, quality pizza in less than 30-minutes. In Japan, DOMINO'S PIZZA was the first home-delivery pizza chain, and is today, the leader in an industry that we created. Our goal is to address the needs of the "New Life-style" of an affluent and industrialized Japanese society, by providing convenience, and timeliness All of our pizzas are made fresh, to order, with the finest ingredients, and special spices, blended to give you an unforgettable dining experience at home.

FROM THE U.S.A.
DOMINO'S PIZZA

保存版

Exhibit 4.3
American pizza companies are doing great business in Japan, but they have found that they can succeed only by adapting to local tastes. United States giants like Domino's and Pizza Hut must compete with local pizza places featuring apples, rice, or squid on pizza crust and even a German sausage and potato pizza with mayonnaise sauce. Domino's, which has about 100 outlets in Japan, is fighting back with gourmet pizzas featuring Japanese-style grilled chicken, spinach, onion, and corn. Industry experts estimate that pizza sales in Japan will reach 300 billion yen (close to $3 billion) over the next few years.

countries consumers' acceptance of a firm's products can be influenced by the firm's country of origin. While "Made in the U.S.A." is a distinct advantage in many countries, in others it has the opposite effect.

A global marketer's product strategy includes packaging decisions related to conditions in the markets it enters. Language differences, color preferences, levels of literacy, and even the meaning of symbols in certain cultures influence packaging strategies. In addition, firms may have to comply with specific labeling information requirements made by the governments in many countries.

Pricing Decisions

A firm's pricing decisions in global markets are crucial, because costs associated with transportation, tariffs and taxes, and even bribes paid to local officials almost inevitably make a product sold in another country more expensive than its cost at home. Yet firms often find conditions in many countries that dictate that products be sold at considerably lower prices. In countries where the economy is underdeveloped, consumers simply can't afford pricey products; in other cases, even if consumers were willing and able to pay the price, government-imposed price controls limit the firm. Sometimes a global marketer is forced to look for ways to lower costs (and prices) because competitors in a host country are subsidized by the government or may even be the government.

Other environmental factors that impact a firm's pricing strategy in a foreign market include the currency exchange rate, inflation rate, and balance-of-trade agreements between its home and host countries. A firm can find itself up against illegal black-marketed goods in some countries, but more typically, firms encounter *gray marketing* practices in which other foreign firms in a country deliberately undercut their prices to gain a foothold in the market.

Distribution Decisions

A firm's domestic distribution strategies can rarely be applied in foreign markets. Marketers used to dealing with relatively few large wholesalers or retailers may be forced to rely instead on thousands of small "mom and pop" stores in some countries, or they may not be able to find a feasible way to package, refrigerate, or store goods for long periods of time in less developed countries. Transportation is an issue in many of these countries, and warehousing facilities may be unsafe or unreliable.

Distribution costs can be high in some countries. The availability of warehouse operations, wholesaling and retailing practices, and the geographic distance between channel partners can all drive costs up. To ease some of the distribution problems of foreign firms, some countries have established **free trade zones,** or designated areas where companies can bring, warehouse, and package goods without paying taxes or customs duties until the goods are moved from the free trade zone area to other areas of the country.

Some firms choose to open corporate-owned stores rather than rely on existing retailers, while others prefer to license or franchise their operations. Many firms solve distribution problems and costs related to government policies in a host country through strategic alliances with a domestic firm.

Promotion Decisions

Promotion strategies in global markets are colored by the local culture. Traditions, values, norms, and even the language spoken varies widely from country to country and sometimes within a single country. Successful global marketers develop promotions and messages that not only acknowledge cultural differences, but convey respect for those differences.

Global marketers must also cope with differences in media outlets that are available to deliver the company's message. The media in a country may or may not be highly developed, and a message that appears in a slickly produced TV commercial in one country may have to be presented in a simple leaflet in another country. Other media issues relate to the level of audience attendance to one media format over another, the number of outlets within a media group, and media strategies that influence the size of the audience. CNN and MTV Europe, for example, strive to reach billions of consumers in many countries, but more typically local media reach only a small portion of a region's population.

THE STANDARDIZATION PERSPECTIVE: ONE MARKET

Advocates of **standardization** argue that many cultures, especially those of relatively industrialized countries, have become so similar that the same approach will work throughout the world. A focus on the commonalties among cultures certainly is appealing. After all, if no changes in a firm's product line had to be made to compete in foreign countries, the firm would realize large economies of scale, since the costs of product development and the creation of promotion materials could be spread over more and more markets. Such widespread, consistent exposure would also help create a global brand by forging a strong, unified image all over the world.

Standardized Product Strategy

Some marketers who are deciding to expand to other countries do not believe that it is necessary to change their products to adapt to local tastes. They feel that providing a consistent, high-quality product experience is all that is required to succeed. The Gillette Company is one firm that believes shoppers all over the world want the same merchandise. As Gillette's CEO recently commented, "The most important decision I made was to globalize. We decided not to tailor products to any marketplace, but to treat all marketplaces the same. And it worked in most countries."[75]

Standardized Promotion Strategy

The same philosophy is also being applied to the crafting of promotion messages, as brands like Coca-Cola and Marlboro spend millions to plaster their names on TV screens, billboards, and T-shirts around the world. The advertising director for the Unisys Corporation, a company that specializes in computers, explained the decision to launch a standardized global campaign: "Now they are seeing the same message, the same company, the same look wherever they go. That really stretches my advertising dollars."[76]

Unisys's decision to adopt a global message illustrates one key to the success of a standardized strategy: It is more likely to work if there are not unique cultural factors affecting

free trade zone: a designated area within a country where outside firms can warehouse and package imported goods without paying taxes or tariffs until the goods are moved from the free trade zone area to other areas of the country

standardization: an international marketing perspective in which the same marketing mix strategies are used in all global markets

the purchase. Such similarities are more likely with business-related products than with consumer goods. It helps if the target customers live in cosmopolitan urban areas where they are regularly exposed to images from different countries, or when they are industrial customers who work for sophisticated, international companies. For such a campaign to succeed, the message should focus on a basic concept that means the same thing everywhere. For example, Unilever has successfully promoted its Impulse Body Spray worldwide by employing the theme "boy meets girl," and Nescafé dwells on the warmth of a shared moment (with a cup of coffee) around the world.[77]

THE LOCALIZATION PERSPECTIVE: MANY MARKETS

The other school of thought is represented by marketers who adopt a **localization** perspective, which focuses on variations across cultures. These marketers feel that each culture is unique, with its own value system, conventions, and regulations. This perspective argues that each country has a *national character,* a distinctive set of behavior and personality characteristics.[78] In addition, sometimes a company has no choice but to alter product content in order to comply with local laws. For example, Heinz 57 Sauce tastes quite different in Europe, simply because of legal restrictions on preservatives and color additives that are not a problem in the United States.[79]

Localized Product Strategy

A strategy that emphasizes adapting products to the tastes of local markets recognizes that in many cases people in different cultures do exhibit strong and different product preferences. Sometimes these differences can be quite subtle, yet still make a difference. That explains why Kellogg, which markets the identical version of its Corn Flakes, and Rice Krispies brands in the United States and Europe, had to remove the green "loops" from Froot Loops, after research showed that Europeans felt they were too artificial-looking.[80]

Local customs and preferences can have a big impact on what people in different parts of the world look for even when they buy a common product like a refrigerator that

ℛEAL PEOPLE, REAL CHOICES:

HOW IT WORKED OUT AT MTV EUROPE

MTV Europe chose option 2. The company retained its pan-European channel, and by using digital compression technology it was able to split its signal and transmit different channel feeds to different key countries such as Germany and Italy. This capability allowed MTV to do some limited customization, including local advertising, for these countries while still retaining most of the pan-European programming and positioning.

MTV retained its goal of developing the channel as a pan-European "brand," but added the objective of meeting the needs of individual territories. In other words MTV "had its cake and ate it too" by continuing to largely broadcast its pan-European programming across Europe, while developing local programming and off-air activities to build brand loyalty. For example, MTV now presents tours by local music groups. These tours are promoted with local marketing partners (usually local press and/or radio stations), who distribute free tickets and promote MTV to readers and listeners.

By maintaining a pan-European strategy and introducing local subtleties, MTV can carefully choose the best music and programming mix for each country or region. And the network still has the power to transport viewers to a "larger place" by bringing international stars into local markets and by broadcasting such shows as the European Music Awards in Berlin, which is the premiere music award show in Europe.

performs a basic function. In parts of rural India, for example, the refrigerator is a status symbol, so people want a good-looking one, which they keep in the living room to proudly show to visitors. When the Electrolux appliance company began selling refrigerators in Europe, it ran into problems: Northern Europeans want large refrigerators because they shop once a week in supermarkets; Southern Europeans want them small because they go through open-air markets daily. Northerners like freezers on the bottom, Southerners on the top. And the British are avid purchasers of frozen foods, so they insist on a unit with 60 percent freezer space.[81]

Localized Promotion Strategy

Fans of an adaptation strategy also feel that most advertising messages must be developed with a local frame of reference; people in different countries do not always share the same ideas about what is funny, glamorous, or admirable. Even Coca-Cola must make minor modifications to the way it presents itself around the world. Coke's highly successful American ad featuring a boy giving his bottle of Coke to football player "Mean Joe" Greene after a game was adapted to other countries—but in these versions soccer stars were substituted.

Chapter 4 Summary

Objective 1. Explain why firms decide to seek global marketing opportunities.

Firms choose to enter foreign markets for several reasons. The principle of comparative advantage means that each country should produce its specialty. A country's market potential is based on its rate of population growth and economic conditions. A decline in domestic demand for particular products encourages some firms to look to foreign markets for growth.

Objective 2. Explain how less-developed, developing, and developed countries provide different global marketing opportunities.

A country's stage of economic development determines a global firm's marketing opportunities. In less-developed countries with subsistence economies, opportunities are usually limited to staples and inexpensive discretionary items. In developing countries such as those in Eastern Europe, Latin America, and the Pacific Rim, an industrial-based economy is evolving and the rising middle class creates great demand for basic consumer goods. Developed countries such as Japan have highly sophisticated marketing systems and offer almost limitless marketing opportunities for goods and services.

In some areas of the globe countries have banded together to form economic communities to promote international trade. These economic communities include the Association of Southeast Asian Nations, the European Union, and the economic alliance produced by the North American Free Trade Agreement.

Objective 3. Understand how elements of the political, legal, and cultural environments influence a firm's decision to enter global markets.

A firm assesses the political risks of entering a foreign market by considering such factors as economic sanctions imposed by the country to restrict trade with another country for political reasons, as well as political upheaval within the country that creates the potential for confiscation of foreign business interests. In some countries political factors can either result in numerous conditions a firm must meet just to enter the global market or lead to excessive controls that inhibit a firm's ability to do business.

In the legal environment global marketers find that some countries have protectionist trade policies that protect domestic industries by erecting barriers to entry in the form of import quotas, tariffs, and embargoes. The General Agreement on Tariffs and Trade, recently revised by the Uruguay Round, has reduced trade restrictions for member countries. Still, global marketers face a variety of problems in many countries including local content laws, human rights violations, bribery practices, and advertising regulations.

Firms also assess a foreign country's sociocultural environment for differences in language, customs, and beliefs that can affect its opportunities. In some countries but not all, the strong appeal of American products makes it easy for U.S. firms to go global.

Objective 4. Explain the different strategies a firm can choose to enter global markets.

Different foreign market entry strategies represent varying levels of commitment for a firm, each accompanied by varying levels of control by the firm. Exporting of goods, which carries little commitment but allows little control by the firm, is typically handled though export merchants, or intermediaries, such as manufacturer's export agents, export management companies, and trading companies. A greater commitment for a firm seeking to manufacture its products in the host country involves choosing a cooperative contractual agreement strategy such as licensing, franchising, or subcontracting (also known as outsourcing).

A firm makes the greatest commitment to a foreign market and gains the greatest control when it chooses to develop a partnership or strategic alliance with one or more companies in the host country. A joint production and marketing agreement is an alliance without equity investment and can create either vertical or horizontal synergy. In a strategic equity alliance such as a joint venture, each firm has an economic investment in the alliance. When firms choose to become business owners in a host country, they may form a merger with another firm or simply purchase a foreign company, both of which require large investments and may be met with negative local sentiment.

Objective 5. Understand the arguments for standardization versus localization of marketing strategies in global markets.

Firms that operate in two or more countries can choose to standardize their marketing strategies—that is, use the same strategies in all countries—or to localize by adopting different strategies for each market. Proponents of the standardization perspective focus on commonalities across countries. Supporters of the localization perspective seek to adapt to the national character of each country.

Review Questions

Marketing Concepts: Testing Your Knowledge

1. What are some of the reasons firms decide to enter the global marketplace?
2. How are countries classified according to their level of economic development? What marketing opportunities are afforded by countries in each stage of economic development?
3. What are economic communities? How have they changed global marketing opportunities?
4. What aspects of the political and legal environment influence a firm's decision to enter a foreign market?
5. What cultural factors in a country influence a foreign firm's ability to succeed there?
6. How is a firm's level of commitment related to its level of control in a foreign market?
7. What strategies can a firm consider if it decides to export goods to foreign markets?
8. What general types of contractual agreements might a firm consider in its decision to become international? What are the types of strategic alliances it may consider?
9. What are the arguments for standardization of marketing strategies in the global marketplace? What are the arguments for localization?

Marketing Concepts: Discussing Choices and Issues

1. Do you think U.S. firms should be allowed to use bribes to compete in countries where bribery is an accepted and legal form of doing business? Why or why not?
2. Some countries have been critical of the exporting of American culture by U.S. businesses. Do you think this attitude is reasonable? Explain your thinking.
3. Do you think franchising is the best option for firms like McDonald's, KFC, and Pizza Hut that decide to go global? Why or why not?
4. Trade regulations and protectionism are important political issues in the United States. What do you think the positive and negative aspects of protectionist policies are for U.S. firms?

Marketing Practice: Applying What You've Learned

1. Assume you are a marketing manager for an American manufacturer of personal computers. Your company is considering strategic opportunities abroad, and your boss has asked you to assess the possibilities for entering the following countries: Canada, Costa Rica, Poland, and France.
   a. Based on what you've read in this chapter, identify the pros and cons of marketing your products in each of the four countries.
   b. Tell which country you think should be the primary target for your company and why.
2. Assume your firm is interested in the global market potential for over-the-counter pain medicines in the following countries: South Africa, Japan, and Mexico.
   a. Prepare a summary of the demographic characteristics and cultural differences you expect to find in these countries.
   b. Tell how the differences might affect marketing strategies for over-the-counter medicines.
3. McDonald's fast food, Ford automobiles, and Pampers disposable diapers are very different U.S. products that are marketed globally.
   a. Outline the reasons each of these companies might choose

      ■ To standardize its product strategies
      ■ To localize its product strategies
      ■ To standardize its promotion strategies
      ■ To localize its promotion strategies

   b. Organize a debate in your class to argue the merits of the standardization perspective versus the localization perspective.

Marketing Mini-Project: Learning by Doing

The purpose of this mini-project is to begin to develop an understanding of a culture other than your own and how customer differences lead to changes in how marketing strategies are implemented in that culture.

1. As part of a small group, select a *country* you would like to know more about and a *product* you think could be successful in that market. As a first step, gather information about the country. Many campuses have international students from different countries. If possible, find a fellow student from the country and talk with him or her about the country. You will probably also wish to investigate other sources of information such as books and magazines found in your library, or access information from the World Wide Web.

2. Prepare a summary of your findings that includes the following:

a. An overall description of the country, including such factors as its history, economy, religions, and so on, that might affect marketing of the product you have selected.
b. The current status of this product in the country.
c. Your prediction for the future success of the product in the country.
d. Your recommendations for a product strategy (product design, packaging, brand name, price, and so on).
e. Your recommendations for promotional strategies.

3. Present your findings and recommendations to the class.

Key Terms

Endnotes

1. Andrew Tanzer, "Sweet Chinese Siren," *Forbes* (Dec. 20, 1993): 78.
2. "The Top 100 Companies," *Business Week* (July 10, 1995): 63.
3. Howard Banks, "America's New Trading Partners," *Forbes* (Nov. 8, 1993): 35.
4. Susan Carey, "Playboy Looks Overseas as U.S. Climate Grows Hostile," *The Wall Street Journal* (Sept. 29, 1993): B4; Tim Smart, "GE's Brave New World," *Business Week* (Nov. 8, 1993): 64.
5. *The World Almanac and Book of Facts 1992* (New York: Pharos Books, 1991).
6. Ricardo Sookdeo, "The New Global Consumer," *Fortune* (Autumn/Winter 1993): 63.
7. Karen Yates, "Advertising's Heart of Darkness," *Advertising Age* (May 15, 1995): I-10, I-15.
8. Bill Saporito, "Where the Global Action Is," *Fortune* (Autumn/Winter 1993): 62.
9. Bill Saporito, "Where the Global Action Is," *Fortune* (Autumn/Winter 1993): 62.
10. Bill Saporito, "Where the Global Action Is," *Fortune* (Autumn/Winter 1993): 63.
11. Kevin Cete, "East Germans Scout for Good Buys in West," *Advertising Age* (Dec. 11, 1990): 40.
12. Neil King Jr., "Kmart's Czech Invasion Lurches Along," *The Wall Street Journal* (June 8, 1993): A12.
13. "Peru: Privatization is Principal Policy for Attracting Foreign Investment," *The Wall Street Journal* (Oct. 27, 1993): B7.
14. Bill Saporito, "Where the Global Action Is," *Fortune* (Autumn/Winter 1993): 63.
15. Nathaniel C. Nash, "A New Rush into Latin America," *The New York Times* (April 11, 1993): 1; Calvin Sims, "KFC Tries for a Turnaround in Chile," *The New York Times* (Dec. 27, 1994): D8.
16. Ricardo Sookdeo, "The New Global Consumer," *Fortune* (Autumn/Winter 1993): 68.
17. Roger Cohen, "A Policy Compass Points East and South," *The New York Times* (Jan. 3, 1994): C3.
18. Louis Kraar, "Asia 2000," *Fortune* (Oct. 5, 1992): 111; Bill Saporito, "Where the Global Action Is," *Fortune* (Autumn/Winter 1993): 63.
19. Pete Engardio, "Asia's Wealth," *Business Week* (Nov. 29, 1993): 100.
20. Ricardo Sookdeo, "The New Global Consumer," *Fortune* (Autumn/Winter 1993): 68, Bill Saporito, "Where the Global Action Is," *Fortune* (Autumn/Winter 1993): 62.
21. Andrew Tanzer, "Sweet Chinese Siren," *Forbes* (Dec. 20, 1993): 78.
22. "When the Action's Worth $50 Billion," *Inc. Magazine's Going Global* (1993): 1.
23. Ibid.
24. Harvey S. James, Jr. and Murray Weidenbaum, *When Businesses Cross International Borders: Strategic Alliances and Their Alternatives* (Westport, CT: Prager, 1993).
25. Ibid.
26. Bill Javetski and Patrick Oster, " 'The Single Market Itself is in Question,' " *Business Week* (Nov. 1, 1993): 52.
27. Bill Saporito, "Where the Global Action is," *Fortune* (Autumn/Winter 1993): 62.

28. Bill Javetski and Richard A. Melcher, "Who Can Put Europe's Humpty-Dumpty Together Again?" *Business Week* (May 31, 1993): 55.

29. Browning, "In Pursuit of the Elusive Euroconsumer," *The Wall Street Journal* (April 23, 1992): B1.

30. Richard Ringer, "Sara Lee's European Strategy Proves a Success," *The New York Times* (Nov. 26, 1993): D12.

31. William C. Symonds, "Border Crossings," *Business Week* (Nov. 22, 1993): 40.

32. Ibid.

33. Debra Hazel, "Mexico: New Land of Opportunity?" *Chain Store Age Executive* (Oct. 1993): 45.

34. William C. Symonds, "Border Crossings," *Business Week* (Nov. 22, 1993): 40.

35. Michael R. Czinkota and Masaaki Kotabe, "America's New World Trade Order," *Marketing Management* (1992): 47–54.

36. "The Harvester Case," *The Wall Street Journal* (Jan. 21, 1982): 22.

37. Cyndee Miller, "Opening the Vietnam Market," *Marketing News* (April 12, 1993): 1.

38. For a review of risk assessment, see Thomas L. Brewer, "Political Risk Assessment for Foreign Direct Investment Decisions: Better Methods for Better Results," *Columbia Journal of World Business* (Spring 1981): 5–12.

39. "PepsiCo Accepts Tough Conditions for the Right to Sell Cola in India," *The Wall Street Journal* (Sept. 20, 1988): 44.

40. Alexander Hiam and Charles D. Schewe, *The Portable MBA in Marketing* (NY: Wiley, 1992).

41. Rich Thomas, "The ABCs of the GATT Pact," *Newsweek* (Dec. 27, 1993): 36.

42. William C. Symonds, "Border Crossings," *Business Week* (Nov. 22, 1993): 40.

43. Michael Oneal, "Does New Balance Have an American Soul?" *Business Week* (Dec. 12, 1994): 86, 90.

44. Thomas L. Friedman, "U.S. Prods Indonesia on Rights," *The New York Times* (Jan. 18, 1994): D1.

45. Philip R. Cateora, *Strategic International Marketing* (Homewood, IL: Dow Jones-Irwin, 1985).

46. "Capital Wrap-Up: Competitiveness," *Business Week* (Nov. 1, 1993): 47.

47. Philip R. Cateora, *Strategic International Marketing* (Homewood, IL: Dow Jones-Irwin, 1985).

48. Celestine Bohlen, "The Latest Signs of Change: Russify that Name!," *The New York Times* (May 25, 1993): A4.

49. Antony Shugaar, "Ads Take High Road in Kenya, on Cinema," *Advertising Age* (April 11, 1983).

50. Matthias D. Kindler, Ellen Day, and Mary R. Zimmer, "A Cross-Cultural Comparison of Magazine Advertising in West Germany and the U.S.," unpublished manuscript, (The University of Georgia, Athens, 1990).

51. Charles D. Schewe and Anne L. Balazs, "Role Transitions in Older Adults: A Marketing Opportunity," *Psychology & Marketing* (March/April 1992): 85–99; Sookdeo, Ricardo, "The New Global Consumer," *Fortune* (Autumn/Winter 1993): 68.

52. David A. Ricks, "Products That Crashed Into the Language Barrier," *Business and Society Review* (Spring 1983): 46–50.

53. Alison Leigh Cowan, "Caterpillar: Worldwide Watch for Opportunities," *The New York Times* (Jan. 4, 1994): C4.

54. Bob Hagerty, "Trainers Help Expatriate Employees Build Bridges to Different Cultures," *The Wall Street Journal* (June 14, 1993): B1, B6.

55. Alecia Swasy, "Don't Sell Thick Diapers in Tokyo," *The New York Times* (Oct. 13, 1993): F9.

56. Marian Katz, "No Women, No Alcohol, Learn Saudi Taboos Before Placing Ads," *International Advertiser* (Feb. 1986): 11–12.

57. Dana Milbank, "Made in America Becomes a Boast in Europe," *The Wall Street Journal* (Jan. 19, 1994): B1.

58. Kevin Kelly and Karen Lowry Miller, "The Rumble Heard Round the World: Harleys," *Business Week* (May 24, 1993): 58.

59. John F. Sherry, Jr. and Eduardo G. Camargo, " 'May Your Life be Marvelous': English Language Labeling and the Semiotics of Japanese Promotion," *Journal of Consumer Research* (Sept. 1987): 174–188.

60. Quoted in Alan Riding, "Only the French Elite Scorn Mickey's Debut," *The New York Times* (1992): A1.

61. Charles Goldsmith and Charles Fleming, "Film Industry in Europe Seeks Wider Audience," *The Wall Street Journal* (Dec. 6, 1993): B1.

62. Martha E. Mangelsdorf, "Building a Transnational Company," *Inc.* (March 1993): 92.

63. Harvey S. James, Jr. and Murray Weidenbaum, *When Businesses Cross International Borders: Strategic Alliances and Their Alternatives* (Westport, CT: Prager, 1993).

64. Alexander Hiam and Charles D. Schewe, *The Portable MBA in Marketing* (NY: Wiley, 1992).

65. Philip R. Cateora, *Strategic International Marketing* (Homewood, IL: Dow Jones-Irwin, 1985).

66. Alexander Hiam and Charles D. Schewe, *The Portable MBA in Marketing* (NY: Wiley, 1992).

67. Calvin Trillen, "Uncivil Liberties: American Fast Food Restaurants Around the World," *The Nation* (April 10, 1989): 473.

68. Harvey S. James, Jr. and Murray Weidenbaum, *When Businesses Cross International Borders: Strategic Alliances and Their Alternatives* (Westport, CT: Prager, 1993).

69. "Continental Airlines and Air France Sign Pact," *The New York Times* (July 28, 1993): D4.

70. Harvey S. James, Jr. and Murray Weidenbaum, *When Businesses Cross International Borders: Strategic Alliances and Their Alternatives* (Westport, CT: Prager, 1993).

71. James Bennet, "Ford Revamps with Eye on the Globe," *The New York Times* (April 22, 1994): D1; John A. Byrne and Kathleen Kerwin, "Borderless Management," *Business Week* (May 23, 1994): 24; Jerry Flint, "One World, One Ford," *Forbes* (June 20, 1994): 40; Jane Perlez, "Toyota and Honda Create Global Production System," *The New York Times* (March 26, 1993): A1; Alex Taylor III, "Ford's $6 Billion Baby," *Fortune* (June 28, 1993): 76.

72. One of the most influential arguments for this perspective can be found in Theodore Levitt, "The Globalization of Markets," *Harvard Business Review* (May–June 1983): 92–102.

73. Sara Hope Franks, "Overseas, It's What's Inside that Sells," *The Washington Post National Weekly Edition* (Dec. 5–11, 1994): 21.

74. Ibid.

75. Louis Uchitelle, "Gillette's World View: One Blade Fits All," *The New York Times* (Jan. 4, 1994): C3.

76. Bradley Johnson, "Unisys Touts Service in Global Ads," *Advertising Age* (Feb. 15, 1993): 3, 59.

77. Ashish Banerjee, "Global Campaigns Don't Work; Multinationals Do," *Advertising Age* (April 18, 1994): 23.

78. Terry Clark, "International Marketing and National Charac-

ter: A Review and Proposal for an Integrative Theory," *Journal of Marketing* (Oct. 1990): 66–79.

79. Sara Hope Franks, "Overseas, It's What's Inside that Sells," *The Washington Post National Weekly Edition* (Dec. 5–11, 1994): 21.

80. Ibid.

81. William Echikson, "The Trick to Selling in Europe," *Fortune* (Sept. 20, 1993): 82.

■ CASE 4-1

MARKETING IN ACTION: REAL PEOPLE AT HÄAGEN-DAZS

Justin King was the head of European Marketing Development at Grand Metropolitan, a U.K. food and beverage firm that's also an international giant. When Grand Met acquired Pillsbury in 1989, it inherited Häagen-Dazs ice cream, a small, relatively unknown brand that was just getting off the ground in the hands of Pillsbury in the United States. The original Häagen-Dazs company, founded thirty years before, had remained a small independent firm in its hometown—the Bronx, New York!—until Pillsbury scooped it up in 1983 and began turning it into an upscale national brand. While the name Häagen-Dazs sounds as if the ice cream is a luxury import, in reality the name is a phony, simply dreamt up by the original owners to sound rich and expensive. But even if the name isn't genuine, the product is. The all-natural ingredients, including 100 percent fresh cream, make it the Cadillac of U.S. ice creams.

Grand Met had initially planned to scrap Häagen-Dazs, but as time passed the company began to see the ice cream product as a global brand just waiting to happen. Today Justin King is managing director of Häagen-Dazs U.K., and the ice cream is one of his biggest success stories. Since 1989 Grand Met has opened franchised Häagen-Dazs stores in Britain, Japan, France, and Germany. In 1993 sales in Asia doubled to $120 million due to a joint venture with Suntory Ltd. In Europe sales in France alone accounted for $30 million. And in the United States its franchised stores numbered over 250, and sales from the stores and supermarkets were topping the 10 percent mark in the world's biggest ice cream market.

Häagen-Dazs' phenomenal global success began in Britain, which makes its rise to the top even more remarkable. In Britain ice cream consumption is only $\frac{1}{3}$ that in the United States. Also, the British have traditionally purchased low-grade, low-calorie local brands of ice cream, some of which do not even contain dairy products. Häagen-Dazs

was also double or triple the price of the local brands. Nevertheless, King saw it as "the right ice cream for the right time" and developed an unorthodox marketing strategy that eventually made Häagen-Dazs a success in Europe and Asia.

This unorthodox strategy does not include any advertising; instead it is a three-part program that relies on sampling and word-of-mouth communication among ice cream lovers. When it is preparing to enter a local market, Grand Met first targets gourmets within the country by placing Häagen-Dazs with just a few high-end retailers. In Britain Häagen-Dazs was first sold in Harrods' department store and then in upscale delicatessens, quality hotels, and restaurants—with the brand name printed on the menus. Next, Grand Met sets up franchises with local entrepreneurs to open posh ice cream parlors in high-traffic areas (fifteen were opened in Britain) to tempt a broader range of potential customers into sampling the ice cream. Finally, the ice cream is distributed to supermarket chains and convenience stores in the country, initially accompanied by point-of-sale taste-testing promotions.

Other than in the United States and London, however, Häagen-Dazs posed a distribution nightmare for local manufacturers. Because of its ingredients, the ice cream needs to be kept frozen at all times, and customers found they barely had thirty minutes to get home and put it into a freezer or they'd end up with Belgium ChocChoc soup that wouldn't refreeze. But Grand Met overcame this potentially disastrous problem with strategies that complemented its overall marketing program. Specially designed carry-home freezer bags, given free with each purchase, not only helped customers get their frozen indulgences home, it helped convince them that the ice cream was really different and special, and the special Häagen-Dazs freezer bags caught the attention of consumers who hadn't yet experienced such delights as Swiss Almond Mocha or Carrot

Cake Passion. Grand Met's special fleet of delivery trucks also attracted a lot of attention, as did the free freezers it supplied to many retailers in Europe. The cold facts of the Häagen-Dazs success story paid off for Grand Met in more ways than one: Because of its difficulties in marketing high-quality ice cream in some countries, potential competitors were less eager to develop copycat products—at least for a while.

Things are changing in the ice cream market in the mid-1990s, but so is Häagen-Dazs. Having established the brand as the world's most indulgent ice cream, Grand Met has had to come to grips with '90s consumers who manage to resist temptation and instead indulge their "urge to splurge" with low-fat frozen yogurt. The company is now offering equally tempting low-fat frozen confections like raspberry-sorbet–coated vanilla yogurt bonbons that were introduced and tested in France and are now making their way to Häagen-Dazs' newly refurbished franchised stores around the globe.

Another problem facing Grand Met is, of course, the competition: Superpremium brands like Ben & Jerry's and Steve's always threaten to steal market share. But Häagen-Dazs is still in the lead, through its new full-scale paid ad-

vertising programs, the smashing success of its low-fat confections, and a new line of "Extras" ice cream that's more indulgent than ever.

Sources: "Häagen-Dazs Pushes Cold Front Across World," *Marketing* (Oct. 4, 1990): 30–31; Mark Maremont, "They're All Screaming for Häagen-Dazs," *Business Week* (Oct. 14, 1991): 121; Robert Dwek, "Extras Puts the Bite on Rivals," *Marketing* (Sept. 23, 1993): 60.

Things to Talk About

1. Why have the efforts for global expansion of the Häagen-Dazs brand been concentrated in the United States, Europe, and Japan, and not in the big markets in the Pacific Rim countries or South America?

2. What hurdles did the company have to overcome to become competitive in Britain?

3. What advantages, if any, did the taste-testing strategy have over media advertising when Häagen-Dazs entered a new market?

4. What elements of the Häagen-Dazs marketing strategy are being carried over to the changing global ice cream market?

5. What secrets to success has Häagen-Dazs discovered?

CASE 4-2

MARKETING IN ACTION: REAL CHOICES FOR MAJOR LEAGUE BASEBALL INTERNATIONAL PARTNERS

Baseball in Europe? Not a chance. But then again, Levi's jeans and Coca-Cola and the Colonel's chicken are global products—so why not baseball? The Major League Baseball International Partners want to make it so. This organization is a partnership consisting of Major League Baseball, NBC, and a British marketing company, Pascoe Nally, Inc.

Major League Baseball International Partners have been marketing and promoting baseball overseas for several years. The motivation for making baseball a global sport is more than just wanting to share a piece of Americana. Rather, it is to expand and increase the sales of league-licensed merchandise—those baseball caps and T-shirts that American fans young and old love to wear. Global sales of these products were $2.4 billion in 1993, but less than $100 million of that came from Europe. The group wants to change that.

The high level of disposable income and an intense liking for sports make Europe an attractive market. Europeans are passionately loyal to soccer, but baseball and soccer are played in different seasons so that, except for cricket in England, baseball would face little competition during its summer season. Europe also already has a few amateur baseball leagues, although they play in tiny stadiums to even tinier crowds. Finally, you can never discount the appeal of the American lifestyle to many people overseas.

Still, there are many factors that might make European baseball a pop fly instead of a home run. Soccer fans are so loyal to their favorite teams that violent fights and near-riot conditions sometimes accompany games. To these hardcore fans, baseball is seen as very tame. Second, compared to soccer, baseball is quite expensive. While soccer games can be played on almost any flat grassy area with only a single ball, baseball requires that expensive fields be built and that teams have lots of balls, bats, gloves, helmets, and other protective gear. Perhaps even more important, Europe has no "history" of baseball. In the United States, schoolyard diamonds, neighborhood sandlots, playgrounds, and official Little League fields are the source of fond memories for most U.S. fans, but in Europe no such "baseball, motherhood, and apple pie" tradition exists on which to build a following.

If baseball could score big time in Europe, league-licensed product sales could climb to over $500 million in the next decade—not exactly peanuts at the old ballpark!

The Major League Baseball International Partners' strategy has focused on encouraging television exposure, including the All-Star game and the World Series, and a weekly television program during the season that includes a tutorial on baseball for European rookies.

As the Partners are well aware, these efforts are not likely to build the kind of loyalty that draws overcapacity crowds to soccer games. On the other hand, keen interest in American sports is not without precedent in Europe. The National Basketball Association has been sending players overseas since the late 1980s, with a series of games played before sellout crowds in Paris, Madrid, Rome, and Barcelona. And European sales of football league-licensed merchandise have increased to between $175 and $200 million through such promotions as the American Bowl game between the Chicago Bears and Dallas Cowboys in London.

To counter the "tame" image of baseball and sell Major League Baseball products that represent more than a fashion statement, the Partners need to develop a knowledgeable following for the game that will ultimately lead to a loyal base of fans. One measure the group considered to build that following involves sending American college coaches and players to schools in Austria, Slovenia, Italy, the Ukraine, France, Finland, and England.

The Major League Baseball International Partners aren't planning to strike out in the contest with soccer. The group is setting its sites on former soccer fans shouting "Hey badda badda badda—swing!" with a British accent, a French accent, an Italian . . .

Source: Erle Norton, "Baseball Hopes to Be Big Hit in Europe," The Wall Street Journal (June 11, 1993): B1.

Things to Think About

1. What is the problem facing the Major League Baseball International Partners?

2. What factors are important in understanding this problem?

3. What are the alternatives?

4. What are your recommendations for solving this problem?

5. What are some ways to implement your recommendations?

CHAPTER

5

Marketing Information and Research:

Analyzing the Environment

*When you have completed your study of this chapter,
you should be able to:*

CHAPTER OBJECTIVES

1. Understand the Marketing Information System (MIS), its importance to marketing decision making, and the types and sources of information needed by marketers.

2. Describe the process of defining the research problem, the criteria for choosing and evaluating the research plan, and some of the issues marketers face when conducting marketing research.

3. Describe the variety of research techniques available to marketers.

4. Discuss how marketers implement research results.

REAL PEOPLE, REAL CHOICES:

MEET BOB BAXTER, A DECISION MAKER AT MERCEDES-BENZ

Bob Baxter is a driving force at Mercedes-Benz of North America. That's a good place to be if you're in the car business: Market research consistently ranks Mercedes as the highest-quality automobile among American consumers.[1] As manager of marketing research, Mr. Baxter is responsible for collecting and analyzing information that gives the automaker input into such issues as pricing, advertising, product positioning, locational decisions for dealers, and customer satisfaction. His department also provides forecasts of economic and industry activity that are used in the company's strategic planning efforts. Mr. Baxter and his colleagues also work closely with Mercedes dealers around the country to ensure that their efforts are maintaining the company's reputation for high-quality cars and service.

Before joining Mercedes-Benz in 1978, Mr. Baxter was manager of consumer research for the Chrysler Corporation. He collected data on consumers' reactions to product styling and features as well as on advertising and other marketing issues. Prior to that position Mr. Baxter was associate director of marketing and research for the Detroit office of the J. Walter Thompson advertising agency. Mr. Baxter has a bachelor of commerce degree from the University of Windsor and an M.B.A. from the University of Michigan.

PUTTING THE FIRM IN THE DRIVER'S SEAT

Information is the engine that drives today's global marketplace. Firms succeed by knowing what consumers want, when they want it, and where they want it—and by knowing what competing firms are doing about it. Whether competing in home markets or foreign ones, a firm's ability to gather and monitor marketing information keeps it on the road. In fact, a sophisticated database of marketing information is a centerpiece in the strategy of cutting-edge firms that pull ahead and stay ahead in the race for customers.

A firm like Mercedes-Benz avoids detours and pit stops in the chase for glory by monitoring luxury car markets around the world. It stays out in front in the highly competitive U.S. market, for example, by finding out just what it takes to tempt American consumers into spending up to $100,000 for their high-quality driving machines. The company relies on consumer research and marketing information from many sources to keep on top of what product benefits, features, and services will get the nod from car aficionados not only in the United States but in its other ports of call as well.

Some information about consumers and conditions in the marketplace is easy to come by. At other times marketers need to conduct in-depth research to make informed marketing decisions. By keeping a sharp eye on day-to-day customer activity, for example, marketing managers can respond very quickly to changes in consumers' needs and buying patterns that mean the difference between success and failure of marketing plans.

Collecting useful information is not a one-shot deal; successful managers gather information from many sources on an ongoing basis. In this chapter we'll look at the kinds of information marketers need and how they gather and use that information to develop marketing strategies that make a difference. We'll also see what factors are involved when a firm decides to conduct marketing research and what research techniques are available to gather the specific information the firm needs to step into the driver's seat.

THE MARKETING INFORMATION SYSTEM

In today's successful firms the people who collect marketing information are the eyes and ears of the organization's marketing efforts. They find out what the firm's present and potential customers are thinking, what strategies competitors are using, and even whether or not the firm's own strategies are working as intended. While some companies try to get by on intuition, most realize that knowledge is power. The more a firm knows about its customers and competitors, the better are its chances for winning the marketing race. Ironically, many firms are blindsided by an overabundance of marketing information, not the lack of it. The trick is to filter out the really useful information and to use it wisely to capture opportunities and gain advantages. Indeed, it is one thing to collect information, and quite another to manage that information to be sure that it is not only in a useful form but available to managers when they need it.

Many firms develop a **marketing information system (MIS)** to continuously gather, sort, analyze, store, and distribute relevant and timely marketing information to managers. The MIS is part of a firm's overall information network that integrates electronic records from all of the firm's functional areas. The purpose of an MIS is to help marketing managers make better decisions. It guides the planning process and leads to meaningful marketing goals and objectives. Having the right information available at the right time also enables managers to make on-the-spot decisions when unforeseen events derail the marketing plan. Many managers see the MIS as a critical marketing tool that can give the firm significant advantages over other firms competing in its markets.

marketing information system (MIS): an organization's system for continuously gathering, sorting, analyzing, storing, and distributing to managers relevant and timely marketing information

An effective MIS is designed to fulfill the specific information needs of the firm's marketing function and to manage the volume of data required to keep the information up-to-date and available when managers need it. A good MIS includes the internal data that marketing needs to detect problems in the firm's marketing effort and to evaluate the performance of specific marketing strategies. It also includes data on competition and other elements in the firm's business environment that affect its ability to compete, and it maintains data on demographic, cultural, and social trends that help identify marketing opportunities.

An information system includes the people and equipment that collect, analyze, process, and store *data*—facts, statistics, and observations—from many sources in a central database. MIS personnel organize and code the data for storage so that they can be retrieved and distributed as relevant *information* in formats suitable for decision making. For example, profit-and-loss statements for a specific product line can be produced on a regular basis by extracting relevant data from accounting, production, shipping, customer service, and marketing records.

A critical component in an MIS is a computer-based subsystem called a **marketing decision support system (MDSS),** that helps marketing managers use the database to make informed decisions. First, the MDSS includes an interactive user interface to help the user access the database and different software applications. Windows, for example, is an interactive interface that uses graphics to allow users to access different computer applications. The second component of the MDSS is the software that helps sort, merge, compile, and analyze the data. Figure 5.1 (page 154) illustrates the key components of an MIS. In this section we'll first look at a firm's information needs, and then we'll see how the data are collected for the MIS database and used in a decision support system.

marketing decision support system (MDSS): a computer-based subsystem of an MIS that helps marketing managers access the MIS database and analyze data to make informed decisions

INFORMATION NEEDS

A well-designed management information system takes into account the specific types of information that marketing management needs. Some of this information is generated on an ongoing basis by the company's information network. Information monitored from other sources is "fed" into the MIS database and is also available to marketing on a regular basis, while other pieces of "outside" information must be requested when a specific need arises.

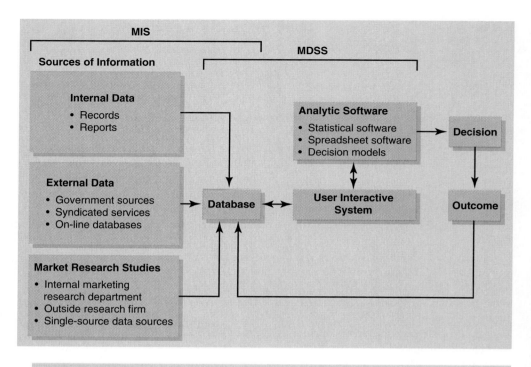

Figure 5.1
Elements of a Marketing Information System

Ongoing Information

Some marketing information needs are ongoing and often immediate. For example, Kmart's MIS uses the company's inventory checkout system in all of its stores and a satellite communications system to provide corporate marketing managers with up-to-the-minute sales data. Most marketing managers use daily sales figures to monitor consumer response to current advertising, couponing and other sales promotions, or price cuts. Current sales data can help managers learn more about customers' brand preferences, and it can also help managers detect problems with products, promotions, and even the firm's distribution system. Marketing managers may use daily or weekly sales data to analyze regional sales by brand or product line, and they may rely on monthly sales reports to measure progress toward marketing's sales and market share goals.

Other ongoing information needs may be tied to marketing expenditures, production and shipping costs, R&D reports, and customer service records. Customer service records and reports from salespeople help marketers to keep on top of customers' concerns about the firm's products and to learn more about their needs and preferences. Historical records also yield information for ongoing needs. For example, a company's sales history can provide valuable clues to past promotions that were particularly effective as well as advertising strategies that stimulated sales in certain geographical regions. Historical cost data on specific promotional campaigns, especially when compared to related sales, may reveal a prior marketing disaster and thus prevent its repetition.

Monitored Information

Marketing managers regularly need some types of information that cannot be obtained by the management information system from company records. This information is obtained by monitoring various sources of information outside the firm and channeling the data into the MIS database. **Marketing intelligence** is information that relates to broad developments in the firm's business environment, including the activities of competitors, that affect the firm. Levi Strauss, for example, tracks environmental changes that could affect the demand for jeans by monitoring indicators of demographic and lifestyle trends; it also monitors changes in government regulations and developments in technology that improve synthetic fibers or manufacturing processes.

Monitored information allows marketers to stay on top of conditions that might af-

marketing intelligence: information gathered from sources outside the firm about developments in the firm's business environment, including the activities of competitors, that affect the firm

Exhibit 5.1
After conducting a very successful sales promotion where it sent a million cases of Diet Pepsi to households of loyal Diet Coke drinkers, PepsiCo decided to include these Coke converts in a database of brand switchers. So it sent the same million households a direct mail piece offering a chance to call an 800 number and "talk" to singer/endorser Ray Charles. First, though, callers had to answer some market research questions using their touch tone phones to enable Pepsi to learn more about Diet Coke drinkers. More than half a million people called in, giving Pepsi a jump on a database that it could use to follow up with these prospects to gain on-going information on their preferences and buying habits.

fect the market for existing products or create demand for new or improved products. Marketing managers typically use up-to-date monitored information on a regular basis to predict fluctuations in sales due to economic conditions, political issues, and events that heighten consumer awareness of such issues as product safety, the health benefits (or risks) of using the product, and the firm's effect on the natural environment. An analysis of trends helps managers to adjust the marketing program by adopting green marketing practices, for example, or by refocusing promotional strategies to emphasize product features and benefits that are currently in demand. Insights into trends also help marketers to plan for the future—to be *proactive,* not just reactive to changes after they occur. For example, knowledge of demographic trends such as a declining birthrate and an aging population allows a firm like Gerber that makes baby food to develop new nutritional products aimed at the unique needs of the elderly.

Requested Information

Sometimes marketing managers need information about consumers that is not tracked by the marketing information system, so new data must be gathered to provide the requested information. This type of information relies on marketing research or formal studies that link marketers directly to consumers to gain data on any of a wide variety of topics such as their lifestyles, demographic characteristics, preferences, attitudes, and buying habits. Marketing research is also needed to determine consumer reactions to products and promotional strategies, for example, by test-marketing a new product before introducing it nationally or pre- and posttesting advertising featuring a celebrity spokesperson before (or after) launching a national campaign.

In Chapter 16 we'll look at other techniques that modern marketers are using to obtain database information directly from consumers. MTV network, for example, has a sample of American viewers who share suggestions about MTV programming online over modems supplied to them by the network. Based on research conducted with this group, MTV managers made the decision to set a new version of its series *The Real World* in London.[2] Later in this chapter we'll see how some marketers rely on full-scale marketing research projects to gain in-depth information on consumers to evaluate the success of current products and marketing mix strategies for pricing, promoting, and distributing them.

COLLECTING THE INFORMATION

Valuable market information comes from many places. As the MIS model in Figure 5.1 shows, some of the data that go into the MIS database are right in the firm's own backyard—that is, they come from internal company sources. Some data come from external sources that the firm monitors, while other data are gathered through research studies. Regardless of their source, data may be broadly categorized based on the purpose for which the data were collected.

primary data: data specifically collected and organized for a particular marketing information need or to solve a particular marketing problem

Primary data are data specifically collected and organized for a particular marketing information need. Many times these data can be obtained relatively easily and inexpensively by seeking information from existing customers. For example, questionnaires attached to billing statements or enclosed in product packages can be used to solicit information that is fed into the MIS. When a person purchases a new computer component, a hair dryer, or refrigerator, for example, the company typically requests the person to mail in the accompanying registration card—which also happens to ask for background information about the buyer.

At other times primary data can only be obtained by conducting research projects designed to address the firm's specific needs. For example, a startup company called Biosite Diagnostics Inc. was trying to market a product that was used for speedier drug testing in hospital emergency rooms. Even though its funds were limited, the company spent $150,000 on two market surveys so it could determine whether its new product had a potential market and, if so, to demonstrate this promise to investors. Biosite found that it was actually lab technicians rather than physicians who made the decision about which test to use in the emergency room, and based on this primary data the company was able to convince its backers that the greater speed of its product compared to competitors was an important factor for this group of decision makers.[3]

secondary data: data used by marketing, but gathered for some purpose other than a current marketing information need

Secondary data are data gathered for some purpose other than the current marketing information need. This type of data is already available and only needs to be accessed and added to the MIS database. While secondary data have the advantages of being fast, easy to obtain, and low in cost, they may not be usable. Marketers must question whether the available secondary data are current and, even more important, how, for what purpose, and by whom the data were collected. For example, information distributed by a trade organization such as the Tobacco Institute may be intended to promote a certain point of view and should be interpreted with care. Data monitored from external sources are always classified as secondary data. The firm's internal data may be either primary or secondary.

Internal Secondary Data Sources

A wealth of marketing information is right under the organization's nose. The MIS model shows that *internal data* include both company records and reports. Company records include such items as sales, orders, customer lists, inventories, costs, quality control, shipping and production schedules, and other activities in all functional areas. Company reports are documents generated for planning or control or decision-making purposes. Some, such as accounting reports, are quantitative in nature. Other reports are qualitative. For example, a salesperson's daily call reports may include the salesperson's assessment of competitive activity or what customers like and dislike about a product.

Most MIS systems are designed to maintain up-to-date records that yield usable secondary data for the marketing function. Some systems are designed to monitor consumer activity and troubleshoot potential problems. For example, United Airlines' information system monitors customers who have connecting flights, and if delays in the first flight will cause them to miss their connecting flight, it automatically rebooks these passengers onto the next available connecting flight.[4] This change is then conveyed to delayed customers before they leave on the first flight to relieve their worries about getting to their destination and to give them time to reschedule appointments or transportation and hotel reservations prior to their eventual arrival.

Company internal reports can be a rich source of both primary and secondary data. For example, reports from the customer service department, from the sales force, from distributors and dealers, and from employees who have been involved in certain marketing activities in the past are specifically requested to obtain needed marketing information. Other ongoing reports in the system, such as production and accounting reports, are not specifically generated for marketing but do provide important secondary data for marketing purposes. At Hewlett-Packard every piece of customer feedback that the company receives—whether from a primary or secondary data source—is assigned to an "owner." This employee is responsible for acting on the information and informing the customer what is being done to address the problem.[5]

Some companies use internal data in combination with external data to generate information that helps marketing predict sales or peak demand for products. For example, Domino's Pizza has a "pizza metering system" that correlates pizza sales in all of its branches with monitored media events. Orders rose 11 percent when Amy Fisher or Joey Buttafucco appeared on the show *A Current Affair,* and when basketball star Michael Jordan retired (at least temporarily) at a daytime press conference, lunchtime pizza orders set a national record.[6]

External Secondary Data Sources

External data provide a second source of marketing information shown in the MIS model. As we've seen, external data are obtained by monitoring sources outside the company. Such monitored information may include data reported in the popular and business press, the results of regular environmental scanning conducted by the government or by private industry, the results of syndicated research studies conducted periodically by private research organizations, and published research on the state of the industry conducted by trade organizations.

Data monitored from outside sources include everything from simple (and usually inexpensive) observations of consumers in action to complicated (and often expensive) reports of market activity. For example, the U.S. government is a major source of important marketing data. The U.S. Bureau of the Census publishes separate reports on specific industries (for example, agriculture, construction, and mining) as well as on housing, population growth and distribution, retail trade, and so on. This type of data can be obtained directly from the Census Bureau very inexpensively or from private companies that summarize and repackage the data and then sell this information to clients.

Other types of external data that can be fed into the MIS database are more costly to obtain. Many times marketers purchase the results of syndicated research studies—that is, research information that is periodically collected by private research organizations and offered for sale to any firm willing to buy it. The Simmons Study of Media & Markets is a syndicated survey that is conducted semiannually; the results are tabulated into thirty-four separate volumes that are then sold to marketers, advertising agencies, and publishers. This information is based on the self-reports of consumers in over 20,000 American households who complete periodic reports that detail their purchases of products from aspirin to snow tires. Many marketers also purchase data from A.C. Nielsen's ongoing study of television program choices, which play a central role in determining how much advertisers pay to have their products advertised on network television as well as which shows will be canceled due to low ratings.

Marketers can also obtain syndicated data from a wide range of other research sources. The *Monitor* service by Yankelovich and Partners, for example, sells marketers information on key social trends by regularly interviewing consumers and reporting on changes in people's priorities, values, and beliefs. The National Crime Study conducted by America's Research Group provides information on the effects of the public's attitude toward crime on retailers. The GeoNetwork supplied by Business Location Research compiles information to allow businesses to choose their location.

Some syndicated research services specialize in predicting the future. They use various methods to forecast trends or changes in lifestyles that will affect the wants and needs of customers in the coming years. One prominent trend forecaster is Faith Popcorn whose company, BrainReserve, sells "TrendPacks" to companies at $12,000 a year. By tracking themes that show up in movies and other mass media, BrainReserve has predicted such

1990s trends as Cocooning (staying home), Cashing Out (quitting the rat race), and Down-Aging (acting youthful).[7]

External data may also be drawn from business directories and the many online databases that have become available in recent years.[8] For a relatively small fee, even small firms that can't afford a separate research department can have access to a variety of sophisticated databases that provide a wide range of information on consumers and other topics related to marketing information needs. As the WorldWide Web continues to expand dramatically, the possibilities for downloading information off the Web are almost limitless.

Several major online database services that are now available provide a variety of secondary data for marketers.

- CompuServe provides full-text articles from over 450 business and trade publications. The service also features Magazine Database Plus, the Associated Press news wire, Newspaper Library, CENDATA (1990 Census data), and SUPERSITE (demographics, sales potential, and neighborhood reports based on the U.S. Census).
- DIALOG offers Worldwide Sales Prospecting data; DIALOG sorts companies by location, size, and industry. The user can request telemarketing reports, mailing labels, company profiles, or Dun & Bradstreet data.
- NEXIS features information from such sources as Dun & Bradstreet, *The New York Times,* CNN, and National Public Radio transcripts.
- Dun & Bradstreet Information Services maintains its own database of business information, including company credit ratings and so on.
- Database America Consumer Files contain information on the mail-order buying habits of 21 million people.
- A British company recently unveiled ConsumerBank, a database with 240 pieces of information each on 40 million European consumers.[9]

Marketing Research Studies

Many marketing managers get lucky and find that most of their information needs can be satisfied by internal or external data in the MIS database. There are times, though, when only the results of marketing research will do, and so the third source of information in an MIS database is *primary marketing research data.* When a firm needs specific data to satisfy a unique information need, it relies on **marketing research,** which is designed to objectively collect, analyze, and interpret data that provide the needed information. While many large firms have extensive marketing research departments to conduct their own research, many others choose to hire research specialists on a consulting basis.

Marketers may select from a wide variety of research suppliers, ranging from one-person consulting operations to huge international firms that generate millions of dollars of revenue a year for their clients. *Customized research data* can be obtained from research firms that provide a range of services from full-scale research projects, in which the consulting firm designs, carries out, and interprets the results of the study, to field service, in which the consulting firm merely gathers the data for a study designed by the marketer. Instead of designing new studies for each project, some research firms help clients reduce costs by offering a standardized methodology that the client firm can buy into to gather the needed information. One such firm, Starch INRA Hooper, for example, has been hired to test the impact of magazine advertisements for so many clients that marketers refer to this process as "Starching" their ads.

Another way that research firms help marketers cut costs is by conducting an **omnibus survey,** in which questions are asked on behalf of several different clients. Each participating company buys questions on the survey and receives only the results of these questions. Omnibus surveys are a way to share the costs of doing research, so they tend to be cheaper and more efficient. They are especially appropriate for a company wishing to ask a limited number of questions of a large, representative sample.[10]

As more and more marketers enter the global marketplace, American and European research firms are aggressively pursuing research opportunities in different countries. The

marketing research: systematic and objective collection, analysis, and interpretation of data for use in making informed marketing decisions

omnibus survey: a research method in which a research firm asks questions on behalf of many clients in a study of a large representative sample of consumers

Gallup Organization, a major research firm, recently opened Gallup China Ltd., where it plans to spend $5 million to $10 million to develop its presence. Its first two clients are the U.S. Chocolate Manufacturers Association and the Washington Apple Commission, which are trying to determine the potential for introducing their products to consumers in this huge but unfamiliar market. So far preliminary results for the Apple Commission are particularly encouraging, because the color red is a favorite of the Chinese![11]

The New Wave: Single-Source Data

One research issue that marketers have been trying to solve for years is determining how their actions in one area (say, inserting coupons into newspapers or advertising on *Seinfeld*) affect outcomes in another (say, the increase in sales that can be attributed directly to the coupons). Short of moving in with a family for a few months, marketers have had no way to determine the actual impact of advertising or other promotional activities on consumer purchasing over time.

Most research techniques that try to gauge the effectiveness of specific advertising messages are less than ideal: For example, researchers have traditionally shown test advertisements in an unnatural situation such as a theater and measured results by asking consumers questions such as "Are you likely to purchase this product?" Today, though, managers' lives are being made a bit easier by **single-source data** research services that use sophisticated technologies to monitor a particular consumer group's exposure to marketing communications and to assess directly the impact of these activities on the defined customer group over time.

The most exciting single-source data methodology involves three separate elements. First, researchers develop a panel of consumer households in certain communities. Member households provide researchers with information on family characteristics and lifestyles, and they agree to have their purchases and television-watching habits monitored. Second, the methodology includes a panel of stores that agree, for a fee, to cooperate in the research effort. They permit researchers to use their checkout scanners to track purchases made by panel members and to control the price and placement of tested products on store shelves. The third part of the methodology is the use of television meters that track all programs the panel families watch.

Once the system is in place, panel families, who have agreed to shop at the panel stores, use an identification number when making purchases. Panel stores' scanners record the purchases and send information, such as the brands purchased on a given date, the package size purchased and the price paid, to researchers. By linking the information on products purchased by a family to television advertising watched, the research firm can assess the effectiveness of the advertising strategies of competing brands in influencing brand purchases, and it gains new data on the buying habits and lifestyles of the panel families.

In these study communities single-source data research firms have also developed *split-cable television* capability, in which different commercials can be broadcast to different segments of the cable television audience. If a client wishes to test different advertising strategies, the research firm can broadcast two alternative versions of a test commercial. One portion of the consumer panel will view version A and the other portion of the panel will view version B. By tracking purchases after these "A-B tests," the research firm gathers data that measure whether consumers who view version A of a commercial buy more or less of the product that do those who view version B.

A-B tests factor in the price of the tested products compared to the price of competing products, the location of the tested product on store shelves, and the quantity available. They also take into account such factors as point-of-sales promotions, couponing, and advertising blitzes by competing firms. These measures help to isolate the effects of the test commercial from other influences on panel members' purchases.

There are currently three major single-source data services: Arbitron's ScanAmerica, Nielsen's ScanTrack, and Information Resources' InfoScan. Although these single-source systems are still a bit rough around the edges, the continuing development of this technology promises to open a new wave of single-source data gathering techniques and perhaps to revolutionize how managers can make use of research information. Stay tuned for future developments.[12]

single-source data: data gathered by research services that use technologies to monitor a particular consumer group's exposure to marketing communications and to track purchases made by the group over time

USING THE DATA

A well-fed database in a marketing information system is of no use to marketers unless they can access and use the data to solve problems or make marketing decisions. As we saw in the MIS model in Figure 5.1, a MIS system includes both the database and a marketing decision support system. The user interface component of the MDSS allows managers to retrieve data from the database for use with system software—database management programs that allow managers to sit at their own computer terminals to sort, merge, and restructure data in the system for analysis.

For example, a sales manager can improve the usefulness of sales reports for a particular product line by sorting and merging data on inventory, returns, back orders, and so on. In the search for reasons for declining sales, a marketing manager might merge sales figures with selected customer service records that show the number and type of complaints received on a weekly or monthly basis. Sales data may be sorted by geographical region and merged with data on customer preferences or general satisfaction with the company. Sales data can also be sorted by product price for comparison with data on the price of competing products. Frito-Lay's marketing management information system (MMIS) generates daily sales data by product line and by region that are used to evaluate the market share of different Frito-Lay products compared to each other and to regional data for the rest of the snack food industry.

The MDDS software also includes analytical tools such as spreadsheets, statistical software packages, and decision models that are essential aids to the marketing decision-making process.[13] Decision models create scenarios based on available data to answer "What if . . ." and "Which is best . . ." questions. These analytic tools allow managers to manipulate the data and variables in the decision situation, for example, by seeing what happens if the price is changed (raised or lowered) or if a new product isn't ready to ship by the planned date.

Zales, the largest retailer of jewelry merchandise, uses its store placement model (SPM) to determine which location for a new store is best. The company's database contains demographic information on Zales' current stores. The characteristics of a potential site are fed in and compared with existing stores. When a close match is found, financial information on the performance of the existing store is output, which allows executives to project how well the proposed store will do under similar circumstances.[14]

ISSUES AND CHOICES IN MARKETING RESEARCH

Some of marketing's most important decisions rely on information gathered by research that specifically addresses the decision maker's concerns. For example, sales personnel rely on research to provide them with feedback on sales performance or to identify likely purchasers. Media planners need information to tell them which specific magazines or television shows will most likely be seen by a market segment. Advertising creatives need feedback to "flesh out" the needs and wants of target consumers. Brand managers want to know how their product is perceived in the marketplace, especially relative to competing brands.

Some marketers conduct limited, low-cost "research projects" by searching the MIS database and finding the needed information waiting to be mined. More typically, the marketer has a problem that requires very specific information and must rely on marketing research to systematically gather the data. Virtually all companies rely on some form of marketing research, though the amount and type of research that is done varies dramatically. In today's competitive business environment, marketing research is a top budget item for cutting-edge firms. Expenditures for marketing research in the United States alone grew to $2.7 billion in 1993, and at least another $1.6 billion was paid to firms who do research in other countries.[15]

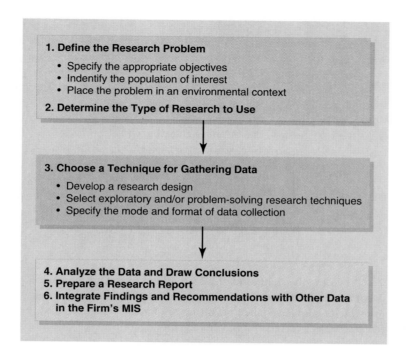

1. **Define the Research Problem**
   - Specify the appropriate objectives
   - Indentify the population of interest
   - Place the problem in an environmental context
2. **Determine the Type of Research to Use**

3. **Choose a Technique for Gathering Data**
   - Develop a research design
   - Select exploratory and/or problem-solving research techniques
   - Specify the mode and format of data collection

4. **Analyze the Data and Draw Conclusions**
5. **Prepare a Research Report**
6. **Integrate Findings and Recommendations with Other Data in the Firm's MIS**

Figure 5.2
The Research Process

Large firms like Coca-Cola and AT&T have extensive marketing research capabilities to conduct their own research. Depending on the information needed and the complexity of the research problem, other companies hire outside research firms to conduct all or part of their research. Marketing managers are responsible for selecting the outside firm, and the manager who requests the information will be involved in one way or another throughout the project. As a general rule most managers prefer to choose a research firm that has a reputation for integrity—that is, an established firm with a solid track record that has earned the trust of clients over the years by doing things the right way and avoiding unnecessary or inappropriate research.

Whether a company conducts the research itself or hires another firm to do it, the goal is still the same: to acquire data that allow managers to make informed marketing decisions. Marketing decisions based on researched information are only as good as the research that provided it. Ideally, marketing research is a series of carefully thought-out steps designed to attain a specific objective. As shown in Figure 5.2, the research process can be divided into three phases. The steps in the first phase, defining the problem and determining the type of research needed, are crucial: Marketing managers provide the input that not only helps researchers structure the study, but keeps the firm from spending its research dollars to collect unnecessary or even useless data.

In this section we'll look at the first two steps in the research process. We'll also examine some of the issues marketing managers face when they decide to embark on a research study, including the research criteria that affect the quality of the study, the ethical issues involved in marketing research, and the unique problems encountered in research with children and in global markets.

DEFINING THE PROBLEM

The first step in the marketing research process is defining the problem (or opportunity) to be addressed by the research. Marketing managers might use research to look for a solution to a specific problem, such as which of two package designs best conveys the desired image for the product, or they might seek more general information for a planning decision. A brand manager planning packaging changes, for example, might want to know what features of a package sitting on a grocery shelf cause people to stop and take a second look. Marketers also use marketing research to identify opportunities for new products or occasionally even to promote existing ones. For example, Amgen Inc., a pharmaceutical firm, commissioned the Gallup Poll organization to conduct a survey among cancer patients receiving chemotherapy. It turned out that nearly half of those who responded were unaware that these treatments carry the risk of severe infections, which provided Amgen an opportunity to promote an infection-fighting drug called Neupogen that it manufactures.[16]

Defining the research issue as precisely as possible allows researchers to set objectives that will result in the right answers to the right questions. It also ensures that the questions are asked of the right consumers and are focusing on the right factors in the problem situation. Defining the problem, then, has three components:

- Specifying the research objectives: What question or questions will the research attempt to answer?
- Identifying the consumer population of interest: What are the characteristics of the consumers involved in the problem situation?
- Placing the problem in an environmental context: What factors in the firm's internal and external business environment might be influencing the problem situation?

Providing the right kind of information for each of these components of the problem is not as simple as it seems. For example, suppose a luxury car manufacturer wants to find out why its sales have fallen off rather dramatically over the past year. The problem—the research objective—could revolve around any number of possible questions: Is the firm's advertising failing to reach the right consumers? Is the right advertising message being sent out to the right consumers? Do the firm's cars have a particular feature (or lack of it) that is turning customers away? Is there a problem with the firm's reputation for providing quality service? Do consumers believe the price is right for the value they get?

The research objective leads to identifying the consumer population that will be studied. The research might focus on current owners to find out what they especially like about the car or the services to develop promotional strategies that emphasize these benefits. Or the research might study nonowners to determine their lifestyles, what they look for in a luxury automobile, their perceptions of the company's cars, or their beliefs about the company itself.

Placing the problem in the context of the firm's environment helps researchers structure the research, determine the specific types of questions to ask, and identify factors that must be taken into account when measuring results. Environmental conditions provide a perspective on the other two components of the problem situation and in some cases can actually influence them. For example, when the economy is tight and sales of luxury cars are generally declining, the population to be studied might be narrowed down to a select group of consumers who are still willing and able to indulge in a luxury vehicle. Alternatively, consumers may be moving away from "glitzy" status-conscious materialism, as in the early part of the 1990s, so that the research question comes down to how promotional strategies can convey honest and basic values that go beyond "snob appeal."

DETERMINING THE TYPE OF RESEARCH TO USE

Sometimes marketers need research information about a clearly defined problem, but at other times the problem may not be clear or obvious. Marketers may not be able to determine exactly what the problem is when they focus on "symptoms," such as declining sales, and not on the underlying problem that's causing sales to drop. If the problem is unclear or unknown, a marketer's best choice is to conduct a small-scale investigation to try to isolate the problem before launching a costly full-scale research project. Two broad types of research that marketers can use depend on how clearly marketing managers can define the problem.

Exploratory Research

Exploratory research investigates or explores a marketing problem that is not yet well defined. It does not seek the answers to specific questions or problems; instead, it is used to generate specific topics and questions for future, more rigorous studies. Because the studies are usually small-scale and less costly than other types of research, marketers often use exploratory research to get ideas for potential new strategies and opportunities.

exploratory research: a type of marketing research designed to investigate or explore a marketing issue or problem that is not well defined by gathering qualitative descriptive information from a small group of consumers

Exhibit 5.2
Beach Patrol, Inc., goes straight to the source when the company wants to come up with winning ideas for new bathing suit designs. Instead of relying solely on input from retail buyers as to what women want, groups of high school and college women in Los Angeles, Florida, and Hawaii are polled on their favorite styles and colors. The company uses this input to determine where to focus its production, and it shares the results with store buyers, who are usually persuaded by this direct input from women who actually buy the suits. This research effort has allowed Beach Patrol to ride the wave of success in the competitive bathing suit market.

Most exploratory research provides qualitative data, where the researcher collects data that add "personality and character" to descriptions of consumers' attitudes, feelings, and buying behaviors. Exploratory research is relatively flexible and unstructured to allow researchers to follow up on each consumer's unique responses in depth. It relies on "open-ended" questions and often involves relatively few consumers. Researchers may interview consumers, salespeople, or other employees about products, services, ads, stores, and so on, or they may simply "hang out" in a store and watch what people do when choosing among competing brands.

Marketing managers frequently rely on exploratory research to develop promotional strategies. Researchers for a manufacturer of Swiss chocolate, for example, interviewed consumers and found that many chocolate lovers hide secret "stashes" around their houses. One respondent confessed to hiding candy bars inside her lingerie drawer! The results of this exploratory research were used to develop an advertising campaign built around the theme: "The True Confessions of Chocaholics."[17]

Problem-Solving Research

Problem-solving research investigates a particular marketing issue or problem. The information needed has already been clearly defined, and the consumers studied are representative of some larger group. Marketers may use this formal research process to collect measurable data on consumers' purchasing behaviors or to determine what effects different strategies will have on their behavior. Because problem-solving research aims to provide decision makers with actionable information, it is usually designed to yield quantitative data, where observations or responses of consumers in the study are specifically defined and measured for analysis.

Problem-solving research allows marketers to test their hunches about the cause of a marketing phenomenon or the results of a particular strategy. For example, a magazine publisher may believe that a cover featuring a well-known comedian will sell more copies than the same magazine sporting a well-known politician. To test this belief, she might arrange to have an issue of the magazine produced with two separate covers and then track newsstand sales to see if the funny guy "pulls" more readership than the serious one (though some people think some politicians are pretty funny as well!).

Problem-solving research typically doesn't provide much in-depth information about any one person's reactions (say, to two different covers on a magazine). Instead it collects data from enough respondents who share important characteristics to allow some *generalizations* to be made about how others who also exhibit these traits would react. Instead of having to ask, say, every college student in the country who eats chocolate bars whether he

problem-solving research: a type of marketing research designed to provide actionable information on a specific issue or problem by collecting measurable quantitative responses or observations of consumers who are representative of a larger consumer group

REAL PEOPLE, REAL CHOICES:

DECISION TIME AT MERCEDES-BENZ

Mercedes-Benz AG is renowned for its high-quality cars around the world. Over the years the Mercedes name has become synonymous with excellence in engineering as well as with status and luxury. Mercedes advertising traditionally had used a serious tone, because buying a car in the $30,000 to $120,000 price range is hardly a casual purchase. In the late 1980s, however, Bob Baxter and his colleagues started to realize that they might have an unusual problem: Research revealed that Mercedes may have done *too* good a job establishing itself as a high-class, sophisticated and *serious* automobile! Indeed, the typical Mercedes owner is a man at least forty-nine years old—perhaps young at heart, but not the ideal age segment if the company wants to expand its cadre of loyal drivers down the road.[18]

In the course of doing some routine qualitative research on customers' feelings about luxury cars, group interviews began to reveal some negative perceptions. While respondents continued to voice their admiration for Mercedes' workmanship, comments that the cars were viewed as unapproachable, aloof, and uncaring started to surface. Similar feedback was obtained from dealers, who reported that customers were reluctant to examine the vehicles. A common reaction was, "May I *really* sit in the car?" Mercedes-Benz had a "personality" problem.

Baxter commissioned another study to determine the extent of the problem. This national survey of high-income consumers compared perceptions of the "personality traits" of Mercedes versus such competitors as Lexus and BMW. Sure enough, the quantitative data from this problem-solving research effort confirmed the problem. For example, while respondents view Mercedes as more "dignified" than competitors, the cars are also seen as relatively more "arrogant" and less "approachable" than either Lexus or BMW.

How should Mercedes-Benz react to these findings? Bob Baxter and his colleagues had several choices:

Option 1. Modify the company's communications strategy to "humanize" the cars while keeping the basic message that Mercedes cars are durable, well-engineered driving machines. Present this message in a less serious tone, so that it is not as threatening to consumers. A potential problem here is that this new advertising will overcompensate by conveying the idea that the cars are "cute"—people do not pay large sums of money for a cute car!

Option 2. Change the basic positioning of the car to make it more approachable. Convince people that Mercedes is not such a "fancy" car, after all. Of course, such a dramatic change in product positioning is difficult to accomplish and might wind up simply confusing buyers.

Option 3. Don't worry about these perceptions. The car is positioned as a serious, high-quality product, well worth the high price. A change in this perception might downgrade consumers' perceptions, making it more difficult to justify charging a premium price for a Mercedes. Besides, these personality issues may just reflect a passing fad. On the other hand, consumers' inability to feel comfortable about a Mercedes might be a competitive disadvantage, especially because the automaker was being challenged by domestic products such as Cadillac and Lincoln as well as by European makes such as BMW, Jaguar, and some models of Volvo, Audi, and Saab.

Now, join the decision team at Mercedes-Benz of North America: What course of action would you recommend to Mercedes management and why?

or she prefers them with nuts or without, a *sample* of several hundred of these chocaholics at selected campuses probably would be sufficient to get an accurate idea of the preferences of the total population of college students. Because marketers rarely have the resources to study everybody in a market segment, the sampling process allows researchers to select a small group of consumers to represent the larger consumer population of interest in a marketing research study.

CRITERIA THAT AFFECT THE QUALITY OF THE RESEARCH

All too often marketers who conduct a research study or pay someone else to do it assume that once a massive amount of data is collected, they will have the "truth." Unfortunately, there are times when research data don't tell the "truth." The collected data may be flawed for some reason; as the expression goes, "Garbage in, garbage out!"[19] Typically, three factors influence the quality of research results.

Reliability

A car is reliable if it starts every time you turn on the ignition. A reliable employee is one who always shows up for work. In research, **reliability** is the extent to which the research measurement techniques are dependable and consistent and will give almost the same results time after time. That means that the results of the research are reproducible with different samples of a population or with the same sample measured at two different times.

Research reliability may be related to how questions are worded. If the wording of a question is ambiguous so that the respondents don't understand it, they may give different responses depending on their mood, level of fatigue, or other factors not related to the topic of the research. When reliability is a problem, marketers cannot know if research results are accurate or inaccurate. On the other hand, being reliable doesn't guarantee that the results are the "truth" or of value. Reliability is kind of like money: Having it is no guarantee of happiness, but the lack of it is always a problem.

reliability: an evaluation criterion that indicates the extent to which marketing research techniques are dependable and consistent and will give the same results time after time

Validity

Validity is the extent to which the research actually measures what it was intended to measure. Validity was part of the problem underlying the famous "New Coke" fiasco, when Coca-Cola replaced "Old Coke" with a new, sweeter formula based on consumers' blind taste test preferences for one anonymous cola over another. Researchers assumed that taste was a valid measure of consumers' preferences for a cola brand and found out the hard way that measuring taste alone is not the same as measuring people's true feelings or their loyalty for a particular brand. Indeed, in a recent blind taste test conducted by Consumers Union, only seven out of nineteen diehard Coke and Pepsi fans could correctly identify their brand of choice when fed four unidentified cola samples—even private label brands like Chek (Winn-Dixie) and Cragmont (Safeway) scored equally well.[20] It's obvious that millions of loyal drinkers are buying a lot more than sugar and carbonated water when they choose one brand over another!

validity: an evaluation criterion that indicates the extent to which marketing research actually measures what it was intended to measure

Representativeness

Representativeness is the extent to which consumers in the study are similar to the larger group in which the marketer has an interest. This criterion for evaluating research underscores the importance of *sampling* to select a subset or small group of consumers that will represent a larger population of interest in a research study. If the sample group is not representative, the study will provide misleading results that marketers cannot use, with any accuracy, to make generalizations about the larger group of interest. The critical issue, then, is how to choose the sample to ensure representativeness.

Three types of sampling procedures are used to select respondents for research surveys. *Random sampling* is the process of randomly selecting names from a list containing all names in a total population. This larger group, or population, might be a city phone book or a membership list of all students who belong to campus sororities. A *stratified* random sample means dividing the total population into categories (age, income, marital status, and so on) before making the random selection. When a simple or stratified ran-

representativeness: an evaluation criterion for marketing research that indicates the extent to which data collected from respondents can be generalized to the larger customer group

dom selection is not practical, researchers create a *systematic sample* (which research has shown gives the same research results as a random sample). In a systematic sampling procedure names are systematically selected from a larger group. For example, a systematic sampling procedure might be to take the fifth name on each of the first two columns of every page of a telephone directory.

Both random and systematic samples can be expensive and time consuming. Often the researcher must instead settle for a *quota sample,* where the researcher specifies the number of respondents with particular characteristics, such as a certain age, income, or marital status, and so on. Once the required number or quota of people in each group is selected, no others in that group are included in the sample. Sometimes the quotas represent each group's proportion of the population, while in other studies the researchers set quotas based on other criteria important to the research. For example, if you were studying the students in your school, you might include 100 each of freshmen, sophomores, juniors, and seniors, regardless of the proportion of each class in the total student population.

Sometimes researchers decide instead to settle for a less scientific (but also less expensive) *convenience sample* by using whoever is available and willing to participate in the study. In some cases they may even use their own employees as "guinea pigs." The 3M Company, for example, first tested its Post-It™ notes on its own people before trying to sell them to other office workers.[21] When Gap Inc. was developing the concept for its new chain of stores called Old Navy, the company gave eight employees who fit the customer profile for these new stores $200 apiece and then interviewed them about how they had spent it (nice work if you can get it!).[22]

CHALLENGES AND OPPORTUNITIES FOR MARKETING RESEARCHERS

Gathering research data is vital to marketing, but actually doing it is not always as easy as it sounds. While it seems like the researcher should just be able to go out and ask questions of people in a target market to guide decision making, any number of issues can stand in the way. One of the most important challenges facing researchers today is contacting potential respondents. Home telephone answering machines, unlisted telephone numbers, and generally pressured lifestyles make many consumer groups difficult to reach. And when they are contacted, many are unwilling to participate because they are "too busy" or "not interested," which is often a way of saying they're distrustful of researchers and resent what they consider to be an invasion of privacy.

Young adults may be easier to reach, but unconventional methods are often needed to get them to open up because researchers sometimes find they are too suspicious or skeptical in traditional research settings. *Details* magazine, for example, holds focus groups in people's living rooms instead of in focus group facilities for this reason. To overcome the problem, researchers may try to find "Generation Xer" respondents waiting in lines to buy concert tickets or hanging out in clubs.[23] Members of minority groups, citizens of other countries, and children also pose special challenges that must be confronted by the determined researcher.

To further complicate matters, changing lifestyles and technological developments are making it much more difficult to track people's behavior. For example, one of the biggest obstacles to further development of marketing activities on the WorldWide Web boils down to the need for research techniques that can let a company know how frequently and by whom a home page is being used and what these browsers are getting out of it.[24]

Superimposed on all of these challenges to gathering data is the ethical question of whether marketing researchers have the right to have this information in the first place. Nevertheless, for those researchers willing to deal with all of the challenges of doing marketing research, opportunities abound.

Ethical Issues in Marketing Research

The ability of marketing researchers to collect useful information depends on the degree to which they earn the trust of those whose opinions they solicit. If people are not willing to participate in the data collection process, marketing managers will not be able to determine their true needs and develop marketing strategies to meet those needs.

Two barriers have prevented researchers from winning this trust in recent years. One is the abuse of this relationship by some unscrupulous marketers who contact consumers under the pretense of doing a research study, when, in fact, their real intent is to sell the respondent something. Selling under the guise of doing research has been termed "sugging." A related strategy is called "frugging"—what is labeled as research is actually fund raising. Consumers do not react well to this kind of deception, and it "poisons the well" for real researchers who try to contact the victims of these procedures later on.

A second concern is privacy: People are increasingly reluctant to divulge personal information to interviewers. According to a 1992 Harris Poll survey, 79 percent of the public are concerned about threats to personal privacy, and 76 percent agree that consumers have lost all control over how personal information about them is circulated and used by companies.[25] After receiving 30,000 complaints, Lotus Development Corporation, for example, was forced to kill plans to sell its *MarketPlace: Households* database software, which contained demographic information on 80 million households. The Blockbuster Entertainment Corp. also ran into trouble when it was accused of trying to sell information detailing customers' video rental habits.[26] Critics charged that a person's movie preferences (whether for action movies, pornography, or cartoons) was his or her own business.

The potential invasion of privacy by market researchers who purchase demographic databases is also an issue for researchers who go "underground" to study consumers in their natural environments. A California couple sued Nissan, charging that the company had planted a "researcher-spy" from Tokyo in their home. The researcher's assignment was to study the living and car purchasing patterns of U.S. consumers, and under the guise of a visiting executive program he rented a room in the couple's home while he observed the behavior of the family and their neighbors. The suit was eventually dropped, but concerns about prying live on.[27]

In 1992 these ethical issues prompted twenty-six of the marketing research industry's major corporations and associations to found the Council on Marketing and Opinion Research (CMOR). The council's purpose is to "promote awareness for and value of marketing research; enhance the marketing research experience; establish a single unified industry voice on restrictive legislation and eroding respondent cooperation rates."[28]

Concerns about ethics and invasion of privacy aren't limited to companies' spying on consumers. The conduct of "research" on the actions of competitors (in this context, a nice word for snooping) is also a matter of some concern. While collecting this type of "market intelligence" is a necessary part of monitoring the business environment, sometimes companies walk a very thin line between monitoring and spying. Some of these activities, like sending employees to competing stores to keep track of what is being offered and for how much, are fairly harmless. Many companies also routinely buy their competitors' products to check them out and sometimes practice "reverse engineering," in which they take a competitor's product apart to see what makes it tick to improve on the competitor's product or process. Other forms of "monitoring" are even more questionable, including picking through the trash in competitors' dumpsters, planting spies in their workplaces, hiring away executives to learn company secrets, posing as a potential supplier, bribing employees, or even posing as college students conducting a class marketing project.

Marketing Research Involving Children

Compared to adults, children are difficult subjects for market research, and the problem is compounded in Europe, where some countries restrict marketers from interviewing children. Kids tend to be undependable reporters of their own behavior, they have poor recall, and they often do not understand abstract questions.[29] Children are more impressionable and, when watching TV, find it harder to tell the difference between objective information and advertising that is intended to create loyalty to a product. In many cases the children themselves cannot directly explain why they prefer one item over another (or they're not willing to share these secrets with grown-ups).[30]

To further complicate things, parents themselves don't always provide accurate explanations of why they chose products for their kids. For example, when mothers were interviewed in focus groups, they claimed they bought a fruit snack made by General Mills because of its "wholesomeness." When researchers hung around supermarkets and observed mothers shopping with their children, however, a different picture emerged: The mothers were actually just giving into their kids as they threw their favorite snacks into the cart.[31]

Despite these problems, though, marketing research involving kids can pay off, and many companies have obtained valuable information by taking seriously the opinions of young "consumers in training."[32] After interviewing elementary school kids, Campbell's Soup discovered that kids like soup, but are afraid to admit it, because they associate it with "nerds." The company decided to reintroduce the Campbell kids in its advertising after a prolonged absence, but they are now slimmed down and more athletic to reflect an updated, "un-nerdy" image.[33]

A particularly helpful type of research with children is product testing. Young subjects can provide a valuable perspective on what products will succeed with other kids. One candy company has a Candy Tasters Club, composed of 1,200 kids aged six to sixteen, that evaluates its product ideas. For example, the group nixed the idea of a Batman lollipop, claiming that the superhero was too macho to be a sucker.[34] The Fisher-Price Company maintains a nursery known as the Playlab. Children are chosen from a waiting list of 4,000 to play with new toys, while staff members watch from behind a one-way mirror.[35]

Researchers have had to be especially creative when designing studies involving younger consumers, and ethical issues related to conducting market research on adults are even more important with children. To win the trust of respondents, a research company called Fresh Kids actually uses kids as moderators who lead discussions among other kids about their product likes and dislikes. These "deputy researchers" wear earphones during the sessions to get guidance from an adult supervisor. Nickelodeon maintains an online panel of eight- to twelve-year-old computer users who give feedback on programming, merchandise options, and package designs. A company called BKG Youth held slumber parties for groups of boys to research attitudes on clothing for Levi Strauss, and the company has also given kids money and then videotaped them on shopping sprees to see how they spend it. These techniques yield valuable information, but marketers must be careful not to cross the fine line between information gathering and exploitation.

Marketing Research Involving Consumers in Other Countries

Information on local consumer preferences and values is a critical need for marketers who enter global markets that, as we saw in Chapter 4, vary widely in different parts of the world. Many global marketers are finding big differences in the sophistication of market research operations and the amount of data available in these countries. Some countries (like the United Kingdom) have a long tradition of cutting-edge research, while in others (like many Third World countries) relatively little information about consumers is available. Even census data from country to country vary both in their overall quality and in how populations are divided into different demographic categories.

These differences in local conditions make it difficult for firms to collect standardized data on consumer preferences and purchasing behavior. The Coca-Cola Company, which does business in more than 155 countries, is just beginning to standardize the type of consumer information it collects, but to date the company has only achieved this goal for relatively few of the many countries in which it operates. Although the Nielsen organization has been gathering retail data in Europe since 1939, one barrier to gathering standardized marketing information in Europe is that new techniques, particularly electronic scanning of grocery purchases, have not yet caught on in many places. In Eastern Europe researchers face an even bigger problem: People's purchasing behaviors tend to be shaped by

Collecting Data on Minority Consumers

Marketers' growing interest in targeting minority consumers is creating opportunities for specialized marketing research to collect data on the buying preferences of specific racial and ethnic groups. These projects have come about because minorities tend to be underrepresented in general consumer surveys. The reason is that they are harder to reach using conventional data collection methods. Telephone interviewing is often ineffective because large numbers of these people have unlisted numbers and are suspicious about giving out personal information to callers. Personal interviews are most effective, but many researchers steer clear of inner-city neighborhoods, which tend to be populated by large numbers of ethnic minorities.

African American consumers in particular are starting to get a lot of attention from marketing researchers. The interest is not surprising, because this market segment is growing at a rate twice as fast as Caucasians. While African Americans spend about $175 billion on goods and services per year, marketers have had surprisingly little information about the factors underlying their purchase decisions. But several major organizations have recently undertaken new research projects to address this lack of knowledge.

A new survey of attitudes expressed by a panel of 1,000 black consumers conducted by a partnership between Yankelovich Partners and the Burrell Communications Group is selling at about $20,000 a copy. The Burrell/Yankelovich MONITOR™ is data collected by conducting hour-long, in-home personal interviews. It provides an in-depth examination of the lifestyle and marketplace behaviors of African Americans and identifies how this segment's attitudes and values are similar to and different from other American populations. And the Simmons Marketing Research Bureau and Essence Communications (a major publisher of black-oriented magazines) is planning to query 10,000 African Americans on a continuing basis.

Sources: Cyndee Miller, "Research on Black Consumers: Marketers with Much at Stake Step Up Their Efforts," *Marketing News* (Sept. 13, 1993): 1; Leon E. Wynter, "Business & Race: Big Survey Firms Join in Ethnic Research," *The Wall Street Journal* (June 14, 1993): B1; personal communication, Burrell Communications.

whatever is available, rather than by subtle consumer preferences for one brand over another.

Legal differences among countries also hinder research efforts to collect data. Some countries are very concerned about citizens' privacy and tightly regulate what information can be obtained. In France, for example, researchers are not allowed access to auto registrations, electoral rolls, lists of apartment owners, or income tax information.[36] When the Discovery Channel initiated an ambitious research program to allow it to grow into a global TV brand (which now has 87 million subscribers in ninety countries), the company discovered that it had to modify its efforts to be sensitive to local laws and customs. For example, Discovery found that it is illegal to mix men and women together in focus groups in Saudi Arabia, while in Spain the tradition of courtesy is so strong that it is difficult to get anyone to say anything negative during discussions (which is not much of a problem in U.S. focus groups!).[37]

A country's communication and transportation networks may not be sufficiently developed to allow researchers to conduct meaningful research. Because communications systems are still primitive in parts of Eastern Europe, for example, one research firm (called SRG International Ltd.) literally relies on the kindness of strangers to conduct its studies there. To get material to interviewers in remote places, the company gives packs of questionnaires to train conductors, stewardesses who work for Aeroflot (the Russian airline), or government officials and then calls ahead with that person's description. A company representative meets the person at the other end and retrieves the materials—assuming the person can be identified![38]

Researchers who are accustomed to using high-tech equipment such as computer-guided telephone banks or electronic supermarket scanners may find that in some places they must be content with paper-and-pencil questionnaires, or even just counting the number of people who walk through a store, because telephone service is just not available in many households. In Mexico, for example, most data collection is still conducted door-to-door—a practice that has been all but abandoned in the United States.

Another problem with conducting marketing research in global markets comes from language differences that exist from country to country and even within a country. For example, there are still large areas in Mexico where native Indian tribes speak languages other than Spanish, so these groups may be bypassed in surveys.[39] Many researchers are trying to minimize the pervasive problems associated with mistranslation of a language by using a process called *back-translation* that requires two steps: First, a questionnaire is translated into a second language by a native speaker of that language. Second, this new version is then translated back into the original language, which helps to ensure that the original meaning has been preserved.

Still, language is only part of the problem. As we saw in Chapter 4, cultures vary widely in their beliefs, priorities, values, and customs. In some countries where telephone service is available, calls from strangers are considered violations of privacy. In other cases cultural differences affect responses to research topics. Both Danish and Spanish consumers, for example, may agree that it is important to have a good breakfast, but the Danish sample may be thinking of fruit and yogurt while the Spanish respondents are referring to coffee and a cigarette!

Nevertheless, firms looking for opportunities in global markets have learned that market research can mean the difference between success and failure in marketing its products in different countries. Research helps global marketers decide how to tailor products to suit local tastes and preferences. Research led Sara Lee to sell its pound cake with chocolate chips in the United States, raisins in Australia, and coconut in Hong Kong.[40] When Domino's Pizza found in Japan that consumers were not interested in large pizzas loaded with tomato sauce and cheese, it developed small pizzas topped with corn and tuna that were more consistent with the Japanese diet.[41]

CHOOSING A RESEARCH TECHNIQUE FOR GATHERING DATA

In the second phase of the research process illustrated in Figure 5.2, researchers decide on the "plan of attack" or research methodology that best meets the needs of the defined problem. All marketing problems cannot be studied using the same techniques, even though some problems can be approached effectively with a number of alternate techniques. The **research design** is the overall plan for actually collecting data in the research project.

Sometimes researchers try to "kill a fly with an elephant gun"; they use some complicated and expensive technique to find answers to a problem that might be as easily understood through simple observation and questioning. In other cases the opposite happens: The researcher may tackle some small aspect of a much larger issue with methods that are wholly inadequate to the problem. In this section we'll review the options marketers and researchers have when it comes to developing a research design that suits the problem to be studied.

research design: the overall research plan that specifies the appropriate research techniques to be used for conducting a research study

EXPLORATORY RESEARCH TECHNIQUES

Because researchers are not concerned that the results of exploratory research are actionable or generalizable to large groups of consumers, they have the luxury of being able to do more in-depth work with a small number of consumers to really understand why they behave as they do. Exploratory research relies on a "grab bag" of techniques that help the researcher understand the marketplace from the consumer's point of view.

Interviewing Techniques

When researchers are conducting exploratory research to help them understand the types of issues they should be concerned with, they often do the obvious: They ask people questions in *consumer interviews*. Sometimes these take the form of a one-on-one discus-

"Our Market Research Reveals Consumers Would Rather Wear A T-Shirt Than A Reptile. Go Figure."
—STICKS
EarAche™ Drummer/Exec. VP Marketing

"You'll freak when you hear this, so don't spew your tofu: 3 outta 4 people want T-shirts as premiums. I mean, T-shirts are cool and everything (our band got stinkin' rich usin' them to make the transition from alternative artists to sellouts). But on the list of stuff people want most, snakes didn't even make top 40. If only people would let their true zen nature emerge, they'd see the snake for what it is: A fashion statement. A workout buddy. A way to meet women. Snakes enhance the quality of life a million times over and people still think T-shirts rule. Maybe it's 'cause they hold up better in the spin cycle."

The EarAche™ 1995 Unofficial World Tour silently sponsored by Fruit of the Loom®

No surprise, T-shirts rank #1 as consumers' favorite premiums—beating caps, jackets, and yes... even reptiles. And with 98% brand awareness, it's no secret Fruit of the Loom® delivers the name your customers know and want. So, screen print or embroider your corporate message on T-shirts and fleecewear by Fruit of the Loom® Cooler than a souvenir cap. More comfortable than a snake.

FRUIT OF THE LOOM®

Exhibit 5.4
Marketing research is an important tool in business-to-business marketing. While some companies conduct research studies to find out more about their business clients, firms like Fruit of the Loom rely on consumer research to promote products that will satisfy their business clients' customers. This Fruit of the Loom ad targeting corporations that offer personalized T-shirts as premiums for customers calls attention to the company's research showing that many different types of consumers prefer T-shirts over all other premium merchandise. It also emphasizes the benefits of linking the corporate name with Fruit of the Loom tees that hold a 98 percent brand awareness rating among researched consumers.

sion, where individuals are asked to share their thoughts directly with a researcher. When a Danish firm unfamiliar with American consumers wanted to introduce a new cigarette brand targeted to blue-collar American males, it sent researchers to interview men in Arkansas, where the brand was to be test marketed. In-depth interviews found that many potential customers felt sexually frustrated and powerless and that they responded to these deep feelings by getting together with their buddies and smoking cigarettes. The company used an ad depicting a brash, confident smoker and challenged these frustrated men to "Make your move."[42]

Often, however, groups of consumers who share some vital characteristics are brought together at one time to voice their opinions. The **focus group** is the most widely used technique for collecting exploratory data. Roughly 140,000 focus groups are held each year in the United States alone. Marketers often get very useful information from these discussions that they use to further refine their strategies. For example, a woman in a group of consumers who were gathered to talk about tooth care observed that tartar felt "like a wall" on her teeth. This imagery was used in ads for Colgate Tartar Control, in which room-sized teeth were shown covered by walls of tartar.[43]

Focus groups typically consist of five to nine consumers who have been recruited to come together to discuss a product, ad, or some other marketing topic. In the discussions participants are asked to *focus* on topics introduced by a discussion leader. Typically these group discussions are taped, and the sessions may be held at special interviewing facilities where they can be observed by the client, who watches from behind a one-way mirror.

Focus group participants often are screened in advance to meet some set of criteria that will make their opinions relevant. These criteria may be demographic characteristics or they may be related to marketplace behavior. For example, participants may be recruited because they use a competitor's product. General Motors used focus groups to dis-

focus group: an exploratory research technique in which a small group of participants is recruited to join in a discussion about a product, an ad, or some other topic of interest to marketers

cover what features of competitors' cars appealed to drivers so that these could be incorporated into its own designs. One result was that GM followed Saab's example by putting fuses in the glove box.[44]

Focus groups are often more productive than individual interviews because group members feed off of each other's comments as they become involved in the discussion (you'd be amazed how much passion people can generate when discussing iced tea, dog food, or deodorant!). Researchers often find it extremely useful to use various "props" to stimulate discussion. Respondents may be shown a picture of a proposed new package design, for example, or a mock-up of a store interior.

Sometimes the security of being in a group allows people to respond more honestly, especially if they feel some bond with other group members. For example, a group conducted with overweight women revealed that the women felt bitterness toward merchants who ignored their needs. This insight prompted the research sponsor to develop a retailing strategy that appealed to this desire for attention.[45]

Projective Techniques

projective techniques: a group of exploratory research techniques that attempt to identify people's underlying feelings by asking them to respond to an ambiguous object, picture, or other stimulus

Many researchers use a variety of exploratory research procedures known as **projective techniques** to get at people's underlying feelings, especially when they feel that consumers will be unable or unwilling to express their true reactions. A projective technique asks the participant to respond to some ambiguous object, often by telling a story about it. For example, a person may be asked, "If your brand of perfume magically came to life, what type of woman would she be? Please describe her personality and tell me what she would do in a typical day." American Express redirected its advertising emphasis away from overachievers after its consumer research indicated that people were intimidated by this approach. One subject, asked to pretend that he was an American Express card come to life, sneered, "You're not really my type—you can't keep up." Later ads instead featured people in laid-back situations, such as deciding to take a spontaneous vacation.[46]

Observational Techniques

observational techniques: exploratory research techniques that attempt to identify people's behavior by observing their everyday activities and gathering in-depth qualitative data to understand that behavior

Some researchers use **observational techniques,** believing that the only way to understand what drives consumers is to observe people in their everyday lives. The aim is to try to gain a better understanding of an activity or process by gathering in-depth qualitative data, which are frequently reported in the form of a *case study.* In business-to-business marketing research, where the consumers are other firms, for example, researchers try to learn as much as possible about how one particular company makes its purchases, includ-

Exhibit 5.5
One projective technique used in exploratory research, called *psychodrawing,* involves asking respondents to a draw picture instead of verbally answering a research question. The goal is to get at feelings that consumers might not be conscious of having. When consumers were asked about users of different brands of cake mixes, they tended to draw Pillsbury users as grandmotherly types, while Duncan Hines users were younger and more dynamic. Exploratory research techniques that yield findings such as this can have a major impact on promotional strategies developed by brand managers.

Who Baked the Cake?

Excellence at Honda

The Honda Accord is one of the best-selling cars in America. Since the car was introduced in 1976 the company has made thousands of changes, big and small, in its design to please its loyal buyers. The Vice President for Research & Development of Honda North America noted, "We believe that the market and the customer will always find the truth."

To figure out just what people want, Honda uses standard research techniques, such as focus groups and surveys. The company also videotapes drivers as they test new cars to see their reactions and determine any problem areas. In an even more ambitious effort, Honda began its ET Phone Home Project in November 1992. Over a three-month period, factory workers who actually build the Accord called over 47,000 recent buyers (about half those who registered cars the previous spring). They asked the customers if they were happy with the cars, and if they could suggest any improvements.

Some of the changes that have resulted from Honda's consumer research have included the installation of a suspension system used on racing cars to improve handling, almost doubling the engine size to 145 hp, and making the wheelbase larger for better rides. Honda also attended to such details as providing one key that operates all four door locks and a holder for a garage door opener. And in its attempts to satisfy owners in every way possible, the company even went so far as changing the shape of the rear side windows so a large soft drink can be passed through them without spilling!

ing as much as possible about the individuals in the firm who are responsible for purchasing. The goal is to identify the key decision makers, to learn what criteria they emphasize when choosing among suppliers, and perhaps to learn something about any possible conflicts, rivalries, and so on that typically go on among these decision makers.

Observational techniques use methods borrowed from anthropologists, who study the dynamics of different cultures by "going native" to study a particular group. An *ethnography* is a detailed report based on a researcher's observations of consumers in a natural setting. The Chicago office of the Foote Cone & Belding advertising agency decided to learn more about the increasing desire of consumers to return to a simpler life, so it chose a small Illinois town that it code-named "Laskerville" as the site of its ethnographic research project (the project was named after one of the agency's founders, Albert Lasker). On several occasions agency researchers visited the town, talking with local residents, reading local newspapers, and attending town functions (even funerals) to determine what issues are important to these consumers. No tape recorders or notes are allowed on these visits, and the town's identity has remained a closely guarded secret—even the agency's CEO doesn't know its real name.[47]

Another research firm gave observational studies a new twist by enlisting consumers to do the research themselves: In Chilton Research Services' project, called "Right There," participants are given an 8mm video camera to record what they really do when at home, school, and work. Bugle Boy, the clothing manufacturer, used some of the results for insights into the language used by teenagers when speaking to each other and the type of clothing "real teens" wear for specific occasions. Natural observation can also create unanticipated marketing opportunities: One tape created for another client showed that most men using a vacuum cleaner need a handle extension, which existing models do not offer.[48]

PROBLEM-SOLVING RESEARCH TECHNIQUES

In contrast to exploratory research, problem-solving research is directed toward finding specific information that will address a current issue confronting the marketer. Problem-solving research can be divided into two categories, depending on the research objective. The objective may be to find the cause-and-effect relationships involved in a problem situation, or it may be merely to describe a phenomenon of interest in the marketplace. Figure 5.3 (page 175) summarizes the set of possible techniques that are available in the researcher's arsenal for each of these research goals.

Causal Research Techniques

causal research: a type of problem-solving research that seeks to identify the cause or reason for a marketing phenomenon of interest

Causal research is problem-solving research that attempts to understand the reason for a marketing phenomenon by ruling out alternative explanations for what has occurred. Suppose, for example, that sales of a brand of hot chocolate mix increased the week after cents-off coupons were mailed to consumers in the Northeast. The brand manager responsible for this promotion might be tempted to conclude that the coupons were the reason for the sales increase, but cannot jump to that conclusion without ruling out other possible reasons for the sales surge. For example, it's possible that a "cold snap" also happened to hit the region at that time, which motivated people to run out and buy hot drink mixes.

In causal research marketers test their conjectures or *hypotheses* that predict the cause of an event or the result of an action. They identify the factors (called *independent variables*) that could be responsible for a phenomenon to determine what outcomes (called *dependent variables*) are affected when the independent variables are changed. To be able to rule out alternative explanations they must carefully design a research **experiment** that tests prespecified relationships among variables in a controlled environment.

experiment: a research methodology in which prespecified relationships among variables are tested in a controlled environment

Causal studies may be performed in *laboratories* or in carefully controlled *field* settings (such as stores, restaurants, or homes) where the researcher is able to exert some control over the environment. In either case the researcher must be able to change the factors (independent variables) that are believed (or *hypothesized*) to cause the phenomenon and be able to hold constant other factors. If a change in the dependent variable is observed after only the independent variable(s) has been manipulated, the researcher can be more confident in concluding that the independent variable(s) in fact has a cause-and-effect relationship with it.

For example, suppose a cocoa marketer wants to test whether a new package design it wants to introduce for its marshmallow-and-cinnamon brand (the independent variable) will increase sales (a dependent variable) as expected. With the cooperation of a store chain, it might select some outlets that are matched in terms of location (and weather!), customer demographics, and so on. One set of stores would feature the hot chocolate flavor with the new package, while another set would continue to sell it in its old package. Marketing managers can then compare sales of the mix for the two sets of stores. If sales rise significantly in stores carrying the new package, the company can conclude with a reasonable degree of confidence that the new package does in fact have an effect on sales of the product.

Descriptive Research Techniques

descriptive research: a type of problem-solving research that seeks to describe a specific issue or problem without looking for the reason or cause of the phenomenon

The major goal of **descriptive research,** not surprisingly, is to describe a specific issue or problem without necessarily explaining the *reason* for the phenomenon. Descriptive research might be used to identify the characteristics of different consumer segments for one or more products in the marketplace. For example, descriptive research is used extensively by broadcasters and publishers to attract advertisers by developing profiles of who is watching a particular TV show or reading a particular magazine—and reminding companies that these are the people they want to reach with their marketing messages. A recent descriptive study showed that the audience for *The New Yorker* magazine had gotten younger and richer since its design was redone and it got a new editor. Based on these results the magazine hopes to lure advertisers such as BMW and Calvin Klein who wish to reach a young, upscale market but who did not consider using *The New Yorker* in the past.[49]

Descriptive problem-solving research gathers measurable quantitative data by seeking answers to unambiguous, specific questions that allow responses to be counted and compared. When choosing how to collect and analyze this type of information, the researcher can choose from several approaches. The most widely used approach is a *cross-sectional design,* which involves the collection of information from a cross-section of consumers in a population at one point in time, as when a random sample of 1,000 consumers are asked by telephone about their preferences for different magazines, radio stations, political candidates, and so on.

One useful cross-sectional technique is called *point-of-sale research,* where shoppers are randomly chosen "on the spot" as they're selecting products and asked about what they're buying and why:

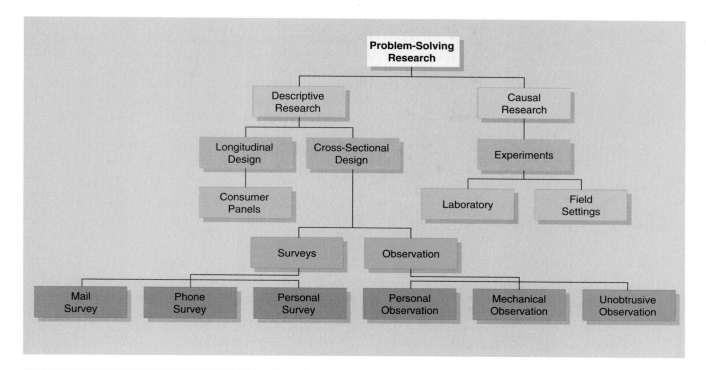

Figure 5.3
Types of Problem-Solving Research

- Why are you buying the premium peanut butter but the economy jelly?
- Is the brand you're buying on your shopping list or are you choosing another?
- Do you know the price of the product you've just selected, and how it compares with the others on the shelf?
- Did you know you were going to purchase this product when you first entered this aisle?

By questioning consumers as their purchase decisions are being made, researchers can sometimes get a more accurate understanding of the real reasons for a purchase. For example, point-of-sale research showed one food manufacturer that its dinner entrees were being used primarily for lunches prepared in office microwaves, suggesting a powerful new way to position the product.

A *longitudinal design* tracks the responses of the same sample of respondents over time. Market researchers who want to collect longitudinal data about consumer behavior often rely on *consumer panels,* where a sample of respondents that is statistically representative of a larger market agrees to provide information about purchases on a regular basis. One of the most prominent diary panels is the 7,500-member MRCA (Market Research Corporation of America) national consumer panel. MRCA panel data showed Coca-Cola that a significant proportion of Diet Coke drinkers also drank Diet 7-Up. As a result, Coca-Cola began putting coupons for Diet Sprite (a Coca-Cola product) on bottles of Diet Coke to get 7-Up drinkers to switch.[50]

The most frequently used (and probably the best) method of collecting data for descriptive studies is the **survey,** a research technique that is designed to collect, summarize, and analyze the responses of a large number of people. Surveys typically ask respondents to complete some type of *questionnaire* that solicits specific information on the study topic.[51] Questionnaires used in surveys may include an open-ended question about products or buying behavior that respondents answer in their own words, but to obtain the necessary quantitative data most questionnaire items are closed-response questions that provide a limited number of specific answer choices for the respondent to check.

One of the most widely used questionnaire formats is a *Likert scale,* where the respondent simply checks or circles a number that indicates how much he or she agrees or dis-

survey: a descriptive research technique used to collect, summarize, and analyze the responses of a large number of people questioned about a research topic

agrees with a statement such as "Sears is a fun place to shop" or "I usually buy the least expensive brand of peanut butter." Crayola adapted this technique for young visitors to its crayon factories by asking kids to rate their liking for new products by choosing among drawings of five smiling or frowning faces instead of on a numerical scale.[52]

A *semantic differential scale* is also a popular questionnaire format consisting of a series of bipolar adjective pairs (for example, good/bad, pretty/ugly) that anchor either end of a set of numbers. The respondent evaluates a concept along the various dimensions:

The atmosphere at Sears is: cold 1 2 3 4 5 6 7 warm

The length of the survey questionnaire and the size of the study population influence the *response mode* to be used to collect responses. Essentially, a researcher who wants to administer a survey to a large number of consumers has three choices: Use the telephone, use the mail, or interview people in person.

Mail surveys are relatively easy to administer and offer a high degree of anonymity to respondents. Mail surveys usually consist of a one-shot questionnaire that is sent to a sample of consumers, often with some incentive to return the survey (the incentive may be a dollar bill attached to the survey, the promise of money-saving coupons, or even a donation to the respondent's favorite charity). Alternatively, the respondents may belong to a consumer panel and receive packets of materials in the mail on a regular basis. Many companies who conduct their own research typically survey their own customers on a regular basis. For example, USAA, a Texas-based financial services company that targets military families, mails 500,000 questionnaires to its customers every year to learn how satisfied they are with these services and to gain ideas for new products.

On the downside, the researcher has little control over the circumstances under which the questionnaire is answered (or, for that matter, who actually answers it). Mail surveys also take a long time and are likely to have a much lower response rate (the percentage of people responding to the survey) than other types of surveys because people tend to neglect them or even toss them in the trash on arrival.

Telephone surveys usually consist of a brief phone conversation where an interviewer reads a short list of questions to the respondent. Technological developments have made *computer-assisted telephone interviewing* (CATI) a popular way to conduct surveys. With CATI the interviewer reads questions from a screen, and the respondent's answers are recorded directly into the computer. While telephone interviewing can yield data from large numbers of consumers very quickly, researchers are limited in that the respondent can't be asked to react to any visual images.

Obtaining responses in telephone surveys has been made more and more difficult in recent years by the proliferation of *telemarketing* activity, where business solicitations are made over the phone, that has eroded the willingness of many consumers to participate in phone surveys. Because the respondent may feel less anonymous speaking directly to an interviewer, telephone surveys may also have a high refusal rate, especially if the survey is about a sensitive subject. Also, telephone surveys cannot include members of the population who do not have telephones in their homes. Finally, increasing numbers of people are using telephone answering machines to screen all of their calls, thus reducing further the response rate.

Personal interviews conducted in the respondent's home were once the preferred technique for gathering data in descriptive research. But this practice has declined markedly in recent years due to escalating costs and security concerns. More typically, today's face-to-face interviews are used in a "mall intercept" study, where participants are recruited in shopping malls or other public areas and are asked to respond to a survey. However, because only certain groups of the population frequently shop at malls, a mall intercept study does not provide the researcher with a representative sample of the population unless the population of interest is "mall shoppers." In addition to being very expensive, the quality of data obtained from mall intercepts can be good or bad. Respondents may be reluctant to answer questions of a personal nature in a public setting, and they may be distracted by activities going on around them, which can distort their responses to visuals such as product package designs or logos.

To gather data in descriptive problem-solving research, researchers may also rely on observation or **unobtrusive measures** that do not require direct human responses. These methods, which rely on evidence of people's purchasing behavior, are used when the researcher suspects that people will probably distort their responses to questions, either because they may not be able to accurately recall their behavior or perhaps may want to portray themselves in a more favorable light. For example, instead of asking a person to report on the products that are currently in his or her home, the researcher might actually go to the house and perform a "pantry check," recording the products that are actually on the person's shelves.

In Argentina one research firm has found that the best route to data collection is literally strewn with garbage: The company sifts through refuse left outside of people's homes, searching for clues about each family's consumption habits. The "garbologists" can tell, for example, which soft drink was consumed with what kind of food, or whether people are drinking more alcoholic beverages on the weekend. As the survey director noted, "The people in this study don't know that we are studying their garbage so the information is totally objective." [53] Smelly, too!

When *personal observation* is employed, people's behavior is observed and recorded. Marsh Supermarkets, for example, positioned observers on a catwalk above its stores to chronicle the routes shoppers used as they wheeled their carts below. This study revealed that people tend to avoid the dry goods section in favor of other areas, which helped the company when it redesigned its store interiors. "Traffic analysis" can really pay off by pinpointing "dead spots" in stores. For example, after Frito-Lay research observers found that shoppers spend twice as much time in the coffee aisle as in the snack foods section, it began to advertise its chips near the coffee cans instead. [54]

Mechanical observation relies on nonhuman devices to record buying behavior. A popular technique, as we saw earlier in the chapter, is *scanning technology,* which can be used to track purchases via the Universal Product Codes on products. Scanning technology can also measure responses to coupon promotions by recording the UPC data now being printed on coupons as well.

Other mechanical observation methods include electronic turnstiles in stores that track how many people have visited the establishment over a certain period. Some grocery stores even use infrared sensors in their ceilings to track the movements of shopping carts. [55] Tandy Corporation's new electronics superstore, The Incredible Universe, goes one step further. To enter the store, each customer is given a bar-coded plastic identification card that must be used while in the store and when revisiting the store. Thus the retailer can track how many times each Incredible Universe customer comes into the store, how long they stay, and where in they store they have been.

Implementing Research Results

Sometimes marketers are content to let the marketing research information they've collected just lay there; they feel a "warm glow" because they have accumulated piles of impressive-looking computer printouts. If the information is actually to be incorporated into marketing decisions, however, it must be analyzed and reported in a way that makes sense and is *actionable* for managers. And the data should be added to the firm's MIS database for future reference. In this section we'll look at the all-important final steps in the marketing research process. We'll consider factors in analysis, reporting, and integrating research results into the marketing planning process.

ANALYZING THE DATA

The data collected in a marketing research project are rarely ready to be applied to a particular marketing decision. The raw data must be sorted, organized, and analyzed to be of use. The format for compiling the data often relies on the type of research method, while the particular techniques used determine how simple or complex the sorting process will be. In problem-solving research the best-case scenario occurs when the data have been collected by computer-assisted telephone interviewing techniques, where responses to specific questions are entered directly into the system as interviewers question respondents. A straight tabulation is easily accomplished by compiling a table listing the number of responses for each interview item. In other situations, particularly when data have been gathered in a causal research experiment, the data must be cross-tabulated to show the results when each of the variables or factors in the study are controlled.

Exploratory research that collects qualitative data presents its own set of compilation problems for researchers. Because the responses are open-ended, researchers must first decide on the categories the majority of responses fall into before they can sort and tabulate them. In some cases categorizing the responses means reading each and interpreting the meaning to assign a category. If the consumers themselves have completed questionnaires or survey forms, researchers must also cope with illegible handwriting and take into account items that have been overlooked or intentionally omitted. Once all of these and other problems have been resolved, each individual response must then be coded for tabulation.

The type of data collected in a research study also influences the way it will be analyzed. Quantitative data may make use of statistical analysis techniques and procedures

Exhibit 5.6
In the highly competitive auto industry, automakers have recognized the need to identify consumer preferences, driving habits, and attitudes about the automobile they own or would like to own to satisfy their targeted customers. All automakers today conduct some form of marketing research, whether using internal resources, specialized syndicated services, or outside research firms that design custom studies. The research projects range from small focus groups of potential customers to comprehensive lifestyle studies of current owners. The Ford Motor Company goes so far as to integrate the company's marketing research efforts in its primary advertising strategy – "Quality Is Job 1" – by highlighting the consumer "experts" it consults when developing the kind of quality its customers can expect.

that produce the impressive-looking tables and charts whose meaning only the initiated can understand. The analysis of qualitative data can also reveal mysterious results if the researcher is not astute in discerning the underlying beliefs, attitudes, or opinions expressed in the responses. Even then researchers may have to examine the data in a variety of ways to draw meaningful conclusions or to identify generalizable trends.

PREPARING THE RESEARCH REPORT

A good research report is intended to be used as feedback to managers. It must present the conclusions from the analysis in a form that makes sense to the marketer requesting the information. Most marketers do not have time to fathom out research jargon. They look for simple writing that plainly states the results and any conditions that limit the generalizability of the findings.

A useful research report identifies the following information in plain language: the problem studied, the limitations of the study, the important findings, and recommendations for action based on the results. Creative researchers may also identify particularly surprising findings that could affect the firm, or they may include conclusions that are not specifically tied to the research problem, but that could mean opportunities for the marketer.

INTEGRATING THE FINDINGS INTO MARKETING PLANNING

The collection and interpretation of research information is hardly a one-shot deal that managers engage in "just out of curiosity," or because they have nothing else to do! Ideally, marketing research is an ongoing problem-solving *process* that should be constantly referred to and updated as the company conducts long-term planning. All the research in the world is worthless unless managers use it to make informed decisions. Ongoing research can provide feedback to planners before products go to market, highlight ways to fine-tune strategies and offerings, and reveal new opportunities.

For example, AT&T uses research feedback to determine where its product development efforts should be heading down the road. The company recently finished a two-year secret research project developed to provide the first comprehensive testing of interactive multimedia, where consumers will have the opportunity to "talk back" to their television

REAL PEOPLE, REAL CHOICES:

HOW IT WORKED OUT AT MERCEDES-BENZ

Based on the research conducted for Mercedes-Benz, option 1 was chosen by communications and senior management in marketing and sales, with one exception: A more serious approach is still used for the top-of-line models in the S-Class, which sell for $65,000 to $130,000. The company elected to change its promotional strategies to "humanize" its other models. Mercedes cars are now open for inspection at auto shows, while in the past they would only be available for a closer look by people deemed to be "legitimate prospects." More important, the tone of Mercedes advertising has been changed to soften Mercedes' unapproachable image.

Bob Baxter and his staff are engaged in ongoing research to ensure that the benefits traditionally associated with Mercedes are still getting through, but in a less intimidating way. A recent commercial for the new Mercedes-Benz C-Class is intended to show that the Mercedes' reputation for fine engineering is now available in a car that costs less than $30,000. The opening shots of a fancy estate imply the car is for the wealthy (and by association expected to be expensive), but later shots show the $30,000 car being driven by a mother who is helping her son, who has a broken arm, deliver newspapers.

screens. The company wired the homes of fifty volunteer AT&T employees and their families in the Chicago area. The "guinea pigs" were linked via remote control to an AT&T network so that their use of different test multimedia services could be monitored. In addition, focus groups met every few weeks to discuss how service could be improved. After observing these families for two years, AT&T was able to get a clearer picture of what "rest stops" people would be looking for on the developing information superhighway. For example, the findings indicated that multimedia services will have to be mindlessly simple and presented as an advanced form of TV, rather than as an extension of the family PC. Researchers also found that kids talked less on the phone when they had interactive TV to talk to instead. They also concluded that the most appealing programs offered a combination of entertainment, transactions, communications, and information. For example, one program that tested very well was a sports program that allowed viewers to buy sports products, relay the show to a friend, and click for additional sports stats.[56]

Chapter 5 Summary

Objective 1. Understand the Marketing Information System (MIS), its importance to marketing decision making, and the types and sources of information needed by marketers.

A marketing information system (MIS) is a system for gathering, sorting, analyzing, storing, and distributing relevant marketing information. A subset of the MIS is the marketing decision support system (MDSS) that helps marketing managers access the MIS database and analyze data to make informed decisions. Marketers generally require ongoing information, which is in the form of company records and reports added to the MIS on a regular basis, monitored information, which comes from regular scanning of the important marketing environments, and requested information, which is not available in the MIS and must be obtained through customized research studies. Information included in the MIS may be primary data that is specifically collected and organized for a particular marketing need and secondary data gathered for some purpose other than the current marketing need. One particularly useful research technique monitors both exposure to television advertising and purchases to provide single-source consumer data.

Objective 2. Describe the process of defining the research problem, the criteria for choosing and evaluating the research plan, and some of the issues marketers face when conducting marketing research.

To make informed decisions, most marketers either conduct their own research or hire an outside firm to conduct marketing research for them. The research process begins with defining the problem to be researched and choosing the type of research that will provide the needed information. When the marketing problem is not yet well defined, exploratory research may be necessary to identify specific questions or issues, which can then be addressed through problem-solving research. Good research methodology will ensure data that are reliable, valid, and representative of the population of interest.

The continued ability of marketing researchers to collect information is strongly tied to ethical research issues, including deceptive practices of unscrupulous marketers, privacy issues, and special ethical concerns in conducting research with children. When operating in a global marketplace, barriers to conducting marketing research may be related to the infrastructure of a country, translation problems, and legal restrictions.

Objective 3. Describe the variety of research techniques available to marketers.

In the second phase of the research process, researchers must select the most appropriate research design. Exploratory research seeks qualitative data through such techniques as individual interviews, focus groups, projective techniques, and observational techniques such as ethnography. Problem-solving research, which is usually quantitative in nature, falls into two categories. Causal problem-solving research seeks to identify the cause or reason why something occurs and involves designing laboratory or field research experiments that can test prespecified relationships. Descriptive studies can attempt to describe an issue or problem at one point in time (cross-sectional design) or over time (longitudinal design). In descriptive studies data are most frequently gathered through mail, phone, or personal interview surveys or can come from personal or mechanical observation techniques.

Objective 4. Discuss how marketers implement research results.

For research data to be useful to marketers, it must be sorted, organized, and analyzed. How data are handled is influenced by the research method (exploratory, causal, cross-sectional, longitudinal, and so on), how the data are collected (phone, mail, or personal interview), and the types of questions asked (open ended versus closed response). Effective marketing managers see research as an ongoing problem-solving process that must be constantly referred to and updated.

Review Questions

Marketing Concepts: Testing Your Knowledge

1. What are some of the reasons a firm needs to have a marketing information system?
2. What types of information are included in an MIS? What are some of the sources of data in the MIS? What is single-source data?
3. What are the phases in the marketing research process? Why is defining the problem to be researched so important?
4. What are the differences between exploratory research and problem-solving research?
5. What is meant by reliability, validity, and representativeness of research results?
6. What is a random sample? How is it different from a quota sample? A convenience sample?
7. What ethical problems are associated with marketing research? What problems does a researcher encounter when conducting marketing research in global markets?
8. What is the goal of exploratory research? What techniques are used to gather data in exploratory research?
9. What is causal research? What is descriptive research? What techniques are used in descriptive research?
10. What are the positive and negative aspects of mail surveys, telephone surveys, and personal interview surveys?
11. What issues are involved in analyzing research data and preparing a research report?

Marketing Concepts: Discussing Choices and Issues

1. This chapter talked about how some marketers attempt to disguise themselves as marketing researchers when their real intent is to sell something to the consumer. What is the impact of this practice on legitimate researchers? What do you think might be done about this practice?
2. Do you think marketers should be allowed to conduct market research with young children? Why or why not?
3. Are you willing to divulge personal information to marketing researchers? How much are you willing to tell, or where would you draw the line?
4. What is your overall attitude toward marketing research? Do you think it is a beneficial activity from a consumer's perspective? Or do you think it merely gives marketers new insights on how to convince consumers to buy something they really don't want or need?

Marketing Practice: Applying What You've Learned

1. Your firm is planning to begin marketing a consumer product in several global markets. You have been given the responsibility of developing plans for marketing research to be conducted in Eastern Europe, in Western Europe, and in China. In a role-playing situation, present the difficulties you expect to encounter, if any, in conducting research in each of these areas.

2. As an account executive with a marketing research firm, you are responsible for deciding on the type of research to be used in various studies conducted for your clients. For each of the following client questions, list your choices.
   a. What do consumers like and dislike about shampoo?
   b. What are the best media vehicles for a local savings and loan to use in its advertising?
   c. How much label information on cereal boxes do consumers read before they make a purchase?
   d. Are consumers more likely to buy brands that are labeled as environmentally friendly?
   e. How do female consumers determine if a particular perfume is right for them?
   f. What types of people read the local newspaper?
   g. How frequently do consumers switch brands of soft drinks?
   h. How will an increase in the price of a brand of laundry detergent affect sales?
   i. How do the different members of a family participate in the purchase of a new car?

3. Your marketing research firm is planning to conduct surveys to gather information for a number of clients. Your boss has asked you and a few other new employees to do some preliminary work. He's asked each of you to choose three of the topics that will be included in the project and to prepare an analysis of the advantages and disadvantages of mail surveys, telephone surveys, face-to-face surveys, or observation for each.
   a. The amount of alcoholic beverages consumed in a city
   b. Young adults' use of illegal drugs
   c. Why a local bank has been losing customers
   d. How heavily the company should invest in manufacturing and marketing home fax machines
   e. The amount of money being spent "over the state line" for lottery tickets.
   f. Reader recall of magazine advertisements
   g. What local doctors would like to see changed in the hospitals in the city
   h. Consumers' attitudes toward several sports celebrities

4. As a marketing researcher, you have been asked by your university to develop a closed-response questionnaire to gather information on college students' perceptions of different universities. Write three questions that would yield the data you need to draw some conclusions and provide the requested information.

Marketing Mini-Project: Learning by Doing

The purpose of this mini-project is to help you become familiar with research techniques used by marketers and to be able to apply these techniques to managerial decision making.

1. With a group of three other students in your class, select a small retail business or fast-food restaurant to use as a

"client" for your project. (Be sure to get the manager's permission before conducting your research.) Then choose a topic from among the following possibilities to develop a study problem:

- Employee-customer interactions
- The busiest periods of customer activity
- Customer perceptions of service
- Customer likes/dislikes about offerings
- Customer likes/dislikes about the environment in the place of business
- The benefits customers perceive to be important
- The age groups that frequent the place of business
- The buying habits of a particular age group
- How customer complaints are handled

2. Develop a plan for the research:

a. Define the problem as you will study it.
b. Choose the type of research you will use.
c. Select the techniques you will use to gather data.
d. Develop the mode and format for data collection.

3. Conduct the research.
4. Write a report (or develop a class presentation) that includes four parts.

a. Introduction: a brief overview of the business and the problem studied
b. Methodology: the type of research used, the techniques used to gather data (and why they were chosen), and the instruments and procedures used, the number of respondents, duration of the study, and other details that would allow someone to replicate your study
c. Results: a compilation of the results (perhaps in table form) and the conclusions drawn
d. Recommendations: a list of recommendations for actions management might take based on the conclusions drawn from the study.

Key Terms

Endnotes

1. "Measuring Quality Perception of America's Top Brands," *Brandweek* (April 4, 1994): 24.
2. Debra Goldman, "Cyber-Chat 101," *Brandweek* (Feb. 6, 1995): 6.
3. Udayan Gupta, "Costly Market Research Pays Off for Biotech Start-Up," *The Wall Street Journal* (Aug. 2, 1993): B2.
4. Dale S. Mills, "Marketing Information Systems' Potential to Senior Management," *Journal of Information Systems Management* (Winter 1990): 76–79.
5. Terence P. Paré, "How to Find Out What They Want," *Fortune* (Autumn/Winter 1993): 39.
6. William M. Bulkeley, "If Clinton Orders Double Cheese and All the Toppings, It's a Crisis," *The Wall Street Journal* (Dec. 7, 1993): B1.
7. S.J. Diamond, "Trend Tracking," *The Los Angeles Times* (March 29, 1993): E1.
8. Christel Beard and Betsy Wiesendanger, "The Marketer's Guide to On-Line Databases," *S&MM* (Jan. 1993): 36.
9. "CMT 'Lifestyle' Launch," *Marketing* (Feb. 3, 1994): 4.

10. "Marketing Guide: 5- Market Research," *Marketing* (April 13, 1989): 31–34.
11. Jennifer Cody, "They Hired Someone to Find Out if People Really Like Chocolate?" *The Wall Street Journal* (Nov. 26, 1993): B1.
12. Martha Farnsworth Riche, "Scanning for Dollars," *American Demographics* (Nov. 8, 1989).
13. Alan J. Greco and Jack T. Hogue, "Developing Marketing Decision Support Systems in Consumer Goods Firms," *J. Cons. Marketing* (Winter 1990): 55–64.
14. Dale S. Mills, "Marketing Information Systems' Potential to Senior Management," *Journal of Information Systems Management* (Winter 1990): 76–79.
15. Kenneth Wylie, "Customer Satisfaction Blooms; Rivalry at Top Grows," *Advertising Age* (Oct. 18, 1993): S-1.
16. Rhonda L. Rundle, "Drug Company Uses Opinion Poll to Sell to You and Me," *The Wall Street Journal* (Sept. 14, 1995): B1.
17. Annetta Miller, "You Are What You Buy," *Newsweek* (June 4, 1990): 59.

18. Kevin Goldman, "Mercedes-Benz Tries Out Humor, Youth," *The Wall Street Journal* (Oct. 10, 1994): B5.

19. Bruce L. Stern and Ray Ashmun, "Methodological Disclosure: The Foundation for Effective Use of Survey Research," *Journal of Applied Business Research* (Fall 1991): 77–82.

20. Alan E. Wolf, "Most Colas Branded Alike by Testy Magazine," *Beverage World* (Aug. 31, 1991): 8.

21. Fahri Karakaya, "Market Research: A Pocket Guide for Managers," *Society for Advancement of Management Journal* (1991): 34–40.

22. Stephanie Strom, "How Gap Inc. Spells Revenge," *The New York Times* (April 24, 1994): 1.

23. Cyndee Miller, "Sometimes a Researcher Has No Choice But to Hang Out in a Bar," *Marketing News* (Jan. 3, 1994): 16.

24. Debra Aho Williamson, "Web Searching for a Yardstick," *Advertising Age* (Oct. 9, 1995): 21, 22.

25. "Summary of 1992 Harris-Equifax Consumer Privacy Survey," *Marketing News* (Aug. 16, 1993): A18.

26. Alan Radding, "Consumer Worry Halts Data Bases," *Advertising Age* (Feb. 11, 1991): 28.

27. Gary Levin, "Anthropologists in Adland: Researchers Now Studying Cultural Meanings of Brands," *Advertising Age* (Feb. 24, 1992): 3.

28. "CMOR: A Key Industry Resource," *Marketing News* (Aug. 16, 1993): A2.

29. Janet Simons, "Youth Marketing: Children's Clothes Follow the Latest Fashion," *Advertising Age* (Feb. 14, 1985): 16.

30. Gary Levin, "New Adventures in Children's Research," *Ad Age* (Aug. 9, 1993): 17.

31. Gary Levin, "Anthropologists in Adland: Researchers Now Studying Cultural Meanings of Brands," *Advertising Age* (Feb. 24, 1992): 3.

32. Horst Stipp, "Children as Consumers"; see Laura A. Peracchio, "Designing Research to Reveal the Young Child's Emerging Competence," *Psychology & Marketing* (Winter 1990): 257–276, for details regarding the design of research on children.

33. Kid Power," *Forbes* (March 30, 1987): 9–10.

34. Dena Kleiman, "Candy to Frighten Your Parents With," *The New York Times* (Aug. 23, 1989): C1.

35. Laura Shapiro, "Where Little Boys Can Play with Nail Polish," *Newsweek* (May 28, 1990): 62.

36. Blayne Cutler, "Reaching the Real Europe," *American Demographics* (Oct. 1990): 38.

37. Wayne Walley, "Programming Globally—With Care," *Advertising Age* (Sept. 18, 1995): I–14.

38. "Europe is Beckoning," *Marketing* (June 27, 1991): 28–30.

39. Jack Honomichl, "Research Cultures are Different in Mexico, Canada," *Marketing News* (May 10, 1993): 12.

40. Julie Skur Hill and Joseph M. Winski "Goodby Global Ads: Global Village is Fantasy Land for Marketers," *Advertising Age* (Nov. 16, 1987): 22.

41. Thomas J. Meyer, "Slicing the Japanese Pie," *American Way* (Nov. 1989): 40.

42. Anthony Ramirez, "New Cigarettes Raising Issue of Target Market," *The New York Times* (Feb. 18, 1990): 28.

43. Jeffrey F. Durgee, "On Cezanne, Hot Buttons, and Interpreting Consumer Storytelling," *Journal of Consumer Marketing* (Fall 1988): 47–51.

44. David Kiley, "At Long Last, Detroit Gives Consumers the Right of Way," *Adweek* (June 6, 1988): 25–27.

45. Judith Langer, "Getting to Know the Consumer Through Qualitative Research," *Management Review* (April 1987): 42–46.

46. Bernice Kanner, "Mind Games," *Marketing Insights* (Spring 1989): 50.

47. Carrie Goerne, "Researchers Go Undercover to Learn About 'Laskerville,'" *Marketing News* (May 11, 1992): 11.

48. Laura Loro, "'This is My Life': Consumers Tape Themselves for Marketers," *Ad Age* (Aug. 9, 1993): 17.

49. Kevin Goldman, "Advertising: New Yorker's Makeover Attracts a Younger and Richer Audience," *The Wall Street Journal* (July 22, 1995): B2.

50. Melvin Crask, Richard J. Fox, and Roy G. Stout, *Marketing Research: Principles & Applications* (Englewood Cliffs, NJ: Prentice Hall, 1995).

51. Terence P. Paré, "How to Find Out What They Want," *Fortune* (Autumn/Winter 1993): 39.

52. Gary Levin, "New Adventures in Children's Research," *Ad Age* (Aug. 9, 1993): 17.

53. Mike Galetto, "Turning Trash to Research Treasure," *Advertising Age* (April 17, 1995): I-16.

54. Michael J. McCarthy, "James Bond Hits the Supermarket: Stores Snoop on Shoppers' Habits to Boost Sales," *The Wall Street Journal* (Aug. 25, 1993): B1.

55. Ibid.

56. John J. Keller, "AT&T's Secret Multimedia Trials Offer Clues to Capturing Interactive Audiences," *The Wall Street Journal* (July 28, 1993): B1.

MARKETING IN ACTION: REAL PEOPLE AT BLACK & DECKER

Traditionally most homeowners have been able to change a light bulb, but not many have been willing (or able) to build a deck or install kitchen cabinets. Today, though, more and more do-it-yourselfers (DIYers as they are known in the trade) are tackling the big jobs thanks to the skyrocketing growth of sophisticated home improvement retailers like Home Depot. And as the range of jobs taken on by serious DIYers has expanded, so has their need for the tools to do it right.

In the summer of 1991 Japan's Makita and Sear's Craftsman lines of tools led the DIYer market. At that time Black & Decker was busy developing its high-priced DeWalt line of tools targeted at professional craftsmen rather than at "Harry Homeowner." As one large chain retailer told Black & Decker, "Look, we're giving business away to your rivals 'cause you don't have what these customers want." To learn what potential customers wanted, Black & Decker first spoke to other retailers and then went straight to consumers to find out what they didn't like about the products already on the market.

Early in the research B&D discovered that the DeWalt line wasn't likely to gain much of a foothold in the price-conscious DIYer market. As Joseph Galli, chief of Black & Decker's U.S. power tool division, observed, "We knew some serious DIYers were going to pay up and buy DeWalt. But others would just go elsewhere, and we're not a company that likes to leave business on the table for our competitors."

Black & Decker began researching consumers by going to Fieldwork Atlanta, an independent marketing research firm, to find fifty male homeowners, ages twenty-five to fifty-four, who owned more than six power tools. The list B&D received included an airline pilot, a bank manager, a veterinarian, and two bachelors. After being contacted, all fifty men agreed to be part of a B&D "living laboratory." During the summer of 1991 these fifty DIYers were questioned about the tools they used and why they had selected particular brands.

In fact, Black & Decker executives "hung out" with them in their homes and workshops. They observed the DIYers while they used their tools and asked why they liked or disliked certain ones and how the tools felt in their hands. They even observed how they cleaned up their work space when they finished. They went with the DIYers on shopping trips, noting what they bought and how much they spent. After this initial exploratory research was completed, the company collected data from hundreds of Black & Decker customers who mailed in warranty cards that also contained questions about their tool usage and needs.

The findings from these research efforts showed B&D, among other things, that DIYers wanted to be able to get advice when they were working on a project and that they hated sweeping up mounds of sawdust after cutting or sanding wood. In terms of product features they wanted a cordless drill that didn't run out of power before the job was done. They also wanted some kind of safety mechanism on their circular saws so that when they're switched off, the blade doesn't keep spinning for another ten to twelve seconds.

Black & Decker then went to work to give customers what they wanted. Engineers created the new product line of eighteen power tools that featured a powerful drill with a detachable battery pack that recharges in an hour rather than overnight. They also came up with a sander and a saw equipped with bags that act as minivacuums sucking up the sawdust before it spews all over, and they built an auto-braking system into their saws so that blades stop spinning within two seconds after the saw is turned off. To make the new product line stand out from both the regular Black & Decker line, which is black, and the DeWalt line, which is yellow, the designers chose to make the tools green with yellow accents. The company also set up a toll-free hotline staffed by experienced DIY advisers seven days a week.

Research was also used to test possible names for the new line of tools. Of the names B&D tested, consumers liked "Quantum" the best, because they felt it conveyed that the tools were a step ahead of the competition and it was easy to pronounce. Because research had shown that consumers had a lot of respect for the Black & Decker name (earlier studies had shown that it was the seventh strongest brand in the United States), the product also carries the Black & Decker name.

At the National Hardware Show (sort of the Academy Awards for the hardware industry), Black & Decker's new Quantum line was given the prestigious Retailers' Choice award. As CEO Nolan Archibald said, "If you simply wait until the other guy comes out with a new model, your competition is already on to the next thing. . . . You're always two steps behind. The whole point behind this product line was to have it driven to market by what the consumers really want." And with sales topping $30 million the first five months on the market, the new line cleaned up a lot more than sawdust.

Source: Adapted from Susan Caminiti, "A Star Is Born," *Fortune* (Autumn/Winter 1993): 44–47.

Things to Talk About

1. What initial problems did Black & Decker's research reveal?

2. What research techniques did Black & Decker use to find out what DIYers wanted?

3. What strategies did Black & Decker develop based on the research findings?

4. How did Black & Decker choose a name for the new product line?

5. What secrets to success has Black & Decker discovered?

CASE 5-2

MARKETING IN ACTION: REAL CHOICES AT GENERAL MOTORS

In the early nineties GM faced several potentially disastrous situations. First, GM's Oldsmobile Division was fighting for its life, and GM was only beginning to recover from embarrassing stumbles in small and mid-size cars, minivans, and sport-utility vehicles. GM had been doing well in trucks and the large luxury-car segments, but making great cars for older people who'd be moving on out of the market was not a very good prognosis for long-term success. What GM needed to do was to "put the customer first, not the sheet metal."

Vince Barabba, who was the general manager of GM's strategic decision center, believed that the answer to GM's problems was research into customer needs. With the right research GM would be able to allocate capital spending and produce vehicles that could not just satisfy but delight customers—and, in the process, make a large profit for GM. So in 1988 Barabba began working with Applied Decision Analysts, a marketing research firm, using *conjoint measurement*—a sophisticated research technique that allows marketers to estimate the relative preferences people have for different vehicle attributes. With conjoint analysis researchers are able to address such questions as how much fuel economy a customer would be willing to trade for bet-

ter acceleration or how much a customer would pay to get more cargo space.

GM used this "needs-based research" to assess the needs and desires of more than a million consumers. This research showed that potential owners of a Chevrolet Lumina, for example, wanted a good-looking car but wouldn't trade off functionality or value for appearance. They wanted more interior space, but because these buyers had economic constraints, the overall size would have to be kept down to keep the price in line. The car would also have to deliver a high level of performance based on miles per gallon and be trouble free to keep maintenance costs down.

Potential drivers of a Pontiac Grand Prix wanted a car that made them feel like they owned the road, and wouldn't sacrifice high style for driving performance. Because these drivers are primarily interested in their own driving pleasure and excitement, roominess and passenger comfort was of little importance. And there were other drivers who wanted something in between. These potential customers had been a prime target for GM's ailing Oldsmobile Division; they wanted a car that had really great styling and room for passengers.

Marketing in Action:
Real Choices at General Motors *(CONTINUED)*

These and other findings revealed overall consumer trends that confirmed the decline of the big-car market and the growth of the small and mid-size car markets. They also had implications for developing new cars that specifically fit the desires of the consumer segments studied. But as the manager of GM's strategic decision center, Barabba questioned whether or not such a strategy would overfragment the company's market. Perhaps the real problem stemmed from GM's inability to focus adequately on the needs of any particular group because of the overabundance of different GM product lines and models. Although a true believer in marketing research, Barabba wondered whether the needs-based research was, in fact, pointing the firm in the right direction or whether more traditional methods should be used to research the attitudes of existing customers.

Things to Think About

1. What is the problem facing GM?
2. What factors are causing the problem?
3. What are the alternatives?
4. What are your recommendations for solving the problem?
5. What are some ways to implement your recommendations?

Why People Buy: Consumer Markets

*When you have completed your study of this chapter,
you should be able to:*

1. Describe how individual (internal) factors influence consumer behavior.

2. Understand the external factors that influence purchasing decisions and buying behavior.

3. Explain the prepurchase, purchase, and postpurchase steps in the consumer decision-making process.

4. Describe the importance of monitoring trends in the marketplace, and identify some of the current trends that are influencing consumers in the 1990s.

REAL PEOPLE, REAL CHOICES:

MEET DAN WELLEHAN, A DECISION MAKER AT SEBAGO INC.

Dan Wellehan aims to win the heart and "sole" of consumers around the world. As president of Sebago Inc. he and his colleagues try to anticipate the footwear tastes of the buying public and develop products that will appeal to well-heeled consumers. The company, originally known as Sebago-Moc, was founded in Westbrook, Maine, in 1946 to manufacture "penny loafers," a new type of footwear that was just beginning to catch the fancy of American consumers. Prior to World War II footwear choices were pretty much limited to laced oxford styles, and Americans were becoming enchanted with the idea of a slip-on shoe—especially one that had a built-in slot to hold a "lucky penny." The company's high-quality, hand-sewn loafers quickly became a weekend favorite among more affluent customers who saw them as the perfect complement to tweed jackets and gray flannel trousers or plaid skirts and cashmere sweater sets. By the 1960s, the penny loafer had become firmly entrenched as part of Americans' image of a classic fall wardrobe, passed on from the socially elite to wannabees in all walks of life.

Mr. Wellehan began working full-time for Sebago in 1960, where his initial responsibilities were in the areas of manufacturing and leather management. Over the years he assumed responsibility for advertising functions, sports promotions, and international sales. Today, as president of the small company, Mr. Wellehan continues to be involved in virtually all aspects of its business. He graduated from the College of the Holy Cross with a major in economics and a minor in classical languages and philosophy. Before joining Sebago he served in the Navy as a line officer on board a destroyer. Three of his six daughters are also employed at Sebago.

KEEPING IN STEP WITH CUSTOMERS

We live in a world overflowing with marketing information designed to turn us on to countless goods and services. Sometimes we respond, but sometimes we seem to be marching to a different drummer. Those marketers who do get through to us have taken a closer look at what makes people tick when it comes to processing marketing information and making a purchase decision.

Astute marketers like Daniel Wellehan and his colleagues at Sebago rely on more than a lucky penny to keep in step with consumers—and a step ahead of the competition. They know that the purchase of a new pair of shoes isn't a simple decision based on the consumer's need for footwear: A consumer's purchase decisions are driven by a variety of complex personal factors, situational events, and sociocultural influences. The extent to which marketers *understand* these factors—and do so better than the competition—is the measure of success in a crowded marketplace.

Insight into the buying behavior of consumers doesn't just happen by observing what they do when choosing among the products in a store. It comes with an understanding of why people do what they do and, more importantly, why each person perceives, interprets, and acts on marketing information in some unique way. It takes into account the effects of individual differences in attitudes, personalities, and lifestyles, as well as the collective influences of family, friends, social groups, and even society as a whole.

Understanding consumer behavior draws from many fields of study—including psychology, sociology, economics, history, and anthropology—that approach consumer issues from different perspectives. In this chapter we'll see how these perspectives are applied in the marketplace. We'll look at the individual influences on consumer choices, consider the effects of social and situational influences, and examine the decision process itself. We'll also see how taking a closer look at why people buy what they do helps marketers predict trends in consumer purchasing.

PERSPECTIVES ON CONSUMER BEHAVIOR

Each of us is constantly confronted with the activities of marketers competing for our attention and our money. Wherever we turn we are bombarded by marketing communications intended to influence our purchase decisions or even the decision to purchase something at all. The most successful marketers recognize that we don't all respond in the same way to *marketing stimuli* or the aspects of marketing mix strategies designed to influence consumers. Each person's response is colored by a variety of internal and external factors.

When buying a new pair of shoes, for example, the style we choose may be based on our attitudes about the importance of stylish footwear in general or even our motivation for wanting a new pair of shoes in the first place. We might be replacing a favorite pair of running shoes, indulging ourselves with a luxurious pair of soft leather boots, or looking for the latest style to maintain our image as a fashion leader. The style we choose is also related to our age group or what we do in our leisure time. It could also be determined by social inflences, such as what our friends are wearing, and situational factors, such as how much time we have to shop for the right style.

Clearly, consumer buying behavior is not merely what happens at the moment a customer hands over money or a credit card in return for some good or service, and marketers who want to understand that behavior look to activities and events that occur before and after the purchase as well. **Consumer behavior** refers to the processes involved when individuals or groups select, purchase, use, and dispose of goods, services, ideas, or experiences to satisfy needs and desires.

Many of the theories about consumer behavior and decision making are based on the idea that marketing stimuli are processed internally by consumers in light of external factors in their lives to arrive at commitment to buy or not to buy. The decision model in Figure 6.1 (page 190), which utilizes this perspective, lists the factors that influence the decision of whether or not to make a purchase and identifies the related choices involved when actually making the purchase. In this section we'll examine the internal factors that influence purchasing decisions.

consumer behavior: the processes involved when individuals or groups select, purchase, use, and dispose of goods, services, ideas, or experiences to satisfy needs and desires

PERCEPTION

Like computers, people undergo stages of information processing in which stimuli are input and stored. Unlike computers, though, we do not passively process whatever information happens to be present. We receive information in the form of *sensations*—the immediate response of our sensory receptors (eyes, ears, nose, mouth, fingers) to such basic stimuli as color and aroma—that we process and store. We add to or take away from these sensations as we assign meaning to them based on our past experiences. **Perception** is the process by which people select, organize, and interpret stimuli to the five senses of sight, sound, smell, touch, and taste.

perception: the process by which people select, organize, and interpret stimuli to the five senses of sight, sound, smell, touch, and taste

The perception process has profound implications for marketers. Take, for instance, how people respond to advertising communications or other marketing information. First, people differ in their ability to "pick up" these messages via sensations. Once a message has been received, its effectiveness hinges on the consumer's interest in paying atten-

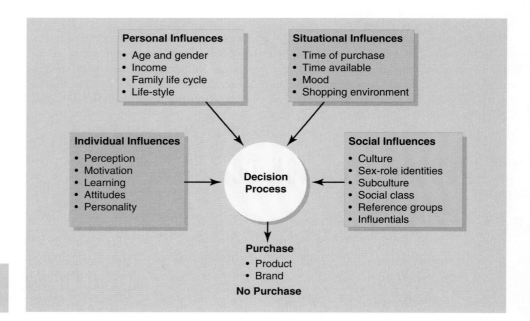

Figure 6.1
Consumer Behavior Decision Model

tion to it. Consumers are often in a state of *sensory overload*, exposed to far more marketing stimuli than they are capable of processing. And the competition for consumer attention is increasing steadily. For example, in 1971 about 2,600 television commercials ran each week; now stations carry more than 6,000 during the same time period.

To further complicate matters for marketers, when people do pay attention to marketing information, the meaning drawn may be quite different from what the marketer intended. Each person tends to organize and interpret marketing stimuli according to his or her unique needs and experiences and the extent to which each stimulus is consistent with other information learned over the years. Perception thus involves exposure to a stimulus, paying attention to it, and then interpreting its meaning in order to respond. The perceptual process thus influences marketing's ability to reach consumers in a crowded marketplace and to develop marketing stimuli that elicit the desired response.

Perceptual Selectivity

Because the brain's capacity to process information is limited, people notice only a very small number of the events or stimuli to which they are exposed, and of these, an even smaller amount are attended to. The process of *perceptual selectivity* means that people attend to only a small portion of stimuli to which they are exposed. Consumers practice a form of psychic economy, picking and choosing among marketing stimuli to avoid being overwhelmed. This selectivity creates a two-part challenge for marketers who want to be noticed.

Exposure is the degree to which a marketing stimulus is within the range of people's sensory receptors. Before anything else consumers must be sitting in front of the television set or within earshot of a radio when a commercial is aired, they must drive by a billboard, or they must flip through the magazine where a print ad has been placed. Because consumers don't all watch the same television programs or read the same magazines, marketing's job is to place the company's messages where targeted consumers will be exposed to them.

Consumers tend to develop *perceptual filters* that determine how much exposure to a particular stimulus they are willing to accept. The advent of the VCR, which has allowed consumers to tape their favorite TV shows, also allows them to fast-forward through the commercials they don't want to see. At other times consumers mentally tune out messages they don't want to hear or see, and they purposefully ignore messages in which they have no interest. *Perceptual vigilence* means that consumers are more likely to look for messages that relate to their current needs. A consumer who rarely notices car ads, for example, will seek them out when he or she is in the market for a new car.

Because consumers are being exposed to so many advertising stimuli, marketers are becoming more and more creative in their attempts to gain exposure for their products.

exposure: the degree to which a marketing stimulus is within range of the consumer's sensory receptors

Q. CAN YOU FIND THE HIDDEN PLEASURE IN REFRESHING SEAGRAM'S GIN?

A. If you think this is just a bubble, look again.

Exhibit 6.1
Many consumers believe that some advertising messages are designed to be perceived unconsciously, so that advertisers are "brainwashing" us into buying their products even when we do not consciously perceive these messages. This technique has been termed *subliminal advertising,* because it involves perception below the level of conscious awareness (*subliminal* means below the threshold of awareness). Although claims that advertisers are placing subliminal messages have been made since the 1950s, there is virtually no scientific evidence that this process even works. Despite the lack of substantiation, protests about this technique continue today and have prompted some marketers to poke fun at the notion of subliminal perception, as in this ad emphasizing the "hidden pleasure" in a glass of its gin.

One solution is to put ads in unconventional places, where there will be less competition. These include the backs of shopping carts, on walls in sports stadiums, at the beginning of movies, and even in restrooms where the marketer has a "captive audience."[1] An executive at Campbell's Soup, commenting on the company's decision to place ads in church bulletins, noted, "We have to shake consumers up these days in order to make them take notice. . . . Television alone won't do that. Now we have to hit them with our ads where they shop and play and on their way to work."[2]

Attention is the degree to which consumers focus on marketing stimuli within their range of exposure. Consumers concentrate on some stimuli but are barely aware of others. *Adaptation* occurs when consumers are overexposed to a marketing stimulus and no longer pay attention to it because it's so familiar. Less intense stimuli (for example, soft sounds or dim colors) can also lead to adaptation because they have less of a sensory impact. The level of attention consumers pay to a marketing message is related to the amount of detail it contains: Simple messages don't contain enough detail to hold people's attention; complex messages contain too much.

Marketers are using a variety of strategies to get noticed and call attention to their products. One expensive strategy involves buying large blocks of advertising space in magazines to dominate consumers' attention. Designer Ralph Lauren, for example, filled fif-

attention: the degree to which consumers focus on marketing stimuli within their range of exposure

teen consecutive full pages in a single issue of *Vanity Fair* for this reason. Other companies are using "bookend ads," where a commercial for a product is split into parts that are separated by commercials for other products. The goal is to hold onto consumers' attention by creating an unresolved problem scenario in the first part and telling the rest of the story in the second part. Other marketers rely on formats that don't fall into predictable patterns to attract attention. These strategies include superimposing a black-and-white object in a color ad or surrounding the object or a small block of type with large amounts of white space.

Principles of Perceptual Organization

When we perceive a stimulus, we don't just do so at random: The information tends to be organized in our minds according to certain principles. These principles have been identified by work in *Gestalt psychology,* a school of thought that maintains that people derive meaning from the totality of a set of stimuli, rather than from any individual stimulus. The German word *gestalt* roughly means whole, pattern, or configuration, and this perspective is best summarized by saying "the whole is greater than the sum of its parts." The gestalt perspective provides several principles relating to the way perceptual stimuli are organized that are particularly relevant to marketers:

- The *principle of closure* implies that consumers tend to perceive an incomplete picture as complete. That is, we tend to fill in the blanks based on our prior experience. Utilization of the principle of closure in marketing strategies encourages audience participation, which increases the chance that people will remember the message. For example, a classic advertising theme for Salem cigarettes said, "You can take Salem out of the country, but you can't take the country out of Salem." After this ad had run for some time, later ads for the cigarette simply read "You can take Salem out of the country but . . ." Readers filled in the rest of the message.
- The *principle of similarity* tells us that consumers tend to group together objects that share similar physical characteristics. That is, they group like items into sets to form an integrated whole. Green Giant relied on this principle when the company redesigned the packaging for its line of frozen vegetables. It created a "sea of green" look to unify all of its different offerings.
- The *figure-ground principle* rests on the idea that one part of a stimulus configuration will dominate (the figure) while other parts recede into the background. This concept is easy to understand if one thinks literally of a photograph with a clear and sharply focused object (the figure) in the center. The figure is dominant, and the eye goes straight to it. In marketing messages that use the figure-ground principle, a stimulus can be made the focal point of the message or merely the context that surrounds the focus. But marketers need to be wary of using splashy graphics and attractive models that dominate the figure to the point where the featured product is virtually imperceptible in the background.

Interpretation

The final stage of the perception process is *interpretation,* which is the meaning that people assign to sensory stimuli. Just as people differ in terms of the stimuli that they perceive, the eventual assignment of meanings to these stimuli varies as well. Two people can see or hear the same event, but their interpretations of it can be like night and day.

Consumers assign meaning to stimuli based on their prior experiences or beliefs. For example, a brand name can communicate expectations about product attributes and color consumers' perceptions of product performance. When Toro introduced a lightweight snow thrower, it was named the "Snow Pup." Sales were disappointing because the word *pup* called up an association with small, cuddly things—not the desirable attributes for a snow thrower. When the product was renamed the "Snow Master," sales went up markedly.[3]

Marketers rely heavily on signs and symbols in marketing messages and sometimes turn to a field of study known as *semiotics,* which examines the correspondence between signs and symbols and the perceived meaning consumers assign to them. According to

UNITED COLORS OF BENETTON.

this perspective, every marketing message has three basic elements: the *object,* which is the product itself (for example, Marlboro cigarettes); the *sign,* which is the sensory imagery that represents the intended meaning of the object (for example, the Marlboro cowboy); and the *interpretant,* which is the derived meaning of the sign or symbol (for example, rugged American individualism). Similarly, the pine tree symbol Procter & Gamble uses on some of its cleaning products conveys a meaning of fresh and clean, while the lion in Dryfus Fund ads provides an association with fearlessness that is carried over to the company's investment approach.

MOTIVATION

Consumers buy what they do for many different reasons. In a marketplace crowded with competing products, consumers themselves may not be fully aware of why they are driven toward some products and away from others. **Motivation** is an internal state that activates goal-directed behavior on the part of consumers to satisfy some need. As we saw in Chapter 1, a *need* is aroused when a consumer recognizes a discrepancy between his or her present state and some desired end state. Once a need has been activated, a state of tension exists that *drives* the consumer toward some *goal* that will reduce this tension by eliminating the need.

The specific products people *want* to satisfy a need are influenced by their unique sets of experiences and backgrounds, and the degree to which a consumer is willing to expend energy to satisfy a need depends on the underlying motivation. *Basic needs,* such as hunger and thirst, must be satisfied by everyone. But the way any two hungry people go about satisfying these needs can be very different: One person wants a Big Mac and coke; while the other wants Chicken McNuggets and coffee. Other needs are *utilitarian* (that is, a desire to achieve some functional or practical benefit, as when a consumer looks for long-lasting flashlight batteries "that keep going and going . . ."), or they may be *hedonic* (that is, an experiential need, involving emotional responses or fantasies, as when consumers choose greeting cards that show they "care enough to send the very best").

Some other motivations that are important to marketers relate to people's needs for achievement, power, status, and affiliation. For example, American consumers may be driven toward products that display their wealth and status, while their Japanese counterparts try to avoid products that make them stand out from the group. Sometimes a person is driven by conflicting motives—caught between the desire for a hot fudge sundae and the rational need to choose frozen yogurt—and marketers like Weight Watchers have turned such conflicts into big business. Consumers can also be driven by motives that

motivation: an internal state that activates goal-directed behavior on the part of consumers in order to satisfy some need

stem from undesirable situations, as when a consumer is forced to replace an old car even though he or she can't really afford a new one. To ease the painful tension created by this type of need, most automakers offer cash-off incentives and easy credit plans.

Recognizing that people aren't always aware of the motives that drive them, many marketers rely on marketing messages that speak to hidden motives or deep-seated needs. Pillsbury, for example, says that "Nothing says lovin' like something from the oven," while Dial soap asks "Aren't you glad you use Dial? Don't you wish everyone did?" Some marketers have also been very successful in their efforts to channel such needs into wants. One Polish entrepreneur single-handedly created a market for electronic hair removers (Polish women traditionally do not shave their legs). Beginning with an ad campaign featuring Miss Poland, he also persuaded a leading Polish fashion designer to announce that hairy legs were out of fashion in Europe and organized local beauty contests to find the best legs. At last report he was selling 30,000 hair removers a month.[4]

Freud's Theory of Motivation

Sigmund Freud had a profound (if controversial) impact on many basic assumptions about what motivates human behavior. He developed the idea that much of human behavior stems from a fundamental conflict between a person's desire to gratify his or her needs and the necessity to function as a responsible member of society. Thus, people may do things unconsciously to satisfy motives of which they are not even aware.

According to Freudian theory, a person's development hinges on the way three systems of the mind interact in childhood. The *id* is entirely oriented toward immediate gratification—it operates according to the *pleasure principle,* guiding behavior by the primary desire to maximize pleasure and avoid pain. The *superego* is essentially the person's conscience, which has internalized society's rules (especially as communicated by parents); it works to prevent the id from seeking selfish gratification. The referee in this subconscious struggle between temptation and virtue is the *ego,* which tries to balance these two opposing forces according to the *reality principle*—that is, by finding ways to gratify the id that will be acceptable to the outside world.

For marketers Freud's work highlights the potential importance of unconscious or hidden motives underlying purchase decisions. The Freudian perspective also hints at the possibility that the ego relies on the symbolism in products to compromise between the demands of the id and the prohibitions of the superego. That is, a person channels his or her unacceptable desires into acceptable outlets by acquiring products that signify these underlying desires. This possibility is the connection between product symbolism and the motivation to purchase it. Most Freudian applications in marketing are related to the sexual meanings of products. For example, some analysts have speculated that for many men a sports car is a substitute for sexual gratification. Indeed, some men do seem inordinately attached to their cars and may spend many hours lovingly washing and polishing them, and many marketers rely on these connotations to promote particular models.

Maslow's Hierarchy of Needs

One influential approach to motivation was proposed by the psychologist Abraham Maslow.[5] Maslow formulated a *hierarchy of needs* that categorizes motives according to five levels of importance. The hierarchy implies that needs at a certain level must be at least partially satisfied before the next, higher level is activated. As illustrated in Figure 6.2, this universal approach depicts individuals starting at the lowest level with basic needs for food, clothing, and shelter and then progressing to higher levels to satisfy more complex needs, such as the need to be accepted by others or to feel good about themselves. Ultimately, people reach the highest-level needs and focus on attaining such elusive goals as spiritual fulfillment.

Maslow's hierarchy of needs does explain in part why people have different needs at different times. It is useful to marketers because it (indirectly) specifies certain types of product benefits people might be looking for, depending on the different stages in their development and/or environmental conditions. For example, the many homeless people around the world are concerned with satisfying the basic need to obtain shelter. For the more fortunate who have a warm and dry place to sleep at night, a house is more likely to satisfy higher-level needs. For some this need might be status and social approval, for others it may be a desire to create a sense of family and belongingness, while some homeown-

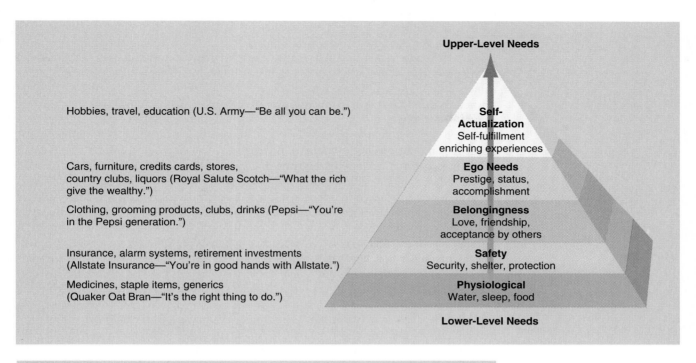

Figure 6.2
Maslow's Hierarchy of Needs and Related Products

ers may place primary importance on the aesthetic enjoyment they receive from decorating and personalizing their abodes.

Compulsive Consumption

For some consumers the expression "born to shop" is taken quite literally. These consumers shop because they are compelled to do so, not because they are motivated to satisfy a need. *Compulsive consumption* is repetitive, often excessive shopping that serves as an antidote to tension, anxiety, depression, or boredom. "Shopaholics," as they are called, turn to shopping much the way addicted people turn to drugs or alcohol.[6] Compulsive consumption is distinctly different from impulse buying, which is temporary and centers on a specific product at a particular moment. In contrast, compulsive buying is an enduring behavior that centers on the process of buying, not the purchases themselves. As one woman who spent $20,000 per year on clothing confessed, "I was possessed when I went into a store. I bought clothes that didn't fit, that I didn't like, and that I certainly didn't need."[7]

LEARNING

Learned associations among feelings, events, and products are important influences on consumer behavior. **Learning** refers to a relatively permanent change in consumer behavior, caused by experience or acquired information. Learning about products can occur deliberately, as when we set out to gather information about different CD players before buying one brand. We also learn even when we are not trying. Consumers recognize many brand names and can hum many product jingles, for example, even for products they themselves do not use. This casual, unintentional acquisition of knowledge is known as *incidental learning*. Psychologists who study learning processes have advanced several theories that affect marketing strategy.

Behavioral Learning

Behavioral learning theories assume that learning takes place as the result of external events or stimuli. In one type of behavioral learning, *classical conditioning*, two stimuli

learning: a relatively permanent change in consumer behavior that is caused by experience or acquired information

behavioral learning theories: theories of learning that focus on how consumer behavior is changed by external events, or stimuli

are experienced close together. After a while the response to one stimulus is transferred to the second. For example, an ad shows a product and a breathtakingly beautiful scene. After we see the ad several times, the positive attitude we have toward the scene is transferred to the product, and we have a more positive attitude toward the product. Similarly, consumers respond to brand names, scents, jingles, and other marketing stimuli based on the learned connections they have formed over time between these stimuli and other pleasant or unpleasant stimuli.

In *operant conditioning* people learn that actions they take result in rewards or punishments, and this feedback influences the way they will respond in similar situations in the future. Just as a rat in a maze learns to choose the option that offers him a piece of cheese rather than an electric shock, consumers who receive a reward, such as a compliment on a new cologne (or a prize in the bottom of the box of cereal), will be more likely to buy that brand again. That feedback acts as a *reinforcement* for the behavior.

One common way to reinforce what consumers learn about goods and services is through *repetition*. Many classic advertising campaigns are built around catchy product slogans or jingles that have been repeated so many times that they are etched in consumers' minds. In other cases brand names like Marlboro and Coca-Cola become fixed in people's minds because they have been repeatedly paired with meaningful symbols like the Marlboro cowboy.

These learned associations have a tendency to transfer to other, similar stimuli in a process called *stimulus generalization*. This phenomenon has important implications for marketers, because it means that they can build on well-learned connections with established products to create similar links with other related goods and services. For example, companies such as Campbell's, Heinz, and General Electric that use a *family branding strategy* rely on the positive image consumers have of their corporate name to create value for different product lines that all display the company name. A related strategy is to create *product line extensions,* where new products share the name of an established brand. Dole, which is associated with fruit, was able to introduce refrigerated juices and juice bars, while Sun Maid went from raisins to raisin bread. Other recent extensions include Woolite rug cleaner, Cracker Jack gourmet popping corn, and Ivory shampoo. These branding strategies will be considered further in Chapter 10.

The process of stimulus generalization also explains the popularity of *licensing* as a marketing strategy. Under this kind of business arrangement one company sells the rights to another company to use its name on an unrelated product. The licensee in turn hopes that the learned positive associations with this name will transfer to its products. Companies as diverse as McDonald's and Harley-Davidson have authorized the use of their names on products manufactured by others.

Cognitive Learning

cognitive learning theories: theories of learning that stress the importance of internal mental processes and that view people as problem solvers who actively use information from the world around them to master their environment

In contrast to behavioral theories of learning, **cognitive learning theory** stresses the importance of internal mental processes. This perspective views people as problem solvers who actively use information from the world around them to master their environment. Supporters of this viewpoint also stress the role of creativity and insight during the learning process.

An important component of the cognitive perspective is *observational learning*. This type of learning occurs when people watch others' actions and note the consequences of their behaviors. They store these observations in memory and at some later point use the information to guide their own behavior, especially when they admire or identify with these people in some way.

The process of imitating the behaviors of other people is known as *modeling,* and the degree to which a model will be copied depends on his or her *social attractiveness.* Attractiveness can be based on several components, including physical appearance, expertise, or similarity to the evaluator. For example, many promotional strategies are centered around endorsements by celebrity athletes, movie stars, and music idols. When a company like Reebok signed basketball star Shaquille O'Neal to a multiyear contract worth close to $20 million before he even set foot on an NBA court, the athletic shoe company did so for a reason: It was counting on the likelihood that "Shaq" would continue to develop into a model for millions of young fans, who would then be motivated to imitate his choice of footwear.[8]

SPOTLIGHT ON ETHICS

Tots, Toys, TV, and Terror

The modeling process is a powerful form of learning. Unfortunately, people's tendencies to imitate others' behaviors can have negative effects. Of particular concern is the potential of television shows, movies, and video games to teach violence to children. Even prominent media executive Ted Turner, who owns the TBS and CNN networks, told Congress that TV is "the single most significant factor causing violence in America."*

Children may be exposed to new methods of aggression by models (for example, cartoon heroes) in the shows they watch. At some later point, when the child becomes angry, these behaviors will be available for actual use. A classic study demonstrates the effect of modeling on children's actions. Kids who watched an adult stomp on, knock down, and otherwise torture a large inflated "Bobo doll" repeated these behaviors when later left alone in a room with the doll, in contrast to other children who did not witness these acts. This modeling process had more disastrous consequences for a real-life family: After watching an episode of Beavis and Butthead on MTV where the two antisocial teens set fire to a trailer, a child did the same thing to his house, killing his little sister in the process.

Some people who are responsible for creating or selling the many violent images to which children are exposed are taking steps to reduce the damage. Toys "Я" Us, the largest U.S. toy retailer, decided to stop selling a CD-ROM video game called Night Trap after receiving numerous complaints about the game. It features scantily clad sorority sisters versus zombies. When the zombies win they suck the girls' blood with a giant syringe. Another popular game made by the same company called Mortal Kombat allows victorious players to rip out an opponent's heart or bash in his brains.† There is a growing movement to introduce violence ratings for video games, though it's unclear how effective this approach will be.

Still, some marketers continue to promote violence to children. A recent ad for Diesel Jeans made by a Swedish ad agency illustrates this attitude. A teenager points a revolver at the reader, while the small print in the ad reads: "MODERN CHILDREN need to SOLVE their OWN problems: teaching kids to KILL helps them deal directly with reality—but they learn SO much quicker when you give them a guiding hand! Make them proud and confident! Man, if they never learn to blast the brains out of their neighbors what kind of damn FUTURE has this COUNTRY of ours got???" The company's director of operations defended the ad by claiming, "It is not promoting killing people, it is promoting jeans. It's an irony. It is not to be taken seriously." After receiving a barrage of complaints, the company's founder finally admitted that the ads were a mistake and has replaced them with an ad campaign promoting love—and blue jeans.‡

---

*Miriam Horn, "Torching Television Violence (Heh Heh)," U.S. News & World Report (Dec. 20, 1993): 91.
†Joseph Pereira, "Toys Я ' Us Says It Decided to Pull Sega's Night Trap from Store Shelves," The Wall Street Journal (Dec. 17, 1993): B5.
‡Don Oldenburg, "On the Offensive: Responding to Ads that Rub You Wrong," The Washington Post (Aug. 2, 1993): B5.

ATTITUDES

An **attitude** is a learned predisposition to respond favorably or unfavorably to stimuli. Attitudes are relatively enduring evaluations of people, objects, and issues.[9] Attitudes help to determine whom a person chooses to date, what music he or she listens to, whether he or she will recycle or discard aluminum cans, or whether he or she chooses to become a market researcher for a living. Attitudes influence consumer behavior by creating a predisposition to respond to a product positively or negatively and by establishing patterns that determine how products will be used. Consumers have attitudes toward very product-specific behaviors (for example, using Crest toothpaste rather than Colgate) as well as toward more general consumption-related behaviors (for example, how often one should brush one's teeth).

According to the **ABC model of attitudes,** a person's attitude has three components: affect, behavior, and cognition. *Affect* refers to the overall feeling the person has about an attitude object. *Behavior* involves the person's intentions to do something or the actual action taken with regard to it. *Cognition* refers to the beliefs and knowledge the person has about it. The ABC model emphasizes the interrelationships among knowing, feeling, and doing.

Depending on the nature of the product, one of these three components—knowing, feeling, or doing—will be the dominant influence in creating an attitude toward a product. Affect is usually dominant for expressive products that we use to say something about ourselves (for example, perfumes). Behavior often determines attitudes for commonly purchased items such as chewing gum, where we often form an attitude based on how the

attitude: a learned predisposition to respond favorably or unfavorably to stimuli, based on relatively enduring evaluations of people, objects, and issues

ABC model of attitudes: a behavioral theory suggesting that an attitude has three components—affect, behavior, and cognition—and emphasizing the interrelationships among knowing, feeling, and doing

product tastes or performs. Cognition is more critical for important or complex products, such as computer systems, that require us to process objective or technical information before we can come to a decision. Because the basic goal of many marketing communications is to influence consumers' attitudes toward a product, the ABC model has important implications for marketers. They can identify consumers' attitudes and either design products that are consistent with them or try to change these attitudes, which is harder to do.

Marketing messages to change attitudes can focus on one of the three components of an attitude. For example, groups like People for Ethical Treatment of Animals have focused on providing hard-hitting information to influence people's attitudes and to discourage them from buying and wearing natural fur coats. The fur industry has countered with ads focusing on women's feelings of resentment at being told what to wear. And both groups have emphasized the behavior component of attitudes by ads depicting a naked woman who'd "rather go naked than wear fur" versus one in which a woman is wearing a fur in a wholesome family scene and enjoying a "very basic luxury."

PERSONALITY

personality: the psychological characteristics that consistently influence the way a person responds to situations in his or her environment

Personality refers to the unique psychological characteristics that consistently influence the way a person responds to situations in his or her environment. Numerous theories have been developed (and debated) about the personality construct and how it accounts for the unique differences in people. One consumer may always be on the lookout for new experiences and cutting-edge products, while another is happiest when he or she is in familiar surroundings, using the same brands over and over. For marketers, these differences underscore the potential value of considering personality differences when crafting marketing strategies.

Personality Traits

One approach to understanding personality is *trait theory,* which focuses on describing and comparing *traits,* or identifiable characteristics, that define a person. For example, people might be compared in terms of how introverted (shy) versus extroverted (outgoing) they are: Some products and advertising messages are more likely to influence one type than another. A cola commercial featuring a solitary figure savoring a glass of soda on an empty beach might appeal to an introvert, while another starring a bunch of "party animals" swilling soda at a party might grab the attention of an extrovert. Some specific traits that are relevant to marketing strategies include *innovativeness* (the degree to which a person likes to try new things); *self-confidence* (the degree to which a person has a positive evaluation of his/her abilities, including the ability to make good product decisions); and *sociability* (the degree to which a person enjoys social interaction and thus may respond to products and situations that relate to social situations).[10]

Self-Concept

self-concept: an individual's self-image that is composed of a mixture of beliefs, observations, and feelings about personal attributes

Many of our purchase decisions are strongly influenced by another personality theory that relates to how we feel about ourselves. **Self-concept** refers to individuals' images of themselves based on who they think they are (the actual self) versus who they would like to be (the ideal self). It is composed of a mixture of beliefs about the self, observations of one's own behavior, and feelings (usually both positive and negative) about personal attributes. The self-concept is influenced by feedback we receive from many sources, including our families, friends, and employers.

Self-esteem refers to the positivity of one's attitude toward oneself. People with low self-esteem do not expect that they will perform very well, and they will try to avoid embarrassment, failure, or rejection. Consumers with low self-esteem tend to be susceptible to marketing messages that show them how to avoid rejection, as is often the case in deodorant commercials where the unlucky hero or heroine suffers the consequences of not using the product. In developing a new line of snack cakes, Sara Lee found that consumers low in self-esteem preferred portion-controlled snack items because they felt they lacked self-control.[11]

On the more positive side, *self-esteem advertising* can influence consumers' attitudes toward products by stimulating positive feelings about the self.[12] This technique has been

If I had a Nissan 240SX . . . it would be a red coupe.

Wait! A silver fastback. And I'd go for a spin up Route 7, the twisty part.

Just me and Astro . . .

no, Amy.

Heck, Christie Brinkley!

Wow! Yeah, me and Christie . . .

in my silver — no, red 240SX . . . driving into the sunset.

Exhibit 6.3
Many goods and services are successful because they reinforce people's tendencies to fantasize about themselves. The marketers use strategies that allow us to extend our vision about ourselves by placing us in unfamiliar, exciting situations where we can "try on" interesting or provocative roles. They help us fill the gap between our perceived actual selves and the ideal selves we would like to be. This marketing technique is sometimes called a *fantasy appeal* and is illustrated in the storyboard for a TV commercial featuring model Christie Brinkley and a young man fantasizing about driving into the sunset with her.

used by Clairol shampoo ("You're not getting older, you're getting better"), Budweiser beer ("For all you do, this Bud's for you"), and McDonald's ("You deserve a break today"). Other strategies rely on consumers' desires to achieve the ideal self. Here, people are influenced by the idea that the "right" clothes, the "right" car, or even the "right" laundry detergent will enhance the self and transform the way others see them.

Do We Buy What We Are?

The notion that consumers buy products that are extensions of their personalities makes intuitive sense. This idea is endorsed by marketers who try to create idealized brand personalities to influence different types of consumers. For example, consider the different "personalities" invented by fragrance marketers: A brand with a "wholesome, girl next door" image like Jean Naté would be hard to confuse with the sultry, exotic personality radiated by Obsession or the sophisticated image of Chanel No. 5.

Some studies have shown that people buy products whose "personality" characteristics match their own. One early study into the congruence between products and people's images of themselves found that car owners ratings of themselves tended to match their perceptions of their cars. Pontiac drivers, for example, saw themselves as more active and flashier than Volkswagen drivers.[13] Others have found a match between consumers and their most preferred brand of beer, soap, and toothpaste, as well as their favorite stores.[14] Overall, studies linking the components of personality to buying decisions have met with mixed results. Better results have been obtained in studies relating personality traits to such consumer behaviors as alcohol consumption or willingness to try new food products.[15]

EXTERNAL INFLUENCES ON CONSUMER DECISIONS

Our identities as consumers are intimately related to the other people with whom we identify. We are all individuals, but rarely do the same products or services appeal to people who differ in age, educational background, income, and so on. Our preferences are shaped by the many groups, large and small, to which we belong. Just as we receive and respond to information delivered in marketing communications, we receive cues from family, friends, neighbors, and even society at large that influence the products and brands we choose to purchase and use.

As we saw in Figure 6.1, consumer purchasing decisions and buying behavior are influenced by many external factors that include personal, social, and situational issues. Understanding these influences on consumer behavior is crucial to identifying marketing opportunities and developing successful strategies for pursuing them. Marketers use many of the personal and social influences—including age, social class, and ethnic affiliation—to categorize consumers (market segmentation) and target specific offerings to them (target marketing). We'll consider these strategies in Chapter 8, and for now we'll first look at how personal and social factors influence consumer behavior. Then we'll review some of the situational factors—time, mood, and the shopping environment—that affect purchasing decisions.

PERSONAL INFLUENCES

The personal influences on consumers are important determinants of their needs and wants. A consumer's decision to go backpacking in the Rockies versus taking a trip to Disney World has a lot to do with the person's age, income, family status, and chosen lifestyle. Goods and services that satisfy the needs of a specific age group are often unwanted by people in other age groups and may even turn them off. Although there are exceptions, it is safe to assume, for example, that most fans of groups like the Stone Temple Pilots or Nine Inch Nails are younger than people who enjoy listening to the likes of Frank Sinatra. As we'll see in Chapter 8, many marketing strategies are based on offering goods and services that appeal to the needs of such different age groups as children, teenagers, young adults, the middle-aged, and the elderly.

Income

Just as people's needs vary at different stages in life, so does their purchasing power to satisfy needs and wants. The typical college student, for example, may have very limited income for both essential and discretionary purchases, while many retired and elderly people are able to indulge in greater discretionary spending than in any other stage in their lives. Overall, American consumers are estimated to wield about $400 billion a year in discretionary spending power, and people aged thirty-five to fifty-five, whose incomes are at a peak, account for about half of this amount.

Of all the personal influences on consumer behavior, income is perhaps the most significant to marketers. As we saw in Chapter 1, demand for consumer goods and services depends on consumers' ability to buy them. While demand for necessities tends to be stable over time, other purchases are closely tied to income levels. Since 1960 the real per capita income of Americans has almost doubled, although this boom has by no means been shared equally among all consumer groups. One reason for the increase in income is that a larger proportion of people of working age have joined the labor force, with close to three-fourths of the adult population now at work. Much of this growth is because women have been surging into jobs in record numbers, and many of these jobs are in high-paying occupations that used to be dominated by men.

The steady increase in the numbers of working women has lead to dramatic changes in the number of middle- and upper-income families. There are now more than 18 million married couples making more than $50,000 a year, and in almost two-thirds of these families it is the wife's paycheck that is propelling the couple up the income ladder. But the news is not all good for marketers. The typical U.S. household is also changing the way it spends its money. The most noticeable change is that a much larger share of the typical budget is being spent on shelter and transportation, and less is being spent on food, apparel, and home furnishings. On the positive side, however, households are spending more on entertainment, reading, and education than in the past.

Family

Our behavior as consumers is heavily influenced by our families and by our current position in the **family life cycle,** the stages through which people pass as they grow older. As small children we learn to buy the brands our family buys, to shop at the stores our family shops at, and to do our shopping systematically or impulsively according to how our family does it. When grown we tend to buy the same brands of appliances, to purchase the same make of automobile, and to support the same political party as our parents. And as our parents become elderly, the roles are reversed and we begin to influence our parents' choices of products and brands.

As we age, our needs change along with our life situations. A family's needs and expenditures are influenced by such factors as the number of people in the family, the ages of family members, and whether one or more adults are in the work force. Newlyweds who focus on setting up housekeeping find that their needs change dramatically when babies begin to arrive on the scene. When the babies are a little older, mothers frequently go to work outside the home, so the family must take into account the need for day care, a working wardrobe for mom, and transportation to get to her job. And so the process goes, until a person reaches old age, where his or her priorities may shift from saving for the kids' college education to buying that retirement home in Florida.

Traditional descriptions of the family have considered two basic stages in the family life cycle: the "full nest" (young and middle-aged couples with several children) and the "empty nest" (where the children have grown and left home). Dramatic cultural changes affecting people's living arrangements, however, have forced marketers to change their conception of the traditional family life cycle. This updated view of the "family" includes such alternative situations as single-parent families, childless couples, couples with adult children living at home, unmarried couples and parents, and homosexual relationships. For marketers these changes mean marked differences in family needs and wants that affect purchases in product categories from food to luxury vacations.

The life cycle perspective also reminds us that many purchase activities are *joint decisions.* A husband and wife today may decide together on a new car or living room sofa, although "masculine" purchase decisions like buying a car or a lawn mower have traditionally been assigned to the husband while the wife assumed responsibility for "feminine" decisions like home decorating choices and food products. With more women working and more men becoming involved in household chores, these traditional assignments are changing, and kids are now getting into the act as well. In other living situations purchase

family life cycle: a means of characterizing consumers within a family structure based on different stages through which people pass as they grow older

REAL PEOPLE, REAL CHOICES:

DECISION TIME AT SEBAGO

Between World War II and the 1960s, operations at Sebago Inc. revolved around the ever-increasing demand for penny loafers, which the company manufactured under its own name—Sebago-Moc—as well as other names for large private-label customers. Unfortunately, although production and sales for the fall buying season were high, they would drop off dramatically until the following season. The company managed to maintain its operations in the off-season by making shoes for the market leader in boating footwear. This company had contracted with Sebago-Moc to make leather boating shoes, which would bear the boating shoe company's name and be distributed by it as well. This product, a basic hand-sewn moccasin secured by a rawhide lace running through a collar and two eyelets, was developed for serious "yachties," who appreciated the shoe's nonslip rubber boating sole.

Although initially only found in high-class yacht chandler's shops, the shoe slowly became part of the "uniform" of the young, prep school males. This *de rigueur* outfit also consisted of a blue oxford button-down shirt, a navy blazer, and a pair of chinos. Like the penny loafer, the "yachting shoe" caught on with the mass market, and by the late 1960s the shoe had been transformed from an obscure, functional item to a mass market fashion statement as young people across the country—even those who had never seen a yacht or even the ocean—tried to imitate the preppie look in droves.

The tendency for people to identify themselves with an idealized image—in this case, the affluent lifestyle symbolized by prep schools and leisure activities like yachting—was paying off for the boating shoe company. Sebago-Moc decided to develop a similar shoe under its own name, but the "SEBAGO-MOC Boat Shoe" did not fare well in the market. Both consumers and retailers strongly associated the name with penny loafers and, ironically, believed that Sebago-Moc had no credibility as the manufacturer of a yachting product! To add to the company's problems, the boating shoe company that had contracted with Sebago-Moc made some management changes, and the new footwear buyer informed Mr. Wellehan that he had located another manufacturer outside of the United States that could produce the shoe with far lower labor costs. Mr. Wellehan was given an ultimatum: Either match the new low price or lose the business.

Mr. Wellehan and his decision team were faced with several difficult choices:

Option 1. To maintain continuity of production and cash flow in the spring, accept the renegotiated pricing for the private-label product. This choice would mean accepting a price that would not even cover Sebago-Moc's overhead, but would enable the company to maintain manufacturing operations year round.

Option 2. Recognize the limitations in consumer perceptions created by the company name. After some twenty-five years, eliminate the term "Moc" from the corporate name and create a new brand identity that would not suffer from the penny loafer association. This choice would involve the creation of a new brand image, entailing new product design, packaging, advertising, and so on.

Option 3. Forget the private-label business and concentrate on producing nothing but penny loafers. Build up more stock during the first six months of the year, and try an advertising campaign that would encourage sales of penny loafers during the spring season as well as fall. Of course, this strategy would mean that a small company would have to try to convince a nation of consumers to change its buying habits. Also, this exclusive focus would put all of Sebago-Moc's eggs in one basket, leaving it vulnerable to that dark day when penny loafers went out of style for preppies and preppy wannabees.

Now, join the decision team at Sebago: Which option would you choose, and why?

decisions may be made jointly by a "committee" composed of housemates or other group members, or they may be divided among different individuals according to a system of specialization wherein each has certain areas of responsibility.

Lifestyles

Lifestyle refers to the pattern of living that determines how people choose to spend their time, money, and energy. It reflects peoples values, tastes, and preferences, and it has a potent influence on purchasing behavior.[16] Consumers choose many goods and services over others because they are associated with a certain lifestyle. Although each person has a set of unique attitudes and personality characteristics that allow him or her to inject some individuality into a chosen lifestyle, people tend to express their group identities by associating with others who are similar in such dimensions as age, interests, income, race, and religion.

A person's lifestyle is a complex mixture of internal and external factors that influences the types of products purchased and the specific brands chosen. It determines whether a person chooses a pair of tennis shoes, running shoes, or penny loafers. It also affects whether a person chooses a no-name polo shirt or one sporting the Izod alligator. Lifestyle marketing strategies often attempt to position a product by adapting it to the lifestyle of a specific consumer group. For example, when Subaru first entered the U.S. auto market in the early 1970s, it had virtually no name recognition and struggled to compete with other, better-known imports. Subaru became the official car of the U.S. ski team and linked itself to the lifestyles of people who enjoy skiing. The company now has the highest market share for imports in several Snow Belt states.[17]

> **lifestyle:** the pattern of living that determines how people choose to spend their time, money, and energy and that reflects their values, tastes, and preferences

SOCIAL INFLUENCES

Humans are social animals. We all belong to groups, try to please others, and take cues on how to behave by observing the actions of those around us. In fact, our desire to "fit in" or to identify with the actions of individuals and groups we admire is often the primary motivation for many of our purchasing decisions. Family members, friends, co-workers, classmates, and celebrities often influence our decisions. In addition we are identified (and identify ourselves) with larger groups, whether African Americans, Democrats, or even Hell's Angels or Deadheads, that also play a big role in guiding our purchases.

Culture

The lasting values and behavior patterns that people learn in childhood are determined by their **culture,** which may be thought of as a society's personality. Culture is the accumulation of shared meanings, rituals, and traditions among the members of a society. It includes both abstract ideas, such as freedom and independence, and material objects and services, such as automobiles, clothing, food, art, and sports, that are valued by a group of people. Culture influences consumers' attitudes, beliefs, and perceptions, and it determines the overall priorities they attach to different activities and products. From a marketing perspective, culture determines *how* people choose to satisfy their needs.

Every culture has a set of *norms,* or rules, dictating what is right or wrong, acceptable or unacceptable to other people within the culture. We learn guidelines about appropriate dress, foods to eat and foods to avoid, how members of one sex should treat the other, and so on. We learn to engage in ceremonies (called *rituals*) such as weddings, funerals, holidays, and graduations that have very specific activities and products associated with them. Very often these cultural expectations are so deeply ingrained that we don't even think about them and are unaware of the influence they have on our purchasing decisions.

Every culture also has a set of ideas about important goals, or cultural values, that it imparts to its members. *Cultural values* are enduring beliefs that some state is preferable to its opposite.[18] These states may not be equally endorsed by everyone, and, in some cases values may even seem to contradict one another. For example, Americans appear to value both conformity and individuality and seek to find some accommodation between them. Other values that have been attributed to American culture include freedom, youthfulness, achievement, materialism, and activity. But culture is never static, and even basic beliefs and values are subject to change over time. Americans' emphasis on youth, for example, is eroding as the population ages.

> **culture:** the learned values and patterns of behavior that stem from the shared meanings, rituals, and traditions among the members of a society and that influence their attitudes, beliefs, preferences, and priorities toward abstract ideas, activities, and products

Exhibit 6.4
The *sex-role identities* of men and women are determined by society's expectations regarding the attitudes, behaviors, and appearance for each sex. These culturally bound guidelines can differ radically from country to country, as illustrated in the Bijan ad shown here, and they can change over time. In American culture changing attitudes about the roles of men and women have minimized the gender-related influences on many purchasing decisions. More and more women are now buying sporting equipment, briefcases, and power tools, while men are beginning to do more shopping for food, clothing, and home furnishings. In two-career families, both sexes are buying more convenience foods, easy-to-care-for clothing, and time-saving goods and services.

Successful marketers monitor cultural shifts and attempt to provide product benefits that are consistent with the values of a culture at that time. For example, the U.S. culture started to emphasize the concept of thinness as an ideal of appearance in the mid-1970s. The premium placed on this goal, which stemmed from underlying values like mobility, wealth, and a focus on the self, greatly contributed to the success of Miller Lite beer at that time. However, when Gablinger introduced a lo-cal beer seven years earlier, in 1968, the product failed. This product was "ahead of its time," because American consumers were not interested in this benefit in the 1960s.

Subculture

While the American culture provides the raw material for many consumer decisions and purchasing patterns, much of the behavior of consumers is profoundly affected by the enormous variations in the social fabric of the United States. A **subculture** is a group within the larger society whose members share a distinctive set of beliefs, characteristics, or common experiences. Each of us belongs to many subcultures. These include age groups, religious groups, ethnic groups, and regional groups (for example, Texans versus New Yorkers). For marketers, some of the most important subcultures are those involving racial and ethnic groups. Many product and communications strategies are developed with specific groups in mind, including such sizable consumer segments as African Americans, Hispanic Americans, and Asian Americans, which we'll discuss in more detail in Chapter 8.

Sometimes even a leisure activity can evolve into a subculture, if this activity involves a well-defined set of behaviors. Consumers in these subcultures—whether "Deadheads" who followed The Grateful Dead band from concert to concert (at least until the band stopped touring in the beginning of 1996 following the death of leader Jerry Garcia), retired people who tour the country in Winnebagos, or members of youth gangs—create their own worlds, often complete with customs, vocabulary, and product insignias. For example, skulls and roses are used to signify the "Grateful Dead" subculture, and items bearing these symbols still hold important meanings for group members even after the band's breakup.

subculture: a group within a society whose members share a distinctive set of beliefs, characteristics, or common experiences

Social Class

The value that a culture puts on such factors as family background, education, occupation, and income defines the class structure within a society. **Social class** refers to the overall rank assigned to groups of people according to the values held by a society. In the United States people who are grouped within the same social class are approximately equal in terms of education and income, and they share many ideas and values regarding the way life should be lived. These people also tend to socialize with others in the same class, and they usually share common tastes in clothing, decorating styles, choices of leisure activities, and so on.[19]

In the United States the social system is not as fixed and rigid as it is in some countries. Upwardly mobile Americans can and do move to higher social classes as their life situations improve. The U.S. social structure is commonly divided into broad classes that range from those at the bottom of the economic ladder (the lower-lower class) to people who are at the very top (the upper-upper class). Unless your last name happens to be Rockefeller or Trump or you are descended from some other very wealthy dynasty, the odds are that you and your family reside in the middle of this system, perhaps in the lower-middle class (where many so-called "working class" consumers are placed) or in the upper-middle class (where many professionals and managers are located).

For marketers, social class identifies large groups of people with much in common. It is also an important determinant of *how much* money a consumer spends, and it influences *how* it is spent.[20] Working class consumers tend to evaluate products in more utilitarian terms such as sturdiness or comfort rather than style or fashionability. They are less likely to experiment with new products or styles, such as modern furniture or colored appliances.[21] Immediate needs, such as a new refrigerator or TV, tend to dictate buying behavior for these consumers, while the higher classes tend to focus on more long-term goals, such as saving for college tuition or retirement.[22]

> **social class:** the overall rank or social standing of groups of people within a society according to the value assigned to such factors as family background, education, occupation, and income

Reference Groups

A **reference group** refers to a set of people that a consumer is motivated to please or imitate. Consumers *conform* or change their beliefs and actions as a reaction to real or imagined pressure to "fit in" with the rest of the group. The "group" can be composed of one other person (for example, a spouse) or a large organization (for example, the American Marketing Association). It can be a person you see everyday, or someone you've never met (for example, a statesman like Martin Luther King or a rock singer like Axl Rose). Because reference groups play an important role in defining individual consumer needs and opinions, they exert a powerful influence on purchasing decisions.

Groups that have a direct influence on an individual consumer are the *membership groups* to which he or she belongs. Small, informal *primary membership groups,* such as family, friends, and co-workers who are involved in an individual's day-to-day activities, can have a major impact on fundamental purchasing decisions and behaviors. Larger, more formal *secondary membership groups,* which include religious organizations, clubs, political parties, professional associations and unions, and so on, tend to influence decisions about specific brands or activities.

Aspirational reference groups are composed of idealized groups that consumers admire and wish to join or to identify with in some way. These may be actual groups like the Dallas Cowboys, or organizations like the Harvard Club, or individuals like Michael Jordan. While consumers may have no direct contact with aspirational reference groups, they have a strong influence on consumer attitudes and preferences, which accounts for the many marketing efforts that rely on superstars and other widely admired people to promote products.

Reference group influences are not equally powerful for all types of products categories and brands. The degree to which reference groups influence purchasing decisions is tied to how socially conspicuous or visible the purchase is to others—that is, whether it will be consumed in public or private—and whether it is a luxury or a necessity. The effects are strongest for *public luxuries* like diamond jewelry, which are highly conspicuous because fewer people own them, and are the least for *private necessities* like undergarments because fewer people will see or notice them. In between these extremes are *private luxuries,* such as electric blankets, ice makers, and home computers, and *public necessities,* like

> **reference group:** a set of people that a consumer is motivated to please or imitate and that influence consumer purchasing to the extent that the purchase is conspicuous to others

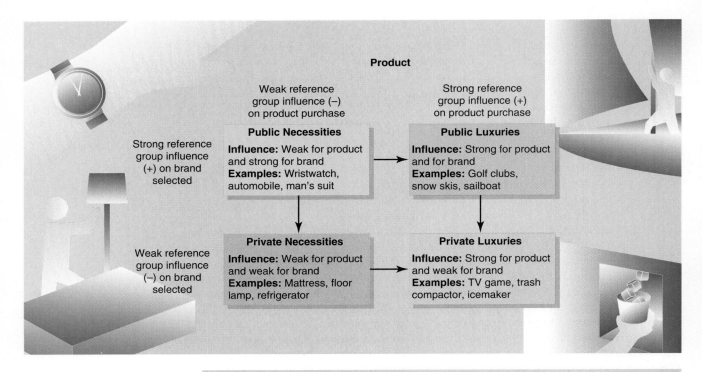

Figure 6.3
Relative Influence of Reference Groups on Product and Brand Choices

Source: Adapted from William O. Bearden and Michael J. Etzel, "Reference Group Influences on Product and Brand Purchase Decisions," *Journal of Consumer Research* (Sept. 1982): 185.

living room furnishings. Figure 6.3 illustrates the relative effects of reference groups on specific product categories according to these dimensions.

Influentials

Some people within a consumer's social or reference groups are particularly influential when it comes to purchasing decisions. An **opinion leader** is a person who is frequently able to influence others' attitudes or behaviors.[23] He or she tends to be a socially active person, with a slightly higher social standing than the rest of the group, and has both an active interest and some expertise in one or more product categories. A fashion opinion leader, for example, is likely to subscribe to a number of fashion magazines, shop in trendy boutiques, and be first to wear the latest styles. This person has a primary influence on clothing choices, but may also be frequently consulted by others for advice about cosmetics, perfumes, and jewelry.

SITUATIONAL INFLUENCES ON CONSUMER BEHAVIOR

Once a consumer decides to make a particular purchase, situational events can cause the person to alter the decision. The shopping environment, the consumer's mood, and the time of day as well as time available are important **situational cues** that affect how products are evaluated and chosen. These situational factors can also prompt a spontaneous decision to make an unplanned purchase or to postpone one that had been planned.

Time

Time is one of the consumer's most limited resources. We talk about "making time" or "spending time," and we are frequently reminded that "time is money." Many consumers believe they are more pressed for time than ever before.[24] This sense of *time poverty* influences purchasing decisions for many goods from microwave ovens to electric

opinion leader: a person who is frequently able to influence others' attitudes or behaviors by virtue of his or her active interest and expertise in one or more product categories

situational cues: events and conditions—such as the shopping environment, the consumer's mood, and the time of day as well as time available—that affect how products are evaluated and chosen at the time of purchase

SPOTLIGHT ON RELATIONSHIP MARKETING

Building Plastic Bonds with Credit Cards

Using a strategy called *affinity marketing,* astute marketers are gaining customer loyalty by emphasizing the bonds between consumers and the important reference groups in their lives. These marketers are promoting products embellished with logos, colors, and images that people identify with these affiliations and that express their affinity for them when purchased. Some auto dealers, for example, attract loyal sports fans by promoting cars and vans in team colors, while Coca-Cola has distributed Coke in cans featuring the Carolina Panthers (football team) logo. Even the U.S. Postal Services practices a form of affinity marketing when it offers stamps depicting such legends as Elvis Presley, James Dean, and Marilyn Monroe.

Banks that offer credit cards have jumped on the bandwagon and are making it easy for customers to express their support and loyalty to reference groups by offering affinity credit cards. These cards not only proclaim the user's affiliation with a particular reference group but also provide a measure of support when the sponsoring group gets a cut of every transaction made with the card. Over 2,700 different affinity cards are available, and they are carried by over 26 million people. According to one estimate, about 6 percent of the 250 million MasterCards and Visa cards in the United States were issued as affinity cards. To date the American Bar Association and the American Medical Association have been the most successful markets for affinity credit cards.

Affinity marketing appeals revolve around consumers' loyalty to five types of affiliations:*

1. **Professionally based affinity,** which stems from membership in professional groups (for example, the American Marketing Association or the American Association of Advertising Agencies) that provide a means for status, networking, and career advancement.

2. **Socially based affinity,** which connects consumers to reference groups organized around common interests and hobbies (these groups can range from owners of Harley motorcycles to stamp collectors).

3. **Value-centered affinity,** which demonstrates both an identification with groups that share a common cause and a commitment to advancing the group's mission (these groups include public interest groups like GreenPeace and Mothers Against Drunk Driving, charitable organizations like the Heart Fund, and community service organizations like the Lions' Club).

4. **Demographics-based affinity,** which links consumers according to some demographic characteristics, such as age, education, or occupation (examples include the American Association of Retired Persons, alumni groups from various colleges and universities, labor unions, and trade associations).

5. **Marketer-generated affinity,** which occurs when marketers successfully create and promote brands (for example, Marlboro cigarettes), made-up characters (The Simpsons), or celebrities (Elvis) demonstrating values and characteristics that build customer loyalty.

Sources: Judith Waldrop, "Plastic Wars," *American Demographics* (Nov. 1988): 6; Elaine Santoro, "Catholic Charities Credit Card Unveiled," *Fund Raising Management* (April 1989): 10; Judith Graham, "Affinity Card Clutter: Number of Tie-Ins Raises Doubts About Continued Use," Special Report: Financial Services Marketing, *Advertising Age* (Nov. 14, 1988): S1; Bart Macchiette and Abhijit Roy, "Direct Marketing to the Credit Card Industry Utilizing the Affinity Concept," *Journal of Direct Marketing* (Spring 1991), 34–43.
*Based on a taxonomy proposed by Bart Macchiette and Abhijit Roy, "Affinity Marketing: What Is It and How Does It Work?" *The Journal of Services Marketing* (Summer 1992), 47–57.

razors that save people time and for services as diverse as photograph processing, take-out pizza, and car repair, where speed of delivery has become an important attribute.[25]

Time pressures can also influence consumers to use brand names or price as cues for quality when time prevents gathering more specific information about different brands. Mothers who have careers may buy their children's entire school wardrobe in one shopping trip to one store in the fall. If the same woman later chooses to put her career on hold in favor of becoming a full-time mother, she has time to engage in comparison shopping and to buy children's clothing at different stores, hoping to get the "best buys" possible. Time constraints can also mean that consumers make spur-of-the-moment decisions when purchasing gifts, household products and gadgets, and food. The time of day also influences food and beverage choices as well as decisions about products that require processing complex information. Few consumers are interested in choosing among brands of wine and beer in the morning, and many feel they are more alert and better able to pay attention to detailed information and instructions later in the day.

Exhibit 6.5
For marketers like McDonald's, both the time of day and the shopping environment are important influences on consumers. The restaurant chain earns 55% of its revenues during lunchtime, serving families with kids. In the morning, when people are in a hurry to get to work, business is brisk, but at dinnertime things are different. The company has tried luring the dinner crowd with test offerings such as pizza, pasta, and skinless roast, but these attempts failed: People have trouble viewing McDonald's as a dinner place, where they want a more relaxed environment. Although about 500 U.S. outlets continue to sell McPizza, for now the company has sent its plans for McDinners back to the test kitchen.

Mood

A person's mood or physiological condition at the time of purchase can also have a big impact on what products are bought and how brands are evaluated.[26] Sometimes these are antecedent states. Hungry shoppers who haven't eaten in a while, for example, spend more time and money in the grocery store, carefully selecting products and brands they see as more tempting and satisfying than others. On the other hand, when shoppers are stressed or tired, shopping becomes a chore to be done as quickly as possible by simply choosing needed products without regard for brand, quality, or price.

Two dimensions of mood are affected by the purchase situation itself. These dimensions are *pleasure* and *arousal,* and they determine whether a shopper will react positively or negatively to products. A person can enjoy or not enjoy a shopping experience. A person can also feel stimulated or not, with the arousal state taking the form of either excitement or distress. A specific mood is some combination of pleasure and arousal, depending on whether the context is positive or negative, and a shopper's mood state biases his or her judgment of goods and services in that direction. Simply put, consumers like things better when they are in a good mood.

The Shopping Environment

Despite all their efforts to "presell" consumers through advertising, marketers increasingly are recognizing the significant degree to which many purchases are influenced by the store environment. Department stores, restaurants, convenience stores, banks—all types of retailers—are increasingly interested in designing the best possible shopping environment. Exterior store design, store layout, store fixtures, colors, lighting, smells, music, and other elements of the store environment can and do affect shoppers' moods and purchasing behavior.

Many consumers become distressed in crowded, congested stores and so do not linger to browse through products they might be tempted to buy, while bright colors and splashy displays that create a feeling of excitement may spur them to buy something new and daring. Diners who listen to loud, fast music in restaurants tend to eat more, and patrons of bars tend to drink more when the music is soft and slow. Soft, pink lighting that is flattering and romantic can influence shoppers' choices in bathing suits, lingerie, jewelry, and perfume, while scents in the store can encourage shoppers to purchase products and brands associated with such nostalgic scents as the clean, comforting smell of baby powder, the homey aroma of apple pies baking, or the sweet, relaxing scent of orange blossoms in the sun.

The layout, fixtures, and displays in a store are particularly influential in supermarkets and grocery stores. About two out of every three supermarket purchases are decided in the aisles, and $\frac{1}{3}$ of unplanned buying has been attributed to consumers' recognition of new needs while in the store.[27] *Impulse buying* occurs when the person experiences a sudden urge to make a purchase that he or she cannot resist,[28] particularly when marketers have conveniently placed these so-called impulse items, such as candy and gum, near the checkout to "cash in" on these urges. Similarly, many supermarkets have installed wider aisles to encourage browsing for impulse items or unplanned purchases, with the widest aisles containing products with the highest profit margin. Items that are purchased regularly tend to be stacked high in narrower aisles to allow shopping carts to speed through.[29]

THE CONSUMER DECISION-MAKING PROCESS

A consumer purchase is a response to a problem: A person recognizes that he or she has a need and must make a decision about how to satisfy it. Because some purchase decisions are more important than others, the amount of effort we put into each differs. Sometimes the decision process is done almost automatically; we seem to make snap judgments based on very little information. At other times coming to a purchase decision begins to resemble a full-time job. A person may literally spend days or weeks thinking about the purchase and may even lie awake at night mulling it over.

Traditionally consumer researchers have viewed consumer decision making as a series of steps in which people calmly and carefully collect information about competing products, determine which products possess the characteristics or product attributes that are important to their needs, painstakingly weigh the pluses and minuses of each alternative, and arrive at a satisfactory decision. While this careful process does occur in some cases, it is not a realistic portrayal of many purchase decisions.[30] Consumers simply do not go through this elaborate sequence for every decision to buy a pack of gum or a can of cola or even a Big Mac. If they did, their entire lives would be spent making such choices, leaving them very little time to enjoy the things they eventually decide to buy.

The factor that determines the extent of problem solving engaged in by a consumer has been called **involvement,** which refers to the importance of the perceived consequences of the purchase to the person. As a rule we are more involved in the decision-making process for products that we feel are risky in some way. *Perceived risk* may be present if the product is expensive or is complex and hard to understand. Alternatively, perceived risk can be a factor when a product choice is visible to others and we run the risk of embarrassment if we make the wrong choice.

When perceived risk is fairly low, the decision process is characterized by *low involvement*—that is, the consumer is not heavily invested in the outcome of his or her decision because it is not seen as especially important or risky (for example, buying a pack of gum). In contrast, under conditions of *high involvement* (for example, buying a house, a car, or a personal computer), the consumer is far more likely to process carefully all of the available information and pay great attention to the details. The consequences of the purchase are important and risky, especially because a bad decision may result in significant financial losses, aggravation, or perhaps embarrassment.

Researchers now realize that consumers actually possess a set of strategies that allow them to tailor their degree of cognitive "effort" to the task at hand. They see consumer problem solving in terms of a continuum: The low-involvement end of this continuum is

involvement: the relative importance of the perceived consequences of the purchase to a consumer

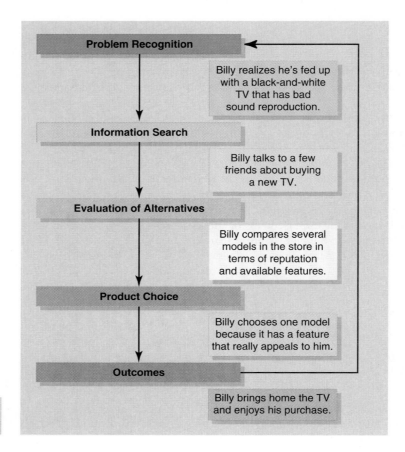

Figure 6.4
The Decision-Making Process

Problem Recognition

Billy realizes he's fed up with a black-and-white TV that has bad sound reproduction.

Information Search

Billy talks to a few friends about buying a new TV.

Evaluation of Alternatives

Billy compares several models in the store in terms of reputation and available features.

Product Choice

Billy chooses one model because it has a feature that really appeals to him.

Outcomes

Billy brings home the TV and enjoys his purchase.

anchored by *habitual decision making,* with *extended problem solving* at the other end, and with decisions characterized by *limited problem solving* falling somewhere in the middle. Decisions involving extended problem solving correspond most closely to the traditional decision-making perspective that involves a series of steps. These steps can be described as (1) problem recognition, (2) information search, (3) evaluation of alternatives, (4) product choice, and (5) postpurchase evaluation. In this section we'll look at each of these steps in the decision process, which is summarized in Figure 6.4.

PROBLEM RECOGNITION

Problem recognition occurs whenever the consumer sees a significant difference between his or her current state of affairs and some desired or ideal state. The consumer perceives there is a problem to be solved, which may be small or large, simple or complex. A woman whose ten-year-old Hyundai is in the repair shop more days than it is out has a problem, as does the man who becomes convinced for some reason that he would have more luck getting dates if he traded in his Hyundai for a new sports car. Although these two people have very different reasons for desiring a new car, each has now embarked on the road to making a purchase decision.

INFORMATION SEARCH

Once a problem has been recognized, consumers need adequate information to resolve it. *Information search* is the process in which the consumer checks his or her memory and/or surveys his or her environment to collect the data required to make a reasonable decision. In some cases we may be so expert about a product category (or at least believe we are) that information search is limited to checking what is stored in memory and no additional search is undertaken. Frequently, however, our own existing state of knowledge is not satisfactory to make an adequate decision, and we must go elsewhere for more information. The sources we consult for advice vary: They may be impersonal and mar-

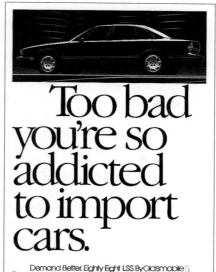

Exhibit 6.6
A product's *country of origin* is an important piece of information that many consumers use to simplify the decision-making process. Some American consumers automatically reject products made in other countries because of their belief that such purchases have a negative effect on the economy; others see country of origin as a measure of product quality (good or bad) that automatically draws them toward or away from products. The ad shown here targets American consumers who tend to use this decision shortcut when choosing certain products, like French wines and Japanese cars.

keter-dominated sources, such as retailers and catalogs; they may be friends and family members; or they may be unbiased third parties such as *Consumer Reports*.[31] The prospective car buyer will most likely pay more attention to all of those car commercials on TV and even venture into a few car showrooms at this stage.

EVALUATION OF ALTERNATIVES

Modern consumer society abounds with choices. In some cases there may literally be hundreds of different brands (as in toothpaste) or different variations of the same brand (as in shades of lipstick), each screaming for our attention.

Identifying Alternatives

How does a consumer decide what criteria are important and narrow down product alternatives to an acceptable number to choose one over the others? The answer varies, depending on the decision strategy used. A consumer engaged in extended problem solving may carefully evaluate several brands, while someone making a habitual decision may not consider any alternatives to his or her usual brand.

The alternatives actively considered during a consumer's choice process are his or her **evoked set,** which is composed of known products and brands already stored in the person's memory, plus those that are prominent in the marketplace. For example, a car shopper may have personal experience that makes the Honda Civic an attractive possibility, but may also identify such alternatives as the Chevrolet Geo and the Chrysler Neon based on marketing messages. A marketer who finds that his or her brand is not in the evoked set of many consumers in the target market has cause to worry. He or she has not done a good enough job of creating awareness for the brand or of convincing consumers in a target market that the product is for them.

> **evoked set:** the set of alternative brands actively considered during a consumer's choice process, which includes known products and brands already stored in the person's memory, plus those that are prominent in the marketplace

Choosing Among Alternatives

Once the relevant options from a product category have been assembled, a choice must be made among them. **Evaluative criteria** are the dimensions (or product attributes and characteristics) consumers use to judge the merits of competing options. The specific evaluative criteria—the *determinant attributes*—people use vary. One car buyer may choose a vehicle because of its comfort and roominess, while another bases the decision on style attributes. Marketers can play a role in educating consumers about which evaluative criteria should be used as determinant attributes. Research by Church & Dwight, for example, indicated that many consumers view the use of natural ingredients as a determinant attribute. The company then began to promote a toothpaste made from baking soda, which it already manufactured for its Arm & Hammer brand.[32]

> **evaluative criteria:** the dimensions (or product characteristics) used to judge the merits of competing options

PRODUCT CHOICE

Once the consumer has narrowed down the possible alternatives to just a few, he or she must actually obtain the product—that is, the intention to purchase a product must be turned into a purchase decision. Consumers often fall back on decision guidelines when making a choice. These are "rules" we have learned (correctly or not) that help us to simplify the process. They are called **heuristics,** or mental shortcuts that lead to a speedy decision.[33] One widely used heuristic is the belief that *price equals quality:* We assume that the higher-priced item must somehow be better, even though this is not always true.[34]

Another commonly used heuristic is *brand loyalty,* where people consistently choose the same product over a long period of time. As you can well imagine, the creation of brand loyalty is a prized goal for marketers. People form preferences for a favorite brand and then may literally never change their minds in the course of a lifetime, making it extremely difficult for rivals to persuade them to switch. In a study of the market leaders in thirty product categories by the Boston Consulting Group, twenty-seven of the brands that were number one in 1930 are still number one today! These brands include such long-standing favorites as Ivory Soap, Campbell's Soup, and Gold Medal Flour.[35]

POSTPURCHASE EVALUATION

Consumer satisfaction/dissatisfaction (CS/D) is determined by the overall feeling, or attitude, a person has about a product after it has been purchased.[36] As we have seen repeatedly in our focus on the "New Era" of relationship marketing, quality and value are key components of customer satisfaction. But CS/D is more than a reaction to the actual performance quality of a product. It is influenced by prior *expectations* of the level of quality that will be obtained for the price paid. Just as consumers use such cues as price, brand name, and country of origin to infer quality, they develop beliefs about product performance based on prior experience and information about the level of quality to be expected.[37]

As a general rule, satisfaction with a product is generated to the extent that it meets or exceeds these expectations. In other words, we assess product quality by comparing it to a *performance standard* that is created by a mixture of information from marketing communications, informal information sources such as friends and family, and our own personal experience with the category. This comparison process reminds us of a simple, yet often overlooked idea: Marketers should not promise the world unless they are prepared to deliver it! Marketers who back up their claims for quality keep customers coming back again and again.

The power of quality claims is most evident when they are not fulfilled, as when a product fails in some way. Here consumers' expectations are dashed, and dissatisfaction results. In these situations successful marketers take immediate steps to reassure customers and retain their loyalty. When a company confronts a problem truthfully, consumers often are willing to forgive and forget. Automobile manufacturers, for instance, have learned to voluntarily conduct a recall when they identify a problem with a model instead of waiting until consumer groups take action. Such was the case when Perrier found traces of benzene in the water it bottled. When the company appears to be dragging its heels or covering up, on the other hand, consumer resentment will grow.

HITTING A MOVING TARGET: TRENDS IN CONSUMER BEHAVIOR

Understanding consumer behavior is a constant challenge for marketers. Once they think they have consumers figured out, they change again. Honing in on consumer tastes and preferences is like aiming at a moving target. Some changes seemingly happen overnight, while others emerge more gradually. Either way, successful mar-

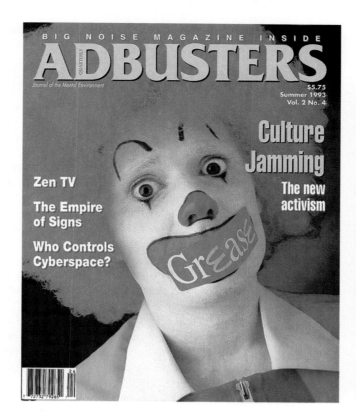

keters understand the importance of being ready to hit that target whichever way it moves.

Fads that are limited to specific consumer groups tend to quickly come and go, but *trends* that affect broad segments of society are more enduring. Trends that influence consumer behavior emerge slowly, and they are consistent with social, cultural, and economic phenomena in society and in the marketplace. The economic and social forces that prompted so many women to seek employment outside the home, for example, continue to change people's attitudes and beliefs about the roles of men and women and alter their expectations of themselves and their perceptions of how they should behave as family members and parents. In response, marketers have altered their strategies and are now targeting men for such products as dishwashing detergent and diapers and aiming promotions for cellular phones and investment services at women. Other marketers have found opportunities in vast new markets for convenience products, household services, and day care.

Shifts in demographic patterns, cultural values, and the way people select and obtain goods and services require constant monitoring if marketing strategies are to keep up with the changing trends in the consumer landscape. Changes in people's values and lifestyles, in their preferences for how leisure time is spent, and in their attitudes toward important social issues such as democracy, materialism, and religion can also yield important clues about their future behavior as consumers. Marketing's goal is to identify these trends early in the game to keep ahead of the competition.

Some of the following trends, which began to emerge in the early 1990s, will continue to influence consumer behavior and marketing strategies well into the mid and late 1990s.

■ As ideals regarding marriages, homosexuality, child rearing, and career choices evolve and uncertainty about the proper roles of men and women in our culture increases, consumers will continue to be influenced by how notions of masculinity and femininity are translated into product concepts and advertising practices by marketers.

■ An increasing emphasis on the value of time as a commodity is influencing consumers to look for new ways to acquire experiences and products in more convenient and accessible forms.

REAL PEOPLE, REAL CHOICES:

HOW IT WORKED OUT AT SEBAGO

Sebago-Moc chose option 2. The company eliminated the word "Moc" from its name and counted on retaining the identity, goodwill, and reputation for quality the "Sebago" part of the name had built up over the years. The company again set its sights on the yachting market and developed a new brand it called "Docksides." It improved on the original design of these boating shoes and developed an advertising campaign aimed directly at the consumer. Even though it had a fairly modest budget, Sebago was able to promote the new shoe in the small number of yachting magazines that were published in the 1970s. Its efforts to reach and satisfy the yachting market were so successful that Sebago Docksides ultimately became the official footwear of the U.S. Sailing Team.

Sebago has earned its reputation as the maker of America's world-class footwear. Today Docksides have a strong international following, and they are sold in some seventy countries around the world. For the yachting and sailing crowd, they are the preferred boating shoe, and for discriminating buyers in all social strata they continue to be the shoe of choice for many leisure activities and casual social events. The company has built its success by developing new footwear products, such as its newer lines of "Drysides" and "Campsides," that have exclusive appeal to narrowly defined market segments. By understanding how people in these segments prefer to spend their leisure time and by designing distinctive shoes suited to these preferences, Sebago gives its customers footwear that makes a statement about who they are and what they like to do. As Mr. Wellehan has discovered, when the shoe fits, consumers wear it . . . and Sebago hopes others will want to join the crowd and wear it too.

"On land or at sea,
Sebago Docksides are a perfect fit."

Whether racing in world-class competitions or just cruising on the weekends, international sailor Gary Jobson demands top performance. He knows that to be the best, you must have complete confidence in your equipment. That's why he wears Sebago Docksides.

SEBAGO
America's World-Class Footwear™

Sebago Docksides, official footwear of the 1992 US SAILING TEAM.

- Advances in technology are making more home-centered activities possible— whether for entertainment (for example, the proliferation of cable stations, home shopping networks, personal computers, video games, and online services) or for work (for example, the trend toward "telecommuting" as more people use their personal computers, the Internet, and faxes to establish offices at home).

- As the influence of diverse ethnic and racial groups continues to grow, consumers are becoming increasingly interested in experiencing foods and products of cultures other than their own.

- Concern for the environment, particularly health-related issues, the use of valuable resources to create products, and problems related to product disposal, will continue to influence many consumers.

- Changing priorities regarding exercise and nutrition, coupled with a premium placed on "antistress," continue to create a demand for services ranging from aromatherapy to personal trainers, as people try to cope with the numerous demands of their roles as parents and workers.

- The complex demands placed on us by modern society are also affecting the "dark side" of consumer behavior, contributing to such problems as addiction, theft, and vandalism.

- As the population continues to age, demand for goods and services tailored to meet the needs of "older" people whose lifestyles are slowing down will continue to increase and will influence the tastes and preferences of many components of American culture in the process.

- Disenchantment with the accumulation of status goods has led many consumers to focus on the acquisition of experiences, whether from travel, high-quality music reproduction, or virtual reality games.

- More and more consumers are searching for goods and services that give the best value for the money, no longer unwilling to buy no-name generic brands and more willing to shop at warehouse stores offering self-service and products by the case.

Chapter 6 Summary

Objective 1. Describe how individual (internal) factors influence consumer behavior.

A number of internal factors influence consumer behavior. Perception is the process by which consumers select, organize, and interpret the marketing stimuli to which they are exposed. To prevent sensory overload, consumers practice perceptual selectivity by choosing which stimuli they will pay attention to and which they will ignore. The principles of Gestalt psychology explain how people organize perceptual input, and each person's prior experiences or beliefs determine the meaning he or she will assign to a marketing stimulus. The study of semiotics tries to account for the ways in which people assign meaning to signs and symbols in marketing messages.

Motivation activates goal-directed behavior to satisfy some need. People are driven to purchase certain products to satisfy basic needs, utilitarian needs, or hedonic needs. Freud's theory of motivation and Maslow's hierarchy of needs provide insights into why consumers are motivated to buy certain types of products. Some consumers engage in compulsive consumption because they are compelled to shop, not because they are motivated to satisfy a need.

Learning is a relatively permanent change in behavior that results from acquired information or experience. Behavioral and cognitive learning theories provide different perspectives on how learning occurs and influences consumers. Behavioral theories hold that people will transfer learned experiences with one branded product to others in the brand's product line. The observational learning component of the cognitive perspective tells us that people learn by imitating or identifying themselves with others in some way and will be influenced to purchase and use similar products.

An attitude is a lasting evaluation of a person, object, or issue. Consumers seek products that are consistent with their attitudes, and marketers often attempt to change these attitudes by focusing on one of the three components—affect, behavior, and cognition—of the ABC model of attitudes. The unique psychological characteristics that consistently influence the way a person responds to situations make up his or her personality. Trait theory focuses on identifiable personality characteristics, such as innovativeness, self-confidence, and sociability, which influence many purchase decisions. Studies have linked these characteristics, as well as a person's self-concept, to buying behavior in which people seek products that enhance or minimize their personal attributes.

Objective 2. Understand the external factors that influence purchasing decisions and buying behavior.

Consumer purchasing decisions and buying behavior are influenced by many external factors that include personal, social, and situational issues. Such factors as age, income, family status, and chosen lifestyle are strongly related to the types of products people buy and the specific brands they want.

The social influences on consumer behavior stem from the culture of the society in which the consumer lives. Consumers' overall priorities for products and activities are significantly influenced by *cultural values* or the enduring beliefs of the culture. Membership in religious, ethnic, racial, and regional subcultures also has a potent impact on purchasing decisions as does the social class to which a person belongs. Consumers are often motivated to purchase products that identify them with the important reference groups in their lives, and they may follow the advice of influential opinion leaders whom they know or respect.

Several situational factors can affect consumers' purchasing behavior. Time (or the lack of it) influences which products and brands are selected, as does the consumer's mood at the time of purchase. Aspects of the physical shopping environment, such as store layout, store fixtures, colors, lighting, smells, and music, influence many product choices and can stimulate impulse buying.

Objective 3. Explain the prepurchase, purchase, and postpurchase steps in the consumer decision-making process.

The degree to which consumers commit themselves to the decision process is determined by the perceived risks associated with the purchase and the relative importance of the perceived consequences to the consumer. Consumers use several strategies to simplify the process, depending on their level of involvement with the purchase. These strategies range from habitual decision making for low-involvement purchases to extended problem-solving activities for high-involvement decisions. Problem recognition, where a consumer realizes that he or she has a need to be satisfied, is the first step in the decision process. Searching for information in memory and in the marketplace reduces the consumer's risk of making a wrong choice. The evoked set of alternatives — those that will be actively considered — are then judged according to evaluative criteria or determinant attributes of the product. Consumers may simplify the process by using mental shortcuts or heuristics such as brand loyalty. Following a purchase, consumer perceptions of product quality lead to satisfaction or dissatisfaction.

Objective 4. Describe the importance of monitoring trends in the marketplace, and identify some of the current trends that are influencing consumers in the 1990s.

A changing consumer landscape means that marketers must continually monitor trends that influence consumer buying behavior to adjust their strategies and stay ahead of the competition. The trends that emerge within a society are consistent with social, cultural, and economic phenomena in the marketplace. Recent trends that are of importance to marketers include changes in the age and ethnic make-up of the population, changing sex-role identities of men and women, an increasing emphasis on time, growing concerns about product disposal, and decreased emphasis on the accumulation of status goods.

Review Questions

Marketing Concepts: Testing Your Knowledge

1. What is perception? For marketers, what are the implications of each component of the perceptual process?
2. How are consumers motivated to buy certain products over others? How have Freudian theory and Maslow's hierarchy of needs contributed to an understanding of consumer behavior?
3. How do the components of the ABC model of attitudes account for consumer decision making and purchasing behavior?
4. What behavioral and cognitive learning theories are important to marketers? How do these perspectives differ when applied to consumer behavior?

5. What is personality? How is consumer behavior influenced by an individual's personality and self-concept?
6. Why is income such an important personal influence on purchasing behavior? How do age and the family life cycle influence consumers? What is the significance of lifestyles in understanding consumer behavior and purchasing decisions?
7. Why is an understanding of social influences such as culture and subculture important to marketers? What is the significance of social class to marketers? What are reference groups, and how do they influence consumers?
8. What are the situational influences on consumer purchasing behavior? How does each affect purchasing decisions?
9. How does the decision process differ under conditions of

high involvement and low involvement? What are the steps in the decision process, and what activities occur in each?

10. Why should marketers constantly monitor trends in the marketplace? What are some of the current trends that affect consumer purchasing behavior?

Marketing Concepts: Discussing Choices and Issues

1. Some consumer advocates have criticized marketing messages that link products to idealized people and situations and encourage the belief that the products will change consumers' lives in the portrayed direction. Tell whether you agree and explain why or why not.

2. This chapter raised the question, "Do we buy what we are?" What answer would you give based on your experience? Provide examples that support your opinion.

3. Do you think there is a connection between the personal influences on consumers (for example, age, income, family status, and lifestyle) and the extent to which they rely on the steps in the decision-making process? Explain your answer for each of the factors.

4. The ABC model of attitudes identifies three components that can be used by marketers to shape people's attitudes about products. Identify the product categories you think are most likely to be affected by each component, and discuss the merits of trying to change people's attitudes about them.

Marketing Practice: Applying What You've Learned

1. Assume you are the director of marketing for a chain of camping and outdoor gear stores. Your firm is expanding, and it is your job to develop general recommendations for store design. Prepare a summary of your recommendations for store design elements that you believe will provide the best shopping environment for your customers.

2. Assume you are an account executive with an advertising agency. Your current client is a firm that makes swimwear. You know that swimwear purchases are often influenced by a variety of social or "other people" factors. Write a report that lists these social influences, explain why each is important, and outline how you might use these influences in developing an advertising campaign.

3. This chapter indicated that consumers go through a series of steps (from problem recognition to postpurchase evaluation) as they make purchases. Write a detailed report describing what you would do in each of these steps when deciding to purchase one of the following products:

a. an automobile
b. a computer
c. a vacation trip

4. You work for a firm that markets frozen foods and are concerned about the effects of current consumer trends, including changing ethnic populations, changing roles of men and women, increased concern for time and for the environment, and decreased emphasis on owning status goods. Others in your firm do not understand or care about these changes. They believe that the firm should continue to do business just as it always has. Develop a role-playing exercise with a classmate to discuss these two different points of view for your class. Each of you should be sure to include

- ■ The importance of each of these trends to your firm.
- ■ Your suggestions for marketing strategies to address these trends.

Marketing Mini-Project: Learning by Doing

The purpose of this mini-project is to increase your understanding of the roles of personal, social, and situational factors in consumer behavior.

1. With several other members of your class, select one of the following product categories (or some other product of your choice):

- ■ perfume
- ■ automobiles
- ■ women's or men's shoes
- ■ fast food

2. Visit three different stores or locations where the product may be purchased. (Try to select three that are very different from each other.) Observe and make notes on all the elements of each retail environment.

3. At each of the three locations, observe people purchasing the product. Make notes about their characteristics (for example, age, race, gender, and so on), their social class, and their actions in the store in relation to the product.

4. Prepare a report for your class describing the situational variables and individual consumer differences you discovered and how they relate to the purchase of the product.

5. Present your findings to your class.

Key Terms

Endnotes

1. "Traffic Now Tuned to Boston's Tunnel Radio," *The New York Times* (Aug. 1, 1982); Alison Fahey, "In the Lobby," *Advertising Age* (Sept. 18, 1989); Kim Foltz, "Ads Popping Up All Over," *Newsweek* (Aug. 12, 1985): 50.

2. Kim Foltz, *The New York Times* (Oct. 23, 1989): D11.

3. Gail Tom, Teresa Barnett, William Lew, and Jodean Selmants, "Cueing the Consumer: The Role of Salient Cues in Consumer Perception," *Journal of Consumer Marketing* (1987): 23–27.

4. Steven Engelberg, "Advertising Pervades Poland, Turning Propaganda to Glitz," *The New York Times* (May 26, 1992): A1.

5. Abraham H. Maslow, *Motivation and Personality*, 2 ed. (New York: Harper & Row, 1970).

6. Thomas C. O'Guinn and Ronald J. Faber, "Compulsive Buying: A Phenomenological Explanation," *Journal of Consumer Research* (Sept. 1989): 144–157.

7. Quoted in Anastasia Toufexis, "365 Shopping Days Till Christmas," *Time* (Dec. 26, 1988): 82; see also Ronald J. Faber and Thomas C. O'Guinn, "Compulsive Consumption and Credit Abuse," *Journal of Consumer Policy* (1988): 109–21; Mary S. Butler, "Compulsive-Buying—It's No Joke," *Consumer's Digest* (Sept. 1986): 55.

8. Patrick Goldstein, "Shaquille O'Neal: He Jams. He Raps. He Acts. He Sells," *Rolling Stone* (Nov. 25, 1993): 52; Stuart Elliott, "The Records May Continue to Fall for Michael Jordan's Career as a Marketing All-Star," *The New York Times* (Oct. 7, 1993): D20.

9. Robert A. Baron and Donn Byrne, *Social Psychology: Understanding Human Interaction*, 5 ed. (Boston: Allyn & Bacon, 1987).

10. Linda L. Price and Nancy Ridgway, "Development of a Scale to Measure Innovativeness," In eds. Richard P. Bagozzi and Alice M. Tybout, *Advances in Consumer Research* (Ann Arbor, Mich.: Association for Consumer Research, 1983); Russell W. Belk, "Three Scales to Measure Constructs Related to Materialism: Reliability, Validity, and Relationships to Measures of Happiness," in ed. Thomas C. Kinnear, *Advances in Consumer Research* (Ann Arbor, Mich.: Association for Consumer Research, 1984); Gordon R. Foxall and Ronald E. Goldsmith, "Personality and Consumer Research: Another Look," *Journal of the Market Research Society* (1988): 111–125; Ronald E. Goldsmith and Charles F. Hofacker, "Measuring Consumer Innovativeness," *Journal of the Academy of Marketing Science* (1991): 209–221; Terence A. Shimp and Subhash Shanna, "Consumer Ethnocentrism: Construction and Validation of the CETSCALE," *Journal of Marketing Research* (Aug. 1987): 280–289.

11. Emily Yoffe, "You Are What You Buy," *Newsweek* (June 4, 1990): 59.

12. Jeffrey F. Durgee, "Self-Esteem Advertising." *Journal of Advertising* (1986): 21–27.

13. Al E. Birdwell, "A study of Influence of Image Congruence on Consumer Choice," *Journal of Business* (Jan. 1964): 76–88; Edward L. Grubb and Gregg Hupp, "Perception of Self, Generalized Stereotypes, and Brand Selection." *Journal of Marketing Research* (Feb. 1986): 58–63.

14. Ira J. Dolich, "Congruence Relationship Between Self-Image and Product Brands," *Journal of Marketing Research* (Feb. 1969): 80–84; Danny N. Belleger, Earle Steinberg, and Wilbur W. Stanton, "The Congruence of Store Image and Self-Image as it Relates to Store Loyalty," *Journal of Retailing* (1976): 17–32; Ronald J. Dornoff and Ronald L. Tatham, "Congruence Between Personal Image and Store Image," *Journal of Marketing Research Society* (1972): 45–52.

15. J.F. Allsopp, "The Distribution of On-License Beer and Cider Consumption and Its Personality Determinants Among Young Men," *European Journal of Marketing* (1986): 44–62; Gordon Foxall and Ronald E. Goldsmith, "Personality and Consumer Research: Another Look," *Journal of the Market Research Society* (1988): 111–125.

16. Benjamin D. Zablocki and Rosabeth Moss Kanter, "The Differentiation of Life-Styles," *Annual Review of Sociology* (1976): 269–297.

17. Chester A. Swenson, "How to Sell to a Segmented Market," *Journal of Business Strategy* (Jan.–Feb. 1988): 18.

18. Richard W. Pollay, "Measuring the Cultural Values Manifest in Advertising," *Current Issues and Research in Advertising* (1983): 71–92.

19. Richard P. Coleman, "The Continuing Significance of Social Class to Marketing," *Journal of Consumer Research* (Dec. 1983): 265–280.

20. J. Michael Munson and W. Austin Spivey, "Product and Brand-User Stereotypes Among Social Classes: Implications for Advertising Strategy," *Journal of Advertising Research* (Aug. 1981): 37–45.

21. Stuart U. Rich and Subhash C. Jain, "Social Class and Life Cycle as Predictors of Shopping Behavior," *Journal of Marketing Research* (Feb. 1968): 41–49.

22. Jeffrey F. Durgee, "How Consumer Sub-Cultures Code Reality: A Look at Some Code Types," in ed. Richard J. Lutz, *Advances in Consumer Research* (Provo, Utah: Association for Consumer Research, 1986).

23. Everett M. Rogers, *Diffusion of Innovations*, 3 ed. (New York: Free Press, 1983).

24. John P. Robinson, "Time Squeeze," *Advertising Age* (Feb. 1990): 30–33.

25. Leonard L. Berry, "Market to the Perception," *American Demographics* (Feb. 1990): 32.

26. Laurette Dube and Bernd H. Schmitt, "The Processing of Emotional and Cognitive Aspects of Product Usage in Satisfaction Judgments," in eds. Rebecca H. Holman and Michael R. Solomon, *Advances in Consumer Research* (Provo, Utah: Association for Consumer Research, 1991); Lalita A. Manrai and Meryl P. Gardner, "The Influence of Affect on Attributions for Product Failure," in eds. Rebecca H. Holman and Michael R. Solomon, *Advances in Consumer Research* (Provo, Utah: Association for Consumer Research, 1991).

27. Donald R. Lichtenstein, Richard G. Netemeyer, and Scot Burton, "Using a Theoretical Perspective to Examine the Psychological Construct of Coupon Proneness," in eds. Rebecca H. Holman and Michael R. Solomon, *Advances in Consumer Research* (Provo, Utah: Association for Consumer Research, 1991); Marianne Meyer, "Attention Shoppers!" *Marketing and Media Decisions* (May 1988): 67.

28. Francis Piron, "Defining Impulse Purchasing," in eds. Rebecca H. Holman and Michael R. Solomon, *Advances in Consumer Research* (Provo, Utah: Assocation for Consumer Research, 1991); Dennis W. Rook, "The Buying Impulse," *Journal of Consumer Research* (Sept. 1987): 189–199.

29. Michael Wahl, "Eye POPping Persuasion," *Marketing Insights* (June 1989): 130.

30. Richard W. Olshavsky and Donald H. Granbois, "Consumer Decision Making—Fact or Fiction," *Journal of Consumer Research* (Sept. 1979): 93–100.

31. H. Beales, M.B. Jagis, S.C. Salop, and R. Staelin, "Consumer Search and Public Policy," *Journal of Consumer Research* (June 1981): 11–22.

32. Jack Trout, "Marketing in Tough Times," *Boardroom Reports* (Oct. 1992): 8.

33. Wayne D. Hoyer, "An Examination of Consumer Decision Making for a Common Repeat Purchase Product," *Journal of Consumer Research* (Dec. 1984): 822–829; Calvin P. Duncan, "Consumer Market Beliefs: A Review of the Literature and an Agenda for Future Research." in eds. Marvin E. Goldberg, Gerald Goro, and Richard W. Pollay, *Advances in Consumer Research* (Provo, Utah: Association for Consumer Research, 1990).

34. Robert A. Baron, *Psychology: The Essential Science* (Boston: Allyn & Bacon, 1989); Valerie S. Folkes, "The Availability Heuristic and Perceived Risk," *Journal of Consumer Research* (June 1989): 13–23; Daniel Kahneman and Amos Tversky, "Prospect Theory: An Analysis of Decision Under Risk," *Econometrica* (1979): 263–291.

35. Richard W. Stevenson, "The Brands With Billion-Dollar Names," *The New York Times* (Oct. 28, 1988): A1.

36. Rama Jayanti and Anita Jackson, "Service Satisfaction: Investigation of Three Models," in eds. Rebecca H. Holman and Michael R. Solomon, *Advances in Consumer Research* (Provo, Utah: Association for Consumer Research 1991); David K. Tse, Franco M. Nicosia, and Peter C. Wilton, "Consumer Satisfaction as a Process," *Psychology & Marketing* (Fall 1990): 177–193.

37. For research on how quality is inferred, see Anna Kirmani and Peter Wright, "Money Talks: Perceived Advertising Expense and Expected Product Quality," *Journal of Consumer Research* (Dec. 1989): 344–353; Donald R. Lichtenstein and Scot Burton, "The Relationship Between Perceived and Objective Price-Quality," *Journal of Marketing Research* (Nov. 1989): 429–443; Akshay R. Rao and Kent B. Monroe, "The Effect of Price, Brand Name, and Store Name on Buyers' Perceptions of Product Quality: An Integrative Review," *Journal of Marketing Research* (Aug. 1989): 351–357.

Marketing in Action: Real People at Nike Corporation

Successful athletic shoe companies like Nike are moving out of the basketball court and onto the rocks. In the early 1990s the market for rugged outdoor footwear, apparel, and equipment was showing signs of becoming the most promising area for growth in the $34.3 billion American sporting goods industry, while sales for traditional sports apparel and footwear were plummeting. Nike Corp., which is headquartered in Beaverton, Oregon, experienced as much as a 25 percent drop in sales of its heavily promoted basketball shoes like the Air Jordan.

Unwilling to sit idly by and watch business decline, Nike's marketing team committed themselves to finding a way to retain the advantage the company had gained as a market leader in athletic footwear. What they found were changing trends in consumer interests, activities, and lifestyles. Those unconvinced only needed to look at the projected growth of outdoor activities between 1989 and 2000, with backpacking expected to increase by 34 percent; hiking, 31 percent; bicycling, 25 percent; cross-country skiing, 17 percent; camping, 16 percent; canoeing and kayaking, 13 percent; and rafting, 11 percent. A study of leisure activities by the Sporting Goods Manufacturers Association found a 25 percent growth in the number of people who hiked and backpacked more than twenty-five days a year.

They also discovered that the aging of the population was the primary factor influencing these trends and other changes in consumer preferences. The baby boomers, who in their twenties had been interested in jogging, running, aerobics, tennis, and "shooting a few hoops," were getting older and had growing families. By the early 1990s the first wave of boomers was switching from individual sports to things that a family could do together, and many more were expected to follow in the coming decade. In addition, the young professionals who were just starting into business in the early 1990s had grown up wearing basketball and running shoes. This group was not willing to give up comfort and was demanding shoe styles that provided the comfort of outdoor shoes in styles that were acceptable for business. The growing numbers of retirees and senior citizens, who had never "adapted" to athletic footwear, were looking for a similar shoe for shopping and leisure activities.

With this understanding of the consumer market, Nike entered the race for its share of the "rough and ready" outdoor recreation market, introducing new styles and changing its promotional strategies. Nike increased its offering of outdoor shoes from a couple dozen styles to seventy-eight different offerings. For consumers interested in a lower-cost Nike, it had a new four-wheel-drive sneaker line, "Air Massa," which was designed as an all-purpose outdoor shoe suited for a variety of sports and leisure activities. For customers willing to pay more, Nike's new offerings included the "Air Krakatoa," a fully waterproof $140 hiking boot with a sole made partially of recycled running shoes. Nike also added outdoor styles to its Fit line of sports apparel.

Nike's promotional strategies for its athletic shoes have centered around million-dollar television campaigns aired during back-to-school periods and featuring sports superstars. But Nike's marketers changed all that for its new outdoor product lines. The products are selectively advertised in magazines like *Backpacker* and *Outside* as well as *Rolling Stone* and *Men's Journal*. The use of sports superstars, which had been so much a part of athletic shoe advertising for decades, was not a part of the new advertising plans.

These tactics scored big gains for Nike. As chairman and chief executive Philip Knight said in 1994, "This category was nowhere for us three or four years ago; this year it will be $200 million in sales . . . and $500 million within three to four years. You will see us be very aggressive in the outdoor category."

Source: Jerry Schwartz, "In Shoes, the Great Outdoors Beckons," *The New York Times* (Feb. 13, 1994): F6.

Things to Talk About

1. How has the sporting goods industry changed during the past few years?
2. What trends are affecting the athletic footwear market?
3. What factors are influencing the changes in consumer preferences?
4. How has Nike responded to the changes in its market to remain competitive?
5. What secrets to success has Nike discovered?

Marketing in Action: Real Choices at Playboy Enterprises, Inc.

Playboy Enterprises, Inc., is one of the best-known companies in America. The organization had its beginnings in the 1950s when founder Hugh Hefner (who still controls 70 percent of the company's common stock) introduced an innovative magazine, produced on a shoestring budget. The shock waves reverberating around this humble issue—which featured Marilyn Monroe on the cover and, you guessed it, in the centerfold—hurtled *Playboy* magazine into orbits of success, bunny and all. The controversy over the morality of the magazine, the ensuing notoriety, and the changing attitudes of the 1960s and 1970s all helped turn the company into an entertainment giant with revenues in excess of $200 million annually.

In the 1960s and 1970s circulation of *Playboy* magazine surged. At the same time one of the hottest status symbol products in New York or Atlanta or in Dallas was a key to one of the local Playboy Clubs, where drinks and meals were served to members by scantily clad Playboy "bunnies." At Christmastime department stores sold key chains and T-shirts and even men's boxer shorts adorned with the sophisticated Playboy bunny logo. But things are changing again in the 1990s. People are getting older, and the clubs have lost their intrigue. In fact the cultural climate has lessened the desire to identify with an organization that some still consider to be morally offensive and that others see to be degrading to women.

Similarly, the maturing market for men's magazines is less interested in centerfolds and more interested in reading articles about issues important to men in the 1990s. This shift has halted the growth of *Playboy* magazine, which kept the enterprise running as interest in the clubs declined, and

reduced the overall profits reported by the company in 1994. Some experts, pointing to the success of new magazines like *Men's Health,* have wondered if Playboy missed its window of opportunity when it abandoned plans to buy and start new men's magazines in the early 1990s.

Despite concerns that any new ventures associated with the Playboy bunny might be met with the same lukewarm reception the magazine has had in recent years, Playboy has opted to shift its focus to entertainment. In the United States it can choose to focus on producing home videos and promoting Playboy-branded videos of popular vintage movies. The company could also decide to pursue its experiments in producing Playboy interviews on CD-ROM and building a home page on the Web to offset the magazine losses and to carve out a market niche for the future. Success, though, depends a lot on the bunny—and how people perceive her.

Source: Adapted from Keith J. Kelly, "Playboy's Fortunes Tied to the Bunny," *Advertising Age* (Oct. 24, 1994).

Things to Think About

1. What are the problems facing Playboy Enterprises, Inc.?

2. What factors are causing the problems?

3. What are the alternatives?

4. What are your recommendations for solving the problems?

5. What are some ways to implement your recommendations?

7

Why Organizations Buy: Business-to-Business Markets

When you have completed your study of this chapter, you should be able to:

1. Describe the general characteristics of business-to-business markets and business buying practices.

2. Tell how business and organizational markets are classified.

3. Explain the elements that determine business buying behavior.

4. Understand the stages in the business buying decision process.

REAL PEOPLE, REAL CHOICES:

MEET BOB WILHELM, A DECISION MAKER AT UNITOG CO.

Bob Wilhelm is vice president and national sales manager of Unitog, one of America's largest industrial uniform companies. The company, which has been in business since 1932, designs, manufactures, and sells, rents, or leases customized uniforms for both large corporate customers and small businesses. Mr. Wilhelm's job is to persuade organizations that the appearance of their employees is as much a part of their corporate image as their advertising, packaging, and facilities. Based in Kansas City, Unitog provides the "people packages" for such organizations as United Airlines, Coca-Cola, Pepsi, Amoco, and the U.S. Postal Service. Mr. Wilhelm is responsible for Unitog's direct marketing, advertising, and sales functions. His goal is to develop new strategies to keep Unitog growing, and one way to do this is by targeting industries that do not typically put their employees in uniforms and convincing these businesses that a uniform program can help to improve their image, sales, and profits.

Bob Wilhelm graduated from Emporia State University with a B.S. in business administration. He began his career with JCPenney in its New York City corporate headquarters as an assistant buyer for the company's retail store and catalog divisions. Wilhelm has been with Unitog for thirteen years, moving from sales representative to his current position as vice president and general manager of Unitog's Brookfield Division. He helped develop new markets, rolled out Unitog's first catalog as the firm got into direct marketing, and introduced "World-Class Service" to the company's mail-order market by providing same-day shipment of orders with priority handling at no extra cost for industrial customers.

BUYING AND SELLING WHEN THE STAKES ARE HIGH

When most people think of marketing, they conjure up images of glitzy ads and commercials for glamorous fashions or the ultimate athletic shoe. However, many marketers know that the real action is more likely to be found in lead pipe, office supplies, safety shoes, meat lockers, or industrial uniforms. These marketers don't try to sell *anything* to consumers. They're doing big business with other companies who buy the goods and services that ultimately wind up in the hands of individual consumers, and by that time they may indeed be more glamorous than a bale of cotton.

An individual consumer may decide to buy two or three T-shirts at one time, each emblazoned with a different design. Fortune 500 companies like Exxon, Pepsi-Cola, and Texaco think in terms of hundreds, even thousands, of uniforms embroidered with their corporate logos to be worn by employees and to be purchased with a single order. Companies like Unitog sell goods and services that satisfy the needs of these customers, but at the same time Unitog has to decide what it needs to buy from other companies to produce the goods and services customers want.

When making purchases, organizations and businesses have many decisions to make, much like a consumer who decides to buy a T-shirt. To begin with, the consumer decides that he or she needs to buy a T-shirt, and this seemingly simple decision sets off a chain reaction of many other decisions: What color? What size? What style? Gaudy or conservative? Long sleeves or short? 100 percent cotton or not? Light weight? Heavy weight? How many? How much? And if the consumer is conscientious, he or she might also shop around for the "best deal," comparing the quality, selections, and prices in different stores. Clearly, making a purchase is not as simple as it seems.

A business buyer makes all of these same kinds of decisions—with an important difference. The purchase may be worth millions of dollars, and both the buyer and seller have a lot at stake. In this chapter we'll look at the big picture of the business marketplace and some of the reasons why the fortunes of buyers and sellers can hang in the balance of a single transaction. Then we'll see how businesses and organizations are categorized and take a look at the products and strategies used by the buyers and sellers in each classification. In the final sections of the chapter we examine the influences on business buying behavior and the purchasing decision process that determines just how much is at stake when a business-to-business transaction is made.

An overview of business and organizational markets

Not all marketing efforts are aimed at satisfying individual consumers' needs and wants. Firms like Unitog exist solely to satisfy the needs of other businesses, while firms like AT&T and Xerox provide goods and services for both consumers and businesses. And the majority of companies—from Betty Crocker to Yamaha—that produce consumer goods don't provide them directly to consumers; they sell them to other firms that serve the consumer market. These firms direct their marketing efforts toward **business and organizational customers** that buy goods and services for some purpose other than for personal consumption. These customers may be manufacturing firms, hospitals and universities, government agencies, or wholesalers and retailers.

Business customers create vast opportunities for marketers and account for far more transactions in the marketplace than consumer purchases. For example, a consumer may browse through several racks of jeans and ultimately purchase a single pair, but the store at which the consumer shops has purchased many pairs of jeans in different sizes, styles, and brands from a wholesaler, who, in turn, has purchased far more pairs from different manufacturers. Each of these manufacturers purchases fabrics, zippers, buttons, and thread from other manufacturers, who purchase the materials needed to make their goods. In addition, all of the firms in this chain need to procure facilities, equipment, utilities, labor, computer systems, office supplies, packing and shipping materials, and countless other goods and services. Thus a single consumer purchase, whether for a pair of jeans or a college education, is the culmination of a series of buying and selling activities among many organizations.

Business-to-business marketing refers to the marketing activities that facilitate sales of goods and services that business and organizational customers need to produce other goods and services for resale and to support their operations. As in consumer markets, business marketers try to develop products that satisfy customers' needs, to deliver product benefits customers want, and to convince customers that they can do so better than the competition. In theory, the same basic marketing principles hold in both consumer and business markets; in practice, significant differences make the process more complex.[1]

- Purchase decisions made by organizations frequently involve many people, including those who do the actual buying, those who directly or indirectly influence this decision, and the employees who will actually use the good or service.

- Organizational and industrial products often are bought according to precise, technical specifications, requiring rational criteria and knowledge about the product category.

- The decision process for some business products is lengthy and may involve price negotiations and complex financial arrangements.

business and organizational customers: business firms and other organizations that buy goods and services for some purpose other than for personal consumption

business-to-business marketing: marketing activities that facilitate transactions involving goods and services that business and organizational customers need to produce other goods and services for resale and to support their operations

- Impulse buying is rare (organizational buyers do not suddenly get an "urge to splurge" on paper clips). Because buyers are professionals, their decisions are based on past experience and a careful weighing of alternatives.
- Many products are purchased directly from the producer, who may even develop goods and services specifically to meet the customer's needs. In many cases both parties depend on each other to stay in business.
- Organizational purchase decisions are frequently characterized by high risk. A buyer's career may be riding on his or her decisions about the choice of products and suppliers and the allocation of company funds.

In this section we'll look at some of the characteristics that distinguish the business market from the consumer market and that contribute to the complexity of the business-to-business marketing process. We'll also see how business demand is created and examine some of the key factors that influence the business buying process.

CHARACTERISTICS THAT MAKE A DIFFERENCE

Some of the characteristics of the business market that complicate the marketing process are what make these markets so attractive in the first place. The size of the market, the volume of purchases, and the concentration of potential customers in specific geographic regions can help or hinder business marketers. The types of products purchased by business and organizational customers also create big differences in market attractiveness compared to consumer markets and often account for many of the differences in marketing practice.

Market Size

Compared to consumers, organizational customers are few and far between. In the United States there are about 100 million consumer households, but under a half million businesses and organizations. Thus business marketers have a narrow customer base and a *limited number of buyers.* Kodak's business division that markets X-ray film to hospitals, HMOs, and other medical groups, for example, has an extremely limited number of buyers compared to its consumer film division, because the millions of consumers who own cameras are potential buyers of Kodachrome film.

Typically a few hundred organizational customers account for more than half of a supplier's sales volume, which gives the customers a fairly high degree of influence over the supplier. It can also mean that a supplier's fortunes depend on maintaining good relationships with each of its customers. On a more positive note, having a limited number of customers increases the marketer's chances of identifying and satisfying the particular needs of each. Like consumers, satisfied organizational customers are loyal customers that keep on coming back, and repeat orders from a few customers are often the mainstay of business marketers.

Size of Purchases

When measured in dollars, the market for business and organizational goods and services is four times larger than the consumer market, and winning or losing a single order can mean the difference between success and failure for a business-to-business marketer. Typically organizational customers purchase items in larger quantities than consumers do, and the dollar volume generated by each customer can be substantial. A company that supplies uniforms to other businesses, for example, buys hundreds of large drums of laundry detergent each year in contrast to a consumer household that buys a box of detergent every few weeks, while purchases of products like X-ray film by one or two large organizations can generate more revenue for a company than hundreds of consumer sales of film for 35-millimeter cameras.

Business buyers also purchase many single items that dwarf individual consumer expenditures, including home mortgage payments and college tuition costs! Organizations purchase many products, such as a highly sophisticated piece of manufacturing equipment or computer-based marketing information systems, that can cost a million dollars or more. Outlays for insurance, travel, and specialized services can also be extraordinary.

Exhibit 7.1
Not all business customers are super-size giants. In the United States there are close to 8 million businesses with less than ten employees and a growing trend toward one-person-owned and -operated enterprises, particularly in service industries. Many of these entrepreneurs – from consultants to locksmiths – rent small offices or work at home. While individual spending by these tiny "firms" is often insignificant, more and more big companies like Xerox are looking at the total numbers and targeting the business buyer who works alone.

Geographic Concentration

Business markets often are characterized by *geographic concentration* — that is, many organizations are located in specific geographic areas, where there is easy access to raw materials, labor, transportation, and technology. For example, the American steel industry is centered in the Pennsylvania area because of the availability of coal and iron ore to be fed into blast furnaces, while many manufacturing firms have located in midwestern states to take advantage of river transportation and electric power. Universities, hospitals, and research centers tend to cluster in cities along the eastern seaboard because of the high concentrations of skilled labor and potential customers.

In consumer marketing, firms look at geographic regions to identify differences in lifestyles and preferences that are crucial to marketing strategy. Business marketers look at the concentration of businesses and other organizations in different geographic areas to determine the market potential for their particular products and to determine the best locations for sales offices and distribution centers. They also choose to locate headquarters and operations in areas where existing resources such as a skilled labor market or raw materials allow them to function competitively, which, of course, is likely to be where similar companies are located.

Types of Products

In business-to-business marketing, products are classified in terms of how they are used by customers. And just to muddy the waters a bit, a single product can be classified in more than one way depending on how different customers will use it. For example, a battery may be used to power a forklift that moves merchandise around in a wholesaler's warehouse, it may be offered for sale to shoppers at Kmart, or it may become part of a new Mustang convertible produced by the Ford Motor Company.

- *Equipment* refers to the items used by an organization in its daily operations. Heavy equipment, sometimes called *installations* or *capital equipment,* includes items such as buildings and robotics used to assemble automobiles. Installations usually are high-dollar items and are used for a number of years. Light or *accessory equipment* used by organizational customers includes computers, photocopy machines, and water fountains. Accessory equipment is usually movable, costs less, and has a shorter life span than capital equipment.

- *Maintenance, repair, and operating (MRO) products* are manufactured goods that are used up or consumed by a business customer in a relatively short time and that do not become a part of other goods and services. Maintenance products include light bulbs, mops, and cleaning supplies. Repair products are such items as nuts, bolts, washers, and small tools. Operating supplies include computer paper and oil to keep machinery running smoothly.

- *Specialized services,* which are acquired from outside suppliers, are essential to the operation of an organization but are not part of the production of a product. Services may be *technical* such as equipment repair or *nontechnical* such as market research and legal services.

- *Raw materials* are products of the fishing, lumber, agricultural, and mining industries that are purchased by organizational customers to process in some way for use in finished products. Whether these raw materials begin as logs, soybeans, or iron ore, they are changed in some way from their original state and sold to others on the journey toward a finished product.

- *Processed materials,* which are the raw materials that have been changed (processed) from their original state, are purchased by organizations to manufacture or create usable products. These materials can be made into a finished product, such as a cement block, or a finished part that will be incorporated into some larger product, such as a pane of glass that will be used in a window or door. Other examples of processed materials are rolled aluminum for cans, flour for bread and other baked goods, and wood pulp for paper.

- *Component parts* are manufactured products or subassemblies of finished items that are purchased for inclusion in manufactured products. Examples include batteries and tires for cars and trucks, silicon chips for computers, and zippers for garments. Some organizational customers need component parts that are *standardized;* they conform to industry standards so that all buyers can use the same items. Companies that play a role in creating these standards often find themselves in a dominant position in an industry, as is the case with Microsoft, which pioneered the DOS operating system for personal computers. In other situations firms require *custom components* that are designed for one buyer's needs such as automobile transmissions and engines intended to be placed into a Ford Mustang, Jeep Cherokee, or Mack truck.

DIFFERENCES IN DEMAND IN BUSINESS MARKETS

When business marketers talk about *demand* they are referring to the amount of a firm's product that is purchased during a specified period of time given a specific price. Demand in business markets differs from consumer demand. Consumer demand can be thought of as a direct connection between a need and the satisfaction of that need. However, the nature of the beast changes in business markets, because business demand is *indirect.* Business-to-business customers don't purchase goods and services to satisfy their own needs. Retailers buy goods to resell in response to consumer demand, while other organizations and firms buy products that are used to produce still more goods and services demanded by consumer markets.

Derived Demand

Business-to-business demand is known as **derived demand** because it is derived from demand for other goods or services that organizations need to respond to consumer demand. Consider a very relevant example: Demand for lumber products is partially derived

derived demand: demand for business or organizational products derived from demand for consumer goods or services

from demand for paper that in turn is derived from demand for newspapers, magazines, catalogs, and textbooks. The demand for textbooks, in turn, is derived from the demand for education. Because of this relationship, the fortunes of the lumber industry are partly tied to college enrollments!

As a result of derived demand, the fortunes of one company may be closely tied to another company in a completely different line of business, and both organizations are affected by environmental factors, such as the health of the economy or the amount of government activity in the marketplace. For example, Boeing, a major aircraft manufacturer, relies on over 4,000 suppliers when building its planes, and if Boeing fails to procure enough contracts from either private airlines or the armed forces to keep its assembly lines moving, the "ripple effect" diminishes the demand for the goods and services of these supplier companies.[2]

Inelastic Demand

Because business demand is derived from the needs for still other goods and services, it is also *inelastic.* That is, business demand is generally not drastically affected by price increases or decreases, at least in the short run. Because businesses and organizations purchase many different items, most of these individual items contribute only a small amount to the firm's finished product. If the price of a single item goes up, business buyers simply pass the price increase on to their customers, or they search for another supplier who can deliver the part more reasonably. For example, if the price of tires or batteries goes up, General Motors will continue to buy enough to meet its customers' demands for automobiles, but will price the autos higher to cover the increased costs it must bear.

When large portions of a final product are dependent on a single material or component part, however, demand may become elastic. For example, steel is a large component of automobiles so that an increase in the price of steel can cause the price of automobiles to increase so greatly that consumer demand drops, thus decreasing the demand for steel.

Fluctuating Demand

Changes in consumer demand often result in even larger increases or decreases in business demand. The *acceleration principle* (also called the *multiplier effect*) explains how a small percentage change in consumer demand can create a large percentage change in total industrial or business demand. For example, even a small percentage (say, 5 percent) increase in demand for air travel may dramatically increase the demand for airplanes, perhaps doubling the number of planes purchased in a single year by large carriers like United Airlines.

Demand for consumer products and derived business demand are linked to the overall economy and fluctuate in similar up-and-down cycles. Economic downturns and decreased consumer demand normally lower derived business demand, which may cause a firm to postpone purchasing equipment or upgrading facilities. In recent years, for example, declining enrollments have caused many universities, perhaps including your own, to adopt a policy of "deferred maintenance" where they are putting off much-needed repairs to their physical plant in the interest of cost cutting.

Shortages and prices also create fluctuations in business demand. Organizational buyers increase demand when they anticipate shortages or price increases and stock up on a product before these market changes occur, or when they take advantage of quantity discounts by placing large orders with suppliers. In cases like these, demand peaks, then flattens until in-stock supplies are nearly depleted. The life expectancy of the product also creates fluctuating demand. Some products, such as installations, tend to be purchased by a customer every ten or twenty years.

Joint Demand

Joint demand occurs when two or more goods are used together to manufacture a product. For example, the manufacturer of automobiles requires tires, batteries, and spark plugs. If the supply of one of these dries up, General Motors will be unable to manufacture as many automobiles and will not buy as many of the other items. Therefore, B. F. Goodrich's sales of tires to General Motors are partly dependent on the availability of batteries and spark plugs and hundreds of other items over which it has no control.

THE BUYING PROCESS

In large firms goods and services are bought by a purchasing department staffed with many trained buyers; in small firms the "department" may consist of a single buyer. In either case the person who purchases a product may never use it. In fact, the buyer doesn't even decide what products need to be purchased. The business buyer's job is to see that the right quality product is delivered at the right time for the right price to the right people in the organization. A big part of this responsibility is determining the best source for obtaining the product and choosing the buying practices and methods to get the best results.

Sourcing: Deciding Whether to Put All Your Eggs in One Basket

One of the most important functions of an organizational or business buyer is locating the best sources of materials, goods, services, and needed supplies. Sourcing decisions include both how many and which suppliers, or *vendors,* can best serve the needs of the organizations.

single sourcing: the business practice of buying a particular product from only one supplier

Single sourcing, or sole sourcing, is the practice of buying a particular product from only one supplier. Single sourcing, which is typically characterized by high levels of interaction between buyer and seller, is particularly important when a firm needs frequent deliveries or specialized products. On the downside, reliance on a single source means that the firm is at the mercy of the chosen supplier to deliver the needed goods or services without interruption. **Multiple sourcing** refers to the more common practice of buying a particular product from several different suppliers. With multiple sourcing suppliers are more likely to remain price competitive. And if one supplier has problems with delivery, the firm has others to fall back on.

multiple sourcing: the business practice of buying a particular product from several different suppliers

Many firms have decided that limiting themselves to a single supplier or to only a few is a real advantage. While at first glance this policy seems risky, it makes a lot of sense in many cases. A firm that buys from a single supplier becomes a very large customer, with a lot of clout when it comes to negotiating prices and contract terms. And having fewer suppliers also lowers administrative costs because the firm has fewer invoices to pay, fewer purchase orders to put into the system, and fewer salespeople to see. In addition, when a firm makes an exclusive commitment to a single supplier, the supplying firm, in turn, is better able to commit more of its resources to product development and service improvement. These commitments lead to close relationships between buyer and seller and create a win-win situation for both.

A firm's commitment to total quality can have a major impact on the number of suppliers it relies on. Quality-focused firms that promise their customers quality beyond expectations seek out materials and parts suppliers who share a similar commitment. A single supplier that delivers quality helps the firm maintain its own quality standards and reduces the costs of frequent inspections to detect inferior or defective items. In 1981, when Xerox began implementing its quality-focused program, the company was purchasing parts for its Marathon high speed copier from more than 2,000 suppliers. Five years later Xerox was down to 350 suppliers for the very same machine.[3] Today it relies on fewer than fifty.[4]

systems buying: a business buying practice in which organizations simplify the decision process by selecting a single supplier to provide everything needed for a complete production or operations system

An outgrowth of single sourcing is a practice called **systems buying,** which reduces the process of making a major purchase to a single decision. The firm selects one supplier to provide a complete package that includes everything needed to produce a particular good or to carry out a particular aspect of its operations. A manufacturer might purchase all of the materials, parts, and equipment from a single supplier. A firm might also purchase a communications and information system from a single supplier who would provide the needed equipment, installation, plus programming, training, data entry, and any other service necessary to operate the system. Systems installations are often called "turnkey operations" because all the purchaser has to do is turn the key to begin operations.

outsourcing: the business buying practice of obtaining outside vendors to provide goods or services that otherwise might be supplied "in house"

Outsourcing occurs when firms obtain outside vendors to provide goods or services that might otherwise be supplied "in house." For example, Associated Data Services is one of a number of companies that supply billing services and customer records maintenance for small independent cable and telephone companies. Companies are outsourcing far more administrative and other services than ever before. A firm like Unitog benefits from this trend when a customer realizes that renting uniforms for its employees—and returning soiled ones to be cleaned—is more efficient than maintaining its own in-house laundry operation.

In the garment industry many manufacturers practice outsourcing when they contract with independent "sewing workrooms" or "shops" to produce the jeans or sweaters or shirts that are then affixed with the manufacturers' well-known labels. If these independent shops need to cut costs, they often pay workers less, perhaps even less than the legal minimum wage. In the United States the Labor Department started a *hot-goods program* to identify sewing suppliers who paid their workers less than minimum wage and required companies such as Patagonia and Guess to monitor lawful payment of wages by their suppliers. As a result of this program Patagonia now inspects time cards at suppliers' shops several times a year to audit wage payments.

Many firms have begun *global or offshore outsourcing,* which is the practice of having some of their manufacturing processes completed in countries with the cheapest sources of labor and/or supplies. Some apparel manufacturers cut their garments in the United States, ship the pieces to Mexico or Taiwan for construction, and then ship the finished products back to the United States for distribution to stores. As we saw in Chapter 4, global outsourcing has the potential to lead to labor abuses and is a recurring ethical problem, especially in the garment industry.

Purchasing Methods

Organizational and business buyers select the best purchasing method for each situation. For standard items like envelopes, nails, or paint thinner, the buyer tends merely to rely on the suppliers' list prices and product catalogs. For purchases such as grain, steel, or cement, buyers typically check the quality or characteristics of what is being purchased by examining a small part of a "lot." *Sampling buying* means buying after inspection of a sample of the product to be purchased and negotiating the price after the sample has been evaluated. In other cases, when products have characteristics that may differ or be unique to each unit purchased, *inspection buying,* where every item is inspected prior to purchase, may be necessary. Inspection buying is frequently used for purchases of used equipment, live animals, or plants. Here again, depending on the results of the inspection, the buyer may haggle over the price.

For many purchases business buyers develop written descriptions of the products needed. *Specification buying* means that a product order is placed based on a written or verbal description that specifies the quality, grade, brand, size, and other details about the product. Most manufactured items, agricultural commodities, and services are purchased "on spec" without inspection of the purchased products.

To get the best deal on products purchased on spec, buyers often request **competitive bids,** or proposals stating the terms of the sale, from two or more suppliers. These proposals include data on product specifications, price, delivery, and other conditions of the agreement, and the firm providing the better offer is awarded the bid. Before the deal is closed, buyers typically negotiate prices and other details of the purchasing agreement, but when neither the buyer nor the seller can determine all of the details in advance, they rely on a formal *negotiated contract* that allows for necessary changes in price, specifications, or timing of delivery as the work progresses. These contracts are common when the cost of products having a high gold or silver content varies with the price of precious metals at any one point in time or when leeway has to be allowed for the completion of a weather-dependent construction project.

For some products, especially services, *dollar contracts* are commonly used. These negotiated contracts guarantee that the buyer will purchase up to a specified total dollar amount during the time period covered by the contract, in return for a percentage discount on these purchases. Prices may also be set by *unit price contracts* that are based on the purchase of a certain number of units of the product during the time period covered by the contract. For example, a hospital may have a contract for purchasing surgical gowns that includes a price based on the purchase of 1,200 cases of gowns per year.

Work and construction contracts concern projects, such as research and development and construction activities, that are intended to result in some tangible goal, such as a new building. Usually the price included in the contract is for finished work or completion of a construction project. Such contracts frequently have requirements for time of completion

competitive bids: a business buying process in which two or more suppliers submit proposals (including price and associated data) for a proposed purchase and the firm providing the better offer is awarded the bid

and penalties for not meeting deadlines or bonuses for completion of work before a certain date.

While a contract may cover a single large purchase or smaller purchases made over a relatively short period of time, many business buyers reward dependable suppliers for their satisfactory service by awarding them long-term contracts. Sometimes, when a buyer has more to gain than the seller, the situation is reversed, and the buyer may have to demonstrate its ability to satisfy the seller and be willing to pay a very high price for a long-term contract. Winning or losing such a contract can have a significant impact on a firm's fortunes. In 1993, for example, the Fox television network obtained a four-year contract for the TV rights for the National Football League for $156 billion.[5] This feat solidified Fox's status as a fourth major network; for CBS, the loss of the NFL contract was an unexpected and devastating blow.

Cooperative Partnerships

One outgrowth of the interdependent relationship between an organizational buyer and seller may be a cooperative partnership that benefits both. A buyer and seller may develop a cooperative purchasing arrangement in which the buyer purchases a particular product from one supplier, who monitors the buyer's inventory or usage patterns and automatically refills orders when the buyer needs them. When a working partnership evolves, a supplier can become intimately involved in a buyer's organization. For example, after studying Boeing Aircraft's manufacturing operations, Ingersol, a machine-tool company, worked with Boeing to redesign its landing-gear parts so they could be produced more efficiently and to lower the cost of the machines Boeing purchased to make them. As a result of this working partnership, Boeing lowered its costs and sped up its production process, and Ingersol won an $8 million contract to produce the machines for Boeing.[6]

Sometimes buyers and sellers form *strategic alliances* or partnerships to achieve mutual goals. As we saw in Chapter 4, strategic alliances allow firms with common goals to share research and development costs, to provide needed capital for a large project, to share production capabilities, and so on. In the computer industry, where competition is fierce and secrets are closely guarded, IBM, Apple, and Motorola joined forces to develop the Motorola PowerPC to compete with Intel's powerful pentium chip.

Firms form trading partnerships when they practice *reciprocity*, which means that a buyer and seller agree to be each other's customers by essentially saying, "I'll buy from you

Exhibit 7.2
More and more business marketers are getting ahead by forming affinity partnerships with organized groups and associations. These partnerships create a win-win situation for everyone involved: In return for a group's endorsement, these companies are offering discounts or special services to group members, and in some cases they're giving back a percentage of sales to the group. AARP, the Association of American Retired People, with its 32 million members, is a prime choice for firms seeking affinity partnerships and has attracted many equally big partners, including Prudential Life Insurance, The Scudder Fund, and FTD Florists.

REAL PEOPLE, REAL CHOICES:

DECISION TIME AT UNITOG CO.

Historically, Unitog has prospered by maintaining its existing customer base, growing through acquisitions, and managing its expenses. To expand its customer base in the past, Unitog had tried a variety of ways to reach prospective customers, including mass media advertising, billboards, direct mail, telemarketing, and direct selling. The company's field sales organization, with over 100 sales "reps" who serviced existing accounts, had targeted smaller accounts, while three national accounts salespeople focused exclusively on very large prospects like Coca-Cola and Amoco.

As national sales manager, Bob Wilhelm faced the question of *how* to attract potential new accounts to beef up Unitog's sales volume. Through market research the company identified a group of medium-size prospective accounts that were currently being targeted by smaller competitors that did not have Unitog's design, distribution, or inventory capacity. This research indicated that national competition to provide uniforms was virtually nonexistent in a select group of industries, including trucking, convenience stores, and building maintenance services, where companies employed 150 to 1,000 people.

Mr. Wilhelm chose as his first target the trucking industry, where factors such as deregulation, increased profitability, and the need for more differentiation among competing firms had increased interest in image-related goods and services. Although the number of prospective accounts within the 150- to 1,000-employee range was small (about 225 firms), the sales potential was roughly $11.2 million. Now he had to figure out the best way to get trucking executives interested in the idea of providing uniforms for their employees. This decision involved choosing the most effective medium to make contact with these prospects and also the best way to deploy Unitog's field sales team and national account representatives to close the sale. Mr. Wilhem identified three options:

Option 1. Develop a radio campaign in cities where major trucking companies were based, coupled with follow-up from one of Unitog's national accounts salespeople. This strategy would create significant recognition and credibility for Unitog in those markets. On the other hand, the cost would be high, and in some cases a radio blitz would reach just a handful of potential customers. Unitog's national account salespeople would benefit from immediate recognition prior to making their calls, but only if the trucking executives heard the company's commercial on the radio.

Option 2. Use a direct mail promotion, followed with telephone contact by a field sales representative to schedule an appointment and with support provided by national accounts personnel as necessary. Direct mail would improve the chances of getting an appointment, and once an appointment was secured, the field salesperson and national accounts sales representative could work together to develop a creative and focused presentation. Although this strategy was cost effective and would provide a training opportunity for the field salespeople, it meant that Unitog would have to take its strongest sellers—the national accounts salespeople—away from some of the "super-size" corporate accounts they were primarily responsible for cultivating.

Option 3. Use a direct mail promotion, followed by telephone contact and an appointment scheduled by a national account sales representative. This strategy could result in the greatest return on invested resources. However, the opportunity to train and develop field salespeople to make more effective presentations to larger accounts would be sacrificed if they were left out of the picture.

Now, join the decision team at Unitog: Which option would you choose and why?

and you buy from me." The U.S. government generally frowns on reciprocal agreements and often determines that agreements between large firms are illegal because they limit free competition. When smaller firms are involved, reciprocity is legal in the United States if it is noncoercive and voluntarily agreed to by both parties. In other countries reciprocity is a common, even expected, practice in business-to-business marketing.

Bartering, which refers to the exchange of goods and services for other goods or services of like value, is a form of reciprocity that is legal in the United States (and subject to income taxes!). Bartering is becoming increasingly popular because it allows businesses to convert excess capacity into something of value by acquiring needed items in return for surplus material that would otherwise go to waste. Although this type of noncash transaction has been practiced since ancient times, as we'll see in Chapter 12, it is occurring on a much larger scale and in more sophisticated forms today.

Yet another type of partnership is known as *reverse marketing,* a practice in which many of the functions of buyer and seller are reversed. Instead of sellers' trying to identify potential customers and then "pitching" their products, the buyers try to find suppliers capable of producing specific needed products and then attempt to "sell" the idea to the suppliers. In these situations the seller's products and operations are shaped by the buyer to satisfy the buyer's needs. Often large poultry producers practice reverse marketing. Firms such as Perdue supply baby chickens, chicken food, financing for chicken houses, medications, and everything else necessary for farmers to lay "golden eggs" for the company. Because of reverse marketing, the farmer is assured a market and Perdue is guaranteed a supply of chickens.

CLASSIFYING BUSINESS AND ORGANIZATIONAL MARKETS

Boeing sells airplanes to Delta Airlines for millions of dollars. Procter & Gamble sells cases of Tide to Certified Grocers, a midwestern wholesaler. The Metropolitan Opera buys costumes and sets and programs. Mac's Diner buys a case of canned peas from B.J.'s Wholesale Club. The U.S. government places an order for 3,000 new IBM computers. The Peoria Public Library buys a Canon copier. The Wallace Construction Company buys lumber and sells houses. These are just a few of the very different purchases and very different buyers and sellers in business-to-business marketing. One way to sort out the many players in the marketplace is to group them into similar categories according to the role they play.

Some organizations produce goods and services; others resell, rent, or lease goods and services; still others, such as the Red Cross, a state government, or a local church, serve the public in some way. These distinctions lead to three broad categories in the overall business market: producers, resellers, and organizations. As illustrated in Figure 7.1, each of these market categories can be subdivided further. For business marketers, the classification of firms is significant: It identifies firms that purchase similar products and that have similar buying practices and expectations of suppliers. The U.S. government also uses a classification system that identifies firms into specific groupings. In this section we'll look first at the government's Standard Industrial Classification system and then at some of the common characteristics of firms in the categories shown in Figure 7.1.

THE STANDARD INDUSTRIAL CLASSIFICATION (SIC) SYSTEM

The **Standard Industrial Classification (SIC) system** is a numerical coding system used by the U.S. Census Bureau to divide businesses into detailed categories. The system was designed to standardize the collection of government data on business activity, and regularly published government reports giving data on the number of firms, the total dollar amount of sales, the number of employees, and a rate of growth for the SIC categories,

Standard Industrial Classification (SIC) system: the numerical coding system used by the U.S. government to classify and group firms into detailed categories according to their business activities and shared characteristics

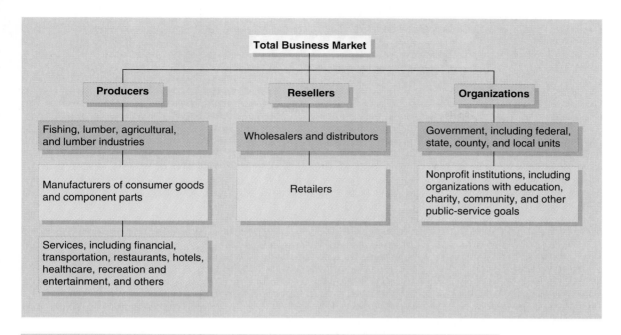

Figure 7.1
The Business Marketplace

broken down by geographic region. These reports have become an essential tool in business-to-business marketing, and many firms rely on them to assess the size of potential markets and to determine how well (or poorly) they are doing compared to their industry group as a whole.

Trade associations and business publications use the SIC system when they report industry studies, statistics, and trends. Dun & Bradstreet and many other private firms offer marketers a wide variety of detailed information on specific firms in SIC categories.

The SIC system uses a different numerical code for each industry. As illustrated in Figure 7.2 (page 236), the SIC system has eleven major divisions that are lettered. Each of these is further broken down into two-digit codes that identify major groups of firms. For example, 28 identifies manufacturers of chemicals and allied products. Next, these major groups are broken down into industry groups (three digits) and specific industries (four digits). The number 284 represents soap, detergents, and cleaning preparations, and 2844 perfumes, cosmetics, and other toilet preparations. As shown in Figure 7.2, further divisions identify product categories and specific products.

To use the SIC system, a marketer might first determine the SIC groups of current customers and then evaluate the sales potential of the overall SIC groups or particular segments based on the number of employees of firms in the groups. For example, a firm like Unitog could evaluate the sales potential of firms having 150 and 1,000 employees in several SIC categories and then set its sights on firms in the category that looks most attractive. In other cases a firm might choose to target firms in a cross-section of categories, as when Sprint devised a campaign, dubbed "Real Solutions," aimed at companies that employ 100 to 500 people.[7]

PRODUCER MARKETS

When we think of business firms, the first type that usually comes to mind is the type of firm that buys goods and services to produce other products. The producer market, or the **industrial market,** as these markets are more commonly called, is composed of individuals or organizations that purchase products to use in the production of goods and services and to support their business operations. In the United States the industrial market is the largest and most diverse of all business-to-business markets. It includes farms, fisheries, forestry and mining operations, as well as construction firms. Two important segments are composed of manufacturing firms and service organizations.

industrial market: the individuals or organizations that purchase products for use in the production of other goods and services to be resold at a profit and for their business operations

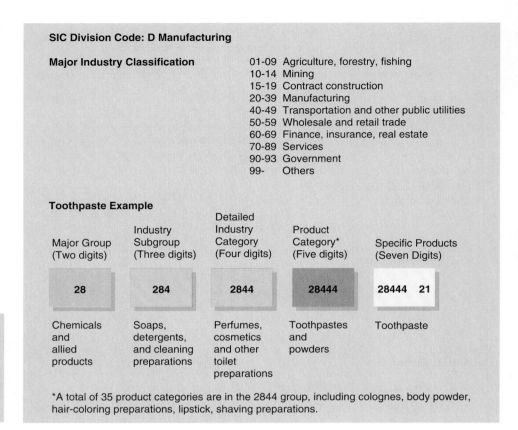

Figure 7.2
Standard Industrial Classification (SIC) System

Source: 1987 Standard Industrial Classification Manual, U.S. Office of Management and Budget; and Census of Manufacturers 1992, U.S. Bureau of Census.

SIC Division Code: D Manufacturing

Major Industry Classification

01-09 Agriculture, forestry, fishing
10-14 Mining
15-19 Contract construction
20-39 Manufacturing
40-49 Transportation and other public utilities
50-59 Wholesale and retail trade
60-69 Finance, insurance, real estate
70-89 Services
90-93 Government
99- Others

Toothpaste Example

Major Group (Two digits)	Industry Subgroup (Three digits)	Detailed Industry Category (Four digits)	Product Category* (Five digits)	Specific Products (Seven Digits)
28	284	2844	28444	28444 21
Chemicals and allied products	Soaps, detergents, and cleaning preparations	Perfumes, cosmetics and other toilet preparations	Toothpastes and powders	Toothpaste

*A total of 35 product categories are in the 2844 group, including colognes, body powder, hair-coloring preparations, lipstick, shaving preparations.

Buying in many large producer firms is typically carried out by a large staff of trained buyers. These buyers tend to focus on economic factors beyond the initial price of the product, including transportation and delivery charges, accessory products or supplies, maintenance, and other ongoing costs. In small organizations, such as a physician's office, purchasing may be handled by anyone available. These buyers typically are not professional purchasers and are more likely to purchase based on personal likes and dislikes.

Manufacturers

Buyers in *manufacturer markets* come in many sizes and varieties, and they are both buyers and sellers. Du Pont buys resins and sells insulation material for sleeping bags. Prince Spaghetti Company buys flour and sells pasta. Spaulding buys rubber and sells basketballs. Alcoa buys aluminum ingots and sells sheet aluminum. Platex buys plastic sheets and sells disposable baby bottles. Ford Motor Company buys batteries and sells cars and trucks. Firms like Ford, which are often referred to as *original equipment manufacturers* (OEM), buy a variety of component parts and use them in larger final products that they manufacture for sale.

Firms in manufacturer markets also purchase products that are not specifically tied to the goods they produce. Aside from office equipment and supplies, manufacturing firms buy forklifts, conveyor belts, cleaning solvents, and countless other products that are needed in manufacturing operations. Suppliers of these products can find huge markets for their wares in manufacturer markets.

Services

Service markets are made up of customers who purchase products for use in the delivery of services. Service markets include major international firms like Citibank and Hilton Hotels, as well as local services like dry cleaners, caterers, and veterinarians. As we'll see in Chapter 11, as the United States has moved from being primarily a manufacturing to a service economy in recent years, service organizations have been growing fast in terms of numbers of customers and dollar volume of service sales. This growth, in turn, has created new opportunities for business marketers. On the downside, customers like Prudential Insurance are few and far between in service markets. A high proportion of organizations are very small, including many that are owned and operated by a single entrepreneur. Identifying and targeting these small potential customers can be challenging for suppliers, and individual purchases are likely to be small and infrequent.

RESELLER MARKETS

A second major type of business-to-business market is the **reseller market.** Reseller markets are composed of individuals or organizations that buy finished goods for the purpose of reselling, renting, or leasing. While resellers do not produce goods and services, they do provide their customers with time, place, and possession utility. Resellers buy goods for resale or leasing, and they also buy goods and services to operate their own businesses.

Many firms choose to lease equipment rather than purchase it outright. *Leasing* means that a customer agrees to rent goods, equipment, or even installations for an extended period of time, usually one year or more. For firms that are short on capital, leasing offers distinct advantages. Firms that lease technology-based equipment also gain the advantage of being able to update their systems and operations every year or two without making major capital investments. Many firms also see leasing as a wise move for equipment that needs frequent servicing or repair. Resellers who also lease equipment gain new customers who might not otherwise make a purchase.

Firms that rent equipment are also finding many opportunities among customers of all sizes who need goods or equipment for an afternoon, a month, or some other short time. Renting is a distinct advantage for firms that need a piece of equipment infrequently or for one-time use. Sometimes firms work out rental contracts for expensive equipment that is used periodically. Hospitals, for example, sometimes rent expensive medical equipment such as lithotryptors, machines that "crush" kidney stones and thus eliminate the need for surgery. One hospital rents the equipment one day a week (the lab is built into a tractor trailer that pulls up to the building), while other hospitals contract to rent other days of the week, thus spreading the cost among several different care facilities and keeping the equipment in daily use for the rental firm.

> **reseller markets:** the individuals or organizations that buy finished goods for the purpose of reselling, renting, or leasing to others at a profit and for maintaining their business operations

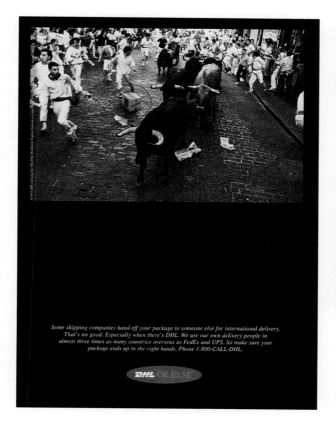

Some shipping companies hand off your package to someone else for international delivery. That's no good. Especially when there's DHL. We use our own delivery people in almost three times as many countries overseas as FedEx and UPS. So make sure your package ends up in the right hands. Phone 1-800-CALL-DHL.

DHL OR ELSE

Exhibit 7.3
The challenges facing firms that do business in global markets can be endless. Suppliers of goods and services in foreign countries have to adapt to local customs, change their ways to suit local business practices, revamp their operations to meet local rules and regulations, and deal with a multitude of uncertainties. For firms like DHL Worldwide Express, an overnight delivery service for business customers the world over, global markets also offer lots of opportunities. This ad assures customers that because DHL uses its own delivery people, their packages will end up in the right hands.

Wholesaler Markets

Wholesalers are individuals and groups that buy goods for resale to retailers and other organizational users. For example, a small grocery store in Blythewood, South Carolina, that carries 10,000 items wouldn't want to place orders with 10,000 or even 1,000 sales reps. And if the store runs out of cooking oil, the owner wouldn't call Cargill, the giant grain trader in Minneapolis, to order soybean oil. Instead the store owner deals with one or a few wholesaler sales reps who resell the products of hundreds of firms and farms to keep the store's shelves stocked.

Wholesalers try to anticipate what their customers will want and may carry hundreds or even thousands of items. A drug wholesaler, for example, may carry as many as 200,000 different products. Many wholesalers who supply retail markets tie into a store's computerized checkout system to monitor the store's inventory and fill orders automatically as stock runs low. As with other resellers, wholesalers purchase goods from producers or other wholesalers and distributors, and their purchasing decisions are impartial. They don't evaluate the quality, benefits, or value of one manufacturer's goods over another's; rather they buy what they can sell, which, of course, is based on their customers' evaluations and product preferences.

As more and more businesses are looking to cut costs, warehouse clubs are flourishing because they cater to the needs of small businesses and organizations that need to buy in bulk. At Sam's Clubs, a division of Wal-Mart Stores Inc., business customers account for 70 percent of sales. Sam's seeks to attract office managers, convenience-store operators, and other small business people who come to warehouse clubs to stock up on products such as soft drinks, paper plates, and computer paper. In 1994 Sam's developed a 225-person sales force to target larger businesses and developed a direct marketing program. Sam's Clubs executives estimate that the company's buying clout and economics of scale allow Sam's to offer prices at 40 to 50 percent lower than the competition.[8]

Sometimes small retailers work together by forming their own group-owned wholesaler operation. For example, the Independent Grocers Association (IGA) is able to obtain many of the price advantages of large grocery store chains by buying as a group. Similarly there are a number of buying groups that have been formed to benefit small member hospitals. Sun Health in the Carolinas is one such group that negotiates with suppliers to obtain the very lowest prices possible to keep costs down for the small independent hospitals that are members of the organization.

Retailers

Retailers are individuals or firms that buy goods to resell to final consumers. Retailer markets include both retail stores and direct marketers such as catalog marketers, home television shopping networks, and direct mail sales organizations. Retailers range from bookstores and auto dealers to florists and jewelers. Retailers buy consumer goods for resale, as well as store decorations and other goods and services for their own operations.

Scanner technology and computer-controlled inventory systems have allowed retail managers to know their businesses better than ever. Even small retailers can monitor what sells and what doesn't on a daily basis. Today's retailers can keep close tabs on what their customers want, and on which product lines are turning a profit and which are not, and this information has brought about changes in the way goods are bought and sold in the retail marketplace. For example, manufacturers of consumer products have traditionally focused on clever TV advertising, hoping to create consumer demand for products that retailers would, in turn, be anxious to stock. As we'll see in Chapter 18, today's manufacturers are relying more on trade promotions, such as discounts and rebates that are aimed directly at the retailers who carry their products.

ORGANIZATIONAL MARKETS

Organizational markets include **government markets** and **nonprofit institutional markets.** Government markets include federal, state, county, and local governments that buy goods and services to carry out public objectives and to support their daily operations. As we'll see in Chapter 11, nonprofit institutions are organizations with charitable, educational, community, and other public-service goals, that buy goods and services to

government markets: the federal, state, county, and local governments that buy goods to carry out public objectives and to support their operations

nonprofit institutional markets: the organizations with charitable, educational, community, and other public-service goals that buy goods and services to support their functions and to attract and serve their members

support their functions and to attract or serve their members. While such organizations buy many of the same products that firms with profit-seeking objectives do, and while their purchases may be as large, or even larger, differences in buying practices do exist.

Governments

Governments make up the largest business and organizational market in the United States and in many other nations as well. In the United States the government market includes more than 3,000 county governments, 35,000 municipalities and townships, 28,000 special district governments, 50 states and the District of Columbia, plus the federal government. There are 11 million local government employees, 4 million state government employees, and 2.2 million federal employees. State and local government markets alone account for 15 percent of the gross national product. Despite ongoing political efforts to curb spending, federal government expenditures for 1994 were over $1.1 trillion and by 1997 are expected to exceed $1.3 trillion.

When the government enters the marketplace, companies sit up and take notice. In 1991 the Air Force awarded Lockheed (and its partners General Dynamics Corporation and the Boeing Aircraft Company) the largest weapons contract ever to build a new generation of fighter planes. The cost of the planes, the F-33, is expected to reach $95 billion.[9] But much of the government's expenditures involve more familiar and less expensive items. More than 4,000 product categories are on the General Services Administration (GSA) Federal Supply Schedule. In one year alone the government purchased more than 5 million bed sheets, nearly 2 million note pads, and 3.5 million paintbrushes![10] The federal government is also a major purchaser of services. For example, the Defense Department recently requested bids from health maintenance organizations to handle the medical care for 800,000 military retirees and dependents in California and Hawaii. The five-year contract is expected to total $3.5 billion or more.[11]

For business marketers, selling goods and services to governments is considerably different than dealing with customers in the private sector. Taking a prospective buyer to lunch may be standard practice in the corporate world, for example, but in government markets this practice may be in conflict with ethical (and legal) standards.[12] Because government purchases are made with taxpayer money, purchases often are governed by stringent regulations. Most government buyers must develop specifications that are highly detailed and often dozens of pages long, use mandatory competitive bidding systems, and by law, in many cases, accept the lowest bid. Negotiated contracts are common for many goods and services purchased by governments. In-state (resident) suppliers are often given preferential treatment during bidding for state government contracts. Government bidding procedures also may give special consideration to firms that are minority-owned or that are located in economically disadvantaged areas.

Laws that require government buyers to obtain competitive bids are generally intended to promote competition among suppliers. To let possible vendors know about purchases that will be made, governments regularly publish information on upcoming bidding opportunities. The *Commerce Business Daily* is published by the federal government every business day and has listings of all federal government bid requests. It includes 500 to 1,000 of these listings every day.

Nonprofit Institutions

Nonprofit institutional markets include nearly 6 million organizations![13] This figure encompasses institutions such as hospitals, churches, universities, and museums. It also includes charitable and cause-related organizations such as the Salvation Army and the Sierra Club. Depending on their profit objectives, some institutions like hospitals, schools, and museums may be classified as either nonprofit organizations or profit-seeking service organizations. Nonprofit institutions tend to operate on low budgets, and in all but the largest, purchases are often made by nonprofessional "part-time" buyers who have other duties, or even by volunteers.

These differences can have a major impact on the quantity, quality, and variety of some purchases, compared to other markets. A private sector hospital, for example, may purchase food products that give patients higher-quality meals with more variety and larger portions than a nonprofit hospital operated by a charitable organization. Because of budget constraints, nonprofits often purchase goods that meet minimum standards and look for suppliers with the lowest prices. Organizations that rely on contributions may also be forced to delay purchasing until funds are available.

Although there are many similarities in the purchasing practices of large nonprofit institutions and government agencies, government purchasing is usually much more structured and regulated, with less room for individual decisions by the buyer. For example, a book publisher can often sell books to a private school by working with a single faculty member or administrator. Books sold to public schools, however, must be approved by a variety of committees, boards, and agencies. They may also undergo rigorous scrutiny by various special-interest groups, such as religious organizations concerned about how the theory of evolution is presented to students.

BUSINESS BUYING BEHAVIOR

The people who do the purchasing for organizations have a lot of responsibility. They spend the company's money and buy the products that keep it running. These people select suppliers and negotiate for the lowest prices, and they are responsible for the quality and delivery schedules that meet the company's needs. The items considered can range in price and significance from paper clips for the secretarial pool to a multi-million-dollar computer system. Obviously these people have a lot at stake when its comes to making purchase decisions.

Most mid- to large-size firms rely on highly trained professionals to do their purchasing. These professionals may be referred to as purchasing agents or buyers. Large corporations may have managers or directors of purchasing who are responsible for a purchasing department staffed by many trained buyers who may also have degrees in fields such as chemistry, physics, and other sciences. Because purchasing personnel control the organization's "wallet," the status of purchasing personnel has been raised in many organizations in recent years. The purchasing agent is no longer considered a paper pusher but is seen as an important contributor to the organization's financial health.

Big firms with several divisions or strategic business units often practice **centralized purchasing,** where company-wide purchasing activities are handled by a single purchasing department.[14] Purchasing decisions for all of the stores in the Wal-Mart chain, for example, are made by a single purchasing group at the company's headquarters. Because centralized purchasing departments buy greater quantities of items, this practice gives the firm more leverage with its suppliers and allows it to obtain volume discounts. People who work in a centralized purchasing office often become expert in the ins and outs of certain types of products, and each may have a specialized role in the purchasing function.

Business buying behavior is often shaped by the people who actually do the buying. Personal factors that are similar to the influences on consumers we saw in Chapter 6 determine how individual buyers interpret and carry out the firm's purchasing policies. Business buying behavior also varies with the complexity of the purchase and the risks involved. The buying situation determines how much time and effort is devoted to a purchasing decision and how many people are involved in the decision-making process. Overall, the need to focus on economic considerations accounts for significant differences in the way these factors affect organizational buyer behavior, as we'll see in this section.

THE BUYER

To the outsider, business buyers appear to be models of cold-blooded rationality, carefully calculating costs and weighing alternatives. But sometimes, like consumers, their buying behavior and purchasing decisions are guided by emotional brand loyalty, by the long-term relationships they have established with particular suppliers, or even by aesthetic concerns. More typically, individual factors such as the buyer's age, income, education, personality, and attitudes can affect their buying behavior, as can marketing communications and the buyer's role in the purchasing process. Other factors, such as the

centralized purchasing: a business buying practice in which all organizational purchasing is performed by a central purchasing department

nature of the organization itself and the buyer's status in it, also have an impact on buyer behavior.

Like consumers, business buyers engage in a learning process and develop an "organizational memory" consisting of shared beliefs and assumptions about the proper course of action.[15] Factors that color a buyer's perceptions of a purchasing situation include the buyer's *expectations* of the supplier—that is, how the buyer perceives the quality and reliability of the supplier's product, the dependability of the supplier to make on-time deliveries, and the competency and behavior of the suppliers salespeople. Another factor is the *organizational climate* of the buyer's own company—that is, how the buyer perceives the company's value system and the way performance is rewarded.

A key factor is the buyer's *attitude toward risk*—that is, whether the buyer perceives the purchasing situation to be risky and whether he or she believes in taking risks.[16] Some buyers are more risk-adverse than others. For example, a buyer who perceives that the company's goal is to control costs may buy an item from the lowest bidder without much regard for other considerations. In the same situation a buyer more prone to risk-taking will risk paying more, recognizing that the lowest-cost purchase may not be the best suited for the requirements of the task. A buyer's attitude toward risk can also lead to buying practices characterized by *inertia,* where the buyer wants to avoid the risk of trying a new supplier, even though the new supplier offers something better.

Successful business marketers try to develop strategies that help the buyer avoid risk. Buyers look to suppliers who provide honest, accurate information about product quality

SPOTLIGHT On Ethics

Drug Kickbacks

Kickbacks or bribes given to customers for business are both an ethical and a legal problem. When a business customer buys a building, a power generator, a fleet of cars, a road, or enough steel to make 20,000 cars, large amounts of money are at stake. To some marketers it might seem perfectly reasonable to reward the person that gives them an order amounting to $2,000,000. But what is a sufficient reward? This question becomes one of where to draw the line between a suitable—and perfectly legal—reward and an illegal kickback or bribe.

At one time or another any number of industries have been accused of engaging in customer bribery, particularly when big rewards and kickback activities are not limited to a few firms but are typical of the industry. In 1994 the Office of the Inspector General at the Health and Human Services Department issued a "Special Fraud Alert" to both health-care providers and patients about the pharmaceutical industry. This alert cited industry marketing practices that offer kickbacks to physicians or pharmacists to promote specific products. The possibly illegal activities included everything from hard cash in the form of research grants or speaking honoraria to golf weekends at expensive luxury resorts.

In one situation a drug company paid pharmacists who persuaded doctors to change their prescriptions from one brand of medication to their own. Another firm paid pharmacists to talk to patients about that company's heart medication. Other firms have awarded physicians points toward free airline tickets each

time the physicians prescribed the company's drug and issued actual cash kickbacks framed as research grants to physicians for keeping minor records on a certain prescription drug's usage. In 1994 a single Minneapolis physician was charged with receiving hundreds of thousands of dollars from a firm for prescribing its growth hormone—all disguised as research grants. And there are other instances where physicians have been given laser printers, fax machines, or even free staff members.

So what's wrong with such practices? First, a federal anti-kickback statute forbids any health-care provider from accepting cash or other types of payment for prescribing drugs funded by either Medicare or Medicaid. And ethical concerns abound when patient treatment includes drugs physicians or pharmacists are being paid to select. When health-care professionals put their own financial self-interests ahead of their patients' needs, they violate patient–provider trust. Patients, in a worst case scenario, may be taking unnecessary medication or, at a minimum, paying higher prices than necessary due to the added expense the pharmaceutical companies incur in paying the prescribers. In an attempt to prevent such abuses and to improve the image of the health-care profession, the Pharmaceutical Research and Manufacturers of America has joined with the American Medical Association to develop guidelines for appropriate relationships between physicians and members of the pharmaceutical industry and their representatives.

Source: Adapted from Elyse Tanouye, "Drug Marketers May Use Illegal Tactics to Sell," *The Wall Street Journal* (Aug. 23, 1994): B1.

and reliability, particularly when a purchase can negatively affect the quality of the firm's products or even create a safety hazard to workers. Buyers also depend on salespeople for information on new products, potential price increases, supply shortages, and other factors that make purchasing decisions less risky. Professional buyers also want to avoid buying situations where a conflict of interest could jeopardize their positions in the company. While bribery is an acceptable part of doing business in many countries, as we saw in Chapter 4, it is illegal in the United States. And many U.S. companies go so far as to prohibit their buyers from accepting anything, even a coffee mug, from a supplier!

THE BUYING SITUATION

Like consumers, business buyers enter some buying situations that are more important than others, and the amount of effort put into each differs. The more complex or risky the purchase decision, the greater the amount of time and effort the buyer will spend searching for information and evaluating alternatives. Complex purchases like a piece of customized equipment, a computer system, or an employee health insurance plan can take months as buyers search for information from a variety of sources. When risks are high, buyers not only seek information on product alternatives but carefully assess the capabilities of several suppliers.

On the other hand, when low-risk purchases are involved, organizational buyers often rely on strategies that simplify the process, just as consumers develop mental shortcuts for making habitual purchases. Using a fixed set of suppliers for routine purchases is one strategy that greatly reduces the information search and effort in evaluating competing alternatives that would otherwise be required.[17] Purchases like computer paper, shipping cartons, cleaning compounds, and many other products are often routinely ordered from trusted suppliers.

buy class: one of three classes used by business buyers to characterize the degree of time and effort required to make a decision in a buying situation

The process of selecting a supplier and evaluating product alternatives can be costly for the buying organization and is a factor in how much time the buyer expends in making a purchase decision. Typically buyers operate within a buy-class framework in which each **buy class** is identified by the degree of effort required to collect information and make a decision. These classes, which apply to three different buying situations, are known as straight rebuys, modified rebuys, and new-task buys.

SPOTLIGHT ON RELATIONSHIP MARKETING

Excellence at American Hospital Supply

To the benefit of both the supplier and the buyer, straight rebuys are often automated, with computers doing the talking. American Hospital Supply (a firm later bought and still doing business as Baxter Laboratories) was a true innovator in creating excellence in customer service. American Hospital Supply (AHS) created its ASAP system in the 1980s. This system provided direct links between customer hospital purchasing departments and AHS's internal order system, first by computer card readers and later via terminals installed in the hospital purchasing departments. With this system customers could generate orders without ever wasting time going through customer service representatives. In addition to the computer terminal, the system also had a dedicated printer that provided immediate customer feedback,

verifying the items and quantities ordered, and giving information about when the order would be shipped, where it would be shipped from, estimated time of arrival, and if there were any items backordered.

The system was so successful that competitors who were almost shut out of the market brought legal action against AHS, arguing that the system constituted unfair trade. Fortunately for AHS, the courts ruled that the system merely provided a competitive advantage and was legal because it was only installed in hospitals at the specific request of the customer. This kind of close cooperation between supplier and business customer is not illegal, just good relationship marketing.

Sources: Personal interviews with Baxter employees and other industry sales management personnel; Baxter Laboratories, "Welcome to an On-Line Presentation of 'ASAP' Electronic Order Entry"; Baxter Laboratories, "Scientific Products System Solutions"; Ron Winslow, "Four Hospital Suppliers Will Launch Common Electronic Ordering System," *The Wall Street Journal* (April 12, 1994): B6.

Straight Rebuy

A **straight rebuy** refers to the purchase of standardized items that are regularly needed by a firm. The buyer has purchased the exact same items many times before and routinely reorders them when supplies are low, often from the same supplier who has provided them in the past. Reordering takes very little of the buyer's time because no new information on product characteristics or suppliers is needed. Buyers typically maintain a list of approved vendors that have demonstrated their ability to meet the firm's criteria for pricing, quality, service, and delivery. Buyers rely on these "in" suppliers whose past performance has been satisfactory, and they are often reluctant to risk placing orders with "out" suppliers as long as prices, deliveries, and services from existing suppliers remain constant.

From the supplier's point of view, straight rebuy situations are the name of the game. Many business marketers go to great lengths to cultivate relationships with customers that will lead to routine purchases, and they will work hard to maintain these relationships over time to avoid losing a highly prized account. Reorders keep a supplier's sales volume up and selling costs down, and the competition for customers can be rugged among firms that market standardized products from petroleum to pencils that customers consume in quantity on a regular basis.

Modified Rebuy

In practice, straight rebuy situations do not last forever. A **modified rebuy** occurs when a firm requires a change in purchases that have been made before. A buyer may "shop around" when an existing supplier's prices, quality, or delivery become less than satisfactory or when the organization has new needs and requirements. A buyer who has purchased numerous copying machines in the past, for example, may evaluate several different lines of high-speed copiers when the company needs to update its copying equipment to handle more capacity.

Modified rebuy situations require more time and effort than routine purchases, but the decision process is nevertheless limited to a few specific details. The buyer generally knows what the purchase requirements are and who potential suppliers are likely to be. For suppliers, modified rebuy situations can mean that those on a buyer's approved vendor list may be dropped as others are considered to take their place. Astute marketers in

both camps routinely call on buyers to detect and define problems that can lead to winning or losing in such situations.

New-Task Buying

When a purchase is made for the very first time, the buying situation is a **new-task buy.** Buying decisions in this classification are characterized by uncertainty and risk, and they involve the most effort because the buyer has no previous experience on which to base a decision. The buyer has to start from scratch to gather information on purchase specifications, which may be highly technical and complex and require detailed input from other members of the firm. In new-task buying situations, the choice of supplier is critical, and buyers typically gather a great deal of information about quality, pricing, delivery, and service from several potential suppliers. How much effort the buyer expends in collecting information and evaluating alternatives depends on the cost of the purchase, its importance to the firm, and the perceived consequences of a wrong decision.

For suppliers, new-task buying situations represent both a challenge and an opportunity. Several suppliers may work closely with a buyer for several months to develop specifications and terms for a major purchase, but only one will ultimately be chosen. While a new-task buy can be significant in itself, many times the chosen supplier gains the added advantage of becoming an "in" supplier for more routine purchases that will follow. A growing retail business that needs an advertising agency for the first time, for example, may seek exhaustive information from several firms before selecting one, but will continue to use the chosen agency's services for future projects without exploring other alternatives.

THE BUYING CENTER

Many organizational buying tasks are so complex or so important that several people may be needed to arrive at a satisfactory decision. Depending on what's to be purchased, these participants may be production workers, supervisors, engineers, secretaries, shipping clerks, or financial officers. In a small organization, *everyone* may have a voice in the decision. The group of people in the organization who participate in the decision-making process or influence the purchase decision in some way is referred to as the **buying center.**

The size of the buying center is determined by the buying situation and the degree of risk involved in the purchase. For routine purchases, a single buyer—the purchasing agent—typically makes the decision without consulting others in the firm. In new-task buys the number of decision makers increases in proportion to the complexity and cost of the purchase. As many as twenty people might actively share the decision—and its associated risks—when a major purchase is to be made.

The Fluid Nature of the Buying Center

While the term *buying center* may conjure up an image of offices buzzing with purchasing activity, it actually refers to an informal cross-functional team of decision makers who work together to gather information and evaluate alternatives for particular purchases. Generally the members of a buying center have some expertise or some interest in the particular decision, and they are able, as a group, to make the best decision for the organization. After the decision is made, the group is dissolved, and when another important purchasing decision is to be made, another set of people will form a buying center.

In many organizations buying centers play a role in some routine purchases as well as modified rebuys and new-task buying situations. Hospitals, for example, frequently make purchase decisions that involve a large number of buying center participants. When making a decision to purchase disposable oxygen masks and tubing, physicians, nurses, emergency room personnel, respiratory therapists, and purchasing agents may work together to determine quantities and select the best products and suppliers. A separate decision regarding the types of pharmaceutical supplies to stock might involve a different cast of characters who would be called in to advise the purchasing agent.

Roles in the Buying Center

Not only are different people in an organization involved in different purchase decisions, but the participants have different roles that vary with the complexity of the decision. In some situations the buyer who makes the purchase may also make the decision, based on information provided by other participants. In other cases the buyer's chief role is to gather information for users of the purchase or a top manager who will ultimately make the final decision. For suppliers the buying center concept complicates the marketing process. A salesperson may have to call on everyone involved and develop strategies that satisfy the interests of each. The salesperson also has to determine who has the most influence on the decision, who plays the key role of decision maker, and who actually makes the purchase.

The buying behavior of each member of the buying center is determined by his or her role in the group. Depending on the complexity of the purchase and the size of the buying center, a participant may assume one of six major roles, several of these roles, or all of them.

- The **initiator** is the member of the buying center who first recognizes that a purchase needs to be made. The act of making the need known to others in the organization begins the buying process. Production employees, for example, may notice that a piece of equipment is not working properly and initiate the purchase process by notifying their supervisor. A sales manager might also initiate a purchase, say for a new telephone system, by relaying the need to higher management. Depending on the position of the initiator in the organization and the type of purchase, the initiator may or may not influence the actual purchase decision.

initiator: the member of a business buying center who first recognizes that a purchase needs to be made and notifies others in the organization

- The **user** of the product is a member of the buying center who will actually use the product after it is purchased. Frequently the user is also the initiator of a purchase, because the people who use an item generally are the first to recognize that a problem or need exists. The user's role in the buying center varies. A secretary may be consulted to determine the features needed in a new copying machine and may participate in the evaluation of the supplier's service after the purchase has been made. A design engineer may be asked to develop the specifications for the purchase.

user: a member of a business buying center who will actually use a business product after it is purchased

- The **gatekeeper** is the member of the buying center who controls the flow of information to other members. Typically the gatekeeper is the purchasing agent who gathers information and materials from salespeople, schedules sales presentations, and controls suppliers' access to other participants in the buying process. In other situations an engineer may fulfill the role of gatekeeper, controlling product information and meeting with suppliers who are capable of meeting product requirements.

gatekeeper: the member of a business buying center who controls the flow of information to other members

- An **influencer** is a member of the buying center who affects the buying decision by dispensing advice or sharing his or her expertise. By virtue of their expertise, engineers, quality control specialists, and other technical experts in the firm generally have a great deal of influence in purchasing decisions involving equipment, materials, and component parts used in production, and in some cases the firm may hire outside consultants like architects or systems analysts whose expert opinions carry a lot of weight. The influencers may or may not be users of the product.

influencer: a member of a business buying center who affects the buying decision by dispensing advice or sharing expertise

- The **decider** is the member of the buying center who makes the final purchase decision. This person may have formal or informal power within the buying center and within the organization to authorize spending the company's money. For a fairly routine purchase, the decider may be the purchasing agent. If the purchase is very large or quite complex, a manager or the CEO of an organization may be the decider. New-task purchases usually involve high-level deciders quite early in the process. For instance, Southwest Airlines' purchase of 63 Boeing 737X aircraft involved its chairman and treasurer early on in the process, because $2.5 billion would be spent![18]

decider: the member of a business buying center who has the authority to make the final purchase decision

- The **buyer** is the member of the buying center who has responsibility for executing the purchase. Although the buyer often has a role in identifying and evaluating alternative suppliers, this person's primary function is implementing the decision of the buying center and handling the details of the purchase. The buyer obtains competing bids, negotiates pricing and service contracts,

buyer: the member of a business buying center who has the formal authority and responsibility for executing the purchase and arranges delivery dates and payment plans. The buyer may be a member of the purchasing department, a purchasing agent, or the director of purchasing.

THE BUSINESS BUYING DECISION PROCESS

Firms buy products for the same reasons consumers do: to satisfy a need and solve a problem. And a decision has to be made on just how to do it. As we saw in Chapter 6, consumers make some purchasing decisions effortlessly, and at other times coming to a decision begins to resemble a full-time job. For organizational buyers making purchasing decisions is a full-time job, but buyers can't spend that much time on each and every purchase if the firm is to have all the goods and services it needs when they are needed. Fortunately, some organizational purchasing decisions can and do proceed more quickly and efficiently than others. A lot depends on how well the members of the buying center work together, how complex or expensive the purchase is, and how much risk is involved if the wrong decision is made.

To manage the many factors and conditions involved in making a purchase, business buyers rely on a number of procedures and practices that also help ensure that the ultimate decision is in the firm's best interests. The business buying decision process typically involves a series of stages similar to the steps in the consumer decision process described in Chapter 6. The business buying process is more complex, however, and each stage may involve several additional steps that take into account business buying practices and procedures. In this section we'll look at the activities involved in the business buying decision process illustrated in Figure 7.3.

PROBLEM RECOGNITION

As in consumer buying, the first stage in the business buying decision process occurs when someone in the organization recognizes that a problem exists and can be solved by a purchase. For routine straight rebuy purchases, this step may result from the exhaustion of the current supply of computer paper, nails, or disposable garbage bags.

Recognition of the need for modified rebuy purchases often comes from the wearing

**Figure 7.3
The Business Buying Decision Process**

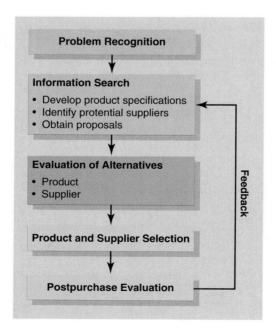

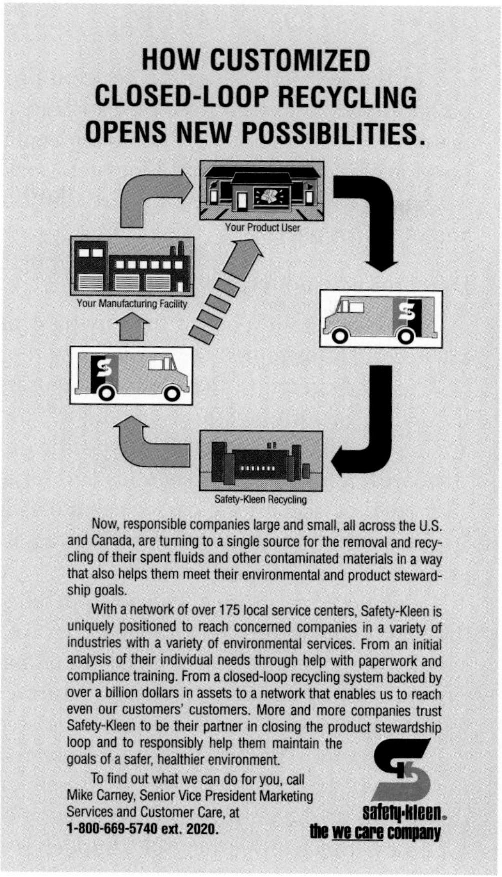

HOW CUSTOMIZED CLOSED-LOOP RECYCLING OPENS NEW POSSIBILITIES.

Your Product User

Your Manufacturing Facility

Safety-Kleen Recycling

Now, responsible companies large and small, all across the U.S. and Canada, are turning to a single source for the removal and recycling of their spent fluids and other contaminated materials in a way that also helps them meet their environmental and product stewardship goals.

With a network of over 175 local service centers, Safety-Kleen is uniquely positioned to reach concerned companies in a variety of industries with a variety of environmental services. From an initial analysis of their individual needs through help with paperwork and compliance training. From a closed-loop recycling system backed by over a billion dollars in assets to a network that enables us to reach even our customers' customers. More and more companies trust Safety-Kleen to be their partner in closing the product stewardship loop and to responsibly help them maintain the goals of a safer, healthier environment.

To find out what we can do for you, call Mike Carney, Senior Vice President Marketing Services and Customer Care, at 1-800-669-5740 ext. 2020.

safety-kleen.
the we care company

Exhibit 7.5
Business marketers often are instrumental in stimulating problem recognition. Salespeople as well as ads in trade publications often focus on how the marketer's goods and services can help a customer solve its problems. Safety Kleen, a company that removes or recycles industrial waste fluids, for example, focuses its advertising on helping firms achieve their environmental stewardship goals and comply with environmental regulations. The company not only solves the problems of waste disposal, but offers to form partnerships with firms to assess these problems and provide compliance training for employees.

out of existing equipment or from changes in technology. At other times a manager may hear about new goods and services that will serve the firm better than the old, or a purchasing agent may be encouraged to make a change by a salesperson who offers a better product at a lower price.

New-task purchases are often related to the desire to enhance the firm's operations in some way, as when the firm aims to improve product quality or to cut costs to remain competitive in the marketplace. Or the firm may decide to introduce a new product that requires new materials and equipment.

A firm's approach to cost control can also initiate a purchase. Many firms conduct a *value analysis,* in which engineering teams carefully study equipment, materials, and component parts to determine whether they can be redesigned, standardized, or changed in some way. The objective is to replace inefficient items with cost-effective substitutes.

In most organizations the initiator prepares a *purchase requisition,* or written request to purchase a product, and submits it to the organization's purchasing department. If the purchase is a straight rebuy, the purchasing department places an order for the product and the decision process is ended. For purchases of standardized or branded products, the purchase requisition may only identify the brand or standard, the quantity, and the date needed. When the purchase is more complex, the purchasing agent needs more information, and a buying center is formed to develop a complete description of the purchase.

At this initial stage in the decision process, the most important decision of all—*to buy or not to buy*—is made. As we saw earlier in this chapter, the overall state of the economy, consumer demand, and other external factors often determine which purchases the firm will make, if any. The organization's *budget cycle* also affects purchasing decisions. Budget cycles are usually set for a period of one year, and budgets usually include a maximum amount that may be spent during a certain period on a particular product category. Near the end of a budget cycle, firms can purchase excess amounts of a product in a given category if there is a budget surplus or if the budget category is depleted, delay all purchases until the beginning of a new cycle.

INFORMATION SEARCH

In the second stage of the decision process for nonroutine purchases, the task of the buying center is to search for information about products and suppliers that will meet the firm's needs. Members of the buying center may individually or collectively refer to reports in trade magazines and journals, seek advice from outside consultants and specialists, and pay close attention to marketing communications from different manufacturers and other suppliers.

Developing Product Specifications

One important goal of the buying center is to identify product attributes that fulfill the need that prompted the purchase in the first place. This process may begin with a general needs description that defines the users' requirements and expectations of the product. When the product needs are highly complex or technical, engineers and other experts are the key players in identifying specific product characteristics and determining whether standardized or customized goods and services are required. For large purchases, costs are calculated by accounting personnel and weighed against the potential benefits to the firm. In short, each member of the buying center provides input that reflects his or her interest and involvement in the purchase.

These efforts ultimately lead to detailed product specifications that may be formally drawn up and agreed to by the members of the buying center. In some cases these specifications may literally describe the "nuts and bolts" of the purchase. Typically they identify the quality, size, weight, color, features, training, warranty, service, quantities, and delivery requirements for the purchase. For products and supplies that will be purchased with a long-term contract, specifications may include the length of the contract, the terms for renewing the contract after an initial period, possible price increases permitted during the length of the contract, reasons for voiding (canceling) the contract, and sometimes even how much inventory the supplier is required to keep on hand to ensure constant supply.

The time required to develop product specifications is determined by the buying task and the complexity of the purchase, but the process can also be delayed by conflicts in the buying center. Each member of the buying center has a different perspective and brings a different level of experience and expertise to the purchasing situation, and differences of opinion can arise. An engineer may insist on quality over cost; the users may be more interested in product features than warranties and service; a manager might focus on in-service training; while a financial officer is generally most concerned with the price. In these situations the purchasing agent may become an important influencer by focusing the group effort on obtaining the best product at the lowest cost.

Identifying Potential Suppliers

The next phase of the information search is to identify the supplier organizations that are capable of providing a product that meets the specifications developed by the buying center. The suppliers with whom the firm already does business are typically considered first to avoid the *switching costs* involved if a new supplier is to be selected. These costs include training the new supplier, the risk of a previous supplier who has been abandoned giving away trade secrets, and the increased risk of a poor-quality product or erratic deliveries by a new vendor that does not have an established "track record."

When existing suppliers are unable to meet the product specifications, the members of the buying center may develop a list of potential suppliers from other supplier salespeople, colleagues in their industry, professional periodicals, or industry directories. The purchasing agent may also conduct a **vendor analysis,** a formal procedure for evaluating and rating suppliers on a variety of dimensions. Suppliers wishing to compete for a specific purchase or wishing to be placed on an approved list are required to complete vendor analysis forms so they can be evaluated. The vendor analysis form may ask the supplier to list previous customers, financial data, information on ownership, facilities, company history, technical expertise, and so on.

vendor analysis: a formal procedure for evaluating product suppliers on a variety of attributes

Exhibit 7.6
When it comes to taking risks and evaluating other companies, business buyers are not alone; suppliers also evaluate and "qualify" potential customers. Before responding to a proposal solicitation or bidding on a contract for a major project, these suppliers turn to many of the same database services that help firms locate potential customers. These services offer financial data that suppliers use to lower the risks of making credit decisions and to increase the efficiency of their targeting strategies. American Business Lists, for example, offer lists of 10 million businesses that are sorted by SIC categories and that provide very detailed information that helps marketers identify, target, and contact potential customers and evaluate their creditworthiness.

The more complex and costly the purchase is, the more time will be spent searching for the best supplier. Several different suppliers may be asked to make formal presentations to the buying center group and to provide samples that can be "test driven." In the case of installations and large equipment, the buyers may speak with or even visit the supplier's other customers to see for themselves how the product performs. In some cases suppliers may be asked to participate in the development of product specifications or to suggest changes in the specifications that will lower the cost and/or improve the item to be purchased in some way.

Obtaining Proposals

The final phase in the buying center's search for information is *proposal solicitation*. The buyer invites qualified suppliers to submit formal or informal proposals or bids. For standardized or branded products, the solicitation may be an informal request for pricing information, including discounts and shipping charges, and confirmation of delivery dates. At other times the request is in the form of a formal *Request for Proposal (RFP)* or *Request for Quotation (RFQ)* that requires suppliers to develop a detailed proposal or price quotation for supplying the product.

Many suppliers believe that formal quotations exaggerate the importance of simply coming in at the lowest price and that the process bypasses customer service, past buyer-seller experiences, and other factors that work in their favor. This objection, however, is often unwarranted. Frequently business is given to a supplier who is not the lowest bidder *if* the chosen bidder has something uniquely better to offer that justifies the higher price.

American Express, for example, has found a way to win bids from competitors without relying on price alone. The company bids for firms' travel business by offering American Express corporate charge cards that employees can use when traveling on business, and its proposals include the offer to provide the corporate customer with monthly reports that detail the company's total travel expenses. For big firms whose executives and salespeople travel frequently, this service can substantially reduce the firm's record-keeping costs. This strategy has helped American Express win $\frac{2}{3}$ of the Fortune 100 travel clients, including a $36 million—yes, *million*—air-travel account, plus the corporate charge account, from W.R. Grace & Co.[19]

EVALUATION OF ALTERNATIVES

In this stage of the business buying decision process, the buying center compares and evaluates the proposals obtained from different suppliers. Several or all of the members of the buying center may participate in developing the evaluative criteria for the particular purchase and rank ordering the determinant attributes, or specific criteria, for judging the merits of each proposal.

Total spending for goods and services can have a major impact on the firm's profitability, so all other things being equal, price is the primary consideration. Pricing evaluations take into account discount policies for certain quantities, returned goods policies (some suppliers charge a percentage of the price when an item is returned for credit), the cost of repair and maintenance services, terms of payment such as discounts for payment within a specified amount of time and penalties beyond a given length of time, and the cost of financing large purchases. For capital equipment, cost criteria also include the life expectancy of the purchase, the expected resale value, and disposal costs for the old equipment. In some cases the buying center may negotiate with the preferred supplier to match the lowest bidder.

PRODUCT AND SUPPLIER SELECTION

While the buying center's choice of products and suppliers is based on cost considerations, more often than not there are occasions when these issues take the back seat in the selection process. For many products attributes such as quality, reliability, durability, service, and delivery outweigh the price.

Quality becomes a chief concern when the product carries the risk of danger to users and others in the organization. In firms that have adopted a TQM approach, the quality, reliability, and durability of materials and component parts are paramount. Reliability and durability rank high for equipment and systems that keep the firm's operations running smoothly, without interruption. For some purchases warranties, repair service, and regular maintenance after the sale are important, as are such issues as whether repairs and maintenance will be done on site or if the item must be returned to the manufacturer and whether loaner equipment will be available during repair or maintenance downtime.

A supplier's ability to make on-time deliveries is the critical factor in the selection process for firms that have adopted an inventory management system called **just in time (JIT)**. JIT systems reduce inventory and stock to very low levels or even zero, but ensure a constant supply through precisely timed deliveries just when needed. In recent years many producer and reseller organizations have adopted the JIT approach and changed their purchasing practices as well as the criteria for selecting a supplier. Because JIT means that materials and components or finished goods arrive just as needed, JIT buyers require strict quality control on the part of suppliers. For manufacturers JIT deliveries of inferior materials or defective parts mean closing down a production line because the firm has no replacements in stock. For resellers defective goods and delayed deliveries mean losing sales because stock is unavailable. For both manufacturers and resellers the choice of supplier may come down to one that is located nearby. To win a large customer, a supplier organization may even have to be willing to set up production facilities close to the customer to guarantee JIT delivery. JIT buyers reduce operating and transportation costs while ensuring higher quality for their firms.[20]

Ultimately, the buying center selects a single supplier—or several suppliers to guard against shortages and delays—and the purchase decision becomes a purchase order. The purchase order may be a simple form processed by purchasing department personnel or a detailed contract that must be verified and approved by management. In addition to the

just in time (JIT): inventory management and purchasing practices used by manufacturers and resellers that reduce inventory and stock to very low levels, but ensure that deliveries from suppliers arrive just when needed

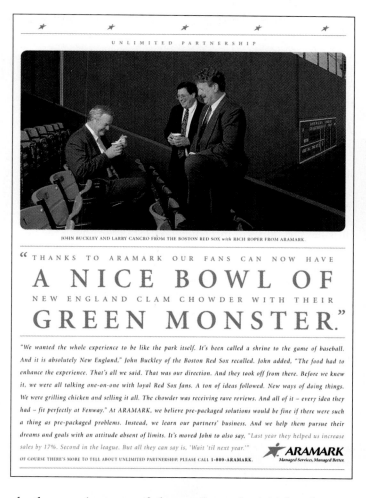

JOHN BUCKLEY AND LARRY CANCRO FROM THE BOSTON RED SOX *with* RICH ROPER FROM ARAMARK.

" THANKS TO ARAMARK OUR FANS CAN NOW HAVE

A NICE BOWL OF

NEW ENGLAND CLAM CHOWDER WITH THEIR

GREEN MONSTER."

"We wanted the whole experience to be like the park itself. It's been called a shrine to the game of baseball. And it is absolutely New England," John Buckley of the Boston Red Sox recalled. John added, "The food had to enhance the experience. That's all we said. That was our direction. And they took off from there. Before we knew it, we were all talking one-on-one with loyal Red Sox fans. A ton of ideas followed. New ways of doing things. We were grilling chicken and selling it all. The chowder was receiving rave reviews. And all of it – every idea they had – fit perfectly at Fenway." At ARAMARK, we believe pre-packaged solutions would be fine if there were such a thing as pre-packaged problems. Instead, we learn our partners' business. And we help them pursue their dreams and goals with an attitude absent of limits. It's moved John to also say, *"Last year they helped us increase sales by 17%. Second in the league. But all they can say is, 'Wait 'til next year.'"*

OF COURSE THERE'S MORE TO TELL ABOUT UNLIMITED PARTNERSHIP. PLEASE CALL 1-800-ARAMARK.

ARAMARK
Managed Services, Managed Better.

UNLIMITED PARTNERSHIP

Exhibit 7.7
Whether a business markets its goods and services to consumers or to other businesses, customer satisfaction is what scores the winning point and guarantees the future. And business marketers, who make it to the big leagues when it comes to satisfying customers, like to let others know about it, as Aramark Managed Services does in the ad shown here. Aramark offers customized services, including food and refreshment services, to a wide variety of organizations. The ad quotes Boston Red Sox marketer John Buckley, who praises Aramark's partnership teams for developing the new food services at Fenway Park that are threatening to replace peanuts and crackerjacks out at the old ball game.

product specifications and other requirements of the purchase, the initial order may include a routine for reorders. To control the costs of maintaining a large inventory or even to "test the waters" with a new product or supplier, many buyers limit the initial quantities purchased. But specifying the reorder routine at the time eliminates the costs of processing many small orders and renegotiating the price and other conditions of the purchase.

POSTPURCHASE EVALUATION

The final step in the business buying decision process is as important to both buyers and sellers as the evaluation and selection steps. Just as consumers evaluate purchases according to the extent that they meet or exceed expectations, an organizational buyer assesses whether the performance of the product *and* the supplier are living up to expectations. The buyer surveys the users of the product to determine their level of satisfaction with the product itself, as well as with the installation, delivery, and service provided by the supplier. The performance review is documented, and the supplier may be added to the approved vendor list for future purchases or dropped from consideration.

In the case of long-term contracts and single-sourcing agreements, the buying firm may monitor the supplier's operations to help them to improve quality and service or to become more efficient to lower production costs and prices. Xerox, for example, sends teams of auditors to suppliers' facilities to determine whether they meet Xerox's efficiency standards for both quality and cost. If suppliers do not make the recommended improvements, they stand a chance of losing a large chunk of the Xerox business.

Many suppliers recognize the importance of conducting their own performance reviews on a regular basis. Evaluations based on the same criteria used by customers can help the firm maintain its relationships with these customers. Measuring up to a customer's expectations can mean winning or losing a big account.

REAL PEOPLE, REAL CHOICES:

HOW IT WORKED OUT AT UNITOG CO.

Bob Wilhelm chose option 2. A four-stage direct mail promotion was mailed to presidents and CEOs of the 225 trucking companies over a four-week period to soften the ground for his army of field sales representatives. The first mailing consisted of a red gift box containing Tabasco sauce with the message, "Spice up your image." One week later prospects received a similar box with hand grips that said, "Pump up your employee morale." The third gift box contained a sewing kit with the message, "Sew up a good deal." The final mailing was a brochure that proclaimed, "With Unitog uniform programs your company's image will travel farther than your trucks."

The mailings came with reply cards and an 800 number that allowed Unitog to track responses. Salespeople were required to contact respondents within five working days of receiving their replies, and the national accounts representatives assisted the field salesperson in developing major presentations for the larger potential customers. This strategy yielded an appointment rate of 20 percent, and the field sales organization sold eight large accounts. One trucking firm president was so impressed by the campaign that he wrote to Mr. Wilhelm: "Your direct-mail campaign has been the best I have ever seen. I intend to share it with my marketing firm as an example of how to make a great impression on potential customers." Based on this effort's success, Unitog is in the process of identifying larger accounts in other niche markets that it feels are just waiting to be put in uniform.

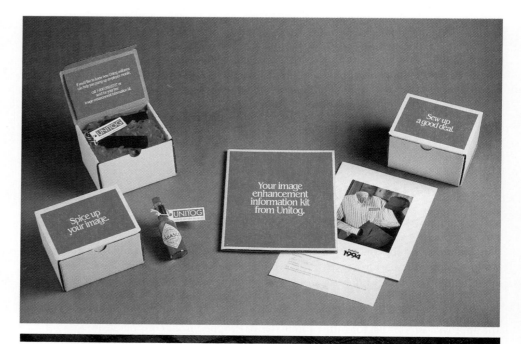

Chapter 7 Summary

Objective 1. Describe the general characteristics of business-to-business markets and business buying practices.

Business-to-business markets include business and organizational customers who buy goods and services for purposes other than for personal consumption. Business and organizational customers are usually few in number, may be geographically concentrated, and often purchase higher-priced products in larger quantities. Businesses purchase equipment, maintenance, repair, and operating products, as well as specialized services, and the materials and component parts needed to produce goods. Business demand is derived from the demand for another good or service, is generally not affected by price increases or decreases, is subject to great fluctuations, and may be tied to the demand and availability of some other good.

Business buying practices include the decision of how a firm will utilize its suppliers, or sources, of the goods and services it needs. A firm's purchasing options include single sourcing, multiple sourcing, or systems buying. A firm can also choose outsourcing or offshore sourcing for services and operations it might otherwise perform itself. Purchasing decisions may be based on detailed descriptions of the product (specification buying), examination of a sample of the product, or inspecting every item. Contracts may be awarded to suppliers based on competitive bids and can involve short-term, long-term, or negotiated contracts.

Objective 2. Tell how business and organizational markets are classified.

The Standard Industrial Classification (SIC) System, a numerical coding system of the federal government, is the most frequently used classification system for business and organizational markets. More generally, business markets can be divided into the three major categories of producers, resellers, and organizations. Producers purchase materials, parts, and various goods and services needed to produce other goods and services to be sold at a profit. Resellers purchase finished goods to resell at a profit, as well as other goods and services to maintain their operations. Governments and other nonprofit organizations purchase the goods and services necessary to fulfill their objectives.

Objective 3. Explain the elements that determine business buying behavior.

Business buying behavior is shaped by the people who actually do the buying. Although business buyers are trained professionals, they are also subject to some of the same personal influences that affect consumer buying behavior. The buying situation determines how much time and effort is devoted to a purchasing decision, and buyers may assign purchases to buy classes that characterize the decision effort. Decision making is minimal in straight rebuy situations, limited in modified rebuys, and extensive in new-task buying. A buying center, or cross-functional team of decision makers, may be formed for a specific purchasing decision. Different members of the buying center usually take one or more roles: initiator, user, gatekeeper, influencer, decider, or buyer.

Objective 4. Understand the stages in the business buying decision process.

The business buying decision process involves a number of stages that are similar to but more complex than the steps followed by consumers when making a purchase decision. A single purchase may involve the recognition of a problem that can be resolved by making a purchase. The recognition stage is accompanied by the submission of a purchase requisition and initiates the subsequent steps of developing product specifications, identifying potential suppliers, requesting and obtaining proposals, evaluating the proposals, selecting a supplier, placing the order, and, finally, formally evaluating the performance of the product and the supplier.

Review Questions

Marketing Concepts: Testing Your Knowledge

1. What are some general characteristics of business-to-business markets? What is the primary difference between business customers and consumers?
2. What types of products are typically bought and sold in business-to-business markets?
3. How is business-to-business demand different from consumer demand? What are some of the factors that cause business demand to fluctuate?
4. What purchasing practices and methods do business buyers typically use?
5. What is the SIC system? What purpose does it serve? Of what use is it to business marketers?
6. How are business-to-business markets generally classified? What types of purchases do the three major types of organizations make?
7. What are the characteristics of business buyers? What are some of the influences that determine individual buyer behavior?
8. Describe the three buy classes.
9. What is a buying center? What are the roles played by the various people in a buying center?
10. What are the stages in the business buyer decision process? What happens in each stage?

Marketing Concepts: Discussing Choices and Issues

1. Do you agree with the idea that business-to-business marketing is more important to a country's economy than consumer marketing? Which one do you think provides better career opportunities for new college grads? Explain your answers.
2. What is your opinion of the government practice that requires large suppliers to do business with a specified number of small disadvantaged firms?
3. Do you think it is ethical for database companies to collect and sell detailed information on firms, including financial data and creditworthiness? Explain your reasoning.
4. Do you think offshore outsourcing by American firms is good for the American consumer? Tell why or why not.

Marketing Practice: Applying What You've Learned

1. With other classmates, form three pairs of debate teams and present a series of formal debates for your class, with each team taking the pro or con side of one of the following statements.
   a. "The buying practice of single sourcing is good for both the buyer and the supplier."
   b. "The buying practice of obtaining sealed competitive bids from potential suppliers is good for both the buyer and the supplier."
   c. "The practice of reciprocity in organizational markets is good for everyone concerned."
2. You are looking for a part-time job and being considered by a small, weekly newspaper. Knowing that you are a marketing student, the editor has asked you to provide a sample article that explains business demand in a way that will be interesting to the owners of small local shops and businesses. Write that article and circulate it among three classmates, asking each to provide brief written comments and suggestions.
3. You've just been hired by a small consulting company that services small- to medium-size firms. One of the company's clients produces custom imprinted T-shirts for local sports teams and other groups and is thinking about switching to a JIT inventory control system. The client, who has ten employees, currently buys the T-shirts in bulk and keeps large quantities of stock imprints and other supplies on hand. Your boss has asked you to prepare a list of issues the owner has to consider. Prepare the list and discuss each point with a classmate who assumes the client's role.
4. As a new director of materials management for a textile firm that manufactures sheets and towels, you are hoping to simplify the buying process where possible, thus reducing costs for the firm. You have first examined each purchase and classified it as a straight rebuy, a modified rebuy, or a new-task purchase. Your next job is to outline the procedures or steps in the purchasing process for each type of purchase. Indicate the type of purchase and outline the steps that must be taken in the purchase of each of the following items.
   a. computer paper
   b. textile dyes for this year's fashion colors
   c. new sewing robotics
   d. new software to control the weaving processes

Marketing Mini-Project: Learning by Doing

The purpose of this mini-project is to gain knowledge about one business-to-business market using the SIC system and other government information.

1. Select an industry of interest to you and use the *Standard Industrial Classification Manual*.
   a. What are the codes for each of the following classifications?
      ■ SIC Division Code (letter)
      ■ SIC Major Group (two-digit)
      ■ SIC Industry Subgroup (three-digit)
      ■ SIC Detailed Industry (four-digit)
   b. What types of products are or are not included in this industry?
2. Locate the *U.S. Industrial Outlook* and/or *Standard and Poor's Industry Surveys* in your library to find the answers to the following.
   a. What was the value of industry shipments (sales) for the United States in the latest year reported?
   b. What were worldwide sales for the industry in the most recent year reported?
3. The U.S. Census Bureau publishes a number of economic censuses every five years covering years ending in 2 and 7. These include the following publications: *Census of Retail Trade, Census of Wholesale Trade, Census of Service Industries, Census of Transportation, Census of Manufactures, Census of Mineral Industries,* and *Census of Construction Industries.* Use the *Census of Manufactures* to determine the value of shipments in your industry for the most recent year reported.
4. *Ward's Business Directory* provides useful industry-specific information. Use it to find the names and addresses of the top four *public* companies in the industry and their sales revenues.
5. *Compact Disclosure* provides information from company annual reports on CD-ROM. Use it to provide the following for the four companies listed in question 4.
   a. the income statements
   b. the net sales, gross profits, and income before tax
6. The *Statistical Abstract of the United States* provides information on the economic, demographic, social, and political structure of the United States. It provides data on the sales of products in consumer markets. Use it to complete the following.
   a. Find a product in the consumer market that is produced by your industry (or is down the chain from your industry; for example, automobiles from the steel industry).
   b. Determine the sales of the consumer product category for the most recent year reported.

Key Terms

Endnotes

1. B. Charles Ames, and James D. Hlaracek, *Managerial Marketing for Industrial Firms* (New York: Random House Business Division, 1984); Edward F. Fern, and James R. Brown, "The Industrial/Consumer Marketing Dichotomy: A Case of Insufficient Justification," *Journal of Marketing* (Spring 1984): 68–77.

2. E. Jerome McCarthy and William D. Perreault, Jr., *Basic Marketing* (Boston: Irwin, 1993).

3. Kate Bertrand, "Crafting 'Win-Win' Situations in Buyer-Supplier Relationships," *Business Marketing* (June 1986): reprinted in V. Kijewski, B. Donath, and D.T. Wilson, eds., *The Best Readings from Business Marketing Magazine* (Boston: PWS-Kent).

4. Laurel Touby, "The Big Squeeze on Small Organizations," *Business Week* (July 19, 1993): pp. 66–67.

5. John Helyar, Meg Cox, and Elizabeth Jensen, "How Fox Grabbed the Football Away from CBS," *The Wall Street Journal* (Dec. 20, 1993): B1.

6. Kate Bertrand, "With Customers, the Closer the Better," *Business Marketing* (July 1989).

7. Terry Lefton, "Spring Positions as Biz Solution," *Brandweek* (July 11, 1994): 6.

8. "Why Sam's Wants Businesses to Join the Club," *Business Week* (June 27, 1994): 48.

9. Richard W. Stevenson, "Air Force Chooses Lockheed's Design for Fighter Plane," *The New York Times* (April 24, 1991): A1.

10. Mark Amtower, "There's Room for Players of All Types and Sizes," *Business Marketing* (July 1994): G-1.

11. George Anders, "Battle of HMOs For Military Job Could Be Model," *The Wall Street Journal* (July 8, 1993): B1.

12. Mark Amtower, "There's Room for Players of All Types and Sizes," *Business Marketing* (July 1994): G-1.

13. Larry C. Giunipers, William Crittenden, and Vicky Crittenden, "Industrial Marketing in Non-Profit Organizations," *Industrial Marketing Management* (1990): 279.

14. For a study that examined factors affecting the time taken to make purchase decisions in organizations, see Ruby Roy Dholakia, Jean L. Johnson, Albert J. Della Bitta, and Nikhilesh Dholakia, "Decision-Making Time in Organizational Buying Behavior: An Investigation of its Antecedents," *Journal of the Academy of Marketing Science* (Fall 1993): 281–292.

15. James M. Sinkula, "Market Information Processing and Organizational Learning," *Journal of Marketing* (Jan. 1994): 35–45.

16. J. Joseph Cronin, Jr. and Michael H. Morris, "Satisfying Customer Expectations; the Effect on Conflict and Repurchase Intentions in Industrial Marketing Channels," *Journal of the Academy of Marketing Science* (Winter, 1989): 41–49; Thomas W. Leigh and Patrick F. McGraw, "Mapping the Procedural Knowledge of Industrial Sales Personnel: A Script-Theoretic Investigation," *Journal of Marketing* (Jan. 1989): 16–34; William J. Qualls and Christopher P. Puto, "Organizational Climate and Decision Framing: An Integrated Approach to Analyzing Industrial Buying," *Journal of Marketing Research* (May, 1989): 179–192.

17. Daniel H. McQuiston, "Novelty, Complexity, and Importance as Causal Determinants of Industrial Buyer Behavior," *Journal of Marketing* (April 1989): 66–79.

18. Jeff Cole, "Boeing Wins Huge Southwest Air Order, Giving 737 Upgrade Plans a Green Light," *The Wall Street Journal* (Nov. 18, 1993): A4.

19. James S. Hirsch, "American Express, the Sleeping Giant, Wakes and Spooks the Travel Industry," *The Wall Street Journal* (Feb. 24, 1994): B10.

20. Faye W. Gilbert, Joyce A. Young, and Charles R. O'Neal, "Buyer-Seller Relationships in Just-in-Time Purchasing Environments," *Journal of Organizational Research,* (Feb. 1994): pp. 29, 111–120.

MARKETING IN ACTION: REAL PEOPLE AT NUCOR

Ken Iverson is CEO of Nucor Corporation, a steelmaker based in Charlotte, North Carolina. Nucor is an American firm that has prospered in an industry that was almost destroyed by lower-priced steel from Japan. Japan's mills had to be rebuilt after they were destroyed during World War II. Ironically, this meant they could take advantage of newer technology than was being used at older U.S. steel mills, enabling Japan to produce the same product more efficiently. Nucor has thrived, though, by building many small, strategically located, steel mills that also use modern steelmaking technology. More important, Nucor has developed an effective business-to-business marketing strategy.

Nucor understands the importance of building lasting relationships between buyers and sellers. Most of Nucor's marketing function is handled by the individual sales and marketing manager with a staff of ten to fifteen people at each individual plant. This means that there is a marketing manager at the plant level who is close to all his customers and who can make on-the-spot decisions. According to Iverson, ". . . most of marketing is getting to where you can service your customer and find out what your customer needs. The idea is to get the marketing down to the lowest practical level—get the people in each plant doing it, not some guy calling the shots from the corporate office." Iverson works individually with each sales manager, meeting with them at least quarterly on a formal basis, but more often in informal settings. And he is always willing to meet with an individual sales managers' customers.

Nucor also understands that in business-to-business marketing, firms must be especially aware of the need for customer satisfaction. The firm regularly invests in marketing research by conducting surveys about possible new products or studying a region being considered for a new plant. In fact, plants themselves are designed based on research findings about the mix of products—hot rolled, cold rolled, and galvanized steel—needed in each geographic market.

Superior customer service is also a major competitive factor. Nucor offers customers in-house engineering assistance such as building a 200-foot joist for the San Antonio Alamodome. Nucor can also offer its customers quick response time, because of their active, concerned sales force, and the best delivery, because they have their own fleet of trucks. In fact, Nucor guarantees delivery at a certain time, or they pay any extra costs their customers incur because of the delay.

And there are other little things. For example, Nucor makes sure its joists are loaded onto trucks for delivery in numbered order; that way the joists can be moved directly from the truck to the building, never having to be placed on the ground—no laydown time or space needed.

Nucor also understands the importance of helping customers as they go through the steps of the buying process. The company focuses advertising messages on what individual customers do with the products they buy. Each Nucor division has its own unique promotion plan. This means that some divisions use advertising more than others: For example, the Vulcraft division, a steel joist company that has had a sustained advertising program going for twenty-two years, has over 50 percent of the market. For Nucor, there is but one purpose for advertising: "to tell the customer why you're there and what you're doing." Iverson says, "We're here to give the customer what he wants. That's our focus everywhere. We may talk about a product, but our efforts are to give a character or a 'personality' to the division in those advertisements, to make the customer comfortable doing business with us."

Another unique aspect of Nucor's customer-oriented marketing program is its pricing strategy. The company prides itself on making manufacturing decisions that lead to cutting-edge products—produced at the most competitive prices. What is different is that Nucor products are always sold at the published price—no special discounts are given to anybody. That way customers see price increases or decreases as real—not just a marketing ploy. And, all customers are charged the same price, regardless of the quantity ordered. Because of this, customers themselves can be more efficient because they are able to maintain the lowest practical inventory.

And what is CEO Iverson's advice to other companies that want to be successful? "Be honest. Today's customers want straight answers and quick responses. And, when necessary, tell them when you can't do it."

Source: Bryan Pack, "Power Marketing From the Top," *Business Marketing* (March 1993): 22–24.

Things to Talk About

1. Why has Nucor been successful when other U.S. steel firms have not?
2. How does Nucor work to build customer relationships?
3. What are some ways Nucor strives to provide customer satisfaction?
4. What are some ways that Nucor is a New Era marketer?
5. What secrets to success has Nucor discovered?

MARKETING IN ACTION: REAL CHOICES AT AMIDA INDUSTRIES

Amida Industries is a privately owned company founded in 1973 with annual sales of over $16 million. Amida's primary business is the manufacture and sale of mobile diesel generator-powered floodlighting towers. Generator-powered floodlighting towers are considered capital equipment and are used for nighttime construction of highways and buildings because they require no separate power source, provide the high levels of light necessary for the construction industry, and are easily moved from one location to another. Amida also produces traffic control arrowboards, engine/generator power systems, and concrete finishing and handling equipment.

Amida enjoys a position of leadership in the floodlight industry and strong product recognition worldwide. The company philosophy is one of providing the most innovative, durable, and reliable equipment to the marketplace. Amida prides itself on its strong engineering capability and its focus on quality, performance, reliability, and safety. The size of the light tower business is determined by both economic factors and by seasonality. Because the construction industry is directly affected by the strength of the economy, tower sales may face dramatic fluctuations during periods of economic growth and downturn. Smaller, but still significant, fluctuations of demand are attributable to changing weather during the seasons of the year. And special conditions, such as the Gulf War or natural disasters, can create sudden increases in sales.

Amida's major competitors are Ingersoll-Rand, Allmand Brothers, and Coleman Engineering. Compared to competitors' products, the major strength of the Amida's light tower is its rugged durable design. But this also makes the Amida product heavier. Amida's product is also more expensive than those of competitors, carrying a premium price but also good value. Amida's advertising message communicates this: "When quality and performance count."

Historically, Amida floodlight towers have been marketed exclusively through a select group of AEDs (associated equipment distributors) who primarily sell and occasionally rent to major contractors and end users willing to pay a premium price for a superior product. The sales function for Amida is handled by one international and five regional sales managers who call on the distributors. While marketing communications are primarily left to the Amida and distributor sales forces, some advertising in trade magazines and journals and exhibits at trade shows are used.

Since the early 1970s, the rental yard business has been a separate and unique part of the "light" construction equipment market and since the mid-1980s has played a major role in the marketing of floodlights. During the late 1980s and early 1990s, there was tremendous growth in the number, size, and importance of rental yards as they became a key player in the distribution process of heavy, general, and light construction equipment. Customers rent light towers for two reasons: to acquire use of the equipment for special projects and to fill in with extra equipment during peak work periods, thus reducing necessary capital expenditures.

Amida initially responded to industry changes by developing an economy floodlight tower that offered fewer features and a cost structure attractive to the price-sensitive rental industry. This strategy, however, caused problems with Amida's loyal and exclusive AED channel of distribution. Amida was encouraged not to sell to the rental industry or run the risk of losing its strong relationships with the established distribution network. As a result, the door was opened for competitors who seized the opportunity to provide the marketplace with low-priced, low-quality floodlights through the rental industry.

The construction recession of 1990 to 1993 added strength to the rental industry as more and more firms moved from buying to renting equipment. At the same time, AED houses, also hurt by the recession, curtailed stocking and aggressively selling the higher-priced Amida product because they felt they were unable to compete with the low-price strategy of the rental industry. Amida, because it had not been aggressively pursuing the rental yards as customers, was unable to compete. As a result, during the early 1990s Amida saw a decline in the volume of floodlight sales, decreasing margins, and a loss of market share.

Amida's dilemma is two-fold. If Amida sells to rental yards, it will have to change current AED contract provisions that guarantee the distributors certain geographic territories, thus losing the support of the AEDs. If they continue to market their products only through the distributors, they face continued loss of market share. And, the rental yards are hesitant to purchase the Amida product because of the high-end pricing strategy. On the positive side is the future of the total market. While generally, the

Marketing in Action: Real Choices at Amida Industries *(continued)*

light tower market is a mature market, an increase in the size of the market is expected in the coming years as road construction projects continue to increase.

Source: This case based on information gained through personal interviews with company personnel for use in student classroom projects.

Things to Think About

1. What are the problems facing Amida Industries?

2. What factors are important in understanding the problems?

3. What are the alternatives?

4. What are your recommendations for solving the problems?

5. What are some ways to implement your recommendations?

Sharpening the Focus: Market Segmentation

When you have completed your study of this chapter, you should be able to:

1. Understand the need for market segmentation in today's business environment.

2. Explain the steps used in identifying attractive target markets.

3. Explain how marketers segment consumer markets.

4. Understand the bases for segmentation in industrial markets.

5. Explain how potential market segments are evaluated and selected.

6. Understand how a firm develops a product positioning strategy.

REAL PEOPLE, REAL CHOICES:

MEET SARAH BURROUGHS, A DECISION MAKER AT BURRELL COMMUNICATIONS

As president and chief operating officer of Burrell Communications Group, Sarah Burroughs is a key decision maker for the country's largest minority-owned advertising agency. Headquartered in Chicago, Burrell has developed black-oriented communications programs for such clients as Dial Corp., Playskool, Prudential Insurance Co., and L'eggs Products. The company has created advertising for McDonald's targeted to black consumers since 1972.

Ms. Burroughs began her advertising career in 1964 at Foote, Cone & Belding/Chicago, where she started out as an analytic assistant/typist and worked her way up through the company's ranks. In 1971 she was promoted to vice president/associate research director, making her the youngest person to be named a vice president in the agency's history. During her successful stint at FC&B she worked on such accounts as Kraft, Sunbeam, and Armour-Dial.

Since going to work for Burrell over twenty years ago, Ms. Burroughs has worked on nearly all of the company's accounts, in addition to managing the agency's consumer research department. She is an alumnus of Lincoln University in Jefferson City, Missouri, where she earned a bachelor of arts degree in history.

HAVE IT YOUR WAY

The goal of the marketer is to satisfy needs, but in our modern, complex society it is often naïve to assume that everyone's needs are the same. Particularly in the United States, the population is a mosaic of many different types of people, from different ethnic and racial backgrounds and with different lifestyles. Although almost every American eats at Burger King, McDonald's, or other fast-food chains periodically, their needs and wants differ in important ways. For example, a salesman who needs to grab a quick lunch on the way to his next customer appointment is most interested in fast drive-thru service. A father who wants to take his kids out for a special treat is attracted to a fast-food restaurant that offers special children's meals, a clean cheerful dining area, and, best of all, a neat playground. The retired couple looking for a place for breakfast on their drive across the country to Branson, Missouri, want a good hearty breakfast at a reasonable price while the college student who insists on healthy eating is only interested in a grilled chicken sandwich and a salad.

Sarah Burroughs and her colleagues know that marketing strategies need to be tailored to the diverse likes and dislikes of consumers who share certain characteristics. Even a "simple" decision like what type of fast food to eat (if any at all) is influenced by many factors that must be considered when a company like Burrell Communications designs campaigns for McDonald's and its other corporate clients.

In this chapter we will first talk about why marketers think target marketing is important. Then we will outline the steps in identifying target markets and many of the different ways marketers often segment consumer and industrial markets. Finally, we'll talk about how to devise a separate marketing mix strategy to satisfy each group's needs and position products to different market segments.

In the remainder of this chapter we'll explore in detail how to identify different market segments in both the consumer and business-to-business markets. Then we'll discuss how to select market segments and how to identify each group's concerns and interests.

Selecting and entering the market

Technological and cultural advances in modern Western society have created a condition of **market fragmentation,** where people's diverse interests and activities have divided them into many different groups with distinct needs and wants. Because of this diversity there are bound to be limits to the degree that the same good or service will appeal to everyone. The flowering of so many different alternatives, whether in music, clothing, cuisine, decorating, or other forms of expression, has spurred the development of goods and services that satisfy very individual tastes.

Consider, for example, the effects of fragmentation in the radio industry. Thirty years ago there were three basic categories of popular music: pop, rhythm & blues, and country. Today, though, there are dozens of musical types, and each *genre* can be heard on specialized radio stations. This level of musical fragmentation has brought about the rapid decline of the so-called Top 40 format. People's tastes are so diverse that it simply is not possible to cater to them all on one station.[1] That explains why the market share of American Top 40 radio stations declined by 40 percent in a three-year period while half of the roughly 1,000 stations featuring that format changed to a more specialized one during the same time.[2] These new formats range from such categories as Churban (a mixture of Contemporary Hit Radio, which is the industry term for Top 40, and urban, which features dance music, rap, and hip-hop) to Alternative (featuring groups with large college audiences, such as U2, Nirvana, and Jesus Jones).

The way we get our information about goods and services has changed too. Advances in communications technology have made it much easier to practice **narrowcasting** (as opposed to *broadcasting*), where the marketing communications presented in magazines or other media are tailored to the needs of small groups of people. For example, printing techniques such as select binding and inkjetting now allow an automotive advertiser to insert ads that reach only magazine readers who own cars that are at least five years old.[3] To the extent that we can sharpen our focus by slicing a total market into smaller ones that share important characteristics, we can do a better job of satisfying customer needs. In this section we will talk about some of the reasons marketers use target market strategies and briefly examine the concepts of market segmentation, targeting, and product positioning.

market fragmentation: a condition in society in which people are divided into many different groups with distinct needs and wants

narrowcasting: the use of marketing communications in magazines or other media tailored to the needs of small groups of people

Satisfying Customers: From Basic Black to the Whole Rainbow

As we saw in Chapter 1, Henry Ford and his Ford Motor Company exemplified the *mass-marketing approach* to production, where one item is manufactured and distributed

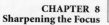

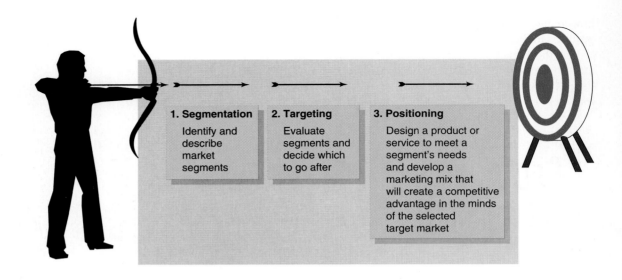

Figure 8.1
Steps in the Target Marketing Process

to many buyers at once. With the development of revolutionary mass-production tech-niques, legions of black Model T's rolled off Ford's assembly lines at a rate never before witnessed in the dawning Industrial Age. Because it standardized its product, Ford was able to provide cars to the masses at an affordable price, helping to liberate working peo-ple from the drudgery of everyday life and transforming American society by giving its citizens tremendous mobility.

Although everyone can use basic transportation, people also value variety—their unique *wants* are shaped by diverse backgrounds, income differences, gender dif-ferences, and all the other differences reviewed in Chapter 6. Today's consumers would be very unhappy if they had only one color choice for their new automobile. But how many colors does Ford or GM or Toyota need to offer? How many different models? How many different options? Marketers must make such decisions by bal-ancing efficiency with effectiveness. *Mass marketing,* in which a firm has one product that is offered to the entire market, is certainly the most efficient plan—it costs much less to offer one product in one size and one color for the entire market. On the other hand, the most effective marketing strategy would be one that develops the perfect product for each individual consumer— the perfect color, size, flavor, and so on. But doing that would not be efficient and would cause products to cost so much that only a few could afford them.

Thus, marketers seek the best compromise between efficiency and effectiveness—to maximize customer satisfaction (and company profits) by developing enough variety in products to meet the needs and wants of different customers but at a price that they can afford. The result is a range of product strategies. On one end marketers may select a *mass marketing strategy,* but in today's sophisticated marketplace, mass-marketing strategies are used for only the most basic products.

Groups of consumers often *share* a set of needs and preferences that set them apart from other groups. Thus, marketers may instead select a **target market strategy** where the market is divided into different segments based on customer characteristics. Once the market is divided, the marketer may choose to go after only one segment (a *concentrated strategy*) or to develop products for several different segments.

As far back as 1920 Al Sloan, a pioneering marketer at Ford's rival General Motors, re-alized that consumers' needs and tastes are different. So Sloan divided the car market into five segments, and he set out to produce a different car for each. The divisions of GM were

target market strategy: a marketing strategy in which a firm seeks to serve the needs of one or more different segments

born, as the Chevrolet, Pontiac, Oldsmobile, Buick, and Cadillac models were created to satisfy the needs of different buying groups.[4] Each division developed its own unique identity, which was forged by a distinctive application of the marketing mix: Models were created to satisfy the needs of buyers ranging from those of modest means to the well off.[5] More recently GM targeted still another segment by adding its new Saturn division to meet the needs of "New Age" buyers who want a fresh alternative to its traditional offerings.

Target marketing happens in three major steps, each of which will be discussed in some detail. For now, though, it is helpful to describe these activities very briefly. To illustrate target marketing in action, we'll consider how these steps would be implemented by a marketing manager for a chewing gum company. These steps are also illustrated in Figure 8.1.

IDENTIFYING CONSUMERS: MARKET SEGMENTATION AND TARGETING

Segmentation: First, the overall market is divided into *market segments,* where each segment has one or more important characteristics in common, characteristics that set it apart from others. Once the relevant market segments have been identified, a *profile* of each segment is constructed. The manager would collect information about heavy gum chewers versus occasional gum chewers and would construct a profile of different user types. These segments might include such groups as "Nervous Nellies," "Tough Guy Wannabees," or "Sewer Breaths."

Targeting: The marketer next evaluates the segments he or she has identified in terms of their relative attractiveness and his or her ability to meet each segment's unique needs. On the basis of this analysis the company decides which segment(s) to target. For example, the Wm. Wrigley Jr. Company, makers of Wrigley's gum, identified cigarette smokers who are finding it harder to smoke in public places as a unique group of current or potential customers and decided to go after them.

REACHING CONSUMERS: PRODUCT POSITIONING

Positioning: After the selection of a target market segment (or segments), a good or service is developed to meet the segment's needs, and the benefits of the offering are communicated and delivered in a way that will appeal to segment members. This is called a *positioning strategy* and involves the creation of a marketing mix that is calculated to closely match the needs of the segment and to provide a *competitive advantage* over rival offerings in the minds of segment members.

For example, Wrigley made some important decisions about how to market its gum, some of which were different from what competitors decided to do. Wrigley maintained its price at five sticks for twenty-five cents, the same price as in 1987. When it developed a promotional strategy, Wrigley resisted the industry trend toward heavy couponing and trade deals (providing support to retailers in return for stocking and featuring the product). Instead, the company stuck to spending 90 percent of its marketing budget on brand advertising, which promotes the theme of providing smokers with an acceptable alternative: "When I can't smoke, I enjoy pure chewing satisfaction."

Finally, the effectiveness of the target marketing strategy must be continually monitored, with adjustments made when necessary. The gum manager will receive reports "from the field" that track how the brand is selling in different regions. He or she will keep tabs on what competitors are doing, and maybe even talk to retailers and customers about the gum's taste, availability, advertising, and so on. You can be sure that Wrigley will keep close tabs on how attitudes toward smoking, regulations about smoke-free offices, and so on are changing in the late 1990s.

STEPS IN IDENTIFYING TARGET MARKETS

market segmentation: a process whereby marketers divide a large customer group into segments that share important characteristics

The target marketing process begins with **market segmentation,** in which a large customer group is divided into segments that share important characteristics. Slicing up the market makes it more manageable and allows the marketer to learn more about the specific needs of selected consumers. As one prominent marketing scholar remarked, "If you're not thinking segmentation, you're not thinking."[6] In this section we'll outline how firms select markets based on customer demand.

DETERMINING CONSUMER DEMAND PATTERNS

Because people's needs are different, marketers must first understand what consumers are looking for before they can try to give it to them. Suppose you were the programming director for your college radio station. Assuming that (especially after taking this course!) you are genuinely interested in playing what your audience wants to hear, you would probably be very interested in knowing something about the musical tastes on campus. In other words, you would want to determine the pattern of consumer demand for your product, which is music. Depending on the particular character of your school, you might arrive at one of the following conclusions after conducting some market research.

homogenous demand: demand in which most people prefer the same product characteristics

1. Most people seem to want to hear the same type of music—pop rock. You are dealing with **homogenous demand.** In this scenario you simply play that one type of music that you know will satisfy your audience's preferences—a mass-marketing strategy.

clustered demand: demand in which most people prefer one of a set of several product varieties

2. Most people seem to have very specific preferences for one of three different types of music: rhythm and blues, heavy metal, and rap. You are dealing with **clustered demand.** Your station programming will satisfy audience wants by providing the three types of music for these three listener clusters or segments—a target marketing strategy.

diffused demand: demand in which most people have very specific preferences that are not the same for everyone

3. Most people have very specific preferences, but these are not the same for everyone. There are a few students who are strongly interested in rap, some that must have country, others that will listen only to alternative rock, and so on. You are dealing with **diffused demand.** In this case you cannot develop programming of specific types of music. Rather, you may choose to randomly play all types of music during your broadcasts, offering a variety of products to please the market.

IDENTIFYING USABLE MARKET SEGMENTS

Just because a demand segment has been identified does not necessarily mean that this classification is a useful one. For a segment to be usable, it should satisfy the following criteria:

1. Are members of the segment similar to each other in their product needs and wants and, at the same time, different from consumers in other segments? Without real differences in consumer needs, firms might just as well use a mass-marketing strategy. On the other hand, it must be possible to develop a product that will be approved by the segment as a whole.

2. Can the segment be measured and understood? Marketers must know something about the size and purchasing power of a potential segment before they can decide if it is worth their efforts. While it may be true that extroverts buy certain products and introverts do not, measuring such personality characteristics of consumers is just not feasible.

3. Is the segment large enough to be profitable, now and in the future? Sometimes a segment is so small that it is ignored because firms cannot provide a unique product at a reasonable price.

4. Can marketing communications be developed to reach the segment? It is easy to select television programs or magazines that will efficiently reach older consumers, consumers with certain levels of education, or residents of major cities. It is unlikely, however, that a media plan can be developed to reach only left-handed blondes. Therefore it may not be reasonable to try to address that segment with a unique marketing plan.

5. Can the marketer adequately serve the segment's needs? Does the firm have the expertise, the resources, the facilities, and so on to be successful in satisfying the segment better than the competition?

DEVELOPING SEGMENT PROFILES

Once a set of relevant and usable segments has been identified, it is helpful to generate a description of each. This *segment profile* often consists of a thumbnail sketch of the "typical" customer in that segment. A segment profile might, for instance, include customer demographics, where the customer is located geographically, lifestyle information, and a description of how frequently the customer buys the product in a typical month. These profiles are useful in evaluating the relative attractiveness of each segment—that is, how well the capabilities and resources of the firm "fit" with the segment.

DIMENSIONS FOR SEGMENTING CONSUMER MARKETS

An important first task in segmenting a market is to decide on one or more meaningful **segmentation variables,** characerics of customers that will allow the total market to be divided into fairly homogenous groups, each with different needs that can be profitably met by a firm. These variables are often used in combination as the marketer continues to break down the larger market into smaller and smaller subgroups. For example, while it used to be sufficient to segment the leisure shoe market into athletes versus nonathletes, a walk through any sporting goods store will reveal that the athlete segment has now been sliced even further, as shoes designed just for jogging, basketball, tennis, cycling, and so on continue to flood the market. Marketers have found it useful to construct segmentation profiles by using information about consumers based on one or

segmentation variables: characteristics of customers that will allow the total market to be divided into fairly homogenous groups, each with different needs that can be profitably met by a firm

Sharpening the Focus 265

more of three dimensions: demographics, lifestyles, and behavior. Let's consider each dimension in turn.

SEGMENTING BY DEMOGRAPHICS

Demographics refers to the measurable characteristics of a population. People can be distinguished in terms of their sex, race, income, age, marital status, and other variables, and these distinctions are vital for identifying the best potential customers for a good or service. Imagine trying to sell baby food to a single male, or an around-the-world vacation to a couple making $15,000 a year!

Age Groups

Consumers of different age groups obviously have very different needs and wants. Levi Strauss has been successful in developing the idea that it is a "brand for life" by introducing products such as Dockers to meet the needs of their consumers as they age. As a Levi's marketing executive explained, "In the 1960s, growth [in the jeans market] was due to adoption of jeans by 15-to-18 year olds. . . . Now these people are 25-49 and Dockers meshes perfectly with what the Levi brand image is about for them."[7] Let's briefly consider how marketers are addressing the needs of different age groups:

- Children have become a very important age segment for marketers. In addition to their obvious appeal as recipients of toys and games, children influence other family purchases as well. By one estimate children aged four to twelve have a say in family-related purchases of more than $130 billion a year.[8] Recognizing the importance of the children's market, Burger King has become the largest publisher of kid's magazines. It sent 3 million copies of new magazines directed to different age segments: "Small Fries" for kids five and younger, "Great Shakes" for six- to eight-year-olds, and "Have It Your Way" for nine- and ten-year-olds. All three magazines contained paid advertising for Anheuser-Busch theme parks, Sprite soda, and Cap'n Crunch cereals.[9]

- The term "Generation X" has been used to describe people who are now in their twenties. While this is an attractive segment for many marketers, they have been struggling to overcome "X'ers" cynicism and sophistication about marketing (for example, a chapter in a book called *Generation X* is entitled "I am not a target market"!).[10] As one twenty-year-old Japanese woman commented, "I don't like to be told what's trendy. I can make up my own mind."[11]

  Cynicism aside, the annual spending power of this age segment is about $125 billion. Over half of "Generation X'ers" still live with their parents, which leaves them with more disposable income and less entrenched brand loyalties. Major marketers are going after them: Ford developed ads to appeal to under-thirty buyers featuring hard rock and quick cuts that look like music videos. Coca-Cola is expanding global distribution of a sports drink called PowerAde and also introduced Nordic Mist and Fruitopia to appeal to this segment.[12]

- "Baby boomers," who are in their thirties and forties, are a segment that has been influenced by Vietnam, Martin Luther King, rock'n roll music, and the sexual revolution. They value individualism, self-fulfillment, and social responsibility. They are also concerned with reducing stress and fighting the aging process. Because of their size and purchasing power, baby boomers are of prime importance to many marketers. Time-Warner recently formed a separate unit to create or acquire magazines that specifically address the interests of baby boomers, including such titles as *In Health, Parenting,* and *Cooking Light.*[13]

■ According to the 1990 Census, there are 31.2 million Americans aged sixty-five or older, a 22 percent increase in this age segment since 1980. Many consumers in their sixties and seventies are enjoying leisure time but are in declining health. Significant events that shaped their values include World War II and the Great Depression. This age group tends to be patriotic, has a strong work ethic, respects authority, and seeks financial security.

Many marketers are focusing on offering goods and services that meet the needs of aging consumers. Some are adding product features that make it more convenient for older people to use these items. For example, Whirlpool now sells kitchen ranges with side controls to allow wheelchair accessibility. Other companies are providing senior citizens with a sense of purpose and a way to spend their considerable discretionary income: Royal Cruise Lines has developed specialized cruises featuring seminars on such topics as financial planning and an introduction to computers that appeal to this group. McDonald's has even focused on the romantic side of people growing old together. One commercial, called "Golden Years," features an older couple who fell in love over a McDonald's meal.[14]

Gender

Many products, from fragrances to footwear, are developed to appeal to either men or women. Segmenting by sex starts at a very early age—even diapers are sold in pink versions for girls and blue for boys. As proof that consumers take these differences seriously, market research has revealed that most parents refuse to put male infants in pink diapers![15] Of course, it would be foolish to assume that all women or all men are alike, so even further segmentation is often required to divide men or women into subgroups that share important characteristics.

Segmenting the Female Market. In particular, dramatic changes in women's life-styles have made it necessary for many marketers to further divide female consumers into smaller market segments. Adult women can be further segmented into at least four groups, depending on their career goals and aspirations:

1. Housewives who do not plan to work outside of the home.

2. Housewives who plan to work at some point. The women in this group may be staying at home only temporarily—until small children grow old enough to enter school, for example—and can't be grouped with those housewives who have voluntarily chosen a domestic life-style.

3. Career-oriented working women who value professional success and the trappings of achievement. In recent years more and more women are "stopping out,"—that is, women who have developed significant careers are choosing to stay home for a number of years to begin a family and be full-time mothers.

4. "Just a job" women who work primarily because they need the money.[16]

Important changes in the needs and behaviors of female consumers are forcing marketers who traditionally assumed that their primary market was male to think again. Most notably, car manufacturers traditionally did not make much of an effort to segment the market by gender, since it was assumed that men were responsible for choosing and purchasing cars. This situation is changing radically and car makers are scrambling to keep up with it. While most car advertising is still male-oriented, women are increasingly depicted as serious buyers. More than six in ten new car buyers under the age of 50 are female, and it has been estimated that women influence 80% of all car purchasing decisions.[6] A new magazine called *American Women Motorscene* was even launched recently to focus exclusively on women car buyers.

Family Structure

Because family needs and expenditures change over time, one way to segment consumers is to consider the stage of the *family life cycle* (FLC) they currently occupy (see Chapter 6). Not surprisingly, consumers in different life-cycle segments have wide-ranging needs.[17] For example, Procter & Gamble recently introduced Folger's Singles to cater to people who live alone and don't need to brew a full pot of coffee at a time.[18]

As we age and move into new life situations, different product categories ascend and descend in importance. Young bachelors and newlyweds are the most likely to exercise; go to bars, concerts, and movies; and to consume alcohol. Families with young children are big purchasers of health foods and fruit juices, while single-parent households and those with older children buy more junk food. Home maintenance services are most likely to be used by older couples and bachelors.

Income and Social Class

The distribution of wealth is of great interest to marketers, because it determines what groups have the greatest buying power and market potential. As we saw in Chapter 4, an explosion of economies in countries from Latin America to Asia is changing the way marketers look at income segments. Consumers in these countries are now beginning to earn incomes that qualify them as attractive market segments for appliances, cars, and cosmetics. For example, while sales of cars in 1993 declined by 4 percent overall, they actually increased by 19 percent in Latin America as incomes rose there.[19]

It should come as no surprise that many marketers yearn to capture the hearts and wallets of high-income consumers. For example, the Italian luxury carmaker Bugatti seems to have no trouble selling autos with sticker prices exceeding $350,000—the company recorded $44 million in sales in 1994.[20] On the other hand, at least some marketers are finding it worth their while to pay more attention to lower-income consumers, who make up about 40 percent of the U.S. market (as defined by households with incomes of $25,000 or less). Discount stores such as Dollar General and Wal-Mart have done quite well for themselves by catering to this segment.[21]

Consumers in different social classes tend to have distinct sets of needs and preferences. While social class and income are related, they are not the same: Many people who earn similar incomes are quite different when it comes to their tastes and values. For this reason marketers often find it necessary to go beyond simple income when seeking to identify market segments. For example, working-class consumers (regardless of income) are more likely to buy domestic products than are middle-class consumers.

Race and Ethnicity

Racial or ethnic categories are important segmentation variables. Membership in these groups often is predictive of media usage, food preferences, the wearing of distinctive apparel, political behavior, leisure activities, and even willingness to try new products.

Racial and ethnic segmentation is affected by country of origin, length of U.S. residency, and socioeconomic status. African Americans, Hispanic Americans, and Asian Americans are the three fastest-growing ethnic groups in the United States. Let's take a closer look at each of these groups.

As demonstrated by McDonald's extensive efforts to appeal to the black community, *African Americans* are a significant racial market segment and account for 12 percent of the U.S. population. If American blacks were a separate nation, their buying power would rank twelfth of any Western country.[23]

The size of the African American market has prompted many companies to sit up and take notice. After Coca-Cola found that African Americans often prefer larger servings of soft drinks, they began using sixteen-ounce containers in their ads directed to this market. In addition, sometimes this segment uses the same product in a different way, as when researchers for Carnation's Instant Breakfast found that African Americans tend to use the product as a breakfast supplement rather than as a substitute.

The *Hispanic American* population is a sleeping giant, a segment that until recently was largely ignored by many marketers. There are now over 19 million Hispanic consumers in the United States. Because of this segment's high birthrate, it is projected that Hispanics will outnumber African Americans as the nation's largest minority group by the year 2015. The number of Hispanics in the United States grew by 30 percent between 1980 and 1988, and the birthrate within this segment is four times the national average.

The growth and increasing affluence of the Hispanic-American population has now made it impossible to overlook, and the Hispanic consumer is now diligently courted by many major corporations. For example, Pepsi sponsors local ethnic festivals in major cities, and the company also signed the music group Miami Sound Machine for its Latin promotions.[7] General Mills recently became the first cereal company to offer a product specifically targeted to Hispanics. It is called *Bunuelitos,* which is taken from bunuelo, a sweet Mexican pastry.[8]

Exhibit 8.1
The recent proliferation of ethnic dolls in America's toy stores reflects society's growing cultural diversity. While non-Caucasian dolls used to appear only in collections of dolls from around the world, all major manufacturers have now introduced ethnic dolls to the mass market. These new entrants include Kira, the Asian fashion doll and Emmy the African-American baby doll. Mattel for several years produced a trio of dolls named Shani (which means "marvelous" in Swahili), Asha, and Nichelle that represent the range of African-American facial features and skin tones. And, while Mattel has sold an African-American version of Barbie for over 20 years, it only recently began to promote the doll in television and print campaigns. Tyco's African-American hairstyling doll sold 250,000 units in 1992. Olmec, the largest manufacturer of African-American-oriented toys, now sells both Martin Luther King and Malcolm X dolls.

In addition to its sheer growth, four other factors make the Hispanic segment attractive to marketers: (1) Hispanics tend to be brand-loyal, especially to brands from their country of origin;[24] (2) they tend to be highly concentrated by national origin, which makes it easy to identify subsegments (for example, Cuban Americans or Mexican Americans); and (3) this market segment is young, with the median age of Hispanic Americans as 23.6 compared to the U.S. average of 32. Finally, (4) the average Hispanic household contains 3.5 people, compared to only 2.7 people for the rest of the United States. For this reason, Hispanic households spend 15 to 20 percent more of their disposable income than the national average on groceries and other household products.[25]

Though their numbers are still relatively small, *Asian Americans* are the fastest-growing minority group in the United States. It has been estimated that there will be 17.1 million Asian Americans by the year 2010, a little less than 6 percent of the total population.[26] Marketers are just beginning to recognize their potential as a unique market segment. This segment is attractive because Asian Americans typically are hardworking and many have above-average incomes. As one Asian American advertising executive noted, "Prosperous Asians tend to be very status-conscious and will spend their money on premium brands, such as BMW and Mercedes-Benz, and the best French cognac and Scotch whiskey." This group also is a good market for technically oriented products. They spend more than average on such products as VCRs, personal computers, and compact disc players.[27]

Despite its potential, this segment is hard to reach, because it is actually composed of subgroups that are culturally diverse and speak many different languages and dialects. The term Asian refers to twelve distinct nationalities, with Chinese being the largest subgroup and Filipino and Japanese second and third, respectively.[28] Still, marketers keep trying: Sears recently became the first major retailer to officially target the Asian American market. Among other actions, it will be taking care to offer an appropriate range of apparel sizes to this segment, because Asians tend to be shorter waisted and have smaller shoulders.[29]

Geography

Recognizing that people's preferences often vary depending on where they live, many marketers use geographic segmentation variables to tailor their offerings to appeal to different regions. Heileman Distilleries is now fifth in sales in the United States largely because of its regional marketing efforts, where distinctive brands are sold in different parts of the country. As the company's marketing vice president explained, "The primary objective of being a regional brand is to make the consumer think that 'this product is mine' . . . People tend to think positively about their hometowns, and a product strongly identified with this aura is likely to strike a responsive chord . . . ."[30] Some of Heileman's successful regional brands include Old Style, Colt 45, Lone Star, Rainier, and Samuel Adams.

There clearly are regional differences in product and life-style preferences. Some leading brands do significantly better in some parts of the country than others: While Kraft Miracle Whip is the nation's best seller in the mayonnaise category, it only turns in a third-place performance in the Northeast.[31] Some of these variations can be traced to life-style differences that influence demand. For example, residents of New York City live up to the stereotype of the fast-paced urban lifestyle. They lead the nation in *per capita* consumption of Scotch, gin, and vodka. Men buy 44 percent more clothes than the average, and women are far above average in purchases of pantyhose and hair spray.

Geodemography: In Search of Beverly Hills 90210. The search for new ways to segment markets more precisely, coupled with the increasing sophistication of data collection and analysis techniques, has enabled marketers to fine-tune their segmentation efforts using geography combined with demographics, hence **geodemography.** A basic assumption of geodemography is that "birds of a feather flock together": People who live near one another share similar characteristics. In geodemography, market researchers use sophisticated statistical techniques to identify geographic areas that share the same characteristics. This allows marketers to construct segments consisting of households that share relevant characteristics. Even more important, with geodemographic segmentation marketers

geodemography: a way to segment consumer markets based on geography combined with demographics

REAL PEOPLE, REAL CHOICES:

DECISION TIME AT BURRELL COMMUNICATIONS

Sarah Burroughs and her colleagues at Burrell Communications have been developing advertising for African American audiences since the company was founded in 1971. The agency is well known for creating ads featuring healthy, positive images of black people.[22] Many of these successful ads were done for McDonald's, one of the company's largest clients.

As a company with a long tradition of involvement with the African American community, McDonald's wanted to let their customers know that the Golden Arches are not just a source for tasty fries and burgers. It is also a business that gives many black youth in urban areas their first shot at employment opportunities. In fact, McDonald's is the largest employer of youth (particularly of African American youth) in the United States. Still, being a "burger flipper" at McDonald's or other fast-food restaurants is viewed negatively by many. McDonald's wanted to let people know that in fact the chain provides an excellent training ground for people who want to move through the ranks of restaurant management, and that McDonald's operators sponsor scholarship programs that provide college educations for many employees who started out as "crew kids."

Burrell Communications Group was given the assignment of building awareness among African American teens of the career opportunities at McDonald's. It was hoped that in the process this campaign would also result in more and better-qualified job applicants for the company. Sarah Burroughs and her staff knew that education and jobs are highly valued by African Americans, so this practical focus would be well received by them. The goal was to communicate to African American youth that crew/entry-level jobs at McDonald's can lead to long-term career opportunities within the company. But how best to implement this approach? The Burroughs team considered several creative alternatives:

Option 1. Create an advertising campaign based on a "real life" situation featuring an African American teenager who works his way up the McDonald's ranks. This would allow young viewers to identify with the person in the ads, and hopefully motivate them to consider a similar career path. On the other hand, there was always the danger that these kids would instead focus on the negative aspects of working at a "scut job" and as a result would tune out before they could be convinced that this hard work would really pay off down the road.

Option 2. Create a corporate "public service" campaign that would provide a lot of factual information about job and training opportunities available at McDonald's. This approach would allow the company to disseminate the maximum amount of information to its target group. On the other hand, a straightforward, fact-filled presentation might not be very effective at grabbing the attention of teenagers, who constituted the primary consumer segment of interest.

Option 3. Build a campaign using a celebrity approach by identifying well-known African Americans who had worked at McDonald's before hitting the big time. This "star appeal" would get teens' attention, and their admiration for these success stories might "rub off" on McDonald's. On the other hand, there was the possibility that teens would not believe that these celebrities actually worked at McDonald's, and this skepticism would drown out the message about job opportunities.

Now, put yourself in Sarah Burroughs' shoes: If you were in charge of developing a marketing communications strategy that would appeal to the market segment consisting of African American teenagers in urban areas, which option would you choose and why?

know what zip codes, census tracts, and even what neighborhood blocks have large proportions of families in each segment.

One widely used geodemographic system is called PRIZM, which was developed by Claritas, Inc. This system classifies every U.S. zip code into one of forty categories, ranging from the most-affluent "Blue-Blood Estates" to the least well-off "Public Assistance."[32] A resident of Southern California might be classified as "Money & Brains" if he or she lives in Encino (zip 91316), while someone living in Sherman Oaks (zip 91423) would be a "Young Influential."[33] This system tells marketers which products, activities, media alternatives, and so on are very likely or very unlikely to be used by people who belong to each category. For example, members of the segment known as "Pools and Patios" are very heavy purchasers of cruise vacations, health club memberships, and Alfa Romeo sports cars, while they are very unlikely to watch roller derby, read *Grit* magazine, and eat canned stews.

SEGMENTING BY LIFESTYLE

Demographic information is useful, but often knowing that members of a consumer segment are, say, female college students in suburban areas does not provide enough information to marketers. For example, we may guess that a typical member of this segment is a user of perfume, but it's impossible to tell from this description if she is a better prospect for, say, Obsession or Charlie.

This is why *lifestyle segmentation* is often such a useful way to better understand differences among consumers who may be outwardly similar to one another, but whose product preferences and needs are like night and day. Life-style segmentation involves the identification of consumer groups on the basis of shared preferences in activities, interests, or opinions.

**Figure 8.2
VALS 2**

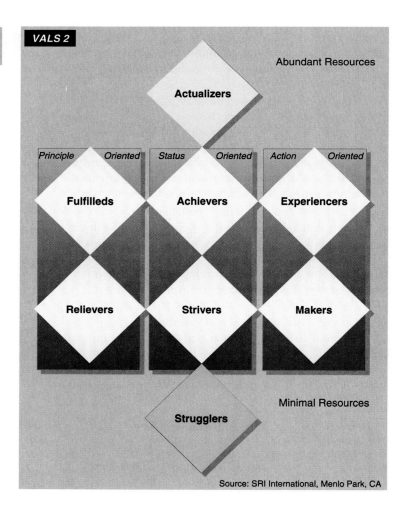

VALS 2

Abundant Resources

Actualizers

Principle   Oriented   Status   Oriented   Action   Oriented

Fulfilleds   Achievers   Experiencers

Relievers   Strivers   Makers

Minimal Resources

Strugglers

Source: SRI International, Menlo Park, CA

Lifestyle Segmentation Systems

Because lifestyle segmentation often requires data about many aspects of consumers' lives, it is common for marketers to buy this information from research companies that specialize in tracking large numbers of consumers, and then use sophisticated statistical techniques to "boil down" this information into clusters of people who seem to share similar outlooks on life and whose buying patterns overlap to a large extent.

VALS 2. One of the most well-known and widely used segmentation systems is VALS 2 (an updated version of a system called VALS, which stands for Values and Life-styles). VALS 2 divides people into eight groups that are determined both by psychological characteristics and "resources," which include such factors as income, education, energy levels, and eagerness to buy.[34]

As shown in Figure 8.2, the groups are arrayed vertically by resources and horizontally by self-orientation. The top group is termed Actualizers, who are successful consumers with many resources. This group is concerned with social issues and is open to change. The next three groups also have ample resources but differ in their outlooks on life:

- Fulfilleds are satisfied, reflective, and comfortable. They tend to be practical and value functionality.
- Achievers are career-oriented and prefer predictability over risk or self-discovery.
- Experiencers are impulsive, young, and enjoy offbeat or risky experiences.

The next three groups have fewer resources:

- Believers have strong principles and favor proven brands.
- Strivers are like achievers but with fewer resources. They are very concerned about the approval of others.
- Makers are action-oriented and tend to focus their energies on self-sufficiency. They will often be found working on their cars, canning their own vegetables, or building their own houses.
- Strugglers are at the bottom of the ladder. They are most concerned with meeting the needs of the moment and thus strongly resemble the survivor and sustainer groups they replaced.

International Lifestyle Segmentation. VALS 2 is by no means the only life-style segmentation scheme available. Researchers in a number of countries have developed lifestyle strategies to apply to their own populations. One classification scheme, developed by McCann-Erickson London, segments British male and female consumers separately. Lifestyle categories in this system include such segments as "avant guardians" (interested in change), "pontificators" (traditionalists, very British), "chameleons" (follow the crowd), and "sleepwalkers" (contented underachievers).

As countries in Eastern Europe convert to free-market economies, many marketers are exploring ways to segment these increasingly consumption-oriented societies. Some Western products such as Marlboro cigarettes and McDonald's are already firmly entrenched in Russia. The D'Arcy Masius Benton & Bowles Advertising Agency, which has offices in Moscow and St. Petersburg, conducted a study of Russian consumers and has proclaimed that the country's 150 million consumers can be divided into five segments, including "Cossacks" (status-seekers who drive BMWs and smoke Dunhill cigarettes), "*Kuptsi*" (people who value practical products, drive Volkswagens, and drink Stolichnaya vodka), and "Russian souls" (passive consumers who drive Russian-made Lada cars, smoke Marlboros, and drink Smirnoff vodka).[35]

SEGMENTING BY BEHAVIOR

People may use the same product for very different reasons, on different occasions, and/or in different amounts. So, in addition to demographics and/or lifestyles, it is often useful to differentiate among consumers in terms of how they *act* toward a brand or

Excellence at Egghead Software

The new emphasis on relationship marketing brings with it a priority on rewarding loyal users. A technique called *frequency marketing* reinforces regular customers by giving them prizes that accumulate in value as the customer continues to patronize the company. "Frequent flyer" programs initiated by the airlines pioneered this concept. Some marketers have introduced "clubs" that allow members to earn bonus points toward future purchases and even invite members to exclusive outings. Egghead Software, a chain of about 200 computer stores, attempts to enhance consumer loyalty by inviting its customers to join the CUE (Custom Updates and Eggstras) Club. In addition to receiving a 5 percent discount on all purchases, members receive a newsletter that is customized to reflect their specific computing needs.*

*"Software Customers Cue Up at Egghead," *Direct Marketing* (Oct. 1992): 3.

---

frequency marketing: a marketing strategy that reinforces regular customers by giving them prizes that accumulate in value as the customer continues to patronize the company

behavioral segmentation: a way to segment consumer markets based on how they act toward, feel about, or use a good or service

product category. **Behavioral segmentation** divides consumers on the basis of how they act toward, feel about, or use a good or service. Because, as the saying goes, "the proof of the pudding is in the eating," many marketers believe that consumers' past behavior is the best way to predict their future actions.

As one basic behavioral distinction, for example, a firm may divide the market into *users versus nonusers* of its product. It may then develop separate efforts to reward current users on the one hand and to win over new customers on the other. For example, the Prudential insurance company considers a number of variables when carving out market segments; one of these is user status (that is, policy owners versus nonowners).

A related concern is *buyer readiness;* in any market, consumers will vary in terms of their current interest in purchasing a product, or even the extent to which they are aware the product exists. Prudential found, for example, that about 40 percent of its sales were actually initiated by buyers rather than agents—these people had independently reached the point where they were ready to make a purchase, without any prompting needed by the company.[36]

Brand Loyalty

Current users can be further segmented in terms of those who are casual customers versus true "die-hards." *Brand loyalty* is a form of repeat purchasing behavior where people make a conscious decision to keep buying the same brand (as opposed to *inertia,* where the purchase is made out of habit or because it is more convenient).[37] Brand loyalists are an extremely valuable asset to a company: At Prudential, for example, about $\frac{2}{3}$ of sales of new insurance policies are to existing policyholders.[38] Brand loyalists often react passionately if a favorite product is withdrawn or modified. If you doubt this, just remember the national outrage that ensued when Coca-Cola changed its tried-and-true formula for New Coke in the 1980s![39]

It is increasingly difficult to locate sizable brand-loyal segments. Many consumers now subscribe to the notion of *brand parity,* which means they don't perceive significant differences among brands in a product category. For example, more than 70 percent of consumers worldwide feel that all paper towels, soaps, and snack chips are alike.[40] Nonetheless, marketers continue to work hard to cultivate a loyal following. As we have seen throughout the book, an effective way to do this is to focus on relationship marketing, where the customer/product bond is nurtured and maintained over time.

Usage Rate

Customers can also be segmented into groups of heavy, moderate, and light users. Many marketers abide by a "rule of thumb" called the *80/20 rule:* About 20 percent of the market accounts for about 80 percent of the product sold. Keep in mind that this is not

Exhibit 8.2
The 80/20 rule does not imply that marketers should ignore lighter users! For one thing, this segment may represent a greater source of profit down the road if they can be converted into heavier users. Developments in the mammoth gambling industry illustrate how a "light user" segment can become more important over time. While gambling used to be associated with a small, somewhat disreputable segment of "heavy users," major casino and hotel chains are now changing their focus to convert the activity into a wholesome middle-class form of recreation. The Excalibur, the largest hotel in Las Vegas, is modeled after a medieval castle and features attractions that look more like Disney World than Sin City. The Mirage hotel sports a man-made volcano and live dolphins. As Steve Wynn, the company's owner explained, "This place is filled with people like me and you—none of whom think of themselves as gamblers. They think of themselves as folks who are on vacation, and while they're here—hey, let's put some money in the slot machine." Quoted in Priscilla Painton, "The Great Casino Salesman," *Time* (May 3, 1993): 52.

intended to be an exact equation, but rather a general guideline that reminds us of the importance of identifying heavy users of a good or service, even if they make up a minority of the total market. For example, a British study of charity donors found that people who gave generously were not very particular about which charity received their money; most charities are in fact competing for the same segment of heavy donors.[41]

Research by New York Telephone found that it is possible to segment consumers in terms of how much leisure calling they do. It distinguishes between "chatterboxes"—young people who seem to live on the phone—and "balanced" users, primarily busy women who don't have the time to spend on idle talk. The company advertises on CNN's early-morning news program to get to "balanced" women, but focuses on entertainment programming like Nick at Nite and MTV when it wishes to communicate with "chatterboxes."[42]

Usage Occasions

Many products are associated with specific occasions, whether time of day, holidays, business functions versus casual situations, and so on. Many businesses, such as restaurants and clothing manufacturers, divide up their markets in terms of the times and situations when their offerings are in demand.

Being associated with an occasion can be a mixed blessing. On the one hand, sales may be almost "guaranteed" at that time (think about how many people cook a whole turkey only on Thanksgiving). On the other hand, a product can become "locked in" to a setting or situation. Ocean Spray is working hard to expand cranberry consumption beyond the holiday season. By introducing new ways to use cranberries, from sherbet and yogurt to cranberry bagels and a line of drinks called "Refreshers," the company has tripled sales over a ten-year period.[43]

...t Segmentation

Benefit segmentation** refers to the process of grouping consumers in terms of the ...ent benefits they want in purchasing and using a product. The Pepsi-Cola Company ...kets Pepsi to those who desire a sweet carbonated beverage and Diet Pepsi to those ... want a low-calorie alternative. In 1993 Pepsi introduced (unsuccessfully) Clear Pepsi ...'New Age" consumers who prefer a more natural drink.

DIMENSIONS FOR SEGMENTING INDUSTRIAL MARKETS

Just as consumers differ from one another in important ways, companies that specialize in selling to other businesses must also segment their markets. Compared to consumer products companies, many industrial companies tend to be more product-oriented, still searching for buyers of whatever items they happen to make without bothering to segment their markets. As we'll see, though, there are some notable exceptions to this form of "industrial marketing myopia."

Although the processes of consumer versus organizational buying share both similarities and differences (as were discussed in the previous two chapters), businesses can be divided up on several dimensions that are somewhat similar to consumer markets.[44]

ORGANIZATIONAL "DEMOGRAPHICS"

Like people, businesses can be segmented using measurable characteristics. These include what industry they are in, the number of companies in that industry, the total quantity of goods produced, and the manufactured value of those goods. In addition to understanding the dynamics of the market in which a company operates, marketers should consider segmentation at the individual company level. Every firm has certain characteristics that influence the types of goods and services it needs and how these choices are made.

SIC Codes

The easiest and most widely used method to categorize firms is to use the Standard Industrial Classification (SIC) system, which was discussed in Chapter 7. While this system is quite useful, it also makes some questionable assumptions. In particular, it gives the impression that all companies in a given category engage in the same activities. This can be misleading; in some categories less than 60 percent of a company's activities may be devoted to the product that defines the category. A retailer, for example, may sell products in a number of different SIC categories but is classified as a single category. For this reason, information about other factors, such as a company's location and size, should be used to further subdivide the market.

Operating Variables

Operating variables include the production technology used, the company's degree of technical, financial, or operations expertise, and whether or not the prospect is a current user or nonuser of the product category or the vendor's brand. General Electric, for example, is rapidly expanding its operations around the world, but it adjusts the degree of sophistication of the products to the capabilities and needs of the local economy. In some countries its primary business is to assemble low-tech goods, while in countries with better-developed economies it is a manufacturer of appliances and other products for export.[45]

Purchasing Approaches

This dimension focuses on the dynamics of the buying center: How centralized is the buying decision? How many people are involved? What specific individuals tend to really call the shots, and what criteria are used when deciding among vendors?

Companies are beginning to do a better job of tracking past purchasing history so that they can develop loyalty among repeat customers. For example, Viking Office Supply has developed a system that allows the company to customize its catalogues so that no two are exactly alike: The company inkjets a message on the front cover, and advertises a product on sale that is calculated to appeal to the recipient based on his or her past purchase history.[46]

End-Use Application

Just as benefit segmentation is often important for consumer products, industrial marketers must consider how their products will be used by different customers. They must focus on identifying different *end-use applications* for these offerings.

The personal computer industry is a good example of how users can be segmented by the end-use setting. Major PC manufacturers have divided the market into three user segments: corporation, small business, and home. Apple tailors its Quadra, Classic, and Performa lines to the needs of each user group, while Compaq sells separate models it calls Deskpro/m, Deskpro/i, and Prolinea.[47]

TARGETING ONE OR MORE SEGMENTS

Once the relevant segments have been identified, the marketer's next task is to select one or more to go after. In this section we'll review how these customer groups should be evaluated and discuss some common selection strategies for effective target marketing.

EVALUATING MARKET SEGMENTS

The firm's goal at this point is to take a hard look at each possible segment and determine which (if any) will be profitable to enter. This requires knowledge about the segment's size and whether the firm believes that this segment will grow or shrink in the future. The choice of segments should also be guided by the firm's overall strategic direction, which was discussed in Chapter 2. A segment may seem quite attractive, but sometimes a firm must avoid the temptation to go after it because it is not consistent with its overall strategic plan. For example, a few years ago Exxon was forced to retreat from the lucrative office-products market because its particular goals and competencies did not "fit" with this market.

Determining Market Potential

As it goes about selecting markets to enter, the firm tries to *forecast* each segment's **market potential**—the maximum demand expected among consumers in that segment for a good or service. To determine market potential, the firm must weigh such factors as the number of consumers in the segment and how much they spend in the product category. This information can then be used to get down to the nitty gritty: What is the sales potential for the firm's product if it targets this segment? To predict this, the firm must estimate the market share it is likely to attract among category users, and multiply that percentage by total market potential. This decision process underscores the idea that the sheer size of a potential market segment is not the only determinant of whether or not to target that segment.

For example, consider a manufacturer of industrial uniforms that is deciding whether to develop a product line of protective clothing for chemical workers or to focus on a newer segment consisting of banks, real estate offices, and other service businesses that want to outfit their staff in "career apparel" (that is, blazers, shirts, and pants designed to convey a consistent, professional image to customers). The market potential for the chemical industry may be several times larger. However, there are also a few established manufacturers who have already cornered much of the business and who command a great deal of loyalty. If the company feels that realistically it can only expect to grab, say, a 2 percent market share in that category, it may decide it is better off going after the newer career ap-

market potential: The maximum demand expected among consumers in a potential market segment for a good or service

market potential: The maximum demand expected among consumers in a potential market segment for a good or service

parel segment, where loyalties have yet to be established. It may be better to be a "big fish in a small pond."

CHOOSING A TARGET MARKETING STRATEGY

Target marketing involves the selection of one or more segments that will be the primary focus of a company's marketing efforts. This section will discuss four basic approaches to deciding which market segment(s) to go after. These approaches are summarized in Figure 8.3.

Undifferentiated Marketing

A company that selects an **undifferentiated marketing strategy** is following in the footsteps of Henry Ford by betting on its ability to appeal to a broad spectrum of people. If successful, this type of operation can be very efficient, especially because costs associ-

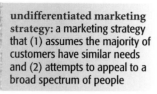

undifferentiated marketing strategy: a marketing strategy that (1) assumes the majority of customers have similar needs and (2) attempts to appeal to a broad spectrum of people

Figure 8.3
Choosing a Target Marketing Strategy

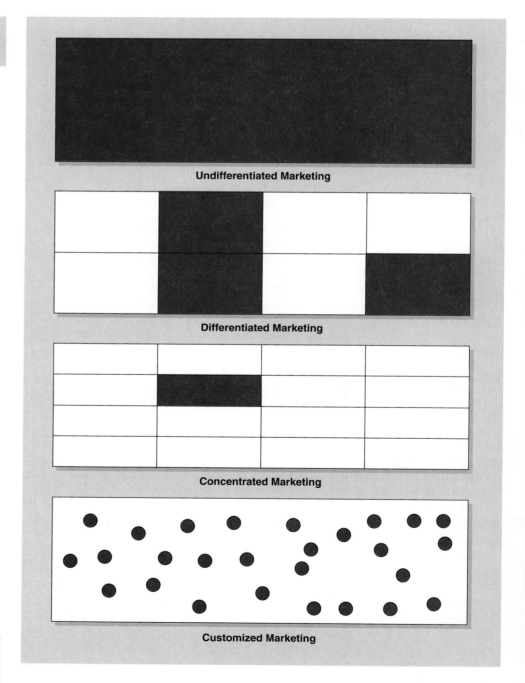

Undifferentiated Marketing

Differentiated Marketing

Concentrated Marketing

Customized Marketing

ated with production, research, and promotion will be minimized. On the other hand, the company must be willing to bet that the large majority of people have similar tastes or needs, or that any differences among them will be so trivial that it will not be worth it to try to distinguish among them. The Ford Motor Company's Model T automobile that we discussed earlier is a classic example of undifferentiated marketing in action.

Still, there are some notable exceptions, often by companies that are bucking the trend toward segmentation by offering "value" to a broader marketplace. Consider, for example, the retailing giant Sears, Roebuck & Co. Even Sears' motto of many years, "Sears has everything," screams out mass marketer. Although Sears has tried to update its image in recent years, it continues to offer a wide range of products (from suits to saws) at reasonable prices to middle America.

Still other companies attempt to market one product to more than one segment. The practice of catering to several segments at once is called *countersegmentation*. For example, Calvin Klein's new fragrance, CK One, is promoted as a "unisex" fragrance that appeals to both men and women.

Differentiated Marketing

A company that chooses a **differentiated marketing strategy** develops one or more products for each of several distinct customer groups. The cosmetics giant L'Oreal is a follower of this philosophy. The company has the resources to offer several product lines at a variety of prices. It targets the luxury market with such brands as Lancôme and Helena Rubinstein, while less expensive offerings like Elseve and L'Oreal are sold by large department stores and discounters.[48]

Concentrated Marketing

When a firm focuses its efforts on offering one or more products to a single segment, it is using a **concentrated marketing strategy.** Although this strategy is more common in organizational settings, it also occurs in consumer markets, especially among companies that are relatively small or have established a reputation for a specific type of product. As in the example of the uniform manufacturer mentioned previously, a small company can do quite well if it offers a specialized product to a segment and convinces segment members that its product holds a competitive advantage over other possibilities—even those sold by "the big guys."

Niche marketing. A **niche market** is a particularly small segment. Although the total size of the market may be small, pursuing a niche strategy can be profitable because there is little to no competition. In particular, small businesses can make big inroads into this type of market; the segment may be so small that larger companies do not have the flexibility or desire to enter.

For example, short men are a consumer segment with big needs, because they often have trouble finding their size in a regular clothing store. One-third of American men are shorter than 5'8", and 13 percent are shorter than 5'6". Noting the bias that many people have against short men, the owner of a Cleveland store that sells only short sizes observed, "Dressing well is one way for short men to overcome discrimination." Because Asians and Hispanics tend to be shorter than Caucasians, some industry people project that the market for this segment will grow as these segments continue to account for increasing proportions of the American population.[49]

Custom Marketing: A "Segment of One"

Ideally marketers should be able to define segments so precisely that they can offer products that exactly meet the needs of every individual or firm. This level of concentration does occur in the case of personal or professional services. We hope that doctors, lawyers, and even haircutters are providing us with a unique product rather than just using a "cookie cutter" approach to service.

Of course, in most cases this level of segmentation is neither practical nor possible when mass-produced products enter the picture. However, advances in computer technology, coupled with the new emphasis on building solid relationships with customers, have focused managers' attention on devising a **custom marketing strategy,** where a separate marketing mix is developed for each customer.

differentiated marketing strategy: a marketing strategy in which a firm develops one or more products for each of several distinct customer groups

concentrated marketing strategy: a marketing strategy in which a firm focuses its efforts on offering one or more products to a single segment

niche market: a particularly small market segment in which a firm may often face little or no competition

custom marketing strategy: a marketing strategy in which a firm develops a separate marketing mix for each customer

This approach is more readily found in industrial contexts, where a manufacturer often works with one or a few very large clients and develops products that only these clients will use. However, some forward-looking consumer-oriented companies are moving toward **mass customization,** in which a basic good or service is modified to meet an individual's needs.[50] For example, Marriott's Honored Guest program tracks the preferences of repeat customers so that when they check in to one of the company's hotels they are assigned a room that best conforms to their individual preferences, such as smoking versus nonsmoking, low floor versus high floor, and so on.[51]

mass customization: a marketing strategy in which a firm modifies a basic good or service to meet an individual customer's needs

SPOTLIGHT ON ETHICS

Can Target Marketing Work Too Well?

Target marketing involves fine-tuning a product's features and image to make it especially appealing to a specific customer segment. Although this process occurs all the time, objections are raised when it encourages consumption of unhealthy products like cigarettes or alcohol. Recent actions by marketers who wanted to target some specific consumer segments raise the issue of whether a marketing strategy can be *too* good—when it encourages people to do things that are bad for them.

The R.J. Reynolds Co. introduced a brand of cigarettes called Dakota in several test markets.* The marketing plan, submitted to the company by an outside consulting firm, specifically targeted the cigarette to eighteen- to twenty-four-year-old women with a high school education or less who work in entry-level factory or service jobs. This segment is one of the few remaining demographic groups in the United States exhibiting an increase in smoking rates, so from a purely economic point of view it clearly has market potential.

The brand was developed to appeal to a segment the company called the "Virile Female." Her favorite pastimes are cruising, partying, and going to hot rod shows and tractor pulls with her boyfriend, and her favorite TV shows are Roseanne and evening soap operas. R.J. Reynolds claimed that the brand was simply aimed at current Marlboro smokers, but over 100 public health officials signed a resolution asking that the product be withdrawn.

R.J. Reynolds also ignited a lot of controversy when it announced plans in 1990 to test-market a menthol cigarette, called Uptown, specifically to African American consumers. Although the marketing of cigarettes to minorities is not a novel tactic, this was the first time a company explicitly acknowledged the strategy. The publishers of African American–oriented newspapers and magazines were caught in the middle, because they stood to receive substantial advertising revenues from the campaign. For example, approximately 10 percent of advertising revenues for *Jet*, a major magazine targeted to African American readers, come from cigarette advertising.

For its part, the company claimed that its actions were a natural result of shrinking markets and the need to more finely target increasingly small segments. Unlike other ethnic groups, which do not seem to display marked cigarette preferences, the tastes of African American consumers are easy to pinpoint. According to the company, 69 percent of African American consumers prefer menthol, more than twice the rate of smokers overall. After market research indicated that African Americans tend to open cigarette packs from the bottom, the company decided to pack Uptowns with the filters facing down.

Reynolds claimed that the product was not designed specifically for African Americans, though it acknowledged that it was likely to attract a disproportionate share of African American smokers. Following a storm of criticism by both private health groups and government officials (including the Secretary of Health and Human Services), the company announced that it was canceling its test-marketing plans. It would not comment on the likelihood that the cigarette would ever be introduced.†

While many corporations are just now waking up to the potential of the Hispanic market, others that sell harmful products such as junk food, cigarettes, and alcohol discovered this market long ago. These industries donate over $1 million a year to Hispanic groups, and critics point to a high concentration of liquor stores and related advertising in Hispanic neighborhoods. Available evidence indicates that Mexican-born men stand a greater chance of dying of cirrhosis of the liver, and that Hispanic men also are more likely to die of lung cancer than are Anglos. The smoking rate of fourth- and fifth-grade Hispanic boys is roughly five times that of Anglo boys.‡

These marketers are effectively using the tools of target marketing. Are these strategies ethical?

---

* Anthony Ramirez, "New Cigarettes Raising Issue of Target Market," *The New York Times* (Feb. 18, 1990): 28.
† "Plans for Testmarketing Cigarette Canceled," *The Asbury Park Press* (Jan. 1990): 20; Anthony Ramirez, "A Cigarette Campaign Under Fire," *The New York Times* (Jan. 12, 1990): D1.
‡ Fernando Gonzalez, "Study Finds Alcohol, Cigarette Makers Target Hispanics," *The Boston Globe* (Nov. 23, 1989): A11.

SELECTING A STRATEGY

A differentiated marketing strategy is the one most commonly pursued by marketers, especially those with the resources to develop more than one marketing mix. However, any of the four targeting strategies can be effective depending on the company's characteristics and the nature of the marketplace. While there are no hard and fast rules that dictate which strategy to choose, the following guidelines often apply:

- An undifferentiated strategy is often appropriate for products that people perceive as basically homogeneous. For example, many commodities such as sugar or salt are largely bought in the same manner by everyone.

- A concentrated or custom strategy is often useful for smaller firms that do not have the resources or the desire to be all things to all people. These companies typically have an advantage over larger firms in that they can stay on top of developments in a specialized market and be flexible enough to develop goods and services that precisely meet the needs of small segments. For larger companies, coming up quickly with new products can be like turning a battleship (see Chapter 10).

- The choice of strategy tends to change as a product moves through the life cycle. In the early stages the firm may need to concentrate on creating awareness for a product and building demand, rather than on persuading people to buy one brand over another. This means that products in new categories, such as cellular phones, often use an undifferentiated strategy. As the category matures and people start to make finer discriminations among alternatives, the company will need to shift to a differentiated strategy.

POSITIONING THE GOOD OR SERVICE TO ONE OR MORE SEGMENTS

The final stage of the target marketing process is to provide consumers who belong to a selected market segment with a good or service that meets their distinct needs and expectations. **Positioning** refers to determining and influencing how a brand is perceived by consumers relative to the competition. The process of developing a product positioning strategy entails a clear understanding of the criteria a target consumer uses to evaluate alternatives in a category, and placing a product in a favorable way along these dimensions. In other words, how does the consumer view the world, and where does your product(s) fit into this picture?[52]

positioning: the marketing practice of determining and influencing how a brand is perceived by consumers relative to the competition

POSITIONING ALTERNATIVES

Positioning involves more than creating a distinctive image for a product. This process also means that marketers must appreciate how their brand will be perceived compared to other brands or products that might serve the same function. There are three basic approaches to setting up one's brand vis à vis the competition.

Like the Competition (But Better)

In many cases a brand competes directly with other products claiming to offer the same benefits. This is a case of *direct competition,* where one tries to do a better job of satisfying customer needs than the other products that are targeted to the same group. For example, Nike and Reebok compete head to head for the privilege of selling the most basketball shoes.

Against the Competition

Another alternative is to take a position that is counter to the competition. Instead of claiming to do the same thing, only better, the brand offers a unique benefit. 7-UP has successfully positioned itself as the "Un-Cola," while Dr. Pepper tries to forge its own unique identity by offering drinkers a different alternative to cola products.

Away from the Competition

Finally, the brand can try to avoid the competition altogether. This occurs when the company adopts a niche marketing strategy. It creates a unique good or service that is made available to a specialized segment, maybe even one that others don't consider desirable.

Consider the strategy of athletic shoe manufacturer K-Swiss. Although it is dwarfed by such industry giants as Nike and Reebok, the company does not feel pressured to constantly keep up with changes in sneaker fashions. It focuses on the blue-blooded end of the market, producing nautical shoes favored by yachtsmen and sailors and tennis shoes that are popular among tennis-playing matrons at country clubs. The company's CEO echoes the concentrated marketing philosophy when he explains, "If it's upscale and snooty, that's just where we want to be."[53]

POSITIONING DIMENSIONS

There are many dimensions that can be used to establish a brand's position in the marketplace. Many of these are related to the segmentation variables we have discussed. Some positioning dimensions include the following:

- Lifestyle image: Grey Poupon mustard is a "higher class" condiment
- Price leadership: L'Oréal's Noisôme brand face cream is sold in upscale beauty shops, while its Plenitude brand is available for $\frac{1}{6}$ the price in discount stores— even though both are based on the same chemical formula.[54]
- Attributes: Bounty paper towels are "the quicker picker upper"
- Product class: The Mazda Miata is a sporty convertible
- Competitors: Northwestern insurance is "the quiet company"
- Occasions: Wrigley's gum is an alternative at times when smoking is not permitted
- Users: Levi's Dockers are targeted primarily to men in their twenties to forties
- Quality: At Ford, "Quality is Job 1"

Bringing a Product to Life: The Brand Personality

Brands are almost like people, in that we can often describe them in terms of personality traits. These descriptions might include words like cheap, elegant, sexy, bold, or wimpy. A positioning strategy tries to create a **brand personality** for a good or service, a distinctive image that captures its character and the benefits it delivers.

Although brand personalities are often more vivid for expressive products like perfume, beverages, or cars, consumers are usually able to form a picture of most products in their minds. Indeed, a favorite tactic of marketing researchers is to ask respondents to describe what a product would be like "if it came to life." People often give clear, detailed descriptions, including such information as what color hair the person/product would have, the type of house he or she would live in, and even whether he or she would be thin, overweight, or somewhere in between.[55] A recent advertisement for *Elle* magazine mirrors this logic: The copy simply proclaims, "She is not a reply card. She is not a category. She is not shrink-wrapped. Elle is not a magazine. She is a woman."

Perceptual Mapping

How does a marketer determine where his or her product actually stands in the minds of consumers? One technique is simply to ask them about what attributes are important to them, how they feel different alternatives rate on these attributes, and perhaps

brand personality: a distinctive image created for a brand that captures its character and the benefits it delivers

how they feel an "ideal" product would rate. This information can be used to construct a **perceptual map,** which is a vivid way to construct a picture of where products or brands are "located" in consumers' minds.

For example, suppose you wanted to construct a perceptual map of women's magazines, as perceived by American women in their twenties. After interviewing readers, you might determine that two dimensions women use when selecting a magazine to read are: (1) Is it "traditional"—oriented toward family, home, and personal issues (for example, offering a heavy dose of recipes, exercise guidelines, and/or decorating tips), or is it "fashion forward"—oriented toward personal appearance and fashion? and (2) Is it for relatively "upscale" women who are either older, established in their careers, and/or more affluent, or for relatively "downscale" women who are younger, just starting out in careers, and/or with lower incomes?

The perceptual map shown in Figure 8.4 illustrates how these ratings might look for a set of current women's magazines. After plotting the feedback you obtained from readers, you would have some guidance if you were planning to develop a new women's magazine. On the one hand you might decide to compete directly with either the cluster of "service magazines" in the lower left or the traditional fashion magazines in the upper right. In this case you would have to analyze the offerings in that cluster carefully to determine what benefits your new entrant might offer that these existing products do not. Condé Nast developed *Allure* to compete against existing fashion magazines. *Allure* is positioned as a magazine that focuses on "deeper" issues related to beauty and appearance (for example, several recent articles have explored the topic of death or disfigurement caused by cosmetic surgery and breast implantation) rather than current fashion *per se.*

On the other hand, you might try to locate an unserved area in this map. There may be room for a magazine targeted to "cutting edge" fashion for college-age women. The identification of an unserved market is the "holy grail" for marketers. With luck, they can move quickly to capture a market. A significant advantage of being the first entrant is that the company gets to define the standards of comparison for the category; it is the baseline against which other, new entrants are measured. This tactic has paid off for companies like Chrysler, which was the first to identify the market for a minivan, and Liz Claiborne, which pioneered the concept of "user friendly" clothing for working women.

perceptual map: a research technique that constructs a graphical representation of where products or brands are "located" in relation to each other in consumers' minds

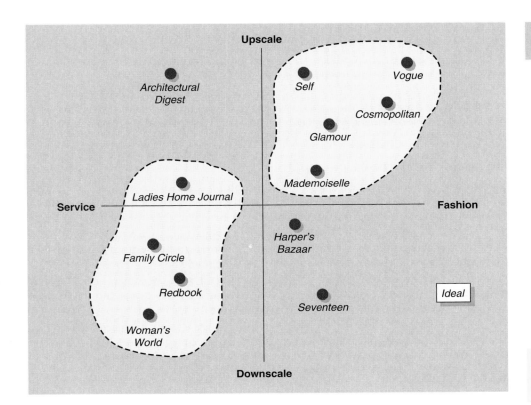

**Figure 8.4
Perceptual Map**

Developing and Implementing a Positioning Strategy

The success of a target marketing strategy hinges on the marketer's ability to identify and then select an appropriate market segment. Once this is accomplished, he or she must devise a marketing mix that will most effectively target the members of that segment. Let's review the four steps necessary to complete this process.

Analyze Competitors' Positions

The marketer must understand the current "lay of the land"—what competitors are out there, and how they are perceived by the target market. This involves doing research such as constructing a perceptual map as described previously. It may also mean stepping back to take a look at the bigger picture: Aside from direct competitors in the product category, are there other goods or services that could also provide the same benefits people are seeking? Recall our discussion of "marketing myopia" in Chapter 1: Consumers are searching for benefits, which they may obtain from a variety of goods or services. For example, when a company like Coca-Cola develops a new soft drink like Fruitopia, it must consider the drink's attractiveness relative to colas, fruit drinks, and even bottled water.

Identify Competitive Advantage

The next task is to offer a product with a *competitive advantage,* the ability to deliver whatever it promises better than the competition. If the company offers only a "me too product," the only way it can induce people to buy it is to sell the item for a lower price—indeed, price leadership is a commonly used positioning dimension. Other than pricing the offering more attractively, here are methods companies use to offer competitive advantages to their customers:

Image advantage: Craft a distinctive "brand personality" through the clever use of symbols, package design, celebrity endorsers, and so on. For example, many product names, whether Calvin Klein or Harley Davidson, are licensed by other manufacturers to provide their own brands with "instant status."

Product advantage: Create a good or service that looks different or offers novel features. For example, Levi's 501 jeans stand out because of their distinctive button fly, which makes this style hard to copy.

Service advantage: Provide unique or superior backup services for what you sell. These "add ons" include delivery, installation, and training. Several luxury automakers, such as Mercedes-Benz and Cadillac, are now trying to differentiate themselves by offering roadside assistance programs to their customers.

People advantage: A company is only as good as the company it keeps: The firm's salespeople, service people, and other representatives can make a product stand out (for better or for worse!). General Motors emphasizes the expertise of its mechanics by featuring the character "Mr. Goodwrench" in its advertising.

Finalize the Marketing Mix

Once a positioning strategy has been decided on, all of the pieces must actually be put into place. When McDonald's decided to target African Americans, it had to be sure that a good number of its restaurants were located in areas where these people live, and that these consumers would respond to its advertising messages and other promotions.

The elements of the marketing mix must be tailored to the selected segment. This means that the good or service must deliver benefits that will be valued by segment occupants. Furthermore, this offering must be priced at a level these consumers will be able or willing to pay, it must be made available at places they are likely to go, and its qualities must be correctly communicated in media to which they're likely to be exposed. We'll explore the specifics of creating a good or service that meets a segment's needs, developing an appropriate pricing strategy, distributing products where they can be easily obtained by the target market, and communicating information about the offering's competitive advantage in later chapters.

Real People, Real Choices:

How It Worked Out at Burrell Communications

Sarah Burroughs and her colleagues chose option 1 to drive home the McDonald's message: They decided to develop a character named Calvin, a "typical" nice kid living in the inner city. The advertising campaign would show how working at McDonald's helped Calvin to chart a positive course for himself. It was felt that this "man in the street" approach would make a big impact on African American teens, who would identify emotionally with the Calvin character. This dramatization would have the added benefit of boosting the morale of McDonald's current employees by making it clear that the company looks to hire "very special people."

Burrell Communications implemented the strategy in several ways. Upbeat television commercials showed Calvin going to work at McDonald's with the approval of his neighbors and friends. These images were supplemented by a newspaper campaign profiling real-life success stories: African American employees who went on to management positions with the company. The company also produced a thirty-minute commercial (called an infomercial) that ran on Black Entertainment Television. The infomercial was called "The Mac Report" and included segments in a news-show format that highlighted the efforts of McDonald's restaurants in communities from "Harlem to Hollywood" to support programs encouraging black education and entrepreneurship.

The campaign was extremely successful. Burrell's commercials generated a lot of spontaneous consumer feedback to McDonald's that indicated they had created very positive images of the company in the minds of both teens and adults. Morale among crew members also improved. In addition, the commercials received several advertising awards.

This campaign demonstrates the wisdom of a successful target marketing strategy: Focus on those segments that you know a lot about, identify what their needs are, and develop products and ideas that not only help to satisfy these needs, but also give something back to segment members. Sarah Burroughs and her colleagues have provided McDonald's with a recipe for success in targeting an important market segment.

Exhibit 8.3
This was one of the newspaper advertisements developed by Burrell Communications to target African American teens. Each ad profiled a real McDonald's employee who had advanced through the ranks of the company.

Evaluate Responses and Monitor Change

Finally, the target marketing process is an ongoing one: The desirability of different segments to a firm changes over time, and the needs of specific segments evolve as well. Marketers need to monitor these changes and adjust their positioning strategies when necessary. Sometimes a product's positioning is totally redone to respond to changes in the marketplace. A classic example of such a "makeover" is Marlboro cigarettes. Believe it or not, this brand was positioned as a women's cigarette when it was first introduced—complete with a red-tipped filter to hide lipstick stains! The brand really took off, however, when its image was "adjusted" to be a male product, complete with the Marlboro cowboy.

Repositioning, which occurs when a brand's original "personality" is altered to appeal to a different segment, is undertaken fairly often. In some cases a marketer may decide that a brand is competing too closely with another of its own products, so sales are being *cannibalized* (that is, the two brands are taking sales away from each other, rather than from competing companies). This was the reason for the decision by Cadbury Beverages to reposition Crush, an orange soda. The brand was targeted to the teen market when it was acquired from Procter & Gamble. However, the company already marketed Sunkist to this segment, so it is taking steps to move Crush toward an all-family position.[56]

Another reason for repositioning crops up when too many competitors are stressing the same attribute. For example, promotional strategies in the airline industry focused on price advantages over the last few years, but now several airlines including American, TWA, and Virgin Atlantic are stressing comfort instead.[57]

Finally, repositioning can occur when the original market evaporates or is unreceptive to the offering. *Details* magazine was initially launched as an "underground nightlife magazine" but was recently relaunched as a fashion and lifestyle magazine for twentysomething males. Formerly criticized for being too raw and bold, it now strives to be more sophisticated so that advertisers wishing to reach younger males will encounter a more conducive environment in which to place their advertising.[58]

Chapter 8 Summary

Objective 1. Understand the need for market segmentation in today's business environment.

Market segmentation and target marketing are important strategies in today's marketplace because of market fragmentation—that is, the splintering of a mass society into diverse groups due to technological and cultural differences. Thus marketers must determine if they can better satisfy customers with a mass-marketing strategy or target marketing based on strategy efficiency and effectiveness.

Market segmentation means to divide a large market into a set of smaller markets that share important characteristics. In target marketing marketers select one or more of these specific groups to serve. The development of a clear and positive image to communicate to members of the target market groups is called positioning.

Objective 2. Explain the steps used in identifying attractive target markets.

In developing a segmentation strategy, marketers first examine consumer demand in relation to the product. If demand is homogenous, a mass-market strategy where only one product is sold to the total market may be best. If demand is clustered or diffused, a segmented marketing strategy may be better. In segmented marketing one or more products are developed for each of several distinct customer groups.

To choose one or more segments to target, marketers examine each segment and evaluate its potential for success as a target market. Meaningful segments have wants that are different from those in other segments, can be identified, can be reached with a unique marketing mix, will respond to unique marketing communications, are large enough to be profitable, have future growth potential, and possess needs that the organization can satisfy better than the competition.

Objective 3. Explain how marketers segment consumer markets.

Marketers frequently find it useful to segment consumer markets based on demographic characteristics including age, gender, family structure, social class, race or ethnic identity, geographic location or, more recently, geodemographics. A second basis, consumer lifestyles, involves measures of psychological and social characteristics. Consumer markets may also be segmented based on how consumers behave toward the product—brand loyalty, usage rates (heavy, moderate, or light), usage occasions, product type purchased, and/or reasons for using a product (benefit segmentation).

Objective 4. Understand the bases for segmentation in industrial markets.

Categories similar to those in the consumer market are frequently used for segmenting industrial markets. Industrial demographics include industry and/or company size, Standard Industrial Classification (SIC) codes, or geographic location. Industrial markets may also be segmented based on operating variables, purchasing approaches, and end-use applications.

Objective 5. Explain how potential market segments are evaluated and selected.

After the different segments have been identified, the market potential of each segment is estimated. The relative attractiveness of segments is also influenced by the firm's selection of an overall marketing strategy. The firm may choose an undifferentiated, differentiated, concentrated, niche, or custom strategy based on the company's characteristics and the nature of the market.

Objective 6. Understand how a firm develops a product positioning strategy.

After the target market(s) and the overall strategy have been selected, marketers must determine how they wish the brand to be perceived by consumers relative to the competition—that is, whether the brand should be positioned like, against, or away from the competition. Through positioning, a brand personality is developed. Brand positions are frequently evaluated with the use of perceptual mapping. In developing and implementing the positioning strategy, firms analyze the competitors' positions, determine the competitive advantage offered by their product, tailor the marketing mix in accord with the positioning strategy, and evaluate responses to the marketing mix selected. Marketers must continually monitor changes in the market that might indicate a need for repositioning of the product.

Review Questions

Marketing Concepts: Testing Your Knowledge

1. What is market segmentation and why is it an important strategy in today's marketplace?
2. List the criteria used for determining whether a segment may be a good candidate for targeting.
3. List and explain the major demographic characteristics frequently used in segmenting markets.
4. Describe the three major ethnic groups in the United States (African Americans, Hispanic Americans, and Asian Americans) and tell how they provide unique market segments for many products.
5. How can consumer behavior be used for segmenting consumer markets?
6. Explain consumer lifestyle segmentation.
7. What are the major bases used for segmenting industrial markets?
8. Explain undifferentiated, differentiated, concentrated, niche, custom, and mass customization marketing strategies.
9. What is product positioning?
10. List the steps in developing and implementing a positioning strategy.

Marketing Concepts: Discussing Choices and Issues

1. Some critics of marketing have suggested that market segmentation and target marketing lead to an unnecessary proliferation or product choices, which wastes valuable resources. These critics suggest that if we marketers didn't create so many different product choices there would be more resources to feed the hungry and house the homeless and provide for the needs of people around the globe. Are the results of segmentation and target marketing harmful or beneficial for society as a whole? Should these criticisms be of concern to firms? How should New Era firms respond to these criticisms?

2. One of the criteria for a usable market segment is its size. This chapter suggested that to be usable a segment must be large enough to be profitable now and in the future and that some very small segments get ignored because they can never be profitable. So how large should a segment be? How do you think a firm should go about determining if a segment is profitable? Do firms ever have a moral or ethical obligation to develop products for small unprofitable segments?

3. Some firms have been criticized for targeting unwholesome products to certain segments of the market—the aged, ethnic minorities, the disabled, et cetera. What other groups deserve special concern? Should a firm use different criteria in targeting such groups? Should the government oversee and control such marketing activities?

4. Marketers are always looking for a better way to segment consumer markets. In the past they have used demographics, lifestyles, geodemographics, and product-related behavior. With a group of classmates, brainstorm to see if you can come up with other possible means for segmenting markets which might be useful to some firms.

Marketing Practice: Applying What You've Learned

1. Assume you have been hired to develop a marketing plan for a small regional beer brewery. In the past the brewery has simply produced and sold a single beer to the entire market—a mass-marketing strategy. As you begin your work for the firm, you feel that the firm could be more successful if they developed a target marketing strategy. The owner of the

firm, however, is not convinced. Write a memo to the owner outlining

a. The basic reasons for target marketing
b. The specific advantages of a target marketing strategy for the brewery.

2. Assume that you are in charge of marketing research for a large regional bank. The marketing director believes that the bank has different types of customers and that these customers have needs for different financial products. She thinks that she can identify a number of attractive segments to target but is unsure what dimensions should be used to segment the market. She has asked you to conduct a survey to identify differences among the bank's customers.

a. Make a list of the questions you will need to ask on your survey.
b. Write a memo outlining the steps you recommend that the marketing director take in using the data from your survey to evaluate and identify attractive segments.

3. Assume that you are the director of marketing for a company that markets personal computers to business and organizational customers. You feel that if your market is segmented, you will be able to satisfy your customers' needs more efficiently and effectively. You must first decide what bases to use for segmenting the market.

a. Develop a list of the potential segmentation variables you might use.
b. Include your thoughts on how useful each might be to your marketing strategy.
c. What are your final recommendations for the bases for segmenting the market?

4. As the marketing director for a company that is planning to enter the industrial market for photocopy machines, you are attempting to develop an overall marketing strategy. You have considered the possibility of using mass-marketing, concentrated marketing, differentiated marketing, and custom marketing strategies.

a. Write a report explaining what each type of strategy would mean for your marketing plan in terms of product, price, promotion, and distribution channel.
b. Evaluate the desirability of each type of strategy.

c. What are your final recommendations for the best type of strategy?

5. As an account executive for a marketing consulting firm, your newest client is a university—*your* university. You have been asked to develop a positioning strategy for the university. With a group of classmates, develop an outline of your ideas, including the following:

a. Who are your competitors?
b. What are the competitors' positions?
c. What target markets are most attractive to the university?
d. How will you position the university for those segments relative to the competition?

Present your results to your class.

Marketing Mini-Project: Learning by Doing

This mini-project will help you to develop a better understanding of how target marketing decisions are made. The project focuses on the market for automobiles.

1. Gather ideas about different dimensions useful for segmenting the automobile market. You may use your own ideas, but you probably will also want to examine advertising and other marketing communications developed by different automobile manufacturers. You may also want to read articles in newspapers and magazines and talk with salespeople at local automobile dealerships about different types of consumers and what cars they buy.
2. Based on the dimensions for market segmentation you have identified, develop a questionnaire and conduct a survey of consumers. You will have to decide what questions should be asked and what consumers should be surveyed.
3. Analyze the data from your research and identify the different potential segments.
4. Develop segment profiles that describe each potential segment.
5. Generate several ideas for how the marketing strategy might be different for each segment based on the profiles.
6. Develop a presentation (or write a report) outlining your ideas, your research, your findings, and your marketing strategy recommendations.

Key Terms

Endnotes

1. Quoted in Stephen Holden, "Breakup of Music Audience Leaves Top 40 Radio Tuned Out," *The New York Times* (March 23, 1993): C13.
2. Stephen Holden, "Breakup of Pop Music Audience . . . ," *The New York Times* (March 23, 1993): C13.
3. Laura Loro, "Media Planners Zoom in for a Consumer Close-Up," *Advertising Age* (July 20, 1992): S18.
4. Grover C. Norwood, "A Target Marketing Primer," *Managers Magazine* (April 1989): 11–14.4.

5. Grover C. Norwood, "A Target Marketing Primer," *Managers Magazine* (April 1989): 11–14.5.

6. Theodore Levitt, as quoted in Grover C. Norwood, "A Target Marketing Primer," *Managers Magazine* (April 1989): 11–14.

7. Quoted in March Magiera, "Levi's Broadens Appeal," *Ad Age* (July 17, 1989): 1.

8. Conway Lackman and John M. Lanasa, "Family Decision-Making Theory: An Overview and Assessment," *Psychology & Marketing* 10 (March/April 1993): 81–93.

9. Scott Hume, "Burger King Claims Crown in Magazines Aimed at Kids," *Ad Age* (March 8, 1993): 6.

10. Douglas Coupland, *Generation X, Tales for an Accelerated Culture* (New York: St. Martin's Press, 1991).

11. Quoted in Karen Lowry Miller, "You Just Can't Talk to These Kids," *Business Week* (April 19, 1993): 104.

12. Raymond Serafin, "Ford Jazzes Up Ads for Young Buyers," *Ad Age* (March 15, 1993): 13; Otto Strong, "New Age Beckons Coke: Soft-Drink Giant to Tap Sparkling Water, Sports Drink Mania," *LA Times* (Sept. 23, 1992): D1; Scott Donaton, "The Media Wakes Up to Generation X," *Ad Age* (Feb. 1, 1993): 16.

13. Scott Donaton, "Media Reassess as Boomers Age," *Ad Age* (July 15, 1991): 13.

14. Charles D. Schewe, "Strategically Positioning Your Way Into the Aging Marketplace," *Business Horizons* (May/June 1991): 59–66.

15. Jennifer Lawrence, "Gender-Specific Works for Diapers—Almost Too Well," *Ad Age* (Feb. 8, 1993): S-10.

16. Rena Bartos, *Marketing to Women Around the World* (Boston, Mass.: Harvard Business School Press, 1989).

17. Charles M. Schaninger and William D. Danko, "A Conceptual and Empirical Comparison of Alternate Household Life Cycle Markets," *Journal of Consumer Research* 19 (March 1993): 580–594.

18. Christy Fisher, "Census Data May Make Ads More Single-Minded," *Ad Age* (July 20, 1992): 2.

19. Rahul Jacob, "The Big Rise," *Fortune* (May 30, 1994): 74.

20. John Rossant, "Bugatti's Back—and Only $350,000," *Business Week* (May 2, 1994): 124.

21. Cyndee Miller, "The Have-Nots: Firms with the Right Products and Services Succeed Among Low-Income Consumers," *Marketing News* (Aug. 1, 1994): 1.

22. Stuart Elliott, "McDonald's Promotes Image Among Blacks," *The New York Times* (July 10, 1993): 41; Jeanne Whalen, "Sarah Burroughs: It's Banner Year for Burrell Agency and Its New President," *Advertising Age* (Nov. 29, 1993): 25; private communication, Burrell Communications, 1994.

23. Monroe Anderson, "Advertising's Black Magic Helping Corporate America Tap a Lucrative Market," *Newsweek* (Feb. 10, 1986): 60.

24. Joe Schwartz, "Hispanic Opportunities," *American Demographics* (May 1987): 56–59.

25. Ibid.

26. "A Window on the Fast-Growing Audience of Asian Americans," *The New York Times* (March 22, 1993): D5.

27. Quoted in Donald Dougherty, "The Orient Express," *The Marketer* (July/Aug. 1990): 14.

28. Donald Dougherty, "The Orient Express," *The Marketer* (July/Aug. 1990): 14.

29. Jeanne Whalen, "Sears Targets Asians," *Advertising Age* (Oct. 10, 1994): 1.

30. Quoted in George Rathwaite, "Heileman's National Impact with Local Brews," *Marketing Insights* (Premier Issue 1989) 108.

31. Brad Edmondson, "From Dixie to Detroit," *American Demographics* (Jan. 1987): 27; Brad Edmondson, "America's Hot Spots," *American Demographics* (1988): 24–30.

32. Michael J. Weiss, *The Clustering of America,* 1 ed. (New York: Harper & Row, 1988).

33. Bob Minzesheimer, "You Are What You Zip," *Los Angeles* (Nov. 1984): 175.

34. Martha Farnsworth Riche, "VALS 2," *American Demographics* (July 1989): 25.

35. Stuart Elliott, "Sampling Tastes of a Changing Russia," *The New York Times* (April 1, 1992): D1.

36. Robert L. Burr, "Market Segments and Other Revelations," *Journal of Services Marketing* (Fall 1987): 59–67.

37. Jacob Jacoby and Robert Chestnut, *Brand Loyalty: Measurement and Management* (New York: Wiley, 1978).

38. Robert L. Burr, "Market Segments and Other Revelations," *Journal of Services Marketing* (Fall 1987): 59–67.

39. Anne B. Fisher, "Coke's Brand Loyalty Lesson," *Fortune* (Aug. 5, 1985): 44.

40. Ronald Alsop, "Brand Loyalty is Rarely Blind Loyalty," *The Wall Street Journal* (Oct. 19, 1989): B1.

41. B.B. Schlegelmich and A.C. Tynan, "The Scope for Market Segmentation Within the Charity Market: An Empirical Analysis," *Managerial and Decision Economics* (June 1989): 127–134.

42. Jonathan Sims, "New York Tel Finds its Targets," *Ad Age* (Feb. 22, 1993): C-14.

43. "How Ocean Spray Gave Cranberries Some Sparkle," *The New York Times* (Nov. 26, 1992): D1.

44. Thomas V. Bonoma and Benson P. Shapiro, *Segmenting the Industrial Market* (Lexington, Mass.: Lexington Books, 1983).

45. Tim Smart, "GE's Brave New World," *Business Week* (Nov. 8, 1993): 64.

46. Patricia A. Scussel, "Segmenting Business Buyers," *Catalog Age* (Feb. 1992): 47.

47. Catherine Arnst, "PC Makers Head for 'Soho,'" *Business Week* (Sept. 28, 1992): 125.

48. William Echikson, "Aiming at High and Low Markets," *Fortune* (March 22, 1993): 89.

49. Patricia Braus, "Selling to Short Men is a Tall Order," *American Demographics* (March 1993): 25–28.

50. Cf. B. Joseph Pine II, Bart Victor, and Andrew C. Boynton, "Making Mass Customization Work," *Harvard Business Review* (Sept./Oct. 1993): 108–119.

51. Philip Kotler, "From Mass Marketing to Mass Customization," *Planning Review* (Sept./Oct. 1989): 10–47.

52. Andre J. San Augustine, William J. Long, and John Pantzellis, "Hospital Positioning: A Strategic Tool for the 1990s," *Journal of Health Care Marketing* (March 1992): 15–23.

53. Quoted in Stephanie Strom, "Athletic Shoes Without the Fads," *The New York Times* (Aug. 6, 1992): D8.

54. William Echikson, "Aiming at High and Low Markets," *Fortune* (March 22, 1993): 89.

55. Martin R. Lautman, "End-Benefit Segmentation and Prototypical Bonding," *Journal of Advertising Research* (June/July, 1991): 9–18.

56. Patricia Winters, "Cadbury Puts Crush Back on TV," *Ad Age* (Feb. 25, 1991): 16.

57. Adam Bryant, "Competition is Shifting from Fares to Chairs," *The New York Times* (March 26, 1993): D15.

58. Scott Donaton, "Magazine of the Year," *Ad Age* (March 1, 1993): S-1.

MARKETING IN ACTION: REAL PEOPLE AT APPLE COMPUTER

A TV ad for Kraft Singles features an adorable child named Emily, who is apparently in love with cheese. The ad becomes silent, and the child begins to communicate to viewers the only way she knows how: through sign language. Emily is hearing impaired.

Emily belongs to an often-ignored market segment, people with disabilities (PWD). There are 49 million disabled consumers—a huge segment by anyone's count. Efforts now are underway to pay more attention to the needs of this group. For example, a new group called the Advertising Coalition for People with Disabilities is a consortium of top companies that work together to encourage companies to include people with disabilities in their marketing campaigns.

Why should businesses see the disabled as an attractive market segment? First, as we note, the group is very large. And with the overall aging of America, more and more people will be classified as disabled in the years to come. Second, the disabled have tremendous spending power. In fact, one out of six consumer dollars is spent by a PWD. According to the U.S. Bureau of the Census, Americans with disabilities have a total income of $700 billion and a discretionary income of $188 billion. Thus, the disabled spend more than the entire U.S. teen population and more than the populations of Alaska, Oregon, Washington, California, and Hawaii combined. Finally, the disabled are incredibly brand loyal. Once a company is recognized as sensitive to the needs of PWDs, word of mouth brings in more business. Even showing the disabled in advertising, while it may provide limited real benefits to the handicapped, brings in business.

Of course, there are some unique problems in directing marketing strategies to this group. First, it is difficult (if not impossible) to select a single best approach. The disabled are not one homogenous segment. Among the hearing-impaired, for example, there is a group that lip-reads and a group that does not. Furthermore, how do you efficiently communicate with the disabled? If your target market includes teenagers, data show that MTV is a good place to advertise. But the disabled are a less obvious group, and there are no clear guidelines on how to reach them.

The Apple Computer Corp. is one company that has developed a special relationship with PWDs. Alan Bright-man heads up Apple's Disability Solutions division. This unit customizes and adapts Apple computers to meet the needs of PWDs. For example, after an accident left a jazz musician paralyzed from the neck down, therapists told him to find another career. Apple thought otherwise; its technicians created a device that allows him to make music with a sip straw.

To reach PWDs, Apple advertises in some of the more than 700 specialized publications that now target disabled readers, and the company works hard to build relationships with over 350 PWD organizations. Alan Brightman and other Apple marketing people also try to get the attention and interest of the therapists and other caregivers who are an important part of the lives of PWDs. Apple salespeople often display their specialized products at meetings attended by therapists to show them how technology can improve the quality of their patients' lives.

Apple has found that when products are developed to meet the needs of the PWD segment, they often benefit other users as well. For example, voice-recognition software products developed for PWDs have applications beyond that market segment. Looking to the future, Apple must determine if it believes pursuing this market segment will be profitable in the long run or if turning a profit should be the reason for targeting PWDs at all. In addition, the company must consider the best ways to identify and communicate with PWDs and their care givers to be sure it is reaching the maximum number of people. Apple has found that helping its disabled customers yields many benefits, but many corporations are still grappling with the best way to address this growing market segment.

Source: Judy Quinn, "Able to Buy," *Incentive* (Sept. 1995) 80–91.

Things to Talk About

1. Why is the PWD segment a good prospect for many marketing strategies?
2. What are some of the problems in marketing to PWDs?
3. What are the benefits a firm may receive from being successful with the PWD segment?
4. How does Apple market to PWDs?
5. What secrets to success has Apple discovered?

MARKETING IN ACTION: REAL CHOICES AT MASTERCARD

MasterCard, founded in 1966, is a nonprofit association of member financial institutions that offer the familiar credit card to their customers. The association's income comes from the charges it imposes on its member banks. For these payments the member banks receive a number of services. These services include the centralized authorization of customer MasterCard purchases and approval of the transfer of payments from the bank to retailers. Advertising that encourages people to charge—and charge often—is also paid for by the association.

Although millions of people were faithfully whipping out their MasterCards to charge purchases from vacation cruises to vacuum cleaners, the member banks began to run into trouble. MasterCard was losing the battle of market share to its plastic competitors. A dramatic repositioning strategy was called for.

Credit card advertising in the 1980s depicted glamorous people having exciting times at expensive resorts in spectacular settings—the ultimate in conspicuous consumption. Consider the slogan used by MasterCard competitor Visa: "It's everywhere you want to be." For a long time American Express trumpeted that "Membership Has Its Privileges," supporting the idea that a person had to be rich and successful to use its credit card. During the same time MasterCard encouraged customers to "Max the moment."

But in the 1990s prestige became harder and harder to sell. Many consumers were becoming disenchanted with the emphasis on spending for spending's sake that was rampant in the 1980s, and credit card companies began scrambling to tone down their focus on "living the good life." American Express, for example, began changing its advertising to distance itself from the selfish, materialistic image it had cultivated in the past decade.

In 1989 Peter Hart took over as president of the association of 27,000 banks that issue MasterCard credit cards. At the time Hart assumed the leadership role, MasterCard had lost $\frac{1}{3}$ of its market share. One problem was that MasterCard had become almost indistinguishable from Visa, except that Visa's name was more recognized. Both could be used at the same stores, both charged the same interest rates, and many banks offered their customers both MasterCard and Visa accounts. An additional problem was Sears' introduction of the Discover card, which was steadily capturing thousands of former MasterCard customers due to aggressive advertising and promotions.

Peter Hart developed a marketing idea for MasterCard that involved a shift toward a benefit segmentation strategy—compete by showing card holders a *different* way to look at the reasons they use a charge card in the first place. Hart felt that to be successful a credit card company needed to get consumers to use its card not just for luxury items and exciting vacations but on a day-to-day basis, as a convenient replacement for cash at the grocery store, the drugstore, the dry cleaner's, and so on. Hart wanted to reposition MasterCard to be "the most useful card for everyday life—the card for everywhere you *have* to be."

Hart's idea was to emphasize the card's value as a way for users to organize their personal finances. The objective was not to steal market share from other credit card companies, but rather to convince customers to use MasterCard for a larger proportion of purchases otherwise made by cash and check, which make up $\frac{4}{5}$ of all customer transactions. To emphasize this change in direction, MasterCard devised a new slogan: "MasterCard. It's not just a credit card. It's smart money."

To further encourage consumers to change the way they used the card, Hart also developed innovative cobranding programs with nonbank companies, including AT&T, General Motors, and General Electric. These arrangements enhanced the card's market position, making MasterCard the credit card alternative with greater value, as these companies offered MasterCard users discounts on their products. Indeed, cobranding has been the fastest-growing segment of the market. For example, in 1992 alone General Motors distributed 4.5 million MasterCards that provided rebates when users purchased GM vehicles.

In 1993 MasterCard began a new advertising campaign focusing on people using the card to charge their groceries so they could track how much they spent on food per month, a far cry from the typical image of a glamorous couple charging scuba lessons at an exotic resort! In addition, individual MasterCard banks have themselves developed unique and successful promotional activities. For example, some institutions now send customers coupons good for discounts in stores such as Kmart and Toys "Я" Us. MasterCard customers also can punch their card number into any telephone in the United States to charge calls, and MasterCard will replace lost or stolen cards in twenty-four hours.

Together these marketing programs have led to a real turnaround for MasterCard. In 1992 the association increased its share of U.S. "charged" dollars for the first time in fourteen years. And the future continues to look bright as more opportunities for everyday credit card use become available. For example, California now lets people renew

MARKETING IN ACTION: REAL CHOICES AT MASTERCARD *(CONTINUED)*

drivers' licenses with a credit card. And before long consumers will even be able to charge their speeding tickets!

But MasterCard must continue to be innovative to succeed in the ever-increasing competition for credit card business. The other credit card companies are learning from MasterCard's benefit segmentation strategy, and they are touting their own value for everyday purchases. And with new marketing opportunities available on the Internet, having a competitive advantage will become more and more difficult for MasterCard. As the United States moves toward becoming a cashless society, credit card companies will continue to do battle to occupy a prominent place in American's wallets. Charge!

Source: Saul Hansell, "The Man Who Charged Up MasterCard," *The New York Times* (March 7, 1993): 3, 8.

Things to Think About

1. What is the problem facing MasterCard?
2. What factors are important in understanding this problem?
3. What alternatives might MasterCard consider?
4. What are your recommendations for solving the problem?
5. What are some ways to implement your recommendations?

CHAPTER

9

Creating the Product

When you have completed your study of this chapter, you should be able to:

1. Explain the various dimensions of a product.
2. Describe the ways in which products are classified.
3. Explain the role of new products in the marketplace.
4. Explain the process of product adoption and the diffusion of innovations.
5. Describe the product life cycle (PLC) concept.

CHAPTER OBJECTIVES

ℛEAL PEOPLE, REAL CHOICES:

Meet Bob Masone, a Decision Maker at Nabisco

As a product manager at the Nabisco Biscuit Company, Bob Masone helps the company take a big bite out of the cookie market. Nabisco sells over $3 billion (in wholesale dollars) of cookies and crackers each year, dominating the category with such brand names as *Oreo, Chips Ahoy!, Ritz,* and *Newtons.* Mr. Masone manages all aspects of the *Newtons* brand, which by itself sells over $300 million a year to wholesalers. As product manager for the brand he is responsible for developing long-term strategies for the brand and implementing all *Newtons* marketing initiatives, including the development of new *Newtons* products and promotional strategies.

Mr. Masone joined Nabisco in 1989 and has worked on both cookie and cracker brands. He has been the *Newtons* product manager since April 1993. Before joining the company he began his marketing career at General Mills. Mr. Masone received a B.S. in accounting from Georgetown University and an M.B.A. in marketing from the University of Michigan.

WHAT IS A PRODUCT? MORE THAN JUST A BOX OF COOKIES

When you think of marketing a product, what comes to mind? A mouth-watering box of chocolates? A hot sports car? A box of laundry detergent? A new notebook computer? These indeed are products, but the marketplace is full of other types of products as well. When you have your best suit dry cleaned, you are buying a product. If you visit a hospital emergency room to have a broken arm put in a cast, you are receiving a product marketed by the hospital. When you help to elect a state senator or a U.S. congressman, you, along with other voters, are choosing one product over others offered in the election. When your firm retains an advertising agency to help it develop a promotional campaign, it is buying a business-to-business product. When you land a hard-to-get ticket to a Bon Jovi or a Janet Jackson concert, this is a product also. Indeed, the term "product" can be applied to virtually *anything* that can be bought, sold, bartered, or rented.

This chapter and the next two will focus on the product, a crucial piece of the "Four Ps" that make up the marketing mix. By **product** we mean a tangible good, a service, an idea or, more often, some combination of these that, through the exchange process, satisfies consumer or business customer needs. Decisions regarding the product that will be offered for sale typically are more complex than they may appear, because in reality there is more to a product than merely a *thing* that comes in a package. For this reason it is actually easier to think of the product as a *bundle* of attributes that includes features, functions, benefits, and uses. For example, Bob Masone's job as a product manager includes developing product ideas for Nabisco—for instance, identifying benefits people might desire in a snack product (such as dietetic, guilt-free, but wonderful-tasting cookies) as well as actual features (like fat-free *Newtons*) that will allow consumers to satisfy these needs.

This chapter will define what we mean when we talk about products and will provide the basic concepts necessary for understanding product strategy. First we will explore exactly what a product is and define the various classifications of consumer and business-to-business products. Then we will talk about new products and how (if the company is lucky!) they are chosen by some members of a target market and then increasingly by

product: a tangible good, a service, an idea, or some combination of these that, through the exchange process, satisfies consumer or business customer needs; a bundle of attributes including features, functions, benefits, and uses

Exhibit 9.1
Lucrative products can take many forms including toys for both kids and grownups. A recent success story illustrates how a lone inventor can make a fortune by dreaming up a new product that does nothing more than get people wet. It all started when Lonnie Johnson walked into the slick conference room of Philadelphia-based Larami Corporation. He smiled mischievously at the assembled executives. Then, he opened his pink, battered Samsonite suitcase and took out a gizmo that looked a bit like a laser gun from Star Trek. Holding out this combination of a hand-held pump apparatus, PVC tubing, Plexiglas, and plastic soda bottles, Lonnie aimed . . . *and fired!* A giant stream of water shot across the room. Larami's president saw the future and shouted: "Wow!" The Super Soaker was born. A year later, Super Soaker had become the most successful water gun in American retail history. By 1993, 27 million units had been sold, and an unknown number of unsuspecting consumers had been soaked.

others in the market. Finally we will discuss how the strategies required to market products successfully change as these goods and services move through stages in the product life cycle to evolve from being "new kids on the block" to tried-and-true favorites.

▪ ▪ ▪ ▪ ▪ BUILD A BETTER MOUSETRAP ▪ ▪ ▪

In Chapter 1 we saw how successful organizations operate in accord with the marketing concept as they seek to satisfy customer wants and needs more efficiently and more effectively than the competition. How do organizations go about satisfying customers? By offering in the exchange process a product that people and organizations want. Thus, the product is the foundation on which an effective marketing strategy is built.

"Build a better mousetrap and the world will beat a path to your door!" While we've all heard that adage, the truth is that just because a product is better *doesn't* mean it will succeed. Only when the product is what customers want and need will it be successful. Classic product failures tell us that no matter how good the promotion, no matter how attractive the price, no matter how efficient the channel of distribution, if the product does not satisfy customer wants and needs, it will fail. If this were not true, we would all be driving Edsels and talking to one another on Picturephones. Because a product can take many forms, we will first examine some of the characteristics of products before considering what features make it more or less likely that a new entrant in the marketplace will become either as popular as the venerable *Fig Newton* or as stale as last week's cookies.

GOODS VERSUS SERVICES

Earlier we defined a product as a good, service, or idea, or some combination of these. A **good** is a tangible product, one that can be seen, touched, smelled, and/or tasted. A good may be a pack of cookies, an audio CD, a house, an automatic dishwasher, or a pair of stone-washed jeans.

A **service** is an intangible product, such as a bank loan, a stay in a hospital, or even an education, that is exchanged directly from the producer to the customer. Services may be performed by *humans* or by *machines* (for example, Automatic Teller Machines or ATMs) and are experienced by customers, not owned. While we generally think of a car as a good and a car wash as a service, most products are neither totally good nor totally service.

goods: tangible products—ones that can be seen, touched, smelled, and/or tasted

services: intangible products that are exchanged directly from the producer to the customer

Exhibit 9.2
"Build a better mousetrap and the world will beat a path to your door?" In reality, you can build a better mousetrap, but if it's not what customers want and need, they will beat a path *away* from your door. Since 1928, the Woodstream Company has built millions of flat wooden mousetraps, but in the 1950s the company decided to see if it could literally build a better one. Woodstream product development people researched mouse eating, crawling, and resting habits. They built prototypes of different mousetraps to come up with the best possible design, and they tested them in actual homes. Finally, the company unveiled the sleek-looking "Little Champ," which was made of black plastic and resembled a miniature inverted bathtub with a hole, just the right size for a mouse to go in. They even developed a "super" model, the "Four Hole Choker" shown here. When the mouse went in and began nibbling on the bait, a spring would snap upward and catch the mouse neatly by the throat, causing almost instant death by strangulation. The mouse could easily be removed by pressing on the spring from the top side of the trap. The trap sold for $0.12 (compared with $0.05 for the "old fashioned" wooden trap.)

The "Little Champ" was a colossal failure because Woodstream Corp. studied mouse habits and not consumer preferences. Woodstream later discovered that typically the husband set the trap at night, but the wife was left with the task of disposing of the dead mouse in the morning. With the old-fashioned trap, this simply meant throwing it away. Unfortunately, the "Little Champ" looked too expensive to just throw away, so the wife had to empty the trap and place it on the cabinet shelf to be re-used. This was a task most women weren't willing to do—and as a result the "better mousetrap" bombed.

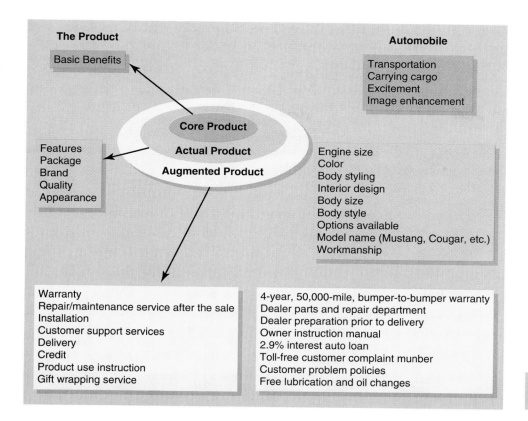

The Product

Basic Benefits

Core Product
Actual Product
Augmented Product

Automobile

Transportation
Carrying cargo
Excitement
Image enhancement

Features
Package
Brand
Quality
Appearance

Engine size
Color
Body styling
Interior design
Body size
Body style
Options available
Model name (Mustang, Cougar, etc.)
Workmanship

Warranty
Repair/maintenance service after the sale
Installation
Customer support services
Delivery
Credit
Product use instruction
Gift wrapping service

4-year, 50,000-mile, bumper-to-bumper warranty
Dealer parts and repair department
Dealer preparation prior to delivery
Owner instruction manual
2.9% interest auto loan
Toll-free customer complaint munber
Customer problem policies
Free lubrication and oil changes

Figure 9.1
Product Layers

As we will see in Chapter 11, most goods and services, in fact, fall somewhere along a good-service continuum. There are usually tangible elements to a service and most goods include some intangible attributes. When a customer buys a new refrigerator, the dealer will unpack and deliver the unit, hook up the waterline to the ice maker, and make sure the refrigerator is level so that the door swings closed. Gateway sells personal computers and provides trouble-shooting services with each sale. Your dentist, in addition to cleaning your teeth and filling a couple of cavities, may give you a toothbrush and some dental floss to take home with you. After you have become an expert on product strategy by reading this chapter and Chapter 10, we'll explore some specific issues related to services in Chapter 11.

LAYERS OF THE PRODUCT CONCEPT

No doubt you've heard someone say, "It's the thought, not the gift itself, that counts." This means that the gift is a sign or symbol that the gift giver has remembered you or is showing you respect. Was the gift presented with a flourish? Was it wrapped in special paper? These special touches add to the meaning of the gift.

Like a gift, a product is more than it seems. A product includes *everything* that a customer receives in an exchange. As Figure 9.1 shows, we can distinguish among three distinct layers of the product. The soul of the product—the *core product*—is made up of the basic benefits provided in the exchange. In addition, the product is also the combination of tangible features (the *actual product*) and intangible attributes (the *augmented product*) the customer receives when he or she purchases the product. In developing product strategies, marketers need to consider how to satisfy customers' wants and needs at each of these three levels. Let's consider each layer in turn.

benefit: the outcome sought by a customer that motivates buying behavior; the value the customer receives from owning, using, or experiencing a product

THE CORE PRODUCT

The single biggest mistake made by managers occurs when they think they are producing and selling a product. They're not. They're producing and selling product benefits. A **benefit** is an outcome sought by a customer that motivates buying behavior. It is what the customer receives from owning, using, or experiencing a product. The *core product* consists of the benefits the product will provide for consumers or business customers. Wise old marketers (and some young ones too) will tell you, "A marketer may make and sell a $\frac{1}{2}''$ drill bit, but a customer buys a $\frac{1}{2}''$ hole."[1]

This timeworn saying (perhaps the closest thing in marketing to a Zen proverb!) is more profound than it seems at first: It reminds us that people are buying an outcome (in this case, a hole). If and when a new way comes along that provides that outcome better or cheaper, the drill maker has a problem. Marketing is about supplying benefits, not products! Table 9.1 illustrates the lengths to which some marketers will go to ensure that their products deliver on the benefits promised.

Why are you or your parents spending thousands of dollars for you to attend college? There are any number of possible reasons: to land a good job, to become an educated person, to enjoy four years of guilt-free partying. Perhaps all of these. In designing product

Table 9.1
Product Testing

With hopes of bringing only successful new products to market and avoiding flops, manufacturers spend millions of dollars testing products to make sure they will meet the quality expectations of consumers. Some of the testing is exotic while other tests are almost humorous. Here are a few examples.

Product	Testing Procedure
Fruit of the Loom men's briefs	Worn by male members of the New Haven (Connecticut) Symphony Orchestra
Chrysler cars	Built a test tunnel where autos face twenty-four hours of gale-force blizzard conditions (snow included). If the car passes that test, it is subjected to simulated desert heat the next day.
Sherwin Williams paint	At the company's fifty-three-acre paint test site in Ohio, over 40,000 panels, painted with both Sherwin Williams and competitors' paints, are subjected to the weather for up to fifteen years (the length of the warranty on some paint).
Apple Computer Powerbooks	To simulate "real life conditions," the computers are drenched with soda, smeared with mayonnaise, and baked in ovens (to mimic the trunk of a car in the summer heat).
Shaw Industries carpet products	Hires workers to pace up and down rows of carpet samples eight hours a day. One worker says she reads about three books a week and has lost forty pounds in the three years she has been a regular carpet "walker."
Mattel's Barbie	When Mattel introduced the new scuba-diving Barbie, product testing required that Barbie must swim and kick for fifteen straight hours to make sure she would last up to a year. Other tests on Barbie make sure that her skin won't crack, which would create unsafe sharp edges, and that pieces of the doll can't be bitten off and swallowed by children.
Procter & Gamble hair care products	P&G pays $1,200 for mannequin heads with realistic hair for testing new hair care products. Each of P&G's fifteen "heads" has a name. When the hair begins to get thin, the "head" is retired.

Source: Faye Rice, "Secrets of Product Testing," *Fortune* (Nov. 28, 1994): 166–172.

strategies, marketers need to understand what benefits consumers and business customers want.

Typically, a product provides a number of different benefits, and these have varying degrees of importance. For example, the primary benefit provided by an automobile is transportation. But an auto also provides psychological benefits. Driving a sporty convertible adds excitement to life. An expensive car may be a statement about status or prestige. As we saw in Chapter 8, segmenting purchasers in terms of their reasons for using a good or service (benefit segmentation) is a common and useful strategy.

All brands in a product category usually provide the same *product category benefits*— that is, they perform some basic function. All cars (when they are working) provide the ability to travel from point A to point B. Customers expect any car they purchase to provide reliable transportation. Products also provide *customized benefits*—benefits that make one brand stand out, providing reasons for customers to choose one firm's product over another. It is because of customized benefits that customers who want economical transportation may drive a Chevrolet Cavalier, others who desire a top-of-the-line, all-terrain vehicle will consider a Range Rover, and still others who want a car that adds excitement to their lives may choose the Mazda Miata.

Sometimes marketers add services to a tangible product to customize benefits. Helping yourself to a dozen fresh eggs at a farmer's stand and placing payment in a cash box involves buying a good that is accompanied by very little service. Had the farmer cleaned up the eggs to improve their appearance or placed the eggs in a container for easier transportation, a degree of service would be added. Delivering the fresh eggs to your door adds more service. If the farmer stayed and cooked the fresh eggs for your breakfast just the way you like them, that service would be an even more noteworthy benefit!

THE ACTUAL PRODUCT

The second level of the product, the *actual product,* is the physical good or the delivered service that supplies the desired benefit. The actual product includes not only the good or service, but also unique features of the product, such as the appearance or styling, the package, and the brand name. Take, for example, an automobile. Cars come with different features to meet the needs and wants of various customer segments. Some have large, roomy interiors. Others use smaller, more economical engines. To attract us to the showroom, automakers offer a vast array of features—high-quality stereo systems, built-in cellular phones, reclining seats, large trunk space—the list is almost infinite. What will be next, self-cleaning ashtrays?

Two important components of the actual product are its packaging and its brand name. *Packaging* is the covering or container that is used to protect a physical good, provide information to customers, promote the good, and add benefits. For Pepsi and Coca-Cola, packaging has become not only an important component of the product but a battlefield between the two soft drink giants. PepsiCo introduced two-liter bottles and six-packs of soda. Coca-Cola Co. revived its patented, contoured glass bottle to evoke nostalgia. PepsiCo introduced the twenty-four-pack cube of eight-ounce cans. Coke announced plans to introduce a plastic contoured bottle. Pepsi introduced thirty-six-can packages for warehouse clubs. And the battle rages on . . .[2] A *brand name* is a symbol that stands for the product's unique character in the minds of customers, and it is often depicted graphically in a distinctive way to reinforce this identity (like the very well-known Coca-Cola logo). We will talk more about the crucial functions of packaging and branding in Chapter 10.

THE AUGMENTED PRODUCT

Finally, marketers offer customers an *augmented product*—the actual product plus supporting features that make it easier or less risky to use. These features can include a warranty, credit, delivery, installation, product repair and maintenance service after the sale, or customer instruction on use of the product. Going that extra mile for customers by offering an augmented product typically is an effective way for a company to stand out from the crowd in a way buyers appreciate. For example, Enterprise Rent-a-Car has competed successfully with industry giants Avis and Hertz by offering an augmented service they don't: free customer pickup service. That's a significant benefit that people appreciate, and a product strategy that's paid off handsomely for Enterprise.[3]

CLASSIFYING PRODUCTS

As we've seen, the term "product" encompasses a wide range of goods and services sought by both consumers and organizations. Of course, these products vary greatly in terms of their price, complexity, importance, frequency of purchase, and on and on. As was discussed in Chapters 6 and 7, differences in product characteristics cause both consumers and business customers to behave differently in making the purchase—how much time they spend in making the decision, how much they search for information, what attributes of the product are important to them, and so on. How one buys a new pair of shoes is quite different (hopefully!) from how one decides on a new car, and neither of these situations bears much resemblance to how a firm selects a pension plan. Because customer purchase behavior differs depending on the type of product being purchased, marketing strategies must differ also.

Generally, products can be classified as either *consumer products* or *business (or organizational) products*. Sometimes this basic classification is based on the characteristics of the product; individual consumers rarely, if ever, buy forklifts, dump trucks, or fire engines (although we do know of one multimillionaire who bought a fire engine to wash down the white fences on his very large estate!). In other cases, though, the same products—such as toilet paper, vacuum cleaners, and light bulbs—are bought by both consumer and business-to-business customers, albeit in very different amounts.

In this section we will outline some of the numerous product classifications. We will first consider differences in consumer products based on how long the product will last and on how the consumer shops for the product. Then we will review the general classifications of business-to-business products.

TYPES OF CONSUMER PRODUCTS

Knowing something about how a consumer goes about buying and using a product is very helpful in marketing decision making. If a product such as a pack of gum or a can of soda is purchased on the "spur of the moment," packaging and other point-of-purchase communications that will influence these decisions are likely to be very important. If a product like a living room sofa will be used for many years, the most wanted features, product quality, and a strong brand reputation will be very important. Consumer products may be understood and classified based on how long they last or based on how consumers buy the products.

Product Classes Defined By How Long a Product Lasts

Consumer goods may be classified as durable or nondurable depending on how long the product will normally last. You expect a refrigerator to last quite a few years, but you know that the gallon of milk in the refrigerator will last only a week or so before it turns into a "science project." **Durable goods** are consumer products that provide benefits over a period of months, years, or even decades, such as cars, furniture, and appliances. In contrast, **nondurable goods** such as newspapers, food, and clothing are used up relatively quickly and thus provide benefits for a shorter time.

Durable goods are more likely to be purchased under conditions of *high involvement*—where the decision is an important one with a fairly high level of perceived risk—as discussed in Chapter 6. That means that when a consumer buys a refrigerator or a computer or a house, he or she will spend more time and energy on the decision process, often gathering lots of information and scrutinizing the various alternatives. Product strategies for durable goods must address the relative importance of various product benefits, the desire for different product features, and the greater importance of warranties, service,

durable goods: consumer products that provide benefits over a period of time such as cars, furniture, and appliances

nondurable goods: consumer products that provide benefits for only a short time because they are consumed (such as food) or are no longer useful (such as newspapers)

Excellence at "Cindy Inc."

In the "old days" (that is, prior to the 1990s!) some beautiful women had careers as highly successful fashion models because they wore clothes well and made apparel manufacturers look good. In today's world, though, so-called supermodels have become a new product category, "household names" who are often better known than the clothes they wear down fashion runways and in the pages of magazines. These top models have become mass-market celebrities with brand-name status. The loyalty they inspire in their fans is changing the face of the modeling game, as savvy sirens (with the help of some clever agents) continue to find new ways to extend the relationship they have built with their fans—and in the process create small empires for themselves.

The dawning of the era of model-as-corporation perhaps began with Cindy Crawford, a well-paid cover girl who catapulted to fame by appearing in a 1988 photo spread in *Playboy*. That exposure paid off big-time, as Crawford went on to land a job hosting *MTV's House of Style*, a widely viewed television series giving an insider's view of the fashion industry. Other developments, such as some highly successful Pepsi commercials (not to mention a now-defunct marriage to actor Richard Gere), firmly established Crawford as a supermodel *par excellence*. She earned $6.5 million in 1994, and her expansion into commercials, exercise videos, TV specials, and fat endorsement con-

tracts with Kay Jewelers, Revlon, and Pepsi earned her the nickname "Cindy Inc." in the modeling industry. Other success stories include:

- **Elle Macpherson:** Her company, Elle Macpherson Inc., is involved in designing a lingerie line for the Australian and New Zealand markets. A chain of Elle Macpherson lingerie boutique stores recently opened in Australia. She is now looking to expand into bed and bath products. Macpherson is also part owner, along with fellow models Naomi Campbell and Claudia Schiffer, of Fashion Cafe, a New York restaurant.

- **Niki Taylor:** She started with a contract from L'Oréal at age fifteen, and in addition to modeling activities is a special correspondent in Miami for NBC and appeared in *Camp Nowhere*, a Disney film.

- **Naomi Campbell:** In addition to her partnership in the Fashion Cafe restaurant, Campbell's novel *Swan* sold 75,000 copies, and she also put out a CD. She has a contract with an Italian clothing manufacturer and is planning to introduce her own cosmetics line.

Source: Joshua Levine, "We Have Shares," *Forbes* (March 27, 1995): 75–78

---

customer support, and so on. Because consumers are likely to engage in an extensive search for information in the decision process, marketing strategies must also ensure that adequate information is available, when, where, and how consumers want it.

Nondurable goods are usually *low involvement* products—that is, the purchase is not generally considered particularly important. The purchase of nondurable goods is typically classified as *habitual decision making*. In these situations price and availability are often more important than product attributes. Branding is especially important in developing product strategies for nondurables as consumers often rely on brand reputation and/or are more likely to be brand loyal. We'll talk more about that in Chapter 10.

Product Classes Defined By How Consumers Buy the Product

Marketers may also classify products based on where and/or how consumers buy the product. Both goods and services are thus labeled *convenience products, shopping products, specialty products,* or *unsought products.*

A **convenience product** is a good or service that consumers purchase frequently, with a minimum of comparison and effort. Examples of convenience products are a can of soda, a loaf of bread, or a taxi ride. Convenience products are usually low-priced and widely available. You can buy a gallon of milk at every grocery store, at "convenience" stores, and at many service stations in any town, city, or rural area in the country. Consumers generally know all they need to know about a convenience product, devote little effort to purchases, and willingly accept alternative brands if their preferred brand is not available in a convenient location.

convenience product: a consumer good or service that is usually low-priced, widely available, and purchased frequently, with a minimum of comparison and effort

Convenience products may be further classified as *staples, impulse products,* and *emergency products.* Milk, bread, and gasoline are staples. They are available almost everywhere, they are considered by most consumers to be basic necessities, and there are few if any perceived differences among brands. While some brands of milk, bread, and even gasoline attempt to differentiate their products through advertising, many consumers are not convinced that big differences exist.

An ice cream sandwich. A copy of *People* magazine. A box of chocolate chip cookies. These are all examples of impulse products—products people buy "on impulse." You stop at the local service station or market to buy a loaf of bread and suddenly you have an uncontrollable urge for chocolate. You are standing in the check-out line at the supermarket and a photo of Michael Jackson with a provocative headline grabs your attention—you've got to read that article (you really should get out more!). Because consumers seldom plan to purchase these items, it is essential that they be available and highly visible. That is exactly why you find candy bars, film for your camera, magazines, and batteries tempting you at the check-out aisle in the grocery store—to stimulate that impulse to buy.

Emergency products are products only needed and purchased, as the name suggests, in an emergency. Bandages, umbrellas, and something to unstop the bathroom sink drain are examples of emergency products. Because of the emergency character of the purchase, price is usually irrelevant. Furthermore, these products are needed when they are needed—not the next day. Therefore, marketers make sure they are widely available. Walk along any street in New York City during a sudden afternoon rainstorm. In store after store, umbrellas suddenly appear for sale—umbrellas that only minutes before were hidden under a counter or in a back room. No one will pay $5.00 for a poor-quality umbrella when the sun is shining, but when it's pouring "cats and dogs," $5.00 suddenly seems like a really good investment.

A **shopping product** is a good or service for which consumers will spend considerable time and effort gathering information on price, product attributes, and product quality, comparing a number of different alternatives before making a purchase. Often consumers have fairly low prior knowledge about currently available alternatives and are only moderately brand loyal. They may visit several retail outlets and devote considerable effort to comparing competing options. A pair of shoes, a color television set, and a housecleaning service are examples of shopping products.

Some products are classified as shopping products because the product choices available are not all alike. For these *attribute-based shopping products,* consumers spend time and energy finding the best possible product selection. In shopping for a new dress the consumer may visit only one or several retailers, examining the selection of dresses, determining what is currently "in style," and trying on different dresses to see which one looks best. The purchase will be made only when the consumer feels she has obtained adequate knowledge of what is available and has found one dress that is the best of all those available—or at least one that looks spectacular.

Other times products are considered shopping products because of differences in price, despite the fact that the different choices available in the marketplace are just about the same. Products such as a portable television or a clock radio are generally regarded as *price-based* shopping products. If the customer is shopping for a nineteen-inch portable color television set, she will probably find that all brands and models are about the same. In this case comparing different retailers' offerings and obtaining information will likely focus on price. Some determined shoppers will visit numerous appliance stores in hopes of saving an additional $10 or $20. The final selection will be made when the customer feels she has obtained as good a buy as possible, all things considered.

Specialty products are goods or services that have unique characteristics and that are very important to the buyer. For this reason a consumer will devote significant effort to acquire these items. Consumers usually know a good deal about specialty products, rely on brands, and spend little if any time comparing alternatives. A favorite restaurant, a Rolex watch, and even a favorite brand of cigarettes are specialty products. Would you accept an imitation for your favorite restaurant? No, you want the genuine article. Consumers won't take substitutes for specialty products, regardless of price and availability.

A fourth category of consumer products is the **unsought product.** Unsought products are goods or services for which a consumer has little awareness or interest until a need arises. For the new twentysomething college graduate with his or her first "real" job,

shopping product: a good or service for which consumers will spend considerable time and effort gathering information and comparing a number of different alternatives before making a purchase

specialty product: a good or service that has unique characteristics, is very important to the buyer, and for which the buyer will devote significant effort to acquire

unsought product: a good or service for which a consumer has little awareness or interest until the product or a need for the product is brought to his attention

a retirement plan, disability insurance, and the services of a lawyer are usually unsought products. It typically requires a good deal of advertising or personal selling to interest people in unsought products—just ask any life insurance salesperson.

TYPES OF BUSINESS-TO-BUSINESS PRODUCTS

In Chapter 7 we discussed the different types or classifications of business-to-business products in detail. In this section we will provide a brief review of these classifications just to refresh your memory.

All types of organizations, manufacturers, government, and not-for-profit organizations purchase *equipment, maintenance, repair, and operating (MRO) equipment* and *business services.* Equipment includes both large installations such as buildings and trucks, often called *capital equipment,* and accessory equipment such as computer terminals and photocopy machines. Maintenance, repair, and operating products refer to items such as light bulbs, computer paper, and cleaning supplies that are essential for the operations of an organization and that are purchased frequently because they are used up. Most organizations also purchase a variety of business services, such as accounting, legal, research, and advertising.

Firms that produce goods also purchase *raw materials, processed materials,* and *component parts* used in their production processes. Raw materials such as iron ore and pulp wood are products of the fishing, lumber, agriculture, or mining industries. Processed materials are goods such as sheets of steel or rolls of paper that have been changed from their original raw material state but that are not yet usable finished products. Component parts are complete finished products such as a battery or a water pump that are used in the production of larger finished products.

NEW PRODUCTS AND THE DIFFUSION OF INNOVATIONS

New products and styles, or **innovations,** constantly enter the market. These new goods or services occur in both consumer and industrial settings. Innovations may take the form of a clothing style (for example, skirts for men), a new manufacturing technique, or a novel way to deliver a service. If an innovation is successful (most are not), it spreads through the population. First it is bought and/or used by only a few people, and then more and more consumers decide to adopt it, until in some cases it seems that almost everyone has bought or tried the innovation and it is now "old hat."

innovations: in marketing, an innovation is a product (a good, service, or idea) that is perceived to be new and different from existing products

Every year thousands of new products appear in the marketplace. What are some of the most exciting new products in recent years? How about these:

- A tastier tomato that has been created through genetic engineering.[4]
- Bike Friday's Pocket Rocket, an American-made high-tech racing bicycle that folds to fit in a suitcase for traveling.
- A Seiko Message Watch: an $80 watch beeper that you wear on your arm, just like Dick Tracy: The watch allows you to get local sports scores, weather, the S & P index, and the Dow Jones industrial average transmitted when the stock market closes.
- For all those consumers who have been driven nuts by a blinking 12:00 when the power goes out, Sony introduced a VCR with a computer chip that will reset its clock by reading the time code broadcast by PBS stations.[5]
- Straight Arrow, maker of a shampoo for horses called Mane 'N Tail, discovered that horse owners were using the product on their own hair. The company introduced two new brands intended exclusively for people but retaining the same essential formula: Equenne is sold in upscale salons while Mane 'N Tail (for people) is aimed at the mass market.[6]

Exhibit 9. 3

Men's fashions have traditionally experienced little change. Ties and jacket lapels get wider or narrower. Jackets have two or three buttons. Shirt collars get longer and shorter. Cuffs and pleats on slacks come and go. Three-piece suits appear and disappear in the marketplace.

In the 1960s, men's fashion designers felt that men were ready for a more dramatic and more exciting change. Enter the Nehru suit, which was fashioned after the traditional clothing worn by leaders of Indian society and named after Jawaharlal Nehru, Prime Minister of India from 1947 to 1964. The suit was made of 100% polyester, which became extremely popular in the 1960s because it never wrinkled. The problem was that it was also extremely hot, uncomfortable, and never seemed to fit the body just right because it always maintained its own shape. Unfortunately for the men's fashion industry, men overwhelmingly rejected the Nehru suit. Manufacturers and retailers lost millions of dollars. Years later, it was rumored that there were warehouses in the garment district of New York where thousands of unsold Nehru suits were still being stored! Let the buyer beware—they may try again!

Which, if any, of these products will be successful? Who will be the first to buy the new products? How fast will the popularity of the products grow?

In this section we will examine what a "new product" really is and discuss the various categories of new products. Then we will talk about how new products come to be accepted (or not) by individuals and by the population as a whole—the *adoption* and *diffusion* processes. Finally we will discuss differences in customers and differences among products that affect the rate of adoption.

THE IMPORTANCE OF INNOVATIONS

Understanding the development of new products is so vitally important that many universities offer entire courses devoted solely to this topic. Why is new product development so important? There are several reasons. First, in today's world technology is advancing at a dizzying pace. Products that were new only a year or so ago are already obsolete. Research-oriented companies like 3M understand the importance of new product development. Sixty thousand different products are marketed by 3M; new product ideas are constantly being developed, and the successful ones go from idea to commercialization in less than three years. Products introduced recently include the Never Rust Wool Soap Pad made from recycled plastic bottles and the O-Cel-O Stay Fresh Sponge that contains an agent that stops the growth of odor-causing bacteria.[7]

The speed of change in technology is nowhere more obvious than in computer technology. Take, for instance, the microprocessor inside a PC. As manufacturers are able to shrink the size of transistor circuits by 10 percent a year, chip makers can develop a new line of chips every three years with four times as many transistors—which in turn improves overall performance by 400 to 500 percent! By about 2005 a memory chip should hold 4 billion bits (or four gigabits)—about the amount of text in two sets of the *Encyclopedia Britannica*. By 2011 the same chip should be able to hold sixty-four gigabits or twenty-seven sets of the *Britannica*. Projections are that by 2020 computers will be as powerful as the human brain and by 2040 will surpass human intelligence.[8] If you wait long enough they'll be able to take this course for you. . . .

The lightning-fast rate of change in many product categories means that if new products are not regularly developed and introduced into the marketplace, manufacturers will soon have nothing to sell, and the entire organization may be doomed to an early death. For example, in the early 1980s Wang Laboratories was a powerhouse in the computer industry. Unfortunately the company failed to anticipate the personal computer revolution and it no longer exists today. A second reason for understanding new products is related to the high cost to firms of developing new products. In the pharmaceutical industry the cost of developing each new drug that enters the market is estimated to be between $200 and $500 million.[9]

Finally, the development of new products is an important contribution to society as a whole. We would never suggest that *everything* new is necessarily good; nevertheless, many of the new products entering the market each year do allow us to live longer, happier, better-quality lives. While there are some cynics who would disagree, most of us feel that our lives are better because of telephones and television and CD players and microwave ovens and computers (except, of course, when these items break down!).

WHAT IS A NEW PRODUCT?

"New and improved!" It seems we run across that description in advertising wherever we turn. When we use the term "new product," what exactly do we mean? The Federal Trade Commission wants to make sure that consumers are not deceived into believing a product is new when it is not. FTC regulations say (1) that a product must be entirely new or changed significantly to be called new, and (2) that a product may only be called "new" for six months.

That definition is fine from a technical perspective. From a marketing standpoint, though, a new product is anything that customers *perceive* as new. It may be a completely new product that provides benefits never available before, or it may simply be an existing product with a new style or some new feature. Even when a firm begins to market a product that has been on the market for a while but that has not been produced by that particular firm, it is still, in a sense, a new product.

The issue of what exactly constitutes a "new" product is quite important to many businesses. It is said that "imitation is the sincerest form of flattery," and decisions regarding how much (if at all) one's product should resemble competitors' are often a centerpiece of marketing strategy (for example, the packaging of "me too" or look-alike products). On the other hand, the product cannot be a total duplicate; patent law is concerned with the precise definition of a new product and protecting that invention from illegal imitation.

A *knockoff* is a style that has deliberately been copied and modified, often with the intent to sell to a larger or different market. For example, *haute couture* clothing styles presented by top designers in Paris and elsewhere are commonly "knocked off" by other designers and sold to the mass market. It is difficult to protect a design (as opposed to a technological feature) legally, but pressure is building in many industries to do just that. Manufacturers argue that, say, a distinctive curve on a car bumper is as important to the integrity of the car as is a mechanical innovation.[10]

TYPES OF INNOVATIONS

Innovations can occur on a symbolic level or a technological level. A *symbolic innovation* communicates a new social meaning (for example, a new hairstyle or car design), while a *technological innovation* involves some functional change (for example, central air conditioning or car airbags).[11] Whether symbolic or functional, new products, services, and ideas have characteristics that determine the degree to which they will probably *diffuse,* or be adopted by many members of a target market. As a general rule innovations that are more novel are least likely to diffuse, because things that are fairly similar to what is already available require fewer changes in behavior to use. On the other hand an innovation that radically alters a person's life-style requires the person to modify his or her way of doing things, thus requiring more effort to adapt to the change. Three major types of innovations have been identified, though these three categories are not absolutes. They refer in a relative sense to the amount of disruption or change they bring to people's lives. Let's consider each type, beginning with innovations that are relatively modest.

Continuous Innovations

A **continuous innovation** refers to a modification of an existing product, as when Cheerios introduces a Honey Nut version of its cereal or Levi Strauss promotes shrink-to-fit jeans. This type of change may be used to set one brand apart from its competitors. Most product innovations are of this type. They are evolutionary rather than revolution-

continuous innovation: a modification of an existing product used to set one brand apart from its competitors

Exhibit 9.4
The zipper is an example of a humble, "low-tech" product that has managed to live an exceptionally long life. Invented in the 1800s, the first zippers were unreliable and came undone easily. After improvement, zippers were advocated as a better way to close high-buttoned shoes, particularly for heavy men who found it difficult to bend over to button their shoes. Originally called the "hookless fastener," only after its success in the Mystic Boot manufactured by B.F. Goodrich Rubber Co. was it renamed the zipper by Goodrich president Benjamin G. Work. While the zipper was readily adopted for use in children's clothing and for sportswear, it took more time to be used in men's trousers where competitors argued that this "newfangled gadget" could result in serious injuries. In 1936 the Prince of Wales adopted the zipper and was the first monarch to "sit on a throne bezippered." Zippers were shown in woman's clothing beginning in the 1930s.

REAL PEOPLE, REAL CHOICES:

DECISION TIME AT NABISCO

When the *Newtons* brand celebrated its 100th birthday in 1991, the cookie had become a familiar part of many American's lives. The brand was, if anything, a bit *too* familiar—as with an old friend or neighbor, consumers took *Newtons* for granted. While they still bought a lot of the fruit-filled cookies (about 55 to 65 million pounds per year), unit sales had stabilized for several years.

Mothers in particular had a strong bond with *Newtons;* company research showed that the cookies were associated by these women with strong childhood memories of their mother taking care of them, so one motivation for buying the product was to return the favor to their own kids. Also, the brand was viewed as a healthy alternative to chocolate snacks. Although over the years Nabisco had tried to appeal directly to kids in its advertising, the primary media target for *Newtons* was female heads of household over the age of thirty-five. While both kids and adults like the taste of the original *Fig Newtons,* they do not crave *Newtons* the way they do chocolate cookies, ice cream, or other dessert alternatives. *Newtons* were seen as a good-tasting snack, but nothing to get too excited about.

The challenge for Nabisco was to revitalize an old, tried-and-true brand. Bob Masone and his colleagues thought about several alternatives that involved either targeting other market segments or developing newer *Newtons* product alternatives that would shake up the market.

Option 1. Regular *Fig Newtons* are consumed by people across the age spectrum, but they make a particularly strong showing among older adults (in the over fifty-five age group). Older consumers have nostalgic feelings about the cookie. They trust *Newtons.* They also love the taste. It is not too sweet like candy or other kid-targeted cookies. Given the brand's popularity among older consumers, the company could refocus its advertising, new product, and promotional strategies to appeal even more to this large age group. On the other hand, it ran the risk of turning off kids and young adults, who might come to view the brand as old-fashioned and out of step.

Option 2. Research showed that many endurance athletes, such as cyclists and runners, eat *Newtons* as a substitute for energy bars. The brand is high in carbohydrates but tastes better than many of those products. Because Nabisco is a mass marketer, the company had never developed a marketing program that specifically targeted this segment. On the positive side, if Nabisco tried to market the product as a great source of energy (an energy bar), it could force consumers to view the brand in a new and different way, which might kick-start sales. On the downside, this option could confuse or even alienate those mainstream American consumers who have come to know *Newtons* as an "everyday cookie."

Option 3. Since the mid 1980s consumers' concerns about eating too much fat in their diets had been increasing. Nabisco had identified this concern as a product development opportunity. The company had worked for several years on a new product line called *SnackWell's.* These low-fat cookies and crackers were not rushed to market, however, because of the initial difficulty in developing tastes that would be acceptable to a finicky American public. Developing a *Fat Free Newtons* brand was an interesting possibility. On the other hand, this strategy ran the risk of cannibalizing the regular *Fig Newtons* business as the new version might simply entice loyal *Newtons* consumers to switch to the new version rather than attracting new buyers.

Now, join the decision team at Nabisco: Which option would you choose, and why?

ary. Small changes are made to position the product, add line extensions, or merely to alleviate consumer boredom.

Consumers may be lured to the new product, but adoption represents only a minor change in consumption habits, perhaps adding to the product's convenience or to the range of choices available. A typewriter company, for example, many years ago modified the shape of its product to make it more "user friendly" to secretaries. One simple change was curving the tops of the keys, a convention that is carried over on today's computer keyboards. The reason: Secretaries complained that the flat surfaces were hard to use with long fingernails.

Dynamically Continuous Innovations

dynamically continuous innovation: a pronounced change in an existing product

A **dynamically continuous innovation** is a more pronounced change in an existing product, as represented by self-focusing 35mm cameras or touch-tone telephones. These innovations will have a modest impact on the way people do things, creating some behavioral changes. The IBM Selectric typewriter, which uses a typing ball rather than individual keys, permitted secretaries to instantly change the typeface of manuscripts by replacing one Selectric ball with another.

Discontinuous Innovations

discontinuous innovation: a totally new product that creates major changes in the way we live

A **discontinuous innovation** creates major changes in the way we live. Major inventions such as the airplane, the car, the computer, and the television have radically changed modern lifestyles. The personal computer has in many cases supplanted the typewriter, and it has created the phenomenon of "telecommuters" by allowing many consumers to work out of their homes. Of course, the cycle continues, as new continuous innovations are constantly being made for computers (for example, new versions of software), dynamically continuous innovations, such as the keyboard "mouse" versus the touchpad, compete for adoption, and discontinuous innovations like wristwatch personal computers loom on the horizon.

ADOPTION AND DIFFUSION PROCESSES

A painting is only a work of art when people view it. A song is not music until someone sings it. In the same way new products can only satisfy customer wants and needs when they are adopted. By **product adoption** we mean the process by which an individual begins to use a good, service, or idea. The term **diffusion** is used to describe how the use of an innovation spreads throughout a society or population.

product adoption: the process by which an individual begins to use a good, service, or idea

diffusion of innovations: the process by which the use of an innovation spreads throughout a society or a population

The adoption and diffusion process is probably one of the most studied topics in marketing. This is because so many groups in our society, both companies and nonprofit agencies, are interested in the diffusion of innovations. Agricultural experts need to find ways to get people (especially people in poorer, less developed countries) to adopt better, more productive farming methods to increase food production. Public health officials want to convince people to practice birth control, improved infant nutrition, sanitary food preparation, and safe sex. Political science scholars seek to understand how propaganda and other political communications influence ideas on various issues. And so there have been literally thousands of studies about this important topic, providing us with very specific recommendations for developing new-product strategies.

STAGES IN A CUSTOMER'S ADOPTION OF A NEW PRODUCT

Whether the innovation is a new electric car, an improved version of Lotus 1-2-3, or a better mousetrap, individuals typically pass through six stages in the adoption process. Figure 9.2 shows how a person goes from being unaware of an innovation to the stages of awareness, interest, evaluation, trial, adoption, and confirmation. As marketers, it is important to understand that a potential customer, going from unawareness to being a loyal user, must pass through each one of these stages. And, at every stage, many people drop out of the process, so the proportion of consumers who wind up using the good or service on a consistent basis typically is a small fraction of those who are exposed to it.

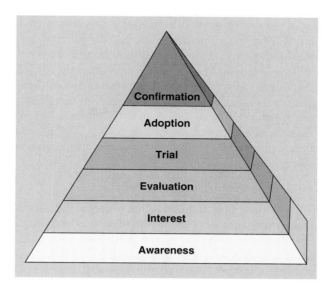

**Figure 9.2
Adoption Pyramid**

Awareness

When an innovation is introduced, very few people know it exists, except the people who work for the company and industry specialists (such as stock analysts and journalists employed by trade magazines) who follow developments in the business. Therefore, *awareness* of the innovation—learning that the innovation exists—is the first necessary step in the adoption process. Consumers and business customers become aware of new products from a variety of sources: advertisements, company or retailer salespeople, trade presentations, news or feature articles published in consumer and trade publications, product brochures, exposure to the product itself, and from other people through word-of-mouth communications. At this point some consumers will say, "So a new widget exists? So what?" and will fall by the wayside, out of the adoption process. We must also realize that no matter what we do there are probably always going to be some consumers who will never become aware of the innovation.

Interest

For some (but not all) of the people who become aware that a new product exists, a second stage in the adoption process is *interest*. By interest we mean that a prospective adopter begins to see how a new product might satisfy an existing or newly realized need—saying, "Hey, that might be for me." Interest builds when an individual imagines how using or owning a product will provide satisfying benefits. Quite obviously many advertisements and other marketing communications efforts are designed to stimulate interest in products. While most prospective customers will move from interest to further evaluation of the innovation, still more consumers will drop out of the process at this point.

Evaluation

When forming an opinion about the possible worth of an innovation, a prospect mentally weighs the costs and benefits of adoption. For complex, risky, or expensive products, *evaluation* is an active learning and analysis phase; people typically think about the innovation a great deal before they make a purchase. For instance, not surprisingly, a $6,000 video conferencing system for personal computers will be carefully evaluated prior to purchase.[12] On the other hand little evaluation may occur with an impulse purchase. For example, consumers may do very little thinking before trying Terra Chips, cousins of potato chips made from yucca, sweet potato, and parsnip.[13] Some, but again, not all of the potential adopters will evaluate an innovation positively enough to move on to the trial stage of the process; others will be lost at this stage as they are not convinced the new product will provide adequate benefits.

A key aspect of the evaluation stage occurs when the potential adopter is made to understand the benefits he or she will receive by deciding to try a new product. For example, the VoiceEM is a $40,000 computer system that makes doctors' jobs easier by transcribing their spoken comments on patients' conditions. No longer must doctors write patient reports by hand, and no longer are their good memories and instincts the only source of ideas for treatment, because the VoiceEM also draws on a computerized knowledge base to assess patient information in these spoken reports and prompts the doctors to check symptoms that might improve diagnoses.[14] When physicians evaluate the purchase of an expensive new product like the VoiceEM, they are "assisted" by the manufacturer as much as possible. Sales reps need to ensure that doctors understand the benefits offered by the innovation, often using other doctors' favorable experiences as a selling point.

Trial

The next stage in the adoption process, *trial,* means that the potential adopter will actually experience what the product has to offer. For new grocery store items trial is often encouraged by *sampling programs* where free samples are given out in the aisles (see Chapter 18). In fact, sampling programs such as this may prompt not just product trial but also awareness, interest, and evaluation for consumers at other stages in the adoption process. Trial is such an important phase in the new product adoption process that marketers spend hundreds of thousands or even millions of dollars striving to provide interested customers with demonstrations, samples, or even the chance to try out the product at home for a short period. A few years ago Apple Computer even allowed potential customers to take a computer home for a "test drive." Based on the trial experience some potential buyers move on to adoption of the new product.

Adoption

With *adoption,* a prospect mentally chooses to use a product and takes steps to make that possible. If the product is a consumer or business-to-business good, this means buying the product and learning about how to use it and maintain it. In the marketing of ideas this means that the individual agrees with the new idea, perhaps expressing this opinion to others. Does this mean that all individuals or organizations that choose an innovation can thereafter be classified as adopters? Not really. Some potential adopters, even after initial adoption, do not go on to the final stage, confirmation. Marketers often provide follow-up contacts and communications with adopters to make sure they are satisfied and remain loyal.

Confirmation

With initial adoption of an innovation, a customer weighs expected versus realized benefits and costs associated with that adoption. Favorable experiences contribute to a new customer becoming a loyal adopter, as his or her initially positive opinion results in *confirmation.* Unfavorable experiences relative to expectations will likely make a customer seek other alternatives, ultimately resulting in rejection of the new product. For example, a customer may initially adopt a new tartar-control toothpaste. After using the product for a while she realizes the new product is cleaning her teeth *too* well and is making them uncomfortable, so she may go back to her old toothpaste. Some marketers feel that *reselling* the customer in the confirmation phase is important—they provide advertisements, sales presentations, and other communications to reinforce a customer's purchase.

INNOVATORS AND ADOPTER CATEGORIES

Some people seem always to be the first to try a new product. Others are so reluctant to give up the familiar one would think they are afraid of anything new. It is important for marketers to recognize and understand the differences among potential customers that affect their readiness to adopt new products. As indicated in Figure 9.3, there are five different categories of adopters: *innovators, early adopters, early majority, late majority,* and *laggards.*[15] To understand how the willingness of consumers to try and use product innovations varies markedly, let's explore how the members of each category differ in terms of their adoption of one specific new product, the microwave oven.

Consumer Products in China

Twenty years ago the Chinese strove to attain what they called the "three bigs": bikes, sewing machines, and wristwatches. This wish list was later modified to become the "new big six," adding refrigerators, washing machines, and televisions. At last count the ideal is now the "eight new things." The list now includes *color* televisions, cameras, and video recorders.*

Very often these new things are of American origin. A Chinese homemaker's shopping list is likely to include a dozen two-liter bottles of Coke, a bottle of Johnson & Johnson baby shampoo, and Nestlé baby formula. Department stores in China's largest cities offer cosmetics by Elizabeth Arden, Revlon, Max Factor, and Coty. Adidas and Reebok sneakers sell for $95 to $130. In the supermarket Quaker oatmeal sells for $4.50, Skippy peanut butter is $4, and M&Ms candy is $.75.

As Chinese consumers increasingly are exposed to images of Western life-styles on television and in the movies, demand for foreign products is booming. Chinese women are starting to insist on using Western cosmetics costing up to a quarter of their salaries while ignoring domestically produced competitors. As one Chinese executive noted, "Some women even buy a cosmetic just because it has foreign words on the package."† That helps to explain why Avon has found the Chinese market so attractive. Entering the market in 1991, Avon had sales of over $8 million within one year!‡

Despite the seeming abundance of American products, however, many marketers approach this huge potential market with a lot of uncertainty. After all, it was only in 1978 that China adopted an "open door" policy that allowed American and other Western goods to enter the Chinese market. Some firms are hesitant to invest in China because of the disapproval of many Western consumers about human rights violations there. There is also the perception that Chinese incomes are very low so it's not worth the risk to try to entice them. Indeed, the average monthly salary is only $130. Coincidentally, though, Nike's top-selling shoe in China sells for $130, so *somebody* is buying nice sneakers!

Even though wages are very low, Chinese workers have a lot of disposable income due to state-subsidized housing and health care. On the average only 13 percent of total income is expended on rent, healthcare, transportation, and education (it is estimated that there is over $200 billion in personal savings in China), leaving a lot of opportunities to put money away for a rainy day—or for a new pair of sneakers. With much of this money waiting to be spent on the latest shoe style or lipstick, it remains to be seen if lingering concerns about important issues like human rights will deter other companies from flooding China with waves of new products.

*David K. Tse, Russell W. Belk, and Nan Zhou, "Becoming a Consumer Society: A Longitudinal and Cross-Cultural Content Analysis of Print Ads from Hong Kong, the People's Republic of China, and Taiwan," *Journal of Consumer Research* (March 1989): 457–72; see also Annamma Joy, "Marketing in Modern China: an Evolutionary Perspective," *CJAS* (June 1990): 55–67, for a review of changes in Chinese marketing practices since the economic reforms of 1978.
†Quoted in Sheryl WuDunn, "Cosmetics from the West Help to Change the Face of China," *The New York Times* (May 6, 1990): 16.
‡Marlene Piturro, "Capitalist China," *Brandweek* (May 16, 1994): 23–27.

Innovators

Innovators are roughly the first 2.5 percent of adopters. This segment is extremely venturesome and willing to take risks with new products, at least in the categories that interest them. They frequently try new ideas and often search out information on new products in publications or other communications sources not typically used by their less enthusiastic peers. Innovators are typically better educated, younger, and better off

innovators: the first segment (roughly 2.5 percent) of a population to adopt a product

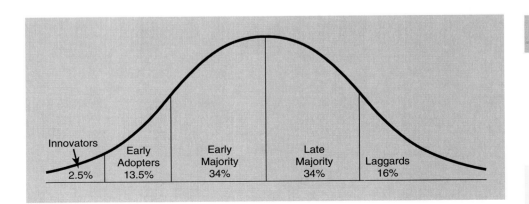

**Figure 9.3
Categories of Adopters**

Innovators 2.5%

Early Adopters 13.5%

Early Majority 34%

Late Majority 34%

Laggards 16%

financially than others in the population. Innovators who were into new technology knew all about microwave ovens when other people were barely aware they existed. Because innovators pride themselves on trying new products, they probably purchased a microwave when they were first introduced to the market way back in the mid-1960s.

Early Adopters

Early adopters, approximately 13.5 percent of adopters, buy product innovations very early in the diffusion process but after the innovators. Early adopters are usually well educated, have higher than average incomes, and are self-confident. Typically they are heavy media users and may be heavy users of a new product category. Others in the population look to early adopters for their opinions on various topics. Because of this, early adopters typically are the key to a new product's success. Marketers often target early adopters in developing advertising and other communications efforts. After reading articles in *Consumer Reports* and other sources of information on new products, early adopters of the microwave made their first purchase in the early 1970s. They probably attended a microwave cooking school offered by an appliance dealer or a microwave specialty store, the only retailers who sold microwaves at that time.

Early Majority

The **early majority,** 34 percent of adopters, avoid being either the first or the last to try an innovation. They are typically middle-class consumers and may be characterized as deliberate and cautious. When a product has been adopted by the early majority, it is no longer considered new or different—it is, in essence, already accepted. Early majority microwave owners made their purchase in the early 1980s, by which time there were ten to fifteen different brands of microwaves sold by a wide variety of retailers.

Late Majority

Late majority adopters, roughly 34 percent of adopters, are older and more conservative. The late majority adopters avoid trying a new product until it is no longer risky. By that time the product has become an economic necessity or there is pressure from peer groups to adopt. Late majority homes did not have a microwave until their friends began asking, "How can you survive without a microwave?" By that time the price of the ovens had been substantially lowered and the innovators, early adopters, and even many of the early majority were purchasing a second or even a third microwave.

Laggards

Laggards, about 16 percent of adopters, are the last in a social system to adopt a new product. Laggards are typically lower in social class and may be characterized as being bound by tradition. By the time laggards adopt a product, it may already be superseded by other innovations. It is unfortunate that the term "laggard" sounds negative. Laggards simply are pro-tradition, rather than pro-change and innovation. Many laggards still do not own a microwave because (1) they feel their traditional stove is adequate, (2) they consider a microwave a waste of money, or (3) they may even be afraid of radiation exposure from a microwave.

PRODUCT FACTORS AFFECTING THE RATE OF ADOPTION

If you could predict which product ideas will be successful and which ideas will fail, you would quickly be in high demand as a consultant by companies worldwide. That's because companies make large investments in new products, but failures are all too common. Estimates of new product success rates range from 46 percent to 65 percent.[16] As you might expect, much research has been devoted to making us smarter about new product successes and failures.

Researchers have identified five characteristics of innovations that affect the rate of adoption. Figure 9.4 summarizes these factors: relative advantage, compatibility, complexity, trialability, and observability.[17] Depending on whether or not a new product has these characteristics, marketers can expect consumer demand to grow more or less quickly. As noted, the microwave oven was first introduced to the market in the mid-1960s but was not adopted by large numbers of consumers until the late 1970s. Examining these five factors helps to explain both why the new product was not adopted during its early years and why adoption speeded up later.

Relative Advantage

Relative advantage is the degree to which a new product is perceived to provide benefits superior to those provided by the product it replaces. In the case of the microwave oven, consumers in the 1960s did not feel that the product provided important benefits that would improve their lives. But by the late 1970s that perception had changed. What differences had occurred in consumer life-styles during those ten or so years? One was that many more women had entered the work force. The microwave oven was not seen as particularly beneficial to the woman who did not work outside her home and who had all day to spend preparing the evening meal. But when that same woman began leaving home at 8:00 or so in the morning and returning home at 6:00 PM, an appliance that would "magically" defrost a frozen chicken and cook it for dinner in thirty minutes provided a genuine advantage.

Compatibility

Compatibility is the extent to which a new product is consistent with existing cultural values, customs, and practices. Was a microwave oven seen as compatible with existing ways of doing things? Hardly. Cooking on paper plates? If you put a paper plate in your conventional oven, you'll likely get a visit from the fire department. And what happens when you bake a cake in a microwave? It's not a crusty brown on top—it's not brown at all. And you have to take it out of the microwave a few minutes before it's done. Take a cake out of your conventional oven before it's done and it's nothing but a "sad" mess for the dog to eat.

Complexity

Complexity is the degree to which individuals find a new product or its use difficult to understand. Many users of microwaves today haven't a clue (and don't care) about how a microwave oven cooks food. But when the product was introduced, everyone was told that food cooked when the microwaves caused molecules to move, rubbing together, creating

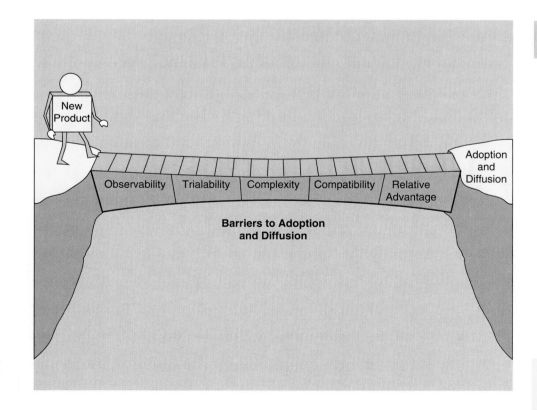

Figure 9.4
Adoption Rate Factors

friction that produced heat—voila! Cooked pot roast. But that explanation was very, very complex and confusing for a traditional homemaker of the Ozzie and Harriet days.

Trialability

Trialability refers to the ease of sampling a new product and its benefits. Marketers took a very important step in the mid-1970s that greatly speeded up adoption of the microwave oven—product trial. Just about every store that sold microwaves invited and encouraged shoppers to attend their microwave cooking school. The prospective customers could come to the store one evening or on a Saturday afternoon, observe while an entire meal was prepared and cooked in the microwave, and then enjoy eating the meal.

Observability

Observability refers to how visible a new product and its benefits are to others who might adopt the innovation. The ideal innovation is easy to see. For example, rollerblades gained instant attention because walkers, runners, and bikers saw rollerbladers zip by them on bike and jogging paths. The microwave was only moderately observable. Only close friends and acquaintances who visited someone's home could see whether or not they owned a microwave.

ORGANIZATIONAL DIFFERENCES AFFECT ADOPTION

Just as there are differences among consumers in their readiness and willingness to try and adopt new product innovations, businesses and other organizations are not alike in their willingness to change to newer industrial products.[18] Innovator firms are likely to be newer, more entrepreneurial organizations in highly technical industries with younger managers. Early adopter firms are likely to be market-share leaders that adopt new innovations to maintain their leadership. Firms that recognize they must innovate to keep up are in the early majority, while late-majority firms tend to be more status quo and production oriented. Firms that are laggards in the adoption process are probably already losing money and are on their way out.

Industrial products, like consumer products, also may possess characteristics that will increase their likelihood of adoption by organizational buyers. Firms too are more likely to adopt an innovation that offers a relative advantage, which for the firm means the opportunity to increase gross margins and profits. From voice mail to automated telephone answering to ATM machines, it is unlikely that firms would have adopted any of these new products unless they provided a way to increase profits. Like consumer products, organizational innovations are more attractive when they are consistent with existing ways of doing things. Relative cost is also a factor; firms are more likely to accept new technology if the improvement is perceived to be large in relation to the amount of investment that will have to be made.

THE PRODUCT LIFE CYCLE

The following items were sold at one time by Sears Roebuck & Co.:[19]

1897—Laudanum (opium) in a four-ounce bottle for $0.29.

1908—A.J. Aubrey Automatic Engraved Revolver for $4.25

1918—House Kit, $1,465 with free building plans

1927—C. Leo ("Gabby") Hartnett Catcher's Mitt for $5.48

product life cycle: concept that explains how products go through four distinct stages from birth to death: introduction, growth, maturity, and decline

While these exact product items are no longer sold (and certainly not at those prices), the products themselves—headache remedies (Laudanum was actually sold to relieve headaches), handguns, housing, and baseball gloves—are still alive and in demand today. In fact, many products have very long lives. You may not always realize the product is the same because often products change their ingredients, features, or price during their lives. The **product life cycle**, sometimes simply referred to as the "*PLC*," is a useful way to ex-

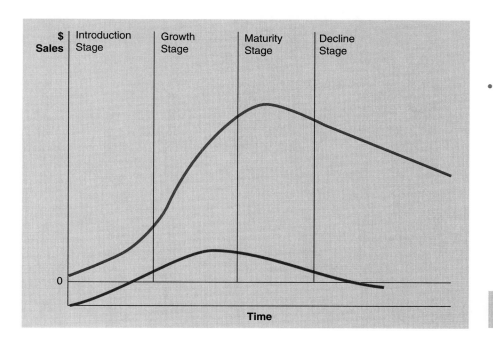

Figure 9.5
The Classic Product Life Cycle

plain how product features change over the life of a product. It is even more useful for helping marketers develop successful, profitable product strategies as the market for a product changes over time.

Note that the concept of the product life cycle does not relate to a single product item or a single brand: Some specific brands have longer "life expectancies" than others. The marketing graveyard is filled with "dead" brands (who remembers a Nash car, Evening in Paris perfume, or singer Julius LaRosa today?), but the product category lives on. On the other hand some brands seem almost immortal: In a study of the market leaders in thirty product categories by the Boston Consulting Group, it was found that twenty-seven of the brands that were number one in 1930 are still number one today. These brands include such perennial favorites as Ivory Soap, Campbell's Soup, and Gold Medal Flour.[20]

The term "life cycle" is borrowed from biology. When you hear "life cycle" you may think of the story of the lowly frog you learned about way back in elementary school. The frog begins life as an egg in a pond, it develops into a tadpole and then a frog, and finally makes its way to frog heaven. While the changes for the product may not occur quite as fast and the product may not change quite as dramatically as the frog, nevertheless the life of a product can also be divided into separate stages.

We will first talk about the stages in what is generally considered the "classic" product life cycle, and then we will discuss how individual product life cycles may be longer, shorter, or look substantially different from this classic model. (Marketing strategies appropriate to each stage of the product life cycle are discussed in Chapter 10.)

THE INTRODUCTION STAGE

The first stage of the PLC, shown in Figure 9.5, is **introduction.** This, as the name implies, is the stage in which a new product is introduced into the market—when customers have a chance to purchase the good or service for the very first time. Often during this early phase a single company is producing the product. Soon, however, if the product is accepted by customers and there is the opportunity for profit, other competitor firms will follow with their own versions.

Sometimes companies work together to launch a product category, as was the case with the audio compact disk, or CD, in the early 1980s. Because of the high cost of both the CD player and the CDs themselves, marketers knew that it would not be easy to convince consumers that they needed this new product. Therefore the four major CD manufacturers, Sony, Warner Music, Capitol-EMI, and MCA, worked together to launch the product, making sure that there were enough recordings available on compact disk to justify early adopters' investing in playback equipment.

introduction stage: the first stage of the product life cycle in which slow growth follows the introduction of a new product in the marketplace

Marketing strategy for the CD initially focused on its relative advantages: perfect sound reproduction, playback control, and freedom from wear and tear. Once playback equipment was purchased, a steady flow of CD hits was necessary to maintain favorable word-of-mouth to prospects who had not yet bought into the technology. Marketers also worked on distribution, addressing details like packaging, shelving design, and sound stations for easy sampling by prospective customers.

During the introduction stage sales of the product begin at zero and (hopefully) increase at a steady but usually a slow pace. Profits during this stage, also shown in Figure 9.5, are negative. Why negative profits? Two reasons. First, the costs for research and development of the new product cause the product to be introduced "in the red." Sufficient quantities of the product must be sold just to break even. Second, heavy spending for advertising and other types of promotion is usually required for introduction of a new product to be successful.

How long does the introductory stage last? For some products such as the microwave oven, the introductory stage may be quite long. How long the introductory stage lasts depends on a number of factors including acceptance by the marketplace and the willingness of producers to continue supporting the product during the interim. In the case of the microwave, sales in countries such as Japan were much stronger, thus contributing to the willingness of manufacturers to continue supporting the product through such a long introductory stage.

Not all products make it past the introductory stage. For a new product to be successful, consumers must first know about the product. Then they must be convinced that the product is something they need. Thus, marketing activities during this phase often focus on informing consumers about the product, how it is used, and what its benefits are. Only about 45 percent of consumer and 69 percent of industrial product introductions are successful. Overall, 38 percent of all new products fail.[21]

THE GROWTH STAGE

growth stage: the second stage in the product life cycle during which the product is accepted and sales rapidly increase

The second stage in the product life cycle, the **growth stage,** is characterized by a rapid increase in sales. During the growth phase profits also increase and peak. But as more and more competitors are attracted by this success, heavy advertising and other types of promotion are required, and the different producers may begin to compete on price, thus driving profits down. During the growth stage most customers are aware of the new product, so the goal is to convince them that one brand is superior to competing brands in the category. Marketers may attempt to develop brand loyalty, or they may seek to capture a particular segment of the market by positioning their product to appeal to a certain group (see Chapter 8). Repeat purchases will occur for nondurables but are unlikely to occur at this stage for durable goods.

Manufacturers' unit shipments of CDs exceeded 100 million units in 1987.[22] CDs had passed the introduction stage and reached the growth stage. The growth stage of audio CDs was accompanied by declining prices, in some cases below $10. A great variety of CDs were available in all categories of music.

THE MATURITY STAGE

maturity stage: the third and longest stage in the product life cycle in which sales peak and level off

The **maturity stage** of the product life cycle is usually the longest stage. During the maturity stage sales peak and then begin to level off and even to decline. Profits continue to decline as well. Competition is more intense than ever as many firms are in the marketplace fighting for a piece of a shrinking pie. During the maturity stage most customers have already accepted the product, and sales are often for replacement of previously purchased items, even for durable goods. Competitors may introduce new models with exciting new "bells and whistles" in an attempt to capture more of the existing market or in hopes of rejuvenating the product's life cycle. Weaker competitors will likely fall out of the market during the maturity stage, leaving the stronger producers to fight each other with renewed distribution and promotional efforts. CD shipments exceeded 400 million units by 1992 and are now in the maturity stage of the PLC.

316

PART 3
CREATING AND
MANAGING A PRODUCT

THE DECLINE STAGE

The **decline stage** of the PLC is characterized by a decrease in product category sales. Decline can be caused by a number of factors: changes in consumer tastes, technological change, shifts in needs, or even changing economic conditions. Often, as product sales decline, discouraged marketers withdraw product support in the form of personal selling effort, merchandising, advertising, and distribution. As recording and communications technology continues to advance, now allowing us to download digital sound bytes over the Internet, it is only a matter of time before the now-mighty music CD enters the decline stage—someday even these new wonders will be piled on the discount rack at secondhand music stores!

decline stage: the final stage in the product life cycle in which sales decrease as customer needs change

VARIATIONS IN THE PRODUCT LIFE CYCLE

We have discussed the product life cycle in its "classic" sense, where there are four distinct stages beginning with birth and ending in death. In reality, marketing (like life) is not so simple. The PLC of many products may deviate from the conventional S-curve, which will affect how a marketer thinks about various marketing decisions.

The Dreamer Curve

A firm's worst fear is that it faces a *dreamer curve* for the product, which means product sales never achieve a growth stage in the PLC. For example, Coke envisioned healthy sales for its BreakMate product. BreakMate is a miniature soda fountain intended for the lunchroom of small businesses, where consumption was too small to justify a vending machine. After spending $30 million to develop the product, sales never took off, mostly because the product is too messy and difficult to maintain.[23]

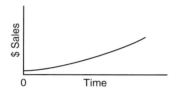

The Contagion Curve

A *contagion curve* is what the dreamers were really hoping for, because it means the product will quickly and completely diffuse into the marketplace. This occurs when a product is a blockbuster hit that takes the market by storm (or, as a radio DJ might put it, "goes up the charts with a bullet.") The movies *E.T. The Extra-Terrestrial* and *Jurassic Park* captured the market in this way.

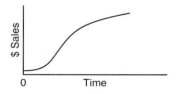

The Fad Curve

A *fad curve* applies to products that rapidly become popular and then lose their appeal just as quickly. Some experts predicted early in the growth phase that Crystal Pepsi and other clear cola products were a fad.[24] Businesses may be able to make money with such products as long as they develop a marketing plan that is paced to the product's sales and its short life. With fads, marketers try to establish market share quickly and then to harvest profits before the fad fades away. As in life, timing is everything!

Clear products are a good example of a short-lived marketing fad. In the early 1990s marketers created dozens of transparent products—colas, dishwashing liquids, deodorants, gasoline, even beer. The craze for clear was so widespread that the TV show "Saturday Night Live" featured a fake ad poking fun at these products: "clear gravy—you can see your meat." By 1994 clear products were "clearly" in decline.[25]

The Redevelopment Curve

A *redevelopment curve* reflects rejuvenated sales of a product that come from product changes or repositioning (see Chapter 8). Roller skates are a product that has undergone a recent rejuvenation. The classic four-wheel roller skates were popular in the 1950s and 1960s, when intrepid skaters tried to knock each other out of the racetrack every Saturday night on TV's roller derby. Then roller skating declined, and the few roller skating rinks around were patronized primarily by very young children. A decade ago, a Minnesota-based company called Rollerblade introduced the inline skate, originally intended as an off-season training device for hockey players. Since that time rollerblading has become the leisure activity of choice for over 12 million Americans, and the product has brought a product category back to life.[26]

REAL PEOPLE, REAL CHOICES:

HOW IT WORKED OUT AT NABISCO

Nabisco chose option 3. *Fat Free Fig Newtons* and *Fat Free Apple Newtons* were launched in February 1992. Fat-free versions of cranberry, raspberry, and strawberry *Newtons* were launched one year later in March 1993. Although initial consumer concept testing indicated that Nabisco had a hit on its hands, this research did not begin to capture the hysteria that actually occurred after the fat-free products (including the *SnackWell's* line) were launched. Part of this frenzy was caused by a severe shortage; Nabisco did not anticipate how quickly the new products would catch on, and the company had to beef up its supply capabilities. Many consumers were even hoarding the goodies—snapping up as many boxes as they could in anticipation of empty shelves the next time they went grocery shopping.

By 1994 the *Newtons* brand had doubled in unit volume from 1991. *Newtons* U.S. unit sales had grown to over 120 million pounds per year. The fat-free varieties accounted for 20 percent of this total. Although some of Nabisco's fears about cannibalization had come true, this outcome was offset because the introduction of fat-free cookies had actually increased the size of the entire cookie category. This product category had been growing at a small rate of about 1 to 3 percent annually, but since the introduction of fat-free cookies the category experienced annual unit volume increases of between 5 and 7 percent per year as new, more health-conscious consumers began to buy cookies. Because competitors were slow to enter this new market (it took two years for rival fat-free cookies to be introduced), Nabisco was able to grab the lion's share of sales. Mr. Masone's current challenge is twofold: (1) to develop and implement the vision for the next generation of *Newtons* products, and (2) to defend the *Newtons* brand against the "me too" new products that are now rushing to meet consumers' demands for tasty, fat-free snacks.

Chapter 9 Summary

Objective 1. Explain the various dimensions of a product.

A product may be a tangible physical good or an intangible service or idea. The core product consists of the basic product category benefits and customized benefit(s) the product provides. The actual product is the physical good or delivered service including the packaging and brand name. The augmented product includes both the actual product and any supplementary services such as warranty, credit, delivery, installation, and so on.

Objective 2. Describe the ways in which products are classified.

Both goods and services may be either consumer or business products. Consumer products are classified according to how long they last and how they are purchased. *Durable* goods provide benefits for months or years, while *nondurable* goods are used up quickly or are useful for only a short time. *Convenience* products are purchased frequently with little effort. *Shopping* products are bought only after customers carefully gather information and compare different brands on their attributes and/or price. *Specialty* products have unique characteristics and are important to the buyer. Customers have little interest in *unsought* products until a need arises. Business products are for commercial uses by organizations and are classified according to how they are used (installations, equipment, maintenance, repair, and operating products, raw and processed materials, component parts, and business services).

Objective 3. Explain the role of new products in the marketplace.

Understanding new products is important to companies because of the fast pace of technological advancement, the high cost to companies for developing new products, and the contributions to society that new products can make. New products are anything consumers perceive to be new and may be classified as to their degree of newness. A *continuous* innovation is a modification of an existing product, a *dynamically continuous* innovation provides a greater change in a product, and a *discontinuous* innovation is a totally new product that creates major changes in people's lives.

Objective 4. Explain the process of product adoption and the diffusion of innovations.

Product adoption is the process by which an individual begins to use a new product, while the diffusion of innovations is how a new product spreads through a population. The stages in the adoption process are *awareness* that the innovation exists, *interest* in how a new product may satisfy needs, *evaluation* of the costs and benefits of adoption, *trial* in which the potential adopter experiences what the product offers, *adoption* in which an individual mentally and physically selects the product, and *confirmation,* which makes the adopter a loyal user of the innovation. Individuals may be classified according to their readiness to adopt new products. The first consumers to know about and to try an innovation are called *innovators. Early adopters* influence many others consumers' adoption. The "follower" group called the *early majority* is neither the first nor the last to adopt. The *late majority* only adopt due to social or economic pressure. *Laggards* may not adopt until all other customers have moved on to an even newer product.

Five product characteristics that have an important effect on how quickly (or if) a new product will be adopted by consumers are (1) *relative advantage,* a new product's ability to provide important benefits; (2) *compatibility* with a consumer's normal way of doing things; (3) product *complexity;* (4) *trialability,* or the ability to sample or try out a new product; and (5) product *observability,* the visibility of the new product to other people. Organizations also exhibit differences in their readiness to adopt new products. Such differences are related to the product's relative advantage, compatibility with existing business practices, and cost relative to benefits.

Objective 5. Describe the product life cycle (PLC) concept.

The four-stage product life cycle (PLC) concept helps explain the diffusion of an innovation. The first or *introduction* stage is characterized by slow growth. The *growth* stage is characterized by increased sales, decreasing prices, high profits, and product improvements. In the *maturity* stage sales level off, new competitors do not enter the market, and the leading firms improve product quality while decreasing prices. During the *decline* stage sales continue to decrease and many firms abandon the product. Examples of PLC curves that are different from the classic PLC are the dreamer curve, the contagion curve, the fad curve, and the redevelopment curve.

Review Questions

Marketing Concepts: Testing Your Knowledge

1. What is a product?
2. What is meant by the core product, the actual product, and the augmented product?
3. List and give examples of the different classifications of consumer products.
4. What is a new product? Why is understanding new products so important to marketers?
5. Explain the different types of innovations based on their degree of newness.
6. List and explain the stages in an individual's adoption of an innovation.
7. List and explain the categories of adopters.
8. What are some of the product factors that affect the speed of adoption?
9. What is the product life cycle concept? Explain the stages in the PLC.

Marketing Concepts: Discussing Choices and Issues

1. In this chapter we talked about the core product, the actual product, and the augmented product. Does this mean that marketers are simply trying to make products that are really the same seem different? When marketers understand these three layers of the product and develop products with this concept in mind, what are the benefits to consumers? What are the hazards of this type of thinking?

2. The phrase "New and Improved" has been used so many times that for many people it is meaningless. Why has this occurred? What challenge does this present to marketers?

3. Discontinuous innovations are totally new products—something seldom seen in the marketplace. What are some examples of discontinuous innovations introduced during the twentieth century? Why are there so few discontinuous innovations? What do you think the future holds for new products?

4. It is increasingly important that marketers develop and introduce new products. One reason is that the PLC for many products seems to be getting shorter and shorter. What are some examples of products that have seen a very short life cycle? Why has this been so? What products in the future do you think will move very quickly to maturity and decline?

Marketing Practice: Applying What You've Learned

1. Assume you have recently been hired by a firm that has developed a new low-calorie, fat-free chocolate candy bar. Because of your knowledge of new product adoption, you know that consumers go through a series of stages in adoption of a new product—awareness, interest, and so on. You also realize that it is important for marketers to "help" customers move from one stage to the next. Develop your recommendations for marketing activities that would be appropriate for each of the stages in the adoption process.

2. As a member of a new product team with your company, you are working with engineers in developing the world's first practical battery-powered automobile. You know that different product characteristics (relative advantage, compatibility, and so on) often influence the speed of adoption of a product. Considering such product characteristics, make a list of suggestions for the engineers (or for the marketing department) that will speed adoption of the new product when it is introduced.

3. Assume you are employed in the marketing department of the firm in example number 2. In developing the new battery-powered car you realize that it is important to provide a core product, an actual product, and an augmented product to meet the needs of customers. Develop an outline of how these three layers of product would be provided in the battery-powered car.

4. You have recently been hired as the director of marketing for a firm that manufactures small kitchen appliances. You have been asked to present your recommendations for three related products: toaster ovens, microwave ovens, and the newer convection ovens (convection ovens cook faster than traditional ovens because they continuously circulate hot air around the food). You believe that understanding the product's position in the product life cycle is an essential first step. Prepare an outline for your presentation in which you describe the current position in the PLC of each of these products, your expectation for the future, and your recommendations.

Marketing Mini-Project: Learning by Doing

What product characteristics do consumers think are important in a new product? What types of service components do they demand? And most important, how do marketers know how to develop successful new products? This mini-project is designed to let you experience making some of these decisions.

1. Create (in your mind) a new product item that might be of interest to college students like yourself. Develop a written description and possibly a drawing of this new product.

2. Show this new product description to a number of your fellow students who might be users of the product. Ask them to tell you what they think of the product. Some of the questions you might ask them are:
   a. What is your overall opinion of the new product?
   b. What basic benefits would you expect to receive from the product?
   c. What about the physical characteristics of the product? What do you like? Dislike? What would you add? Delete? Change?
   d. What do you like (or would you like) in the way of packaging of the product?
   e. What sorts of services would you expect to receive with the product?
   f. Do you think you would try the product? How could marketers influence you to buy the product?

3. Develop a report based on what you found. Include your recommendations for changes in the product and your feelings about the potential success of the new product.

Key Terms

Endnotes

1. Theodore Levitt, "Marketing Myopia," *Harvard Business Review* (July-Aug. 1960): 45–56.

2. Eleena De Lisser, "Pepsi Puts Spotlight on New Packaging," *The Wall Street Journal* (Aug. 11, 1993): B1, B6.

3. Gabriella Stern, "If You Don't Feel Like Fetching the Rental Car, It Fetches You," *The Wall Street Journal* (June 9, 1995): B1 (2).

4. Peter Coy and William D. Marbach, "Developments to Watch," *Business Week* (May 17, 1993): 81.

5. "The Best New Products," *Business Week* (Jan. 9, 1995): 114–119.

6. Pam Weisz, "HBA Companies are Making Hay with a Little Horse Sense," *Brandweek* (May 16, 1994): 32.

7. Kevin Kelly, "The Drought Is Over at 3M," *Business Week* (Nov. 7, 1994): 140–141.

8. Otis Port, Neil Gross, Robert Hof, and Gary McWilliams, "Wonder Chips: How They'll Make Computing Power Ultrafast and Ultracheap," *Business Week* (July 4, 1994): 86–92.

9. George Anders, "Vital Statistic: Disputed Cost of Creating a Drug," *The Wall Street Journal* (Nov. 9, 1993): B1.

10. Edmund L. Andrews, "When Imitation Isn't the Sincerest Form of Flattery," *The New York Times* (Aug. 9, 1990): 20.

11. Elizabeth C. Hirschman, "Symbolism and Technology as Sources of the Generation of Innovations." In *Advances in Consumer Behavior,* 9 ed. (Provo, Utah: Association for Consumer Research, 1981).

12. William M. Bulkeley, "PictureTel to Introduce $6,000 System To Make PCs Work as Video Telephones," *The Wall Street Journal* (July 16, 1993): B8.

13. Toddi Gutner, "Chip Mania," *Forbes* (July 19, 1993): 197–198.

14. Gene Blinsky, "At Last! Computers You Can Talk To," *Fortune* (May 3, 1993): 88–91.

15. Everett Rogers, *Diffusion of Innovations* (New York: Free Press, 1983).

16. Christopher Power, Kathleen Kerwin, Ronald Grover, Keith Alexander, and Robert D. Hof, "Flops," *Business Week* (Aug. 16, 1993): 77.

17. Everett Rogers, *Diffusion of Innovations* (New York: Free Press, 1983).

18. Thomas S. Robertson and Yoram Wind, "Organizational Psychographics and Innovativeness," *Journal of Consumer Research* 7 (June 1980): 24–31.

19. Paul Gray, "An Ode to The Big Book," *Time* (Feb. 9, 1993): 66.

20. Richard W. Stevenson, "The Brands With Billion-Dollar Names," *The New York Times* (Oct. 28, 1988): A1.

21. Robert J. Thomas, *New Product Development* (New York: Wiley, 1993).

22. Larry Armstrong, "What's Wrong with Selling Used CDs?" *Business Week* (July 26, 1993): 38.

23. John R. Emshwiller, "Coke's Soda Fountain For Offices Fizzles, Dashing High Hopes," *The Wall Street Journal* (June 14, 1993): A1, A8.

24. David Lavinsky, "When Novelty Wears Off, Soft Drinks Clearly Will Fail," *Marketing News* (March 15, 1993): 4.

25. Kathleen Deveny, "Anatomy of a Fad: How Clear Products Were Hot and Then Suddenly Were Not," *The Wall Street Journal* (March 15, 1994): B1, B8.

26. Michael R. Solomon, *Consumer Behavior: Buying, Having, and Being,* 3 ed. (Upper Saddle River, NJ: Prentice Hall, 1996).

MARKETING IN ACTION: REAL PEOPLE AT GILLETTE

The Gillette Corporation has dominated the men's shaving market for decades, but until very recently its profitability in the women's razor market was at best razor-thin. This situation changed when Gillette's chairman and chief executive officer Alfred Zeien, a twenty-six-year veteran with Gillette, began to focus on developing new products. In fact, Zeien's goal for the company is "getting there first with the best." Under Zeien's leadership, Gillette introduced twenty-two new products in 1993 and has tried to exceed that each succeeding year.

Gillette is a tremendously successful company, and its razors and blades are sold around the globe. However, many people don't realize that Gillette is truly a diversified consumer products company with sales of over $5 billion. Other Gillette products include personal-care items such as deodorant and shaving cream, pens (Paper Mate, Waterman, and Parker) toothbrushes (Oral B), and electric appliances (Braun). During the first half of the 1990s Gillette experienced yearly profit increases of 17 percent.

According to Zeien, Gillette has "a tradition of a love of products and respect for technology." Research labs are the heart of the business to Zeien—the key to its future. R & D at Gillette is viewed not as an expense but as a type of capital investment. More important, the company doesn't just give lip service to research. Each year the company spends an amount on R & D equal to what shareholders get in dividends. According to Zeien, "From technological advancements derive the product opportunities. The best measure of a company is not what it's accomplished, but how well it's improved the prospects for the future." The success of Gillette's Sensor razor serves as evidence supporting this philosophy. Since it was introduced into the highly competitive razor market in 1990, Gillette's razor and blade sales have increased 54 percent in the United States and 71 percent worldwide.

For many years, until Gillette turned its attention to women's shaving needs, Gillette's women's razor was just a pink version of the men's razor. As such it did not meet the real shaving needs of women. The first step in producing a product just for women was to understand better what women wanted in a razor. Gillette researchers spent nine months talking to women about their problems with existing products and what they wanted and needed. What they discovered was that the handles of men's razors slipped in women's hands in the shower or bath. Furthermore, the shape of a man's razor made it difficult to maneuver over the curved surfaces of legs. In general, women wished that shaving their legs could be more comfortable.

Gillette incorporated this information into its design process, and in 1992 the Gillette Sensor for Women was introduced—the first razor designed specifically for women. The Sensor for Women has a broad, ridged handle that fits into the palm of a woman's hand, making it easier to use on all sides of a leg. In addition, the new women's Sensor also has a broad lubricant strip coated with aloe to leave the skin feeling soft and smooth. Of course, Gillette did not abandon the proven shaving technology used in its men's razors, and the women's Sensor also has the same patented pivoting blade cartridge used in the men's Sensor. What would demand be for the Sensor for Women? In-home tests, conducted around the country prior to the women's Sensor introduction, showed that Gillette needed the capacity to produce 30 million of the new women's razors annually.

So has the Sensor for Women been successful? Very. Sales during the first eighteen months were almost as high as those for the men's Sensor when introduced—about $12 million.

But Gillette continues to look to the future. The research that Gillette conducted prior to introducing the Sensor revealed an interesting point. Men who cut themselves shaving blame the blade and throw it out. Women blame themselves for being careless. This means that women are less likely to change blades than men—and thus less likely to buy new blades, a major source of Gillette's profits. Gillette marketers see this finding as an opportunity to increase profits in the women's razor market if women can be convinced to change blades more often.

Source: Rita Koselka, "'It's My Favorite Statistic,'" *Forbes* (Sept. 12, 1994): 162–176.

Things to Talk About

1. What type of innovation is the Sensor for Women? Continuous? Dynamically continuous? Discontinuous?

2. How did Gillette use research to develop the Sensor for Women product?

3. What factors affected the rate of adoption of the Gillette Sensor for Women?

4. How would you describe the life cycle of women's razors?

5. What marketing strategies are appropriate for a product such as the Sensor in this stage?

6. What secrets to success has Gillette discovered?

MARKETING IN ACTION:
REAL CHOICES AT GM'S HUGHES AIRCRAFT

Is General Motors going into the TV business? At the huge automaker's annual meeting in 1994 it was a wide-screen television and a pizza-size satellite dish rather than shiny new cars that captured stockholders' attention. This new product innovation was GM's DirectTV, which offered crystal-clear television images and CD-quality sound to jaded TV viewers.

DirectTV was the creation of engineers at GM's aircraft division, Hughes Aircraft Co., who had spent their careers building huge communications systems for the navy and NASA. Eddie Hartenstein, GM's DirectTV president, described GM's $750 million investment in the project as "the biggest thing since color television."

From the beginning DirectTV was a risky venture. Over half a dozen similar systems had failed. In fact, Hughes Aircraft had just axed a similar project, SkyCable satellite-TV, a joint venture with NBC News Corp and Cable Vision Industries.

Up to the introduction of DirectTV, the major supplier of satellite TV was Primestar. Primestar is owned by Primestar Partners, a consortium of six cable operators. Introduced in 1990, Primestar was intended for rural areas where cable was not available. Primestar initially offered only ten channels and afforded only poor reception because of its analog signal. In addition, many consumers were turned off by satellite TV because of the big, unsightly dish required for reception. In 1994, however, when digital technology became more affordable, Primestar upgraded sixty-seven channels, and the service started to catch on among finicky viewers.

To succeed as a product innovation, DirectTV had to overcome some technological challenges. First there would have to be a new generation of satellites capable of beaming reams of digital data into home receivers, which also had yet to be developed. And each home had to have a sophisticated decoder box to receive the signal. The problem facing GM's engineers was to develop these devices at prices low enough to be considered acceptable by consumers. And all this had to be done quickly to beat other competitors to the market.

A second important point revolved around what programming must be offered to entice customers to sign up. Would 50, 100, 150, or more channels do the trick, and what type of programming needed to be available? Current cable subscribers were used to receiving such standard offerings as The Disney Channel, the traditional movie channels such as HBO, and recent hit movies on pay-per-view. DirectTV had to offer that and much more—hit movies that played regularly, enough sports for the most avid fans, and other programming that sizzled. Programmers tied to cable would be hesitant to jeopardize those relationships by making a deal with DirectTV.

Another major question was how the product should be sold. Should there be a base price for equipment and then a monthly fee for programming, or would customers be more likely to sign up if there was only a monthly fee with no initial investment required? Research showed that consumers were unlikely to be willing to pay above about $700 for an initial investment in the service. Primestar had used the lease approach and rented equipment to its subscribers.

The purchase-lease decision was also important in terms of recouping GM's investment. Sales of the new product had to generate enough revenue to pay for the very expensive venture. No one was sure whether or not, in the long run, cable and fiber optics might do an even better job of delivering more programming. DirectTV's future was uncertain in an era where new technologies are constantly being introduced to a media-saturated public.

Finally, DirectTV marketers were unsure about the most likely consumer market for the new product. Would traditional cable subscribers be willing to switch or would the major market be only among those consumers who were unable to currently get cable service? Would the early adopters be only the relatively few "videonuts" who were eager and willing to obtain the latest and the best in television? Would DirectTV eventually spread to the mass audience required to keep the business running?

Source: Eric Schine and Kathleen Kerwin, "Digital TV: Advantage, Hughes," *Business Week* (March 13, 1995): 66–68.

Things to Think About

1. What is the problem facing DirectTV?

2. What factors are important in understanding this problem?

3. What are alternatives GM might consider?

4. What are your recommendations for solving the problem?

5. What are some ways to implement your recommendations?

10

Managing the Product

When you have completed your study of this chapter, you should be able to:

1. Explain some of the different product strategies a firm may choose.

2. Describe some of the typical ways organizations are structured for new and existing product management.

3. Describe how firms go about developing new products.

4. Explain how products are managed throughout their life cycle.

5. Discuss how branding creates product identity, and describe different types of branding strategies.

6. Explain the important part packaging and labeling play in developing effective product strategies.

REAL PEOPLE, REAL CHOICES:

MEET DENNIS CARTER, A DECISION MAKER AT INTEL

Dennis Carter makes product decisions that affect the "brains" of most of the personal computers manufactured in the world, very possibly including your own. As a vice president and general manager of corporate marketing at Intel Corporation, he is responsible for Intel's marketing communications, advertising, public relations, and corporate and end-user marketing programs. Among other things Intel makes the microprocessors that power personal computers made by IBM, Compaq, Dell, and many other computer industry giants.

Mr. Carter joined Intel in 1981 as product marketing engineer and software marketing engineer. In 1985 he became technical assistant to Intel's president, a position he held for four years. He was promoted to marketing manager for the End-User Marketing Group in 1989, and then promoted to general manager of the End-User Components Division in 1990. He became director of marketing in 1991 and was elected an Intel vice president in 1992.

Prior to joining Intel Mr. Carter worked as an engineering manager for Rockwell International, where he was responsible for product designs of collision avoidance avionic systems and radar altimeters. Prior to that he served as an instructor of electrical engineering technology at Purdue University. He earned bachelor of science degrees in electrical engineering and physics from Rose-Holman Institute of Technology. In 1974 he received a master's degree in electrical engineering from Purdue University, and in 1981 he got an MBA from Harvard University.

CHIPPING AWAY AT THE COMPETITION: CREATING AND NURTURING QUALITY PRODUCTS

Although plenty of other firms make microprocessors, Intel sells 80 percent of all the chips that power PCs. In 1995 Intel shipped more than 35 million Pentium chips, making it number one in the industry. Analysts predict that Intel will continue to prosper, perhaps reaching an annual sales mark of $50 billion by the end of the decade.[1]

What makes one product fail and another enjoy unbelievable success? The answer is product management. Firms that do a good job at developing and implementing effective product strategies will enjoy increases in sales and profits in the short term. Even more important, they can be assured of enjoying financial stability over the long haul—all this because winning product strategies allow an organization to meet customer wants and needs. Just as Intel's chips play a key role in allowing computers to do wondrous things, a sound product strategy is the driving force behind a successful marketing plan.

It's worth repeating what we said way back in Chapter 2: Firms that succeed plan well. Product planning plays a big role in the quarterly or semiannual *operational plans* we discussed in that chapter. The strategies outlined in the product plan spell out how the firm expects to develop a product that will meet marketing objectives. And it's important to remember that while a product plays a key role in marketing strategies (you can't distribute or promote something that doesn't exist), it is still only one piece of the pie; product decisions must always be integrated with the other elements of the marketing mix. How will this product be distributed? What sort of promotion is likely to be developed for the product? What will the pricing structure be? Each of these decisions says something about what the product is, or at least about what it wants to be.

In this chapter we will look at how companies manage products. We will examine how planners develop product objectives and the factors influencing product strategies, and consider how strategies are developed both for new and existing products. Finally we will discuss branding and packaging, two of the more important tactical decisions made by product planners that "breathe life" into a product by giving it a unique identity in the marketplace.

USING PRODUCT OBJECTIVES TO DECIDE ON A PRODUCT STRATEGY

When marketers develop product strategies, they are making decisions about product benefits, features, styling, branding, labeling, packaging, and so on. But what do they want to accomplish with these decisions? Clearly stated product objectives provide focus and direction. Product objectives should support the broader marketing objectives of the business unit in addition to supporting the overall mission of the firm. For example, the firm's objectives may be related to return on investment or overall profits. As an outgrowth of this emphasis, marketing objectives may focus on market share and/or unit or dollar sales volume. Product objectives need to specify how product decisions will support or contribute to that market share or level of sales.

Take, for instance, a company like Lever Brothers. Overall organizational objectives will likely refer to overall return on investment. Objectives for the various strategic businesses might relate to market share—for example, increase laundry detergent market share by 2 percent. And the product strategy may be based on a goal of rolling out a new brand or a new product line to add new customers for Lever Brothers products.

As with overall marketing objectives, planners must keep in touch with consumers and/or business customers so that objectives accurately reflect customer needs. Equally important in developing product objectives is an up-to-date knowledge of competitive product innovations. Above all, product objectives should consider the *long-term implications* of product decisions. Planners who sacrifice the long-term health of the organization to reach short-term sales or financial goals are being irresponsible.

A classic example of the negative impact of a short-term focus is the story of the Ford Pinto. To keep product costs down and profits up, Ford Motor Company knowingly designed the Pinto without adequate protection for the gas tank. As a result, many consumers lost their lives in rear-end crashes when the Pinto gas tanks exploded. In the long run, Ford suffered financially due to huge damages awarded in courts to injured parties and also lost consumer confidence that took years to renew.

To be effective, product-related objectives must possess these characteristics:

- They must be measurable.
- They must be clear and unambiguous.
- They must be feasible.
- They must indicate a specific time frame.

Consider, for example, how a frozen entrée manufacturer might state its product objectives:

- "In the upcoming fiscal year, modify the product's fat content to reflect the trend toward healthier foods."

- "Introduce three new items to the product line to take advantage of increased consumer interest in Mexican foods."
- "During the coming fiscal year, improve the chicken entrées to the extent that consumers will rate them as better-tasting than _____'s comparable line of chicken entrées."

In some cases product planners will focus their objectives on one or more individual products at a time. In other situations it is necessary to look at a group of product offerings as a whole. In this section we will briefly examine these different situations. We will also look more closely at one important product objective: product quality.

Exhibit 10.1
The Volkswagen Beetle is an interesting story of a successful product that triumphed over great obstacles. When first introduced into the United States, almost every dealer in the country was offered the opportunity to sell the Beetle but most refused, feeling the car was too ugly to sell. Many of those dealers were probably kicking themselves later—over 21 million Beetles eventually were bought by true believers who adored the car's simple engineering and funky image. In 1977 Volkswagen removed the Beetle from U.S. markets because it could not meet new EPA standards for auto emissions. Still, the Beetle has remained a popular car on American highways—so popular, in fact, that before the year 2000 Volkswagen plans to introduce a "concept car" model of the Beetle. This newer version will look like the older Beetle but will be equipped with air bags and will have a front-mounted engine that does meet emissions standards. Based on consumer response when a prototype of this concept car was shown at an auto show, Volkswagen dealers are excitedly awaiting the introduction with visions of sales levels similar to those of the old Beetle.

OBJECTIVES FOR INDIVIDUAL PRODUCTS

Some product strategies focus on individual product items. The objectives developed for guiding individual product strategies are often quite different for new products, mature products, regional products, or products that are clearly in decline.

For new products, not surprisingly, the objectives relate to successful *introduction* of the product to the marketplace. Microsoft worked for years to develop Windows 95, a product first scheduled for introduction several years earlier. To meet early sales objectives, Microsoft spent millions to promote the introduction. The accompanying media hype caused millions to reserve their copies of the product weeks ahead of time or to stand in line for the new software, which was dramatically delivered at midnight to selected distributors.

Alternatively, a firm may try to introduce a brand that has been successful in a local or regional market to a national market. Dr. Pepper was originally a regional soft drink sold only in Texas and Mexico, Rolling Rock beer originated in western Pennsylvania, and Goya Foods, a major marketer of Hispanic food products, is currently pushing for sales in Anglo grocery stores.[2]

Sometimes product strategies are designed to meet objectives for rejuvenating a product by developing new uses for it. The Florida Orange Growers were successful in making dramatic increases in consumption of their product by promoting orange juice as ". . . not just for breakfast anymore." Makers of tofu, considered a "yucky" food product by many finicky Americans, focused on the product's health benefits and provided consumers with lots of new recipes to make the product more tasty.

OBJECTIVES FOR MULTIPLE PRODUCTS

While a small firm might "put all its eggs in one basket" by focusing on only one product, typically an organization markets a set of related products. This means that some strategic decisions affect two or more products at once—the firm must think in terms of its entire *portfolio* of products (see Chapter 2). Product planning means developing *product line* and *product mix* strategies that encompass multiple offerings. These dimensions are illustrated in Figure 10.1 (page 330).

Product Line Strategies

A **product line** is a firm's total product offering designed to satisfy a single need or desire of a group of target customers. For example, Procter & Gamble markets a line of three different liquid dish detergents (LDDs). Dawn is targeted to consumers who want a liquid that cuts grease, Ivory is for customers to whom mildness is important, and Joy is for people who are concerned that their dishes are shiny. The number of separate items offered within the same category is referred to as the *length* of the product line. Decisions regarding how long this line should be have important strategic implications.

product line: a firm's total product offering designed to satisfy a single need or desire of target customers

When a firm has a large number of product variations in its product line, it is said to carry a *full line*. With a full line strategy it is possible to please a lot of different customer segments, thus increasing total product line sales. Often the items in a product line are coordinated; that is, they are purposefully designed to use the same logo, the same colors, the same packaging, and so on, so that customers can see that all of the items are part of the same product line. General Electric is an example of a full line marketer, it sells a full line of home appliances including refrigerators, freezers, dishwashers, washers, dryers, and stoves, all bearing the same logo and sharing similar design characteristics.

A company that adopts a *limited line strategy* markets a smaller number of product variations. If sales of these fewer variations are quite high, the firm may be able to take advantage of economies of scale in manufacturing and in other elements of the marketing mix. Sometimes having a limited product line can actually improve the image of a firm—it is perceived to be a specialist and has a very clear, specific position in the market. Curtis Mathes for many years maintained such an image by selling its televisions in company stores and bragging in its advertising that it sold the most expensive TV on the market but that the price was "darn well worth it." The downside of a limited line strategy is that it does mean a loss of some sales, because inevitably many customers will choose competi-

Laundry and Cleaning Products	Personal Care Products	Food and Beverage Products	Pulp and Chemicals
Bold	Attends	Crisco	
Bounce	Bain de Soleil	Duncan Hines	
Cascade	Camay	Fisher Nut	
Cheer	Charmin	Folgers	
Comet	Clearasil	Hawaiian Punch	
Dawn	Cover Girl	Jif	
Downy	Crest	Pringles	
Dreft	Head & Shoulders	Sunny Delight	
Mr. Clean	Ivory		
Spic and Span	Luvs		
Tide	Metamucil		
	Oil of Olay		
	Old Spice		
	Pampers		
	Pantene		
	Pepto-Bismol		
	Pert		
	Puffs		
	Scope		
	Secret		
	Sure		
	Vicks		
	Vidal Sassoon		
	Zest		

Length of Product Line

Depth of Product Mix

Tide
  Regular detergent
  Tide Ultra powder
  Tide liquid
  Tide with bleach

Figure 10.1
Product Line and Mix

tors' products that offer still other benefits. Also, the limited line strategy is not likely to be particularly attractive to distributors and retailers, who would prefer carrying many different products but dealing with only one or a few suppliers.

In developing product strategies, organizations may decide to *extend* their product line—that is, add more items to an existing product line. Popular clothing retailers Patagonia, Lands End, and The Gap have added children's clothing. Hushpuppy, maker of shoes designed for comfort, has added women's dress shoes with heels. Taco Bell now offers Border Lites, and Baskin Robbins sells sugar-free and fat-free dessert items. General Mills created the well-known brand Cheerios, the "whole grain toasted oat cereal" that has the top market share for any dry cereal on the grocers' shelves. In an attempt to increase dry cereal sales while building on the popularity of Cheerios, General Mills introduced Multi Grain Cheerios, the "taste of whole grain corn, oats, rice, and wheat" and, for those wanting a sweeter cereal, Apple Cinnamon and Honey-Nut Cheerios.

If the company does decide to stretch its product line, it must decide on the best direction in which to extend itself. If a firm's current product line includes middle and lower-end items, an *upward line stretch* would add new "top of the line" items, those with a higher price, greater quality, and more "bells and whistles." General Electric, for example, introduced its Profile series of kitchen appliances, which offered special features and was priced considerably higher than other GE appliances. Of course the firm always runs the risk that consumers will not be convinced that the new upper-end items really are of sufficient quality. For example, the retailer JCPenney has tried to upgrade its image by adding designer clothing lines in recent years, but the jury is still out as to whether shoppers really believe that the mass-market merchandiser now carries more upscale items.

Conversely, a *downward line stretch* means that the firm completes a line by adding items at the lower end. Holiday Inn's newer Holiday Inn Express hotels are a downward line stretch. If a downward stretch is selected, the firm must be careful that the lower-priced line items do not adversely affect sales of higher-priced, upper-end offerings, or that the new items do not "cheapen" the upscale image that has been carefully cultivated. Wouldn't it be great if Rolex came out with a lower-priced line of watches? We'd all buy one. Unfortunately, such a strategy would surely devastate sales of Rolex premium watches.

In some cases, when the existing product line is quite limited, the product strategy may call for a *two-way stretch,* where line items are added at both the upper and lower ends. Marriott Hotels, for example, has added Fairfield Inns and Courtyard at the lower end and Marriott Marquis Hotels at the upper end.

A *filling out* strategy may mean adding sizes or styles not previously available in a product category. PepsiCo tried this with its eight-ounce Pepsi Mini cans and its wide-mouth Big Slam.[3]

In a few cases the best overall product strategy is to *contract a product line.* This may be the case when the firm finds itself overextended, and too many products are being produced relative to the amount of sales. Some of the items may not be profitable and are not "carrying their weight" for the company. In such cases a product line contracting strategy saves resources and allows firms to focus on other new items that may have a greater chance to succeed.

To further explore these strategic decisions, let's return to the "glamorous" world of dish detergents. What does Procter & Gamble do if the objective of the LDD division is to increase P&G's market share? One possibility would be to expand its line of LDDs. If the line extension meets a consumer need currently not being met by P&G's existing products, this would be a good strategic objective. On the other hand, whenever a product line or a product family is extended there is the danger of **cannibalization,** which occurs when sales of an existing product are lost (or eaten up) when a new item in a product line or product family is introduced and customers simply switch from the old product to the new one. That explains why the Carnation Company canceled plans for "Lady Friskies," a contraceptive dog food, after tests indicated it would simply reduce sales of regular Friskies.[4] When a product line is extended, the hope is always that the new line item will generate more new sales than it will cannibalize.

cannibalization: the loss of sales of an existing product when a new item in a product line or product family is introduced

Product Mix Strategies

While product planning for a single product item or even a specific product line is important, marketers often must deal with entire groups of products. A firm's **product mix** is the total set of all products offered for sale by a firm—including all product lines sold to all customer groups. Industry giant Procter & Gamble markets over 2,300 brand varieties, including laundry and cleaning products such as Bold, Bounce, Cascade, Cheer, Mr. Clean, Spic and Span, and Tide, personal products such as Bain de Soleil, Camay, Charmin, Clearasil, Crest, Head & Shoulders, Ivory, Luvs, Metamucil, Old Spice, Pepto-Bismol, Scope, Vicks, and Zest, and food and beverage products such as Crisco, Duncan Hines, Folgers, Jif, and Pringles.[5]

In developing a product mix strategy, planners usually consider the *breadth of the product mix* and the *product mix consistency.* By breadth, marketers mean the number of different products produced by the firm. Consistency refers to how closely related the items are in terms of technology, end use, channels of distribution, price range, or customer market. If the product mix is fairly consistent, managing it will probably be more

product mix: the total set of all products offered for sale by a firm, including all product lines sold to all customer groups

efficient and far less difficult. For example, Romanoff International, marketer of the leading brand of caviar, expanded its product mix to include Texas Best Barbecue Sauce, Jack Daniels mustard, a line of meat marinades, and a host of other specialty food items. Its chances of successfully marketing such a diverse group of products were improved because all use the same channel of distribution — all are sold through food brokers to grocery chains and independent specialty food stores.

While the term *length* is usually used in referring to a product line, marketers may also refer to the *length of the product mix,* the total number of different product items including all of the items in each product line. The *depth of the product mix* refers to the number of different versions of each product — that is, the number of different forms of Crest, the number of different flavors of GatorAde, or the number of different Downy fragrances being produced.

In today's marketplace many firms have large, vastly diverse product mixes. Sometimes customers don't even know that the different products are produced by the same company because they are sold with different names. The Ralston-Purina Company, for instance, produces food for cats, dogs, horses, chickens, goats, rabbits — almost every animal not living in the wild. At the same time it sells Rice, Wheat, and Corn Chex dry cereals, Beech-Nut baby food, Energizer batteries, and Hostess Twinkies — something for just about everyone!

When does it make sense for a firm to change its product mix? Above all, objectives for changing the marketing mix should consider the wants and needs of customers. Companies that lose contact with customers are likely to be doomed to failure. Just because a firm is successful with one product does not mean that people will buy anything it puts on the market. Cadillac discovered this when it introduced its low-priced Cimmaron model. Cadillac is perceived as an expensive, big-car company, and the company discovered that consumers who want a high-end small car will more likely look elsewhere.

QUALITY AS A PRODUCT OBJECTIVE

More and more often organizations' product objectives relate to *product quality.* Product quality refers to the overall ability of the product to satisfy customers, to meet their performance expectations, and to provide the benefits they seek in the manner they prefer. It is important to remember that this means that quality is tied to customer *expectations* of how a product will perform and not necessarily to some technological level of perfection.

Why is product quality such an important product strategy objective? The direct benefits of high product quality are the ability to charge a higher price for the product and to sell more of the product than the competition. Thus, product quality is directly related to marketing objectives for higher sales and market share and to overall organizational objectives for increased profits. Figure 10.2 illustrates the close relationship between consumers' perceptions of a brand's quality and the sales of that brand. According to an ongoing survey of perceived brand quality by the Total Research Corporation, some of the most highly rated brands today include Kodak film, Disney World, Mercedes-Benz cars, Hallmark greeting cards, and Fisher-Price toys.[6]

As we saw in Chapter 3, quality has many meanings. In some cases product quality means *durability* — we say that a pair of athletic shoes that lasts a long time is of higher quality than one that develops huge holes after its owner shoots hoops in them for only a few weeks. *Reliability* is also an important aspect of product quality. According to its long-running advertising campaign, the Maytag repairman has been lonely for decades because high-quality Maytag appliances never give their owners problems. For other products quality means a high *degree of precision.* Higher-quality stereos provide clearer music reproduction with less distortion. Quality, especially in business-to-business products, is also related to *ease of use, maintenance, and repair.* Yet another crucial dimension of quality is *product safety;* consumers typically are forced to trust companies when they certify a product will operate safely. Ensuring that a product performs as it was designed is not

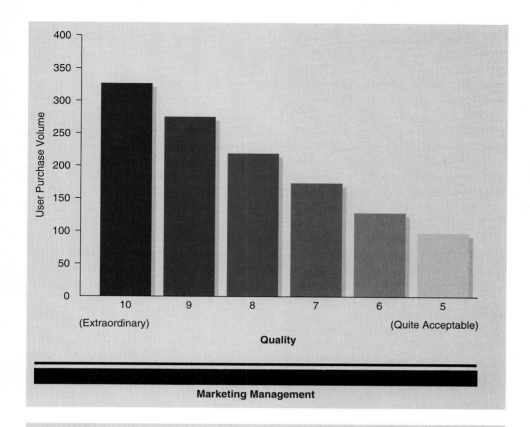

Figure 10.2
The Quality/Sales Relationship

only ethically imperative, it is also economical in the long run. For example, in 1995 the National Highway Traffic Safety Administration caused Japanese car makers to fix or replace poorly designed seat belts on over 8 million autos, a remedy that cost the seven Japanese manufacturers about $250 million.[7] Finally, the quality of products such as a painting, a movie, or even a television program relates to the *degree of aesthetic pleasure* they provide. Of course, evaluations of aesthetic quality differ dramatically among people—one person's quality program may be *Masterpiece Theater,* while another would use the same term to describe *Beavis and Butthead!*

Often marketing planners focus product objectives on one or both of two key aspects of quality: *level* and *consistency.* A product's perceived level of quality is often determined by customers through comparisons with other brands belonging to the same product category. Quite obviously a hand-crafted Rolls-Royce automobile is of higher quality than an assembly-line-produced Ford Mustang, but this is probably irrelevant to a person who is considering buying a Mustang, because he or she will more likely compare it to other sports cars in the same price range than to a super-expensive luxury car driven only by high-society tycoons and extremely successful marketing majors.

Consistency of quality means that customers receive the same level of quality in a product time after time, thus endowing the product with a reputation for always performing at the same high level. Consistent quality is also one of the major benefits of organizations adopting total quality management practices. Consumer perceptions can be changed overnight by a single instance of inconsistent product quality. For example, many people in the United States feel that the quality of service provided by the United States Postal Service is extremely poor. In fact, the Postal Service provides high-quality service in most instances, but news stories of mail lost for thirty or forty or fifty years in some postal employee's attic and word-of-mouth anecdotal evidence of lost or delayed mail have overshadowed this record of good service in the minds of many.

DUOFOLD
SPECIAL EDITION

The distinctive Duofold Special Edition Orange captures the classic style and brilliant color of the original 1920s Duofold. These exquisite writing instruments appeal to those with a nostalgia for the finer things of yesteryear. A distinctive handset motif marks it as a special edition.

Each Duofold is precision machined from a solid block of hand-cast acrylic and trimmed with heavy 23K gold plate. There are two choices of fountain pens, both featuring 18K gold nibs for perfect balance of strength and flexibility, and a choice of 24 nib grades. A matching roller ball combines the smooth flow of a fountain pen with the convenience of a ball point. A ball pen and pencil, echoing the design of the original 1920s Duofold Pencil, complete the set.

♦ PARKER ♦
DUOFOLD

Exhibit 10.2
In some product categories customers seek styles that support their self-image or provide them with some form of distinction. Reading glasses, automobiles, and clothing are examples. When this happens product lines may be extended to meet these customer wants. Parker Pen recognized that premium writing instruments fit this description, so the company added a number of new styles, including the Pearl and Black style. This style included ball pens, mechanical pencils, and fountain pens in a marble-looking, hand-cast acrylic with 23K gold-plated trim.

Organizing for effective product management

Students sometimes ask, "How many people typically work for a big company in marketing?" The answer, of course, is "It depends." As we discussed in Chapter 2, how the marketing function is organized or structured is crucial to the successful implementation of the marketing function. And nowhere is this more obvious than in the organization of product management. In this section we will look at the different ways firms may choose to manage both existing and new products.

MANAGEMENT OF EXISTING PRODUCTS

In a small firm such as Romanoff International, the caviar company discussed earlier, the marketing function is usually handled by a single marketing manager. Even though Romanoff produces a wide variety of different products, this lone manager (with the assistance of the owner of the company) is responsible for new product planning, advertising, working with the company's few sales representatives, marketing research, and just about everything else. Romanoff simply is not big enough to afford a larger marketing management team.

In larger firms, however, where there are many products with sales in the tens of millions of dollars, there are usually a number of managers responsible for different brands, different product categories, or different markets. How the firm organizes for product management has an important influence on the potential success of its product strategy. Depending on the organization, product management may be structured with *brand managers, product category managers,* and/or *market managers.* Let's take a look at how each type operates.

Brand Managers

Sometimes a firm has several different brands within a single product category. For example, General Foods, a subsidiary of Philip Morris Companies, Inc., produces quite a few different brands of coffee including Brim, Maxim, Maxwell House, International Coffees, Sanka, and Yuban. In such cases a separate **brand manager** (sometimes called a *product line manager*) may have the responsibility for each individual brand. Procter & Gamble for many years was well known for its brand management structure. Each brand manager acts independently, planning the marketing strategy for a new or existing brand. The brand manager is generally responsible for coordinating all marketing activities for his or her brand: positioning, identifying target markets, research, distribution, advertising, sales promotion, packaging, and evaluating the success of these decisions. Problems with the brand management system often center on the increasing levels of competition among the firm's brands. Acting independently, the brand managers may fight for increases in short-term sales for their own brand. They may attempt to boost sales by relying too heavily on coupons, cents-off packages, or other price incentives. Because customers become used to purchasing a discounted product, they will refuse to buy the product when it is not on special, thus jeopardizing the firm's long-term profitability.

Product Category Managers

Some larger firms have such diverse product offerings that there is a need to coordinate the different product lines within separate product categories. Philip Morris Companies, Inc. is such a firm. Philip Morris is best known for its eleven brands of cigarettes. But Philip Morris also markets six brands of beer and a variety of food products including Yuban and Maxwell House Coffee, Cool Whip, DiGiorno pasta products, Oscar Mayer meats, and Jell-O. In such cases organizing for product management may include **product category managers** who coordinate the mix of product lines within the more general product category and who consider the addition of new product lines. In recent years both Procter & Gamble and Lever Brothers have changed their management structure, becoming more centralized. Brands are consolidated under product category managers who are responsible for profit and losses within the category.[8]

Market Managers

A somewhat newer and different management structure is based on the markets served by the organization rather than on the products it makes. Some firms have developed a **market manager** structure where different managers focus on specific customer groups. Such a structure is especially useful when firms offer a variety of products that serve the needs of a wide range of customers. For example, firms such as Raytheon sell some products directly to consumer markets (for example, the firm's Amana appliances division or its D.C. Heath publishing company), others to manufacturers (Raytheon operates a number of businesses that provide energy and environmental services—for example, Cedarapids makes road paving equipment, and the Beech Aircraft division is the world's largest producer of aircraft for the general aviation market), and still others to the government (Raytheon makes Hawk, Sidewinder, and Patriot missiles under contract to the U.S. government).[9]

Which type of management structure is best? As with much of marketing the answer is, "It depends." Different products, different customers, and different competitive situations all contribute to making each management structure decision unique. As Procter & Gamble and Lever Brothers and a host of other companies have discovered, what is best today may not be best tomorrow as markets continue to change.

ORGANIZING FOR NEW PRODUCT DEVELOPMENT

In Chapter 9 we discussed the tremendous importance of new products to the long-term health of an organization. Because launching new products is such an important activity, the management of new product development must be carefully organized. In some instances new product development is handled by a single individual. In other cases teams of people or even planners from more than one firm work together to plan new product launches.

ENTREPRENEURS

entrepreneurs: individuals who assume risks in owning, organizing, and managing their own businesses

Sometimes new products are developed by intrepid individuals working alone on a great idea or invention, maybe even toiling away in the wee hours in a lonely garage (that's how Apple Computer got started). Individuals who not only create a new product but who also start up their own businesses with the product are called **entrepreneurs.** One of the more celebrated entrepreneurs in the United States is Bill Gates of Microsoft. Like many entrepreneurs he started out with an idea and a willingness to work hard and take risks. In 1975, at the age of typical college juniors, Bill Gates and Paul Allen formed a partnership, licensed their version of BASIC to Altair microcomputers, and named their business venture Microsoft. Microsoft reached $1 million sales in 1978 and $100 million by 1984. By 1992 *Forbes* magazine named Bill Gates the richest person in America, worth around $7 billion.[10]

New Product Managers

Within larger organizations, new product development almost always involves many people. One person, however, may be assigned the role of *new product manager.* A new product manager is someone who has the knowledge and skills necessary to develop and introduce new products successfully. Often individuals who are assigned to manage new product development are especially creative people with entrepreneurial skills. Some firms are even using the term "intrapreneurship" for their efforts to stimulate creativity and encourage innovation within the big-company environment.

Venture Teams

A study by *Inc.* magazine found that of successful start-up businesses, 54 percent had two founders and 40 percent had three or more. Only 6 percent were one-person efforts. Even Bill Gates had Paul Allen and others on his team.[11] Although this study looked at small business start-ups, large companies also rely on experienced individuals working together to successfully develop new products.

venture teams: a group of people within an organization who work together focusing exclusively on the development of a new product

The challenge in large companies is to get specialists in different areas to work together in units known as **venture teams,** where members focus exclusively on the new product development effort. Sometimes the venture team is located away from traditional company offices, perhaps in a totally separate building called a *skunk works.* This odd term suggests that the group avoids opponents of change within the firm who might stop a project that would upset the status quo. Often having team members with different areas of knowledge provides a diversity of perspectives that contributes to creativity. Venture teams may include design and manufacturing engineers as well as marketers.

Whirlpool, the appliance company, is a true believer in the venture team concept—a team it put together won $30 million for the company. In the early 1990s refrigerators accounted for 21 percent of electricity consumption by U.S. households. A consortium of utilities sought to reduce electricity consumption by offering a $30 million dollar prize for the best design. The seven-person Whirlpool team developed a refrigerator that was 25 percent more energy efficient and did not use ozone-depleting chlorofluorocarbons.[12] Runner-up Frigidaire also used a team approach and discovered that time devoted to new product development was cut in half—to nine months.[13]

Partnering by Companies

Today it is increasingly common for companies to cooperate with one another to create new products. Cooperation between companies is commonly referred to as *partnering.* Two forms of partnering are joint ventures and alliances.

A *joint venture* is a business formed by two or more companies that agree to pool certain resources for some common purpose. In Chapter 4 we discussed how firms engaged in global marketing strategies form joint ventures to introduce products into international markets. Domestic joint ventures also are frequently formed for the purpose of developing new products that will benefit both firms. For example, Sega of America teamed up with Time Warner and Tele-Communications, forming a joint venture to start a cable network that offered interactive video games.[14] Usually companies form joint ventures when they cannot accomplish both the technical and commercial development of a new product by themselves. They pool their financial resources, technology, access to markets, or special know-how to further the purposes of the joint venture.

When companies want to cooperate, but do not want to create a separate business entity, they form an alliance. An *alliance* is an agreement by two or more companies to work together on some common business objective. For example, American Cyanamid and MedImmune Inc. signed a letter of intent to develop and market four drugs. MedImmune has one drug with significant sales growth potential, but only a fifteen-person sales force. American Cyanamid has 1,000 sales representatives and will give MedImmune $30 million to help cover MedImmune's development costs.[15]

DEVELOPING STRATEGIES FOR NEW AND EXISTING PRODUCTS

Developing strategies for the product plan means deciding "how to" achieve the product objectives: how to design a new product that will increase the organization's market share; how to extend a product line so as to attract segments of the market not previously served; how to harvest a product with declining sales. In this section we will talk about how firms develop and manage new products. Then we will discuss different types of product strategies that are appropriate for existing products in different phases of the product life cycle.

THE NEW PRODUCT DEVELOPMENT PROCESS

Jogging in a Jug, an unorthodox arthritis treatment made from cider vinegar and fruit juices, was the brainchild of an almost-bankrupt farmer who used an old formula handed down from his grandmother to cure his own arthritis. This success motivated him to try to market the concoction, and he convinced two local supermarkets to take a few cases on consignment (they paid nothing unless the cases sold). The cases sold quickly . . . a successful test market! The product was launched, and within two years Wal-Mart, Kroger, and Food Lion carried Jogging in a Jug.[16]

This type of "seat of the pants" success story still occurs in the 1990s, but such a feat is getting tougher to accomplish. Successful new product introductions have become more and more difficult for a variety of reasons. First, the costs of research and development are often so huge that they limit new product development. The fast pace of technological developments has shortened the product life cycle, which means that firms have less time to recover their research and development costs. And there are simply too many new products being introduced to go on limited shelf space, making it very expensive for firms to obtain retailer support.[17] What all this means is that well-designed new product strategies that reduce the time it takes to get good products to market are more important than ever.

New product development typically occurs in three stages: the visionary phase, the planning and development phase, and the test and improvement phase. In the *visionary phase* a firm generates ideas and screens them, trying to identify the ideas that will work best for the firm, given its situation and business mission. The *planning and development phase* involves turning an idea into a product that customers want and the company can manufacture. The *test and improvement* phase involves trying out marketing strategies in test markets, getting customer reactions, and improving the marketing plan and product prior to full commercial launch. Let's take a more in-depth look at each step in this process.

Idea Generation

New product ideas come from many different sources. Sometimes these brainstorms arise by assessing customers' needs. When customers complain they may also offer suggestions for new products that might do a better job. For example, when NEC Corporation designers were developing a new notebook computer, they observed how people used their current models. They realized that frequently people were talking on the phone or writing or doing something else as they opened up their laptop. To accommodate this activity the UltraLite Versa was designed with a single center latch that can be opened with one hand.[18]

Salespeople, service providers, and others who have direct customer contact also provide insights about what works and what doesn't. Marketing research activities such as focus groups may also be useful to firms in their continual search for new product ideas. New ideas also come from anticipating what product benefits will be important to customers. The VCR came from visualizing a benefit that had never been experienced by consumers. In the Dark Ages before the time of video cassette recorders (VCRs), the only chance a viewer had to catch a favorite television program was when the network chose to broadcast it. Imagine the surprising benefit these "ancient" consumers experienced when they first realized that VCRs gave them the power to record and save their favorite television programs even when they were not at home!

Screening Product Concepts

New product ideas are expanded into more complete *product concepts*—more specific descriptions that include the major product features and benefits. Next comes **screening**—that is, examining the chances that the ideas generated will achieve technical and commercial success. Does the product meet unfulfilled needs of a segment of buyers? This stage is extremely important because it is then that marketers (and engineers) start with a large number of concepts and go about weeding out those that have little or no chance of success. Ideas that are selected will use up large amounts of company resources, so they had better be good. Those that are abandoned may be lost forever.

One of the most popular methods for screening product concepts is through the use of *intention-to-purchase measures.* Typically a survey is designed that includes one or more carefully defined product concepts. Each product concept is evaluated by survey respondents in terms of how likely they would be to purchase the product, given the products currently on the market. Based on these data marketers are able to estimate the percentage of the target market that would be interested in each product concept.

Business Analysis

Once a product idea has been selected for further consideration, the next step is to *really* get serious by conducting a *business analysis.* Can the product be developed into a profitable contribution to the organization's product mix? What is the potential demand for the product? What expenditures of resources will be required? It is at this point that the fantasies of creative inventors are exposed to the harsh spotlight of financial reality. The marketing graveyard is littered with products that sounded "interesting" but that failed to catch on, including jalapeño soda, aerosol mustard, and edible deodorant![19]

Firms use various *forecasting techniques* to assess the probable customer demand for a new product. Sometimes they develop pessimistic, realistic, and optimistic demand estimates over a reasonable time framework to assess the full range of possible outcomes they might expect. Sometimes vastly different estimates are necessary because of the uncertainty in the market. For example, estimates of the 1995 market for interactive media, based on CD-ROMs, ranged from $4 billion (pessimistic estimate) to $14 billion (optimistic estimate).[20]

Equally important to assessing demand is developing estimates of the costs of the marketing efforts necessary to stimulate demand and achieve desired distribution levels. This approximation may include costs required for establishing or training a sales force, recruiting distributors, advertising, sampling, conducting sales promotions, and communicating through press releases and direct mail.

Planning and Development

If it survives the scrutiny of a business analysis, a new product concept then undergoes commercial and technical development. *Commercial development* means putting together a marketing plan and involving potential customers in the process of improving customer benefits. The marketing plan builds on the initial projections made during product screening. Forecasts are adjusted to fit more precise information about the market and how customers will respond to the product. Also, planned price, advertising, and

screening: the process of examining the prospects of a product concept achieving technical and commercial success

distribution policies are taken into account. *Technical development* involves actually designing the product and planning how it will be manufactured.

The better a firm understands how customers will probably react to a new product idea, the better are the eventual chances of commercial success. *Involving prospects* means getting individual consumers or organizations that are likely to be future customers to participate in evaluating product benefits during the development stage. In fact, new product development is most successful when prospective customers are *continually* involved in new product development.

One example of continual involvement of prospects can be found in this very textbook. As we mentioned in Chapter 1, marketing professors from colleges and universities across the United States were recruited early in the developmental stage of this book to serve on an advisory panel. As we made decisions about our product—what to include, where to include it, and how much of a topic should be included—we surveyed our panel of experts to get their ideas about what they felt their students needed to know and how this material should be presented. Hopefully this interactive process results in a product that better meets the needs of customers (or at least is less likely to put them to sleep!).

Technical development sometimes involves application for a patent. A **patent** is legal documentation granting an individual or a firm exclusive right to use a particular invention. Patents are granted by the U.S. Patent Office to individuals and firms that create a unique product design or manufacturing process. Because patents give inventors exclusive rights, a patent may reduce or eliminate competition in a market for many years, allowing a firm "breathing room" to recoup investments in technical development. For example, for many years G.D. Searle Pharmaceuticals (now owned by Monsanto) held the patent for its NutraSweet brand of artificial sweetener; this exclusive right to make and sell the product allowed the company to reap huge profits. Now that the patent has expired, Searle faces competition from other similar products, and life is no longer as sweet.

patent: legal documentation saying that an individual or firm has exclusive rights to use a particular invention

Test Marketing

The next step in new product development is *test marketing*. Test marketing typically means that the firm conducts a field experiment to test the effectiveness of the product offering under realistic market conditions. The complete marketing plan for the new product is tried out—distribution, advertising, sales promotion, point-of-purchase displays, and so on—but in just one city or in a small geographic area.

Test marketing can take several forms. *Simulated market tests* attempt to imitate a consumer's shopping or consumption situation. Most commonly simulated market tests are run in a storelike setting created by researchers to study how product variables affect consumers' decisions to purchase a new product. For grocery items and other nondurable consumer goods, this test provides useful information at a relatively low cost. Similarly, some planned advertisements are tested by showing them in theaters to consumers who provide their evaluations of each possible message.

Selected consumer tests are commonly used by industrial firms to test their products. Perhaps you have heard the term *beta testing* in connection with software development. Beta testing refers to a software developer, such as Lotus, giving a loyal customer a new version of software to use. This user supplies Lotus with feedback about bugs that are discovered when the new version is tried out.

When choosing a geographical region or city for test marketing purposes, marketers typically try to locate a place that is the most representative of the country. They want a place that will allow them to predict how the mass market will react to product designs or promotional ideas. The expression "Will it play in Peoria?" refers to the traditional designation of that city as most representative of the American heartland. More recently, Tulsa has replaced Peoria as the most typical city in America. It most closely matches the national average in terms of age distribution, racial mix, and housing prices. Other popular test cities include Charleston, South Carolina; Midland, Texas; and Springfield, Illinois.[21]

There are a number of benefits and some problems associated with test marketing. By offering a new product to a sample of customers, marketers can evaluate and improve the marketing program. In fact, test marketing may be the only way to see if all of the technical and commercial elements work. Sometimes test marketing leads to product improvement. In other cases test marketing may warn marketers of probable product failure, allowing the firm to save millions of dollars by "pulling the plug" before the doomed item is introduced for real.[22]

However, test marketing is extremely expensive; it may well cost hundreds of thousands of dollars to conduct a product launch even in a single city. Another hazard of a test market is that it allows the competition to get a free look at the new product, its introductory price, and the intended promotional strategy. In competitive markets this sort of visibility can be deadly to a new product's success, because it allows other companies to adjust their own strategies in advance of product introduction.

As a result of the high costs of test marketing, some research organizations such as Burke Marketing Research have developed computerized models for conducting test market simulations. The process involves first gathering some basic research data on consumer perceptions of the product concept, the physical product, and the advertising and other promotional activity. A computer simulation model is then able to predict the potential success of the new product much less expensively (and more quietly) than a traditional test market. As research firms such as Burke continue to improve their ability to predict accurately the success or failure of a new product with simulated test markets, "real" test markets may become a thing of the past.

Launching a New Product

A *product launch* is the process of commercializing a product by implementing a complete marketing program. If test marketing has gone well, it is likely that marketers will decide to commercialize the new product full-scale. This is a big decision, especially if the new product will be launched nationally.

Launching a new product requires full-scale production, distribution, advertising, sales promotion, the whole works. For this reason full-scale commercialization of a new product cannot happen overnight. A launch requires advance planning and careful preparation. Advertising typically is arranged months before implementation with print, network, cable, and radio outlets. Sales promotions, such as coupons, are developed. Point-of-purchase displays are commissioned in preparation for delivery to distribution outlets. Manufacturing produces sufficient quantities of the product. Employees who will provide customer services receive extensive training and preparation. Others who will participate in the marketing program, such as salespeople, distributors, and retailers, are informed of the product and trained to present it in the most effective way to customers.

As launch time nears, preparations gain a sense of urgency—it's almost like count-

Excellence at AST

The practice of relationship marketing requires anticipating customer needs and developing new products that give people what they want—perhaps even before they realize they want it. Take, for example, the basic personal computer (PC). It seems that PC users want more computing power and greater ease of use. So the only way to keep customers happy is to add computing power and build in greater ease of use continually, right? Wrong!

Consider PCs from a different perspective, that of an office manager. PCs are on nearly every desk. A small business might count PCs in the dozens. A Fortune 500 firm might count PCs in the thousands. Now consider the power consumption of dozens

or thousands of PCs humming away on office desks everywhere. Here is a great place for business managers to prune operating costs: Simply reduce PC energy consumption.

AST, a PC supplier, anticipated customer demand for an energy-conserving PC before these machines became a fixture on virtually every desk. Introduced in 1993, AST's "green" PC used an estimated 40 percent less power.* In addition, they were available with fifteen-inch, low-radiation monitors, another emerging interest of PC customers. Effective relationship marketing (that is, exceeding customer expectations) also turned out to be good stewardship of the environment.

---

* Mike Hogan, "Bravo for Green Thinking from AST," *PC/Computing* (Aug. 1993): 80.

---

down in the control room at NASA. Marketers build enthusiasm among those who will launch the product. Special motivational programs are explained to salespeople and distributors. The marketing department, indeed, the whole company, is excited as the first product is shipped. Soon the media announces to prospective customers why they should buy and where they can find the new product. All elements of the marketing program, ideally, come into play like a carefully rehearsed symphony. The product is launched!

MANAGING EXISTING PRODUCTS OVER THE LIFE CYCLE

We have focused so far on new product strategies because successful new product introductions are the lifeblood of organizations. However, launching a product is only the beginning. Equally if not more important are effective marketing strategies for products that are no longer new. Continuous adjustments to marketing strategy occur throughout the product life cycle in response to changes in demand, technology, competition, regulations, and the economic and cultural environment in which the company must operate.

In Chapter 9 we discussed the stages of the product life cycle (PLC). As a product moves through each stage of the PLC, consumers change, the competitive picture changes, and to be successful, marketing strategies must change as well. Therefore the PLC provides a very useful framework for discussing strategy adjustments as products move from birth to death.

The Introductory Stage

The introductory stage is the time when a new product is put on the market. Usually when the product introduction is for a durable good such as the first microwave ovens or the first personal computers, this means that one basic product is made available to customers. When introducing nondurables such as Snapple fruit beverages or Healthy Choice Ice Cream, the introduction may include a variety of flavors, fragrances, or other variations. In either case the goal is to get first-time buyers to try the product.

Pricing may be high to recover research and development costs, or it may be low so as to attract large numbers of consumers to try the new product. (These and other pricing strategies will be discussed in detail in Chapters 12 and 13.) Distribution is typically somewhat selective due to the high costs of developing mass distribution for a new product and the reluctance of many retailers to devote valuable shelf space to an unknown performer.

The Growth Stage

During the growth stage in the product life cycle, the goal of each individual producer of a product is to establish its product in the marketplace and encourage brand loyalty. During this phase new competitors will be entering the marketplace. This creates the need to introduce product variations, possibly designed to attract specific segments of the market, to grow market share. Thus a firm may seek either to improve the product or to expand the product line.

Marketers may be able to increase sales of their offering by reducing prices, as by this time research and development costs have usually been recovered. Distribution may become less selective as there is a greater need for mass distribution to boost sales.

The Maturity Stage

During the maturity stage of the product life cycle, many firms are competing in the market so that the weaker firms typically drop out. Often an individual firm will have many different items in its product line. To remain competitive and to maintain market share, it is usually essential to tinker with the marketing mix to adapt to changing conditions.

Often firms engage in significant *product modification* at this time. Product differentiation may involve using a new technology to change an existing product, or it may mean that a firm simply applies existing technology to change a product. Producers of potato chips and other snack foods have modified their products to meet consumers' changing wants and needs. One ounce of regular potato chips has about 150 calories and eight grams of fat. Newer reduced-fat or fat-free potato chips do away with some or all of the fat (and many would say with taste as well!). Taking the opposite product improvement strategy, one ounce of Chickasaw's Dirty Potato Chips have 170 calories, eleven grams of fat, and 240 milligrams of sodium![23] This approach applies to services as well. For example, Aspen, Vail, and other Colorado mountain resorts have differentiated their product lines by adding golfing, tennis, music festivals, and many other nonski vacation products.[24]

Sometimes modifications are made because consumers want some new benefit or simply greater variety. Coca-Cola and Pepsi both regularly introduce new varieties of soda to rejuvenate sales in the mature cola market. Pepsi was also very successful with its freshness dating idea to invigorate a mature brand. In March 1993 Pepsi began testing freshness dating on Diet Pepsi followed by a national roll-out in April that included a $25 million marketing campaign. Today freshness dates are on all Pepsi beverage cans and bottles, including iced tea and juices.[25]

Sometimes changes are made in the basic design of a product to make it more useful. Today most of the total sales of personal computers are for more powerful replacement units, made necessary by the introduction of increasingly sophisticated software that requires greater memory to run. In other instances the product may be improved aesthetically. Because some people dislike the smell of pine oil, Texize Pine Oil Cleaner sought to increase its customer base by developing a lemon-scented pine oil cleaner. Downy fabric softener now comes in four different fragrances, each identified by a different color bottle cap.

Attracting new users of the product may be another strategy pursued during the maturity stage. *Market differentiation* refers to introducing an existing product to a market that currently does not use the product. For example, an English firm, Land of Telephones' Future, introduces new products to the English market first and then later targets the United States. Many U.S. firms find that new markets such as those in Eastern Europe are prime targets for a product whose sales are lagging in the United States. In this case market differentiation involves two culturally and geographically distinct markets.[26]

Using a market differentiation strategy, firms may also seek to rejuvenate the product by developing new uses for it. Arm & Hammer baking soda is a classic example of a product that was rejuvenated after it had been in the maturity stage for decades. Now baking soda is used to make your refrigerator, your freezer, your garbage disposal, your cat litter, and your laundry smell fresh and clean—and many people brush their teeth with it as well (hopefully using a new box!).

During the maturity stage firms will normally try to sell their product through all suitable retailers, because product availability is crucial in a very competitive market. Consumers will not go far to find one brand when there are many others conveniently available. Pricing may be adjusted downward to meet or undercut the competition.

The Decline Stage

During the decline stage of the PLC, industry sales start to drop off. While a single firm may still be profitable, the market as a whole begins to head toward zero profits as some firms experience financial losses and eventually abandon the business. During the decline stage, at least at the beginning, there are usually a large number of competitors with no one having a really distinct product. The market is full of me-too products, each clawing for market share and trying to hang on with minimal investment.

A major product decision in the decline stage is whether to keep the product at all. In some cases new technology has made a product obsolete. Or fashion or style changes have tolled the death knell for a once innovative product. In any case the product is simply no longer profitable. Thus it drains resources from the firm—resources that could be better used to develop or introduce newer products. In such cases, such as with Crystal Pepsi, it may be best simply to drop the product from the firm's product mix if it fails to perform up to expectations. If the decision to drop the product is made, elimination may be handled in one of several different ways. Sometimes it makes more sense to phase the product out by cutting production in several stages and then slowly allowing existing stocks to run out. In other instances it is better just to drop the product immediately.

Sometimes a firm may choose to maintain the product in the market. This is likely to occur when a firm that is the established market leader anticipates that there will be some residual demand for the product for a long time to come. Thus the firm expects to continue to sell a limited quantity of the product with very little or no output in resources. Some classic products still on the market with little or no marketing support include laundry aids, bluing and starch, and Vicks VapoRub.

CREATING PRODUCT IDENTITY: BRANDING DECISIONS

How important is branding? Well, of the over 17,000 new products or line extensions introduced each year, 25 percent or more than 4,250 are new brands. About $127.5 billion is spent on introducing new brands every year. Despite these heroic efforts, between 80 and 90 percent of all new brands fail.[27] Yes, branding is an extremely important (and expensive) element of product strategy.

In this section we will examine what a brand really is and how brands are protected by law. Then we will discuss the importance of branding and how firms make branding decisions.

WHAT'S IN A NAME (OR A SYMBOL)?

How do you identify your favorite brand of soda? By its name? By the logo (how the name appears)? By the shape of the bottle? By the color of the container?

A **brand** is a name, a term, a symbol, or any other unique element of a product that identifies one firms' products and sets them apart from those of other producers. Branding provides the essential identification needed by products whether they are distributed regionally, nationally, or internationally.

Functions of a Brand

Whether a brand name, a logo, or a trade character, branding serves a number of important functions. Why are brands so important? A 1995 survey of senior executives provides part of the answer. When asked how brands contribute to the effectiveness of their companies, 65 percent said they provided an umbrella for goods and services, and 58 percent said they contributed to corporate identity.[28]

brand: a name, a term, a symbol, or any other unique element of a product that identifies one firms' products and sets them apart from those of other producers

Branding reflects the positioning or the personality of the brand. Think about the logo for Pepperidge Farm products: The old-fashioned type style says homemade quality. In addition, brand names can also contribute to awareness and knowledge of the purpose of the product. The Drano brand of drain opener serves this function extremely well.

Sometimes brand marks are created to resemble the product; for example, Bell Telephone uses an image of a bell to represent itself. On the other hand, the brand mark may be a symbol for a product because of either conventional or agreed-on associations. For example, the lion in Dreyfus Fund ads provides the conventional association with fearlessness that is carried over to the company's approach to investments. In each case the brand name or imagery used to represent the product plays a very important role in positioning the product and communicating a desired image to the audience.

Choosing a Brand Name or Character

There are several important considerations in selecting a brand name, brand mark, or trade character. First, it must have a positive connotation and be memorable. The brand should be developed in such a way that consumers automatically recall and respond in a positive manner to the brand. To appreciate the ability of a brand name to create expectations of what a product can do, remember the story about Toro's snow thrower we discussed in Chapter 6. With the name "Snow Pup" sales were disappointing, but when the product was renamed the "Snow Master," sales jumped.[29]

There are also some important graphic considerations for a brand symbol, name, or logo. It must be recognizable regardless of the package size on which it appears. No matter how small or how large, the triangular Nabisco logo in the corner of the box is always a familiar sight. The best brand logos also reproduce well both in black and white and in color. While the color of "Big Blue," IBM's logo, is important, using a unique type style allows easy recognition of the brand even when seen in black and white. Graphics specialists would also say that a brand must have visual impact. That means that from across the store, while hurrying down a grocery store aisle, or while quickly flipping the pages in a magazine, the brand will catch your attention and be recognized—even in a fraction of a second.

In today's global markets smart marketers also feel it is important to consider whether or not a brand can be used successfully in different regions and in different countries. It may not be wise to devote time and resources to introducing and supporting a brand that does not "travel well" to other countries.

Brand Names

A brand name is probably the most used and most recognized form of branding. A good brand name may position a product, describe how it works, or alternatively may be ambiguous, allowing advertising to create an image effectively for the new brand (for example, Exxon, Ajax, and Lotus). Brand names such as Caress and Shield help to position these very different brands of bath soap by telling us something about the benefits they provide. Cereals often have names that are extremely descriptive, from old favorites like Corn Flakes, Frosted Flakes, Lucky Charms, and Rice Krispies to newer entrants into the marketplace like Nut 'n Honey, Frosted Mini-Wheats, Booberries, and Almond Delight.

How does a firm select a good brand name? A guideline used by brand designers is that the name should pass four "easy" tests: *easy to say, easy to spell, easy to read,* and *easy to remember.* Consider how easy it is to communicate with these P&G laundry product names: Tide, Cheer, Dash, Bold, Gain, Downy, and Ivory Snow.

The name should also pass another test by "fitting" in four ways: A good brand name *fits the target market, fits the product's benefits, fits the customer's culture,* and *fits legal requirements.* These guidelines suggest that a good name is consistent with the overall product positioning that will appeal most to target consumers *and* the name can be legally protected. Once again let's use P&G brands to illustrate.

- Who would use Oil of Olay or Lava—men, women, or both?
- What are the benefits of Spic 'n Span, Mr. Clean, and Fixodent?

Finally, a brand must fit certain legal requirements. In particular, the name can't duplicate someone else's registered brand name or a name for a product category that is in

common use. For example, McDonald's filed suit against McSleep Hotels to prevent infringement of the company name.[30]

Trademarks

The legal term used for a brand name, brand mark, or trade character is **trademark.** Brand identification may obtain legal protection by becoming a legally registered trademark, thus preventing the use of the name or mark on imitation products. In the United States trademark protection was established by the Lanham Act of 1946 and updated by the Trademark Revision Act of 1989. The symbol for legal registration is a capital R in a circle:® In addition to names or symbols, other distinctive aspects of a product can receive legal trademark protection. A color can be granted protection if it is determined to be a unique product feature. For example, Owens-Corning won trademark protection for its pink insulation, though Pepto Bismol was not allowed similar protection for its pink stomach medicine.[31] In 1995 Harley-Davidson petitioned the U.S. Patent and Trademark Office for exclusive rights to its engine sound, claiming that a lot of its owners buy their "hogs" just for its unique noise. If granted, this sound would join other legally protected trademark sounds, such as the distinctive NBC television network chimes and the roar of the MGM studios' lion.[32]

It is possible for a brand to be protected even if it has not been legally registered. *Common-law protection* exists if a name has been used and established over a period of time (rather like a common-law marriage). This form of protection extends as far geographically as the name is known. For a local business that does not anticipate expanding outside its local area, common law will protect the name in that one area, even if at a later date a large company tries to establish a national trademark. In the 1980s the grocery chain Food Town changed its name to Food Lion because it wanted to open stores in states where the name Food Town was already being used. The common-law protection prevented Food Town from using that name, so the firm identified a similar name that could be used in any state in the nation.

Obtaining legal protection for a trademark is a lengthy process involving large legal fees. First, the organization wishing to register a trademark must make an application that provides evidence that the brand is distinct and that the product is used, transported, and/or purchased across state lines. The trademark then becomes a registered federal trademark only after the application has been reviewed and approved. To retain protection of the brand, however, firms must continue to market the branded product. If not

trademark: the legal name for a brand name, brand mark, or trade character; trademarks may be legally registered by a government, thus obtaining protection for exclusive use in that country

REAL PEOPLE, REAL CHOICES:

DECISION TIME AT INTEL

In 1991 Intel was going great guns, selling thousands and thousands of its 386 microprocessors as the demand for personal computers skyrocketed among both corporations and end consumers. But, while it's said that imitation is the sincerest form of flattery, Intel wasn't thrilled that many other chip manufacturers had also taken to referring to their microprocessors by the number 386. This usage had become so commonplace that the number no longer was identified with the Intel product. Widespread usage of the number made it difficult for the company to make buyers understand why they should choose one company's 386 chip over those made by others. When Intel tried to halt this practice, the courts ruled against the company, finding that 386 should be considered a part number and thus could not be trademarked. This ruling presented a big marketing challenge, because it deprived Intel of the ability to differentiate the part from that made by competitors or to describe to consumers the benefit of choosing an Intel product.

Dennis Carter and his associates at Intel needed to find some other way to implement an *"ingredient branding strategy."* This meant that they had to convince their customers that one chip brand was preferable to others, even though they could not see or touch the product Intel sold, because it was buried deep inside the computer they chose. It's hard enough to devise an effective branding strategy for a visible product—how about imparting a distinctive image to a product that most people don't even know is inside the machine? Dennis Carter considered three options:

Option 1. Encourage manufacturers to use the Intel brand name, but protect it at the same time by developing a logo that would be unique to microprocessors but that still featured the Intel name. The company had already begun promoting itself with the phrase, "Intel—the computer inside," so that campaign could be leveraged here. In addition, an invented logo could be licensed and used in a variety of ways. A licensing decision also meant that Intel could develop cooperative advertising campaigns with the computer manufacturers who used the chip. This meant that two or more companies could share the costs of promoting a computer product. Still, this choice presented a lot of risk since it meant developing brand identification where none currently existed. It was also a very complex and novel way to designate a computer "ingredient," and Mr. Carter had no way to know how such an unusual strategy would be received by manufacturers or end consumers.

Option 2. Continue with the status quo. Go on marketing the chip by its part number, but be sure that the product is always referred to as the Intel 386 chip. This strategy would allow Intel to continue to build brand equity because the corporate name would continue to be associated with the part and used in the firm's advertising. It would also be a simple solution, because manufacturers and customers could continue to designate the specific part number they desired. On the other hand, it seemed quite possible that the Intel designation would get lost in the shuffle; by the time the product made its way to the end user, it would probably be simply referred to as the 386, and Intel's unique link to the chip would be erased in people's minds.

Option 3. Devise an entirely new brand name. This would allow the Intel microprocessor to take on a unique identity and clearly set it apart from the competition. And, as Intel makes other products as well, this strategy would permit the company to highlight its chip. One brand possibility the company considered was the Intellect 386, a bit of a play on words that would retain some connection with the Intel name. There was a negative side to this strategy, though: A new brand name would have no existing brand equity at all, and promotional efforts would have to focus on building recognition and positive associations in customers' minds from scratch.

Now, join Intel's decision team: If you were vice president of corporate marketing for Intel Corporation, which option would you choose, and why?

used after a period of years, the trademark will cease to be the property of the registering company.

Firms also must protect a brand name from becoming common language. When brand names have been used for a very long time, they sometimes become associated with a product category and are used to describe any product in that category. In legal terms they became part of the "public domain." A long time ago aspirin was a brand name, but Bayer lost exclusive rights to it when common use made it a generic name for the product category. Similarly, people used to say, "I'm going to xerox this." Xerox spent millions of dollars reminding customers that they should say, "I'm going to *photocopy* this." Other brands with this problem include Kleenex, Formica, and Teflon.

Federal trademark protection of brands not only protects them from being used by other firms but creates requirements that the brand be used only in certain ways. Specifically, trade names must always be capitalized and must be followed by a generic name. Brand names are never pluralized, never used as verbs, and are not possessive. For example, it is actually incorrect simply to say "Kleenex"; the correct usage is "Kleenex facial tissues." And people don't wash their laundry with Tide; they use Tide laundry detergent. While companies do not pay "trademark police" to eavesdrop on consumers' conversations about their products, they do regularly inform members of the press when their brand name has been used incorrectly and may actually take legal action to protect the brand.

A registered trademark means that others cannot use that mark on their product if it would confuse shoppers—that is, if it is a product in the same or a similar product category. The same name or mark, however, may be used by a product in a completely different type of business—one that would never be confused by the consumer. A new Chrysler

SPOTLIGHT ON GLOBAL MARKETING

Brand Pirates

Trademarks are only protected in a single country. If you as a marketer want to protect your trademark internationally, you must obtain protection in each and every country where you want to market the product. There are a number of horror stories of unethical individuals who registered major U.S. brand names in other countries and then demanded money from the legitimate owner of the brand for its use in that country. The International Trademark Association provides a media guide, a hot line, and a list of 4,000 registered trademarks to aid in the protection of trademarks. The total cost of brand piracy to U.S. marketers was estimated to be $8.57 billion in 1994.

Some countries in Southeast Asia are notorious for encouraging counterfeit trade. Older laws in Indonesia simply stated first come, first registered. It was under that old law that an Indonesian firm, PT Makmur Perkasa Abadi, registered trademarks used by Pierre Cardin and Levi Strauss. Newer regulations require that the company seeking to register a trademark show that they have a right to it.* According to the International Intellectual Property Alliance, as much as 95 percent of the software sold in Thailand is pirated.†

Some industries are fighting back. The Motion Picture Association is running an ongoing campaign where a trailer in movies shown in the cinema and on videocassettes gives consumers in Belgium, Germany, Italy, and the U.K. a toll-free hot line to report piracy. The Software Publishers Association, representing 1,200 U.S. software manufacturers, is conducting an "education and enforcement" campaign in Singapore, where software pirating cost U.S. marketers $33 million in 1994.

* Junda Woo and Richard Borsuk, "Asian Trademark Litigation Continues," *The Wall Street Journal* (Feb. 16, 1994): B8.
† Todd Pruzan, David Butler, Deborah Klosky, Elisabeth Malkin, Dagmar Mussey, Jack Russell, Douglass Stinson, and Chris Wellisz, "Modern Day Pirates a Threat Worldwide," *Advertising Age* (March 30, 1995): 13–14.

automobile provides an example of the same brand name used (legally) for two totally different products. Chrysler recently launched the Cirrus automobile, using the same name as the MasterCard's Cirrus ATM network. The concern for MasterCard is that if the Cirrus turns out to be an Edsel, it will hurt the reputation of the MC Cirrus network.[33]

THE IMPORTANCE OF BRANDING

Brands that exhibit staying power are treasured by marketers, and for good reason. People who form preferences for a favorite brand may literally never change their minds in the course of a lifetime. We call this preference brand loyalty, and it is the first and foremost benefit of branding. **Brand loyalty,** which we discussed in Chapter 6, is a form of repeat purchasing behavior driven by a conscious decision to continue buying a product with a particular trademark. Conscious decisions to make repeat purchases differ from **inertia,** which refers to purchases made out of habit merely because this takes less effort. Conscious preference may be based not only on objective reasons but also on emotional attachment, particularly if the brand is heavily advertised.

Marketers spend huge amounts of money to create brand loyalty. Advertising, new product development, and promotions contribute to brand development. In addition, a firm earns the privilege of a customer's loyalty by providing a consistent set of benefits. If successful, this investment creates **brand equity.** Brand equity is the value of a brand related to the brand's ability to attract future customers reliably.

BRANDING STRATEGIES

Brands significantly affect a marketing program's success. Therefore, branding strategies are a major part of product decision making. Table 10.1 summarizes some major brand strategies.

brand loyalty: a form of repeat purchasing behavior based on a conscious decision to continue buying a product with a particular brand or trademark

inertia: a form of repeat purchasing behavior based on habit because this takes less effort

brand equity: the value of a brand related to the brand's ability to attract future customers reliably

Exhibit 10.5
Consumers sometimes form a lifetime preference for a brand such as the Ford Mustang. The Mustang model has significant *brand equity.* This Mustang ad prominently displays the Mustang brand symbol on the 1964 Ford Mustang and on the 1994 Ford Mustang. The company is trying to evoke continuity in brand preference and provide a nostalgic appeal at the same time. This campaign targeted over 6 million people who have bought the celebrated car since it first appeared in 1964. The marketing program was quite successful, causing Ford to increase production by almost 50 percent.

WHAT IT TAKES TO TURN AN *AMERICAN DREAM* INTO *REALITY.*

BUCKLE UP—TOGETHER WE CAN SAVE LIVES.

MANY *Americans have dreamed of owning a sports car, yet up until 1964, when the Mustang was introduced, sports cars were out of the reach of most people. It took INGENUITY to make that dream a reality. And over the years ingenuity and quality have become Ford Motor Company hallmarks. From its beginning, in 1903, right up to today, Ford Motor Company has found more ways to say QUALITY than anyone else.*

THE 1964½ FORD MUSTANG WITH THE 1994 FORD MUSTANG

· FORD · FORD TRUCKS · *Ford* · LINCOLN · MERCURY ·

QUALITY IS JOB 1

Brand Type	Strategy	Examples
• National or manufacturer brand	A brand name owned by the manufacturer of the product	Keebler, Hunts, Tide
• Regional brand	A manufacturer brand that is only distributed regionally	Maurice's Barbecue
• World brand	A manufacturer brand that is distributed globally	Coca-Cola
• Private distributor or store brand	A brand name used for products sold by a certain retailer or other distributor	Sears: Craftsman Revco
• Private nonstore brand	A brand that is owned by a distributor but sold in a number of different retail outlets	President's Choice
• Family brand	A brand that is used with a number of different product items and/or different product lines	General Electric, Johnson & Johnson, Oldsmobile
• Individual brand	A brand used for one product only	Tide

Table 10.1
Different Branding Strategies

Individual Brands versus Family Brands

Sometimes a product strategy dictates that a separate brand be used for each product item—*an individual brand strategy.* Individual brands, also called *subbrands,* are names and symbols applied to individual products for the purpose of communicating clearly and concisely what the consumer can expect from the product. In other cases multiple items are marketed under the same brand name—*a family or umbrella brand strategy.* The Pittsburgh-based H.J. Heinz Company, with over 3,000 products, uses both family and individual brands for its Weight Watchers product line. The Weight Watchers name is a **family brand,** which means it is shared by a line of individual brands. In this case the Weight Watchers brand establishes that the product bearing the name is a food for consumers who try to maintain a healthy diet and control their calorie intake. Under the Weight Watchers umbrella brand are different individual brands, including Smart Ones, Brick Oven Style pizza, Ultimate 200, Stir-Fry, Breakfast-on-the-Go, and Sweet Celebrations.[34]

Family brands make it much easier to introduce new products, especially when a firm has developed a high level of brand equity. Consumers know what to expect from any product carrying the family brand. The downside to this strategy is that if the consumer has negative associations with one member of the family, these can transfer to other members as well. Nestlé encountered this problem when consumer activists who opposed the company's practice of selling powdered baby formula in less developed countries (which often was mixed with contaminated water and resulted in illness) urged a boycott of *all* Nestlé products, whether they had anything to do with babies or not.

More and more companies are capitalizing on the power of well-known brand names by creating **brand extensions**—existing brand names applied to new product categories. For example, Reese's, the maker of Reese's Peanut Butter Cups candy, is now marketing a line of peanut butter. Grey Poupon, a product of the Nabisco Foods Group, has added salad dressings to its traditional mustard offerings. Bull's-Eye steak sauce is a brand extension of the Bull's-Eye barbecue sauce.[35]

Power and Niche Brands

Power brands are the leading brands in their product categories. Brands that dominate their markets may exceed their nearest competitor's profits by 50 percent or more.[36] According to an international survey of brand power in Japan, Europe, and the United States, the following brands are the most powerful in the world: Coca-Cola, IBM, Sony, Porsche, McDonald's, Disney, Honda, Toyota, Seiko, and BMW.[37]

family brand: a brand that is shared by a group of individual products or individual brands

brand extensions: new products that are marketed with the brand name of existing products, often in a different product category

power brand: the dominant brand in a product category

Marketers like to transform family brands into power brands. When successful, the power brand not only enhances the image of individual products, but also greatly improves the success of new product introductions. Many experts are surprised, for example, that the Coke and Pepsi power brands are rarely used to introduce new products. By contrast, Sony's line of consumer electronics shows the success of individual products that are linked to a power brand.

Niche brands are brands that successfully compete (at least in a small way) with power brands by appealing to a narrow segment of the market. Niche brands are successful because they provide customized benefits that uniquely satisfy consumers in a way that can't be matched by a power brand. Of course sales are lower for niche brands, but profits can be far higher. For example, Tom's of Maine markets a line of personal care products to consumers who desire all-natural ingredients, including mouthwash, dental floss, and toothpaste. The company will never sell as much toothpaste as its huge competitors such as Crest and Colgate, but it continues to meet the needs of a small and loyal contingent.[38]

National and Store Brands

As we will see in Chapter 14, retailers today often are in the driver's seat when it comes to deciding what brands will be sold in their stores. In addition to choosing among the brands owned and sold by various producers, called **national or manufacturer brands,** retailers decide whether or not to offer their own version. **Store brands,** also called **private-label brands,** are the retail store's or chain's exclusive trade name. The A&P grocery chain, for example, prominently displays its own Ann Page products next to those of national brands. Wal-Mart sells Sam's cookies inside the store and has a Sam's Cola vending machine right outside the store entrance.

Store brands are attractive to retailers for two reasons. First, they generally have a higher margin—that is, the store can make a larger profit. Higher margins and higher profits are possible because the brands are not advertised or promoted as heavily as national brands. By avoiding such costs retailers can offer consumers a very attractive price yet still make more money per unit than they make on a national brand. One company that has been extremely successful manufacturing private-label brands is Cott Corporation, which makes dozens of store-brand sodas that strongly compete with Coca-Cola and PepsiCo products. Wal-Mart alone sells over one billion cans of soft drinks made by Cott. Though Cott and other small bottlers have been dismissed as " . . . parasites . . . a tiny bug waiting to be crushed" by Coca-Cola's president, many other industry players take them quite seriously.[39]

A second reason for choosing to offer a store brand concerns the image that the retailer wants to convey to consumers. Ann Taylor is a nationwide chain of over 200 stores selling fashionable clothing for professional women. Ann Taylor stores carry their own line of clothing at a more attractive price than the competition. In addition, all of the items in the line are designed to be sold in the Ann Taylor stores to Ann Taylor customers, thus maintaining a consistent product image.[40]

Private-label brands had 19.7 percent of market share in supermarkets in 1993, 8.6 percent in drugstores, and 9.1 percent for mass merchandisers. Some product categories are heavily dominated by private labels; for example, about 63 percent of beer and ale products sold in supermarkets are private brands, as are 35 percent of ice cream purchases.[41] Private labels are even more successful in the United Kingdom than in the United States. In the U.K. they tend to dominate the grocery store shelves and are highly profitable for retailers, who post profit margins eight times as high as their U.S. counterparts. Private labels make up about 36 percent of grocery store sales in the U.K.[42]

Licensing

Another way that new products are developed using existing brands is through **licensing.** Typically a licensing agreement means that one firm sells another firm the right to use a brand name for a specific purpose and for a specific period of time.

Sometimes licensing agreements are between two producers of similar products. For example, Jack Daniels, the company that makes the famous bourbon, has licensed its name to Romanoff International for producing Jack Daniels bourbon-flavored mustard. Much more well known, however, are licensing agreements between the sports and enter-

niche brands: small brands that successfully compete with power brands by appealing to a narrow segment of the market

national or manufacturer brands: brands that are owned by the manufacturer of the product

store or private-label brands: brands that are owned and sold by a certain retailer or distributor

licensing: agreement in which one firm sells another firm the right to use a brand name for a specific purpose and for a specific period of time

tainment industries and manufacturers of products. The blockbuster movie *Jurassic Park* made news for the number of different products marketed with licensing agreements from the moviemaker. As the movie was shown on the screen, the stores filled with Jurassic Park candy, Jurassic Park key chains, Jurassic Park miniature figures, Jurassic Park clothing, and so on. A year later the shelves of the same stores were filled with *Lion King*, toys and backpacks. In 1995 the most popular licensing agreements were for Walt Disney's *Pocahantas*.

Co-Branding

Skippy peanut butter turns up in Delicious cookies. Oreo Cookies are in Pillsbury Cookie mixes, and M&M's candies are in Keebler cookies. Strange marriages? These are examples of **co-branding.** Co-branding, which has been called one of the "preeminent marketing strategies of the early and mid-'90s," means that two brands form a partnership in marketing a new product.[43]

Co-branding has grown at an annual rate of about 40 percent a year. The credit card industry led the way in pioneering this strategy by teaming up with other companies to offer cards that provide discounts on products and services. One example is the GM Card created by a deal between General Motors and Household Bank. Customers can receive earnings of 5 percent of purchases charged to their GM Visa card up to a maximum of $1,000.00 per year; earnings can then be applied against the purchase of a GM vehicle. Co-branding accounted for over $\frac{1}{3}$ of the nearly $5 billion in credit card volume in 1993.[44] Primarily due to co-branding, MasterCard added 8.6 million cards in 1992 compared to only 2.7 million the previous year.[45]

Co-branding ideally benefits both partners. First, the two brands together can enjoy greater recognition power than either would experience alone. In a time when new products must rigorously vie for retail shelf space, such power may be essential. Additionally, co-brand partners can split the cost of advertising and trade promotions. Co-branding makes sense for a brand when the perceived value of the two brands together will be greater than either single brand sold alone.

co-branding: an agreement between two brands to work together in marketing a new product

CREATING PRODUCT IDENTITY: PACKAGING AND LABELING DECISIONS

How do you know if the soda you are drinking is a "regular" or a "caffeine free"? How do you keep your low-fat grated cheese fresh after you have used a little of it? Why do you always leave your bottle of Elizabeth Taylor's White Diamonds perfume out on your dresser so everyone can see it? How can you tell which chocolate chip cookie is more fattening (and tastes better too)? The answer to all these questions is effective packaging and labeling. These decisions play several different but important functions. In this section we will talk about the strategic functions of packaging and some of the legal issues regarding package labeling.

FUNCTIONS OF PACKAGING

A **package** is the covering or container for a product. While the most obvious function of a package is that it contains the product, a package can (and should) do far more—otherwise everything we buy would simply come in a plain brown wrapper! Let's review the diverse roles a package plays in product management.

package: the covering or container for a product that protects the product, facilitates product use and storage, and supplies important marketing communication

Containment and Protection

Packaging plays an important protective role. For example, packaging for computers, televisions, and stereos protects the units from damage during shipping, storage, and life "on the shelf" prior to purchase. Cereal, potato chips, or packs of grated cheese would not be very tasty if packaging did not provide protection from moisture, dust, odors, and insects.

Use and Storage

Another function of effective packaging is that it allows for easy and efficient use and storage of the product. One example of creative customer-oriented packaging is Hungry Jack Microwave Ready pancake syrup. The product comes in a short, fat jug that fits into the microwave, has a handle that stays cool, a special closure that automatically releases steam, and a label that says "hot" when the syrup is ready to serve.[46]

Communications

Over and above these utilitarian functions, the package plays an important role in marketing *communication*. Effective product packaging uses colors, words, shapes, designs, pictures, even packaging materials, to provide brand and name identification for the product. Well-designed packaging communicates product benefits in a clear and memorable way.

Packaging has become an even more important means of communication in recent years for several reasons. First, television and other advertising media are losing their effectiveness as we continue to be bombarded by more and more messages competing for our limited attention. Second, consumers have less time to shop and gather information about products, so they rely more heavily on the package to provide what they need to know. A recent study showed that consumers spend an average of twenty minutes in the store per visit and look at about twenty products *per second* during that time. This makes the retail shelf the best "mass medium" available for marketers at a reasonable cost. Because in many cases the container serves as a "salesperson" for the product, having a package that catches the consumer's eye is a vital concern. For example, Snapple has facilitated brand recognition by selling its juices in uniquely shaped bottles.[47] The company claims that its distinctive package has been at least partly responsible for boosting sales nearly 50 percent in the first six months after it was introduced.[48]

A second factor that has made packaging an important communications tool is the huge increase in brand extensions that have saturated the market. *Family packaging* means that the same basic package design is used for all products within a family brand. Using family packaging allows the packaging to transfer brand equity to the extension product. Whether the new product is a low-fat cheese, a low-fat entrée, or low-fat mint chocolate chip ice cream, Healthy Choice has accompanied its family branding strategy with family package design. The now-familiar green package with the black Healthy Choice logo is easily recognizable in the dairy case or the frozen food case—anywhere new brand extensions need to be. It's just as easy to recognize that SnackWell's cookies and crackers have been joined by SnackWell's chips and other snack foods.

In addition to communicating a product's identification and benefits, packaging provides specific information consumers want and need. Typically packaging includes information about the specific variety, flavor or fragrance, directions for use of the product, suggestions for alternative uses (for example, new recipes), warnings about hazards with using the product, and product ingredients. Often packaging will also include information about the product warranty and give a toll-free telephone number for consumers to make comments or voice complaints to the manufacturer.

A final communication element on packaging is the *universal product code (UPC)*— that set of bars or lines printed on the side or bottom of most items sold in grocery stores and other mass merchandising outlets. While the UPC code may not tell the consumer anything about the product, it is an essential means of communication for the seller of the product. The UPC is a national system of product identification. Each product has a unique ten-digit number assigned to it. At check-out counters electronic scanners can read the UPC—the set of bars—on the label and automatically transmit the product code to a computer that controls the sales register. At the same time the information about the sale is fed into main store data files where it automatically updates inventory records. Retailers can also use the information gathered in this way to evaluate the effectiveness of advertising and promotion, to make shelf-space allocation decisions, and to develop pricing policies.

PACKAGING DECISIONS

Planning effective packaging means making many small decisions that add up to create the total package. To devise an effective and eye-catching package, marketers need to decide on the set of objectives they hope to accomplish. Then other specific decisions must be made about the material to be used, the color, the basic design, the exact information to be included, and so on.

Packaging Objectives

While all of the functions of packaging we discussed are important, decision making often requires that compromises be made. The package that would be least expensive may not provide adequate protection. The package that is the easiest to use may be almost impossible to store. And the package that is designed to communicate the brand image may increase the cost of the product beyond what is reasonable.

In addition to general communications, storage, and usage objectives, marketers often have other goals in mind in designing a packaging strategy:

- to create awareness of the product at the point of purchase
- to communicate product attributes
- to generate product trial
- to communicate promotional information

The Kiwi brand of shoe polish illustrates how packaging performs different functions, even for a humble, infrequently purchased product. Made by Sara Lee, Kiwi has a 90 percent share of the consumer shoe-polish market in the United States and is sold in over 130 countries.[49] The Kiwi package is a metal can $2\frac{3}{4}$ inches in diameter and $\frac{3}{4}$ inch deep that *contains* the paste wax and its chemical odor and *protects* the wax from contamination. To help consumers locate the right color wax, each can is colored to suggest the color of the paste wax inside. The circumference, top, and bottom have red and white Kiwi lettering; the top pictures the brand symbol, the Kiwi bird. Directions on the can's bottom explain how to give shoes a high shine and *promote* an alternative use, staining unfinished furniture or polishing finished furniture. The universal product code on the side enables retailers to retrieve a computerized price. For some customers, the Kiwi can has an afterlife storing small household items. Retailers like the can because it works well in a wide variety of display racks.

Package Design

Once the packaging objectives have been formulated, the next step is the actual design of the package. Specially trained designers create both the functional and the aesthetic elements of the package. Functional design often focuses on consumer convenience. Should the package have a zip-lock closing, an easy-to-pour spout, be compact for easy storage, be short and fat so it won't fall over or tall and skinny so it won't take up much shelf or refrigerator space?

Even functional decisions are not always so simple. Planners must also consider the packaging of other brands in the same product category. Take, for example, dry cereal. Traditionally all cereal has been packaged in tall rectangular boxes. What happens if one manufacturer suddenly starts packaging its cereal in a reclosable plastic jug? How about a square reclosable carton like that used for orange juice? Even if a new design is easier to use, consumers may not be willing to accept such a radical change. There may also be serious resistance to new package shapes by retailers who would have to adjust their shelf space allocations.

The choice of packaging material also has both functional and aesthetic aspects. The image of a fine liqueur may be enhanced by enclosing it in a velvet or silk bag. The image of masculinity is often evoked when wood is used as the packaging material. Shiny gold or silver packaging transmits an image of quality and opulence. Good packaging is made not only for storing and using the product but to facilitate disposal after the contents have been used up. Evian natural mineral water comes in a collapsible 1.5-liter bottle made of recycled plastic for this reason.[50]

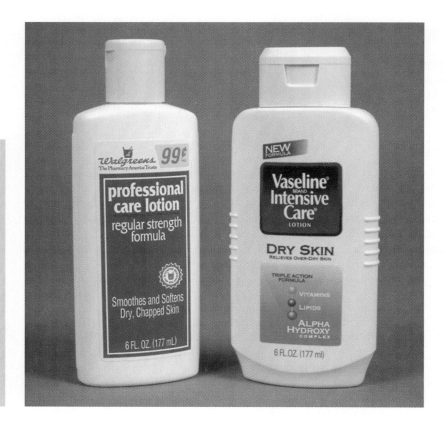

Of course, in deciding about the physical materials to be used in packaging, marketers must consider cost as well as the communications impact. A wood package will cost more than paper, and glass is more expensive than plastic. In recent years the cost of all package materials has escalated dramatically. The cost of paper, in particular, has seen enormous increases in just the past three or four years.

Firms seeking to act in a socially responsible manner also consider the environmental impact of packaging. Increasingly firms are developing innovative *green packaging*— packaging that is less harmful to the environment. For example, refills for a number of products used in spray bottles are being sold in plastic pouches, which contain far less plastic and take up less space in landfills. Products such as laundry detergent and fabric softener are coming in concentrated forms so that smaller packages are required. Manufacturers of televisions, stereos, and telephones have found that they can protect their products just as well with cleverly designed cardboard inserts as they can with less environmentally friendly plastic foam.

The visual impact that the package will have is also the result of design decisions. What color should be used? White to communicate purity? Yellow because it reminds people of lemon freshness? Brown because the flavor is chocolate? Purple because the desire is to create an exciting, luxurious brand image?

What about the shape of the package? Square? Round? Triangular? In the shape of an hourglass? Like an old-fashioned apothecary jar so it can be reused as an attractive storage container?

And finally, what verbal and visual information should be included? Should there be a picture of the product on the package—should cans of green beans always have a picture of green beans on the front? A picture of the results of using the product—such as beautiful hair? A picture of the product in use—perhaps a box of crackers shows the crackers with delicious-looking toppings arranged artistically on a fine silver tray. Should there be a recipe on the back? Should a coupon be included? Information about a sweepstakes?

LABELING REGULATIONS

Package communications or labeling is controlled in the United States by the Federal Fair Packaging and Labeling Act of 1966. This law aims at making labels more helpful to

ℛEAL PEOPLE, REAL CHOICES:

HOW IT WORKED OUT AT INTEL

Intel chose option 1: The company developed its "Intel Inside" logo that can now be seen on computers everywhere. Computer manufacturers found that this co-branding option enhanced the value of their brands, because many people had positive associations with the Intel name. In a three-year period more than $1 billion worth of advertising carried the "Intel Inside" logo. The brand is now very widely recognized, and company research shows that it is as well known as the Windows name in the computer industry—not bad for an obscure ingredient!

consumers by providing more useful information. The requirements of the Nutrition Labeling and Education Act of 1990 have forced food marketers to make sweeping changes in how they label products. By August 18, 1994, most foods sold in the United States were required by the FDA to have new food labels telling how much fat, saturated fat, cholesterol, calories, carbohydrates, protein, and vitamins are in each serving of the product as well as percentages of the "daily value" so that consumers can determine if the amount is high or low. The labels must also contain standardized serving sizes so that different brands can be compared (without a calculator); each brand of peanuts or peanut butter or salad dressing must use the same size serving when reporting calories and fat grams. New regulations also require marketers to comply with stricter rules in describing their products. Juice makers, for example, now are required to state how much of their product is real juice rather than sugar and water.[51]

Marketers must also make sure that labeling provides accurate information for consumers. New Balance Athletic Shoe Inc. and Hyde Athletic Industries (maker of Saucony shoes) have been successful making athletic shoes in the United States. But in 1994 the FTC said that the claims of "Made in the USA" were deceptive because components are imported and only the sewing and gluing of the shoes is done in the United States. Other companies with questionable labeling are Converse, Inc., whose All-Stars are constructed from uppers made in Mexico; Dell Computer, which assembles computers in Texas from components made in Asia; and General Motors, which advertises that the Camaro is "from the country that brought you rock and roll" when in fact the cars are built in Quebec, Canada.[52]

Chapter 10 Summary

Objective 1. Explain some of the different product strategies a firm may choose.

Product objectives support a firm's broader marketing objectives and, ideally, focus on customer needs. Objectives for individual products may be related to introducing the product, rejuvenating an existing product, or harvesting a declining product. Other strategies focus on entire product lines, different product items that satisfy the same customer need. Thus marketers may select a full-line or a limited-line strategy. Marketers may determine that the best strategy is to extend the product line with an upward stretch, a downward stretch, or a two-way stretch. Sometimes firms may seek either to fill out a product line or to contract a line. In other cases objectives relate to a firm's product mix—all of the products offered by the firm. Product mix objectives may be concerned with the breadth or consistency of the mix, the length or total number of different items in the mix, or the depth (the number of different versions of each product) of the mix. Product objectives often address product quality or the product's ability to satisfy customers. Product quality is tied to customer expectations of product performance and can mean durability, reliability, degree of precision, ease of use and repair, safety, or degree of aesthetic pleasure. Product quality objectives are likely to focus on the level and the consistency of product quality.

Objective 2. Describe some of the typical ways organizations are structured for new and existing product management.

One way that firms manage existing products is with individual brand managers who supervise all the marketing activities for a single brand. Other firms may include product category managers to coordinate the activities of individual brands. Sometimes firms feel that it is best to focus on specific customer groups and structure product management with a number of market managers. New products are sometimes both created and managed by entrepreneurs. In large firms new product managers can develop marketing for the many different new products the firm develops, or new products can be managed by venture teams, groups of specialists from different areas who work together for a single new product. Finally, new product development may be the result of partnering, in which two (or more) different companies form an alliance and work together to create a new product.

Objective 3. Describe how firms go about developing new products.

New product development typically includes a visionary phase and a planning and development phase followed by testing and improvement. In the visionary phase new product ideas can be generated by identifying customer needs, by recognizing product benefits that will be needed in the future, or by determining how existing products can be improved. Product screening assesses the potential success of new product concepts. Through a business analysis, demand and costs are estimated. Planning and development often involves prospective customers and includes creating a marketing plan. Obtaining a patent is often an important part of technical development. The effectiveness of the new product may be assessed in an actual or a simulated test market. Finally the product is launched and the entire marketing plan is implemented.

Objective 4. Explain how products are managed throughout their life cycle.

Managing an existing product requires understanding its status in the PLC. In the introductory stage the goal is to get customers to try the product. During growth, firms focus on establishing brand loyalty and can make product improvements. In maturity, significant product modification can occur, and new users can be attracted with market differentiation strategies. During the decline stage firms must decide whether to keep the product or to phase it out.

Objective 5. Discuss how branding creates product identity, and describe different types of branding strategies.

A brand is a name, logo, trade character, or some other recognizable element that is used to identify or position a product or to convey product attributes. A brand should be selected that has a positive connotation, is memorable, reproducible, and recognizable, and can be legally protected. Brand *names* need to be *easy* to say, spell, read, and remember and should *fit* the target market, the product's benefits, the customer's culture, and legal requirements. To protect a product legally, the brand name or symbol or other distinctive aspects can receive legal trademark protection. Brands are important because they help to develop and maintain customer loyalty and create value or brand equity. Firms may develop individual brand strategies or market multiple items with a family or umbrella brand strategy. Well-known brand names are often used with new product categories to create brand extensions.

Brands that are the leaders in their product categories are called power brands. Niche brands are very small brands that compete successfully in a small way by appealing to a narrow market segment. National or manufacturer brands are owned and sold by producers. Private-label or store brands carry the retail or chain store's trade name. Store brands offer the retailer higher profit margins, provide lower cost to the consumers, and convey the desired store image to customers. In licensing agreements a firm sells another firm the right to use a brand name with another product. In co-branding strategies two brands form a partnership in marketing a new product that combines the value of both existing brands.

Objective 6. Explain the important part packaging and labeling play in developing effective product strategies.

A package is the covering or container for a product and serves to protect a product and allow for easy use and storage. In addition, the colors, words, shapes, designs, pictures, and materials used in package design communicate a product's identity, benefits, and other important product information. Package designers must consider cost, product protection, and communication in creating a package that is functional, aesthetically pleasing, and not harmful to the environment—green packaging. Package labeling in the United States is controlled by a number of federal laws aimed at making package labels more helpful to consumers.

Review Questions

Marketing Concepts: Testing Your Knowledge

1. List and explain some of the typical objectives for individual product strategies.
2. Explain what is meant by a full-line strategy and a limited-line strategy. How might a firm stretch or expand its product line?
3. What is a product mix? Explain what is meant by the breadth, depth, length, and consistency of a product mix.
4. Why is quality such an important product strategy objective? What are the important dimensions of product quality?
5. Describe some of the different ways firms organize the marketing function to manage existing products. What are the ways firms organize for the development of new products?
6. Describe the three phases of new product development.
7. What are the benefits of branding a product? What are the characteristics of a good brand name?
8. How do firms legally protect their brands?
9. List and explain the different branding strategies.
10. What are the functions of packaging?
11. What are the important elements of effective package planning?
12. What should marketers know about package labeling?

Marketing Concepts: Discussing Choices and Issues

1. Quality is an important product objective, but quality can mean different things for different products—durability, precision, aesthetic appeal, and so on. What does quality mean for the following products?
   a. automobile
   b. pizza
   c. running shoes
   d. hair dryer
   e. deodorant
   f. college education
2. Many times firms take advantage of a popular well-known brand by developing brand extensions because they know that the quality reputation or brand equity of the original or parent brand will be transferred to the new product. But the transfer can go the other way. If a new product is of poor quality, it can damage the reputation of the parent brand, while a new product of superior quality can enhance the parent brand reputation. What are some examples of brand extensions that have damaged and that have enhanced the parent brand equity?
3. Sometimes marketers seem to stick with the same old packaging ideas year after year, regardless of whether they are the best possible design. Following are a list of products. For each one discuss what, if any, problems you have with the package. Then think of ways the package could be improved. Why do you think marketers don't change the old packaging? What would be the results if they adopted your package ideas?
   a. dry cereal
   b. laundry detergent
   c. frozen orange juice
   d. a gallon of milk
   e. potato chips
   f. a loaf of bread
4. Maintaining a profitable monopoly through patents can also pose an ethical problem. Burroughs Wellcome chose to defend its patented monopoly on AZT, an important AIDS treatment. The firm's monopolistic pricing forced patients to pay as much as $2,500 per year for treatments. Generic-drug makers offered to sell AZT at a much lower price if they could license the drug.[53] Does Burroughs Wellcome have a moral responsibility to society to offer the drug at a lower, though profitable, price?

Marketing Practice: Applying What You've Learned

1. You may think of your college or university as an organization that offers a line of different educational products. Assume that you have been hired as a marketing consultant by your university to examine and make recommendations for extending their product line. Develop alternatives that the university might consider for each of the following product strategies:
   a. an upward line stretch
   b. a downward line stretch
   c. a two-way stretch
   d. a filling-out strategy

   Describe how each might be accomplished. Evaluate each alternative.
2. Assume you are the vice president of marketing for a firm that markets a large number of specialty food items (such as gourmet sauces, marinades, and relishes).
   a. Your firm is interested in improving its marketing management structure. You are considering several alternatives: implementing a brand manager structure, having product line managers, or focusing on marketing managers. Outline the advantages and disadvantages of each type of organization. What is your recommendation?
   b. Your firm is also interested in aggressively pursuing the development of a number of new products. You have been asked to develop recommendations for organizing for this new product development. Prepare a report outlining your recommendations for organizing for new product development.
3. Assume you are working in the marketing department of a major manufacturer of athletic shoes. Your firm is introducing a new product, a line of disposable sports clothing. You wonder if it would be better to market the line of clothing with a new brand name or to use the family brand name that has already gained popularity with your existing products. Make a list of the advantages and disadvantages of each strategy. Develop your recommendation.
4. Assume you have been recently hired by Kellogg's, the cereal manufacturer. You have been asked to work on a plan for redesigning the packaging for Kellogg's cereals. In a role-playing situation, present the following report to your marketing superior:
   a. a discussion of the problems or complaints customers have with current packaging
   b. several different package alternatives
   c. your recommendations for changing packaging or for keeping the packaging the same.
5. Firms go to great lengths to develop new product ideas. One way that new ideas are generated is through brainstorming, where groups of individuals get together and try to think of

as many different, novel, creative, and hopefully profitable ideas for a new product as possible. With a group of other students, participate in brainstorming for new product ideas for one of the following (or some other product of your choice):

a. an exercise machine
b. computer software
c. a new type of university

Then, with your class, screen one or more of the ideas for possible further product development.

Marketing Mini-Project: Learning by Doing

In any supermarket in any town you will surely find examples of all of the different types of brands discussed in this chapter: individual brands, family brands, power brands, niche brands, national brands, store brands, and co-branded products. This mini-project is designed to give you a better understanding of branding as it exists in the marketplace.

1. Go to a typical supermarket in your community.
2. Select two product categories of interest to you: ice cream, cereal, laundry detergent, soup, paper products, and so on.
3. Make a list of the brands available in each product category. Identify what type of brand each is. Count the number of shelf facings (the number of product items at the front of each shelf) for each brand.
4. Arrange to talk with the store manager at a time that is convenient with him or her. Ask the manager to discuss
   a. how the store decides which brands to carry
   b. whether the store is more likely to carry a new brand that is an individual brand versus a family brand
   c. what causes a store to drop a brand
   d. the profitability of store brands versus national brands
   e. other aspects of branding that she/he sees as important from a retail perspective
5. Present a report to your class on what you learned about the brands in your two product categories.

Key Terms

Endnotes

1. Brent Schlender, "Why Andy Grove Can't Stop," *Fortune* (July 10, 1995): 88–98.
2. Cara S. Trager, "Goya Foods Tests Mainstream Market's Waters," *Advertising Age* (Feb. 9, 1987): S-20.
3. Eleena de Lisser, "Pepsi Puts Spotlight on New Packaging," *The Wall Street Journal* (222): B1.
4. Peter H. Farquhar, "Managing Brand Equity," *Journal of Advertising Research* (Aug./Sept. 1990): RC7–RC12.
5. Gary Hoover, Alta Campbell, and Patrick J. Spain, *Hoover's Handbook of American Business 1994* (Austin, Texas: The Reference Press, 1994).
6. T.L. Stanley, "How They Rate," *Brandweek* (April 3, 1995): 45–48.
7. Larry Armstrong, "Avoiding a Total Recall," *Business Week* (June 5, 1995): 37.
8. Pam Weisz, "Lever Plans P&G-Like Moves," *Brandweek* (Jan. 10, 1994): 1, 6.
9. Gary Hoover, Alta Campbell, and Patrick J. Spain, *Hoover's Handbook of American Business 1994* (Austin, Texas: The Reference Press, 1994).
10. Stephen Manes and Paul Andrews, "Gates," *PC/Computing* (Feb. 1993): 263–276.
11. Leslie Brokaw, "The Truth About Start-Ups," *Inc.* (March 1993): 56–68.
12. James B. Treece, "The Great Refrigerator Race," *Business Week* (July 15, 1993): 78–81; "Whirlpool Wins Prize of $30 Million to Build Efficient Refrigerator," *The Wall Street Journal*, (June 30, 1993): B8.
13. Zachary Schiller, "Frigidaire's Run for the Cold Cash," *Business Week* (July 15, 1993): 81.
14. Mark Landler, Bart Ziegler, and Ronald Grover, "Media," *Business Week* (May 10, 1993): 61.
15. "American Cyanamid and MedImmune Inc. Reach Pact on Drugs," *The Wall Street Journal* (July 16, 1993): B5.
16. Warren Midgett, "Jogging in a Jug," *Forbes* (July 19, 1993): 70–71.
17. Roman G. Hiebing and Scott W. Cooper, *Instructor's Manual, The Successful Marketing Plan* (Lincolnwood, Illinois: NTC Business Books, 1992).
18. Gary McWilliams, "A Notebook That Puts Users Ahead of Gimmicks," *Business Week* (Sept. 27, 1993): 92, 96.
19. James Dao, "From a Collector of Turkeys, A Tour of a Supermarket Zoo," *The New York Times* (Sept. 24, 1995): F12.
20. Jolie Solomon, Michael Meyer, Seema Nayyar, and John Schwartz, "A Risky Revolution," *Newsweek* (April 26, 1993): 44–45.
21. Steve Lohr, "Forget Peoria. It's Now: Will it Play in Tulsa?" *The New York Times* (June 1, 1992): D1.

22. "Test Marketing a New Product: When It's a Good Idea and How to Do It," *Profit Building Strategies For Business Owners* (March 1993): 14.

23. Toddi Gutner, "Chip Mania," *Forbes* (July 19, 1993): 197–198.

24. Gordon Wiltsie, "Fat Tire Frenzy," *Ski* (May/June 1993): 64–69.

25. Emily DeNitto, "Pepsi's Gamble Hits Freshness Dating Jackpot," *Advertising Age* (Sept. 19, 1994): 50.

26. Daniel Pedersen, "Here's to Your Future, Chum," *Newsweek* (April 12, 1993): 45.

27. John Bissell, "What's in a Brand Name? Nothing Inherent to Start," *Brandweek* (Feb. 7, 1994): 16.

28. Stuart Elliott, "Advertising," *The New York Times* (June 21, 1995): D9.

29. Gail Tom, Teresa Barnett, William Lew, and Jodean Selmonts, "Cueing the Consumer: The Role of Salient Cues in Consumer Perception," *Journal of Consumer Marketing* (1987): 23–27.

30. Diane Schneidman, "Use of 'Mc' in Front of Travel Firms' Names Leads to Lawsuits," *Marketing News* (Nov. 20, 1987): 17.

31. Maxine S. Lans, "Supreme Court to Rule on Colors as Trademarks," *Marketing News* (Jan. 2, 1995): 28.

32. Anna D. Wilde, "Harley Hopes to Add Hog's Roar to Its Menagerie of Trademarks," *The Wall Street Journal* (June 23, 1995): B1.

33. Douglas Lavin, "A Cloudy Issue: Will ATM Users Be Confused by a Car Called Cirrus?" *The Wall Street Journal* (Feb. 16, 1994): B1.

34. Julie Liesse, "Weight Watchers Looks to New Items to Spark Rebound," *Advertising Age* (Feb. 22, 1993): 36.

35. Julie Liesse, "Brand Extensions Take Center Stage," *Advertising Age* (March 8, 1993): 12.

36. Richard W. Stevenson, "The Brands With Billion-Dollar Names," *The New York Times* (Oct. 28, 1988): A1.

37. Laura Clark, "Porsche Top Auto Brand Name; Honda, Toyota, BMW Follow in U.S., Japan, and Europe Survey," *Automotive News* (Dec. 12, 1988): 62.

38. C.R. Hartmann, "Mass-Marketing Natural Toothpaste," *D&B Reports* (Sept./Oct. 1989): 58–59.

39. William C. Symonds and Paula Dwyer, "A Third Front in the Cola Wars," *Business Week* (Dec. 12, 1994): 66–68.

40. Susan Caminiti, "How to Win Back Customers," *Fortune* (June 14, 1993): 118.

41. Alison Brower, "Shoppers . . . by the Numbers," *Brandweek* (May 2, 1994): 56.

42. Elena DeLisser and Kevin Helliker, "Private Labels Reign in British Groceries," *The Wall Street Journal* (March 3, 1994): B1.

43. Betsy Spethmann and Karen Benezra, "Co-Branding or Be Damned," *Brandweek* (Nov. 21, 1994): 21–24.

44. Ibid.

45. Terry Lefton, "Co-Branding Redefines an Industry," *Superbrands* (Oct. 18, 1993): 80–81.

46. Wayne Simpson and Terry Lefton, "Seeing Double," *Brandweek* (Oct. 17, 1994): 31–36.

47. Terry Lefton, "Packaging All They Can Get Into What's On the Shelf," *Brandweek* (Oct. 3, 1994): 34–39.

48. Karen Benezra, "Coke Queries on Contour Can," *Brandweek* (Nov. 7, 1994): 4.

49. Milton Moskowitz, Robert Levering, and Michael Katz, *Everybody's Business/A Field Guide to the 400 Leading Companies in America* (New York: Doubleday, 1990).

50. "A Collapsible Bottle From Evian," *The New York Times* (Feb. 2, 1995): O3.

51. Laura Bird, "New Labels Will Tell Real Story on Juice Drinks," *The Wall Street Journal* (May 3, 1994): B1, B6.

52. Michael O'Neal, "Does New Balance Have an American Soul?" *Business Week* (Dec. 12, 1994): 86, 90.

53. Edward Felsenthal, "Wellcome Wins Patent Ruling in AZT Case," *The Wall Street Journal* (July 23, 1993): B1, B6.

MARKETING IN ACTION:
REAL PEOPLE AT FEROLITO, VULTAGGIA & SONS

Arizona—not the state but the brand of iced tea— has become a beverage success story, reaching $300 million in annual sales. This upstart drink product owes much of its success to its clever packaging, as we will see.

The company that markets Arizona brand beverages is New York-based Ferolito, Vultaggia & Sons. The founders of the company, John Ferolito and Don Vultaggia, both worked in New York, driving beer trucks and building a business as distributors.

Little about the company follows traditional operations. It has no advertising agency, does no formal product research, and pays no big fees to get retailers to stock its beverages. The two founders early on conducted their own unique type of marketing research. They leased a white limo and drove store owners around New York City asking them about their customers' buy-ing habits! The company founders brought this unique insight into consumers to their selection of the product's packaging.

Arizona tea first reached retailers' shelves in a twenty-ounce liquor-style bottle and a twenty-four-ounce can with graphics inspired by the American Southwest. Even Arizona competitors have raved about the packaging. According to one competitor (who went so far as to copy the sizes of the cans), the packaging is the "ultimate promotional item: It creates its own theme and purchase intent." In fact, many people feel that this brand is responsible for changing how the beverage industry (and other industries) looks at packaging.

So what about Arizona's packaging is so special? The market was immediately attracted to the unique colors of the Arizona tea can. Its pastel packaging tones caught consumers' eyes in the stores (though a graphic designer warned the company that the color scheme wouldn't work). Customers also found the size of the cans a selling point. Although retailers questioned the wisdom of the company's decision to sell twenty-four-ounce cans that could not be reclosed, people haven't hesitated to bring the product to the cash register. In fact, some consumers have crafted the larger cans into miniature sailboats and airplane models, which they've sent along to company headquarters.

When Ferolito, Vultaggia & Sons followed up their original success with the launch of Arizona Iced Tea packaged in a twenty-ounce liquor-style bottle, this product outdrew the original can. Why a bottle? In part the company had to respond to the shortage of available cans. It seems that the Stroh Brewery had cornered the supply of large cans for its own tea brand (which, by the way, died a quiet death).

By 1994 Arizona had reached third place in the ready-to-drink tea market, with a 12 percent market share, trailing only Lipton and Snapple. Some experts expect Arizona will end up a billion-dollar brand.

Ferolito and Vultaggia's original line of iced tea has since been joined by the Cowboy Cocktails line of juice-based drinks, lemonades, and a no-fat chocolate drink, and the company has extended its packaging strategy to these new products. The company is considering adding other products, including a 100-percent-fruit-juice line, bottled waters, vodka, and a dark cola that would compete with Coke & Pepsi.

The Arizona package is so popular that the design has been licensed to lollipops and freeze pops, and it appears on beach towels, shirts, and other products. Arizona's innovative marketing strategy has succeeded in putting its brand on the map in a hurry.

Source: Gerry Khermouch, "Grand Can Yen," *Brandweek* (Nov. 7, 1994): 23–29.

Things to Talk About

1. Arizona tea was developed by a pair of true entrepreneurs. Explain how they developed a product differently than a large corporation might have developed it.

2. Do you think the brand name for Arizona tea has helped it succeed? Why or why not?

3. How has the package for Arizona tea set it apart from its competitors? How would you rate the Arizona tea package on satisfying the use and storage function? The communications function?

4. What do you think are the objectives of the package design for Arizona tea?

5. What secrets to success have Ferolito and Vultaggia discovered?

CASE 10-2

MARKETING IN ACTION: REAL CHOICES AT PROCTER & GAMBLE

Aleve is one of Procter & Gamble's new products in the $2.7 billion category of analgesics—that is, pain relievers. Although Aleve is new to the consumer market, it has been a prescription drug for some time. This expensive new OTC (over-the-counter) product is giving P&G a bit of a headache: Aleve has not become the success that P&G wants it to be. P&G marketers must seriously consider whether the company's future includes Aleve.

Aleve was introduced into the marketplace with much fanfare by Procter & Gamble in 1994. First-year sales of the product topped $100 million, but marketing expenditures to introduce the medication exceeded this amount. Often, though, companies spend an amount equal to or in excess of first-year sales to gain a toehold in a crowded market.

Just weeks after being introduced in June 1994, Aleve had a 6.5 percent monthly share for the month of August, and in 1995 it was the fourth-ranked pain reliever with a 5.45 percent share. As good a start as Aleve had, however, its opening performance did not meet P&G's expectations, and the product's market share is not growing.

Historically, P&G has chosen not to stay in a product category unless it can be a leader—the company is simply not willing to be a minor player. For example, when Citrus Hill orange juice failed to gain more than a 10 percent share, P&G dumped the brand after ten years of attempting to invigorate sales. What will the company do with Aleve and its mere 5 percent market share? And P&G's market share may drop below 3 percent after its patent expires in January 1997 and other companies can market their own versions. Many firms would be happy with even a 3 percent share in such a huge market, but P&G would consider the product a failure.

Even with its patent intact, Aleve is fighting off fierce competition from existing competitive products and their heavy promotional efforts. One analyst suggests that the product category is saturated. There just aren't enough differences among Aleve, Tylenol, and other similar products. And more products continue to enter the market.

What does the future hold? Research suggests that P&G pushed sales up with a strong promotion only to find its customers moving to other products. Consumers simply don't remain with Aleve. Still, Aleve does have brand recognition, and it completes a portfolio of health-care products for P&G. If P&G does decide to keep Aleve, the company must come up with a new prescription for success.

Source: Michael Wilke, "Aleve Is No Pain Category Killer," *Advertising Age* (Oct. 23, 1995): 52.

Things to Think About

1. What is the problem facing Procter & Gamble in the analgesics category?
2. What factors are important in understanding this problem?
3. What alternatives might Procter & Gamble consider?
4. What are your recommendations for solving the problem?
5. What are some ways to implement your recommendations?

11

Broadening the Focus: The Marketing of Intangible Products

When you have completed your study of this chapter, you should be able to:

1. Describe the characteristics of services.

2. Explain how marketers create and evaluate service quality.

3. Explain marketing strategies for intangibles.

4. Explain the marketing of people and ideas.

5. Discuss some of the differences between the marketing mix for goods and for the marketing of intangibles.

REAL PEOPLE, REAL CHOICES:

MEET RICH MACKESY, LUTHERAN HEALTH SYSTEMS

Rich Mackesy is the vice president for strategic integration at Lutheran Health Systems (LHS), a large not-for-profit, nondenominational health-care organization based in Fargo, North Dakota. Lutheran Health Systems owns or operates over seventy nursing homes, hospitals, clinics, and home-care agencies in the midwestern and western United States. Mr. Mackesy's responsibilities include strategic planning and service development.

Rich Mackesy began his fourteen-year health-care career with a freestanding hospital in a New York City suburb at a time when marketing professionals were not common in the hospital industry. He also worked for a large multispecialty physician group practice in central Florida prior to joining LHS in 1990. He holds a B.A. from the State University of New York, an M.B.A. in marketing from The Ohio State University, and an M.H.A. (master's of health administration) from the University of Minnesota. Mr. Mackesy is also chairman of the Alliance for Healthcare Strategy and Marketing, the national professional organization for marketing and strategy professionals in the health-care industry.

THE MARKETING OF EXPERIENCES

What do a medical exam, an airplane ride, a Pearl Jam concert, a bank account, a stiffly pressed shirt, a college education, and a game-winning touchdown have in common? Each is a product that is produced and consumed. However, unlike a can of peas or a Porsche, these products are composed of experiences as well as physical goods.

True, each event requires one or more products, or *tangibles,* to deliver the experience (after all, you can't have a concert without instruments, a touchdown without a football, or a college education without textbooks such as this one!). However, these objects are secondary to the primary product that is being purchased, which is some act that produces knowledge, enjoyment, or satisfaction. While patients at the health-care facilities Rich Mackesy oversees use plenty of tangibles, from sophisticated laboratory equipment to bedpans, the real value of the benefits provided are intangible, such as a doctor's diagnostic skills or a nurse's bedside manner. All of the fancy medical equipment in the world is useless unless it is operated by people who deliver health care in a competent and sensitive fashion. Indeed, even though new breakthroughs in health care are reported in the press almost everyday, in a sense the health-care industry is the mature stage of the product life cycle—at least for routine medical problems. Many consumers don't see that many differences among competitors, or they are skeptical about what hospitals do and how much they cost; while others are fiercely loyal to one facility because their personal physician is affiliated there. Health-care marketers need to be good "operators" to succeed in this competitive environment.

This chapter will consider some of the challenges and opportunities facing marketers like Rich Mackesy whose primary offerings are *intangibles*—products that cannot be held in your hand, eaten, or driven. The marketer whose job is to build and sell a better football—a tangible—must deal with different issues than someone who must sell enough tickets to a football game—an intangible—to pack the stadium on Sunday, just as the manufacturer of surgical supplies is in a different boat than is the surgeon confronting a complex operation (and perhaps a scared patient).

WELCOME TO THE SERVICE ECONOMY

When you think about it, many of the "things" that are marketed are more likely to be intangible than tangible. Many of these intangible products, in fact, are services, which will be a central focus of this chapter. Before we get into the details of what a service is and how it can differ from a product, though, it's worth noting one important reason why you should be especially interested in learning about services: If you pursue a marketing career, it's very likely that, like Rich Mackesy, you will be employed in some aspect of services marketing! At the very least, you are an active consumer of intangibles, whether this involves a medical exam or going to the Lollapalooza Festival. That's why it's especially worthwhile to learn the importance of these activities.

Services have always been a significant part of consumers' lives, and they continue to gain in importance as the economies of industrialized nations evolve toward a services-oriented rather than a goods-oriented economy. Technological developments are making it more efficient for these countries to focus on the production and export of information and expertise, whereas less-developed economies that offer lower production costs concentrate on manufacturing and agriculture. Services contribute an average of more than 60 percent to the gross national product of all industrial nations.[1] The United States is the largest exporter of services, accounting for over 20 percent of total world exports. France is the second largest exporter (over 8 percent of total services), followed by the United Kingdom, Germany, and Japan.[2] Services currently generate 74 percent of the U.S. gross domestic product and account for 79 percent of all jobs. According to the Bureau of Labor Statistics, service occupations will be responsible for *all* net job growth through the year 2005.[3] Got your interest?

In this section we will first look at the growth of the services industry. Then we will examine the marketing concept in the marketing of intangibles such as health care and how marketing strategies apply to such industries.

SERVICES ARE WHERE THE ACTION IS

As the modern world continues to evolve, these changes bring with them an even greater need for service businesses. We need more and more professionals to help us navigate the decisions we need to make in the purchase of computers, communications, legal issues, and financial transactions. Social changes, such as the large numbers of working women and retired senior citizens, fuel demand for day-care services and nursing homes. As people have more leisure time and income, they are more interested in travel, education, and services that provide convenience, such as lawn care and even dog walking. New services constantly are springing up to address these needs: even playgrounds for grown-ups! This new entertainment concept has been made a reality at Block Party facilities, which are being tested by Blockbuster Entertainment. The centers includes video game arcades, virtual reality machines, and rooms filled waist-deep with plastic balls. No children are allowed unless accompanied by an adult.[4] Who knows what will be next?

By the year 2000 an estimated 88 percent of working Americans will be employed in the service sector, which includes such industries as banking, health care, insurance, transportation, and utilities.[5] Some of the largest American diversified service companies include American Telephone & Telegraph, Walt Disney, Marriott International, Hospital Corporation of America, and Time Warner.[6]

Do Services = McJobs?

The transition to a service economy is not all positive. Some people, especially those in their teens and twenties, are concerned that this change will eliminate attractive job opportunities, as workers are forced to take low-paying service jobs in the fast-food industry and elsewhere. The author Douglas Coupland, in his widely read book *Generation X*, refers to these as McJobs!

While these fears may be true to some extent, the service economy also creates many opportunities for young people. Of the total number of people employed in service industries, $\frac{1}{2}$ will be involved in the creation and selling of information, such as data processing and telecommunications.[7] And many students who choose marketing as a career will wind up working in such services-related areas as sports, financial services, and entertainment.

EXPANDING THE MARKETING CONCEPT

The marketing of a health-care organization like Lutheran Medical Systems illustrates the extent to which the marketing concept, which was originally applied almost exclusively to tangible industries such as soft drinks and cars, is now being embraced by a diverse array of other enterprises, from artists to attorneys.

Health-care practitioners are a good example of professionals who are beginning to adopt the marketing concept as competition for their services heats up, along with the costs of delivering quality care and maintaining a medical practice. For example, various medical groups that used to rely on doctors' recommendations have started advertising directly to consumers. The American Physical Therapy Association ran ads in such magazines as *Good Housekeeping, Ladies' Home Journal, Working Mother,* and *Essence.* The group was trying to target female baby boomers, whom they see as the primary health-care decision makers for both their children and their aging parents.[8] In addition to professional associations, individual health-care professionals are becoming more aggressive in setting marketing objectives and adopting the marketing concept. Table 11.1 illustrates how three different types of health-care practitioners can devise marketing strategies to improve their practices.

Competition for health-care services has made many health-care professionals realize that it is useful to adopt the same type of long-term strategic planning perspective that was outlined in Chapter 2. The following examples illustrate this strategic thinking:[9]

Table 11.1
Health-Care Marketing Strategies

	Psychologist	Orthodontist	Chiropractor
Marketing Objective	Add ten billable hours per week	Attract five new adult patients; increase awareness of practice in community to generate referrals	Increase new patients by 50% within one year
Target Markets	Inactive clients	Primary market: Women 25–55, middle income and above Secondary market: Male executives over 40	25–50-year-olds, 65% blue collar, 60% female within a four-mile radius of my office
Benefits Offered	Feel happy Solve problems	Beauty Professional self-confidence	Relief of back, neck, shoulder, head pain; convenience
Strategy	Write a letter to former patients; remind them that if they have learned the basics of turning their lives around, they may just need some short-term assistance now	Talk to 200 people in two days at a local health fair; Position myself as the community specialist in cosmetic dentistry	Change location to a new shopping center—locate between a supermarket and a fitness center that attracts a large female clientele. Give seminars at the health club and place articles in its newsletter

Source: Adapted from Alan L. Bernstein, *The Health Professional's Marketing Handbook* (Chicago: Year Book Medical Publishers, 1988).

- *Market penetration:* A hospital-based glaucoma clinic desires to get physicians and senior citizen groups to double referrals to get a bigger share of business in its current operating area.
- *Market development:* A family counseling agency opens a new branch in an adjoining county, providing the same services as in its main location.
- *Product development:* A referral service operated by a United Way agency increases its availability to twenty-four hours a day.
- *Diversification:* A Red Cross chapter adds training on the Heimlich maneuver (for freeing blocked tracheal passages) to its emergency training programs. The agency then markets these programs to employees of restaurants, who are required to know the procedure.

Health-care professionals are also learning to pay more attention to the quality of their interactions with their "customers." While many physicians used to display a superior, all-powerful attitude, many are now realizing that psychological factors play an important role in inspiring confidence, getting patients to comply with medical procedures, and increasing patient retention. They are learning to involve the patient by explaining the reasons for their diagnoses and demonstrating that they care about his or her individual welfare. Some recommendations to create better rapport with patients include keeping a social profile on every patient, looking him or her straight in the eye to build trust, and explaining the function of every diagnostic tool used. As even "hard-core" traditionalists like physicians begin to buy into the marketing concept, it's more and more likely that this way of thinking will influence your own career prospects. Let's see why.

DOES MARKETING "WORK" FOR INTANGIBLES?

Some producers of intangibles have been slower than others to accept the idea that what they do can or should be marketed. Many people who work in, say, health care or the arts resist the notion that the quality of what they produce and the demand for their services are affected by the same market forces driving the fortunes of paper products or canned peas.

Although there are indeed important differences in the *types* of marketing strategies that should be developed and implemented (it's not too cool to run a "Midnight Madness" sale for a root canal, a face-lift, or liposuction, or to use a fashion model to advertise a symphony orchestra), nonetheless many of the same basic strategic steps can be taken to ensure that the organization does the best job it can of meeting the needs of patients or patrons. Consider, for example, how the marketing director of a community theater company, dance troupe, or symphony might develop a comprehensive marketing plan, just as his or her counterparts do at firms like Procter & Gamble. Let's take a quick look at how some basic marketing concepts would apply in an arts context, and then focus more closely on differences between goods and services in terms of how these and other principles would be applied.[10]

Mission Statement

As we saw in Chapter 2, the organization should begin by developing a mission statement and setting organizational goals. These goals should be as concrete as possible, such as "increase the number of season ticket holders by 20 percent over the next two years."

Situation Analysis

The situation analysis should include an assessment of threats and opportunities. The arts marketer must remember that he or she is trying to win the consumer's discretionary dollar; the competition for this patronage includes not only other dance companies or theaters, but other forms of entertainment as well—everything from a Hootie and the Blowfish concert to a Tom Hanks movie to a pro wrestling match.

This analysis should also attempt to define the organization's current audience as precisely as possible. Some performing arts organizations survey attendees as they leave a show. Others insert a questionnaire in programs. One issue that is typically crucial is to describe the demographic differences between season ticket holders and other attendees.

The Arts Product Life-Cycle

Like goods, aesthetic products also have a life cycle, as was discussed in Chapter 9. The arts organization's goals must be developed in light of which part of the PLC it is currently in:

- *Introduction:* In this stage the company or art form is new to the community. The primary goal is to make people aware of its existence, so an initial promotional campaign is often called for.
- *Growth:* If the group gets a favorable response, it must then begin to develop loyalty among patrons. A major goal at this stage is to convert single-ticket buyers into season ticket holders.
- *Maturity:* At this stage audience levels have stabilized. The group should consider offering specially priced performances and developing new markets. Special attention must be paid to competitors, including other forms of entertainment such as sports teams or the local zoo. Sometimes product modifications can be attempted to differentiate the offer. For example, some operas now provide captioning to encourage attendance by people who get easily frustrated when they can't understand what the characters are singing about.
- *Decline:* If the organization is not meeting its objectives, it must consider withdrawing from the market. However, this action should only be taken after trying mature stage strategies!

WHAT IS A SERVICE?

Now that (hopefully) we've convinced you that marketing is just as important for an intangible service such as a dance company as it is for a company that sells ballet slippers, it's time to explore precisely what we mean by services. Services are acts, efforts, or performances that can't be handled or examined prior to purchase and that are exchanged from producer to user without ownership rights. A service is typically an act that accomplishes some goal, whether that is providing pleasure, information, convenience, or some other form of utility. Like other intangibles (which we'll discuss later in the chapter), a service is something that you can't hold on to or put in a pretty box. Nonetheless, like the air we breathe, services are everywhere and are a very important part of our lives.

THE NATURE OF THE SERVICE ACT

Because a service offering can take the form of a massage, a museum, or a mortgage, it seems that it would be very hard to lump different services together in any meaningful way. However, it is both possible and desirable to do so. Marketing managers who work in one specific service industry often can benefit by understanding the strategies that work and don't work in other businesses facing similar issues. Unfortunately, many service managers have spent their entire careers in one industry, such as hotels or airlines, so they assume that the challenges facing them are unique. However, by examining some of the underlying characteristics of services, we can identify areas of similarity that help us to understand and improve the quality of service that is delivered.

There are many ways to classify services, such as whether the service firm has a formal relationship with the consumer (for example, a college) or not (for example, a movie theater), whether the service is delivered on a continuous basis (such as insurance) or on separate occasions (such as auto repair), or whether the consumer goes to the firm to obtain the service (as with a barber) or the firm goes to the consumer (as in lawn care).

We know that a service usually consists of some task, activity, or deed. We can go further in understanding the nature of service acts by distinguishing between service acts that are directed toward people versus toward their possessions (the *orientation* of the service act). We can also identify differences in the *result,* or benefit, of the service act.[11]

Orientation of the Service Act

Services directed toward people include such activities as an aroma therapy massage, a limousine ride to a party, and a dental checkup. Such services usually require the customer to be present when the service is rendered. This means that the customer has to have direct contact with the people performing the service. Satisfaction will be affected by the service facility, the way in which the service is delivered, the types of interactions the person has with service providers, and even by the other people using the service. For example, the likelihood that you'll patronize a local bar or club will be influenced by such factors as the decor of the place, the type of music that is played, the friendliness of the staff, and whether or not the other people who go there are the types with whom you want to hang out.

Services directed toward possessions, on the other hand, often are performed in the customer's absence. You don't have to be present to get your stereo repaired, your new suit altered, or a new paint job on your classic 1965 Mustang. Issues such as location, convenience, and speed of delivery often are important. These types of services may be easier to evaluate and compare, especially if they result in the delivery of some finished good like a starched shirt or an attractive lawn. Because they are done *for* the person rather than *to* him or her, more objective features such as price and availability can be used to select one provider over another.

Result of the Service Act

By definition a service act is always intangible. However, the result of the act may or may not be something that leaves physical remains. Services often do provide such a "product trail," whether they are performed on people or on their possessions. A trip to the dentist for a painful root canal procedure makes this obvious! So in many cases services involve the maintenance or improvement of "products" we already own, whether these are pets, cars, shirts, or even our own teeth, hair, or manicured fingernails.

In other cases, though, the benefits of a service act are much harder to discern. The service may provide the person with an experience that he or she alone can evaluate. Education is such a service product, as is a play, a college football game, or even a ride on a scary roller coaster or a simulated walk through space in a virtual reality arcade. In addition to the fun stuff, many services are directed toward maintaining or adding to the value of a person's intangible possessions, whether building up (and hopefully not down) a stock portfolio, ensuring that a person will be worth something to his/her dependents in the event of death, or keeping a person out of jail if he or she is accused of a crime.

As we'll see a bit later, these types of services often are difficult to evaluate, and people are likely to rely heavily on supporting cues, such as the professional image projected by the service provider (would you want to be defended by an attorney wearing a cheap polyester suit?), the corporate image of the provider's firm, and well-known brand names and logos that breathe life into an abstract concept (for example, Prudential Insurance uses the Rock of Gibraltar to signify that its services are reliable and enduring).

CHARACTERISTICS OF SERVICES

Regardless of whether they affect ourselves or our possessions, or whether we can touch, see, or taste the results after they have been rendered, *all* services share four characteristics that make them distinct from physical products: intangibility, perishability, inseparability, and variability. Let's take a brief look at each dimension.

Intangibility

Service intangibility, as we have seen, means that customers can't see, touch, or smell good service. Unlike the purchase of goods, services cannot be inspected or handled before the purchase is made. Because you're basically marketing something that isn't there, this can be a problem. Consumers look for reassuring signs before purchasing—this means that marketers of intangibles have to go out of their way to provide these signals. That's why the appearance of the service provider and of the facility can make or break a service business. As we'll see later on, the need to make a service tangible creates numerous strategic possibilities, especially for a marketer who wants to set his or her particular service product apart from the competition.

Perishability

Service perishability means that services can't be stored—it's a case of use it or lose it. When tables go unfilled at a McDonald's restaurant and the drive-through window isn't busy, there will be no way to make up for the lost opportunity to exchange product for money. The burgers will keep (for a while, anyway), but the services of store workers won't. Perishability refers to more than food spoilage, though. Similar issues are encountered by dentists and doctors who are out of luck if a patient doesn't show up at the scheduled time, and by an airline that is forced to fly a half-empty plane across the country. Unlike canned goods or building supplies, time cannot be warehoused and reused at a later date!

Variability

Compared to mass-produced, standardized goods, service variability means that the same service activities are performed in different ways from one day to the next. Even the same service performed by the same provider for the same customer can vary from time to time. The excellent General Tso's chicken dish you ordered at your favorite Chinese restaurant last week may be only mediocre this week, and you'll never get *exactly* the same cut from your favorite hairstylist.

Several factors cause variability in service quality. It is difficult to standardize services because service situations, service providers, and customers all vary so much. Your experience in college classes is an example. A college can control situations to some degree; course catalogs, course content, and classrooms are fairly predictable. Professors, however, vary so much in their training, their life experiences, and their personalities that there is little hope of making teaching uniform (not that this would necessarily be very desirable in this case anyway). And students with different backgrounds and interests vary in their needs, so the lecture that one group finds fascinating might be slept through by another. Even the time of day in which the service is delivered can make a big difference—if you've ever had a class that runs from very late afternoon through dinnertime, you know just what we mean.

Inseparability

While a good can be manufactured way ahead of time and even sit on a shelf for years before it is sold and consumed, most services are produced, sold, and consumed at the same time. Both the customer and the service provider must be present at the same time for the service to be delivered; it's hard to take notes on a lecture when the professor doesn't show up! In some cases, of course, the service can be sold prior to being produced and consumed, as when one buys a hot ticket to the Lollapalooza concert months before actually attending the event. Still, the expertise, skill, and personality of a service provider, or the quality of a firm's facilities and equipment, cannot be detached from the offering itself. This inseparability makes the nature of the encounter between the service provider and the customer crucial—the most expertly cooked meal can be ruined by a surly or incompetent waiter.

Inseparability also means that the consumer often plays an active role in the production of the service, as when enthusiastic audience members sing along with a band at a concert. Indeed, many service businesses are looking for ways to encourage even more customer participation, because consumers can be a cheap source of labor![12] And although many people like the personal touch of being waited on, rising costs, time pressures, and the inferior quality of service they may actually receive have led many to welcome the chance to serve themselves, whether at salad bars, gas tanks, or bank machines. This trend has been termed *disintermediation* (translation: eliminating the middleman). In the United States, for example, about 80 percent of gasoline is pumped by drivers rather than by attendants.

THE GOODS/SERVICES CONTINUUM

Despite all this talk about tangibles versus intangibles, in reality it is often very difficult to point to a product and say for sure that it's definitely an intangible service versus a tangible good: Most products are actually a *combination* of goods and services. Everything we buy is either a good or a service or some combination of goods and services. So while we're in the process of defining what an intangible product is, we need to recognize that the distinction between goods and services is really a relative one—to what extent is the product characterized by tangible versus intangible properties? The purchase of a "pure good" like a Porsche still has service components, including the selection of a trained mechanic and the use of a comfortable customer lounge while waiting for the car to be tuned up. The purchase of a "pure service" like a makeover at a department store cosmetics counter still has product components, including the various lotions, powders, and lipsticks that were used by the cosmetologist to create the "new you."

Still, we can distinguish among products that are dominated by either goods or services. The service continuum shown in Figure 11.1 illustrates that some products are

**Figure 11.1
The Service Continuum**

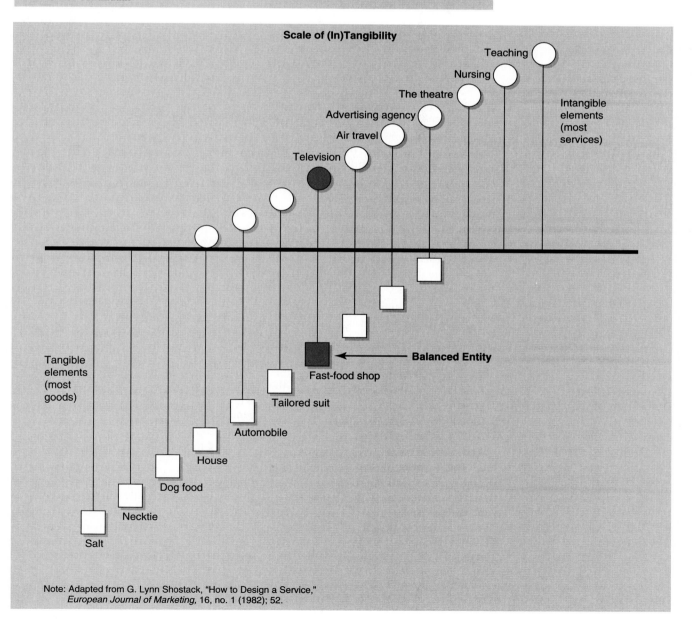

Scale of (In)Tangibility

Teaching

Nursing

The theatre

Advertising agency

Air travel

Television

Intangible elements (most services)

Balanced Entity

Fast-food shop

Tangible elements (most goods)

Tailored suit

Automobile

House

Dog food

Necktie

Salt

Note: Adapted from G. Lynn Shostack, "How to Design a Service," *European Journal of Marketing,* 16, no. 1 (1982); 52.

dominated by either tangible or intangible characteristics (such as salt versus teaching), while others tend to include a mixture of goods and services (for example, flying on an airplane). As the product approaches the tangible pole of this continuum, there is fairly little emphasis on service. The physical product itself is the focal point. As the product gets near the intangible pole, the physical product recedes in importance, and typically the person or people providing the service play a key role in shaping the service experience. Toward the middle of the continuum, however, both goods and services contribute substantially to the quality of the product. Very often this is because these products are facility-based—they rely on the ability of people to operate equipment and/or staff a store satisfactorily to deliver quality service. Let's consider each of these three positions as we move from products dominated by tangibles to those dominated by intangibles.

Product-Related Services

Many tangible products are accompanied by supporting services, even if this means only that the company maintains an 800 telephone line for questions or provides a thirty-day warranty if the product is defective. The strategy of including a service with the sale of a physical good is termed *embodying*.[13] This is becoming an increasingly popular option in industries such as computers, especially for companies that are trying to break into new international markets that are saturated by cheap products, but where customers have little guidance available for using them.

Just putting out a product without providing for adequate support can be deadly, as computer makers are starting to find out. As millions of people are buying their first computers, they are finding it difficult to navigate the maze of setup instructions and next to impossible to cope with machines that unexpectedly go down or crash. Indeed, a recent survey by *PC Magazine* found that 28 percent of its readers required technical support within the first year of using a personal computer—but in grading the service performance of manufacturers, about $\frac{2}{3}$ received Cs and Ds. The companies with the resources to provide superior service find that this support can be a potent marketing tool as they compete against "clone" manufacturers. As an executive at Compaq observed, "The bad guys give us an opportunity to differentiate."[14]

Equipment- or Facility-Based Services

As seen in Figure 11.1, some products require a mixture of tangible and intangible elements to work. Many of these, such as hospitals and restaurants, fall in the middle of the continuum because they need elaborate and expensive equipment or facilities to deliver a product. *Facility-driven services,* such as automatic car washes, amusement parks, museums, movie theaters, health clubs, tanning salons, and zoos, must be concerned with three important factors:[15]

- *Operational factors:* Technologies must be designed to move customers smoothly through the process. Clear signs and other guidelines must be provided to show customers how to use the service. In particular, efforts must be made to minimize waiting times, which are a major source of annoyance to customers. Marketers have developed a number of "tricks" to give impatient customers the illusion that they aren't waiting as long. Disney World bends lines around corners so people can't judge how long the wait is. One hotel chain, responding to complaints about the long wait for elevators, simply installed mirrors in the lobby: People's natural tendency to examine their appearance gave them something to do until the doors opened, and protests went down.[16]
- *Locational factors:* These are especially important for frequently purchased services such as dry cleaning or retail banking, that are made at a fixed location. Issues regarding store location are discussed at length in Chapter 15.
- *Environmental factors:* Facility-based services are the most likely to have a lot in common with other retailers. One trend, in fact, is for such services to adopt a more "retail-like" philosophy, as service managers realize they must create an attractive environment to lure customers to their facility. Banks, for example, are creating signature looks for their branches through the use of lighting, color, and graphics. Bank employees at Banc One Corporation in Columbus,

Ohio, even hold annual sidewalk sales, where they grill hot dogs and lure customers into the bank with specials on loans and credit cards.[17]

People-Based Services

At the intangible end of the continuum are people-based services, like the Great American Backrub store in Manhattan. To experience this service customers come in off the street, sit in a specially designed chair, and get a massage that lasts exactly $8\frac{1}{2}$ minutes for $7.95. The owner of the store explained, "To get Americans to buy massages I realized you had to solve three problems. You had to come up with something that was quick, inexpensive, and most important, you had to find a way to do it without asking people to take their clothes off." Some masseuses give as many as thirty back rubs a day to stressed-out executives and weary shoppers.[18]

The large majority of service settings, for better or worse, still require us to interact with people. The central role played by service employees in making or breaking a service reminds us of the importance of the **service encounter,** the interaction between the customer and the service provider.[19] Our interactions with service providers can range from the most superficial (for example, buying a movie ticket) to situations where we tell a stranger our most intimate secrets (for example, a psychiatrist or a bartender). And people are often literally part of the service offering we buy, whether this product is the skill of a haircutter, the training of a doctor, or the home furnishings taste of an interior decorator. As people have less and less time, interest, and/or capability to perform various tasks, the role of people-based services is increasing. About 60 percent of consumers hire an attorney to do their legal work, about half pay someone to repair their cars, appliances, and do their tax returns, about a quarter hire someone to mend their clothing, and over 10 percent hire a lawn service.[20]

service encounter: the actual interaction between the customer and the service provider

Exhibit 11.1
Bar associations are sensitive about flamboyant promotions that they feel belittle the image of lawyers. They are concerned about TV ads like the one for a Texas lawyer who is sitting at his desk when a car comes crashing through his ceiling. He reaches under the wreckage for a telephone and says, "Hurt in a car accident? Haven't got your check yet? Call me." This colorful attorney defends his ads this way: "People want to be entertained, whether it's selling lawyers or selling soap. God knows, lawyers are boring enough. If you make it so that all they can do is stand in front of a lot of books and say, 'I'm a lawyer, call me,' people will switch the channels as fast as they can."

Because many services are so labor-intensive (whether that labor involves giving a vaccination, painting nails, or commissioning an architect to design a new headquarters building for a company), consumers' images of a service business often depend on the person who actually delivers the service. An airline may invest millions of dollars in providing top-quality planes, devising efficient route systems, and training pilots, but a passenger's evaluation of the company may be ruined by one nasty encounter with a rude ticket clerk.

On the other hand some service businesses are experimenting with ways to turn "high contact" services into "low contact" ones by eliminating the need for customers to actually enter the "service factory." For example, many financial and travel services are transacted by mail, phone, or computer—the customer may have no idea what his or her travel agent or mortgage broker even looks like! Even some universities are reducing the need for students to come to class by offering courses on radio and television. In these situations the outcome of the service is still very important, but the customer may not be very interested in the process by which it is delivered. Still, in many cases it's the "personal touch" that distinguishes one service product from another—especially for services at the intangible end of the continuum.

This personal dimension is especially important for professionals such as physicians and attorneys who essentially *are* the service they sell. However, many professionals have been reluctant to think of their services in marketing terms. This perspective is often not considered dignified or ethical, and some professional groups have even prohibited members from advertising. For example, even though the Supreme Court ruled in 1977 that lawyers have a constitutional right to advertise their services, this practice remains controversial. Several states regulate the contents of legal advertising (Mississippi requires lawyers who tout their "juris doctor" degree to disclose that *all* lawyers have one).

DELIVERING AND EVALUATING QUALITY SERVICE

The Saturn Corporation is serious about its goal "to be the friendliest, best-liked car company in the U.S." The company has found that good service can turn lemons into lemonade. When some of its cars were recalled for faulty wiring, this potentially negative event instead became a publicity bonanza. Customers who were affected by the recall found that dealerships extended their hours to take care of the problem, provided door-to-door pickups, and provided free car washes, coffee, doughnuts, and soft drinks while repairs were being done. Many dealers even threw free barbecues and other festivities to turn an otherwise aggravating experience into a pleasurable one. Although these actions are not cheap, the company hopes the investment will pay off by creating fiercely loyal customers who receive better quality service than they expected.[21] But words are cheap: Everyone likes to *say* that they deliver quality service. Let's take a closer look at what we mean by quality in this context. In this section we'll consider some of the factors people look for when deciding if they've received good or shabby treatment at the hands of service providers.

JUDGING SERVICE QUALITY

Saturn's service strategy illustrates the *power of expectations*. Satisfaction or dissatisfaction is more than a reaction to the actual performance quality of a good or service. It is influenced by prior expectations regarding the level of quality.[22] When an offering is delivered the way we expected, we may not think much about it. If, on the other hand, it fails to live up to expectations, we will not be happy. And if performance like the goodwill displayed by Saturn happens to exceed our expectations, we are pleased and will probably continue to reward the company with our business. That's what Saturn is banking on.

Quality is Relative

Quality service implies that the customer is satisfied with the intangible product he or she pays for and feels that the exchange has been of value. However, satisfaction is relative; the service recipient compares the current experience to some prior set of expectations. That's what can make delivering quality service so tricky—what may seem like excellent service to one grateful person may be merely mediocre to someone else who's been "spoiled" by their past encounters. So it can be useful to identify what people's expectations are and then work hard to exceed them.

For example, the Marriott Corporation is working on improving aspects of its service where guests *expect* to have problems. Many people complain about the time spent checking in at a hotel, so Marriott launched a new program called "1st 10" that eliminates a trip to the front desk. Pertinent information, such as the guest's time of arrival and credit card number, is collected when the reservation is made. This reduces average check-in time to $1\frac{1}{2}$ minutes, which greatly exceeds most peoples' expectations.[23]

Customer expectations are usually communicated by word of mouth rather than by direct experience with the service, so they are not always realistic in the first place.[24] In some cases there is little service marketers can do to soothe ruffled feathers: Exaggerated customer expectations account for about $\frac{3}{4}$ of the complaints reported by service businesses! However, providing customers with logical explanations for service failures and compensating them in some way can still reduce dissatisfaction.[25]

Ironically, the employees who often have the biggest impact on service perceptions are among the lowest-ranking individuals in the company! This makes it extra important for management to engage in **internal marketing,** where employees at all levels are educated about the firm's offerings and persuaded that they are of high quality. If the service provider doesn't believe in what he or she is doing, this attitude will quickly be conveyed to the customer.

The Ritz-Carlton chain is legendary for anticipating guests' desires, and one reason is the extensive internal marketing the company does. As one industry expert observed, "They have figured out what guests want in a hotel, and they have learned how to exceed their expectations." New employees receive an intensive two-day orientation, 100 additional hours of training, plus a daily appearance inspection. In 1992 the chain became the first hotel to win the Malcolm Baldrige National Quality Award. To ensure that attentiveness to guests' needs remains at a peak, the company regularly surveys customers and even hires outside auditors to pose as guests.[26]

internal marketing: marketing activities aimed at employees in an effort to inform them about the firm's offerings and their high quality

Evaluative Dimensions

Because services are intangible, their quality is usually much harder to evaluate than in the case of goods, which can be seen, tasted, touched, or smelled. Because they are not produced until the time they are consumed, it is difficult to make a prepurchase evaluation of quality; most service businesses do not offer a free trial. Because services are variable it is hard to predict if one will get the same quality as last time. Because they're perishable you don't often have the luxury of taking a long time to make up your mind and do comparison shopping. Compared to goods, then, we can expect that the choice process for services is somewhat different, especially for services that are highly intangible, like those on the right end of the continuum in Figure 11.1.[27]

It's helpful for marketers to understand what criteria consumers are using to judge a service, especially when they discover that they are not stressing the right dimensions. For example, a service such as an airline is used by both personal and business travelers, but each group may not select an airline for the same reasons. United Airlines realized that because business travelers are more likely to make their travel plans on the spur of the moment, they are more likely than casual flyers to choose a carrier because of its schedule frequency. The carrier increased its market share of business travelers (a more lucrative segment, because business travelers are more likely to pay full fares!) by advertising its frequent flights, promoting this convenience as "Business One" service.[28] In general it's helpful to think about three dimensions that customers can use to choose among products:

- *Search qualities* refer to attributes that the consumer can examine prior to purchase. These include color, style, price, fit, smell, and texture. Not surprisingly, tangible products are the most likely to be evaluated according to these characteristics.

- *Experience qualities* refer to product characteristics that can only be determined during or after consumption. For example, we can't really predict how good a vacation we'll have until we have it, or whether our new haircut will make us want to hide in a dark room for a few weeks until the hair grows back.

- *Credence qualities* refer to attributes that are difficult to evaluate even *after* we've experienced them. This dimension is common to many service businesses. For example, most of us don't have the expertise to know if our car has *really* been repaired properly, or if our doctor has made a correct diagnosis.[29] These services are the most difficult to evaluate, and to a great extent we simply have to trust the service provider and pray for the best. Most professional services possess credence qualities. That is why tangible cues of professionalism, such as an appropriate appearance, diplomas, or an organized office are so critical to purchase satisfaction.

MEASURING SERVICE QUALITY

Because the customer's experience of a service is so crucial to determining whether he or she will continue to use it, service marketers feel that identifying and measuring the aspects of a great or a disastrous service experience is the "Holy Grail" for the services in-

---

SPOTLIGHT ON RELATIONSHIP MARKETING

Excellence at Southwest Airlines

While the airline industry is racking up billions in losses, an upstart company called Southwest Airlines is demonstrating the power of relationship marketing. As CEO Herbert Kelleher explains the airline's success, "We dignify the customer." At first blush it's hard to see how Southwest does this, because the carrier has no first-class section, serves no food other than peanuts, potato chips, and cookies, and does not transfer passengers' luggage to other airlines. What it does do is charge about ⅓ the price of its competitors for a ticket.

To reflect its emphasis on customer service, the company insists on capitalizing the word *Customer* in ads, brochures, and even its annual report. The airline, which specializes in short flights that can't be economically served by the big guys, also has an executive vice president whose only job is to oversee contacts with the public. CEO Kelleher claims, "The bigger we get, the smaller I want our employees to think and act."

By paying attention to the quality of the service encounter its passengers experience, Southwest makes up for its lack of "frills."

Frequent flyers get birthday cards from Southwest, and they can also interview people who are applying for flight attendant positions. When five medical students who flew weekly to an out-of-state school complained that their flight got them to class fifteen minutes late, Southwest moved up its departure time by—you guessed it—fifteen minutes. The 1,000 or so customers who write to the company every week get a personal response within four weeks. This effort demands more than 1,500 man-hours a week from forty-five employees, including the CEO. Southwest continues to involve its employees in its efforts to woo customers. One group of employee volunteers is working on games and quizzes to be used during flight delays, while another group is looking at humorous ways to present FAA safety demonstrations.*

---

* Richard S. Teitelbaum, "Where Service Flies Right," *Fortune* (Aug. 24, 1992): 115–116.

dustry. Indeed, it's been estimated that about $\frac{1}{3}$ of the business of marketing research firms is now devoted to measuring customer satisfaction *after* the sale.[30]

Consumer responses can be gathered in a variety of ways, using both qualitative and quantitative methods (see Chapter 5). For example, some companies hire "mystery shoppers" to check into hotels or fly on airlines and report on how they were treated (sometimes these shoppers work for a research firm, but some airlines reportedly recruit these "spies" from among their most frequent flyers). Other firms maintain ongoing customer panels who are periodically asked about their experiences, while a similar approach is to locate "lost customers"—identifying former patrons to find out what parts of the service turned them off to the company. Let's quickly review a couple of measurement techniques that can be used to provide some insights on service satisfaction.

Gap Analysis

Gap analysis is a measurement tool that focuses on the difference between a customer's expectation of service quality and what actually occurred. By identifying specific places in the service system where there is a wide gap between what is expected and what is received, service marketers can get a handle on what aspects of their service need improvement. This approach has been taken by many companies to pinpoint problems. Some major gaps include the following:[31]

- Management doesn't understand what the customer's expectations are: Service organizations tend to lag behind other firms in their use of marketing research that would help them to understand what customers are looking for (as discussed in Chapter 5). They are more likely to have an operations orientation, as exemplified by a bank that closes its branch lobbies in the middle of the day to balance transactions because that's more efficient, even though it's less convenient for customers.

- Management fails to establish a quality control program. Successful service firms, like American Express and McDonald's, tend to establish formal quality goals. American Express analyzed customer complaints and found that they were most likely to center around responsiveness, accuracy, and timeliness. The company established 180 specific goals to correct these problems, and developed a process to monitor how fast phones were being answered, bills were mailed, and so on.

- Employees do not deliver the service at the level specified by the company. Teamwork is crucial to service success. Merrill Lynch put over 2,500 of its operations personnel into quality teams of eight to fifteen employees each to identify ways that service delivery could be improved. Unfortunately, many companies do a poor job of specifying precisely what employees are expected and are not expected to do, which creates conflict and uncertainty.

- The firm makes exaggerated promises or does not accurately describe its service when it communicates with customers. When the Holiday Inn hotel chain developed an advertising campaign based on the promise that guests would receive "No Surprises," many operations personnel opposed the idea—they knew that *no* service organization, no matter how good, can anticipate every single thing that can go wrong. Sure enough, the campaign was unsuccessful.

gap analysis: a marketing research methodology that measures the difference between a customer's expectation of service quality and what actually occurred

The Critical Incident Technique

The **critical incident technique** is another way to approach the same problem.[32] By collecting and closely analyzing customer complaints, the service firm can identify *critical incidents,* specific face-to-face contacts between consumers and service providers that cause problems and lead to dissatisfaction. These incidents can generally be divided into two categories. The first type involves situations where customers' expectations cannot be met by the service organization. For example, the customer might make an unreasonable demand, such as this one of a flight attendant: "Come sit with me. I don't like to fly alone." In the second type of situation the firm is capable of meeting these expectations but fails to do so. For example, the customer might complain to a flight attendant, "My seat won't recline."[33]

critical incident technique: a method for measuring service quality in which customer complaints are used to identify *critical incidents,* specific face-to-face contacts between consumers and service providers that cause problems and lead to dissatisfaction

STRATEGIES FOR DEVELOPING AND MANAGING SERVICES

Because services differ from tangible goods in so many ways, decision makers who work in service businesses may find themselves grappling with an interesting problem: They're marketing something that isn't there! As a result some special touches may be required to develop and fine-tune marketing strategy for a service. In this section we'll review some of these issues and suggest ways that marketers can deal with the unique challenges posed by intangible products.

CORE AND AUGMENTED SERVICES

Recall that when we buy a product, whether tangible or intangible, we are actually buying a benefit. In the case of a physical good this benefit may be whiter teeth or efficient computer power. As we've seen, many services provide a benefit that's harder to identify and evaluate, such as reduction in lower back pain after treatment, or improved performance from one's employees after hiring a management consulting firm. This basic reason for purchasing an intangible product is the **core service.** The core service is usually a benefit that is obtained as a result of having a deed performed. For example, H&R Block stresses the peace of mind that results from having one of its tax preparers take charge of your tax return.[34]

Just to make the life of a services marketer a bit more complicated, though, we must note that not only do most services involve the use and purchase of goods, they also typically entail the provision of more than one service! These other activities that support the core service or enhance its value are called **augmented services.** Because in many cases the core service offered by competitors is basically the same, a common strategic option is to provide competitive advantage by creating one or more augmented services unique to a company's service product.

To understand the distinction between core and augmented services, think about the core service you are buying when you purchase an airline ticket: Safe transportation from Point A to Point B. However, when they are trying to convince you to choose their company, airlines rarely emphasize the basic benefit of arriving intact at your destination. Instead, they typically stress augmented services, such as earning frequent flyer miles, speedy

core service: the basic benefit that is obtained as a result of having a service performed

augmented services: the core service plus additional services provided to enhance its value

**Figure 11.2
Core and Augmented Services**

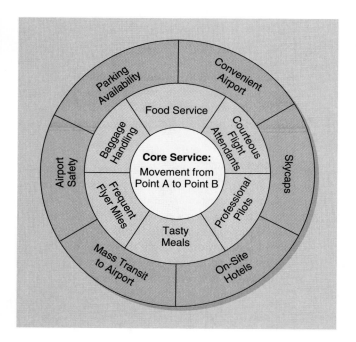

checkout, tasty meals, or reliable baggage delivery. Figure 11.2 illustrates a set of core and augmented services for an airline.

The use of augmented services to increase market share is particularly important in mature industries, such as the airline industry, where the core service has essentially become a commodity that every competitor is capable of delivering.[35] Carriers are stepping up efforts in particular to attract business flyers, who pay full fare. The McDonnell-Douglas Corporation is designing new planes with an "office in the sky," featuring a stand-up booth with a fold-down table to allow passengers to send a fax, make a call, use a computer, and then return to their seats for cocktails.[36] Let's take a look at some forms these augmented services can take.

Innovative Features

One obvious way to compete by offering superior augmented services is to develop new, innovative features that other companies do not offer. Northwest Airlines scrapped its regular meal service in favor of a moving buffet where passengers can take as much as they want. Midway Airlines features a bathroom for women only, American Airlines and British Airways offer showers in the arrival lounge, and United boards passengers beginning with people in window seats instead of from the back of the plane to the front. Japan Airlines installed an electronic massage chair in first class.[37]

Unique Delivery

Another way to stand out from the competition is to find a better way to deliver the core service to customers. Typically such a delivery system provides greater convenience by making it easier to obtain the service. Some entrepreneurs operate mobile units, vans that come to your house to provide services ranging from changing the oil in your car to grooming your pooch. Although it is now commonplace, at one time the provision of drive-through lanes to make bank transactions or order fast food was an augmented service that created a competitive advantage. Going one step further, a Chicago funeral home even offers drive-through service, where viewers can see a loved one on a screen without taking the time to leave their cars. The owner notes, "The working person doesn't have time to come in."[38]

Bundling

Another strategic option is **bundling,** where augmented services are packaged together (sometimes with tangible goods as well) to provide added value. For example, Bay-Banks Inc. in Boston copied the fast-food industry and started offering "value packages,"

bundling: a services marketing practice in which services are packaged together (sometimes with tangible goods as well) to provide added value

Exhibit 11.2
Japan is a "service-intensive" country, where consumers expect to be treated like royalty regardless of how routine the transaction may be. A typical scene at a Japanese service station exemplifies the level of augmented service provided: the motorist is greeted by several uniformed attendants shouting welcomes. They help guide the car into position, wipe the windows, fill the tires, even check the ashtray. If they have to they will stop traffic to allow the car to get back on the road, bowing energetically as the car leaves the station.

including a combination of checking, savings, and credit services bundled together for a flat monthly fee.[39] The Chicago White Sox organization sells a "Soxpack," which includes a ticket, a hot dog, chips, a drink, a program, and a souvenir for $12.[40] (We will talk more about bundling as a pricing strategy in Chapter 13.)

CUSTOMIZED VERSUS STANDARDIZED SERVICE

Many services, confronted with the problem of variability discussed earlier, try as much as possible to achieve a level of **standardized service,** where every customer receives almost exactly the same outcome. However, some businesses have gone the other direction: They promote themselves on their ability to provide **customized service,** where each customer receives a unique product that has been tailored to meet his or her specific needs. That's the logic behind Burger King's promise to "Have It Your Way." Indeed, as many organizations continue to narrow their focus from mass markets to serving very narrowly defined target groups (see Chapter 8), this emphasis on micromarketing is accelerating the push toward customizing service whenever possible. The promise to liberate the customer from the "cookie cutter" approach to standardized service is becoming one of the key strategic developments of the 1990s.

Managers are constantly grappling with the trade-off between consumers' desires for customization and the economic advantages of standardization. People like to feel that they are getting personal treatment in the form of customized service, but this special attention is often expensive. For example, Progressive Corp. is an innovative insurance company that provides customized service in an industry where many customers resent being "treated like a number." A Progressive claims adjuster arrives on the scene of an accident in an air-conditioned van equipped with chairs, a desk, and cellular phones. The company developed what it calls an Immediate Response program that offers the client a settlement for the market value of a wrecked car, even before the tow trucks have cleared the wreckage. This fast process reduces costs, builds goodwill, and reduces liability suits. Adjusters are trained in insurance regulation, negotiation skills, and even grief counseling, since part of their job involves dealing with the relatives of dead crash victims.[41]

Many service businesses have found that people are willing to pay extra for the luxury of obtaining an offering that exactly fits their needs and tastes, so we often find that customers are presented with the options of either buying a standardized offering or having one tailored to their needs. While most men are content to buy suits "off the rack," many appreciate the added touch of a fine tailor, or even have their clothes made from scratch. Computer stores will configure systems for buyers, and some business schools design executive education programs that address the specific needs of individual companies.

In many cases the ability of a service business to make a customer feel special or to provide an intangible product that is tailored to a specific person or company is transforming services strategy. As discussed in Chapter 7, mass customization means that a service is designed to fit an individual customer's needs. The trend toward mass customization of services is demonstrated by the British arm of the Prudential Insurance company. The Pru devised a system to let clients switch pension contracts, design their own payment schedules, and make flexible monthly contributions.[42]

One factor that is fueling the development of mass customization strategies is the increasing sophistication of information technologies. Powerful computer database systems allow an organization to learn more about an individual customer's needs by tracking his or her responses to different offerings over time, and to modify its approach based on that feedback (this procedure, known as *database marketing,* will be discussed in detail in Chapter 16, so stay tuned).

Technology also gives customers greater input into designing their own service options. For example, Weyerhauser responded to the desire for customization by installing computers in home repair stores that allow shoppers to custom design their own home decks; printouts conveniently include a list of the goods they will need to purchase to complete this service.[43] In other cases, though, mass customization can be realized through simpler, "low tech" means. For example, many restaurants have introduced do-it-yourself salad bars or dessert bars that let diners "design" their own meals.

standardized service: a service designed and delivered in a manner in which every customer receives almost exactly the same outcome or product

customized service: a service designed and delivered so that each customer receives a unique product that has been tailored to meet his or her specific needs

IMPROVING SERVICE DELIVERY

Another avenue that can be taken to provide competitive advantage is to focus on how well the service is actually delivered after it has been purchased. This means gaining an understanding of what happens to the customer once the service process has been initiated, and also attempting to structure the service so that it can efficiently and comfortably accommodate customers. In this section we'll review some of the factors that help to determine how well the service "works."

The Service System

When a customer purchases a service, he or she enters a **service system,** a set of interrelated procedures and facilities that work together to produce the service product. Many different operations are often involved in the creation and delivery of a service, only some of which are actually visible to the customer. The service typically consists of a series of *contact points* between employees and the customer.[44] To the extent possible these contacts should all be consistent and positive.

To appreciate the importance of these contact points, consider the experience of Fidelity Investments, the largest mutual fund company. Fidelity studied its customers and found out that more than anything else, customers value polite treatment—even more than investment performance! Now representatives go through a course on phone etiquette, they work in teams, and the reward system has been changed. Though customers sign up with Fidelity Investments to buy shares in a mutual fund, personalized telephone service is what builds long-term customer loyalty.[45]

Unfortunately, many firms do not understand the link between better training and better service. Also, some firms fail to develop policies that retain employees, so they see training as a waste because employees tend to leave the firm. A quality-focused firm will continually improve the reliability of services, especially those used as part of relationship marketing. Firms constantly plan improvements to their programs to combat these sources of *service failure:*

- *Customer and provider differences:* Differences among customers make the task of planning services quite complex. Service providers have different skills and learning abilities; it is not always possible to plan training programs that handle every deficiency of service providers.

- *Fatigue:* Like factory workers, service providers get fatigued, so performance goes down as the extent of contact hours with customers goes up. (Disney provides "off stage" time to service personnel at its theme parks to combat fatigue.)

- *Communication problems:* Communication problems interfere with the ability of a service provider to provide exactly what the customer wants. Communication interference can arise from small differences in language, different interpretations of situations and requests, and interference or noise related to the situation.

Services as Theater

Each service contact can be thought of as a dramatic performance, complete with actors, props, and costumes. Service providers have "scripts" to read, but so do customers. Part of the challenge of being a services marketer is to ensure that both employees and customers are reading from the same script. When each party has different expectations regarding what he or she is supposed to do in the service setting, trouble can result. For example, a professor who feels that his role is simply to show up and deliver a lecture may encounter a group of "dissatisfied customers," because his students' expectations of his responsibilities and their obligations may be quite different.

As shown in Figure 11.3 (page 384), a *service performance* usually takes place in two regions, the *front stage* and *backstage.* Think of the activities that occur in a fancy restaurant. Waiters, wine stewards, and the maître d' "perform" for diners by reciting daily specials, opening bottles with a flourish, or even bringing flaming delicacies to the table with-

service system: the set of interrelated procedures and facilities that work together to produce the service product

REAL PEOPLE, REAL CHOICES:

DECISION TIME AT LUTHERAN HEALTH SYSTEMS

In the 1960s Lutheran Health Systems bought a community hospital in a predominantly rural state, and it has continued to operate this facility since that time. The closest competing hospital of comparable size is almost an hour's drive away. A larger institution is located well over an hour from Lutheran's site. The major regional referral centers (four large medical centers) are all located in a major metropolitan area that is more than a two-hour drive from the community.

Over $\frac{1}{3}$ of the local population works for one major employer, a company that is closely associated with the federal government. In response to federal regulation this employer began to offer multiple managed-care health plans during the 1980s. It was generally believed that client satisfaction did not differ significantly among users of the different plans. While LHS enjoyed sole-provider status in the area, about 15 percent of this firm's employees nevertheless chose a health plan that was not available at the LHS location. These people elected to drive the two hours to the major referral center if they needed care because they could save about $100 per month in health-care premiums. This group was composed of young, reasonably healthy people who (research indicated) did not predict that they would need health care imminently and as a result were willing to put up with the inconvenience to save money on health-care costs.

LHS decided that the pricing discount it would have to offer to capture this small segment wasn't worth the revenue it would lose. However, LHS also predicted that the rival health plan would systematically attempt to steal away even more employees as time went on. LHS decided to escalate its integration of hospital services with other community providers, such as physicians and nursing homes, in an effort to reduce costs and solidify its dominance of the health-care delivery system in the community. With no local presence LHS felt that the competing organization would not be able to increase its market share much beyond its current 15 percent.

Shortly thereafter LHS learned that the competing organization had arranged to purchase the practices of six of the ten primary care physicians in the community; these six physicians accounted for over $\frac{1}{3}$ of the hospital's inpatient and outpatient business. Additionally, two of the remaining physicians were seriously contemplating selling their practices to LHS's rival. Rich Mackesy and his colleagues at LHS knew they had to take quick action to head off this threat. They identified three possible options:

Option 1. Outbid the competing organization for the physician practices it had targeted. Although nearly finalized, a much larger bid might win over the doctors. However, the expense of starting a bidding war would increase total operating costs by nearly 10 percent over and above the usual 7 percent per year increase being experienced in the health-care industry. LHS would have to consider carefully the impact of this outlay on consumers, because the increase in expenses would have to be passed on to them in the form of higher premiums.

Option 2. Recruit new physicians into the community who would be aligned with the LHS organization. There was adequate community demand and need for increasing the number of doctors. This approach would not eliminate the threat posed by the rival organization, but it would provide consumers with a broader choice of primary care physicians. On the other hand, the cost of recruiting physicians could pose a problem, as expenses associated with locating, moving, and assisting a physician in setting up a new practice in the community could be expected to run up to $100,000. In addition, new physicians must establish strong relationships with their patients. This requires considerable time and effort and reduces the productivity of the new physician during the time the practice is getting off the ground.

Option 3. Do nothing about the physician issues but concentrate on lowering the overall costs of hospital care. This would establish the hospital as the lowest-cost provider of hospital care and therefore have immediate appeal to both the major employer as well as the managed care plan. The need to transfer patients out of the community would therefore be a more expensive and thus less desirable option for the competing organization. The downside to this alternative is the questionable speed in which this option could be implemented. The bulk of the cost structure associated with hospital care is salary and benefit expenses (which represent from 50 to 60 percent of overall hospital expenses). Redesigning care delivery is often a multiyear project that must contend with such obstacles as the need for expensive technology, education and training of the nursing staff, and the preferences of physicians that practice at the hospital. In addition, one typical casualty of cost-cutting effort is that jobs are often lost through attrition or downsizing. This often leaves the hospital with a major public relations problem as it attempts to justify these cuts to the community.

---

out burning down the restaurant. Crucial parts of the service occur in both the front and the back of the service setting.

The front is the setting for the performance that the customer sees. The restaurant will take great care to ensure that tables are clean and elegantly set, and that appropriate music is playing softly in the background. Backstage, where the food is prepared, is another story. The elegant waiter with the French accent may slip back into the kitchen to grab a smoke, make jokes about the diners (and maybe even revert to his "real" accent!). Managers often try to separate the front from the back, though this is not always possible.[46]

In addition, a service often is not obtained all at once. It frequently involves a sequence of steps, so service marketers must pay great attention to this process to anticipate the points at which problems may arise. A look at the flowchart of a hotel service in Figure 11.3 reminds us of the many different operations that must go on, both behind the scenes and in front of the customer, for a service to be delivered.

Demand Management

Another way to improve the efficiency of the service system is to try to avoid excessive demands on the system. Most services confront peaks and valleys of demand; a restaurant, for example, may be depressingly empty at 3:00 in the afternoon, but have to turn away customers at 8:00 on a Saturday night. **Demand management** refers to procedures that attempt to smooth demand by encouraging service usage during slack times and/or discouraging patronage during peak times. For example, the airline industry has developed elaborate computerized models that allow carriers to price tickets according to the likely demand for seats—to the point where it is not unusual for two people sitting right next to each other to have paid vastly different amounts for their tickets, depending on how close to the actual flight their seats were purchased.

Demand management is crucial to service delivery, because the perishability problem means that management cannot build up an inventory. Some service businesses are more affected by this problem than others. If an airline doesn't sell a seat on a particular flight, that product is history. On the other hand, an insurance policy that is not bought today can still be bought tomorrow. Services such as accounting, transportation, hotels, and restaurants are particularly likely to be affected by demand fluctuations. Domino's Pizza was known for its heroic efforts to battle perishability by promising to deliver pizza within thirty minutes. The company dropped this promise, though, after a jury awarded more than $78 million to a woman who was hit by a driver rushing to make a delivery.[47]

Sometimes demand management is accomplished by tinkering with what is offered to customers, and when. McDonald's successfully filled its restaurants during slow breakfast hours by expanding its menu to include breakfast finger food. Of course sometimes there are limits to how well this strategy can work: When the fast-food chain tried to increase

demand management: procedures that attempt to smooth demand by encouraging service usage during slack times and/or discouraging patronage during peak times

Figure 11.3
Flowcharting a Hotel Visit

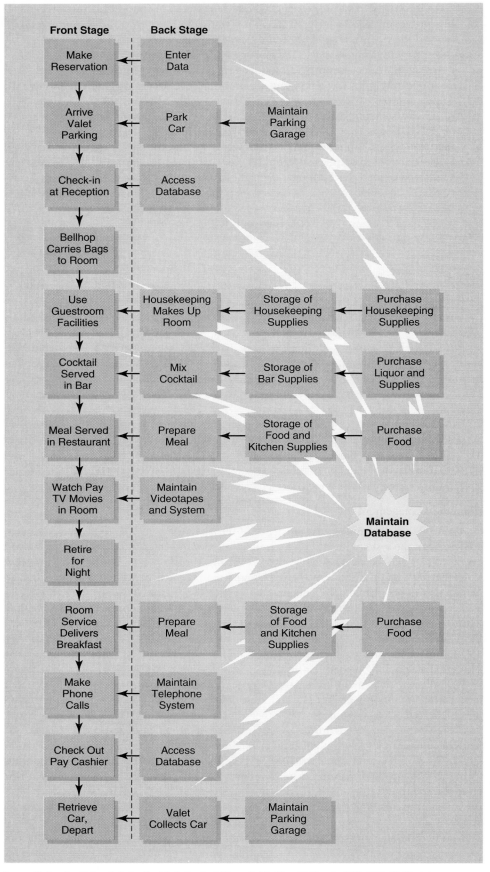

Source: Christopher H. Lovelock, *Services Marketing,* 2 ed (Upper Saddle River, NJ: Prentice Hall, 1991): 22, Fig. 2.4.

demand during the dinner hour by introducing pizza, pasta offerings, and a skinless roast chicken entrée, the attempt fizzled. Company research found that many people simply don't regard McDonald's as a dinner destination.[48]

Capacity management is the process by which the offering is adjusted in an attempt to match demand. In some cases this is relatively easy to do, especially if the periods of peak demand are predictable. For example, the electric company knows that demand for its service will rise systematically as the temperature goes up. A related strategy is to promote customer traffic during times of low demand. In the summer the Winter Park Ski Resort in Colorado opens its lifts to mountain bikers, who tear down the sunny slopes. Ski areas that used to be ghost towns in the summer now are starting to come alive as they develop new approaches to capacity management.[49] Similarly, this explains why it's cheaper to use AT&T phone service on the weekends. Other tactics include scheduling downtime during a low-peak period, using part-time employees, renting or sharing equipment with other facilities, and cross-training employees (for example, grocery stores may use stockers at cash registers during the "graveyard shift," when few people are in the store).

capacity management: the process by which the offering is adjusted in an attempt to match demand

CREATING PHYSICAL EVIDENCE

The intangibility of services also creates strategic opportunities, as organizations search for ways to represent the benefits they offer in some physical form. The most common solution is to create a tangible symbol of service excellence: Associate an intangible service with one or more tangible objects. These objects are called *physical evidence;* they are tangible cues used by consumers to infer the underlying qualities of an intangible product. Services vary in the extent to which the need to make the offering tangible is important. As a general rule of thumb, the more intangible the service (for example, insurance), the more crucial it is to create physical evidence to reassure people that the service is a good one.

Physical evidence takes many forms, including the firm's building and equipment, its employees, and its advertising. Some firms rely on metaphors in their advertising, where the characteristics of a symbol are transferred to the service. Allstate insurance communicates security by claiming, "You're in good hands with Allstate," while Travellers' insurance uses an umbrella to reinforce the idea that its service will protect you. In other cases, outfitting employees in distinctive uniforms allows them to be easily identified and to stand out from competitors (as we saw in Chapter 7). Like branded goods, the familiar "service package" also reduces risk by increasing credibility and by assuring buyers that a reliable company stands behind the service. In addition, just as a product package is carefully designed to create a "brand personality," the uniform communicates—it speaks volumes about the values and standards of the company it represents.[50]

One of the most powerful ways to create physical evidence for a service is to adopt a *branding strategy,* much like a marketer of a tangible product might do. Services marketers such as McDonald's, the tax preparation firm H&R Block, and the Century 21 realty company have essentially branded their services to create a unique identity for themselves. Developing a clear image for a brand name makes consumers feel as if they "know" the service. The United States Tennis Association adopted a branding strategy: In the first phase of a $1.1 million TV and print ad campaign created by Lintas:New York, promotional messages all carry the tag line, "The U.S. Open: A USTA event." A second phase showcases the USTA's local activities and serves to increase brand awareness in another TV spot.[51]

The adaptation of a conventional branding strategy to a set of services is nicely illustrated by British Airways, which decided to develop seven distinct types of flights, each run by its own brand manager:[52]

- ■ *Concorde:* The corporate flagship brand, offering five-course gourmet meals served on bone china, a commemorative gift, and complimentary helicopter transfer at New York
- ■ *First Class:* Provision of exclusive first-class facilities and preferential treatment throughout the travel experience. Spacious seats, valet parking at Heathrow (London), complimentary bar service, postcards with free postage
- ■ *Club World:* Catering to the business traveler, including free amenity kit with shaving supplies, comb, shoehorn, et cetera

- *Long-Haul Economy:* Quality, care, and value for money
- *Club Europe:* A time-efficient, hassle-free travel experience that recognizes the distinctive needs of the European business traveler. Includes rapid check-in, terminal lounge, increased wardrobe facilities
- *Europe Economy:* The value-for-money leisure travel product across the European continent. Includes children's services, low fares
- *Super Shuttle:* "Turn up and take off" with no need to reserve a seat, complimentary newspapers

TARGETING AND POSITIONING STRATEGIES

Like any other product, perhaps the most crucial strategic decisions for a service revolve around its definition in the market: Who are the target customers for the service, and how is the service perceived by them? These issues were the focus of Chapter 8, so although we won't belabor them here they are important enough to deserve a bit of a review, especially insofar as they apply to defining the market position of an intangible.

Targeting: Defining the Service Customer or Audience

Just as there are few (if any) physical goods that appeal to everyone, it is also true that not all people or organizations are interested in receiving a given service. Residents of a nursing home probably won't be good candidates for body piercing, a small retailer probably can't afford to hire a sophisticated management consultant, college students won't be lining up any time to buy tickets to a Frank Sinatra concert, and so on.

And in some cases members of a market segment may not be the best customers for a service, whether they want it or not. It may be that the segment cannot be served profitably. Bus companies often close down routes that simply don't generate enough ridership. Or it may turn out that the customer is simply too demanding or difficult to work with, and the amount of "handholding" he or she will need is simply not worth the investment. There are a few companies, for example, that are widely known to be so difficult that many advertising agencies will not bother to compete for their accounts.

Fortunately these examples are the exception rather than the rule: Most services can identify a target customer that they can serve well, and sometimes an organization may develop a separate strategy for multiple segments. To understand how this process works, consider how an arts organization, such as a local dance company or theater troupe, might go about identifying and targeting desirable market segments.

The organization can usually identify a small, hard-core group of supporters and a larger group of occasional attendees. It should classify the audience by light, medium, and heavy attendance and determine whether these groups differ in terms of psychographics, demographics, and benefits sought. People attend for different reasons, such as to support the organization, to see a particular performance, or because it is a social event.

Depending on the characteristics of the target audience and their motivations for purchasing an arts experience, marketers need to tailor their approaches to maximize their chances of reaching these diverse segments. For example, people who currently are patrons of other arts organizations can probably be reached by purchasing mailing lists containing their names. Tourists can be reached via Chambers of Commerce and hotel associations. Newcomers to a community get information from real estate agents. College students learn of arts events in their dormitories, student centers, and in English and drama classes.

Additionally, each segment requires a customized strategy to ensure that it is easy for people to obtain tickets when and where they want them: Regular arts patrons will probably be more interested in buying season tickets, while tourists and newcomers will be more attracted to tickets for a single performance. Professional groups can be reached by staging special parties (for example, "lawyers' night") that combine business with pleasure, while senior citizens might be lured by receiving discount passes in exchange for volunteering to work as ushers.[53] Like marketers of tangible goods, arts executives need to search for the right "hook" that will attract each type of audience member and fill seats.

Arts organizations often find that they have two basic marketing goals: (1) attracting new attendees and (2) retaining the loyalty of current attendees.[54] Separate strategies need to be developed for each target market. The development of a loyal group of enthusiastic subscribers, who will hopefully volunteer their time and contribute money to the group as well as faithfully attend its productions, is a process that depends on building a good relationship between the group and the person over time.[55] Here are some different goals that will help to determine the type of activities on which the organization should focus:

- *Audience maintenance:* If the goal is to encourage current customers to continue to buy tickets, the group should try to strengthen its relationships by developing newsletters for subscribers, giving them advance notice of future productions, or writing them letters to thank them for their patronage.

- *Audience enrichment:* A related goal is to enhance the experience of attendees. This often means a focus on improving augmented services, including improvements to the physical facility (for example, parking, lighting, and even temperature in the auditorium), as well as adding symposia, workshops, and other events related to the group's productions.

- *Audience expansion:* If the goal is to increase the number of people who attend performances, the arts organization needs to promote itself by reaching out for "fresh blood." The most likely prospects are people who are similar to those in the current audience, so the organization needs to conduct some research to generate a profile of the people who now attend its shows.

- *Audience development:* A big challenge faced by many arts organizations is to convince people that their offering is something they would enjoy. Many people resist patronizing the arts. The comments of one marketing survey respondent about attending theatrical performances are typical: "Those things are too rich for my blood. I don't think it's any fun. I'd be bored. That's for uppercrust people, the ones that have their noses in the air."[56] The organization needs to cultivate prospects by exposing people to its offerings who would not ordinarily attend. A common strategy is to encourage the development of school programs, corporate events, and group sales.

SPOTLIGHT ON MULTICULTURAL MARKETING

The Florida Marlins

By executing a careful targeting strategy, the Florida Marlins baseball team has a big hit on its hands. The team, owned by Blockbuster Entertainment, is spending more than $1 million to market itself to Hispanic fans. Central and South America as well as south Florida are being blitzed with TV and newspaper ads proclaiming the Marlins the "Team of the Americas." Sales agents are already in place in Puerto Rico and the Dominican Republic, with other countries to follow. This unique ethnic service identity is a natural for this upstart team. Florida's Dade County is already 52 percent Hispanic, and Florida has for years been a popular summer vacation spot for Latin Americans. The team's strategy is clearly working: A third of the season ticketholders are Hispanics.

American Airlines, which flies to over forty Latin American and Caribbean cities, quickly set up a promotional tie-in with the Marlins. They are jointly offering travel packages, TV and radio advertising, and stadium promotions that will put more Hispanics in airplane and ballpark seats.

The Marlins intend to sign as many Hispanic players as possible to build a bond with Hispanic fans. Owner Wayne Huizenga is making sure Dade County's Joe Robbie Stadium, where the Marlins play, has a distinctly Latin flavor. The concession stands offer not just popcorn and Cracker Jacks but *media noche,* a Cuban cheese and pork sandwich, and *arepa,* fried mozzarella on cornmeal pancakes. To be sure fans get the point, every time a Marlin hits a home run the team's Colombian-born play-by-play announcer can be counted on to scream, "Hasta la vista!" *

---

* William Stern, "Buy Me Some Arepa and Media Noche," *Forbes* (May 24, 1993): 184.

Positioning: Defining the Service to Customers

As we saw in Chapter 8, positioning is a process of creating a specific image for a product and differentiating it from competitors. Researchers have identified five dimensions of service delivery that generally are used to position a service vis à vis competitors:[57]

- *Tangibles:* Services often rely heavily on physical evidence to communicate such a position. Such cues as the facility (clean versus dirty, modern decor versus traditional), the brand name (Burger King versus the Hard Rock Cafe), distinctive colors used (the dependable dark brown of UPS versus the bright purple and orange of Federal Express), trademarks, logos, and symbols (the lion of the Dreyfus Corporation versus the bull of Merrill Lynch) help to send messages about attributes of the service.

- *Responsiveness:* Some services emphasize the speed and care with which they respond to customers' requests. For example, print shops like Kinko's and PIP

Exhibit 11.3

When the Disney organization tried to export its particular brand of American fantasy experience to its new facility outside of Paris, the company discovered that service products must sometimes be repositioned when they are exported. The theme park struggled from the outset. Because visitors spoke many languages, they had to hear performers say awkward things like, "How is everyone tonight? Ca va?" then order from a menu that turned such American delicacies as "Cattleman's Chili" to "Pepperoncino alla Cowboy" on the Italian menu and "Chili auf Cowboyart" on the German menu.

Other problems arose when Disney tried to impose its wholesome U.S. practices on the unwilling French. Its dress code, which requires women to wear "appropriate undergarments" and keep fingernails short was not a big hit. Its no-alcohol policy was a bigger disaster, because the French practically regard the consumption of wine with their meals as a constitutional right (Disney eventually changed the policy). To make matters worse, unlike Americans who are willing to put off lunch to visit the attractions, the French refused to delay their traditional 1:00 lunch, so Disney had a big capacity problem at its restaurants.

The company lost $203 million in its first six months of operation. Things got so bad that a Spanish newspaper ran a cartoon of Mickey Mouse panhandling near the Eiffel Tower. Disney's numerous adjustments to its marketing strategy are beginning to pay off as the park is now starting to catch on with tourists. Nonetheless, Disney's harsh lesson shows that even Mickey Mouse is not infallible when it comes to exporting services to other cultures.

promote their twenty-four-hour service and their efforts to preserve the client's valuable original documents.

- *Empathy:* An organization that is perceived to understand the needs of its customers and genuinely care about their welfare often has a leg up on the competition. Recall the long-standing motto of State Farm insurance: "Like a good neighbor, State Farm is there."

- *Assurance:* Finally, an organization can emphasize the knowledge or competence of its employees. This is a good strategy to minimize risk, especially for services where the customer finds it difficult to evaluate the quality of service received. For years Texaco proudly proclaimed, "You can trust your car to the man who wears the star."

MARKETING PEOPLE AND IDEAS

While all services are intangible, not all intangibles are services. The marketing concept also applies to other types of products, even to items that people don't typically think of in those terms. Like personal computers, automobiles, and headache remedies, people and ideas also compete for market share. Let's elaborate on that statement a bit.

MARKETING PEOPLE

In many situations people are packaged and promoted, bought and sold. If you don't believe that, you've never been on a job interview, or spent a Saturday night in a singles bar! Although many of us find it distasteful to equate people with products, nonetheless we often act as if this were the case. A sizable number of people go so far as to hire personal image consultants to devise a marketing strategy for them, and others undergo plastic surgery, physical conditioning, or cosmetic makeovers to improve their market position.[58] In fact researchers have found that dating is often equated with shopping, and that prospective partners are described in product-like terms.[59] Let's briefly touch on a few prominent categories of people marketing.

Politicians

Whether they agree with it or not, many people would readily acknowledge that modern politicians are created and marketed. These efforts were pioneered way back in the presidential campaign of Dwight Eisenhower, when advertising executive Rosser Reeves repackaged the bland candidate by inventing jingles and slogans and staging man-on-the-street interviews to improve Eisenhower's market position.[60]

A political campaign is really a marketing campaign; politicians and their "brand managers" (that is, campaign consultants) make use of market research to identify voters' needs and "test market" campaign position, use advertising and public relations to maximize awareness and sway evaluations, and work hard to position the candidate favorably against his or her opponents.[61] The political process is like other marketing exchanges, except in this case the candidate gives out promises and favors in return for votes.[62]

Celebrities

From movie stars and rock stars to superstar athletes and fashion models, the famous and near-famous jockey for market position. Sometimes celebrities even take on sacred status: For example, about 700,000 people make the annual pilgrimage to Graceland, the home of Elvis Presley. As one minister put it, "This has the makings of a new religion. Elvis is the god, and Graceland is the shrine . . . some even say he is rising again."[63]

Like politicians, celebrities often are carefully packaged by agents, record company executives, and so on.[64] They even are given "brand names" to help position themselves. The suggested criteria for choosing stage names strongly resemble those recommended for naming packaged goods, including memorability (for example, Evel Knievel), suitability (for example, fashion designer Oscar Renta reverting to his old family name of de la Renta

Exhibit 11.4
One of the most famous political ads in history was run in 1964 by the Democrats during the presidential campaign of Lyndon B. Johnson. The television commercial juxtaposed a child plucking the petals from a daisy with a bomb explosion as Lyndon Johnson talked about loving one another—an effort to drum up paranoia about the willingness of Barry Goldwater, his conservative Republican opponent, to resort to nuclear warfare in a crisis. As a mushroom cloud rose to the heavens, a voiceover of LBJ said, "These are the stakes. To make a world in which all of God's children can live. Or to go into the darkness. We must either love each other. Or we must die. Vote for President Johnson on November 3. The stakes are too high for you to stay at home." The ad made a huge impact, and it also demonstrated that controversial political advertising is often designed to be used for publicity purposes as well. Bill Moyers, who worked on the campaign, wrote to President Johnson: "While we paid for the ad only once on NBC last Monday night, ABC and CBS both ran it on their news shows Friday. So we got it shown on all three networks for the price of one."

because it sounded more elegant), and distinctiveness (for example, Steveland Morris Hardaway being given the name Stevie Wonder when he began his recording career). Indeed, we can even identify distinct strategies that have been used to "sell" a celebrity (or aspiring star): [65]

- *Pure selling approach:* An agent presents a client's qualifications to various managers (for example, a singer's tapes and photos are sent to talent scouts at record companies). The person is like an existing product that must be sold on the best possible terms.

- *Product improvement approach:* The agent works with the client to modify his/her characteristics to increase market value. In some cases this means changing the person's repertoire or image to correspond to changes in the public's tastes. For example, Madonna's image changed over three consecutive albums from East Village punk to lacy virgin to Marilyn Monroe clone, and she continues to mutate with each succeeding release. [66]

- *Market fulfillment approach:* The agent scans the market to determine what needs have not been satisfied. After identifying a need, the agent locates a person or a group that meets a set of minimum qualifications and develops that person into a product desired by the market. The creation of "stars" is evident in the worlds of film (Marilyn Monroe, Pia Zadora), music (The Monkees, New Kids on the Block), fashion (designer Tommy Hilfiger), and art (Julian Schnabel).

social marketing: the promotion of causes and ideas that are generally thought to be good for society and for people

MARKETING IDEAS

Social marketing refers to the promotion of causes and ideas such as responsible drinking, energy conservation, and population control. [67] For example, a major campaign to combat drug use was undertaken by the Partnership for a Drug-Free America, a group organized by the American Association of Advertising Agencies. This campaign was the largest *pro bono* effort (meaning the ad agencies involved donated their services) in history. As one involved executive noted, "We are approaching the problem posed by the $110 billion illegal drug industry from a marketing point of view. What we're doing is competing with drug pushers for market share of nonusers."[68]

Cause Marketing

Businesses are also getting into social marketing as a way to encourage constructive behavior while promoting a positive public image. This strategy is known as **cause marketing,** where corporate identity is linked to a good cause through advertising, public service, and publicity. The company will often align itself with a credible nonprofit group and make a long-term commitment to an issue of urgency. Companies are now spending close to $1 billion a year on cause marketing.[69] This strategy originated in the early 1980s when American Express sponsored a large campaign to help restore the Statue of Liberty.[70] Some recent examples of cause marketing include the following:[71]

- *Sears, Roebuck & Co.:* sponsored a forty-city concert tour by Phil Collins to raise $1 million for the homeless.
- *Kraft General Foods:* donates twenty-five cents for scholarships for African American students when coupons are redeemed for Stove Top stuffing and other Kraft products.
- *American Express:* donated two cents per transaction to Share Our Strength, an anti-hunger group. The campaign raised $5 million.
- *Midas:* With Project Baby Safe, drivers who buy a Century car seat receive a certificate worth the amount they spent in Midas services.
- *Dannon yogurt:* launched a new line of yogurt called Dannon Danimals, decorated with elephants and bears. Dannon gives 1.5 percent of the sales price of each package to the National Wildlife Federation.

While supporters of cause marketing point to the role of this strategy in boosting product sales or improving a poor public image, detractors claim that these campaigns are often done just for publicity reasons. They argue that if companies are so sincere about helping out, why don't they just contribute the money they're spending on cause-related ads to the cause itself? Benetton, the Italian clothing company, has come under fire for its controversial campaigns that pair shocking photos with social issues. A recent photo of a blood-soaked uniform belonging to a Croatian soldier brought passionate accusations from many Europeans that the company was exploiting the Yugoslav civil war for business purposes.[72]

Nonprofit Organizations

One very important characteristic of the marketing of intangibles is that many of the offerings are not intended to make a profit. Some are directed at providing social services, such as education, health care, or charity. Some provide cultural experiences, such as museums, symphonies, and dance companies. Others are interested in changing people's behavior or attitudes, such as environmental organizations like the Sierra Club. Still others advocate a certain political or religious philosophy and attempt to gain members or converts. Thus a church or a political party can be thought of as aiming to expand its "share of mind" rather than its market share.

Although nonprofit organizations such as churches, colleges, philanthropies, or dance companies have always attempted to succeed in their respective marketplaces, many have been reluctant to embrace the marketing concept. Nonprofit organizations face several obstacles to effective marketing:

- Although they cannot exist without adequate numbers of worshippers, students, donors, or patrons, in many cases they have equated marketing with profit making, and they have avoided efforts to develop offerings that meet the needs of their respective consumers. Marketing (the "M word") is still a taboo subject to some people in nonprofit organizations.
- Nonprofits often exhibit a production orientation rather than a marketing orientation: They feel their role is to produce an offering that they have decided is "best" for the public. They may have an "arm's length" relationship with the

users of their service: Think about a museum that calls its customers "visitors," implying a temporary, polite connection—look, but don't touch. These managers feel that it is sufficient to offer the best product they can, and hope that people will recognize this quality and flock to them. In particular, some people in artistic areas reject the idea that an audience's needs should be considered when a work of art is created. What do you think?

- Nonprofits often must serve several target markets or "publics," and sometimes these groups have conflicting interests. For example, a science museum would like to encourage more visitors from among the general public. It may also generate a lot of its "business" by visits from organized groups, such as school field trips. The museum must also cater to the needs of wealthy patrons and corporations who will underwrite its activities, members of the scientific community who may use it as a teaching and research resource, as well as local and federal authorities who may be responsible for grants, zoning ordinances, or even legislation that will affect its ability to mount exhibitions of controversial topics (for example, endangered species). Some groups, like the scientific community or wealthy patrons, may object to marketing strategies that stress "fun" exhibits over serious ones that have true scientific merit.

- Nonprofit groups typically have much less to spend on marketing efforts. They may be living hand to mouth, with precious little to spare for promotional activities. Their efforts are more likely to revolve around obtaining funding from the government or businesses and generating favorable publicity than on developing elaborate marketing research programs or sophisticated advertising campaigns.

- The objectives of a marketing campaign may be harder to identify. Sometimes these goals may be simple enough, such as "increase attendance at our museum by 20 percent next year." In other cases, though, the effects are harder to measure and may be more evident in the long term than during the next quarter. For example, a public education campaign to encourage people to eat healthier foods may not have any apparent effects for quite some time.

In more recent years this outlook has changed dramatically. Churches that are viewed as cold and unapproachable have lost "market share" to those that offer benefits people are looking for. Universities, faced with dwindling enrollments, have had to tailor their offerings to the needs of the market; some have even started to advertise themselves aggressively or to alter their distribution strategies by offering classes off campus (Long Island University even offers courses to commuters on the Long Island Railroad!). Philanthropies such as the United Way or the Sierra Club develop sophisticated fund-raising strategies, using the latest marketing research techniques to analyze their target markets.

Religion

Even the clergy are increasingly adopting secular marketing techniques. Televangelists rely on the power of television to convey their messages. So-called megachurches are the latest trend; they typically feature huge steel and glass structures, acres of parking, and slickly produced services with pop-style music, live bands, and professional dancers that draw audiences of worshippers that number in the thousands. Some even offer aerobics classes, bowling alleys, and multimedia Bible classes inspired by MTV to attract "customers" who were turned off by more traditional approaches to religion.[73]

A lot of religious advertising attempts to create *primary demand;* it is intended to motivate people to get more involved with religion. Episcopal congregations, for example, have begun running TV commercials to woo back lapsed worshippers. The Episcopal Radio-TV Foundation is a nonprofit Atlanta group that produces TV and radio programming. The foundation is targeting women between twenty-five and forty-five years old. Research showed they were the most likely prospects to return to church and to bring their families as well. Local congregations raised money to broadcast the ads as paid advertising. The ads show majestic landscapes and tell viewers what religion can do for them. One, featuring a mountain scene, has a narrator say, "If God can create these peaks and valleys, God is bound to understand yours." The effectiveness of campaigns like this one are difficult to measure, because most churches don't take attendance. But the "product sell" approach might help reverse membership declines.[74]

The use of marketing techniques is not unanimously endorsed by religious practitioners. While some clergy are enthusiastically defining the best target market for a church, using direct mail to reach prospects, and adding such features as live bands, multimedia presentations, and workshops on family issues to make church services more interesting to baby boomers, other reject this approach. One official at a divinity school commented, "Church is not supposed to be a place where everybody's needs are met. It's supposed to be a place where we're transformed by God's grace into something we're not."[75]

In other cases one "brand" of religion attempts to convert "users" of another brand—a practice called proselytizing. For example, while Hispanic Americans are predominantly Catholic, millions of Hispanics are leaving the Roman Catholic Church. It is estimated that about one in five Hispanics now practices some form of evangelical Protestantism. This change is ascribed to two factors: The evangelical Protestants have adopted sophisticated marketing techniques, such as providing local clergy with profiles of Hispanic communities in a campaign to convert large numbers of Hispanic Catholics, and the style of U.S. Catholicism is alien to many Hispanics. It tends to be more rational and bureaucratic and is not viewed by many as being responsive to the more emotional and mystical Hispanic religious experience. For example, the belief in miraculous healing that is prevalent in Latin American Catholicism does not tend to be emphasized in American churches.[76]

INTANGIBLES AND THE MARKETING MIX

The marketing mix for services and other intangibles tends to be different than for goods. Factors such as packaging, labeling, or distribution of product samples are obviously not relevant. On the other hand, personal recommendations and publicity will tend to be even more important for a service. The marketer has to consider the elements of the marketing mix that he or she can control, and use these tools very carefully.

For example, the Hartford Stage Company in Connecticut combined elements of the marketing mix to realize its goals. First it moved from an old theater to a new larger one that was more convenient for its audience. The company also found that people are more likely to attend a play if a total evening is planned for them. It designed a total entertainment package, giving each subscriber a two-for-one dinner, discount theater tickets, and free parking, plus a free newsletter and priority notices about upcoming shows. In a single campaign that cost only $10,000 to implement, season subscriptions jumped from 7,500 to 17,000.[77] To close out the chapter, let's see how even small organizations in industries like the arts that are not usually "marketing minded" can incorporate aspects of the marketing mix into their planning process.

PRODUCT

The core service for a theater company is the consumer utility received from the show—his or her level of enjoyment. The augmented service includes seat comfort, the playbill, and even parking availability. Product utility is derived from both the performance itself and the environment in which it is delivered. The playgoer is not buying a play, but a satisfying aesthetic experience. He or she will not enjoy the performance, no matter how well done, if the room is too stuffy or other audience members smoke or make wisecracks during the show. In addition, the marketer cannot overlook the other benefits of consuming an arts offering: The *possession utility* of an event may come from the knowledge or self-enrichment it provides, or in some cases simply the snob value of being seen at a performance!

PRICE

Because services are so hard to evaluate, consumers often rely heavily on price as an indicator of quality. (We will discuss the price-quality relationship more fully in Chapter 12.) Price is also used to smooth demand for the offering. Here are some examples of pricing strategies as applied to the performing arts:[78]

- **Customer-based pricing:** Discounts to students and senior citizens
- **Location-based pricing:** The quality of seat location is an aspect of the product for which people are willing to pay. Theaters typically charge more for a front center orchestra seat than a seat "up in heaven" in the rear balcony.
- **Time-based pricing:** Some performance times are more desirable than others. Tickets usually are priced lower for Wednesday matinees than for Saturday evening shows.
- **Product-based pricing:** Some types of performances are more in demand than others. Many theaters charge more for musicals than for dramas.

PLACE

Because a performance, like other services, is usually produced and consumed at the same time, where and when factors are crucial. *Place utility* is derived from the location — the theater must be convenient, safe, and comfortable. In addition, *time utility* must be considered: Is the scheduling convenient? One theater company boosted Friday evening

REAL PEOPLE, REAL CHOICES:

HOW IT WORKED OUT AT LUTHERAN HEALTH SYSTEMS

Lutheran Health Systems chose option 2. Rich Mackesy and his colleagues calculated that it would take at least two years to adequately reduce costs to make option 3 a viable possibility. Cost restructuring was pursued, but in a more deliberate and organized fashion. Option 1 was ruled out due to the prevailing need in the health-care industry to cut costs, not raise them.

An additional four physicians were recruited within six months. The need for these physicians was clearly documented by LHS and supported by community research and input (hospitals must abide by strict requirements when engaging in physician recruitment). Lutheran Health Systems continued to maintain relationships with the six physicians who sold their practices (the other two never did sell after all).

The new physicians were heavily promoted in the community. Open houses, community lectures, and interaction with civic and social organizations enhanced their visibility to the employer's work force. During the next employee enrollment period the physicians rotated through the employer's worksite, meeting prospective enrollees and reminding them that the competing plans required exclusive use of the other six physicians in town.

Despite a reduction in patient volume at the hospital, it continues to thrive. The new physicians have provided valuable new health care choices to the community. One year after purchasing the physicians' practices, the competing organization was not granted the ability to continue to offer its product to this employer. The employer decided instead to offer an exclusive arrangement with the two other remaining plans in town. The efforts of the competition have been minimized . . . for now.

attendance simply by changing curtain time from 8:00 to 8:30, so people could have a leisurely dinner before the show.

PROMOTION

Promotional strategy should be tailored to the market segment one is trying to reach. The arts marketer typically does not have a huge promotional budget, but much can be done by taking advantage of contacts with community groups and local media. Promotions need to be targeted to three different segments: enthusiasts, interested, and nonattenders. *Enthusiasts* are loyal patrons; they mostly need information about upcoming productions, which can be provided through simple direct mail pieces. The *interested* group represents potential audience members who need to be persuaded to spend their entertainment dollars on one form of entertainment versus another. The promotion message thus needs to focus more on incentives for attending, which can be provided by creative advertising and special events.

The third group, *nonattenders,* are people who need to be educated as to why they should consider coming at all. The promotional objective for this group is different still; they will more likely be receptive to personal contact or to group promotions that draw them into the theater (sometimes kicking and screaming). This group must first be made aware of the delights of attending the theater before they can be persuaded to do so voluntarily.[79]

Chapter 11 Summary

Objective 1. Describe the characteristics of services.

Services are products that are intangible and that are exchanged directly from producer to customer. Generally services are acts that accomplish some goal and may be directed either toward people or toward an object or possession. Important service characteristics include (1) intangibility (they cannot be seen, touched, or smelled); (2) perishability (they cannot be stored); (3) variability (they are never *exactly* the same); and (4) inseparability from the producer (most services are produced, sold, and consumed at the same time). In reality most products are a combination of goods and services. Some services are product-related—that is, tangible products are marketed with supporting services. Some are equipment- or facility-based—elaborate equipment or facilities are required for creation of the service. Other services are people-based, meaning that people are actually a part of the service marketed.

Objective 2. Explain how marketers create and evaluate service quality.

The satisfaction of service customers—that is, the perception of service quality—is related to prior expectations. Because services are intangible, evaluation of service quality is more difficult and is generally based on customer perceptions. Both qualitative and quantitative research methods may be used to measure customer satisfaction. Gap analysis measures the difference between customer expectations of service quality and what actually occurred. Using a critical incident technique, service firms can identify the specific contacts between customers and service providers that create dissatisfaction.

Objective 3. Explain marketing strategies for intangibles.

In developing strategies for services, marketers focus on both the core service—the basic benefit received from the service—and on augmented services—innovative features, unique delivery systems, and the bundling of services together. While many marketers seek to provide standardized services (in which services are all alike), others offer customized services in which each customer receives a unique product. In mass customization strategies technology allows large numbers of customers to design their own unique service products. Services strategies may focus on productivity management, attempts to improve what happens once the service process has begun. Demand management refers to strategies aimed at equalizing demand for services, crucial because of the perishability of services. Capacity management means that service strategies must adjust the service offering to match peak demand. Because of the intangibility of services, marketers may design buildings, equipment, employees, advertising, or brand strategies to provide tangible symbols of service excellence. As with strategies for marketing physical goods, service strategies include targeting segments of service customers and positioning the service to differentiate it from competitors' offerings.

Objective 4. **Explain the marketing of people and ideas.**

    Sometimes marketing intangibles means packaging, promoting, and selling people such as politicians and celebrities. Social marketing, the promotion of causes and ideas, includes cause marketing in which corporations use advertising, public service, and publicity to link themselves with a good cause in hopes of boosting sales. Nonprofit organizations also develop marketing strategies to "sell" social services, cultural experiences, ideas such as environmental protection, or a political or religious philosophy. The marketing of religion, aimed at both increasing primary demand and at individual "brand" choice, has gained in popularity as evidenced by the increased use of religious broadcasts and religious advertising.

Objective 5. **Discuss some of the differences between the marketing mix for goods and for the marketing of intangibles.**

    In marketing intangibles some important marketing mix elements such as packaging and labeling are not relevant. The intangible product is the utility received. Price is very important in services marketing as an indicator of quality. Because a service is produced and consumed at the same time, place and time utility are especially important. Promotion, as with the marketing of goods, must focus on different market segments.

Review Questions

Marketing Concepts: Testing Your Knowledge

1. What are services? What are the important characteristics of services that make them different from goods?
2. Explain how different types of products fall along the goods-services continuum. Give examples of how the differences create unique marketing challenges.
3. How do consumers evaluate product quality? How do marketers work to create service quality?
4. Describe some of the ways marketers measure service quality.
5. How do marketers create augmented services to increase market share?
6. Explain the advantages and disadvantages of customized and standardized services.
7. What are some of the ways marketers work to improve the delivery of services?
8. How might marketers make services more tangible?
9. What are some of the ways in which people are marketed?
10. What are some of the unique problems faced in marketing of ideas by nonprofit organizations?

Marketing Concepts: Discussing Choices and Issues

1. By the year 2000 88 percent of all Americans will be working in service industries. How do you think this will change the field of marketing?
2. Sometimes service quality may not meet customers' expectations because services are inseparable from the service provider and because of the variability in the performance of the service from one time to the next. What problems have you experienced with quality in the delivery of the following services? What do you think is the reason for the poor quality?
   a. hotel accommodations
   b. dry cleaning
   c. a haircut
   d. your college education
3. There have been a lot of criticisms of the way politicians have been marketed in recent years. What are some of the ways marketing has helped our political process? What are some ways the marketing of politicians might have an adverse effect on our government?
4. Many firms have found it makes good sense to link their identity to a good cause. There are, however, firms who are concerned that linkups with some causes may not be in their best interest. For example, if you support groups that help battered women, it might mean that your company name is seen with a picture of battered women, not a particularly appealing idea. Should firms only align themselves with "attractive" causes? Is there a problem with supporting important but unpleasant causes?

Marketing Practice: Applying What You've Learned

1. Because of increased competition in their community, you have been hired as a marketing consultant by a large group of family physicians. You know that the characteristics of services (intangibility, perishability, and so on) create unique marketing challenges. You also know that these challenges can be met with creative marketing strategies. Outline the challenges for marketing the physicians created by each of the four characteristics of services. List your ideas for what might be done to meet each of these challenges.
2. As an entrepreneur you plan to open a car wash. You feel that your chance of being successful is best if you can create a product that is superior to that offered by competing businesses. Put together a list of ways in which you can augment the basic service offering (features, delivery, bundling, and so on) to develop a better product. List the advantages and disadvantages of each possibility. Tell which you feel are best.
3. You are currently a customer for a college education, a very expensive service product. You know that a service organization can create a competitive advantage by focusing on how the service is delivered after it has been purchased—making sure the service is efficiently and comfortably delivered to the customer. Develop a list of recommendations for your school for improving the delivery of their service. Consider both classroom and nonclassroom aspects of the educational product.

4. Assume you have been hired as a campaign manager for a local candidate for mayor. In other words, you have been asked to create and manage a plan for marketing a person. Prepare an outline for your marketing plan. First list the special problems and challenges associated with marketing a person rather than a physical product. Then outline your ideas for product, price, and promotion strategies.

5. Assume you have been recently hired by your city government to head up a program to create 100 percent compliance with recycling regulations. Your first responsibility is to develop a presentation for the City Council in which you will outline the problems in "selling" recycling and your recommendations for improvement of the problem. Develop an outline for the presentation. Be sure to focus on each of the Four Ps in your presentation.

Marketing Mini-Project: Learning by Doing

Any time you are a customer for a service—when you get a new haircut, visit the emergency room for a broken finger, or have your teeth cleaned—you experience a great many different elements of the product, many of which you normally do not even notice. The purpose of this mini-project is to increase your awareness of the variety of aspects of the service encounter that can either help or hurt the success of the service business.

1. Select a service that you will purchase in the next week or so.
2. As you experience the service, write down the details of every aspect of the encounter. Some of the things you might wish to describe are

   a. People: the number of people you come in contact with; how they look, what they wear, how they talk, what they say, their attitudes, how they treat you, level of expertise, apparent training, adequate explanations, questions answered, and so on

   b. Physical facilities: appearance, temperature, sounds (music, noise, and so on), cleanliness, roominess, arrangement and style of equipment, furniture, lighting

   c. Location: safe, easy to find, ease of parking, close to other attractive businesses

   d. Amount of time: phone contact time, waiting time, service completion time

   e. Hours: convenient, varied

   f. Actual service delivery: quality, consistency, your expectations

   g. Transaction: ease of payment, appropriate billing, receipt

   h. Other customers: attitudes, appearance, how they are treated

   i. Tangible aspects of the experience: anything you took with you, logos, uniforms

   j. Search qualities: ability to evaluate the service prior to purchase

   k. Credence qualities: ability to judge the service after receipt

3. Based on your experience, develop recommendations for improving the service encounter.

Key Terms

Endnotes

1. Lee D. Dahringer, "Marketing Services Internationally: Barriers and Management Strategies," *Journal of Services Marketing* (Summer 1991): 5–17.
2. Ibid.
3. Ronald Henkoff, "Service is Everybody's Business," *Fortune* (June 27, 1994): 48.
4. Eben Shapiro, "Entertainment Giants Push Playgrounds for Grown-Ups," *The Wall Street Journal* (June 8, 1995): B1.
5. Walter Wingo, "What's Ahead for Tomorrow," *Nation's Business* (Sept. 1987): 72–74.
6. "The 100 Largest Diversified Service Companies," *Fortune* (May 30, 1994): 200.
7. Walter Wingo, "What's Ahead for Tomorrow," *Nation's Business* (Sept. 1987): 72–74.
8. Emily DeNitto, "Ads Fit the Bill for Medical Groups," *Advertising Age* (July 5, 1993): 12.
9. Robert Rubright and Dan MacDonald, *Marketing Health & Human Services* (Rockville, MD: Aspen Publishers, 1981); Philip Kotler, *Marketing for Nonprofit Organizations* (Upper Saddle River, NJ: Prentice Hall, 1975).
10. Based on a discussion in Gene R. Laczniak, "Product Management and the Performing Arts," in eds. Michael P. Mokwa, William M. Dawson, and E. Arthur Prieve, *Marketing the Arts* (New York: Praeger Publishers, 1980).
11. Adapted from Christopher H. Lovelock, *Services Marketing*, 2 ed. (Upper Saddle River, NJ: Prentice Hall, 1991).
12. Faye Rice, "The New Rules of Superlative Service," *Fortune* (Autumn/Winter 1993): 50.
13. Lee D. Dahringer, "Marketing Services Internationally: Barriers and Management Strategies," *Journal of Services Marketing* (Summer 1991): 5–17.
14. Quoted in Jim Carlton, "Support Lines' Busy Signals Hurt PC Makers," *The Wall Street Journal* (July 6, 1995): B1.
15. Lon W. Turkey and Douglas L. Fugate, "The Multidimensional Nature of Service Facilities: Viewpoints and Recommendations," *Journal of Services Marketing* (Summer 1992): 37–45.

16. David H. Maister, "The Psychology of Waiting Lines," in eds. J.A. Czepiel, M.R. Solomon, and C.F. Surprenant, *The Service Encounter: Managing Employee/Customer Interaction in Service Businesses* (Lexington, MA: Lexington Books, 1985).

17. Eleena DeLisser, "Banks Court Disenchanted Customers," *The Wall Street Journal* (Aug. 30, 1993): B1.

18. Michael T. Kaufman, "About New York: The Nail Salon of the 90's: Massages for the Clothed," *The New York Times* (Dec. 1, 1993): B3.

19. Cf. John A. Czepiel, Michael R. Solomon, and Carol F. Surprenant, eds., *The Service Encounter: Managing Employee/Customer Interaction in Service Businesses* (Lexington, MA: D.C. Heath and Company, 1985).

20. Jan Larson, "Getting Professional Help," *American Demographics* (July 1993): 36.

21. Ray Serafin, (1993) "Saturn Recall A Plus—For Saturn!" *Advertising Age* (Aug. 16, 1993): 4.

22. Gilbert A. Churchill, Jr. and Carol F. Surprenant, "An Investigation into the Determinants of Customer Satisfaction," *Journal of Marketing Research* (November 1983): 491–504; John E. Swan and I. Frederick Trawick, "Disconfirmation of Expectations and Satisfaction with a Retail Service," *Journal of Retailing* (Fall 1981): 49–67; Peter C. Wilton and David K. Tse, "Models of Consumer Satisfaction Formation: An Extension," *Journal of Marketing Research* (May 1988): 204–212; for a discussion of what may occur when customers evaluate a new service for which comparison standards do not yet exist, see Ann L. McGill and Dawn Iacobucci, "The Role of Post-Experience Comparison Standards in the Evaluation of Unfamiliar Services," in eds. John F. Sherry, Jr. and Brian Sternthal, *Advances in Consumer Research* (Provo, Utah: Association for Consumer Research, 1992).

23. Faye Rice, "The New Rules of Superlative Service," *Fortune* (Autumn/Winter 1993): 50.

24. Cynthia Webster, "Influences Upon Consumer Expectations of Services," *Journal of Services Marketing* (Winter): 5–17.

25. Mary Jo Bitner, "Evaluating Service Encounters: The Effects of Physical Surroundings and Employee Responses," *Journal of Marketing* (April 1990): 69–82.

26. Edwin McDowell, "Ritz-Carlton's Keys to Good Service," *The New York Times* (March 31, 1993): D1.

27. Keith B. Murray, "A Test of Services Marketing Theory: Consumer Information Acquisition Activities," *Journal of Marketing* (Jan. 1991): 10–25.

28. Michael J. McCarthy, "Airlines Retool Services to Attract More Full-Fare Fliers," *The Wall Street Journal* (Oct. 27, 1993): B1.

29. Valarie A. Zeithaml, "How Consumer Evaluation Processes Differ Between Goods and Services," in Christopher H. Lovelock, *Services Marketing* 2 ed. (Upper Saddle River, NJ: Prentice Hall, 1991).

30. Kenneth Wylie, "Customer Satisfaction Blooms; Rivalry at Top Grows," *Advertising Age* (Oct. 18, 1993): S-1.

31. Valarie A. Zeithaml, Leonard L. Berry, and A. Parasuraman, "Communication and Control Processes in the Delivery of Service Quality," *Journal of Marketing* (April 1988): 35–48.

32. Jody D. Nyquist, Mary F. Bitner, and Bernard H. Booms, "Identifying Communication Difficulties in the Service Encounter: A Critical Incident Approach," in eds. John A. Czepiel, Michael R. Solomon, and Carol F. Suprenant, *The Service Encounter: Managing Employee/Customer Interaction in Service Businesses* (Lexington, MA: D.C. Heath, 1985).

33. Jody D. Nyquist, Mary F. Bitner, and Bernard H. Booms, "Identifying Communication Difficulties in the Service Encounter: A Critical Incident Approach," in eds. John A. Czepiel, Michael R. Solomon, and Carol F. Surprenant, *The Service Encounter: Managing Employee/Customer Interaction in Service Businesses* (Lexington, MA: D.C. Heath, 1985).

34. Jan Larson, "Getting Professional Help," *American Demographics* (July 1993): 34.

35. Christopher H. Lovelock, *Services Marketing* 2 ed. (Upper Saddle River, NJ: Prentice Hall, 1991).

36. Michael J. McCarthy, "Airlines Retool Services to Attract More Full-Fare Fliers," *The Wall Street Journal* (Oct. 27, 1993): B1.

37. Adam Bryant, "An Airborne Battle of Services," *The New York Times* (Oct. 19, 1994): D1.

38. Quoted in Isabel Wilkerson, "New Funeral Options for Those in a Rush," *The New York Times* (Feb. 25, 1989): A16.

39. Eleena DeLisser, "Banks Court Disenchanted Customers," *The Wall Street Journal* (Aug. 30, 1993): B1.

40. Gary Levin, "Baseball's Opening Pitch: Winning Over New Fans," *Advertising Age* (April 5, 1993): 1–2.

41. Ronald Henkoff, "Service is Everybody's Business," *Fortune* (June 27, 1994): 48.

42. Paul Meller, "The Pru Adopts Personal Touch," *Marketing* (Feb. 18, 1993): 23.

43. "Weyerhauser Installs Computer Design Centers in Home Repair Outlets," *Marketing News* (May 22, 1989): 32.

44. Christopher H. Lovelock, *Services Marketing* 2 ed. (Upper Saddle River, NJ: Prentice Hall, 1991).

45. Gilbert Fuchsberg, "Gurus of Quality Are Gaining Clout," *The Wall Street Journal,* reprinted in E. Jerome McCarthy and William D. Perreault, Jr., *Applications in Basic Marketing/Clippings from the Popular Business Press* (Boston: Irwin, 1990).

46. Michael R. Solomon, Carol Surprenant, John A. Czepiel, and Evelyn G. Gutman, "A Role Theory Perspective on Dyadic Interactions: The Service Encounter," *Journal of Marketing* (Winter 1985): 99–111; Erving Goffman, *The Presentation of Self in Everyday Life* (New York: Doubleday, 1959).

47. Michael Janofsky, "Domino's Ends Fast-Pizza Pledge After Big Award to Crash Victim," *The New York Times* (Dec. 22, 1993): A1.

48. Gretchen Morgenson, "Look Who's Coming to Dinner," *Forbes* (March 1, 1993): 104–106.

49. Marj Charlier, "Bikers Give Ski Resorts Summertime Life," *The Wall Street Journal* (July 7, 1994): B1.

50. Michael R. Solomon, "'Packaging' the Building Maintenance Worker," *Services* (July 1995): 14–19.

51. Jeff Jensen, "Tennis Serves Up Branding Plan," *Advertising Age* (Sept. 13, 1993): 10.

52. Torin Douglas, "The Power of Branding," *Business Life* (April/May 1988), reprinted in Christopher H. Lovelock, *Services Marketing* 2 ed. (Upper Saddle River, NJ: Prentice Hall, 1991).

53. Michalann Hobson, "Making the Marketing Plan and Mix Work," in ed. Joseph V. Melillo, *Market the Arts!* (New York: Foundation for the Extension and Development of the American Professional Theater, 1983).

54. Robert A. Peterson, "Marketing Analysis, Segmentation, and Targeting in the Performing Arts," in eds. Michael P. Mokwa, William M. Dawson, and E. Arthur Prieve, *Marketing the Arts* (New York: Praeger Publishers, 1980).

55. Robert A. Peterson, "Marketing Analysis, Segmentation, and Targeting in the Performing Arts," in eds. Michael P. Mokwa, William M. Dawson, and E. Arthur Prieve, *Marketing the Arts* (New York: Praeger Publishers, 1980).

56. Sidney J. Levy, "Arts Consumers and Aesthetic Attributes," in eds. Michael P. Mokwa, William M. Dawson, and E. Arthur Prieve, *Marketing the Arts* (New York: Praeger Publishers, 1980): 29.

57. A. Parasuraman, Valarie A. Zeithaml, and Leonard L. Berry, "SERVQUAL: A Multiple-Item Scale for Measuring Consumer Perceptions of Service Quality," *Journal of Retailing* (Spring 1988): 12–40; Valarie A. Zeithaml, A. Parasuraman, and Leonard L. Berry, "Strategic Positioning on the Dimensions of Service Quality," in *Advances in Services Marketing and Management*, vol. 2, eds. Teresa A. Swartz, David E. Bowen and Stephen W. Brown (Greenwich, CT: JAI Press).

58. Michael R. Solomon, "The Wardrobe Consultant: Exploring the Role of a New Retailing Partner," *Journal of Retailing* (Summer 1987): 110–128.

59. Aaron Ahuvia and Mara B. Adelman, "Market Metaphors for Meeting Mates," unpublished manuscript, Northwestern University, 1991.

60. Irving J. Rein, Philip Kotler, and Martin R. Stoller, *High Visibility* (New York: Dodd, Mead & Company, 1987).

61. Philip Kotler, "Overview of Political Candidate Marketing," *Advances in Consumer Research*, vol. 2 (1975): 761–769.

62. Ibid.

63. Quoted in Richard Corliss, "The King is Dead—Or is He? The Elvis Cult Has the Making of a New Religion," *Time* (Oct. 10, 1988): 90.

64. Michael R. Solomon, "Celebritization and Commodification in the Interpersonal Marketplace," unpublished manuscript, Rutgers University, 1991.

65. Adapted from a discussion in Irving J. Rein, Philip Kotler, and Martin R. Stoller, *High Visibility* (New York: Dodd, Mead & Company, 1987).

66. Charla Krupp, "Can Cyndi Lauper Bring Back the Headdress?," *Glamour* (Jan. 1987): 138.

67. Seymour H. Fine, *Social Marketing: Promoting the Causes of Public and Nonprofit Agencies* (Boston: Allyn & Bacon, 1990).

68. Quoted in Cecelia Reed, "Partners for Life," *Advertising Age* (Nov. 9, 1988): 122.

69. Geoffrey Smith and Ron Stodghill II, "Are Good Causes Good Marketing?" *Business Week* (March 21, 1994): 64.

70. Yumiko Ono, "Advertisers Try 'Doing Good' to Help Make Sales Do Better," *The Wall Street Journal* (Sept. 2, 1994): B8.

71. Geoffrey Smith and Ron Stodghill II, "Are Good Causes Good Marketing?" *Business Week* (March 21, 1994) 64; Jan Larson, "Sweet Charity," *Marketing Tools* (May 1995: 69–72; Yumiko Ono, "Advertisers Try 'Doing Good' to Help Makes Sales Do Better," *The Wall Street Journal* (Sept. 2, 1994): B8.

72. Peter Gumbel, "Benetton is Stung by Backlash Over Ad," *The Wall Street Journal* (March 4, 1994): A4; Geoffrey Smith and Ron Stodghill II, "Are Good Causes Good Marketing?" *Business Week* (March 21, 1994): 64.

73. Gustav Niebuhr, "Where Religion Gets a Big Dose of Shopping-Mall Culture," *The New York Times* (April 16, 1995): 1.

74. Laura Bird, "And They're Very Good at Praying for Success," *The Wall Street Journal* (Oct. 15, 1993): B1.

75. Quoted in Associated Press, "New Church Uses Marketing to Appeal to Baby Boomers," *Marketing News* (April 12, 1993): 11.

76. Roberto Suro, "Switch by Hispanic Catholics Changes Face of U.S. Religion," *The New York Times* (May 14, 1989): 1.

77. Micheal [*sic*] House, "The Marketing Mix," in ed. Joseph V. Melillo, *Market the Arts!* (NY: Foundation for the Extension and Development of the American Professional Theater, 1983).

78. Micheal [*sic*] House, "The Marketing Mix," in ed. Joseph V. Melillo, *Market the Arts!* (NY: Foundation for the Extension and Development of the American Professional Theater, 1983).

79. Roger A. Strang and Jonathan Gutman, "Promotion Policy Making in the Arts: A Conceptual Framework," in eds. Michael P. Mokwa, William M. Dawson, and E. Arthur Prieve, *Marketing the Arts* (New York: Praeger Publishers, 1980).

MARKETING IN ACTION: REAL PEOPLE AT CRESTED BUTTE

The Crested Butte Mountain Resort may not compare in size to the major Colorado resorts such as Vail and Aspen, but its unique marketing plan is giving the once-struggling facility a much-needed "ski lift." With an industry trend toward increasing consolidation, small family-owned resorts like Crested Butte are fast becoming an endangered species. In fact, about 25 percent of these businesses have closed in the past ten years due to financial difficulties.

The success of Crested Butte is a good example of how a service firm can hire talented people and capture national attention with innovative marketing—all on a shoestring budget. Located sixteen miles away from Aspen, Crested Butte offers only 1,100 acres of ski trails, many of which are so difficult that only the most expert skiers dare attempt them. But Crested Butte's gutsy owners have found that aggressive marketing is the key to success. Here's the story.

The Rocky Mountain ski industry has increasingly been dominated by major corporations such as Aspen Skiing Co., Vail Associates Inc., S-K-I Ltd., and the Ralston Purina Corp. Typical of the successful ski resorts is Aspen, which offers four mountains, 3,700 acres of ski trails, and an international reputation as a mecca for "the beautiful people." It's very hard to compete against that as a tourist destination.

Ten years ago Crested Butte was a small, little-known hill with only 450 acres of routine ski trails. The resort is owned by Howard "Bo" Callaway and Ralph O. Walton, two Georgians (related by marriage) who bought Crested Butte in 1970. The motivation to purchase the property was revenge rather than financial gain: Both had been "chewed out" by Aspen ski-lift operators, and this was a way to get back!

For fourteen years the resort lost money on skiing but made up for it on land sales. But in 1984 land sales dried up while the ski resort losses increased to $1.5 million. Something had to be done, so the owners thought hard about possible adjustments to their marketing strategy.

Callaway and Walton examined other similar business situations and realized that their number one marketing problem was Place: The resort is a five-hour drive from Denver, so access was difficult. The owners went to American Airlines and begged the carrier to provide direct air service connecting Crested Butte to major cities. They even guaranteed American a 15 percent profit if it opened these routes. Unfortunately, the plan's success was far less than anticipated, and within a year American was losing money and began to cancel some flights. To salvage the scheme

Callaway sent a letter to previous Crested Butte guests living in Dallas and Chicago. The resort offered these customers a one-week package deal—airfare, lodging, and lift tickets for $199—and nearly all of this money would go directly to American Airlines to persuade the carrier to stay in the game a bit longer. Because the mailing received a rousing 10 percent response, American remained interested in keeping the Dallas and Chicago flights for another year. However, this desperate plan also increased the resort's annual loss to $2 million.

Crested Butte did not give up. Callaway set up a program to track reservations for twelve separate periods of the year in sixty-four different geographical markets. If reservations from Dallas for a certain period—say, the week before Christmas—fell below expectations, then a special promotion would be offered in that market using direct mail and radio ads. If sales were up, then the resort could raise the price of its package deals in that market.

Next the resort hired John Norton away from Procter & Gamble to be in charge of its marketing. Norton set up a group sales unit and sent salespeople to talk to travel agencies. Under his direction Crested Butte began positioning itself as the ski resort with a "funky" character and a real Western setting. The resort's advertising slogan became, "Heaven Forbid We Should Ever Become Like Aspen or Vail" and "Crested Butte—What Aspen Used to Be and Vail Never Was."

Still, the resort needed to offer its customers more. So in 1987 Crested Butte looked for a way to build new ski slopes. The only land available was rocky, with slopes so difficult that only about 10 percent of skiers could navigate them. Crested Butte took the plunge and developed the new terrain anyway. The 400-acre addition of "extreme" slopes, which dwarfed the very expensive, small areas offered by competitors like Aspen, gave Crested Butte a unique personality. Giant signs were erected warning skiers of the difficulty of the slopes in five languages.

But Crested Butte still had one problem. The facility was losing money between Thanksgiving and Christmas. The answer: It offered free skiing between the two holidays, a program made affordable because the lodging and restaurant owners gave part of their revenues to the ski resort in return. This program was so successful that lodging at the Crested Butte resort between Thanksgiving and Christmas is booked solid with 9,000 skiers swarming over slopes designed for 6,500 on the busiest days.

What are the results of these marketing strategies? By

the 1988–89 season the resort was making a $250,000 profit, and by 1990–91 profits were up to $1.3 million. And Crested Butte now has received the ultimate compliment: imitation. Other resorts, such as Steamboat in Colorado and Jackson Hole in Wyoming, have copied Crested Butte's airline guarantee program. By carefully honing its "product" image, Crested Butte demonstrates how an intangible product can navigate the marketing terrain without taking a dangerous tumble in the powder.

Source: Marj Charlier, "How an Obscure Ski Hill Carved a Niche Among Resorts," *The Wall Street Journal* (Jan. 20, 1994): B1–B2.

Things to Talk About

1. What problems did Crested Butte face in the early 1980s?
2. How did Crested Butte marketers use bundling as a marketing strategy?
3. Explain how Crested Butte has worked to manage demand for its product.
4. How has Crested Butte's positioning strategy allowed the resort to achieve success in a niche market?
5. What secrets to success has Crested Butte discovered?

CASE 11-2

MARKETING IN ACTION: REAL CHOICES AT ILLINOIS POWER CO.

Who says working in a "nonglamorous" business like public utilities can't be electrifying? Big changes now underway in this 200-billion-dollar business are sending shock waves that are a wake-up call for many power executives. Utility companies are finding that suddenly they will have to compete for customers just as if they were selling computers, sneakers, or perfumes. Almost overnight they will have to defend their turf from other producers of electricity as well as from wholesale power brokers that buy electricity, mark it up 5 or 10 percent, and then sell it to businesses or to other utility companies.

This adjustment is coming about due to a fundamental shift in the way the industry is structured. Because of changing government regulations in the late 1990s, both homes and businesses will be allowed to hook up with power suppliers from anywhere in the country, just as people now can hook up with any long-distance telephone carrier. No longer will consumers be at the mercy of the one

company in their area that provides electric power. Instead they will be able to choose from many different companies—evaluating each supplier in terms of price, service, or other "product attributes."

Currently the price of electricity across the country varies tremendously—from three cents per kilowatt-hour in Missouri to four times that rate in New York. But soon consumers will be able to shop around for the best power bargains, and (at least in theory) utility companies will have to lower their prices to remain competitive. The Federal Energy Regulatory Commission has already made some of these changes, and states will be developing deregulation plans during the next few years that will invite utility companies from around the country to offer their services locally.

These changes are a mixed blessing for the utility industry. Opportunities to enter new markets abound, but at the same time innovative methods of doing business must

MARKETING IN ACTION: REAL CHOICES AT ILLINOIS POWER CO. (CONTINUED)

be identified to attract additional customers and prevent current ones from being lured away by the competition. As one *Advertising Age* writer observed, "With the promise of deregulation surging through the industry, electric utilities are looking to the power of marketing."

Marketing? That's an alien concept to many in the utility industry. Suddenly executives are attending conferences on marketing and seeking to learn more about brand loyalty. Many are taking a new look at how pricing decisions affect demand and even at the importance of developing a packaging and branding strategy. Some utilities are luring marketing executives away from packaged goods firms, and others are hiring advertising agencies for the first time.

Illinois Power Co. is one of the many public utilities trying hard to adapt to a new way of doing business. Illinois Power is located in Decatur, Ill., and provides electricity to homes and businesses in a large portion of the state. To improve its marketing efforts Illinois Power hired Ralph Tschantz, a veteran of PepsiCo and Keebler Co., as its new VP of marketing.

Illinois Power expects its marketing spending to increase as much as seven times from the current level, including dramatic growth in its advertising budget. According to Jim Buck, communications strategist at Illinois Power, initial marketing efforts will be aimed at businesses rather than at residential customers. In the meantime, it is expected that residential customers will actually see *higher* rates in the short term because of the increased costs of marketing. Of course the utility can afford to maintain this pricing strategy only until threatened by outside competitors that inevitably will try to gain market share by offering lower-priced power. Tschantz also knows that part of his job will be to "educate" longtime utility executives about the desirability of investing money in these newfangled marketing efforts.

A lot of questions about applying the marketing concept to an intangible product like electricity need to be resolved at Illinois Power. One option for attracting both business and residential customers is branding—not nec-

essarily an easy task for an intangible product like electricity. Still, many in the industry agree on the strategic importance of building name recognition for a utility company to turn an intangible into something more concrete that will help consumers make a choice. Some people have suggested that utilities also will have to differentiate themselves from the competition by devising novel new products or even by "bundling" electricity with other products or services such as outside lighting equipment, security devices, or appliance repair services.

Another important part of the picture is consumer awareness. Most consumers have no idea that a major change in the way they obtain electricity is in their future. It is never too early to begin public relations programs that educate customers about the complicated choices they are going to be asked to make.

But for Illinois Power this all means charting new territory. There are no examples of which marketing activities will work and which will not, no guidelines for which activities should come first, and no way of knowing how large marketing budgets must be if the company is going to continue to thrive and grow in this new age of competition. Only time will tell if Ralph Tschantz can devise marketing strategies that will allow Illinois Power to see the light.

Source: Andrew Wallenstein, "Utilities Look for Brand Heat," *Advertising Age* (Oct. 9, 1995): 1, 12.

Things to Think About

1. What is the problem facing Illinois Power Co.?
2. What factors are important to understanding this problem?
3. What alternatives might Illinois Power consider?
4. What are your recommendations for solving the problem?
5. What are some ways to implement your recommendations?

C H A P T E R

12

Pricing the Product

When you have completed your study of this chapter, you should be able to:

CHAPTER OBJECTIVES

1. Explain the importance of pricing and how prices can take both monetary and nonmonetary forms.

2. Describe how customer demand influences pricing decisions.

3. Describe how marketers use costs, demands, and revenue to decide on the price of a product.

4. Describe the important psychological aspects of pricing.

5. Understand some of the legal and ethical considerations in pricing.

REAL PEOPLE, REAL CHOICES:

MEET RANDALL POINDEXTER, A DECISION MAKER AT BOJANGLES' RESTAURANTS, INC.

Randall Poindexter's job is to find the recipe for marketing success at Bojangles', a chain of fast-food restaurants. Bojangles' was founded in Charlotte, North Carolina, in 1977 and specializes in cajun spiced chicken and made-from-scratch buttermilk biscuits. Currently the company operates 224 restaurants (110 company-owned and 114 franchise-owned) in seven states. Bojangles' key strengths, which give them a competitive advantage, are their unique flavor profile, their fresh products, and the fact that they serve their breakfast products all day. As vice president of marketing for the chain, Poindexter's responsibilities include overseeing new store openings, developing individual market media plans and TV/radio creative ads, and setting pricing strategies.

Mr. Poindexter began his professional career in 1978 as a sales executive with Pitney Bowes. In 1980 he moved into advertising with the Martin Agency in Virginia Beach, serving several retail clients. At this time he became involved in promotional work for Burger King and went on to join Chart House, Inc. (a major franchisee of Burger King with over 300 units) as director of marketing for their Burger King restaurants in Virginia. In 1981 he moved to Houston where he was responsible for marketing for 200 of the company's Burger King restaurants. Chart House then promoted Mr. Poindexter to direct all marketing efforts for one of its other subsidiaries, Luther's Bar-B-Que. In 1983 he joined Kentucky Fried Chicken Corporation in Atlanta as field marketing manager, and in 1988 he became division marketing manager for KFC Management Company in Charlotte. A year later Mr. Poindexter was named division marketing director for KFC Management Company's largest region in Atlanta, with responsibilities for 1,275 restaurants in fifty-two marketing areas located in thirteen states and control of an advertising budget of $38.5 million.

Mr. Poindexter joined Bojangles' Restaurants, Inc. in 1990 as vice president of marketing. He holds B.S./B.A. degrees in marketing and real estate from East Carolina University.

"YES, BUT WHAT DOES IT COST?"

You may have heard the expression "There's no such thing as a free lunch." That's certainly a saying with which Mr. Poindexter would agree—his job is to offer lunches (and other meals) to thousands of customers every day at prices that are attractive enough to lure them away from rivals like Burger King and McDonald's yet still allow Bojangles' to operate profitably.

At Bojangles' people gladly hand over their dollars to receive a tray of fried chicken and other goodies. Many but certainly not all goods and services are provided to customers in return for currency, whether dollars, pesos, or pounds. True, *every* exchange relationship involves a cost, or something we give up in order to obtain a desired product, but this "something" can take forms other than currency. Even in those situations where no money is charged (as in a free lunch), there will be other forms of payment demanded in the form of time, votes, or perhaps returning the favor by buying lunch the next time. And what we pay for something says a great deal about what we think of it. A product's value is communicated by its price tag. That's why the issue of what to charge for a product is not just something to be debated by economists, it's a central part of the marketing mix (and one of the famous Four Ps that marketers like to talk about).

In this chapter we will first answer the basic question, "What is price?" Then we will see how price is related to product demand, to costs, and to other environmental influences. We will also discuss some of the psychological aspects of pricing. Finally we will present some of the important legal and ethical considerations of pricing practices. Then, in Chapter 13, we will move on to consider how marketers try to adjust their pricing decisions to meet strategic objectives.

WHAT IS PRICE?

There is a popular saying, "If you have to ask how much it is, you can't afford it!" Despite this folk wisdom, how often do you buy something without asking about the price? If only we didn't have to worry about price, we could all drive dream cars, take trips to exotic destinations, and live like royalty. However, as consumers we need to consider a product's price. **Price** is the outlay customers must make to obtain a desired product in an exchange. This part of the transaction can be in the form of money, goods, services, favors, votes, or anything else that has *value* to the other party. In this section we will examine the concept of price from various perspectives and discuss how price is interrelated with other marketing mix variables. We will also see how pricing strategies are vitally important to an organization's health.

> **price:** the amount of outlay — that is, money, goods, services, or deeds — that is given in exchange for a product

NONMONETARY AND MONETARY PRICES

As we explained in Chapter 1, marketing is about the exchange of things of value. We usually think of this exchange meaning that people exchange money for a good or a service. But price refers to exchanges of both *monetary* and *nonmonetary* value.

Bartering

Long before societies printed currency, people exchanged one good or service for another. This practice, called **bartering,** still is widespread, even in our cash-oriented society. For example, someone who owns a home at a mountain ski resort may exchange a weekend stay for having their car repaired or for dental work. While no money changes hands during these transactions, value still is exchanged — indeed, the Internal Revenue Service understands this very well and requires a taxpayer to report the value of a good or service received in exchange for another good or service as income!

Since 1982 when the Internal Revenue Service recognized bartering as legitimate trade, organized bartering has become an important way of obtaining goods and services, especially for small businesses and professionals.[1] In fact, during the last ten years bartering has become a flourishing industry in the United States, and more than 300,000 companies rely on barter for a portion of their business.[2] This practice has become so widespread that many small businesses and professionals belong to one of over 600 barter trade exchanges that have been established to make these transactions more efficient. These exchanges typically offer their members *barter dollars,* which they earn by performing services for other members and can then redeem from others the same way.

> **bartering:** the practice of exchanging a good or service for another good or service of like value

The advantage to small businesses is that they don't have to use their cash reserves or increase their debt to receive the goods and services they need, plus they can often dispose of excess inventory and obtain new customers. For example, an office supply company might need to have its parking lot paved but doesn't have the cash for the job. What the company does have is excess inventory of file cabinets. With the barter exchange it can trade extra file cabinets to other members and in return get the needed paving done by another exchange member firm.

In international trade a form of bartering may be required by foreign government regulations. Some countries, interested in improving their balance of trade payments, require that imported goods be paid for with other goods, not with money. Say a firm sells computer equipment to Saudi Arabia. Instead of money the firm might receive payment in the form of barrels of oil, which it could then turn around and sell in yet another market.

Intangible Costs

If we examine the exchanges of intangibles, we find examples of other types of prices or costs. What is the cost of wearing seat belts? A wrinkled suit may be a high price if a disheveled appearance stands in the way of landing a big account. What is the price people have to pay for attractive, unlittered highways?

One of the difficulties in social marketing and the marketing of people or ideas is the perceived *cost-value relationship.* Marketers often have a very difficult time convincing people that the value they receive is worth the price they have to pay for such products. It should be obvious that wearing seat belts has great value in terms of injuries or deaths prevented. Unfortunately, many people think they are immune to auto accidents and so the value of a seat belt is simply not worth the wrinkled suit. As one author put it, it's so difficult to sell "brotherhood like soap."[3]

In addition, it's important to consider *opportunity cost,* or the value of something that is given up to obtain something else. For example, the cost of going to college involves more than "just" tuition (and of course the hard work and stress of pouring over the books)—it also includes the income that the student does not earn because he or she has to go to school instead of working full-time (no, we're not trying to make you feel guilty . . .).

Even monetary prices are sometimes disguised or at least referred to in terms that give an air of greater respectability. For example, a college education is received in return for *tuition.* A lawyer or accountant charges a *professional fee.* Students who join a chapter of the American Marketing Association pay *dues* (which all marketing students should do, hint, hint). When someone subscribes to a newspaper or a magazine, they are billed a *subscription rate.* A student who lives on campus may pay a *housing fee,* but another person who lives off campus probably pays a monthly *rent.* A campus fraternity may spend a Saturday washing cars for a *donation.* No matter what it is called, though, it's still a price.

THE IMPORTANCE OF PRICING DECISIONS

How important are good pricing decisions? Pricing is probably the least understood and least appreciated element of the marketing mix. We all like to talk about advertising and other promotional elements. It's fun to think about changing technology and how firms invest in new product development. Even decisions about channels of distribution seem to be more exciting than setting the right price. But developing good pricing strategies is critical to an organization's health.

The U.S. airline industry is a good example. Between January 1, 1990, and December 31, 1992, the airline industry lost over $10 billion, more than it had earned in its entire previous history. One major reason was pricing policies. During the decade prior to 1992, costs such as labor and fuel more than doubled, while price wars among airlines lowered the price per mile per seat nearly 25 percent (accounting for inflation of the dollar).[4]

Price Creates Profits

First of all the one and only source of income and of profits for most organizations is through the price charged for products. The $8.7 billion cereal market is an example of price playing a major role in driving sales. For many years the cereal market focused so much on promotions that more than 60 percent of all cereal purchases were made with a coupon or some other type of discount. The pricing strategy thus was one of "pricing up and discounting back." This was quite costly in that the manufacturers pay not only the discount received by the consumer but the additional costs of printing, distributing, handling, and redeeming the coupons. A fifty-cent coupon can actually cost a manufacturer seventy-five cents. In 1994 General Mills cut the prices of about 40 percent of its cereals (an average of 11 percent) while eliminating cereal couponing and other promotions that were costing the company more than $175 million annually in its quest for added sales.[5] In 1996 Post announced similar price reductions for its cereals.

Because of a few greedy firms, profit has become a dirty word in some circles. A firm only profits by pleasing customers, who gladly pay the firm's price to get the value they see in a firm's product. If a firm doesn't make a profit, then the firm has not only failed shareholders, it has also failed its customers. Furthermore, profits are necessary for job creation. New jobs result from investing profits

- ■ in R&D for new products,
- ■ in communications and promotion to launch products, and
- ■ in factories and equipment to produce products.

Profits also are essential for a firm to attract investors and lenders that provide capital necessary for growth and development. When a firm is unable to sell enough product to cover its costs and generate a profit for its shareholders, the firm soon loses vital resources that make it a going concern. Put simply, without profits the firm has no choice but to *exit the market*.

Price Influences Customers

Even during the best of economic times more than 50 percent of consumers rank "reasonable price" as the most important consideration in a purchase. "Reasonable prices" also count most when consumers decide where to shop.[6] Price is even more important during recessions, when consumers on average have less money to spend. In the early 1990s recession, for example, the importance of price went up eight percentage points relative to other influences on purchase decisions![7]

Consumers aren't the only buyers who focus on price. Purchasing agents for firms often put a high priority on getting a favorable price. At least one study has found that price is second only to quality as the most important supplier selection factor. These buying professionals know that when all else is equal, getting a low price keeps costs down and helps make their firm's product more competitive.[8]

Reduced prices stimulate consumer interest in one brand over another. In the 1970s Xerox thought it was quite successful until Japanese firms began selling office photocopiers at a price *below* Xerox's costs! The Japanese firms had found ways to reduce costs by increasing quality—by developing materials, components, and work procedures free of defects (this total quality management approach was discussed in Chapter 3). In the 1990s IBM and Apple discovered that mail-order and telephone-order computer firms could take away market share with their lower prices on personal computers. IBM and Apple were forced to cut their own costs so they, in turn, could afford to make drastic price cuts to match the fierce competition.

Price Affects Market Share

Price cutting as a way to build or maintain market share is a strategy that has been practiced by firms as diverse as software marketer Borland International (which slashed the price of its Quatro Pro spreadsheet software from $495 to $99), RJR Nabisco (which cut the price of Marlboro cigarettes by forty cents per pack), and Reebok International Ltd. (which launched four new versions of its Shaq Attaq shoe priced from $60 to $130—the original Shaq Attaq is priced at $135).[9]

It may seem confusing that price became a competitive weapon at the time of the quality revolution. For years everyone thought higher quality meant greater expense. With the old idea of creating quality through increased inspection and product rework, quality *is* expensive. However, total quality management programs actually reduce costs because there is far less waste and less need to fix problems caused by defective manufacturing. Firms that were slow to create a quality-focused culture found that their products had more deficiencies than the competition and higher prices as well. A quality-focused firm not only squeezes deficiencies out of its products but also reduces the costs associated with low quality. When a firm's costs are lower than the competition's, low price can be used to win customers.

PRICING AND THE MARKETING MIX

Remember as we noted in Chapter 2 that all elements of the marketing mix are interdependent. Pricing decisions, like product decisions, are always interrelated with all other marketing mix decisions.

Price and Place

Take, for example, place decisions. Pricing decisions must be studied from the viewpoint of each channel partner's situation (that is, the other businesses—manufacturers, wholesalers, or retailers—that are involved in getting the product into the consumer's hands. This process will be discussed in Chapter 14). Will the pricing plan allow the channel partner to be successful in reselling the product to end-customers? Is the *margin* (the difference between the product's cost and selling price) the channel partner earns too low to cover costs? Or is it so high that it invites discounting, perhaps hurting the product's image?

Marketers want channel partners to perform various marketing, selling, and physical distribution tasks. By taking into account the costs of these functions, the marketer can figure out the margin a channel partner needs to operate at a profit—a margin that covers shipping costs, inventory costs, customer credit, overhead, and marketing and selling costs. In any case manufacturers are legally restricted from forcing channel partners to resell a product at a given price, for such control would hamper competition and hurt consumers. So a pricing plan must appeal to channel partners on its own merits.

Consider the plight of QMS Inc., a company that makes high-quality laser jet printers, which are purchased by retailers for resale to end-users at a marked-up price. The retailer, a distribution channel partner, incurs costs to stock, display, and sell the QMS printers. Imagine what happened when QMS tried to get its channel partners to sell the printers at a markup that was *less than the retailer's costs:* Disaster! Retailers refused to stock and display the QMS printers, causing QMS printers to pile up at the factory. QMS lost money the year of that decision, and the firm was forced to ask its bankers for more money to cover the costs of an unwanted inventory buildup.[10]

The relationship between place and price also means that the retail channels selected must be in line with the price and the image of the product. For example, a shopper would not expect to find a Rolex watch in Sears or Wal-Mart any more than he or she would expect to see Timex watches on display at upscale Tiffany's jewelers in New York.

Price and Product

Pricing decisions are also interrelated with product factors. Quite obviously a product's price must pay for the cost of production and other costs of doing business. Higher-priced products often reflect the increased costs of better manufacturing and of service guarantees. But the price is also an important communication tool, providing customers with information about product quality, status, or prestige. Curtis Mathes advertises its televisions as the highest quality in America, thus justifying the higher price it charges for the sets.

The stage of the product's life cycle also affects pricing. Early in the life cycle a single firm may be the only producer of a highly desirable product. This firm, essentially a monopoly supplier, is able to charge a premium price. Later, as competitors enter the market, prices are often reduced. For example, Novell Inc. sold NetWare 4.0, which links as many as 1,000 PCs into a common network, for as much as $48,000 early in the growth phase of this product. As the market grew and matured, Microsoft decided to enter the market, selling a product similar to Novell's—but for $35,000 less![11]

In addition, a number of companies have tried to "breathe new life" into older brands by cutting prices and repositioning the brands as higher-grade alternatives to the often-favored low-priced store brands. Procter & Gamble, for instance, in 1993 and 1994 slashed prices by 12 to 33 percent on such brands as Joy dishwashing detergent, Era liquid laundry detergent, Luvs disposable diapers, and Camay beauty soap.[12]

Price and Promotion

Pricing is perhaps most strongly related to promotional activities. First, promotion costs must be covered. If a heavy television advertising campaign is planned for the introduction of a new product, then price planning must ensure that these promotional costs

Putting College "On Sale"

College education has become a buyers' market, and universities are responding. Since 1980 private college tuition has jumped from an average of $3,200 to over $11,000, while tuition at Ivy League schools and other exclusive institutions runs around $20,000. At the same time the number of high school graduates has decreased, from about 3 million in 1980 to only 2.5 million in 1994. By the 1991–1992 school year some schools had experienced a severe drop in enrollments, caused by the decline in the number of seventeen- to eighteen-year-olds. At the same time, due to a recessionary economy, endowments were earning lower returns. Thus many schools were forced to increase tuition and to work harder than ever to attract affluent students who could afford to pay full tuition.*

Many colleges are seeking to get students who can pay at least part of their own tuition by offering scholarships, not based on financial need, to attract top students. At George Washington University over half of the undergraduate students get some kind of discount. In fact, nationwide, fewer than half of all college students pay full tuition. Many colleges will meet the financial offers of competing schools if the student seeks to negotiate. And there are other creative programs to attract students. At Lehigh University top students can get a fifth year of undergraduate or graduate education at no charge. MBA tuition has been cut 22 percent, and MBA graduates get a $\frac{2}{3}$ discount on any course they want to take after graduation.

Other schools are experimenting with innovative pricing strategies. Muskingum College, a small private school in Ohio, slashed tuition for the 1996–97 school year by a whopping 29 percent in hopes of attracting more students.† The University of Rochester, a private institution in New York State, offered a $5,000 grant to any New York State resident who enrolled in 1995. The University of Detroit Mercy, another private university, offers out-of-state students $1,950 to match what the state will give to Michigan residents who enroll at the college. Some colleges such as Susquehanna University in Pennsylvania and Clarkson University in New York are offering students a four-year degree for the price of three years. And some state universities are trying to forge a lasting relationship by "locking in" students when they're still in diapers; several states have begun to offer parents the opportunity to prepay tuition at today's prices. This gives Mom and Dad ten years or more to convince their kid to attend a school in-state!‡

---

* Sarah Lubman, "A 'Student of Value' Means A Student Who Can Pay The Rising Cost of College," *The Wall Street Journal* (Jan. 5, 1994): B1, B2.
† Laura Meckler, "Small, Private Ohio College Slashes Tuition by 29 Percent," *Montgomery Advertiser* (Nov. 26, 1995): 4A.
‡ Shawn Tully, "Finally, Colleges Start to Cut Their Crazy Costs," *Fortune* (May 1, 1995): 110–114; Peter Applebome, "Colleges Luring Students With Discounts in Tuition," *The New York Times* (Dec. 25, 1994): 1, 28.

---

will be covered, at least in the long term. Just as important is that the advertising's creative strategy and media strategy must justify the cost of the product. For example, an ad for an expensive fragrance should clearly communicate luxury, quality, and status to convince shoppers that they will indeed receive something of value in return for surrendering a hefty portion of their income for some liquid in a bottle.

HOW DEMAND INFLUENCES PRICING DECISIONS

One of the first concepts that marketers need to understand before developing pricing strategies is demand. **Demand** is the amount of a product that customers would be willing to buy at different prices, all other things being equal.

demand: the amount of a product that customers will be willing to buy at different prices, all other things being equal

DEMAND CURVES

Marketers often estimate demand for possible target markets. By plotting a *demand curve* a marketer can see how different prices affect the quantity of product customers will purchase.

The Typical Demand Curve

In Figure 12.1 you can see that the typical demand curve is downward sloping. As the price of the product goes up, the number of units that customers will be willing to buy goes down. If prices decrease customers will buy more. This is known as *The Law of Demand*. For example, if the price of bananas in the grocery store goes up, a customer will probably buy fewer of them (unless he or she happens to own a pet monkey who is indifferent to price changes!). If the price increases too much the person will be forced to eat his or her cereal without bananas. If there is a special this week on bananas, on the other hand, the shopper might even buy several bunches and feast on banana splits (with or without a monkey).

Marketers should also realize that there is an *income effect on demand*—that is, an effect on demand caused by changes in income even if price remains the same. For most goods, called *normal goods*, as income increases the quantity demanded increases. For those few goods called *inferior goods*, as income increases quantity demanded decreases.

Demand for Prestige Products

While this type of price/quantity relationship is typical, there is not always a negative relationship between cost and amount purchased. To the contrary, occasionally there are situations where (otherwise sane) people desire a product more as it *increases* in price! For *prestige products* such as luxury cars, jewelry, country club memberships, and accommodations at exclusive resorts, an increase in price may actually result in an *increase* in the quantity demanded. Thus the demand curve actually slopes upward for prestige products. If the price is lowered the product is perceived to be less desirable and demand may decrease.

Figure 12.1 also shows what is called the "backward bending" demand curve associated with prestige products. But the higher-price/higher-demand relationship has its limits. If the firm increases the price too much, making the product simply out of range for buyers, demand will begin to decrease, as shown by the downward slope at the top portion of the backward bending curve.

External Influences on Demand

The demand curves shown assume that all other factors stay the same. But what if things don't remain the same? What if the product is improved? What happens when there is a great new advertising campaign? What if a stealthy photographer for the *National Enquirer* catches one of the stars of *Melrose Place* using the product at home? The result would be an upward *shift* of the demand curve. Figure 12.2 shows how a demand curve may shift from D_1 to D_2 after a change in promotion or some other market occurrence. So, without changing price, the quantity demanded can increase.

**Figure 12.1
Demand Curves
for Traditional
and Prestige Products**

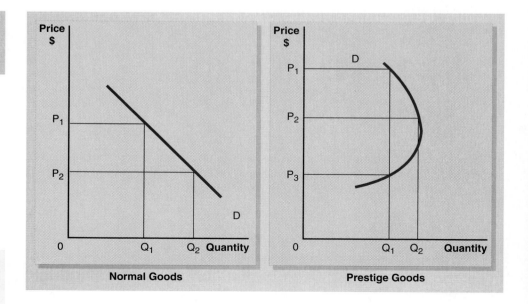

Normal Goods

Prestige Goods

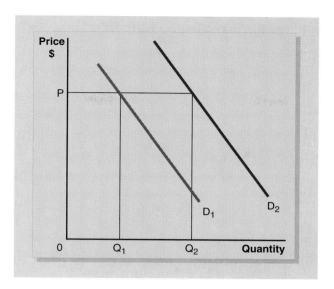

Figure 12.2
Shift in Demand Curve from Changes in Advertising.

In the real world, factors other than the price and other marketing activities influence demand. If it rains, the demand for umbrellas increases and the demand for tee times on a golf course goes down. There is little demand for garden tools and fertilizer in the winter, and the demand for houses and furniture decreases during a recession. In addition, the development of new products may influence demand. While phonographs are still produced and sold, the introduction of the cassette tape and later the compact disk dramatically reduced the demand for vinyl records (except among a loyal band of audio connoisseurs!).

Estimating Demand

Understanding demand is extremely important to marketers. Generally, demand is higher for products that offer good value. But just what is good value—ah, that's the "million dollar question"! The short answer is that it is whatever customers *think* is good

Exhibit 12.1
The economy also affects demand. For example, starting in 1990, the recession combined with the increase in new car prices caused an increase in demand for used cars at the very time when people were holding onto their cars longer. As a result, used-car prices went up 8.6% as compared to 2.5% for new cars and 2.7% for consumer prices overall.

price elasticity of demand: a measure of the sensitivity of customers to changes in price; the percentage change in unit sales that results from a percentage change in price

value. In 1993 a survey of U.S. consumers asked what products were perceived to offer the best value. The top items named were poultry, videotape rentals, fruits and vegetables, television sets, and red meat.[13]

Providing value determines what price a company can charge. Consider, for example, a company called Lone Star, which makes a very unique concrete mix called Pyrament. Compared to normal concrete Pyrament is super strong—seven inches of Pyrament replaces ten inches of normal concrete. Also, while normal concrete needs seven to fourteen days to cure, Pyrament cures in *four hours*.[14] Lone Star has *earned the privilege* of charging a very high price for its concrete product. The company has been successful at creating *benefit sensitivity* instead of *price sensitivity*. This means that consumers view a product's unique benefits as more important than price when making a purchase decision. Many quality-conscious contractors are willing to incur the extra expense to obtain the benefits offered by Pyrament, to the extent that they willingly pay between $120 and $180 per ton, as compared to $60 to $80 per ton for regular concrete!

Often companies need to estimate product demand. Such estimates may be essential for planning product production, and, of course, all marketing planning and budgeting must be based on reasonably accurate estimates of potential sales. In some cases, especially when a company has a large share of the market, it will seek to identify demand for an entire product category. PepsiCo, for example, will estimate the entire demand for colas or for soft drinks in its domestic and its international markets. A small business, such as a start-up premium coffee supplier, will estimate demand only in markets it expects to reach through its marketing program. Of course, the coffee company may want to estimate not only the demand for its brand of coffee but also the demand for all coffee and for substitute products such as tea or other beverages within the limited markets it serves.

THE PRICE ELASTICITY OF DEMAND

In addition to understanding what type of relationship there is between price and the quantity demanded, marketers also need to know how sensitive customers are to *changes* in the price. In particular it is critical to understand whether a change in price will have a large or a small impact on the quantity demanded.

How much can a firm increase or decrease its price before seeing a change in sales? If the price of a pizza goes up $1, will people switch to subs or burgers? What about $2? $3? $5? **Price elasticity of demand** is a measure of the sensitivity of customers to relative changes in price: If the price changes by 10 percent, what will be the percentage change in demand for the product? In the simplest terms, price elasticity is calculated as follows:

$$\text{Price elasticity of demand} = \frac{\text{percentage change in quantity}}{\text{percentage change in price.}}$$

Procter & Gamble learned about price elasticity the hard way. In 1993 P&G launched a price war for its disposable diapers. P&G's strategy was to grow the market share for Luvs, P&G's lower-priced brand that had been repositioned as a middle-price, no-frills brand. The aim of this strategy was to slow the growth of private-label disposable diapers while increasing the sales of Luvs. P&G's price reduction did slow the growth of less-expensive private-label disposable diapers. The hitch was that in the process Luvs also cannibalized sales of its premium-priced Pampers brand.[15]

Elastic and Inelastic Demand

When a change in price results in a large change in quantity demanded, demand is said to be *elastic*. For example, if the price of an automobile increases 10 percent and sales for new automobiles decrease by 20 percent, the demand is elastic. When demand is elastic, changes in price and in total revenues work in opposite directions. If the price is increased, revenues decrease, while a decrease in price will cause an increase in total revenues. With elastic demand the demand curve becomes more horizontal.

On the other hand if a change in price results in little or no change in the quantity demanded, marketers face *inelastic demand*. When demand is inelastic, price and revenue

changes go in the same direction—increases in price result in increases in total revenue. With inelastic demand the demand curve becomes more vertical. These relationships are shown in Figure 12.3.

External Influences on Demand Elasticity

Price elasticity and sales are affected by other factors, a very important one being the availability of *substitute* goods or services. If a product has a close substitute, its demand will be elastic. For example, Coke and Pepsi may be considered close substitutes by all but the most die-hard cola loyalists. If the price of Pepsi goes up, many people will simply put Coke in their shopping carts instead.

Price elasticity also depends on the market time period being considered. The longer the time period, the greater the likelihood that demand will be more elastic (or less inelastic). Here again, the role of substitutes comes into play because longer time periods make it possible for substitutes to become available. If the price of oil increases, there may not be much immediate change in the quantity demanded. However, in the long term there may be significant changes as substitutes become more available. For example, consumers may select alternative means for heating homes (for example, electric or solar heat), utility

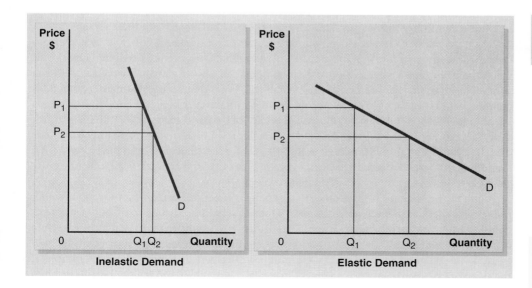

Inelastic Demand   **Elastic Demand**

Figure 12.3
Price Elastic and Inelastic Demand Curves

Exhibit 12.4
If demand is price-inelastic, can marketers just keep raising prices over and over again so that revenues and profits will just grow larger and larger? And what if demand is elastic? Does it mean that prices can never be raised? The answer to both of these questions is "no." Price elasticity of demand is never that simple—thankfully. Whether demand is price elastic or price inelastic depends on the product's location on the demand curve. In the 1950s and 1960s, the price of gasoline was very low—less than $.50 a gallon. Competing service stations often had "gas wars" during which the price per gallon might go down to $.19 a gallon. In those years, if the price of gasoline had increased 10 or 15 cents a gallon, demand would have been reduced—demand was elastic at the low price. In the 1990s, gasoline prices are seldom less than $1.00 a gallon. An increase of 10 or 15 cents is an everyday occurrence—making gasoline demand price inelastic.

companies will build nuclear power plants, and auto manufacturers will work even harder to develop satisfactory electric automobiles.

Generally, the demand for necessities is more likely to be inelastic, while the demand for luxuries is elastic. Even very large price increases do not cause us to buy less food or to give up our telephone. But if the price of imported caviar or a maid service is increased 30 or 40 or 50 percent, demand is more likely to decrease significantly. When consumers experience economic hardships, as occur during periods of recession, necessities may become luxuries. In such situations price increases may indeed cause many consumers to substitute Hamburger Helper for steak and even (shudder!) to give up their phones.

As noted earlier, changes in consumer income affect demand. For most items, an increase in income will result in increased demand—that is, demand is income-elastic. This will usually be more noticeable for luxury items such as caviar and expensive French wines. For items considered necessities such as salt, toilet tissue, and toothpaste, demand is income inelastic—changes in income do not have much impact on demand. It is interesting to note that for some items, income elasticity of demand changes with the passage of time. If income decreases, the demand for new automobiles may decrease (elastic demand) in the short run as consumers put off buying that new car. In the long run, however, demand is less affected (inelastic demand) because the old car begins to have mechanical problems.

Finally, the changes in prices of *other* products affect the demand for an item, a phenomenon called *cross-elasticity of demand.* This is likely to occur in two quite different situations: when two products are either substitutes or complements for each other. When products are *substitutes* for each other, as we've seen, an increase in the price of one will increase the demand for the other, assuming its price remains the same. For example, if the price of bananas goes up, consumers may switch to buying more strawberries or blue-

Exhibit 12.5
Warner-Lambert successfully marketed a drug product called Lopid, which lowers a person's cho-lesterol level. Because Lopid was patented, it had no competition until the patent expired. In such cases, demand isn't closely linked to price—especially for many people whose prescription costs are covered by health insurance and who never pay the actual amount of the drug. In this situa-tion, the drug company has a virtual monopoly. This lock on the market raises some serious ethi-cal issues, because the firm is selling a needed medication at whatever price it decides.

Until Lopid's patent expired, physicians had no other drugs to substitute. Lopid was a finan-cial success, despite the tremendous product development and FDA approval costs. Lopid's patent expired in 1993, allowing competitors to challenge Warner-Lambert with identical formulas under different brand names. Because physicians and consumers could choose lower-priced Lopid imita-tors, Warner-Lambert was eventually forced to lower its price.

Still, the issue remains: Should a drug marketer charge the highest price the market will bear—and the overworked health-care system will pay? A high price would seem to meet the needs of shareholders and employees. Or, should the marketer choose to price the patented prod-uct only to cover costs and to obtain a more modest profit that would make the drug more afford-able and available to people who are not covered by health insurance?

berries or apples. However, when products are *complements*—that is, when one product is essential to the use of a second—then an increase in the price of one decreases the de-mand for the second. For example, if the price of gasoline goes up, consumers may spend less time in their cars, and thus the demand for tires also will decrease.

COSTS, DEMAND, AND REVENUE: DECIDING ON A PRICE

Setting prices is a complicated business. Should a firm raise the price of a product? If it does, it will make more money on each one sold. But will the company sell the same amount? Will it sell more? How likely is it that it might even sell less (hint: this would not be a good thing)?

Before marketers can develop pricing strategies, it is necessary that they understand the relationships among costs, demand, and revenues for their product. Typically mar-keters use two basic types of analysis for pricing decisions. The first uses *costs* as the basis

REAL PEOPLE, REAL CHOICES:

DECISION TIME AT BOJANGLES'

In the spring of 1995 Mr. Poindexter and his colleagues at Bojangles' considered a new pricing strategy. They had discussions on whether they should modify their lunch pricing strategy to include "combo" pricing. This pricing strategy packages sandwiches and individual dinners with a side item and a medium drink. These are then sold together at a price that is about 15 to 20 percent less than the total cost if each item was bought separately, giving the customer a big savings. At the time this "combo" pricing strategy was considered, Bojangles' lunch sales were down slightly, due to the intensely competitive environment. Almost all of Bojangles' competitors had combo menus, and many had invested in substantial media support.

Combo pricing can provide several benefits to a fast-food chain. Service is improved because it takes less time to fill a predetermined lunch order. Customers can be "traded up" to more profitable menu items such as fries and drinks, which feature a higher profit margin than do sandwiches. For example, by adding the drink and side item, which have higher profit margins, into a combo package, you can still give a 15 to 20 percent savings to the customer and maintain a reasonable food and paper cost. And, of course, the average lunch bill per customer would increase (as well as the overall penny profit) as the special offer would motivate more people to buy the lunch package instead of just an *à la carte* menu item. However, combo pricing does carry a major risk. When customers who order combos are primarily those who were buying the menu items separately at full price, the strategy doesn't benefit the company. Those people just pay less for lunch by taking advantage of the special offer, and sales and profits decrease. This problem is a prime example of cannibalization, where sales of a new product "eat into" sales of an existing one!

Mr. Poindexter considered these options:

Option 1. Keep all sandwiches and individual dinners priced *à la carte* and assume most customers will continue to purchase the side items and drinks at the full retail price. This option would ensure that the price of the average lunch order stayed at its current level. The downside to this choice was that Bojangles' would be at a competitive disadvantage, because most competitors had a lunch combo program.

Option 2. Package all sandwiches and individual dinners as combos and price them at a 15 to 20 percent advantage to the customer versus the *à la carte* prices. The upside of this choice would be increased volumes of two very profitable menu items (side items and drinks). The downside of this choice was, would there be enough customers trading up to the more expensive combo order to offset the 15 to 20 percent savings? More importantly, would the combo strategy generate incremental customer transactions?

Now, join the decision team at Bojangles'. Which option would you choose and why?

---

for price. The second incorporates economic theory into pricing based on *demand*. In this section we will talk about different types of costs that must be considered in pricing. Then we will show how the two types of analyses are used in making pricing decisions.

TYPES OF COSTS

Not surprisingly, a product's cost is one logical place to start when determining what to charge for it. If a firm prices a product lower than the costs for producing the product, quite obviously it will lose money. How much the price exceeds the costs determines the amount of profit the firm may earn, everything else being equal. Price also helps to determine the quantity that will ultimately be sold.

Before looking at how costs influence pricing decisions, it is necessary to understand the different types of costs a firm incurs. If a college student wants to build a bookcase for his or her room, the only costs would be for the lumber, nails, and paint (plus, of course, the time the student would spend pounding nails instead of pounding the books at the library). If, however, after the student graduates he or she decides to build a factory and own a business producing bookcases for sale, this young entrepreneur would have to worry about other costs as well. Supposing that this factory idea does turn into reality, let's consider how these costs would affect pricing decisions.

Variable Costs

First, a firm incurs **variable costs** in producing a product. Variable costs are the costs that vary, or fluctuate, depending on how many units of the product are produced. What would the variable costs be for producing the bookcases? Well, of course there would be the lumber and nails and paint, but there would also be the need to hire factory workers. Some examples of variable costs at different levels of production are shown in Table 12.1. If the firm produces only 100 bookcases, the cost per unit is $50.00 and the total variable cost is $5,000. If production is doubled to 200 units, the cost per unit remains the same at $50.00 and the total variable cost now is $10,000.

Usually, calculating variable costs is not really quite that simple. As the amount produced increases or decreases, the variable cost per item produced may also go up or down. For example, if the capacity of the factory was doubled, therefore doubling the number of bookcases that could be built, the company would probably be able to negotiate a better price on the lumber it buys, thus reducing variable costs for materials. In our example in Table 12.1, the cost per unit of producing 500 bookcases is reduced to $40.00 each and total variables costs now are $20,000.

And there are other complexities in the accuracy of calculating variable costs. A firm generally cannot hire a quality furniture craftsman to work a limited number of hours. Therefore it probably will have to pay the worker for forty hours a week whether he or she builds five bookcases or fifteen bookcases. And some workers do a better job than others, some work faster, some are slower. Therefore, in reality firms calculate the *average variable cost,* which is the total spent on raw materials, labor, and so on divided by the number of items produced.

Fixed Costs

Fixed costs are costs that do *not* vary with the number of units produced—the costs that would remain the same whether the firm produces 1,000 bookcases this month or none. Fixed costs include rent or the cost of owning the factory, electricity, the cost of equipment (hammers, saws, planers, paint sprayers, and so on) used in the production of the product, expected repair costs, and depreciation of buildings and equipment.

Combining variable costs and fixed costs yields **total costs** for a given level of produc-

variable costs: the costs of production that are tied to and vary depending on the number of units produced; variable costs typically include raw materials, processed materials, component parts, and labor

fixed costs: costs of production that do not change with the number of units produced

total costs: the total of the fixed costs and the variable costs for a set number of units produced

Table 12.1
Variable Costs at Different Levels of Production

Costs for Producing 100 Bookcases		Costs for Producing 200 Bookcases		Costs for Producing 500 Bookcases	
Wood	$13.25	Wood	$13.25	Wood	$9.40
Nails	.25	Nails	.25	Nails	.20
Paint	.50	Paint	.50	Paint	.40
Labor (3 hours × $12.00 hr)	36.00	Labor (3 hours × $12.00 hr)	36.00	Labor ($2\frac{1}{2}$ hours × $12.00 hr)	30.00
Cost per unit	$50.00	Cost per unit	$50.00	Cost per unit	$40.00
Cost for 100 units	$5,000	Cost for 200 units	$10,000	Cost for 500 units	$20,000

SPOTLIGHT ON GLOBAL MARKETING

Pricing a Jeep in Japan

Pricing of products for international markets often must cover some additional costs. These costs frequently make a product's final selling price higher in foreign markets than in the country where the product is produced. That can make it very hard for global marketers to compete with domestic products, especially when local firms receive government support in the form of subsidies and tax breaks that allow them to keep costs down.

Consider as one example the plight of the Chrysler Corporation when the American car maker tried to sell its Jeep Cherokee model to Japanese drivers at a competitive price. The Jeep Cherokee leaves the Chrysler Corporation plant in Toledo, Ohio, en route to Japan with a factory price tag of $19,100. By the time the vehicle is displayed in a showroom in Tokyo, its price has mushroomed to $31,372—an increase of nearly 65 percent! How did this happen?

First there is the exchange rate. The car is priced in yen at the exchange rate expected to be in effect at the time the car is sold to a Japanese consumer. If the dollar falls the price must be adjusted for the exchange rate. After leaving the factory the Cherokee goes to a port in Baltimore where adjustments are made to adapt it to Japanese regulations. This adaptation, called "homologation," adds $1,100 to the price of the car. It costs $200 to ship each Jeep to Japan and another $682 to pay tariffs at Japanese customs. The Japanese importer, Chrysler Japan, takes its profit of approximately $1,569. The car is then transported to the distributor where employees inspect the car, checking for scratches and missing parts such as floor mats and cigarette lighters, remove the protective shipping wax, polish the car, and install some optional equipment. This, combined with the profit taken by the distributor, adds an additional $1,925 to the price.

Finally the car is shipped to a retail showroom where it is assigned a sticker price of $31,372. This price includes a profit for the dealer of $5,463. The high profit for the dealer is partly due to the exceptional level of service that Japanese drivers expect. If the car breaks down a dealer employee goes to the customer's home, picks up the car for repairs, and returns the car to the customer. Often a replacement vehicle is provided free of charge. This series of steps helps to explain why one sees very few American cars on Japanese roads!

Source: Sheryl WuDunn, "An Uphill Journey to Japan," *The New York Times* (May 16, 1995): D1, D5.

---

tion. While fixed costs remain the same, the *average fixed cost* will decrease as the number of units produced increases. Over a range of output, *average variable costs* will also decrease; hence average total costs will decrease at some level of output. As output increases further, however, average variable costs, after earlier decreases, may actually begin to increase as marginal costs increase because of the inefficiencies created by having a larger number of variable inputs sharing the same fixed space. These variable costs ultimately increase faster than average fixed costs are decreasing, with the net result that average total costs also increase.

BREAK-EVEN ANALYSIS

break-even analysis: a method for determining the number of units that will have to be produced and sold at a given price to break even—that is, to neither make a profit nor suffer a loss

Break-even analysis is one technique marketers use to examine the relationship between cost and price. Basically, break-even analysis allows marketers to identify how many units of a product will have to be sold at a given price (or at a number of different prices) to start making money. At the break-even point revenue or income from sales is *just* equal to costs.

Figure 12.4 uses our bookcase manufacturing example to demonstrate break-even analysis. In this example the total fixed costs are $200,000 and average variable costs are assumed to be constant. The figure shows the total costs (variable costs plus fixed costs) and total revenues if various quantities are produced and sold. The place where the total revenue and total costs lines intersect is the *break-even point*. If sales are above the break-even point the company makes a profit. At any level below that point the firm will suffer a loss.

Marketers usually want to calculate the break-even point to determine how many of their products they will have to sell at what price to make a profit (or at least not to lose any money). The first step in doing that is to calculate the *contribution per unit*—the difference between what a firm sells a product for (the revenue per unit) and the variable costs. This figure is the amount the firm has after paying for the wood and nails and paint

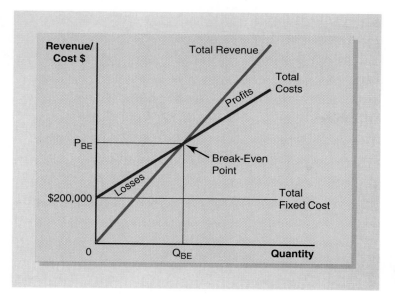

Revenue/Cost $

PBE

$200,000

0

Losses

Profits

Total Revenue

Total Costs

Break-Even Point

Total Fixed Cost

QBE

Quantity

Figure 12.4
Break-Even Analysis

and labor to contribute to meeting the fixed costs of production. For our example we will assume that the firm sells its bookcases for $100.00 each. Using the variable costs of $50.00 per unit that we had before, contribution per unit is $50.00. Using the fixed cost for the bookcase manufacturing of $200,000, we can now calculate the firm's break-even point in units of the product.

$$\text{Break-even point (in units)} = \frac{\text{total fixed cost}}{\text{contribution per unit to fixed cost}}.$$

$$\text{Break-even point (in units)} = \frac{\$200,000.00}{\$50.00} = 4,000 \text{ units}.$$

Thus we see that the firm must sell 4,000 bookcases to meet its fixed costs and to break even. In a similar way we can calculate the break-even point in dollars. This shows us that to break-even, the company must sell $400,000 worth of bookshelves:

$$\text{Break-even point (in dollars)} = \frac{\text{total fixed cost}}{1 - \dfrac{\text{variable cost per unit}}{\text{price}}}.$$

$$\text{Break-even point (in dollars)} = \frac{\$200,000.00}{1 - \dfrac{\$50.00}{\$100.00}} = \frac{\$200,000}{0.5} = \$400,000.$$

After the firm's sales have met and passed the break-even point it begins to make a profit. How much profit? Per-unit profit after the break-even point is the same as the contribution per unit before break-even. Thus if the firm sells 4,001 bookcases it will make a profit of $50. If it sells 5,000 bookcases it will make a profit of 1,000 × $50, or $50,000.

Often a firm, whether a small mom-and-pop business or a large corporation owned by hundreds of individual shareholders, will set a *revenue goal*—a dollar profit figure it desires to earn. So the break-even point may be calculated with that target return included in the figures. Thus, if our bookcase manufacturer (or perhaps his or her spouse!) feels it is necessary to realize a profit of $50,000, the calculations would be as follows:

$$\text{Break-even point (in units with dollar return included)} = \frac{\text{total fixed cost} + \text{target profit}}{\text{contribution per unit to fixed costs}}.$$

Table 12.2
Profit Maximization
with Marginal
Analysis

Quantity (Q)	Total Fixed Costs	Total Variable Costs	Average Variable Cost	Total Cost	Average Total Cost
0	$300	$ 0	$ 0	$ 300	
1	300	170	170	470	$470
2	300	282	141	582	291
3	300	348	116	648	216
4	300	396	99	696	174
5	300	425	85	725	145
6	300	438	73	738	123
7	300	441	63	741	106
8	300	448	56	748	94
9	300	468	52	768	85
10	300	500	50	800	80
11	300	528	48	828	75
12	300	588	49	888	74
13	300	689	53	989	76
14	300	938	67	1238	88
15	300	1200	80	1500	100

$$\text{Break-even point (in units)} = \frac{\$200,000.00 + \$50,000}{\$50.00} = 5,000 \text{ units.}$$

Sometimes the target return or profit goal is expressed as a *percentage of sales.* For example, a firm may say that it wants to make a profit of at least 10 percent of the sales price. In such cases this profit is added to the variable cost in calculating the break-even point. In our example the company would want to earn 10 percent of the selling price of the bookcase, or 10% × $100.00 = $10 per unit. We would simply add this to the variable costs of $50.00 and calculate the break-even point as before. The contribution becomes

$$\text{Contribution per unit} = \text{selling price} - (\text{variable costs} + \text{target profit})$$
$$= \$100.00 - (\$50.00 + \$10.00) = \$40.00$$

$$\text{Break-even point (in units)} = \frac{\text{total fixed cost}}{\text{contribution per unit to fixed costs}}.$$

$$\text{Break-even point (in units)} = \frac{\$200,000.00}{\$40.00} = 5,000 \text{ units.}$$

While break-even analysis is very useful, it does not provide an easy answer for pricing. It is easy to calculate how many units must be sold to break even and to make a profit, but without knowing whether demand will equal that quantity at that price, big mistakes can be made. Therefore, it is often useful for marketers to estimate the demand for their product and then to perform what is called a marginal analysis. Let's see how that's done.

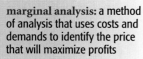

marginal analysis: a method of analysis that uses costs and demands to identify the price that will maximize profits

MARGINAL ANALYSIS

Economists often examine pricing using **marginal analysis.** Marginal analysis provides a way that marketers can look at both costs and demands at the same time. Specifi-

Marginal Cost	Price	Total Revenue	Marginal Revenue	Total Profit
$470	$170	$ 170	$170	– $300
112	165	330	160	– 252
66	160	480	150	– 168
48	155	620	140	– 76
29	150	750	130	25
13	145	870	120	132
3	140	980	110	239
7	135	1080	100	332
10	130	1170	90	402
32	125	1250	80	450
28	120	1320	70	492
60	115	1380	60	492
101	110	1430	50	441
249	105	1470	40	232
262	100	1500	30	0

cally, marginal analysis examines the relationship of **marginal cost** (the change in total costs from producing one additional unit of a product) to **marginal revenue** (the change in total income or revenue that results from selling one additional unit of a product). Marginal analysis allows marketers to identify the output and the price that will generate the maximum profit.

Figure 12.5 provides an easy way to look at the various cost and revenue elements considered in marginal analysis. The figure shows the demand curve and the average cost,

marginal cost: the increase in total cost that results from producing one additional unit of a product

marginal revenue: the increase in total revenue (income) that results from producing and selling one additional unit of a product

Figure 12.5
Graphic Presentation of Marginal Analysis

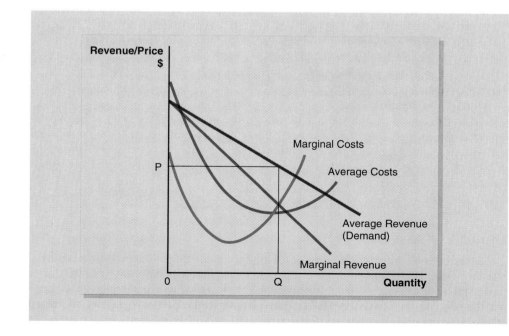

the marginal cost, and marginal revenue curves. Table 12.2 (pages 420–421) shows the data that might result from marginal analysis including profits at different price levels. If only one unit is produced the average cost per unit is the same as the marginal cost per unit. However, after the first unit the cost of *producing each additional unit* (marginal cost) at first decreases and then increases. Think of these costs as added overtime labor costs, inefficiencies caused by crowding on the shoproom floor where the good is produced, added maintenance, and so on.

As the price of a product goes down, the amount that will be sold (the demand) increases (assuming that demand for the product does not follow the prestige curve we discussed earlier). Thus total revenues increase even though prices decrease. Notice, however, that the amount of added revenue for each additional unit sold, the marginal revenue, decreases at each lower price level.

Profit is maximized at the point where marginal cost is *exactly* equal to marginal revenue. To find the selling price at which profit will be maximized, look in Table 12.2 at where marginal cost equals marginal revenue. In this example both marginal cost and marginal revenue are $60 at the twelve-unit level. Based on the demand in this example, the firm will sell 12 units if the price per unit is set at $115. Thus, given these costs and this demand, the firm will maximize profits if it sells twelve units at $115.00. If the firm continues to lower the price, more units of the product can be sold, but profits will decrease.

One word of caution in using marginal analysis: While the procedure is quite simple and straightforward, in the real world things are never that easy. Production costs may vary unexpectedly due to shortages, inclement weather, unexpected equipment repairs, and so on. And because we are dealing with the often fickle consumer, predicting demand is never an exact science.

PSYCHOLOGICAL ISSUES IN PRICING

Much of what has been said about pricing is based on the economist's notion of a customer who evaluates price in a logical, rational manner. For example, the concept of demand is expressed by a smooth demand curve, which assumes that if a product's price is lowered from $10.00 to $9.50 and then from $9.50 to $9.00 and so on that customers will simply buy more and more.

In the real world, though, prices cause emotional reactions in people. Consumers may use price to decide if a product is good quality or "cheap," and they may even use this information to evaluate themselves and others (for example, by paying a lot of money for status symbols or priding themselves on always finding bargains). In this section we will look at the psychological aspects of pricing and how marketers may use an understanding of these factors when developing their pricing strategies.

BUYERS' PRICING EXPECTATIONS

Often consumers base their perceptions of price on what they perceive to be the *customary or fair price*. For example, for many years a candy bar or a pack of gum was priced at five cents. A different price was not customary and therefore was perceived as too high or too low. To avoid violating buyers' expectations when their costs went up, candy manufacturers shrunk the size of the bar but could still say they hadn't changed the price! In today's more volatile market, however, variations in price are so prevalent that there are few customary prices compared to the "good old days."

Internal Reference Prices

Sometimes a consumer's perception of a product's price is influenced by an *internal reference price.* That is, based on past experience the consumer has a set price or a price range that he or she refers to in evaluating a product's price in the marketplace. For example, the reference price may be the last price paid, or it may be the average of all known prices. No matter what the brand, the normal price for a loaf of bread is about $1.50. In some stores it may only be $1.39 and in others it is $1.59, but the average is $1.50. If consumers find a loaf of bread priced much higher than this, say $2.99, they will feel it is overpriced and will probably not buy it.

In some cases marketers rely on consumers' expectations about what a product "should" cost by employing *reference pricing strategies*. Typically a retailer might display a product next to a higher-priced model of the same or a different brand. The consumer must choose between the two products with different prices. Two quite different results can occur as the result of this technique.

On the one hand, if the prices of the two products are fairly close, it is likely that consumers will feel the product quality is similar; this is called an *assimilation effect*. She might think, "The price is about the same, they must be alike. I'll be a smart shopper and select the one that saves me a few dollars." Thus the customer chooses the item that is lower priced because the low price looks more attractive next to a high-priced alternative than it does in isolation. This helps to explain the common sight of store brands of deodorant, vitamins, pain relievers, and shampoo stacked beside a national brand—often accompanied by a shelf sign pointing out how much shoppers can save by purchasing the store brand.

On the other hand, if the prices are not close enough a *contrast effect* may result. In this case the consumer feels that the difference in price means that there is a large difference in the quality of the two products: "Gee, this one is so much lower priced. It probably is not nearly as good. I'd probably be unhappy if I bought that one. I'll buy the more expensive one." An appliance store may place an advertised $300 refrigerator next to a $699 model to make it obvious to the customer (hopefully) that he or she could *never* be happy with the "bottom of the line" model.

Price-Quality Inferences

Consumers make *price-quality inferences* about a product when they use price as a cue or an indicator for quality. By inferences we mean that something is believed to be true without any direct evidence. And so, if consumers for one reason or another are unable to judge the quality of a product through examination or prior experience with it, they will often assume that the higher-priced product is in fact the higher-quality product.

A shopper can easily buy a bottle of very good olive oil for $7 or a little more. But some brands of Italian-import olive oil sell for $10 or $25 or even $65. And some customers *gladly* seek out the higher-priced olive oil because the olives used in the more expensive brand have been "first pressed" and "cold pressed," meaning that they haven't been squashed twice or more, and they haven't been heated up. In reality, producers admit that most customers can't actually taste the difference, but they skillfully price the olive oil to encourage the psychological link between the perceived benefits and the price.

Does it make sense to believe that a product is better quality just because it has a larger price tag? The answer is clearly: sometimes. In many cases it is true that a higher-priced product is better quality. Many of us have bought a bargain-priced pair of sneakers, a private-label brand of cereal, or a less expensive brand of cellophane tape, only to be disappointed in the quality and wish we had bought the more expensive brand. These experiences lead the most rational decision makers to use price as a cue for quality when quality cannot be directly judged, especially when they have little prior experience in evaluating the item.

PSYCHOLOGICAL PRICING STRATEGIES

Because the amount charged for a good or service says a lot about its value and meaning, setting a price is part science, part art. Psychological aspects of price thus are important for marketers to understand in making pricing decisions.

Odd-Even Pricing

In the U.S. market normal prices are $1.99, $5.98, $23.67, or even $599.99. Seldom do we see merchandise in a supermarket or a department store priced in even dollars—$2.00, $10.00, or $600.00. The reason is that marketers have assumed that there is a psychological response to odd prices that differs from the responses to even prices.

Research on the difference in perceptions of odd versus even prices has been inconclusive and has produced no substantive evidence that the use of odd prices is superior to even prices. But that doesn't mean that marketers should change this practice. Because consumers at this point in time are so accustomed to odd prices, it is likely that changing to even dollar prices would be met with suspicion. In other words, odd pricing has become the normal practice, and even-dollar pricing would be considered unusual or strange.

At the same time there are some instances where even prices are the norm or perhaps even necessary. Theater and concert tickets, admission to football games, and lottery tickets tend to be priced in even money. Professional fees are normally expressed as even dollars. In fact, if a doctor or dentist charged $39.99 for a visit, the patient might think the quality of medical or dental care was less than satisfactory because it felt like the service was "bargain-priced"! Many luxury items such as jewelry, golf course fees, and resort accommodations use even dollar prices to set them apart from less costly substitutes.

Price Lining

Marketers often apply their understanding of the psychological aspects of pricing in a practice referred to as **price lining.** Price lining means that marketers set a limited number of different specific prices, called *price points,* for items in a product line. If you want to buy a new refrigerator, you will find that most manufacturers have one "stripped down" model for about $400.00 —with an exact price of $379 or $389 or even $419. A better but still moderately priced model will be around $600.00. A good refrigerator will be about $800.00, and a large refrigerator with lots of special features will be around $1,000.00. Some appliance manufacturers have come out with new models, branded and marketed as special premium lines, with price tags of $1,200 or more.

Why is price lining a good practice? From the marketer's standpoint price lining is a way to maximize profits. In theory, a firm would make the most profit by charging each individual customer the highest price that the customer was willing to pay. If one person would be willing to pay $550 for a refrigerator, that would be the price. If another would only pay $500, that is what she would be charged. If a third would be willing to pay $900, that would be his price. But charging each consumer a different price is really not possible. Having a limited number of prices that generally fall at the top of the ranges customers find acceptable is a more workable alternative.

Firms that use price lining assume that demand is inelastic within certain ranges but that if prices go above that range, demand will change to become elastic and customers will balk. Figure 12.6 shows an assumed demand curve for a product for which price lining is a good strategy and demonstrates how firms that practice price lining set prices at the top of ranges or *price bands.* Customers tend to resist buying a product if it is not

**Figure 12.6
Price Lining**

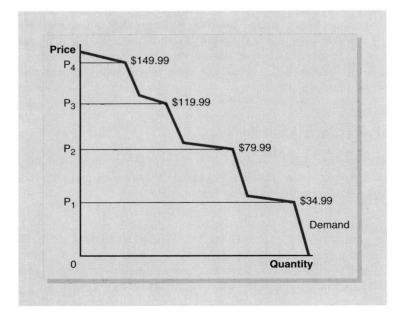

within a range they find acceptable. Returning to the refrigerator example, landlords who rent apartments to lower-income tenants are willing to pay no more than $400 to supply each kitchen with a refrigerator. Moderate-income families will pay up to $600 for this appliance, middle-class families will consider a refrigerator priced between $650 and $800, young professionals will want a better refrigerator to keep their white wine and brie chilled and will pay up to $1,000, while larger upper-class families will pay even more for a SubZero top-of-the-line unit. Price lining provides the different ranges necessary to satisfy each segment of the market.

LEGAL AND ETHICAL CONSIDERATIONS IN PRICING

The free enterprise system is founded on the idea that the marketplace will regulate itself. Prices will rise or fall according to demand. Supplies of goods and services will be made available if there is an adequate profit incentive. In an ideal world this would be all that is necessary. But unfortunately our world includes a few greedy and unscrupulous businesspeople. For that reason federal, state, and local governments have found it necessary to enact legislation to protect consumers from businesses and to protect businesses from other businesses. In this section we will talk about deceptive prices, unfair prices, discriminatory prices, price fixing, and some of the more important regulations that concern pricing.

DECEPTIVE PRICING PRACTICES

Sometimes unscrupulous businesses advertise or promote prices in a way that is purposefully deceptive. The Federal Trade Commission, state lawmakers, and private bodies such as the Better Business Bureau have developed guidelines for price setting and price advertising to prevent this from happening. Retailers (or other suppliers) should not claim that their prices are lower than a competitor's unless the price difference has been verified. A going-out-of-business sale should actually be followed by going out of business. A fire sale is only a fire sale when there really has been a fire, and so on.

Deceptive pricing practices mislead consumers and take advantage of them. For example, **bait-and-switch pricing** is a tactic where a retailer will advertise an item at a very low price—the *bait*—to lure customers into the store. But once the customers are there, watch out. It is almost impossible to buy the advertised item—salespeople like to say (privately) that the item is "nailed to the floor." What happens is that the salespeople do everything possible to get the unsuspecting customers to buy a different, more expensive, item—the *switch*. They might tell the customer something like, "The advertised item is really poor quality. It doesn't have important features. There have been a lot of problems with that one. I can tell you're a real smart shopper—you know poor quality when you see it."

There are other guidelines against deceptive illegal and/or unethical pricing practices. For example, marketers may not claim a price is reduced if it is not, and the product must actually have been offered at a regular price. (This practice is sometimes called *superficial discounting*.) For example, the Better Business Bureau accused Montgomery Ward of improper behavior when it compared the regular price of a pair of diamond earrings, $1,199, with Ward's sale price of $399—the BBB found no evidence that Ward's had ever actually sold the earrings at the "regular" price.[16]

Not every advertised bargain is a "bait and switch." Some retailers advertise items at ridiculously low prices and are glad to sell them at that price because they know that once in the store, customers will buy a second and a third item at regular price. This practice is called **loss leader pricing** and is aimed at building store traffic. Some states do have laws that restrict loss leader pricing, but because consumers benefit, often these regulations are not enforced.

bait-and-switch pricing: an illegal marketing practice in which an advertised price special is used as bait to get customers into the store with the intention of switching them to a higher-priced item

loss leader: an advertised item that is offered and sold at or below cost in order to increase store traffic

UNFAIR SALES ACTS

unfair sales acts: state laws that prohibit suppliers from selling products below cost to protect small businesses from larger competitors

Some states have passed legislation called **unfair sales acts** (sometimes called *unfair trade practices acts*). These are laws or regulations prohibiting wholesalers and retailers from selling products below cost. Many of these regulations even include a set percentage markup below which the retailer or wholesaler may sell the products. This percentage is most commonly 6 percent for retailers and 2 percent for wholesalers. Firms can, however, sell below this level if they have proof that their operating costs are low enough to allow them to do so without losing money. Is it right for the government to tell a business owner that he cannot sell a product below a certain price? While it may seem unreasonable, such laws are sometimes necessary to protect small independent retailers from large giants like Wal-Mart, Sears, or Kmart.

The *Sherman Act* is a federal regulation that also addresses unfair pricing practices by prohibiting prices that are below cost and are aimed at driving a competitor out of business, a tactic called **predatory pricing.** Wal-Mart, for instance, has a meet or beat the competition policy "without regard to cost," which results in store managers getting into trouble for predatory pricing. In 1993 three independent pharmacies accused Wal-Mart of attempting to drive competitors out of business with predatory pricing tactics. The retailers felt that Wal-Mart's pricing of a range of items from toothpaste to over-the-counter medicines was unfair. The three pharmacies were awarded $289,407—triple the $96,469 damages Wal-Mart caused these pharmacies in the view of the court.[17]

predatory pricing: low pricing policies designed to drive competitors out of business

In general, predatory pricing accusations are hard to prove because the accusing party must prove that the prices charged were indeed below cost. For example, in 1992 Continental and Northwest Airlines charged that American Airlines had tried to drive them out of business by slashing prices below cost. American Airlines was acquitted on the charges.[18]

PRICE DISCRIMINATION

The *Robinson-Patman Act* includes regulations against **price discrimination** when it involves interstate commerce. Price discrimination means selling the same product to different buyers (retailers and wholesalers) at different prices if such practices would lessen competition. In addition to regulating the price charged, the Robinson-Patman Act specifically prohibits offering such "extras" as discounts, rebates, premiums, coupons, guarantees, and free delivery only to certain selected customers.

price discrimination: the illegal practice of offering the same product to different business customers at different prices and thus lessening competition

There are exceptions to this law, however. First, Robinson-Patman does not apply to final customers, only resellers. Even then price differences can be legal if they can be justified by costs. A discount to a large customer is legal if it reflects the quantity of the sale and the resulting efficiencies such as savings in transportation. But the quantity discount must be available to *any* customer who chooses to buy in that quantity. In other instances lower prices may be acceptable because a product has become "out of style" or is perishable. Differences in prices are also allowed if there are substantial physical differences in the product sold. Thus a name brand of appliance or clothing may be available through a large national retail chain at a lower price because that model is only sold through that chain.

One example of suspected discriminatory pricing can also be found in the pharmaceutical industry. In 1994 four major grocery store chains filed suit against sixteen drug makers for discriminatory pricing—one of over forty such lawsuits facing the industry at that time. The grocery stores charged that the pharmaceutical firms were charging hospitals, health maintenance organizations (HMOs), and mail-order prescription companies lower prices than the grocery chains.[19]

PRICE FIXING

price fixing: the collaboration of two or more firms in setting prices, usually to keep prices high

Price fixing occurs when two or more companies conspire to keep prices at a certain level. For example, General Electric Co. and DeBeers Centenary AG were charged with fixing the prices in the $600-million-a-year world market for industrial diamonds used in cutting tools for construction, oil drilling, and other work.[20] This type of illicit agreement can take two forms: horizontal and vertical.

Horizontal Price Fixing

Horizontal price fixing occurs when competitors who sell the same kind of product jointly determine what price they will charge. Usually this kind of price fixing is aimed at keeping prices high. The Sherman Act makes this practice illegal. A celebrated case affecting students involved collaboration among some Ivy League colleges to avoid competition on financial aid to students. While a Justice Department legal action temporarily stopped the practice, that ruling was overturned in 1994. Another example of horizontal price fixing is when contractors work together to decide who will be low bidder on a contract, taking turns so that all benefit by the higher prices. Marketers and salespeople need to be careful that they do not innocently share price lists or information on prices, which could make their firms appear guilty of price fixing.

Vertical Price Fixing

Sometimes manufacturers or wholesalers attempt to require retailers to charge a certain price for their product. This is called *vertical price fixing.* If the retailer wants to carry the product it has to charge the "suggested" price. The *Consumer Goods Pricing Act* limited this practice in 1976. Thus retail stores are free to set whatever price they choose for a product, without interference by the manufacturer or wholesaler. Today retailers cannot be required to adhere to list prices.

There are exceptions, of course. Manufacturers or wholesalers are free to set prices when they own the retail outlet. The same is true for consignment selling, where retailers do not actually ever own the product but simply agree to offer it for sale and to accept a percentage of the selling price for their efforts. Also, it is legal for a manufacturer to give a suggested retail price and to preprint prices on products, just so long as the retailer is not required to actually sell the item at that price.

OTHER GOVERNMENT PRICING REGULATIONS

There are other ways that state and federal government regulations and programs influence pricing. In some states *unit pricing* is required—the price per unit (ounce, pound, and so on) must be posted next to the item on the retailer's shelf. This enables consumers to compare the price of products by a common unit. With unit pricing consumers can tell which of the competing brands or different-size packages is the best buy.

REAL PEOPLE, REAL CHOICES:

How It Worked Out at Bojangles'

Randy Poindexter and his colleagues chose option 2. They decided to package all sandwiches and individual dinners as combos despite the 15 to 20 percent price savings to the customer compared to the *à la carte* purchases of these items. This decision resulted in higher sales for Bojangles' lunchtime business, as well as improving the chain's overall speed of service.

However, Mr. Poindexter and his team had to convince Bojangles' store-level personnel of the wisdom of the plan. Many managers felt that lunch customers were already purchasing drinks and side items *à la carte,* and the combo campaign was merely cutting into that business. Eventually these people in the "front lines" came to understand that combo pricing did in fact increase lunch sales. The improvement in speed of service alone contributed to the bottom line, because this innovation allowed the store to serve more customers. Bojangles' also increased the awareness of the pricing decision by developing a "variety combo" advertising campaign that included television, radio, outdoor, and print messages. The result was a win-win situation for the customer and Bojangles'.

The federal government provides *price supports* for some agricultural products. What this means is that if the market price is below a certain level, the government will give the producers (the farmers) the difference between that amount and the market price that they receive.

At times governments have put restrictions on prices due to national emergency situations. This was true during World War II, during the Korean Conflict, and again in the 1970s when President Ford initiated a nationwide price freeze because of the potentially disastrous inflationary economy.

As a final note we would like to say that these laws are necessary only because of a few unscrupulous suppliers. Many manufacturers, wholesalers, and retailers develop ethical pricing policies simply because it is the right thing to do. For example, when a hurricane in Florida damaged 75,000 homes, there was an enormous demand for plywood. Some suppliers quickly raised prices on the wood they had in stock to take advantage of the disaster. Home Depot, a large chain of home improvement and hardware stores, however, refused to budge from its prestorm prices. The company knew that after the crisis had passed consumers would remember which stores were the price gougers and which were the good neighbors. Price gougers see scarcity as a chance for big, short-term profits. Relationship marketers see scarcity as a chance for creating long-term goodwill. In this example admirable marketing policy was also good business.[21]

Chapter 12 Summary

Objective 1. Explain the importance of pricing and how prices can take both monetary and non-monetary forms.

Price, the amount of outlay of money, goods, services, or deeds given in exchange for a product, may be monetary (for example, dues, tuition professional fee, rent, donations, and so on) or nonmonetary (for example, a vote for a candidate, or contribution of time or effort). Pricing is important to firms because it creates profits, influences customers to purchase or not, and can be a competitive weapon useful in gaining market share.

Objective 2. Describe how customer demand influences pricing decisions.

Demand is the amount of a product customers are willing to buy at different prices. For most products lower prices increase demand, but with some prestige products demand increases as price goes up. Price elasticity of demand is the sensitivity of customers to changing prices. With elastic demand changes in price create large changes in demand, while when demand is inelastic price increases have little effect on demand and total revenue increases.

Objective 3. Describe how marketers use costs, demands, and revenue to decide on the price of a product.

Marketers often use break-even analysis and marginal analysis to help in deciding on the price for a product. Break-even analysis uses fixed and variable costs to identify how many units will have to be sold at a certain price in order to begin making a profit. Marginal analysis uses both costs and estimates of product demand to identify the price that will maximize profits. In marginal analysis profits are maximized at the point where the revenue from producing one additional unit of a product equals the costs of producing the additional unit.

Objective 4. Describe the important psychological aspects of pricing.

Consumers are not completely rational and may express emotional or psychological responses to prices. Based on past experience, customers may use an idea of a customary or fair price as an internal reference price in evaluating products in the marketplace. Sometimes marketers use reference pricing strategies in which one product is displayed next to another with a different price. Reference pricing may result in assimilation (the two products' qualities are perceived to be similar) or contrast (customers assume the different prices represent large differences in product quality) effects. A price-quality inference means that consumers use price as a cue for quality. Marketers also know that customers respond to odd prices differently than to even-dollar prices. Marketers can apply their understanding of the psychological aspects of pricing with price lining strategies, a practice of setting a limited number of different price ranges for a product line.

Objective 5. Understand some of the legal and ethical considerations in pricing.

Most marketers seek to avoid unethical or illegal pricing practices. Deceptive pricing practices include illegal "bait and switch" pricing, loss leader pricing, and superficial discounting. Many states, in attempts to keep the marketplace competitive, have passed unfair sales acts, laws that make it illegal to sell products below cost or, in some states, to sell at a price less than a certain percentage above cost. Federal regulations protect against predatory pricing—selling below cost to drive a competitor out of business. Similarly, price discrimination (selling to different customers at different prices) is illegal unless it is justified by the seller's costs. Federal laws also make it illegal for two or more companies to conspire to keep prices at a certain level. Horizontal price fixing occurs when firms that sell the same product conspire to set prices, and vertical price fixing refers to members of a channel cooperating to control a product's final selling price.

Review Questions

Marketing Concepts: Testing Your Knowledge

1. What are some examples of monetary and nonmonetary prices?
2. Explain how pricing decisions are important to firms.
3. How are pricing decisions interrelated with other elements of the marketing mix?
4. How is demand influenced by price? What is elastic demand? What is inelastic demand?
5. What external influences affect demand elasticity?
6. Explain variable costs, fixed costs, average variable costs, average fixed costs, and average total costs.
7. What is break-even analysis? How is break-even analysis used by marketers?
8. What is marginal analysis? How is marginal analysis used by marketers?
9. Explain these psychological aspects of pricing: price-quality relationship; odd-even pricing; internal reference price; the practice of price lining.
10. Explain these unethical or illegal pricing practices: bait and switch; predatory pricing; price discrimination; price fixing.

Marketing Concepts: Discussing Choices and Issues

1. Many very successful retailers use a loss-leader promotion strategy in which they advertise an item at a price below their cost—and sell the item at that price—to get customers into their store. They feel that these customers will continue to shop with their company and that they will make a profit in the long run. Do you consider this an unethical practice? Who benefits and who is hurt by such practices? Do you think the practice should be made illegal as some states have done?
2. As the scope of marketing expands from producers of goods and services to marketing of such intangibles as ideas and people, the concept of pricing must also be expanded. What is the price and the benefit of marketing programs for a political candidate, keeping your cholesterol level down, donating blood to the Red Cross, or wearing a seat belt? Why do marketers sometimes find it more difficult to sell these "products" than to sell a pair of sneakers?
3. Retailers sometimes display two products that are similar but that have different prices next to each other, hoping for an assimilation effect or for a contrast effect. Give some examples of products that you have noticed displayed in this manner. What factors do you think make it more likely that one effect versus the other will occur? Do such practices help or hurt the consumer?
4. Agricultural price supports are often hotly debated in Congress. Farmers say they can't get along without them. Opponents say that agricultural prices need to be left to the natural pressures of supply and demand. In what ways are price supports good for farmers? For consumers? For our country? What are some ways they hurt us? If you were in Congress, how do you think you would vote?

Marketing Practice: Applying What You've Learned

1. Assume you have been hired as the assistant manager of a local store that sells fresh fruits and vegetables and some homemade baked goods. As you look over the store you notice two things about the prices of the products. All of the products are priced using even numbers: $1.00 a pound for green beans, $2.00 each for cantaloupes, $3.00 for a loaf of cheese bread. You also notice that sometimes two different offerings of the same item are priced very close to each other. Small tomatoes are $1.25 a pound, and large tomatoes are $1.40 a pound. Large apples are $4.00 a bag, and small apples are $3.50 a bag. You feel that by understanding the psychological aspects of pricing you can develop pricing policies that will increase store sales. Outline your recommendations for price changes and explain why each suggestion is important.
2. Assume you are the assistant director of marketing for a firm that manufactures a line of hair care products (shampoos, conditioners, and so on). This morning your boss came into your office and announced that she is going to recommend a dramatic price increase. You respond by asking, "Well, I guess that means we need to totally revamp our marketing plan."

   To this she replies, "No, all we're going to do is to raise the price. We're not going to mess with anything else."

   After she leaves you think, "I've got to convince her that we can't make pricing decisions without considering the other elements of the marketing mix. It's all interrelated."

   In a role-playing situation with one of your classmates, explain to your boss why you think the marketing department should consider the implications of the price increase on the other marketing mix elements, what you feel these implications are, and what recommendations for change might be suggested.
3. Again, assume that you are the assistant director of marketing for a firm that manufactures a line of hair-care products. This morning your boss came into your office and announced that she is going to recommend a dramatic price decrease. "If we decrease the price, we should be able to sell a lot more of our products and actually increase our total revenue and our bottom line as well."

   You respond by asking, "That's true if indeed our demand is elastic. But do we know that? Demand for our product may be fairly inelastic."

   To this your boss replies, "Elastic-ballistic. What difference does it make? Everyone knows that if you cut prices you sell more and you make more money."

After she leaves you think, "I've got to convince her that we have to know the effects of price changes on demand before we can make a move that could be a disaster."

Again, in a role-playing situation with one of your classmates, explain elastic and inelastic demand to your boss. Discuss your recommendations for measuring the elasticity of demand for your product.

4. Assume you and your friend have decided to go into business together manufacturing wrought iron bird cages. You know that your fixed costs (rent on a building, equipment, and so on) will be $60,000 a year. You expect your variable costs to be $12.00 per bird cage.

a. If you plan on selling the bird cages to retail stores for $18.00, how many must you sell to break even—that is, what is your break-even quantity?

b. Assume that you and your partner feel that you must set a goal of achieving $10,000 profit with your business this year. How many units would you have to sell to make that amount of profit?

c. What if you feel that you will be able to sell no more than 5,000 birdcages? What price will you have to charge to break even? To make $10,000 in profit?

Marketing Mini-Project: Learning by Doing

The purpose of this mini-project is to help you become familiar with how consumers respond to different prices by conducting a series of pricing experiments.

For this project you should first select a product category that students such as yourself normally purchase. It should be a moderately expensive purchase such as athletic shoes, a bookcase, or a piece of luggage. You should next obtain two photographs of items in this product category, or better, two actual items. The two items should not appear to be substantially different in quality or in price.

NOTE: You will need to recruit separate research participants for each of the activities listed in the next section.

Experiment 1 — reference pricing

a. Place the two products together. Place a sign on one with a low price. Place the other with a high price (about 50 percent higher will do). Ask your research participants to evaluate the quality of each of the items and to tell which one they would probably purchase.

b. Reverse the signs and ask other research participants to evaluate the quality of each of the items and to tell which one they would probably purchase.

c. Place the two products together again. This time place a sign on one with a moderate price. Place a sign on the other that is only a little higher (less than 10 percent higher). Again, ask research participants to evaluate the quality of each of the items and to tell which one they would probably purchase.

d. Reverse the signs and ask other research participants to evaluate the quality of each of the items and to tell which one they would probably purchase.

Experiment 2 — odd-even pricing

For this experiment you will only need one of the items from Experiment 1.

a. Place a sign on the item that ends in $.99 (for example, $59.99). Ask research participants to tell you if they think the price for the item is very low, slightly low, moderate, slightly high, or very high. Also ask them to evaluate the quality of the item and to tell you how likely they would be to purchase the item.

b. This time place a sign on the item that ends in $.00 (for example, $59.00). Ask different research participants to tell you if they think the price for the item is very low, slightly low, moderate, slightly high, or very high. Also ask them to evaluate the quality of the item and to tell you how likely they would be to purchase the item.

Develop a presentation for your class in which you discuss the results of your experiments and what they tell you about how consumers view prices.

Key Terms

Endnotes

1. Bob Ortega, "Swap the Sweat of Your Brow For a Suite Right on the Beach," *The Wall Street Journal* (June 16, 1995): B1, B9.

2. Marsha Bertrand, "Let's Make a Deal," *Nation's Business* (Feb. 1995): 27–29.

3. Michael L. Rothschild, "Marketing Communications in Nonbusiness Situations or Why It's So Hard to Sell Brotherhood Like Soap," *Journal of Marketing* (Spring 1979): 11–20.

4. Kenneth Labich, "What Will Save the U.S. Airlines," *Fortune* (June 14, 1993): 98–101.

5. Tim Triplett, "Cereal Makers Await Reaction to General Mills' Coupon Decision," *Marketing News* (May 9, 1994): 1–2.

6. Leslie Vreeland, "How to Be a Smart Shopper," *Black Enterprise* (Aug. 1993): 88.

7. Gary Levin, "'Price' Rises as Factor for Consumers," *Advertising Age* (Nov. 8, 1993): 37.

8. Melissa Campanelli, "The Price to Pay," *Sales and Marketing Management* (Sept. 1994): 96.

9. Christopher Ferrell, Zachary Schiller, Richard A. Melcher, Geoffrey Smith, Peter Burrows, and Kathleen Kerwin, "Stuck! How Companies Cope When They Can't Raise Prices," *Business Week* (Nov. 15, 1993): 146–155.

10. Allan J. Magrath, "Ten Timeless Truths About Pricing," *Journal of Consumer Marketing* (Winter 1991): 166.

11. Jim Carlton, "Microsoft Takes Aim at Novell by Cutting Software Price $35,000," *The Wall Street Journal* (Sept. 22, 1993): B6.

12. Jonathan Berry, Zachary Schiller, Richard A. Melcher, and Mark Maremont, "Attack of the Fighting Brands," *Business Week* (May 2, 1994): 125.

13. Keith Hammonds, "Consumers Report," *Business Week* (Feb. 22, 1993): 46.

14. Allan J. Magrath, "Ten Timeless Truths About Pricing," *Journal of Consumer Marketing* (Winter 1991): 163.

15. Gabriella Stern, "P&G Gains Little from Diaper Price Cuts," *The Wall Street Journal* (Oct. 28, 1993): B12.

16. Paul Farhi, "The Everlasting Sale—Retailers' Nonstop 'Specials' Stir a Question: When is a Markdown Real?" *The Washington Post* (June 20, 1993): H-1.

17. Bob Ortega, "Wal-Mart Loses Predatory-Pricing Case in Arkansas Court but Plans to Appeal," *The Wall Street Journal* (Oct. 13, 1993): A-3.

18. Kathryn Jones, "Wal-Mart on Trial on 'Predatory Pricing' Charges," *The New York Times* (Aug. 24, 1993): D1.

19. Dave Kansas, "Four Grocery Chains Sue 16 Drug Firms, Mail-Order Concern in Pricing Debate," *The Wall Street Journal* (March 7, 1994): B6.

20. William M. Carley and Amal Kumar Naj, "Price-Fixing Charges Put GE and DeBeers Under Tough Scrutiny," *The Wall Street Journal* (Feb. 22, 1994): A1, A9.

21. Steve Lohr, "Lessons from a Hurricane: It Pays Not to Gouge," *The New York Times* (Sept. 22, 1992): D1.

MARKETING IN ACTION:
REAL PEOPLE AT CHARLES SCHWAB

Charles Schwab & Company, the discount brokerage firm, has indeed brought Wall Street to Main Street—and become very successful in so doing. The major component of its success has been Schwab marketers' understanding its customers and offering them its services at a price that stimulates demand.

At one time all trading of stocks and bonds for individuals was done by full-service brokerage firms, organizations that both provided investment advice and facilitated transactions. The brokers at the stock firms understood the mysterious world of finance and "managed" customers' portfolios. Those who managed better were more successful. But the consumer market for financial transactions has recently changed in two significant ways.

First, many traditional investors have become more knowledgeable. Throughout the 1980s and 1990s the general public's interest in financial markets, and its sophistication, has dramatically increased. This increase has been both evidenced and encouraged by an accompanying growth in business and financial media. Magazines such as *Fortune, Forbes, Business Week,* and *The Economist* have seen large increases in circulation. Television offerings of financial programs have gained proportionately in popularity; CNN is even offering a separate financial cable network. Online services like American Online and CompuServe have made it easy (and fun) for the individual investor to obtain vast amounts of information on companies and investment opportunities. This new, more sophisticated investor was very endearingly portrayed during the mid-1990s with national media coverage of groups of "little old ladies" (such as the Beachtown Ladies) who beat some of the top investment experts in picking stocks for their investment club portfolio.

These older, experienced investors became more and more confident of their own abilities to manage their money—to decide what and when to buy and sell. They realized, too, that they might be paying for services they really weren't using. The demand for a broker that would get out of the way and simply facilitate the investor's trading activities began to grow.

Second, the number of individuals seeking to invest in the stock market has increased. Baby boomers have become increasingly concerned about their financial future. Overall increases in stock values (called a bull market) have made more conservative investments, such as certificates of deposit and bank savings accounts, less and less attractive. As a result more and more individuals have become interested in entering the public markets, if they can do it with little risk and without high costs.

Enter San Francisco-based discount brokerage firm Charles Schwab. Realizing that demand was price elastic for both groups, Schwab marketers created low-priced products that meet customers needs while still making a profit.

For the older investors Schwab made it possible for customers to make their own trades and investments. Because customers did their own research and stock analysis Schwab could operate with a much lower cost structure than could full-service brokerage firms. Planners soon realized it could save even more money by letting technology do some of its work. Thus in 1989 Schwab introduced touchpad telephone trading for its customers. In 1993 the firm introduced StreetSmart for Windows, which allowed users to trade stocks using the software and a computer modem. Then in 1994 Schwab offered Custom Broker, a phone, fax, and paging service for the company's most active trading customers. The savings from Schwab's initiatives were passed along to its customers in the form of lower commissions. For example, a small trade that might cost the customer $75.00 from a full-service house would cost less than $40.00 when handled by Schwab.

For the new investor, another important innovation has been OneSource, a group of no-load funds (funds that do not require customers to pay brokerage fees). OneSource offered the investor the low risk of mutual funds without commission fees. This product has been termed a "financial Wal-Mart" and has made Schwab one of the top three distributors of mutual funds.

Of course, other discount brokerage firms have arisen. But by 1995 Schwab had acquired 44 percent of the discount brokerage business, which accounted for 14 percent of all retail stock trades. All the while, Schwab has remained an extremely profitable company. For example, since 1990, Schwab's own shareholder value has increased by nearly 400 percent to more than $1.5 billion. Also, Schwab has a profit margin of 90 percent for all trades over the pricing break-even number of 22,400 daily trades. The company typically meets or exceeds this level. In fact, in February of 1994 it averaged 38,000 per day. Not bad for discounting.

Source: Slywotzky, Adrian J. "Taking the Low Road," *Sales & Marketing Management,* (Jan. 1996) pp. 53–61.

Things to Talk About

1. How has the consumer market for financial invest-ments changed in recent years?

2. Describe the price elasticity of demand in the new in-vestor markets.

3. How has Charles Schwab cut costs?

4. What is Schwab's break-even point? What happens with sales above this break-even point?

5. What secrets to success has Charles Schwab & Com-pany discovered?

CASE 12-2

MARKETING IN ACTION: REAL CHOICES AT LAMBORGHINI

"If you have to ask the price, you can't afford it!" That sums up the Italian car company Lamborghini. In 1995 the Lamborghini Diablo VT sold for $239,000, and the Diablo SE for $255,000. And most buyers simply wrote out a check for that amount and drove away.

Who is the customer of the Lamborghini? According to Robert Braner, president and CEO of Lamborghini USA, Lamborghini owners are "people affluent enough to afford the better things in life. They don't feel peer pressure, and whether or not they need something isn't the question. It's a matter of the way they perceive the quality of a product, which is why they'll pay $2,800 to $3,200 for an Armani suit."

Of course, the Lamborghini is not just an ordinary car. The Diablo VT has a 492 horsepower engine with a top speed of 202 miles per hour and can go from zero to 60 mph in 4.1 seconds. But buyers are also interested in the car's exotic design and how it fits into their life-style. A *New York Times* review of the car described it as a "kinetic sculpture, proof of affluence, and amusement park ride wrapped into one."

Until 1987 the Italian car maker sold its product through individual distributors and dealers who imported the supercars, one at a time, when ordered by specific cus-tomers. Then in 1987 Chrysler Corp. bought Lamborghini. Unfortunately, soon after the purchase Chrysler's own problems distracted the firm from the Italian acquisition, and Chrysler never really pushed the sportscar. After the retirement of CEO Lee Iacocca in 1993, Chrysler's enthusi-asm for the supercar deteriorated even further, and in 1994

Chrysler sold Lamborghini to MegaTech, a group of In-donesian investors.

Automobili Lamborghini USA, based in Jacksonville, Florida, is the American arm of the firm. In 1993 Lam-borghini sold only thirty-three cars in the United States. Sales increased to eighty-nine cars in 1994 after the In-donesian purchase. In 1995 U.S. sales were expected to be about 100 cars. But the goal for the firm is much higher—between 1,500 and 2,000 cars a year.

Historically Lamborghini had done little if anything to market its car. But a new marketing plan called for spend-ing in excess of half a million dollars on U.S. marketing. Much of that amount would be spent on advertising in business, travel, and upscale life-style publications aimed at creating more awareness of the car. With so few Lamborgh-inis sold, people in the United States rarely get a chance even to see one. In addition, the company planned a direct mail campaign that would be targeted to 50,000 individuals with median household incomes of $1.5 million. And arrangements were made for the Diablo VT to be used as the pace car for the PPG Indy Car World Series, giving the car exposure at fifteen different race sites.

But many at Lamborghini thought the automaker needed to do even more if it was to meet its U.S. sales goals. Some contended that Lamborghini should look at its pric-ing strategy. They felt that the value consciousness of the 1990s had caught up even with the Lamborghini market and potential customers were considering how affordable the cars really were.

One suggested alternative pricing strategy was leasing.

A twenty-four- to sixty-month lease of the Diablo VT at $2,999 a month with a $52,000 down payment would make the price of the Lamborghini more palatable. Furthermore, the flexible lease (from twenty-four to sixty months) would show that the car retains its value. Others felt that to increase sales Lamborghini must offer more popularly priced products. A possibility was to offer a sport-utility vehicle priced in the $75,000 to $100,000 range and/or a sports car that would sell for under $200,000.

But both of these suggestions raised some potential questions. First, was the demand for the Lamborghini really price elastic? Would either the lower-priced sports car or the leasing option really increase demand? In fact, it could be argued that for prestige products such as the Lamborghini, demand might actually decrease if prices were cut. And what about the psychological effect of changing price structure. Would such a move jeopardize customers' beliefs about the quality of the vehicle?

Source: Serafin, Raymond, "Even Lamborghini Must Think Marketing," *Advertising Age* (May 1, 1995): 4.

Things to Think About

1. What is the problem facing Lamborghini?
2. What factors are important in understanding this problem?
3. What alternatives might Lamborghini consider?
4. What are your recommendations for solving the problem?
5. What are some ways to implement your recommendations?

Pricing Methods

When you have completed your study of this chapter, you should be able to:

1. Discuss the pricing objectives that marketers typically have in planning pricing strategies.

2. Understand some of the environmental factors that affect pricing strategies.

3. Describe some commonly used pricing strategies.

Real people, real choices:

Meet Lisa Adelman, a Decision Maker at MCI Communications

Lisa Adelman is one of the people who helps determine just how big our long-distance phone bills will be every month. Based in Atlanta, she is a pricing analyst in the Marketing Analysis Group of MCI Business Markets. Her primary responsibility is to provide rate comparisons and product price analyses to MCI's Small Business Product Marketing Group for both domestic and international customers.

Lisa has been with MCI since the end of 1993, and since joining the company she has begun to work on complex issues related to interstate and international pricing. Before joining MCI, she worked as an assistant account executive at an advertising agency in Atlanta. She received a B.A. in economics with a concentration in marketing from the University of Pennsylvania in 1992 and is now enrolled as a marketing major in the evening MBA program at Emory University.

Deciding on a pricing strategy: move and counter-move

An old Russian proverb goes something like this: "There are two kinds of fools in any market. One charges too much. The other doesn't charge enough."[1] Marketers are never really sure which type of fool they are, because there is seldom any one-and-only, now-and-forever, best pricing strategy. Instead, pricing has more of the continuous decision-making character of a game of chess. For every move, the organization must be thinking two or three moves ahead—always considering what its opponent's counter-move will be.

In other words, never assume that a pricing decision is written in cement. Costs increase. Sales decline. The competition changes its prices. Price reductions may keep a market from being attractive to possible new competitors, or they can sabotage the competitors' expensive product introductions. In 1993, when a new local airline, Mahalo Air, Inc., offered tickets from Honolulu to other Hawaiian islands for $25, other airlines followed, forcing Mahalo Air to reduce its tickets to $10; this new company had challenged the competition to a "pricing game" it may not have been fully prepared to play to its conclusion.[2]

Because the selection of a long-distance carrier depends so much on whether the company's prices are attractive compared to those of the competition, businesses like MCI are constantly looking at possible rate adjustments to keep them ahead in the "telephone wars." As they jockey for position in the minds of users, each company periodically makes a move on the "battlefield" and then sits back and waits to see how the others respond to its latest volley.

When MCI's marketing people get feedback from its salesforce about which products are selling and which are not, they ask Lisa's group to give them some answers and to figure out what (if any) rate adjustments might breathe life into some stagnant products—and in the process make some inroads against such competitors as AT&T and Sprint. In the telecommunications industry, "products" are volume calling programs tailored to the needs of specific businesses. Products typically come in the form of "packages" that vary in rate charged, discounts applied, time of day calls can be made, and so on. For example, MCI's most popular package for small businesses is called Preferred; for a small monthly fee, these customers get specific day/evening/night/weekend rates, a Key Member discount of 10 percent to numbers dialed most often, and a discount on all calls made to the most frequently called area codes.

Lisa's group is likely to address several issues: Should we adjust our volume discounts? Should we adjust the day rates while leaving the evening and night/weekend rates alone, or vice versa? Should we adjust the monthly fee? These decisions have to take into account not only economic issues but also the way a particular phone service is positioned in the industry (for example, the "Preferred" product is positioned to business customers who spend between $50 and $2000 per month on telephone charges). Once Lisa's group and the Product Marketing group agree on an action they believe would address the problem, she presents a case for making a change (including a profitability analysis) to MCI's financial people, who are known within MCI as the Business Analysis Group. These analysts have to approve the changes before new rates or discounts can be filed with the FCC (Federal Communications Commission).

In this chapter we will look at how companies like MCI develop and manage pricing strategies. We will examine the different pricing objectives for pricing policies, look at some of the factors that influence price decisions, and consider the different pricing strategies that might be used for new and existing products. Finally, we will discuss some of the specific practices that are used to put pricing strategies in action.

Deciding on pricing objectives

Developing a pricing strategy involves disciplined planning. Figure 13.1 shows the steps in the pricing planning process that will be reviewed in this chapter. The first step is to develop pricing objectives: what the pricing decisions must accomplish. Having clear objectives gives focus and direction to price planning, making it more likely that the marketer will end up with an effective pricing strategy.

Pricing objectives must support the broader objectives of the firm (such as maximizing shareholder wealth) as well as its overall marketing objectives (such as increasing its market share within a product category). Objectives should focus on how pricing can best contribute to these goals.

Consider, for example, the very different pricing decisions made by two major rivals in the breakfast cereal market. Between 1983 and 1988, major cereal producers increased net prices (prices after deducting the cost of coupons and other promotions) more than 6 percent per year. This strategy worked well for quite a few years, but all good things must come to an end. During the early 1990s, the sales of low-priced supermarket brands showed major increases, until in 1994 they captured 9 percent of the market. In 1993, the top two makers of ready-to-eat cereals announced very different pricing strategies. General Mills *cut* prices on the biggest boxes of three of its major brands. Its objective was to build a reputation for an every day low price, combined with a reputation for better ingredients. In contrast, archrival Kellogg responded to the private label threat by announcing an average 2.6 percent price *increase* on its cereals. The firm planned to soften the $5-a-box sticker shock with discount coupons that consumers could use to cancel out price increases. Kellogg's objective was to win customers by rewarding them with frequent price-oriented promotions.[3] Although these two responses were quite different, each was carefully calculated to

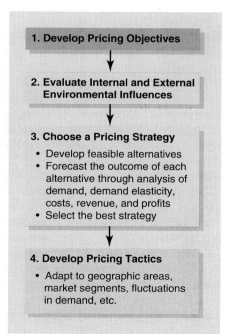

Figure 13.1
Steps in Developing Pricing Strategies

Table 13.1
Pricing Objectives

Type of Objective	Examples
Flexible	Utilize a lower price relative to the competition in the Southeast region.
	or
	Increase prices during the strong tourist months of May through September, then lower prices during the off-season.
Sales	Institute changes in pricing strategy to support an increase in sales of 5 percent.
Profit	During the first 6 months, set a price to yield a target profit of $200,000.
	or
	Set prices to allow for an 8 percent profit margin on all goods sold.
Competitive effect	Alter pricing strategy during the first quarter of the year to increase sales during the introduction of a new product.
	or
	Maintain low end pricing policies in order to discourage new competitors from entering the market.
Customer satisfaction	Simplify the pricing structure to simplify the decision process for customers.
	or
	Alter price points to be more consistent with customer expectations.
Image enhancement	Alter pricing policies to reflect an increased emphasis on the quality image of the product.

achieve an objective, and these actions demonstrate that pricing decisions are not inflexible. In this section we will first talk about how pricing objectives must be flexible to be effective. Then we will examine some specific types of pricing objectives.

FLEXIBILITY OF PRICE OBJECTIVES

In addition to being measurable, feasible, and clearly stated in terms of a specific time frame, it is important that pricing objectives be flexible. Often it is necessary to develop different pricing objectives (and strategies) for different geographic areas and for different time periods. For instance, there may be different levels of competition in different parts of the country. If so, it may be necessary to lower prices in the areas with the heaviest competition. Such is the case in areas where health maintenance organizations (HMOs) dominate the health care field. As these HMOs vie for patients, the costs of health care from both the HMO and non-HMO providers go down.

Some geographic regions may have greater potential for sales, making it wise for firms to have higher, penetration-level goals. For example, in areas where new housing starts are booming, mortgage lenders may offer lower rates in an attempt to dominate the market. Market conditions also change during different parts of the year. It may be necessary to charge one price for summer and a different one for winter, because supply is fixed and demand is changing. Villa rental rates in Naples, Florida and at Telluride, Colorado are much higher during the winter than during the summer, whereas rates on Hilton Head Island and on Cape Cod are higher during the summer vacation months. Table 13.1 provides some examples of different types of pricing objectives.

SALES OBJECTIVES

Often, the objectives of pricing strategies are to maximize sales (either in dollar sales or in units) or to increase market share. Does setting a price that is intended to increase sales or market share *(sales objectives)* simply mean pricing the product lower than the competition? Sometimes. For example, before Russia entered the business, launching a typical 3-ton telecommunications satellite into geostationary orbit was fixed by a cartel at $60 million. The Russians, however, knocked $25 million off the price in order to get into the game.[4]

Of course, price cutting is not always the answer. Marketers need to be careful that their sales objectives don't lead to strategies that provide benefits in the short term at the expense of long-term goals. Decreasing prices in order to boost sales in the current quarter or year can cause customers to become more price-sensitive. The end result is a downward shift in the demand curve; demand at the original price actually drops, because buyers have been "trained" to look for the product at a lower price.[5] This pattern can be witnessed in department stores almost every Christmas, as savvy shoppers wait for prices to drop before scooping up those last-minute gifts.

When Southwest Airlines started doing business in 1970, all other airlines were setting prices on a *cost-plus basis*—that is, simply adding a certain percentage to the airline's cost for making each flight. Southwest instead developed a policy of offering the lowest prices available in order to increase market share. Most of Southwest's routes are fairly short, so when the airline decides how much to charge for a ticket, it considers how much a passenger would pay if he or she were to take a bus, a train, or a rental car to the same destination. When passengers decide on the best way to make these quick trips, modes of land transportation provide the sort of close substitutes discussed in Chapter 12 and thus create greater price elasticity of demand. Southwest also monitors such factors as demand, no-show rates, and seasonality to offer low prices to customers. These policies have made Southwest the low-price leader in the airline industry.[6]

PROFIT OBJECTIVES

Profit objectives usually focus on a target level of profit growth or a desired net profit margin. Profit objectives are important to firms that see profit as what motivates shareholders and bankers to invest in a company. When the product is assumed to be a fad and marketers know the life of the product will be very short, a profit objective is essential to allow the firm to cover its investment in a short period of time. It must "harvest" profits before customers lose interest and move on to the next pet rock or hula hoop.

COMPETITIVE-EFFECT OBJECTIVES

Competitive-effect objectives are the hallmark of a pricing plan specifically directed at having a certain effect on the marketing efforts of the competition. Sometimes a firm may deliberately seek to preempt or reduce the effectiveness of one or more competitors.

In 1993, for example, Toys "Я" Us sought to preempt Wal-Mart and Kmart from selling their usual share of toys to holiday shoppers. To achieve this goal, it launched an early-November program offering nearly $500 worth of price-off coupons on toys. The move surprised the competition, which had little time to react. This "Christmas surprise" enabled Toys "Я" Us to generate a significant portion of its holiday sales from one single price-off coupon program.[7]

CUSTOMER SATISFACTION OBJECTIVES

Many quality-focused firms believe that profits result from making customer satisfaction the primary objective. They believe that by focusing solely on short-term profits, a company loses sight of winning customers and keeping them. These firms instead develop pricing objectives based on pleasing customers over the long term.

GREAT BUCS
FOR LESS
BUCKS.

Consider the value
of a Buc.
The Florsheim Buc.

Florsheim quality
pairs up with
premium leather
styling, for a look
that's right with all of
today's looks. So
whether it's business
or the beach, this
shoe always fits in.
Especially since we
have so many styles to
choose from, all for
about $65 a pair.

For the Florsheim
dealer nearest you,
call 1-800-446-3500.

FLORSHEIM

There's More To Florsheim.

Exhibit 13.1
Pricing can be an important communications tool. Consumers often make inferences about product quality on the basis of price. Therefore, if the product's image is one of high quality, the price should support that image. This ad for Florsheim shoes reflects the footwear company's *image enhancement objective*.

The difference between short-term and long-term pricing philosophies is illustrated by recent events in the auto industry. Most people hate to buy a new car. They often feel that the dealers are out to get them, that car salespeople are untrustworthy hucksters, and that there is no way they can win in the auto marketplace. In contrast, with Saturn's value pricing strategy, customers are given one price and one price only—no haggling, no negotiating, no "deals." This strategy has not only been successful for the company but has also created a new brand of car salespeople at dealerships, salespeople who use low-pressure sales tactics and who emphasize customer satisfaction and service after the sale.

The negative side of value pricing for car dealers is that it reduces margins, thus making each sale less profitable. Dealers have to be convinced that the long-term benefits outweigh these negatives. And indeed, other General Motors divisions and other companies, such as Ford, are experimenting with "no-dicker sticker prices," where the (lowered) list price is the one the customer actually pays. Oldsmobile's 1995 advertising campaign summed up this approach: "Simplified pricing. A new way of doing business from Oldsmobile."[8]

EVALUATING THE PRICING ENVIRONMENT

It should be clear by now that pricing decisions are not made in a vacuum. In fact, the second step in developing pricing strategies is to examine and evaluate the pricing environment. In this section, we will talk about the most important of these external influences—the economic environment, competition, consumer trends, and uncontrollable costs—and consider how they affect pricing strategies.

THE ECONOMY

Trends in the economy play an important role in directing pricing strategies. The business cycle, inflation, economic growth, and consumer confidence all help to determine whether one pricing strategy or another will succeed. But the upswings and downturns in a national economy do not affect all product categories or all regions equally. Marketers need to understand how economic trends will affect their particular business.

Trimming the Fat: Pricing in a Recession

In times of recession, consumers become very price-sensitive. They switch to generic brands, often sacrificing some benefits to get a better price. Discount stores and warehouse outlets, positioned as offering every day low prices, appeal to recession-weary customers. Even wealthy households that are relatively unaffected by the recession tend to cut back on conspicuous displays of their affluence — if for no other reason than to avoid negative attention. Price sensitivity tends to persist for a time even after a recession ends.[9] Pricing strategies aimed at maintaining a pre-recession level of sales must address the loss of market share to private labels and must appeal to consumers' desire for low price.

Recessions are a time when firms trim the fat, cutting costs and reducing the scale of their operations. Layoffs are common, because demand shrinks during recessions. And people who are out of work or who fear losing their jobs put off buying big-ticket items such as new cars. Toyota saw its car sales dip during the recession of the early 1990s, but the company also saw the pickup truck market grow. It decided to take advantage of this situation and made plans for a new truck line, the T100. Unfortunately, Toyota's pickup didn't meet the needs of the market. The T100 was too large for the yuppie market that wanted a compact truck for "urban adventures." On the other hand, the pickup was underpowered for the full-size segment that wanted a heavy-duty 8-cylinder work horse. In addition, the T100 price had to cover a $2500 import fee not required of U.S. automakers. While Fords and Chevys sold like ice cream cones on a hot summer day, Toyota sold far fewer of the new pickups than the 50,000 it had projected.[10]

Increasing Prices

Economic trends also influence a firm's ability to increase prices because they affect what consumers see as acceptable or unacceptable price ranges for a product. For example, inflation causes customers to see price increases as normal. They become more accustomed to paying higher prices. But customers often become fearful of the future during times of inflation, wondering whether they are going to have enough money to meet their basic needs for food and shelter. As a result they may cut back on purchases.

During years of rampant inflation, customers *expect* prices to go up. In some countries, every year seems to be a year of inflation. However, really high inflation rates are unusual, and customers in most developed countries expect prices to remain fairly stable. Nevertheless, sometimes it is necessary to charge more even when prices are generally stable. When demand is price-inelastic, there is a price range over which customers will accept price increases. Whether customers will accept the increase depends on the product's differential benefit, which determines how attractive competing alternatives appear to customers. Raising prices when demand is price-elastic is far less likely to work. In such cases, the best strategy is often to develop a differential benefit in order to decrease the likelihood that demand will decrease.

Implementing differential price increases, or raising prices selectively, is a price policy that works for American Lock & Supply, Inc. This wholesale distributor of locks and other door hardware increases prices in many different ways. No longer are volume discounts the only way to offer different prices to different customers. Customers that pay their bills get a lower price; laggards pay a higher price. Customers that require customized service pay more than those satisfied with routine services.[11]

Reducing Prices

Reducing prices? No company in its right mind would do that. Prices always go up, don't they? Just about every kid grows up hearing some story from parents or grandparents about the good ol' days when "A hamburger cost 10 cents and a hot dog was a nickel." Except for short-term price-off sales, it seems like prices always march onward and upward.

That impression is an illusion, for the most part. Inflation—the persistent weakening of a currency—disguises the constant-dollar fact of life: Prices tend to *decrease* over time.[12] Price declines may also go along with the learning curve of production, a principle that says production costs go down as manufacturing experience increases; that is, costs are a function of *cumulative* output. And when costs go down, firms find that they are able to maintain a required level of profit and actually reduce their prices.

Lowering the price of a product probably makes sense when the goal is to expand market to new purchasers who couldn't buy at a higher price. Reducing prices also may be appropriate if the goal is to increase overall demand with a product that is price-elastic. And price reductions may enable a firm to steal market share from the competition.

Exhibit 13.2
Advances in technology can influence pricing strategies in important ways. New production techniques can often lower costs by improving manufacturing efficiency. Technology can also improve a product's differential benefits so that it provides greater customer value. For example, personal computer companies continuously strive to develop more efficient manufacturing techniques that will enable them to sell increasingly powerful machines at lower costs. They have managed to reduce their prices to the point where large numbers of customers no longer even focus on price when choosing among competing systems. On the other hand, many PC firms, such as CompuAdd Computer Corp., that offered low price and little else are no longer in business. CompuAdd's demise occurred because its competitors were able to sell their higher-priced computers as a result of technological advances. These other companies were able to launch technology-driven product improvements that appealed to customers so strongly that they were willing to pay slightly higher prices to get more advanced computers. CompuAdd's obituary is a reminder that pricing moves must be coordinated with other elements of the marketing mix, such as product characteristics.

Sometimes a firm finds itself in a situation where competitors are offering something the firm cannot offer, such as superior service, fast delivery, or the like. In such cases, competing by offering a lower price can increase sales, and this decrease may not be matched by competitors who instead offer a higher level of service and as a result incur higher costs to deliver the product to the customer.

The behavior of consumers in Japan illustrates how changes in expectations can force changes in pricing strategies. Unlike consumers in the United States, the Japanese were used to paying high retail prices all the time. High prices resulted from an inefficient, multilayered distribution system. However, the recession of the early 1990s opened the door to discount retailing. Specialty retailers bought directly from manufacturers and were thus able to sell goods at no more than two-thirds of what department stores were charging. As the Japanese discovered the benefits of buying at discount prices, the trend gained momentum, and bargain hunting may finally have become a consumer sport in Japan.[13]

The Competition

Decision makers must constantly worry about what the competition will do in response to their pricing actions. They know that consumers' expectations of what constitutes a fair price are influenced by what they are being charged by the competition. MCI,

Exhibit 13.3
Price is sometimes used to position a product. A low price may be used to establish the product as a bargain brand, whereas a high price helps to position the product as a premium brand.

Spoetzl Brewery was the last of the small, independently owned regional beer makers in Texas. Priced below Miller Lite, it was positioned to compete on price, and it wasn't having much success. Then Spoetzl got a new owner and a turnaround began. The first step was to improve the product so that it could have a stronger appeal to customers than low price. Investing in new equipment and making other changes resulted in a unique, customer-satisfying, premium-tasting beer.

Then the six-pack price was *raised* from $3.00 to $4.50, which positioned the product above Budweiser and Miller Lite but below the super-premiums. The strategy worked: Higher prices combined with improved taste repositioned the brew. Sales revenues tripled, and the eighty-year-old brewery returned to profitability. Cheers!

for example, continuously monitors the calling rates charged by AT&T, Sprint, and smaller companies to avoid being "caught" with significantly higher rates.

Pricing strategies are usually influenced by the type of competitive environment in which an industry operates—that is, whether it is an oligopoly, monopolistic competition, or pure competition (see Chapter 3). Generally, firms that do business in an oligopoly adopt *status quo* pricing objectives in which pricing (like other variables of the marketing mix) is linked to the competition. Such objectives are attractive to oligopoly firms because avoiding price competition enables all players in the industry to remain profitable. For example, the American beer industry has been primarily an oligopoly in which the major portion of the market is controlled by a few firms, such as brewing giant Anheuser Busch. Historically, when one firm cut (or increased) its prices, the others simply followed along.

In a state of monopolistic competition, it is possible to differentiate products and to focus on nonprice competition. This was the situation Trans World Airlines (TWA) faced in 1993. TWA, with a 6.4 percent market share, saw little hope of overtaking its competitors with its low-price image, partly because its costs were not much lower than those of the other major airlines, so a big price difference couldn't be sustained. In order to compete, TWA needed to reposition itself. Marketers developed the theme reflected in the slogan "TWA. The most comfortable way to fly." Passengers flying coach across the United States or to Europe would gain footrests, 50 percent more leg room, and other new benefits. The new strategy focused not on a lower price but on more value for the same price as the competition, and it placed TWA head-to-head with the leaders.[14]

The retail trade is an example of monopolistic competition. A shopper can buy Bloomingdale's private-label brand of sweater only at Bloomingdale's, and competitors Macy's and Bergdorf Goodman's offer their own sweaters. The sweaters are not national brands and thus are not 100 percent comparable, so consumers are likely to make their selection by considering nonprice factors such as color and style. Therefore, each firm prices its sweater on the basis of its cost without much concern for matching the exact price of competitors' sweaters.

For those firms that operate in a market that is more like pure competition, price is a major component of competitive strategy. The price of soybeans or corn or fresh peaches is directly influenced by supply and demand. When bad weather hurts crops, prices go up. And prices for almost all kinds of fish have increased dramatically in recent years as health-conscious consumers are turning away from beef and other red meat in favor of the lower fat content in chicken and fish. Other factors such as pollution and the overfishing of certain areas have decreased the supply of fish at the same time, which has also affected prices.

CONSUMER TRENDS

As we noted in Chapter 6, the cultural and demographic characteristics of consumers that determine how individuals think and behave have a large impact on all marketing decisions. Thus marketers who continually monitor the consumer environment are able to make better pricing decisions. Here are a few trends that affect price sensitivity:

■ Many consumers are no longer interested in the trappings of fancy stores, especially when the products within are marked up too high. These finicky types are what the Grey Advertising agency calls "precision shoppers"; picking and choosing carefully, they no longer shy away from lesser-known house brands and are flocking in droves to warehouse stores that offer inexpensive self-serve products sold by the case in drab surroundings.[15] Marketers of everything from autos to suits are scrambling to find ways to offer value and build bonds with customers who are weary of glitzy promotions and overpriced goodies. With the new emphasis on "value," more understated, inexpensive products, ranging from the Sensor razor from Gillette to clothing from the Gap, are benefiting from this trend.

■ In the last decade, sales of products such as Godiva chocolate, Filofax binders, and BMW cars soared as consumers strove to acquire tokens of success. Today, though, disenchantment with the accumulation of status goods has led many consumers to focus instead on the acquisition of *experiences*, such as travel to exotic locales, high-quality music reproduction, and virtual reality games. Filo-fax was recently bought for a quarter of its 1987 value, and BMW now sells a $20,000 model—for an "affordable good time."[16] Even an indulgence like Go-diva chocolate is being repositioned as an "accessible luxury" in the cost-conscious nineties.[17]

■ Many of the women who have been pursuing career goals since their twenties are hearing the ticking of their biological clocks as they enter their late thirties and forties. But couples who have babies later in their lives are often better off financially than younger parents, and they are far more willing to spend whatever it costs to give their babies the best. For producers of products for babies and children, this means that price sensitivity is extremely low among "yuppie" moms and dads.

■ Working couples place great value on convenience products and services that minimize time and effort spent in purchasing. Although couples where both partners work *and* couples where only one partner works average two weekly trips to the market and spend about the same ($57.00 per trip), working couples spend 15 percent less time in the market. This means they are willing to pay a premium for take-out food or prepared dinners. As one consequence of the time pressures facing many consumers, for example, the car is becoming a popular dining room. The practice of eating on the run has become so widespread that one out of every ten meals bought in a restaurant is eaten in a car!

DOMESTIC AND INTERNATIONAL COSTS

A firm's ability to control costs has a direct effect on its price planning. Costs are determined by both internal and external factors. Some competitors pay more attention to keeping costs low, and others have developed a corporate culture that is especially "lean and mean." Unfortunately, still other firms don't know how to make their operations efficient, so they cut costs by making people and machines work harder. The result is worn-out machines and weary people who create deficient products that drive away customers in the long run, no matter what price is charged.

Some competitors gain an advantage simply by carefully choosing where they locate their operations. They may achieve lower costs by getting tax relief from a local government that wants to attract the firm to its region. Labor costs may be reduced by locating in a region where unions are poorly organized or in *right-to-work states* (states where laws prevent people from being forced to join a union in order to work at a plant that is unionized). Distribution costs may be reduced by finding a geographic location that minimizes travel distances, weather delays, or warehousing costs.

Often there are other unique environmental issues that affect pricing decisions by firms conducting international trade. One of the most important cost factors in global pricing is the *currency exchange rate*, the amount of foreign currency received in return for another nation's currency. In the 1992 model year, for example, the Dodge/Plymouth minivan had over ten times the market share of Toyota's Previa model. This lopsided situation was partly due to the strength of the yen relative to the dollar (meaning that a U.S. dollar bought fewer yen and so it took more dollars to buy Japanese products). This unfavorable currency rate (from the Japanese perspective) increased the Previa's price by 13.7 percent over the previous year, compared to an increase of only 5.8 percent for the American-made Dodge/Plymouth minivan. Because this favorable cost differential deflated the value of Japanese imports, American car manufacturers were able to gain market share and increase profits as the Japanese companies were battered by conditions in the currency market.[18]

Another important source of cost differentials in global marketing is the competitor's national or local government. Governments sometimes provide a **price subsidy** that reduces the domestic company's costs, either in the form of an outright payment or as tax relief. For example, America's number-one exporter, Boeing, competes directly with Europe's Airbus Industry, the number-two producer of planes. Four member companies of the Airbus consortium (British Aerospace PLC, Aerospatiale SA of France, The Deutsche

price subsidy: government payments made to producers that reimburse the producer who sells a product below some set price level; the subsidy can be in the form of either a cash payment or tax relief

Dumping

Global influences make managing prices more challenging than ever before. The American steel industry, for example, has been threatened by drastically lower prices in other countries. In 1993, U.S. customers told Connecticut Steel that Japanese and Canadian manufacturers were quoting steel wire rod prices far below those offered by Connecticut Steel and other U.S. manufacturers. How could this be?

The explanation is that the foreign rod makers found that they had excess capacity after selling their goods domestically – that is, in their home-country market. To use up their extra capacity, they sold their product in the United States at a price lower than that charged in their home markets. Selling goods in another country isn't wrong. However, when companies sell their products in a foreign market for a lower price or for lower net revenues (a price less than the price in the domestic market plus the cost of shipping) than they sell it domestically, this practice is called **dumping**. Dumping damages local producers, such as Connecticut Steel, that cannot afford to sell steel wire rod at a loss.

How can this problem be dealt with? The U.S. Commerce Department listens to petitions from U.S. companies that claim they are harmed by dumping. If the petitions are judged to be valid, then a duty (import tax) is imposed on offenders. For example, as a result of petitions by Connecticut Steel and other U.S. steel wire rod producers, an 11 percent duty was placed on Canadian steel rod producers and a 48 percent duty was levied on Japanese manufacturers.

"Antidumping Duties Are Tentatively Set on Wire-Rod Makers," *The Wall Street Journal*, 222 No. 102 (Nov. 23, 1993): B1.

Aerospace unit of Germany's Daimier-Benz AG, and Construcciones Aeronauticas of Spain) jointly own Airbus.[19] For one customer, Airbus priced a fifty-plane order at $28 million per plane, or $4 million less than each plane cost to build! Because Airbus is considered such an important industry to both the economy and the defense of Europe, the governments of Great Britain, France, Germany, and Spain made up the difference in order for Airbus to get the order. Boeing's costs were actually 18% less than Airbus's actual costs, but subsidies wiped out Boeing's advantage, causing it to lose the order.[20] Although the United States government also subsidizes Boeing, the amount is not enough to offset such a large advantage.

PRICING STRATEGIES

The third step in price planning is choosing a pricing strategy. There is no one clear answer at this stage (surprise!). Some strategies are superior for certain products with certain customer groups in certain competitive markets; other strategies are required in other markets. And there may be more than one strategy that would be successful in any given situation. Will it be best for the firm to try to undercut the competition or simply to meet the prices that competitors charge? Is the best alternative one that simply considers costs, or should the company involve itself in the more complex process of pricing strategies based on demand?

Pricing analysts usually consider a number of different alternatives and try to forecast the outcome of each choice. The break-even analysis and marginal analysis procedures explained in Chapter 12 are almost always included in this process. Research may be conducted in order to estimate demand and demand elasticity. Using costs and demand data, planners estimate the revenues and profits that are likely to result from each alternative.

In this section we will look at some of the most commonly used pricing strategies. Some of these strategies are based on costs, some on demand, and others on competition. A few are even based on customer considerations (now there's a novel idea!).

PRICING STRATEGIES BASED ON COST

Marketing planners often choose one of several pricing strategies based on the costs involved in producing the product. *Cost-based strategies* are simple to calculate and relatively safe—they ensure that the price will cover the costs of production and will usually yield at least some profit. The simplicity of these approaches makes basing pricing decisions on costs the most widely employed technique.

Cost-based pricing methods, however, also have a lot of drawbacks. They do not consider a number of important factors, such as the characteristics of the target market, demand, plant capacity, competition, stage in the product life cycle, and the image of the product. In addition, although the calculations for price are fairly simple and straightforward, it may be difficult to calculate costs accurately. Think about firms such as 3M, General Electric, Texas Instruments, and Nabisco. These firms produce a number of different products. How does the analyst allocate the costs for the plant, the capital equipment, design engineers, maintenance, and marketing personnel so that the plan accurately reflects the cost of production for each individual product?

Cost-Plus Pricing

The most common approach to pricing a product is known as **cost-plus pricing,** where in a price is set by adding a "markup" to the cost of producing or buying the product. The goal of this approach is to set a price that will ensure the revenue received from selling the product will cover all the costs associated with the product and also provide the desired profit or return on investment.

> **cost-plus pricing:** a method of setting prices in which the seller totals all the costs for the product and then adds an amount for overhead and profit

To find the price that will satisfy this goal, two steps are necessary. The first is to estimate the cost per unit of output; the second is to add a markup to this cost. The first step requires that the unit cost can be estimated reasonably well and that the level of output will not change a lot during the time period being considered.

For this and the other pricing examples, we will consider an entrepreneur who manufactures a small line of jeans. We will assume that the manufacturer of the blue jeans has a fixed cost of $200,000 for producing 40,000 pairs of jeans, or $5.00 per pair. Variable costs for the jeans are $20.00 per pair.

Once the product's variable costs, fixed costs, and the desired profit are accounted for, the price is easily calculated:

$$Price = cost(1 + markup)$$

In the case of our blue jeans, assuming that the manufacturer wants a profit of $200,000, or 20 percent of the cost, the calculation is

$$Price = \$25.00(1 + 0.20) = \$25.00 \times 1.2 = \$30.00$$

Hewlett-Packard (HP) for many years used cost-plus pricing when figuring out how much to charge for the electrical equipment the company sold to engineers. HP managers would determine how much it cost to produce the equipment, decide how much profit would satisfy the company's objectives, and *voilá:* There was the price!

Cost-plus pricing can also be used to price services. A commercial printer, for example, may produce the annual report for a major corporation, a brochure for the local chapter of the Red Cross, and a cookbook to be sold by the city's Junior League. It must tailor each customized printing job to the requirements of the customer. Service firms may have greater flexibility with pricing and may find that cost-plus pricing, though it is a useful place to begin, must be adapted to individual situations. For example, it may be necessary to adjust the cost-plus price by taking into account an estimate of what each customer is willing to pay and what the competition might offer on a similar quote.

The most common form of cost-plus pricing is straight *markup pricing,* in which price is calculated by adding a set percentage to the cost. This technique is especially popular with retailers and wholesalers because it makes price so easy to calculate. The marketer simply determines the cost per unit of the product and the percentage necessary to cover expenses and the desired level of profit.

Actually, two different methods—markup on cost and markup on selling price—are used, the latter being more popular. In *markup on cost pricing,* a percentage of the cost is added to the cost to determine the selling price. With *markup on selling price,* the calculation includes the desired percentage of the selling price.

Markup on cost:

$$\text{Price} = \text{cost} + (\text{cost} \times \text{markup percent})$$

Let's say our retailer buys the jeans from the manufacturer for $30.00 per pair. If the retailer requires a 40 percent markup on cost, the calculation is

$$\text{Price} = \$30 + (\$30 \times 0.40) = \$30 + \$12 = \$42$$

Note that in the calculations, the markup percentage is expressed as a decimal; that is, 20 percent = 0.20, 25 percent = 0.25, 30 percent = 0.30, and so on.

Markup on selling price:

$$\text{Price} = \frac{\text{cost}}{1.00 - \text{markup percent}}$$

Thus, using the same product cost and a price with a 40 percent markup on selling price would yield

$$\text{Price} = \frac{\$30}{1.00 - 0.40} = \frac{\$30}{.60} = \$50.00$$

As you can see, markup on selling price results in a higher final price. The markup on selling price is more frequently used, because the markup percentage is also the gross margin. That is, a 40 percent markup on selling price means that a firm has a 40 percent margin—40 percent of all sales are available for covering overhead and for profit.

Price-Floor Pricing

The cost-based pricing methods we have looked at do not take into account any factors except costs and profits. **Price-floor pricing** is a method for calculating price that considers both costs and what can be done to ensure that a plant can operate at its capacity.

price-floor pricing: a method for calculating price in which, to maintain full plant operating capacity, a portion of a firm's output may be sold at a price that only covers marginal costs of production

Price-floor pricing can be used only in certain unique situations. Sometimes, the state of the economy or other temporary market conditions make it impossible for a firm to sell enough units of its product, at a price that covers fixed costs, variable costs, and profit goals, to keep its plants operating at full capacity. Price-floor pricing allows the marketer to determine the lowest price at which it makes sense to increase production to full capacity. In such circumstances, it may be possible to sell part of the units produced at a lower price, one that covers only the marginal costs or production. If the price-floor price can be set above the marginal costs—that is, if marginal revenues are greater than marginal costs—then the firm can use the difference to increase profits or to help cover its fixed costs.

For example, assume our jeans firm, operating at full capacity, can produce 50,000 pairs of jeans. The average variable costs per unit are $20.00, and the price that covers fixed costs, variable costs and a desired level of profits is $30.00 per pair. But at this price, the firm can sell only 40,000 units. Using price-floor pricing, the firm could sell the additional 10,000 pairs of jeans at $20.00 and maintain operations at full capacity.

If it adopted this approach, the firm would not make anything on the additional units, but it would not lose anything either. If it could sell the additional 10,000 pairs at

Will Shoppers Shell Out More Greenbacks for Green Products?

Only a decade ago, price planning virtually ignored whether consumers would be willing to pay more for "green" products—products that are friendly to the environment. Today, the appeal of green marketing can't be overlooked. Marketers are challenged to find ways to make green products less expensive or to produce green products that customers will want and need.

One survey found that eight out of ten consumers were willing to pay higher prices in order to avoid harming the environment. Two-thirds of those in the survey said they would pay 15 to 20 cents a gallon more for gasoline that causes much less pollution than current blends. But don't let statistics like these mislead you: What consumers say and what they do are often quite different. The actual market share of green products does not reveal overwhelming consumer support. To the contrary, few consumers believe that a personal sacrifice—like paying more for green products—will help unless everyone else pitches in as well. A common sentiment is "I'd gladly pay the higher price if everyone *else* did."

Sometimes green products can be more appealing because they offer consumers a tangible benefit that is friendly to their wallets as well as to the earth. For example, consumers are very willing to recycle soft drink bottles when they have to pay a deposit on each bottle purchased. From Wal-Mart to Lord and Taylor, retailers have learned that by selling the cardboard boxes used to deliver goods to their stores to be recycled, company profits can be substantially increased.

There are even cases where "going green" can help keep product costs down. For example, Procter & Gamble is testing Tide Refill for powder detergents; a refill carton slips into the original box. Besides a 50 percent reduction in waste, packaging costs may also decline. P&G may have found a packaging approach that permits a lower price and reduces waste at the same time. Downy fabric softener refills are sold in a concentrated form packaged in a paper milk-carton type of package. The Resolve carpet cleaner refill package is a lightweight plastic pouch. All of these packages not only ease the burden on the environment but also make the products less expensive to produce, which spells cost savings for the consumer. When companies can cut costs (and pass the savings on to customers through reduced product prices) and protect the environment at the same time, they surpass customer expectations—one way new era firms can build long-term customer relationships.

$25.00, then it would not only cover the variable costs but would also increase its total profits 10,000 × $5, or $50,000—not a bad deal. On the other hand, several risks accompany price-floor pricing. Selling the additional 10,000 pairs of jeans at a lower cost could cannibalize full-price sales. And if the lower price were offered to some retailers and not others, it might anger those not included and undermine customer loyalty.

Firms that produce their own national brands and that also manufacture private-label brands sold through various retailers and distributors may use price-floor pricing for the private-label part of their business. Thus Frigidaire may use 70 percent of its manufacturing capacity to build refrigerators to be sold with the Frigidaire name while it also produces refrigerators to be sold by Sears under the Kenmore name.

PRICING STRATEGIES BASED ON DEMAND

In **demand-based pricing** the selling price is based on an estimate of volume that can be sold at different prices. In order to use any of the pricing strategies based on demand, firms must conduct research to determine how much different target markets are willing to pay. In other words, they need to know the amount that is likely to be purchased (the demand) and the price elasticity of demand at different price ranges.

demand-based pricing: a method for setting price that is based on an estimate of demand at different prices

One important strength of demand-based pricing strategies is that they generally ensure a firm that it will be able to sell what it produces—that there will be demand for the good or service at the determined price. A major disadvantage is the difficulty of accurately estimating demand.

To estimate demand at different price levels, marketers often use customer surveys in which consumers are asked whether they would buy a certain product and how much of it they would buy at various prices. Experienced researchers, however, know that what consumers say they will do and how they behave in the marketplace are often quite different. Therefore, more accurate estimates of demand are obtained by some type of field research. For instance, a firm might actually offer the product at different price levels in different test markets and measure how much is sold at the different prices.

Demand-Backward Pricing

Demand-backward pricing starts with a customer-pleasing price and works backward to costs. Costs are seen as fixed with cost-based pricing. Not so when firms practice demand-backward pricing, in which they use creative cost-management strategies in order to produce the product at a cost that will allow them to sell it at the demand-determined price and still have the required level of profit. In other words, they work *backward* by first determining the price at which they need to sell the product and then designing the product in such a way that they can produce it (and still make a profit) at this price.

The pricing strategy used by Boeing illustrates demand-backward pricing. Boeing sought to persuade the big passenger carriers, such as American Airlines and United Airlines, to trade in their old planes for new ones. First, Boeing figured the demand-driven price by considering not only the purchase price but also the operating costs that its customers would take into account when deciding whether to replace inefficient old jets. Given this price ceiling, Boeing concluded that costs must drop about 30 percent per plane to get customers to trade in their older jets for new ones. Boeing was able to accomplish this by scaling down operations and reducing the costs of materials and labor so that the company would be able to produce a new plane at this lower price.[21]

Chain-Markup Pricing

Chain-markup pricing is a pricing strategy that extends the logic of demand-backward pricing from the ultimate consumer all the way back through the channel of distribution to the manufacturer. A firm first determines the maximum, or the ideal, end-user price on the basis of estimates of demand. Next the percentage margins that the retailer, wholesaler, and/or distributor will require to cover overhead and profits are estimated. Finally, the required cost of manufacturing is obtained.

For example, assume that, on the basis of estimates of demand, a firm finds that the best price to charge consumers for a pair of jeans is $60.00. But the channel of distribution includes both retailers and wholesalers. Past experience tells the marketer that the retailer will require a 40 percent markup on its purchase price in order to make a profit. To make carrying the product attractive to wholesalers will require that they have a 20 percent gross margin. And the manufacturer requires a 12 percent profit margin. Thus the cost of production can be no more than the following calculations specify.

Final selling price	$60.00
Less retailer margin of 40%	(24.00)
Selling price for the wholesaler	36.00
Less wholesaler margin of 20%	(7.20)
Selling price for the manufacturer	28.80
Required profit for the manufacturer (12%)	(3.46)
Maximum cost of production	$25.34

But what happens if, no matter how hard it tries, the firm cannot manufacture a good-quality pair of jeans for $25.34? Abandon the product? Cut out members of the channel of distribution and sell directly to consumers through catalogs? Well, those are certainly possibilities. Some firms find that *off-shore outsourcing* (contracting with foreign firms that can produce the product cheaper as a result of lower labor costs) of some or all of the production process enables them to meet the required cost limits. At other times, a firm may find that changing elements of the marketing mix can shift the demand curve upward (as we discussed in Chapter 12). For example, the firm might improve the product or add special features to it. It might try to change demand by increasing its advertising budget for the item. Boosting demand makes possible a higher end-user price so that the essential costs of product and profit can be covered.

Exhibit 13.4
Most demand-based pricing methods are focused on customer needs and wants. Products are produced only if they can be manufactured at a cost consumers are willing to pay. But sometimes demand-based pricing can be used to take advantage of a captive market. *Insult pricing* is a term for a not-so-consumer-friendly pricing strategy used in the convenience store industry. Some convenience stores charge extremely high prices for items that consumers might suddenly have need for at 2:00 in the morning when other stores are closed. The price of diapers, dog food, and diarrhea medicine may be 40, 50, or even 60 percent higher than at the local supermarket—an "insult" to the desperate customer. Fortunately, as more and more supermarkets are choosing to stay open twenty-four hours a day, many consumers have found they can avoid being "insulted" in the wee hours of the morning.

PRICING STRATEGIES BASED ON THE COMPETITION

In some situations, the prices charged by competitors are more important than costs and demand. This occurs when the offerings of rival companies are so similar that a firm is not able to differentiate its product clearly and justify a big price difference. Pricing based on the competition is fairly simple. And basing a price on the competition often makes sense because it represents the sum of all industry wisdom: Maybe the other companies have already determined, through their own research and experience, what people are willing to pay for an item.

Pricing based on the competition can be tricky, though. If a firm raises its price, then other firms may follow the leader, or they may choose to maintain the lower price, thus capturing additional market share. If a firm lowers its price, competitors are quite likely to retaliate with a price that is lower still. Bearing these considerations in mind, marketers must select the pricing strategy that gives the maximum benefit at the minimum risk of loss to the firm.

Price Leadership

In the "good old days" before non-U.S. automakers invaded the domestic market, pricing decisions for American cars were straightforward: Industry giant General Motors would announce its new-car prices, and Ford and Chrysler would follow suit with similar prices. At that time, GM was a **price leader.** As the most powerful firm in its industry, the giant company established prices that prevailed for other companies in the industry as well. A firm that chooses a *price leadership* strategy follows the leader by setting similar prices. Usually, a price leadership strategy is found in an industry with relatively few producers—that is, an oligopoly. In such an industry, it is in the best interests of all firms to avoid price competition. But it is illegal for competitors to get together and set prices (price fixing). Price leadership strategies are popular because they provide an acceptable way for firms to agree on prices without ever talking with each other.

price leader: the firm that sets price first in an industry; other major firms in the industry follow the leader by setting similar prices

REAL PEOPLE, REAL CHOICES:

DECISION TIME AT MCI

In the spring of 1995, the president of Lisa Adelman's division instructed the group to raise rates by 3.9 percent for all products and all time periods. The reason for this increase was to provide needed revenue to the company. Once the new rates were filed, the Marketing Analysis Group would have to wait and see how the competition (primarily AT&T) would react: Would AT&T follow suit and raise its rates by 3.9 percent as well? This response was crucial to the final filing: MCI did not want to risk having its rates higher than AT&T's, even for a short time. This discrepancy would discredit all of its claims to offer savings and harm its reputation as a lower-cost provider. Over the past several years, AT&T's rates typically have been 3 percent to 5 percent higher than MCI's, so Lisa's group anticipated that AT&T would choose simply to go along with the rate increase—an action that would provide their rival with extra revenue as well.

AT&T waited until the last possible moment to file in order to have its rate change go into effect on the same day as MCI's. This tactic was predictable, but the specific response was not: AT&T did raise its rates, but to a level even greater than MCI's increase. To make things even more confusing, rates for AT&T's various products were not raised evenly across the board. Some of its products received an increase of between 6.9 percent and 7.6 percent, while others were raised by only 3.9 percent to 4.5 percent.

Now Lisa Adelman and her colleagues faced the challenge of determining how MCI should respond to AT&T's move. They had only 24 hours to notify the company's Tariffs and Regulations Department so that it could file the new rates with the FCC in time to meet the effective date for the rate increase. They considered two options:

Option 1. MCI could keep the 3.9 percent filing intact. When the rate changes for MCI and AT&T became effective, MCI could boast of offering significant savings, but with no particular pattern compared to AT&T's products. At a later point, MCI could decide whether it wanted to adjust its rates further to be more consistent with AT&T's pricing schedule. The down side to this choice is that the amount that customers would save compared to AT&T's rates would not be the same in different countries, so MCI could not legally claim in its advertising that all customers would save by choosing MCI over AT&T.

Option 2. MCI could withdraw its filings in order to give the company a few days' breathing room to analyze each product's price differential against AT&T. Then, once all the new rate changes had been decided on, it could file them to be effective as soon as possible. Choosing this option, however, would mean that MCI's new rates would reach the market later than AT&T's, and MCI would lose valuable revenue every additional day it waited to take action, because the lower rates would still be in effect.

Now, join the decision team at MCI: which option would you choose, and why?

Meeting the Competition: Parity Pricing

The basic idea of **parity pricing** is to keep the price about equal to the key competitors' prices, thus eliminating price as a consumer's point of comparison. Because everyone's product prices are about the same, the shopper must make a decision on the basis of other factors, such as image, ease of use, and availability. This situation can occur when there is no established price leader. Parity pricing was recently seen in the diaper market. In January 1993, Kimberly-Clark, maker of Huggies disposable diapers, dropped its prices and reduced the number of diapers in its packages. This move was aimed at overtaking the slender market-share lead held by Pampers, a Procter & Gamble Co. (P&G) brand. In April 1993, P&G responded by reducing Pampers' price so that the cost per diaper was about the same.[22]

A variation on parity pricing strategy is *pegged pricing,* which means setting prices relative to an important industry reference point. For example, in the mid-1990s Japanese automakers would set their U.S. prices, and then Detroit's automakers would set theirs. In the minds of many consumers, the price of Japanese autos was important, because this information signaled what a well-made car was worth in a particular price class. This relationship endured until 1994, when an unfavorable exchange rate forced Japanese automakers to increase their prices drastically. To grab market share, General Motors, Ford, and Chrysler kept their prices about $2000 lower per car than the average price on Toyotas, Hondas, and other Japanese imports—the pegging price. As Japanese prices went up, so did the prices of U.S. automakers. The $2000 margin below the pegged price enabled the American companies to build market share *and* harvest tremendous profits.[23]

Limit Pricing

When a firm introduces a new profitable product into the marketplace, it makes an attractive target for potential competitors. A **limit pricing** strategy means that a firm sets a price low enough to discourage competition from entering the market but still high enough to make a profit. Its hope is that other firms will think the payback on the costs of entering the market is too low to be attractive. In practice, it is nearly impossible to discourage all potential competitors. Take the airline industry. Even though the passenger airline industry lost billions through the mid-1990s, low-price niche airlines such as Kiwi and ValuJet keep emerging in search of profits.

Limit pricing also works well in protecting a firm's existing market share. The Coca-Cola Company illustrates this strategy. The sale price of a 2-liter bottle of Coca-Cola Classic in the United States costs consumers less than a half-penny per ounce more than store brands selling at rock-bottom prices. Coca-Cola marketers believe private-label soft drinks appeal solely to price-driven consumers. To blunt the share growth of private brands, Coca-Cola has systematically forced down costs and kept prices low.

> **limit pricing:** a pricing strategy in which a firm sets a price low enough to discourage competition from entering the market but still high enough to make a profit

PRICING STRATEGIES BASED ON CUSTOMERS' NEEDS

When firms develop pricing objectives aimed at satisfying the needs of customers, they are less concerned with short-term successes, choosing instead to focus on keeping customers for the long term. New Era firms that are truly dedicated to customer satisfaction look at the wants and needs of customers in developing pricing strategies.

Every Day Low Prices: Value Pricing

Firms that practice **value pricing,** or **every day low pricing (EDLP)** as it is often called, develop a pricing strategy that provides ultimate value to consumers. *Value* is defined as the "ratio of benefits to the sacrifice necessary to obtain those benefits," but what this really means is that in the customer's eyes, the product's cost is justified by what is received in return.[24]

When firms base price strategies on cost, they are operating under the old production orientation, not a marketing orientation (see Chapter 1). Value-based pricing begins with customers, then considers the competition, and then determines the best pricing strategy. Smart marketers know that the firm that will win is not necessarily the one with the lowest prices but rather the one that delivers the most value.

In practice, when EDLP strategies are used, products are perceived as offering strong benefits compared to similar products in their price range. Marketers hope that increasing what consumers get for their money will make them see the price as very reasonable and encourage them to remain loyal to that brand, rather than snapping up whatever happens to be on sale this week. This is often not the case now; shoppers have been "trained" to choose products because they are "on special" rather than because they are superior to others. For example, about one-fourth of all snack foods sold in supermarkets are bought with a cents-off deal.[25]

The changing pricing strategies of Procter & Gamble during recent years provide examples of value pricing. Procter & Gamble had watched its Charmin toilet tissue, Dawn dishwashing liquid, Pringles potato chips, and many other well-established brands lose customers. Shoppers were still buying these products, but only when their prices were reduced during sales and special promotions. To build loyalty, in 1992 P&G switched to an EDLP strategy. The company reduced prices by 12 percent to 24 percent on nearly all U.S.

> **value pricing,** or **every day low pricing (EDLP):** a pricing strategy in which a firm sets prices that provide ultimate value or price/benefit ratio to customers

TWO GREAT COMPANIES, ONE SHINING NEW BATTERY NAME.

GREAT BATTERIES. GREAT SAVINGS. GREAT ECOLOGY.

General Electric and Sanyo have come together to create a powerful new line of batteries and money-saving chargers: Rechargeable, alkaline, lithium, and cordless phone batteries, radio control hobby and camcorder battery packs, as well as battery chargers for our complete line of AA, AAA, C, D and 9 volt rechargeable battery sizes.
GE/SANYO RechargAcell™ batteries save you money because they're rechargeable up to 1,000 times and are available in our Mailback Recycle System™ packaging that allows you to send your old rechargeables back to be recycled. QUESTIONS? Call the GE Answer Center® (800) 435-4448 — 7:00 A.M. to 8:30 P.M. EST.

Manufacturer's Coupon   Expires February 28, 1994

SAVE $1.00
on GE/SANYO Rechargeable Batteries

Exhibit 13.5
The *cost of ownership* is the price paid for a product, plus the cost of maintaining and using the product, less its resale (or salvage) value. Sanyo uses a cost-of-ownership strategy in drawing attention to the low cost of using its batteries. Because the batteries can be reused 1000 times, the cost of ownership is reduced, and perhaps consumers will see the initial price in a more favorable light. The Sanyo ad also appeals to consumers who believe recycling is a good thing to do. And it offers a price promotion to stimulate consumers to try the product. The cost of the "money-saving" charger, which might raise the perceived ownership cost, is not stated. Reference to the charger is cleverly connected to lower ownership costs.

brands by cutting the amount it spent on trade promotions: Like the Saturn pricing policy we discussed earlier, P&G essentially said, "This really *is* our best price, and it's a good value for your money. Buy the item now rather than waiting for it to go on sale next week. That's not the way we do business anymore."

Value pricing has worked in at least some product categories. For instance, liquid laundry detergent prices were cut 9 percent in 1992 and an additional 15 percent in 1993. Since then, P&G's market share in this category has gone from 42 percent to 47 percent.[26] Remember that EDLP does *not* mean "bargain basement" pricing. It merely means the product rarely gets sold through off-price promotions. The price shoppers see today is the price they'll see tomorrow. Because P&G combined EDLP with reductions in overhead, manufacturing costs, and marketing costs, the price on P&G brands declined significantly, yet profit margins went up.[27]

The ultimate fate of EDLP with firms like P&G, however, remains questionable. In 1993, P&G modified its EDLP policy with Tide after losing market share.[28] In 1995, the intense competition among the major producers of disposable diapers, P&G, Kimberly-Clark, and Drypers caused P&G to abandon EDLP in this product category and return to in-store coupons for Pampers and to mail couponing for its Luvs brand. In 1996, however, P&G made an even more dramatic move toward EDLP when it stopped distributing any coupons in the Buffalo, Rochester, and Syracuse, New York, markets.[29] If these tests are successful, then P&G and other large manufacturers of package goods are likely to expand the no-coupon EDLP concept.

Negotiated Pricing

Every year, the April issue of *Consumer Reports* includes an auto buyers' guide. In that issue, shoppers can find all sorts of advice and information about bargaining car dealers down to a thin margin over costs. Most consumers don't realize that the price of *almost anything* is negotiable! In the United States, persistent customers can get a lower price on hotel rooms, stereo equipment, clothing, catering services, guitars, taxi rides, and many other products.

Marketers use various strategies to influence bargaining outcomes. Car dealers have long used *the good cop/bad cop* strategy. This ploy tries to get the customer to accept the trust and friendship of a car salesperson (the good cop), who pretends to be fighting for his or her best interests against the nasty, price-gouging manager (the bad cop). The idea is to make the consumer feel that the good-cop salesperson is offering the best deal, so he or she had better grab it. While the good cop/bad cop tactic is still popular in TV shows like *NYPD Blue,* it's falling out of favor in car showrooms as haggle-weary customers are throwing their business to car dealers that promise the best price without the aggravation.

As in consumer marketing, when the complexity of a sale and its value to a business customer go up, so does the chance that some price bargaining will be involved. Bargaining is even more likely in sales to business customers, because face-to-face agreement making is more common. For example, hospitals compete for business from health maintenance organizations. Aggressive competition has driven the ordinary cost of, say, liver transplants down from $500,000 to between $135,000 and $375,000.[30]

Business marketers are concerned with how salespeople bargain with business customers, and salespeople are usually given plenty of training in price negotiation. For example, good salespeople need to know how to achieve the following basic outcomes.[31]

- Both parties feel their interests were addressed.
- Both feel the process was fair.
- Both feel they preserved face (maintained the respect of role partners).
- Both would bargain again with each other.
- Both will work toward fulfilling the agreement.

An alternative to bargaining is **bidding,** which means offering a price that a business or government customer will evaluate and compare to competing offers. For example, Aetna Life & Casualty Co. won a health care services contract worth $3.5 billion from the Department of Defense.[32] Losing competitors hotly contested the award to Aetna, caus-

bidding: offering a price that a business or government customer will evaluate and compare to competing offers

Exhibit 13.6
In the United States, haggling over price is a popular sport only in some car showrooms and in flea markets, but energetic bargaining is a time-honored means of matching price to demand elsewhere in the world. For instance, shopping for groceries or any other product in India's village markets would be incomplete without some haggling on almost every purchase. In fact, the sense of satisfaction that consumers often feel at getting a good deal is an integral part of the shopping experience. Bargaining also gives sellers greater pricing flexibility. Wealthy-looking tourists pay top dollar, and locals usually get the best price. Throughout the world, buyers and sellers talk over price until there is a meeting of the minds.

ing the General Accounting Office to reopen bidding. This successful appeal illustrates that even formal bidding procedures occasionally include give and take much like bargaining.

Two-Part Pricing

In two-part pricing there are two separate parts to the price of a product. For example, when someone joins a golf club, he or she typically pays a monthly or yearly membership fee but also has to pay a user fee for each round of golf. America On Line, Compuserve, and other suppliers of internet connections offer a flat rate for so many hours of connection time per month. Then customers who use additional connect time are charged a per-hour rate.

Payment Pricing

Sometimes marketers seek to make their price seem like a better deal through payment pricing.[33] In payment pricing, the total cost is not given, but rather the price is stated as a monthly rental fee or as "three payments of $39.99 each." Marketers of costly durable goods such as automobiles, stoves, and refrigerators often promote payment pricing. For example, many customers now opt to lease rather than buy a car. The monthly lease amount is an example of payment pricing, which tends to make people less sensitive to the total price of the car.[34]

Pricing by Priority

Pricing by priority means that the seller sets a schedule of prices for the product and then serves first those buyers who elect to pay the highest price. Customers who are willing to pay the next highest price are then served, and on down the line. A priority pricing schedule will work only when there is limited product and customers are concerned that if they wait, the product will not be available. Airline fares are an example of pricing by priority. Passengers who are willing to pay the full price almost always find a seat available. People willing to risk losing out on a seat, though, can choose to wait until a time closer to the departure date and take a chance that discount seats may become available.

NEW-PRODUCT PRICING

Intel's pricing of its 486 microprocessor computer chip and of its successor, the Pentium chip, illustrates the importance of a new product's price in determining its chances for success in the marketplace.[35] A 486 CPU (central processing unit) computer chip carries millions of microscopic transistors that enable a personal computer (PC) to perform Windows-based applications and that make PCs important business tools. The 486 more than doubled the processing power of a PC equipped with the old 386 chip. Intel initially thought the competition was way behind in developing competing computer chips and thus set a high price for its 486 chip.

However, nothing stays still for long in the computer industry. When the Pentium chip—which in turn more than doubled the processing speed of the fastest versions of the 486—was introduced, Intel knew that Motorola was working with IBM and Apple to develop the PowerPC chip that would compete with Intel's product. In contrast to the 486 chip's high introductory price, Intel deliberately set the price of the Pentium chip low in order to sell more in a short period of time and thus slow the sales of the PowerPC chip when it was introduced.[36]

As we noted in Chapter 9, new products are vital to the growth and profits of a firm. But new products also present some unique pricing challenges. When a product is new to the market or when there is no established industry price norm, marketers may use a skimming price strategy, a penetration pricing strategy, or (for a short, introductory period of time) trial pricing.

Skimming Price

It is unlikely that many college students (unless, of course, they grew up on a farm) know that milk in its natural form, without being homogenized, separates; the cream rises to the top leaving nonfat milk below. If your grandmother wanted to make ice cream for a fourth of July picnic or serve whipped cream on top of the Christmas fruit cake, instead of buying a carton of whipping cream in the grocery store, she would simply "skim" the rich cream off the top of the whole milk.

In pricing, setting a **skimming price** means that a firm skims the "richest" product sales off the top by charging a very high premium price for a new product, as Intel did with its 486 chip. If a product is highly desirable and offers unique customer benefits, demand is price-inelastic during the introductory stage of the product life cycle. In such cases, a skimming pricing policy enables a firm to recover the cost of research, development, and the promotion necessary for a successful introduction. Firms that focus on profit objectives in developing their pricing strategies often set skimming prices for new products.

Certain circumstances make a skimming price more likely to be successful. First, the product has to provide some important benefits to the target market that make customers feel they "gotta have" the product, no matter what the cost. When introduced in the late 1960s, hand-held calculators were this kind of product. These magic little devices could add, subtract, multiply, and divide at the push of a button. It seems hard to believe, but when they were first introduced, the simple calculators sold for about $200.00!

Second, for skimming pricing to be successful, there should be little chance that new competitors will enter the market in a short period of time. With highly complex, technical products, it may be quite a while before competitors can develop and test new products and get them into production. This is also the case for patented pharmaceutical products that have a lock on the market. In other cases, there may be such a small market for the product that competitors looking at the situation will realize that if more players take to the field, none can be profitable.

Finally, a skimming pricing strategy is most successful when the market consists of several customer segments with different levels of price sensitivity. There must be a substantial number of initial product customers who have very low price sensitivity. After a period of time, the price can be reduced and a second segment of the market, with a slightly higher level of price sensitivity, will purchase, and so on.

Penetration Pricing

Penetration pricing is just the opposite of skimming pricing—that is, a new product is introduced at a very low price, as Intel did with its Pentium chip. There are several reasons why a firm might decide to engage in penetration pricing. First, the low price will encourage more customers to purchase the new product, thereby increasing demand and sales in the early stages of the product life cycle. Thus if the marketing objective is to beef up market share, penetration pricing makes sense.

Second (and often more important), a low price may discourage competitors from entering the market. In general, the firm that is first to introduce a new product has an important advantage; experience has shown that a *pioneering brand* often is able to maintain dominant market share for the life of the product. Competitors looking at the market may feel that the potential for developing a profitable alternative is not very good. Bayer aspirin and Hoover vacuum cleaners are examples of brands that were first to market and have retained a leading share for decades. Keeping prices low may even act as a *barrier to entry* to potential competitors. When prices are kept low enough, the cost of developing and manufacturing a new competitive product is simply too great relative to the potential return.

Trial Pricing

Trial pricing is pricing a new product low for a limited period of time in order to lower the risk for customers.[37] In trial pricing, the idea is to win customer acceptance first and make profits later. Often, trial pricing is seen as an alternative to giving away samples of a product in order to get people to try it.

CA-Simply Money, a personal-finance software package, was initially offered to mail-order customers at a trial price of $7.00, the cost of shipping and handling. Later the software was priced at $69.95. Similarly, Microsoft introduced the Access database program at the short-term promotional price of $99; the suggested retail price was $495. Marketers from both of these firms sought a high rate of trial, believing that the strong benefits of using the product would create loyal customers and favorable word-of-mouth communi-

skimming price: a very high, premium price that a firm charges for its new, highly desirable product

penetration pricing: a pricing strategy in which a new product is introduced at a very low price to encourage more customers to purchase it

trial pricing: pricing a new product low for a limited period of time in order to lower the risk for customers

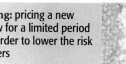

cation about it to other prospective users. Trial pricing also works for services. Health clubs and other service providers frequently offer trial memberships for special introductory one-time prices. The hope is that the customer who is induced to try the service at a low price will be converted to a loyal regular-price customer.

PRICING FOR MULTIPLE PRODUCTS

Often, a firm sells several products that consumers typically buy together. As we saw with Bojangles' Restaurants in Chapter 12, someone who buys a burger or a pizza or a taco for lunch usually purchases a drink, fries, or a salad to go along with it. When a person buys a paper-cup dispenser for a bathroom, a package of cups is not far behind.

Price Bundling

Price bundling is selling two or more goods or services as a single package for one price. A music buff can buy tickets to an entire concert series for a single price. An advertiser may purchase space in a group of magazines at a total package price. A PC typically comes bundled with a monitor, a keyboard, and software. Even an "all-you-can-eat" special at the local diner is an example of price bundling.

Price bundling offers advantages for buyers. With a single decision and a single purchase, the customer minimizes the hassles that may be involved with buying everything separately. And price bundling often provides a price savings. As with the Bojangles' combo plan, it is typical for the price of a bundle of goods to be set lower than the price of purchasing the items separately.

From a marketing standpoint, price bundling also makes good sense. If products are priced separately, then it is likely that customers will buy some but not all of the items. They might choose to put off some purchases until later, or they might shop around and buy some of the items from a competitor. By offering the bundle of products at a single low price, the firm increases total sales volume and thus profits, even at the lower price. For example, Microsoft's pricing decisions helped sustain its profit margin when other firms were barely breaking even. One of the software giant's tactics is to bundle several of its products together, which increases the sales of these items, reduces some selling expenses, and makes it hard for competitors to match the bundled offer.[38]

Captive Product Pricing

Captive pricing is a pricing tactic used when a firm has two items that *must* be used together. The firm sells one very low-priced item and then makes its profit on another, high-margin item. The second item is typically essential to the operation of the first item. Movie theaters employ captive pricing when they charge a very high price for a bucket of buttered popcorn (in some cases, more than admission to the movie itself!) to accompany the show.

PRICING TO MEMBERS OF THE CHANNEL

Whether a firm sells to businesses or to consumers, most pricing structures are built around list prices. A **list price** is the price the end customer is expected to pay. List price is determined by the manufacturer. But as we'll see in the next two chapters, the manufacturer seldom sells to the ultimate customer because most goods are sold by retailers or distributors in a channel of distribution. Often, however, pricing to members of the channel is temporarily discounted. Discounts should not be simply a means of price competition. Rather, most discounts to members of the channel are designed to meet a specific goal of the manufacturer. In this section we will consider some of these pricing-related objectives.

Quantity Discounts

Firms that sell to distribution channel members or end-user business customers often offer **quantity discounts,** or reduced prices for purchases of larger quantities of a product. Marketers commonly use quantity discounts as a way to encourage larger purchases from distribution channel partners. Consumer products also may use quantity pricing. For in-

price bundling: selling two or more goods or services as a single package for one price

captive pricing: a pricing tactic for two items that must be used together; one item is priced very low, and the firm makes its profit on another, high-margin item that is essential to the operation of the first item

list price: the price the end customer is expected to pay, as determined by the manufacturer

quantity discounts: a pricing strategy of charging reduced prices for purchases of larger quantities of a product

The only razor that senses and adjusts to the individual needs of your face.

Gillette Sensor: the shave personalized to every man. It starts with twin blades, individually and independently mounted on highly responsive springs. So they continuously sense and automatically adjust to the individual curves and unique needs of your face.

Innovation is everywhere. You can feel it in the textured ridges and the balance of the Sensor razor. You appreciate it in the easy loading system and the convenient shaving organizer.

Even rinsing is innovative. The new blades are 50% narrower than any others—allowing water to flow freely around and through them, for effortless cleaning and rinsing.

All these Sensor technologies combine to give your individual face a personalized shave—the closest, smoothest, safest, most comfortable. The best shave a man can get.

The Best a Man Can Get

stance, the man who buys a twenty-four-issue subscription to *Men's Fitness* magazine saves $49 over the single-issue newsstand price.

Sometimes, offering quantity discounts can create problems for the manufacturer. For example, a Canadian publisher developed a fine, four-volume set of encyclopedias. Figuring that more books displayed on the shelves of book stores would result in higher sales, the publisher created a pricing structure with steep quantity discounts. The publisher planned a list price of $175 per set. Small, independent book stores bought in quantities priced at $125 per set, whereas large chain stores purchased in larger quantities at $75 or $80 a set. The problem arose when the chain stores decided to give up some of their margin to increase sales and sold the sets at $99—a price below what the independents had to pay just to obtain the merchandise![39]

Cash Discounts

Using money costs money (as anyone who's ever taken out a mortgage or a college loan understands). When a firm borrows money, it is charged interest for every day it has the use of the money. On the other hand, if a firm has excess cash, then it is able to invest that cash and make money from its money. For this reason, many firms try to entice their customers to pay their bills quickly by offering *cash discounts*. For example, a firm selling to a retailer may state that the terms of the sale are "2 percent 10 days, net 30 days." This means that if the retailer pays the producer for the goods within ten days, then the amount of the bill will be reduced by 2 percent. If the total bill is $10,000, the net payable within the ten days is only $9800. The whole $10,000 is due within thirty days, and the payment is considered late after the thirty days are up.

Seasonal Discounts

Seasonal discounts are price reductions offered only during certain times of the year. Products such as snow blowers, lawn mowers, and skiing and water-skiing equipment are seasonal products—that is, they are used only at certain times of the year. If products are sold only during a few months of the year, then the manufacturer must either build a very large plant that has to be shut down during the "off season" or build a very large warehouse to store inventory until the season comes along again. Both of these options are unattractive, so in order to entice retailers and wholesalers to buy "off season" and store the product at their location until the right time of the year, a firm may offer seasonal discounts.

On the other hand, manufacturers can offer discounts when their products are "in season"—ensuring that retailers will have their product on hand when consumers go on the prowl for a great new snowboard or a shiny jet-ski.

Geographic Pricing

Geographic pricing is the practice of charging different amounts for products depending on how far they must be shipped. Characteristics of the product, the customer, and the competition sometimes make it advisable to charge all customers the same price, but in other situations it makes better sense to vary the prices charged to customers in different locations. Several pricing methods are employed when a firm negotiates terms with distributors, wholesalers, or retailers.

- *F.O.B. pricing:* Often pricing is stated as F.O.B. factory or F.O.B. delivered. F.O.B. stands for *free on board,* which means the supplier will pay only to have the product loaded onto a truck or some other carrier. Also—and this is important—*title passes to the buyer* at the F.O.B. location. *F.O.B. factory* or *F.O.B. origin* means that the cost of transporting the product from the factory to the customer's location is the responsibility of the customer. *F.O.B. delivered* means that the cost of both loading and transporting to the customer is included in the selling price and will be paid by the manufacturer.

  F.O.B. factory pricing creates many different delivered prices, because the purchase price for each customer changes with shipping costs. On the other hand, with F.O.B. delivered pricing, every customer pays the same price. Another option is somewhat of a combination of F.O.B. factory and F.O.B. delivered. Sometimes a seller's terms indicate that title to the product is transferred at the seller's location but the seller will pay the freight. This plan is called *F.O.B. factory, freight prepaid.*

  Sellers often prefer *F.O.B. factory* pricing because of its simplicity. The marketer doesn't have to take into account the costs of shipping to different customers at different distances from the factory. It also allows more flexibility in how a product gets shipped, because pricing does not depend on shipping by one method. In addition, the fact that title is transferred before shipping shifts the risk of damage to the transit company and the customer.

- *Zone pricing:* Another geographic pricing practice is *zone pricing.* Like F.O.B. factory pricing, zone pricing means that distant customers pay more than customers who are close to the factory. But in the case of zone pricing, there are a limited number of different prices charged. The seller establishes geographic zones based on the distance from the factory to the customer's location. All customers who are located in one zone pay one price, and all customers in a different zone pay a different price (much like the pricing structure for a subway fare in Washington, D.C. or Atlanta).

  Zone pricing simplifies pricing, and that is important in some markets. It would be nearly impossible for United Parcel Service to charge one price if a package shipped from Los Angeles went to Miami, a different price if it went to Fort Lauderdale, another if it went to Naples, Florida, and so on and on. Therefore, UPS charges different rates for shipping packages from any single location to different zones across the country. The shipper in Los Angeles pays the same for his package to go to any of the Florida locations but considerably less for shipment to Seattle or Las Vegas, which are in nearby zones.

- *Uniform delivered pricing:* In *uniform delivered pricing* an average shipping cost is added to price. Thus the same charges for shipping are added to the prices for customers who are ten miles away and for those that are two or three thousand miles from the shipping point. Catalog sales, home television shopping, and other types of nonstore retail sales generally use uniform delivered pricing. Such direct retailers add a standard shipping and handling fee to the price of every item sold. This single-zone approach is acceptable to customers only when shipping costs are small and don't vary much. Otherwise, a competitor will use zone or F.O.B. pricing and appear to offer a lower price, simply because these methods provide a closer match to actual shipping costs.

- *Freight-absorption pricing:* In *freight-absorption pricing* the seller absorbs the total cost of transportation. Freight-absorption pricing is more likely to be applied to very high-ticket items where the cost of shipping is negligible compared to the sales price and the amount of profit per unit. In other instances, a seller may absorb the cost of shipping in order to obtain the business, believing that the extra income from increased sales will cover the freight charges it has to pay.

- *Base-point pricing:* In *base-point pricing* the seller figures shipping costs from designated locations called bases. A customer pays shipping charges from that base-point, which is not always the location from which the product is actually shipped.

    Sometimes firms use base-point pricing to keep their costs low while remaining competitive. Suppose that a seller has eight to ten distribution centers around the country. Its competitor also has eight or ten distribution centers located generally in the same areas. For our example, we will assume that both firms have distribution centers in Chicago. To be competitive, it is necessary that our seller's charge for shipping be no greater than that of the rival firm. Now suppose that the competitor has the product available in its Chicago location, whereas our seller stocks the item only in its Dallas location. Must our seller carry every item in every one of its distribution centers or risk losing business to a competitor who just happens to have the needed item closer to the customer? No. Base-point pricing solves this problem. The company remains competitive by charging the customer only for shipping from Chicago, not for the actual miles the product travels. In some instances, however, base-point pricing has led to customers paying for *phantom freight*—freight fees that do not exist. Because courts have ruled that such charges are illegal, base-point pricing is not often used today.

REAL PEOPLE, REAL CHOICES:

HOW IT WORKED OUT AT MCI

Lisa Adelman and her colleagues chose option 1: They decided to keep their original flat 3.9 percent rate increase filing intact despite the apparent randomness of AT&T's increases. This decision gave MCI the revenue boost it needed, while at the same time enabling the company to claim, in its comparative advertising against AT&T, that its customers will enjoy greater savings: up to 9 percent over AT&T's rates. MCI's advertising department capitalized on this difference by sending out ads and direct-mail pieces boasting of these new savings. On the down side, the Business Analysis Group was not thrilled with this decision (even though they ultimately approved it). They thought that AT&T's raising its rates by more than 3.9 percent, gave MCI a perfect opportunity to gain even more revenue. Lisa's group convinced them that staying with the original pricing strategy met the company's goals without jeopardizing the trust of its customers. By continuing to be a customer-driven company, MCI illustrates that lasting marketing benefits are not always 100 percent congruent with short-term economic goals. This logic rings true to us!

Chapter 13 Summary

Objective 1. Discuss the pricing objectives that marketers typically have in planning pricing strategies.

Effective pricing objectives are designed to support corporate and marketing objectives and are flexible. Pricing objectives often focus on sales (to maximize sales or to increase market share), or they may specify a desired level of profit growth or profit margin. At other times, firms may develop pricing strategies designed to preempt the competition or to increase customer satisfaction.

Objective 2. Understand some of the environmental factors that affect pricing strategies.

Like other elements of the marketing mix, pricing is influenced by a variety of external environmental factors. Economic trends such as inflation and the stages of the business cycle (recession, recovery, and so on) strongly affect a firm's ability to increase or decrease prices. Price strategies are also related to the firm's competitive environment, that is, whether the firm does business in an oligopoly, a monopoly, or a more competitive environment. Changing cultural and demographic consumer trends must also be considered in the development of pricing strategies. Finally, firms must adjust to differences in the costs faced in various domestic and international markets.

Objective 3. Describe some commonly used pricing strategies.

The most commonly used pricing strategies are based on cost. Though easy to calculate and "safe," cost-based strategies do not consider demand, the competition, the stage in the product life cycle, plant capacity, or product image. Cost-based strategies include cost-plus pricing, (either markup on cost or markup on selling price) and price-floor pricing.

Pricing strategies based on demand require that marketers estimate the elasticity of demand in order to be certain they can sell what they produce. Such strategies include demand-backward pricing, which starts with a customer-pleasing price and works back to cost, and chain-markup pricing, which begins with an end-user price and works back through the channel.

Strategies based on the competition may represent industry wisdom but can be tricky to apply. A price leader strategy is often used in an oligopoly, where it is best for all to avoid competition. In parity pricing, a firm sets the same price as competitors. Limit pricing exists when a firm sets a low price for a new product to discourage new competitors.

Firms that focus on customer needs in developing pricing strategies may consider every day low price (EDLP) or value pricing strategies, negotiated pricing policies, two-part pricing, payment pricing, or pricing by priority. If a new product has unique customer benefits and demand is inelastic, then a firm may charge a high skimming price in order to recover research, development, and promotional costs. If the firm needs to encourage more customers and discourage competitors from entering the market, then it may use a very low penetration price. Trial pricing means setting a low price for a limited time.

For multiple products, marketers may use price bundling, wherein two or more products are sold and priced as a single package. Captive pricing is often chosen when two items must be used together; one item is sold at a very low price and the other at a high, profitable price.

Pricing for members of the channel may include quantity discounts to encourage larger purchases, cash discounts to encourage fast payment, and seasonal discounts to spread purchases throughout the year or to increase off-season or in-season sales. Geographic pricing tactics address differences in how far products must be shipped. F.O.B. factory pricing indicates that the seller will pay only to have the product loaded for shipment. In zone pricing, a firm sets a limited number of different prices based on shipping distances. Uniform delivered pricing means that the same shipping cost is added to the product price no matter how far the product is actually shipped. In freight-absorption pricing, the seller absorbs the costs of transportation. In base-point pricing, shipping charges are based on a base-point distance, which is not necessarily the actual distance shipped.

Review Questions

Marketing Concepts: Testing Your Knowledge

1. What are some of the more frequently used pricing objectives?
2. What are some ways in which changes in the business cycle, the competitive environment, and consumer trends affect pricing strategies?
3. Explain cost-plus pricing and price-floor pricing.
4. What are the advantages and disadvantages of pricing strategies based on demand?
5. Explain how a price leadership strategy works and how it helps all of the firms in an oligopolistic industry.
6. What is every day low pricing?

7. For new products, when is skimming pricing more appropriate and when is penetration pricing the best strategy?

8. Explain how marketers may use price bundling or captive pricing for multiple product pricing.

9. Why does it make sense for marketers to use quantity discounts, cash discounts, and seasonal discounts in pricing to members of the channel?

10. What are the advantages and disadvantages of F.O.B. factory pricing, zone pricing, uniform delivered pricing, freight-absorption pricing and base-point pricing?

Marketing Concepts: Discussing Choices and Issues

1. Governments sometimes provide price subsidies to specific industries; that is, they reduce a domestic firm's costs so that they can sell products on the international market at a lower price. What reasons do governments (and politicians) use for these government subsidies? What are the benefits and disadvantages to domestic industries in the long run? To international customers? Who would benefit and who would lose if all price subsidies were eliminated?

2. With a price leadership strategy, firms are able to avoid price competition and yet not be guilty of illegal collusion—getting together to set prices. Although it is legal, is a price leadership strategy ethical? How does a price leadership strategy hurt and how does it help the industry? What benefits does it provide and what problems does it pose for customers?

3. Every day low pricing strategies have met with limited success. What do you think are the advantages and disadvantageous of EDLP? Are some products more suited to EDLP than others? Why have customers not been more responsive to EDLP? What do you think will be the future of EDLP?

4. Two-part pricing, payment pricing, and pricing by priority are pricing tactics that are designed to make price more palatable to customers and to better meet their needs. But do these policies always benefit consumers? What are the advantages and disadvantages of these pricing approaches for the average consumer? For business customers?

Marketing Practice: Applying What You've Learned

1. Assume that you are the director of marketing for a large Rocky Mountain ski resort. It is essential that the resort maintain a very high occupancy rate during the skiing season. Pricing is a very important part of your marketing strategy because the demand for rooms at your resort is very price-elastic. For this reason, you feel you should develop contingency pricing plans for use during changes in the economic environment (inflation and recessions, for example). List the economic conditions that might warrant changes in the pricing strategy, and give your recommendations for each possibility.

2. As the vice president for marketing for a firm that markets computer software, you must regularly develop pricing strategies for new software products. Your latest product is a software package that enables any computer (DOS or Apple) to read any file, whether DOS or Apple, and automatically convert to the user computer's operating system. You are trying to decide on the pricing for this new product. Should you use a skimming price, a penetration price, or something in between? With a classmate taking the role of another marketing professional with your firm, argue in front of your class the pros and cons for each alternative.

3. Assume that you are working in the marketing department of a firm that manufactures furnaces and air conditioners. Previously, your firm has limited its operations to manufacturing units for other OEM companies. Now your firm is expanding. You will be manufacturing your product for sale with your own brand name and will be selling to heating and air-conditioning distributors across the country. Part of the plans for the new venture include how to cover the costs of shipping units to the customers from your plant in Blackville, South Carolina. You, of course, can consider F.O.B. factory pricing, zone pricing, uniform delivered pricing, freight-absorption pricing, and base-point pricing. Write a report presenting the advantages and disadvantages of each of these alternatives. What is your recommendation?

Marketing Mini-Project: Learning by Doing

Organizations develop pricing strategies to meet pricing objectives. These objectives may be related to sales, profit, the competition, customer satisfaction, or the image of the product. The purpose of this mini-project is to help you understand how different pricing objectives are important in marketing planning.

Many universities today are having trouble filling up their existing dormitory space as more and more students choose to live off-campus in houses or in apartments. For this project you will be identifying your university's existing pricing objectives and developing recommendations for changes.

1. First, with two or three of your classmates, seek to talk to someone who participates in your university's pricing of dormitory space. (It may be the vice president for student affairs, the dean of students, the director of student life, or the vice president for business and finance.) In interviewing this person, try to find out
   a. The current prices charged for dormitory space
   b. What the pricing objectives for dormitory space are
   c. How the prices are calculated
   d. The part that costs, demand, customer satisfaction, and competitive housing prices play in setting the dorm prices

2. Next talk with students in your school to find out
   a. Students' attitudes toward the prices charged for dormitory space
   b. What a customer-pleasing price for dormitory space would be
   c. The type and price of alternative housing used by students
   d. Any other relevant student attitudes toward dormitory housing

3. Develop a report that includes your findings and what recommendations you would make to your university. Be sure to focus on the pricing objectives currently in use and the alternative objectives that might be considered. What pricing strategies do your findings seem to suggest? Present your results to your class.

Key Terms

Endnotes

1. Steward Washburn, "Pricing Basics: Establishing Strategy and Determining Costs in the Pricing Decision," *Business Marketing* (July 1985), in eds. Valerie Kijewski, Bob Donath, and David T. Wilson, *The Best Readings from Business Marketing Magazine* (Boston: PWS-Kent, 1993).

2. Michael J. Ybarra, "Price-Cutting Airline Does No-Frills Hula," *The Wall Street Journal* (Dec. 29, 1993): B2.

3. Andrew E. Serwer, "What Price Brand Loyalty?" *Fortune* (Jan. 10, 1994): 103–104; Richard Gibson, "General Mills to Cut Prices of 3 Cereals and Curb Discounts," *The Wall Street Journal*, 222, no. 116 (Dec. 14, 1993): A10; Richard Gibson, "Kellogg Boosts Prices on Many Cereals; Average 2.6% Rise May Meet Resistance," *The Wall Street Journal*, 223, no. 27 (Feb. 8, 1994): A3, A8.

4. Peter Fuhrman, "Race to the Marketplace," *Forbes*, 152, no. 10 (Oct. 25, 1993): 42–44.

5. Thomas T. Angle, "Game Theory Should Guide Pricing Strategy, But Be Sure to Pick the Right Playing Field," *Marketing Management*, 2, no. 1 (1993): 36–45.

6. Melissa Campanelli, "The Price to Pay," *Sales and Marketing Management* (Sept. 1994): 96–102.

7. Joseph Pereira, "Early Coupon Campaign by Toys 'R' Us May Spark Price War Among Discounters," *The Wall Street Journal*, 222, no. 85 (Oct. 29, 1993): B1.

8. Eric Hollreiser, "For GM Units, Value Pricing Comes, Goes," *Brandweek* (Jan. 2, 1995): 6; Michelle Krebs, "Moving Out the Cars with a 'No-Dicker Sticker,'" *The New York Times* (Oct. 11, 1992): F12.

9. Rahul Jacob, "The Economy: Girding for Worse," *Fortune* (Oct. 18, 1993): 10.

10. Larry Armstrong, Karen Lowry Miller, and David Woodruff, "Toyota's New Pickup: Oops," *Business Week* (Feb. 15, 1993): 37–38.

11. Michael Selz, "Small Firms Use Variety of Ploys to Raise Prices," *The Wall Street Journal*, 221, no. 117 (June 17, 1993): B1.

12. Bill Saporito, "Why the Price Wars Never End," *Fortune* (March 23, 1992): 68–78.

13. Yumiki Ono, "As Discounting Rises in Japan, People Learn to Hunt for Bargains," *The Wall Street Journal*, 222, no. 128 (Dec. 31, 1993): 1, 8.

14. Jennifer Lawrence, "TWA Embraces Quality, Drops Low-Price Image," *Advertising Age* (March 1, 1993): 8.

15. Jacob Rahul, "Beyond Quality and Value," *Fortune* (Autumn/Winter 1993): 8.

16. Kim Foltz, "As Baby Boomers Turn 40, Ammirati and BMW Adjust," *The New York Times* (Jan. 26, 1990): D17.

17. Judann Dagnoli, "Godiva Tones Down Luxury Image," *Advertising Age* (Jan. 20, 1992): 54.

18. Joseph Spiers, "The Pickup in Car and Truck Sales Won't Stall Out Anytime Soon," *Fortune*, 127, no. 12 (June 14, 1993): 19–20.

19. Brian Coleman, "Airbus to Build Transport Jet for the Military," *The Wall Street Journal*, (Sept. 6, 1994): A3.

20. Shawn Tully, "Can Boeing Reinvent Itself?" *Fortune*, 127, no. 5 (March 8, 1993): 67.

21. Ibid.

22. Michael Janofsky, "P&G, the Diaper Leader, Strikes Back," *The New York Times* (April 15, 1993): D1, D7. Anonymous, "Procter & Gamble Co.," *The Wall Street Journal*, 221, no. 110 (June 8, 1993): B4.

23. Mike Meyers, "Big 3 Get Chance to One-Up Japan," *Times Union*, (Feb. 11, 1994): A1, A14.

24. Zachary Schiller, "'Value Pricing' Pays Off," *Business Week*, 3343 (Nov. 1, 1993): 32–33.

25. Karen Benezra, "Frito-Lay Dominates, While Others Pick Up Loose Chips," *Brandweek* (Feb. 7, 1995): 31–32.

26. Zachary Schiller, "Ed Artz's Elbow Grease Has P&G Shining," *Business Week* (Oct. 10, 1994): 84.

27. Melissa Campanelli, "What's in Store for EDLP?" *Sales & Marketing Management* (Aug. 1993): 56–59.

28. Jack Neff, "Diaper Battle Puts EDLP on Injured List," *Advertising Age* (Aug. 14, 1995): 3, 33.

29. Raju Narisetty, "P&G Bets on Low Prices 'Every Day' to Cut Out Need for Company Coupons," *The Wall Street Journal* (Jan. 8, 1986): B5.

30. Robert Lenzner, "Abramson to Clinton: Thanks, But No Thanks," *Forbes* (Jan. 3, 1994): 50–57.

31. Allan J. Magrath, "Ten Timeless Truths About Pricing," *Journal of Consumer Marketing* (Winter 1991): 5–13.

32. Jim Carlton, "Bids Reopen on Health Pact for Military," *The Wall Street Journal*, 222, no. 127 (Dec. 30, 1993): A3, A4.

33. Michael D. Mondello, "Naming Your Price," *Inc.*, (July 1991): 159.

34. Douglas Lavin, "Goodbye to Haggling: Savvy Consumers Are Buying Their Cars Like Refrigerators," *The Wall Street Journal* (Aug. 20, 1993): B1, B3.

35. Sebastian Rupley, "The PowerPC Revolution," *PC/Computing*, (February 1994): 129–131; Marc Dodge, "New Power Chips," *PC/Computing* (Feb. 1994): 116–117.

36. Jim Carlton, "Apple to Launch Macintosh PowerPCs Priced at Level to Gain Market Share," *The Wall Street Journal* (March 14, 1994): B4.

37. Michael D. Mondello, "Naming Your Price," *Inc.*, (July 1992): 159.

38. Richaard Brandt and Gary McWilliams, "The Shooting War in Software," *Business Week*, 3345 (Nov. 8, 1993): 86–88.

39. Michael D. Mondello, "Naming Your Price," *Inc.*, (July 1992): 166.

MARKETING IN ACTION: REAL PEOPLE AT RANGE ROVER

Land Rover North America, the U.S. marketing arm of the British manufacturer of Land Rover and Range Rover vehicles, has used a price lining strategy combined with an understanding of consumer needs to build a successful marketing program. In fact, Land Rover marketers have found that their only problem is making enough vehicles to satisfy demand.

Both the Range Rover and the famous Land Rover vehicles are made by the United Kingdom's Rover Group. The Range Rover is a luxury, four-door sport-utility vehicle. It combines off-road capability with such comforts as leather seats and polished wood trim. Even though advertising for the Range Rover focuses on the vehicles off-road ability, people rarely if ever take Range Rovers off the highway because of their high price tag.

The Range Rover County Classic, the basic Range Rover model for 25 years, was introduced into the United States in 1987. Its selling price in 1995, the last year it was produced, was $46,125. At the end of 1995, the County Classic was replaced with the Range Rover 4.0 (actually introduced in 1995) and the Range Rover 4.6 (introduced in 1996). The Rover 4.0 is basically a modernized version of the County Classic, with a 190-horsepower engine and 16-inch wheels. It sells for about $55,000. The Ranger Rover 4.6 is identical to the 4.0 except that it boasts a 225-horsepower engine and 18-inch wheels, and it sells for $62,000. All Range Rovers have V-8, 4-liter engines and full-time four-wheel drive (which means you never have to "shift into four-wheel").

The classic all-terrain Land Rover has been a standard commodity for decades in Hollywood's safari films and travelogs, but the same is not true with its presence on American highways. Because of poor sales, the Land Rover was pulled from the United States market in 1974. But in 1992, Land Rover North American again introduced the Land Rover into the challenging and crowded U.S. auto market.

The Land Rover model introduced in 1992 was the Defender 110, a boxy, five-door aluminum-bodied vehicle that seated 9 and guaranteed durability. It was a far cry from the luxury Range Rover, with a price tag just under $40,000.

Then in October 1993, Land Rover rolled out the Defender 90. The Defender 90 was even further from the upper-crust image of the Range Rover, instead projecting an image of fun. Like a Jeep Wrangler, the Defender 90 is an open-air, no frills, four-wheel-drive vehicle. Even carpeting is optional. Yet the 90 is powerful. It has the same big V-8 engine as the Range Rover County Classic model.

Although the Defender 90 does offer some extra equipment, such as disc brakes, it comes with only a five-speed manual transmission with high- and low-range gear ratios for use on or off the highway. To attest to its all-weather, all-terrain ability, the Defender 90 was even fitted with water-resistant stereo speakers. Dealer-installed options include alloy wheels, brush bars, mud flaps, a rear seat, taillight protectors, running boards, winch, air conditioning, carpeting, auxiliary lights, and a roof rack. Factory options include two different convertible tops (a full top with sliding glass windows for the side doors and a roll-up, plastic window for the back, or a half-top with no sides that serves as a sun-shade, called a "Bimini" top). The base price for the Defender 90, at $27,900, was nearly three times that of the Jeep Wrangler but far below that of the other Land Rover models.

Unfortunately, the Defender 110 was discontinued in 1993 but was replaced the same year with the introduction of the 1994 model of a new Range Rover, the Discovery. The Discovery is a compact, sport-utility vehicle with standard dual air bags, anti-lock brakes, and a price that ranges between $30,000 and $38,000. The Defender 90 remains available, but only in a hard-top version.

What were the results of the price lining policy at Land Rover? The company sold 4300 vehicles in the United States in 1993, 12,000 in 1994, and 20,025 in 1995. It hopes to be able to produce 28,000 in 1996 to keep up with what seems to be an ever-growing demand.

Source: *Automotive News*, "Discovery Coming in April" (Jan. 10, 1994): 6; Lynwood Bolles, Hendrix Imports, Charlotte, NC, 1/23/96; Henry, Jim, "Land Rover Rolls Out Defender 90," *Automotive News* (Sept. 13, 1993): 20; Raymond Serafin, "Land Rover Back in U.S.," *Advertising Age* (July 13, 1992): 4.

Things to Talk About

1. Explain the price lining strategy used by Land Rover.

2. Why do you think these price points have been effective?

3. Who would you imagine are the customers for the different Land Rover offerings?

4. What changes in the consumer market contributed to the increases in Land Rover sales?

5. What secrets to success has Land Rover discovered?

CASE 13-2

MARKETING IN ACTION: REAL CHOICES AT SOUTHWEST AIRLINES

It's not just the makers of disposable diapers and laundry detergent who are jumping on the every day low price (EDLP) bandwagon. A number of airlines are becoming EDLP carriers, a move that is expected to transform the industry as both large and small carriers compete for low-fare travelers.

Southwest Airlines was the first airline to implement EDLP fares; and so far it has been the most successful. Its strategy has been to reduce costs in order to offer low fares day in and day out. According to Keith Taylor, Southwest's director of revenue management, "We've had a simplified, low-fare structure for 21 years, and we've kept that in place. What's happening is that a lot of carriers are trying to emulate us from a low-fare strategy. We try to keep costs as low as we can, and when passengers decide they want to travel with low fares and quality service, they come to Southwest." Southwest has been so successful with low fares that it was the only U.S. airline that was consistently profitable between 1991 and 1994. Southwest's success can be seen in its revenue passenger miles (each revenue passenger mile represents one paying passenger flown one mile.) In 1994, Southwest flew 21.6 billion revenue passenger miles, up 14.8 percent from 18.8 billion in 1993.

An important indication of cost cutting and of the profitability of Southwest is its load factor. The load factor is the percentage of seats filled. To cover costs, the industry average requirement is a 67 percent load factor. Southwest's required load factor for covering costs is closer to 45 percent. Southwest's actual load factor was a very profitable 67.3 percent in 1994 and 68.4 percent in 1993.

How does Southwest keep costs down? For one thing, Southwest uses only one type of plane, the Boeing 737. Other major airlines may have 15 or 20 different planes. Using only one plane cuts costs for repairs and maintenance substantially.

As the airline industry has become more and more competitive, other airlines have attempted to follow Southwest's EDLP strategy. For example, between October 1993 and February 1994, Continental Airlines nearly tripled the number of no-frills Peanuts Fares to 875 daily departures,

more than half of the airline's 1599 flights. Another major airline, Delta, has abandoned its obsolete management practices and has been quite successful at cutting costs in a variety of ways, including reducing staff, cutting travel agents' commissions, using students to staff reservation offices on college campuses, and standardizing its stationery (letterhead, envelopes, and so on).

Other EDLP competition comes from a number of new regional airlines. These include Kiwi International Airlines in New Jersey, Midway Airlines flying out of Chicago, and Reno Air located in Reno, Nevada.

It is in this increasingly competitive environment that Southwest must consider its future. Although the airline would like to increase its number of flights in the hope of becoming the first national low-fare carrier, it must consider whether such growth is possible. One problem with larger airlines is that they are saddled with high fixed costs that are not part of the current Southwest financial structure. By increasing in size, would Southwest increase its per-mile costs substantially above what they are now? And although Southwest has secured its position in its current routes, would attempts at expansion cause its market to overlap those of the new EDLP competitors so that new routes would not be profitable?

Sources: Adam Bryant, "Three Airlines Chart Austerity Course," *The New York Times* (June 14, 1995): D1, D4; Jennifer Lawrence, "Major Airlines Look for Lift from Low Pricing," *Advertising Age* (Feb. 14, 1994): 8; Bridget O'Brian, "Continental's CALite Hits Some Turbulence in Battling Southwest," *The Wall Street Journal* (Jan. 10, 1995): A1, A5.

Things to Think About

1. What is the problem facing Southwest Airlines?
2. What factors are important in understanding this problem?
3. What alternatives might Southwest consider?
4. What are your recommendations for solving the problem?
5. What are some ways to implement your recommendations?

CHAPTER

14

Channel Management, Physical Distribution, and Wholesaling

CHAPTER OBJECTIVES

When you have completed your study of this chapter, you should be able to:

1. Explain what a distribution channel is and describe its functions in the marketing mix.

2. Describe some of the distribution channel members and the different types of distribution channels.

3. Discuss the different types of decisions that must be made in distribution planning.

4. Describe the types of decisions made in physical distribution planning.

REAL PEOPLE, REAL CHOICES:

MEET CECELIA GARDNER, A DECISION MAKER AT FIRST UNION NATIONAL BANK

Cecelia Gardner is senior vice president and project manager for consumer reengineering at First Union National Bank. Until last year, First Union was an $85 billion financial institution with 1200 branches in the southeastern United States. Now it has grown even bigger; its merger with First Fidelity, a northeastern bank, has increased its asset size to $125 billion. The bank has about 2000 branches, and Ms. Gardner is well aware that stiff competition in the banking industry, and changes in technology that are removing the need for customers to visit branches at all, mean that First Union has to stay on top of consumers' preferences regarding where banking services are available. Part of her job is to "reengineer" the bank so that it will be where consumers want it to be in the year 2000.

Cecelia Gardner began her career in banking with First Union in 1978. After receiving a B.A. in psychology from the University of South Carolina, she started as a file clerk at the bank. Before being appointed project manager for consumer reengineering, she went through First Union's management training program and then held numerous jobs with the company, including branch manager, consumer credit sales manager, and general banking group executive. Ms. Gardner holds an MBA from Winthrop University.

PRODUCT AVAILABILITY: A BENEFIT YOU CAN BANK ON

Cece Gardner and her colleagues at First Union Bank are very much aware of a major criterion that people use to choose among competing banks. No, it's not how many billions of dollars the bank holds in deposits, the cheerfulness of the tellers, or even which banks are less likely to be robbed. The answer is the same as the answer realtors give when asked what three factors sell a house: "Location, location, and location."

Because the convenience of visiting a bank branch is such an important consideration, forward-thinking banks such as First Union have begun to view *place*, one of the 4Ps of the marketing mix, as a major source of competitive advantage. In 1994, for example, there were about 2100 bank branches operating out of American supermarkets. This is not because bank marketers feel more comfortable working in the icy ambiance of the refrigerated section: Supermarkets are where the people are; between 10,000 and 30,000 people pass through a typical supermarket each week. In addition, many customers who visit the grocery store on a regular basis hardly ever enter a bank branch—they have their paychecks automatically deposited, and they use the ATM (automatic teller machine) to get cash. By including these nontraditional banking locations in their place strategy, banks have found a way to make contact with consumers who are too busy shopping for a loaf of bread or a carton of milk to stop into the bank building for that latest deal on a car loan or mortgage.[1]

This chapter is about the science (and a bit of art) of getting goods and services to people where and when they want them—conveniently, efficiently, and affordably. Every product, whether a savings account offered by a bank, a cup of coffee, a car, or a college education, must make its way from a producer to a consumer. Just as we take for granted the air we breathe because it is always around us (unless you're stuck on a New York City subway at rush hour!), we tend to *assume* that as long as we have the money to buy a product, we can magically obtain it by simply dropping into a store, calling an 800 number, or accessing a Web home page.

In reality, a lot of work goes on behind the scenes to accomplish this feat; products move through one or more channels of distribution, and each channel is composed of many interlocking players and activities that must be coordinated before we can purchase that coffee or that college degree. In this chapter we will first examine what a channel of distribution is, how different channels operate, and what types of people and organizations compose these channels. Then we will describe how firms go about planning the distribution function, the issues involved in managing channels, and some of the ethical and legal considerations that arise in distribution. Finally, we will examine the important area of physical distribution—the nuts and bolts of moving the product through the channel.

THE IMPORTANCE OF DISTRIBUTION: YOU CAN'T SELL WHAT ISN'T THERE!

For many years, place was the poor stepchild of the marketing mix. It's not as glitzy as promotion, as impactful as price, or as visible as product. But those days of obscurity are over. Increasingly, marketers are finding that distribution is a hot topic. In today's marketplace, they are finding that they must work harder to get their products to finicky consumers who no longer have the leisure time available to "shop 'til they drop" for goods and services. Evolving lifestyles and technologies such as telecommuting and selling on the Internet are changing the way people shop, work, and live. Advances in transportation make it feasible for even smaller, regional companies to expand their operations to other parts of the globe.

Still more important, distribution may be the final frontier for competitive success. After years of hype, many consumers no longer believe that "new and improved" products really are new and improved. Nearly everyone, even upscale manufacturers and retailers, tries to gain market share through aggressive pricing strategies. And advertising and other forms of promotion are so widespread that they have lost some of their impact. Of the four Ps, place may be the only one remaining where there is an opportunity to develop a significant competitive advantage.

To appreciate the renewed emphasis on place, consider these recent developments.

- Takeout dinner is not just pizza anymore. In many cities customers can now have a variety of menu items, prepared by the best restaurants, delivered to their door. In 1994, McDonald's began experimenting with delivering food to hotels in 20 cities across the country. McDonald's sees its growth in two areas: off-premises consumption (take-out) and nontraditional locations such as airports, train stations, hospitals, and kids' meals on airplanes.[2]
- Winn Dixie, a large southern supermarket chain, has begun home delivery of groceries.
- KinderCare Learning Centers, Inc. has increased its attractiveness to working parents by locating its Lombard, Illinois, center at the commuter train station.
- Dean College of Franklin, Massachusetts, has begun offering courses on board Boston commuter trains. Impossible to take notes on a moving train? Dean College's professors hand out jiggle-free notes to students.[3]

In this section we will define a channel of distribution. Then we will talk about the importance of distribution to marketing planning, the functions of channels of distribution, and how distribution interacts with other elements of the marketing mix.

WHAT IS A DISTRIBUTION CHANNEL?

channel of distribution: an organized network of firms that work together to get a product from producer to consumer or business customer

In this context a channel is *not* a place you find by clicking the TV remote. A **channel of distribution** is an organized network of firms that work together to get a product from producer to consumer or business customer. A channel of distribution consists of, at a minimum, a producer and a customer. Most channels also include one or more *channel intermediaries*—wholesalers, retailers, agents, brokers, distributors, and dealers—who in some way help move the product to the consumer.

The purpose of the channel of distribution is to facilitate the flow of products. Consider the channel for the sporting goods department at a typical Wal-Mart store. Wal-Mart buys goods from a number of different sporting goods manufacturers. The manufacturers ship their goods, using a variety of transportation modes, to Wal-Mart distribution centers. From the distribution centers, the goods travel to Wal-Mart's retail stores, where they are snapped up by thousands of anglers, soccer players, and other "weekend warriors."

FUNCTIONS OF DISTRIBUTION CHANNELS

Why is distribution an important part of marketing planning? As a student, you have completed both group projects and individual assignments. And you probably know from experience that there are pros and cons to each kind. Cooperating with others can reduce individual effort, but each group member has only partial control over the content of the final project.

The same trade-off occurs for marketers who work with other organizations in a channel of distribution. From the producer's standpoint, working with people in other or-

Exhibit 14.1
Would love and romance be the same without flowers? The availability of fresh flowers year round is a tribute to the efficiency of global distribution. The story begins in the Netherlands, where the delicate flowers are grown in a greenhouse. Men and women shod in wooden shoes harvest the flowers, placing them on a conveyor belt for sorting by electronic eyes. By 4:30 A.M. flowers begin arriving in carts for a 6:30 A.M. auction. Buyers assemble in a huge but dim and chilly building—the ideal environment for cut flowers—outside of Amsterdam where the bidding continues until all the flowers have been sold. U.S.-bound flowers are readied for air transport. On their arrival at Kennedy Airport in New York, the Department of Agriculture inspects them for insects and disease. Next an importer takes possession of the flowers, which are transported by truck or plane to a network of over 170 wholesalers around the country. From there they are distributed to local florists, who make them available that same day to budding lovers everywhere.

ganizations means losing some control over how and to whom products are sold. On the other hand, there are economies of scale to be had from mass distribution that simply are not available to a single producer. It is just not practical to set up separate retail outlets to sell M&M's candies or Lysol toilet bowl cleaner. Producers also work with intermediaries because they lack the financial resources to develop retail outlets and distribution centers themselves. Perhaps most important, channels of distribution perform a number of functions more effectively and efficiently than a single organization can. These include customer service functions, physical distribution functions, communications functions, and facilitating functions. Let's consider each in turn.

Distribution Functions That Help Customers

One way intermediaries facilitate the flow of goods from producers to customers is by providing a number of important customer services. First of all, retailers and wholesalers provide *time, place,* and *ownership utility* for customers—they make desired products available when, where and in the sizes and quantities in which customers want them. In addition, retailers and other intermediaries often provide valuable product information, usage instructions, and even financing to help customers obtain these items. Because most wholesalers and retailers allow customers to return goods that don't function properly or that are unsatisfactory in some way, they reduce the risk to the customer. Most of us like to shop at Wal-Mart or Macy's or Circuit City because we know that if we are not happy with the product, all we have to do is to take it back to the store, where cheerful customer service personnel are happy to give us a refund (at least in theory!). These same customer services are even more important in business-to-business markets where larger quantities of higher-priced products are routinely purchased.

Physical Distribution Functions

A second category of functions carried out by channels of distribution are those classified as *physical distribution functions.* The most obvious reason for using intermediaries is that they increase the efficiency of the flow of goods from producer to customer. How would people buy groceries without our modern system of wholesalers, dealers, and retailers? They would have to get their milk from a dairy, their bread from a bakery, their tomatoes and corn from a vegetable market, and their flour from a flour mill. In fact, a shopper might have to go to 20 or 30 or 50 different locations in order to buy weekly staples. And forget about specialty items like Twinkies and Coca-Cola. The companies that make these items would have to handle literally millions of transactions to sell to every individual who craved a junk food fix.

Distribution channels, by performing these functions efficiently, actually reduce the cost of purchases. For example, *freight forwarders* are distribution specialists that combine smaller quantities of goods belonging to many different firms into one large, economical shipment. Freight forwarders handle about three-quarters of all shipments from U.S. ports to foreign markets, so they are especially crucial for global transportation.

Effective channels of distribution provide the following physical distribution functions.

- *Breaking bulk:* Wholesalers and retailers purchase large quantities (usually cases) of laundry detergent, shaving lotion, and toilet paper but sell individual customers only one or a few at a time. In this way, efficiency in production and shipping is provided for the producer, and the customer can purchase only what he or she needs (and can afford to buy and store).

- *Accumulating bulk:* Sometimes channel intermediaries do the opposite—they accumulate bulk. A large floral wholesaler may buy from a number of different growers to obtain the quantities of flowers its largest customers need.

- *Creating assortments:* Supermarkets, department stores, drugstores, and convenience stores provide a variety of products in one location for the convenience of customers. In a similar manner, industrial distributors such as office supply companies, hospital supply and equipment firms, and building supply and lumber yards provide their business customers with an assortment of goods made by many manufacturers.

- *Reducing transactions:* One of the most important types of efficiencies provided by intermediaries is reducing the number of different transactions nec-

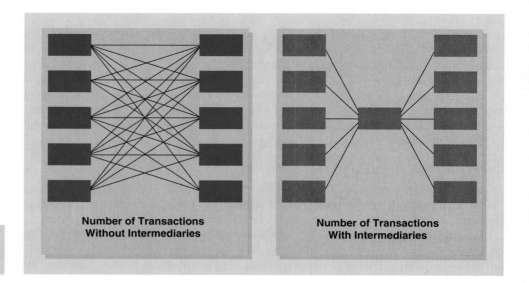

Number of Transactions Without Intermediaries

Number of Transactions With Intermediaries

Figure 14.1
Reducing Transactions via Intermediaries

essary for goods to flow from the many different producers to large numbers of customers. Figure 14.1 shows a simple example with just five producers and five customers. If each producer sold its product to each individual customer, 25 different transactions would have to occur. But with a single intermediary who buys from all 5 producers and sells to all 5 customers, the number of transactions is cut to 10. If there were 10 producers and 10 customers, an intermediary would reduce the number of transactions from 100 to 20.

■ *Transportation and storage:* Often intermediaries handle important transportation and storage functions. For example, supermarket chains and other large retail organizations such as JCPenney, Wal-Mart, and Kmart provide cost savings for their customers by buying products in quantity, storing in their own distribution centers, and delivering on a weekly basis to their own stores. Why stuff a closet with a year's supply of paper towels or dog food when a local store can perform this function instead?

Communications Functions

In addition to providing help in physically moving and storing products, intermediaries assist with communications functions. These agents often gather and disseminate information from manufacturers and help to inform consumers about important developments.

The typical wholesaler or distributor works with many different manufacturers. The manufacturer's sales force provides wholesalers with information about new products and product features to entice them to carry the product. The intermediary thus helps to "edit" the many (some would say *too many*) choices available to retailers and consumers by choosing to carry only some of the available product options. Once the decision to carry the product is made, the intermediary continues to perform a communication function by selling the product directly to customers or to other channel members. In addition, retailers, wholesalers, and distributors often work either with the manufacturer or independently to promote a product. Retailers are big users of newspaper, radio, and outdoor advertising, where they often feature individual products. Industrial distributors often find it good business to exhibit at regional or national trade shows, where they display different manufacturers' products. And it goes without saying that the sales personnel employed by retailers and other intermediaries provide a very important communications function. We'll explore the vital role of product communications in great detail in the last section of this book.

Intermediaries also facilitate communications with producers. Because these retailers and business product distributors are the ones who actually come in contact with customers, they are able to find out what customers like, what they dislike, what problems they have, what new product features they want, and what the competition is doing in the marketplace. These intermediaries may also provide producers with their own feedback about elements of the marketing mix. For example, retailers in Germany who carry the Benetton line recently went so far as to sue the Italian clothing manufacturer over what they viewed as the inappropriate and offensive advertising (it featured AIDS victims, blood-soaked soldiers, and other controversial images) that the company was using to promote its products.

Facilitating Functions

In addition to their key roles in assisting with physical distribution and communications, intermediaries perform a number of other duties, called *facilitating functions,* that may not be as visible to the end consumer. For example, many times retailers, dealers, and distributors provide repair and/or maintenance service for products they handle. An appliance, television, stereo, and computer dealer may serve as an authorized repair center. Auto dealers both repair cars and provide auto maintenance services. Businesses often cover the maintenance and repair of their computers and other equipment through maintenance contracts with the equipment dealers. And essential supplies—from disposable vacuum cleaner bags to toner for the photocopier—are often easily purchased from an intermediary.

Producers, wholesalers, and distributors who sell to retailers or business customers may also build an important relationship in the distribution channel by providing valuable services to them. For example, intermediaries may help retailers select a store site, plan store layout, and plan inventory, and they may even provide management training programs for channel members. Accounting systems or billing services may also be offered by wholesalers and distributors.

Safety Equipment Co. is an industrial distributor: a wholesaler that sells industrial-safety supplies to firms.[4] For its best customers, such as Tampa Electric Co., Safety Equipment guarantees next-day delivery. To assist Tampa Electric's purchasing department, Safety Equipment files monthly performance reports and publishes a customized product catalog. It has also arranged fire inspection surveys at power plants and safety equipment seminars for the utility's employees. Safety Equipment profiles customers' preferred products, delivery schedules, and technical assistance needs. By performing these important facilitating functions, Safety Equipment ensures that its best customers remain that way.

Yet another facilitating function is the provision of credit. Gasoline credit cards enable drivers to fill up at any company-owned or independent gas station where that brand is pumped. Sears, JCPenney, and a host of other department stores have their own credit operations that enable them to provide credit to their customers with little or no risk. When credit is easily available, customers are more likely to trade with the retailer, so everybody wins.

Finally, international distribution channels often make global marketing easier. Even small companies can export goods, provided they find a firm that is a local distributor in the chosen foreign market. Distributors can present a producer's product to local customers in the most appealing way. As we saw in Chapter 4, even large companies rely on distributors, who know local customs and laws that often surprise and confuse foreign producers.

DISTRIBUTION CHANNELS AND THE MARKETING MIX

Distribution decisions can play a key role in positioning a good or service—sometimes the place where a product can be obtained gives it a distinct position in its market. For example, Enterprise Rent-a-Car largely avoids the cutthroat airport rental car market by instead seeking locations in residential areas and local business centers. This distinctive strategy is designed to appeal to those customers who prefer to rent a car for quick trips instead of putting mileage on their own vehicle. By adopting a unique distribution approach, Enterprise can cater to an underserved market and, in the process, build an infrastructure of rental locations that will be hard for other rental car companies to compete against if and when they decide to target this segment as well.[5]

How are decisions regarding place interrelated with other elements of the marketing mix—the other three Ps? For one thing, place decisions are strongly tied to pricing. Marketers who plan to distribute their products through mass merchandisers such as Kmart and Wal-Mart have different pricing objectives and strategies from those who want to sell to specialty stores. In cases where the manufacturer actually has contact with its end customer (what we will term a *direct channel* in a later section), advertising, personal selling, and other forms of promotion are targeted toward the buyer. But with one or more channel intermediaries, firms usually direct advertising and other forms of promotion to the members of the channel. Often they need a strong sales force that calls on dealers, distributors, and retailers. For example, a high-end furniture manufacturer like Ethan Allen needs to convince legions of interior decorators to recommend its ensembles to their clients when they are presented with a decorating plan.

As a final note, whereas promotion and pricing decisions can be changed quite easily and quickly, channel decisions are more likely to be long-term. It is never easy to obtain new retail outlets, find new distributors, set up new dealers, or convince new wholesalers to carry and push a product. Just as a great deal of effort is involved in turning an aircraft carrier, once a distribution channel has been established, it often is difficult and time-consuming to change it.

Dramatic changes in the structure of some distribution channels, from health care to hardware, are bringing about fundamental changes in the way these products are thought of. Depending on one's perspective, developments such as managed health care are either streamlining the process or depersonalizing it. With the use of computers and communications networks, businesses are linking suppliers and consumers directly, often passing over traditional "middlemen" in the process. In the travel industry, three companies have installed over 12,000 electronic ticket machines (ETMs) in office buildings, hotel lobbies, and airports, thus enabling customers to bypass travel agents.[6] Insurance companies such as Allstate Corp can contract with a single large auto glass firm to serve its policyholders at a lower rate than can independent local dealers.[7] In each case, the market position of a good or service is influenced as much by *how* it is delivered as by *what* is delivered.

THE COMPOSITION AND STRUCTURE OF CHANNELS

When you decide one day to treat yourself to a new Bon Jovi T-shirt (or Nine Inch Nails, or KRS-One, or even Hootie and the Blowfish), you can obtain this prize in one of several ways. You may be able to pick one up at your local tape store, at your college bookstore, or perhaps at the Wal-Mart down the road. In some cases, you may choose to order a shirt directly from the band or its fan club. Or you might buy an "official concert T-shirt" being hawked by vendors during a stadium show. Alternatively, you might get a "deal" on a bootlegged, unauthorized version of the same shirt being sold from a suitcase by a shady guy standing *outside* the stadium. It's even possible to find T-shirts and album covers being sold by those cheerful folks on the Home Shopping Network! Each of these distribution alternatives traces a different path from producer to consumer. In this section, we'll review the functions of people who populate distribution channels, and we'll see how these channels differ in structure.

CHANNEL INTERMEDIARIES

We have talked in general about channel middlemen, often referring to them as wholesalers, but there is really a wide variety of different types of consumer and business-to-business channel intermediaries. Some of these are independent, others are owned by the manufacturer, and still others are owned by retailers. Table 14.1 summarizes the important characteristics of each; let's take a brief look at each type.

Table 14.1
Types of Intermediaries

	Intermediary Type	Description	Major Advantage
Manufacturer Owned	Sales branches	Wholesaler type; in different geographic areas; maintain some inventory; may have product maintenance/service capabilities.	Provide service to customers in a specific geographic area.
	Sales offices	No inventory; in different geographic areas.	Reduce selling costs and provide better customer service.
	Manufacturers' showrooms	Products attractively displayed for customers to visit.	Customers and salespeople can visit at a central location to examine merchandise.
Independent Intermediaries	***Merchant Wholesalers***	Buy goods (take title) from producers and sell to organizational customers.	Allow small producers to serve customers throughout the world while keeping costs low.
	Rack jobbers	Full function; limited line; call on retailers.	Provide display units, check inventories, and replace merchandise.
	Cash-and-carry wholesalers	Limited function; limited line; small retailers purchase at wholesaler's location.	Provide low-cost merchandise for retailers too small for other wholesalers' sales reps to call on.
	Drop shippers	Limited function; take orders from and bill retailers; products drop-shipped from manufacturer; take title to product but do not have physical possession of it.	Facilitate transactions important to both manufacturer and retailer.
	Mail-order wholesalers	Limited function; sell through catalogs, telephone or mail order.	Provide products for small organizational customers at a reasonable price.
	Truck jobbers	Limited function; sell perishable food and tobacco items.	Provide delivery and some sales functions for perishable items.
	Merchandise Agents and Brokers	*Do not take title.*	*Same as merchant wholesalers.*
	Manufacturers' agents	Independent salespeople; carry several lines of noncompeting products; have contractual arrangements with manufacturer.	Supply sales function for small and new-to-the-market companies.
	Selling agents	Handle the entire output of one or more products.	Handle all marketing functions for small manufacturers.
	Merchandise brokers	Identify likely buyers and bring buyers and sellers together.	Facilitate transactions in markets with lots of small buyers and sellers.
	Export/import agents	Handle sales agent function in international transactions.	Same as selling agents.
	Export/import brokers	Handle merchandise broker function in international transactions.	Same as merchandise brokers.
	Commission merchants	Primarily in agricultural products markets; take possession of products without taking title; receive a commission on the sales price.	Serves as a sales agent for the producer.

Manufacturer-Owned Intermediaries

Sometimes manufacturers choose to "have their cake and eat it too" by setting up their own channel intermediaries. In this way, they are able to have separate business units that perform all the functions of independent middlemen, while at the same time maintaining complete control over the channel. Manufacturer-owned intermediaries include the following:

- *Sales branches* are wholesaler-type facilities owned and run by a manufacturer. Typically, sales branches are located in different geographic areas in order to provide service to customers in those areas. Sales branches usually maintain a certain amount of product inventory so that they can provide immediate delivery. Often they have their own managers and sales forces. Sales branches may also have product maintenance or service capabilities if it is important to avoid delays that might result if repairs are handled only at a central location. Health-care firms such as Baxter Laboratories, which markets a wide variety of products for hospitals, usually maintain regional sales branches for this purpose.

- *Sales offices,* like sales branches, are typically located in strategic geographic areas in order to be closer to customers. In the case of a sales office, however, there are no inventories. Manufacturers set up local sales offices in order to reduce selling costs and to provide better service to customers. Consumer goods companies like Procter & Gamble often set up sales offices to improve the access of local salespeople to other members of the channel.

- *Manufacturers' showrooms* are producer-owned facilities that customers visit to see the firm's products attractively displayed. Clothing manufacturers and furniture companies usually have such showrooms where salespeople can work with retail buyers to select and order merchandise. These showrooms provide either temporary or permanent year-round display areas within a large merchandise mart. An example of such a facility is the internationally famous Furniture Merchandise Mart in High Point, NC. Some furniture manufacturers maintain year-round showrooms in the market, and nearly all manufacturers of furniture and accessories open showrooms during the spring and fall "market weeks," when thousands of retailers from around the world invade the town to place their orders for next year.

Independent Intermediaries

Independent intermediaries do business with many different producers and customers; they are not owned or controlled by any one manufacturer. A major difference among these intermediaries is whether they *take title* to the products they handle. Middlemen who take title actually buy and own the product at some time. Other intermediaries simply facilitate the transfer of the goods from the producer to the customer (or some other intermediary) without ever actually owning the merchandise themselves. Let's review first the types of intermediaries who do take title to the products they distribute and then those who do not.

merchant wholesalers: intermediaries who buy goods from producers (take title to them) and sell to other producers, wholesalers, and retailers

Merchant wholesalers buy goods from producers (that is, they take title to the goods) and sell to other producers, wholesalers, and retailers. Merchant wholesalers may be generally classified as *full-function wholesalers* or *limited-function wholesalers.* Full-function wholesalers have their own sales force that calls on businesses and institutions. Such distributors also provide delivery, credit, product use assistance, repairs, and other services. Indeed, the marketing and wholesaling expertise of merchant wholesalers, along with the variety of functions they perform, enables many small producers to serve customers effectively throughout the United States and around the world.

Large merchant wholesalers have the lowest costs and the highest sales per employee. Their success stems from a greater capacity to invest in employee development, information technology, and expensive capital improvements. For example, Arrow Electronics has 3500 on-line computer terminals worldwide, offering information on every item in stock.[8]

Specific types of merchant wholesalers include the following:

- *General-merchandise wholesalers,* sometimes called full-line wholesalers, are full-function wholesalers who carry a wide variety of products but offer limited depth in each product line. General-merchandise wholesalers often carry such products as cosmetics, detergents, tobacco, and drugs.
- *Limited-line wholesalers* are full-function wholesalers who carry only one or a few product lines, such as heating and air conditioning equipment or beauty shop supplies.
- *Rack jobbers* are full-function wholesalers who regularly call on retailers. They typically carry a limited line of products. Rack jobbers are important to retailers because they provide "racks" or other display units, check inventories, and replace merchandise in the display units.
- *Cash-and-carry wholesalers* are limited-function wholesalers. As suggested by the name, they do not provide delivery or credit. It is simply not practical for rack jobbers or other full-function wholesaler salespeople to call on the many small "mom and pop" retailers who need limited quantities of goods. The cash-and-carry allow these business customers to buy goods in small quantities. Because services such as delivery and credit are not provided, the small retailers can purchase the products they need at a price low enough to remain profitable.
- *Drop shippers* are limited-function wholesalers who take orders from retailers or business customers. Drop shippers forward the order to the manufacturer, who then ships the product directly to the customer. The drop shipper bills the customer for the product and then pays the manufacturer (after deducting money to cover overhead and profit.) This means that the drop shippers take title to the product, even though they never actually have the product in their physical possession or in any way handle the product.
- *Mail-order wholesalers* are limited-function wholesalers who sell through catalogs, telephone, or mail order without ever having any face-to-face contact with retailers or business customers. Mail-order wholesalers typically do business with customers who are too small to be profitable customers for full-service wholesalers and in certain product categories where profit margins are very low because of intense competition. Thus a small-town purchasing agent may buy shovels and mower blades from a mail-order wholesaler, and even larger customers may find it less expensive to buy pens, legal pads, and laser printer paper from a catalog.
- *Truck distributors,* sometimes called *truck jobbers,* are limited-function wholesalers who make regular deliveries of perishable items (including dairy products, fresh fruits and vegetables, snack foods, baked goods, and tobacco products) to retailers. Truck jobbers make deliveries and perform some limited sales functions.

The second major type of wholesaler consists of *merchandise agents,* brokers who specialize in one or more distribution functions but who do *not* take title to the products themselves. Merchandise agents are independent firms that typically perform personal selling on behalf of firms they represent. A small number of merchandise agents represent buyers and fulfill a purchasing function.

Specific types of merchandise agents include the following:
- *Manufacturers' agents* are independent salespeople who carry the product lines of noncompeting manufacturers. Over two-thirds of manufacturers' agents do business as a single-person agency.[9] On average, they carry the products of about nine different manufacturers. Manufacturers' agents are generally specialized by customer and product type. For example, an independent manufacturers' agent in the fashion industry (called "a rag salesman") may sell ski wear and all-weather coats in the summer and bathing suits in the winter to the same retail stores. For large firms entering a new market and for many small firms, manufacturers' agents are handy substitutes for a full-time sales force. Manufacturers' agents are really entrepreneurs who run their own small businesses. They typically work in accor-

Exhibit 14.2
A truck jobber from a local bakery calls on supermarkets. Typically, he or she will first check the stock of bread on the shelf, remove any outdated items and provide a record for store credit, and suggest how much will be needed before the next visit. Then the jobber will bring that amount into the store, provide the store personnel with a delivery itemization, and place the bread attractively on the shelf. If the bakery has any special holiday or seasonal items, the jobber may also be responsible for making a sales pitch to the grocery's bakery manager to promote these goodies.

dance with a contract through a manufacturer and are not directly supervised by a manufacturer's sales manager.

- *Selling agents* handle the entire product line of one or more producers. Selling agents often handle all the marketing functions for a small manufacturer and have complete authority to make pricing, promotion, and distribution decisions on behalf of the producer.

- *Merchandise brokers* assist in the sale of products by identifying likely buyers and sellers, bringing them together, and helping them make a purchase agreement. Brokers generally represent either the buyer or the seller, but not both, and receive a fee for their services. Brokers are typically used in industries such as real estate and used equipment, where there are a lot of small sellers and buyers.

- *Export and import agents* serve as manufacturers' agents in international transactions. Similarly, export and import brokers operate much as merchandise brokers, but for international transactions.

- *Commission merchants* typically are found in agricultural markets such as grain, livestock, and produce. Commission merchants take possession of the products without taking title. The commission merchant serves as a sales agent for the agricultural producer and receives a commission on the selling price. Because the fee received by the commission merchant is a percentage of the selling price, the producers are confident that the agent will try to get the highest price possible.

CHANNEL STRUCTURE

Distribution channels come in all shapes and sizes. The bakery around the corner where you buy your favorite homemade cinnamon rolls is a member of a channel, as are the baked goods section at the local supermarket, the *espresso* bar at the mall that sells *biscotti* to go with your double mocha *cappuccino,* and the bakery outlet store that sells day-old rolls at a discount (almost as good as new!).

Figure 14.2 summarizes the different forms a distribution channel may take. An important way to describe and compare distribution channels is by looking at **channel levels,** or the number of distinct units (producers, intermediaries, and final customers) that populate a channel of distribution. The producer and the customer are always involved, so the shortest possible channel has two levels. Adding a retailer adds a third level, a wholesaler adds a fourth level, and so on. Different channel structures exist for consumer and

channel levels: the number of distinct units that populate a channel of distribution

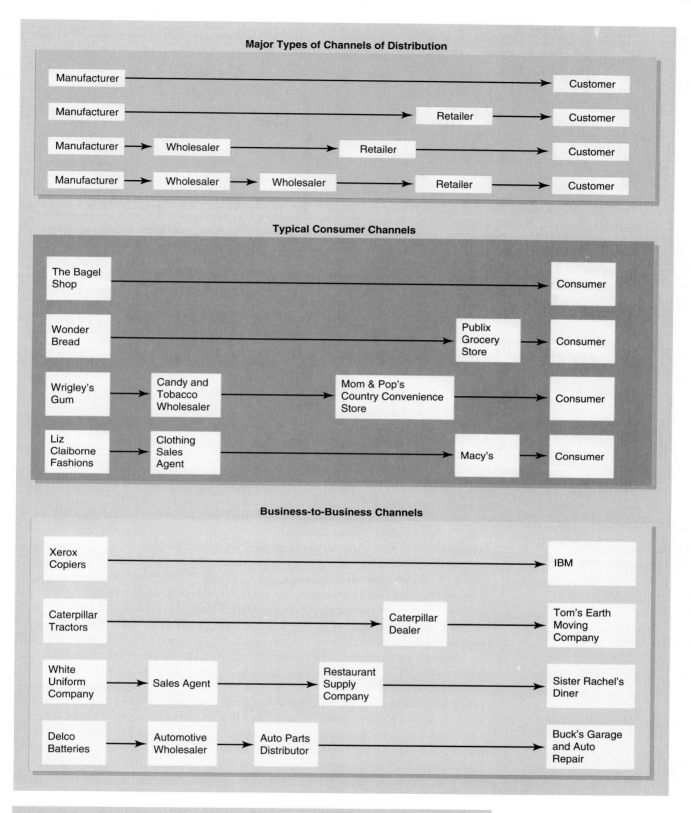

Figure 14.2
Different Types of Channels of Distribution

SPOTLIGHT ON RELATIONSHIP MARKETING

The Japanese *Keiretsu*

Building strong relationships among channel members is often crucial to the success of all member firms, but the Japanese have elevated this practice to an art form – often to the frustration of non-Japanese firms seeking a toehold in this huge and lucrative market. Companies in Japan often join together into a larger cluster to form a *keiretsu,* which is an interlocking network of firms that deal exclusively with one another. Within a *keiretsu,* trust is very high, commitment is very strong, and cooperation predominates. Almost like a fraternity, it's an exclusive club that rewards its members and punishes those who don't belong.

The *keiretsu* is a natural extension of the Japanese cultural preference for doing business on the basis of strong personal ties, rather than relying on formal legal contracts developed by a pack of lawyers. This level of cooperation is both envied and feared by businesses elsewhere. They envy the apparent order a *keiretsu* imposes on markets. Fear derives from the belief that *keiretsu* pool resources and know-how to gain technological advantage and protect mutual interests by keeping outsiders from becoming suppliers. Over the next few years, as other countries (particularly the United States) continue their quest to break into Japanese domestic markets to sell more cars, computers, toys, or fast food, the ability of the *keiretsu* to withstand intense political and economic pressure from outside will be sorely tested. The challenge to these firms is to discover a way to develop relationships of their own – a kind of international keiretsu.

Source: Larry Holyoke, William Spindle, and Neil Gross, "Doing the Unthinkable," *Business Week* (Jan. 10, 1994): 52–53.

---

for business-to-business markets. We'll start by describing the ones we commonly encounter in consumer markets.

Consumer Channels

Consumer distribution channels are pathways that deliver goods and services to end users. After we review these structures, we'll compare them to those used by producers who supply organizations with the products they need to do business.

In a **direct channel,** the producer and the customer are the *only* members of the channel; that is, there are no intermediaries or middle levels. When you buy a quart of strawberries at the farm where they are grown, when you purchase a handmade quilt from the quilter, and when you buy a mug of beer from a local microbrewery, you are participating in a direct channel. (Remember that a channel of distribution begins with the finished product, not with the raw materials that go into making that product.)

When producers market their own products through catalogs, via 800 numbers, or by operating a factory outlet store, they are employing a direct channel. Shiseido, a major Japanese cosmetics manufacturer, operates about 25,000 of its own stores in its homeland. This channel strategy enables the company to focus exclusive attention on its line of cosmetic products.[10]

Why do some manufacturers decide to sell directly to their customers rather than delegating this task to channel intermediaries? One major reason is economics: Although the use of middlemen often creates greater efficiency and reduces the cost to the final customer, there are some instances where the direct channel makes it possible to serve the customer better at a lower cost. In fact, there are situations where this may be the *only* way to sell the product at a reasonable price, because using intermediaries may increase the price above what consumers are willing to pay.

Another reason is control. When the producer handles distribution, it maintains control of pricing, service, delivery — all the elements of the transaction. Conflict with wholesalers and retailers over price, level of service, promotion, product selection, and many other issues is eliminated. Marketers realize that most distributors and dealers carry many products. Because of this, it can be hard to get the wholesalers' or dealers' sales force to push a single product without offering expensive incentives. Direct distribution means a producer works directly with customers, gaining insights into their needs, complaints, and trends. The producer in a direct channel can also alter marketing strategies much more quickly when such changes are necessary.

direct channel: a channel of distribution in which there are no intermediaries or middle levels

When intermediaries are included in the channel of distribution, the producer must make a commitment to the middlemen (and hope that they make a return commitment to the producer). Once such commitments are made, it is difficult to change them. Using a direct channel allows for a degree of flexibility that is lost in indirect channels.

Finally, direct distribution is sometimes the only way to stimulate customer interest in a new product. Later, when sales of the product are growing, it is possible to get wholesalers and retailers to carry the new product.

A manufacturer who reaches end users through intermediaries—wholesalers, dealers, distributors, agents and/or retailers—is practicing **indirect distribution.** Why do producers choose indirect channels? Customers may be more familiar with existing stores, so rather than trying to identify a specific manufacturer, they are more likely to look there first for what they need. In addition, middlemen help producers in all the ways described earlier: By performing physical distribution, communications, and facilitating functions, channel members make producers' lives easier by increasing their efficiency and their ability to reach their customers. In addition to a direct channel, Figure 14.2 shows three different indirect channel designs, beginning with the shortest indirect channel and ending with a longer, more complex one.

So which is better, a direct or an indirect channel? As with many questions in marketing, the correct answer is "It depends." Most consumer products that have a large potential market and lots of competition are probably best sold through indirect channels. But if the market for the product is somewhat limited, and if there are important benefits to be gained by maintaining complete control of getting the product to the customer, then the marketer should at least consider developing an effective direct channel.

The *manufacturer–retailer–consumer channel* shown in Figure 14.2, is the shortest indirect channel. This channel is frequently used when products are distributed through very large retailers such as Wal-Mart and Sears. Because they are able to buy in very large volume, these retailers can demand a very low price, which they can pass on to shoppers. Also, the size of these retail giants means that they have the capability to provide the physical distribution functions such as transportation and storage that wholesalers frequently handle for smaller retail outlets.

The *producer–wholesaler–retailer–consumer channel* is the most common form of distribution channel in consumer markets. In developed countries, where there are millions of consumers throughout a wide geographic area who use an individual product, and where there are tens of thousands of products, this type of channel is the most efficient. It enables consumers to purchase many different products conveniently at the least cost possible.

Take for instance such food products as ice cream, cheese, and hot Mexican salsa. A single factory supplies four or five regional wholesalers, which service 400 or more retailers, such as grocery stores, which in turn serve up to 8000 customers each. In this channel, the regional wholesalers combine the products of numerous producers to supply grocery stores. In turn, because the grocery stores do business with many wholesalers, this arrangement creates an even broader selection of products from which shoppers can choose. This type of distribution system is often the most obvious "place difference" between industrialized nations and developing countries, where consumers are instead more likely to buy goods directly from individual farmers and craftspeople in large open markets.

Business-to-Business Channels

Business-to-business distribution channels, as the name suggests, are networks designed to facilitate the flow of goods from a producer to an organizational or business customer. Generally, business-to-business channels parallel consumer channels in that they may be direct or indirect. In business-to-business channels, there are less likely to be retailers (though the growth of office supply superstores such as Staples and warehouse operations such as Sam's Club that supply small businesses are changing the landscape of business-to-business channels). However, business markets also include other types of intermediaries not generally found in consumer channels.

Direct channels are found in business-to-business markets even more frequently than in consumer markets. One reason is that many industrial products are such high-cost items that the producer can develop its own sales force and sell directly to customers at a lower cost than if intermediaries were used. American Express, for example, uses its own sales force to market its credit card directly to corporations.

Producers often utilize other types of intermediaries when distributing products to business and organizational customers. The simplest form of indirect channel in industrial markets occurs when there is a single middleman—an *industrial distributor*—that provides products for business customers. Sometimes this type of intermediary is also called a *jobber* or a *dealer*.

Distribution Channels for Services

Because of the intangibility of services, there is no need to be concerned about storage, transportation, and the other functions of physical distribution (see Chapter 11). Thus the distribution channels for services tend to be relatively straightforward. In most cases, the flow of the service is directly from the producer to the consumer or to the business customer. However, many services do involve an important intermediary—an *agent* who helps the parties complete the transaction. Examples include insurance agents, stock brokers, and travel agents. These intermediaries are important because they provide communications and customer service functions. Generally, agents work for independent businesses that receive a commission, which is a percentage of the selling price of the service. Because the service provided is so strongly tied to the person or people who perform it, customers often remain with the same service provider over very long periods of time, even if the provider changes firms. Clients may remain loyal to a particular real estate agent or stockbroker no matter where that person is employed.

Turmoil in the travel industry illustrates the pivotal role played by service businesses that facilitate transactions—and the influence they wield in determining which company will get the customers' business. Historically, travel agencies received a percentage commission for their work (deducted from the amount paid to the airline, not added to the price paid by the customer.) In 1995, airlines made radical changes in the ticket distribution system when they instituted a $50 commission cap on ticket sales by travel agencies in an effort to reduce distribution costs (which were running around 40 percent compared to 2 to 9 percent in other industries). Not surprisingly, travel agents were not happy with this change, and it remains to be seen whether it will stick; a few airlines are already violating the policy to encourage travel agents to write tickets on their planes and thus make a higher commission.[11]

In addition, even though managers in service industries do not have to worry about the best way to store and ship tangible goods, distribution remains an important area of competitive advantage. Hospitals, ski resorts, amusement parks, banks, and colleges alike must establish locations where the service is performed, and these organizations must ensure that the materials and personnel needed to deliver the service—whether tongue depressors, cotton candy, deposit slips, or faculty members—are available and up to the job.

International distribution offers even broader markets for services. Playboy Enterprises, for instance, airs its programming for cable and pay TV in such far-away markets as Bulgaria and Latin America.[12]

Like tangible-goods industries, service industries must choose among competing channels. The entertainment industry, for example, no longer is limited to on-stage or in-person distribution. Sports teams, rock performers, Broadway musicals, Italian opera companies, and Russian ballet companies provide entertainment through videos, via CDs, on pay-per-view cable networks, and even on the Internet. Higher education (and public education also) has begun exploring new ways to become more cost-competitive. More and more schools are using distance-learning facilities that provide two-way audio and video communication to offer their courses and degrees. And even top-ranked schools such as the Georgia Institute of Technology are offering mail-order degree programs using video tapes.

Dual Distribution Systems

Figure 14.2 depicts only very simple, single distribution channels. In the real world, of course, life is rarely that simple: Producers, dealers, wholesalers, retailers, and customers alike may actually interact with more than one type of channel. We refer to this as participation in *dual* or *multiple distribution systems*.

The pharmaceutical industry provides a good example of a multiple distribution system. Prescription medicines are distributed in at least four different channels. First, drug manufacturers sell to hospitals, clinics, and other organizational customers directly. These customers buy in quantity, purchase a wider variety of products, and often require different product packaging because in hospitals, pills are dispensed one at a time—not in a bottle of 50. In the consumer market, more and more of us are finding that we can obtain our medications at lower prices by shopping at the pharmacies located in mass-merchandisers such as Kmart and Wal-Mart, or from large drugstore chains such as Eckerds, Phar-Mor, and Drug Emporium. In these cases, an indirect consumer channel includes the producer who sells direct to the retailer, who in turn facilitates purchase by the consumer. Some of us would rather purchase our prescriptions in a more personal manner from the local drug store (which is supplied by a drug wholesaler rather than by the manufacturer), where we can still get an ice cream soda while we wait and that may even deliver our medicine and send us a bill at the end of the month. However, many independent pharmacies are suffering as increasing numbers of consumers choose convenience and low price over personalized service and decide to abandon this traditional distribution channel. An increasingly popular alternative for many consumers is to purchase their prescriptions through mail-order firms that offer even lower prices than the mass merchandisers—a fourth channel.

DISTRIBUTION PLANNING

Good distribution decisions make products available to customers in the right quantities when and where they are wanted. From the consumer's point of view, this seems to occur by magic. We don't give much thought to what had to go on behind the scenes to ensure that we will encounter fully stocked shelves during a shopping trip.

The distribution planner knows otherwise: Many decisions have to be made so that these products appear where and when they are needed. Do customers want products in large or small quantities? Do they insist on buying them locally or will they purchase from a distant supplier? How long are they willing to wait to get the product? What types of product-related services do they demand?

Distribution planning, like planning for other elements of marketing, is best accomplished by following a series of orderly steps as shown in Figure 14.3 (page 484). In this section we will first look at the objectives of distribution strategies. Then we will examine elements of the internal and external environments that affect place decisions.

DISTRIBUTION OBJECTIVES

The first step in deciding on a distribution plan is to develop appropriate objectives. As always, the primary consideration is to identify how distribution can best support the organization's overall marketing goals. How can distribution work with the other elements of the marketing mix to increase profits? To increase market share? To increase volume of sales?

Distribution objectives are often related to the desired amount of **market penetration,** the number of wholesalers or retailers who will carry the product within a given market. At first glance that may seem an easy decision: Do everything possible to penetrate the market totally. But guess again. If the product is being distributed through too many outlets—that is, if the market is *overpenetrated*—there may be inefficiency, duplication of efforts, and even cannibalization of sales. On the other hand, if the market is *underpenetrated*—that is, if there are not enough outlets—then sales (and profits) cannot be maximized. Thus a distribution objective may be either to increase or to decrease the amount of market penetration.

Another concern is geography. Do we need to have the same level of concentration in different regions of the country? Do we need the same penetration rates in large markets as in small ones? Often, because customers, competition, and other environmental factors

market penetration: the number of wholesalers or retailers who carry a product within a given market

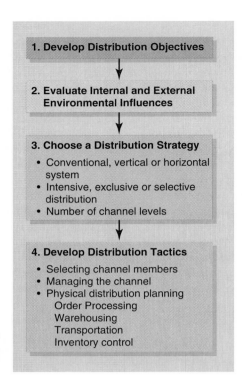

**Figure 14.3
Steps in Distribution
Planning**

vary in different geographic regions, it may be wise to develop different distribution objectives for separate regions or areas of the total market.

Finally, distribution objectives should clearly specify the time frame for accomplishing each objective. Should the objectives be accomplished in a few months, in a year, or over a period of several years? Because of the long-term nature of distribution strategies, it is important to proceed slowly and carefully. If an error is made when an advertising campaign is developed, the agency can tinker with the result in a few weeks or months. In contrast, adjusting poor distribution decisions may take several costly years. Also, distribution strategies often require large inputs of both financial and other resources. It is a mistake to expand distribution so fast that production cannot keep up. It is always easier to get a new customer than to recover one that has been lost to a product shortage. Growth of distribution must also not outstrip the organization's financial resources. Most firms finance part of their operations with short-term and long-term borrowing, which of course costs money (as you well know if you've ever gotten a car loan or a mortgage!). More than one firm has found that it has grown too fast—it has grown itself into bankruptcy!

Here are a few possible distribution objectives:

Increase market coverage 30 percent among independent drug retailers in the top 100 markets over the next year.

Fully penetrate the southeastern market by distributing to at least one store per 50,000 population in that region.

Identify and develop contractual arrangements with at least one manufacturer's agent in each state within 6 months.

ENVIRONMENTAL INFLUENCES ON DISTRIBUTION PLANNING

Effective distribution planning can occur only when marketers have considered important factors in the internal and external environment (see Chapter 3). The organization must consider such issues as its own ability to form and influence distribution channels, how the competition gets its products to market, and the ability of customers to access these channels and perhaps even to consider channels that are not currently being fully utilized. In addition, distribution decisions must consider the nature of the product

REAL PEOPLE, REAL CHOICES:

DECISION TIME AT FIRST UNION NATIONAL BANK

Historically, banks have invested heavily in brick and mortar as their primary distribution channel. They build a branch (typically in a free-standing building) and wait for depositors to show up. Now, changes in consumers' lifestyles (such as scarcity of precious time to run to the bank), coupled with improved technology that permits transactions and information transfer to occur over phone lines and in other locations, are fundamentally transforming the way banking services are distributed. In addition, depositors are leaving banks in droves; in the past ten years, mutual fund assets have grown by two million dollars, and much of this came from the banking industry. As forward-looking banks consider different channels for delivery that will lure customers back to the bank, they must also redefine the role of the branch.

In September 1994, First Union engaged Arthur Andersen Consultants to work with its own staff. The goal: to reengineer the retail bank so that customers can obtain fast, easy, error-free banking service where, when, and how they want it. This project involved a thorough analysis of the entire retail banking operation, including coming up with innovative ways to market multiple products to diverse customer groups via multiple delivery channels.

Extensive research was conducted in the fall of 1994. Over 3600 customers and non-customers participated in a comprehensive survey designed to determine what benefits they sought in a bank. In early 1995, a team of 55 First Union bankers joined the team to begin the internal assessment and design stages of the reengineering project.

Although banks typically segment the market on the basis of customer demographics, the team's research revealed another way: It identified segments based on consumers' priorities regarding banking services, regardless of their age, sex, and so on. The five segments were

1. *Speed:* The customer who is willing to trade off price and convenience for speed. This segment accounted for 17 percent of the market studied.

2. *Price:* The customer who is willing to forgo a relationship with a bank in favor of simply obtaining the services at the best price. This was the largest segment, which included 38 percent of consumers.

3. *Place:* The customer who places the highest value on where and how he or she transacts business made up 17 percent of the market.

4. *Relationship:* The customer who places the highest value on the quality of his or her relationship with the banker accounted for 16 percent of the market.

5. *Price/speed:* The customer who wants it all: banking services at the best price and as fast as possible. When a trade-off is inevitable, though, price is more likely to drive the buying decision. This group made up 11 percent of the market.

Ms. Gardner's team has been challenged with creating the bank that will attract each of these segments. The team has been developing and testing different concepts to determine how much of the market would switch to each new possibility. Today, First Union customers transact 66 percent of their banking business in person, 8 percent by phone, and 26 percent through the ATM.

First Union hopes to convince customers to migrate to alternative delivery channels such as telephone and personal computer, and it projects that within four years the amount of business done over the phone will increase by 50 percent and that customers will do over 10 percent of their business via personal computer and other electronic delivery systems. The company hopes to reduce its dependence on costly "brick and mortar" delivery of banking services, although other banks have found that many consumers do

not change old habits readily. In fact, the team's research showed that 22 percent of the population will continue to want to use a branch in the future. The team explored many delivery channels, and eventually the list was narrowed down. The team also felt that the alternative forms of delivery were not mutually exclusive; different combinations of two or more methods might be considered. Here are some of the individual options the team continued to consider.

Option 1. Retail center: A free-standing facility offering in-person sales and service. This configuration is very different from the traditional branch, because most of the operational and administrative functions will be centralized outside the retail center. Instead, the retail center will be primarily a sales center, where self-service vestibules will move the customer to alternative channels. This option appeals to individuals and small business in the "place" and "speed" segments. The retail center offers familiar physical locations and a customer-oriented staff and will create a more efficient environment where transactions will be faster and more user-friendly. On the other hand, this brick and mortar delivery system is very expensive.

Option 2. Telephone bank: A center that offers full-service banking by phone. The center concept includes telemarketing, relationship management, service, and sales units. This version appeals to people who value price, speed, and convenience. It does not appeal to those in the "place" segment who value the personal touch of a teller or bank officer.

Option 3. Mobile sales force: An external sales force prospecting for new business and delivering to customers who want business conducted at their place of choice. This concept appeals to people who value in-person contact, convenience, and advisory services. On the other hand, the mobile sales force is very expensive. Ms. Gardner and her colleagues believed that motivated First Union representatives must be a presence in the market when the company begins to make the transition to a reduced branch structure, though it is likely that over time this sales force will be reduced to a more sustainable level.

Option 4. Home banking: Considerable reliance on multifunctional automatic teller machines and home PCs. The ATM network will be greatly expanded to help cover the markets where branch closures occur. Self-service offers a lower-cost alternative to traditional banking that requires no personal interaction. This option appealed to higher-educated, high-balance customers, so long as ATMs could be enhanced to perform more of the transactions performed by tellers, including express bill payment. The challenge here is to replace the familiar teller with machines that are seen as user-friendly and superior to face-to-face transactions.

Now, join the First Union decision team: If you had to recommend a solution for streamlining First Union's delivery services, which option would you recommend, and why?

and other elements of the marketing mix. For example, physical characteristics of the product itself are important: Is the product perishable? Bulky? Fragile? It's a lot easier to ship cans of soda or beer over long distances than it is to send the delicate potato chips that people eat along with them.

In Chapter 9, we classified products as either convenience, shopping, or specialty goods. Each of these product types calls for different considerations in distribution strategies. Convenience products need maximum exposure. When consumers have an emergency, the product must be nearby. Marketers of convenience products usually want widespread, low-cost distribution. Although a long-running cigarette ad campaign proclaimed, "I'd walk a mile for a Camel," most people will not go very far out of their way to buy smokes, drinks, or newspapers.

In contrast, factors other than instant availability are relevant to most other kinds of products. Because people spend time comparing different brands when purchasing a shopping product, distribution decisions need to ensure that the item is located near other, similar products. If most competitors distribute their electric drills through mass-merchandisers, a manufacturer has to make sure its brand is there also. In the case of specialty products, it may be acceptable to have only limited distribution. Indeed, restricted access to the product may well be part of its appeal and market position if it's viewed as an "exclusive" product that isn't available to just anyone (that's why bouncers at trendy nightclubs encourage people to leave who don't look cool enough or rich enough).

Existing channel relationships and traditions are also important. Is a ready-made channel available or will a new channel have to be created? What middlemen are available, and are those available willing and able to perform the functions that might be required—promotion, customer contact, storage, credit? Another consideration is whether it is best to use the same or different intermediaries from those used by competitors; sometimes, to ensure customers' undivided attention, it is preferable to make items available only in outlets that don't carry the competitors' products.

As with any of the aspects of marketing planning, distribution decision making is successful only when marketers understand their customers. Not only do marketers need to consider who is buying and why are they buying, but they must also know the *distance* from the producer to the market, the *number* and *density* of customers in the market, and the *functions* that a distributor must perform to meet customer needs. If there were only a handful of potential customers in a certain region, it would be disastrous to attempt to set up a company sales office there. Although it makes sense for brokers to handle real estate sales and even the sales of used manufacturing equipment, customers buying new high-tech telecommunications equipment want to deal with a manufacturer's rep who can provide installation, product usage instruction, and product maintenance and service.

Finally, by studying the distribution strategies of competitors, marketers can learn from their successes and failures. How can distribution make the firm more competitive in the marketplace? How can a distribution plan enable the firm to satisfy customer needs better than the competition? If the biggest complaint of customers is delivery time, then developing a system of strategically located sales branches that allow same-day delivery can make the competition pale by comparison.

Planning distribution strategies really means making two decisions: *what type* of channel to use and *how many* intermediaries—that is the number of levels in the channel and the number of intermediaries at each level. In the next section we will discuss different types of marketing systems and strategies.

SELECTING A DISTRIBUTION CHANNEL

Participants in a distribution channel belong to an interrelated system, where the actions of one member often affect the outcomes of others. Generally speaking, these systems take one of three forms: conventional, vertical, and horizontal marketing systems.

Conventional Marketing Systems

A **conventional marketing system** is a multiple-level distribution channel in which channel members work independently of one another. Conventional systems involve little between-levels cooperation. Members seldom work together to build demand, reduce costs, or improve customer satisfaction. Each firm essentially pursues its own objectives without giving much thought to overall channel coordination.

The activities of Du Pont, America's number-one chemical producer, illustrate the working of a conventional channel. Du Pont makes chemicals that are used in many industries; a Lycra biking outfit and nylon windbreaker contain Du Pont chemicals, as does the paint on cars. Each specialized chemical follows a different channel, and Du Pont can't really control all these channels, which are very complex and involve many different channel members. Coordination takes place between individual firms, but not within the entire channel system.

Vertical Marketing Systems

A **vertical marketing system** (VMS) describes a channel in which there *is* cooperation at the manufacturing, wholesaling, and retailing levels. Firms in a VMS work together and depend on each other like links in a chain. There are three types of vertical marketing systems.

conventional marketing system: a multiple-level distribution channel in which channel members work independently to perform channel functions

vertical marketing system (VMS): a channel of distribution in which there is cooperation among members at the manufacturing, wholesaling, and retailing levels

Table 14.2
Established and
Emerging
Franchises: A
Sampler

Company Name	Description	Start-up Costs
Software Exchange Franchising Corp.	Sells second-hand software disks purchased from personal-computer users	$42,000–$81,000
Kid to Kid Franchise System	Sells used children's clothing	$88,000 up
Microplay Franchising	Sells used video games	$140,000
Record Swap Franchises, Inc.	Sells a mix of recycled and new audio disks.	$150,000
Toy Traders Franchising, Inc.	Used toys	$50,000
Heartland Properties, Inc.	Assisted living for the elderly (not nursing home care)	$600,000
Mad Science Group, Inc.	After-school programs and birthday party entertainments that make science fun	$57,000
California Closet Co.	Custom closets	$75,000 and up
McDonald's	Hamburger restaurants	Start-up costs estimated at $500,000
Subway	Sandwich shops	$34,400
Dunkin' Donuts	Doughnut Shops	$120,000–280,000
Baskin-Robbins	Ice cream shops	$134,000–150,000
Hardee's	Hamburger restaurants	$700,000–$1.7 million
Arby's	Roast beef restaurants	$525,000–850,000
Domino's Pizza	Pizza delivery	$76,500–187,500

Source: Adapted from Jeffrey A. Tannenbaum, "Franchisers Are Finding Some New Twists on Old Ideas," *The Wall Street Journal* (April 24, 1995): B2; Veronica Byrd, "Hamburgers or Home Decorating? Businesses That Sell," *The New York Times* (Oct. 4, 1992): 10.

1. *Administered VMS:* An administered VMS consists of independent firms working together. Voluntary cooperation is enforced by a channel leader. The dominant member is able to assume leadership and direct cooperation because of its expertise and power to give or withhold rewards. Often an administered VMS experiences more turmoil than other channel systems, because the channel leader has no legitimate authority by which it can control the channel members. On the other hand, because there are no contractual or ownership relationships among the channel members, the administered VMS may be better able to adapt to changing opportunities in the marketplace.[13]

2. *Contractual VMS:* In a contractual VMS, cooperation is legally enforced. Independent firms sign contracts that spell out how they will cooperate. There are three types of contractual VMSs.

   a. **Wholesaler-sponsored voluntary chains:** Because independent retailers have difficulty competing with large national chains, wholesalers sometimes organize retailers into a voluntary chain. Retail members of the chain typically use a common name, cooperate in advertising and other promotion, and even develop their own private-label products. Examples of wholesaler-sponsored chains include IGA (Independent Grocers' Alliance) food stores and Ace Hardware stores.

   b. **Retailer cooperatives:** Sometimes retailers themselves organize a cooperative marketing system. A retailer cooperative is a group of retailers that has

Multilevel Marketing

In recent years many people have been captivated by the controversial concept of **multilevel marketing**, which is essentially a *pyramid scheme* whereby independent contractors earn commissions on the products they sell and on the sales of others whom they recruit into the business. Like a chain letter, this structure succeeds only so long as participants are able to convince new people to join up. New members typically join as independent distributors who buy inventory from the company and then in turn attempt to recruit others to do the same. Although this arrangement can work quite well for a while, once a market has been saturated and there are no more additional people to recruit, the last people in the chain can get stuck—sort of like the "odd one out" in a game of musical chairs.

Large firms that operate on this concept, such as Mary Kay Corp. and Amway Corp., have been the subject of lawsuits and investigations while at the same time attracting a host of professionals who often leave lucrative jobs as lawyers, stockbrokers, or school teachers to make more money while attaining an entrepreneurial lifestyle. Many multilevel marketing firms foster an almost cult-like atmosphere as they recruit and motivate members to sell, sell, sell. Firms such as Amway and Mary Kay attract and retain people in their organization with the use of songs, conventions, and motivational audio and video tapes. Whatever they're doing, it's working: It is estimated that in 1994 over three million people were involved, and about one-fourth of those were working at it full-time.

Defenders of multilevel marketing argue that the plans have offered opportunities for many hard-working individuals to make millions; others feel that people are recruited with promises of big money that rarely materialize. These critics cite numerous instances where new recruits invest large sums to buy inventory they are unable to sell. The reputation of multilevel marketing has also been damaged by small scam companies disguised as legitimate multilevel firms. In 1992, the Direct Selling Association adopted an ethics policy requiring its members to buy inventory back from distributors for at least 90 percent of the purchase price, and the trade group prohibits false or inflated claims about products and earnings.

Source: Stephanie Mehta, "Visions of Wealth and Independence Lead Professionals to Try Multilevel Marketing," *The Wall Street Journal* (June 23, 1995): B1–B2.

---

established a wholesaling operation in order to help individual small businesses compete more effectively with the large chains. Each retailer owns shares in the wholesaler operation and is obligated to purchase a certain percentage of its inventory from the wholesaler. Examples of retailer cooperatives are Associated Grocers and True Value Hardware Stores.

c. **Franchises:** Franchises are contractual arrangements in which a franchisor (a manufacturer or a service provider) allows an entrepreneur to use the franchise trade name and marketing plan for a fee. Franchises account for $246 billion a year in sales, 12.7 percent of retail sales—from steel bungee-jumping towers (Air Bongo) to gun shops (Strictly Shooting).[14] Some longstanding and some new franchise operations are listed in Table 14.2. Franchises are a popular way for entrepreneurs to get a start in dozens of fields: restaurants, motels, hair salons, print shops, laundry and dry cleaning, automotive goods and services, and on and on.

Buying a franchise rather than starting from scratch often confers certain advantages. Just using the name of the franchiser gives the entrepreneur advertising clout, purchasing power, and name recognition.[15] Typically, the franchiser provides a variety of services for the franchisee, helping to train employees, giving access to lower prices for needed materials, and helping pick a location with visibility. In return, the franchiser receives a percentage of revenue from the franchise owner. Usually the franchisees are allowed to use the franchiser business format, but they are also required to follow that format to the letter.[16] For example, a McDonald's franchisee is seldom allowed to change the menu or the physical decor of the restaurant. It's important that customers know that they can get the same Big Mac in New York City that they will find in Moncs Corner, South Carolina, and in Shanghai.

3. *Corporate VMS:* In a corporate VMS, a single firm handles manufacturing, wholesaling, and retailing functions. Thus the firm has complete control over

multilevel marketing: a pyramid type of channel of distribution in which independent contractors earn commissions on the products they sell and on the sales of others whom they recruit into the business

all channel operations (a structure known as vertical integration). Retail giant Sears Roebuck & Co., for example, sells brands such as Kenmore appliances that in reality are manufactured by Sears itself.

Horizontal Marketing Systems

In a **horizontal marketing system,** two or more firms at one channel level work together for a common purpose. United Airlines and Lufthansa, for example, cooperate to increase the appeal of their separate businesses. To increase passenger volume for both airlines, they share a common flight code that places connecting flights between the two carriers higher on travel agents' screens. To increase customer benefits, they also share frequent-flier programs and airport clubs.[17]

Horizontal marketing systems can help to increase the attractiveness of an entire industry—as the saying goes, "A rising tide lifts all boats." Semiconductor manufacturers in the United States jointly fund research and development efforts. Retailers serving tourists at many beach towns co-sponsor activities, events, and services that increase overall tourist traffic and satisfaction. By pooling resources, participants in a horizontal marketing system reduce costs and increase customer benefits. Sometimes these relationships are a little *too* cozy, however, and as we'll see shortly, these types of horizontal cooperation are illegal.

HOW MANY CHANNEL MEMBERS SHOULD BE INCLUDED?

Distribution strategy decisions also mean determining how many wholesalers and retailers are needed to achieve marketing goals. This decision determines a product's market exposure, the scope of distributor functions, and the ideal customer service level. The three basic alternatives are intensive, exclusive, and selective distribution. First, we will compare the two options that are most different from each other: intensive and exclusive distribution. Then we will discuss selective distribution.

Intensive distribution means selling a product through all suitable wholesalers or retailers who will stock and sell the product. In contrast, **exclusive distribution** means limiting distribution to a single outlet in a particular region. Marketers use intensive distribution for chewing gum, soft drinks, cigarettes, office supplies, and other goods consumed frequently. By comparison, pianos, cars, executive training programs, and television programs typically are sold through exclusive distribution arrangements.

Table 14.3 summarizes some of the factors that help guide the marketer's selection of distribution partners. The five decision factors shown there—company, customers, channels, constraints, and competition—help to determine the best fit between the type of distribution system and the marketing situation. For example, consumers buy soft drinks regularly, and they buy what is easy to get. Pepsico, Inc. makes its cola drink available nearly everywhere food and drinks are purchased. High customer density makes this costly strategy worthwhile.

As Table 14.3 shows, exclusive distribution fits situations where the firm's mission is to meet specialized demand, where there is low customer density and service and cooperation are important, where the cost of serving customers is high, and where individualized attention to customers contributes to customer satisfaction. Nonoverlapping market coverage enables wholesalers and retailers to recoup the costs associated with long selling processes for each customer and, in some cases, extensive after-sale service. Exclusive distribution fits situations where products carry high price tags, because the wholesaler or retailer gets significant pay-back on the high level of service given to individual customers.

Of course, not every situation neatly fits Table 14.3. For example, consider professional sports. Customers don't shop around for games like they shop for pianos; they may even go to a game on an impulse. And they don't require much individualized service. Nevertheless, professional sports employ exclusive distribution. The cost of serving customers is very high because players are well paid and stadiums expensive. Profitability depends on exclusive distribution. Just as the *constraints* factor drives exclusive distribution in professional sports, any one of the five decision factors in Table 14.3 might loom large in a distribution decision.

Don't confuse the deliberate decision to adopt an exclusive distribution strategy with the problem of incomplete market coverage. For example, professional football has teams in most major metropolitan areas. By covering the entire United States (and a good part

Decision Factor	Intensive Distribution	Exclusive Distribution
Company	Oriented towards mass markets.	Oriented toward more specialized markets.
Customers	High customer density. Price and convenience are priorities.	Low customer density. Service and cooperation are priorities.
Channels	Overlapping market coverage.	Nonoverlapping market coverage.
Constraints	Cost of serving individual customers is low.	Cost of serving individual customers is high.
Competition	Based on a strong market presence, often through advertising and promotion.	Based on individual attention to customers, often through relationship marketing.

of Canada), the National Football League (NFL) has helped American football become a national sport. Not so for hockey. Until the Minnesota North Stars moved south and became the Dallas Stars, NHL teams mostly served Canada and the wintry portions of the U.S. Incomplete market coverage meant that hockey was a regional sport with too few fans to justify the broadcast of games on national television networks.[18]

SELECTIVE DISTRIBUTION

The alert reader (especially if he or she is also a sports fan) may note that there are some exceptions to the distribution of sports teams we have noted. For example, New York has two football teams and two baseball teams, Chicago fields two baseball teams, and so on. Market coverage that is less than intensive distribution, but more than exclusive

distribution, is called **selective distribution.** Selective distribution fits those situations where demand is so large that exclusive distribution is inadequate, but selling costs or some other decision factor makes intensive distribution a poor fit. Although a White Sox baseball fan may not believe that the Cubs franchise is necessary (and vice versa), the Chicago market is large enough to support both teams.

Selective distribution is suitable for many products, including consumer goods sold in retail stores. To maintain a quality image, a producer chooses retailers that will provide better product displays and more customer service. Selective distribution enables the producer to choose only those wholesalers and retailers that have a good credit rating, provide good market coverage, serve customers well, and cooperate effectively. Wholesalers and retailers like selective distribution, because sales aren't shared with many other outlets, resulting in higher sales and profits. In return for higher profits, the producer obtains a higher level of cooperation and greater control over marketing the product.

MANAGING THE CHANNEL OF DISTRIBUTION

Once a channel strategy has been developed and the channel members are aligned, the day-to-day job of managing the channel begins. Good channel management makes the difference between a successful and an unsuccessful distribution plan. Just as in any other "family" where diverse interests and priorities must be accommodated, it is important that marketers understand channel leadership and how to achieve channel cooperation while avoiding excessive conflict.

Channel Leadership

The measure of an effective channel of distribution, as with all marketing strategies, is better business performance and higher levels of customer satisfaction. In a channel, such success often depends on a firm at one level of distribution taking a leadership role. The **channel leader,** sometimes called a *channel captain,* is the dominant firm that in general controls the channel. The leader establishes operating norms and processes that reduce channel conflicts, minimize costs, and enhance delivered customer value.

A firm becomes the channel leader because it has *power* relative to other channel members. This power can be derived from several different sources.

Exhibit 14.4
In order to develop effective channels, manufacturers may try to recruit qualified channel partners. They might assess prospective partners' goals and guiding values, reputation, marketing and financial performance history, growth potential, quality of leadership within the firm, and cooperativeness. What type of customer does the outlet serve? What types of other products are carried? What expertise does the intermediary possess? Published directories that list various types of suppliers, wholesalers, and retailers may be useful in identifying potential partners, as is print advertising such as this appeal by Hallmark.

- A firm has *economic power* because of its size and its ability to control resources. For example, Microsoft has gained a leadership role in the computer industry because of the widespread use of its software.

- A firm has *legitimate power* because it has legal authority to call the shots. McDonald's Corporation wields such power over its thousands of franchisees.

- A firm may have *expert power* because it has demonstrated that it has the knowledge required to do an effective job. Procter & Gamble gained influence as an industry expert in the manufacture and marketing of many personal care and household products.

- *Reward or coercive power* accrues to firms that engage in exclusive distribution and are able to control the channel because they have the ability to give profitable products to, and take them away from, the channel intermediaries. For example, automobile dealers are quite willing to accept a variety of restrictions imposed by a manufacturer in return for the privilege of offering the latest models BMWs, Jeeps, or Corvettes. In some instances, the intermediaries work even harder to achieve excellence as outlets because of special incentives provided by the channel leader. For example, dealers who sell more of a product may receive priority in delivery of their order over less successful intermediaries.

A firm at any level of distribution may emerge as a channel leader. When retailers were much smaller than they are now, manufacturers tended to assume leadership in consumer goods markets. Procter & Gamble, for instance, developed customer-oriented marketing programs, tracked market trends, and advised retailers on the mix of products most likely to build sales. As large retail chains evolved, giant retailers began to assume a leadership role. Wal-Mart, for instance, developed a clear market image and a strong customer following. Wal-Mart provides leadership to suppliers in the markets it serves.

Channel Cooperation

Because producers, wholesalers, and retailers depend on one another for success, cooperation helps everyone. Cooperation between firms at different levels of a distribution channel emerges from both formal and informal agreements. Formal agreements require more of a commitment from each party. For example, Levi Strauss & Co. developed an inventory system called LeviLink that ties a retailer's cash registers directly to Levi Strauss's inventory system. Because this system provides timely, detailed information about purchase patterns and inventory levels, Levi Strauss can ship product directly to retailers, avoiding added costs of warehouses and distribution centers. Further, the retailer requires a smaller staff to manage inventory purchases.[19] Everyone wins.

This kind of cooperation requires a long-term commitment so that the substantial investment in technology can be recouped. However, cooperation occurs in small ways, too. Federated Department Stores, for example, asked its suppliers to upgrade the quality of hangers on which they ship clothes. This simple improvement saves Federated time and money when its employees unpack the items for display in the store.[20]

Channel cooperation is also stimulated when the channel leader takes actions that help make its partners more successful. Good dealer profit margins, dealer training, cooperative advertising, and expert operational advice are invisible to end customers but are important motivating factors in the eyes of wholesalers and retailers.[21] Haggar Apparel, for example, found ways to help retailers improve the speed and accuracy of reorders. Compaq Computer runs training classes for retailers that carry its PCs.

Channel Conflict

Of course, relations among members in a channel are not always full of sweetness and light. Because each firm has its own objectives, channel conflict may threaten the distribution strategy. *Vertical conflict* occurs between firms at different levels of the same distribution channel. Incompatible goals, poor communication, and disagreement over roles, responsibilities, and functions cause conflict. For example, a producer may want an intermediary to carry only its brands, whereas the intermediary feels it would be more successful if it were to carry a variety of brands, including private labels. Producers want consumers and business customers to be loyal to them, whereas the intermediaries want to "own" the customers themselves.

Horizontal conflict occurs between firms at the same level of a distribution channel. For example, the same brands of computers, stereos, and televisions may be sold by independent appliance or computer dealers, by large appliance chains such as Circuit City and Best Buy, and by warehouse merchandisers such as Sam's Wholesale Clubs. A surprising source of horizontal competition may come from a retailer's own suppliers in the form of factory outlets. For example, Nike men's socks selling for $4.25 at JCPenney's sell for half that price at a Nike outlet store. Not surprisingly, Penney's doesn't appreciate the competition created by its own supplier![22]

ETHICAL AND LEGAL ISSUES IN DISTRIBUTION

When a firm engages in illegal distribution practices, the marketer loses in a number of ways. The effort spent in building a distribution system is lost, competition gains ground, and courts may impose high fines on a guilty firm. To avoid costly setbacks, marketers must understand the basic legal constraints of channel arrangements. Here are some of the most common offenders:

Exclusive Dealing Contracts

A producer would often prefer that channel partners sell only its own products, rather than having them stacked next to the competition. Sometimes a producer requests a written agreement to that effect, called an *exclusive dealing contract.* However, such an agreement is illegal in the United States if it restricts competition. This is the case in most situations in which the producer is large and dominates the market whereas the wholesaler or retailer is small. To determine whether the deal is illegal, the courts usually focus on three questions.

1. Does the dealer have 10 percent or more of the market (meaning that 10 percent or more of the sales in the market would be blocked off from competitors' products)?
2. Are the sales revenues involved sizeable?
3. Is the producer larger—and thus more intimidating—than the dealer?

Producers like Coca-Cola meet all of these qualifications. If Coca-Cola tried to tell retail grocers that they could not carry Pepsi if they want to carry Coke, this threat would almost certainly be considered illegal.

Exclusive Territories

In some situations it is preferable to grant an exclusive selling territory to a wholesaler or retailer. When an exclusive territory exists, the intermediary is confident that investments of financial resources, effort, and time in selling the product will not be lost because of competition. *Exclusive territories* may or may not be illegal, depending again on whether they restrict competition. There are three circumstances under which exclusive territories are usually considered legal.

1. It would be difficult to get retailers or wholesalers to make the investment necessary to handle the product without such guarantees. Furniture manufacturers such as Thomasville feel that their customers are best served when they can visit retail locations where most of their line is on display. Thus, in order to become a dealer, a retailer must purchase (and display) $100,000 or more of the company's line. Such requirements could not be imposed without the granting of exclusive territories.
2. In order for customers to have confidence in the quality of the product, it is necessary to maintain high levels of consistency among outlets. McDonald's and other franchisers maintain strict control of their outlets by granting exclusive territories. In this way, a person who gets a "Big Mac attack" knows that any McDonald's he or she happens to be near at the time will feature the same clean dining area, a familiar assortment of Big Macs and fries, and clean restrooms.
3. Exclusive distribution is essential to maintain the image of the product. A Harley-Davidson motorcycle might lose some of its cachet if someone could

pick one up in Wal-Mart. When the fashion designer Halston introduced a new line designed specifically to be sold by JCPenney, the upscale department store Bergdorf-Goodman promptly dropped Halston's regular lines of apparel from its inventory.

Tying Contracts

Tying contracts, also called *full-line forcing,* occur when a producer requires that a wholesaler or retailer purchase one or more of its *other* products in order to obtain supplies of a highly desired product. That is, access to popular items is *tied* to buying other inventory. Tying contracts are legal only if the products in question must be used at the same time in order to function properly or in the case of small firms trying to enter a market. Such contracts are especially popular—and often appropriate—in franchising agreements, where tying contracts ensure consistency in the products that franchisees offer.

Unauthorized Distribution

An application of U.S. copyright laws prohibits importing and distributing copyrighted material without permission of the copyright owner. For example, a Miami-based importer distributed Amarige, an upscale French perfume, without authorization of the French firm's U.S. subsidiary. The importer attempted to distribute the boot-legged fragrance to discount stores. It was determined that this action would diminish the perfume's luxury image and divert profits from the U.S. subsidiary, which had invested large sums of money to promote the perfume.[23]

Legal Constraints on Horizontal Marketing Systems

Court-enforced constraints on horizontal marketing systems are straightforward. Obvious *collusion,* wherein executives of competing firms conspire to manipulate the market, is illegal. For example, the actions of the international oil cartel, OPEC, that restrict oil production to maintain high crude oil prices would be illegal *if* the cartel's members were U.S. domestic firms. Cooperation that restricts supply to control prices or that controls prices directly is illegal. In other words, a CEO at, say, United Airlines cannot simply call up his or her counterparts at American, Delta, and Continental and get everyone to agree to double ticket prices.

Global competition has changed some of governments' views on horizontal marketing systems. Today, national governments recognize that domestic firms compete with other nations' industries, and some countries emphasize the development of a coordinated *industrial policy* whereby taxation, tariffs, and regulations are formulated to favor home-country production in designated industries. Although in recent years the Japanese have been sharply criticized for protecting their position in the automobile industry, other countries also routinely take actions to support their own favorites (for example, the U.S. textile industry is heavily subsidized by the government).

Gray Markets

Although not illegal, American marketers are increasingly facing the problem of counterfeit or *gray products* on U.S. retailers' shelves.[24] Quite obviously the knock-off Rolex and Cartier watches sold on the streets of New York and Los Angeles are illegal, but the "gray market" Lava soap made in Latin America, Colgate toothpaste from Venezuela, and Chiclets gum from Beirut are not. What exactly are gray products? They are branded products that are legally produced but were intended for sale in some other country.

One source of gray products in the U.S. can be traced to the attempts of American marketers to internationalize by licensing the manufacture of brand-name products in various countries around the globe. Because the products made in South American, Eastern European, and other developing countries are so much cheaper, they can be shipped to the United States and sold at a substantial savings compared to their "made in America" counterparts. And U.S. Customs regulations do not specifically prohibit the importing of American brands licensed to foreign manufacturers.

It is estimated that the sale of such products costs American manufacturers between $5 and $8 billion a year. But the costs can be much higher than just lost sales. For example, when British-made Shield soap was imported into the United States, Lever Brothers lost not only sales but also many customers. Because the British version of Shield was made for the hard British water and was highly perfumed, Americans who bought the less expensive version were turned off to the brand.

The Japanese have developed a new twist on gray markets by double importing. Because the value of the yen is high and because the Japanese government subsidizes the export market for many products, Japanese marketers can go to Los Angeles, buy the export versions of Japanese products, and ship them back to Japan where they sell for 20 to 30 percent less than the "made for Japan" versions. And this market isn't just for electronics. The biggest Japanese gray market is for camera film. Japanese retailers sell the made-for-America Fuji film for half the price of the product labeled in Japanese.

PHYSICAL DISTRIBUTION

Marketing textbooks tend to depict the practice of marketing as 90 percent planning and 10 percent implementation. In the "real world," many managers would no doubt argue that this ratio should be reversed. Marketing success is very much the art of getting the timing right and delivering on promises. That's why marketers place so much emphasis on efficient physical distribution, the movement of goods from manufacturer to customer in the most timely, efficient, and cost-effective way to meet customers' expectations for time and place utility. Indeed, the success of retailing giants like Wal-Mart is largely due to the skill with which they handle distribution decisions. In the 1970s, the Arkansas-based company established highly automated distribution centers, which cut shipping costs and time. Also, Wal-Mart used an advanced computer system to track inventory and speed up check-out and reordering. These two distribution innovations, along with founder Sam Walton's plan to locate stores at the edge of rural towns, created the largest, fastest-growing, and most profitable retailer in the United States.[25]

In this section, we will first talk about what physical distribution is. Then we discuss the importance of physical distribution and some of the important aspects of physical distribution decision making.

WHAT IS PHYSICAL DISTRIBUTION?

Physical distribution is, very simply, the process of getting product benefits in the hands of customers at the *best time* in the *right place* and at the *lowest possible cost*. Figure 14.4 shows that physical distribution includes the following activities:

- Order processing—transferring title and handling paperwork related to distribution
- Materials handling and warehousing—storing goods before they reach final customers
- Transportation—physically moving the goods from one location to another
- Inventory control—determining what amounts and types of goods should be kept on hand prior to sale

In most of these decisions, the marketer must strike a compromise between low costs and high customer service. It would be nice to transport all goods quickly by air, but that is certainly not practical. Keeping down costs may result in back orders, stock-outs, special costly production runs, and high-cost fast-freight shipments when customer demand exceeds inventory. In physical distribution as in other marketing decisions, marketers need to study what customers want and what the competition is doing.

Many current physical distribution techniques have evolved from methods initially devised for getting supplies to the battlefield. Consider the expression "an army travels on

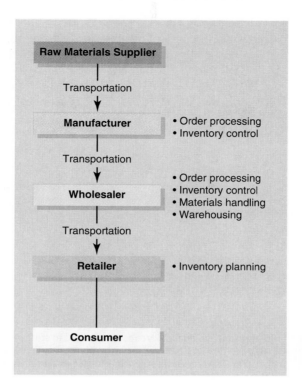

Figure 14.4
The Physical Distribution Process

its stomach": The most competent, heavily armed fighting force cannot prevail if its lines of supply are cut.

Similarly, a retailer or distributor travels on its inventory: The most beautiful, spacious store cannot function if it is too cumbersome or expensive to stock. Perhaps this is why Sears hired the general who managed the military supply chain during the Persian Gulf War to head up its effort to improve physical distribution! Physical distribution involves looking at transportation, storage, order processing, selling, distribution, packaging, purchasing, and customer service as pieces in a big puzzle, the coordinated flow of goods from producer to consumer.[26] Let's examine some of these pieces in more detail.

Order Processing

Order processing includes the activities that occur between the time an order comes in and the time a product goes out the door. After an order is received, it is sent to an office for record keeping and then on to the warehouse to be filled. When the order reaches the warehouse, it is checked to see whether the item is in stock. If it is not, the order is placed on *back-order status*. That information is sent back to the office and then back to the customer. If the item is available, it is located in the warehouse, packaged for shipment, and scheduled for pickup by either in-house or external shippers.

Fortunately, many firms have automated this process. Once an order has been placed in the system, all the other steps occur automatically. Inventories are continuously updated in computer data bases so that both the sales representative who calls on a customer and the individuals who take orders know immediately whether the product is in stock. In more sophisticated warehouses, many of the steps in locating and packaging the order are handled through robotics. And the order is scheduled for pickup via electronic communications with shippers.

Materials Handling

Materials handling is the moving of products into, within, and out of warehouses. When goods come into the warehouse they must be identified, checked for damage, sorted, and labeled. Next they are taken to a location for storage. Finally, they are recovered from the storage area for packaging and shipment. All in all, the goods may be handled over a dozen times.

Procedures that limit the number of times a product must be handled decrease the likelihood of damage and reduce the cost of materials handling. In many facilities, the process has been automated allowing products to be identified quickly and easily, added into inventory records when they arrive, and taken out of inventories when they are shipped.

Warehousing

Whether we speak of fresh-cut flowers, canned goods, or computer chips, at some point goods must be stored. Storing goods allows marketers to match supply with demand. For example, lawnmowers may be needed only in the summer but are produced year round. Toys and other gift items are big sellers at Christmas, but toy factories operate 12 months of the year. **Warehousing**—storing goods in anticipation of sale or transfer to another member of the channel of distribution—enables marketers to provide time utility to consumers by holding on to products until they are needed.

Developing effective physical distribution means deciding how many warehouses are needed, where they should be located, and what types of warehouses to use. The location of the warehouse(s) is related both to the location of customers and to transportation access. If customers are widely dispersed, it may be necessary to locate warehouses in several different areas of the country. If the product is usually shipped by air, warehousing may instead be situated close to airports. The number of warehouses is often related to the level of service the customers require. If customers generally require fast delivery (today or tomorrow at the latest), then it may be necessary to store products in a number of different locations where they can be delivered quickly. In other instances, one or a few centrally located storage facilities are adequate.

Transportation

Physical distribution decisions also involve what forms, or *modes*, of transportation to use to move products among channel members, and from channel members to customers. Again, making transportation decisions entails a compromise between minimiz-

warehousing: storing goods in anticipation of sale or transfer to another member of the channel of distribution

ing cost and providing the service customers want. As shown in Table 14.4 (pages 500–501), modes of transportation, including railroads, pipelines, water transportation, motor carriers, and airways, differ in the following ways:

- *Dependability:* the ability of the carrier to deliver goods safely and on time
- *Cost:* the total charges for moving a product from one location to another, including any charges for loading, unloading, and in-transit storage
- *Speed of delivery:* the total time for moving a product from one location to another, including loading and unloading
- *Accessibility:* the number of different locations served by the carrier
- *Capability:* the ability of the carrier to handle different types of goods
- *Traceability:* the ability of the carrier to locate goods in shipment

Each mode of transportation has strengths and weaknesses that make it a good choice for different transportation needs. Table 14.4 (pages 500–501) summarizes the pros and cons of each type.

Railroads. For many years railroads were the major freight carrier in the United States. Railroads are best for carrying heavy or bulky items such as coal and other mining products, agricultural products, forest products, steel, automobiles, and large machines over long distances. Railroads are about average in their cost and provide moderate speed of delivery. Railroads are readily accessible, because rail networks are highly developed in many countries. Since the development of the interstate highway system in the United States, however, railroads have fallen out of favor as the carrier of choice for many industries.

Water. Ships and barges, like railroads, carry large, bulky, nonperishable goods and are very important in international trade. Water transportation is quite low in cost but is very slow and is limited to inland and oceanic water routes. Weather can be a problem: Rivers freeze over in the winter in colder climates, and storms can upset transoceanic

Exhibit 14.6
Rail transportation provides dependable, low-cost service to many locations, but trains simply cannot carry goods to every community in the country, and they can't go over the oceans. These problems with rail transportation have been solved in recent years by innovations developed in the industry. *Piggyback services* make it possible to use low-cost rail transportation for shipping to a larger number of destinations: Truck trailers are loaded onto trains and carried as close to their destination as possible. Truck, train, and ship transportation have been similarly combined to provide *fishyback services.* Combining truck and air transportation is called *birdyback service.* Problems of excessive handling and damage have been reduced by *containerization,* wherein large quantities of goods are sealed in large protective containers—some as big as a truck—for transit.

**Table 14.4
A Comparison of
Transportation
Modes**

Transportation Mode	Dependability	Cost	Speed of Delivery
Railroads	average	average	moderate
Water	low	low	slow
Trucks	high	high for long distances; low for short distances	fast
Air	high	high	very fast
Pipeline	high	low	slow
Internet	high	low	very fast

shipping. Because of a number of environmental disasters such as the oil spill caused by the *Exxon Valdez,* the transportation of oil and other chemicals by tankers is increasingly being scrutinized.

Trucking. As the bumper sticker displayed on the back of many eighteen wheelers proclaims: "America's needs move by truck." This claim is more than just hype: Trucks or motor carriers are the most important carrier for consumer goods, especially for shorter hauls. Motor carrier transportation is extremely flexible; trucks can travel on almost any road to literally every location in the country. Trucks are also able to carry a wide variety of products, including perishable items that may be transported in *reefers*—refrigerated tractor-trailers.[27]

Although costs are fairly high for longer-distance shipping, trucks are very economical for shorter deliveries. Delivery is fast in most instances, and because trucks provide door-to-door service, product handling is kept at a minimum, thus reducing the chance for product damage. In Japan, a wide range of special deliveries—from live fish to whale bacon to temple bells are handled by *takuhaibin* (home delivery services), which make 1.2 billion deliveries annually. Delivery trucks are equipped with refrigeration, two-way radios, printers for delivery data, and satellite navigational screens.[28]

Air. Air transportation is both the fastest and the most expensive transportation mode. It is ideal for moving high-value items such as some mail, electronic goods, fresh-cut flowers, and live lobsters. Air transportation is provided by passenger airlines, by air-freight carriers, and by express delivery firms such as Federal Express and Airborne Express.

Even though the specific charges for air transportation are higher, the total cost of distribution may actually be lower in the long run. Because air transportation allows goods to be shipped quickly, with limited handling, and because the ride is smoother than land-bound methods, products are less likely to be damaged, stolen, or vandalized, and costs for packaging materials are reduced as well. In addition, air transportation—especially the overnight services provided by express delivery firms—are becoming more and more important in the development of international markets. Ships remain the major mover of international cargo, but air transportation networks are rapidly making the world a smaller place.

Pipeline. Pipelines are used to carry petroleum products—oil and natural gas—and

Accessibility	Capability	Traceability	Best for These Types of Products
high	high	low	heavy or bulky goods, such as automobiles, grain, steel
low	moderate	low	bulky, nonperishable goods, such as automobiles
high	high	high	a wide variety of products, including those that need refrigeration
low	moderate	high	high-value items, such as electronic goods and fresh flowers
low	low	moderate	petroleum products and other chemicals
potentially very high	low	high	services such as banking, information, and entertainment

a few other chemicals. Pipelines primarily flow from oil or gas fields to refineries. They are very low in cost, require little energy, and are not subject to disruption by weather. Quite obviously, the versatility of pipelines is very low. Individual pipelines can be designed only to carry one or two products; transportation goes in only one direction and only to places where the pipelines are located. And transportation by pipelines is very slow and limited in quantity to the capacity of the pipe. Most pipelines are owned by the oil companies or other firms that use them.

The Internet. Although scientists have not yet figured out how to transport goods electronically (except on the TV show *Star Trek*), marketers of services such as banking, news, and entertainment are increasingly taking advantage of rapidly evolving electronic communications networks. The Internet, created by the U.S. Department of Defense way back in the 1960s to link government laboratories, contractors, and military installations, was designed to operate without any central control so that it could survive a nuclear attack. The Internet has since been "conquered" by civilians, millions of whom are joining each year to share information, opinions, and products. We are only beginning to realize the potential of the Net to deliver goods and services to people who simply place their orders from their home keyboards while browsing in cyberspace.

The Internet is revolutionizing many distribution channels. Even though only 5 percent of homes were connected to the Internet in 1995, competitors are already fiercely jockeying for position in this booming $1.3-billion-a-year industry. The trendiest part of the Internet is the WorldWide Web, where virtually anyone can set up shop by offering a home page for web browsers. Small entrepreneurs as well as firms like Reebok, AT&T, and Miller Brewing are rushing to set up websites to promote their brands with games and other services.[29]

One final note on the modes of transportation: In recent years, the increased efficiency and innovative equipment used by many of these transporters have blurred the distinctions among the different modes of transportation. JIT delivery can be handled just as efficiently by rail as by truck. Furthermore, the use of intermodal transportation (such as piggyback and fishyback services) offered by third-party contractors is changing the transportation picture. As such innovations emerge, the common stereotypes of the various means of transportation grow less and less applicable.

Inventory control

Inventory control means developing and implementing a process to ensure that the firm always has available the types and quantities of goods needed to meet customers' demands—no more and no less. Firms store goods (create an *inventory*) for several reasons. First, the pace of production may not match cyclical demand. For example, it may be more economical to produce water skis year-round, but few water skis are sold during winter in the northern states.

Second, it may be more economical to order a product in quantities that don't exactly parallel demand. For example, retail gas stations usually receive truckloads of gasoline, holding their inventory in underground tanks. Also, consumers may prefer shopping at a location with a large variety of styles in inventory, as at car dealerships, piano stores, and department stores. Finally, the consequences of stock-out may be very negative. Hospitals must keep adequate supplies of blood, IV fluids, drugs, and other supplies on hand to meet emergencies, even if some items become outdated without ever being used.

Inventory control has a major impact on the costs of physical distribution. If supplies of products are too low, then expensive emergency deliveries may have to be made—or the company may lose customers to its competitors. If inventories are above the level required, then the firm incurs unnecessary storage expenses and the risk of damage or deterioration. Inventory control involves deciding when to buy and how much to buy at a time.

Firms sometimes engage in practices that serve their own purposes but that in the process increase the costs of inventory management. In *trade loading,* manufacturers seek to induce wholesalers and retailers to stock up on products that they can't sell right away in order to achieve monthly or quarterly sales goals. Trade loading achieves short-term sales and profits at the producer's level but cause members of the channel to hold more inventory. Experts estimate that at one time, trade loading added about $20 billion to $30 billion in promotion costs, storing costs, and handling costs. Ultimately, American consumers paid this annual bill through inflated grocery store prices. In recent years, trade loading has declined as producers, wholesalers, and retailers have all placed greater emphasis on cost controls.

As we discussed in Chapter 7, to minimize inventory storage costs, many companies have begun using just-in-time (jit) inventory systems. Pioneered by the Japanese, JIT systems reduce storing and handling costs by carefully matching supply and use—order quantities are kept small and orders are placed more frequently. Manufacturers in particular try to utilize JIT, often requiring that suppliers make deliveries daily or even several times a day, just in time for production. JIT requires a close supplier–user relationship. Suppliers cannot have lapses or delays in deliveries and often locate facilities near their customers.

Another innovation that has improved efficiency in inventory management is **electronic data interchange (EDI).** EDI uses information technology to track goods in transit. With EDI systems, electronic scanners capture bar code information on goods, which are then tracked by computer. Because EDI provides a standardized format, the information can be shared between computers. Thus EDI links among suppliers, transporters, and customers are becoming more and more common, even in global trade.

Increasingly, manufacturers are turning to *quick-response replenishment systems* to ensure that their products get to where they are needed. As noted earlier, VF Corporation, maker of Lee and Wrangler jeans and Vanity Fair women's undergarments, is at the forefront of this new technology. VF makes sure customers find what they're looking for by use of a computerized "market-responses system," which keeps records on what consumers buy so that VF can rapidly restock stores with popular items. As a result, VF jeans arrive within three days after an order has been placed by a retailer, compared with the more typical delivery time of a month. The system is hooked to the computers of large retail customers such as Wal-Mart and JCPenney. Every night, retailers transmit sales data collected at register scanners straight to VF, where restocks are performed automatically.[30] This is the future of distribution planning.

inventory control: a process developed to ensure that the types and quantities of goods needed to meet customers' demands are always available

electronic data interchange (EDI): a method for tracking goods in transit through the use of information technology; in EDI systems, electronic scanners capture bar code information on goods, which are then tracked by computer

REAL PEOPLE, REAL CHOICES:

HOW IT WORKED OUT AT FIRST UNION NATIONAL BANK

To narrow down the list of delivery options, the team conducted a thorough cost/benefit analysis to project the incremental revenue potential and the cost of developing each possibility. The team then retained outside consultants to help it find the best way to change the way people will bank in the year 2000. Ms. Gardner and her colleagues concluded that all four channels should be activated and that the transition from in-person to alternative delivery cannot occur unless all four are fully operational. They spent several months developing the design details of each delivery channel to prepare for a pilot test in 1996.

Chapter 14 Summary

Objective 1. Explain what a distribution channel is and describe its functions in the marketing mix.

A distribution channel is an organized network of firms that work together to get a product from a producer to a customer. Channels provide time, place, and ownership utility for customers. Channel members handle the physical distribution function for products, including the breaking and accumulation of bulk, creating assortments, reducing the number of transactions necessary for the flow of goods, transportation, and storage. Intermediaries in channels of distribution also perform a variety of both communications and facilitating functions.

Objective 2. Describe some of the distribution channel members and the different types of distribution channels.

Manufacturer-owned channel members include sales branches, sales offices, and manufacturers' showrooms. Merchant wholesalers are independent intermediaries who take title to a product. They include both full-function wholesalers such as general-merchandise wholesalers and rack jobbers and limited-function wholesalers such as cash-and-carry wholesalers, drop shippers, mail-order wholesalers, and truck distributors. Merchandise agents and brokers are independent intermediaries who do not take title to products. They include manufacturers' agents, selling agents, merchandise brokers, export and import agents, and commission merchants.

Channels vary in length from the simplest two-level channel to longer channels with three, four, or more channel levels. Consumer distribution channels include direct distribution, wherein the producer sells directly to consumers, and indirect channels, which may include a wholesaler and/or a retailer. Business-to-business channels are often direct but may include industrial distributors, jobbers, or dealers. Distribution channels for services are usually direct, but services such as insurance and travel include an agent who helps complete the transaction. In reality, many firms are part of more than one type of channel; that is, they participate in dual or multiple distribution systems.

Objective 3. Discuss the different types of decisions that must be made in distribution planning.

Distribution planning begins with developing objectives, which often involve the amount of market penetration. Next, marketers must consider environmental factors (such as the characteristics of the product, existing channel relationships, intermediary availability, the number and density of customers, customer needs, and the distribution channels of competitors) before they select the type of channel and the number of channel members. Conventional marketing systems include multiple levels of intermediaries that work independently. Vertical marketing systems (VMSs) are channels in which there is cooperation at the different levels. VMSs include administered and contractual VMSs, wholesaler-sponsored voluntary chains, retailer cooperatives, franchises, and corporate VMSs. Horizontal marketing systems are composed of firms at one channel level who work together.

Distribution planning also includes decisions about the number of channel members at each level. Intensive distribution means including all possible intermediaries, exclusive distribution means having only one intermediary per region, and selective distribution means including a few—but not all—outlets in a region.

The day-to-day management of the established channel means that one firm takes a leadership role. That is, the firm, by virtue of economic, legitimate, expert, reward, or coercive power, becomes the channel leader or captain. Channel leaders work to make all members more successful in order to ensure channel cooperation. Channel conflict, among firms either at different levels or at the same level, may occur when firms have different objectives.

Marketers must seek to avoid illegal distribution practices in their distribution planning. Some of the more common offenses are exclusive dealing contracts, exclusive territories, tying contracts, unauthorized distribution, collusion among competing firms at the same channel level, and the sales of gray products.

Objective 4. Describe the types of decisions made in physical distribution planning.

Physical distribution involves moving goods from the manufacturer to the customer in the most efficient and effective manner possible. Physical distribution includes order processing, materials handling, warehousing, transportation, and inventory control. When order processing is automated, all of the steps occur automatically. Effective physical distribution means deciding where and how many warehouses are needed for storage of goods until they are ready for sale or transfer to another channel member. Another physical distribution decision involves the mode of transportation to be used. Railroads, pipelines, water transportation, trucks, air transportation, and even the Internet offer different levels of dependability, cost, speed of delivery, accessibility, capability, and traceability.

Inventory control, another important part of distribution planning, means developing a process to make sure that the firm always has available the types and quantities of goods to meet customers' demands. Inventory control can have a big impact on costs. Trade loading to meet short-term sales goals increases product costs. Just-in-time inventory systems reduce costs by requiring more frequent small orders. Inventory management has also been improved by EDI (electronic data interchange) which enables firms to track goods in transit using bar codes. With quick-replenishment systems, products are automatically restocked for retailers as soon as customers buy them.

Review Questions

Marketing Concepts: Testing Your Knowledge

1. What are the functions of a channel of distribution?
2. List and explain the types of manufacturer-owned and independent intermediaries.
3. What is a direct channel? An indirect channel?
4. What types of channels are used for the distribution of services?
5. What are vertical marketing systems? Horizontal marketing systems?
6. What is the job of a channel leader?
7. What activities are involved in physical distribution?
8. How do just-in-time inventory systems reduce costs?
9. How does electronic data interchange improve physical distribution?
10. What are the advantages and disadvantages of shipping by rail? By air? By ship? By truck?

Marketing Concepts: Discussing Choices and Issues

1. Have you ever heard someone say, "The reason products cost so much is because of all the middlemen." Do middlemen increase the cost of products? Would consumers be better off or worse off without middlemen?

2. Many entrepreneurs choose to start a franchise business rather than "go it alone." Do you think franchises offer the typical person good opportunities? What are the positive and the negative aspects of purchasing a franchise?

3. There are some legislators who would like to make "gray market" goods illegal. Do you think gray market goods should be sold? If so, should there be any controls on them?

4. As colleges and universities are looking for better ways to satisfy their customers, an area of increasing interest is the distribution of their product—education. Describe the characteristics of your school's channel(s) of distribution. What types of innovative distribution might make sense for your school to try?

Marketing Practice: Applying What You've Learned

1. Assume you have recently been hired as director of marketing for a medium-size furniture manufacturer. Your firm specializes in making small tables and chests, each of which is made unique with a hand-painted design. As your firm is beginning to expand into new regions of the country, you must consider whether an intensive, selective, or exclusive distribution system is best for your product.

a. Develop an outline listing the pros and cons of each type of system for your product.

b. Decide which you will recommend, and tell why it is preferable.

2. As the one-person marketing department for a small candy manufacturer (your firm makes high-quality hand-dipped chocolates containing only natural ingredients), you are considering making changes in your distribution strategy. Your products have previously been sold through a network of food brokers who call on specialty food and gift stores. But you think it might be good for your firm to develop a corporate VMS—that is, vertical integration. In such a plan, a number of company-owned retail outlets would be opened across the country. The president of your company has asked that you present your ideas to the company executives. In a role-playing situation with one of your classmates, present your boss with your ideas, including the advantages and disadvantages of the new plan compared to the current distribution method.

3. Assume that you have recently been given a new marketing assignment by your firm. You are to head up development of a distribution plan for a new product line: a series of do-it-yourself instruction videos for home gardeners. These videos would show consumers how to plant trees and shrubbery and bulbs, how to care for their plants, how to prune, and so on. You know that in developing a distribution plan, it is essential for you to understand and consider a number of internal and external environmental factors. Make a list of the information you will need before you can begin developing the distribution plan. How will you adapt your plan on the basis of each of these factors?

Marketing Mini-Project: Learning by Doing

In the United States, the distribution of most products is fairly easy. There are lots of independent intermediaries—wholesalers, dealers, distributors, and retailers—who are willing to cooperate to get the product to the final customer. Our very elaborate interstate highway system combines with rail, air, and water transportation to provide excellent means for moving goods from one part of the country to another. In many other countries, the means for distributing products are far less efficient and effective. This project is designed to help you better understand the importance of distribution decisions in marketing success.

For this mini-project, you and one or more of your classmates should first select a consumer product, probably one you normally purchase. Then use library sources and/or other people (retailers, manufacturers, dealers, classmates, and the like) to gather information to do the following:

1. Describe the path the product takes from the producer to you. Draw a model to show each of the steps the product takes. Include as much information as you can about transportation, warehousing, materials handling, order processing, inventory control, and so on.

2. Select another country in which the same product or a similar product is sold. Describe the path the product takes from the producer to the customer in that country.

3. Determine whether the differences between the paths in the two countries cause differences in price, availability, or quality of the product.

4. Present your findings to the class.

Key Terms

Endnotes

1. G. Bruce Knecht, "Banks Bag Profits with Supermarket Branches," *The Wall Street Journal* (May 20, 1994): B1, B8.

2. Edwin McDowell, "McDonald's and Hotels Plan Food Delivery Test," *The New York Times* (June 23, 1994): D5.

3. Bob Jones, "Know Your Place," *Entrepreneur* (June 1994): 52–55.

4. Michael Selz, "Firms Innovate to Get It for You Wholesale," *The Wall Street Journal* (July 23, 1993): B1–B2.

5. Gabriella Stern, "If You Don't Feel Like Fetching the Rental Car, It Fetches You," *The Wall Street Journal* (June 9, 1995): B1(2).

6. Keith Alexander and Andrea Rothman, "Will Travel Agents Get Bumped by These Gizmos?" *Business Week* (June 28, 1993): 72.

7. Zachary Schiller and Wendy Sellner, "Making the Middleman an Endangered Species," *Business Week* (June 6, 1994): 114–115.

8. Robert F. Lusch, Deborah Zizzo, and James M. Kenderdine, "Strategic Renewal in Distribution," *Marketing Management,* 2 (Nov. 2, 1993): 20–29.

9. "The Single-Person Sales Agency; Solo Agents Like Their Independent Life," *Agency Sales Magazine* 22 (March 1992): 21–29.

10. "Taking Aim," *The Economist* (April 24, 1993): 74.

11. Catrin Blair, "Business Travel: The Distribution Revolution," *Fortune* (May 29, 1995): 32–38.

12. Susan Carey, "Playboy Looks Overseas as U.S. Climate Grows Hostile," *The Wall Street Journal,* 222 (Sept. 29, 1993): B4.

13. Brent H. Felgner, "Retailers Grab Power, Control Marketplace," *Marketing News,* 23 (Jan. 16, 1989): 1–2.

14. Michele Galen, Laurel Touby, Lori Bongiorno, and Wendy Zellner, "Franchise Fracas," *Business Week* (March 22, 1993): 68–73.

15. Andrew E. Serwer, "Trouble in Franchise Nation," *Fortune* (March 6, 1995): 115–129.

16. Jeffrey A. Tannenbaum, "Chain Reactions," *The Wall Street Journal* (Oct. 15, 1993): R6.

17. Robert L. Rose and Bridget O'Brian, "United, Lufthansa Form Marketing Tie, Dealing a Setback to American Airlines," *The Wall Street Journal* (Oct. 4, 1993): A4.

18. Cristine Gonzalez, "An Icy Sport Heads South to Make (It Hopes) Its Fortune," *The Wall Street Journal* (Oct. 4, 1993): B1, B4.

19. Richard S. Teitelbaum, "Designs Inc.," *Fortune* (Feb. 8, 1993): 127.

20. Christina Duff, "Nation's Retailers Ask Vendors to Help Share Expenses," *The Wall Street Journal* (Aug. 4, 1993): B4.

21. Allan J. Magrath, "The Gatekeepers," *Across the Board* (April 1992): 43–46.

22. Kevin Helliker, "Thriving Factory Outlets Anger Retailers as Store Suppliers Turn into Competitors," *The Wall Street Journal* (Oct. 8, 1991): B1, B6.

23. Stephanie Strom, "Givenchy Wins a Major Round in Discount Fight," *The Wall Street Journal* (Sept. 4, 1993): 37.

24. Dan Koeppel, "Brands Dressed in Gray," *Adweek's Marketing Week* (March 20, 1989): 20–24.

25. Wendy Zellner, "When Wal-Mart Starts a Food Fight, It's a Doozy," *Business Week* (June 14, 1993): 92–93.

26. Stephanie Strom, "Logistics Steps Onto Retail Battlefield," *The New York Times* (Nov. 3, 1993): D1.

27. Christopher Palmeri, "Reefer Man," *Forbes* (April 25, 1994): 82–84.

28. Jennifer Cody, "Ding-Dong, Here's a Thank-You Fish; Is There Any Reply?" *The Wall Street Journal* (July 12, 1994): A1, A12.

29. Stephanie Losee, "How to Market on the Digital Frontier," *Fortune* (May 1, 1995): 88.

30. Joseph Weber, "Just Get It to the Stores on Time," *Business Week* (March 6, 1995): 66–67.

MARKETING IN ACTION:
REAL PEOPLE AT VF CORPORATION

VF Corp. isn't a trendsetting clothing manufacturer, and it doesn't plan to be. This giant apparel company, which manufactures Lee and Wrangler jeans and Vanity Fair women's undergarments, avoids risk and has been quite successful being a "second to market" type of company. VF's "follower" strategy was in evidence during the recent hoopla in the industry about push-up bras. Only after competitor Sara Lee Corporation introduced its new Wonderbra in the United States in 1994 and American shoppers eagerly snapped it up did VF get around to introducing its own version, called It Must Be Magic. The secret of VF's success is not its innovative, daring designs. It's something not nearly so glamorous but every bit as important: the company's state-of-the-art distribution system.

A key aspect of VF's marketing strategy has been a focus on selling timeless apparel staples and using advanced technology to ensure that these classics are available when and where shoppers want them. CEO Lawrence R. Pugh believes that this low-risk strategy has made VF successful and has enabled the firm to avoid the financial ups and downs that can be disastrous to clothing makers. Retailers like doing business with VF because the apparel maker gives customers what they want, and even more important, VF ensures that customers can find what they're looking for. These efforts led Tom Cole, logistics chief at Federated Department Stores, to call VF the "vanguard in retailer–vendor partnerships."

VF is a leader in computerized market response systems. Such systems basically keep tabs on what shoppers buy and allow VF to restock store shelves faster than the competition. For example, it can take up to a month for a retailer to get in a shipment of new Levi's jeans, but VF's high-tech distribution system enables the company to get Lee and Wrangler jeans on store shelves within three days after an order is placed.

The story of VF's ascent to distribution leadership centers on CEO Pugh. Pugh, who became chairman of VF in 1983, began experimenting with new market response systems as early as 1989. To get a workable system off the ground, VF first had to connect its computers with the computers of major retailing partners such as Wal-Mart and JCPenney. Wal-Mart alone sells millions of pairs of Wrangler jeans each year through its 2100 outlets, so this cooperative effort was more complex than it may sound.

However, VF was determined to make this idea work, and now the mechanism is in place. Every night, Wal-Mart collects sales data from its store scanner systems and sends these data straight to VF. With this information, VF is able to restock all 2100 stores automatically. Thus if a Wal-Mart customer buys a pair of jeans on Monday morning, VF gets that information on Monday night. If the same size and style are in stock, the jeans are shipped on Tuesday and arrive at the store on Wednesday. If the style is not in stock, VF's computers automatically order a replacement and a new pair of jeans goes out to the store within a week—a far cry from VF's old three-month waiting period for back-ordered products.

Speed is not the only benefit to retailers who are plugged into VF's distribution system. Because only products that sell are restocked, retailers are less likely to be stuck with dozens of pairs of unpopular sizes or styles. Stores get more sales out of the same amount of inventory, because they can stock only those sizes and styles that customers "vote" for with their dollars.

How has this attention to high-tech detail paid off for VF? Since 1991, the company has enjoyed an annual compounded growth rate in sales and income of nearly 20 percent. For 1994, net earnings were $274.5 million, an increase of 11.4 percent from the previous year. In fact, VF is the biggest player in the $7.9 billion U.S. jeans market. Its market share rose from just under 26 percent in 1989 to 30 percent in 1994, while Levi's share slipped from 21 percent to under 17 percent—in part because of slowness in replenishing retailers' stock.

Of course, nothing stays the same for long in the highly competitive apparel industry. Other manufacturers are learning the moral of this distribution tale and are developing their own quick-response systems, threatening VF's edge. To meet this challenge, CEO Pugh is working with retailers to move beyond restocking. Specifically, VF is developing its Trendsetter system, which will track groups of goods, such as jeans and shirts of specific sizes. For example, it may be that stores that typically sell fifty pairs of jeans in size 10 will sell only half as many shirts of the same size. With this information, retailers will better be able to forecast ideal supply levels and will be less likely to have to deal with over- or underordering certain sizes.

Source: Joseph Weber, "Just Get It To the Stores on Time," *Business Week* (March 6, 1995): 66–67.

MARKETING IN ACTION: REAL PEOPLE AT VF CORPORATION *(CONTINUED)*

Things to Talk About

1. Compare the distribution system used by VF Corp. to these used by other members of the apparel industry.
2. How is VF Corp.'s distribution strategy an example of relationship marketing?
3. In what ways is VF's quick-response distribution system important to retailers?
4. Who do you think is the channel leader in this system?
5. What secrets to success has VF Corp. discovered?

CASE 14-2

MARKETING IN ACTION: REAL CHOICES AT PEAPOD

Who says grocery shopping has to be a time-wasting hassle? If Peapod succeeds with its vision, the company may radically change the way the $400 billion U.S. grocery industry operates. Based in Evanston, Illinois, Peapod turns its customers' PCs into grocery carts. For the busy 1990s householder with a sixty-hour-a-week job and a family to feed, Peapod provides a virtual supermarket. Shoppers can place their orders from home and have them conveniently delivered without ever leaving the house.

Here's how the system works: Each day, supermarkets who are partners with Peapod transmit computerized price updates on over 18,000 items from toothpaste to tofu. At-home shoppers can scan entire categories of products, just as they would if they were in the store walking down the grocery aisles. Items can be selected from broader categories (snacks), from more narrow categories (pretzels), or by brand name (Rold Gold). Regular users of the system can save even more time simply by calling up their own personal shopping lists. Because shoppers can sort items in the computer database by cost per ounce or per pound or check to see what's on sale today, it's easy to comparison-shop for the most economical brand or size. Customers can indicate whether they are willing to accept a substitute product if their selected brand is out of stock, and they can even specify precisely what they want—a *ripe* avocado, two *green* bananas, or six *large* apples.

The Peapod distribution system also offers other ways to make shoppers' lives easier. Because customers are increasingly interested in the fat, sugar, and salt content of foods, Peapod plans to upgrade its software to provide information on the nutritional content of products. And the service takes credit cards, checks, or online payments. It even accepts coupons! The customer simply places an order, specifies a method of payment, indicates a preferred delivery time, and waits for the order to show up at the door. Once Peapod receives the order, it is forwarded to the closest grocery store partner, where the specified items are collected by Peapod employees. These items are checked out at special Peapod counters and taken to a holding area where refrigerated and frozen goods can be safely stored until Peapod delivers them.

Peapod was founded by brothers Andrew and Thomas Parkinson, both veterans of Procter & Gamble. The business is based on the close partnerships Peapod has developed with two grocery chains, Jewel/Oscar in Chicago and Safeway in San Francisco. For now at least, these food retailers feel that the losses they may incur in sales of impulse purchases to in-store customers will be more than offset by what they will gain in sales volume as more people choose to use the Peapod system.

Peapod has a great idea, but the jury is still out on whether the company will succeed. Some critics suggest that it is just a novelty distribution system doomed to failure like many other computer shopping ventures. In fact, Peapod's owners have yet to make a profit, even after five years of operations. However, Microsoft chairman Bill Gates has predicted that one-third of food sales will be handled electronically by the year 2005. If this high-tech soothsayer is correct, Peapod is off to a good start toward cornering this market.

Indeed, to date Peapod has few competitors. Although this may seem like a plus, it also may mean that other firms simply are hesitant to invest in such a risky venture. Currently Peapod has a customer base of 10,000 households in Chicago and San Francisco. Although consumer surveys repeatedly say that shoppers are unwilling to pay extra for the privilege of shopping online, Peapod customers tend to be loyal and don't seem to wince at paying the $29.95 start-up fee, a $4.95 monthly service fee, and a $6.95 base charge per order plus 5 percent of their grocery bill. But to become profitable, Peapod may have to make changes in its marketing strategy: raise its prices even more, increase its volume to spread fixed costs over a larger number of customers, or perhaps cut the level of service it now provides.

Only time will tell whether enough harried shoppers will be willing to write a bigger check to save time at the checkout.

Source: Susan Chandler, "The Grocery Cart in Your PC," *Business Week* (Sept. 11, 1995): 63–64.

Things to Think About

1. What is the problem facing Peapod?
2. What factors are important in understanding this problem?
3. What alternatives might Peapod consider?
4. What are your recommendations for solving the problem?
5. What are some ways to implement your recommendations?

15

Retailing and Direct Marketing

When you have completed your study of this chapter, you should be able to:

CHAPTER OBJECTIVES

1. Explain the position of retailing in the marketplace—that is, how retailing has evolved and how it continues to change.

2. Describe how retailers may be classified by type or selection of merchandise.

3. List and explain the major choices that must be made in developing a retailing strategy.

4. Explain some major nonstore direct-marketing activities in today's marketplace and mention some possibilities for the future.

5. List and describe some environmental trends that will affect the future of retailing.

ℛEAL PEOPLE, REAL CHOICES:

Meet Göran Carstedt, a Decision Maker at IKEA

IKEA is the world's largest-volume furniture chain, with 125 outlets in 24 countries.[1] The company is based in Sweden, but about 80 percent of its sales come from beyond Scandinavia. Its business idea is "IKEA shall offer a wide range of home furnishing items of good design and function, at prices so low, that the majority of people can afford to buy them."[2] The company was founded by Ingvar Kamprad, who arrived at the name by combining his initials with the first letters of the Swedish farm, Elmtaryd, and parish, Agunnaryd, where he grew up.[3]

Göran Carstedt joined the IKEA organization in 1990, when he was named president of IKEA North America, which is headquartered outside of Philadelphia. Prior to entering the world of retailing, he had spent most of his career in the Swedish auto industry. After receiving a Ph.D. from the University of Umeå in 1974, Mr. Carstedt joined Volvo as manager of market planning in the Car Division. He was president of Volvo France for several years, and from 1985 until he joined IKEA he was president of Volvo Svenska Bil AB, the Swedish Volvo sales organization for cars, trucks, buses, spare parts, financial and computer services, and car rental. He also served as an executive member of the Swedish bidding committee for the 1994 Winter Olympics. Since September of 1995, Mr. Carstedt has been president of IKEA Europe, and he also oversees the company's newly established corporate marketing staff.

ℛETAILING: SPECIAL DELIVERY

Shop 'til you drop! For many people, obtaining the product is half the fun (others, of course, would rather be dragged over burning coals than spend time in a store). **Retailing** is the final stop on the distribution path; it is the process by which goods and services are sold to consumers for their personal use. Very often the *way* we obtain something is a part of *what* we are buying, so the retailer has the ability to add or subtract value from the offering by virtue of its image, inventory, service quality, location, and pricing policy. The retailer puts the final brush strokes on the picture that is presented to consumers: This role makes the retailing process an extremely important and visible element of the marketing system.

The ability of a retailer to create value is exemplified by IKEA. It's more than a store for many shoppers; it's a way of life. The company's inexpensive, Scandinavian designed furniture especially appeals to young people (and to the "young at heart"). The huge stores feature such amenities as child care, restaurants with authentic Swedish food, and the free use of tape measures, pencils, and strollers. Satisfied customers can even borrow car racks to take merchandise home.

Furniture is displayed in attractive room settings to help shoppers visualize what it will look like once they get it home. The reactions of one devoted customer on discovering IKEA sum up the store's appeal: "I opened the catalogue—and in one . . . instant, I saw a door swinging wide and a beautiful white light spilling over a land of knotty pine coffee tables with copies of *The Atlantic* scattered on them, leather couches the color of wonderful old saddles, Turkish "kelim" carpets, blond bookcases glowing with track lighting, exotic leafy plants nestling in gently glazed terra-cotta pots. . . . this was my true 'inner' living room. It was as 'me' as if I had decorated it myself. It was IKEA-land."[4]

As this daydreamer discovered, retailers play a key role in assembling and presenting products—often from many different manufacturers—in ways that make them appeal-

retailing: the final stop in the distribution channel by which goods and services are sold to consumers for their personal use

ing and accessible. This chapter will explore the many different types of retailers, comparing and contrasting them along some key dimensions. It will consider the strategic decisions that retailers must make as they position themselves in the minds of increasingly choosey shoppers. How much and what type of merchandise to carry? At what prices? Where should the store be located? Alternatively, should merchandise be sold in a store at all? How about catalogs, television shopping, the WorldWide Web? We'll look at the dynamics of both store retailing and nonstore retailing, but first we'll start with an overview of where retailing has been and where it's going.

RETAILING: A MIXED [SHOPPING] BAG

Although we often think of large department stores when we hear the term *retailer,* in reality *any* person or organization that offers something for sale to a consumer is a retailer. About one of every seven U.S. workers is employed in retailing—they certainly are not all working in department stores! Indeed, in such categories as sporting goods and gifts and novelties, small merchants with less than $1 million in annual sales accounted for over 70% of new job growth over the last decade.[5]

Part of what makes retailing such an exciting area is that the same good or service can be obtained in so many different ways. As we saw in the last chapter, customers seeking to buy, say, Hootie and the Blowfish T-shirts may find them for sale at a department store, a small clothing store, a warehouse outlet, a mail-order catalog, or on TV. They may even be offered bootlegged ones from a street vendor selling shirts that "fell off a truck" on their way to the store. Retailers as diverse as mammoth department stores and sidewalk vendors are clamoring for the attention and dollars of shoppers. In fact, retailers vary greatly in size of the store, number of outlets, type of ownership (corporate, franchise, or personal), service level provided, and whether the shopper physically goes to the store or the store "comes to the shopper" by providing products that can be ordered over the telephone, through the mail, or even in a vending machine.

Retailers make the final, crucial connection between the producer and the consumer; they make it possible for the actual marketing exchange to occur. Retailers provide many benefits to consumers. Some save people time or money by providing an assortment of merchandise under one roof. Others search the world for the most exotic delicacies, giving shoppers access to goods they would otherwise never see or even hear about. And many retailers even offer us entertainment: They provide us with interesting and stimulating environments (some would say *too* stimulating!) in which to spend our leisure time—and, they hope, our money.

In this section we will first look at how retailing changes over time. Then we will provide an overview of the different types of stores operated by retailers. In a later section, we'll see how nonstore retailing is developing to provide alternative ways for the shopper to obtain goods and services.

THE EVOLUTION OF RETAILING

As long as people have been bartering or selling their wares, there have been middlemen to facilitate this process. Retailers have taken many forms over time, ranging from the simple peddler who hawked his wares from a horse-drawn cart to a majestic urban department store, from the intimate boutique to the huge "hyperstore" that sells everything from potato chips to snow tires.

Today merchants have to be more creative and resourceful than ever in order to convince consumers that *their* version of retailing is the desirable way to procure goods and services. As consumers grow increasingly pressed for time and overburdened with choices, this task is getting more difficult: The typical consumer spent only four hours a month in a mall in 1990, compared to ten hours in 1985. Newer competitors like Wal-Mart, warehouse clubs, and specialty stores continue to present new challenges to shopping malls, just as these malls challenged downtown department stores a generation ago.[6]

As economic, social, and cultural developments change the face of society, different types of retailers develop—often replacing older, outmoded forms. How can we predict what the dominant forms of retailing will be tomorrow or ten years from now? Over the years, several attempts have been made to explain how retailing forms evolve over time.

The Wheel of Retailing

wheel-of-retailing hypothesis: a theory that explains how retail firms change, becoming more "upscale" as they go through their life cycle

One of the oldest explanations for these changes is the **wheel-of-retailing hypothesis.**[7] This theory states that new types of retailers find it easiest to enter the market as low-price competitors. After they gain a foothold, they gradually trade up, improving their facilities, increasing the quality of the merchandise they carry, and offering such amenities as parking and gift-wrapping. This "upscaling" of course, is not free—it also results in greater investment and operating costs. As a result, the store must raise its prices, which makes it vulnerable to still newer entrants, who are competing on price rather than image and service . . . and so the wheel continues to turn.

The turning of the wheel is evident in the history of department stores. So-called budget floors were invented in the late nineteenth century, and they attained legendary status in 1909 when Filene's opened its "automatic bargain basement" in Boston. Its innovation was to feature dated price tags that put price markdowns on a fixed schedule. The passion to grab bargains was so frenzied that shoppers were known to disrobe in the aisles in order to try on clothes quickly before someone else snapped them up! By the 1950s, however, most department stores gave up their "basements" as they tried to develop more upscale images. In so doing, they opened the door to newer discounters like Kmart.[8] And so the wheel turns.

The Retail Life Cycle

retail life-cycle theory: a theory of retailing that focuses on the various life-cycle stages from introduction to decline

Although the wheel of retailing has a certain appeal, significant exceptions reduce the ability of this theory to predict new retailing developments. For example, in modern times we can point to planned shopping centers that are built "from scratch" to be elegant and upscale. A more useful approach is to regard retailing institutions as similar to products: They are born, they live, and eventually they die. Like the product life cycle discussed in Chapter 9, **retail life-cycle theory** categorizes retailers in terms of the conditions they face at different points in their "lives."[9]

In the *introduction* stage, the new retailer often is an aggressive entrepreneur who takes a different approach to doing business. This may involve competing on the basis of low cost, as the wheel of retailing suggests. Or it may entail offering a distinctive assortment or a different way to purchase items (such as television shopping). In this initial stage, profits are low because of high development costs.

As the business enters the *growth* stage, the concept catches on and sales and profits go up. On the other hand, a new concept doesn't stay new for long—others start to copy it, and competition increases. The need for a larger staff and more complex management processes begins to erode profitability. This happened with the *superstores* (called *category killers* because they dominated certain product lines, such as electronics) that were created in the 1970s, and a similar pattern emerged for TV shopping in the 1980s.

In the *maturity* stage, market share stabilizes and profits decline. The industry has overexpanded, management is more complex, and competition from newer types of retailers makes it more difficult to maintain customer loyalty. This pattern occurred for department stores, which were introduced in the 1860s, and for cafeterias, which date from the 1940s.

Finally, there is the *decline* stage. The retail business becomes obsolete, because newer forms of doing business are clearly more in step with societal developments. The retailer does not have to fold his or her tent at this stage; marketers who anticipate these changes can postpone decline by changing with the times. For example, many full-service gas stations have adapted to today's consumer by offering self-service gas. They have also added variety stores to their retail mix to accommodate drivers who want to save time by buying a tank of gas and groceries at the same location. Similarly, as we'll discover later in the chapter, some traditional department stores such as Macy's and Saks Fifth Avenue are now aggressively exploring the possibilities offered by catalogs and television shopping.

Exhibit 15.1
The Woolworth Corporation, whose aging discount stores once had "decline stage" written all over them, is taking dramatic steps to ensure that its stores do not become a part of the retailing graveyard. The company has reinvented itself by devising and following a new strategic course that revolves around the opening of new, exciting specialty stores all over the world, while closing older operations that no longer fit in with its long-range plans.

The company now runs more than forty specialty chains, each with a distinct merchandise assortment, image, and target market. The Foot Locker chain alone now accounts for about one-fifth of Woolworth's sales. The company also owns such chains as Champs sports, Lady Foot Locker, Afterthoughts Accessories, Northern Reflections (cold-weather outerwear), Going to the Game (sports memorabilia), Best of Times (watches), Kid's Mart, Williams the Shoeman, and Northern Traditions in Canada.

Woolworth plans to open 800 new stores and close 300 old stores each year between now and the end of the century and hopes to operate a total of 13,000 stores by the year 2000 with sales of about $20 billion. In 1983, general merchandise stores accounted for 71 percent of sales, but now specialty stores contribute 47 percent of sales. Stores located abroad now account for 40 percent of company sales.

CLASSIFYING RETAILERS BY THE TYPE OF MERCHANDISE THEY SELL

One of the most important strategic decisions a retailer has to make is *what* to sell— its *merchandise mix*. This choice is not as easy as it may appear. It is similar to settling on a market segment: If a store's merchandise mix is too limited, it may not have enough potential customers, whereas if the mix is too broad, the retailer runs the risk of being a "jack of all trades, master of none"—it will stock a little bit of everything, but it won't do anything quite as well as a specialist. Because the issue of precisely what the retailer sells is central to its identity, we will describe some major types of retailers in terms of their merchandise mix.

Product Lines: What Is Sold

The Census of Retail Trade, conducted by the U.S. Bureau of the Census, classifies all retailers by SIC codes (the same system we described in Chapter 7 that is used to classify industrial firms). The first two digits in a code provide a very broad breakdown of store type (for example, apparel and accessory stores are coded SIC 56). SIC codes also break retailers down further into lines of trade; thus the code numbers 562 and 563 denote apparel and accessory stores that sell women's ready-to-wear, accessories, and/or furs. In many cases, a retailer's major competition comes from others in its category, with the important exception of general merchandise stores, which stock items from many code categories. Table 15.1 (pages 516-519) summarizes the SIC breakdown for retailers.

Table 15.1
SIC Groupings for Retail Establishments

Major Group Number	Industry Number	Includes
52: Building Materials, Hardware, Garden Supply, and Mobile Home Dealers	5211: Lumber and Other Building Materials Dealers	Brick and tile dealers Cabinet/kitchen installation Fencing dealers
	5231: Paint, Glass, and Wallpaper Stores	Glass stores Wallcovering stores
	5251: Hardware Stores	Handtools Door locks
	5261: Retail Nurseries, Lawn and Garden Supply Stores	Christmas trees (natural) Garden supplies Nursery stock
	5271: Mobile Home Dealers	Mobile homes and equipment
53: General Merchandise Stores	5311: Department Stores	
	5331: Variety Stores	
	5399: Miscellaneous General Merchandise Stores	Catalog showrooms Country general stores
54: Food Stores	5411: Grocery Stores	Convenience food stores Frozen food and freezer plans (except meat) Supermarkets
	5421: Meat and Fish (Seafood) Markets, Including Freezer Provisioners	Fish markets Frozen food and freezer plans—meat Meat markets
	543: Fruit and Vegetable Markets	Fruit stands Produce Markets
	544: Candy, Nut, and Confectionery Stores	Candy stores Confectionery produced for direct sale on the premises Nut stores Popcorn stands
	545: Dairy Products Stores	Cheese stores Dairy products stores Ice cream (packaged) stores
	5461: Retail Bakeries	Bagel stores Bakeries Cookie stores Doughnut shops Pretzel stores and stands
	5499: Miscellaneous Food Stores	Health food stores Spice and herb stores
55: Automotive Dealers and Gasoline Service Stations	5511: Motor Vehicle Dealers (New and Used)	
	5521: Motor Vehicle Dealers (Used Only)	Antique autos Pickups and vans, used only
	5531: Auto and Home Supply Stores	Auto accessory stores Speed shops Tire dealers
	5541: Gasoline Service Stations	Filling stations Marine service stations Truck stops

Table 15.1 (continued)
SIC Groupings for Retail Establishments

Major Group Number	Industry Number	Includes
	5551: Boat Dealers	Motorboat dealers Marine supply dealers
	5561: Recreational Vehicle Dealers	Campers for mounting on trucks Recreational vehicle parts and accessories
	5571: Motorcycle Dealers	All-terrain vehicles Bicycles, motorized
	5599: Automotive Dealers, Not Elsewhere Classified	Aircraft dealers Dunebuggies and go-carts Snowmobiles
56: Apparel and Accessory Stores	5611: Men's and Boy's Clothing and Accessory Stores	Apparel and accessory stores Haberdashery stores Tie shops
	5621: Women's Clothing Stores	Bridal shops Clothing, ready-to-wear Maternity shops
	5641: Children's and Infants' Wear Stores	Children's wear Infants' wear
	5651: Family Clothing Stores	Jeans stores Unisex clothing stores
	5661: Shoe Stores	Athletic shoe stores
	5699: Miscellaneous Apparel and Accessory Stores	Bathing suit stores Custom tailors Riding apparel stores Umbrella stores Uniforms Wig, toupee, and wiglet stores
57: Home Furniture, Furnishings, and Equipment Stores	5712: Furniture Stores	Beds and springs Kitchen cabinets Juvenile furniture Outdoor furniture Waterbeds
	5713: Floor Covering Stores	Carpet stores Linoleum stores
	5714: Drapery, Curtain, and Upholstery Stores	Slipcover stores Upholstery materials stores
	5719: Miscellaneous Homefurnishings Stores	Aluminumware stores Bedding Brushes Crockery Fireplace accessories
	5722: Household Appliance Stores	Air-conditioning units Household freezers Refrigerators Sewing machines
	5731: Radio, Television, Consumer Electronics, and Music Stores	Antenna stores Hi-fi equipment Video camera stores

(continued)

Table 15.1 (continued)
SIC Groupings for Retail Establishments

Major Group Number	Industry Number	Includes
	5734: Computer and Computer Software Stores	Computer printer stores Peripheral computer equipment
	5735: Record and Prerecorded Tape Stores	Disks, music and video Video tape stores
	5736: Musical Instrument Stores	Piano stores Sheet music stores
58: Eating and Drinking Places	5812: Eating Places	Automats Beaneries Carry-out restaurants Frozen custard stands Oyster bars Dinner theaters
	5813: Drinking Places	Beer gardens Cabarets Discotheques Wine bars
59: Miscellaneous Retail	5912: Drug Stores and Proprietary Stores	Apothecaries
	5921: Liquor Stores	
	5932: Used Merchandise Stores	Antiques stores Secondhand book stores Rare manuscripts Pawnshops
	5941: Sporting Goods Stores and Bicycle Shops	Ammunition Exercise apparatus Pool and billiards tables
	5942: Book Stores	Religious book stores
	5943: Stationery Stores	Pen and pencil shops School supplies
	5944: Jewelry Stores	Clocks Silverware
	5945: Hobby, Toy, and Game Shops	Ceramics supplies Hobby shops Kite stores
	5946: Camera and Photographic Supply Stores	
	5947: Gift, Novelty, and Souvenir Shops	Balloon shops Curio shops
	5948: Luggage and Leather Goods Stores	Trunks
	5949: Sewing, Needlework, and Piece Goods Stores	Fabric shops Notion stores Quilting supplies
	5961: Catalog and Mail-Order Houses	Book clubs Mail-order cheese Record clubs Television mail-order (home shopping)

Table 15.1 (continued)
SIC Groupings for Retail Establishments

Major Group Number	Industry Number	Includes
	5962: Automatic Merchandising Machine Operators	Coin-operated machine selling merchandise
	5963: Direct-Selling Establishments	House delivery of purchased milk Ice cream wagons Magazine subscription sales Newspapers, home delivery Party-plan merchandising
	5983: Fuel Oil Dealers	
	5984: Liquefied Petroleum (Bottled Gas) Dealers	
599: Retail Stores, Not Elsewhere Classified	5989: Fuel Dealers, Not Elsewhere Classified	Coal dealers Wood dealers
	5992: Florists	
	5993: Tobacco Stores and Stands	
	5994: News Dealers and Newsstands	
	5995: Optical Goods Stores	Opticians
	5999: Miscellaneous Retail Stores, Not Elsewhere Classified	Architectural supplies Art dealers Artificial flowers Auction rooms Autograph and philatelist supply stores Cake decorating supplies Fireworks Hot tubs Orthopedic and artificial limb stores Pet shops Religious goods stores Rubber stamp stores Tent shops Tombstones Trophy shops

Source: *Standard Industrial Classification Manual,* U.S. Office of Management and Budget.

Product Type: Gross Margin and Turnover

Another important distinction is how the characteristics of the particular products a store carries affect its ability to make a profit. Two such dimensions—gross margin and turnover—are key factors.

Gross margin is the amount a retailer makes on an item. It is revenue minus the cost of goods sold, calculated as a percentage of sales. **Inventory turnover** (or *stock turn*) is the average number of times a year a retailer expects to sell its inventory. For example, a candy store owner can expect to sell the "same" pack of gum hundreds or thousands of times a year (well, not really the same *pack,* but rather the same item *type*). In contrast, a jewelry store owner may sell only a few hundred diamond rings a year. However, the retailer who

gross margin: revenue minus the cost of goods sold, calculated as a percentage of sales; the amount a retailer makes on an item

inventory turnover: the average number of times a year a retailer expects to sell its inventory

Exhibit 15.2
One very broad distinction has traditionally been made between *food* and *nonfood* retailers. However, even this partition is evaporating as supermarkets add hardware and other nonfood items to their inventories and some department stores feature gourmet food sections. The decision to carry a combination of food and nonfood items to increase profitability is termed **scrambled merchandising.** One of its more visible applications is in the growing number of linkages between retailers and fast-food chains, including alliances between Kmart and Little Caesar's pizza, Jamesway and Burger King, and McDonald's and Wal-Mart. Similarly, gasoline retailers are reinventing themselves; many now feature convenience stores where customers can buy flowers, drop off dry cleaning, or eat a taco while they gas up.

This strategy is exemplified by Blockbuster Entertainment Group, which is defining its merchandise mix in terms of products a customer might want when spending an evening at home watching a videotape, rather than in terms of traditional food versus nonfood product categories. In addition to stocking thousands of movies on videotape, the chain offers couch potatoes one-stop shopping by selling such items as 80 different confections, candy, and blank videotapes. Blockbuster is now selling private-label popcorn in all stores to enhance further the alternatives it offers to its customers.

scrambled merchandising: a retail strategy in which a store carries a combination of food and nonfood items in order to increase profitability

sells the rings is making a significantly larger profit on each sale than the person who is selling the gum, so he or she can make the same profit by selling many fewer rings. As a rule, stores that sell big-ticket items such as cars, furniture, and jewelry operate on a higher margin than do supermarkets or discount stores, which rely on selling greater volume (that is, higher stock turn) in order to compensate for razor-thin margins.

Retailers often confront a basic trade-off between margin and volume, and they sometimes must adjust their merchandise mix as their strategy evolves. This situation was faced recently by Gap, Inc., an innovative company that made its name by selling inexpensive jeans and T-shirts, which have relatively low markups and thin profit margins. But when competitors began imitating this strategy, the company decided to refocus on selling more fashion items such as hats, handbags, and skirts, where profit margins are fatter. The Gap was thus able to boost profits by modifying its merchandise mix to include more higher-margin items.[10]

In some cases retailers try to develop a "portfolio" of products with low and high margins. They reason that by making a relatively large profit on some items, they can use these revenues as a buffer against price wars in other areas that may erode profitability. For example, many mass merchandisers, supermarkets, and warehouse clubs are getting more interested in the $35 billion pharmacy business and are beginning to crowd out the traditional small pharmacy. Retailers expect to lure shoppers into the store by featuring a pharmacy, and they hope that these customers will shop for related health care items while they are there.[11]

CLASSIFYING RETAILERS BY THE SELECTION OF MERCHANDISE THEY SELL

A retailer's **merchandise assortment,** or the range of products sold, can be described along two dimensions: breadth and depth. **Merchandise breadth** is the number of different product lines available. **Merchandise depth** is the variety of choices available for each specific product. Assortment can thus be either broad or narrow, deep or shallow. When these two dimensions are combined as in Figure 15.1, we can see how quite different types of retailers can be compared in terms of the selection of inventory they stock.

Convenience Stores

Convenience stores are neighborhood outlets that carry a limited number of frequently purchased items, including basic food products, newspapers, and sundries. They cater to consumers who are willing to pay a premium for the ease of buying staple items close to home. In other words, they meet the needs of those who are pressed for time, who buy items in small quantities, or who shop at irregular hours. As the label suggests, these shoppers are buying convenience.

Supermarkets

Supermarkets are food stores that carry a wide selection of edibles and related products. The modern supermarket was born in the 1930s with the opening of the King Kullen store in Brooklyn, NY. At the time, the large size and scale of the operation were a radical departure for retailers, who (aided by such inventions as the automobile and the refrigerator) could now offer shoppers a wide selection of goods under one roof at lower prices than the "mom and pop" food stores with which they competed.

merchandise assortment: the range of products sold

merchandise breadth: the number of different product lines available

merchandise depth: the variety of choices available for each specific product

convenience stores: neighborhood retailers that carry a limited number of frequently purchased items, including basic food products, newspapers, and sundries, and cater to consumers who are willing to pay a premium for the ease of buying close to home

supermarkets: food stores that carry a wide selection of edibles and related products

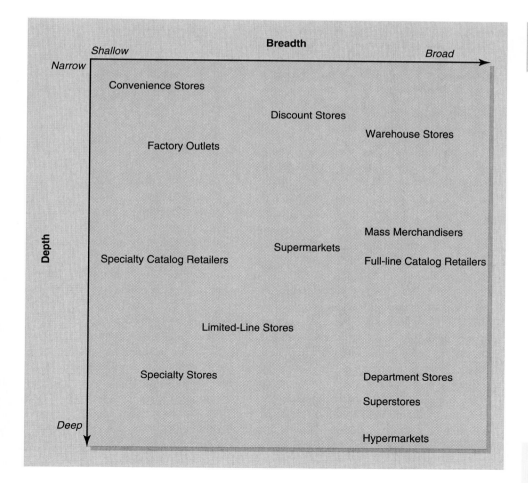

Figure 15.1
Breadth and Depth of Merchandise Assortments

specialty stores: retailers who carry only a few product lines but offer good selection within the lines they sell

discount stores: retailers who offer a wide variety of inexpensive brand-name items in a self-service, "no-frills" setting

off-price retailers: retailers who buy excess merchandise from well-known manufacturers and pass the savings on to customers

Specialty Stores

Specialty stores are characterized by narrow and deep assortments. They do not carry a lot of product lines, but they usually offer good selection within the lines of goods or services they do sell. Specialty stores are well represented in such areas as clothing, electronics, toys, and furniture, and in such services as hairstyling and tailoring. One store in The Mall of America in Minnesota sells nothing but magnets! Specialty stores have the advantage of being able to tailor their assortments to the specific needs of a targeted consumer group, and they frequently offer a high level of knowledgeable service. They have been responsible for creating some of the most exciting and innovative retail environments. Stores like The Limited, with outlets in malls around the country, are able to stay on top of trends and offer their own, private-label merchandise to "fashion-forward" shoppers.

Discount Stores

Discount stores offer a fairly wide variety of inexpensive items, with an emphasis on the availability of brand-name merchandise in a self-service, "no-frills" setting. Traditional discount stores such as Korvette's and Target had their heyday in the 1950s and 1960s, when they sprung up as an alternative to relatively plush department stores. Many have since gone out of business or have upgraded their image by adding more services and nicer facilities (as predicted by the wheel of retailing). Some discount stores, such as Loehmann's, promote themselves as **off-price retailers;** they buy excess fashion merchandise from well-known designers and pass the savings on to customers.

The *warehouse club* is a newer version of the discount store. These establishments do not even pretend to offer any of the amenities of a store; a bargain mentality is reinforced by merchandise that is displayed (often in its original box) in a warehouse-like facility. These clubs typically carry a broad assortment of food and nonfood items (often sold in bulk or large family sizes), but the selection available for any one category is often narrow (and may fluctuate depending on what "deals" the club made at the time of purchase). The typical warehouse shopper is likely to have a large family and a relatively high income (so he or she can afford to "stock up" on staples during one shopping trip).[12]

The *factory outlet store* is still another type of discounter. These stores are owned by a manufacturer and are used to sell off defective merchandise or excess inventory. The outlet industry does about $7 billion in sales annually.[13] Although their assortment is not very wide because each store carries only products made by one manufacturer, a recent trend is for different factory outlet stores to cluster together and offer a variety of products in a mall-like setting. Outlet malls reported sales of $235 per square foot in 1990, which compares quite well to the $182 reported at conventional regional malls and the $219 at super regional malls.[14] Some high-end retailers such as Macy's, Bloomingdales, and Nordstrom's are now opening their own clearance centers in outlet malls.

Department Stores

Department stores sell a fairly broad range of items, and the selection tends to be fairly deep. The grand stores that dominated urban centers in the early part of this century must have been something to see. As they developed over time, their interiors grew more splendid and the goods they offered more wondrous. In their heyday, these stores sold airplanes, auctioned fine art, and recreated entire luxury apartments on their furniture floors. Lord & Taylor even offered its customers a mechanical horse to ensure the perfect fit of riding habits.

Department stores were a significant force in shaping popular culture. Merchants even played a major role in creating America's holiday traditions. As early as 1910, Philadelphia's Strawbridge & Clothier store featured "Krisskringleville," complete with Santa Claus and a merry-go-round. In 1939 Montgomery Ward's began giving away books describing the exploits of a reindeer who was first called Rollo, then Reginald, and finally Rudolph—his signature song was recorded by Gene Autry in 1949. One retailer, Ohio merchant Fred Lazarus, Jr., even persuaded President Teddy Roosevelt in 1939 to proclaim that Thanksgiving would always be celebrated on the fourth Thursday of November in order to increase the number of Christmas shopping days!

In recent years department stores have encountered serious problems. On the one hand, they have been hurt by specialty stores that have lured shoppers away with deeper, more "cutting-edge" fashion selections and better service. They have also been squeezed by mass merchandisers and catalogs that offer many of the same items at lower prices. Department stores are searching for different strategies to compete, including pruning their assortments to concentrate more on "soft goods" such as clothing and home furnishings and less on "hard goods" such as appliances. For example, Macy's dropped its appliances department altogether and used the space to create its highly successful "Macy's Cellar," which features tastefully displayed cooking items and food. Other stores are modeling themselves after specialty stores by borrowing the "boutique" concept. For example, Montgomery Ward's has redesigned many of its outlets to be "stores within a store," where different departments are decorated and run almost as though they were separate stores.

Mass Merchandisers

Mass merchandisers, such as Sears, Kmart, and Wal-Mart, offer a broad assortment of items. Although they do not usually feature the depth of assortment found in department stores, they emphasize well-known brand names at low prices. The mass merchandise approach to retailing is exemplified by the long-standing motto of Sears, Roebuck & Co.: "Sears has everything." After an unsuccessful attempt to change its identity to that of a more upscale department store, Sears recently reverted to its roots: It now promotes itself as "Brand Central," where shoppers can find well-known makes of electrical appliances, stereos, and so on.

Hypermarkets

Hypermarkets combine the characteristics of warehouse stores and supermarkets. Originally introduced in Europe, these are huge establishments several times larger than other stores (a typical supermarket might occupy 40,000–50,000 square feet, whereas a hypermarket takes up 200,000–300,000 square feet!). They offer one-stop shopping for virtually everything from grocery items to electronics, and they often feature many services such as restaurants, beauty salons, and children's play areas as well. Hypermarkets such as Carrefour in France combine high-technology check-out scanning equipment, coordinated store graphics, and a massive selection to create a retail environment that draws shoppers from many miles away. The Pick 'n Pay store in Johannesburg, South Africa, is so large that it sells more than the equivalent of $1 million in merchandise every day.[15]

department stores: retailers who sell a broad range of items and a good selection within each product line

mass merchandisers: retailers who offer a very large assortment of items

hypermarkets: retailers with the characteristics of both warehouse stores and supermarkets; hypermarkets are several times larger than other stores and offer virtually everything from grocery items to electronics

Developing a Store Positioning Strategy: Retailing as Theater

It's hard to remember a time when an athletic shoe was just a sneaker. Nowadays they seem to be self-contained technological marvels, complete with magic pumps and other gizmos to boost the height of our jumps. The places where we buy these items have changed as well—they are a far cry from the old days, when tired shoe salesmen (who tended to bear an uncanny resemblance to Al Bundy in the TV show "Married with Children") waded through box after box of shoes as kids ran amok across dingy floors. Now, stores like Woolworth's World Foot Locker scream out high technology and vibrant fashion. The store is ablaze with neon and features a huge tiered tower in the center with rotating levels. The shoes are displayed in clear acrylic walls so they appear to be floating.[16]

Like Foot Locker, many retailers recognize the importance of using visual and other sensory cues to create a store environment that reflects and perpetuates a desired image. These merchants would no doubt agree that much of retailing really *is* theater: In an age when a customer could just as easily pick up the phone to buy many items, he or she must be given a reason to make a trip to a store instead.

Shoppers, then, are an audience that must be entertained. The "play" can be carefully engineered by employing clever props and stage sets *(store design)* and actors *(salespeople)* that work together to create a desired "scene." As one marketing strategist commented, "The line between retail and entertainment is blurring. Retailers are responding to a well-known fact: The longer a consumer stays in a store, the more he buys. If it's not exciting, he won't stay in the store."[17] This section will review some of the tools that are available to the retailing "playwright" who wants to create an effective environment in which to sell.

STORE IMAGE

When people think of a store, they often have no trouble portraying it in the same terms they might use in describing a person. They might refer to it as exciting, depressed, old-fashioned, tacky, or elegant. The **store image** is the way a retailer is perceived in the marketplace—its market position relative to the competition.

store image: the way a retailer is perceived in the marketplace relative to the competition

It is essential for a retailer to understand what its image is and whether changes should be made to keep up with the competition. Consider Frederick's of Hollywood, for example. For many years people associated this company with "naughty" lingerie that was the stuff of many men's fantasies in the 1940s and 1950s. In more recent years, however,

Exhibit 15.4
The Forum Shops at Caesars Palace in Las Vegas illustrate how entertainment blends with shopping. The mall is laid out as an ancient Roman street, featuring a painted-sky ceiling with a computerized system that changes colors from dawn to dusk. Garish statues include robots that come alive every hour and put on a show. Gladiator battles also occur nightly to amuse shoppers.

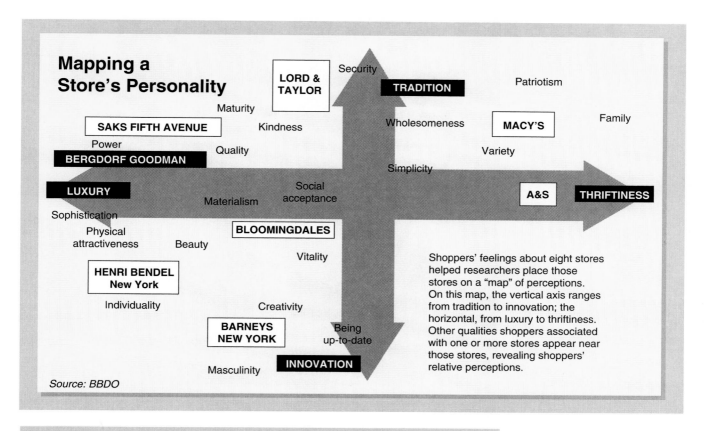

Mapping a Store's Personality

LORD & TAYLOR

Security

TRADITION

Patriotism

Maturity

SAKS FIFTH AVENUE

Kindness

Wholesomeness

MACY'S

Family

Power

Quality

Variety

BERGDORF GOODMAN

Simplicity

LUXURY

Materialism

Social acceptance

A&S

THRIFTINESS

Sophistication

Physical attractiveness

Beauty

BLOOMINGDALES

Vitality

HENRI BENDEL
New York

Individuality

Creativity

BARNEYS NEW YORK

Being up-to-date

Masculinity

INNOVATION

Shoppers' feelings about eight stores helped researchers place those stores on a "map" of perceptions. On this map, the vertical axis ranges from tradition to innovation; the horizontal, from luxury to thriftiness. Other qualities shoppers associated with one or more stores appear near those stores, revealing shoppers' relative perceptions.

Source: BBDO

Figure 15.2
Mapping a Store's Personality

the company found sales lagging despite an upsurge of interest by women in intimate apparel. Although women were ready and willing to buy these products, they were more interested in the tasteful, romantic assortment offered by such stores as Victoria's Secret than in the revealing undergarments reflecting the tacky pin-up girl mentality of days gone by. To keep up with the times, Frederick's of Hollywood set about to update its image. Stores were redesigned, its merchandise mix was upgraded, and "questionable" items were eliminated. Frederick's is on its way to becoming "de-sleazified."[18]

In developing a desirable store image, the resourceful retailer has a number of choices to make. Ideally, all of these elements should work together to create a clear, coherent picture that meets consumers' expectations of what that particular shopping experience should be, much like a "play" that consumers want to see again and again. Figure 15.2[19] illustrates one attempt to identify and compare the store images of eight different department stores in the New York City area.

Atmospherics is the use of color, lighting, scents, furnishings, and other design elements to create a desired setting. Butcher shops often display meat under ultraviolet lamps to make it look redder (and thus fresher), and bakeries have been known to vent smells from their kitchens onto the street to attract passers-by with the tempting scent of freshly baked goodies. The Ralph Lauren flagship store on Madison Avenue in New York carefully cultivates a sophisticated, refined image through the artful use of atmospheric elements. The store is located in a renovated mansion, and merchandise is carefully laid out on expensive antiques. Cocktails and canapes are served in the evening. Even the cleaning staff carry their supplies in Lauren shopping bags.[20] As Lauren's designers well know, the use of atmospherics is most effective when all the elements are artfully coordinated. Let's look at some of the specific tools that can be used to create this "hit play."

atmospherics: the use of color, lighting, scents, furnishings, and other design elements to create a desired store image

Store Design

There is no single right or wrong way to create a retailing "play"; the elements should be engineered to correspond to management's desired image. A bank lobby may need to

Exhibit 15.5
Some manufacturers are coming to view the store environment as an opportunity to showcase their best products. Instead of relying on independent retailers to decide which of their products they will carry along with those of their competitors, companies such as Speedo, Sony, Nike, Levi Strauss & Co., Walt Disney Co., and Warner Bros. have opened **concept stores** that carry only their own brands, usually in stylish or *avant garde* settings. The Speedo store features mannequins that appear to be diving from a ceiling that is made of swimming pool tiles. At Niketown stores in Portland, Oregon, and in Chicago, surfboards double as shelves, bounding tennis balls can be heard on the sound system, and a pneumatic tube shoots shoes from the basement as they are needed. Even Rubbermaid has opened a concept store, called Everything Rubbermaid, in the firm's home town of Wooster, Ohio!

Sony Style in Manhattan features both electronic merchandise and offerings from the company's entertainment division. Customers can play futuristic video games or listen to performers in the Sony stable, such as Mariah Carey or Bruce Springsteen, wail away on new models of the Sony Walkman. As a company executive observes, "Sony Style is more than a store—it's a showcase for the Sony Corp. It is a place where consumers can learn about and play with Sony products."

Source: Quoted in "Brand Name, High-Profile Stores Create a Splash," *Chain Store Age Executive*, 22 (Feb. 1994): 4.

concept stores: retailers that carry only their own brands, usually in stylish or *avant garde* settings

convey an image of solid respectability and security. In contrast, a used bookstore or retro clothing boutique might deliberately strive for a feeling of disorder bordering on chaos to signal to the intrepid shopper that undiscovered treasures lie buried beneath piles of merchandise. The specific design decisions that must be made include the following:

■ *Store layout:* This refers to the physical arrangement of merchandise in the store. The placement of fixtures such as shelves, racks, and cash registers is important, because store layout determines *traffic flow*—how shoppers will move through the store and what areas they will pass or avoid. A *grid layout,* usually found in supermarkets and discount stores, consists of rows of neatly spaced shelves that are at right angles or parallel to one another. This configuration is useful when management wants to move shoppers systematically down each aisle, being sure that they pass through such high-margin sections as deli and meat. Figure 15.3[21] illustrates how a grid layout in a supermarket helps to regulate traffic flow. In contrast, a *free-flow layout* is more often used in department and specialty stores because it is more conducive to browsing. This arrangement is more unstructured—it may include merchandise displayed in

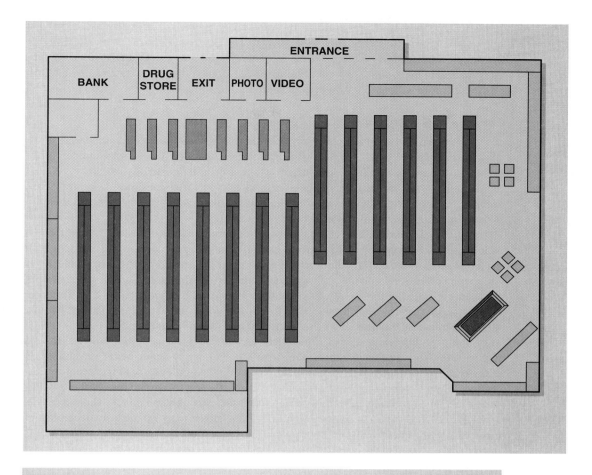

Figure 15.3
Supermarket Layout
A typical aspect of a supermarket's layout strategy is to place staple goods in more remote areas. The designers know that traffic will move to these areas, and they try to place impulse goods (items people tend to buy without having planned to, such as candy and gum) in spots shoppers will pass on their way elsewhere. This explains why the racks near cash registers are always laden with sugary treats that beckon to us (and to our children) as we wait to check out!

circles or arches, or perhaps in several self-contained areas or boutiques around the floor, each with its own distinct image and merchandise mix.

■ *Fixture type and merchandise density:* Generally speaking, clutter is associated with lower-class stores. In more upscale stores, greater space is allocated to sitting areas, dressing rooms, and elaborate displays of merchandise. A basic design decision such as having carpeting rather than concrete floors can also do a lot to "classify" a store.

■ *Sound type and density:* An elegant restaurant softly playing Mozart in the background is worlds apart from a raucous place like The Hard Rock Cafe, where loud rock 'n roll is essential to the atmosphere. Sound can be used to repel as well as attract customers. One owner of a 7-11 convenience store in Canada discovered the power of music when he figured out how to get rid of groups of teenagers who were loitering in his store. He piped in "classics" from the l940s and 1950s, and soon they were gone! [22]

■ *Color and lighting:* Red, yellow, and orange are warm colors (fast-food chains use a lot of orange to stimulate hunger), whereas blue, green and violet are cool and are used to open up "close" places and to signify elegance and cleanliness. Red is perceived as negative and tense as well as physically arousing; blue is calm, cool, and positive. In one study that examined shoppers' reactions to red versus blue environments, a store decor done in blue stimulated purchases and made people want to browse longer. [23]

The type of lighting can influence store image as well. Soft-lights make one feel serene, whereas bright lights convey excitement. The power of lighting even extends to the dressing room. Fashion designer Norma Kamali replaced fluorescent lights with pink ones after management found that pink lighting tended to be more flattering and made female customers more willing to try on bathing suits.[24]

The Actors: Store Personnel

Store personnel should be carefully selected to complement a store's image. Each employee has a part to play, complete with props and costumes. Think, for example, of the activities that occur in a fancy restaurant, where a meal is "presented" to diners. Waiters and wine stewards, wearing their "black and whites," "perform" for diners by reciting daily specials, opening bottles with a flourish, and even bringing flaming delicacies to the table without burning down the establishment.

Providing outstanding service has become a major headache for retailers, and the lack of it is a major reason why many consumers dread the prospect of shopping. Although the presence of knowledgeable sales personnel is viewed as crucial to the large majority of shoppers, consumers generally rate the quality of service they receive from retail personnel as low.[25] In one recent survey, 62 percent of Americans interviewed said that sometime in the past six months, they had decided to buy a product in a store but then left without making a purchase because sales clerks were not available to help them.[26]

After a prolonged period of time where service levels were allowed to deteriorate in many stores, the employees' contribution to store image is again being recognized by many retailers, who now view a committed and competent sales force as a competitive necessity. This philosophy is exemplified at Wal-Mart, where employees—called associates—are urged to build pride in their accomplishments and to dedicate their efforts to service excellence. The company provides a clear career path for dedicated employees; more than a third of its assistant managers began as sales associates.[27]

However, this renewed dedication to service doesn't come cheap. As a general rule, increasing the amount and quality of service adds significantly to a retailer's costs, so choosing the optimal service level is an important strategic decision. It depends on store characteristics, the level of service offered by competitors, the type of merchandise (Are alterations or delivery required?), and the store's price image. For example, adding a service that increases costs by $10,000 per year for a store operating on a gross margin of 20 percent would have to increase sales by at least $50,000 ($10,000/0.2) for this service level to be feasible. As a result some retailers, especially those who deal in high-volume, mass-merchandise categories, may find it preferable to keep staffing at a minimum in order to compete more effectively on price.

Important cultural differences also exist in expectations of service quality. At one extreme are the Japanese. A visitor to a Japanese store is greeted by an enthusiastic, polite employee who bows profusely. Elaborate gift wrapping is an art form that is considered almost as important as the gift itself. Many stores feature spacious art galleries and gardens.[28] In contrast, until very recently the concept of service was virtually nonexistent in Eastern bloc countries. Stores were viewed as places to hunt for items that were in scarce supply rather than as attractive places to spend leisure time. Many salespeople still are not used to the concept of a "customer" who must be treated politely. This attitude was demonstrated by one veteran saleswoman in Kmart's Prague store, who hid in her pocket her Kmart badge proclaiming "I'm Here For You." She explained, "It offends me . . . it looks as though I'm here not just for business but for the amusement of certain customers." She feared that the slogan, interpreted in the West as a sign of friendliness, would instead be viewed by Czech shoppers as an invitation to sexual harassment.[29]

Pricing Policy: How Much for a Ticket to the Show?

A store's pricing policy goes well beyond mere economics; this decision influences shoppers' perceptions of the "type" of store it is. As consumers have become more price-sensitive, retailers of all kinds have redoubled their efforts to control costs. Smaller retailers are banding together to form buying cooperatives that enable them to take advantage of quantity discounts. Department stores are increasing their offerings of less expensive, private-label merchandise that is produced specifically for them. At IKEA, items are shipped compactly and stacked flat on pallets to reduce storage space. To avoid extra costs of reloading and repacking, customers take the goods they want to buy from the pallets to the check-outs on trolleys. These savings allow IKEA to charge prices that are often 25 to 50 percent lower than those of their competitors.

When consumers form an image of a store in their minds, the *price points,* or ranges where most merchandise is sold, often make up a major component (note that in Figure 15.2, the horizontal axis ranges from luxury to thriftiness). As we have seen, higher overhead costs typically cause department and specialty stores to differentiate themselves in terms of the depth or quality of their assortments, whereas discount stores and mass merchandisers compete on a price basis. For example, a chain of off-price stores in the Northeast called Daffy's advertises with such slogans as "Friends Don't Let Friends Pay Retail."

In recent years department stores in particular have been hurt by consumers' desires for value, which sent them flocking in droves to outlet malls and warehouse stores. The response of many department stores was to run frequent sales—a strategy that often backfired because it "trained" many seasoned shoppers to postpone buying until merchandise was drastically marked down. Some stores have reduced the number of sales they run and instead have lowered prices across the board. Nordstrom's is positioned as an upscale store, but its sales staff is given freedom to implement lower prices if necessary. In one celebrated case, a customer fell in love with a pair of slacks that were on sale, but the store did not have her size. The employee took some petty cash from her manager, bought the pants at full price at a rival store, and sold them to the customer at the marked-down price.[30] Now that's service!

BUILDING THE THEATER: STORE LOCATION

As we stated in the previous chapter: Ask a realtor to list the three most important factors in selling a home, and he or she will tell you, "Location, location, and location." The same is true in retailing. For example, a big part of Wal-Mart's retailing success is not what it is, but *where* it is. The chain's decision about where to open a new store is based on its strategy of being the first mass merchandiser to locate in small and rural markets. When choosing a site, Wal-Mart's planners consider such factors as major traffic routes, proximity to highways, and the presence of other retailers in the area. By carefully selecting "undiscovered" areas, the company has been able to negotiate cheap leases in areas with expanding populations.[31] This section will review some important aspects of where a retailer locates.

Types of Store Locations

There are four basic types of retail locations. A store can be found in a business district, in a shopping center, as a free-standing entity, or in a nontraditional location (a place where retailers are not customarily found). *Note:* These types do not include versions of nonstore retailing, such as purchases by telephone or mail, which will be addressed later in the chapter.

- *Business districts:* The most traditional place to find a store is in a business district, usually an urban area containing a concentrated number of retailers. A *Central Business District (CBD)* is an unplanned shopping area where public transportation systems converge. A *secondary business district* is a smaller area with at least one department or variety store at a major intersection. Finally, a *neighborhood business district* evolves to satisfy convenience-oriented neighborhood shopping needs. It often features dry cleaners, drug stores, and fast-food stores. American retailers have been deserting impoverished center cities in droves for the past 20 years, but these downtown areas are now staging a comeback, luring such companies as Filene's, Montgomery Ward & Co., Target Stores, and Toys "Я" Us with promises of cheap real estate and access to large markets.[32]

- *Shopping centers:* A shopping center is a centrally owned and/or managed planned shopping district. It features one or more *anchor stores*—usually major department stores that initially attract shoppers, who then discover the other small, specialty stores in the center. Shopping centers offer the advan-

Exhibit 15.6
The fortunes of what were once majestic and vibrant downtown shopping areas have soured in recent years, falling victim to lack of parking, age of stores, congestion, and decaying conditions in many urban centers. On the bright side, some major cities are revitalizing their downtown areas, and some have developed planned business districts that resemble a cross between a shopping area and a theme park.

These sophisticated, exciting developments are exemplified in Boston's Fanueil Hall, New York City's South Street Seaport, Union Station in St. Louis, and the Harborplace in Baltimore. The Rouse Corporation has been behind many of these "festival marketplaces"; this innovative development firm has been credited with contributing to the resurgence of the American downtown as a cultural and retailing center.

tages of 1) heavy traffic flows (especially valuable for small stores that would not attract so many people if they were on their own), 2) the sharing of costs (such as advertising and promotion) among tenants, and 3) a clean and usually safe environment.

Shopping centers can be described in terms of their total amount of square footage.

1. A *neighborhood shopping center* features convenience goods and is generally about 50,000 square feet in area.

2. A *community shopping center,* or *strip mall,* features a greater diversity of merchandise, including both soft goods (such as clothing) and hard goods (such as hardware). These centers occupy about 150,000 square feet of space. About two-thirds of all shopping centers in the United States are neighborhood or community types, and these centers account for about one-third of all retail sales. Strip malls are gaining in attractiveness as harried shoppers grow increasingly willing to trade off elegance and variety for speed and convenience. Small-mall shoppers are most likely to be female homemakers with children who have a specific shopping purpose in mind. Capitalizing on this trend, The Gap is locating many of its new stores in strip malls.

3. A *regional center* contains one or more department stores not less than 100,00 square feet in size.

4. A *super-regional center* has at least three major department stores. These huge centers usually have between 600,000 and 1,400,000 square feet of store space. Although they make up only 1 percent of the total number of shopping centers, they account for over 10 percent of retail

sales (excluding autos) in the United States. It seems likely that large malls will continue to evolve as entertainment centers and for recreational shopping, featuring a greater mix of movie theaters, restaurants, and hobby and bookstores.[33]

■ *Freestanding retailers:* Some stores (usually larger ones) are freestanding, located by themselves in a separate building. The Toys "Я" Us chain, for example, has a policy of locating only in freestanding locations off of main roads. Because of the expenses encountered by mall-based music stores such as Musicland and Sam Goody, Tower Records pioneered freestanding record and tape stores. The company's new retailing concept, the giant Media Play stores, sell music, books, and video games in a separate location rather than in a mall.[34] This strategy has the advantage of offering distance from direct competition, lower rents, and adaptability; the store has more freedom to alter its selling space to accommodate its own needs. On the other hand, the store had better be popular because it cannot rely on the drawing power of neighbor stores to provide it with customer traffic.

■ *Nontraditional store locations:* Innovative retailers are constantly experimenting with new ways to reach consumers who may not be willing or able to take the time to travel to conventional locations. The Baskin-Robbins ice cream chain even takes advantage of a "captive audience" by putting shops on U.S. Navy ships! In addition, computer kiosks are now beginning to pop up in high-traffic locations such as airports and public buildings. Over two million of these automated "satellite stores" are expected to be in use in the United States before the end of the twentieth century.[35]

The Store Location Decision Sequence

Store location is a key strategic decision. It affects economic aspects of a company's ability to operate effectively (such as whether the store will be prevented from turning an adequate profit because overhead costs are too high), turnover (whether there is sufficient traffic passing by or through the store to support sales goals), and store image (shoppers may assume that a store located in a swanky section of town carries pricey, high-quality merchandise).

Excellence at Dollar General Stores

When it comes to locating stores, most large chains avoid low income housing projects like the plague. They are reluctant to enter such areas because of fear of losing too much inventory to theft, anxiety about ensuring the safety of their employees, and concerns about the profit potential of targeting low-income areas.

Dollar General decided otherwise. This discount store chain targets families earning less than $25,000, and at least 1500 of the items in its inventory cost $1.00 or less. The stores are located in the South and Midwest, usually in rural areas that are too small to attract larger competitors.

Dollar General is headquartered in Nashville, Tennessee, and management decided to take the risk and open store number 2899 in a housing project on the east side of the city. Its executives gambled that if local residents felt a commitment to the store, they would work to ensure that it prospered and was safe. Thus Dollar General set out to build a strong relationship with project residents. All of the employees except the manager live in the project, and each splits his or her time between working in the store for four hours and attending classes covering high school subjects and job skills. Federally funded day care enables employees with several children to continue to work at the store.

This effort to build a strong relationship with the neighborhood has paid off for Dollar General. Profits are higher than those of a typical company store, and theft is only 2 percent of sales. In addition, executives are learning valuable lessons about marketing in low-income urban areas, finding out what sells (bleach and slippers) and what sits (picnic coolers and kitchen appliances). More important, the store has earned the goodwill of the community and has become a treasured institution to grateful residents who now have a decent place to shop.

Source: Laurie Grossman, "Desolate Housing Project Provides Profits and Lessons," *The Wall Street Journal* (April 5, 1995): B1–B2.

In the past, retailers simply chose to build a store on a site where an adequate number of people either walked or drove by. Sam Walton used to fly over an area in a small plane until he found a spot where he'd like to build a Wal-Mart. No more. Now, such factors as long-term population patterns, the location of competitors, and the demographic make-up of an area must be considered as well. The choice of where to open a new outlet ideally reflects the company's overall growth strategy: The place selected should be consistent with long-term goals and should be the spot where the company can best support the outlet. For example, a chain with stores and an extensive warehouse system in the Northeast may not be wise to open a single new store in California. Such a store would be an "orphan" cut off from the company's supply lines.

A location decision is actually a sequence of choices as the retailer steadily narrows down the options. First, a market must be selected (say, the Washington, DC, metropolitan area). Second, the retailer should conduct an area analysis, evaluating alternative territories within the market (comparing, say, Bethesda, Maryland, and Springfield, Virginia). Finally, site evaluation involves a very specific assessment of possible specific properties within an area (such as an available property on Wisconsin Avenue in Bethesda versus one on East-West Highway).[36]

Choosing a Retail Site

Reilly's law of retail gravitation: a theory to explain how a store's trading area is affected by its proximity to a population center

One of the earliest attempts to address the store location issue was known as **Reilly's law of retail gravitation,** which tried to explain how a store's *trading area* (the size of the region from which its customer base is drawn) is affected by its proximity to a population center. It proposed that, when faced with the choice of going to one of two stores in different locations, people tend to shop in a larger city if its distance away is equal to, or even greater than, that of a store located in a smaller area, because they believe the store in the larger city will offer a superior product selection. In other words, shoppers will be willing to expend greater effort to get to stores in more developed areas, because they feel that the payoff, in terms of what will be available to them there, will be worth the trouble.

Although this logic may have been valid in earlier times, Reilly's law is probably applicable today only in rural areas. For most consumers, though, city population doesn't always determine shopping facilities, because most suburban areas (at least in the United

REAL PEOPLE, REAL CHOICES:

DECISION TIME AT IKEA

IKEA came to North America in the early 1980s, first to Canada and then to the United States. As Göran Carstedt puts it, IKEA North America's strategy is to appeal to the American customer ". . . by speaking English with a Swedish accent." IKEA's unique recipe for success caught on quickly, and the company now sells about $700 million worth of products per year in North America. IKEA stores are usually found outside city limits but close to main truck roads to keep costs down.

Such phenomenal success is bound to be copied, and that's just what happened. An American-owned clone of IKEA, called STØR, opened three stores in the Los Angeles area (STØR was a made-up name intended to imply that the company was Swedish!). Although IKEA entered the U.S. market on the East Coast, management believed it needed to go head-to-head with STØR in the L.A. marketplace. If STØR was too successful, IKEA feared it would expand to other locations and create problems later.

In November 1990, IKEA opened a store in Burbank. A second store opened in Fontana in February 1992. Meanwhile, IKEA decided to acquire STØR, and it did so in January 1992. The company closed one of its former rival's smaller stores, which was located in a very successful shopping center called the Del Amo Fashion Center in Torrance. It also reopened the two STØR facilities in City of Industry and Tustin as IKEA stores in May 1992.

But Göran Carstedt still had a problem: Although IKEA now had four stores operating in the L.A. area, not one of them was close enough to attract the customers who had shopped at the STØR in Torrance. IKEA began to shop around for sites near Torrance, keeping in mind the company's strategy of locating in a highly visible area, preferably right off a major highway—in this case, the San Diego Freeway. The overall objective was to have five stores in place by the end of 1992. A number of potential sites were identified, but each had drawbacks:

Option 1. The STØR site in Torrance. The problem was that it was only 110,000 square feet, much smaller than IKEA needed.

Option 2. Three properties in the same area were possibilities. However, one was on a dump site, and the other two were contaminated. There might be delays in getting construction started if one of these were chosen.

Option 3. A site was available at Carson Mall, a strip mall with three department stores. On the positive side, the shopping center was located at an exit of the San Diego Freeway, the most heavily traveled highway in the world. About 250,000 cars pass by this intersection every day! On the negative side, Carson Mall suffered from a poor image. It had a bad reputation in the community as an unsafe place to shop. The company hired a local research firm to conduct a telephone survey of area residents, and it found that only 60 percent of the residents they surveyed said they would shop at IKEA if it were located at the Carson Mall. To make matters worse, only 14 percent said that they had shopped at the Carson Mall in the last three months.

Now, join the IKEA decision team: If you were president of IKEA North America, which option would you choose, and why?

States) now offer branch stores and numerous shopping malls. Also, shoppers are willing to travel farther for some types of products than for others; a 20-mile trek may be justified to buy the "perfect" kitchen table but probably not to buy groceries to keep in that same kitchen. Finally, mileage *per se* is no longer a good indicator of the time and effort required to reach stores. Modern interstates enable us to cover many miles in a short time,

CHAPTER 15
Retailing and
Direct Marketing 533

whereas urban traffic congestion may mean that traveling just a few miles is a major ordeal!

Modern location planners look at many factors when selecting a site. They often try to determine whether an area needs a new store in the first place. Put simply, locations can be evaluated in terms of whether they are *saturated, understored,* or *overstored.* Try as Wal-Mart may to seek out understored areas, there simply aren't that many to be found in developed countries anymore (this helps to explain why major U.S. retailers are expanding to other countries—a trend that will be discussed at the end of the chapter).

Depending on the store's targeted consumer segment, different criteria may be emphasized. For example, a new, growing community would hold obvious appeal for toy and hardware stores, whereas upscale dress stores and travel agencies might find a better home in a more established, older area. Planners also consider such market supply factors as the size of existing stores and how much retail growth is occurring in the area. A site evaluation would also consider such specific factors as traffic flow, number of parking spaces available, ease of delivery access, visibility from the street, local zoning laws, and such cost factors as the length of the lease and the amount of local taxes.

Cost, of course, is often a major consideration, particularly in crowded urban areas. A location decision is first and foremost a real estate decision—in some cases, the land on which a store sits is more valuable than the store itself! For example, retail space is extremely expensive in Hong Kong, largely because Japanese retailers have bid up local properties to the point where local businesspeople find it hard to afford a lease.[37]

Stores often have no choice but to enter a saturated area, relying on their ability to offer a competitive advantage over existing stores in order to lure shoppers to the new facility. In an unusual twist, this is an issue that has been faced by Dorian's, a large department store chain in Mexico. The retailer's main challenge has been to persuade Mexican shoppers that they can do better by shopping locally than by patronizing rival stores across the U.S. border.[38]

One widely used measure of an area's potential is the *buying power index (BPI).* Each year, the trade magazine *Sales & Marketing Management* publishes its *Survey of Buying Power,* which provides data on an area's buying income, retail sales, and population. Planners also consider such population characteristics as age profile (Is the area witnessing an influx of new families moving in?), community life cycle (Is the community relatively new, stable, or in decline?) and mobility (How often are people moving in and out of the area?).

NONSTORE RETAILING AND DIRECT MARKETING

The familiar "Avon Ladies," who sell cosmetics and other beauty products to millions of women around the world in the comfort of the customers' own homes, are a potent reminder that not all retailing activity occurs in stores. Reflecting the changing times, Avon is continuing to explore new ways to give customers access to its products. The company's recent undertakings reflect some of the new possibilities that are dramatically changing the retail landscape, Avon's new "Four Ways to be Beautiful" program now provides customers with four separate ways to order the same merchandise: They can place their orders by phone, by fax, by catalog, or through a sales representative. Avon is currently testing a thirty-minute infomercial to sell its products on television and is even experimenting with "beauty boutiques" in Mexico and Japan, where customers can buy Avon products at the same distribution centers used by sales reps to obtain merchandise.[39]

Avon's success at giving customers alternatives to traditional store outlets illustrates the increasing importance of **nonstore retailing**—any method used to complete an exchange that does not require a customer visit to a store. Americans spend almost $60 billion through catalogs, TV shopping channels, and other nonstore alternatives. Although

nonstore retailing: any method used to complete an exchange with a product end user that does not require a customer visit to a store

that's less than 3 percent of the country's $2.1-trillion-a-year retail marketplace, nonstore shopping is expected to account for 15 percent of total sales by the end of the decade.[40] Much of nonstore retailing consists of **direct marketing,** which involves two basic steps: 1) exposing a consumer to information about a good or service through a nonpersonal medium such as a letter, a print ad, a radio or TV commercial, or a home page on the WorldWide Web, and 2) convincing the customer to take action by responding with an order via mail, telephone, fax, or computer.

A lot of other exciting marketing developments also involve activity outside of stores. These emerging techniques do not necessarily result in an actual transaction and hence are not strictly considered retailing. For example, many forward-thinking marketers are pioneering innovations with interactive media that enable consumers to get product information or provide feedback via computers, faxes, and so on. In fact, we feel that the emerging practice of *database marketing,* which involves the use of computer technology to create long-term relationships with customers where they live, work, and play, is so important that we've devoted most of the next chapter to it. For now, though, we'll focus our discussion strictly on the retailing of goods and services in nonstore venues.

Many consumers love the idea of avoiding stores: Although available store space has increased 4 percent per year on the average over the last decade, sales per square foot have declined by almost 3 percent annually. This means that traditional retailers who want to entice shoppers into their stores will have to find new ways to reach them. As Stanley Marcus, the head of famed retailer Neiman Marcus, observed, "You lose everything if you don't think like the customer. If customers don't want to get off their butts and go to your stores, you've got to go to them."[41] This section will review some of the ways retailers are doing just that.

The U.S. Census of Retailing divides nonstore retailing into three categories:

- *Mail-order houses* (the number of catalogs distributed in the United States has nearly tripled in the last decade; 15 billion were mailed in 1990).
- *Direct-selling establishments,* where retail sales occur either on an in-person basis or by telephone. It is estimated that about $9 billion worth of sales are transacted via direct selling every year in the United States, and about $39 billion globally. Japan is the largest direct-selling country.
- *Automatic merchandising machine operators* (a fancy term for vending machines).

MAIL ORDER

In 1872, store owner Aaron Montgomery Ward and two partners put up $1600 to mail a one-page flier that listed their merchandise with prices, hoping to spur a few more sales.[42] The mail order industry was born. Today, consumers can buy just about anything through the mail (in a later section, we'll discuss electronic versions of direct marketing).

Catalogs

The first primitive catalogs came on the scene within a few decades of the invention of moveable type in the fifteenth century, but they've come a long way since then.[43] The early catalogs pioneered by Montgomery Ward and other innovators such as Sears, Roebuck were designed for people in remote areas who lacked access to stores. Today, the catalog customer is more likely to be an affluent career woman who has access to more than enough stores but who does not have the time or desire to go to them. According to the Direct Marketing Association, in a recent year over half of the American adult population ordered from a catalog at least once.

Of course, many catalogs are published by established retailers such as Bloomingdales and JCPenney, but others are start-ups by ambitious entrepreneurs who cannot afford to operate a storefront. For example, a housewife named Lillian Hochberg began by selling handbags from her kitchen table. Today, the Lillian Vernon catalog mails out more than 137 million copies each year.[44] Research on the American and Canadian mail-order consumer revealed that the typical catalog shopper is a woman who is better educated, wealthier, and more likely to be married than a noncatalog shopper. People thirty-five to forty-four years old account for one-quarter of all catalog shoppers, and consumers who go this route are also more likely to be comfortable with new technologies and to go out more to eat or see live entertainment or a movie.[45]

As the dislike of shopping increases for many people, catalogs are springing up to present alternatives. New catalogs are glossy, sophisticated, and visually appealing. Spiegel, for example, recently mailed a new mega-catalog called *Shops* to three million of its regular customers. The 300-page book features thirteen of the cataloger's specialty catalogs, such as *Crayon Kids* boutique, *Body & Soul* athletic wear, and *Home Source* home furnishings, all rolled into one. The mail-order giant is striving to create a sort of mall for nonstore shoppers, who can then have their cake and eat it too as they browse through specialized "stores" while relaxing at home.[46]

Catalog mania extends well beyond clothing and cosmetics purchases. For example, the Computer Shopper has helped to legitimize the mail-order computer market. Dell and Gateway 2000, direct-selling computer companies, both have annual sales of over $1 billion. Recent catalog entries by computer giants IBM and Compaq are signs that ordering even a complex and expensive purchase such as a computer by mail is becoming routine for many shoppers—mail-order computer sales tripled (to $7.9 billion) between 1987 and 1992.[47]

Direct Mail

Innovative marketers are finding new ways to use the mail to generate interest in their products and to compile lists of qualified potential buyers. Saab Cars U.S.A. has started a direct-response program to sell cars, using letters and a $2000-off coupon. In a pilot program, the company spent $200,000 on thank-you letters and, in the process, helped generate sales of $62 million of new Saabs. As an executive who worked on Saab's direct-response program observed, "Obviously, Saab has a pretty well-defined target audience and a fairly unique appeal. Since it's not intended for everybody, direct-response marketing has a very clear role to play."[48]

Despite the growing popularity of catalogs and direct-mail advertising, only about 5 percent of U.S. retailers use any kind of direct mail, and on average they spend about 2 cents out of every advertising dollar on it. In contrast, direct mail accounts for about 15 percent of the total advertising budget of European companies. For example, Bijttebier, one of Belgium's largest wholesalers and importers of tableware and cutlery, put together

SPOTLIGHT On Global Marketing

Excellence at Patagonia and Lands' End

The catalog boom is certainly not unique to the United States. In fact, Japanese consumers buy more products through direct selling than people in any other country (mail-order sales in 1990 were the equivalent of $11 billion). To tap into this market, L.L. Bean, Lands' End, Tweeds, and nine other catalog marketers collaborated on a mega-catalog of made-in-America goods aimed at the Japanese market. Fifty thousand copies of the "American Showcase" catalog originally were shipped to Japan, and the initial sales were so encouraging that another 500,000 followed.

Catalog marketers are convinced they've discovered the Promised Land. They are rushing to set up toll-free twenty-four-hour international phone and fax lines, and some employ Japan-ese-speaking telephone operators in the United States to take these calls. The catalogs themselves are becoming more "user-friendly" for eager Japanese buyers by adding inserts with sizing and ordering information in Japanese. Lands' End has gone a step farther by producing an entire catalog in Japanese.

Patagonia, Inc. is trying to lower the costs of overseas sales (phoning or faxing orders, postage, duty, currency conversion) by actually setting up a mail-order operation in Tokyo. Employees are English-speaking Japanese nationals, and customers pay for their orders in Japanese yen. Patagonia and other catalogers have encountered one problem as they try to establish outposts in Japan: Unlike most American companies, Japanese businesses consider customer lists proprietary and won't sell them, so these mail-order pioneers will have to build their lists from scratch.

Source: Art Garcia, "It's in the Mail!" *World Trade*, 56 (April 1992): 7; "Japan Is Dialing 1 800 BuyAmerica," *Business Week*, 61 (June 12, 1995): 2.

a direct marketing program for brides-to-be. The company signed up one of every three brides-to-be in Belgium.[49]

DIRECT SELLING

Direct selling can be an effective approach, especially for products that require a demonstration. One popular form of direct selling is a *home shopping party,* where a company representative makes a sales presentation to a group of people who have gathered in the home of a friend or acquaintance.[50] This technique can be very effective, partly because people who attend feel some obligation to buy and because they may get caught up in the "group spirit," buying things they would not normally purchase on their own. Most people associate this technique with the Tupperware Party, but it is also used to sell other products—even lingerie![51]

Door-to-Door Sales

Door-to-door selling is one of the oldest forms of retailing. Thousands of persistent salespeople comb neighborhoods, selling everything from Bibles to vacuum cleaners. This form of nonstore retailing is alive and well in some countries such as China, but it is declining markedly in the United States because of high labor costs, the large numbers of homes that are empty during the day, and the increasing reluctance of those who are at home to admit strangers.

Finding that many of its female customers are no longer home during the day, even Avon has expanded its distribution network to the office, where representatives make presentations during lunch and coffee breaks. Similarly, Tupperware features "rush-hour parties" at the end of the workday and now finds that about 20 percent of its sales are made outside of private homes. An employee of Mary Kay cosmetics, which has also adopted this strategy, offered another explanation for its success: "Working women buy more in the office because they are not looking at the wallpaper that needs replacing. They feel richer away from home."[52]

Telemarketing

The use of *telemarketing,* wherein prospective customers are contacted by phone, is on the rise. Especially compared to door-to-door selling, this method is cheaper and easier. Recent surveys indicate that one out of six Americans felt it difficult to resist a telemarketing pitch. On the other hand, about one in three said they felt they had been cheated at one time by a telephone sales representative.[53]

When it is abused, telemarketing embodies the most negative aspects of marketing. Many consumers resent being interrupted at home for unsolicited sales pitches or requests for donations. Sometimes this practice can be more than annoying; it can be downright illegal. The F.B.I. recently concluded a three-year effort called "Operation Disconnect," in which the agency arrested more than 100 people for fraudulent telemarketing. About one-third of the victims were elderly people. Many of the telemarketing scams involved credit card deals, scholarships, and vacation packages, and nearly 20 percent involved the sale of vitamins over the phone. The deception usually started with a phone call or a postcard telling people they had won a prize or were eligible for a sweepstakes. They were then asked to pay the marketer between $50 and $5000 to deliver the prizes, which never appeared or, if they did, were almost worthless.[54] Congress is now considering enacting much more stringent rules to regulate the telemarketing industry.

AUTOMATIC VENDING

Coin-operated vending machines are a tried-and-true way to sell convenience goods, especially cigarettes and drinks. These machines are appealing because they require minimal space and personnel to maintain and operate.

Some of the most interesting innovations can be found in state-of-the-art vending machines, which now dispense everything from Hormel's microwaveable chili and beef stew to software. French consumers can even purchase Levi's jeans from a machine called "Libre Service," which offers the pants in ten different sizes. Their frenetic lifestyles make the Japanese avid users of vending machines. These machines, a cluster of which can be found on many street corners, dispense virtually all of life's necessities, plus many luxuries people in other countries would not consider obtaining from a machine. The list includes jewelry, fresh flowers, frozen beef, pornography, business cards, underwear, and even the names of possible dates.[55] Back in America, one company has introduced a computerized vending machine that dispenses cans of beer to thirsty golfers on the golf course: The machines feature a surveillance system so that someone can check to be sure a golfer is old enough—and sober enough—to buy a drink![56]

THE ELECTRONIC MARKETPLACE

Some of the most exciting developments in nonstore retailing can be found in the growing electronic marketplace—the use of television and computers to communicate product information and make transactions. While in some ways this form of retailing is still in its infancy, virtually every major corporation's eagerness to become involved in this enterprise shows how important it will be in the future. Whether this means mailing an *electronic catalog* on videotape or CD/ROM to promote resorts or exercise equipment like NordicTrac or creating a home page on the World Wide Web, the electronic marketplace is here to stay.

Television

The potential of the television as a sales tool has been recognized since its introduction, when the first shows were sponsored by major corporations. The advent of cable and the possession of at least one TV by almost every American household has only accentuated this potential.

■ *Television sales:* As early as 1950, a channel called Television Department Stores brought the retailing environment into the TV viewer's living room. Television sales picked up in the 1970s when two companies, Ronco Incorporated and K-Tel International, began to hawk such products as the "Kitchen Magician," the "Mince-O-Matic," and the "Miracle Broom" on television sets around the world.[57]

Today, these primitive sales pitches have largely been replaced by slick *infomercials*—half-hour or hour-long commercials that resemble a talk show but in actuality are intended to sell something. More than forty major companies have used this format, including heavyweights from American Airlines and Apple Computer to Visa and Volkswagen. According to the National Infomercial Marketing Association, gross sales of products advertised on infomercials in 1993 were about $900 million, and sales have probably topped $1 billion since. A recent survey by *TV Guide* found that 72 percent of respondents had watched at least one infomercial and that about one-third had actually made a purchase as a result.[58]

■ *Home shopping networks:* Developments in marketing and technology have now made it possible for shopping junkies to indulge themselves without leaving their living rooms. France's Minitel system, the world's largest videotext service, uses a telephone to link users with a host computer. The system offers home shopping, travel, games, and many other services. About 6 million French consumers have Minitel terminals in their homes.[59]

In the United States, home shopping channels posted $2 billion in sales in 1992. The QVC channel alone sells products at the rate of $39 per second around the clock.[60] To date, the typical American home shopping customer is slightly lower on the social ladder than the typical store shopper, but if some powerful companies have anything to do with it, this profile is going to change. Upscale retailers and manufacturers like Saks Fifth Avenue, Bloomingdales, Sharper Image, Nordstrom, and Calvin Klein are all planning home shopping efforts, and Macy's is going so far as to start its own shopping channel! On QVC, callers can now buy Von Furstenberg silks and jewelry from comedienne Joan Rivers. The primary buyers of these products are professionals and managers with little time to shop, exactly the market that many upscale retailers target.[61]

Computers

As increasing numbers of households buy computers for personal use, computer shopping is starting to go mainstream. As one industry executive observed, "The target audience is still pretty much gearheads, technically astute people."[62] However, this description is expected to change as more people become familiar with computers and the Internet and as such interface programs as Windows 95, Mosaic, and Netscape make it easier for "regular people" to navigate in cyberspace.

- *On-line services:* The most sophisticated nonstore retailing via computer is currently to be found on such online services as Prodigy, CompuServe, and America Online. For example, Apple Computer, America Online, and Medior, an interactive software-development company, formed a partnership known as 2Market, an interactive online service initially featuring about thirty merchants and catalog titles, including Lands' End, 800-Flowers, Chef's Catalog, Spiegel, Sony Music, and Time Warner's Warner Brothers Studio Store.[63] The dollar volume on the Electronic Mall operated by CompuServe is growing by 30 to 40 percent a year.[64]

- *The World Wide Web:* Much of the action on the Internet can be found on the **World Wide Web,** a service that links computers called Web servers all over the world and that enables companies and individuals to establish "home pages" where "Web surfers" (an estimated 10 million worldwide and growing rapidly) can visit, learn, and buy.[65] PolyGram records opened a web site in 1995 (www.polygram.com) that allows users to listen to song samples from hot new artists, obtain concert information, download photos of favorite artists, and locate record stores in their area that carry PolyGram releases. The site will also enable the user to link directly to online record stores, where purchases can be made over the Net.[66]

- *CD-ROMs:* More than a third of all desktop PCs now have connected to them a CD-ROM drive, which allows a computer to read a compact disk.[67] Some marketers are taking advantage of this new multimedia capability by developing computerized sales presentations on CD/ROM. These include electronic catalogs wherein the viewer can learn more about the product, desktop presentations, and disk-based advertising to make it easier to update information and increase user interaction. In the auto industry, disks that explain available options are now being mailed to potential customers. Some include spreadsheets that permit consumers to compute the car's monthly payments and a simulator so that they can take a test drive.[68]

World Wide Web: a service that links computers all over the world and allows companies and individuals to establish "home pages" where they can visit. learn, and buy

RETAILING: WHAT'S IN STORE FOR THE FUTURE

This is a very exciting—and challenging—time to be in retailing. The development and evolution of retailing will be fueled by several fundamental changes. In this final section, we'll briefly review a few of these.

DEMOGRAPHIC CHANGES

As we noted in Chapter 8, keeping up with changes in population characteristics are at the heart of many marketing developments. Retailers can no longer afford to stand by and assume that their customer base is the same as it has always been. They are coming up with new ways to sell their products to diverse groups. For example, some direct-marketing companies are developing catalogs targeted to gays and lesbians, including such recent entries as *Made in Gay America, Shocking Gray,* and *H.I.M.*[69] As the chairman of British retailing giant Marks & Spencer, which owns the venerable Brooks Brothers clothing stores, recently observed, "We can't run our business on a 55-year-old man who wears a three-button Brooks Brothers suit and only comes in twice a year."[70] Instead, retailers need to refine their merchandise mix constantly to meet the needs of a changing market. Let's take a quick look at a few of the major demographic factors that are altering the face of retailing.

Working Women

The dramatic increase in the number of working women has made the problem of "time poverty" even more acute. To survive, conventional retailers have to offer the same kind of convenience and speed that makes nonstore retailing so attractive to many of these busy people. Some retailers are already adapting to these changes by expanding their hours of operation (many people have time to shop only at night) and by adding drive-up windows to meet demands for convenience and security. This innovation is being tried by dry cleaners, pharmacies, liquor stores, and lumberyards. For example, at the Home Base Warehouse, 200 cars a day drive up for lumber supplies.[71]

In areas from financial services to interior decorating and clothing, enterprising individuals have turned this time shortage into a business opportunity by offering their services as shopping consultants. Many people are interested in forming a relationship with an objective professional who understands their individual needs and will make purchase decisions on their behalf. One growing area is wardrobe and image consultation: Almost one-fifth of the female executives polled in a national survey reported that they had employed the services of an image counselor when selecting or purchasing apparel.[72] Many major department stores are jumping in to fill this need as well by offering the services of their own in-house consultants at no charge.

Age Segmentation

Retailers are increasingly recognizing that consumers in different age groups vary dramatically in terms of what they look for in a retail environment—and have also developed a healthy respect for the spending power of both young people and senior citizens. Here are three examples of age-specific retail segmentation strategies:

Exhibit 15.8
In Orange County, California, there is a shopping center called the Lab that shoppers have dubbed the anti-mall. This is shopping with an edge: It's targeted to mall rats aged eighteen to thirty who are fed up with conventional layouts featuring the same old assortment of stores like Waldenbooks and the Bombay Co. Instead, the Lab features a record store called Tower Alternative, a florist named Weeds, and a clothing store known as Philosophy of Comfort. In contrast to the slick façade of traditional centers, it features pieces of concrete walls, a fountain made of oil drums, a concrete stage, and an open-air living room filled with furniture from a thrift shop.

- Stride Rite has opened Great Feet superstores targeted specifically to six- to eight-year-olds. The boys' selling area is designed to resemble a basketball court in a schoolyard.[73]

- In a calculated appeal to baby boomers who wish to browse through reading matter in a leisurely, upscale atmosphere, the Barnes & Noble chain is developing bookstores designed to be comfortable places that make browsers feel welcome. Some even include coffee bars inside the store to encourage a lengthy visit.[74]

- A health club chain called Take Time, Inc. opened fitness centers for people over the age of fifty. Exercisers do the Charleston to the accompaniment of big-band music, and they can buy a work-out video starring singer Pat Boone.

Ethnic Diversity

Although members of every ethnic group can usually find small, local retailers that cater to them, larger operations must begin to tailor their strategies to the cultural makeup of specific trading areas. National Convenience Stores, which owns a chain of convenience stores called Stop N Go, recently revamped some of its outlets when its research showed that large numbers of customers were Hispanic. These stores now feature Mayan murals and sell Mexican delicacies.[75] Similarly, the Winn-Dixie supermarket chain promotes dishes native to individual Hispanic countries with the theme *"Winn-Dixie tiene el sabor de mi pais"* ("Winn-Dixie has the flavor of my country").[76] In the catalog area, Spiegel teamed up with *Ebony* magazine to create *E Style*, a catalog targeting black women. This project was launched after consumer research showed that black customers did not feel that retailers were adequately serving their needs.[77]

TECHNOLOGICAL AND ENVIRONMENTAL CHANGES

At the Tandy Corporation's Incredible Universe mega-store in Oregon, every customer who enters the registration area gets a scannable membership card for efficient check-out and delivery.[78] Tandy is helping to bring high technology to the store level.

Technological Developments

Exciting new developments like this are constantly being introduced by retailers. Some of the most profound changes are not even visible to shoppers, such as advanced electronic **point of sale (POS) systems,** which contain computer brains that collect sales data and are hooked directly into the store's inventory control system. Systems now being introduced even have multimedia capability; they can entertain waiting customers by giving messages about local events, showing ads on a screen, or transmitting classified ads prepared at the store.[79] Other firms are experimenting with wireless networks that enable shoppers and employees to record purchases with hand-held devices. Shoppers soon will be able to scan in their own items as they drop them into the cart, eliminating the need for check-out lines.[80]

Other technological innovations will radically change the way we shop. The president and CEO of JCPenney International makes the following predictions about what retailing will be like in the year 2010.[81] Each consumer will have a personal preference card, so a store will know your tastes, clothing sizes, and even your current household decor. When you are shopping for furniture, a design consultant will call up a 3-D image of your living room and show you how your new purchases will actually look in the room. And forget about endlessly trying on clothes—holographic imaging will let you "see" yourself in a new suit or dress. What's more, your clothes will work hard to make sure you're comfortable. You'll be wearing climate-controlled fabrics that adjust to outside temperatures!

Already, we are witnessing developments like these:

- First Direct is a British bank with half a million customers and no branches. All bank business is transacted completely by phone.[82]

- Food retailers like Safeway and A&P and drugstores like Eckerd Drug give customers the options of shopping by phone, fax, or computer.[83]

point of sale (POS) systems: retail computer systems that collect sales data and are hooked directly into the store's inventory control system

- Sears, Roebuck & Co. installed Florsheim kiosks to give shoppers access to computerized displays that transmit information about shoe styles and sizes that the stores don't carry.[84]

Environmental Developments

Both traditional retailers and nonstore retailers are taking steps to minimize the damage they do to the environment. This is good citizenship and also good business: Consumers' environmental concerns extend beyond recycling supermarket shopping bags. Many shoppers will be looking for stores that are kind to the earth. Anticipating this demand, Wal-Mart recently unveiled a new, environmentally friendly store format. Its "eco-store" carries the usual Wal-Mart assortment, but the facility is brighter and less cramped. It is built with wood beams instead of steel, it has skylights for natural light, and the store's air-conditioning system doesn't use CFCs. The store's theme is recycling, and it lets the public use an on-site recycling center. Customers are encouraged to discard packaging at a recycling station before they leave the store, and an environmental meeting room is open to the local community.[85]

Direct marketers also are grappling with reducing the waste created by the mountains of catalogs and direct-mail pieces now produced, mailed, and ultimately discarded. As one modest step to curb the volume of waste products caused by the direct-marketing revolution, France's Minitel system now encourages the use of shredded paper trimmings instead of polystyrene peanuts.[86] Recognizing that the industry must take steps to police itself, the Direct Marketing Association has even started to give awards to environmentally conscious members. The Fingerhut Corporation, an award winner, encourages customers to return duplicated or incorrect mailing labels by offering $5 gift certificates for doing so.

GLOBAL CHANGES

As the world grows smaller, retailers will continue to expand around the globe. Improved communications and distribution channels enable companies large and small to practice *global sourcing,* where they buy merchandise worldwide. One good example of this sophisticated access is IKEA, which has developed a unique system of global networking: Unlike most companies that pick and choose among the products of many different suppliers, IKEA does the reverse: It designs its furniture in-house and then contracts with suppliers around the world to manufacture the items. This allows IKEA to keep firm control of design and quality and to buy components wherever they are the most economical at the time.

Global Expansion

American and European firms are slowly waking up to the idea that they must expand internationally to continue to see their sales expand. As markets are getting saturated in their home countries, merchants like Marks & Spencer, Disney, and Toys "Я" Us are trying to turn their stores into global brands, so that they can sell higher-margin private-label goods and gain leverage with suppliers. Some retailers, such as Kmart, that do venture aggressively into international locales have found it much easier to do so with local partners who know the market.

The world's largest Wal-Mart is in Mexico City; the company operates 67 stores in Mexico and, with partners, is opening stores in Brazil and Argentina. Many American retailers, including Home Depot, Staples, and The Gap, have succeeded in the Canadian market since the U.S.–Canada Free Trade Agreement went into effect in 1989.[87] Overall, restaurant chains such as McDonald's and KFC and specialty apparel retailers such as T.J. Maxx, The Gap, and Foot Locker have been the most globally oriented, while other segments such as grocery chains have lagged far behind.[88]

American discounters have found fertile ground in Europe, a market where consumers traditionally have had to put up with high prices, limited selection, and abbreviated shopping hours (many stores close on Sundays, and in some countries they begin to close their shutters on Saturday afternoon). Now these markets are getting more competitive, as countries like Germany begin to relax their very restrictive laws regulating retailing and advertising.

*R*EAL PEOPLE, REAL CHOICES:

How It Worked Out at IKEA

Mr. Carstedt and his colleagues chose option 3. They decided to go into the Carson Mall, but only on the condition that the mall owner do a major renovation. The owner agreed to spend $12 to $17 million to do a complete rehabilitation of the Center, which was renamed Southwest Plaza. This involved installing windows in the roof to open up the enclosed space to natural light, redoing the exterior façade, and adding a fourth department store, an additional 50,000 square feet of retail space, and a multiscreen movie theater. This IKEA store is now the second-biggest IKEA store in the Los Angeles area. IKEA is using its strong presence in the Los Angeles market as a platform to enter such new markets as Seattle, San Francisco and San Diego.

Global Cross-Fertilization

As retailers around the world continue to develop a presence in other countries, they bring with them innovations and management philosophies that will change the way local firms do business as well. Many American companies will be influenced by innovative European retailing concepts that are already beginning to change the way we shop. Three influential companies at the moment are

- Conran's (U.K.). This home furnishings store has profited by targeting middle-class young people, who are drawn to its simple designs displayed in realistic settings.

- Benetton (Italy). This apparel company targets those fourteen to thirty years old, who snap up its functional and fashionable ready-to-wear clothing around the world. The company's extensive use of computer-aided design keeps costs down, while it constantly monitors demand for colors and style and shapes its manufacturing process to be consistent with consumers' buying patterns.[89]

- IKEA (Sweden). As we've seen, IKEA's success is largely due to its concept of warehouse retailing based on economies of scale, where customer participation in assembling and transporting merchandise is a key factor in controlling costs. IKEA appeals to people it calls *prosumers;* they are willing to get involved in both the production and the consumption of its products. Customers are supplied with catalogs, tape measures, pens, and notepaper so that they can make their choices without the aid of salespeople (though help is available if requested). Labels carry each item's name, price, dimensions, materials, and available colors. Furniture purchased at IKEA is picked up by the customer, who then takes it home and assembles it (delivery and assembly are available for an extra fee).[90]

Chapter 15 Summary

Objective 1. Explain the position of retailing in the marketplace—that is, how retailing has evolved and how it continues to change.

Any person or organization that offers something for sale to a consumer is a retailer. Retailers continually change to meet the needs of a variety of consumers, saving them time and money and providing desirable merchandise assortments. The wheel-of-retailing hypothesis suggests that new retailers compete on price and then move upscale, leaving room for other new low-price entrants. The retail life-cycle theory suggests that retailing institutions are introduced, grow, reach maturity, and then decline.

Objective 2. Describe how retailers may be classified by type or selection of merchandise.

Retailers are classified by SIC codes based on the product lines sold. Retailers may also be classified according to whether they carry items that have high or low gross margins and/or high or low turnover rates. Categorizing retailers by the merchandise assortment they carry—that is, by its breadth and depth—results in their classification as convenience stores, supermarkets, specialty stores, discount stores, department stores, mass merchandisers, and hypermarkets.

Objective 3. List and explain the major choices that must be made in developing a retailing strategy.

In developing a retailing strategy, marketers seek to develop a desirable store image through the use of many different elements. Color, lighting, scents, furnishings, and other design elements—called atmospherics—are designed to appeal to specific market segments. Store design decisions include 1) store layout (which determines traffic flow and influences the desired customer behavior in the store), 2) the use of store fixtures and open space, 3) the use of sound to attract (or repel) certain types of customers, and 4) the use of color and lighting, which can influence customer mood as well as store image. The number and type of store personnel and the pricing policy for products sold in the store also contribute to shoppers' perceptions. Major types of retail locations include central business districts, secondary or neighborhood business districts, shopping centers, freestanding retailers, and new, nontraditional locations.

Objective 4. Explain some of the major nonstore direct-marketing activities in today's marketplace and mention some of the possibilities for the future.

Nonstore retailing includes traditional mail-order shopping, direct-selling operations, and vending machines as well as newer forms of direct marketing such as television shopping and telemarketing. Mail-order retailers send billions of catalogs and direct-mail advertisements to consumers. Home shopping parties, door-to-door sales, and telemarketing are popular direct-selling techniques. Vending machines offer customers the ultimate in convenience, dispensing both necessities and luxury items. The growing electronic marketplace utilizes the power of more traditional television infomercials, home shopping networks and the growing popularity of computer online services, the World Wide Web, and CD-ROM sales presentations.

Objective 5. List and describe some of the environmental trends that will affect the future of retailing.

A number of environmental trends will continue to drive the evolution of retailing. These include demographic changes such as an aging population and increasing affluence among ethnic groups, time poverty resulting from increased numbers of working women, and technological developments such as advanced POS systems that enable retailers to provide more personal service. Environmentally conscious consumers look for retailers who are environmentally sensitive. Market globalization will continue to offer new opportunities for retailing innovation.

Review Questions

Marketing Concepts: Test Your Knowledge

1. How does the wheel of retailing explain changes in retail outlets? How does the retail life-cycle concept explain these changes?
2. How are gross margins and turnover rates used to classify retailers? Describe the differences in merchandise assortments for convenience stores, supermarkets, specialty stores, discount stores, department stores, mass merchandisers, and hypermarkets.
3. What is store atmospherics? How can the elements of atmospherics be used to increase the store's success? How are store personnel a part of store image?
4. What are some of the different types of store locations? What are the advantages and disadvantages of each?
5. How do retail store location planners evaluate potential store sites?
6. Describe the three major types of nonstore retailing.
7. Describe the retail mail-order industry.
8. Explain the different forms of direct selling.
9. Describe some of the changes that are expected in the growing electronic marketplace.
10. What are some of the environmental trends that will have a major impact on the future of nonstore retailing?

Marketing Concepts: Discussing Choices and Issues

1. Some people nostalgically believe retailing was better in the "good old days." What are some of the ways in which modern retailing makes your life better? What are some negative aspects of modern retailing?
2. Retailers use store atmospherics to create a certain image. Describe some ways in which creative marketers might use atmospherics to create an image for (a) an antique store, (b) a vintage-clothing store, (c) a bank in a Hispanic neighborhood, and (d) a bookstore.
3. Some people have suggested that retailers have gone too far in using lighting, color, and even smells to entice shoppers to buy. What do you think? Can the use of atmospherics be unethical?
4. As the twenty-first century dawns, the potential of electronic media is in its infancy. How do you think electronic media will change retailing in your lifetime?

Marketing Practice: Applying What You've Learned

1. All your life you've wanted to be an entrepreneur—to own your own business. Now, you're ready to graduate from college and you've decided to open a combination coffee shop/bookstore in a location near your college. You know that to attract both the college student market and other customers from the local community, it will be necessary to design the store image carefully. Develop a detailed plan for store atmospherics for your retail store.
2. In your job with a marketing consulting firm, you often are asked to make recommendations for store location. Your current client is a local caterer who is planning to open a new retail outlet for selling takeout gourmet dinners. You are examining the possible types of locations: the central business district, a shopping center, a freestanding arrangement, or some nontraditional location. Outline the advantages and disadvantages of each type of location for your client. Present your recommendations to the class.
3. Assume you are the vice president of marketing for Elegant Evenings, a chain of women's lingerie stores. Your firm sells exclusive designer lingerie in boutiques located in shopping malls across the country. With a changing marketplace, your firm is considering whether it should develop some type of nonstore retailing operation. Specifically, you are considering the opportunities for marketing your products via 1) catalogs, 2) direct mail, 3) television infomercials, 4) a television home shopping network, 5) the World Wide Web, and 6) CD-ROM.

    In a role-playing situation with one or more of your classmates, debate the benefits of the different types of direct retailing for this firm.
4. Assume you are the director of marketing for a national chain of convenience stores. Your firm has about 200 stores located in forty-three states. The stores are fairly traditional both in design and in the merchandise they carry. Because you want to be proactive in your marketing planning, you are concerned that your firm may need to consider significant changes in anticipation of demographic, technological and global changes in the marketplace. You think it is important to discuss these things with the other executives at your firm. With one or more of your classmates, develop a presentation that includes
    a. A discussion of the demographic changes that will affect your type of store.
    b. A discussion of the technological changes that will affect your type of store.
    c. A discussion of how global changes may provide problems and opportunities for your organization.
    d. Your recommendations for how your firm should meet the challenges it will face in each of these areas.

Marketing Mini-Project: Learning by Doing

This project is designed to help you understand how store atmospherics play an important role in consumer perceptions of a retail store.

1. First, select two retail outlets where students in your college are likely to shop. It will be good if you can select two outlets that are quite different in store image but which sell some of the same types of products.
2. Visit each of the stores and write down a detailed description of the store atmosphere: colors, materials used, lighting fixtures, product displays, store personnel, and so on.
3. Survey some of the students in your college. Develop a brief questionnaire to determine how respondents perceive the two stores you are studying. You may want to ask about such things as the quality of merchandise, prices, competence and friendliness of the store personnel, and the attitude of management toward customer service.
4. Develop a report of your findings. Compare the descriptions of the stores with the results of the survey. Try to explain how the different elements of the store atmosphere shape each store's unique image.

Key Terms

Endnotes

1. "The IKEA Figures 92/93" (company literature).
2. "IKEA Facts 92/93" (company literature).
3. "The Swedish Invasion," *Discount Merchandiser* (July 1990): 52.
4. Sandra Tsing Loh, "IKEA! Cry of a Lost Generation," *Buzz*, 9 (January/February 1993): 68.
5. Michael Selz, "Small Retailers Fare Well Despite Chains' Onslaught," *The Wall Street Journal* (September 12, 1994): B2.
6. Jonathan R. Laing, "The New Ghost Towns: A Vicious Shakeout Takes Its Toll on Shopping Malls," *Barron's*, 4 (March 16, 1992): 8.
7. Stanley C. Hollander, "*The Wheel of Retailing*," *JR* (July, 1960): 41.
8. Christina Duff, "Brighter Lights, Fewer Bargains: Outlets Go Upscale," *The Wall Street Journal* (April 11, 1994): B1.
9. William R. Davidson, Albert D. Bates, and Stephen J. Bass, "The Retail Life Cycle," *Harvard Business Review* (November–December 1976): 89.
10. Mitchell Russell, "The Gap Dolls Itself Up," *Business Week* (March 21, 1994): 46.
11. Kate Fitzgerald, "Retailers Prescribe Pharmacies," *Ad Age*, 2 (March 15, 1993): 3.
12. Julie Liesse, "Welcome to the Club," *Ad Age*, 2 (February 1, 1993): 3.
13. Debra Hazel, "The Factory Outlets' Best of Times: Belz's and Other Centers Beat the Recession," *Chain Store Age Executive* (November 1992): 39–42.
14. Adrienne Ward, "New Breed of Mall Knows: Everybody Loves a Bargain," *Ad Age* (January 27, 1992): 55.
15. Roger D. Blackwell, Wayne Talarzyk, and James F. Engel, *Contemporary Cases in Consumer Behavior*, 3rd ed. (Hinsdale, IL: Dryden Press, 1990), 389–402.
16. "A Wide World of Sports Shoes: Fixtures Enhance Appeal of World Foot Locker," *Chain Store Age Executive* (January 1993): 176–181.

17. Quoted in Wendy Marx, "Shopping 2000," *Brandweek*, 2 (January 9, 1995): 20.
18. Marianne Wilson, "The De-Sleazification of Frederick's," *Chain Store Age Executive* (September 1989): 94–96.
19. Stephanie From, "Image and Attitude are Department Stores' Draw," *NY Times* (August 12, 1993): D1.
20. Sallie Hook, "All the Retail World's a Stage: Consumers Conditioned to Entertainment in Shopping Environment," *Marketing News* (July 31, 1987): 16.
21. *Consumers Reports* (September 1993).
22. "Lobbyists Against Noise Pollution Pick Up Some Unexpected Allies," *The Wall Street Journal* (June 1, 1990): B1.
23. Joesph A. Bellizzi and Robert E. Hite, "Environmental Color, Consumer Feelings, and Purchase Likelihood," *Psychology & Marketing*, 9 (September/October 1992): 347–363.
24. Deborah Blumenthal, "Scenic Design for In-Store Try-Ons," *The New York Times* (April 9, 1988): 56.
25. "Service: Retail's No. 1 Problem," *Chain Store Age* (January 1987): 19.
26. Elaine Underwood, "Mall Busters, Like Crime, a Boon for Home Shopping," *Brandweek*, 2 (January 17, 1994): 18.
27. Van Johnston and Herff Moore, "Pride Drives Wal-Mart to Service Excellence," *HR Magazine*, 3 (October l991): 79.
28. Stephanie Strom, "Bold Stroke in Japan's Art of Retailing," *The New York Times*, 2 (April 23, 1993): D1.
29. Quoted in Jane Perlez, "In East Europe, K-mart Faces an Attitude Problem," *The New York Times*, 2 (July 7, 1993): D1.
30. Brian Silverman, "Shopping for Loyal Customers," *Sales & Marketing Management*, 2 (March 1995): 96.
31. Kate Fitzgerald, "All Roads Lead to . . . ," *Ad Age* (February 1, 1993): S-1.
32. Gregory A. Patterson, "All Decked Out, Stores Head Downtown," *The Wall Street Journal*, 2 (February 15, 1994): B1.
33. Chip Walker, "Strip Malls: Plain but Powerful," *AD*, 4 (October 1991): 48.

34. Christopher Palmeri, "Media Merchant to the Baby Boomers," *Forbes*, 2 (March 15, 1993): 66.

35. Evan I. Schwartz, "The Kiosks Are Coming, the Kiosks Are Coming," *Business Week* (June 22, 1992): 122.

36. Avijit Ghosh and Sara L. McLafferty, *Location Strategies for Retail and Service Firms*, Lexington, MA: Lexington Books, 1987.

37. Tan Lee Hock, "How the Japanese Are Winning the Retailing War," *Asian Finance* (January 15, 1989): 26–27.

38. Bruce Fox, "Dorian's Tries to Keep Shoppers in Mexico," *Chain Store Age Executive* (February 1992): 23–24.

39. Pat Sloan, "Avon Looks Beyond Direct Sales," *Ad Age* (February 22, 1993): 32; Seema Nayyar, "Avon Calling, by Fax, Phone, and Infomercial," *Brandweek* (February 22, 1993): 22–23.

40. Stratford Sherman, "Will the Information Superhighway be the Death of Retailing?" *Fortune*, 5 (April 18, 1994): 99.

41. Quoted in Stratford Sherman, "Will the Information Superhighway Be the Death of Retailing?" *Fortune*, 5 (April 18, 1994): 110.

42. Frances Huffman, "Special Delivery," *Entrepreneur*, 3 (February 1993): 81.

43. Paul Hughes, "Profits Due," *Entrepreneur*, 4 (February 1994): 74.

44. Frances Huffman, "Special Delivery," *Entrepreneur*, 3 (February 1993): 81.

45. Jo Marney, "Research: Consumers Now Driven by Need, Not Want," *Marketing* (Canada) (March 1, 1993): 7.

46. Melissa Dowling, "Spiegel 'Malls' the Mailbox," *DM* (May 27, 1992).

47. Bradley Johnson, "Giants' entry in Mail Order Adds Weight to Magazine's Heft," *Ad Age* (March 1, 1993): S-15.

48. Stuart Elliott, "A Mail Campaign Helps Saab Find, and Keep, Its Customers," *The New York Times* (June 21, 1993): D7.

49. Murray Raphel, "Where's the Retail Direct Mail Revolution?" *Direct Marketing* (December 1992): 42–45.

50. Len Strazewski, "Tupperware Locks in New Strategy," *Advertising Age* (February 8, 1988): 30.

51. Peter Wilkinson, "For Your Eyes Only," *Savvy Woman*, (January 1989): 68.

52. Quoted in Kate Ballen, "Get Ready for Shopping at Work," *Fortune* (February 15, 1988): 95.

53. Linda Lipp, "Telephones Ringing Off the Hook," *Journal & Courier* (May 19, 1994).

54. Denise Gillene, "FBI Launches 12-State Telemarketing Sweep," *LA Times* (March 5, 1993): D1.

55. James Sterngold, "Why Japanese Adore Vending Machines," *The New York Times*, 2 (January 5, 1992): A1.

56. Michael Janofsky, "A Bartender with Buttons Serves Brew to Go," *The New York Times*, (July 8, 1993): D1.

57. Alison J. Clarke, "'As Seen on TV': Socialisation of the Tele-Visual Consumer," paper presented at The Fifth Interdisciplinary Conference on Research in Consumption, The University of Lund, Sweden (August 1995).

58. Tim Triplett, "Big Names Crowd the Infomercial Airwaves," *Marketing News*, 2 (March 28, 1994): 1.

59. "How Videotex Offers Special Potential in France," *Business Marketing Digest*, 17 (1992): 81–84.

60. Stratford Sherman, "Will the Information Superhighway be the Death of Retailing?" *Fortune*, 5 (April 18, 1994): 99.

61. Scott McMurray, "Television Shopping Is Stepping Up in Class," *The New York Times* (March 6, 1994): F5.

62. Quoted in Gerry Khermouch, "Chiphead Connection," *Brandweek*, 4 (March 14, 1994): 18.

63. Kevin Goldman, "Advertising On-Line Catalog Service Takes Shopping to Cyberspace," *The Wall Street Journal* (November 18, 1994): B-5.

64. Gerry Khermouch, "Chiphead Connection," *Brandweek*, 4 (March 14, 1994): 18.

65. John W. Verity, "The Internet: How It Will Change the Way You Do Business," *Business Week*, 9 (November 14, 1994): 80.

66. "WWW.Polygram.Com Goes Live!" *The Digital Enquirer* (March 1995): 1–2.

67. Tim Triplett, "The CD-ROM Revolution," *Marketing News*, 2 (September 12, 1994): 1.

68. Thayer C. Taylor, "Fight Mail Costs with Your PC," *S&MM*, 3 (March 1993): 16.

69. Stuart Elliott, "As the Gay and Lesbian Market Grows, a Boom in Catalogues That Are 'Out, Loud and Proud,'" *The New York Times* (September 10, 1993): D17.

70. Quoted in Sunita Wadekar Bhargava, "What's Next, Grunge Bathrobes?" *Business Week*, 2 (June 21, 1993): 64.

71. "Window Shopping at the Drive-in," *Nation's Business* (February 1993): 43.

72. Michael R. Solomon, "The Wardrobe Consultant: Exploring the Role of a New Retailing Partner," *Journal of Retailing* (Summer 1987): 110–128; Joseph Z. Wisenblit, "Person Positioning: Empirical Evidence and a New Paradigm," *Journal of Professional Services Marketing*, 4 (1989): 51–82.

73. Cyndee Miller, "Retailers Do What They Must to Ring Up Sales," *Marketing News*, 3 (May 22, 1995): 1.

74. Kate Fitzgerald, "What's Next Chapter in Bookstore Battle?" *Ad Age* (April 12, 1993): 12.

75. Steve Dwyer, "C-Stores Are Catching the Wave in Target Marketing Techniques," *National Petroleum News* (May 1991): 26–30.

76. David J. Wallace, "How to Sell Yucas to YUCAs," *Ad Age* (February 13, 1989): 5–6.

77. Cyndee Miller, "Major Catalogers, Niche Players Carve Up Mail-Order Market," *Marketing News*, 2 (September 27, 1993): 1.

78. Marianne Wilson, "Incredible Universe Blasts Off," *Chain Store Age Executive* (November 1992): 106–110.

79. Robert E. Calem, "Coming to a Cash Register Near You: Multimedia," *The New York Times* (July 31, 1994): F7.

80. Gary Robins, "Wireless POS Systems," *Stores*, 2 (February 1994): 47.

81. Alfred F. Lynch, "Training for a New Ball Game: Retailing in the 21st Century," *The Futurist* (July/August 1992): 36–40.

82. Saul Hansell, "500,000 Clients, No Branches," *The New York Times*, 2 (September 3, 1995, Sec. 3): 1.

83. Cyndee Miller, "Retailers Do What They Must to Ring Up Sales," *Marketing News*, 3 (May 22, 1995): 1.

84. Wendy Marx, "Shopping 2000," *Brandweek*, 2 (January 9, 1995): 20.

85. Kate Fitzgerald, "It's Green, It's Friendly, It's Wal-Mart 'Eco-Store,'" *Ad Age*, 2 (June 7, 1993): 1.

86. Mollie Neal, "Marketers Develop a Green Consciousness," *Direct Marketing* (February 1993): 35–37.

87. William C. Symonds, "Invasion of the Retail Snatchers," *Business Week*, 2 (May 9, 1994): 72.

88. Stephanie M. Shern, "Going Global," *Chain Store Age Executive* (February 1994): 38–39; Carla Rapoport, "The New U.S. Push into Europe," *Fortune* (January 10, 1994): 73–74.

89. Madhau Kacker, "International Flow of Retailing Know-How: Bridging the Technology Gap in Distribution," *JR* (Spring 1988): 41–67.

90. Richard Norman and Rafael Ramirez, "From Value Chain to Value Constellation: Designing Interactive Strategy," *Harvard Business Review* (July–August 1993): 65–70.

MARKETING IN ACTION:
REAL PEOPLE AT THE BOMBAY CO.

The Bombay Co., founded by Brad Harper, sells replicas of eighteenth- and nineteenth-century English furniture, mostly small pieces such as butler's tables, plant stands, and night stands. The company started as a strictly mail-order business, advertising its products in magazines and shipping the goods to customers—and it was losing money. But then Harper met Robert Nourse, a former marketing professor with a doctorate from Harvard University. And Nourse saw potential. After all, the company had nice styles of furniture sold at very reasonable prices. Nourse bought the Canadian rights to the Bombay Co. for $1 and 4 percent royalties (the agreement was written over lunch on a paper napkin.)

But Nourse felt that malls, with high levels of traffic, were a better way to market the Bombay line. Although mall rent was high, the fact that people could buy the products on impulse and carry them right to their cars and homes—a far cry from the current six to twelve-week waiting time to get furniture delivered—would generate high levels of sales. Also, Bombay sold its furniture unassembled in boxes (or, in the industry lingo, as "knock downs"), which kept inventory storage space to a minimum.

Nourse's first store was modeled after Fountain Court at Henry VIII's palace. It was an immediate success. When Nourse sold his Canadian rights to Tandy Brands, Inc. in 1981, he maintained control of the operation, and in 1983 he was made president of the whole Bombay Co. In 1991 he became CEO. Since Nourse took over, Bombay Co. has been extremely successful. By the end of 1992 sales were $232 million, making Bombay Co. the sixteenth-largest home furnishing company in North America. Today, Bombay's average sales per square foot are $340, compared with the $110 industry average for furniture stores.

What is the strategy that has made Bombay Co. such a success? First, CEO Nourse is just plain picky about the malls his stores go into—they must have upscale clientele and high levels of traffic. Locations near the food court are ideal because traffic is especially heavy there.

Next, Bombay Co. tailors the entire retail concept to the malls, which means the stores don't carry large, more expensive items (such as sofas) that tend to have a lower turnover rate. Instead, the focus is on giving the customer furniture at reasonable prices. Although direct comparisons are impossible because all of Bombay's items are produced exclusively for the chain, the products sell for 30 to 60 percent below competitors' prices. Nothing goes for more than $500, most items cost less than $150, and the average sale is $80.

Nourse believes that an important part of the company's success, and an important factor in keeping down costs, is the strong relationships developed with its more than 130 vendors. Prices are kept low because the company vertically integrates by retaining control of its products from factory to store. A large percentage of production is done in contract factories in Asia, which mass-produce furniture to Bombay Co. specifications. Nourse and Bombay staff often consult with these partners, making sure that designs are attractive and can be efficiently produced. The close-knit nature of Bombay's sourcing network may be one reason why no one has attempted to copy it.

Bombay also stays ahead by ensuring that its styles are kept up to date. In an average year, 25 percent of furniture and 50 percent of wall decor are replaced in each Bombay store to keep the stock fresh. Store layouts are all designed by visual merchandisers in Bombay's Fort Worth headquarters so that each individual outlet reflects the current inventory and theme.

In addition, Bombay Co. works hard to cultivate a loyal customer base. The 1.2 million active customers on its mailing list receive the company's catalogs seven times a year (including two for Christmas.). Store personnel are trained to greet a customer within twenty-nine seconds after he or she enters the store. And Bombay stands behind its merchandise by offering an unconditional guarantee on everything it sells. Nourse thinks that the best time to make people customers for life is when they want a refund. He comments, "We'll take the thing back with no hassle, no questions, no guff about 'Where's the receipt?' The cost of that is peanuts compared with what you gain in customer loyalty." As he observes, "When you treat customers like a million dollars, they'll come back." So far, this former professor has shown that he can take his own exam—and pass with flying colors.

Source: Anonymous, "Survival of the Smartest," *INC.* (Dec. 1993): 78–88.

Things to Talk About

1. Describe how the Bombay Co. would be classified as a retail operation.

2. How has the positioning strategy of the Bombay Co. been important to its success?

3. How has store location been important for the growth of the Bombay Co.?

4. What demographic changes have contributed to the success of the Bombay Co.? How do you think current and future demographic trends may affect the company?

5. What secrets to success has the Bombay Co. discovered?

CASE 15-2

MARKETING IN ACTION: REAL CHOICES AT STARBUCKS

In the mood for a double-mocha half-decaf cappuccino with skim milk foam? Howard Schultz is the man who started the specialty coffee craze and who has persuaded millions of Americans to ask for something like that instead of simply ordering a plain cup of joe. In 1987, this Brooklyn native bought a small Seattle-area coffee bean store called Starbucks. The original three founders of the store named it after the coffee-drinking first mate in Herman Melville's novel *Moby Dick,* saying that they wanted to "scour the seven seas" to find the best coffee beans in the world.

But the enterprising Schultz had a slightly different idea: He began opening stylish coffee bars where customers could savor exotic coffee drinks. Today the company operates over 500 trendy coffee bars around the country. Schultz wants to make Starbucks the McDonald's of the coffee business by continuing to expand his retail operation into mass markets. But with increasing competition from all directions, that may not be as easy as brewing a leisurely cup of coffee on a lazy Sunday morning. Starbucks, like many retailers, must continue to modify its merchandising mix if it wants to sustain its dramatic growth. The big question is how that evolution should be directed.

Schultz has made Starbucks a success because he believes in his product. In fact, Schultz says, "Our dream was to create a national retail brand. The fact that we are passionate about coffee and about people is one of the unique things about us. Something about coffee transcends the beverage. Someone once said that as opposed to meeting someone over a glass of wine, meeting someone over coffee shows coffee to be the beverage of truth."

Starbucks typically gives its loyal customers a choice of thirty coffee blends—from Arabian Mocha to Sanani to Indonesian Sulawesi to Yukon Blend. And there are other products for sale: Starbucks private-label espresso makers, water filters, plunger pots and other kinds of coffee-making and -storing products. To maintain quality, all coffee is roasted in-house. Starbucks' own team of designers works to maintain the upscale image of all the stores.

Except for a few airport kiosks, all Starbucks stores are company owned and operated. Although the company gets about 15,000 inquiries about franchises a year, Schultz believes the company cannot franchise and still adhere to its high standards. "We decided early on that one aspect we had to protect and preserve would be the very fragile relationship between our customers and our people behind the counter—to both attract customers and [reward] our employees for exceeding our customers' expectations." The strategy has paid off. In 1994, *New York* magazine awarded the company its "Best Service in New York," "Best Espresso," and "Best Latte" awards.

Since 1987, Starbucks has become the leader in the $2.1-billion specialty coffee industry. Schultz has staffed Starbucks with experienced managers hired from bigger chains (Taco Bell, Wendy's, Burger King, and Blockbuster). Schultz says "I believe in the adage: Hire people smarter than you are and get out of their way." Starbucks stores are now in New York, Boston, Minneapolis, Atlanta, Dallas, and Houston, in addition to the earlier West Coast locations. And there are plans to expand abroad.

But lately Starbucks has encountered problems. Sales at some recently opened stores have slowed down. Annual growth in revenues has dropped from around 20 percent in previous years to less than 10 percent. Of even greater concern is increasing competition as other entrepreneurs try to capitalize on Americans' renewed love affair with the coffee bean. The Fort Lauderdale-based Brothers Gourmet Products, Inc. is opening an 80-store chain of Brothers Coffee Bars. Seattle's Best Coffee plans to franchise nearly 500 stores nationwide during the next five years. Mom-and-pop espresso stands are popping up on every corner, and even older, more humble firms like Dunkin' Donuts are climbing on the caffeine bandwagon and steadily improving their coffee offerings. These new developments are giving the coffee company a real wake-up call.

Sources: Russell Shaw, "Grounds for Success," *Sky* (April 1995): 60–74; Dori Jones Yang, "The Starbucks Enterprise Shifts into Warp Speed," *Business Week* (Oct. 24, 1994): 76–79.

Things to Think About

1. What is the problem facing Starbucks?
2. What factors are important in understanding this problem?
3. What alternatives might Starbucks consider?
4. What are your recommendations for solving the problem?
5. What are some ways to implement your recommendations?

CHAPTER

16

Connecting with the Consumer:
Promotional Strategy, Database Marketing, and Integrated Marketing Communications

*When you have completed your study of
this chapter, you should be able to:*

1. Explain the steps in managing the promotion mix.

2. Compare the traditional model of communications with interactive promotion strategies.

3. Explain the popularity of database marketing and how databases are developed and managed.

4. Explain integrated marketing communications, how an IMC program can be implemented, and why some marketers resist IMC.

REAL PEOPLE, REAL CHOICES:

MEET TOM EPPES, PRESIDENT, PRICE/MCNABB FOCUSED COMMUNICATIONS

As president of Price/McNabb, Tom Eppes is on the cutting edge of marketing communications. Based in Charlotte, North Carolina, Price/McNabb is a $45 million company that spent three years in an intensive restructuring process to turn itself into a fully integrated marketing communications company. Unlike a traditional advertising agency, Price/McNabb develops communications programs for clients that *combine* the promotional elements of advertising, public relations, database marketing, and sales promotion. These pieces work together to present a unified message to narrowly defined target customers, whose responses to these messages are carefully monitored by a marketing database. Price/McNabb's business comes from McDonald's franchisees, the Square D Corporation, Centura Bank, the Biltmore Estate, and other companies.

Tom Eppes is a graduate of the University of Southern Mississippi. He began his career as a reporter and then became public information director for a Mississippi state agency. After working as a press secretary on a few political campaigns, Eppes decided to return to journalism. During a flight to New York where he was to interview for a newspaper job, he happened to sit next to the president of Days Inns of America. By the time the plane landed, Eppes had been offered a job heading the motel chain's public relations efforts. (Moral: choose your airplane seats wisely!) When he was hired in 1985 to head up the public relations division of Price/McNabb, he was convinced that agencies can develop more effective, hard-hitting marketing campaigns if they go to the trouble to come up with a "razor-sharp definition" of the target customer and then devise messages using the mixture of media that is most relevant to that customer.

TAILORING MARKETING COMMUNICATIONS TO CUSTOMERS

Tom Eppes is a leader in the emerging trend toward integrated marketing communications. He knows that to reach customers who are overwhelmed by the many messages competing for their attention, it is essential to get to know buyers and talk to them in language they can understand. Sometimes it's as simple as matching up products with people's preferences: When McDonald's found that it was behind in the Southern breakfast market, Price/McNabb pointed out that folks in that region were more likely to start off their day with a fresh-baked biscuit than with an Egg McMuffin. Other times this effort involves the careful combination of messages, including paid ads broadcast or appearing in print media, sponsored "happenings," store displays, and direct mail.

And if the marketer can actually track responses to these messages and develop a dialog with the customer over time, so much the better! That's what Price/McNabb is doing for Drexel Heritage, a client that was initially reluctant to adopt this approach to sell fine furniture. Beginning with customer lists supplied by a dozen Drexel dealers and adding information about these customers from other sources, such as car registration rolls and magazine subscriptions, Price/McNabb was able to develop a profile of Drexel's highest-margin customers in each market. Price/McNabb is now able to target customers in each market who match these best-customer profiles and undertake a one-to-one marketing effort to woo these new buyers.

Promotion is the coordination of efforts by a marketer to inform or persuade consumers or organizations about goods, services, or ideas. As one of the famous "four P's" of the marketing mix, promotion plays a vital strategic role for virtually every type of business, whether (for example) the organization's goal is to sell suits to executives, to sell wool or cotton to clothing manufacturers, or even to arouse consumer or government action to reduce or increase the tariffs attached to imported textiles.

You've probably heard a lot of talk about the communications revolution in progress that some call the *information superhighway*. If things work out as predicted, this high-tech road will be built from digitized information that will allow many different forms of entertainment and information (including telephone conversations, movies, catalogs, and bank transactions) to be converted into electronically transmitted binary code and then provided to you in the "driver's seat" of your own television or personal computer.

Perhaps we can think in terms of a *promotion superhighway* as well. As telephone, cable, and entertainment companies unite to offer new ways to talk to consumers in their homes, in their cars, or even at the beach on their portable fax/modems, the face of promotion is changing in exciting ways.[1] While some firms are taking the lead by riding on the highway, others may just be waiting to get run over, but the routes we take to let people know about our goods and services will never be the same again.

This chapter will provide an overview of the communications tools that Tom Eppes and other marketers use to connect with consumers. After reviewing some of the basic elements of marketing communications, we will take an exit ramp onto the promotion superhighway by discussing emerging perspectives on how to connect with consumers in the 1990s and beyond. We will focus on two fascinating changes in how promotion strategies are being carried out: database marketing and integrated marketing communications. **Database marketing** involves the creation of an ongoing relationship with a set of customers who have an identifiable interest in a product and whose responses to promotion efforts become part of future communications attempts. The organization that applies an **integrated marketing communications** (IMC) strategy coordinates every type of communication in its promotion arsenal—from advertising to company letterhead—to reach these people with a message that is clear, that is consistent, and that maintains this positive relationship with them over time.

promotion: the coordination of efforts by a marketer to inform or persuade consumers or organizations about goods, services, or ideas

database marketing: the creation of an ongoing relationship with a set of customers who have an identifiable interest in a product and whose responses to promotional efforts become part of future communications attempts

integrated marketing communications (IMC): a strategy in which an organization coordinates the different types of communication, from advertising to company letterhead, to reach customers with a message that is clear, that is consistent, and that maintains this positive relationship with them over time

ELEMENTS OF PROMOTION

Virtually everything an organization says and does is a form of communication. The ads it creates, the packages it designs, and even the uniforms its employees wear contribute to the picture people have of the company and its products. In fact, in a broad sense it can be argued that *every* element of the marketing mix is actually a form of communication: After all, the price of a product, where it is sold, and the very nature of the product itself contribute to the impression of the item created in people's minds.

As we'll see in a later section devoted to integrated marketing communications, forward-thinking strategists who recognize these interrelationships are working hard to coordinate all of these dimensions when they try to create a distinctive and consistent image for their product. For the time being, though, we'll concentrate specifically on traditional communications techniques that can be used to transmit the intended picture. Whether the goal is to inform, remind, persuade, or create a positive image, marketers need to work with all the elements in their "communications palette" to be sure that the resulting company portrait corresponds to strategic goals.

Marketing communications can be categorized along two basic dimensions: (1) whether the messages are transmitted via the mass media or are communicated person-to-person, and (2) whether the source is clearly identified as the marketer or the origin of the messages is unclear or is assumed to be an objective third party. These categories are shown in Table 16.1 (page 554).

Table 16.1
Types of Marketing
Communications

		SOURCE	
		Identified as Marketer	**Not Identified as Marketer**
METHOD OF TRANSMISSION	**Mass Media**	Advertising, Sales promotion	Public relations
	Personal	Personal selling	Word of mouth

THE DESTINATION: GOALS OF PROMOTION

No matter how messages are communicated, promotion strategies are developed for a reason. Whether executed in the form of television commercials, billboards, T-shirts, or home pages on the World Wide Web, marketing communications attempt to accomplish specific goals.

■ Promotion *informs* consumers about new goods and services and where they can be obtained. Products are designed to meet existing needs, and promotion provides valuable information to consumers about the best way to satisfy those needs. Promotion messages can increase efficiency by reducing the time required to search for what we want or need.[2]

A recent business-to-business campaign by Georgia-Pacific Corp., a leading paper manufacturer, illustrates how promotion activities can be used to inform the market of a company's needs. The company was running short on raw materials (trees), so its agency designed a campaign to generate leads for buying lumber. Using the tagline "A tree is for life. Pass it on," the company developed marketing communications that offered information about growing trees and selling them. As a result, Georgia-Pacific received 754 leads on possible tree suppliers in fourteen weeks, and it continues to receive suggestions at the rate of about fifty new leads a week.[3]

Exhibit 16.1
One way in which established products remind customers to use them is by dressing them up for holidays and other special occasions. Many companies promoted special versions of their products for the 1996 Olympics. During the Christmas season, marketers fill store shelves with products such as Ho Ho Holiday Rice Krispies, Milk-Bone Holiday Flavor Snacks, and Hershey's Kisses in red and green foil. As one marketing research executive observed, "When a product, even a commodity product or an everyday product bought through the year, dresses itself up . . . [i]t says, 'Remember, I am something you need.'"

- Promotion *reminds* consumers to continue using familiar products. You may think that devoting valuable resources to reminding loyal customers to keep on doing what they're doing is "preaching to the converted." However, this form of promotion is necessary to maintain customer loyalty and to provide ammunition against competitors' inevitable attempts to steal faithful users. NBO Stores, a men's clothing chain in the northeastern United States, mails postcards to its customers throughout the year to remind them to shop there. For example, the company mailed Christmas cards to 130,000 customers who had not shopped at the store in the last two years, and 1.5 percent of these "lapsed shoppers" returned to the store as a result.[4]
- Promotion *persuades* consumers to choose one alternative over others. In today's competitive marketplace, buyers need a reason to select a product from a crowded field of suitors, so a product must somehow be differentiated from other possibilities in a favorable way. Promotion strategies that make these differences clear are essential for a brand to break free from the pack.
- Promotion *builds* relationships with customers. By communicating with buyers over a period of time and creating involvement with the organization, a sound promotion strategy helps forge a bond that may last a lifetime.

THE PROMOTION MIX

The major elements of communication that can be controlled by the marketer are known as the **promotion mix.** These alternatives include advertising, sales promotions, publicity and public relations, and personal selling. The term *mix* implies that a company's promotion strategy is usually focused on more than one element, so part of the challenge is to combine these different communications tools in an effective way.

In this section we'll briefly describe the elements of the promotion mix, each of which will be covered in detail in later chapters. Some of the pros and cons of each element are also presented in Table 16.2 (page 556).

promotion mix: the major elements of marketer-controlled communications, including advertising, sales promotions, publicity and public relations, and personal selling

Personal Appeals

The most immediate way for a marketer to make contact with a customer is simply to tell him or her directly about how wonderful the product is. This intimate communication is often an important part of the promotion mix. It takes the form of *personal selling*, which entails direct contact between a company representative and a customer. This interaction can occur in person, over the phone, or even (but perhaps more commonly a few years in the future) over an interactive computer link.

Wherever the conversation takes place, the goals of the salesperson are to inform the customer about his or her product, to persuade the customer that this choice is superior, and/or perhaps to develop an enduring relationship with the customer so that the salesperson will be seen as a long-term source of information and help with future needs.

Salespeople are themselves a valuable communications medium, because customers can ask questions and the salesperson can address objections and relay product benefits. In a sense, the salesperson is also a walking advertisement for the company: Even his or her appearance speaks volumes about the organization he or she represents. Finally, salespeople often provide valuable additional services to customers and help to strengthen their bond with the company.

Personal selling can be tremendously effective, especially for "big-ticket" consumer items and for industrial products where the "human touch" is essential. It can be so effective that some marketers, if given a choice, might well abandon other forms of promotion and simply dispatch a salesperson to every customer's house or office! Unfortunately, this form of promotion is also the most expensive, and it can be difficult to ensure that all salespeople are delivering the same message with the same impact. In addition, even the very best salesperson would be hard pressed to sell products on behalf of a company that had failed to establish a desirable image through its other promotion activities. For these reasons, it is necessary to also consider other forms of promotion that either substitute for or complement personal selling activities. Chapter 19 provides a detailed discussion of the role of personal selling in a company's marketing strategy.

Table 16.2
A Comparison
of Elements
of the Promotion Mix

Promotional Element	Pros	Cons
Advertising	The marketer has control over what the message will say, when it will appear, and who is likely to see it.	Often expensive to produce and distribute. May have low credibility and/or be ignored by audience.
Sales promotion	Provides incentives to retailers to support one's products. Builds excitement for retailers and consumers. Encourages immediate purchase and trial of new products. Price-oriented promotions cater to price-sensitive consumers.	Short-term emphasis on immediate sales rather than a focus on building brand loyalty. The number of competing promotions may make it hard to break through the promotional clutter.
Public relations	Relatively low cost. High credibility.	Lack of control over the message that is eventually transmitted, and no guarantee that the message will ever reach the target. Hard to track the results of publicity efforts.
Personal selling	Direct contact with the customer gives the salesperson the opportunity to be flexible and modify the sales message to coincide with the customer's needs. The salesperson can get immediate feedback from the customer.	High cost per contact with customer. Difficult to ensure consistency of message when it is delivered by many different company representatives. The credibility of salespeople often depends on the quality of their company's image, which has been created by other promotion strategies.

Mass Appeals

Most of the company or product information we receive is delivered to many other people as well. Whether in the form of an announcement that is mailed to a few hundred local residents or a television commercial that is seen by millions, most marketing messages are delivered as mass communications.

■ *Advertising: Advertising* is nonpersonal communication that is paid for by an identified sponsor using mass media to inform or persuade an audience.[5] Advertising is for many the most familiar and visible element of the promotion mix. As we'll see in Chapter 17, this form of promotion runs the gamut from a line in the Yellow Pages to a lavish, multimillion-dollar television campaign.

Because it can convey such rich and dynamic images, advertising is often used to create and reinforce a distinctive brand identity. This helps marketers to realize their goal of persuading customers to select their product, as well as building bonds with buyers by presenting familiar brand images and logos time after time. Because the marketer controls the content of an ad, this promotion element is also very useful in communicating factual information about the product or reminding consumers that it has been a while since they used their favorite brand.

On the other hand, advertising sometimes suffers from a credibility problem, as cynical consumers tune out messages they think are biased because they are intended to sell them something. Advertising can also be very expensive, so great care must be taken to ensure that ad messages are not "wasted" but instead are noticed and absorbed by those consumers to whom they are directed.

■ *Sales promotion:* What does an official Rolling Stones tour jacket have in common with a cents-off coupon for Tide laundry detergent? Both are forms of *sales promotions,* marketing activities that are used to stimulate immediate sales by providing extra value or generating interest in a product. Sales promotions provide a form of mass appeal because they target groups of consumers or retailers to receive special offers or merchandise, invite these people to participate in some activity, or call attention to some event or product feature.

As we will see in Chapter 18, sales promotions can either be trade-oriented or consumer-oriented. A trade promotion often consists of some incentive to a retailer to stock or feature one's products, such as an attention-getting floor display. Some consumer promotions create interest in the form of a contest or a special event, such as an in-store appearance by a celebrity to promote the product. In 1996, a very visible promotional effort by Diet Coke capitalized on the enormous popularity of the TV sitcom "Friends" when the company distributed bottle caps with each of the show's main characters' names on them. Each week, a different character was shown drinking a bottle of Diet Coke in a commercial immediately after the show, and holders of caps with that person's name won a prize. Other promotions motivate consumers to buy a product by providing them with cents-off coupons or additional gifts if they buy the featured item. Sales promotions are valuable when promotion goals revolve around the need to inform consumers about a new product or when strategists want to remind people that they should continue to buy an old favorite.

Sales promotions give retailers incentives to move a company's products out the door, and they help to create excitement among consumers who are otherwise bored or overloaded with product advertising. On the other hand, some marketers are concerned that excessive reliance on sales promotions at the expense of advertising will reduce consumers' brand loyalty by getting them accustomed to choosing products that happen to be in the limelight or on sale rather than those that represent long-term value.

A recent promotion campaign for Nestlé's Raisinets candy illustrates how an assortment of consumer-oriented sales promotions can work together to build interest in a brand. Listeners to advertisements run on radio station KDWB in Minneapolis–St. Paul received invitations to an exclusive movie premiere sponsored by Nestlé. KDWB disc jockeys gave away passes to the movie, and the first 101 KDWB listeners carrying Raisinets wrappers to the theater got in free. Each moviegoer also entered a drawing for station T-shirts and suntan kits stamped with the Raisinets slogan, "Catch Some Rays." The grand prize was a vacation for two to "Catch Some Rays" in person. Using an assortment of promotion techniques ensured that the "Catch Some Rays" theme was reinforced in several different ways and reached consumers in situations where they would be receptive to the message.[6]

■ *Publicity and public relations:* As is also discussed in Chapter 18, *public relations* consists of marketing efforts or activities to portray an organization and its products positively by influencing the perceptions of various *publics,* including customers, government officials, and shareholders. These activities include writing press releases, staging events that will reflect favorably on the organization or that will influence the opinions of legislators or stock analysts, commissioning surveys of people's feelings about issues related to a product, and even putting a positive "spin" on negative news reports. Unlike sales promotions, public relations components of the promotion mix typically are not intended to stimulate a short-term increase in sales but instead to craft a positive image for the product or organization in the long term.

The big advantage of public relations is that when messages are successfully placed, they are more credible than if the same information appeared in a paid advertisement. As one marketing executive observed, "There's a big difference between hearing about a

SPOTLIGHT ON ETHICS

Blurring the Boundaries Between Editorial and Commercial Messages

It's getting a lot harder these days to tell whether a message is meant to entertain us or to sell us something, which means that the black-and-white distinction between paid advertising and sales promotions and nonpaid public relations and publicity is getting steadily grayer. Marketers are gradually erasing the line between a commercial and a show or news program. This poses some problems for consumers, who understandably have trouble separating biased product information from supposedly objective reporting.

Commercial messages increasingly are produced to appear like entertainment or news shows, thus boosting their credibility among consumers who may not realize that the actors are being paid to hawk a product during the show. The Turner Broadcasting System considered but rejected plans to run commercials resembling news interviews on its CNN and Headline News networks. A network spokesman commented, ". . . we believe advertorial advertising blurs the line between advertising and journalism." *

Despite these occasional objections, the boundaries between promotion and objective reporting are being crossed regularly. Let's look at some of the many variations on this technique.

■ *Program tie-in:* A sponsor agrees to buy advertising time in exchange for product exposure in the program. The CBS network recently arranged for a shot of a Coke vending machine to appear in a program called TV 101.†

■ *Program-length commercial:* Also known as an infomercial, this very popular technique is a paid message broadcast to a TV audience in a format resembling that of a legitimate program. Infomercials have been packaged as consumer news shows, as sitcoms, as talk shows with celebrity hosts, and as a series of endorsements from satisfied customers. These testimonials can be misleading; in some cases, what looks like an enthusiastic studio audience is really populated with paid actors.†

■ *Masked-art message:* A work of art or literature features brand-name products. Clairol made such an arrangement with Bantam romance novels. Each novel in the series featured a description of the heroine's hair color that matched shades in a new line of Clairol hair dyes, and the books also included coupons for the products.†

■ *Masked news:* A marketer distributes information about its products that masquerades as a news item. For example, a pharmaceutical company inserted reports about some of its products in copies of *USA Today* newspapers that were distributed to doctors attending an American Gastroenterological Association conference. These inserts were printed in the same style as the newspaper to give the impression that they were really a part of the paper.†

■ *Masked spokesperson:* An expert or celebrity who has a vested interest in a product advises others to use it. Wyeth-Ayerst Laboratories gives doctors 1000 miles in the American Airlines frequent-flyer program for every patient they put on a hypertension drug made by the company.†

■ *Product placement:* A brand-name product appears in a show for a fee (sometimes as much as $50,000!). The match between product and entertainment vehicle is often made by a placement specialist, who is hired by the product sponsor to review upcoming scripts for desirable opportunities. Perhaps the great product placement success story still belongs to Reese's Pieces; sales jumped by 65 percent after the candy appeared in the film *E.T.: The Extra-Terrestrial.*‡ In some cases scripts have actually been rewritten to feature a product. The movie *Rocky III* was changed to include a scene where Sylvester Stallone endorses Wheaties, and a scene in *Cocoon: The Return* was re-shot so that Quaker Instant Oatmeal could be displayed more prominently.†

*Stuart Elliott, "Advertising: Turner Officials Pull Back from Allowing CNN to Run Commercials that Imitate News Interviews," *The Wall Street Journal* (Oct. 6, 1993): D18.
†Siva K. Balasubramanian, "Beyond Advertising and Publicity: Hybrid Messages and Public Policy Issues," *Journal of Advertising* (Dec. 1994): 29–46.
‡Benjamin M. Cole, "Products That Want to Be in Pictures," *Los Angeles Herald Examiner* (March 5, 1985): 36.

product from a pitchman and from your trusted local anchorman."[7] On the other hand, the marketer has very little control over what information does get out or the form in which it will appear. In addition, it is hard to gauge how effective these efforts really are.

One important component of public relations is *publicity,* which calls attention to the organization in the form of interviews, favorable product reviews, personal recommendations, or media coverage of sponsored events. Publicity can help to build interest in a good, service, or event, such as when a local newspaper reporting on an upcoming concert features an interview with the band's lead guitarist around the time that tickets go on sale. Public relations experts also try to minimize the effects of negative publicity. For example, they might help to craft a response to explain why a band member was arrested on drug charges or to "put a good face" on reports that a company's much-touted new product would not be released on schedule. Finally, public relations experts try to maximize the impact of unexpected events that somehow involve the product in a favorable way. For example, athletic shoe manufacturer L.A. Gear benefited from a news report about a little girl in Tennessee who got lost and who was eventually found by rescue workers who followed the lights on her L.A. Twilights sneakers.[8]

PRODUCT AND PACKAGE DESIGN

As we saw in Chapters 9 and 10, a product is itself a form of communication. In addition to satisfying a need, its shape, color, and style help create a unique identity, and often these decisions are made with a specific target consumer in mind. For example, Honda Motor Company introduced to the Japanese market a model called the City that was deliberately designed to attract young drivers. The car featured a very high roof that made it stand out from others. This design, called "Tall Boy," gave the City the appearance of a toy, a quality that appealed to the childishness of Japan's young consumers at that time.[9]

A product's appearance is often a key feature that helps to determine whether it will stand out from the competition and whether customers will regard it as crude or sophisticated, modern or traditional, cheap or expensive, and so on. For example, consumer electronics manufacturer Goldstar commissioned a product design firm to create a new VCR player to help the company reposition itself as a higher-quality line, which in turn would justify higher prices.[10] This strategy illustrates how different elements of the marketing mix work together to communicate a message about the product.

In addition to the product itself, its package also tells a story. As we noted in Chapter 10, a package performs many important functions, such as protecting the product and allowing it to be efficiently transported. However, the package is also a communications tool. At the time of purchase, it can remind, inform, and persuade. At the time of use, it informs and reminds again, reinforcing the purchase decision.[11]

As a result of the intense competition for shoppers' attention, packaging is playing an even greater role in communicating product information and breaking through advertising clutter. Packaging is also increasing in importance because of the explosion of brand extensions in recent years—the package provides a "hook" that allows the new product to benefit from the name recognition of its parent.[12]

An interesting packaging strategy by Quidel Corporation provides a powerful illustration of how the same product can communicate very different messages. The company markets two pregnancy tests that are identical except for the packaging. Conceive brand features a smiling infant on the pink box and sells for $9.99. RapidVue features just brick-red lettering against a mauve background and sells for $3.00 less. Conceive is packaged to appeal to couples who *want* to have a child, whereas RapidVue is intended for those who are hoping for a negative test result![13]

WHEN CONSUMERS DO THE PROMOTING: WORD-OF-MOUTH COMMUNICATIONS

Ironically, some of the most persuasive marketing communications do not come from marketers at all. **Word-of-mouth communication,** or product-related information informally transmitted from one consumer to another, is often the single most influential

word-of-mouth communication: product-related information informally transmitted from one consumer to another

factor in informing people about a product and creating the desire to buy—or not buy—the good or service.

Word-of-mouth communication is *not* part of the promotion mix, because marketers can't easily control it, plan for it, or budget for it. Still, it is often a key factor that determines how a product is received in the market. When your friend tells you about how much she loved a new movie, restaurant, or car, you are likely to give her opinion considerable weight. After all, she's probably similar to you in a lot of ways, and she's not working on commission for the company, so she has no reason to distort her evaluations (unless she's secretly participating in a "member get a member" promotion, where customers receive discounts if they steer new prospects to the company!).

Word-of-mouth communication is a sword that cuts both ways. It can make or break a product, depending on whether people have good or bad things to say about it. And negative reports don't even have to be true to be damaging: Companies are often confronted with rumors that their products contain nasty ingredients or cause unpleasant side effects. For example, Nestlé had to spend more than $250,000 in a public relations effort to reassure consumers in Indonesia after a rumor spread that their products were made with pork fat, which is forbidden to the 160 million Muslim consumers in that country.[14]

Although marketers like to encourage positive word of mouth, they usually can't do much to create it other than making good products and hoping for the best. However, some clever public relations activities can help this process along. Chrysler launched its LH-series cars (Concorde, Dodge Intrepid, and Eagle Vision) in 1993 by lending them on weekends to 6000 community leaders in twenty-five cities. Ninety-eight percent of these people said they would recommend the models to friends, and the company sold out its entire production run for that year.[15] To encourage the use of its brand, Southern Comfort sent a series of personalized mailings to 28,000 bar owner/managers from celebrities such as Woody Harrelson, who played a bartender on "Cheers." The company also sponsored a bartender recipe contest that netted 3500 entries; presumably contestants would be eager to showcase their contribution by serving it to bar patrons.[16]

Managing the promotion mix

The marketing manager has many different promotion tools available, and his or her challenge is to identify the specific combination that will meet the company's objectives in the most effective and cost-efficient way. It is often hard to predict how effective each element will be, so this is easier said than done! Think of the manager as an artist who must choose just the right blend of pigments to produce a picture of the organization and its product that is pleasing to the public. To create such a picture, numerous decisions must be made about the best way to blend these elements.

In order to avoid winding up with a picture of the organization that is just a jumble of unrelated events and themes, the smart manager first develops a "sketch" of what he or she wants the picture to look like. A **promotion plan** is a framework for developing, implementing, and controlling the firm's promotion activities.[17] Just as with any other strategic decision-making process, the development of this plan includes several stages, as shown in Figure 16.1. Let's review each step.

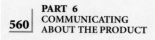

promotion plan: a document that outlines the strategies for developing, implementing, and controlling the firm's promotion activities

ESTABLISH PROMOTION OBJECTIVES

The whole point of developing a promotion strategy is to connect the marketing plan to consumers—to let them know that the organization has a product that has been developed to meet their needs in a timely and affordable way. It's bad enough when a product is developed that people don't want or need, but perhaps a bigger marketing sin is to have a product that they do want but to fail to inform or convince them of this!

Promotion Objectives Do Not Equal Marketing Objectives

It is important to remember that promotion objectives are *not* the same as marketing objectives. The marketing objectives spelled out in the marketing plan are typically stated in terms of concrete, measurable outcomes such as market share or volume of sales ex-

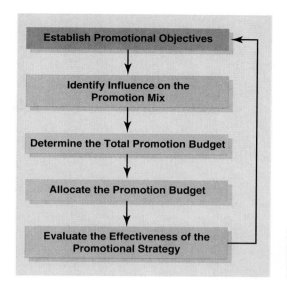

Figure 16.1
Stages in Developing the Promotion Mix

pected by the end of the next year. If these goals are realized, it will be because the company's promotion efforts work *along with other elements* of the marketing mix, such as product planning and pricing, to reach them.

Promotion objectives need to be defined in terms of the specific *communications tasks* that will deliver the desired message to the target audience. In some cases the primary goal is merely to build awareness for a new product, in others it is to provoke an immediate response, and in still other situations it is to instill a feeling of goodwill toward the company over a period of time. And although promotion is an extremely important part of the marketing mix, it can't do the job by itself. The best public relations campaign, sales pitch, or coupon in the world can't compensate for a poorly designed product, a boring package, or a product that isn't sold in the places where targeted consumers shop.

Rome Wasn't Built in a Day: Moving from Awareness to Purchase

As creative as some advertisements and salespeople are, it is unlikely that any promotion element could single-handedly cause a consumer who has never heard of a product suddenly to become aware of it, to decide he or she prefers it over competing products, and to buy it on the spot. (A possible exception is novelty or impulse items, where the product is bought on a whim.) More typically, the task of promotion is to move consumers along a path that starts with awareness, eventually leads to a purchase, and then helps to ensure that people will continue to buy the product in the future.

Think of this promotion road as an uphill climb, where each step is a bit harder than the one before. Relatively less effort is required at the early stages to accomplish such objectives as building awareness and getting people to understand what the product does. As the grade of the hill begins to get steeper, though, the later steps, which involve forming a preference for the product and actually buying it, get tougher. During this climb, many people drop out, so only a fairly small proportion of the target market is actually brought to the top of the hill to become loyal customers. Each step on this path entails different promotion objectives to "push" people to the next level.

To understand how this process works, consider how a company has to adjust its promotion objectives as it tries to establish a presence in the market for a new men's cologne called Hunk. Let's say that the primary target market for the cologne is single men aged eighteen to twenty-four who are very conscious of their appearance and who are into health, fitness, and working out. The company will want to rely to a greater extent on some promotion methods (such as advertising) and less on others (personal selling would not play a large role, *unless* the company decided to distribute the product through such channels as direct-sales organizations). Here are some steps the company might take that are consistent with the specific promotion objective that is relevant to each step of the process. These are summarized in Figure 16.2 (page 562).

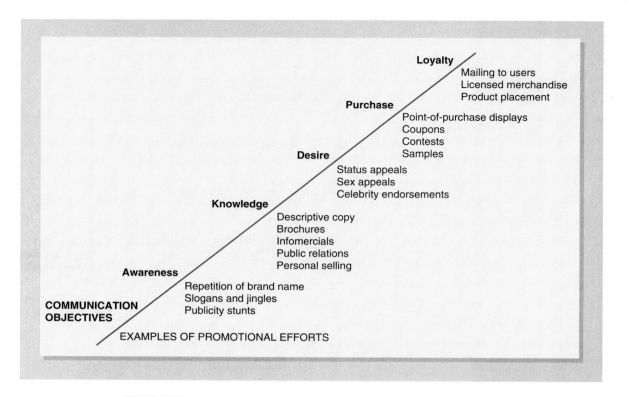

Figure 16.2
Up the Promotion Road

■ *Create awareness:* The first step is to make members of the target market aware that there's a new brand of cologne on the market. This would probably be accomplished by simple, repetitive advertising in magazines, on television, and/or on the radio that would prominently feature the brand name. The company might even undertake a *teaser campaign,* where interest is heightened by not revealing the exact nature of the product (perhaps newspaper ads simply proclaim, "Hunk is coming!"). The promotion objective might be to create an 80 percent awareness of Hunk cologne among men eighteen to twenty-four years old in the first two months.

■ *Inform the market:* The next step is to tell prospective users what benefits the new product has to offer—how it is positioned relative to other fragrances (see Chapter 8). Perhaps the cologne has a light, slightly mentholated scent that vaguely resembles that of liniments used in weightrooms after a workout session. Promotion would focus on communications that emphasize this position. The objective at this point might be to communicate the connection between Hunk and muscle building so that 75 percent of the target market is interested in the product.

■ *Create desire:* Once many members of the target market know about the brand, the next task is to create favorable feelings toward the product and to convince at least some portion of this group to prefer it over other colognes. Communications at this stage might emphasize splashy advertising spreads in magazines, perhaps including an endorsement by a well-known celebrity "hunk" like Arnold Schwarzenegger. The specific objective might be to create positive attitudes toward Hunk cologne among 50 percent of the target market and brand preference among 30 percent of the target market.

■ *Encourage trial:* As the expression goes, "the proof of the pudding is in the eating": The company now needs to get some of the men who have formed a preference for the product actually to splash it on. A promotion plan might encourage trial by mailing samples of Hunk to members of the target market, inserting "scratch-and-sniff" samples in body-building magazines, placing elaborate displays in stores that dispense money-saving coupons (perhaps a life-size cutout of Arnold Schwarzenegger holding a bottle of Hunk), or other sales promotions such as sponsoring a contest where the winner gets to have Arnold Schwarzenegger as his personal trainer for a day. The specific objective now might be to encourage trial of Hunk cologne among 25 percent of men eighteen to twenty-four years old in the first two months.

■ *Build loyalty:* Of course, the *real* "proof of the pudding" is loyalty: convincing customers to keep buying the cologne after they've gone through the first bottle. This allegiance certainly cannot be taken for granted. In addition to continuing to woo new users, subsequent promotion efforts must maintain ongoing communications with current users to reinforce the bond they feel with the product. As before, this will be accomplished with some mixture of strategies, such as periodic advertising, special events and gifts for users, and maybe even the development of a workout clothing line bearing the fragrance's logo. The objective might be to develop and maintain regular usage of Hunk cologne among 10 percent of men in the eighteen to twenty-four year age bracket.

IDENTIFY INFLUENCES ON THE PROMOTION MIX

Unfortunately, there is no such thing as one perfect promotion mix that the manager can pull off the shelf for every good or service. This mix must be carefully tailored to each unique situation: A combination that is perfect in one instance may be a total disaster in another. In order for the manager to make an intelligent decision, he or she must take into account how various characteristics of the situation are likely to influence which promotion tools will be more (and which less) effective.

Push versus Pull

One crucial issue in determining the promotion mix is whether the company is relying on a push strategy or a pull strategy. A company implementing a **push strategy** is seeking to move its products through the channel by convincing channel members to offer them. On the other hand, the company relying on a **pull strategy** is counting on consumers to learn about and express desire for their products, thus convincing retailers to respond to this demand by stocking these items.

If the company wants to push its products, it is more likely to use a combination of sales promotions and personal selling directed toward channel members. A pull strategy seeks instead to create desire with advertisements and promotions targeted to the final buyer rather than to the retailer.

Type of Product

What is being sold influences how it should be sold. Even though some salespeople claim they are good enough to "sell ice to Eskimos," some products lend themselves to personal contact whereas others are best sold in other ways. Industrial goods and services, as well as big-ticket consumer items, are likely to have a greater emphasis on personal selling in their promotion mix. Many consumer products, such as cologne, tend to rely more on advertising—especially since a certain brand is selected because of an image that has been created for it over time by the careful crafting of media messages.

Products that are heavily image-oriented, such as apparel, rely on fashion advertising and on sales promotions such as in-store appearances by designers and celebrities to make the desired impression. Price reductions and other similar sales promotions work best for frequently purchased packaged goods, where consumers don't see much of a difference among brands and are more likely to be influenced by the appeal of a bargain. Public relations efforts carry more of the load for large firms that are trying to create a positive image in the broader marketplace for the entire company as well as for its specific set of products.

Stage of the Product Life Cycle

The promotion mix must vary over time, because some elements are better at accomplishing the marketer's objectives at different times than are others. As we saw in the Hunk cologne example, the stage of the product life cycle influences the promotion mix.

push strategy: a promotion strategy in which a company tries to move its products through the channel by convincing channel members to offer them

pull strategy: a promotion strategy in which a company tries to convince consumers to want their products in anticipation that retailers will stock the items demanded

In the *introduction phase,* the realistic marketer knows that he or she cannot magically create a base of loyal users overnight. Instead, the objective is to build awareness of the product among consumers and to rely on a push strategy by convincing retailers to take a chance by stocking the new item. Advertising is the primary promotion tool for creating awareness, and a publicity campaign to generate news reports about the new product may help as well. Many marketers have successfully used a consumer sales promotion, such as giving away free samples to stimulate excitement and encourage people to try the product. Trade promotions give retailers reasons to gamble by devoting valuable shelf space to an unfamiliar item.

In the *growth phase,* promotions must start to focus on communicating specific product benefits. People (one hopes) have heard of the product at this point, so what they need to know is why they should choose it over others. Advertising typically increases, whereas sales promotions that encourage trial often decline because people are more willing to try the product without being offered an incentive to do so.

The opposite pattern often occurs during the *maturity phase,* by which time many people have tried or are using the product. As sales stabilize, the goal is to persuade people to switch from a competitor's product—often under conditions where they see few important differences among competitors and are buying out of habit. Sales promotions, particularly coupons and special price deals, increase.

All bets are off during the *decline phase.* As sales plummet, the company may dramatically reduce spending on all elements of the promotion mix. Sales are driven by the continued loyalty of a small group of users, who keep the brand alive until it is sold to another company or discontinued as part of a harvesting strategy (see Chapter 2). This may create a kind of self-fulfilling prophecy: People no longer hear about the product, so they stop buying it. This continued decline in sales further discourages the company from investing any more money in promotion, and the product may be left to wither on the vine. Alternatively, the company may decide to try to revive the brand and dedicate a modest budget to bringing it back from the dead.

Buyer Readiness

The promotion mix must be tailored to the market's level of interest and knowledge about the product. This level can range from consumers being unaware that the product exists to their being ready to make a purchase any minute. The stages in consumer decision making were described in Chapter 6. As a general rule, advertising and public relations are more influential in building awareness and providing knowledge about a product. As the buyer gets closer to making a decision, sales promotions and personal selling are often needed to close the sale.

Type of Buyer

Promotions must be developed with the needs of different types of buyers in mind. Business and organizational buyers, for example, rely on both company salespeople and specialized trade publications for information and assistance in ordering and using complex products. In contrast, consumers often are swayed by "glitzy" mass-media messages that employ celebrity endorsers or attractive models to give the product a certain aura.

DETERMINE THE TOTAL PROMOTION BUDGET

In an ideal world, setting the budget for promotion would be simple: Spend whatever it takes to accomplish the stated objectives. In reality, though, the budget is determined by "real-world" factors, one of which is the tendency to view communications costs as an *expense* rather than as an *investment* that will lead to greater profits in the future. One consequence of this logic is that when sales are declining or the company is operating in a difficult economic environment, it is often tempting to cut costs by reducing the money spent on advertising, promotions, and other "soft" activities whose contributions to the bottom line are hard to quantify.

Although sophisticated mathematical models have been developed to aid in the development of a budget, these approaches are not widely used and suffer from several limitations:

- Economic approaches to budgeting rely on *marginal analysis,* where the organization spends money on promotion as long as the revenues generated by these efforts continue to exceed the costs of the promotions themselves. This perspective assumes that promotions are always intended solely to increase sales, when in fact these activities may have other objectives, such as creating awareness or enhancing the overall image of the firm.

- These methods also assume a direct relationship between sales and promotion. This assumption ignores the effects of other aspects of the marketing mix, such as how widely the product is distributed and how it is priced relative to the competition. Because many other factors may influence consumers' choices, analysts continue to struggle with ways to demonstrate a direct effect between marketing communications and purchases.

- Finally, it is hard to know how best to measure the relationship between different promotion activities and sales. One problem is that the effects of promotions are often *lagged* over time. For example, a firm may have to spend a lot on promotion when it first launches a new product without seeing any return on this investment for quite a while.

Because of these limitations, most firms rely on rules of thumb when they actually get down to the business of setting a promotion budget. These procedures can be divided into basic types: top-down and bottom-up techniques.

Top-Down Techniques

As the name implies, top-down techniques involve spending decisions that originate in the upper echelons of a firm and filter down to lower levels. The overall dollar amount that the organization wishes to devote to promotion activities is established by top management, and this amount is then divided among departments. The problem is that the total amount allocated is not often based on any systematic analysis of the firm's objectives. Instead, it is usually arbitrarily based on some criterion, whether duplicating what was done last year or even (especially in small companies) giving promotion the "*leftovers*"—whatever remains after other expenses have been covered. (Not surprisingly, this decision-making rule is called the *all-you-can-afford method.*)

- *Percentage-of-sales method:* The most commonly used top-down procedure is the *percentage-of-sales method,* in which the promotion budget is based either on last year's sales or on estimates for this year's sales. The percentage specified is often based on an industry average, a figure that can usually be obtained from trade associations. An advantage of the percentage-of-sales approach is that it reminds the organization of the connection between spending on promotion and resulting profits.

    Unfortunately, this method may be self-defeating, because it implies that promotion outlays are *caused* by sales rather than viewing sales as the *outcome* of promotion efforts. If sales are low, perhaps more should be spent on promotion, not less! Another drawback is that basing budgets on what has happened in the past fails to take into account factors in the current environment that make next year's prospects different from last year's (such as a change in economic conditions or a rival's introduction of a new product).

- *Competitive-parity method:* The *competitive-parity method* is a fancy way to say, "Keep up with the Joneses." In other words, match whatever competitors are spending. Some marketers feel this approach is justified, because the decision simply mirrors the best thinking of others in the business.

    Again, this method is often less than satisfactory. It frequently results in each player simply maintaining the same market share year after year—each is looking to the other for guidance! This method also assumes that the same dollars spent on promotion by two different firms will yield the same results, which ignores the fact that good promotions depend on good ideas and creative executions that can't be guaranteed by money alone. Firms certainly need to monitor their competitors' promotion activities, but they must combine this information with their *own* objectives and abilities.

Bottom-Up Techniques

The problem with top-down techniques is that budget decisions are based more on established practices than on promotion objectives. A better approach is to begin at the beginning: Identify promotion goals and allocate enough money to accomplish them. That is what bottom-up techniques attempt to accomplish. For example, some marketers construct a *payout plan* that attempts to predict the revenues and costs associated with a product over several years and matches promotion expenditures to this pattern (spending more on promotion in the first year to build market share, for example, and then relatively less in later years once this initial goal has been achieved).

■ *Objective-task method:* This bottom-up logic is also at the heart of the *objective-task method,* which is gaining in popularity. Using this approach, the firm first defines the specific communications goals it hopes to achieve, such as increasing by 20 percent the number of consumers who are aware of the brand. It then tries to figure out how much and what kinds of promotion efforts it will take to meet that goal.

This is the most rational approach; it obliges managers to specify what their objectives are and attach a dollar amount to them. On the other hand, this is often very hard to do. How can you predict in advance exactly how much it will cost, say, to convince 30 percent of a target market to try a new product in the next six months?

ALLOCATE THE PROMOTION BUDGET

Once the organization decides how much to spend on promotion, it must divide its budget among the elements in the promotion mix. Can promotion objectives be met best if 80 percent of the budget goes to advertising or should the budget be split evenly between advertising and sales promotion?

In today's marketplace, consumer promotions are playing a bigger role in marketing strategies. As MasterCard's vice president of promotions observed, marketers who once relied on promotions solely to create a short-term response now see them as "a permanent, integral part of the brand."[18] The shift began during the economic downturn of the early 1990s when profit pressures forced companies to focus on ringing up sales. Today, consumer promotions have displaced media advertising as the backbone of marketing communications; since the beginning of the decade, the share of marketing budgets devoted to promotions has replaced that devoted to media advertising as the biggest-ticket item.[19] For example, Nestlé, the giant Swiss company, shifted about 20 percent of its advertising budget into sales promotion and direct-response efforts over a two-year period after the company determined that its promotion dollars would be more effective there.[20]

Attempts to reach consumers where they work and play are causing many marketers to put more of their communications dollars into sponsorship of live events, such as sports and concerts, and to concentrate more on interacting with shoppers by developing elaborate in-store messages (called *point-of-purchase advertising*). After McDonald's found that its best customers are sports fans, for example, the company decided to sponsor the 1994 World Cup soccer games as its first global promotion.[21]

These allocations must eventually be split further. For example, an advertising budget must be divided among spending for radio advertising, television advertising, print advertising, and so on. NBO Stores divides its promotion budget approximately as 40 percent, 30 percent, and 30 percent split among newsprint, TV, and direct mail.[22]

Decisions regarding the best use of promotional resources must be faced by for-profit and not-for-profit organizations alike. For example, Partnership for a Drug-Free America is a group dedicated to educating people about drug abuse. Although the organization is best known for its eye-catching advertisements (such as a picture of a fried egg sizzling in a pan with the caption "This is your brain on drugs"), it is now turning to other media to drive home its messages. In cooperation with the Toy Manufacturers of America, it is placing bumper stickers on toy cars and trucks with messages like "Drugs Are a Dead End." It is producing videos that play as people pump gasoline, and it is working with a major school supplies company to produce book covers with anti-drug messages and distribute them to high school students all across the country.[23]

Several factors influence how companies divide up the promotion pie.

- *Organizational factors:* Characteristics of the specific firm influence how monies are allocated. These include the complexity and formality of the company's decision-making process, preferences within the company for advertising versus sales promotions or other elements in the promotion mix, past experiences (good and bad) with specific promotion vehicles, as well as the "comfort level" of the firm's advertising and promotion agencies with developing different kinds of marketing communications.

- *Market potential:* Consumers in some markets will be more likely to be interested in buying the product than will consumers in other markets. For example, the marketers of Hunk might find that men in blue-collar occupations would be more likely to be interested in the product than men in professional occupations. It makes sense for marketers to allocate more resources to promote their products in areas where they expect resulting sales to be higher.

- *Market size:* As a rule, larger markets are more expensive places in which to promote. The costs of buying media exposure (such as spots on local television) are higher in major metropolitan areas, and the segment to which messages are being targeted may be more spread out and thus harder to reach. On the other hand, the sheer density of highly populated areas makes it easier to reach large numbers of consumers at the same time.

CREATE AND IMPLEMENT THE PROMOTION MIX

Once the promotion objectives and budget have been determined, it is time to create the promotion mix elements. This means deciding which elements should be used and creating a plan for those selected.

Not all elements of the promotion mix are equally appropriate for all marketing situations. A personal sales call may be essential in marketing major pieces of industrial equipment, but it would be silly for Colgate to hire door-to-door salespeople to promote toothbrushes and toothpaste. Likewise, consumer sales promotion techniques such as coupons and premiums are very important to Procter & Gamble's sales of Tide and Dawn and Ivory soap, but those same activities would cheapen the image of Rolex or Mercedes. In addition to specifying which of the promotion mix elements to use, marketers must decide how much emphasis to place on each. A promotion strategy for a new brand of beer may require spending millions of dollars on prime-time television advertising, whereas introducing a new electric motor drive for use in construction of large buildings requires only some minimal advertising in professional periodicals.

The next step is to plan and execute the advertising, sales promotion, or whatever promotion will be used. In Chapters 17, 18, and 19, we will discuss the types of activities included in these strategies and how the different promotion plans are created.

EVALUATE THE EFFECTIVENESS OF THE PROMOTION MIX

The final step in managing the promotion mix is to decide whether the plan is working. The marketer needs to determine whether the promotion objectives have been adequately translated into marketing communications, whether the right mix has been used to reach the target market, and even whether the original target market is in fact the appropriate one to aim for.

It would be nice if a promotion manager could simply report, "Our new $3 million promotion campaign for our revolutionary glow-in-the-dark surfboards resulted in $15 million in new sales!" Unfortunately, life is not so easy. Because there are so many other factors at work in the marketing environment, it is very difficult to isolate the effect of any particular one on sales. For example, those $15 million in new sales may have been caused by such other events as a manufacturing problem encountered by a rival board manufacturer, a coincidental photograph of an up-and-coming movie star riding one of the boards, or even renewed interest in surfing among burned-out baby boomers looking for a new thrill.

Still, there are ways to monitor and evaluate the company's promotion efforts. The catch is that the effectiveness of some forms of promotion is easier to determine than that of others. As a rule, sales promotions are the easiest to evaluate; these activities occur during a fixed period of time and can be directly tied to sales. For example, coupon redemption rates quickly reveal whether customers are responding to the promotion by clipping and using the coupons. And if purchases peaked during the time a sweepstakes was running, then it is fairly safe to conclude that this event had the desired effect.

Advertising effectiveness is a bit harder to gauge. Research can be done to measure brand awareness, recall of product benefits communicated through advertising, and even the image of the brand before and after an advertising campaign. Some of these techniques are discussed in Chapter 5. The performance of salespeople in different territories can be analyzed and compared, though again it is often difficult to rule out other factors that make some salesforces more effective than others. Public relations activities are perhaps the hardest to assess because they are cumulative. They rely on inducing favorable media exposure over time, so the effects are more subtle. In Chapter 18 we will consider techniques that can be used to evaluate these efforts.

THE PROMOTION SUPERHIGHWAY: MORE THAN ONE ROUTE TO SUCCESS

Now that we've identified the set of tools with which marketers can construct a promotion strategy, it's time to explore the specific ways in which the paths between producers and consumers are built. We'll start by considering the factors that are necessary for communication to occur. Then we'll take a detour down a slightly different road, presenting new developments in promotion activities that are changing the way this process works. As we'll see, the traditional approach can be thought of as a one-way street, where marketers talk to customers and hope they are listening. The newer perspective is more like a two-lane highway, where marketers solicit input from customers and use this information to pave the road to business success.

THE TRADITIONAL COMMUNICATIONS MODEL: THE WELL-TRAVELED ROAD TO PROMOTION

Marketers are used to talking to passive groups of consumers on a "one-way, dead-end" street, using one method of communication at a time. The traditional perspective on communications views the consumer as the final link in a chain of events: A message is transmitted via some medium from a sender to a receiver who (it is hoped) is paying attention and understands what the sender is trying to say. Regardless of the form messages take (whether a lively TV commercial for Pepsi, a hat with a Caterpillar tractor logo on it, or a sales pitch from a Mary Kay representative), they share some basic characteristics. Each is designed to capture the attention of the receiver, invoke his or her needs, and offer a way to satisfy them.

Any way that marketers reach out to consumers, from a simple highway billboard to a customized message sent via electronic mail to a busy executive, can be understood by considering the basic pieces of the communications process. The *communications model* specifies that a number of elements are necessary for communication to be achieved. These are a source, a message, a medium, and a receiver.

The communications model is shown in Figure 16.3. Each element involves the need to make important decisions about how the message will be executed, who will do it, and what it will look like. In this section, we will review these elements and consider the types of decisions that must be made for effective communications to occur.

Encoding: Creating Meaning

It is one thing for a marketer to create an idea of a product's image in his or her mind and quite another to find a way to express that idea so that other people get

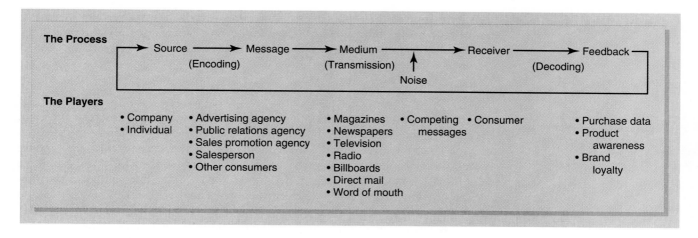

Figure 16.3
The Communications Model

roughly the same picture when they hear the brand name or see the bottle. The process of translating an idea into a form of communication that will convey meaning is called **encoding.**

There are many ways to encode the same underlying idea. Finding the best way is one of the great challenges that marketing communicators face. For example, competing marketers may want to convey the idea that their new fragrance is designed to be worn by fashionable, sophisticated women. One manufacturer may encode this idea by naming a perfume after a glamorous movie star like Elizabeth Taylor. Another may encode the same idea by designing a uniquely shaped perfume bottle. A third may rely on dramatic colors, poses, and captions in ads to convey the same idea.

To do a better job of choosing the specific symbols that will convey the desired product qualities, some marketers use principles from the field of *semiotics,* or the study of how symbols communicate meaning.[24] For example, consider how financial services companies like to represent themselves with different animal symbols. The Dreyfus Corporation uses a lion in all of its marketing communications. The company expects that consumers' associations of this animal with such characteristics as fearlessness and being "king of the jungle" will transfer to their feelings about Dreyfus. Of course, this lion has to fight it out with other companies' mascots, such as the Merrill Lynch bull and the ram used by T. Rowe Price.

The Source

The **source** is the organization or individual sending the message. Of course, a bank, an airline, or a university cannot speak for itself, so marketers must choose a real person (such as company president Dave Thomas for Wendy's fast-food restaurants), hire an actor or model (such as Cindi Crawford for Pepsi), or create a character (such as Mr. Peanut for Planters Peanuts) who will *represent* the source.

The choice of a spokesperson is not as easy as it seems. Common sense tells us that the same words uttered by different people can have very different effects. The source can be chosen because she or he is an expert, is good-looking, is famous, or even is a "typical" consumer who is both likeable and trustworthy. In general, a message source must be either attractive or believable to create the desired impact.

How to decide which characteristic of a source is most important? One principle is that there should be a match between the source and the type of product being promoted. Experts are effective at changing attitudes toward technical or complex products such as computers that have high *performance risk* (that is, they may be complex and not work as expected). Celebrities and physically attractive models are more effective when they focus on appearance-related products or items such as jewelry and furniture that have high *social risk;* their use will affect others' impressions of the owner. Finally, "typical" consumers, who are appealing sources because of their similarity to the recipient, tend to be most effective when endorsing everyday products that are *low in risk,* such as cookies.[25] It also

encoding: the process of translating an idea into a form of communication that will convey meaning

source: an organization or individual that sends a message

helps if the source's "claim to fame" is somehow consistent with the product. When former baseball pitcher Jim Palmer endorsed Jockey International products, his athleticism was instrumental in reassuring men that it was acceptable for them to wear skimpy underwear in unusual colors.[26]

The Message

The **message** is the communication in physical form sent from a sender to a receiver. The message should ideally accomplish four objectives (though a single message can rarely do all of these): It should get Attention, hold Interest, create Desire, and produce Action. These communications goals are known as the *AIDA model.* (We'll talk more about the AIDA model in Chapter 17.) Here we'll review some different forms the message can take and suggest how the information in the message can best be structured to get the point across.

■ *Type of appeal:* There are many different ways to say the same thing. This means that marketers must choose what type of appeal they will use when encoding the message. To illustrate how different choices can result in very different communications compare two strategies selected by rival car companies to promote very similar automobiles. A few years ago, Toyota and Nissan both introduced a large luxury car that sold for over $40,000. The two companies chose very different ways to communicate their products' attributes. Toyota's advertising for its Lexus model used a *rational appeal,* which focused on the objective reasons to choose one alternative over others. Toyota created ads that emphasized the large number of technical advancements incorporated in the car's design. Print ads were dominated by copy describing these engineering features. This approach is often effective for promoting products that are technically complex and that represent a substantial investment.

In sharp contrast, Nissan's controversial campaign for its Infiniti model used an *emotional appeal,* an attempt to arouse feelings in the consumer that will translate into liking for the product. The new car was introduced with a series of print and television ads that did not discuss the vehicle at all. The ads instead focused on the Zen-like experience of driving and featured long shots of serene landscapes. As one executive involved with the campaign explained, "We're not selling the skin of the car; we're selling the spirit."[27]

The goal of an emotional appeal is to establish a connection between the product and the consumer, a strategy known as *bonding.*[28] Many companies turned to this strategy after realizing that consumers do not find many differences among brands, especially those in well-established, mature categories. Ads for products ranging from cars (Lincoln Mercury) to cards (Hallmark) focus instead on emotional aspects.

Fear appeals, however, highlight the negative consequences that can occur unless the consumer changes a behavior or an attitude. This strategy is widespread, with fear appeals used in over 15 percent of all television ads. Fear appeals seem to be most effective when the consumer is already afraid of the problem discussed in the ad. The threats are not generally excessive, and a solution to the problem should be presented (otherwise, consumers will tune out the ad because they can do nothing to solve the problem). An example of fear appeals is a series of posters that were placed around Holland, each with a picture of young men with mutilated hands or faces as the result of playing with fireworks.

■ *Structure of the appeal:* Marketers may be thought of as storytellers who supply visions of reality similar to those provided by authors, poets, and artists. These communications take the form of stories, because the product benefits they describe are intangible and must be given tangible meaning by expressing them in concrete form.

One important way to describe different types of stories is to classify each as either a *drama* or a *lecture.*[29] As you are well aware from sitting through many college courses, a lecture is like a speech. The source speaks directly to

the audience in an attempt to inform them about a product or idea—or persuade them to buy it. In contrast, a drama is similar to a play or movie. Whereas a lecture holds the viewer at arm's length, a drama draws the viewer into the action. The characters address the audience only indirectly; they interact with each other about a good or service in an imaginary setting. Thus ads for the Infiniti attempted to transform the "driving experience" into a mystical, spiritual event.

Many marketing messages are similar to debates or trials, wherein someone presents arguments and tries to convince the receiver to shift his or her opinion accordingly. The way the argument is presented can be very important. Let's look at several.

1. *One versus two-sided arguments:* Most messages merely present one or more positive attributes about the product or reasons to buy it. These are known as *supportive arguments.* An alternative is to use a *two-sided message,* wherein both positive and negative information is presented. Even though research has indicated that two-sided ads can be quite effective, they are not widely used.[30]

2. *Drawing conclusions:* A related issue is whether the argument should draw conclusions or should merely present the points, permitting consumers to arrive at their own decisions. Should the message just say "Our brand is superior"? Or should it add "You should buy our brand"? The answer seems to depend on the consumer's motivation to process the ad and on the complexity of the arguments. If the message is personally relevant, people will pay attention to it and spontaneously draw conclusions. However, if the arguments are hard to follow or the person's motivation to follow them is lacking, it is safer for the ad to make those conclusions explicit.[31]

3. *Comparative advertising:* In 1971, the Federal Trade Commission issued guidelines that encouraged advertisers to name competing brands in their ads. This action was taken to improve the information available to consumers in ads.[32]

In **comparative advertising,** a message identifies two or more specifically named or recognizably presented brands and compares them in terms of one or more specific attributes.[33] For example, Schering-Plough claimed that "New OcuClear relieves three times longer than Visine," and Bristol-Myers Squibb stated that "New Liquid Vanish really does clean tough rust stains below the water line better than Lysol."

The Medium

No matter how the message is encoded, it must then be transmitted via a **medium,** a communications vehicle used to reach members of a target audience. This vehicle can be television, radio, magazines, personal contact, a billboard, or even a product logo printed on free coffee mugs distributed at a local gas station. Marketers have many forms of media to choose from when deciding how to transmit their messages. The pros and cons of these alternatives in terms of relative cost, ease of use, and the like are considered in later chapters. For now, keep in mind that insofar as possible, the attributes of the medium should be matched to those of the product. For example, magazines with high prestige are more effective at communicating messages about overall product image and quality, whereas specialized, "expert" magazines do a better job of conveying factual information.[34] In an attempt to exert even more control over the viewing environment, some marketers are distributing glossy magazines to supplement conventional advertising media. This strategy virtually ensures a friendly environment, because ads appear in a medium produced by the advertisers. Recent examples include *Colors* from Benetton, *Elements* from Timberland, and *Profit* from IBM.[35]

The Receiver

Communication cannot occur unless a **receiver** is there to intercept the message. Assuming that the customer is even paying attention (a big assumption in our overloaded, media-saturated society), the meaning of the message is interpreted in light of that individual's unique experiences. The process of assigning meaning to the message by a receiver is called **decoding.** We hope that the target consumer will decode the message the way we intended, though this does not always work out so well. For example, you may think that a college student has to love an ad that uses a hit song from Pearl Jam as background, but the person who has just broken up with someone who played the band's CDs constantly may have another opinion!

One important factor that determines whether a message will get through is the receiver's level of *involvement* with the message and/or the product that is the object of the message. The chances of grabbing the receiver's attention are improved when the source is someone he or she likes or knows, when the message is creatively executed, and when the medium is one that the receiver is motivated to spend time looking at or listening to. Furthermore, it helps if the subject of the message is something that is personally relevant. The most enticing shampoo ad in the world probably won't be noticed by a bald man!

Noise

The communications model also acknowledges that messages have to compete with many other things to get through to a receiver. They often are blocked by **noise,** which is anything that interferes with effective communication. Noise may be caused by competing messages or by other things going on in the environment at the time the message is transmitted, such as a receiver whose attention is diverted from listening to a radio ad because she's having a conversation with a friend.

Feedback

To complete the communications loop, **feedback** is received by the source. The source uses the reactions of the receiver to gauge the effectiveness of the appeal and ideally to fine-tune the message so that it will do a better job of conveying the intended ideas in the future.

Although it is often hard to identify a single factor that shapes customers' reactions to a product, marketers try to collect feedback by evaluating such factors as changes in the brand's sales volume after a promotion campaign, people's awareness or knowledge of a brand before and after they have been exposed to a message, and even whether people can recall being exposed to the message at all.

Two drawbacks of traditional promotion methods are that feedback is often difficult to measure and that customers' reactions to the message are not sufficiently integrated into ongoing promotions. That is where newer techniques based on more interactive feedback come in. Let's take a look at how these approaches are transforming promotion activities from a one-way road to a two-lane highway.

REDRAWING THE COMMUNICATIONS ROAD MAP: INTERACTIVE MARKETING

Most forms of promotion involve mass communication, wherein a message is simultaneously transmitted to a large number of people. A television commercial is broadcast to thousands or even millions of people at a time, a newspaper that reports some news about a company-sponsored event is sold throughout a metropolitan area, and cents-off coupons are mailed to thousands of households. Even a "flesh-and-blood" salesperson often delivers a standard "pitch" to anonymous shoppers without knowing very much about their individual characteristics and needs.

The problem with many traditional promotion strategies is that it's very difficult to determine whether the message is having the desired effect and even whether it is getting through to the target market. Some proportion of receivers may pay attention to the message, and of this number a smaller percentage will be interested enough to consider acting on what they hear or see. Consumers are exposed to so many different marketing communications urging them to BUY NOW! that most messages simply get lost in the clutter. Because of these difficulties, we are witnessing a profound change in promotion practices, as many organizations are choosing to build a new road to connect them more intimately with recipients that they have some reason to believe will want to hear from them and—most important—to talk back to them. This road is called **interactive marketing,** wherein customized marketing communications elicit a measurable *response* from receivers.

Interactive marketing techniques range in sophistication from an automated teller machine (ATM) at a bank, which to some extent tailors the content of each communication to the needs of a particular customer, to an automated clipping service on the Internet that provides each account holder with information about research topics that he or she has specified in advance.[36] Indeed, the ATM is just the first salvo in the banking industry's battle to make financial services truly interactive. One recent demonstration of these efforts is a demo CD/ROM produced for Wells Fargo Bank. The disk demonstrates how Wells Fargo's online home banking can save time and depicts humorous real-life situations. There are interactive examples of how the product works that illustrate the ease with which transactions can be made. Of the people who reviewed the disk, 20 percent ordered the service.[37] Let's take a closer look at the components of interactive marketing.

Customizing the Message: De-Mass Marketing

To improve the abilities of organizations to offer goods and services that better match the characteristics of targeted individuals, the mass market is steadily being sliced into smaller and smaller pieces. Promotion messages increasingly are being tailored to the needs of specific consumers, who in turn will be more responsive to information that is directly relevant to their interests (the discussion on micromarketing in Chapter 8 also addresses these developments). Even the Coca-Cola Company, which has long been known for extravagant network productions, is beginning to abandon its strategy of running big-budget mass market commercials. One recent campaign, produced by Creative Artists Agency, has twenty-four ads in many moods and styles developed for twenty different TV networks. These range from one done in a "quick-cut" style for MTV to a spot intended to appeal to teenage boys and called Spaceship, which imitates "Star Trek: The Next Generation."[38]

In a truly interactive marketing environment, promotion efforts will look more like door-to-door selling than like television advertising. They will focus on one customer at a time and try to sell that customer as many products as possible. Rather than competing

interactive marketing: a promotion practice in which customized marketing communications elicit a measurable response from individual receivers

for market share, the interactive marketer competes for *share of customer*. This new philosophy was nicely described by an executive who is in charge of exploring interactive marketing applications for Leo Burnett, a major advertising agency:

> There's a metaphor here: Because of technology, what advertising started as—one guy with a bullhorn standing 300 yards from the crowd, who had to yell to sell, had to keep his sales pitch real general for the whole audience—technology brings him closer and closer to the crowd. He can lower his voice now, and talk to the really key customers; and they can talk back, because he's close enough to talk to them without having to yell. So you lower your voice, you target your audience better, you become less manipulative in your advertising.[39]

To appreciate this trend toward fine-tuning communications, consider that in 1993 alone, the long-distance telephone company MCI ran more than fifty different commercials on American television stations—not counting specialized spots on Chinese, Hispanic, and Russian TV.[40] MCI's logic is simple: Expensive network television commercials are seen by millions of people, but many of these viewers are probably not very much interested in the product advertised. Indeed, they may be using the opportunity of a commercial break to grab a snack! In contrast, the average commercial on the many specialized cable channels that are being developed, such as the Military Channel and the Therapy Channel, may reach only 30,000 people. However, those who do make the effort to tune in are much more likely to be interested in what they see. As a result, advertisers can buy a TV spot cheaply and communicate with a motivated audience that will be more receptive to what they are selling.

As we saw in the earlier discussion of the communications model, a recipient's level of involvement with a message helps determine how receptive he or she will be to what is said. The greater the extent to which a recipient can identify with the message, the greater the probability of his or her making a response. Now, to round out our understanding of what interactive marketing is all about, we need to make an important distinction between two *levels* of response, or feedback.

Levels of Interactive Response

The key to understanding the dynamics of interactive marketing is to consider exactly what is meant by a response. Recall that the goals of promotion include, *but are not limited to,* a purchase. Other objectives include building awareness, informing, reminding, and developing a long-term relationship. Therefore, a transaction is *one* type of response, but forward-thinking marketers realize that customers can interact with them in other valuable ways as well. For this reason it is helpful to distinguish between two basic types of feedback.

- *First-order response:* In Chapter 15, we saw that direct-marketing vehicles such as catalogs and home shopping television shows increasingly are playing a major role in nonstore retailing. These techniques are interactive—if successful, they result in an order, which is definitely a response! Let's think of a product offer that directly yields a transaction as a *first-order response*. In addition to providing revenue, sales data are valuable sources of feedback that enable marketers to gauge the effectiveness of their promotion efforts.

- *Second-order response:* However, a marketing communication does not have to result immediately in a purchase to be an important component of interactive marketing. Promotion messages can prompt useful responses from customers, even though these recipients do not necessarily place an order immediately after being exposed to the communication. Customer feedback that is generated in response to a promotion message but is not in the form of a transaction is a *second-order response.*

A second-order response may take the form of a request for more information about a good, service, or organization, or it might be a "wish list" from the customer that specifies the types of product information he or she would like to get in the future. This response may even be in the form of recommendations for other potential customers: MCI's Friends and Family program, for example, offers a 20 percent discount to customers who give them the names of people they call regularly. The phone company then targets these people with promotion messages to get *them* to switch to MCI.

A second-order response program called the Pepperidge Farm No Fuss Pastry Club illustrates how one firm communicates directly with users without trying to make an immediate sale. The club boasts more than 30,000 members who have been recruited through a combination of promotion efforts, including a magazine mail-in offer, an offer on packages of Pepperidge Farm products, publicity created by news reports about the club, and a sign-up form available in grocery stores. Pepperidge Farm uses surveys to determine members' attitudes toward issues related to its business, and the company also collects valuable information on how these people actually use frozen puff pastry products.[41] Though the company's immediate goal is not to generate the first-order response of selling frozen pastry, it knows that the second-order responses received from club members will result in loyal customers over time—and will lead to many more first-order responses down the line as a result.

We usually assume that one goal of any promotion campaign is to get more customers. Interactive marketers often operate with the opposite goal in mind: to *reduce* their customer base! No, they have not lost their sanity—they know that their efforts will be most effective when they are communicating only with customers who are interested in what they have to promote. The amount of effort required to sell the same item gets progressively greater as the target's interest in it gets lower. Thus a second-order response may take the form of a request not to receive any more information at all! An expression of no interest is valuable information because it enables the firm to concentrate its resources on those customers who are the most likely to consider buying.

Interactive marketing allows the company to screen, or qualify, potential buyers, then follow up with other promotion messages directed only to people it has reason to believe will consider making a purchase. For example, a common practice is to call or write to potential customers with a request that they indicate whether they have any interest in learning more about the product. Those who respond affirmatively are then contacted by a salesperson, who knows in advance that the prospect will be expecting his or her call. This two-step approach is especially useful for smaller firms that cannot afford large promotion budgets. These companies can maximize the efficiency of a small salesforce by first sending targeted direct mail to prospects and then following up with carefully timed phone calls to deliver a "one-two" sales punch.[42]

In other contexts, interactive marketing may involve sending messages to people in an effort to involve them in a grassroots political or social movement, soliciting ideas for new products or improving current ones, or even inviting feedback on new ways to use existing products. As one very relevant example of interactive marketing, note that this book benefited from many suggestions made by an Electronic Advisory Panel of professors from over twenty universities, who contributed via the Internet their ideas about what should go into a marketing textbook.

Interactive Promotion Vehicles

When they hear the word *interactive*, many people think of sophisticated CD/ROMs or surfing on the Internet. Although advances in computers and telecommunications technology make interactive marketing easier, in reality this interactive capability is available in virtually *all* promotion vehicles, including rudimentary space ads in newspapers, response cards used to activate product warranties, and sweepstakes entry forms.

The following are some examples of different types of interactive promotion media and of how marketers are beginning to incorporate the feedback they receive from these messages into improved, finely tailored offerings that better match the needs of individual customers.

■ *Mail:* Some companies maintain an active mail correspondence with their customers. One popular technique is to create a fan club for the product; in addition to organizations devoted to the adoration of Barbie dolls and Mustang cars, there are even clubs for lovers of peanut butter and catfish! A typical program is run by McCormick Canada, which uses its McCormick Dinner Club to promote new ways to use its line of spices. More than 70,000 Canadian homemakers receive three mailings a year, including newsletters, recipe cards, coupons, and new-product samples.[43]

- *Television:* To promote its 1995 Tercel model, Toyota tried its first infomercial to help it stand out from such competitors as Civic, Neon, and Saturn. The program features comments from young Tercel buyers to attract the target audience (people eighteen to thirty-five years old). About 7000 people in two test markets responded to an invitation to call a toll-free number for more information about the car. In one test version initially shown only in the Los Angeles area, callers were offered two movie tickets and dinner for two at a restaurant as an incentive to inquire about the car. When that offer pulled twice as many responses as other versions, Toyota decided to include a similar one when it rolled out the infomercial nationally.[44]

- *Radio:* A little-used technology called the *radio data system* (R.D.S.) allows a radio station to transmit data on the unused portion of its frequency, known as a subcarrier. The system has been adopted in Europe by the British Broadcasting Corporation and is slowly coming to America. R.D.S. is the concept behind Coupon Radio, a car radio system now being tested that lets listeners "capture" information and give stations and advertisers feedback about their choices. If the system is found to be viable, then a driver who hears, for example, a new song he or she likes would be able to request more information about the musicians. Respondents could also get the names and addresses of retailers that sell an advertised product.[45]

- *Telephone:* The technique of telemarketing is widely used to solicit product purchases and charitable donations. However, the telephone can also be used to generate second-order responses: requests for information that are actually initiated by the customer. For example, NBO Stores averages about 100 incoming calls a day on its toll-free number, which provides its customers with information about the closest retail location to them and describes specific store events.[46] The Butterball Turkey Talkline has become the brand's principal marketing tool; the company receives about 25,000 calls during the Thanksgiving season from anxious cooks who want personal cooking advice from a home economist. Butterball then stays in touch with callers through the year by sending them recipe booklets and Butterball calendars.[47] Other companies contact potential customers by phone with the intention of convincing them to preview a product at home and decide later whether they want to make a purchase—this selling strategy is called a *soft offer.*[48]

- *Computer media:* As we saw in Chapter 15, home shopping networks are already providing an alternative to purchasing products in stores. However, the potential for second-order responses is just beginning to be realized. QVC Networks, for example, is working on plans to turn the home computer into a shopping tool by developing software that consumers can use to scan databases for the latest information on products from videocassette recorders to mutual funds. These "shopping assistants" could be given specific orders, for example, to find lamps under $50 or all sporty cars painted cherry red. As QVC's executive in charge of interactive technology observed, "The key is personal relevancy. The carpet-bombing mentality of advertising does not make much sense here."[49]

- *Kiosks:* Passport Plus, an interactive multimedia travel information system developed for high-traffic public areas by Lunar Communications, is offering to carry ads placed by travel agencies for as little as $75 per month. So far, two kiosks have been set up in the Philadelphia area, including one at Drexel University, and more are planned elsewhere in the Northeast. They feature touch screen controls that users, at no charge, can manipulate to view multimedia displays and print out information on travel destinations, as well as advertisements for related businesses. In the future, telephones will be built into the kiosks to enable users to contact advertisers directly. On college campuses, the kiosks will feature a spring-break module highlighting resort destinations.[50]

Intouch Group makes an interactive music sampling kiosk called the iStation. In 300 retail locations, the installation offers online information and sound bites from more than 37,000 albums. Consumers can also listen to cuts from a

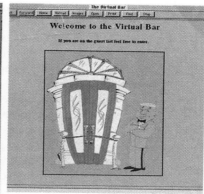

Exhibit 16.3
Vibe, the hip-hop culture magazine published by Time Inc., created a home page on the Internet and is selling advertising space on it. About 40 percent of the magazine's content appears online. Users can also download images and pieces of music. To appease users who resent commercialization of the Internet, the graphic interfaces were designed to be nonintrusive and to appear only if the user clicks a certain area. The offering from DeKuyper cordials invites users to enter an online barroom. Users can click on different areas to hear various messages. The walls are decorated with logos from different Jim Beam products.

CD from store shelves by passing its bar code over the laser. Users sign up for a free silver card for limited sessions or for a gold card at $5.95 per year that includes a subscription to a related magazine plus purchase discounts. Users must register with the company, providing information about their musical preferences, ethnic background, and electronics usage in the home. The company then uses the data it obtains to send targeted mailings that inform subscribers of upcoming concerts and releases tailored to their musical preferences.[51]

THE BEDROCK OF THE PROMOTION SUPERHIGHWAY: DATABASE MARKETING

As we have seen, the promotion superhighway is a two-way road. The key to reaching and pleasing customers in the 1990s is interactivity. But how is this accomplished? For many marketers, the answer is *database marketing,* interactive marketing activities that utilize a customized database of customers who have an identifiable interest in the product. Of course, maintaining a database is not a new idea (see Chapter 5), but what *is* new is using the database as the core of the company's marketing activities rather than as a simple repository of information.

The secret to a sophisticated interactive marketing strategy is the development of a customer database that allows the organization to learn about the preferences of its customers, to fine-tune its offerings to their needs, and slowly but surely to build an ongoing relationship with them. As a result, the database evolves over time; it is continually updated to reflect both the first-order and the second-order responses of the firm's customers. In this section we'll take a closer look at how database marketing is being used to build bonds with database members.

NBO Stores is an excellent example of database marketing at work. NBO, with a customer list of one million people, uses direct mail between six and eight times a year to between 150,000 and 800,000 households each time. The company has obtained (or *captured*, to use the industry term) these names from several sources, including credit card *reverse appends* (deriving names and addresses from names and credit card numbers), phone numbers requested at point of sale (the telephone company is able to provide about 50 percent of the addresses that correspond to those numbers), clothing alteration tickets, check authorization forms, calls to an 800 number, and request pads placed at NBO's registers for customers who want to sign up. The database entry for customers on the list contain about thirty pieces of information about those people, including when they shop in NBO stores and what types of clothes they buy.[52]

Like NBO, many major companies have become convinced that traditional promotion strategies simply aren't sufficient to create and cement brand loyalty among fickle consumers in the 1990s. Slowly and quietly, marketers such as Philip Morris USA and Procter & Gamble have begun to build huge databases to help them stay in touch more intimately with their customers. Marketing giant Procter & Gamble has been a leader in developing targeted communications strategies. The company has mounted an extensive effort to build databases of several target groups, such as new mothers.[53] Kraft General Foods sends nutrition and exercise tips to a list of more than thirty million consumers on the basis of information they provide when they send in coupons or respond to other promotions.[54] Waldenbooks has a Preferred Reader Program consisting of a database of four million names. This list, which contains information about the types of books bought by members, can then be used to develop separate promotions for, say, mystery lovers and fans of romance novels.[55] Similarly, the key to greater efficiency at Dell Computer Corp. resides in its sophisticated corporate database. Manufacturing, finance, marketing, and sales units across the company link to the database and continually feed it information. Because the database is organized by market segments, Dell marketers can manipulate and analyze the data available on each customer segment to identify the best prospects for direct mailings.[56]

ADVANTAGES OF DATABASE MARKETING

All organizations may be able to use database marketing, but some types of companies can benefit more from a database than others. Those firms that are likely to get the most out of it are

- Companies that need to analyze lack of response or reactivate one-time buyers
- Companies with tight, highly defined market niches
- Companies that need to sell many products to survive
- Companies in highly competitive market niches looking for a competitive advantage[57]

Although the costs of developing and maintaining a customer database can be substantial, they are often well worth it. When Heinz wanted to steal dog owners away from Nabisco's Milk-Bone for its Meaty Bone dog biscuits, it ran a TV commercial that included an offer of a free Meaty Bone Taste Challenge Kit and a toll-free 800 number to call to get it. Callers received a trial-size box of biscuits, a 50-cent coupon, and a special canine place mat that told puppies to choose between competing brands by placing a paw over the picture of their preferred biscuit. Happily for Heinz, their canine customers chose Meaty Bone by a 2-to-1 margin, and sales rose more than 10 percent. As a company executive noted, "It's as if we poured the names of all our potential customers into a funnel. Thanks to that 800 number, we now know the people most likely to buy from us, and we can send them coupons and questionnaires."[58] In this section, we'll consider some of the advantages of database marketing compared to conventional promotion techniques.

Database Marketing Is Interactive

Recall that interactive marketing requires a response on the part of the consumer. He or she must take some action, such as filling out an order form or calling an 800 number for product information. For example, a mail piece sent to women cat owners by H.J.

Heinz's Amoré cat food asked the provocative question "Does he sleep with you?" If the woman completes a brief survey that tells the company more about her pet food preferences, she receives a personalized thank you note that mentions her pet by name.[59] She is also entered into the company's database so that she will receive future communications about her feline friend. This type of interactivity gives marketers more than one opportunity to develop a dialog with the customer—and possibly to create add-on sales by engaging the customer in a discussion about the product and about related items or services in which he or she might be interested.

Database Marketing Builds Relationships

Because they are directed to specific consumers, interactive communications have some important advantages over other techniques. Interactive promotions help build alliances with consumers because they enable marketers to open a line of communication with people and continue to supply them with product information and advice that they have indicated they would like to have. For example, Warner-Lambert, makers of the allergy remedy Benadryl, included a toll-free telephone number in a television commercial for people who wanted more information on allergy treatments. At the end of the campaign, Warner-Lambert had received calls from about 17,000 viewers. The company thus provided a service for these consumers and also had a healthy start on compiling names for a database of allergy sufferers.[60]

The beauty of database marketing is that it allows the marketer to develop programs that build and continue over time. These programs are more flexible, because each phase can be modified in light of consumers' responses to what went before. In turn, information from the current wave can be used as input to future programs. As noted by the CEO of Colgate-Palmolive, "We're using direct marketing as a mechanism to increase our overall penetration, as a sampling device, a word-of-mouth device and to supplement our overall marketing program."[61] Here are some specific ways in which database marketing helps to build valuable long-term relationships:

■ *Database marketing rewards loyal users.* The single best predictor of who will buy a product in the future is knowing who bought it in the past. Because sophisticated database marketers know who has already purchased from them, they can keep in touch with these consumers. They can also reward loyal customers by notifying them of upcoming deals and mailing them money-saving coupons.

NBO Stores found that 30 percent of its customer list generated 70 percent of the company's business. Of that 30 percent, there are about 3300 men who spend $1000 a year and about twenty men who spend $4000 a year. NBO created a group it informally called the 3300 Club; collectively, this relatively small group of men have spent $4.7 million at NBO stores. To continue pleasing this group, NBO sends the men on the 3300 list more frequent mailings, from birthday reminders to announcements about the arrival of new merchandise. As one NBO executive explained, "They are members of a club, but they don't know they are members."[62]

■ *Database marketing locates new customers.* In some cases, a marketer can create new customers by directing its communications to nonusers who are considered likely prospects. These consumers may possess characteristics similar to those of current users, or they may simply live near these people. For example, Dial sent coupon mailings about rust stains to neighbors of people in Des Moines, Iowa, and Omaha, Nebraska, who use its Sno Bol toilet bowl cleaner. That boosted the brand's sales volume by 81 percent in a twelve-week period.[63]

This is how Club Med found new guests for its resorts: It developed a list of prospective customers and sent each a postcard that looked as though it were sent by a personal friend staying at the resort.[64] To create its list, Club Med sent its consulting firm information about clients who had recently bought one of its travel packages. The agency then tried to figure out what characteristics those individuals had in common. They compared zip codes to see which communities they came from. Then, by searching through various computer databases, the agency was able to determine everything from the average age (thirty-five) to the average annual income ($60,000) of its most likely travelers.

REAL PEOPLE, REAL CHOICES:

DECISION TIME AT PRICE/MCNABB

The Biltmore Estate is a national historic attraction located in Asheville, North Carolina. Set on 8000 picturesque acres in the western North Carolina mountains, the French Renaissance chateau, with 250 rooms and more than four acres of floor space under roof, is the largest private home in America. The Biltmore House plays host to over 750,000 visitors annually. One of the highlights of the attraction is the annual Christmas Celebration, a tradition that was begun by George Vanderbilt (grandson of the builder of America's railroads) after the house was constructed in 1885. Promotion for the event had typically been carried out exclusively in mass media with a heavy emphasis on television advertising. This approach had been successful at building attendance for more than a decade.

More recently, though, Scrooge was starting to show his face: Entering the 1994 Christmas season, ticket sales had leveled off. Attendance at similar attractions around the country was down, and to add to this general problem, there was inertia in the marketing campaign: The same message and strategy had been essentially repeated every year. The "Christmas elves" at Price/McNabb were brought in and assigned the marketing objective of increasing admissions and revenue by 5 percent during the tourist attraction's 1994 season (the estate's centennial year).

Price/McNabb's IMC perspective led the agency to try to understand the estate's patrons *before* it began to formulate a communications strategy. Research showed that the mass media approach did not efficiently accomplish some important communications objectives: (1) It did not attract people who previously had visited the estate. (2) It failed to take advantage of the fact that a Christmas season visit to Biltmore had become a family tradition among many annual pass holders. (3) It didn't recognize a widely held belief that residents of nearby cities were unwilling to travel to Asheville during Christmas because of fears about unpredictable winter weather. Price/McNabb's research identified four individual segments of potential Christmas visitors, each of which required a unique message in terms of pricing, days of week for use, incentives to refer others, and on-site promotions.

Armed with this knowledge, Tom Eppes and his team faced a choice: Should the agency continue to rely on mass media advertising, knowing that the mass media strategy had on the whole yielded steady business growth for more than a decade? Or should it try a different approach to get the message across in a fresher way? The team considered three options:

Option 1. Continue with television and other mass media advertising, increasing budgets to produce fresh, creative material and boosting the frequency of advertisements prior to and during the Christmas season. Television is *the* traditional ad medium, and Christmas obviously is the time of the year when viewers are interested in holiday-oriented messages. TV also reaches a huge audience. On the other hand, it is extremely expensive to produce TV ads and to buy air time on hot shows. Also, TV advertising is still largely a shotgun approach; its accuracy in reaching a specific target audience is questionable.

Option 2. Continue with television and other mass media advertising, supporting it with promotions and special admission discounts. Television advertising had worked in the past, and adding promotions or discounts to the message probably would be effective in boosting ticket sales. On the other hand, expense would still be a major problem. Promotions that are not targeted to potential high-margin customers are likely to result in increased attendance by less affluent segments. It's a bit like offering coupons to people who will shop in your store only if they have a coupon or if something is on sale.

Option 3. Abandon mass media as the primary delivery vehicle in favor of direct mail to select targets. This approach would allow Biltmore to communicate individually with each customer segment, providing the appropriate information that would be likely to motivate that specific type of person. That's a more cost-effective way to reach potential customers. However, travelers depend on detailed information to plan their trips, and publicity is a proven way to deliver all the facts an individual or family needs with high credibility. Using radio as a supplementary medium gives added weight, immediacy, and emotional relevance to the message in a way that direct mail often cannot.

Now, join the decision team at Price/McNabb: Which option would you choose, and why?

■ *Database marketing stimulates cross-selling.* Another way in which database marketers can maximize the service they offer to customers is by offering them related products. If a person has expressed interest in a particular product category, the odds are that he or she will also be a good candidate for similar items. This helps to explain why consumers are often bombarded with mail offers for computer software, magazines, or clothing after purchasing a similar product over the phone or through a catalog. As we saw in Chapter 10, a related strategy is for companies to embark on *co-branding programs* with other companies, as when credit card companies offer special versions of their cards bearing the logos of other organizations (such as a Visa card offered in conjunction with Ford Motor Company).[65]

Database Marketing Is Measurable

A common complaint voiced by marketers is that they can't pinpoint exactly what impact a promotion message had on the target market. Who can say for sure that a $100,000 commercial really motivated people to switch colas? How do we know that a person's attitude toward recycling was changed by a billboard on the highway? Would a prospect have bought that new computer system even without the repeated urging of a persuasive salesperson? Because the database marketer knows exactly who received a specific message, he or she can measure the effectiveness of each communication. Responses are trackable; the marketer can assess the proportion of message recipients who responded, compare the relative effectiveness of different messages, and compile a history of which consumers are most likely to respond over time.

One of the great advantages of database marketing is that the firm can track how well specific promotions worked and determine whether some market segments are more or less responsive to its efforts than others. Farm equipment manufacturer John Deere targeted 20,000 farmers who were loyal to other brands. Using a list of farmers who owned competing equipment, the company sent prospects a series of four mailings spaced over eight weeks, each with an inexpensive gift related to the theme of saving time and money by replacing existing equipment (one gift was a stopwatch). The campaign brought 5800 farmers into the showroom, a 29 percent response rate. Nearly 700 of these consumers bought new equipment, resulting in a total of more than $40 million in new business. Because John Deere knew exactly who had received and responded to its messages, it could tell exactly how effective the campaign was.[66]

BUILDING THE DATABASE

In 1982, Vipont Pharmaceutical, Inc. was an unknown start-up company selling $13,000 worth of oral hygiene products. Seven years later, the company had grown to $37 million in sales, and in 1990 it was bought by Colgate-Palmolive for $94 million. The company's founders attribute their success to database marketing. Let's see how Vipont went about constructing a workable customer list from scratch.

The company was initially having trouble reaching dentists because it couldn't afford a sales force. At first, it started to compile customer information on index cards so that it could solicit reorders at the appropriate time. Later on, Vipont installed a toll-free number to take orders, and the company began to keep a record of incoming calls on the cards as well. As management got more sophisticated, the company eventually switched to a computer, graded customers by how much they bought, and designed promotions to target different customers and measure results.[67] Vipont "captured" names for its database by tracking responses it got to its 800 phone number. Vipont's actions illustrate the three steps needed to build a customer database: 1) *identify* customers or prospects, 2) *communicate* with targets using appropriate messages and media, and 3) *capture* the responses received and record this information to fine-tune further efforts.[68]

Other capturing methods that can be used include providing a response coupon with the company's print ads or with point-of-sale information, relying on the salesforce to report leads, starting a customer club or newsletter, and buying a commercial database. In addition, the marketer should actively solicit feedback from the customer; instead of ignoring comments or complaints, the marketer should carefully record them. Ideally, every response received from a customer should be entered into the system, and every communications contact with the recipient—whether in the form of an ad, a phone call, or an announcement on the Internet—should include some way for that person to respond.[69]

This strategy was demonstrated by Hewlett-Packard when the company wanted its customers to upgrade to new equipment. First, the company updated its customer list for accuracy. Then it segmented the list into four groups according to volume of prior purchases. The lists were coded by job title so that messages could be tailored to different people. Each person on the list received a customized letter offering an appropriate incentive to update his or her equipment.[70]

Data Sources

A marketer can obtain lists of names from many sources, but the *quality* of a list is usually the single most important determinant of success. In this context, *quality* refers to the proportion of prospects contacted who will eventually be converted into customers. In general, "quality" prospects are people who are likely to be interested in the product and who are willing to make such a purchase by mail or phone. The single best predictor of purchase is whether the person has bought a similar product recently.

> ■ *Buying and renting lists:* A variety of government and commercial agencies provide information that can be used to develop lists of potential customers. Both the U.S. Census Bureau and the U.S. Postal Service are examples of government sources. Private sources include numerous syndicated data services, such as the Simmons Market Research Bureau, that are discussed in Chapter 5.

Many companies obtain more focused lists of prospects from professionals called *list managers and compilers,* who keep records of people who exhibit many different characteristics. These lists are usually rented for a defined (usually one-time) usage. If the marketer has luck with a list and wants to use it again, he or she continues to rent the list. The renter often uses a list broker to obtain lists from various managers and compilers.

Two basic types of lists are compiled lists and response lists. A **compiled list** is a purchased list made up of names taken from secondary sources, perhaps even the phone book. The people on the list may share some desirable characteristic (for example, a furniture manufacturer may obtain a list of people in a state who have applied for wedding licenses in the past year—presumably newlyweds would be good candidates for new furniture purchases), but their willingness to buy is unknown. In contrast, names that are purchased from a **response list** have an identifiable interest in the product *and* have a history of responding to direct marketing promotions. Response lists are more effective, but they are also more expensive to rent.

> ■ *Creating in-house lists:* A drawback to importing lists from other sources is that the individuals or organizations on these lists are not (at least not yet) the firm's customers. True database marketing involves more than mailing an ad-

compiled list: a purchased (or rented) list that is made up of names taken from secondary sources

response list: a list of individuals or organizations that have an identifiable interest in the product and a history of responding to direct marketing promotions

vertisement to people on a list; it goes a step further by maintaining a continuous record of the connections members of the list actually have with the firm. Building a really effective database requires the use of **transactional data**—an ongoing record of who is using the firm's services or buying its products. Some businesses, such as hotels and airlines, have the appropriate data already. They are able to record the names and addresses of customers, their method of payment, frequency of use, and even preferences for service. Hotel chains such as Hilton now routinely record each guest's preferences for non-smoking rooms, double beds, and so on, and this information is used to assign that person the type of room he or she desires on the next trip without the guest even having to ask.

Even if it has to start from scratch, though, it is usually more effective (though also more expensive) for a company to build a list by starting with its own customers and trying to find out as much about them as possible. For example, NBO started its list in 1989 by running a sweepstakes to win a BMW. To enter, customers filled in their names and addresses at the time they charged their purchases. The event yielded over 250,000 names, though some time passed before NBO even did anything with the names. Eventually, the company hired an outside service company to match credit card numbers back to the names and addresses. That matching procedure continues to add roughly 10,000 new names per month to the NBO list.[71] NBO uses only names it has generated from customer transactions and advertising responses. The retailer has tested bought lists, but it has found its own to be superior: The list is so good that 20 percent of the names on it provide NBO with 60 percent of its trackable sales![72]

■ *Integrating transactional data with other information:* Typically, a company will collect its own information on customers and then enhance it with other data, such as demographic or psychographic information purchased from syndicated services like Simmons, Polk, MRI, Donnelly, or the U.S. Census. Adding information on other dimensions is called *overlaying* the database.[73] For example, an auto manufacturer trying to increase sales of its four-wheel drive vehicles might overlay its prospect file with data on customer households in the area who own a car that is at least five years old and/or people who belong to an organization such as the Sierra Club. It could then design a mailing specifically for this group, reminding them that it's time to get a new car that will allow them to go off the road and enjoy nature. NBO gets a better picture of its shoppers by overlaying its list with data supplied by Donnelly Marketing. That tells the company that its typical customer is thirty to sixty-four years old, earns an income over $40,000, has a college education, and is likely to have a child under eighteen at home.[74]

Protecting Lists: Consumer Privacy

The growing use of sophisticated databases is not sitting well with many consumers, who are concerned about possible violations of privacy. After receiving 30,000 complaints, Lotus Development Corporation killed plans to sell its MarketPlace: Households software data base, which contained demographic information on 80 million households. At around the same time, New England Telephone & Telegraph cancelled plans to sell a list of 4.7 million of its customers.[75]

Although the American Civil Liberties Union is pushing for a watchdog group to protect privacy rights, the direct-marketing industry claims self-regulation is working. Executives point to the Direct Marketing Association's Mail Preference Service and Telephone Preference Service, which enable consumers to specify that their names be removed from mailing lists or that they not be called by telemarketers. Still, problems remain: Only about half of all mailers participate in this service, and many consumers are unaware of its existence.[76] However, experiences from other countries show that it is possible to regulate the use of consumer information and still continue to use databases profitably. For example, Germany has very restrictive laws but still supports a $29 billion mail-order industry.[77]

PUTTING IT ALL TOGETHER AND HITTING THE OPEN ROAD: INTEGRATED MARKETING COMMUNICATIONS

In the typical promotion campaign, there is little effort to coordinate the messages consumers receive. An advertising campaign is run independently of a sweepstakes, which in turn has no relation to a series of billboard ads.

More recently, though, some innovative marketers, such as Tom Eppes and his colleagues at Price/McNabb, are beginning to realize that *all* marketing activities involving contact with the public are a form of communication. These contacts range from the appearance of the product itself to the promotional messages about it, and they also include many other cues that are sometimes overlooked, such as the uniforms employees wear and even the company's letterhead. As shown in Figure 16.4, the IMC perspective recognizes that consumers get their information from many sources and different media vehicles, rather than just one. Each and every contact the marketer has with the customer, no matter how trivial, is a form of communication! Although the marketer may view communications as different activities (advertising, publicity, sales promotion, and so on), the customer views communications as a single marketing activity.

DRIVING IN MULTIPLE LANES: COORDINATING PROMOTION MESSAGES AND ACTIVITIES

This broader view of the communications process has spurred the development of an exciting new perspective on promotion strategy. *Integrated marketing communications* (IMC) is the coordination of messages and media to maximize the effectiveness of a promotion strategy in reaching targeted consumers on a continuous basis. In a recent survey of marketing executives, IMC was rated as likely to be the most important factor in marketing strategy in the next few years—more important than consumer lifestyle changes, economic trends, new retail formats, or globalization![78]

Taking the Driver's Perspective

The IMC philosophy recognizes that the customer absorbs information about a good, service, or organization from many sources, not all of which are formal promotion messages or even necessarily under the marketer's control. Thus the basic idea is to take the recipient's perspective by trying to anticipate every opportunity or situation in which he or she will be exposed to information about the good, service, or organization and to ensure, where possible, that all these different exposures communicate the desired message

Figure 16.4
The Integrated Communications Perspective

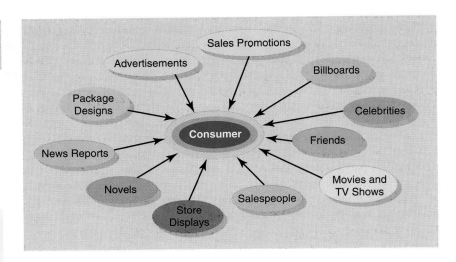

and elicit the intended response.[79] In other words, promotion planners must think in terms of the whole forest rather than just individual trees when it comes to designing marketing communications. Indeed, a study conducted by Campbell Soup found that when it tied its in-store advertising to its television advertising, the store displays generated over 15 percent more sales than normal.[80] This approach still relies on elements in the promotion mix, but it emphasizes that these must all be used in concert to reach targeted consumers both in and out of the home. For example, Folgers Coffee (a Procter & Gamble brand) is targeting Hispanics by sponsoring "*Primera Hora,*" a national morning news and talk show that is shown on the Telemundo television network. "Shelf-talkers" in stores promote the show, along with the Folgers Hispanic ad theme, "*Despiertan lo mejor en ti*" ("Wake up to the best in you").[81]

Highway Under Construction: The Emerging IMC Perspective

The IMC perspective is still new and evolving. At many companies it is more of an idea than a reality. However, many advertising agencies, promotion companies, and manufacturers are beginning to develop their own ideas of what an IMC strategy should look like. These approaches tend to share a number of characteristics.

- They focus on the customers' need for communications rather than on the message.
- They rely on the use of a customer database to focus their messages precisely.
- They strive to send consistent messages utilizing diverse communications vehicles.

SPOTLIGHT ON RELATIONSHIP MARKETING

Excellence at Microsoft

Microsoft is a leader in the personal computing industry. The company's marketing goal is to establish close, long-term customer relationships. If this plan succeeds, current users will not only want to buy Microsoft products; they will also recommend these products to others. Jim Minervino, director of end-user marketing, observes: "The customer buys a product—it's great, now the relationship begins. It's sort of like a first date. You can just first date a thousand people or you can decide to have a relationship."

To build these relationships, Microsoft follows an IMC strategy. Its objectives include promoting the use of its Windows operating system, enhancing its position as the industry standard for operating systems, getting owners of its word processors and spreadsheet programs to trade up to new versions, and getting novices to choose Microsoft products when they are ready to buy.

The IMC strategy has been successful. About 30 percent of Microsoft's applications sales are to customers trading up to new versions, and another 30 percent are to current users who are buying additional programs. To attract novice computer customers, Microsoft targets "influential" computer users: the less than 20 percent of Microsoft customers who influence 40 to 50 percent of the company's sales by recommending its products to others.

This customer loyalty is partly due to the impressive database of Microsoft users the company has built up. This wealth of information enables the company to stay in contact with its customers. Microsoft's database contains 8.5 million users, up from fewer than 1 million five years ago. Those customers receive direct-mail advertising with software user tips, product upgrade deals, and new-product information. Connections with the company are further reinforced by including the company's Microsoft Windows Showcase catalog inside product boxes. Microsoft also publishes a quarterly newsletter that it mails to three million registered owners of its applications software. That makes it the industry's highest-circulation computer publication.

Although the company's advertising agency (Ogilvy & Mather, Los Angeles) conducts multiple product campaigns, each has a similar look, and advertising usually includes an 800 number for customers to get further information and make contact with the company. The company's annual marketing budget is about $90 million, and about one-third of this amount is spent on direct mail, another $25 million on packaging and point-of-sale material. To connect with its customers even more, Microsoft holds numerous customer seminars, hosts trade shows, and contributes generously to retailer cooperative-advertising campaigns. As another sign of its commitment to keeping its relationships healthy, Microsoft spends more than $100 million annually on customer service. By maintaining continuous contact with loyal users, Microsoft turns what could be a single date into a long-term commitment.

Source: Bradley Johnson, "In a Millisecond, Microsoft Boots Up Marketing Database," *Ad Age* (Nov. 8, 1993): S-6.

- They plan for carefully timed message deliveries to provide a continuous stream of consistent information to recipients.
- They utilize several elements of the promotion mix, as well as product design and packaging, to communicate.

THE IMC PLANNING MODEL: BEGIN WITH THE DRIVER, NOT THE ENGINE

A company that wants to implement an IMC strategy still must start with a promotion plan. However, the planning procedure is a bit different from the traditional approach.[82] This sequence is outlined in Figure 16.5. Let's take a quick look at the steps that are involved during the development of an IMC promotion strategy.

Start with a Customer Database

An IMC plan starts with a marketing database that contains as much information as possible on current customers and prospects. This is an important departure from traditional promotion planning, because it means that the *customer*, rather than the firm's profit or sales goals, truly is the focus of the communications strategy. Starting with the customer is a more realistic approach. It recognizes that in today's competitive markets, where customers are oversaturated with information and less likely to believe everything they hear, no one firm has the power to single-handedly transform the market by devising a catchy jingle, a tempting pricing strategy, or an irresistible sales pitch. Firms are much more dependent on developing a base of long-term, satisfied customers.

Classify Consumers by Deeds, Not Words

A second difference is that what customers think matters less, and what they *do* matters more. In other words, classification of consumers is not driven so much by their attitudes toward the product as by their past behavior toward it. An important component of the marketing database is that it uses data from past purchases to differentiate among *loyal users* of the brand, *loyal users of competing brands,* and *brand-switchers* who don't have a strong allegiance to one brand over another (these customers may even be lapsed users of the brand who need to be enticed back from other brands). Separate communications strategies may then be developed to appeal to each group.

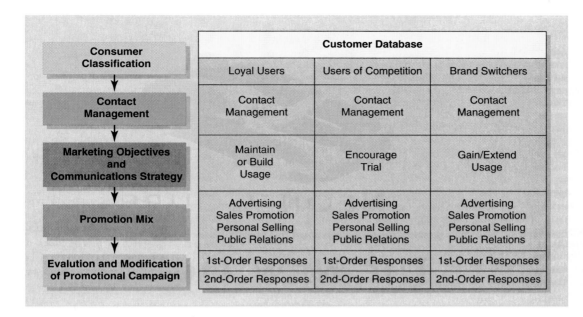

Figure 16.5
An IMC Planning Model

Contact Management

The next step in the IMC planning process is called **contact management,** which involves planning communications exposures to occur where and when the targeted customer is most likely to receive them. Whereas the primary goal of those devising promotion strategy used to be crafting a persuasive message, a bigger concern of IMC planners now is identifying the times, places, or situations where marketing communications are most likely to reach each of the three customer types we have identified. The advertising agency D.D.B. Needham is typical of the evolving IMC approach to contact management: Planners at Needham now use a technique they call media mapping, wherein consumers are asked to identify what specific media (from billboards to TVs in bars) they pay attention to over a period of time. This information helps Needham place messages where and when they are most likely to reach the target audience.

contact management: a communications strategy that seeks to provide communications exposures where and when the targeted customer is most likely to receive them

Communications Strategy and Marketing Objectives

The communications situation will then determine the type of message that should be developed. This decision is based on the communications objectives and on what response from recipients is required (for instance, the planners may want to induce 30 percent of the target market to try the product, or they may want to convince 10 percent of users of a competing brand to switch). The characteristics of the specific group being targeted and the exposure situation also influence what type of message will be most effective and *when* the message is most likely to be seen, heard, or read by people in the target market.

Evaluating IMC Communications

Just as with any promotion effort, the effectiveness of an IMC campaign must be measured and monitored on an ongoing basis. However, the way to accomplish this objective is not so clear. Most traditional measures of marketing communications try to focus on one specific message at a time. For example, a firm might assess consumers' awareness of a new product before and then after they are exposed to an advertisement or sweepstakes. Presumably, any change that is observed during this time period is attributable to the promotion.

The IMC perspective takes a much broader view of the world: Learning about a good or service comes from many sources, and beliefs about the item develop over time. For these reasons, traditional measurement techniques that focus on the impact of one single

message communicated at one time are not adequate to assess the impact of an entire communications program. Instead, the following dimensions should be considered.[83]

- *First-order responses:* Recall that transactional data, consisting of first-order consumer responses to an offer, form the backbone of a marketing database. The firm can thus track transactions over time to assess the effectiveness of the campaign.

- *Second-order responses:* Customers' second-order responses, such as requests for more information, numbers of visits to a dealer, members enrolled in an association, and so on, can also be tracked to determine whether interest has been stimulated by the campaign.

- *Attitudes toward the brand and/or organization:* Although they don't always accurately predict purchases, customers' attitudes toward an item are important pieces of information—especially when changes in attitudes are tracked over time. We can't necessarily expect a dramatic change in attitude overnight, but if an IMC strategy is effective, then these efforts should change consumers' level of recognition of a product, package, or logo and should form closer bonds between the firm and the customer that can be assessed by using some of the research techniques discussed in Chapter 5.

ROADBLOCKS ON THE IMC SUPERHIGHWAY

The idea that one should coordinate the elements of the promotion mix seems so sensible. So what's the big deal? Why aren't all communications strategies mapped out this way? The answer is that for several reasons, many marketers have been resisting the IMC approach or are having trouble implementing it.[84] Here are some of the barriers that marketers are discovering:

- The approach requires changes in the way promotion strategies are planned and implemented. Many companies are financially driven; planning is oriented toward realizing dollar or volume objectives rather than securing long-term customer loyalty. In addition, the attitude persists that marketing efforts cause customers to buy the firm's products, rather than customers being created when the firm offers them something they want or need. Also, there is a general resistance to change in organizations; people are most comfortable doing what they have been trained to do. Many executives specialize in a single aspect of promotion, such as advertising or sales promotion; they were not trained in other aspects of promotion.

- The IMC approach assigns relatively more importance to aspects of promotion other than advertising, which has long been considered the "glamorous" part of marketing. Some executives are reluctant to divert part of their communications budget from splashy ads and toward coupons, give-aways, or T-shirts.

- Communications is often assigned relatively low priority in marketing companies. Promotion strategies are typically developed at lower levels by brand managers and associate brand managers. The IMC approach requires management to view other aspects of the marketing mix (such as packaging or pricing decisions) as part of the communications strategy, so the participation of upper-level executives in promotion decisions is now required. A successful IMC approach requires a company-wide commitment, from the CEO on down, to putting customers first and communicating interactively with them through many different channels.

- There is a "turf battle" going on. Many advertising agencies are trying to jump on the bandwagon; they feel that they should be the ones to provide "one-stop shopping" for promotion services.[85] Virtually every major agency now has a separate direct-marketing arm. Big agencies are also trying to buy other companies that specialize in other aspects of promotion. For example, Ogilvy & Mather bought Adams & Rinehart, a public relations firm, and A. Eicoff & Co., an infomercial producer, to provide diversified services to its clients.

On the other hand, many marketers doubt that ad agencies will be able to change so quickly. As one executive put it, "You can teach an elephant to dance, but the likelihood of it stepping on your toes is very high."[86] These marketers believe that developing an IMC strategy is their responsibility, and they are trying to work with different specialists to develop a coordinated strategy. For example, company executives who worked on a campaign for Reebok's Black Top basketball shoe used four separate agencies to put together a

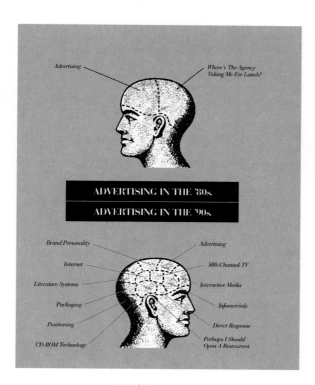

CKS|Partners

Integrated Marketing Communications

Cupertino 408 366-5100 | Silicon Valley 408 343-4800 | San Francisco 415 905-8200 | New York 212 741-5480
Washington D.C. 202 822-6200 | Portland 503 790-2450 | London 011 441 344-382114

Exhibit 16.6
Progressive communications companies in the 1990s are attempting to expand their role in the promotion process well beyond traditional advertising. This ad for a California firm illustrates the broader definition of promotion possibilities in the age of interactive marketing.

REAL PEOPLE, REAL CHOICES:

How It Worked Out at Price/McNabb

The identification of important differences among consumer segments led Price/Mc-Nabb to choose Option 3: Tom Eppes and his staff abandoned television and other broad-based media advertising for the first time since the marketing of "Christmas at Biltmore" began. Instead, the team delivered a unique message to each customer segment through a combination of direct mail and tightly focused radio spots. These efforts were complemented by a high-profile public relations program. The direct mailings included invita-

To help you and your family experience the historic spirit of Christmas,
we would like to offer you the following during this holiday season:

$3 off the admission of each guest in your party
for a daytime visit or Candlelight Christmas Evening
Sunday through Thursday through December 31, 1994.

For Candlelight Christmas Evening reservations, call 1-800-289-1895.
(Reservations are required; Candlelight Christmas Evenings are not held on Mondays)

For more information call 1-800-543-2961.

Please bring this card with you when you visit.
We look forward to seeing you during this holiday season.

tions offering small cash discounts on the price of admission for all people who accompanied the person presenting the invitation. Each invitation was numbered, which enabled the agency to identify which people redeemed the offer (and were therefore likely to respond to other discount offers).

The IMC approach produced exceptional sales results: The season's marketing efforts exceeded expectations by over 200 percent for the total season and by over 300 percent for the month of December. However, this perspective also produced a longer-lasting effect: It provided a foundation to begin tracking customer behavior and building a customer information file for use in future marketing campaigns. One approach that Price/McNabb used to "capture" data was to create a Centennial Guest Registry—a kiosk that enabled the agency to build a database of people who signed in and who might be interested in other centennial events at the Biltmore House.

The information gleaned from this tracking process produced valuable insights related to (1) attendance patterns during specific times of the day and week, (2) the effectiveness of various discount levels offered for admission tickets, (3) attendance by geographic region, and (4) the effectiveness of on-site retail promotions such as the sale of souvenirs and of a discount offered via direct mail for a specific restaurant associated with the Biltmore House. Price/McNabb's efforts to develop an integrated communications strategy for the Biltmore Estate demonstrate the extra marketing mileage a company can get when it coordinates many elements on the promotion superhighway.

program: an advertising agency, a sales promotion agency to run local tournaments, a design firm to create point-of-sale material, and a media-buying service.

In fact, in a survey by the American Association of Advertising Agencies, 85 percent of clients said they wouldn't trust their agencies to coordinate integrated marketing. Some companies are going so far as to create a communications "czar," often called a *marcom manager* (for marketing communications) who plans the overall program. The marcom manager coordinates the activities of individuals who formerly had little contact with one another, such as those responsible for media relations, advertising, marketing strategy, data management, and the creative people who write and produce marketing communications. By crossing over what used to be "no-passing zones" on the information superhighway, the marcom manager sits squarely in the driver's seat and coordinates the company's efforts to provide the consumer with a smooth ride.

Chapter 16   Summary

Objective 1. Explain the steps in managing the promotion mix.

Marketers use a variety of communications tools to connect with consumers. Through promotional strategies, marketers inform consumers about new products, remind them of familiar products, persuade them to choose one alternative over another, and build strong relationships with customers.

The four major elements of marketing communication are known as the promotion mix. Personal selling provides face-to-face contact between a company representative and a customer. Advertising, the most visible element, is used to create brand identity. Sales promotions stimulate immediate sales by providing incentives to the trade or to consumers. Publicity and public relations activities seek to influence the attitudes of various publics. Marketers also communicate with customers through product and package design. Word-of-mouth communication from one consumer to another is often the most influential factor in consumer decisions.

The promotion plan begins with objectives, which are usually stated in terms of communications tasks such as creating awareness, knowledge, desire, product trial, and brand loyalty. Which promotion mix elements are used depends on the overall strategy, (a push strategy or a pull strategy), the type of product, the stage of the product life cycle, the degree of buyer readiness, and the type of buyer. Promotion budgets are often developed using such rules of thumb as the all-you-can-afford method, the percentage-of-sales method, the competitive-parity method, and the objective-task method. Monies from the total budget are then allocated to various elements of the promotion mix in accordance with the characteristics of the organization, the market potential, and the size of the market. Next the specific strategies for the various elements of the promotion mix are planned and executed. Finally, marketers monitor and evaluate the promotion efforts to determine whether objectives are being reached.

Objective 3. Compare the traditional model of communications with interactive promotion strategies.

The traditional communications model includes a message source who encodes an idea into a message and transmits the message through some medium. Marketing messages exploit a variety of appeals and message structures. The message is transmitted using one of several different communications media and is finally delivered to a receiver, who decodes the message and may provide feedback to the source. Anything that interferes with the communication is called noise.

Today, marketers are focusing on interactive marketing, wherein customized marketing communications elicit a measurable response from specialized market segments. Product purchases provide first-order responses, but marketers also seek second-order responses such as requests for information or suggestions for product improvements. Important interactive marketing media vehicles include mail, television, radio, telephone, computer media, and kiosks.

Objective 4. Explain the popularity of database marketing and how databases are developed and managed.

Database marketing is interactive marketing that utilizes a customized database. Database marketing enables marketers to develop dialogs and build relationships with customers. Database marketing programs are flexible, reward loyal users, locate new customers, offer related products to existing customers (cross-selling), and track customer responses.

Quality databases may be lists purchased or rented from government or private sources. Response lists of individuals who have responded to direct-marketing programs before are generally superior to compiled lists. In-house lists of a firm's own customers, which include transactional data, are usually the most effective. Marketers should be careful to protect their lists and maintain customer privacy.

Objective 5. Explain integrated marketing communications, how an IMC program can be implemented, and why some marketers resist IMC.

Integrated marketing communications (IMC) programs enable marketers to communicate with consumers on a continual basis by coordinating the promotion messages and media. IMC uses customer databases to deliver a continuous stream of consistent messages where and when customers will be receptive to them. The effectiveness of the IMC strategy may be assessed through transactional data, by customers' second-order responses, or by customer attitudes. Some marketers resist IMC because it requires changing accepted ways of doing things, it deemphasizes advertising, it puts added emphasis on communications, and it requires major changes in advertising agencies.

Review Questions

Marketing Concepts: Testing Your Knowledge

1. What are the elements of the promotion mix? What other forms of marketing communications are important to marketers?
2. Why should promotion objectives be phrased in terms of communications tasks? What are some examples of communications task objectives?
3. Explain each of the following budgeting methods: (a) marginal analysis, (b) all-you-can-afford, (c) percentage-of-sales, (d) competitive-parity, and (e) objective-task.
4. Describe the traditional communications model.
5. Explain how the source of a message affects the effectiveness of the communication.
6. Discuss how the following may be effectively used in marketing communications.
   a. One-sided versus two-sided messages
   b. Drawing conclusions
   c. Comparative advertising
7. What is interactive marketing?
8. Why is database marketing growing in popularity? What are some ways in which marketers develop quality databases?
9. What is integrated marketing communications (IMC)? What is contact management and how is it a part of IMC?
10. Why do some marketers resist IMC?

Marketing Concepts: Discussing Choices and Issues

1. Increasingly, marketers are seeking new ways to communicate with consumers. Advertising is being placed on bathroom walls, in high school cafeterias, and even in the halls of university classroom buildings. Develop debate arguments for and against this proliferation of commercial messages.
2. Still another reason to build a database is to advance a politi-

cal or social agenda by identifying and mobilizing a core of supporters. For example, Philip Morris has built a 26-million-name database that the tobacco company uses to rally customers to the cause of smokers' rights.[87] What are the ethical issues related to this usage of databases?

3. Increasingly, consumers are becoming concerned that the proliferation of databases is an invasion of the individual's privacy. Do you feel this is a valid concern? How can marketers use databases effectively and, at the same time, protect the rights of individuals?

4. In France and some other European countries, comparative advertising is illegal. What do you think are the reasons for such laws? Do you think comparative advertising is a bad thing?

5. There are some who argue that IMC is just a passing fad in marketing communications. What do you think?

Marketing Practice: Applying What You've Learned

1. As a marketing consultant, you are frequently asked by clients to develop recommendations for promotion strategies. Outline your recommendations for the use of different promotion mix elements for one of the following clients: a) a new brand of laundry detergent, b) a familiar brand of cereal, c) a political candidate, or d) equipment for a new manufacturing facility.

2. As the director of marketing for a small firm that markets specialty salad dressings, you are in the process of developing a promotion plan. With one or more of your classmates, develop suggestions for each of the following. Then, in a role-playing situation, present your recommendations to the client.
   a. Promotion objectives
   b. A method for determining the promotion budget
   c. The use of a push strategy or a pull strategy

3. Assume you are an account executive with an advertising agency. Your assignment is to develop recommendations for advertising for a new client, a health and fitness center. Give your recommendations for
   a. What types of appeals to use

b. How to use interactive marketing
c. How to develop a database for interactive marketing

4. As a member of the marketing department for a manufacturer of sports equipment, you have been directed to select a new agency to do the promotion for your firm. You have asked two agencies to submit proposals. One agency recommends an integrated marketing communications plan, and the second agency has developed recommendations for a traditional advertising plan. Write a memo to explain each of the following to your boss.
   a. What is different about an integrated marketing communications plan
   b. Why the IMC plan is superior to merely advertising
   c. Why some agencies resist changing from traditional promotion planning

Marketing Mini-Project: Learning by Doing

This mini-project is designed to help you understand how organizations use database marketing.

1. With a group of fellow students, contact a local small business. (This might be a restaurant, a dry cleaner, a hardware store, a bookstore, or the like.) Ask the managers there whether they make use of any database marketing activities such as the ones discussed in this chapter.

2. Obtain the cooperation of the business owner or a manager in working with you to develop recommendations for a new database marketing plan or for improving the existing plan. Your recommendations might include the following:
   a. How to obtain names for an initial or expanded database
   b. What information should be included in the initial database
   c. What information should be regularly added to the database
   d. How the business might use the database for communicating with existing customers, obtaining new customers, increasing the sales volume for existing customers, planning for future expansion, monitoring and improving customer satisfaction, and making changes in the business strategy.

Key Terms

Endnotes

1. Jolie Solomon, "Big Brother's Holding Company," *Newsweek* (Oct. 25, 1993): 38.

2. William Leiss, Stephen Kline, and Sut Jhally, *Social Communication in Advertising: Persons, Products, & Images of Well-Being* (Toronto: Methuen 1986); George Stigler, "The Economics of Information," *Journal of Political Economy* (1961): 213–225.

3. Nancy Arnott, "Getting the Picture: Integrating the Trees into the Forest," *Sales & Marketing Management* (June 1994): 78–82.

4. Elaine Santoro, "NBO Markets with Style," *Direct Marketing* (Feb. 1992): 28–31.

5. William Wells, John Burnett, and Sandra Moriarty, *Advertising: Principles and Practice* 2 ed. (Upper Saddle River, NJ: Prentice Hall, 1992).

6. Ed Shane, "Playing the Local Song," *American Demographics* (Sept. 1989): 51–53.

7. Laura Bird, "First Advertorials; Now Advernewscasts," *The Wall Street Journal* (Sept. 24, 1993): B1, B14.

8. Ibid.

9. Katsumi Hoshino, "Semiotic Marketing and Product Conceptualization," *Marketing and Semiotics: New Directions in the Study of Signs for Sale, Berlin: Mouton de Gruyter* (1987): 41–56.

10. "Draw Out the Best from Designer," *Marketing* (Aug. 25, 1994): 35.

11. Frank Tobolski, "Package Design Requires Research," *Marketing News* (June 6, 1994): 4.

12. Terry Lefton, "Packaging All They Can Get into What's on the Shelf," *Brandweek* (Oct. 3, 1994): 34–39.

13. Rita Koselka, "Hope and Fear as Marketing Tools," *Forbes* (Aug. 29, 1994): 78–79.

14. Sid Asbury, "Pork Rumors Vex Indonesia," *Advertising Age* (Feb. 16, 1989): 36.

15. Patricia Sellers, "The Best Way to Reach Your Buyers," *Fortune* (Autumn/Winter 1993): 15.

16. Thomas L. Harris, "PR Gets Personal," *Direct Marketing* (April 1994): 29–32.

17. George E. Belch and Michael A. Belch, *Introduction to Advertising & Promotion: An Integrated Marketing Communications Perspective* 2 ed. (Homewood, IL: Irwin, 1992).

18. Quoted in Jonathan Berry, "Wilma! What Happened to the Plain Old Ad?" *Business Week* (June 6, 1994): 54–55.

19. According to data presented in the *Donnelly Marketing Surveys of Promotional Practices, 1990–1993* and reported in *Business Week* (June 6, 1994): 54.

20. Patricia Sellers, "Winning Over the New Consumer," *Fortune* (July 29, 1991): 113.

21. Patricia Sellers, "The Best Way to Reach Your Buyers," *Fortune* (Autumn/Winter 1993): 15.

22. Jim Frain of NBO Stores, personal communication (Aug. 1994).

23. Joseph B. Treaster, "From Toys to TV, Drug Fight Grows," *The New York Times* (March 16, 1991): A8.

24. David Mick, "Consumer Research and Semiotics: Exploring the Morphology of Signs, Symbols, and Significance," *Journal of Consumer Research* (Sept. 1986): 196–213.

25. Hershey H. Friedman and Linda Friedman, "Endorser Effectiveness by Product Type," *Journal of Advertising Research* (1979): 63–71.

26. "Jim Palmer Pitches 'Style' for Jockey," *The New York Times* (Aug. 29, 1982): F23.

27. Michael Lev, "For Car Buyers, Technology or Zen," *The New York Times* (May 22, 1989): D1.

28. "Connecting Consumer and Product," *The New York Times* (Jan. 18, 1990): D19.

29. John Deighton, Daniel Romer, and Josh McQueen, "Using Drama to Persuade," *Journal of Consumer Research* (Dec. 1989): 335–343.

30. Linda L. Golden and Mark I. Alpert, "Comparative Analysis of the Relative Effectiveness of One- and Two-Sided Communication for Contrasting Products," *Journal of Advertising* (1987): 18–25; Kamins, "Celebrity and Noncelebrity Advertising in a Two-Sided Context"; Robert B. Settle and Linda L. Golden, "Attribution Theory and Advertiser Credibility," *Journal of Marketing Research* (May 1974): 181–185.

31. Frank R. Kardes, "Spontaneous Inference Processes in Advertising: The Effects of Conclusion Omission and Involvement on Persuasion," *Journal of Consumer Research* (Sept. 1988). 225–233.

32. George E. Belch, Michael A. Belch, and Angelina Villareal, "Effects of Advertising Communications: Review of Research," *Research in Marketing* (Greenwich, CT: JAI Press, 1987).

33. Cornelia Dröge and Rene Y. Darmon, "Associative Positioning Strategies Through Comparative Advertising: Attribute vs. Overall Similarity Approaches," *Journal of Marketing Research* (1987): 377–389; Darrell D. Muehling and Norman Kangun, "The Multidimensionality of Comparative Advertising: Implications for the FTC," *Journal of Public Policy and Marketing* (1985): 112–128; Beth A. Walker and Helen H. Anderson, "Reconceptualizing Comparative Advertising: A Framework and Theory of Effects," in eds. Rebecca H. Holman and Michael R. Solomon, *Advances in Consumer Research* (Provo, Utah: Association for Consumer Research, 1991); William L. Wilkie and Paul W. Farris, "Comparison Advertising: Problems and Potential," *Journal of Marketing* (Oct. 1975): 7–15; R.G. Wyckham, "Implied Superiority Claims," *Journal of Advertising Research* (Feb./March 1987): 54–63.

34. Gert Assmus, "An Empirical Investigation into the Perception of Vehicle Source Effects," *Journal of Advertising* (Winter 1978): 4–10; for a more thorough discussion of the pros and cons of different media, see Stephen Baker, *Systematic Approach to Advertising Creativity* (New York: McGrawHill, 1979).

35. Stuart Elliott, "Advertising: In Addition to Buying Space in Established Magazines, Some Marketers Become Publishers," *The New York Times* (May 5, 1993): D24.

36. John Deighton, "Interactive Marketing Technology: Implications for Consumer Research," presented at ACR 1994.

37. Daniel S. Levine "Top 100 — InterActive Media, #27: New Ad Technologies Make InterActive," *San Francisco Times* (Dec. 21, 1994): B15.

38. Patricia Sellers, "The Best Way to Reach Your Buyers," *Fortune* (Autumn/Winter 1993): 15.

39. Beth Spethman, "Closer and Closer to the Crowd," *Media Week* (Oct. 17, 1994): 24–27.

40. Patricia Sellers, "The Best Way to Reach Your Buyers," *Fortune* (Autumn/Winter 1993): 15.

41. Thomas L. Harris, "PR Gets Personal," *Direct Marketing* (April 1994): 29–32.

42. Martin Everett, "Cases in Point," *Sales & Marketing Management* (Aug. 1994): 85–86.

43. Thomas L. Harris, "PR Gets Personal," *Direct Marketing* (April 1994): 29–32.

44. James Bennet, "Toyota's Tercel Infomercial Draws a Significant Response from Its Youthful, Hungry Audience," *The New York Times* (Dec. 20, 1994): D21.

45. Michael Wilke, "A Radio Entrepreneur Reaches for the Interactive Age," *The New York Times* (Sept. 4, 1994): F7.

46. Elaine Santoro, "NBO Markets with Style," *Direct Marketing* (Feb. 1992): 28–31.

47. Thomas L. Harris, "PR Gets Personal," *Direct Marketing* (April 1994): 29–32.

48. Linda Lipp, "Telephones Ringing Off the Hook," *Journal & Courier* (May 19, 1994): A8.

49. Doug Abrahms, "QVC Poised for Leap from Cable to On-line," *Washington Times* (June 16, 1994): B7.

50. "Company Offers Interactive Aids at Kiosk Sites," *Travel Weekly* (Oct. 24, 1994).

51. Alice Z. Cuneo, "With an 'i' Toward Music Lovers," *Advertising Age* (Aug. 29, 1994): 18.

52. Jim Frain of NBO Stores, personal communication (Aug. 1994).

53. Gary Levin, "P&G Tells Shops: Direct Marketing Is Important to Us," *Advertising Age* (June 22, 1992): 3.

54. Robert Shaw and Merlin Stone, "Database Marketing," *Business Week* (Sept. 5, 1994): 56.

55. Lisa Benenson, "Bull's-Eye Marketing," *Success* (Jan./Feb. 1993): 43–46.

56. Tom Eisenhart, "Dell, Polaroid Use Databases to Target Customers, Link Internal Units," *Business Marketing* (May 1992): 24–26.

57. Curt Barry, "Building a Database," *Catalog Age* (Aug. 1992): 65–68.

58. Patricia Sellers, "Winning Over the New Consumer," *Fortune* (July 29, 1991): 113.

59. Martin Everett, "This One's Just for You," *Sales and Marketing* (June 1992): 119–126.

60. Stan Rapp, "From Mass Marketing to 'Direct Mass Marketing,'" *Direct Marketing* (May 1990): 63, 95.

61. Howard Schlossberg, "Marketers Moving to Make Data Bases Actionable," *Marketing News* (Feb. 18, 1991): 8.

62. Elaine Santoro, "NBO Markets with Style," *Direct Marketing* (Feb. 1992): 28–31.

63. Gary Levin, "Package-Goods Giants Embrace Databases," *Advertising Age* (Nov. 2, 1992): 1.

64. Bruce Horovitz, "The Future of Advertising," *Los Angeles Times* (Oct. 6, 1991): D1, D18.

65. G. Bruce Knecht, "American Express Embraces Co-Brands," *The Wall Street Journal* (Feb. 17, 1994): B1.

66. Martin Everett, "This One's Just for You," *Sales and Marketing* (June 1992): 119–126.

67. Lisa Benenson, "Bull's-Eye Marketing," *Success* (Jan./Feb. 1993): 43–61.

68. Rob Jackson and Paul Wang, *Strategic Database Marketing* (Lincolnwood, IL: NTC Business Books, 1994).

69. Don E. Schultz, Stanley I. Tannenbaum, and Robert F. Lauterborn, *Integrated Marketing Communications: Pulling It Together & Making It Work* (Lincolnwood, IL: NTC Business Books, 1993).

70. Martin Everett, "It's No Fluke," *Sales & Marketing Management* (April 1994): 67.

71. Elaine Santoro, "NBO Markets with Style," *Direct Marketing* (Feb. 1992): 28–31.

72. Jim Frain of NBO Stores, personal communication (Aug. 1994).

73. Annalise Roberts, database consultant, personal communication.

74. Elaine Santoro, "NBO Markets with Style," *Direct Marketing* (Feb. 1992): 28–31.

75. Alan Radding, "Consumer Worry Halts Data Bases," *Advertising Age* (Feb. 11, 1991): 28.

76. Cyndee Miller, "Privacy vs. Direct Marketing," *Marketing News* (March 1, 1993): 1.

77. Ibid.

78. Scott Hume, "Integrated Marketing: Who's in Charge Here?" *Ad Age* (March 22, 1993): 3.

79. Don E. Schultz, Stanley I. Tannenbaum, and Robert F. Lauterborn, *Integrated Marketing Communications: Pulling It Together and Making It Work* (Lincolnwood, IL: NTC Business Books, 1993). Melanie Wells, "Purposeful Grazing in Ad Land," *Advertising Age* (April 11, 1994): S-12.

80. John P. Dickson, "Coordinating P-O-P and TV for Increased Display Productivity" (Fort Lee, NJ: Point-of-Purchase Advertising Institute, Inc., undated report).

81. Junu Bryan Kim, "Market Forces Integrated Messages," *Advertising Age* (Jan. 24, 1994): S-2.

82. Don E. Schultz, Stanley I. Tannenbaum, and Robert F. Lauterborn, *Integrated Marketing Communications: Pulling It Together & Making It Work* (Lincolnwood, IL: NTC Business Books, 1993).

83. Don E. Schultz, Stanley I. Tannenbaum, and Robert F. Lauterborn, *Integrated Marketing Communications: Pulling It Together & Making It Work* (Lincolnwood, IL: NTC Business Books, 1993).

84. Don E. Schultz, Stanley I. Tannenbaum, and Robert F. Lauterborn, *Integrated Marketing Communications: Pulling It Together & Making It Work* (Lincolnwood, IL: NTC Business Books, 1993).

85. Adrienne Ward Fawcett, "Marketers Convinced: Its Time Has Arrived," *Ad Age* (Nov. 8, 1993): S-1.

86. Joshua Levin, "Teaching Elephants to Dance," *Forbes* (March 15, 1993): 100.

87. Jonathan Berry, "Database Marketing," *Business Week* (Sept. 5, 1994): 56.

MARKETING IN ACTION: REAL PEOPLE AT PORSCHE

If you spend $20,000 on a new car, you expect service from the dealer, but if you spend $50,000 or more, you expect SERVICE. George Cabanting, manager of warranty and service systems for Porsche Cars North America, and other marketers at Porsche have found that by creatively using a vastly improved database, dealers are giving their affluent, finicky customers the type of personal service they demand. What's more, improved customer satisfaction has led to improved sales for the upscale car company. Porsche appreciates the importance of maintaining the customer–dealer relationship between purchases, and its reliance on a customer database enables the company to stay in the driver's seat in the competition for upscale car sales.

Porsche Cars North America is secretive about its customer demographics, but it's a good bet that these owners are pretty affluent—some Porsche models sell for up to $140,000! Despite this high price tag, the Porsche Club of America has a membership of 36,000 owners. Still, membership in this club is fairly exclusive. Only 4000 to 5000 Porsches are manufactured each year, and there are only 217 Porsche dealers in the entire American market. With this elite, high-class image, it is especially important that Porsche let both customers and dealers know they are very important to the company.

During the early 1990s, the entire auto industry was suffering sales declines as a result of a seemingly endless recession, and Porsche was no exception. At that time Porsche maintained several different databases, one for each department. For example, there was a database of new-car buyers and a different database for customers who came to dealerships for service. By merging the databases into one, Porsche hoped to improve its marketing and its customer service activities and to jump-start sales in the process. As Cabanting observes, "It's better for customer relations. When someone calls us, we can call up information on the database right away and we have access to the person's entire purchase history. It's a more personalized service now."

Since the merged database of 500,000 customer names was developed, dealers have continued to update the files. Every time a customer visits a dealer for service or repair, the dealer enters the customer's name, address, and warranty ID number into the database. The system can thus track the sales and repair history for every customer. The current database includes over 650,000 names, 275,000 of whom are current Porsche owners. Others in the database are former owners, and others are simply consumers who have participated in dealer promotional events during the past several years—prospects whom Porsche would like to convert into owners.

The database has become an important marketing tool for dealers and for the company. Several times a year, the company mails customers special parts and service offers, including coupons for savings during the promotion period. Some of these are accompanied by giveaway promotions, parties for Porsch drivers, and other dealer incentives. The mailings are handled by the national Porsche headquarters but include the name of the individual dealer. The company develops the artwork and handles the mailing, and the dealers are responsible for the costs of printing and mailing to customers in their areas. And if individual dealers want to do their own mailings using the database, Porsche provides financial assistance in the form of earned credits on future orders of auto parts.

Porsche has also made use of the database in its marketing research activities. Participants in Porsche's Customer Commitment program, which surveys customers about their sales and service experiences, are recruited from this list. The results of these customer service surveys are, in turn, used in Porsche's dealer recognition program. Those dealers singled out by customers as offering outstanding service are allowed to display in their ads a special logo noting their recognition for superior performance, and they receive special perks such as first-class airline seats and the best hotel rooms at the annual dealer meeting.

Since improving its database, Porsche has seen significant increases in its customer loyalty rate (the percentage of Porsche owners who buy yet another Porsche later on). The prior loyalty rate of 60 percent has increased to 74 percent. Car sales also have improved. During the first quarter of 1995, sales were up 68 percent, the highest first-quarter increase since 1990. In 1994, when there was an overall 6 percent decrease in total car sales in the United States, Porsche sales increased a whopping 52 percent over sales in 1993.

Customers also report improvements in service. As one customer said, "The service at my dealership has gone from adequate to absolutely terrific. I get reminders in the mail when the dealer thinks I need to go in for service. And after I get it serviced, I get a phone call from a market research bureau asking me to rate the service I received. I think that's impressive." Like many other firms, Porsche has discovered that investing in a sophisticated customer database results in improved marketing mileage down the road.

Source: Regina Eisman, "Porsche," *Incentive* (June 1995): 54–55.

Things to Talk About

1. How and why did Porsche develop its national database?
2. What are the advantages of database marketing for a company like Porsche?
3. Explain how Porsche's database marketing program begins with the customer.
4. In what different ways does Porsche use its database in its marketing strategy?
5. What secrets to success has Porsche discovered?

■ CASE 16-2

MARKETING IN ACTION: REAL CHOICES AT STAPLES

Like many others before him, entrepreneur Thomas Stemberg turned disaster into opportunity. In early 1980, when Stemberg was forced out of his job with a large supermarket chain, he became a consultant operating out of his home. Finding that he had trouble buying computer supplies one Saturday and feeling that he was being "ripped off" by office supply companies, Stemberg opened Staples, the first office supply discount store. Since 1986, Staples has grown to nearly 400 stores in twenty-one states and Canada. Annual sales are nearly $3 billion. That's a lot of paper clips!

But the office supply industry is not standing still. Staples was successful almost from the beginning, but that success invited others into the market: Office Depot and OfficeMax Inc. became fast-growing competitors, and warehouse clubs such as Wal-Mart's Sam's Clubs began stocking office supplies as well. The market, once wide open, is starting to get a little too crowded for comfort.

In order to remain the industry leader, Staples must continue to reinvent itself. Stemberg thinks that the way to do that is improved service: "We need to become more intimate with our customers. We're way better at service than we were two years ago, but I don't think we're nearly as good as we need to be." What does customer intimacy mean? For Staples it means not only offering great prices on its products but also providing customers with the best solutions to their problems—to cultivate relationships that will enable the company to recognize each customer's unique needs.

Doing that requires better tracking of each customer to be sure that his or her needs are being met. Stemberg and his colleagues have decided that this information is at their fingertips if they can only figure out the best way to use it: Historically, Staples has been structured as a "membership club" type of retailer where membership is free. To join the club, business customers provide information about their companies and in return receive membership cards entitling them to discounts on certain items. But what's most important for Staples is that the membership system provides a database with information on each customer. And each time the customer uses the card, Staples collects more information about the member's purchase behavior. (While the membership program has been abandoned in some areas, Staples still collects information about customers who want to be on Staples' mailing list.)

Staples is trying to make effective use of this database. According to Jim Forbush, Staples's vice president of marketing, "Our database is more than a simple contact tool. It provides the underpinning for relationship marketing." Staples uses the information it collects on new members for several purposes. For example, the chain analyzes zip codes to determine where to open new stores, and it follows up by mailing catalogs and promotional letters to its club members.

Still, Stemberg believes that the Staples database could be mined much more effectively. Could the database be used for more specialized, finely targeted mailings to businesses with different supply needs? Could it somehow help

MARKETING IN ACTION: REAL CHOICES
AT STAPLES *(CONTINUED)*

to recover business from customers who stop buying or whose level of purchases suddenly drops? Staples VP Forbush feels that the database can help Staples to "know who customers are, their behavior, how they feel, and their needs and wants. With that knowledge, we could determine the target with the greatest potential." If Staples can figure out how to do more with the information being collected, the chain will be able to file itself under "P" for Profits.

Sources: Norm Alster, "Penny-Wise," *Forbes* (Feb. 1, 1993): 48–50; "Staples Attached to Its Database," *Direct Marketing* (Oct. 1992): 4, 6; Rahul Jacob, "How One Red Hot Retailer Wins Customer Loyalty," *Fortune* (July 10, 1995): 72–79.

Things to Think About

1. What is the problem facing Staples?
2. What factors are important in understanding this problem?
3. What alternatives might Staples consider?
4. What are your recommendations for solving the problem?
5. What are some ways to implement your recommendations?

17

A dvertising

When you have completed your study of this chapter, you should be able to:

CHAPTER OBJECTIVES

1. Explain advertising's role in marketing communications.

2. List and describe the major types of advertising.

3. Explain the major factors that shape an advertising campaign.

4. Tell how advertisers develop creative strategies.

5. Describe the major advertising media and explain the important considerations in media planning.

6. Explain how advertisers evaluate the effectiveness of an advertising campaign.

7. Discuss some of the important aspects of advertising in international markets.

REAL PEOPLE, REAL CHOICES:

MEET HIROSHI TANAKA, A DECISION MAKER AT DENTSU ADVERTISING

Hiroshi Tanaka is marketing director at Dentsu, Inc. in Tokyo. Although Dentsu is not a "household name" to many Western students, this Japanese company is the largest advertising agency in the world. Tanaka's clients have included Nestlé, American Express, Philip Morris, Minolta, Kikkoman, and SmithKline Beecham.

Tanaka joined Dentsu Inc. as an account executive in 1975, after obtaining a B.A. degree in Spanish studies at Sophia University in Tokyo. He worked as a media planner/buyer at various Dentsu offices. Along the way, he studied in the United States as an overseas trainee, earning an M.A. degree in journalism from Southern Illinois University at Carbondale in 1984. In addition to his work for Dentsu, Mr. Tanaka has a strong interest in research on global marketing and consumer behavior, and he teaches marketing at several colleges in Japan.

"IT'S THE REAL THING"

Dentsu turns ideas into action around the world. Whether crafting messages on behalf of DuPont, TDK Electronics, Toyota, Suntory, or Fuji, this communications giant is responsible for creating many of the images seen and heard in numerous markets. The company maintains a network of twenty-eight domestic and seven overseas offices that, along with forty-eight overseas subsidiaries, offer services ranging from consumer research to the production of advertising communications in thirty-two countries.[1]

Advertising is the most visible part of marketing. Wherever we turn, we are bombarded by ads, commercials, and billboards screaming "BUY ME!!!" Advertising can be fun, glamorous, annoying, informative, or simply ignored. It can take many forms, ranging from a glitzy TV commercial to a hand-lettered pamphlet distributed in mailboxes, from a catchy radio jingle to a one-line listing in the Yellow Pages. At its best, advertising helps consumers make informed choices and enables marketers to let their customers know how their products will meet the customers' needs. At its worst, advertising creates unrealistic expectations about goods and services and how they will change our lives. Advertising is a powerful tool that can be used either to enlighten or to exploit consumers.

In this chapter we will look briefly at the history of advertising, at advertising's role in marketing, and at the different types of advertising. Then we will examine the parts of an advertising campaign: advertising objectives, creative strategy, media strategy, and evaluation of the effectiveness of advertising. Finally, we will look at how advertisers face the challenges of international markets.

ADVERTISING: "YOU'VE COME A LONG WAY, BABY!"

No matter what form it takes, all types of advertising share some basic characteristics. We can define **advertising** as nonpersonal communication paid for by an identified sponsor using mass media to persuade or inform an audience.[2] By nonpersonal communication, we mean that the message is usually not delivered in the form of face-to-face, two-way communication. Advertising is intended to bring about some change in its audience, whether to create awareness of a product, to change the way we think about it, or to get us to run out and buy it immediately.

Advertising differs from other parts of the promotion mix. It differs from personal selling in that, even though many ads use "real people" or celebrities to try to make us feel as though we were having a conversation with an individual, some *mass communication medium* is used (television, radio, newspapers, billboards, or even banners flown from airplanes). And it differs from publicity in that the source of an advertising message is known to us, and the sponsor has paid for the message. Before considering the important functions played by advertising and how these communications are created and executed, we will briefly review advertising's history and discuss some of the factors that are changing the way advertising is done in the 1990s.

THE EVOLUTION OF ADVERTISING

A long-running Virginia Slims cigarettes advertising campaign says, "You've come a long way, baby!" The same could be said of advertising itself. Advertising has been with us a long time. In ancient Greece and Rome, announcements about products and happenings were inscribed on walls and on tablets. Until fairly recently, most people could not read, so a lot of advertising resembled a primitive version of the TV evening news: Criers on street corners would simply shout out the latest developments.

The intent of most of this advertising was usually to inform people about the availability of products, rather than to persuade them to choose one type over another.[3] When movable type was invented in the fifteenth century, things began to change. The printing press made mass communication possible, and with it came the means to get a message out to large numbers of people. The earliest known ad was an offer to sell a prayer book, which was placed in 1477.

From that point on, the art of *copywriting* began to develop, as merchants used the power of print to describe and sell their products. Here is copy written by the American patriot Paul Revere in 1768 to sell his own brand of false teeth.

> Whereas many Persons are so unfortunate as to lose their fore-teeth by Accident, and otherways, to their great detriment not only in looks, but in speaking both in Public and Private:— This is to inform all such, that they may have them re-placed with artificial Ones that look as well as the Natural, and answers the End of Speaking to all Intents, by PAUL REVERE, Goldsmith, near the Head of Dr. Clarke's Wharf, Boston.[4]

Advertising is such a pervasive part of our lives that we tend to take it for granted. What would the world be like without humorous television commercials, radio jingles that you can't keep from humming, and the Goodyear blimp hovering over a football stadium? Probably it would be a much quieter place, though perhaps not so interesting.

Mass advertising as we know it didn't really begin until the mid-1800s. The first advertising agencies didn't create ads at all; these firms were media brokers that earned a living by charging a fee in return for negotiating rates with newspapers for placing other people's messages. As magazines came on the scene, they gave companies an incentive to create more elaborate messages and the ability to enhance these messages with attention-getting artwork and photos. Advertising with eye-catching graphics began to attract viewers' attention around 1895, and the rest is history. A brief chronology of this history appears in Figure 17.1 (page 602).

Advertising has a fascinating history as a marketing tool, and many even consider it an art form. The following are some notable milestones in the development of commonly used advertising techniques.

1905 • Around 1905, some executives began to see the potential of advertising to sell products. The famous copywriter John E. Kennedy observed, "Advertising is salesmanship in print." The "reason-why" copy style, where readers are told explicitly why they should buy, is born.

1910 • By around 1910, the soft-sell approach that relies on the consistent presentation of a stream of positive images (without necessarily a hard-sell "Buy now!" message in each ad) is developed. This technique was pioneered by car advertisers (particularly Cadillac and Buick).
After World War I, the J. Walter Thompson agency focused on the use of brand names to create a unique product identity. The agency also introduced the idea of using status appeals in advertising and began to develop modern marketing research techniques.

1920 • In the 1920s, the Young & Rubicam agency pioneered the use of ads with intriguing headlines to grab reader's attention. The agency also hired pollster George Gallup to conduct research that would be used in the creative process.

1930 • By the early 1930s, a few executives started to test the effectiveness of one ad against another. Radio ads gained in popularity. This created a need for people with vivid imaginations who could write copy that would appeal to listeners rather than readers.

1940 • World War II demonstrated the power of mass advertising, as techniques were refined and applied to such concerns as bolstering civilian morale, conserving resources for use in the war effort, fund raising by selling war bonds, and military recuitment.

1950 • After World War II, prosperity brought with it a rash of "me-too products" in the 1950s. To make a brand stand out, adman Rosser Reeves invented the concept of the **unique selling proposition (USP)**: Give consumers one clear reason why your product is better. This philosophy gave rise to such well-known slogans as "M&M's melt in your mouth, not in your hand."
• Although NBC, the first regular broadcast network, was founded as far back as 1939, television did not start to become a major advertising vehicle until the 1950s.

1960 • The 1960s were the "golden age" of advertising. Many of the most creative advertising campaigns were born during this time, and some of these are still well known today. Three advertising executives had an especially large influence during this decade. Bill Bernbach focused on emotional ads that pulled at people's heart strings to sell products. His campaign for Volkswagen came to symbolize the "creative advertising" emphasis of this era. In one typical ad, the car is labeled a "lemon" became a strip on the glove compartment is blemished and must be replaced. David Ogilvy developed distinctive images and stories for fictional characters, such as the Hathaway shirt man with the eye patch. Leo Burnett developed a whole stable of mythical characters that created strong brand images, such as the Jolly Green Giant, Tony the Tiger, and the Marlboro Man.

1970 • The 1970s and 1980s saw the advertising industry put more emphasis on performance and profit. Many marketers began to shift advertising dollars to sales promotions in order to generate short-term sales, and agencies began to merge in order to offer a broader range of client services to companies doing business around the world.

1990 • Advertising continues to evolve in the 1990s. New media techniques are allowing messages to be presented in exciting ways, and interactive technologies are beginning to enable consumers to become more involved in determining what information they can see and hear. One recent example of these changes is *Blender*, a bimonthly pop-culture magazine on CD-ROM. This advertising-supported title features news, reviews, interviews, and features on topics ranging from movies to music. *Blender* lets readers click into an interview on a group like Nefertiti and then tap into biographical information, video snippets and even music samples. Participating companies buy megabytes of disk space instead of the traditional pages of ad space.

Figure 17.1
A Time-line of American Advertising History: A (Very!) Brief History of Modern American Advertising

Sources: Abstracted from a more extended discussion in William Wells, John Burnett, and Sandra Moriarty, *Advertising: Principles and Practice*, 2 ed. (Upper Saddle River, NJ: Prentice-Hall, 1992); "Pop-culture mag spins on CD-ROM," *Crains New York Business* (Oct. 17, 1994); Charles Goodrum and Helen Dalrymple, *Advertising in America: The First 200 Years* (New York: Harry N. Abrams, 1990).

THE IMPORTANCE OF ADVERTISING TO THE MARKETING FUNCTION

Advertising is an essential means of communicating with customers, and it is a major component in most marketing plans. It can be a very powerful way to inform people about new products, to remind them to keep using "tried and true" goods and services, to make consumers aware of specific features and benefits, and to develop a distinctive image for a product, service, or organization.

Although some people argue that advertising is an unnecessary activity that only makes products cost more, these messages actually play a beneficial role in our society. Because advertising can increase demand, it tends to encourage the production of more goods, thus making possible economies of scale in production, which in turn lowers the price of these items. By advertising heavily, advertisers give signals about product quality—they must be doing something right to be able to afford the ads.[5] At the retail level, advertising promotes efficiency, even when stores' ads do nothing more than indicate where low-price, high-variety stores are located. The resulting increase in customer traffic enables stores to offer wider selections and to invest in cost-reduction technologies that help make them more efficient.

Furthermore, advertising is often unparalleled in its ability to create desire for these goods or services by transporting us to imaginary worlds where users of these items are happy, beautiful, or rich. And because the marketer has total control over what is said, how it is said, and when it is said, advertising allows the organization to communicate its message in a favorable way and to repeat the message as often as it deems necessary.

Advertising's Role in the Promotion Mix

As attention-getting as an ad may be, it is important to remember that advertising is only one aspect of the organization's overall promotion mix. Consumer-directed advertising is more likely to play a central role in this mix when a *pull* strategy (rather than a *push* strategy) is being used. A company chooses a pull strategy when it wants to create desire for the product in its target market, thus motivating consumers to seek out specific brands when they shop. On the other hand, trade advertising directed to wholesalers, retailers, and other members of the distribution channel can also play an important role in convincing these agents to stock or to feature the item.

Recall from the discussion of integrated marketing communications in Chapter 16 that the different elements of the promotion mix should be coordinated to deliver a consistent, persuasive message to the target market. This axiom, which marketers sometimes forget, certainly applies to advertising. The most riveting ad ever created can't accomplish a product's promotion objectives by itself. Ideally, the imagery and message *support* other promotion efforts, such as when an advertisement motivates a customer to seek out more information from a salesperson or when an event intended to create publicity for an organization is announced on flyers, radio, and television. Advertising is likely to play a central role in the promotion mix under any of the following conditions.

- The good or service is simple and/or inexpensive, and it doesn't require two-way communication to explain how it works.
- The good or service is at an early stage in its life cycle, and the goal is to build primary demand. (Intensive advertising that provides necessary information about it is required to convince customers of the need for the product.)
- The good or service is well-established and is competing for acceptance with other mature brands. (Advertising that focuses on building and reinforcing brand image and differentiating the product from its competition is required to attain or hold high market share.)
- The good or service is a personal product or one that is valued primarily for its symbolic rather than its functional qualities. (Advertising is often an effective way to create a desirable "brand personality.")

CHAPTER 17
Advertising | 603

Limitations of Advertising as a Form of Promotion

Advertising is a very popular form of promotion, but it is by no means perfect. The advertising industry fell on some hard times from the late 1980s to the mid-1990s, as economic and cultural factors forced many marketers to reassess the best way to communicate with their customers. Revenues then began to rise again, helped along by such factors as the 1996 presidential election, the Olympics, and a healthy economy.[6] Still, ad executives continue to face fundamental issues that threaten to change the way marketing communications strategies are carried out.

From 1976 through 1988, it seemed that advertising agencies could do no wrong. Total U.S. ad spending consistently grew faster than the economy as a whole. The industry's success was partly due to the growth of new product categories such as personal computers and CD players that needed to be heavily promoted when they were introduced to the market. As ad revenues soared, the agencies reaped millions from their standard 15 percent commissions on media billings. Such growth spawned advertising empires such as Rupert Murdoch's and Robert Maxwell's multinational media conglomerates.

At the end of the decade, the party began to end. Total ad spending grew just 5 percent in 1989 and 3.8 percent in 1990 as consumer spending slowed. In addition, some major marketers simply didn't have the money to spend on advertising. Leveraged buyouts, which were all the rage in the late 1980s, left many giant consumer goods companies saddled with huge debt. This belt tightening, which continued into the mid-1990s, can be explained by a number of factors.

Erosion of Brand Loyalty. Marketers began to realize that cynical consumers were tired of the constant barrage of marketing messages. Their brand loyalty eroded as they began to view products more as commodities that were distinguished only by price. Advertising agency DDB Needham Worldwide Inc. found that 62 percent of consumers polled in 1990 said they bought only well-known brands, whereas 77 percent did so in 1975. When consumers buy solely on the basis of price, image-oriented advertising that stresses intangible qualities such as sex appeal and style is not very effective.

Technology Gives Power Back to the People. Modern technology has given consumers remote controls for their television sets, cable television with its proliferation of station choices, and VCRs with which to record and play back programs or watch movies. Thus television advertising no longer reaches the captive audiences it did in previous decades, when marketers had confidence that viewers were watching one of the three TV networks.

Greater Emphasis on Point-of-Purchase Factors. Many companies have realized that numerous purchase decisions are made when the consumer is actually in a store. Thus there has been a shift in emphasis away from advertising and toward other elements of the promotion mix, such as in-store sales promotions and publicity events.

The Rules Are Changing in the Industry. Advertising has always been a competitive industry, and executives in advertising agencies are now finding that they must also compete with people in other industries. Some once-loyal clients are turning to computer wizards and even to talent agencies for help in developing communications programs.

Advertising Is Expensive! Nearly $400 billion per year is spent on advertising in the United States alone. Retail advertisers spend the most per year (almost $8 billion), followed by car manufacturers (almost $6 billion). Procter & Gamble, which leads all American companies in advertising expenditures, invests over $2 billion a year in advertising! Other companies that spend well over a billion dollars a year include Philip Morris, General Motors, PepsiCo, and Sears, Roebuck and Co.[7]

The Advertising Environment Is Very Cluttered. Part of the problem is that advertising is *too* popular—there are so many messages competing for customers' attention that it is extremely difficult for any one message to get noticed. About 40,000 magazines and journals are published every year, and there are more than 10,000 radio stations. The average household can view thirty-five TV channels. The number of network TV commercials has tripled from about 1800 in 1965 to nearly 5400 per year. During prime time, commercials account for 10.5 minutes of each programming hour.[8]

Some Consumers Are Turned Off by Advertising. Some advertising messages are so persistent or even obnoxious that people tune them out altogether. One survey found that 60 percent of consumers agreed that "advertising insults my intelligence."[9] Other people feel that ads simply have little or no credibility; they assume that product claims are untrue or exaggerated, that the spokesperson in the ad is just touting the product for the money, or even that advertising sends the wrong messages about what is important to people.

Important Trends Affecting the Advertising Industry

These discouraging factors have forced advertising agencies to focus more on providing their clients with efficiency and value. They are taking bold steps to demonstrate that advertising can still deliver powerful, persuasive messages to vast numbers of consumers in a cost-efficient manner. Here are some of the ways they're doing this:

Technology. First, many agencies are banking on new technology (such as electronic mail, cable, and interactive media) to deliver advertising messages, often with a goal of personalizing the message. For example, the Chrysler Corporation recently introduced Command, a system designed to coordinate the various databases the company uses to learn about customers. This system will enable Chrysler to fine-tune its advertising by customizing its messages in terms of the receiver's driving habits and even his or her favorite car color! [10]

Global Reach. Second, advertisers are trying to establish brand images globally. Fast and clear satellite transmission improves global marketing, and many executives now understand that to compete in the 1990s and beyond, they must broaden their focus as consumers in one country are increasingly exposed to and influenced by what happens to people elsewhere (see Chapter 4). For example, Dentsu's advertising for Lexus cars in Japan (where the model goes by the name Windom) attempts to appeal to higher-income Japanese by depicting a young law professor at Yale as the ideal driver of the car.

Diversity. Organizations are working hard to reflect the cultural diversity of their target markets. At the same time, they are trying to be more sensitive to how people are portrayed, especially now that consumers are being more vocal in protesting messages they feel are inappropriate. Ads that have drawn protests from special-interest groups in recent years include[11]

- Ads for Calvin Klein apparel featuring waif model Kate Moss were attacked by a group called Boycott Anorexic Marketing, which objects to ads that glamorize excessive thinness in women. Klein's campaign featuring scantily clothed preadolescents was also shelved, but only after the firm received a massive amount of free publicity related to the controversial messages it was sending.
- A commercial for Black Flag insecticide was modified after a veterans group protested the playing of taps over dead bugs.
- Nike ads starring cartoon character Porky Pig drew fire from the National Stuttering Project, which argued that advertisers who make fun of stuttering make it difficult for stutterers to get respect.
- A public service ad from Aetna Life & Casualty encouraging people to get vaccinated for measles that depicted a wicked witch with a chin wart and green skin drew fire from a "witches' rights group." (Members of such groups consider themselves adherents to a legitimate—and benign—religion.)

Integrated Communications Strategies. Finally, as we noted in Chapter 16, an emphasis on integrated marketing communications is reminding many that advertising strategies must work in harmony with other aspects of a company's overall marketing strategy. The goal is to create advertising that doesn't just look and sound good but also sends consistent messages about products, services, and ideas that will make people sit up and take notice in a cluttered, complex environment. Easier said than done!

TYPES OF ADVERTISING

As we stated earlier, advertisers will spend almost $400 billion this year to bring their messages to American consumers. That's about $4300 for every household in the United States, or $1600 per person. Though nearly every business advertises, some businesses are bigger spenders than others. Restaurants, toy manufacturers, and household cleanser companies spend as much as one-fifth of their revenues on advertising; specialized industrial firms spend considerably less. On average, all U.S. businesses spend between 1 and 3 percent of what they earn on advertising. About 79 percent of this total is allocated to consumer ads, the rest being earmarked for business-to-business messages. Three out of five ad dollars are locally controlled and spent by small businesses.[12] Of course, all this activity is directed toward many different types of advertising communications, from pushing soap powder, beer, and cars to promoting corporate services, plugging charities, and selling political candidates. In this section we will consider three basic types of advertising.

PRODUCT ADVERTISING

When most people are asked to give examples of advertising, they recall the provocative poses in Calvin Klein ads, Michael Jordan flying through the air for Nike, or perhaps attractive men and women drinking beer on a beach. These are all examples of *product advertising,* which is intended to persuade people to choose a specific good or service. Product advertising is the most common form of advertising, whether on a local, national, or global level.

As we saw in Chapter 16, these product-related messages may or may not be intended to result in some immediate action. A *first-order response advertisement* is geared toward stimulating a purchase, as when a local concert promoter announces on the radio that the group Green Day will be appearing in the area for two shows only. A *second-order response advertisement* is instead designed to create or enhance brand image. This type of message usually takes the form of a "soft-sell" approach that is intended to instill a favorable impression of the good or service in people's minds. The advertiser hopes that those "good vibes" will influence consumers later, when they are choosing among competing offerings.

BUSINESS-TO-BUSINESS ADVERTISING

Business-to-business advertising is widely used by manufacturers to communicate with businesses and not-for-profit organizations. Producers of goods and services, retailers, wholesalers, and even governments rely on this form of communication. Business-to-business advertising increased by 9 percent from 1991 to 1992 to more than $4 billion, compared to an increase of only 4 percent in overall ad spending during the same period.[13]

Much of this promotion is in the form of **trade advertising:** product advertising directed at people and businesses who buy products related to a specific trade or industry. Trade advertising often emphasizes how profitable a company's products will be to the seller who agrees to stock them. It is used to increase the distribution of products by persuading more retailers to carry them and also to persuade retailers to give the advertisers' products more support and visibility once they are in the store. Trade ads are the third most important information source for new products (the first two are discussions with colleagues and technical manuals).[14] Though personal selling typically is the most important component in the business-to-business promotion mix, advertising plays a crucial supporting role that makes the salesperson's job much easier. Advertising can give the potential buyer additional information, and it also creates an image in the buyer's mind of the company that the salesperson represents.

trade advertising: product advertising directed at people and businesses who buy products related to a specific trade or industry

INSTITUTIONAL ADVERTISING

Rather than focusing on a specific good or service, *institutional advertising* promotes the activities, "personality," or point of view of an organization. It seeks to create or maintain a positive overall image in the minds of consumers. Let's consider a few variations of institutional advertising.

Corporate Image Advertising

The "picture" that comes to people's minds when they think of an organization such as IBM, Levi Strauss, or even the Catholic Church or the United States Government is that group's *corporate identity,* the overall image of the group held by members of society. A

SPOTLIGHT ON RELATIONSHIP MARKETING

Excellence at Borden

Although most advertising campaigns come and go, some have been tremendously successful at winning a place in consumers' hearts over a long period of time. The specific ads may change with the times, but the characters created by Madison Avenue live on. These make-believe people and animals have become a part of our cultural heritage, and because consumers identify so strongly with them, this bonding process enables the sponsor to build a relationship with its customers by offering products that are "tried and true."

Still, even old friendships need to be updated. With consumers' allegiance to brand names going down, some established companies are reaching back into their advertising past, reviving characters that they hope will be recognized and welcomed by the consumers who grew up with them. Campbell Soup Co. is bringing back the plump "M'm M'm good!" Campbell Kids (slimmed down for the 1990s), and Planter's has brought Mr. Peanut out of retirement.

After being "put out to pasture" for 20 years, fifty-seven-year-old Elsie the Cow is returning as the lead "spokes-bovine" for a $20 million marketing campaign by Borden Inc. Of course, Elsie got a makeover to make her a "90s kind of cow." Grey Advertising, Borden's agency, shaved a few years off her age, trimmed her horns, dressed her in pants, freshened her daisy, and put her in charge of her own supermarket. Elsie's children, Beulah and Beauregard, are now Bea and the Beaumeister, with headphones and a skateboard close by. Her husband Elmer (of Elmer's Glue fame), now sports a wardrobe from L.L. Bean and is more sensitive and helpful around the house.

Borden is trying to revive the relationship between Elsie and her human fans in a bid to rejuvenate sales of its dairy products, which have been dropping dramatically. The latest campaign teaser is in the form of billboards asking, "Guess who's on the mooove?" The next round of billboards provides the answer: "It's Elsie! (And she's more mooovelous than ever.)" All of the advertising will repeat the company's long-running theme, "If it's Borden, it's got to be good." Borden is betting that nostalgic consumers will be "udderly" delighted to see their old bovine friend once again and that this emotional linkage will breathe new life into the relationship Borden has formed with its customers over the years.

Source: Adam Bryant, "Advertising: Elsie and Family Return to Help Revive Borden's Flagging Dairy Fortunes," *The New York Times* (March 10, 1993): D22.

---

company that markets many different products, such as Beatrice Foods, often attempts to create a "halo effect," whereby consumer goodwill toward the parent company translates into greater liking for its individual products. Other institutions, such as not-for-profit universities and hospitals, also are more likely to promote all their features than to dwell on one only.

Although many companies dramatically scaled back their corporate advertising in the last decade, corporate ad spending is rebounding to historically high levels. About $654 million was spent on corporate advertising in 1994. There is considerable acknowledgment in the business community that corporate image is a key point in competitive advantage. As the chairman of one corporate identity firm observed, "An organization's corporate identity can inspire loyalty, shape decisions, aid recognition and attract customers. It is vital to effective employee recruitment and to the way people work together inside a company. And it is directly related to profitability. A corporation's identity, if it is perceived negatively, can work against even the best marketing innovations and strategic initiatives."[15] Unlike many older campaigns that consisted largely of "fluff" ("We're Company X. Look how wonderful we are!"), newer messages are more likely to carry a corporate branding emphasis that is more marketing-oriented. These newer ads tend to offer one cohesive message, such as the campaign for Cigna Corporation, which carries the theme "The business of caring."[16]

Benetton, the Italian clothing manufacturer and retailer, has applied a highly unusual advertising strategy to craft a unique corporate image and to call attention to pressing social issues. Benetton's controversial ads have included pictures of a war cemetery, an oil-soaked sea bird, the bloody uniform of a Croatian soldier, and a dying AIDS patient. An ad showing a man with a tattoo that read "H.I.V. Positive" provoked an outcry in Germany, where retailers who carry the line banded together to refuse to buy any more merchandise. They claimed that bad publicity was hurting their sales and had in some cases resulted in smashed store windows and death threats. A lawyer who represented the retailers complained that Benetton "is using human tragedy and suffering to sell clothes; I think that's totally cynical and without feeling." Benetton was ordered to pay damages to French people infected with the H.I.V. virus as a result of the same ad.[17]

Retail Advertising

Retail advertising is usually local. It typically consists of brand-related product information that focuses on the items a store carries. This form of advertising often emphasizes the store's location, hours, and price and the availability of certain products.

The primary goal of retail advertising, especially that placed by local retailers, is to build store traffic rather than to increase the consumer's brand awareness. Although an ad may take pains to announce that a store has a popular item in stock or perhaps on sale, the retailer hopes to use this information as leverage to enhance the overall image of the store. Much retail promotion is in the form of *co-op advertising*, where a manufacturer shares the costs of local advertising with a retailer (see Chapter 18). Co-op is an effective way to enhance consumer awareness of a product or brand in a local market by linking it with stores that feature the item.[18]

Public Service Advertising

Public service advertisements (PSAs) sell causes rather than products or companies. They typically champion an issue that is clearly in the public interest, such as increasing literacy or discouraging drunk driving. Advertising agencies often take on one or more public service campaigns on a *pro bono* basis (at no charge). For example, the agency Wells Rich Greene BDDP produced a successful campaign on drunk driving called "Friends Don't Let Friends Drive Drunk."[19] There are several benefits to doing this work: In addition to the public service it provides, these campaigns are good for the agency's image, they enable ad executives to experiment with innovative creative ideas, and they can be a valuable way to give newer employees account experience.

One variation of public service advertising is **advocacy advertising,** or cause advertising. This is an attempt by an organization to influence public opinion on an issue because it has some stake in the outcome.[20] For example, the R.J. Reynolds company ran an ad titled "Of Cigarettes and Science" that tried to refute arguments about the relationship between smoking and health. These ads are often aimed at a small group of influential people and are sometimes intended as a sign that a company is prepared to fight for a cause.

advocacy advertising: a type of public service advertising provided by an organization that is seeking to influence public opinion on an issue because it has some stake in the outcome

THE ADVERTISING CAMPAIGN

No matter what type of advertising is needed, the messages that greet us on the radio, on TV, in the newspaper, and so on do not magically appear by themselves. Recall our earlier discussion of the communication process in Chapter 16: This model reminds us that any message requires a source, a medium, and a receiver. Advertising is all about creating and sending these messages, so it is not surprising that the process of creating ads can be long and complex, involving many players. An **advertising campaign** is a coordinated, comprehensive communications plan that is tied to promotion objectives and results in a series of messages placed in different media over a specified time period. In this section, we will describe the duties of the major players who must work together to make a campaign happen and will discuss how the nature of a campaign depends on the objectives of the advertiser.

advertising campaign: a coordinated, comprehensive communications plan that is tied to promotion objectives and results in a series of messages placed in different media over a specified time period

PLAYERS IN THE ADVERTISING GAME

Any campaign begins with an advertiser, or *client.* This can be a manufacturer or a service provider (Salomon skis or Joe's barber shop), a distributor or retailer (Amway or Bloomingdale's), or an institution (the U.S. Army). Individuals are often advertisers as well, whether they are promoting a professional service (a lawyer), selling a product on their own (a used car), or even marketing themselves (a personal ad).

In some cases, firms maintain an *in-house agency* that actually creates the company's advertising. This practice, which occurs when a company wants closer control over its advertising, is typical among large retailers who regularly need to make local newspaper or radio deadlines. Some companies that make highly technical products also prefer to create their own advertising, because specialized knowledge is needed to discuss the complicated issues involved.

More typically, the company hires one or more advertising agencies to create and execute the firm's communications. If the company works with more than one agency on its various brands or divisions, one agency is designated the *agency of record*. This company coordinates media-buying decisions among the various accounts and keeps a record of all advertising that is actually executed on behalf of the company.

An *advertising agency* creates a communication on behalf of a client and delivers it to a target market as efficiently and creatively as possible. An agency can be one person working out of a cramped office or a huge company like Dentsu with thousands of employees worldwide. An agency may specialize in one aspect of the advertising process (such as media buying) or may offer a full range of services to clients. The five largest full-service American agencies (ranked in order of descending gross income) are the Leo Burnett Co., J. Walter Thompson Co., Grey Advertising, McCann-Erickson Worldwide, and DDB Needham Worldwide. With the exception of Leo Burnett (which is based in Chicago), these agencies are headquartered in New York City and serve their clients with offices around the globe.[21]

In addition to internal functions, such as *traffic control* (the tracking of projects to meet deadlines, accounting, production, and personnel), agency services usually include account management and creative, research, and media planning. Table 17.1 (page 610) shows how the different functions in an ad agency work together to produce an advertising campaign. An advertising agency is composed of people from a variety of specialties who work together to create an effective campaign. Let's look at the major players.

Account Management

The *account executive* is the "soul" of the operation. He or she is in charge of developing the overall strategy for the client and making sure that the advertising that is created will meet the client's needs. The account exec supervises the day-to-day activities on the account and is the primary liaison between the agency and the client (which is usually represented by the brand manager). The account exec often has to be a good politician in that he or she must be certain the client is kept happy while also ensuring that people within the agency are working well together to execute the desired strategy.

Creative Services

Creatives are the "heart" of the communications effort. These are the people who actually dream up and produce the ads. They include the agency's *creative director* (who is in charge of ensuring that the agency's strategy is expressed in the most interesting and effective way), copywriter, art director, and producer. Creatives are the artists who breathe life into marketing objectives and craft messages that (hopefully) excite, arouse, or interest consumers.

Research and Marketing Services

Researchers are the "brains" of the operation. They collect and analyze information that will help account executives develop a sensible strategy. They assist creatives in designing and evaluating ad executions by doing copy testing to gauge consumer reactions to different versions of ads and by providing copywriters with information about the target group. *Media researchers* evaluate the standing of different media vehicles in terms of their ability to deliver the desired consumer group. In some cases, the research department is a part of the agency's media department.

The importance assigned to research varies among agencies and countries. Some agencies (such as DDB Needham and Young & Rubicam) tend to be research-driven; others are more likely to rely on "gut instinct" when developing campaigns. European agencies are not as likely as American firms to have a separate research department.

Table 17.1
Development of an
Advertising Campaign:
From Soup to Nuts

The following sequence of events is representative of what occurs when a small- to medium-size agency pursues and obtains a new account, in this case for a print advertising campaign.

- Initial contact with potential client.
- Meeting with client to determine what is needed; general direction desired of agency.
- Presentation date is set.
- Internal meeting is held, usually attended by account exec, art director, copywriter, and traffic manager.
- Brainstorming sessions are held.
- Concepts to be presented are agreed on.
- Copywriter works on headlines, subheads, and copy outline.
- Art director works on layouts.
- Account executive works on proposal and budget.
- Account executive reviews art and copy outline.
- Account executive presents concepts to potential client (sometimes accompanied by copywriter and art director).
- Agency waits to hear from potential client whether it won the account (two to five agencies are usually invited to pitch the account).
- If the agency gets the account, it learns which concept the client has chosen and what changes are asked.
- Agency prepares materials to be used (brochures, ads, fact sheet, premiums, and so on).
- Project begins.
- Traffic manager develops production schedule.
- Media research is conducted and recommended media schedule is submitted.
- Ad placement occurs once approval of media schedule is received from client.
- Photo shoots are set up, stock photography is located, and illustrations are created.
- Copy outline and art layouts are started.
- Layout and copy outline are submitted to client, and feedback is received.
- Draft copy is written and submitted to client for feedback.
- Copy approval process continues with revisions.
- Client approval is received.
- Galleys are produced for client approval.
- Mechanicals are started by production manager and submitted for client approval; periodic revisions are made.
- Final client approval is received.
- Color separations of the artwork are made and sent to printer.
- After coming off press, the job goes through a drying process and is bound, scored, collated, shrinkwrapped, and so on.
- Printed piece is usually completed in one to six weeks and delivered to the client or to a mailing house.

Source: Adapted from information provided by Leigh Grissler, traffic manager, Schuler, Sadowski & Bloodgood agency, Somerville, NJ, personal communication, 1993.

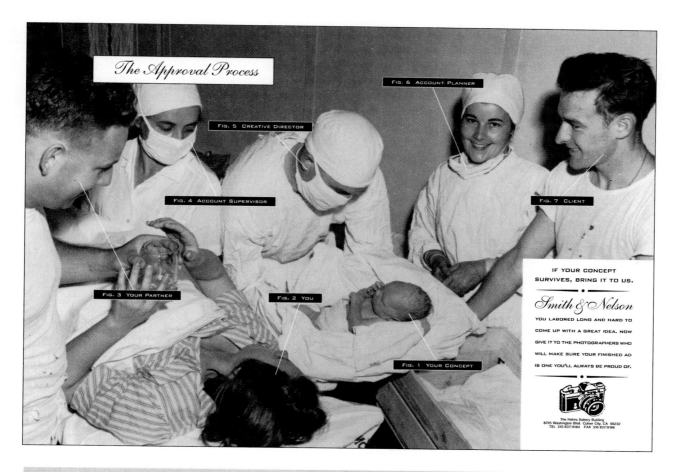

Exhibit 17.1
This trade ad for an advertising photography firm humorously illustrates the "birth" of an advertising concept, highlighting some of the major players who participate in the creative process.

The Account Planner

The position of *account planner* is fairly new, and it is gaining in popularity. The planner is not attached to a department but instead works with researchers and creatives to be sure that ads will appeal to the target market. This person talks to consumers in the field about a product and then shares their opinions with the client and creatives. Account planners, such as Hiroshi Tanaka of Dentsu, analyze the current market situation and are instrumental in developing a communications strategy that specifies the key message to be employed by the creative team, the media that will be used to do this, and so on.

The contributions of an account planner were evident in a recent British campaign for Oxy acne medication, a product of SmithKline Beecham Consumer Brands. Most acne cream ads take place in settings where teenage girls talk with their friends about how well the medication works. After interviewing many target consumers, however, the account planner found that these girls were concerned about their complexions primarily when going out on Saturday date nights. The findings resulted in a series of successful ads, like one where a girl is hiding in the bathroom of a disco on date night, talking to a friend while standing with a bucket over her head.[22]

Media Planning

The *media planner* helps determine which communications vehicles will be the most effective at accomplishing the campaign's advertising objectives. He or she recommends the most efficient means of actually delivering the message to the target audience. The media buyer evaluates what options are available and how much each will cost. This information is eventually incorporated into a media schedule that maps out the specific times and places where the message will appear.

ESTABLISHING ADVERTISING OBJECTIVES

The overriding objective of all advertising is to communicate. This means that advertisements should catch people's attention, be easily understood, be credible, and be memorable. How best to accomplish those goals depends on characteristics of the intended receiver: An ad that uses the latest "hip hop" slang to attract high school students will probably be viewed as confusing or even obnoxious by their parents.

Marketers must decide what it will take to reach the target market and what they hope to accomplish by doing so. The objectives set for a campaign must be consistent with the overall marketing plan. As we noted in Chapter 16, these may take the form of increasing awareness of a brand name, stimulating a certain percentage increase in sales of the product, or even just reaching an acceptable percentage of the target market with one's message. The most crucial issue in planning an advertising campaign is knowing precisely who the target will be. All other decisions should flow from the answer to this question, because target groups differ greatly in what types of products they want, what messages will persuade them, and particularly where they are likely to see those messages in the first place.

For advertising to work, the basic reasons for developing the campaign need to be tied to the marketing plan. Ideally, all of the specific advertising executions will be consistent with this plan. One basic strategic issue revolves around what the advertising is supposed to accomplish in terms of reinforcing or changing the way consumers think about or act toward the product, service, or idea.

The Product Life Cycle: Creating Primary versus Selective Demand

Advertising objectives must be closely related to the communications needs of a product at a particular point in time. The product-life-cycle concept reminds us that the promotion mix must be periodically adjusted from the time a product is introduced to the market to the time it "matures."

Especially in the early part of a product's life cycle, an important goal of advertising is to create awareness by getting people's attention and motivating them to think about the good or service and how it would fit into their lives. Initially the goal is to build *primary demand* for the entire product class, rather than worrying about which brand is perceived as superior. This was the case when personal computers were first introduced; consumers had to be convinced of the need to buy a PC before they could be persuaded to buy an IBM instead of an Apple.

Once a product has been established, advertising focuses on building *selective demand,* which involves creating desire for one brand over others in its category. At this stage of the game, the idea is usually to increase the brand's market share by persuading users of competing products to switch or by reaching out to new market segments. In

Exhibit 17.2
Trade associations often commission advertising that will help build primary demand for the goods or services produced by its members. The highly popular "California Raisins" campaign is a good example of an industry's efforts to convince people to eat more raisins.

some cases, simple reminder advertising is needed to be sure that people actually remember to use the product instead of just taking it for granted and letting it occupy a dusty place of honor on the shelf.

Recall that a brand's *position* reflects how it is perceived by target consumers relative to other brands in its category. If the desire is to reinforce an existing position, the challenge for the campaign is to keep coming up with images that maintain it, while at the same time keeping the consumer from getting tired of the same old messages. Many successful, long-running campaigns do this by subtly changing some elements of an ad but keeping the same basic characters or themes. For example, H&R Block keeps reminding us of ever more reasons to choose the firm for income tax preparation. On the other hand, if the goal is to *reposition* the product by changing the image it calls up in people's minds, advertising is used to replace an old brand personality with a new one. Dr. Pepper has changed its advertising in an effort to reposition itself from a "quirky" soft drink meant for particularly adventurous types to a mainstream beverage. In contrast to its many years of ads that showed somewhat unusual people bucking the trend by choosing Dr. Pepper, the newer ads evoke images of small-town America, such as an "All-American" dad playing with his daughters in a field of daisies.[23]

Aesthetic versus Practical Objectives

Many people are fascinated by quirky or dynamic advertising. Who can fail to be intrigued by the spectacle of a television commercial that features futuristic computer-generated images, revered athletes performing superhuman feats, or even a supermodel caressing a can of soda?

There is, however, a down side to this appreciation of the aesthetics of advertising, which is that these promotion messages must also work for the product. An advertising message must inform, remind, or persuade. And ironically, many really creative ads don't do that as well as one might think. These elaborate productions may make the advertising agency that created them look good within the industry, but if after being exposed to these captivating images, people cannot identify the sponsor or remember what the specific message was, then the advertisement did not accomplish its marketing objectives.

What's more, even memorable ads are not *necessarily* effective ads. Alka-Seltzer's famous campaign slogan, "I can't believe I ate the whole thing," is still recalled fondly by many, but during the time it ran, rival Pepto-Bismol sales were steadily going up: The ads were funny to listen to, but people in pain wanted serious medicine.[24] Similarly, a lot of people remember the campaign starring Joe Isuzu, the lying car salesman. Isuzu's ads scored as the most remembered by viewers for two years. During the same time, unfortunately, sales of Isuzu cars went steadily down.[25] As one advertising executive explained, "Joe Isuzu reminded you of everything you wanted to forget about a car salesman. The humor got in the way. All you remembered was that car salesmen were dishonest, and the car salesman you remembered most was from Isuzu."[26]

The lesson here is that image advertising can be very effective, but too often the advertising gets so far removed from what is being advertised that consumers can't connect it to the product. As one consultant observed, "There is so much emphasis on the creative aspect of the ads, sort of 'Aren't we clever?' that the message is lost."[27] Advertisers often walk a fine line between creating a "great ad" and coming up with an ad that contributes to an increase in brand awareness, stimulates repeat purchases, generates leads for salespeople, or achieves whatever other marketing objectives are tied to the campaign. In the next section, we'll examine how advertising professionals go about creating messages that get noticed and that *also* communicate as they should.

CREATIVE STRATEGY

It's one thing to know what a company wants to say about itself. But it's quite another to figure out exactly what to say and how to say it so that advertising objectives will be accomplished. The creative process has been described as the "spark between objective and execution"; it involves the translation of objectives into memorable, attention-getting messages. The term *creative strategy* refers to the process that occurs when a concept is translated into an actual advertisement. As we saw in Chapter 16, for an advertising message to be effective, it should satisfy four requirements that are commonly lumped together in a formula known as **AIDA**.

- Attention. The most persuasive argument in the world will have no effect if the receiver is not motivated to read it, watch it, or listen to it. An advertisement must generate attention, which is no mean feat in the current environment where so many other messages are also competing to be noticed. The techniques used to draw attention include vivid colors, novel settings, humorous situations, and highly attractive people.

- Interest. Once the receiver has noticed the message, he or she must be motivated to follow through and process the information that is presented. Interest is often enhanced by emphasizing how the product is relevant to the viewer's life. Good market segmentation plays an important role here: If the message is targeted to the wrong market, it is unlikely to hold the interest of those people.

- Desire. The next step is to instill desire for the good or service. This is often accomplished by showing images of happy, successful people who have used the product and whose lives have changed for the better.

- Action. Finally, the ideal advertisement will move the receiver to action. This may involve making an actual purchase, but often it may entail contacting the company for more information or discussing the purchase with a friend.

No single advertisement is likely to satisfy all these requirements, but the goal of an advertising campaign is to present a series of messages over time and to repeat them enough that the recipient will progress through these *AIDA stages*. To do this, advertising creatives (art directors, copywriters, photographers, and others) must come up with a "Big Idea": a concept that enables them to express aspects of the product, service, or organization in a tangible form that is attention-getting and memorable.

A *creative platform* is a document that lays out the strategy decisions for a specific ad.[28] It includes the basic elements of the advertising strategy, such as target audience and objectives. It also outlines the message strategy, including the ad's selling premise (the logic of the message). Although coming up with an attention-getting way to say something profound about cat food or laundry detergent is more of an art than a science, most advertising messages can be categorized in terms of what is said (the appeal) and how it is said (the execution).

WHAT TO SAY: THE APPEAL

Advertisers have come up with many ingenious (and some not so ingenious) ways to express a concept. Some do it with dramatic color or powerful images; others bombard the audience with facts. Some feature scantily clad women (or men); others feature stern-looking experts (even professors from time to time!). Some ads are funny, some are stupid, some really grab you, and some are so irritating you may swear you'll never buy the product they're pushing.

An **advertising appeal** is the central idea of the message. It is how the advertiser chose to sum up the qualities of the product and let receivers know why they should like it. Advertisers often use the same appeal over time and in different formats to hammer it home. This strategy entails the development of a *theme* that (if successful) becomes uniquely attached to the product, such as "Bounty, the quicker picker-upper" and "Cachet: As individual as you are."

Most appeals can be described in terms of whether their overall emphasis is on facts or feelings. Some rely on cold, hard information to promote a product, whereas others try to build appeal by linking the product to desirable images and symbols. In the two examples just offered, Bounty paper towels are promoted in terms of their performance ability, whereas the theme for Cachet perfume implies that the scent will "magically" smell different on every woman.

A basic issue for advertisers often boils down to "Do we sell the steak or the sizzle?" In other words, do we focus on characteristics of the product itself with an informational campaign (the steak), or do we try to develop a vivid "brand personality" by creating psychological meanings for the product based on its packaging, color, supposed sex appeal, and so on (the sizzle)? There are many types of appeals, but most can be characterized as being either hard sell (the steak) or soft sell (the sizzle).

The Steak: Hard Sell

A hard sell is an appeal that reflects a product-centered strategy; it presents information about the item in order to influence the receiver's beliefs about how the product functions or what tangible benefits it can deliver.

Reasons Why: The USP. Some of the most effective hard-sell appeals simply present a **unique selling proposition (USP)** — they give consumers one clear reason why one product is better ("M&M's melt in your mouth, not in your hands"). Sometimes this information is delivered in the form of a *promise,* which is a statement about what the product will do for its owner.

Comparative Advertising. Another form of hard sell is *comparative advertising,* in which two or more brands are compared by name. For example, in a recent campaign, Coors claimed that 58 percent of beer drinkers participating in taste tests preferred its Extra Gold brand to number-one Budweiser.[29]

Comparative ads run the risk of turning off consumers who don't like the negative tone. This is especially a problem in cultures that don't take kindly to impolite messages. In 1991, for example, Tokyo's five major TV networks refused to continue airing a Pepsi comparative ad that featured singer M.C. Hammer, claiming that Japanese consumers feel uncomfortable with the comparative approach.[30] In France, comparative advertising that refers to a competitor by name is illegal.

The Sizzle: Soft Sell

A soft-sell appeal is more indirect. It attempts to create an emotional response in the receiver that will translate into desire for the product. For example, television commercials for Hallmark cards typically feature a scenario involving some kind of relationship (lovers, a child with grandparents, two long-lost friends reuniting) that makes most viewers feel "warm and fuzzy." Other appeals that are based on emotional responses were discussed in Chapter 16. To review, these include

Fear Appeals. Fear appeals highlight the negative consequences of using or not using a product. This approach is used in over 15 percent of all television ads.[31] The arousal of fear is a common tactic for public policy messages, such as those created to convince people to use a designated driver when drinking.

Celebrity Endorsements. Many marketers hope that the "star quality" of famous people will rub off onto the products they endorse. The use of *celebrity endorsers* is a common but expensive strategy. It is particularly effective for mature products that need to differentiate themselves from competitors. That's why celebrities are so widely used as weapons in the battle between Coke and Pepsi. Pepsi's sponsorship of Michael Jackson reportedly cost $5.5 million, and the company has also enlisted actor Michael J. Fox, pitcher Dwight Gooden, and Madonna in its efforts. Coke's stable of endorsers includes hockey player Wayne Gretzky, singer George Michael, the rap group Run-DMC, and model Elle MacPherson.[32]

Sex Appeals. Many ads appear to be selling sex rather than products. In a recent Guess jeans ad, a shirtless man lies near a woman wearing panties and an open blouse that just covers her breasts. An ad for Timex's glow-in-the-dark wristwatch proclaims, "Make Your Husband Really Shine in Bed." A naked woman on a couch sells Obsession for men. Joop jeans uses provocative (and confusing?) copy: "In the uterus of love, we are all blind cavefish."[33]

Humorous Appeals. Humor can be tricky, because what is funny to one person may be offensive or stupid to another. Different cultures also have different senses of humor. For example, a Japanese ad featured a famous actress dressed as a tampon—that probably wouldn't go over well in many other countries![34] Humor is most effective when the brand is clearly identified, when the jokes are appropriate to the product (undertakers might want to avoid this type of appeal), and when the ad does not make fun of the consumer.

YOUR TODDLER
IS SICK, IRRITABLE
AND AGITATED.
NOW, TRY TO TELL HER
WHERE THE
THERMOMETER
NEEDS TO GO.

It's hard enough to get a squirm-
ing kid to sit still for several minutes.
Much less with a thermometer in
the mouth, under the arm, or in the
worst-of-all-possible places.

But that's all changed now. The
Thermoscan® Instant Thermometer
takes an accurate, easy-to-read temperature at the ear—in only one short
second. With virtually no worries
about injury or spreading germs.

(No wonder ear thermometers
are used to take millions of temperatures each year in doctors' offices
and hospitals.)

So get a thermometer your whole
family will be happy with for years.

The first name in fast temperatures
THERMOSCAN
INSTANT THERMOMETER

Exhibit 17.3
As this ad for a new kind of children's thermometer illustrates, humor can be an effective way to break through advertising clutter, especially when it addresses a problem with which many people (such as anxious parents) can sympathize.

HOW TO SAY IT: THE EXECUTION

Some of the most important choices facing the creative team concern the actual "nuts and bolts" of constructing an advertising message. In the world of advertising, how something is said is as important as what is said. Many different approaches can be used for the same product, from a bland "talking head" to a montage of spectacular animated special effects. The specific technique that is used to present the message is the **execution format.**

To some extent, the selection of an execution format depends on practical considerations. One crucial factor is the sponsor's advertising budget: A local car dealer can't afford to hire Steven Spielberg to recreate the set of Jurassic Park in order to announce a sale on used vehicles! Another factor concerns the ability of a particular medium to showcase the creative ideas. Obviously, a creative team producing a newspaper space ad can't do quite as much as a team shooting a television commercial, or even as much as the many sound effects available to radio advertisers, who can rely on listeners' imaginations to create vivid pictures to accompany what they are hearing.

Still, every advertisement is an opportunity to depict some piece of the world, and an important distinction can be made between formats that present product-centered information in a straightforward manner and those that present a story. As noted in Chapter 16, this is the difference between a lecture and a drama.[35]

Lecture Formats

No college student needs to be told what a *lecture* is! The source speaks directly to the audience in an attempt to inform them about a product or idea and/or persuade them to buy it. Because a lecture clearly implies an attempt at persuasion, the audience will regard it as such. Assuming that listeners are motivated to do so, they will weigh the merits of the message along with the credibility of the source. Because it is oriented toward a factual presentation, this form of execution works best with hard-sell appeals. The commonly used lecture formats include

Demonstration. The product is shown "in action" as proof that it performs as it claims to. In some cases, the virtues of the product are driven home by comparing it to an inferior competitor.

Problem Solution. The message focuses on a need and points out how the product can satisfy it. For example, a commercial for a cold remedy may illustrate how quickly the medicine works to relieve a stuffy nose. The problem solution format sometimes introduces *scientific evidence* to support the claim.

Testimonial. A celebrity, an expert, or a "typical person" states how effective the product is.

---

execution format: the specific technique used to present an advertising message

Drama Formats

In contrast, a *drama* is similar to a play or movie. Whereas an argument holds the viewer at arm's length, a drama draws the viewer into the action. The characters address the audience only indirectly; they interact with each other about a product in an imaginary setting. Many advertising communications take the form of stories because the product benefits they describe are intangible and must be given tangible meaning by expressing them in a form that is concrete and visible. Other advertisements take the form of poems that rely on the use of imagery or fantasy to communicate. Dramas attempt to be experiential—to involve the audience emotionally. Here are some dramatic formats:

Metaphor. A metaphor involves the use of a comparison, and the reader is told that A is B ("United Airlines is your friend in faraway places"). Metaphors enliven language by linking meaningful images to everyday events. Just as in the stock market "white knights" battle "hostile raiders" using "poison pills," in advertising Tony the Tiger leads us to equate cereal with strength and the Merrill Lynch bull sends the message that the company is "a breed apart."[36]

Allegory. Many ads take the form of an allegory, and an abstract trait or concept is personified as a person, animal, vegetable, or mythical character. Modern allegories include the "marriage" of two neighboring telephone area codes and the invention of a character named "Rusty" who protects cars from dirt and rust on behalf of Rusty Jones wax.

Storyline. This format tells a story about the product itself. For example, an animated television commercial for Levi Strauss dramatically illustrated how the company's founder (guess what his name was?) began making blue jeans with rivets in them to supply miners and cowboys with pants that were more durable.

Slice-of-Life. A slice-of-life format presents a (dramatized) scene from everyday life so that viewers can identify with the situation (sort of like a product-related soap opera). For instance, MCI Communications had a lot of luck with its successful "Friends and Family" campaign that used actual operators to make its pitch.[37] Many of these ads use professional actors ("I'm not a doctor, but I play one on TV"), but another approach is to use actual employees or customers for realism. Let's look at two controversial slice-of-life ads to see how powerful these depictions can be.

- A commercial for South African Air that ran in the United States, Europe, Hong Kong, and Singapore recreated an unusual event that occurred aboard a 747 en route from London to Johannesburg: A passenger, assisted by flight attendants, gave birth to a baby boy. In the ad the pilot announces, "Ladies and gentlemen, this is your captain. We'd like to welcome a new passenger on board." The ad was intended to soften the unfeeling image of South Africa and to symbolize the birth of the new, post-apartheid South African state. One ad critic complained, "I don't see flight attendant-assisted birth as an appropriate selling tool, unless you're trying to promote Lamaze Airlines." Still, the commercial has won awards, and research shows it was noted and liked by an impressive number of viewers.[38]

- An ad for Spray 'n Wash Stain Stick from Dow Chemical shows a mother and her Down syndrome child. The mother comments, "The last place we need another challenge is the laundry room." One advertising critic described the spot as "the most crassly contrived slice-of-life in advertising history." On the other hand, the National Down Syndrome Congress applauded the ad and awarded Dow its annual media award.[39]

Lifestyle. A lifestyle format depicts a person or persons calculated to be attractive to the target market in an appealing setting. The advertised product is depicted as being part of this scene, so by implication, if the person buys it, then he or she will also attain the lifestyle. For example, a commercial shown on MTV might depict a group of "cool" California skateboarders who take a break for a gulp of milk—"It does a body good." A *fantasy format* is a variation of the lifestyle approach, wherein the viewer is encouraged to imagine that he or she is transported to a novel or exotic situation. In one appeal to a common male fantasy, Coors promoted its Keystone beer by depicting "regular guys" imagining themselves in such situations as being the photographer for a sports magazine's swimsuit issue or playing in a major league baseball game.[40]

MEDIA STRATEGY

Recall from the communications model that any message must be delivered over one or more media for communication to occur. Advertisers have a wide range of media choices, inasmuch as virtually every aspect of the marketing mix, from packaging to pricing, doubles as a form of communication about the product.

Media selection is a very important issue, because the characteristics of the communications vehicle have a major influence on whether the message is received and what meaning it is assigned. There is no such thing as one perfect medium; the choice depends on such factors as the specific audience one is trying to reach, the objective of the message, and (of course) the budget that is available.

In order to maximize the effectiveness of the advertising message, the media planner must do his or her best to match up the profile of the target market with that of specific media vehicles. For example, African-American consumers are more likely than other Americans to be avid radio listeners, so planners trying to reach this segment might allocate a larger share of their advertising budget to buying time on radio stations.

This section will focus on two crucial issues: (1) the characteristics of different media alternatives that make them attractive or unattractive in terms of their relative ability to deliver the advertising message efficiently to the target market and (2) the choices available to the media planner in terms of how to schedule these messages in such a way as to get them noticed without putting people to sleep because of too much repetition.

TYPES OF MEDIA

What does a 52-inch TV with Dolby Surround-Sound have in common with a matchbook? Each is a communications medium that permits a source to place a message in front of a potential receiver. Depending on the intended message, each has its advantages and disadvantages. Obviously, a glitzy TV commercial is capable of saying much more than an ad for a restaurant printed on a matchbook. On the other hand, the four most commonly read words in the English language are "Close cover before striking." People do tend to read the print on matchbooks!

Although newspapers continue to lead the pack in terms of overall advertising spending, the use of this medium is basically stagnant. In contrast, the amount spent on television advertising is growing, and much of the increase is coming from cable stations rather than the major networks. Let's take a look at the major types of media. (Some of the major pros and cons of each type are summarized in Table 17.2.)

Broadcast Media

As the name implies, broadcast media enable the communicator to send a message to many people simultaneously by electronic means. Broadcast media include television and radio.

Television. Because of television's ability to reach so many people with a vivid message, this medium is a favorite choice for regional or national companies. Television can be further divided into network, local, and cable. A *network* is made up of affiliate stations that agree to carry programming supplied by the company during a certain part of the day. In return, the local stations receive a percentage (usually 12 to 25 percent) of the advertising revenue paid to the national network.

It is no secret that the long-standing television networks ABC, NBC, and CBS are in trouble. The television networks' share of the U.S. viewing audience has declined to about 60 percent from 87 percent ten years ago, and the average prime-time show attracts 15.8 million viewers instead of 24.1 million.[41] People simply have many more alternatives than they used to, including upstart networks such as Fox, numerous cable stations, pay-per-view, and videotape rentals. Although many viewers complain, as did Bruce Springsteen in his song "57 Channels and Nothin' On," that these choices haven't really improved the quality of television, they certainly have made it more difficult for an advertiser to reach a really large and desirable audience by buying commercial time on the major networks.

Table 17.2
Pros and Cons of Media Vehicles

Vehicle	Pros	Cons
Newspapers	Wide exposure provides extensive market coverage. Flexible format permits the use of color, different sizes, and targeted editions. Useful for comparison shopping. Allows local retailers to tie in with national advertisers.	Most people don't spend much time reading the newspaper. Readership is especially low among teens and young adults. Short life span—people rarely look at a newspaper more than once. Very cluttered ad environment. The reproduction quality of images is relatively poor.
Television	Extremely creative and flexible. Network TV is the most cost-effective way to reach a mass audience. Cable TV allows the advertiser to reach a selected group at relatively low cost. A prestigious way to advertise. Messages have high impact because of the use of sight and sound.	The message is quickly forgotten unless it is repeated often. The audience is increasingly fragmented. Although the relative cost of reaching the audience is low, prices are still high on an absolute basis—often too high for smaller companies. A 30-second spot on a prime-time TV sitcom costs well over $250,000. Rising costs have led to more and shorter ads, which cause greater clutter.
Radio	Good for selectively targeting an audience. Is heard out of the home. Relatively low cost, both for producing a spot and for running it repeatedly. Radio ads can be modified quickly to reflect changes in the marketplace. Use of sound effects and music allows listeners to use their imagination to create a vivid scene.	Listeners often don't pay full attention to what they hear. The small audience of most stations means ads must be repeated frequently. Not appropriate for products that must be seen or demonstrated to be appreciated.
Direct response	Ads can target extremely narrow audiences. Messages can be timed by the advertiser at his or her convenience. Easy to measure the effectiveness of ads.	High cost per exposure. Target lists must be constantly updated. Ads lack credibility among many consumers.
Magazines	Audiences can be narrowly targeted by specialized magazines. High credibility and interest level provide a good environment for ads. Advertising has a long life and is often passed along to other readers. Visual quality is excellent.	With the exception of direct mail, the most expensive form of advertising. The cost of a full-page, four-color ad in a general-audience magazine typically exceeds $100,000. Long deadlines reduce flexibility. The advertiser must generally use several magazines to reach the majority of a target market.
Outdoor	Most of the population can be reached at low cost. Good for supplementing other media.	Hard to communicate complex messages. Hard to demonstrate a product's effectiveness. Controversial and disliked in many communities.

Source: Adapted from J. Thomas Russell and W. Ronald Lane, *Kleppner's Advertising Procedure,* 11 ed. (Upper Saddle River, NJ: Prentice-Hall, 1990); William Wells, John Burnett, and Sandra Moriarty, *Advertising: Principles and Practice,* 3 ed. (Upper Saddle River, NJ: Prentice-Hall, 1995).

Exhibit 17.4
How much impact can a commercial have if it's shown only one time? In the third quarter of the 1984 Super Bowl, Apple introduced the Macintosh computer with a commercial created by Chiat/Day that made advertising history. Borrowing the imagery of a drab, conformist state from George Orwell's novel *1984*, a young woman hurled a mallet at a big screen to kill Big Brother, symbolically breaking the tyranny of huge corporations (that is, IBM) and bringing computer power to individuals. The commercial, which cost $400,000 to produce and $500,000 to broadcast was shown only once, but it became a feature story on nightly news programs and is still widely considered the most powerful commercial ever made and a tribute to the creative potential of advertising.

Network television is a very expensive advertising vehicle. Although it has the capacity to reach millions of people at once, advertisers pay dearly for this access. A commercial shown during prime time costs upwards of $150,000, not including the costs of producing the spot, which can run well over $100,000. A 30-second commercial aired on the Super Bowl now costs over $1 million! It is also getting harder to get a complex message across via this medium. Most commercials today are only 30 seconds long, and many now last a meager 15 seconds—you'd better speak quickly if you want to make a point in that amount of time! Still, network television can't be beat in terms of its prestige value to advertisers and the impact one really good commercial can have. This medium still accounts for over 25 percent of all national advertising dollars spent in the United States, and a well-done commercial can be very cost-efficient if it does a good job of communicating in a memorable way.

Many advertisers prefer to buy local television time rather than network time. They may not have the budget to play in the networks' league, or they may be promoting a product that is available only regionally. *Spot TV* involves the purchase of advertising time from a local station. Spot commercial time is often purchased by time of day (called a *daypart*) rather than being allocated to a specific program. Local broadcast advertising tends to be more varied, and most of the advertisers are likely to be local retailers. The advertiser must buy time on a station-by-station basis, so this strategy often is not efficient for a larger advertiser.

A third broadcast alternative is *cable television*, which has experienced tremendous growth. Advertising revenues for the cable television industry topped $5.2 billion by the end of 1995.[42] The explanation for this growth is simple: Well over half of all U.S. households now receive cable, and this medium is often attractive because many channels specialize in a specific programming format (MTV) or audience (Black Entertainment Television) that makes it easy to reach a particular market segment.

Radio. Radio has been used as an advertising medium since 1922, when a New York City apartment manager went on the air to advertise apartments for rent. One of the advantages of radio advertising is that commercials can be changed quickly because production usually requires only an announcer and a recording engineer.[43] Radio's strong community appeal has always depended on local personalities, local news, and the emotional power of music. Radio is gaining popularity as an advertising medium because of its low cost and its ability to target specific consumer segments. It is particularly effective when advertisers link their radio ads to print advertising, in-store promotions, and special events.

Ninety-nine out of every hundred U.S. households have a radio, and the average home has 5.6 of them. Radio listening has grown in popularity because it meshes well with a fast-paced lifestyle. Radio listeners tend to listen habitually, at predictable times, to stations with narrowly targeted formats. Radio advertising revenues almost tripled between 1980 and 1992, from $3.5 billion to $8.7 billion.[44]

A radio campaign can reinforce a brand's other advertising efforts by adding local flavor. A campaign run only in Texas by Pepsi, for example, featured Texas bands such as Asleep at the Wheel and the Thunderbirds. Texas bottlers wanted their customers to feel at home with Pepsi, so their radio campaign carried the theme "Today's Texas Taste." The use of radio to market national products locally is increasing.[45]

Print Media

Print media consist primarily of newspapers, magazines, and directories. Let's take a quick look at each type.

Newspapers. The newspaper is one of the oldest media. Retailers in particular have relied on newspaper ads since before the turn of the century to inform readers about sales and deliveries of new merchandise. Unfortunately, people just don't read the paper as much as they used to. Many get their news from TV or the radio instead. The total circulation of morning and evening papers declined from almost sixty-three million in 1985 to just over sixty million in 1992.

This drop in readership has forced papers to rethink their relationships with marketers. Some are exploring alternative ways to deliver information and are getting into electronic publishing, database marketing, and other emerging forms of communication. For example, some papers are selling their subscriber lists to direct marketers and are actually delivering catalogs and samples along with newspapers to their readers every morning.

Newspapers can be described in terms of their frequency of publication (most come out daily or weekly, and daily editions are usually found in larger towns and cities). They typically are produced in one of two sizes: A *tabloid* has five or six columns and looks similar to an unbound magazine. The standard *broadsheet paper* is twice as large as a tabloid. Another way to classify newspapers is in terms of circulation. A few papers, (such as *USA Today*) have national distribution, but most are regional. Within the paper, there are three types of advertisements:

- *Classified advertisements* are commercial messages arranged according to interest or topic, such as Help Wanted, Cars for Sale, and Personals.
- *Display ads* can appear anywhere in the paper except on the editorial page.
- *Supplements* are inserts to the paper that often appear on Sundays (for example, *Parade* magazine is distributed along with most newspapers in the United States). Local supplements are produced by one paper or a group of papers in the same area. A *free-standing insert* (FSI) is a "loose insert" consisting of a preprinted ad that the paper allows to be inserted, for a fee, in its regular edition.

Magazines. Until radio came into its own in the 1920s, magazines were the only way to reach a national audience. Later on, though, such mass market magazines as *Life* and *Look* were forced to fold. These magazines could no longer generate enough advertising revenue, as advertisers followed consumers defecting to television. Still, magazines are an important advertising medium—approximately 92 percent of adults read at least one magazine per month.

Magazines have adapted to changing times by focusing on more specific segments. New technologies such as selective binding allow publishers to personalize their editions, and desktop publishing enables magazines to close their pages just before going to press, eliminating the long lead time that used to be a serious drawback for advertisers who wanted to hit their market with timely information.

A quick look at any newsstand will confirm that there is now at least one magazine that specializes in every interest you can think of—plus some topics you never knew existed! The circulation of *Bicycling* and *European Travel & Life* will never rival that of *Newsweek* or *Time,* but these focused vehicles have the advantage of appealing to a very selective readership: people who are likely to have a serious interest in seeing advertising for certain products (bicycle gear, for example). A magazine—especially an upscale one such as *Architectural Digest* or *Vogue,* is also a very useful vehicle that allows the advertiser to make a statement about the high quality of the good or service. If it's advertised in such splendid company, it must also be high-class!

Directories. Directory advertising is the most "down-to-earth," information-focused advertising medium. The best-known directory is the Yellow Pages, which is designed to provide answers to very specific questions. It is a highly credible source, because it contains primarily factual information and very little advertising puffery. The name comes from the classified section of the 1883 telephone book printed in Cheyenne, Wyoming, when a printer ran out of white paper and substituted yellow. Today, this medium has revenues of more than $9.5 billion. More than 6000 Yellow Pages directories are now published in North America. These listings are generally used just before the consumer makes the decision to buy, so the advertiser has the opportunity to influence the buyer immediately prior to the decision. In a typical week, 60 percent of all American adults refer to the Yellow Pages.[46]

Out-of-Home Media

Because many consumers spend a good part of their days on the go, many advertisers work hard to reach them where they work, where they play, and on the way. Out-of-home media are communications vehicles that reach people in public places, such as billboards, blimps, and transit ads placed on buses and subways.

Outdoor Advertising. Outdoor advertising was the first advertising medium, dating back to stone carvings in Egypt and painted walls in Rome. It seems that billboards are everywhere. In 1991 the $1.6 billion spent on outdoor advertising, however, accounted for only 2.2 percent of all media expenditures.

As advertisers are finding it harder to reach a mass audience through television and as the development of computer technology has increased the ability of boards to feature eye-catching messages, outdoor is doing better in recent years. Outdoor advertising works best when there is a simple, straightforward message and a lot of details are not necessary to tell the story.[47]

Outdoor advertising is also evolving as an art form and is being used to make personal statements. A few recent applications:

- In Houston, four men rented a billboard with the message "4 Middle Class White Males, 32–39, Seek Wives." These "advertisers" got responses from almost 800 women.[48]

- So-called "aerosol advertising" is catching on in New York City. This is the commercial use of graffiti on buildings. Street artists are commissioned by local stores and services to paint large murals that blend in with the graffiti landscape.[49]

- An uproar followed the announcement that Space Marketing Inc. of Roswell, Georgia, in cooperation with the Lawrence Livermore National Laboratory and the University of Colorado, planned to launch a mile-wide display satellite. The spacecraft would be made of a thin plastic film that would reflect sunlight back to Earth from aluminized letters or symbols. The chairman of a United Nations committee on the environment observed that "The ultimate disaster for astronomical science is now clearly identified: commercial adver-

Exhibit 17.5
Many people have a negative view of billboards because they are felt to be ugly barriers to our enjoyment of scenic beauty. An anti-billboard group called Scenic America has waged a campaign to ban boards near state parks, wildlife refuges, schools, and churches. In response to this negative image, the Gannett Outdoor Group introduced a campaign urging creatives to produce billboards that will be artistic statements rather than a blight on society. These billboards for a fast-food restaurant certainly fall into that category.

The Visual Pollution Control Act of 1991 was defeated in the Senate, but in December 1991, President Bush signed the Intermodal Surface Transportation Efficiency Act (ISTEA), which bans construction of new boards on scenic highways. On the other side of the street, the Outdoor Advertising Association of America has begun a campaign to encourage the use of billboards, claiming, "It's not a medium, it's a large."

tising from space." More recently, advertising space was rented on a NASA rocket to promote the Arnold Schwarzenegger film "Last Action Hero."[50]

Place-based Media. Advertisers are showing more interest in hitting consumers with messages that are relevant to the activity in which they are engaged at the time the communication reaches them. Place-based media, whether in the form of signs or of closed-circuit video presentations such as "The Checkout Channel" and "The Airport Channel," attempt to reach a "captive audience."

The ability of signs to break through the clutter of television advertising is evident in the mushrooming of ads placed in sports stadiums. For example, on average there are fifty-nine signs displayed in a National Basketball Association arena. These placards are primarily intended to be seen by TV viewers; the companies that place the signs often guarantee sponsors that their signs will receive a certain minimum amount of air time during televised games.[51]

Advertising messages also appear in the sky above the stadium. It's been over seventy years since the chairman of the Goodyear Tire & Rubber Company turned his hobby into a marketing tool. Now many companies have blimps floating around the country. In 1992 Anheuser-Busch measured the impact of its Sea World blimp shaped like Shamu the whale. The equivalent television advertising would have cost $10 million.[52]

On-screen advertising in theaters is another form of place-based media that has been controversial but is a growing practice. About 6600 movie screens now show ads before the feature show. The verdict is still out regarding consumer acceptance of these messages. Both Disney and Warner Bros. prohibit the showing of ads before their movies, but as such major advertisers as AT&T, Reebok International, and Sega of America continue to buy space, the pressure to accept this practice will probably intensify.[53]

Direct and Interactive Media

As we saw in Chapter 16, the communications landscape is undergoing some dramatic changes as direct mail and interactive technologies are allowing advertisers to reach their audiences with an immediacy and intimacy that in the past could be provided only

REAL PEOPLE, REAL CHOICES:

DECISION TIME AT DENTSU

A concentrated, seasonal campaign is at the heart of the advertising strategies of virtually all Japanese packaged-goods companies. Once or twice a year, these manufacturers "blitz" the market with heavy doses of TV and newspaper ads, accompanied by consumer and trade promotions. The advertising created for these campaigns must work doubly hard, for these messages must not only remind consumers about the products but also ensure that retailers and wholesalers give them a high profile in stores.

Nakano, a Japanese vinegar manufacturer, is almost 200 years old. Most people know it by its popular "Mitsukan" brand name. Vinegar is a central part of Japanese cuisine, being heavily used in such staples as rice balls and sushi.

In the spring of 1993, Mitsukan decided to implement a new advertising campaign for two of its products: One of these products was Omusubi-yama, an additive for homemade rice balls. Mitsukan controlled almost 70 percent of the market in this category. Because it was an established product in the category, the key to marketing Omusubi-yama was differentiating it from the competition. The company asked Dentsu and a competitor to present proposals for a campaign. Hiroshi Tanaka led a research team that had to come up with ideas for a campaign theme. Here are some themes they considered:

Convenience.

Option 1. One obvious way to promote Omusubi-yama would be to emphasize the traditional focus on convenience. Sushi vinegar enables Japanese homemakers to prepare sushi easily, and this emphasis on ease of preparation has been successfully used in past campaigns for this product.

Family.

Option 2. When Tanaka and his colleagues were considering different ways to pitch the account, they were struck by changes that were occurring in Japanese society. Japan was in an economic recession, and consumers were starting to put more emphasis on saving money. At the same time, they noticed an important shift in consumers' working habits. Although Japanese fathers are well known for being workaholics, they were starting to come home earlier from work—the Japanese were beginning to rediscover the value of "family." This change had created the demand for more inventive family dinners, encouraging greater experimentation by Japanese housewives. Therefore, another possibility would be to promote the other ways that sushi vinegar could be used, such as in salad dressing. This approach would also highlight the family theme by emphasizing the relationship between delicious food and family dinners.

Quality.

Option 3. Another possibility would be to emphasize the quality of the product. This approach would highlight how carefully the product is made, focusing on the carefully selected ingredients that are used as well as the brewing technology behind the creation of Mitsukan sushi vinegar.

Now, join the Dentsu decision team: If you were in charge of the Mitsukan account, which option would you recommend, and why?

by actual salespeople. Direct media appear in both broadcast and print form, including television shopping, computerized services and electronic mail, FAX advertising, and messages on the Internet, as well as catalogs, letters, and flyers. Even the Yellow Pages are being used increasingly as a direct-mail medium. In addition to coupon insertions, telephone directory databases are being transformed into CD/ROM format and will eventually feature full-motion videos on products, stores, and services.

Even radio is becoming more interactive, as innovative advertisers are experimenting with putting toll-free numbers in ads so that consumers can call for more information about products and with providing 900 numbers so that they can enter sweepstakes to win prizes donated by advertisers.[64] In the Netherlands, listeners to radio station RTL see the words "RTL Pepsi" glow on the radio display where the station number usually appears. And four times an hour, the message "Be young, have fun, drink Pepsi" pops up on the dial![55]

MEDIA PLANNING

Media planning consists of deciding how to place a message before a target audience in the most effective fashion. The process includes deciding which audience(s) to reach and where, when, how long, and how intense or frequent the exposure should be. These choices fall to media planners who specialize in understanding the pros and cons of the available alternatives. In some cases, *media-buying services* are used (especially by smaller agencies) to plan and buy media—particularly television spots.

Analyzing and Comparing Media Effectiveness

For each prospect, there is an ideal time and a place where he or she will be most receptive to learning about a product. This opening is called an aperture. Identifying the aperture is the goal of the media planner.[56] The planner's task is to create a **media schedule** that specifies what media will be used and when (including how often) the messages will be sent. A hypothetical media schedule for the promotion of a new video game is shown in Figure 17.2. Note that much of the advertising activity for this product is timed to reach its target audience in the months just before Christmas.

The media schedule reflects the planner's judgment of which media will best achieve the firm's advertising objective(s) and which specific media vehicles will do the most effective job of reaching the target market. The media planner considers such information as

- The match between the demographic and psychographic profile of the target audience and that of the people a media vehicle reaches.
- Sales patterns to analyze media in terms of area differences and month-by-month differences, as well as distribution of the brand (it's not terribly efficient to buy advertising in areas where the product is unavailable). In some cases, a product may be extremely popular in some markets yet lose out to competitors in others. The planner may want to concentrate advertising in markets that need help, or, alternatively, the strategy may be to reinforce the brand's market position in areas where it already does well.
- The advertising patterns of competitors.
- The amount of attention viewers or readers will pay to material appearing in each vehicle. For example, readers of specialized computer magazines such as

media planning: the process of developing media objectives, strategies, and tactics for use in an advertising campaign

media schedule: the plan that specifies what media will be used and when the messages will be sent

	Jan	Feb	Mar	Apr	May	June	July	Aug	Sept	Oct	Nov	Dec
Medium												
Television												
Specials											■	
Saturday cartoons						▬▬▬▬▬▬▬▬▬▬▬▬▬▬						
Newspaper												
Co-op advertising	▬▬▬▬▬▬▬▬▬▬▬▬▬▬▬▬▬▬▬▬▬▬▬▬											
Direct Mail					▬▬▬							
Magazines												
Mag 1		■	■	■	■	■	■	■	■	■	■	■
Mag 2	■	■		■		■		■		■	■	■

Figure 17.2
A Media Schedule

Byte are likely to spend time seriously examining computer ads, whereas the majority of readers of *Newsweek* may barely notice the same ad.

■ The capability of a medium to convey the desired information. For example, a new clothing style that "must be seen to be believed" probably wouldn't make much of an impression in a radio ad, and the benefits of owning a new computer with a lot of technical improvements might not come across very well in a 30-second TV commercial.

■ The quality of the media environment. The planner must consider such factors as how cluttered the medium is with competing ads and other distractions, the compatibility of the product with editorial content (frozen pizza manufacturers generally avoid buying commercial time on TV shows that feature a lot of bloody violence—guess why?), and the overall tone or mood of the other material (a light-hearted ad for a new snack food might not be well received in a somber documentary on world hunger).

The choice of where the advertisement will appear is a crucial one. A marketer's message can be placed on a billboard in Times Square, inserted on television between episodes of "Beavis and Butthead," towed through the sky from an airplane, or all of the above. In some ways, however, choosing a medium to carry one's advertising message is a bit like comparing apples and oranges: Will a consumer respond more favorably to the message after seeing a glitzy (and very expensive) television commercial and will the response be worth the cost? Or will the viewer instead use that occasion to get up and fix a sandwich? Will that same person really read a detailed ad in a magazine or just flip right over it in search of that article on the future of techno music?

When comparing different media, the media planner must first consider the size of the audience a vehicle will deliver and whether the characteristics of the people who will see or hear it match the profile of the desired target market. Media planners have access to very detailed profiles of people who are exposed to specific magazines, newspapers, radio stations, and television shows. Syndicated services, such as the Simmons Study of Media & Markets, provide statistical breakdowns that enable planners to match media with consumers.

Exposure. When analyzing media, the planner is interested in assessing *advertising exposure:* the degree to which an advertising message placed in a specific vehicle will be seen or heard by members of a target market. Media planners think in terms of *impressions;* an impression is one person's opportunity to be exposed to a message. Impressions measure the size of the audience for one media vehicle or for a combination of media vehicles. For example, if five million people watch "Melrose Place" on TV, then each time an advertiser uses that program, it receives five million impressions (this assumes that everyone is watching the commercial, which is not likely!). If the advertiser's spot ran four times during the program, total viewer impressions would be twenty million. Planners usually work in terms of *gross impressions*—the sum of audiences of all media vehicles in a time period—regardless of how many different people saw the ads or how many times each person was exposed.

Planners evaluate the exposure a message will have if placed in a certain media vehicle by considering two factors: reach and frequency. **Reach** is the proportion of the target market that will be exposed to the media vehicle. A high level of reach is particularly important for widely used products, where it is vital to get the message to as many consumers as possible. **Frequency** is the average number of times a given person in a target group will be exposed to the message. Media planners usually feel frequency is more important in the case of products that are complex or are targeted to relatively small markets.

Gross Rating Points. Say a media planner who is working on the Levi Strauss 501 jeans account and wants to get her message to college students finds that 25 percent of people in that group read at least a few issues of *Rolling Stone* in a year (reach). She may also estimate that these students, on average, will see eight of the twelve ads that will be run by Levi Strauss (frequency). These estimates allow the planner to calculate the magazine's **gross rating points (GRPs).** This measure enables her to compare the effectiveness of *Rolling Stone* with that of other possible vehicles by examining each vehicle's total exposure as a percentage of audience population. The estimated GRPs for the magazine are

reach: the proportion of the target market that will be exposed to the media vehicle

frequency: the average number of times a person in a target group will be exposed to the message

gross rating points (GRPs): a measure used for comparing the effectiveness of different media vehicles; average reach times frequency

Exhibit 17.6
Marvel Comics sells itself to potential advertisers by touting its reach among kids six to seventeen years old.

found by simply multiplying reach times frequency. In this case,

$$\text{GRP} = 25 \text{ (reach)} \times 8 \text{ (frequency)} = 200$$

Cost per Thousand. Although some media vehicles clearly have a superior ability to deliver exposure, they may not be so cost-effective. Many more people are going to see a commercial if it airs during half time in the Super Bowl than if it airs during a rerun of a Tarzan movie at 3 o'clock in the morning. On the other hand, the advertiser could run late-night commercials every night for a year for the cost of one 30-second Super Bowl spot!

To compare the relative cost-effectiveness of different media and of spots run on different vehicles in the same medium, media planners use a measure called **cost per thousand (CPM),** which allows them to compare vehicles that have different exposure rates. Specifically, CPM is the cost of delivering a message to one thousand people or homes or circulated copies of a media vehicle. A media vehicle's popularity with consumers determines how much advertisers who want to be featured there can be charged. This is why television networks are so concerned about having shows that get good ratings every season—their advertising rates are determined by how many viewers they are able to deliver. Similarly, magazines and newspapers try to boost circulation (in some cases by mailing free copies) to justify higher rates for ad space. CPM is calculated as follows:

cost per thousand (CPM): a measure used to compare the relative cost-effectiveness of different media vehicles that have different exposure rates; the cost to deliver a message to one thousand people or homes or circulated copies of a media vehicle

$$\text{CPM} = \frac{\text{cost of message unit} \times 1000}{\text{number of exposures}}$$

A more precise measure is the *weighted CPM*, which adjusts the measure to reflect only those people exposed to the medium who fall into the target market the advertiser wants to reach. For example, suppose that *Rolling Stone* has a circulation of about 1,202,082 readers, of whom 250,000 are college students. The magazine charges $48,930 for a full-page, four-color ad. The weighted CPM is

$$\text{Weighted CPM} = \frac{\$48,930 \times 1000}{250,000} = \$195.72$$

The media planner might wish to compare this CPM with that offered by some other magazine. For example, *Outside,* which advertises itself as a magazine "for men and women who lead active year-round lifestyles" has a circulation of 371,504 and charges $25,420 for a full-page four-color ad. If 50 percent of these readers were college students, the CPM would be

$$\text{Weighted CPM} = \frac{\$25,420 \times 1000}{185,752} = \$136.85$$

The CPM for *Outside* is lower, but fewer college students will be reached. The media planner must decide which is more important—cost or reach—within the overall media plan.

Media Scheduling

Once the planner decides where to advertise, she or he must also make decisions about when: How often should the ad be shown? What time of day? Frequently for a few weeks, or occasionally for a long time? When the media schedule is selected, planners are making decisions about the overall pattern the advertising will follow. Let's look at three typical patterns.

Continuous Schedule. Maintaining a steady stream of advertising throughout the year is most appropriate for products that are bought on a regular basis, such as shampoo or bread. The American Association of Advertising Agencies, an industry trade group, reports that continuous advertising sustains market leadership. The group found that even if total industry sales fall off, present market leaders will get the largest portion of business as a result of the awareness that is maintained through advertising.[57] On the down side, some messages suffer from *advertising wearout* if they are seen too often; bored receivers stop paying attention after a few exposures.

Pulsing Schedule. A *pulsing schedule* means that some advertising is continuous throughout the year, but the advertising is run more heavily at some times than others. This involves intensively advertising during periods when consumers are most receptive to the message, such as increasing spending for toy ads in the months before Christmas.

Pulsing is particularly appropriate for products that are affected by *seasonality;* they are more likely to be bought at some times than at others. This may be due to environmental factors (people are more likely to buy charcoal for outdoor barbecues in the spring and summer than in the winter), holidays (roughly 40 percent of retail sales occur during the Christmas shopping season), or special events (sales of wedding gowns and tuxedos peak in May and June, when people are most likely to attend proms and weddings).

Flighting Schedule. Flighting is an extreme form of pulsing, wherein advertising appears in short, intense bursts alternating with periods of little or no activity. Flighting can buy as much brand awareness as a steady dose of advertising at a much lower cost, if the messages carry over from the last flight.

EVALUATING THE EFFECTIVENESS OF ADVERTISING

John Wanamaker, a famous Philadelphia retailer, once complained, "I am certain that half of the money I spend on advertising is completely wasted. The trouble is, I don't know which half."[58] Because advertising is so expensive, marketers are constantly searching for ways to tell whether they're getting their money's worth. They need to know whether their messages are meeting their objectives and what effect these communications are having on sales. Some of the techniques used to assess message effectiveness are discussed in Chapter 5.

The problem with evaluating the effectiveness of advertising is that ad spending often moves in concert with a company's profits, and sometimes it's hard to tell the cause from the effect. IBM, Adolph Coors, and Chrysler all saw their profits fall in the first quarter of 1991, and all three reduced their advertising budgets. On the other hand, profits at Philip Morris Companies rose 22 percent in the same period. The company boosted its ad spending for Kraft Miracle Whip, Maxwell House coffee, and other brands by an average of 5.1 percent. This tendency raises an interesting chicken-and-egg question: Does more advertising result in greater profits, or do greater profits simply lead to more advertising?

To some extent, advertisers can take heart: Research findings generally support the wisdom of spending money on advertising.[59] Advertisers that increase spending, either modestly or aggressively, achieve greater gains in market share than those that cut their advertising investment. A number of major studies by media companies and trade groups such as the American Association of Advertising Agencies and the Advertising Research Foundation show that advertising increases result in significantly more sales and that increased product usage is directly linked to advertising exposure.

Most advertising research is not done to determine whether advertising works but rather to find out which particular ad executions work better than others. Research of various kinds is conducted during all phases of a campaign, both to provide feedback before the campaign is launched (pretesting) and to evaluate how well the campaign actually performed in the marketplace (posttesting).

PRETESTING

A lot of the research that goes on in the early stages of the campaign revolves around gathering basic information that will help planners clearly define the product's market, consumers, and competitors. This information is taken from quantitative sources, such as syndicated surveys, and from qualitative sources, such as focus groups, that are described in Chapter 5.

As the campaign takes shape, though, it is necessary to predict how well the specific advertising executions being developed will actually perform. **Copy testing** is a procedure that measures the effectiveness of ads. The object is to determine whether the ad is being received, comprehended, and responded to in the desired manner.

- *Concept testing* helps strategists to determine whether initial ideas will work. Respondents are asked to evaluate different creative ideas or rough copies of ad layouts.
- A rough version of a commercial may be created for evaluation purposes. The test commercial may take the form of an *animatic* or *storyboard,* which is a taped or static series of drawings that show what will happen in the finished ad.
- *Finished testing* involves showing an actual television commercial to test audiences, who rate it in terms of what they can recall about the product and/or whether the ad motivated them to think about buying the product. Similar measures are taken after the commercial has actually aired, as described in the next section.

copy testing: a procedure that measures whether an ad is received, comprehended, and responded to in the desired manner

POSTTESTING

Advertisers often need more solid evidence that a campaign is doing what it set out to do. In today's cluttered media environment, it is extremely difficult to come up with advertising that really stands out and influences consumers' feelings about the product. Viewer retention of television commercials has slipped dramatically in recent times. In 1986, 64 percent of those surveyed could name a TV commercial they had seen in the previous four weeks. By 1990, just 48 percent could.[60]

A number of tests are commonly used to get a handle on which ads are remembered, liked, and understood. Two major ones are the *Starch Report* for magazines and *Burke*

Day-After Recall for television. Both of these services interview consumers to determine who read or saw the ads and what they came away with afterward.

Three ways to measure the impact of an advertisement are unaided-recall, aided-recall, and attitudinal measures. *Unaided-recall* measures ask respondents to a telephone survey or personal interview whether they can remember the advertisements they saw or read within a specified period of time. An *aided-recall* question provides more "help" by giving respondents clues before they answer. For example, consumers might be shown a list of brands and asked to choose which items were advertised. Unaided recall is a more powerful measure of an advertisement's impact, but in some cases a good aided-recall score is satisfactory, assuming that the respondent will also be able to see the choices laid out before him or her at the time of purchase (as is the case with supermarket products).

Finally, attitudinal measures probe a bit deeper by measuring people's beliefs or feelings about a product before and after being exposed to messages about it. If, for example, after being exposed to Pepsi's messages about the "freshness dating" that now appears on the company's products, people are more likely to feel that freshness of soft drinks is an important issue, then the advertising campaign may be considered successful.

Adapting advertising to international markets

As we saw in Chapter 4, advertising agencies are taking dramatic steps to expand their reach in order to serve clients' needs around the world. Saatchi & Saatchi, a British agency, tried to become the first global agency in 1984 by acquiring agencies in other countries and developing campaigns with a global focus. In some cases, networks of independent agencies, such as Affiliated Advertising Agencies International, have been formed to offer this global reach to clients.

Multicountry advertising usually develops in one of two ways: In some cases, a campaign is initially developed with the intent of distributing it globally. Coca-Cola pioneered this approach by assembling a task force of employees from around the world who developed a basic communications strategy and decided how it should play out in each country. In other cases, such as advertising created for McDonald's, a successful campaign is modified if necessary and then transferred to other countries. Let's take a closer look at each approach.

A Consumer Is a Consumer: The Standardization Perspective

Advertising history was made on January 24, 1992, when the first worldwide telecast of an advertising message appeared on the Cable News Network. It was a pitch for Coca-Cola, the best-known brand on the planet. The same commercial was telecast simultaneously in about 130 countries, including such exotic locales as North Korea, and Mongolia, where television viewers were seeing a Coke commercial for the first time. A senior Coke executive proclaimed, "We have never created before in our history an ad designed explicitly to air in every country of the world." After the commercial made its worldwide debut, it was pulled off the global networks, dubbed in six languages, distributed to Coca-Cola's twenty-two operating divisions, and aired on a country-by-country basis.[61] This Coke commercial was the most significant example yet of a much-debated marketing practice: global advertising. Many companies market their products in more than one country, and the best way to advertise in several cultures has been the subject of much debate.

On the one hand, companies such as Coca-Cola feel that many cultures, especially those in industrialized countries in Europe and the United States, share so many similarities that essentially the same advertising campaign will work well for all of them. This side

SPOTLIGHT ON ETHICS

Exporting Cigarette Advertising

The vivid imagery created by advertisers to sell American cigarettes has done its job: These products are in great demand around the world. The Marlboro Man, created by Leo Burnett in the 1960s, is a cowboy who personifies the image of America for many. A more recent "smooth character" that has stirred up controversy is Old Joe, the hip camel created in 1974 for a French Camel cigarettes campaign. The Smooth Character campaign has been so successful at rejuvenating an old brand (at a cost of about $23 million per year) that Camel is one of only a few full-priced cigarette brands that has seen its market share increase in recent years.

This may be a case where advertising works *too* well. According to a widely publicized study on children aged three to six published in the *Journal of the American Medical Association,* more than half of the kids studied were able to match the Joe Camel logo with a photo of a cigarette. Six-year-olds were almost as familiar with Old Joe as they were with Mickey Mouse.[*] Many health experts and parents are concerned about the powerful role advertising has had in teaching kids that smoking is cool.

R.J. Reynolds is taking aggressive steps to counter criticism about its Joe Camel campaign. The company has attacked the methodology used in the aforementioned study and has commissioned its own research that it claims counters these findings (for instance, RJR claims that only 3 percent of kids who recognize the Joe Camel figure say smoking is an acceptable habit). The company has also attempted to generate favorable publicity by sponsoring a public service campaign intended to discourage underage smoking.[†]

As tobacco companies are facing increasing resistance to their products in the United States, they are focusing more of their advertising efforts on teaching consumers around the world to smoke American-style. In Eastern Europe, for example, 700 billion cigarettes are sold per year. Eastern Europe is a market that is 40 percent larger than the U.S. market, and, unlike in the United States, smoking has never been widely disapproved of. One recent survey in Czechoslovakia found that over half of the country's surgeons were smokers!

This explains why Philip Morris International has invested nearly $1 billion in that area since the fall of communism. Images of the Marlboro Man and Old Joe are everywhere. One billboard proudly proclaims, "L&M: The Way America Tastes." As smoking rates declined in the United States (by nearly 3 percent a year between the mid-1980s and the mid-1990s), this stepped-up advertising seemed to be convincing even more Eastern Europeans to smoke. One Czech health official observed, "Until the arrival of the transnational tobacco companies and the beginning of aggressive advertising, the prevalence of smoking was decreasing."[‡]

Some governments are trying to restrict these advertising efforts. The Moscow City Council has taken steps to ban tobacco and alcohol ads, but there are doubts about whether the ban can or will be enforced.[§] The tobacco companies and the advertising industry are fighting the restrictions by arguing that they inhibit free speech: At this point in Eastern Europe, few politicians want to be seen as arguing against that. Thus at least for the time being, the Marlboro Man and his cronies continue to spread their smokey message around the world.

[*]Eben Shapiro, "FTC Staff Recommends Ban of Joe Camel Campaign," *The Wall Street Journal* (Aug. 11, 1993): B1.
[†]Maria Mallory, "That's One Angry Camel," *Business Week* (March 7, 1994): 94.
[‡]Quoted in Richard W. Stevenson, "Tapping a Rich Smoking Frontier," *The New York Times* (Nov. 12, 1994): D1.
[§]Michael Janofsky, "A Red Flag in Moscow on Tobacco and Liquor Ads," *The New York Times* (July 20, 1993): D1.

of the debate is appealing, because if it is true, a lot of time and expense can be saved; the same marketing communications strategy can be used in each market where the firm does business.

Multinational advertising agencies often feel that a standardization strategy enables the company to focus on developing and communicating a uniform brand image. When the Mars company introduced its Pedigree dog food, it used exactly the same media strategy and message appeals around the world. Even so, slight alterations usually have to be made. In this case, the ads used golden retrievers in the United States and poodles in Asia to reflect differences in the types of dogs people value.[62]

Indeed, there are some global brands (such as Coca-Cola, Marlboro, Gillette, Rolex, and Nissan) that are advertised in very similar ways around the world. Standardization tends to be easier in trade advertising, where ads are more likely to convey specific information that is needed by industrial buyers rather than communicating a status image, sex appeal, and so on. It is also successful for products that are strongly identified with a country with which people want to identify. The products that are often bought because they signify American culture include Marlboro, Levi Strauss, and Coca-Cola.

REAL PEOPLE, REAL CHOICES:

HOW IT WORKED OUT AT DENTSU

Hiroshi Tanaka and his colleagues chose Option 2: Because Mitsukan had already introduced a number of products targeting families, the Dentsu team decided that the campaign theme should be focused on "family ties." They also decided to stress the connections between Omusubi-yama and rice, which is a central part of the Japanese diet (see Exhibit 17.7).

The next step was to find the ideal "mother" and "father" figures to use in the advertising campaign. In Japan, popular celebrities are even more central to effective advertising executions than in other countries, so this is a key choice. Dentsu chose Masayuki Kakefu, a retired baseball player and now a TV entertainer, to be the father. Yoshiko Tanaka, an actress who is very popular among Japanese housewives, was picked to play the mother. The campaign was created, along with an accompanying sales promotion effort that included a "cushion futon" (Japanese traditional bedding) used by the family and sold to consumers.

The "family ties" campaign went on air for three months and was very successful. As one indicator of its success, more than 700,000 requests were received for the futon premium (by far exceeding the pre-campaign projection of 600,000 units). The client's sales also rose dramatically; they were up about 10 percent from the previous year. Market share for the brand also increased from 56 percent to 64 percent. The brand's success was largely due to the advertising campaign, which created a favorable impression among consumers and also motivated Omusubi-yama's sales force to work harder to get stores to stock the product.

VIVE LA DIFFÉRENCE! THE LOCALIZATION PERSPECTIVE

On the other hand, many marketers feel that advertising must be tailored to the unique aspects of each culture. This side of the debate stresses that every country has a unique set of values and preferences and that most ads developed to appeal to consumers in one country will be "alien" to people elsewhere. One noticeable difference across cultures is intolerance toward sexual content and nudity: Although many Americans pride themselves on their "progressive" attitudes, many would blush if they saw some of the commercials that are popular in Europe or Japan! At the other extreme, a condom advertisement was rejected by the conservative Indian government because the tagline read "For the pleasure of making love."[63]

Messages that focus on universal values, such as love of family, tend to travel fairly well, whereas those that focus on specific consumer lifestyles do not. Compared to those in the United States, for example, British commercials tend to contain less information, employ a soft sell, and attempt to entertain rather than persuade.[64] In fact, a recent American campaign for Boboli, a line of Italian bread shells and pizza sauce sold by Kraft General Foods, was rejected for the British market because the ads were "too American" (that is, too hard-sell).[65]

DOES GLOBAL ADVERTISING WORK?

The practice of global advertising has met with mixed results. A few large companies have had success with standardized advertising, but most have found that the often subtle differences from country to country demand that advertising appeals be tailored to each culture for maximum effectiveness.

Exhibit 17.7
This television commercial for Omusubi-yama rice ball additive ran in the spring of 1994. Here is the dialog:

Wife: "Omusubi-yama is delicious!"

Husband: "It makes our family happy."

Wife: "Now that it has 30 percent more salmon."

Husband: "It makes us even more happy."

Wife and Husband: "It is a new Omusubi-yama!"

One problem is that consumers in different countries simply have too many different customs, and do not necessarily even use the same product in the same way. For example, Kellogg discovered that in Brazil, cereal is more likely to be eaten as a dry snack than as part of a big breakfast, and Procter & Gamble had to discontinue a Japanese ad campaign for Camay soap—the ads featured men complimenting women on their appearance, a behavior the Japanese consider too forward.[66]

Perhaps the solution is to compromise, as American Express did in a recent $100 million global campaign that targeted almost thirty countries. To promote its green card around the world, AmEx created a series of testimonials featuring successful businesspeople from many places. Each spot follows the same formula but substitutes a local businessperson; the endorser discusses his or her business philosophy and then gives credit to the card for making it easier to run the company. As an AmEx executive observed, "You have to be conscious of local attitudes and economics. But, in fact, 80 percent of the emotional element of our brand is the same around the world."[67] This strategy highlights the advice we gave in Chapter 4: "Think globally and act locally."

Chapter 17 Summary

Objective 1. Explain advertising's role in marketing communications.

Advertising is nonpersonal communication from an identified sponsor using mass media to persuade or influence an audience. Advertising informs, reminds, and creates consumer desire. In recent years, advertising's importance in the promotion mix has decreased because of an erosion of brand loyalty, changing media technology, increasing costs of advertising, changing consumer attitudes toward advertising, and increased emphasis on integrated marketing communications.

Objective 2. List and describe the major types of advertising.

Consumer product advertising is used to persuade consumers to choose a specific product or brand. Trade advertising promotes products to people and businesses in a specific industry. Institutional advertising is used to promote an entire organization (corporate image advertising), to promote a local store (retail advertising), to express the opinions of an organization (advocacy advertising), or to support a cause (public service advertising).

Objective 3. Explain the major factors that shape an advertising campaign.

Advertising begins with the client or advertiser, who may be a manufacturer, a distributor, a retailer, or an institution. Some companies have in-house advertising departments, but most rely on the services of advertising agencies to create ads (or other promotions) and arrange for their delivery to the target market. Typical agency personnel and departments include account management, creative services, research and marketing services, account planners, and media planners. Early in the product life cycle, the major objective for an advertising campaign can be to build primary demand for an entire product class. Once the product is established, campaign objectives can relate to creating selective demand for one particular brand. Setting aesthetic objectives rather than practical ones can lead to ineffective ads.

Objective 4. Tell how advertisers develop creative strategies.

A creative strategy is the process whereby objectives are translated to messages that hopefully will create attention, interest, desire, and action. Some frequently used types of advertising appeals are the unique selling proposition (USP), comparative advertising, fear appeals, celebrity endorsements, slice-of-life ads, sex appeal advertising, and humorous ads. Advertisers may choose a lecture format or a drama format to present the advertising message.

Objective 5. Describe the major advertising media and explain the important considerations in media planning.

A media plan determines where and when advertising will appear. Broadcast media include television and radio. As a result of increasing television viewing alternatives, the TV audience has become fragmented, yet advertising time on network television remains very expensive. Radio has a strong local appeal, and radio ads can be changed quickly. Print media are newspapers, magazines and directories. Newspapers are a primary medium for retailers, despite declining readership. Magazines have become more specialized in recent years, allowing advertisers to reach very specific target markets. Directory advertising such as the Yellow Pages is a highly credible source of information for consumers. Out-of-home media include outdoor advertising (primarily billboards) and place-based media. High levels of future growth are expected for direct and interactive media.

In comparing the ability of different media vehicles to deliver the desired target market, media planners use measures of reach and frequency to calculate the vehicles' gross rating points (GRPs). The comparative cost-effectiveness of different media vehicles is evaluated using the cost per thousand (CPM). Media planners must also decide when to deliver the messages and whether to use a continuous, pulsing, or flighting schedule.

Objective 6. Explain how advertisers evaluate the effectiveness of an advertising campaign.

Although it is clear that advertising does increase sales, advertisers need to conduct research to determine whether specific advertisements are effective. Pretesting or copy testing of advertising before it is placed in the media may include concept testing, testing of TV advertising animatics or storyboards, and finished ad testing. Later, advertisers may also conduct posttesting research to make sure the ads are doing well.

Objective 7. Discuss some of the important aspects of advertising in international markets.

A standardization strategy may be used in advertising an international brand. Here, the same ad campaign is used in different cultures and emphasizes similarities among consumers. The localization perspective, on the other hand, focuses on differences among cultures and calls for modifying the ad campaign.

Review Questions

Marketing Concepts: Testing Your Knowledge

1. What is advertising and what is its function in marketing?
2. How does the advertising industry of the 1990s differ from that of earlier decades?
3. What are the different types of advertising that are most often used?
4. List and describe the various departments in an advertising agency.
5. When is the goal of advertising likely to be to build primary demand? Secondary demand?
6. What are hard-sell advertising appeals? What are soft-sell appeals?
7. Describe the different types of advertising execution formats?
8. What are the strengths and weaknesses of newspapers, magazines, television, radio, outdoor, and place-based media for advertising?
9. What information does a media planner use in developing an effective media schedule?
10. How can advertisers make sure their advertising is effective before it is placed in the media? After the audience has been exposed to the advertising in the media?
11. What is the difference between a standardization perspective and a localization perspective in international advertising strategy?

Marketing Concepts: Discussing Choices and Issues

1. Some people have criticized advertising for unnecessarily increasing product costs. Others argue that advertising is beneficial and actually provides value for consumers. What are some arguments on each side? How do you feel?
2. In recent years, for various reasons, many advertisers have been decreasing the amount spent on advertising. What are the reasons for this change? What do you think will happen to advertising spending during the next five to ten years?
3. Advertisers who spend millions of dollars for Superbowl ad spots may be more interested in achieving esthetic goals—that is, having the most highly rated ad—than in selling products. Does it make sense for advertisers to focus on esthetic goals rather than marketing goals? Explain.
4. Some critics say that many ads seem to be selling sex rather than products. Do you agree or disagree with this criticism? In a role-playing situation with another member of your class, argue your position on the subject.

Marketing Practice: Applying What You've Learned

1. As an account executive for an advertising agency, you have been assigned to a new client, a manufacturer of a popular brand of shampoo. As you begin development of the creative strategy, you are considering different types of appeals: (a) USP, (b) comparative advertising, (c) a fear appeal, (d) a celebrity endorsement, (e) a slice-of-life ad, (f) sex appeal, and (g) humor. Outline the strengths and weaknesses of using each of these appeals for advertising the shampoo.

2. Advertisers may use the same ad campaign in different cultures, or they may decide that the different countries require different campaigns as a result of variation in values, tastes, government regulation, and so on. With one or more classmates, select a country from among (a) Sweden, (b) Saudi Arabia, (c) Romania, (d) Mexico, and (e) France. Locate information about the country in your library or talk with someone from the country. With the group, develop some suggestions for advertising a brand of perfume in the country. Include the type of appeal you would use and what sort of execution. Present your plan to the class.

3. Assume you are working in the media department of an advertising agency. You have been asked your opinion on which media to use for advertising for a local retail clothing store.
   a. Write a memo that compares newspapers, magazines, television, radio, and outdoor as vehicles for this media plan.
   b. Write a memo assessing the appropriateness of each of these media for advertising a national brand of cat food.

4. A list of different media vehicles, the size of their audience, and the cost of advertising follows.
   a. Use the information to calculate the CPM for each of the media vehicles.
   b. Assuming a total target market of 5,000,000, what is the reach for each media vehicle?
   c. Develop a media plan that will provide 200 GRPs a week.

Media Vehicle	Audience	Ad Cost
TV evening news	1,500,000	$5,000.00 (30-second commercial)
Daily newspaper	2,800,000	$1,000.00
Local country radio station	300,000	$250,000 (30-second commercial)
Local rock radio station	400,000	$350,000 (30-second commercial)
Local split run of *Newsweek* magazine	900,000	$30,000

Marketing Mini-Project: Learning by Doing

The purpose of this mini-project is to give you an opportunity to experience the advertising creative process.

1. With one or more classmates, create (imagine) a new brand of an existing product (such as a laundry detergent, toothpaste, perfume, soft drink, or the like).
2. Decide on an advertising appeal for your new product.
3. Create a series of at least three different magazine ads for your product, using the appeal you selected. Your ads should have a headline, a visual, and "copy" to explain your product and/or to persuade customers to purchase your brand.
4. Present your ads to your class. Discuss the advertising appeal you selected, and explain your ad executions.

Key Terms

Endnotes

1. Dentsu Inc., *Annual Report,* 1993.
2. William Wells, John Burnett, and Sandra Moriarty, *Advertising: Principles and Practice,* 2 ed. (Upper Saddle River, NJ: Prentice-Hall, 1992).
3. Ibid.
4. Charles Goodrum and Helen Dalrymple, *Advertising in America: The First 200 Years* (New York: Harry N. Abrams, 1990).
5. Rob Norton, "How Uninformative Advertising Tells Consumers Quite a Bit," *Fortune* (Dec. 26, 1994): 37.
6. "TV Ad Picture Looks Good," *Marketing News* (Jan. 15, 1996): 1.
7. "100 Leading National Advertisers," *Advertising Age* (Jan. 2, 1995): 12.
8. William Wells, John Burnett, and Sandra Moriarty, *Advertising: Principles and Practice,* 3 ed. (Upper Saddle River, NJ: Prentice-Hall, 1995).
9. *Ibid.*
10. Gary Levin, "'Keeping in Touch' Easy with Database," *Advertising Age* (March 28, 1994): S-8.
11. Kevin Goldman, "From Witches to Anorexics, Critical Eyes Scrutinize Ads for Political Correctness," *The Wall Street Journal* (May 19, 1994): B1.
12. Kip Cassino, "An Advertising Atlas," *American Demographics* (Aug. 1994): 44–55.
13. Laura Bird, "Business-to-Business Pitches Lack Pizazz," *The Wall Street Journal,* (Oct. 1, 1993): B5.
14. Ibid.
15. Wally Olins, "How a Corporation Reveals Itself," *The New York Times Forum* (Oct. 14, 1990): F13, quoted in Marion G. Sobol, Gail F. Farrelly, and Jessica S. Taper, *Shaping the Corporate Image: An Analytical Guide for Executive Decision Makers* (Westport, CT: Quorum Books, 1992).
16. Stuart Elliot, "An Increase in Corporate Campaigns Points to a Continuing Recovery for Madison Avenue," *The New York Times* (Jan. 18, 1995): D5.
17. Nathaniel C. Nash, "Benetton Touches a Nerve and Germans Protest," *The New York Times* (Feb. 3, 1995): D1.
18. Mark Vogel and Walter J. Fiorentini, "Redefining Co-op," *Sales & Marketing Management* (May 1993): 63–65.
19. Kevin Goldman, "Wells Rich Isn't Private on Public Service," *The Wall Street Journal* (Dec. 21, 1993): B5.
20. Bob D. Cutler and Darrel D. Muehling, "Another Look at Advocacy Advertising and the Boundaries of Commercial Speech," *Journal of Advertising* (Dec. 1991): 49–52.
21. "U.S. Agency Brands Ranked by Gross Income," *Advertising Age* (Jan. 2, 1995): 13.
22. Kevin Goldman, "IBM-Account Fight Lifts Planner Profile," *The Wall Street Journal* (Oct. 26, 1993): B8.
23. Kevin Goldman, "Dr. Pepper Wraps Ads in Stars and Stripes," *The Wall Street Journal* (Oct. 4, 1993): B3.
24. Charles Goodrum and Helen Dalrymple, *Advertising in America: The First 200 Years* (New York: Harry N. Abrams, 1990).
25. Ibid.
26. Quoted in Kevin Goldman, "Knock, Knock. Who's There? The Same Old Funny Ad Again," *The Wall Street Journal* (Nov. 2, 1993): B10.
27. Carol Moog, president, Creative Focus, quoted in Kevin Goldman, "The Message, Clever As It May Be, Is Lost in a Number of High-Profile Campaigns," *The Wall Street Journal* (July 27, 1993): B1.
28. William Wells, John Burnett, and Sandra Moriarty, *Advertising: Principles and Practice,* 3 ed. (Upper Saddle River, NJ: Prentice-Hall, 1995).
29. Greg Prince, "Confrontation, Innovation, Gimmickry Mark First Month of New Year's Advertising," *Beverage World* (Periscope edition) (Jan. 31, 1991): 1.
30. Juliette Walker, "Pepsi-Coke Spat Raises Questions about Ad Policies," *Japan Times Weekly,* International edition (June 24–June 30, 1991): 7.
31. Lynette S. Unger and James M. Stearns, "The Use of Fear and Guilt Messages in Television Advertising: Issues and Evidence," in eds. Patrick E. Murphy *et al., 1983 AMA Educators' Proceedings,* (Chicago: American Marketing Association).
32. Douglas C. McGill, "Star Wars in Cola Advertising," *The New York Times* (March 22, 1989): D1.
33. Michael Janofsky, "Naked Bodies. Oh-my-goodness Words. They Attract Plenty of Attention, But Can They Hold It?" *The New York Times* (Oct. 4, 1993): D8.
34. Damon Darlin, "Myth and Marketing in Japan," *The Wall Street Journal* (April 6, 1989): B1.
35. John Deighton, Daniel Romer, and Josh McQueen, "Using Drama to Persuade," *Journal of Consumer Research* (Dec. 1989): 335–343.
36. Barbara B. Stern, "Medieval Allegory: Roots of Advertising Strategy for the Mass Market," *Journal of Marketing* (July 1988): 84–94.
37. "Candice Bergen Leads the List of Top Celebrity Endorsers," *The Wall Street Journal* (Sept. 17, 1993): B1.
38. Stuart Elliott, "South African Air Gets Results from a Much-Debated Commercial," *The New York Times* (Jan. 11, 1995): D18.
39. Kevin Goldman, "Ad with Disabled Child Stirs Controversy," *The Wall Street Journal* (Sept. 3, 1993): B8.
40. Ira Teinowitz, "Coors Keys on Fantasy," *Advertising Age* (Sept. 11, 1989): 114.

41. Patricia Sellers, "Winning Over the New Consumer," *Fortune* (July 29, 1991): 113–114.

42. Carrie Goerne, "Some See Cable TV Law as Threat to Ad Growth," *Marketing News* (Nov. 9, 1992): 1.

43. Phil Hall, "Make Listeners Your Customers," *Nation's Business* (June 1994): 53R.

44. Rebecca Piirto, "Why Radio Thrives," *American Demographics* (May 1994): 4.

45. Ed Shane, "Playing the Local Song," *American Demographics* (Sept. 1989): 51–53.

46. Information provided by Yellow Pages Publishers Association, Troy, Michigan.

47. Lisa Marie Petersen, "Outside Chance," *Mediaweek* (June 15, 1992): 20–23.

48. Shakira Hightower, "On the Next Oprah: Women Who Found Their Mates on Billboards," *The Wall Street Journal* (Aug. 19, 1993): B1.

49. Michel Marriott, "Too Legit to Quit," *The New York Times* (Oct. 3, 1993): 8V.

50. Malcolm W. Browne, "City Lights and Space Ads May Blind Stargazers," *The New York Times* (May 4, 1993): C1.

51. John Helyar, "Signs Sprout at Sports Arenas as a Way to Get Cheap TV Ads," *The Wall Street Journal* (March 8, 1994): B1.

52. Joshua Levine, "Lighter Than Air," *Forbes* (Oct. 10, 1994): 120.

53. Marcy Magiera, "On-Screen Ads Unspool New Tactics," *Advertising Age* (Dec. 13, 1993): 10.

54. Donna Petrozzello, "Interactive Ads May Be on Rise," *Broadcasting & Cable* (Oct. 17, 1994): 52.

55. Patricia Sellers, "The Best Way to Reach Your Buyers," *Fortune* 4 (Autumn/Winter 1993): 15.

56. William Wells, John Burnett, and Sandra Moriarty, *Advertising: Principles and Practice,* 3 ed. (Upper Saddle River, NJ: Prentice-Hall, 1995).

57. Bristol Voss, "Measuring the Effectiveness of Advertising and PR," *Sales & Marketing Management* (Oct. 1992): 123–124.

58. This remark has also been credited to a British businessman named Lord Leverhulme. See Charles Goodrum and Helen Dalrymple, *Advertising in America: The First 200 Years* (New York: Harry N. Abrams, 1990).

59. The research findings reported here are abstracted from Bristol Voss, "Measuring the Effectiveness of Advertising and PR," *Sales & Marketing Management* (Oct. 1992): 123–124.

60. Mark Ladler, "What Happened to Advertising?" *Business Week* (Sept. 23, 1991): 66–72.

61. Melissa Turner, "Coca-Cola Goes Global With New Commercial," *Atlanta Constitution* (Jan. 24, 1992): 1.

62. Zachary Schiller and Rischar A. Melcher, "Marketing Globally, Thinking Locally," *International Business Week* (May 13, 1991): 23.

63. David Alexander, "Condom Controversy: Suggestive Kama-Sutra Ads Arouse India," *Advertising Age International* (April 27, 1992): I-12.

64. Terence Nevett, "Differences between American and British Television Advertising Explanations and Implications," *Journal of Advertising,* XXI (Dec. 1992): 61–72.

65. Stuart Elliott, "A Relatively Gentle American Campaign for Pizza Fixing Is Still Too Hard Sell for British Tastes," *The New York Times* (Aug. 10, 1993): D19.

66. Julie Skur Hill and Joseph M. Winski, "Goodby Global Ads: Global Village Is Fantasy Land for Marketers," *Advertising Age* (Nov. 16, 1987): 22.

67. Jon Berry, "Don't Leave Home Without It, Wherever You Live," *Business Week* (Feb. 21, 1994): 76.

MARKETING IN ACTION: REAL PEOPLE AT AMOCO CHEMICAL

Sanford Schulert nearly lost his job over an ad he developed to bolster Amoco's corporate image. Fortunately, the ad turned out to be a big hit, and ever since, Schulert has continued to create the right chemistry for an industrial products firm.

Schulert is director of marketing communications in charge of advertising at one of Amoco Corporation's three major business sectors, Amoco Chemical. His job is to convince industrial purchasing agents that Amoco is a company to be trusted "for innovation, technological prowess, and reliability." How has Schulert done this? The answer is advertising—but not just any advertising. In an environment where the typical ad is bland and highly technical, Schulert has turned instead to promotional messages that are off-beat, unexpected, and colorful.

Schulert's challenge is to make Amoco's product stand out—not an easy task because the product is basically indistinguishable from the chemicals sold by competitors. To create a competitive advantage, Schulert feels the advertising must focus on the fact that buying from Amoco means buying the resources of Amoco, not just the chemical itself. Ideally, then, Amoco's advertising should communicate a feeling of trust, technical innovation, and expertise. Trying to convey this feeling, Schulert came up with a unique ad. It showed an IMSA GT race car with an engine made of an Amoco plastic. The headline read, "Incredible. Now there's a car engine made of plastic." The hitch was that Amoco had to spend $130,000 to build the car in order to make this claim valid! Fortunately for Schulert, the ad worked. The car became the subject of countless news stories, and Schulert was vindicated.

Although Amoco Corporation's chemical division was established in 1954, it took almost twenty years before anyone at the company realized that building a positive corporate image might be important. One reason why advertising is so important to Amoco is that most chemical buying is done by committee. On average, only 20 percent of the members of the committee ever see an Amoco salesperson, so advertising is essential to reach the other 80 percent.

When Richard Leet became head of marketing for Amoco Chemical, he was stunned to find out that many potential customers had never even heard of the company. Schulert was brought in to polish up Amoco's image. His first ad was the one that nearly cost him his job. More than ten years later, Schulert's surprising ads continue to shape the image of Amoco Chemical in the minds of customers and prospective customers. Subjects of the ads have ranged from children driving cars to the Stars and Stripes sailing crew racing in the America's Cup. Each execution illustrates a novel way in which Amoco chemicals play an important part in people's lives. Amoco's current theme is "The Chemistry's Right at Amoco."

Amoco Chemical's advertising efforts appear to have paid off. In 1980, a study by *Chemical & Engineering News* showed that only 20 percent of the company's target market had a favorable opinion of the firm. That percentage has since doubled. What's more, for over ten years, Starch readership scores of *Business Week* ads have shown that Amoco's ads are among the most read and best remembered in the magazine. And Amoco Chemical's income increased from $2.5 billion in 1980 to $4 billion in 1995. Nobody is arguing that this increase is due solely to advertising, but these efforts certainly haven't hurt. Even so, Schulert still has to defend his programs. Some skeptics at Amoco still wonder about the millions spent on image advertising with nothing tangible to show for it. Schulert's continuing task is to develop a "personality" for an industrial company—and to convince his colleagues that it's worth the effort to do so.

Source: Weld F. Royal, "Good Chemistry," *Sales & Marketing Management*, (April 1995): 111–114.

Things to Talk About

1. Why is corporate image advertising important to Amoco Chemical?

2. How has Amoco Chemical used its image advertising to build customer relationships?

3. Why is corporate image advertising more important to a company such as Amoco Chemical than to a firm that manufactures trucks or cereal or photocopy machines? How would you respond to those in the company who feel that advertising money would be better spent in other ways?

4. Do you think the novel nature of Amoco Chemical ads has been important in their success? Why or why not?

5. What secrets of success has Amoco Chemical discovered?

CASE 17-2

MARKETING IN ACTION: REAL CHOICES AT POSTUM

Postum is a 100-year-old coffee substitute that many of today's consumers have never even heard of. If some stubborn marketers at Kraft have their way, though, that may change soon. They are engineering a comeback for Postum and are hoping that advertising can convince a new generation to give the venerable old product another try.

Postum was the first product sold by the Post Cereal Company (Post was later absorbed by General Foods, which was then bought by Kraft Foods). Made from roasted wheat, bran, and molasses, the powder is added to hot water to make a tasty (to at least the two million people who buy the product each year) morning beverage. For a hundred years, the brand has dominated the market for coffee substitutes, with an 87.7 percent share. Postum marketers feel that much of that success can be traced back to early advertising efforts. In 1934, a newspaper ad showed how a husband suffering from indigestion, headaches, and sleeplessness was a "new man" after his wife switched from coffee to Postum. The ad also featured "Mr. Coffee-Nerves," a cartoon character, who grumbled, "Postum, curse it, has driven me out of another home!" This character has been out of work for some time, though: Since 1983 there has been no advertising of any kind for Postum.

Tate Lucy is senior brand manager for Postum at Kraft Foods. When talking about the brand, Lucy uses such phrases as "a very stable franchise" and "a lot of loyal users." But another term for Postum is "ghost brand"—an older, unadvertised product that survives because a small group of steadfast fans continue to buy it. Even though Postum pretty much "owns" the coffee substitute market, sales of Postum have not increased in recent years and, in fact, have shown a slight decline. Whereas annual sales of popular coffee brands typically run into several hundred million dollars, Postum's yearly sales have been in the range of $7 million to $8 million.

Kraft would like to try to increase the usage of the brand—in short, to find out whether Postum can be re-

vived. In recent years, as more and more products have been introduced to the market, grocery store shelf space has become increasingly scarce. For package goods producers, this means that even venerable older brands must either grow or die. And many at Kraft feel that Postum deserves a chance. After no advertising or other marketing support for over a decade, though, no one is quite sure what the potential for the brand really is in the 1990s.

Postum's target is the consumer at least fifty-five years old. Currently, product users are almost exclusively in the sixty-five-plus range, but Lucy thinks advertising can effectively persuade slightly younger consumers to add Postum to their current portfolio of drinks. He feels that "coffee, tea, or Postum?" should be the question consumers ask themselves when thinking of hot beverages. According to Lucy, as people age, "they tend to look for hot beverage alternatives," and he intends to make Postum high on the list.

The only question is how best to convince these consumers to become Postum drinkers. Advertising worked a hundred years ago, and there is reason to believe it will work again. But what media, what message, and what budget? Can the company afford to spend $1 million on a market of less than $8 million? It's do or die for Lucy. Can he craft a wake-up call to revive this dormant brand?

Source: Stuart Elliott, "Advertising," *The New York Times* (April 19, 1995): D7.

Things to Think About

1. What is the problem facing Postum?
2. What factors are important in understanding this problem?
3. What alternatives might Postum marketers consider?
4. What are your recommendations for solving the problem?
5. What are some ways to implement your recommendations?

18

Sales Promotion and Public Relations

When you have completed your study of this chapter, you should be able to:

1. Explain the use of sales promotion and its importance in the marketing function.

2. Describe some of the various types of trade and consumer sales promotions frequently used by marketers.

3. Outline the steps in developing a sales promotion program.

4. Explain the role of public relations.

5. Describe the steps in developing a public relations campaign.

MEET VICTORIA FELDMAN, A DECISION MAKER AT KWE ASSOCIATES

Victoria Feldman is vice president of KWE Associates, a public relations firm based in New York City that specializes in the travel and hospitality industries. KWE's clients have included Visa, American Airlines, Royal Caribbean Cruise Line, and the Ritz-Carlton Hotel Company. The company has also done extensive tourism-related work on behalf of Finland, Grenada, Ecuador, and Bermuda.

Feldman began her marketing and communications career in market research for Shell Oil, and she later entered the public relations field as manager of public relations for the Venice Simplon-Orient Express and the company's affiliated hotels and cruise ship. Since joining KWE Associates in 1989, she has executed public relations programs for Visa U.S.A., Adirondack Beverages, and the Royal Caribbean Cruise Line, among others. Most recently, she directed media relations and special events for Royal Caribbean's launch of its newest, $325 million vessel, *Legend of the Seas*. Feldman is a *magna cum laude* graduate of Boston College, with a bachelor of science degree in marketing.

THERE'S MORE TO LIFE THAN ADVERTISING!

When asked, "How does a company let consumers know about its products and entice them to buy them?," many people automatically think of lavish TV commercials or informative print ads. Advertising is, of course, a widely used method of communication, but marketers also have many other tools available to them. Victoria Feldman and her colleagues who specialize in public relations know this well—they routinely create promotional programs for clients, such as arranging for news coverage of quirky events like 24-hour golf in Finland to call attention to a good or service without actually sponsoring an advertising message.

This chapter will focus on two important elements in the promotion mix: sales promotions and public relations. Both are crucial to many marketing strategies, and each can be implemented separately or—ideally—coordinated with a firm's advertising activities. At the same time, they present an interesting contrast: Whereas sales promotion activities often consist of short-term efforts to bring about a fairly quick result (such as temporarily boosting market share), public relations efforts often are ongoing or long-term attempts to hone the image of a company, person, or product. Because both types of promotion are widely used ways to communicate the value of an offering, each can play an important role in building relationships with customers. In addition, the two types of promotion often work together: A sales promotion may be designed to draw attention to a company and make it stand out in a crowded market, and public relations specialists often are on hand to be sure the right people are aware of what is going on. As an introduction to these various activities, consider how the following companies are getting in touch with their customers where they shop and where they play.

■ In 1993, Reebok International initiated its Reebok Bodywalk program to reach the seventy million Americans who walk for exercise. The company instituted a heavy point-of-purchase campaign at retail outlets, including mini-boutiques set up to feature its products. Also, catering to the walker's tendency to wear a portable stereo during exercise, the company linked up with Warner Brothers Records to sell a Bodywalk audiotape featuring samples of Warner's latest artists spliced into workout guidelines and instructions.

■ To reach kids, Nestlé U.S.A. sponsored a Sweetarts/Nickelodeon Easter Egg Hunt. To target older customers, the company's baking products were featured in recipes demonstrated on shows such as the Nashville Network's "Cookin' USA" and the Family Channel's "Let's Eat with Burt Wolfe." [2]

■ Mennen, maker of Speed Stick deodorant, Skin Bracer after-shave and Baby Magic lotion, donates a small percentage of the coupons consumers redeem for its products to the U.S. Marine Reserve's Toys for Tots program. That comes to about $300,000 per year. [3]

■ RJR Nabisco's Winston cigarette division spends $4.5 million a year sponsoring Nascar stock car races. [4] Philip Morris's Miller Lite beer has joined the legions of companies that promote beach volleyball. [5]

■ Life Savers' Bubble Yum brand is taking a virtual reality game on a shopping mall tour. Four participants don headsets that electronically move them through a maze of falling chunks of gum. [6]

AN OVERVIEW OF SALES PROMOTIONS

Sales promotions are short-term programs to build interest in, or encourage purchase of, a good or service during a specified time period. [7] Like advertising, a sales promotion is often targeted to a particular segment of either consumers or organizations. Sales promotions are usually developed to complement other promotion activities, such as when a contest is held to motivate salespeople by awarding a trip to Hawaii to top performers, or when a sweepstakes or in-store appearance by a celebrity is intended to yield valuable headlines for the sponsoring company. Many, though certainly not all, sales promotions are price-oriented; they are designed to entice greater immediate purchasing by either retailers or consumers. They are used in many consumer marketing applications as well as in business-to-business marketing strategies. Sometimes they are even used as a tool for social change. In one highly effective application, about fifty retail music chains in 1992 were involved in a voter awareness campaign called "Rock the Vote." The stores distributed more than 60,000 pieces of promotion material to music shoppers to encourage them to register to vote. [8]

In this section, we'll briefly discuss the use of sales promotions by companies. Then we'll examine the importance of sales promotions to the marketing function.

sales promotions: short-term programs to build interest in, or encourage purchase of, a good or service during a specified time period

THE EVOLUTION OF SALES PROMOTIONS

The amount of money and effort allocated to sales promotions in the promotion mix has been rising steadily. Today, over 75 percent of U.S. companies' promotional budgets are devoted to sales promotions rather than to advertising.

Sales promotions in the 1990s are becoming more complex and expensive, and they may even involve multiple companies. A recent promotion by Pepsico illustrates this evolution: The company distributed forty million discount cards during its recent "Gotta Have It" promotion. Consumers who bought Pepsi multipacks could use the cards, which look like credit cards, to purchase merchandise at discounts ranging from $10 off Reebok sneakers sold at Foot Locker to $100 off Norwegian Cruise Line voyages. As a spokesman for Pepsi observed, "Reebok was happy . . . MCI, which offered special discounts to new customers as part of the promotion, was getting 2000 calls a day. So our partners in this told us it was a success." Pepsi itself attributed a sales gain of $250 million to the promotion. [9]

A fierce battle is still raging between advertisers and sales promotion specialists over the best way to allocate marketing dollars. Although the use of sales promotion tactics continues to increase, there are some signs that this trend is slowing. The most notable omen comes from marketing giant Procter & Gamble, which, as we discussed in Chapter 13, is moving away from a heavy reliance on coupons and other short-term price reductions and toward an every day low pricing strategy where its products will be discounted on a more regular, predictable basis. Still, sales promotions in all of their various forms continue to play a vital role in contemporary marketing strategies.

THE IMPORTANCE OF SALES PROMOTIONS TO THE MARKETING FUNCTION

Budgets for sales promotions have been growing steadily at many companies, often at the expense of advertising allocations. Why this shift in emphasis within the promotion mix? One answer is that while the amount of time people spend interacting with all media—newspapers, magazines, radio and television—has remained fairly constant, the number of separate outlets available to them has exploded. Television grew from three networks to more than sixty channels, thanks to cable. New magazine titles crop up like weeds. As a result, the cost of advertising has risen dramatically as companies spend ever more money in pursuit of increasingly fragmented audiences. For network advertisers, the cost per thousand viewers (the standard measure of efficiency), is now five times what it was in 1970.[10]

Another factor is that brand loyalty has deteriorated. The current emphasis on value for the dollar means that many people are more swayed by price-based appeals than by long-term advertising campaigns that slowly but surely forge a favorable brand "personality."[11] Many forms of sales promotions, such as coupons and product giveaways, emphasize savings more than superiority of the product.

Because they can be very focused and can have an immediate impact, sales promotions targeted to a specific consumer segment can be particularly effective for reaching smaller markets, such as members of specific ethnic and racial groups. Consumption in almost all consumer product categories is rising faster among minorities, as incomes rise, than among whites. Furthermore, minorities tend to exhibit greater brand loyalty when they are properly courted. The Hispanic division of Quaker Oats sponsored a $25,000 Magic Wish sweepstakes for Cap'n Crunch brand, and Univision sponsored a Hispanic festival in New York City that drew more than 1 million attendees. Martell Cognac sponsors jazz musician Al Jarreau (58 percent of cognac in the U.S. is consumed by African-Americans, many of whom use it as a mixer). To celebrate the Chinese New Year in San Francisco, the *San Francisco Chronicle* and other companies sponsored an Asian festival. The event was televised and syndicated, and coverage reached more than 1 million Asians in more than 20 markets nationwide.[12]

Finally, the results of sales promotions can be more directly measured by comparing sales before, during, and after promotions. As with the direct marketing activities described in Chapters 15 and 16, marketers can get a better sense of whether they are really getting their money's worth.

Using Sales Promotions to Meet Marketing Objectives

Because it often involves a combination of marketing communications, physical displays, and actions by a sales force, the development and planning of a sales promotion are usually shared by advertising and sales managers. In some cases, an outside agency is retained to implement a specific project as well. For example, some companies specialize in conducting sweepstakes or other games on behalf of clients.

A sales promotion sponsored by Taster's Choice instant coffee illustrates how the impact of a company's advertising can be enhanced by further increasing consumers' involvement with the campaign via a coordinated sales promotion effort. The brand capitalized on the publicity created by its well-known advertising campaign involving the mysterious saga of a pair of coffee-borrowing neighbors who always appear to be on the verge of a romantic relationship. A consumer essay contest was run on the theme "What's brewing for our couple?" Contestants were asked to submit essays describing what the next step in the serial advertising campaign should be. Entries were judged on creativity, romantic appeal, writing skill, and, of course, flattering references to Taster's Choice. The grand-prize winner won a trip for two to Paris. In addition, booklets offering synopses of the commercials in the long-running series were attached to store displays (in Britain, a novel based on the exploits of the couple has already been a best seller).[13]

The specific nature of the promotion should depend on the objectives the company is trying to achieve. A promotion can be undertaken for many reasons:

Obtaining distribution or shelf space for a product

Generating dealer enthusiasm

Increasing the volume of product bought by a retailer

Creating greater brand awareness among consumers

Featuring a particular item

Encouraging consumers to try the product

Boosting short-term sales

Advantages of Sales Promotions

Sales promotions are useful for building interest in products throughout their life cycles. They can encourage trial of new products, as when a shopper is handed a free sample of a new brand of microwave pizza while strolling through the supermarket. On the other hand, promotions are widely used to stimulate sales of established, mature products, as when Pepsi attempts to steal sales from Coca-Cola by giving shoppers discounts on a range of products.

In most cases, it is unrealistic to expect that sales promotions will create a long-term change in market share—the goal instead is to create a short-term sales burst for the brand. However, there are exceptions: Some sales promotions are intended to "hook" consumers on a good or service in the hope that they will develop loyalty to it over time. For example, MasterCard is trying to build brand equity among college students by sponsoring a music and comedy talent search program at 225 colleges nationwide. A recent study by the company showed that two-thirds of card users continue to use as their primary card the same credit card they acquired in college.[14] (Choose your plastic carefully!)

A trade promotion is often a powerful way to cement relationships with retailers and wholesalers, because it allows the marketer to reward them for choosing to carry the product. Business promotions are useful in creating awareness of a firm and keeping its name and products in front of other companies with whom the organization does business (or hopes to). Some promotion efforts are also paying off for firms that practice database marketing (see Chapter 16); they collect valuable information from all of those rebate forms, mail-in offers, and sweepstakes that people fill out every day.

Promotions may influence consumers who would otherwise have a very low probability of buying.[15] Because these messages tend to reach people at a time when they're in a buying mood (at the store rather than sprawled in front of the TV set), they are more likely to result in action. Also, the consumers most likely to be influenced by sales promotions are those who are relatively fickle as opposed to those who are brand-loyal; they are swayed by what they perceive to be a good value for the money and will probably abandon the brand for another as soon as it goes "off deal."

In general, promotions work best when they present a tangible benefit to the consumer, such as giving something away or stressing attractive and innovative product displays. One study conducted in supermarket bakery sections found that an in-store sales promotion that featured a bakery item and lasted for one week netted as much volume for the bakery section as did two months of unadvertised discounting alone.[16]

Exciting sales promotions help to keep store traffic high, which in turn makes it easier for retailers to generate high turnover and thus higher profits. In addition, many promotions occur behind the scenes; they involve partnerships between manufacturers and retailers and often serve the purpose of cementing good working relationships in the channel of distribution. Other promotions, such as company sales contests, are internally focused; they are intended to motivate the firm's salespeople and others to build better relationships and maximize customer satisfaction.

Disadvantages of Sales Promotions

On the other hand, many marketers (including many of those employed by advertising agencies!) argue that reliance on sales promotions instead of advertising can have negative consequences. Some of the opponents' arguments:

■ Sales promotions dilute brand equity. They condition people to choose brands on the basis of short-term gimmicks or price reductions, rather than building brand loyalty through many years of usage and fostering deep-seated bonds with the product. Whereas advertising builds loyalty to a brand, sales promotions break it down.

■ Consumers learn a bad lesson. Marketers "poison the well" by teaching consumers always to expect brands to be on sale. Because many sales promotions are based on temporary price breaks, consumers come to assume that the products they want will always be on "special," so they won't buy a regularly priced brand.

■ Promotions have at best a temporary effect. Any positive effects of sales promotions will be experienced only in the short term. Again, because they are often based on price breaks, sales promotions rarely stimulate repeat purchases.

■ Marketers are preaching to the converted. The positive effects of sales promotions are an illusion that results from "borrowing from Peter to pay Paul." Sales promotions dilute sales from future purchases; the consumer would have bought the product (at regular price) anyway at some later time and is just using this opportunity to stock up.[17]

TYPES OF SALES PROMOTIONS

Sales promotions can take the form of cents-off coupons, toys in the bottom of cereal boxes, sweepstakes that dole out millions of dollars in fabulous prizes, or even a trip to Hawaii for the retail salesperson who sells the most of a specific line of vacuum cleaner, computer, or mutual fund. Some sales promotions are intended to tempt consumers to go out and buy an item because it's on sale ("Quantities are limited!" "Contest ends tomorrow!"). Others go on behind the scenes; they are designed to inform or persuade retailers about a company's goods or services. Some examples of sales promotions are given in Table 18.1. In this section, we'll consider the whole range of sales promotion possibilities, starting with trade promotions.

Table 18.1
Types of Sales Promotions

Technique	Primary Target	Description	Example
Trade show	Industry	Many manufacturers showcase their products to convention attendees.	The National Kitchen and Bath Association organizes several shows a year. Manufacturers display their latest wares to owners of kitchen and bath remodeling stores.
Incentive program	Sales force	A prize is offered to employees who meet a pre-specified sales goal or who are top performers in a given time period.	Mary Kay cosmetics awards distinctive pink cars to its top-selling representatives.
Point-of-purchase displays	Trade and consumers	In-store exhibits make retail environment more interesting and attract consumers' attention.	The Farnam Company: As somber music plays in the background, a huge plastic rat draped in a black

(continued)

Table 18.1
Types of Sales Promotions (continued)

Technique	Primary Target	Description	Example
			shroud lies next to a tombstone to promote the company's Just One Bite rat poison.
Push money	Trade	Salespeople are given a bonus for selling a specific manufacturer's product.	A retail salesperson at a formalwear store gets $1.00 every time he or she rents a particular tuxedo for a prom or wedding.
Specialty advertising	Trade	A company builds awareness and reinforces its image by giving out items with its name on them.	Beer companies send liquor store owners posters of attractive women wearing company T-shirts.
Cooperative promotions	Trade	Companies team up to promote their products jointly.	CompuServe and Universal Pictures ran a promotion for the mystery/thriller film *Sneakers*. CompuServe users were invited to break a series of codes contained in a special "Sneakers" file and win a trip to Hollywood.
Coupons	Consumers	Certificates for money off on selected products, often with an expiration date, used to encourage product trial.	Colgate-Palmolive offers 79 cents off a bottle of Teen Spirit deodorant.
Refunds/rebates	Consumers	Shopper receives money back from the manufacturer after mailing in a certificate; encourages trial.	Receive $3.00 after sending in a receipt to prove purchase of Smirnoff vodka.
Samples	Trade and consumers	Retailers might get a demonstration product to help in sales presentations; consumers get a free trial size of the product.	A small bottle of Pert shampoo arrives in the mail.
Contests/sweepstakes	Trade and consumers	A sales contest rewards wholesalers or retailers for performance; consumers participate in games or drawings to win prizes; builds awareness and reinforces image.	The Publishers' Clearing House announces its zillionth sweepstakes.
Bonus packs	Consumers	Additional product is given away with purchase; rewards users.	Maxell provides two extra cassettes with purchase of a pack of ten.
Events	Consumers	A company sponsors or underwrites a public "happening," sometimes for charity; reinforces corporate image.	The Kool Jazz Festival.
Gifts with purchase	Consumers	A consumer gets a free gift when a product is bought; reinforces product image and rewards users.	A free umbrella comes with the purchase of Lagerfeld's Photo cologne.
Continuity plans	Consumers	Customers accumulate prizes as they purchase increasing quantities; used to build brand loyalty.	Green stamps.

Source: Some material adapted from Ajay Bhasin, Roger Dickinson, William A. Robinson, and Christine G. Hauri, "Promotion Investments That Keep Paying Off," *Journal of Consumer Marketing,* (Winter 1989): 31–36; "One Sneaky Campaign," *Incentive,* (Nov. 1992): 93.

TRADE PROMOTIONS

Marketers spend roughly twice as much on activities targeted to industry members and retailers than on promotions that consumers directly experience.[18] Trade promotions can be roughly divided into two types: First, there are efforts to make retailers' lives easier by giving them a break on what they pay for a product or on advertising. Second, there are efforts to generate product awareness and orders by creating opportunities for the retailer and other members of the distribution channel to be exposed to one's products. Let's take a look at each type.

Working with the Retailer

Manufacturers often promote special arrangements that encourage retailers to plug their brands. Fierce competition for valuable shelf space has given retailers much more power than they used to have, and often they are able to receive large price concessions or advertising support from manufacturers. However, relatively little of this "generosity" is passed on to the consumer: Manufacturers spend about $18 billion on promotions, but only one-third of that amount gets translated into discounts for shoppers.[19] This competition has been especially tough for smaller manufacturers, who claim that the dominance of the shelves by major companies is stifling the introduction of new products and costing consumers money. However, here are two ways in which manufacturers work with local retailers to make their jobs easier:

Providing Local Advertising Support or Sales Training. Cooperative sales promotions are often useful to local retailers, who may not benefit directly from all the money that is spent on national advertising. For example, the Keebler Company recently began WELF Radio, an eighteen-market, four month, local radio promotion to support its Ripplin's and Tato Skins brands. In exchange for local retailers' in-store support, such as end-aisle displays, the local merchants receive the second half of a sixty-second radio spot to advertise their stores.[20]

In addition, some marketers work with retailers to help them sell the products that consumers come to the store to search for. Kraft General Foods runs several programs—with titles such as Dairy Case 2000—in which sales teams help grocers rearrange shelves and displays to maximize profits. In a two-year period, VF Corp. increased revenues in its Vanity Fair lingerie division by 25 percent to some $300 million by building alluring displays, training salespeople how to sell bras and camisoles, and giving lessons in customer service.[21]

SPOTLIGHT ON ETHICS

The Notorious Slotting Allowance

Probably the most controversial form of trade promotion is a slotting allowance: a direct payment to a retailer in return for stocking an item. Some industry critics charge that paying a slotting allowance means that supermarkets are putting their shelf space up for ransom. If companies want to place a new product in a grocery chain, they must give owners discounts, special deals, and usually a slotting fee (essentially a bribe) of $30,000 or so.* In some cases, a manufacturer might have to pay a slotting fee as high as $70,000 to get a grocery chain to carry its new product line.

Retailers, however, insist that slotting allowances help cover the high cost of introducing new products onto already crowded shelves. The number of items stocked by a typical supermarket (about 26,000) has doubled in the last ten years. To cope with the avalanche, retailers are considering imposing annual renewal fees to keep products on their shelves, and even *failure fees* for new products that fall short of minimum sales targets.† Some critics argue that this widespread practice is a violation of antitrust laws, though it is yet to be proved that slotting fees are harmful to competition.‡ Thus the jury is still out: Is a slotting allowance a bribe or a necessary evil?

*Patricia Sellers, "Winning Over the New Consumer," *Fortune* (July 29, 1991): 113.
†Lois Therrien, "Want Shelf Space at the Supermarket? Ante Up," *Business Week* (Aug. 7, 1989): 60–61.
‡Joseph P. Cannon and Paul N. Bloom, "Are Slotting Allowances Legal Under the Antitrust Laws?" *Journal of Public Policy and Marketing* (Spring 1991): 167–186.

Giving a Break on Prices. A manufacturer can choose to reduce a retailer's costs through sales promotions that provide a **price allowance,** or a discount on its products. A *merchandise allowance* reimburses the retailer for in-store support, such as paying for the cost of an in-store shelf display. A *case allowance* provides a discount to the retailer based on the volume of product ordered. A *slotting allowance* is actually a direct payment to the retailer for stocking a product. Finally, a manufacturer may even reward individual dealers for making a special effort to sell its products: *Push money* is sometimes paid to a salesperson every time he or she sells an item (for this reason, the shopper cannot assume that the recommendation of a salesperson is unbiased).

price allowance: a type of trade sales promotion in which a manufacturer reduces prices to retailers

Sales Force and Industry Promotion: Boosting and Boasting

Other types of sales promotions are intended to make a manufacturer's products more visible to industrial customers. These promotions are designed to reward current business partners, to motivate salespeople, and to generate new business leads. Whether in the form of an elaborate exhibit at a convention or a coffee mug with the firm's name on it mailed to customers, these efforts attempt to make the company "top of mind" when distributors or retailers decide which products to stock and push to their customers. They also support the company's salespeople by polishing the firm's image and providing tangible rewards to those who are most successful at placing its products in the hands of retailers and customers.

Trade Shows. The more than 9000 industry trade shows that are held in the United States per year are major vehicles for manufacturers to show off their product lines to wholesalers and retailers.[22] An additional thousand or so fairs occur in Europe. About 11 percent of trade shows, such as the New York Auto Show, are open to the public. These shows tend to be larger than trade shows, drawing an average of 54,460 attendees (compared to an average of 9975 attendees for trade shows).

Large trade shows are often held in big hotels or convention centers. They may include thousands of companies that rent space and set up elaborate exhibits where they showcase their new products, give away samples and product literature, and attempt to generate sales leads. One company has even created a robot, named Gus, that can be programmed to talk with visitors at a trade show about a client company. Because Gus can read, clients can send information to be scanned into the robot. Chrysler Canada Ltd. was one of the first major companies to rent Gus for a show.[23]

A trade show allows the marketer to showcase its products efficiently by presenting an exhibit that is visited by many buyers from around the country. For example, 80,000 people attended the International Manufacturing Technology Show in 1994. Major trade shows are held in such cities as Paris, Mexico City, Cologne, and Singapore.[24] These shows enable a company's salespeople to compile a list of good prospects that they can contact later (virtually all attendees are to some extent serious buyers, or they wouldn't have spent the time and money to attend the show).

Exhibit 18.1
Trade shows enable companies of all sorts to showcase their products, sometimes in strange ways. In 1995 Oscar Mayer's Weinermobile debuted at the Chicago Auto Show. The twenty-seven foot fiberglass hot dog on wheels will promote Oscar Mayer meat products around the country.

For a trade show promotion to be successful, the marketer should do a lot of work in advance to ensure that its products are presented in their best light and that the contacts made at the show will be followed up.[25] Exhibits at major shows are often elaborate productions that mount complicated high-tech displays, feature numerous product giveaways, and in some cases offer refreshments and even prominent entertainers. For example, the Kenworth trucking company hired the musical group Alabama for a trade show. Visitors to the Kenworth booth received free concert tickets and got to meet band members. In addition, the group made a special limited-edition cassette of their hits accompanied by a photograph of the band posing in front of a Kenworth truck.[26]

Specialty Advertising Programs. We have all seen them: coffee mugs, visors, T-shirts, key chains, and countless other "doo-dads" emblazoned with a company name. These products are examples of **specialty advertising,** which employs useful or decorative items imprinted with an organization's identification, message, or logo. Unlike licensed merchandise intended for sale (such as a Dallas Cowboys cap), a specialty item is distributed free.

Traditionally, businesses gave away such items as pens, rulers, and calendars to build goodwill and serve as reminders for their goods and services. Many companies now are discovering that far more creative uses of ad specialties can help them to generate new business as well. The targeted nature of the specialty advertising medium means that there will be little wasted coverage, and the personal touch inherent in gift giving makes specialty advertising a high-impact tool when used in conjunction with other media—a good way to help build relationships. These "throw-away" items may seem trivial, but expenditures on specialty goods currently total about $4 billion per year. That's a lot of coffee mugs!

A specialty advertising campaign undertaken by the CIT Group, a financial services firm, illustrates the role this form of promotion can play in business-to-business marketing. The company first sent targeted businesses a signed Willie Mays baseball in a display box that had room for two more balls. Recipients who responded to that mailing received a second ball autographed by Stan Musial. After an appointment was made with a CIT salesperson, executives got a third ball autographed by Mickey Mantle to complete the set. The campaign generated a 93 percent response rate and brought the CIT Group $60 million in new revenues. Play ball![27]

Incentive Programs. In addition to motivating distributors and customers, some promotions are designed to light a fire under the firm's own sales force. A sales contest is a way for a company to reward its best performers. Most firms offer some kind of *incentive program* to recognize superior achievements, such as meeting or exceeding specific sales objectives. These incentives may come in the form of cash bonuses, trips, or prizes. One very visible motivator is the trademark hot-pink car awarded to top-performing representatives of Mary Kay cosmetics—it's hard to be modest about your performance when you're spotted in one of those on the highway!

CONSUMER PROMOTIONS

Coca-Cola tours the United States with a semitrailer that converts into a 25,000-square-foot interactive entertainment center. The "Coca-Cola Road Trip" includes a performance stage anchored by two huge Coca-Cola bottles, as well as a video wall with interactive video and sports games, an observation deck 16 feet high, a scoreboard with field lights for nighttime entertainment, a soft-drink stand and a retail store with Coca-Cola merchandise.[28]

Coke's efforts illustrate how major companies are creating unusual and attention-getting forms of promotion. Expenditures for consumer promotions are growing steadily, and industry experts predict further growth for such strategies as in-store promotion, direct-mail couponing, targeted coupon promotions, and product sampling.[29] We'll review two broad categories of consumer-oriented sales promotions: attention-getting promotions that are designed to create excitement or enhance brand awareness by giving away product-oriented materials, and price-based promotions that are designed to encourage purchase by offering temporary price reductions.

Attention-Getting Consumer Promotions

Attention-getting consumer promotions stimulate interest by involving the consumer in the company's marketing efforts. Consider, for example, some of the recent promotions staged in the highly competitive airline industry. After Northwest Airlines announced that passengers could fly cheap to Memphis on Elvis's birthday (January 8), American Airlines countered by offering a $20 discount to passengers who came to the airport dressed as The King. Not to be outdone, United Airlines awarded a first-class upgrade to anyone who could sing the words to Elvis's song "Jailhouse Rock."[30] USAir gives funeral directors a free round-trip ticket if they ship 30 bodies on its planes to funeral homes. Midway Airlines held a briefcase contest, giving prizes to winners in such categories as ugliest briefcase and briefcase that looked most like its owner.[31] Continental Airlines promoted its discounted "Peanuts Fares" by inviting families with the last name Nutt to ribbon-cutting ceremonies at four airports where the service was being inaugurated.[32]

Giveaways. Product giveaways are a particularly impactful (though expensive) form of promotion. Recently, for example, Diet Pepsi took direct aim at its largest competitor, Diet Coke, by sending a million cases of its low-calorie cola straight to the homes of known Diet Coke drinkers. In Pepsi's view, the promotion was an unqualified success: "We received 400,000 written responses from consumers—staunch, loyal Diet Coke drinkers," claims a Pepsi spokesman. "Nearly half of them said they will be drinking Diet Pepsi in the future."[33]

Exhibit 18.2
One effective way to attract shoppers' interest is to stage in-store events in order to make shopping a bit of an adventure. Russell's Shoe Carnival, Inc., in Evansville, Indiana, is a chain where magicians and clowns roam balloon-filled aisles and fifties rock 'n' roll music blasts over the sound system. In 1992 Shoe Carnival's thirty-nine stores sold $127 million worth of Rockports, Reeboks, and Hush Puppies: an impressive $3.4 million per store. At $278 in sales per square foot, the stores generate 64 percent more sales than the average American shoe store. The owner attributes his success to his ability to create excitement in small towns where entertainment options are limited. As he notes, "In some of these towns, we are the Friday night fights and the Saturday afternoon matinees."

Exhibit 18.3
Giveaways can be used by smaller companies that cannot afford to pay the slotting fees charged by supermarkets to get their products on shelves. Practicing a form of "guerilla marketing," tiny Smartfoods, Inc. of Marlboro, Massachusetts, dressed college students in costumes resembling giant bags of popcorn to give away samples of its unique white cheddar cheese popcorn product. The walking bags skied down slopes, paraded on beaches, and invaded college campuses handing out samples. This stunt resulted in terrific press coverage for the brand, and the company was later acquired by Frito-Lay for $10 million.

Although many giveaways are focused on ordinary consumer products such as food, beverages, and personal health care items, even prescription drug manufacturers have started to get into the act. Gifts include $70 electronic blood pressure monitors, $10 electronic pedometers, price breaks on prescriptions and refills, coupons for $50 off over-the-counter pharmacy products, newsletters, magazines, and even telephone reminders to take your medicine. Drug makers and pharmacists have an obvious incentive: Together they lose approximately $2.8 billion per year in revenues because patients forget to refill prescriptions or just stop taking medication. Pharmaceutical manufacturers would also like to create brand loyalty. Surveys show that four out of five doctors will consider prescribing a drug requested by a patient; drug companies hope the premiums will inspire patients to make those requests.[34]

Contests and Sweepstakes. A *contest* involves some test of skill, whereas winning a *sweepstakes* is based only on chance. Both types of promotions are often successful at garnering consumer attention and interest, though a contest is more likely to appeal to a smaller number of people who have some skill they want to showcase. Sweepstakes entrants, in contrast, typically are attracted by large cash awards. (And no, by law, you don't have to buy anything to be eligible to win.) For this reason, sweepstakes involve many more consumers, but contests are useful for reaching people who are very much involved with a good or service. In addition, contests can actually help the company further develop its products. For example, when Xerox held a design competition among its customers of desktop publishing systems, the company was able to learn about the software these expert users needed to make its products work better.

Contests and sweepstakes are most effective when they are directly related to a company's advertising themes or products. Coca-Cola's Hi-C drink, which is targeted to preteens, sponsored a sweepstakes with a grand prize sure to interest many consumers in this age group: A trip for two to the set of the show "Beverly Hills 90210."[35] A contest run on behalf of the band Smashing Pumpkins by Virgin Records involved an on-line scavenger hunt, where contestants had to log on to America Online to get clues leading them to the prizes: CDs and videos featuring the band.[36]

Premiums. **Premiums** are items that are offered to people who have bought a product. A premium is often a novelty item that may or may not be related to the original product, such as the free removable tattoos, called "Barqtoos," given away in packs of Barq's root beer. Barq's recently received the Super Reggie Award for the best sales promotion campaign from the Promotion Marketing Association of America. In its "Soviet Union Going Out of Business Sale," Barq's offered authentic memorabilia, such as stamps and enameled pins, from the defunct Soviet Union in exchange for proofs of purchase.[37]

Some premiums, such as the ever-popular "surprise" in the bottom of Cracker Jacks, are provided with the product; others are sent through the mail to those who request them. As far back as 1940, the Quaker Oats Co. awarded pairs of silk stockings to women who sent in a Silk Stocking Certificate, 25 cents, and a proof of purchase from any Quaker Oats package.[38]

In-packs and *out-packs* give a gift either inside the package (Cracker Jacks) or attached to it (a disposable razor attached to a can of shaving cream). A *near-pack* is a separate product offered at the time the featured product is purchased (gas stations often give away National Football League mugs to customers who fill up their tanks).

As the name suggests, a *free-in-the-mail premium* is given free, usually in exchange for proofs of purchase and a small handling charge. A *self-liquidating premium* is offered at a cost, so the marketer recoups the cost of the promotion. Premiums are often useful to get attention for a brand or to remind people to buy it. For example, shoppers who get Pillsbury's free book of pizza recipes may be more inclined to buy the company's refrigerated pizza dough when they're in the mood for a home-made slice.[39]

The latest craze in premiums is the use of pre-paid phone cards to enhance brand identification. Many companies are jumping on the phone card bandwagon, offering cards emblazoned with pictures of sports heroes, products, and even rock bands. Phone cards offer many advantages for marketers: They are compact in size, the sponsor can control the dollar value of the promotion, brand logos or graphics provide opportunities for repeat exposure, and the issuer can track card usage and build databases by determining where calls originate. As an added bonus, a growing number of hobbyists are buying, saving, and trading the cards, ensuring that they will be around for some time to come.[40]

Exhibit 18.4
Cooking contests are an effective and popular way to let creative, loyal customers "show their stuff" with a product. This proud winner and his wife hold his prize from one such contest, sponsored by Jim Beam bourbon, for submitting the best recipe made with the company's product (the man in the middle is Beam's Master Distiller Emeritus, Booker Noe, grandson of the legendary Jim Beam). The oldest cooking contest of them all is the Pillsbury Bake-Off, which has been attracting avid bakers since 1949. The contest enhances Pillsbury's image as an essential company for baking products, and it confers great prestige on the winner, who must survive a grueling selection process.

point of purchase (POP): an element of sales promotion that includes displays and signs for use in the retail outlet

Point of purchase (POP) is an element of sales promotion that includes displays and signs for use in the retail outlet. As a result of the erosion of brand loyalty and the increasing emphasis on value for the money, reliance on POP promotions by major marketers is skyrocketing.[41]

One reason why POP is becoming so important is that customers in the 1990s want more information on the products they plan to buy. Meanwhile, retailers and manufacturers find that delivering detailed messages to such discriminating buyers is more costly and complex. A good place to get the company's message out is at the in-store purchase point. To break through the clutter, marketers are challenged to come up with new and innovative product displays that will grab people's attention.[42] Let's take a look at some of the ways they're doing this.

In-Store Sampling. How many people at one time or another have managed to scrape together an entire meal by cruising up and down the aisles of their local supermarket in search of free food samples? There is nothing as persuasive as a favorable in-store experience with a new product. Even record companies are getting into the sampling act: Geffen Records sent free cassettes of some new releases to almost five hundred coffeehouses, vintage clothing shops, hair salons, and even cafe/laundromats to get listeners to check them out.[43] On the other hand, samples generally are feasible only for low-cost items, and many nonfood samples (such as trial sizes of health and beauty products) are wasted because people do not use them.

Many grocery retailers prefer in-store activities that put something in consumers' hands to other forms of sales promotions.[44] Procter & Gamble's new interactive product-sampling hot line is being promoted in conjunction with in-store sampling tied to Ivory

Exhibit 18.5
The POPAI/DuPont Consumer Buying Habits Study monitored 50,000 purchases made by four thousand shoppers at one hundred supermarkets and found that POP influences 81 percent of all buying decisions that are made in the store.[92] As one trade executive noted, "People go to the store knowing they want to buy, say, ketchup, but they don't decide which brand until they get there." To illustrate the importance of POP, consider that almost 80 percent of total packaged soft drinks are purchased as the result of a promotion. One study found that when soft drinks are accompanied by in-store displays and signs, sales increase by *445 percent! This company specializes in providing customized electronic signs in store aisles to get shoppers' attention when they are deciding what to buy.*

Exhibit 18.6
Beer companies increasingly rely on eye-catching point-of-purchase displays to make their brands stand out in a highly competitive product category. This display for Miller Genuine Draft, featuring a bottle inside a "blizzard," won a Gold Award in the 1994 Outstanding Merchandise Achievements Awards bestowed by the Point of Purchase Advertising Institute.

Clear dishwashing liquid and Cheer with Color Guard Bleach.[45] NutraSweet is encouraging consumer trial of its new NutraSweet Spoonful product by giving out samples in almost five thousand supermarkets in a single weekend.[46] Nestea gave away six million cans of iced tea in sixty cities in what is believed to be the largest ready-to-drink beverage sampling campaign in history.[47]

Displays and Signage. Store displays often act as a stimulus to consumers, serving either to remind them of a purchase or to give them a reason to look twice at a product. Product displays are commonplace in the United States, and they are also gaining in popularity in Europe. One recent European survey found that 60 percent of British advertisers believe displays are becoming more important to communication strategy, and that Dutch respondents feel displays are the single best way to stimulate consumer activity.[48]

Effective displays are often tied to other promotion activities or seasonal events. For example, in the summer months, Anheuser-Busch pushes its beers with displays tied to barbecues and Labor Day block parties.[49] Displays can range from a simple poster to an elaborate creation, such as the mechanical Dancing Can used in a recent Coors Light promotion.[50] In-store displays can be used to store extra merchandise, to add visibility to sales items, to cross-merchandise related items, or to stimulate impulse purchases. In addition, *signs* in the form of window banners, in-store banners, or flags can help to create a colorful in-store theme and draw attention to a display.

In-Store Media. In-store advertising has been around since at least 1972, when shopping cart ads were first introduced. Today, however, the typical grocery store is also the base of other, more sophisticated forms of in-store media, including both audio and video components.

The latest in audio in-store promotions can be found at the Seattle-based Muzak Limited Partnership, the folks who bring you those bland background tunes in elevators and dentists' offices. Muzak, with $65 million in sales last year, is leveraging its main competitive advantage: telecommunication receivers made to Muzak's specifications and placed in some 200,000 businesses across the country. Because each site has a unique receiving code, Muzak's computers can target its twelve music channels—and audio advertisements—to stores according to geographic area, ethnic community, type of chain, or time of day. If a marketer wants to push its brand of refried beans in Hispanic markets, then Muzak can broadcast its message in Spanish to grocery stores in Latin communities in California, Florida, or Texas. If a firm wants to advertise snow shovels in November, then Muzak can send its ads only to stores located in snowy regions. One recent test of Muzak's system at forty stores in the Phoenix area showed that Muzak ads, combined with visual displays, produced double-digit sales increases in some cases.

In-store video is also catching on: Nowadays, shoppers can't avoid watching TV even when they are in a store. Several point-of-purchase networks are online or in test. The largest network, ActMedia, sells ad space in 26,000 stores to such companies as Kellogg and Procter & Gamble, much as TV networks sell commercial time. As ActMedia's CEO observes, "Does it make any sense to spend millions of dollars talking to people in their living rooms and cars and then let them wander around a supermarket with 30,000 product choices without something to remind them to buy your product?" Campbell Soup, which has used all of ActMedia's programs, reports sales increases of 7 to 10 percent from various in-store promotions. Grocers are happy because they pay nothing for ActMedia's displays and receive commissions of 10 to 25 percent on the ad programs that marketers buy.[51]

Price-Based Consumer Promotions

Most sales promotions aim right where consumers live: their wallets. They emphasize short-term price reductions or refunds, thus encouraging people to choose a brand—at least while the deal is on!

Coupons. Open any Sunday newspaper and the avalanche of coupons that falls out makes it clear where many marketers invest their sales promotion money. **Coupons,** or certificates redeemable for money off on a purchase, are by far the most common type of price promotion. Indeed, they are the most popular form of sales promotion overall.

Over *three hundred billion* coupons are distributed annually. Health and beauty aid products account for the most coupon usage, followed by breakfast cereals.[52] The large majority (about 80 percent) of manufacturers' coupons are distributed in **free-standing inserts (FSIs),** which are placed in newspapers and magazines.[53] These FSIs are rapidly replacing more traditional newspaper coupons, called *run-of-paper (ROP)* coupons.[54]

Although most people use them to some extent, the effectiveness of couponing strategies is a matter of debate. On the one hand, coupons are claimed to influence significantly the likelihood of brand trial, insofar as they tempt consumers to buy new or unfamiliar products in order to save money.[55] Coupons are also more likely to affect purchases during a major shop rather than a "fill in" shop, where people are more interested in saving time by snapping up a few familiar brands than in saving money.[56] On the other hand, the potential for waste is enormous: About 85 percent of American households use coupons, but less than 3 percent of those distributed are redeemed.[57] In the United Kingdom, coupon redemption has fallen by half in the past ten years.[58]

Price Deals and Rebates. In addition to coupons, manufacturers frequently offer a temporary price reduction to stimulate sales. This **price deal** may be printed on the package itself or announced in a *price-off flag* or banner on the store shelf. Alternatively, a **rebate** may be offered. This is a short-term offer that enables the consumer to get back part of the product's original cost by mail directly from the manufacturer. Sometimes marketers try to do some good while engaging in a price promotion by featuring a *cause-related refund,* offering to donate money to a charity every time someone buys their products. For example, Ben & Jerry's Homemade donates a percentage of its profits on certain ice cream products to help preserve the Brazilian rain forest, and Levi Strauss & Co. gives to AIDS-related causes.[59]

Especially when consumers are not loyal to other brands, they can be motivated to try a new product if it is favorably priced. The risk of this practice is that regular-price sales can be cannibalized if the price promotion mostly affects the brand's regular purchasers: They would have bought the product anyway, but they will now reap the benefits of the price reduction.

Price deals are most likely to be employed for frequently purchased food products, but they turn up in other categories as well. For example, in the United Kingdom the Lotus software company counted on impulse purchases by offering a steep discount in order

coupons: printed certificates redeemable for money off on a purchase

free-standing inserts (FSIs): preprinted advertising pages which are placed in newspapers and magazines

price deal: a temporary price reduction offered by a manufacturer to stimulate sales

rebate: a short-term offer that enables the consumer to get back part of the product's original cost by mail directly from the manufacturer

Excellence at Vons Co.

Couponing has reached a saturation level in the United States, and marketers that issue them tend to follow a *parity strategy:* They do it only to stay even with everyone else. Part of the problem is that consumers are showered with so many coupons that they find it hard to make good use of them.* Marketers are scrambling to find new ways to make coupon distribution more efficient and less wasteful. Vons, an innovative grocery store chain in California, looks at price promotions as an opportunity to build relationships with its long-term customers by giving them discounts on the items they are most likely to need without bombarding them with tons of paper that they don't need.

A program called Target Vons cross-indexes customer purchase information by product category to enable grocery suppliers to distribute their coupons to only the most appropriate cus-tomers. Members of the store's VonsClub present a card at the check-out and get instant electronic discounts on promotion items—no coupons necessary. Over time Vons has accumulated extensive data on each individual's purchasing patterns, and the store sends a monthly mailing of individually printed coupons to each member. Coupons for McCormick & Co. baking products, for example, go only to those members who have previously bought cake mixes, and Beech-Nut coupons were sent to every household that had purchased a baby product in the preceding eight weeks.† By devoting considerable resources to developing and refining Target Vons, the grocery chain encourages shoppers to rely on the store to keep track of their needs and find ways to keep satisfying them.

*Kathleen Deveny and Richard Gibson, "Awash in Coupons? Some Firms Try to Stem the Tide," *The Wall Street Journal* (May 10, 1994): B1.
†Larry Armstrong, "Coupon Clippers, Save Your Scissors," *Business Week* (June 20, 1994): 164.

---

to encourage users to experiment with a new spreadsheet product it was introducing there. According to the company's European brand manager, "When people see and use the product then they realize they need it. . . . Word of mouth recommendations will grow the market once the initial offer ends."[60]

Special Packs. On many occasions, marketers choose to give the shopper more of the product instead of lowering its price. These offers are often effective in getting consumers to make an impulse purchase, thus increasing sales.[61] Kellogg is an industry leader in the use of coupon advertising that features bonus deals. The company frequently distributes coupons that offer two boxes of cereal for the price of one, or three for the price of two.[62]

A **bonus pack** is a special container that gives the consumer more of the product than usual for the same price. On a typical trip to the supermarket you might buy a box of eight Kellogg's PopTarts for the price of six, a 15 percent larger bonus pack of Pillsbury's Hungry Jack pancake mix, and a box of fifty free packets of Equal shrink-wrapped to a regularly-priced box of 200 packets.

> **bonus pack:** a special container that gives the consumer more of the product than usual for the same price

Manufacturers often use bonus packs to lower the potential success of new competitive product introductions by getting consumers to "stock up." For example, you might buy four bars of Dial bath soap for the price of three or eight bars of Shield for the price of six.

A *reusable container* is a premium that continues to be used even after the product that came in it is used up. For example, a special edition of Maxwell House coffee comes in a "decorative" can that can be used as a planter.

Exporting Promotions around the Globe

Although some marketers feel that many consumers in the United States and Western Europe are too sophisticated for such gimmicks as a free soda pop glass with every fill-up, the potential is much greater in developing nations. "The noise level for promotions like these is much too high in the U.S.," says Paul Clayton, director of sales and marketing in Asia for Goodyear Tire & Rubber. "In the developing world, you can run a much simpler, cheaper promotion and get astonishing results." Among Goodyear's successful promotion efforts are a kids' calendar contest and a backpack giveaway.[63]

Soft drink makers also tailor promotions to each developing nation. In Mexico, Pepsi runs Pepsi Numeros, a lottery-like game, that is so popular that the winning numbers are televised throughout the country every night. For twelve Pepsi caps and 20 *rupees* (about 75 cents), Indian customers get a cassette tape of American pop hits. Pepsi's vice president of public affairs says it has been the best-selling tape on the subcontinent.[64]

There are many advantages to promoting in developing nations. Labor-intensive programs that are prohibitively expensive in the United States or Europe are possible in India and Taiwan. In southern India, Jos. E. Seagram & Sons hired hundreds of villagers to carry sand to form a beach for a wine cooler party. There are also potential disadvantages. As one researcher notes, "You have to have a real understanding of the culture . . . or else you could plan a gaudy promotion in the midst of a religious procession. That would be unforgivably bad form."[65]

THE SALES PROMOTION PROCESS

Like any other promotion activity, sales promotions need to be carefully planned and implemented to be effective. This section will briefly describe the issues that must be considered. The sales promotion planning process is summarized in Figure 18.1.

ESTABLISH SALES PROMOTION OBJECTIVES

Ideally, the goal of every sales promotion should be to cement the product's position in the marketplace. This means that the promotion should do more than just give away something for a short period. It should encourage the target of the promotion to regard the product favorably over the long term as well. Specific objectives of the promotion depend on the audience on which it focuses.

■ *Trade promotion objectives:* Among retailers, this goal is accomplished by encouraging decision makers to select the item, to stock it in larger quantities, and/or to feature it prominently in retail advertising and on store shelves.

Figure 18.1
The Sales Promotion Planning Process

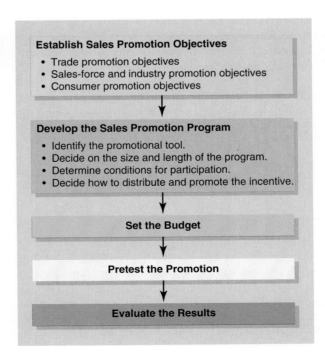

Establish Sales Promotion Objectives
- Trade promotion objectives
- Sales-force and industry promotion objectives
- Consumer promotion objectives

↓

Develop the Sales Promotion Program
- Identify the promotional tool.
- Decide on the size and length of the program.
- Determine conditions for participation.
- Decide how to distribute and promote the incentive.

↓

Set the Budget

↓

Pretest the Promotion

↓

Evaluate the Results

- *Sales force and industry promotion objectives:* Among salespeople, sales promotions build morale and enthusiasm by demonstrating the level of support given to the product and by rewarding the sales force for selling even more of it. Sales promotions can also be very helpful in creating or maintaining awareness of a company's line of products.

- *Consumer promotion objectives:* Among consumers, promotions may be intended to stimulate impulse buying, to encourage loyal users to "load up" on the product by buying it in larger than normal quantities, to reward loyal customers for continuing to buy the product, to lure users of competing products away, or to build long-term market share by prodding people to try a product that is new or is unfamiliar to them.

DEVELOP THE SALES PROMOTION PROGRAM

Once the marketer has determined what objectives the firm hopes to accomplish, specific decisions must be made about the actual program. Let's consider some of these choices.

Identify the Promotion Tool

We have reviewed a number of the many promotion devices that are used to appeal to trade partners, to the sales force, and to consumers. The choice of a specific one should be related to the campaign's objectives. For example, if the objective is to encourage users of a competing product to try the item, a sampling program might be called for. If the objective is to increase loyal users' interest in the brand, the firm might sponsor a contest or sweepstakes. If the company wants to increase the amount of shelf space allocated to the brand in grocery stores, it might give a price break to retailers and/or award prizes to salespeople who are the most successful in increasing the volume of orders.

Because promotion activities frequently focus on immediate, attention-getting activities, many marketers are discovering the virtues of *cross-promotion,* wherein two or more

Exhibit 18.7
Sampling Corp. of America provides one way for marketers to induce potential consumers to try their products. The company specializes in distributing goody bags stuffed with product samples, coupons, and pamphlets to schools around the United States. The goal for participating companies such as Procter & Gamble is to introduce students to products targeted to their grade levels with the hope that over time they will become loyal users. For instance, because hair care is a big priority for junior high school students, the bags they receive include P&G's Vidal Sassoon products.

goods or services combine forces to create interest by using a single promotion tool. For example, Volkswagen U.S. and Atlantic Records capitalized on the popularity of music featured in the automaker's TV spots. Powered by its use in a commercial, a song by Irish folk/New Age band Clannad climbed the U.S. charts. The two companies negotiated a deal to tag TV spots to identify the artists, song, and record labels used, and they are also labeling CDs and cassettes to say they include a track used in the VW commercial. Each tape also comes packaged with an informational insert about VW that includes its logo and an 800 number to call for more information.[66]

Retailers and media can also work together to create excitement and arouse consumer interest. In France, for example, *Paris Vogue* magazine worked with the French department store LePrintemps to devise a fragrance promotion called Sensaura that would get the attention of jaded French shoppers. This promotion took the form of a multimedia kiosk that used a touch screen to guide shoppers through a series of questions about their lifestyle preferences. Each person then received a personality analysis and the names of two perfumes that fit her lifestyle. The consumer could then receive a free sample of one of the fragrances from the perfume counter. The promotion was highly successful: At times people waited in line for half an hour to use the kiosk.[67]

Decide on the Size and Length of the Program

No one wants to give something away and get nothing in return. On the other hand, "You have to spend money to make money." The company has to decide what *incentive level* will be sufficient to meet the promotion's objectives. If a contest awards a prize of a few dollars or a framed certificate, will anyone bother to enter? Firms often find it useful to analyze the results of past promotions to determine what incentive levels were effective. In addition, the company has to decide how long the program will run and must establish a schedule for producing promotion materials, distributing them, and perhaps awarding prizes. This is not easy. A sales promotion needs enough time for potential participants to become aware of it, but if it drags on too long it will become "old news" and lose its punch.

Determine Conditions for Participation

Planners must decide who will be eligible to participate in the promotion. They may decide to limit participation to customers who send in a set number of proof-of-purchase seals from boxes of the product or to develop a sales contest only for "rookies" who have been with the company for less than two years.

Decide How to Distribute the Incentive and Promote the Program

A promotion will not work if no one knows about it. Planners must decide how to communicate the offer to participants. Their choices may range from putting an announcement on a box to distributing coupons in Sunday newspaper supplements, or, for some lavish promotions for national brands, even producing television commercials announcing a contest or sweepstakes. For example, when Frito-Lay sponsored a promotion that involved giving away six million bags of new Nacho Cheese Doritos around the country in one day, a primary objective was to energize the company and get its employees excited about the new product as well. For this reason, the company turned to its own people to distribute the free goodies, and a full-page ad in *USA Today* featured actual employees who had worked on the brand.[68]

SET THE BUDGET

Planners must decide how much to spend on the promotion. Sales promotions are increasingly playing a central role in the marketing strategies of many companies, and budgets are rising as well. In the past, sales promotions got whatever was left after the company budgeted for advertising expenditures, but it is fairly common now for the reverse to happen: The company first decides how much it wants to spend on sales promotions (especially trade promotions) and later budgets for advertising. Table 18.2 provides a glimpse of the costs of different sales promotions offered by one set of companies.

PRE-TEST THE PROMOTION

Although the large majority of companies don't do it, ideally the promotion should be *pre-tested* to make sure it is effective and works as planned. For example, a national contest or sweepstakes can be tried in one or two test markets to determine whether it generates enough consumer interest or even whether the game works as intended.

Some pre-testing might have averted a big headache for the Pepsi-Cola Company in the Philippines, after a botched promotion resulted in rioting outside Pepsi plants and the torching of more than 30 Pepsi delivery trucks. The promotion offered to pay up to about $37,000 to holders of specially marked bottle caps. As the result of a computer error, however, the wrong number was announced, and half a million people claimed the prize! When Pepsi refused to pay, the trouble began. Pepsi offered to pay each cap holder 500 pesos (about $18.50) as a "gesture of goodwill" and spent about $11 million to settle claims and repair its shattered image.[69]

Company/Program	Activity	Cost
3M Sound Products	Customized audio messages broadcast via satellite	$30–$40 for a single 30-second message, broadcast over a 30-day cycle
ActMedia	Ads inserted into the center of aisle directories. Electric motor can incorporate a moving component	$195,000 per cycle
ADDvantage Media Group	Shoppers' Calculator includes a calculator and advertising and is mounted on grocery cart handles	$38,000 to $50,000 per 4-week cycle
Advanced Promotion Technologies	Interactive electronic delivery system featuring financial services, instant credits, recipes, coupons, and video	$1300 per check-out lane connection charge, plus $.06 to $.10 charged per triggered instant credit event (such as dispensing a recipe)
Advance Marketing, Inc./AMI In-Store	Promotion offers and peel-off instant redeemable coupons delivered via retailer-issued packaging such as bakery, deli and produce bags	$15 to $48 per thousand coupons distributed
Bullock Communications, Inc.	Shopper-activated audio shelf talker that mounts on the edge of the shelf at the product display	$25 to $50 per 4-week cycle
Catalina Marketing Corp.	Electronic coupon triggered at check-out by scanned UPC code	Up to $.09 per coupon issued

Table 18.2
Representative Costs of In-Store Promotions in 1995

Source: "In-Store Promotion," *PROMO: The International Magazine for Promotion Marketing* (Jan. 1995): 79–81.

EVALUATE THE RESULTS

Because the (ideal) sales promotion is tied to specific, short-term objectives, the firm should be able to tell whether these were achieved. One popular assessment technique is simply to compare sales before, during, and after the sales promotion. A common pattern for consumer promotions is that sales rise during the promotion and then fall immediately afterward—it takes some time for people to use up the excess inventory they accumulated during the promotion! Because of this tendency, a more accurate approach is to wait until some time after the promotion has concluded to determine whether any significant effects occurred. In addition, consumer research can be performed to determine which consumers were most likely to participate in the promotion and how (or whether) their attitudes toward the product or company changed as a result. For example, some recent research indicates that people who choose to participate in promotional games are younger and better educated than those who do not play such games and that they are more likely to participate in other games of chance, especially the lottery.[70]

PUBLIC RELATIONS

Although a marketer may work hard to communicate the wonders of a particular product, in the long run it is often even more important to cultivate a positive overall image for the company. And it is not only the end consumer who must be favorably impressed: It is also crucial that other *publics,* such as shareholders, retailers, suppliers, and legislators, have good feelings about the company and what it does. **Public relations** efforts attempt to influence the way consumers, stockholders, and others feel about brands, companies, politicians, celebrities, not-for-profit organizations, and even governments. This section will provide an overview of how public relations activities, such as those performed by Victoria Feldman's firm, fit in with the organization's overall promotion mix.

public relations: activities of organizations aimed at influencing the way consumers, stockholders, and others feel about brands, companies, politicians, celebrities, not-for-profit organizations, and even governments

THE ROLE OF PUBLIC RELATIONS IN THE PROMOTION MIX

Public relations is crucial to an organization's ability to create and manage a favorable long-term image. It is especially valued by marketers who understand the importance of also satisfying noncustomer groups (those who can affect the fortunes of an organization apart from individual purchase decisions, such as government regulators and the investment community).

Public Relations Deserves More Respect

Public relations typically is not allocated nearly as much funding as advertising or sales promotion, and it frequently is not well coordinated with the rest of the promotion mix. Publicity campaigns are often carried out by public relations specialists who are not associated with the firm's marketing department. This relationship is improving somewhat as more marketers buy into the idea of integrated communications strategies (see Chapter 16), but most firms still have a long way to go.

Part of this confusion boils down to a turf battle: Marketers and public relations experts are divided over whether public relations should be merged into the marketing function or kept separate.[71] On the one hand, some people argue that marketing and public relations both attempt to serve the interests of outside groups, recognize the need for market segmentation, and acknowledge the value of communications in influencing market attitudes, perceptions and images. On the other hand, PR "purists" argue that a merger would reduce the ability of the organization to communicate effectively with groups *other* than consumers (employees, communities, government, stockholders, and donors) that also have strategic importance for organizations.

This dispute is being resolved to some extent as companies are making the distinction between *corporate public relations* and *marketing public relations* functions. The former focuses on the traditional duties of public relations, such as interacting with employees and government officials, whereas the latter is intended to support promotion efforts directly.

©1994 Ben & Jerry's Homemade,

Some firms are forming a separate organizational unit for *public affairs,* which comprises government relations, employee communication, corporate philanthropy, and community relations programs.[72]

Managing Information, Both Good and Bad

The basic rule of public relations is "Do something good, and then talk about it." However, public relations is also important when the company does something bad: Often the goal is to manage the flow of information about a topic so that it does not become an issue in the first place, as when companies try to control the negative effects of product failures, rumors, or other embarrassing or harmful events.[73] Unfortunately, marketing history is filled with public relations disasters that have done serious damage to firms' images. Here are a few examples:

- Uptown cigarettes and PowerMaster malt liquor, two new products intended to be targeted to African-Americans, were killed before launch because of the public outcry about the exploitation of minorities.

- Much of Volvo's reputation for being the safest car on the road is probably due to public relations rather than advertising. However, the automaker shot itself in the foot when its ad agency produced a commercial that gave the impression that the car could withstand more damage than competitors. When word got out that a demonstration of this durability had been faked, the ensuing scandal was a blow to the company's reputation.

Pepsi is pleased to announce... ...nothing.

As America now knows, those stories about Diet Pepsi were a hoax. Plain and simple, not true. Hundreds of investigators have found no evidence to support a single claim.

As for the many, many thousands of people who work at Pepsi-Cola, we feel great that it's over. And we're ready to get on with making and bringing you what we believe is the best-tasting diet cola in America.

There's not much more we can say. Except that most importantly, we won't let this hoax change our exciting plans for this summer.

We've set up special offers so you can enjoy our great quality products at prices that will save you money all summer long. It all starts on July 4th weekend and we hope you'll stock up with a little extra, just to make up for what you might have missed last week.

That's it. Just one last word of thanks to the millions of you who have stood with us.

Drink All The Diet Pepsi You Want. Uh Huh.

Exhibit 18.9
In the peak of the summer selling season in 1993, PepsiCo was rocked by claims that hypodermic needles had been found in cans of Pepsi and Diet Pepsi. After two people in Washington State claimed to have found the needles, officials were swamped with similar panicked claims from consumers in more than twenty states. The company assembled a crisis team of executives to map out a response. Pepsi supplied video footage of its bottling process to news stations to show that it would be impossible for foreign objects to be inserted. The Commissioner of the Food and Drug Administration backed the company's claim that there was no danger, and Pepsi refused to recall the drinks. Eventually more than a dozen arrests were made for filing false reports as people sought to climb on the publicity bandwagon, and the Food and Drug Administration was never able to confirm a single report of tampering. Pepsi's calm, coordinated response to the accusations saved the day, and a disaster was avoided.

■ A growing number of merchants were displeased with high fees charged by American Express. Some of them boycotted the company to get their point across, and the resulting publicity forced American Express to modify its fee structure.[74]

■ When a user of Intel's much-heralded Pentium processor reported in 1995 that it made errors in some obscure mathematical calculations, the company reacted by downplaying the problem. Instead of moving instantly to correct the flaw, the company provided a technical explanation of why the problem occurred. This action did not reassure the "typical" consumer, who was not interested in technical arguments, or the businessperson who feared that his or her company's operations would be affected. The company initially refused to replace the chip, instead requiring users to demonstrate that they needed a new one for specific applications. Although the problem with the chip has been fixed, the jury is still out on whether the damage to Intel's reputation has been repaired as well.[75]

Publicity: If You've Got It, Flaunt It!

Public relations strategies often involve attempts to secure favorable publicity. **Publicity** is unpaid communication in the mass media regarding a company, product, or event. Because it is not identified as a paid advertisement, people often assume this sort of information is more objective and accurate. Public relations may be confused with publicity,

publicity: unpaid communication in the mass media regarding a company, product, or event

Sponsor	Stunt
Wild 107 FM (San Francisco)	Deejay blocked traffic on the Bay Bridge for two hours during morning rush hour while he got a haircut (chosen as winner of the "most poorly timed, dumbest, or most tasteless stunt" award by the local chapter of the Public Relations Society of America).
KYNG FM (Dallas)	The Fort Worth public library was left in a shambles after the radio station announced that it had hidden $5 and $10 bills in library books. More than 3000 books were thrown on the floor by frenzied money seekers. The station claimed it wanted to boost interest in the library.
British Knights	Hosted "World's Smelliest Socks Contest." About 4600 people sent in their stinky socks to win free sneakers.
Publishers of the book *Marketing Warfare*	Hired a World War II tank to carry the authors down Fifth Avenue in Manhattan.
Milton Bradley	Sponsored National College Pigsty Search, a contest for the messiest dorm room.

**Table 18.3
"Wild and Wacky"
Publicity Stunts**

Sources: Michael J. Ybarra, "Some Publicists Are Good, Some Are Bad, and Some Just Talk Funny," *The Wall Street Journal* (Feb. 28, 1994): B1; "Cash in the Library? Not a Total Fiction," *The New York Times* (April 7, 1994): A16; Lee Berton, "Smelly Socks and Other Tricks from the Public-Relations Trade," *The Wall Street Journal* (Nov. 30, 1993): B1; James Barron, "A Winemaker, a Bird, and the Publicity Game," *The New York Times* (Dec. 2, 1993): B1; "Masses of Messes," *Asbury Park Press* (Dec. 14, 1994): A2.

but the two are not the same. Many public relations activities occur at the corporate level, are carried out by corporate communications specialists, and have little to do with communicating about specific products. However, product-specific publicity often is a part of the promotion mix as well. Table 18.3 provides some examples of "wacky" stunts engineered by publicists to break through the promotional clutter and get people's attention.

FUNCTIONS OF PUBLIC RELATIONS

Public relations activities occur at many levels of the organization. As we saw in Chapter 16, every employee and product of a firm, from its annual report and company stationery to its corporate headquarters building, represents that organization and plays a role in influencing impressions about it. Public relations specialists work to ensure that the flow of information about a firm's employees, activities, and products is consistent with its objectives and that the organization's image is presented in as positive a light as possible. Because the goal of public relations is to manage the entire image of an organization, in a sense these specialists are at the vanguard of integrated communications strategies: They increasingly are paying attention to such components of corporate identity as brochures, logos, and company uniforms to ensure that *everything* connected to the organization projects an appropriate and consistent image.

Public relations campaigns have the advantage of being very timely (they can be tied to ongoing news coverage), and they can be conducted in concert with advertising, direct mail, or sales promotion.[76] The many marketing areas in which public relations strategies can be used include the following:

Introduce New Products to Manufacturers. Companies often find it useful to "prime the pump" before rolling out a new product by making sure that potential buyers understand its benefits and even anticipate its release. Weyerhaeuser's introduction of Cellulon, a new biotechnology product, was accompanied by press materials that clearly explained the technical product and its applications to each of twelve markets.[77]

Introduce New Products to Consumers. Similarly, public relations efforts can help a company that is using a "pull strategy" by creating consumer demand for a new product.

REAL PEOPLE, REAL CHOICES:

DECISION TIME AT KWE ASSOCIATES

In honor of the seventy-fifth anniversary of its independence, Finland proclaimed 1992 "Homecoming Year." The Finnish Tourist Board, which had been working with KWE Associates since 1987, retained the firm to develop a campaign that would help promote tourism in the Scandinavian country. Finland was a relatively little-known travel destination among U.S. travelers, and the agency had already helped the country to create a unique identity by positioning it as an exciting, off-beat place that offers one-of-a-kind adventures to jaded American visitors. These activities ranged from ice breaker cruises, reindeer races and twenty-four-hour golf to outdoor opera and jazz festivals. In a special effort to attract foreign visitors of Finnish ancestry, the country established genealogy centers to help descendants trace their roots.

The overall marketing challenge in this commemorative year was to increase tourism arrivals to Finland. This was a difficult assignment, because the agency had to combat the "double whammy" of the Gulf War (which slowed international travel in general) and the U.S. recession (which made American tourists more reluctant to take elaborate vacations). Victoria Feldman's task was to identify the market segments most likely to choose to travel to Finland and to determine how these prospects could be reached most cost-effectively. She narrowed the universe of travelers down to the three groups described in the following options.

Option 1. Target Americans of Finnish descent specifically. Although these people had never been courted by Finland before, they could be assumed to be relatively knowledgeable about the country and would perhaps be more likely to choose Finland over other European destinations. They could also be reached through Finnish-American networks such as specialized organizations and media. Of course, given the relatively small number of Americans claiming Finnish ancestry (compared to, say, those with Irish or Italian roots), this group represented a rather limited market in the United States. And some effort would be involved in tracking them down and determining the best way to communicate with them.

Option 2. Target people who have already decided to go to Europe but have not yet settled on a specific destination. This is an attractive segment, because these travelers are probably familiar with what Europe has to offer and have already decided to spend money on a European vacation. These people would be accessible through traditional public relations methods, such as placing in travel magazines articles that chronicle interesting tourist attractions and providing promotional material to travel agents. On the other hand, targeting this group would mean going up against fierce competition from the tourism efforts of virtually every other European country, including better-known destinations such as France and Italy.

Option 3. Target people who have decided to take a vacation but have not decided where they will go. These travelers have not yet committed themselves to any particular destination, so they might be more open-minded and willing to consider an off-beat place like Finland. On the other hand, their knowledge of Finland *per se* would be limited, and the effort to educate them about the country might be significant. These "undecideds" also might not be willing to spend the money to travel to such an exotic locale, and their sense of adventure might be limited to exploring more familiar countries.

Now, join the decision team at KWE Associates: Which option would you choose, and why?

When Chrysler Corp. rolled out its trio of big LH sedans late in 1992, the market was already waiting, thanks to the careful building of awareness by Chrysler's PR teams. Working months ahead of the car's public introduction, Chrysler's PR teams had exposed journalists to the LH project through factory and laboratory tours and open discussions with designers.[78]

Influence Government Legislation. Much public relations activity goes on behind the scenes, as lobbyists and communications specialists try to create a favorable legislative environment for companies and their products. In a news conference announcing a new children's vaccine program, President Clinton called drug prices shocking and claimed the prescription drug industry spends $1 billion more on advertising and lobbying than on research and development. In an attempt to reach opinion makers, the Pharmaceutical Manufacturers Association initiated a $5 million to $8 million print campaign in February 1993, arguing that drugs represent just 5 percent of national health care expenditures and save lives.[79]

Ease Public Acceptance of Corporate Changes. Consumers are often confused or resistant when a corporation reorganizes, merges with another company, or even changes its name. Public relations experts try to ensure that people understand what the changes mean and accept them enthusiastically. The public is especially leery of change at financial institutions. This concern led United States Bank (USB), a $50 million institution planning a name change, to launch the first comprehensive PR campaign in the bank's sixty-nine year history. By taking a proactive stance in announcing its name change, the bank cast itself in a positive light and not only averted losing current customers but also benefitted from a substantial growth in deposits.[80]

Enhance the Image of a City, Region, or Country. Cities, regions, and countries zealously protect their images, because image is often crucial in determining whether tourists will choose a place as a vacation destination or a company will decide to locate a manufacturing facility there. Whether supported by a local Chamber of Commerce or by a sophisticated international public relations firm, these areas endeavor to communicate their best side to potential visitors. The Chinese government, for example, works very hard to present an acceptable image to outsiders. It established an office in charge of "overseas propaganda" designed to present China to best advantage to the rest of the world. As a public relations exercise, the eleventh Asian Games hosted in Beijing were right on target. The media covered Games-related activities extensively, focusing on internal harmony and high morale as well as on tourist attractions and on the tight security designed to make visitors feel safe.[81]

Encourage Recruitment and Patronage at Not-for-Profit Institutions. Many not-for-profit institutions, such as museums and dance companies, have limited promotion budgets and rely to a large extent on goodwill in the community for survival. Even colleges must work hard to be sure their reputations make them attractive to prospective students (especially in an era of declining enrollments, where competition for tuition dollars is as fierce as any bowl game!) Faced with declining interest in MBA programs and demographic changes, even the top business schools are hiring PR firms to publicize their merits. At least ten of *Business Week* magazine's top forty business schools mail videotapes to prospective students. The Wharton School sends accepted applicants interactive floppy disks in an attempt to hook students by providing everything from details on what life is like in Philadelphia to student profiles.[82]

Enhance the Image of a Company by Linking It to Activities That Benefit Society. "Cause marketing" links corporate identity with good causes by combining public service, advertising, and public relations efforts to make a long-term commitment to an issue of urgency. The Coors Brewing Co. launched a five-year, $40 million program aimed at teaching illiterate American adults, and in the United Kingdom, Texaco contributed to the government's efforts to improve road safety with an £8 million campaign: "Children should be seen and not hurt."[83]

PLANNING A PUBLIC RELATIONS CAMPAIGN

To conduct an effective public relations campaign, a company must do more than have its executives take journalists to lunch to try to get favorable press coverage. A public relations strategy involves three steps: research and planning, execution, and evaluation.

Research and Planning: Deciding What to Talk About

The organization must first justify the need for the program and define the problem. It can then develop a benchmark for measuring changes in consumers' attitudes and proving the value of the program to the company. The American Society of Internal Medicine, for instance, found that many people confused the term *internist* with *intern*. The organization used this information to launch a campaign that offered tips on how to be a good patient while educating the public about what internists do.

After determining the particular issue of interest, the next step is to decide what the organization should do about it. The campaign plan should include the following elements:

- A statement of the problem
- A situation analysis
- The development of program goals and objectives
- Specification of target audiences (publics), messages to be communicated, and specific program elements
- A timetable and budget
- Discussion of how the program will be evaluated

For example, the International Apple Institute, a trade group devoted to increasing the consumption of apples, had to choose from one of several objectives before it could plan a public relations campaign. Should the campaign get consumers to cook more with apples, to drink more apple juice, or to buy more fresh fruit? Because fresh apples brought a substantially higher price per pound than applesauce or apple juice, the group decided to push the fresh-fruit angle. It used the theme "An apple a day. . . ."

Execution: Doing Something Good and Talking About It

There are many ways to get a positive message out to the public, ranging from a news conference to the sponsorship of a tennis tournament. In some cases the organization can simply try to get media exposure for something that already exists, such as the achievements of an employee who has done some notable charity work or a new product that contributed to saving someone's life. In other cases the organization must make news, often by sponsoring some event of local interest, such as an art exhibit, a contest, or a factory tour.

Doing Something Good: Event Sponsorship. Event sponsorship is an extremely popular form of public relations. Each year, an estimated 4500 firms spend some $3.7 billion on event sponsorship, including everything from sports (two-thirds of all event promotions) and rock concerts to museum exhibits and the ballet. Event sponsorship has been growing at better than 17 percent a year since the late 1980s. "With event marketing, we're touching customers in their life-style, when they are more relaxed," says the national director of sponsorships and promotions for AT&T's consumer long-distance division, which arranged for AT&T to be a major sponsor of the National Basketball Association.[84] Here are some other recent and planned sports sponsorships:

- Gillette Co. will spend $8 million on a one-month promotion blitz for the Gillette 3-point Challenge. The college basketball theme program is the first leg of an expanded multisport promotion series.[85]
- Anheuser-Busch has become a major league baseball sponsor for the pre-season and the World Series. A major fall promotion for Budweiser brands will be tied to the World Series. A responsible-drinking ad campaign related to baseball is also in the works. In return for its sponsorship, Anheuser-Busch has the right to use major league baseball insignia and terms such as "World Series" in ads and promotion materials.[86]
- Strategic planners acknowledge that it will take time to bring full-scale Indy 500 racing to markets such as the Philippines, Malaysia, India, and countries in Latin America. To prepare the populace, Goodyear has held a rally race for women on the outskirts of New Delhi every year since 1988. Using local cars, about 100 women race over open roads and across fields. The race regularly draws thousands of spectators.[87]

Exhibit 18.10
A canoe/kayak endurance race was held to boost sales of Finlandia vodka. The promotion ties Finlandia's positioning (the water used in making the vodka comes directly from a glacial spring) to water sports. The company's strategy is to find a sport "on the ground floor" and become associated with it. It had already done this in 1978 for José Cuervo tequila, when it transformed beach volleyball into a sport with stars, TV coverage, and more than $6 million in prize money. That effort also increased sales from 629,500 cases in 1978 to two million in 1992; Cuervo outsells competitors by a 4-to-1 margin.

Doing Something Even Better: Cause Marketing. As many consumers are searching for socially responsible companies to patronize, some firms are accelerating their public relations efforts to be sure not only that they are involved in constructive causes but also that they receive proper credit for their good works. Some companies are beginning to engage in what has been called point-of-purchase politics, wherein they link their products to social issues such as homelessness (Hanes apparel), AIDS (Heublein), rain forest preservation (Ben & Jerry's ice cream), and animal testing (The Body Shop). The Members Only apparel company has been especially active in this area. The company has funded $100 million worth of advertising to combat drug abuse and to encourage voter registration. One recent TV commercial includes images of past dictators such as Hitler and Mussolini to remind people that the way to avoid the creation of future dictators is to vote.[88]

Cause-related marketing also has its downside: Critics sometimes question the motives of these campaigns, arguing that companies may invoke social issues as a roundabout way to promote their own causes. For example, Procter & Gamble's distribution of free teaching kits on environmentalism to thousands of money-starved public schools has come under fire for advancing the company's own business interests. Among other "pearls of wisdom," the kit informs students that disposable diapers are as good for the environment as cloth, that incineration is similar to recycling, and that timber clear-cutting helps to stimulate growth and feed animals. The company denies the charges, noting that it has furthered children's education since 1912 (when students were taught to use Crisco oil while learning how to cook).[89]

Talking about It. The most common way for public relations specialists to communicate is to issue a **press release,** which is a description of some event that is sent to newspaper and magazine editors in the hope that it will be published as a news item. Here are some of the most common types of press releases:

press release: a description of some event that is sent to newspaper and magazine editors in the hope that it will be published as a news item

- *Timely topics* deal with topics in the news.
- *Research stories* summarize research projects conducted by the organization's personnel.
- *Coming events* promote activities sponsored by the organization.
- *Consumer information releases* provide information to help consumers make better product decisions.
- *Institutional releases* report activities, services, and accomplishments of part of the organization or the entire firm.
- *Features* include articles about people associated with the organization who have done something of interest.
- *Past events releases* summarize events that have already occurred.

Of course, submitting a release does not guarantee that it will be published. Editors are bombarded with these items and often reject them because they are not directly related to readers' lives or are seen as merely promoting the organization. The challenge, then, is to write a release that provides a service to readers while simultaneously promoting the company.

For example, a public relations executive who worked for a paper cup company periodically wrote effective releases based on how germs spread through the use of common glasses and how disposable glasses limit the spread of germs. Press releases that provide

Exhibit 18.11
One recent sales promotion in the medical field by the pharmaceutical company Boehringer Ingelheim (Canada) Ltd. illustrates how a company can forge relationships with customers while doing a good deed—and getting valuable publicity for it!—at the same time. To build corporate image and increase sales of some of its respiratory medicines for children, Boehringer Ingelheim sent cute, near life-size dolls wearing customized respirator masks to 575 Canadian pediatricians. The dolls, known as My Buddy, encouraged physicians to help children with asthma and other respiratory disorders learn how to use respirator masks. The dolls enabled patients to play out some of their fears about putting a mask over their mouths and noses. The immediate awareness of the respirator-equipped doll within the medical community and the surrounding publicity made the campaign one of Canada's most successful sales promotion efforts. By performing a valuable public service, this type of promotion makes long-term partners out of suppliers and users and gives a firm's public relations experts something positive to talk about.

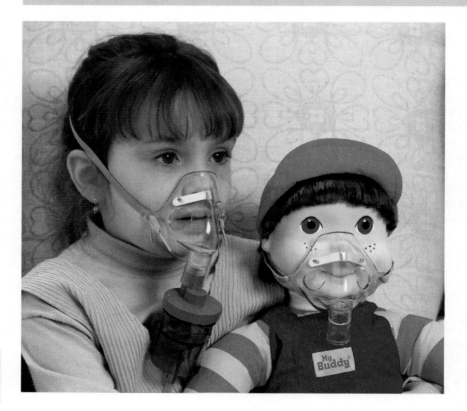

some service to the reader are likely to be picked up by the media, as are releases (called hometowners) that emphasize local news. Small-circulation newspapers are particularly likely to print releases that feature a "hometown hero."[90]

A newer version of the traditional press release is the *video news release (VNR)*, wherein the company's story is told on screen rather than on paper. VNRs often are slickly produced and may be inserted directly into television news programs, especially by program managers at smaller stations. The pressure on news editors to stay within budget puts increased value on free, professionally prepared footage to support business stories and accounts of new products and technology breakthroughs. In one survey of European television stations, 58 percent of broadcasters said they used at least one VNR in a typical month.[91]

Evaluation: Deciding What Worked

One of the barriers to greater reliance on public relations campaigns is that it is hard to gauge the effectiveness of these approaches. After all, who can say precisely what impact a series of appearances by company executives on talk shows or the firm's sponsorship of a charity event has on actual purchases? In contrast, a marketer can tell immediately whether a direct-marketing piece that hits consumers over the head with product information is effective, simply by counting the orders the piece generates.

However, it *is* feasible to tell whether a public relations campaign is getting the company the exposure it seeks. Many companies, such as Hewlett-Packard, have set up systems to evaluate their PR efforts. These systems monitor the amount and type of coverage the company receives in selected media. For example, a company might hire a clipping service to collect copies of newspaper articles mentioning the company or its products from around the country. Alternatively, it might conduct an ongoing consumer *tracking study* to determine how attitudes toward the company, product, or issue are changing over time. Some of the most common measurement techniques are described in Table 18.4. In some cases, these measurements and others are provided (often at significant cost) by specialized companies, such as the Delahaye Group, Inc., that provide sophisticated assessments of media coverage and comparisons with the coverage received by competitors.

Table 18.4
Measuring the Effectiveness of Public Relations Efforts

Method	Description	Pros	Cons
In-house assessment conducted by a public relations manager	Analyze media coverage in publications, looking for number of mentions and prominence of mentions.	Relatively inexpensive, because the major cost is the manager's time.	Cannot guarantee objectivity in the analysis; crucial to specify "up front" what the relevant indicators are.
Awareness and preference studies	Assess company's standing in the minds of customers relative to competition.	Good for broad-based strategy setting or to demonstrate the progress of a large program.	Difficult to connect results to specific PR events and to identify which actions had what level of impact on awareness; very expensive.
Counting of press clippings	The basic measurement tool in PR.	Provides a quantifiable measure of press coverage; relatively inexpensive.	Quantitative only; does not consider the *content* of the press coverage.
Impression counts	Measure the size of the potential audience for a given article.	Because a similar measure is used to assess advertising effectiveness, provides a common measure for comparison.	Usually limited to the circulation of selected publications, so this method does not include pass-along readership; can be expensive.

Source: Adapted from Deborah Holloway, "How to Select a Measurement System That's Right for You," *Public Relations Quarterly* (Fall 1992): 15–17.

REAL PEOPLE, REAL CHOICES:

HOW IT WORKED OUT AT KWE ASSOCIATES

Victoria Feldman chose Option 1. Finnish-Americans became the primary target for KWE Associates' public relations campaign to increase tourism in Finland. The agency began the task of identifying prospects by using U.S. Census data to identify key geographic areas where Finnish-Americans were concentrated. These areas included Detroit, Duluth (Minnesota), Lake Worth (Florida), and Worcester (Massachusetts). KWE then developed a year-long strategic plan and a timetable of PR activities, including news releases and media tours in key markets. The agency also created a target list of key Finnish-American publications and invited journalists to visit Finland for feature story coverage to promote Homecoming Year. Targeted newspapers received an "editor advisory" with Finnish-American population statistics for their markets.

In the fall of 1991, a press conference for the travel press was held in New York City to announce specifics of the travel program. In January 1992, KWE produced and distributed a video news release to over 800 television stations nationwide. The agency continued to garner publicity for Homecoming Year through such activities as arranging a media tour for the program coordinator in key markets where interviews were arranged with major city newspapers, ethnic newspapers, and local television stations and radio stations in nine selected cities. KWE also coordinated a press trip to Finland for editors from these markets. News of Finland's Homecoming Year, including television, radio, and print placements, reached more than thirty-eight million people nationwide with significant penetration in the top ten targeted Finnish-American markets. As a result of this public relations campaign, overall arrivals to Finland from the United States during this period increased by nearly 20 percent. In addition, travel by the targeted segment of Finnish-Americans exceeded the campaign's goals by 100 percent. By working creatively with the mass media to generate a "buzz" about Finland, Victoria Feldman and her associates were able to accomplish their marketing objectives without incurring the significant costs associated with traditional advertising. Who says reindeer races can't be profitable?

Chapter 18 Summary

Objective 1. Explain the use of sales promotion and its importance in the marketing function.

Sales promotions are short-term programs designed to build interest in, or encourage purchase of, a good and/or to complement other promotion activities. Sales promotion has become more important in recent years because advertising has become very expensive and less effective, brand loyalty has deteriorated, sales promotion activities are particularly effective for smaller markets, and marketers can measure the results of sales promotions. Sales promotions enhance marketing efforts by creating short-run changes in product sales, by cementing relationships with retailers and wholesalers, and by encouraging high levels of store traffic. Sales promotions also have some less attractive characteristics: They dilute brand equity, they teach consumers always to look for special offers, their effect is only temporary, and they often reach only current users.

Objective 2. Describe some of the various types of trade and consumer sales promotions frequently used by marketers.

Sales promotions aimed at industry members and retailers are called trade promotions. Sometimes trade promotions mean manufacturers work to help make retailers more successful by providing local advertising support, conducting sales training, or giving the retailer a price allowance. Trade promotions aimed at the sales force and at members of the industry include trade shows where manufacturers can showcase their products for many buyers from around the country, specialty advertising, and incentive programs such as sales contests.

Consumer sales promotions may be classified as attention-getting activities, point-of-purchase (POP) activities, or price-based promotions. Attention-getting promotions involve the consumer in the company's marketing efforts and include giveaways, contests and sweepstakes, and premiums delivered to the consumer in, on, or near the package or through the mail. POP activities include in-store sampling, product displays and signs, and in-store media. Price-based consumer promotions include coupons, which are most often delivered via newspaper free-standing inserts (FSIs), price-offs, rebates, and special packs such as bonus packs.

Objective 3. Outline the steps in developing a sales promotion program.

A first step in planning a sales promotion program is to develop objectives. Marketers also must decide on the best sales promotion tools to use, the size and length of the program, eligibility requirements, and the specifics about distribution and promotion of the program. The final steps are to decide on the budget, pre-test the promotion, implement the program, and evaluate the results.

Objective 4. Explain the role of public relations.

The purpose of public relations is to create or manage the image of an organization among various publics—that is, shareholders, employees, retailers, suppliers, and the like. Effective public relations is important to the long-term health of an organization, because it not only communicates good news about the organization to the various publics but also works to control the effects of negative information or events. A major public relations tool is publicity: unpaid communications through the mass media used to introduce new products to manufacturers and consumers, influence legislation, ease acceptance of corporate changes, encourage recruitment and patronage at not-for-profit institutions, and enhance the image of a company, place, or group.

Objective 5. Describe the steps in developing a public relations campaign.

A public relations campaign begins with examining the current attitudes of various publics, determining the problem or issues of interest, and then planning what action to take. A PR campaign may include sponsorship of an event, cause-related marketing activities, and/or development of print or video news releases about timely topics. As with other promotion tools, careful implementation and evaluation are important also.

Review Questions

Marketing Concepts: Testing Your Knowledge

1. What is sales promotion and why is it an important part of marketing strategy?
2. What are the advantages and disadvantages of sales promotions?
3. Explain the different types of trade promotions frequently used by marketers.
4. Explain the different types of consumer promotions frequently used by marketers.
5. Outline the steps in developing a sales promotion program.

6. What is public relations and what is its role in the promotion mix?
7. Explain how public relations and marketing may have conflicts.
8. What are the functions of public relations?
9. What are the typical activities of a public relations department?
10. What are the steps in planning a public relations campaign?

Marketing Concepts: Discussing Choices and Issues

1. In recent years many firms have reduced the amount spent on advertising while increasing sales promotion budgets. At the same time, firms such as Procter & Gamble have reduced spending on coupons and other sales promotion in favor of EDLP strategies. Why have these changes occurred? What are the potential benefits and problems of such changes for marketers? For consumers? What is your opinion of these changes in promotion strategy?
2. Companies sometimes teach consumers a "bad lesson" with the overuse of sales promotion. As a result, consumers expect the product always to be "on deal." What are some examples of products where this has occurred? How do you think companies can prevent this?
3. The $4 billion specialty advertising industry has been called the stepchild of advertising. What are the benefits of specialty advertising? Where do you think specialty advertising works best? Should specialty advertising get more respect?
4. In many firms and in the minds of many marketers, there is a conflict between public relations and marketing. Is PR a part of the marketing function? Should PR be merged into marketing within the organization or should it remain a separate function?
5. Two public relations activities that have been criticized are lobbying or other attempts to influence legislation and cause marketing. What are the criticisms of each of these activities? When do you think these types of activities are good? When may they not be in the best interests of consumers or of businesses?

Marketing Practice: Applying What You've Learned

1. Assume you are a member of the marketing department for a firm that produces several different brands of household cleaning products. Your assignment is to develop recommendations for trade and sales promotion activities for a new brand and an older brand of dish liquid.
   a. Develop an outline of your recommendations for sales promotions for the new dish liquid.
   b. Develop an outline of your recommendations for sales promotions for the older brand of dish liquid.

2. Timing is an important part of a sales promotion plan. When is the best time to mail out samples, to offer trade discounts, to sponsor a sweepstakes? Assume the introduction of the dish liquid in question 1-a is planned for April 1. Place the activities you recommended in question 1-a on a 12-month calendar. In a role-playing situation, present your plan to your supervisor. Be sure to explain why you have included certain types of promotions and the reasons for your timing of each promotion activity.
3. As part of the marketing department for a firm that is introducing a new brand of healthy snack foods called "Snak-Smart," you have been asked to develop a point-of-purchase promotion plan. Outline your recommendations for point-of-purchase promotions. Make sketches of the signs and/or displays you wish to use.
4. Assume that you are a public relations professional working for a firm whose business is the incineration of hazardous waste. Outline your recommendations for a public relations strategy for the coming year. Be sure to list and describe all the different types of PR activities you would include.

Marketing Mini-Project: Learning by Doing

Most colleges and universities have a public relations department, sometimes called a university relations or college information department. The purpose of this project is to enable you to learn more about what a real PR department does and understand how PR helps an organization such as a university.

1. With one or more of your classmates, arrange to talk with the public relations staff at your school. You will probably want to find out about
   a. The different responsibilities of the department
   b. How the department fits into the overall organization of the school
   c. The background and skills of the individuals in the department
   d. How the public relations function is viewed both by those in the department and by the school administration in general
2. Find out how others on your campus feel about the public relations function at your school. Talk with a variety of different students, faculty members, and staff. Ask them
   a. What they know about the public relations function on campus
   b. What they think the PR department does very well
   c. Whether there are additional activities or changes in existing programs they would recommend for the PR department
3. Present your findings to your class. If possible, invite members of the PR staff to your class for the presentation.

Key Terms

Endnotes

1. Matthew Grimm, "Reebok, Evian and Warner Team to Put More Power in Walking," *Brandweek* (Sept. 14, 1992): 73–76.
2. Jonathan Sims and Sasaki James, "Cable Diversity Attracts Nestlé," *Advertising Age* (Feb. 22, 1993): C-14.
3. Leland Montgomery, "The 'Gotta Have It' Syndrome," *Financial World* (April 13, 1993): 40–43.
4. Ibid.
5. Ibid.
6. Riccardo A. Davis, "Bubble Yum Kicks Off Virtual Reality Game," *Advertising Age* (March 22, 1993): 3.
7. Howard Stumpf and John M. Kawula, "Point of Purchase Advertising," in ed. S. Ulanoff, *Handbook of Sales Promotion.* (New York: McGraw-Hill, 1985); Karen A. Berger, *The Rising Importance of Point-of-Purchase Advertising in the Marketing Mix* (Englewood, N.J.: Point-of-Purchase Advertising Institute).
8. Susan Nunziata, "Rock the Vote Promo Gains Support of 50 Music Chains," *Billboard* (July 18, 1992): 3.
9. Quoted in Stephen Kindel, "Cutting Through the Clutter," *Financial World* (April 13, 1993): 36–38.
10. Leland Montgomery, "The 'Gotta Have It' Syndrome," *Financial World* (April 13, 1993): 40–43.
11. Robert Buzzell, John Quelch, and Walter Salmon, "The Costly Bargain of Trade Promotion," *Harvard Business Review* (March/April 1990): 142.
12. Howard Schlossberg, "Event Sponsorships Prove Reliable in Targeting Ethnics," *Marketing News* (Jan. 18, 1993): 8.
13. Stuart Elliott, "Contest Is Next in Coffee Caper," *The New York Times* (June 21, 1993): D7.
14. Terry Lefton, "MasterCard Credits Campus Talent," *Brandweek* (March 28, 1994): 14.
15. Scott A. Neslin and Robert W. Shoemaker, "An Alternative Explanation for Lower Repeat Rates after Promotion Purchases," *Journal of Marketing Research* XXVI (May 1989): 205–218.
16. Ed Weller, "The Place to Sell Is in the Store," *Progressive Grocer* (Nov. 1992): 116.
17. John Philip Jones, "The Double Jeopardy of Sales Promotions," *Harvard Business Review* (Sept./Oct. 1990): 145–152.
18. Scott Hume, "Trade Promotion and Share Dips in '92," *Advertising Age* (April 5, 1993): 3.
19. Spencer L. Hapoienu, "Product Glut Sparks Struggle for Shelf Space; Small Companies Protest Slotting Allowances," *Marketing News* (Jan. 16, 1989): 2.
20. Ed Shane, "Playing the Local Song," *American Demographics* (Sept. 1989): 51–53.
21. Patricia Sellers, "Winning Over the New Consumer," *Fortune* (July 29, 1991): 113.
22. Melinda Grenier Guiles, "Wooing Press and Public at Auto Shows," *The Wall Street Journal* (Jan. 8, 1990): B1.
23. *A Guide to the U.S. Exposition Industry* (Denver, CO: Trade Show Bureau Resource Center, 1994); Cyndee Miller, "It Walks, It Talks, It Even Collects Consumer Data—It's Gus," *Marketing News* (Jan. 6, 1993): 26.
24. *A Guide to the U.S. Exposition Industry* (Denver, CO: Trade Show Bureau Resource Center, 1994).
25. Bruce Bendow, "Promoting Exports to Europe, Part II: Using Trade Fairs and Advertising," *International Trade Forum* (April–June 16, 1992): 6.
26. Sandra Pesmen, "Want to Be No. 1 in Your Industry and Trade Show? Team Up with a Celebrity," *Business Marketing* (March 1992): 54–55.
27. Charles S. Madden and Marjorie J. Caballero-Cooper, "Expectations of Users of Specialty Advertising," *Journal of Advertising Research* (July/Aug. 1992): 45–52; Kevin Doyle, "Getting the Message Across," *Incentive* (Feb. 1992): 67–70; Howard Schlossberg, "Financial Services Firm Hits a Grand Slam with Direct Marketing Campaign," *Marketing News* (Feb. 1, 1993): 13.
28. Patricia Winters and Scott Donaton, "Coke Takes to Highway to Grab College Crowd," *Advertising Age* (March 29, 1993): 8.
29. Scott Hume, "Trade Promotion and Share Dips in '92," *Advertising Age* (April 5, 1993): 3.
30. Adam Bryant, "When It Comes to Offbeat Promotions to Woo Passengers, Where Will the Airlines Draw the Line?" *The New York Times* (Jan. 24, 1994): D9.
31. Ibid.
32. Andrea Adelson, "Airline Gives Family a Crack at Fame," *The New York Times* (June 23, 1994): D5.
33. Leland Montgomery, "The 'Gotta Have It' Syndrome," *Financial World* (April 13, 1993): 40–43.
34. Doug Podolsky and Richard J. Newman, "Prescription Prizes," *U.S. News & World Report* (March 29, 1993): 56.
35. Terry Lefton, "Hi-C, '90210' Turn on the Juice," *Brandweek* (Jan. 18, 1993): 7.
36. Blair R. Fischer, "Record Companies Give Sampling a Spin," *Promo: The International Magazine for Promotion Marketing* (Jan. 1995): 17–18.
37. "Fall of Soviet Union a Win for Barq's," *Advertising Age* (March 22, 1993): 37.
38. "Quaker Club Was a Sheer Winner," *PROMO: The International Magazine for Promotion Marketing* (April 1994): 116.
39. Don E. Schultz, William A. Robinson, and Lisa A. Petrison, *Sales Promotion Essentials,* 2 ed. (Lincolnwood, IL: NTC Business Books, 1993).
40. Kerry J. Smith, "It's For You," *PROMO: The International Magazine for Promotion Marketing* (Aug. 1994): 41; Sharon Moshavi, "Please Deposit No Cents," *Forbes* (Aug. 16, 1993): 102.
41. *The Point-of-Purchase Advertising Industry Fact Book* (Englewood, N.J.: The Point-of-Purchase Advertising Institute, 1992).
42. John Mason, "The Point of P-O-P; Tomorrow's P-O-P Stars," *Sales & Marketing Manager Canada* (Dec. 1991): 8–12.
43. Blair R. Fischer, "Record Companies Give Sampling a Spin," *Promo: The International Magazine for Promotion Marketing* (Jan. 1995): 17–18.
44. Julie Liesse, "Sampling Beats In-Store TV, Grocery Execs Say," *Advertising Age* (March 8, 1993): 32.
45. Jennifer Lawrence, "P&G Hooks Up with Interactive Product-Sampling Hot Line," *Advertising Age* (Oct. 5, 1992): 3.
46. Betsy Spethmann, "NutraSweet Samples to Spice Up Word of Mouth," *Brandweek* (April 12, 1993): 9–12.
47. Glenn Heitsmith, "Nestea Takes a Sampling Plunge," *Promo* (April 1994): 1.
48. Robert Dwek, "POPAI Predicts Strong Future," *Marketing* (Feb. 4, 1993): 10.
49. Betsy Spethmann, "Big Three Brewers Heat Up on Displays," *Brandweek* (March 15, 1993): 5.
50. Geoffrey Brewer, "Dancing for Dollars," *Incentive* (July 1992): 49–51.

51. Patricia Sellers, "Winning Over the New Consumer," *Fortune* (July 29, 1991): 113.

52. Scott Hume, "Kellogg Tops Cents-Off Derby," *Advertising Age* (Feb. 1, 1993): 25.

53. Scott Hume, "Coupons Set Record, But Pace Slows," *Advertising Age* (Feb. 1, 1993): 25.

54. Ann Marie Kerwin, "ROP Coupon Share Continues to Fall; FSI Coupons Grow," *Editor & Publisher* (March 20, 1993): 24–26.

55. Robert M. Schindler, "A Coupon Is More than a Low Price: Evidence from a Shopping Simulation Study," *Psychology & Marketing* (Nov./Dec. 1992): 431–451.

56. Barbara E. Kahn and David C. Schmittlein, "The Relationship Between Purchases Made on Promotion and Shopping Trip Behavior," *Journal of Retailing* (Fall 1992): 294–315.

57. Scott Hume and Patricia Strand, "FSI Coupon Redemption Hits Wall," *Advertising Age* (March 18, 1991): 41.

58. Ken Gofton, "Seeking Redemption," *Marketing,* (March 12, 1992): 25–26.

59. Don E. Schultz, William A. Robinson, and Lisa A. Petrison, *Sales Promotion Essentials,* 2 ed. (Lincolnwood, IL: NTC Business Book, 1993).

60. Mat Toor, "Lotus Targets Impulse Buyers," *Marketing* (Feb. 25, 1993): 3.

61. This section is based on material presented in Don E. Schultz, William A. Robinson, and Lisa A. Petrison, *Sales Promotion Essentials,* 2 ed. (Lincolnwood, IL: NTC Business Books, 1993).

62. Scott Hume, "Kellogg Tops Cents-Off Derby," *Advertising Age,* (Feb. 1, 1993): 25.

63. Nancy Hass, "Back to the Future," *Financial World* (April 13, 1993): 42.

64. Ibid.

65. Ibid.

66. John P. Cortez, "'VW Song' Strikes Chord, Results in Cross-Promotion," *Advertising Age* (March 1, 1993): 4.

67. Debra Aho, "France Says 'Oui' to Interactive Kiosk," *Advertising Age* (Nov. 8, 1993): 25.

68. Jennifer Lawrence, "Tracy-Locke Division Works for the Big Event," *Advertising Age* (May 17, 1993): S-2, S-7.

69. "Pepsi Caps the Damages on a Promotion Gone Flat," *The New York Times* (Aug. 18, 1993): D3.

70. Beverly A. Browne, Dennis Kaldenberg, and Daniel J. Brown, "Games People Play: A Comparative Study of Promotional Game Participants and Gamblers," *Journal of Applied Business Research* (Winter 1992–1993): 93–99.

71. William Briggs and Marilen Tuason, "Let the Games Begin," *IABC Communication World* (March 1993): 16–20.

72. Mike Reynolds, "From PR to PA: A Natural Fit," *Communication World* (Jan./Feb. 1995): 27–31.

73. Willie Vogt, "Shaping Public Perception," *Agri Marketing* (June 1992): 72–75.

74. William N. Curry, "Customer-driven Isn't Enough; You Have to Be Publicly Driven," *Marketing News* (April 12, 1993): 6, 14.

75. Elizabeth Corcoran, "How to Win Friends and Influence People (Not)," *The Washington Post National Weekly Edition* (Dec. 26, 1994–Jan. 1, 1995): 21; Don Clark, "Intel Finds Pumped-Up Image Offers a Juicy Target in Pentium Brouhaha," *The Wall Street Journal* (Dec. 5, 1994): B5.

76. David Drobis, "Building Brand Equity with Public Relations," *Management Review* (May 1993): 52–55.

77. Judy A. Gordon, "Print Campaign Generates Sales Leads for Biotechnology Product," *Public Relations Journal* (July 1991): 21.

78. Lindsay Chappell, "PR Makes Impressions, Sales," *Advertising Age* (March 22, 1993): S-18, S-32.

79. Patricia Winters, "Drugmakers Portrayed as Villains, Worry About Image," *Advertising Age* (Feb. 22, 1993): 1, 42.

80. Jennifer Kearns, "Case Study Name Change," *Bank Marketing* (June 1992): 20–23.

81. Ni Chen and Hugh M. Culbertson, "Two Contrasting Approaches of Government Public Relations in Mainland China," *Public Relations Quarterly* (Fall 1992): 36–41.

82. Lori Bongiorno, "B-Schools Are Taking a Crash Course in Hoopla," *Business Week* (April 19, 1993): 38.

83. Robert Dwek, "Doing Well by Giving Generously," *Marketing* (July 23, 1992): 16–18; Don Oldenburg, "Big Companies Plug Big Causes for Big Gains," *Business & Society Review* (Fall 1992): 22–23.

84. Stephen Kindel, "Gentlemen, Flash Your Logos," *Financial World* (April 13, 1993): 46–48.

85. Matthew Grimm, "Gillette Back Heavy in Sports," *Brandweek* (March 15, 1993): 3.

86. Patricia Winters, "A-B Scores Unusual Tie-In with Baseball," *Advertising Age* (March 1, 1993): 30.

87. Nancy Hass, "Back to the Future," *Financial World* (April 13, 1993): 42.

88. Stuart Elliott, "When Products Are Tied to Causes," *The New York Times* (April 18, 1992): 33.

89. David E. Kalish, "P&G's Lessons on Environment Provoke Criticism," *Marketing News* (March 14, 1994): 7.

90. Linda P. Morton, "Producing Publishable Press Releases," *Public Relations Quarterly* (Winter 1992–93): 9–11.

91. Bruce Whitehall, "Video News Releases: Faster Track to TV, Exposure?" *Business Marketing Digest* (Second Quarter 1992): 15–22.

92. *POPAI/DuPont Consumer Buying Habits Study* (Englewood N.J.: Point-of-Purchase Advertising Institute, 1986).

CASE 18-1

MARKETING IN ACTION: REAL PEOPLE AT BUDGET RENT-A-CAR CORP.

Five years ago, only about half of Budget Rent-A-Car's customers were referred to the company by travel agents. John Power, Budget's senior vice president for marketing and sales, wanted to boost this figure. He and his colleagues set out to design a series of sales promotion programs that would entice agents to recommend Budget more frequently when their clients expressed interest in a rental car. These efforts have not only increased rentals for Budget, they have also helped the company establish stronger, more enduring relationships with thousands of these vitally important middlemen.

The first promotion Budget developed was Book Smart, a program that rewards travel agents for booking Budget cars. Book Smart offered discount rental coupons to travel agents to pass along to any customers they chose, which makes *them* look good to their clientele. Also, Book Smart ran a scratch-off sweepstakes for agents, awarding a grand prize of use of a Lincoln Town Car for a year. Following these two promotional efforts, travel agency bookings increased by 14 percent.

That was a good start, but Budget wanted a still greater share of these referrals. Therefore, Budget expanded the Book Smart program with even more creative trade promotions, such as the Masters of Business Acquisition (MBA) program. It awards agents a $30 bonus every time they enroll a new corporate account, plus a 10 percent commission for bookings on all existing corporate accounts. Another addition to Book Smart, Budget's Commitment to Satisfaction program, takes a more unusual approach. This promotion helps travel agents increase the level of satisfaction of their customers—even if the customer doesn't use Budget. To do this, Budget provides travel agents with discount coupons to be given to any customer who makes a complaint about *any* car rental company. The coupon gives the customer a free one-day rental with Budget and an invitation to join the company's frequent-renter program. If the complaint concerns Budget, then the customer is also personally contacted by a Budget representative to solve the problem.

Since the trade promotion program was begun in 1991, over 25,000 agents have enrolled in Book Smart. Travel agents now book 70 percent of Budget's business,

with a rate of growth substantially higher than overall growth in the rental industry. Book Smart agencies contribute five times more average sales than nonparticipating agencies.

Yet another promotion aimed at travel agents is the Road Scholar program. According to Power, "We found through our research that travel agents weren't familiar with the booking of car rentals in general." Road Scholar is first and foremost an educational program. That program has great credibility, because it was jointly developed with the American Society of Travel Agents. The Road Scholar program also rewards agents with credits redeemable for savings bonds, free rentals, cash, or travel to industry events. To be eligible for these incentives, Road Scholar participants must have increases in sales each year, and the top performers are named to the "Dean's List."

Budget's success with trade promotions has inspired the company to continue its efforts to develop still more motivational programs. The firm even asks travel agents to participate in focus groups to provide suggestions for future programs that would cause them to refer still more clients to Budget. These ongoing relationship-building efforts with travel agents have, in essence, created an extension of Budget's own sales force. As the company prepares to move into other countries and Budget begins to woo travel agents around the world, the value of investing in trade promotions will not soon be forgotten.

Source: Regina Eisman, "Budget," *Incentive* (Sept. 1995): 58–59.

Things to Talk About

1. What were Budget's reasons for beginning its Book Smart program?

2. How have Budget's sales promotion programs benefitted the travel agents?

3. What are the benefits to Budget of having more than one trade promotion program?

4. What do you see as the advantages and disadvantages of the sales promotion programs to Budget?

5. What secrets of success has Budget Rent-A-Car discovered?

MARKETING IN ACTION:
REAL CHOICES AT HAWKEYE BANK

It seems as though a new newspaper headline about bank consolidations, mergers, mega-mergers, and acquisitions has appeared daily over the last decade. However, although consumers don't mind reading about these developments happening to other people, they tend to be less than thrilled when their own bank undergoes change. When United States Bank, a $50 million financial institution that has been in business in Cedar Rapids, Iowa, for over seventy years, planned to change its name, not surprisingly there was concern about how to make the switch without alarming customers.

United States Bank was founded in 1922 in a Czech neighborhood, and it still maintains a high profile among the Czech community. Approximately one-fourth of USB's customers are older, conservative people—people who don't welcome change just for change's sake. The bank currently operates three branches, one in the original Czech neighborhood, a second in downtown Cedar Rapids, and a third in another residential neighborhood.

In 1982, the bank was purchased by a Des Moines-based holding company called Hawkeye Bancorporation. Because USB retained its name and there were no changes in the bank staff during this transition, customers didn't even seem to notice the change in ownership. But recently, all twenty-two banks owned by Hawkeye had voted to adopt a common name: Hawkeye Bank.

Bank officials knew that it was important to develop a program that would communicate this change to employees and customers. They felt that it was also important that the bank reinforce its image as a locally owned, well-managed, service-oriented bank and assure customers that the new name would in no way change the bank's culture or its conservative approach to business. And it was hoped that the name change would also increase the bank's visibility and customer traffic at all three USB locations.

This change had to be implemented carefully. Employees had to be knowledgeable about it so that they could reassure long-time customers. The bank's business customers and its most important individual customers had to be handled with care. If effectively implemented, the communications program could even increase enthusiasm among employees and community residents and generate increased business. The only question was when and how to do all this—and do it right.

USB bank officials recognized that there is a lot to consider in making such a change. Quite obviously, there was concern about the reactions of employees. Because employees *are* the bank in the minds of customers, creating a positive attitude toward the new name and making clear that no other changes would adversely affect employees was very important. And, of course, bank managers were concerned about how to announce the change to current and potential customers. They were especially concerned about their many elderly customers, who might accept the change less readily than younger consumers. It was important to maintain the trust of these customers not only for the sake of existing accounts but also because these people were influential leaders in the Czech community and served as role models and opinion leaders for younger customers. If the bank lost them, other customers would surely follow their lead and go elsewhere.

Bank managers also knew that Cedar Rapids had not been exempt from recent problems in the nation's banking industry that had tarnished the image of financial institutions in general. When one local bank became insolvent, some customers had had difficulty withdrawing their funds, an experience that left many in the community worried about the safety of their money. Again, the elderly, many of whom could clearly remember the bank failures of the Great Depression, were the most concerned.

To add to the problem, two other banks in the community had recently been purchased by out-of-state holding companies. The fact that these two institutions were also in the process of changing their names made USB especially aware of the problem of timing. After considering everything, officials at USB decided it would be best to move forward very quickly, making the name change first, before other banks did so. Thus they needed a plan and they needed it immediately.

Source: Jennifer Kearns, "Name Change," *Bank Marketing* (June 1992): 20–23.

Things to Think About

1. What is the problem facing USB?
2. What factors are important in understanding this problem?
3. What alternatives might USB consider?
4. What are your recommendations for solving the problem?
5. What are some ways to implement your recommendations?

19

Personal Selling and Sales Force Management

When you have completed your study of this chapter, you should be able to:

CHAPTER OBJECTIVES

REAL PEOPLE, REAL CHOICES:

MEET KATHLEEN CARROLL-MULLEN, A DECISION MAKER AT GENERAL ELECTRIC

When Kathleen Carroll-Mullen was elected vice president of the student chapter of the American Society of Mechanical Engineers at Manhattan College, she was surprised to find that the best part of the job was recruiting guest speakers for the organization. The satisfaction she received interacting with people in the engineering industry led her to consider a job in sales. After a brief stint as a summer intern in industrial purchasing for Consolidated Edison, Kathleen took a job as an entry-level sales representative for General Electric, and from there she never looked back.

In her role as an account manager, Kathleen was constantly learning. She had to learn everything she could about the six industrial companies that were her assigned accounts, and in turn she had to let her clients know all the ways in which GE's expertise in providing generators, motors, integrated electrical systems, and related services would meet their needs. Much of her time was spent making on-site visits to customers around the world. Kathleen soon discovered she was spending a lot of time in airplanes, and she used this opportunity to study technical proposals, plan meetings, and chart paths for developing relationships on key accounts. Once Kathleen set her sights on winning an order, few account managers could match her energy, business smarts, and tenacity. She earned the GE Navigator Award for being the top key account manager in her sales region. Kathleen recently was promoted and is now program manager–National Accounts for GE Supply.

THE BIRTH OF A SALESPERSON

Kathleen Carroll-Mullen discovered firsthand that even the marketing of highly technical products such as gas turbine generators and adjustable-speed motor drives requires the personal touch. Her work for General Electric highlights the crucial role played by personal selling in the promotion mix of many companies, from mom-and-pop retail stores to huge corporations.

This chapter will take a close look at how personal selling works. Many of us assume that being a salesperson means hawking sneakers or jeans to strangers at the local mall, but in reality the marketing world is populated with highly sophisticated salespeople who work hard to develop long-term relationships with demanding customers whose orders can run into millions of dollars. We will first look at just what personal selling really is, and examine its role in the marketing function and the promotion mix. Next we'll talk about different types of personal selling and learn about the selling process. We will also discuss how firms manage the sales function, and we will consider ethical and legal issues that arise when salespeople compete to land those big orders.

personal selling: the part of the promotion mix that involves direct contact between a company representative and a customer

AN OVERVIEW OF PERSONAL SELLING

Personal selling is the part of the promotion mix that involves direct contact between a company representative and a customer in an effort to inform him or her about a product or service and/or to persuade him or her to make a purchase. As we've seen in prior chapters, there are many dimensions of the promotion mix that enable marketers to communicate about a product or service and persuade customers to choose it. Unlike promotional efforts involving mass communication, however, selling is "up close and personal." It involves understanding the customer's needs, providing information that persuades the customer that a product will satisfy those needs, and often providing service to the customer after the sale. Although most personal selling is done by salespeople whose job is to sell company products, *all* employees who come in contact with customers—whether cashiers, delivery people, or repair people—engage in some form of selling because they represent the organization to the public.

For many people, the terms *personal selling* and *marketing* are synonymous. As one well-known sales training consultant put it, "Nothing happens until somebody sells something." This emphasis is a bit exaggerated in that selling is only one part of an organization's marketing strategy. Still, for many organizations, personal selling is often the most important source of revenue. This form of promotion is particularly crucial for many business-to-business marketers. As Kathleen Carroll-Mullen's contributions to GE demonstrate, some industrial products and services are simply too complex or expensive for the firm to allow impersonal communications to carry the weight of the sales effort. Firms such as GE, IBM, and Xerox rely on a strong sales force.

Personal selling is not limited to businesses; many not-for-profit organizations and even governments also maintain a personal sales function. Hospitals employ patient coordinators or service representatives who show prospective patients such as expectant mothers the facilities, seeking to get their business in the profitable areas of the hospital. Even universities in a sense employ salespeople: University admissions counselors and students who lead campus tours for prospective freshmen are not pushing their schools just for the fun of it.

In this section we will discuss the nature of personal selling and talk about how selling has evolved into an important part of the total marketing effort. We will also discuss some of the strengths and weaknesses of sales within a firm's total promotion mix.

IT'S NOT JUST A JOB, IT'S AN ADVENTURE . . .

Personal selling has special importance for students, because many graduates with a marketing background will enter sales jobs after they are "paroled" from school. It is estimated that between 1990 and 2000, American businesses will need to add to their rosters from 25 to 34 percent more retail sales workers, from 14 to 24 percent more manufacturers' and wholesale sales representatives, and 35 percent more service sales representatives.[1]

Those who stay with a sales career often are very well paid, particularly in business-to-business selling for large companies. Today the average starting salary is around $25,000 for salespeople with a bachelor's degree and is over $35,000 for new sales personnel with an MBA. As the salesperson climbs the ranks, the picture is even brighter: The average salary is over $66,000 for top-level salespeople and over $75,000 for sales supervisors. To appreciate the importance of a salesperson to his or her firm, consider that an average field salesperson

- Earns about $70,000 per year
- Brings in about $1.1 million in sales
- Spends over 180 days a year in the field making an average of four calls per day
- Incurs travel and other expenses of over $15,000 per year[2]

THE EVOLUTION OF PERSONAL SELLING

International "jet setters" such as Kathleen Carroll-Mullen represent a new breed of salesperson: a far cry from the image many people have of a rather scruffy fellow knocking on doors to push encyclopedias. Let's take a quick look at how the sales function has evolved over the years.

Personal selling is one of the oldest forms of promotion. Indeed, the term *salesman* was mentioned in the writings of the ancient Greek philosopher Plato![3] Salespeople in the Middle Ages were peddlers who sold fruits and vegetables to townspeople and then bought manufactured goods in towns and returned to sell them to people in the farming communities.[4]

transactional selling: a form of personal selling that focuses on making an immediate sale with little or no attempt to develop a relationship with the customer

relationship selling: a form of personal selling in which the salesperson seeks to develop a mutually satisfying relationship with the customer so they can work together to satisfy each others' needs

The Industrial Revolution created demand for more—and more sophisticated—salespeople. At that time, economies of scale in production made possible the manufacture of a greater volume of goods and thus created a need for salesmen to reach more and more customers in wider geographic regions. Unlike the peddlers, who were independent entrepreneurs, these salesmen were hired by manufacturers to sell the goods they produced.

During the first and second world wars, most industrial effort was aimed at producing goods for the military, so there was relatively little need for salespeople. In the period between the wars, however, firms struggling through the Great Depression became desperate for sales, and many developed very aggressive sales forces. Remember that at this time the marketing concept as we now know it was in its infancy. The philosophy was that a good salesperson could push *anything* onto *anybody*.

After World War II, industrial capacity was converted from the production of war goods to that of consumer goods. Consumers who had done without many products during the war years were initially eager to buy products from fast-talking salespeople. But the success of these hard-sell tactics was short-lived. Beginning in the mid-forties, customers began to demand a more customer-oriented approach. Thus was born the professional salesperson—one who is honest and who focuses on satisfying customer needs as well as providing revenue for the firm.

Unfortunately, many people still harbor the stereotype of the vacuum cleaner salesman who won't take his foot out of the door until the homeowner buys a machine. During this century, personal selling has done much to redeem itself as a profession as it has moved from a transactional "hard-sell" approach to a relationship marketing approach. Let's take a look at each type.

Transactional Marketing: Putting on the Hard Sell

The *hard sell* is a high-pressure form of selling. We've all been exposed to (and probably angered by) at least one of these hard-sell techniques:

- A used-car salesperson tries to convince a couple that if they don't buy a certain car today (right this minute!) they will lose their chance because another customer is also considering the car.
- A door-to-door salesperson insinuates that if a woman doesn't purchase the vacuum cleaner, she is not a good wife and mother.
- An electronics salesperson puts down the competition by telling shoppers that if they look elsewhere, they will be offered an inferior sound system that will fall apart in six months.

These hard-sell tactics are typical of **transactional selling,** a form of personal selling that focuses on making an immediate sale—a single transaction—with little or no attempt to develop a relationship with the customer. Hard-sell techniques typically are used to sell products that consumers buy only once or a few times in their lives, such as encyclopedias, refrigerators, and televisions.

Many times salespeople feel compelled to engage in transactional selling in order to meet sales quotas or, as we will discuss later in this chapter, because of commission compensation plans that encourage them to make as many one-time sales as possible. Although the hard sell can be effective in the short term, it can be poison over the long haul. Transactional selling often makes us feel compelled to buy something we were not planning to buy. As customers, the hard sell makes us feel manipulated and resentful. This technique also contributes to the negative image many of us have of salespeople. As we'll see, though, in many cases this reputation is undeserved. The truly professional salesperson plans for the long term and works hard to build a relationship with customers.

Relationship Selling: Countering the Tarnished Image

Many modern salespeople are working hard to overcome the tarnished hard-sell image of their profession. Today's professional salesperson is much more likely to practice relationship selling than transactional selling. In **relationship selling,** the salesperson seeks to develop a mutually satisfying relationship with the customer, one in which the salesperson and the customer work together to satisfy each others' needs. Especially in the world of business-to-business marketing, this orientation simply makes more sense: Most selling situations are characterized by long-term relationships because it is far more cost-effective to keep current customers happy than to continually find new customers.[5]

The objectives of relationship selling include winning, keeping, and developing customers. *Winning* a customer means converting an interested prospect into someone who is convinced that the value offered exceeds the total costs of owning the product or using the service. *Keeping* a customer means ensuring that the product or service received delivers what was promised. *Developing* a customer means helping him or her satisfy needs not only through the current purchase but also through future purchases.

Relationship-oriented salespeople such as Kathleen Carroll-Mullen call on customers on a regular basis, even when the customer is not ready to make a purchase. They spend time with the customer to learn about his or her specific needs, and they take a personal interest in the customer's welfare. These professionals try to suggest ways in which the customer can improve his or her business, even if it means recommending a competitor's product! The salesperson who practices relationship selling realizes that both she or he and the company will be best served by a style of selling that will stimulate repeat purchases.[6]

Relationship selling is more likely to occur in industrial marketing settings, but it is becoming more common in retail settings as well. This practice may take the following forms:

■ A sales associate in a men's clothing store keeps a file of the likes and dislikes of customers and calls when new merchandise they might like arrives.

■ A buyer at a formal wear shop offers to look for a dress for a special occasion for a customer when she goes to New York.

SPOTLIGHT ON RELATIONSHIP MARKETING

Excellence at Saturn Corp.

The auto industry has built its selling programs around promotions, discounts, rebates, bait-and-switch advertising, and a high-pressure good guy/bad guy approach. A new selling style, built around fixed, no-haggle prices, full book price for trade-ins, and patient explanations of cars' features, has been pioneered by General Motor's small-car subsidiary, Saturn Corp.* Given the hard sell that many people have experienced in pressure-filled car-buying episodes, Saturn dealers have created a differential benefit by encouraging more of a consultant–client relationship with customers.

A key aspect of the Saturn program is salesperson compensation. Saturn encourages dealers to pay their salespeople salaries instead of commission. More than half pay salaries only, and the remainder have salary-plus-bonus plans with bonuses tied both to sales and to measures of customer satisfaction.†

But Saturn went a step farther. On June 24 and 25, 1994, Saturn hosted the "Saturn Homecoming." Saturn invited its nearly 700,000 owners to come to the Saturn factory in Spring Hill, Tennessee, to visit the birthplace of their cars and get to know other Saturn owners. Corporate communications manager Bill Betts said, "We're constantly trying to establish relationships with our customers. The Homecoming party is another way of building these relationships, and it shows that we treat our customers differently than any other car company."

Activities for the weekend included a tour of the manufacturing complex. Camp Saturn provided arts and crafts activities, games, storytelling and entertainment for children aged three to twelve. For guests aged thirteen to eighteen there was "Excel," a course of physical challenges designed to build trust and team spirit. The cost for the weekend was $34 for adults and $17 for children; a portion of the proceeds went to the Make-A-Wish Foundation. Celebrity guests included country singer Winona Judd and gold medal speed skater Dan Jansen.‡

The result of this new sales strategy? Saturn's customer satisfaction level was recently ranked just below those of luxury carmakers Lexus and Infiniti and above those of Mercedes-Benz and Lincoln, whose cars are priced more than $20,000 above the Saturn. A report by J.D. Power & Associates found that Saturn owners were particularly pleased with the treatment of customers. There has been a similar response in sales. Sales by Saturn dealers have been more than twice the industry average. To meet the ferocious demand, some dealers were even forced to sell the staff's personal cars when inventory got too low!

* Warren Brown, "Running Rings Around the Competition: Saturn Dealers Court 'Be-Back' Customers, Cut Haggling—and Increase Car Sales," *Washington Post* (Aug. 8, 1992): B1; Jack Falvey, "The Selling of Saturn," *Sales and Marketing Management* (Oct. 1994): 26.
† David Woodruff, "May We Help You Kick the Tires?" *Business Week* (Aug. 3, 1992): 48.
‡ Andy Cohen, "It's Party Time for Saturn," *Sales and Marketing Management* (June 1994): 19.

- An assistant manager in an auto parts store offers to install an alternator for a man who is on his way out of town on a Sunday afternoon.
- The manager of a dry cleaner tells customers that if they can't get by during business hours to pick up clothing needed for a special occasion, they can call him and he will meet them at the store.

THE IMPORTANCE OF PERSONAL SELLING TO THE MARKETING FUNCTION

For most firms, some form of personal selling is essential for a transaction (the sale) to occur, so this type of promotion is an important part of an organization's overall marketing plan. Perhaps the best way to appreciate the importance of personal selling is to compare it to advertising, another vital activity that often complements the sales effort. Table 19.1 lists some of the factors that make personal selling relatively more or less important in an organization's promotion mix.

One Message Per Customer, Please

Unlike most forms of advertising, personal selling allows for flexible, precisely targeted, one-on-one marketing communications. For example, firms such as Nike spend millions of dollars advertising their shoes on television. Nike has no way of knowing whether members of the TV audience have long or short feet, walk on pavement or sand, or play basketball for fun or are on a high school team. They simply deliver the same message to all of their potential customers who share some basic set of characteristics such as age or income.

The retail sales associate, on the other hand, can talk with each customer, learn what he or she needs in a shoe, and recommend the shoe that will best satisfy those needs. Of course, the many exciting developments in interactive communications and database marketing are blurring the distinction between mass advertising and personally tailored sales appeals. Still, many customers value the personal attention one can get only from a flesh-and-blood salesperson.

Customers Talk Back

Most advertising is one-way communication. Although two-way communication through interactive television or via the Internet promises a better way for marketers to solicit customer feedback, there is currently little opportunity for a marketer to receive

Table 19.1
Factors That Influence the Firm's Emphasis on Personal Selling

Factors That Increase the Emphasis on Personal Selling	Factors That Limit the Emphasis on Personal Selling
The marketer is engaging in a push strategy.	The dollar amount of individual orders will be small.
The decision maker has higher status within the organization.	The customer has a poor image of salespeople.
The purchase is a "new task" for the customer.	The marketer is selling personal products.
The product is highly technical or complex.	There are many small customers.
The customer is very large.	
The product is expensive.	
Custom goods or personalized services are involved.	
There are trade-in products.	

feedback on the response to its advertising or to answer customers' questions. In direct customer–salesperson interactions, the salesperson can listen to customers and can address objections as well as communicate product benefits.

More Than Just Communications

Especially for such products as inexpensive, frequently purchased packaged goods like detergents or chewing gum, advertising is quite sufficient to provide information, persuade, and perhaps even entertain customers. In many other cases, though, successful firms must not only communicate but also provide a variety of services. The sales function enables the firm to provide this extra level of support. Salespeople for companies such as Xerox that sell expensive, highly technical equipment often also provide product installation and set-up, instruction in use of the product, and product maintenance as well.

In retail selling it is not uncommon to find bored sales clerks waiting on customers if and when the mood strikes them. But Nordstrom Inc., a Seattle, Washington-based retailer, has enlarged the role of sales associates, who call themselves "Nordies." The Nordies go to unusual lengths to learn about, advise, and please customers, thus winning their loyalty. They have even been known to locate merchandise at a competitor's store if the item is unavailable at Nordstrom's! This emphasis on consultative relationships has paid off handsomely for the store; its annual sales of $370 per square foot certainly compare well to the $160 industry average.[7]

Feedback on Marketing Strategy

Have you ever tried talking back to your television set? Many of us have, but it's unlikely that the people at the TV station or the advertiser heard us! Because advertising is one-way communication, no information is returned to the sponsoring firm. In contrast, the salesperson is an invaluable source of feedback and can act as the firm's eyes and ears in the field. If some aspect of marketing strategy is not working, the salesperson will be the first to hear about it!

Salespeople who know their customers are also able to provide valuable information about changes in customer needs, marketplace developments, and so on. They are thus an important source of specific competitive intelligence. Because the innovations, successes, and failures of the competition directly affect the personal (and financial) success of the salesperson, members of the sales force are eager to learn as much as they can about what the competition is doing. They naturally pay attention to which competitors' salespeople are calling on customers, what new competing products have been delivered to their customers, and what new literature is lying on the purchasing agent's desk.

THE ROLE OF PERSONAL SELLING IN THE PROMOTION MIX

As important as it may be, personal selling is only one element of the promotion mix. All the elements of the promotion mix are interrelated. The ideal promotion strategy creates advertising, sales promotion, publicity and public relations, and personal selling plans that work together in a synergistic fashion wherein the whole is greater than the sum of the parts. As a result, personal selling strategies are designed to support other promotion activities, and the personal sales function in turn is enhanced by the other elements of the promotion mix.

The job of the salesperson is often made easier by publicity and advertising. The customer who has regularly seen a supplier's advertisements or has read about a company's new products is more likely to welcome the salesperson's call. Interactive advertising that provides a toll-free number for interested consumers to call for more information provides a list of potential customers for the salesperson. In return, information the salesperson obtains from customers about what ads they have seen and about their response to the advertising is important in evaluating the success of the advertising and publicity efforts and in developing new advertising.

The interdependence of the personal sales function and trade promotion is even stronger. Trade shows enable the salesperson to visit with hundreds of customers and prospective customers in a few days at one location and help to generate leads for the salesperson who calls on wholesalers and retailers (see Chapter 18). And it is the persuasive communication of the salesperson that encourages customers to take advantage of promotions such as trade allowances and contests.

Factors That Make the Sales Function More Important

As we have seen, personal selling can play a central promotional role in some situations, whereas in others its contribution is virtually nonexistent: When was the last time you saw a salesperson pressing the flesh in a grocery store? Generally, a personal sales effort is more important when a firm engages in a *push strategy,* where the goal is to push the product through the channel of distribution. As a vice president at Hallmark Cards observed, "We're not selling *to* the retailer, we're selling *through* the retailer. We look at the retailer as a pipeline to the hands of consumers."[8]

These firms need a strong personal sales force that works closely with wholesalers, dealers, distributors, and/or retailers to persuade them to feature the company's offerings. In addition, a number of characteristics of both the customer and the product determine how much emphasis personal selling should receive in the promotion mix.

Customer-Related Factors. In industrial buying contexts, the status of the decision maker helps to determine how influential a salesperson will be. If upper-level management is part of the decision process, the personal touch is often essential to making a deal. And with larger business-to-business customers, there is often a more competitive sales environment that calls for personal attention and the development of close salesperson–buyer relationships.

For both consumers and industrial customers, the buyer's experience in making the decision also affects the importance of contact with a salesperson. Relatively inexperienced buyers may need more assistance. Thus firms that sell products that consumers buy infrequently, such as computers, riding lawn mowers, and a college education, often place greater emphasis on personal selling. In other situations, some consumers simply have greater confidence in their ability to make purchase decisions. For those experienced shoppers, relationships with a salesperson may be unimportant or may even be considered undesirable.

Product-Related Factors. Characteristics of the product or service itself also contribute to the relative emphasis placed on the sales function. As a rule, the more expensive or complex the product, the greater the need for a salesperson to explain, justify, and sell it. This is also the case where the product or service must be customized to fit the specific needs of the buyer. For example, it's hard to imagine ordering a yacht or an office computer system through a catalog! Finally, in some product categories, negotiation is an important part of the sales process. Then the salesperson is responsible for developing a unique pricing strategy for each potential purchaser.

Limitations of Personal Selling

If personal selling is so effective, why don't firms just scrap their advertising and sales promotion budgets and hire more salespeople? Personal selling has some drawbacks that can limit its role in the promotion mix.

A major limitation is cost per contact compared to other forms of communication. Television advertising, for example, can communicate with millions of viewers in thirty seconds, whereas a salesperson may be lucky to call on two or three customers in a whole day. The estimated cost of a sales call may range from as low as about $12.00 per contact in service businesses to as high as over $400.00 for firms such as airplane manufacturers that have only a few key customers around the globe.

The median cost per call for consumer-goods, industrial, and service industry salespeople is over $200.00.[9] In comparison, although the cost of a national television commercial may seem exorbitant, the cost per contact is relatively low. A thirty-second prime-time commercial may run $300,000 to $400,000, but with millions of viewers, the cost may be only $10 or $15 per thousand viewers, or only a cent or two per individual contact. Personal selling costs include both salaries and travel and entertainment (T&E) expenses and average 10.5 percent of total sales in consumer-goods industries and 15.3 percent of total sales in service industries.[10]

Characteristics of the customer and the product may also make personal selling a less attractive form of promotion. Many consumers and business customers have a poor image of the salesperson. For many personal products, consumers would rather purchase the product in relative privacy, without being in contact with a salesperson. And for convenience goods, there are literally millions of customers, far too many for companies to use salespeople efficiently.

Personal Selling and Integrated Marketing Communications

As we noted in Chapter 16, integrated marketing communications enables a firm to deliver coordinated messages to narrowly defined target markets through a variety of channels. The IMC concept recognizes the sales force as the heavy hitter in the communications arsenal. Within an IMC strategy, sales force calls are aimed carefully and only at prime targets. For instance, a firm that sells groundskeeping equipment to municipalities may designate a salesperson to call on the maintenance departments of large city governments while a telemarketing program targets smaller communities. Then when a telemarketer identifies a small community that is planning a major purchase, the company sales rep calls on the customer and works with city personnel on the order.

One firm that has implemented an IMC strategy to enhance its sales function is Fluke Corporation, a maker of electronic test equipment. Fluke needed to know what product information it should send to the different individuals at prospective customer firms and when this information should be mailed. The first step was to develop a database the company called a "Customer Information System" from fifteen existing departmental computer files. The database included names, products purchased, frequency and volume of purchases, results of contacts, and likelihood of new business. Using the database, Fluke can provide customer profiles to its sales force and to the distributors, jobbers, and dealers that handle its products. The prime benefit to Fluke is that its salespeople can now deliver a unique message to each prospective customer.[11]

As more firms buy into the IMC concept, we will see some changes in the basic character of the sales force. The focus of an IMC program is on the customer, not on the product, so the sales manager becomes a *customer manager,* and salespeople are not just salespeople but real links between the customer and the organization. With an IMC strategy salespeople will work with manufacturing to develop products that better meet customers' needs.[12] Thus the integrated marketing communications concept makes sales forces more efficient and effective. It also requires them to take more responsibility for working with customers to devise long-term solutions to their needs.

TYPES OF PERSONAL SELLING

The job description of a salesperson varies widely. Pharmaceutical companies employ salespersons called *detail reps* who promote their products to physicians, hospitals, and other health care customers. A sales associate at a department store such as Macy's offers expertise and advice as she helps retail shoppers make selections. General Electric's salespeople call on contractors who purchase large quantities of equipment for major construction projects such as airports, skyscrapers, and manufacturing plants. The customer service representative for MCI telephones potential customers and tries to persuade them to change long-distance carriers. Even the person who rings up orders at the local pizza parlor can be considered a salesperson.

Different personal sales jobs require that the salesperson engage in different sales activities and work with different types of customers. Salespeople also conduct their work in widely varying selling environments, from fast-food restaurants to nuclear power plants, from the comfort of their own offices to the homes of farm families, or while visiting the offices of customers from Chicago to Shanghai. In this section we'll look at how the job of selling differs based on the selling function, the sales environment, and the customer type.

FROM GETTING TO TAKING: PERSONAL SELLING FUNCTIONS

Personal sales functions differ in how the salesperson interacts with the customer. There are also differences in the amount of creativity required for the selling job. Some salespeople are *proactive;* they identify potential customers and try to influence them to make purchases. Other salespeople are *reactive;* they try to meet the needs of customers who already know what they want. Still others in the sales organization do not actually sell at all but instead provide support to the firm's salespeople. Table 19.2 gives some examples of how sales personnel meet the customer's needs in different purchase situations, ranging from a new purchase to a routine one (these types of organizational purchase decisions were discussed in Chapter 7).

Order Getting

order getter: a salesperson who works creatively to develop relationships with customers or to generate new sales

A salesperson who works creatively to develop relationships with customers or to generate new sales is an **order getter.** Order getters have two goals: to maintain a company's existing business and to generate new business. Order getters find new customers, provide customers with information about their products, persuade customers of the benefits of their products or services, and close the sale. Most business-to-business salespeople—those who call on business or organizational customers—are order getters. However, some retail salespeople who are aggressive and committed to creating business also are order getters, whether they sell encyclopedias door-to-door, push men's suits in a fine department store, or tempt shoppers with state-of-the-art home theater systems in electronics boutiques.

Sophisticated order getters often do more than sell products; they also act as *account managers* by arranging for others within the organization to provide help and expertise in satisfying the customer's needs (these people are sales support personnel; we'll talk about them shortly). Order getters become more involved in working relationships with customers than do order takers. Because order getters are more likely to handle nonroutine purchases, they typically must be more knowledgeable and skilled about product characteristics, customers, and selling practices.

Table 19.2
Sales Tasks Vary by Customer Needs

Purchase Type	Selling Tasks		
	Order Getting	**Order Taking**	**Sales Support**
New Purchase	Order getter works with physician to select equipment and software for a clinic's accounting and payroll tasks.	Order taker on phone enters office manager's request for a bulk purchase of floppy disks.	Telephone technical support technician helps physician's accountant obtain replacement part for computer system.
Modified Purchase	Order getter helps physician to order back-up computer memory and a fail-safe computer system power supply.	Order taker on phone enters office manager's reorder of a larger quantity of floppy disks.	Telephone technical support technician helps physician's accountant resolve monitor glare and radiation with an attachable monitor filter.
Routine Purchase	Order getter helps physician order a second computer to handle a second clinic.	Order taker enters office manager's reorder of floppy disks.	Telephone technical support person tells accountant at the second clinic how to install purchased software.

Order Taking

Salespeople whose primary function is to facilitate transactions that are initiated by the customer are called **order takers.** Most retail salespeople are order takers, but wholesalers, dealers, and distributors may also employ counter salespeople who work at the firm's place of business and who assist customers and make sure they buy the correct merchandise. When customers call catalog companies to place an order, the individual who answers the phone is an order taker.

Trade salespeople take orders but also provide other services to customers. They may restock shelves in retail stores, obtain more shelf space, set up displays, or provide product demonstrations. For example, these services are routinely performed by route salespeople who deliver bread or milk to grocery stores and restaurants.

Although order takers tend to perform more routine duties than do order getters, this does not mean they are unimportant. Order takers also handle customer complaints, check inventory levels and product availability, and provide information about delivery schedules. The order taker may not need the extensive technical expertise and persuasive skills of the order getter, but it is vital that he or she provide courteous, efficient service. All it takes is one negative encounter with a rude clerk to dismantle years of careful image building!

Having made the distinction between order getters and order takers, we must not assume that a salesperson has to be one or the other. In fact, most salespeople fall somewhere in the middle of a continuum ranging from a thoroughly creative salesperson to one who handles only routine orders. And one consequence of the conversion to relationship marketing is that many companies are working harder to convert their order takers into order getters. For example, the catalog company's order taker becomes an order getter when, after callers have placed their orders, he or she tells them about a special offer the company is making. Even the counter salesperson at a fast-food restaurant is frequently coached to ask customers, "Do you want fries with that?"

Sales Support Personnel

Sales support personnel are company representatives who provide support or assistance to the sales force but are not involved in actually making sales. Three types of support personnel are important to know about.

The Technical Specialist. One particularly crucial type of sales support, especially in industrial settings where complex products and services are needed, is provided by the *technical specialist.* He or she contributes expertise in the form of product demonstrations, recommendations for complex equipment, setup of machinery, or in-service education. Technical specialists typically have advanced training; they often hold an engineering or science degree and have completed specialized company training programs. Technical salespersons known as *sales engineers* have engineering degrees or expertise. Sales engineers participate in the creative selling process and also have the expertise to provide technical advice to their customers.

The Missionary. Another type of support is rendered by **missionary salespeople,** who practice a kind of indirect selling. These specialists promote the firm and try to stimulate demand for a product, but they do not actually complete a sale. A manufacturer of such products as hospital or construction equipment whose products are sold through distributors or dealers often fields its own missionary sales force.[13] In the pharmaceutical industry, missionary salespeople known as *detailers* keep physicians up to date on the latest medicines. By answering questions and providing informational pamphlets and samples, missionary salespeople give valuable assistance to physicians and influence what drugs they will prescribe.

Missionary salespeople can also be found calling on retailers in situations where the product reaches the store through a wholesaler. Though a wholesaler may actually deliver the manufacturer's product, the wholesaler does not necessarily give retailers guidance on how to market the manufacturer's products. Consequently, the manufacturer employs missionary salespeople to visit the retailer and provide marketing suggestions. Effective missionary salespeople in these situations substantially improve product sales, because they help the retailer properly present a product to customers.

order taker: a salesperson whose primary function is to facilitate transactions that are initiated by the customer

sales support personnel: company representatives who provide support or assistance to the sales force but are not involved in actually making sales

missionary salespeople: salespeople who promote the firm and try to stimulate demand for a product but do not actually complete a sale

The Sales Team. Sometimes the job of selling is better accomplished when creative salespeople and sales support personnel work together. A **sales team** is a group of individuals who have different skills or expertise and who work together in selling an organization's products to customers. A sales team might include technical personnel, customer service personnel, top management (especially when very large sales or very large customers are involved), financial experts, and logistics planners. The concept of team selling was pioneered by DuPont, which uses teams of sales representatives, technicians, and factory managers to solve customers' problems and develop new products.

Xerox has gone so far as to name its sales effort "Team Xerox," and its sales teams include sales, administrative, and manufacturing personnel—and even customers.[14] For example, Xerox maintains a sales team dedicated solely to serving the needs of AT&T, one of the company's biggest corporate clients. The team includes over two hundred Xerox salespeople, and finance, administration, and service specialists also report to the team.

The sales team or whole-company approach to selling is beginning to be seen in the field of traditional retailing as well. Although layers of management above store managers are usually removed from customers, this isolation is clearly not the case at Wal-Mart. Wal-Mart applies its own version of team selling to retailing. Upper-level managers at Wal-Mart are constantly on the move, visiting outlets and talking to customers. Wal-Mart recognizes that even in retail selling, it is possible to make managers part of a sales team. By truly knowing customers and having everyone focus on the unique needs of retail customers in different markets, Wal-Mart has become the largest retailer in the United States.

A salesperson plays the role of manager and leader in team selling, setting goals and developing a selling strategy. For example, Masterclip Graphics has a successful relationship selling program whereby it derives 70 percent of its software sales from major accounts, typically Fortune 500 companies. Though itself a small company, Masterclip wins orders from large companies by shrewdly deploying a mix of sales and support personnel, depending on the stage of the selling process and the demands of the situation. As the buyers' needs develop, a salesperson will bring in an applications specialist to help with planning, for example, or ask a hardware specialist to check the software–hardware fit.[15] In short, a salesperson at Masterclip Graphics actively works as a team leader, calling on other team experts as needed.

THE SALES ENVIRONMENT

Sales jobs also differ in terms of the *selling environment:* the circumstances under which the salesperson and the customer come together. One important distinction is whether the salesperson works "inside" or "outside" his or her organization.

Outside Selling

Outside selling is conducted by salespeople who visit face-to-face with customers away from the selling company's place of business. Outside salespeople are often called *field salespeople* because they don't spend much time at company headquarters. Field salespeople generally are independent in choosing what they try to accomplish each day, are not closely supervised, travel a great deal, and experience a wide mix of customer situations.

Having an outside sales force is quite costly for firms, so not all firms engage in outside selling. Firms are more likely to have field salespeople when the dollar amount of each sale is quite large or when the company's product or service is so complex that the salesperson must demonstrate it on-site to prospective customers. It is also a good idea to have a field sales force for selling situations in which the decision maker is the president, the CEO, or some other high-ranking individual.

Inside Selling

Inside selling is selling (other than in-store retail selling) conducted at the organization's place of business. Inside selling is often an order-taking operation; for example, a person who works at the counter taking orders for an electrical parts distributor is an inside salesperson. Inside salespeople may use telephones, fax machines, computer links, and mail services to perform selling activities with customers.

Because the cost of field salespeople is so great, inside salespeople who use the telephone are increasingly important in many companies. *Telemarketing* is selling in which person-to-person communication takes place via the telephone or fax machine. Over 480,000 companies representing about $60 billion in business sell by telephone each year.[16] Telemarketing may be *inbound* or *outbound:* Catalog companies such as L.L. Bean, Speigel, and Victoria's Secret are conducting inbound telemarketing when their customers call to place orders. AT&T checks customer sales records and uses outbound telemarketing to offer customers special long-distance service packages that will save them money.

CONSUMER VERSUS INDUSTRIAL SELLING

Sales jobs also differ in terms of the types of customers and their reason for purchase. Whereas some customers purchase for their own consumption, others buy on behalf of their organizations. Salespeople engaged in retail selling and those engaged in business-to-business selling face different challenges.

Retail Selling

Retail selling involves the selling of goods and services to individuals or groups who purchase for personal consumption. Many students are likely to have firsthand knowledge of this type of sales job. It is estimated that there are 4,754,000 retail sales workers in the United States alone.[17] As we noted in Chapter 15, retailing includes both *in-store retailing* and *nonstore retailing.* In-store retailing embraces department stores, specialty stores, supermarkets and hypermarkets, auto dealerships, appliance stores, and outlets ranging from the corner candy store to a giant Wal-Mart. In the past few years, though, increasing numbers of retail salespeople have found themselves working for a nonstore retailer, whether they sell encyclopedias door to door or work as a host on television's "Home Shopping Network," as an Avon representative, or as a broker for Merrill Lynch.

Retail store sales typically involve a high level of supervision and less individual initiative. Because retail selling may involve a wide array of products, salespeople must be well informed about the products and creative in helping customers. Compensation for entry-level retail salespeople is often low, but the picture brightens as a salesperson moves up to supervisory positions.

Business-to-Business Selling

Business-to-business selling involves the selling of goods and services to individuals or groups who purchase for some reason other than personal consumption. This includes retailers that purchase for resale, industries that purchase in order to produce other goods or services themselves, and organizations that simply need products to operate. It is estimated that there are 1,944,000 salespeople and over two million additional representatives selling insurance, real estate, and financial securities and services to businesses large and small.[18]

business-to-business selling: the selling of goods and services to individuals or groups who purchase for some reason other than personal consumption

THE SELLING PROCESS

The world of selling is seldom boring. Every customer, every sales call, and the personality and skills of every salesperson are unique. With some customers, the salesperson may need to spend time talking about a favorite football team or the customer's recent vacation before making a pitch. Other customers may be more impatient and grant the salesperson only ten minutes to make a short, fact-filled sales presentation. Some salespeople are successful primarily because of their knowledge and expertise; others "own" their territories because of the strong relationships they have built with their customers by virtue of having worked in the same territory for a long time. Regardless of these differences, most salespersons understand and engage in a series of activities that are necessary to bring about a transaction. Many experts suggest that these activities should be developed by thinking about the mental steps that constitute a buying decision, commonly known as the AIDA model (described in Chapter 17):

- The *attention* of the prospect is best maintained by a well-planned presentation.
- *Interest* is motivated if the salesperson understands the prospect's needs.
- *Desire* is based on a belief that the product's benefits will satisfy the prospect's problems or needs.
- *Action* (purchase) occurs when the salesperson asks the prospect to buy.

creative selling process: the process of seeking out customers, analyzing needs, determining how product attributes might provide benefits for the customer, and then communicating that information

The **creative selling process** involves seeking out customers, analyzing customer needs, determining how product attributes might provide benefits for the customer, and then communicating that information to the customer. As shown in Figure 19.1, there are seven steps in this process. In this section, we'll first examine these steps and then look at the different selling approaches that firms use.

PROSPECTING AND QUALIFYING

prospecting: a part of the selling process that includes identifying and developing a list of potential or prospective customers

Prospecting is the process of identifying and developing a list of potential or prospective customers. Prospects are people or businesses who are likely candidates to become customers. The first step in prospecting is *lead generation,* the development of a list of people or businesses who might be prospects.

Firms have a number of sources for new customers. In some cases *sales leads* are readily available from customer lists or telephone directories, or names for cold calls can be obtained from commercially available databases. In addition, the local library usually contains directories of businesses, including those published by state and federal agencies. Libraries also contain directories of associations that will provide membership listings to those who join. Another source of prospects may be no farther away than the local newspaper. For example, prospects for wedding gowns and reception facilities can be located simply by reading engagement announcements.

Sometimes company marketing activities are effective in generating names. Many companies use advertising in trade or consumer publications to obtain prospects. For example, an ad in *Ski* magazine may prompt an 800-number call to Vail's lodging desk, where a telephone salesperson begins the selling process with the prospect. Trade shows also deliver a high concentration of prospective customers who are interested in a specific class of products (see Chapter 18).

Cold calling involves contacting prospective customers without prior introduction or permission. Of course, it always helps to know someone rather than starting off cold. *Re-*

Figure 19.1
Steps in the Creative Selling Process

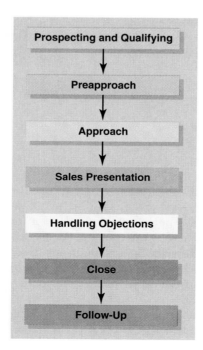

Prospecting and Qualifying

↓

Preapproach

↓

Approach

↓

Sales Presentation

↓

Handling Objections

↓

Close

↓

Follow-Up

ferrals come from an acquaintance or associate who suggests a prospective customer. Current customers who are satisfied with their purchase often give referrals—yet another reason to maintain ongoing relationships!

Another popular way to get contacts is through *networking:* using friends, acquaintances, co-workers, and others to help identify prospective customers. In some cases, visibility in the community or profession is the best way to find prospects. Accountants, lawyers, insurance salespeople, consultants, politicians, and others try to keep visible so that they can identify prospects for their services. Salespeople and service professionals often find it beneficial to be active in trade associations or in local community groups where they can expand their range of contacts.

The mere fact that someone is willing to talk to a salesperson doesn't mean that he or she will turn out to be a good sales lead. After identifying potential customers, salespersons need to **qualify** the prospect by determining (1) whether he or she meets the necessary criteria to be a customer and (2) how likely he or she is to become a customer. Many salespeople classify leads by assigning them a "grade" of A, B, or C. An "A" prospect is the most likely to provide favorable pay-back, a "C" prospect the least. Sometimes qualifying results in prospects being turned over to the firm's telemarketing operations, because although they are potential customers, their sales potential does not warrant the time and expense of a field call.

Qualifying usually involves gathering several different types of information about the prospect. First, does the potential customer need the product? Does the prospect match the characteristics of current customers? Is the prospect likely to respond to cost savings or other unique benefits offered by the company?

Second, is the potential sales volume large enough to make a relationship with the customer profitable? Many times a firm knows that accepting small orders and working with very small customers will, instead of being profitable, actually *cost* the company money!

Finally, does the potential customer meet the financial requirements to become a customer? Can a prospect afford the purchase? If a prospect must borrow money, is the prospect's credit history acceptable? What is the credit rating of the prospect? This concern is entirely legitimate. A survey of readers of *Inc.* magazine indicated that 86 percent of the respondents had had a customer go bankrupt and that 78 percent had had more than one such experience.[19]

> **qualify(ing):** a part of the selling process that determines how likely a prospect is to become a customer

PLANNING THE SALES CALL: THE PRE-APPROACH

The **pre-approach** consists of developing information about prospective customers and planning the sales interview. This step in creative selling often determines the success (or failure) of the remainder of the selling process.

Once a prospect is qualified as a valid potential customer, more effort can be devoted to learning about his or her specific situation and needs. Particularly in the case of business marketing, it is far preferable to learn as much as possible about the qualified prospect before initiating any attempt to make a sale. Important purchases are not made lightly, so it is foolish for a salesperson to call on a qualified prospect blindly. Information obtained about the circumstances of a purchase reveals the extent to which a customer can benefit from a purchase. IBM salespeople, for example, do not even attempt to make a sale of business equipment if a customer will not save money overall after having made the purchase.

Often, information about a prospect is available from a variety of sources. The public library may yield background information about the company. In the case of larger companies, financial data, names of top executives, and other information about business can be found in such publications as *Standard and Poor's 500 Directory* or the *Million Dollar Directory.* More information may be available from library collections of annual reports or through *Compact Disclosure,* which is an easy-to-use source of summary information taken from publicly traded firms' annual reports. Information on local firms may be available from commercially produced state business directories. Commercial databases, such as McGraw-Hill's *Publications Online* provide another means for learning about a customer's purchase situation. "The inside scoop" on a prospect, however, frequently comes

> **pre-approach:** a part of the selling process that includes developing information about prospective customers and planning the sales interview

Considering how our phone systems affect revenues, perhaps we should consider a new design.

How would you like a phone system that's designed not only for making calls, but for making money? One that lets you pick up any line, even your bottom line?

Sound interesting? Then a ROLM system will sound downright fascinating.

In the case of C.R. England & Sons, Inc. trucking company, ROLM helped them haul in a 26% increase in annual revenues. Then there's Acme Premium Supply Company. A ROLM system supplied them with a 25% increase in annual sales.

With customer after customer, we hear the same story. They can handle more calls in less time without adding people.

ROLM is part of the Siemens family. The world's largest private communication systems manufacturer.

Lost customer calls are being recovered. And the sales just keep rolling in.

It's not simply that ROLM can offer more sophisticated features than other PBX vendors. We can. But we also take a more intelligent approach to putting those features together. We take time to study your

business. Find out how it all works. Then we develop a customized solution that helps your business work faster. Leaner. More profitably.

Call us at **1-800-ROLM-123** to learn more. We'll send you a free video featuring a number of ROLM business success stories.

Once you see for yourself how our phone systems are ringing up sales, we're sure you'll find our design is just fine as is.

ROLM
A Siemens Company

Exhibit 19.2
Database marketing also offers an excellent source for generating sales prospects. Companies such as Rolm often add a coupon or a phone number to an ad offering valuable information to the prospective customer. When potential customers reply, Rolm can capture the names of people who are genuinely interested in its product for the firm's database and can pass this information on as leads to its sales force.

from more informal sources. Noncompeting salespeople are often happy to tell colleagues about customer characteristics. Other customers may also be rich sources of information about prospects.

The second part of the pre-approach is planning the initial prospect contact. Sometimes it is helpful to develop a written plan for converting a qualified prospect into a customer. Developing a careful plan for the sales call has several benefits. Perhaps most important, it gives the salesperson self-confidence.

INITIATING THE SALES INTERACTION: THE APPROACH

After the groundwork has been carefully laid, it is finally time to begin to make contact with the prospect. The **approach** is the first step of the actual sales presentation. During these important first few minutes when the salesperson initiates contact with the prospective customer, several key events occur. The salesperson tries to learn more about customer's needs, create a good impression, and build rapport. At the same time, the customer is deciding whether the salesperson has something of benefit to offer.

The old saying, "You never get a second chance to make a good first impression" rings true in this context: If this first impression is not favorable, the customer may erect barriers that prevent the relationship from continuing. The personal appearance and activities of the salesperson in the first few minutes are critical. The successful salesperson is neat, is well groomed, and wears appropriate business dress. The salesperson absolutely must not chew gum, avoid eye contact, use poor grammar or inappropriate language, criticize the competition, mispronounce the customer's name, or act bored.

Approaches based on the salesperson's knowing about the customer and/or the needs of the customer get attention and create interest. When the salesperson knows that the customer is planning an expansion, that the customer is currently using a competitor's

approach: the first step of the actual sales presentation, in which the salesperson tries to learn more about customer's needs, create a good impression, and build rapport

product that is priced higher, or even that the customer just won an amateur golf tournament, he or she has a greater chance of making a successful approach.

A salesperson may open the presentation with a statement, a demonstration, or a question since different types of openings may be better for different sales situations and for different customers. Statements such as "You certainly have a great new facility here" compliment the customer. Other times, mentioning a referral source is best: "Barbara Price with Amida Industries suggested that I call on you." Asking a question such as "Would you be interested in getting better-quality printer ribbons at a lower price?" is often an effective opening, and this approach is even more dramatic when the salesperson simply places a new product on the customer's desk and says nothing, letting the novelty or quality of the product speak for itself.

MAKING THE SALES PRESENTATION

In the **sales presentation,** the salesperson seeks to communicate the product's features and the benefits it will provide. Developing an effective sales presentation is not a simple task. The salesperson's bag of tricks can include a number of different presentation elements. Table 19.3 describes some of the mistakes most commonly made in sales presentations.

The most effective sales presentations are those that are tailored to the specific needs of the customer. In *adaptive sales presentations,* information learned about a customer is used to select product and service features that will appeal to the customer. For example, the director of operations for a company called Measurex Latin America encourages his salespeople to learn about a customer's situation and then emphasize in sales presentations those aspects of Measurex's product that are superior to the competitions' and of great importance to the customer. He focuses on drawing attention to purchase criteria where his firm has a differential benefit. When a customer agrees that these purchase criteria are important, the approach ensures a more favorable evaluation of the firm's products.[20]

sales presentation: the part of the selling process in which the salesperson seeks to persuasively communicate the product's features and the benefits it will provide

Table 19.3
Nine Deadly Mistakes in Sales Presentations

1. **Lack of focus in the presentation.** You must decide in advance the purpose of the presentation on the basis of the customer's problems.

2. **Failure to adapt the presentation to the unique needs of the customer.** Find out as much as you can about the customer before the presentation.

3. **Focusing on product facts rather than on customer benefits.** Know what the customer's problems are.

4. **Giving too much information—too many details.** Each presentation should have one clearly defined idea you are seeking to get across.

5. **Not allowing customers to ask questions.** It's more important for the customer to talk and ask questions than for the salesperson to talk.

6. **Not listening to the customer's comments and failing to adjust the presentation to respond to those comments.** Plan the presentation around getting the customer to talk.

7. **Lack of enthusiasm, energy, and animation in delivery of the presentation.** Have fun in delivering your presentation.

8. **Using poorly designed visuals or using too many visuals.** Visuals should complement the presentation, not dominate it.

9. **Failure to clarify what will happen next.** Summarize what all parties involved will be expected to do and when.

Source: Adapted from Alan Rosenthal, "How to Improve Presentations," *Business Marketing* (June 1992): 40–41.

Elements of the Successful Sales Presentation

The most effective sales presentations include a number of different elements. First and foremost, the presenter needs to be enthusiastic about what he or she is selling: It is very unlikely that the salesperson who seems to lack interest in either the product or the customer will ever move much merchandise. To be persuasive, the communication must also be logical, believable, simple, personal, and diplomatic.

The *participation* of the buyer can be encouraged during the sales presentation by asking questions or, if practical, allowing the customer to try the product. For example, a music store in Florida did some research and found that its main clientele, elderly retirees, did not desire a musical instrument so much as companionship. The store's salespeople now sell organs by encouraging passersby at the mall to join in group singing sessions. If they buy an instrument, free weekly group lessons come with the package.[21]

Proof statements, such as data on past sales, testimonials of other buyers, guarantees, or independent research results, also make the salesperson's pitch believable. For example, medical and pharmaceutical companies often encourage physicians to participate in research on their products and then provide copies of articles reporting research results to their colleagues.

People retain information far more effectively when it is associated with a visual image or when they can smell it, taste it, or hear it. Most salespeople use some type of *visuals* such as charts or photographs to sustain interest. *Demonstration* of the product that proves what the salesperson is saying may be the best way to persuade a customer. As you shop for a new car, the salesperson offers you a test drive. If you are shopping for a luxury car, you may be offered a car for the weekend. Corporate jets are sold by putting a corporate pilot in the driver's seat and a corporate officer in a passenger seat on a routine business trip.

Sales Presentation Techniques

Different sales jobs require different levels of creativity in developing sales presentations. For some sales situations, the successful salesperson knows that she must provide a unique presentation for each customer, one that is creative, adaptive, and relationship-oriented. In some sales situations, though, this customization may not be necessary—the same presentation may work for all customers. Sales presentations can be described in terms of the amount of creativity and customization they require and in terms of how much they allow the prospect to participate in the process. Some examples of sales "scripts" typifying each approach are provided in Table 19.4. Let's start with the most "automatic" kind of approach.

The Canned Sales Approach. The least adaptive type of sales approach is the highly structured **canned sales presentation,** which consists of a standard, memorized sales script in which the salesperson explains the major points of the product. This technique is also called a *stimulus-response approach,* because presentation provides a series of verbal stimuli to which the customer is expected to respond in the desired manner. For example, a salesman might say, "You are interested in making more money, aren't you?" or "You do want to feed your family good food, don't you?" knowing that the answer is always going to be "yes." A door-to-door vacuum cleaner or aluminum siding salesperson is likely to use a memorized sales presentation.

Although many people are put off by canned presentations, they do have some benefits. One is that reciting a speech that has been proven effective over time can build confidence for novice salespersons. Another benefit is that the company can be sure that the same message is delivered to all customers. Also, this approach can help the salesperson retain control over the interaction, because the customer is "allowed" to talk only in certain places where responses are planned.

The Selling Formula Approach. The *selling formula approach* is a method of selling in which a structured or ordered plan for achieving a sale is used. The salesperson follows a sequence of ordered steps, typically beginning with an assessment of the individual customer's needs. On the basis of this knowledge, the salesperson gives a "formula" presentation designed in advance to address those specific needs. Compared to a canned presentation, this technique provides some flexibility and allows some degree of buyer–seller interaction. The formula method is simple and can be adapted to a variety of selling situa-

canned sales presentation: a standard, memorized sales presentation

Table 19.4
Sample "Scripts" for the Four Sales Approaches

Approach	Typical Script
Canned or memorized	SALESPERSON: If something happened to you, you'd want to make sure your family were taken care of, wouldn't you? PROSPECT: Yes SALESPERSON: You'd want to make sure your family could stay in your home and that your kids could go to college, wouldn't you? PROSPECT: Yes. SALESPERSON: Don't you think they'd feel better knowing that you had life insurance to provide that for them? PROSPECT: Yes.
Formula	SALESPERSON: *(attention and interest)* Ms. Robbins, you've said before that you don't have room to carry our new line of sleeping bags, although you admit that you may be losing some sales by carrying only one brand with very few different models. If we could determine how much business you're losing, I'd be willing to bet you'd make room for our line, wouldn't you? PROSPECT: Yes, but that's easier said than done. SALESPERSON: *(interest and desire)* I'd suggest a trial. Find room to squeeze our line in for one month. If you're not satisfied with the sales after that, we'll take all the unsold merchandise back and give you a complete refund. Furthermore, we'll even pay half of the cost of some local newspaper advertising to let people know you're carrying our brand. What do you think? PROSPECT: *(moving toward conviction)* Well, maybe. SALESPERSON: May I enter your order for six of each of our different model bags now? PROSPECT: *(action)* That's fine. When will they be delivered?
Need satisfaction	SALESPERSON: *(need identification)* Do you have a particular car in mind? PROSPECT: No, but I want to make sure it's good looking. I like a really sporty car. SALESPERSON: So you think you'd like a cute little sports car? PROSPECT: No, I have a little two-seater now, but it's just not big enough, and my wife and I are expecting a baby in a couple of months. I have to have something that will hold three of us. SALESPERSON: *(need awareness)* Let me see if I have this right. You want something that is good looking but still has room for a family? PROSPECT: That's almost right. It also has to be comfortable. SALESPERSON: *(need fulfillment)* Let's go over here and look at this model. It is good looking but it also has room for a family. And even more important, it has several important safety features. PROSPECT: You know, I think that's exactly what I'm looking for.
Problem solution	SALESPERSON: With your present situation, does your hospital always have enough equipment when you get lots of critical patients? PROSPECT: No, and that's a real problem. SALESPERSON: So, if you don't have enough equipment, what does that mean about your patients' care? PROSPECT: We sometimes can't do as much for our patients as we'd like to, or we have to send them to another hospital. SALESPERSON: What if I could show you a way to get the extra equipment, but only when you need it, at a much lower cost than if you owned the equipment? PROSPECT: That would be great. SALESPERSON: Why don't you let me make a thorough analysis of exactly what your needs are, and then I will be better able to make a proposal for a cost-effective solution. I'll probably need to spend a couple of days talking with your staff in different departments. Then I can get back with you in a week or so. PROSPECT: Fine.

tions, such as straight rebuy and modified rebuy situations. It is effective with existing customers and may be used with new customers if the salesperson has a lot of information about the prospect. A formula approach may be necessary when the expected pay-back from a particular customer does not warrant the investment required for a more adaptive and proactive effort.

The Need Satisfaction Approach. The most creative and demanding approach to selling is the *need satisfaction approach.* This is a method of selling in which the salesperson fully understands the needs of the customer and develops sales appeals that are based on product benefits related specifically to the needs and wants of the customer. The need satisfaction approach is far more "labor-intensive," because it requires the salesperson to construct a different sales presentation for each individual customer.

This technique typically includes three stages, each related to the needs of the customer. The first stage is *need identification,* wherein the salesperson asks questions to identify the needs or problems of the buyer. For example, the salesperson may ask, "What do you need in a software product?" or "How much office space will you need?" The second stage is the *need awareness* stage, in which the seller restates the buyer's needs or problems and clarifies the situation. Finally, during the *need fulfillment* stage, the salesperson shows how his or her product will solve the problem or satisfy the need of the buyer.

The Problem Solution Approach. In certain complex selling situations, understanding the customer's needs may be quite complicated. In such cases, a *problem solution approach* to sales may be required. The salesperson first conducts a detailed study of the buyer's situation and problems and then makes detailed recommendations for meeting the buyer's needs. Only then is a formal written and oral proposal presented to the potential customer. Advertising accounts, research studies, and construction contracts are usually handled by using problem solution presentations.

Exhibit 19.3
Firms that practice relationship marketing know that salespeople must understand their customers' problems and needs in order to ensure customer satisfaction. Aetna, for instance, provides training about customers' businesses and then makes this training a selling point in its ads.

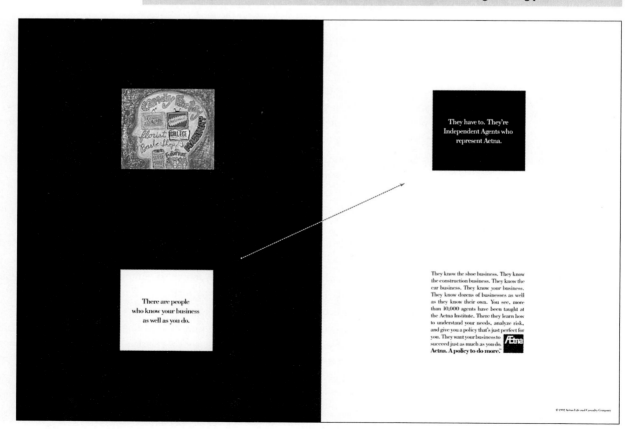

Overcoming Customer Objections

It is a rare situation indeed when a customer willingly accepts whatever the salesperson has to say and immediately places an order. Most people generate at least some *objections,* or problems they see with the product or service. The effective salesperson anticipates these objections and is prepared to overcome them with additional information or persuasive arguments.

A salesperson cannot always tell whether an objection is meant to end the selling process or simply to test the idea of a purchase. Consequently, the first two steps of handling objections are crucial: (1) Let the customer know you respect his or her concerns and the questions raised by the objection. (2) Inquire further about the objection to make sure you—and the customer—really understand what is at the heart of the objection. Ironically, the salesperson should *welcome* objections because they show the prospect is interested enough to think about the possibility of making the purchase! Objections are a positive sign to experienced salespeople, because objections signal that a prospect has moved from attention through interest to evaluation. Handling the objection successfully may move a prospect to the decision phase. Nevertheless, fear of objections is one of the "turn-offs" for novice salespeople.

For example, a purchasing agent might say, "If something goes wrong with this bar-code reader, how can I be sure it will get fixed right away?" The purchasing agent does not get involved in fixing bar-code readers. Really, the purchasing agent wants to make sure that the users of the product will be satisfied with the purchase and not later come back and say, "You sure did mess up that purchase! We can't get this @^*&+#$ bar-coder fixed for 60 days!" By answering this objection, a salesperson not only raises the buyer's comfort level with the purchase but also coaches the buyer about what to say to others who raise similar issues.

Closing the Sale

A common mistake made by salespeople is that they work very hard to open the door for the prospect but forget to invite him or her to walk through it. **Sales closing** is the stage of the selling process in which the salesperson actually asks the customer to buy the product. There are several tried-and-true ways to accomplish this crucial step. How many of the following have been tried on you?

sales closing: the stage of the selling process in which the salesperson actually asks the customer to buy the product

- In a *trial close,* the salesperson acts as though the purchase is inevitable and all that remains is to wrap up the details, as when he or she asks, "What quantity would you like to order?"

- An *options close* asks the customer to choose between alternatives: "Would you like the pin-striped suit, the double-breasted, or both?"

- A *last objection close* asks the customer whether he or she is ready to purchase, provided that this final concern can be addressed. "Are you ready to order if we can show you a 20 percent cost savings associated with using this software?"

- An *assumptive close* goes a step further; the salesperson acts as though the purchase has already been made: "I'll have this shipped . . ." or "I'll call in the order. . . ."

- A *summary-of-benefits close* occurs when the salesperson presents a summary of the major benefits of interest to the customer.

- A *standing-room-only close* means that the salesperson indicates that if the customer does not buy now, then he may not have the opportunity in the future. A similar technique is called the *urgency close,* wherein the salesperson indicates that if the customer does not order very soon, then he or she will be sorry because the price is going up or the store is about to sell out of the item.

- A *negotiation close* means that the salesperson seeks to find a mutually agreeable compromise in order to get the sale.

- A *silent close* occurs when the salesperson simply remains silent, waiting for the customer to indicate that she or he wishes to order.

Once a customer has made a decision to buy, it is time to stop talking! The salesperson who is too talkative after the close runs the risk of saying something that will cause the customer to reconsider the purchase. The most appropriate way to end a closing is to reassure the customer that he or she has made a good decision and to say "Thank you!"

ℛEAL PEOPLE, REAL CHOICES:

DECISION TIME AT GENERAL ELECTRIC

As Kathleen Carroll-Mullen was checking her mail at the GE sales office in New Jersey, she came upon a letter from a purchasing agent for an Asian plastics company requesting a quotation (called an RFQ) for stated equipment and electrical motors in a Louisiana plant. She estimated that the purchase would fall in the $100,000 range: not small, but not key account material either. The agent closed the letter by mentioning a new chemical processing plant project and inviting GE to provide some information about that as well . . . *a possible opportunity?*

Kathleen made a few phone calls and learned that the firm had three power generation plants located in Delaware, Texas, and Louisiana. Although the company had purchased a $6 million power generation turbine from GE some years ago, it had relied on one of GE's competitors for almost all its power generation equipment in Asia and the United States. There wasn't much hope that GE could overcome this close working relationship. Even small orders were infrequent.

When Kathleen called the U.S. purchasing office for the firm, she learned that the company wanted to build a $2–3 billion chemical processing plant. *Not the sort of project for a rookie account manager, she thought, especially because the competing company was expected to be the primary supplier.* Back at the office, senior salespeople said, "Kathleen, don't spend time on projects that are likely to go to another supplier. Move on to something else . . . Don't waste your time and energy—or that of our engineers!" Still, Kathleen was tempted: Was this an opportunity worth pursuing or just a distraction that would sidetrack her career? She considered these alternatives:

Option 1. Go for it. Go all out on the $100,000 RFQ. Develop a plan that makes this the first step in winning a share of the chemical project. As a "rookie" account manager, Kathleen had some time to devote to this possibility, but on the other hand, her superiors might have preferred her to spend it elsewhere. The division had scarce resources, and this effort might divert GE's attention from other projects.

Option 2. Wait and see. Don't develop a proposal. Just show interest and collect some more information until GE's prospects for winning the account look better. GE had existing key accounts, including DuPont, Scott Paper, and Hess Oil, that were priorities. The company had targeted the petrochemical, pulp and paper, and power generation industries for its efforts, and this plastics manufacturer did not really fit into these areas of emphasis.

Option 3. Test the waters. Draft a routine proposal in response to the $100,000 RFQ to get a foot in the door but avoid unnecessary investment in this long-shot customer. The time and effort might be better used to improve margins with existing key accounts instead of trying to increase market share.

Now, join the decision team at GE: Which option would you choose, and why?

FOLLOWING UP AFTER THE SALE

In transactional sales, the salesperson often gets the order and blithely walks away without ever having any future contact with the customer. This huge mistake is never made by a relational salesperson! This new breed of marketer understands that a purchase is a beginning, not an end. **Sales follow-up** includes immediate activities such as arranging for delivery, payment, and purchase terms as well as later follow-up, in which the salesperson makes sure that the order has been received, the customer is satisfied, and all is working well and that setup, instruction, and in-service training have been properly completed.

Servicing after the sale involves solving problems that crop up, facilitating actions such as invoicing and delivery, and providing information where needed. Sometimes salespeople also provide application assistance or other technical support, but more often such tasks are the responsibility of specialists. Effective trouble-shooting is the distinguishing feature of quality-focused firms that take customer satisfaction and relationship principles seriously. Bought an expensive Disney World pass and now you can't figure out where you are or where to go next? Ask *anyone*, even an employee who is having a bad day, and you will receive courteous assistance. Experiencing a malfunction with a new Gateway PC? A trained, responsive technician is an 800-number away. Having trouble making a profit using Kodak's pre-press imaging equipment? A team of quality improvement experts will work with a client and find *hundreds of thousands of dollars worth* of improvements in the way the firm operates. In relationship selling, customer satisfaction is an on-going concern, even after the customer's money is in hand.

Follow-up also enables the salesperson to *bridge* to the next purchase. Once a relationship develops with a customer, there is no end to the selling process. Even as one cycle of purchasing draws to a close, a good salesperson is laying the foundation for the next purchase. Preparing for the next purchase entails maintaining contact with customers and informing them of new product introductions, gathering information about future purchase requirements, and seeking referrals.

SALES MANAGEMENT: DEVELOPMENT AND IMPLEMENTATION OF THE SALES FUNCTION

The sales force plays a vital role in many organizations, but it is also an expensive and time-consuming aspect of doing business that must be carefully managed. Increased foreign competition, the need to compete in global markets, changes in technology, shorter product life cycles, demands for greater environmental responsibility, and the acceleration of equal-opportunity hiring practices have all led to a need for greater sophistication in the firm's selling function. **Sales management** is the process of planning, implementing, and controlling the personal selling function of an organization.

The quality of the selling function is the direct responsibility of the *sales manager*. The major tasks of the sales manager are outlined in Figure 19.2 (page 702). In this section we will discuss the tasks of the sales manager, which are

- Setting sales force objectives that support the firm's values, principles, and goals
- Creating a personal selling strategy that fits the firm's marketing plans
- Managing a human resource development plan that includes recruiting, selecting, and training the sales force
- Directing salespeople by providing advice, motivation, and evaluation

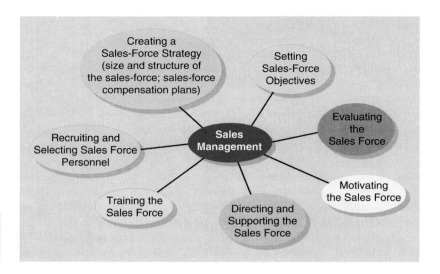

Figure 19.2
Elements of the Sales Management Process

SETTING SALES FORCE OBJECTIVES

As we discussed in Chapter 2, most successful organizations engage in strategic planning at various levels of the organization. A first step in strategic planning for the sales manager is developing objectives for the sales force. Sales force objectives are generally derived from the overall objectives of the total organization and those of the marketing function. They state what the sales force is expected to accomplish and when, and they provide a basis for evaluating overall sales force performance. Meeting the sales objectives should be challenging, but definitely possible.

Sales objectives may be stated at two different levels. More general strategic objectives, such as those that involve desired market share or level of profit, typically reflect organizational or marketing objectives. To support these general objectives, specific performance objectives may be developed. ("Acquire one hundred new customers," "Generate $100 mil-

SPOTLIGHT ON GLOBAL MARKETING

Microsoft in Mexico

Mexico is one of the many fast-growing global markets for U.S. products. Even before the North American Free Trade Agreement (NAFTA) took effect in January of 1994, the pro-business government eased regulations and privatized key industries such as banking and communications. One firm that has benefitted from expansion into Mexico is Microsoft, which has won yearly increases in sales of 100 percent or more. But entering the Mexican market is not without its problems. The country's economy is hurting badly, and the peso has lost much of its value.

To survive in this troubled economy, Microsoft learned that it is best to sell through Mexican distributors and independent reps or to hire local salespeople. Microsoft has fifty sales and marketing employees in Mexico, most of whom are Mexican nationals. Graft is also a problem in Mexico, especially in the rural areas where there is less government supervision. It is not uncommon for government workers to insist that businesses pay them to receive building and other permits. Another form of graft is *payola* to middlemen, who demand payment in return for access to certain corporate customers.

Can American firms win in such a corrupt environment? Microsoft has done so and feels that any firm can if it offers a superior product that customers must have. Even more important, the firm must stand behind what it sells. Mexicans often feel service is as important as price in purchasing goods and services. They want service and attention before, during, and after the sale. The major enemy of good service is Mexico's infrastructure. It is difficult to provide the same level of service as in the United States in a country with unreliable or unsatisfactory communications, transportation, and warehouse space. Thus Microsoft can never rest on its laurels. Its sales force must constantly fight to create and maintain quality relationships with customers.

Source: Geoffrey Brewer, "New World Orders," Sales and Marketing Management (Jan. 1994): 58–63.

lion in sales," or "Reduce travel expenses by 2 percent"). Productivity goals might also include a targeted number of calls per salesperson or sales per customer. Some firms also state goals for customer satisfaction, for new-customer development, for new-product suggestions, for training, and even for community involvement. The importance of goals was made very evident to Da Vinci Systems, a firm that sells electronic-mail systems. After four straight months of salespeople's not meeting sales targets, a consultant recommended creating daily, measurable goals for the sales force. The firm saw results almost immediately.[22]

Sales objectives also provide an outline for development of the specific goals for the individual salesperson. These goals are tied to the person's **territory**—the set of customers and prospects for whom a salesperson or sales team is responsible. Such goals typically include quotas in terms of dollar or unit sales that the person should close within a specified time period.

Sales objectives are likely to differ among salespeople in the same organization, because each person's territory has distinguishing features that may make it easier or harder to work. For example, a sales rep in North Dakota may have to drive hundreds of miles to visit prospects, whereas his or her counterpart in Minneapolis may be a cab ride away from a sales call. The sales manager works with individual salespeople to develop objectives for each person's territory.

territory: the set of customers and prospects for whom a salesperson or sales team is responsible

Specifying Goals for Salespeople

Goals for individual salespeople fall into two categories. *Performance goals* are measurable outcomes. Using performance goals has the advantage of allowing salespeople some latitude in determining how those goals are achieved. Performance goals, such as total sales and total profits, work better in situations where purchase orders are received on a regular basis and when the time spent moving a customer from an inquiry to a purchase order is measured in weeks or months, not years.

Behavioral goals specify the activities or behaviors that must be accomplished over a period of time. For example, a salesperson may have goals for the number of prospects identified, the number of visits to qualified prospects, and the number of sales presentations made that represent the final phase of the selling process. In other lines of business, the number of responses to RFQs (requests for quotations) might be a more appropriate behavioral measure. Behavioral goals can be used in most selling situations but are essential when sales are very large but infrequent.

Selling Task Analysis

A *selling task analysis* is a systematic investigation of the specific activities necessary in order for a salesperson to be successful. After a marketing plan has been developed, a selling task analysis provides information for designing the structure of the organization, creating job descriptions, and developing a plan for human resource management practices and policies. Sources of information include experienced sales associates, industry experts, and customers.

Here are a few of the questions that must be addressed in a selling task analysis:

- What are the characteristics of buying behavior for the particular product or service?
- What steps are required to develop a customer?
- What must a salesperson know in order to perform selling tasks associated with the company's product?
- How much contact with a prospect or customer is necessary to develop purchase orders?
- Where are customers located and what territorial responsibility will minimize travel time and cost but also provide adequate sales potential for a salesperson?
- What types of support, such as office help and technical support, will be required to enhance a salesperson's effectiveness?

A careful analysis can go a long way in pinpointing areas where the sales force can be more efficient. For example, the pharmaceutical firm Hoescht Roussel recently cut nine regions down to six and eliminated 125 sales positions, saving over $10 million a year in expenses while focusing on making calls on higher-volume customers. Lower-volume customers will instead be reached with direct mail and telemarketing.[23] American Business Information, Inc., a supplier of such business services as mailing lists and databases on tape or CD-ROM decided a few years ago that the firm needed to focus less on local business and more on obtaining national accounts. Today, it targets about 3000 large customers with a national account division composed of five regional managers and twenty-five salespeople.[24]

CREATING A SALES FORCE STRATEGY

A *sales force strategy* is a plan for how a firm's resources will be allocated for the purpose of fulfilling the selling task. This plan specifies the overall sales approach that will be used, the size of the sales force and how it will be deployed in the field, and how salespeople will be compensated.

Structure of the Sales Force

What is the best way to organize the sales force? In most nonretail selling situations, each individual salesperson is given the responsibility for a set group of customers called a territory. This structure enables the salesperson to develop an in-depth understanding of customers and their needs and build strong relationships. The question of structuring the sales force, then, involves how customers are assigned to different salespeople or how territories are developed.

The most common way to structure territories is by *geographic specialization,* where the salesperson is assigned a customer base within a specific region. This arrangement minimizes travel and other field expenses by locating a sales associate in a designated location based solely on geographic boundaries. The salesperson calls on all customers in that geographic area. Individual territory salespersons report to regional or divisional sales managers.

If the product line is technically complex or quite diverse, however, it may be impossible to master the technical details of a long product line. In such cases the best structure is called *product specialization,* where each salesperson is responsible for a small class of products. If a customer buys products from more than one class of products, two or more salespeople will call on the customer at different times. Product specialization enables salespeople to devote more time to developing expertise with a smaller number of products. This arrangement may mean that an individual salesperson is not able to develop relationships as effectively with the customer and may result in higher selling costs, because it is necessary for more than one salesperson to call on the same customer. Air Products & Chemicals, for example, recently realigned its sales force from a geographic focus to one based on product lines.[25]

Still another setup is *industry specialization,* wherein salespeople focus on a single industry or a small number of industries and become industry experts. Industry specialization enables a salesperson to understand a customer's business thoroughly, which makes relationship selling more effective. IBM, in becoming less product-driven and more market-driven, has recently changed from a geographic sales force structure to one focusing on fourteen different industries. In making the change, IBM executives cited a need to have salespeople who "speak the language of its customers and understand their industries."[26]

Task specialization defines a sales force according to what tasks are assigned to individual salespeople. Some salespeople may be responsible for obtaining new customers, while others work at maintaining relationships with existing customers or telemarketing. Task specialization is helpful in situations where it takes a highly motivated individual to generate new business but a highly methodical person to maintain existing customers.

Size of the Sales Force

Sales force strategy also includes decisions about the size of the sales force. Because both sales revenues and sales costs are determined by the number of people pounding the pavement, determining the optimal number of salespeople is important. A larger sales force may increase sales, but it will also increase costs significantly. Sales managers may use one of several different methods for calculating the optimal size of the sales force.

Using a *workload approach,* the number of customers is simply multiplied by the number of times a year a salesperson should call on each customer. Dividing that figure by the number of calls a salesperson can reasonably make during a year (allowing for travel time) yields an optimal sales force size. For example, say a firm that sells office supplies and equipment has 300 key accounts that require 2 calls per month, or 24 calls each year. It also has 1500 smaller accounts that need to be called on only once a month, or 12 times a year. The total number of calls per year is $(24 \times 300) + (12 \times 1500) = 25,200$ calls. If a salesperson can make approximately 600 calls per year, the number of salespeople needed is $25,200/600 = 42$ salespeople.

With the *incremental productivity approach,* more and more salespersons are added so long as profits from the additional sales generated are greater than the amount needed to compensate the extra people and support their expenses. Referring to the example above, if calling on key accounts twice as often, or 48 times a year, would increase sales and profits, the optimal sales force size might be $(48 \times 300) + (12 \times 1500) = 32,400/600 = 54$ salespeople.

Compensating Salespeople

From the perspective of the salesperson, the most important part of the sales force strategy is probably the development of a compensation plan. As much as salespeople love to sell, they also enjoy being rewarded fairly for their efforts! Compensation plans typically include a number of fringe benefits such as retirement funding, tuition for education, a company car, profit sharing, vacation time, and health, life, and disability insurance. Salespeople also typically receive some form of *expense allowance.* This is money advanced or reimbursed to salespeople for travel, lodging, food, postage, and other travel and sales expenses. In the United States, travel expenses per salesperson per year range from $1200 to $50,000 with a median of $16,100 for consumer sales, $24,000 for industrial sales, and $15,600 for service industry sales.[27]

From the company perspective, the perfect compensation plan is one that will attract and retain top salespeople, provide both motivation and personal satisfaction for the sales personnel, and maximize company sales and profits. Typically, compensation plans include a salary, sales commissions, sales bonuses, or some combination of these. How best to combine these in order to motivate salespeople to produce the best results is a matter of some debate.

Straight commission is a salesperson compensation plan based solely on a percentage of each sales dollar secured through selling efforts. The straight commission plan ensures salespeople that they will be compensated in direct proportion to their actual sales success. On the down side, this means that if sales are low, income is also low. But with higher levels of sales, there are no limits to earning potential, and many salespeople on straight commission earn $100,000, $200,000 or more annually.

Commissions might seem to be the ideal form of compensation, because they provide strong incentive to increase sales. However, there are important drawbacks to this method. One is that it motivates some salespeople to encourage purchases that are not really necessary. Sears, Roebuck & Co. found this out the hard way in 1992, after it was discovered that employees in Sears Auto Centers were recommending unnecessary work on customers' cars. This scheme allowed them to increase their pay after compensation plans were switched from salaries to commissions.[28]

Another problem is that it is harder to transfer someone to a different territory, because the salesperson loses the valuable customer base he or she has worked so hard to build up. Also, emphasis tends to be placed on serving large customers over small customers, because commissions are earned more easily with large customers. Finally, sales commission compensation tends to reduce teamwork and divert attention from quality improvement efforts.

Under a *commission-with-draw* plan, earnings are still based on commission. However, the salesperson also receives a minimum weekly or monthly payment, or "draw," that may be charged against future commissions if current sales are inadequate to cover the draw. The draw is especially important in recruiting new salespeople, because it guarantees them an income while they are learning their job and building customer relationships.

With a *straight salary* compensation plan, the salesperson is paid a set amount of money regardless of sales performance. Straight salary plans appeal to salespeople who see themselves as professional relationship managers working in a consultant-like capacity. This arrangement provides financial security for the salesperson but limits rewards for exceptional sales performance. With a straight salary plan, the sales manager has greater control over the activities of the sales force, but he or she must also have more skill in tracking sales force performance and in trouble-shooting when performance falls below acceptable levels.

To gain the advantages of both sales commission and straight salary plans, many firms use a *combination plan,* where compensation includes salary plus some incentive such as a bonus for exemplary performance or for sales above a predetermined sales quota. Table 19.5 outlines the features of a straight commission plan, a straight salary plan, and a combination plan.

To encourage relationship selling and discourage transactional selling, many companies have changed their compensation plans to reflect the focus on relationship building. Some firms (such as General Electric, AT&T, and even some car companies like Chrysler

Table 19.5
Advantages and Disadvantages of Salesperson Compensation Plans

Compensation Plan	Advantages	Disadvantages
Straight salary, travel expenses paid by company	Company has greater control over activities of salesperson. Salesperson has secure income.	May create salesperson complacency and not generate maximum level of sales. Limited income capability for salesperson.
Salary plus bonus, salary plus commission, or salary plus bonus and commission, travel expenses paid by company	Company maintains control over salesperson activities, but salesperson has greater motivation because of opportunity to increase earnings over base pay.	May not generate greater sales if salesperson does not see opportunity for significant income increase. Salesperson may focus on sales that will create larger bonus and neglect customer satisfaction and relationship building.
Straight commission with draw, salesperson pays travel expenses	Because of direct correspondence between sales and income, salesperson is highly motivated. Even if sales are "slow" during certain periods or for new salespeople, the draw allows salesperson to have a minimum income. Company has limited sales expense if salesperson is not productive.	Company loses much control over activities of salesperson. May create short-term focus on dollar volume rather than customer satisfaction and relationship building. Circumstances beyond salesperson control (such as competitive activity or economic downturns) may limit salesperson compensation and discourage salesperson. Salesperson may seek other employment.
Straight commission, salesperson pays travel expenses	Salesperson is highly motivated. Company has no sales expense unless sales are made.	Company loses control of salesperson activities. Short-term focus on sales. If sales are below expectations, salesperson may become discouraged and seek other employment.

and Toyota) are beginning to develop compensation plans in which salespeople are rewarded for bringing about customer satisfaction.[29] A recent study showed that 10 percent of companies surveyed relate customer satisfaction to some portion of sales force compensation, and 11 percent said they plan to implement such a plan in the next year.[30] It would seem that they have good reason for doing so: A senior executive at IBM estimates that every percentage-point variation in customer satisfaction results in a gain or loss of $500 million in sales over a five-year period.[31]

RECRUITING AND SELECTING SALESPEOPLE

It's not much of an exaggeration to say that the quality of a sales force can make or break a firm. An organization that chooses inferior people to represent it to the outside world faces the prospects of high turnover rates, poor customer relationships, and many management headaches—including the possibility of significant sales losses. That is why searching for the right set of people to do the job has high priority for sales managers. It also explains why campus recruiters are so careful to screen applicants, subjecting them to many probing questions before handing out precious job offers!

Recruitment

The purpose of sales force recruiting is to attract an adequate pool of job candidates. The desirable characteristics of the applicant pool of course depend on what is being sold. The first step in recruiting a sales force is to conduct a *job analysis* by developing a clear statement of job qualifications—aptitude, skills, knowledge, personal characteristics—based on the selling tasks required to do the job right.

In the past, most firms just recruited aggressive, hard-working people with a college degree. Today, many firms recruit salespeople with backgrounds in business and computer systems, and some firms hire only individuals with specialized backgrounds such as chemistry or engineering. Certainly Kathleen Carroll-Mullen could not perform as she has for General Electric without knowing a lot about turbines and electrical systems. Other employers say they need people who are strategic thinkers, those who have knowledge of different company processes and systems and who offer interpersonal expertise.[32] One salesperson consultant says that being a good salesperson "boils down to one thing: a positive attitude." A sales manager recently claimed he can tell whether candidates will be successful salespeople by asking them to describe their earliest childhood memory. If the memory is positive, the person has the right attitude.[33]

For example, suppose the selling task requires helping multilingual small business owners identify and procure telecommunications systems appropriate for their businesses. This was the task faced by M. Colleen Mullens, who was responsible for AT&T's Business Communications Service in San Francisco. Customers included Asian, Hispanic, African-American, and women entrepreneurs. Creating a sales force with language skills and cultural knowledge suitable to the selling job required an aggressive recruiting plan that would make AT&T visible and attractive to groups likely to include potential recruits. Of course, a very simple but important step was actively recruiting multilingual individuals, many of whom are first- or second-generation Americans. Another important program that encourages diversity at AT&T is an employee group called HISPA, which identifies and mentors Hispanic employees who need educational assistance.[34]

The sales manager has a variety of sources available to locate job applicants. Within the company, people use referrals from current and former employees. Outside sources include public and private employment agencies, newspaper and magazine ads, radio and television advertising, colleges and universities, student interns, and even walk-in applicants.

Selection

Selection is the process of evaluating job applicants and offering employment to those individuals deemed capable of doing the job. Companies use various methods to screen potential salespeople. Interviews, of course, play an important part in evaluating a candidate because they reveal communication skills, interpersonal skills, and information about interests and capabilities. Paper-and-pencil tests are helpful for determining quanti-

Exhibit 19.4
Although sales reps are three times more likely to be men than women, more and more women are choosing personal sales as a career. Currently, 26 percent of salespeople in the United States are women, up from 7 percent ten years ago. This increase is especially noticeable in the previously male domain of auto dealerships. It is estimated that 25,000 of the 184,000 new-car salespeople now working in auto dealerships are women. Saturn Corp. has led the way in focusing on women as both auto buyers and salespeople. A recent ad campaign criticized some dealers' salespeople for ignoring women customers and assuming women are interested only in a car's "frills." In a television commercial, one woman Saturn customer says she liked the way Saturn treated women so much that she became a Saturn salesperson herself.

One reason for this transformation on the showroom floor is that women now are likely to be decision makers when choosing a vehicle; they currently are responsible for about 45 percent of car purchases. This trend is being felt in Europe as well, where some car dealers are going so far as to hand their female customers a bouquet of flowers or a glass of champagne when they sign on the dotted line! Another reason is related to the slow death of the hard sell: Some sales experts believe that women, who tend to be more interpersonally oriented, are better at consultative selling such as that practiced in Saturn dealerships. As one female car salesperson observed, "I think women tend to be more thorough, more detail-oriented. Rather than concentrating on just trying to sell a car, they're paying more attention to the needs of the buyer." Indeed, a recent survey among car buyers found that they ranked female salespeople higher in such areas as honesty, sincerity, and concern.

tative skills and competence in other areas not easily assessed through interviews or a job application. Phone calls to references can reveal aspects of the candidate's character that cannot be learned any other way.

TRAINING SALESPEOPLE

Once the firm has obtained the "raw materials," it needs to train those individuals to be effective salespeople. Although some believe that a successful salesperson is born, not made, even the most skilled communicator needs to learn about what he or she is selling, just as a "natural athlete" still needs to put in hours of practice to perfect his or her skill. A survey of over five hundred business professionals indicated that salespeople make frequent mistakes choosing prospects and that they may use evasive or deceptive tactics, talk too much, fail to ask questions, be insincere, focus too much on the product, and try too hard to convince and persuade.[35]

Most firms provide training for new members of the sales force as well as ongoing training for experienced salespeople. Sales training provides an opportunity for salespeople to learn about the organization and its products and to develop the skills, knowledge, and attitudes necessary for high levels of performance. For example, training programs at

Exhibit 19.5
Every summer, almost 4000 college students converge on Sales School, a program run in Nashville by a publisher called the Southwestern Company. But this isn't anything like the school you're used to. It involves five days of intensive study during which students attend pep rallies, meetings with sales managers, and training sessions where they learn everything from handling their business records to coping with rejection. Then they pound the pavements for three months, selling books door to door. The program works; it's the only way the company sells its books. Students endure the grueling program because they claim it prepares them like nothing else for life as a salesperson. In this photo, students cheer for a Sales School faculty member, who puts on a concert intended to double as a motivational rally.

Xerox focus on what the customer thinks, on consultative selling techniques, and on ways to identify problems. The Xerox Document University, a training facility with 109 acres of campus, 250 classrooms and a curriculum of 180 courses, offers training for both employees and customers of Xerox. The company provides an 11-week training program for new salespeople and continuing training throughout the salesperson's career.[36]

A survey of 1500 sales managers and sales reps indicated that the top sales skills for long-term success are believed to be (1) pre-call planning, (2) approach and involvement, (3) qualifying the prospect's needs, (4) managing time, and (5) overcoming objections.[37] Many training programs focus on newer sales strategies, such as ways to build long-term relationships with customers and team-selling techniques. The introduction of quality improvement programs in many firms has led to greater emphasis on customer satisfaction and relationship building in sales training programs.

Sales training programs may include both on-the-job and classroom components. Classroom training often employs role-playing and business simulation exercises in addition to lectures and discussions of the material. For example, Merck Pharmaceuticals trains new salespeople over twelve months in pharmaceuticals and in sales techniques and provides refresher courses for the entire sales force.[38]

DIRECTING AND SUPPORTING THE SALES FORCE

The typical salesperson can be thought of as a territory manager who is responsible for developing customers, planning travel, and managing his or her time and efforts. Although most salespeople like to work independently, general supervision and direction are essential to an effective sales force. The sales manager may, for instance, work with salespeople to develop individual sales quotas and sales call norm goals. A *sales quota* is a stated dollar or unit sales figure based on sales forecasts. A *sales call norm* is the average number of customer calls made per day. Both measures are used to develop expectations of how the salesperson should be performing, and a comparison of these goals with actual results is useful in evaluating the salesperson's performance.

Salespeople usually are required to report regularly on their progress. They are encouraged to develop monthly, weekly, and daily *call plans*—written plans specifying which customers will be called on and when. Salespeople typically submit daily or weekly *call reports* that detail the results of their calls. These reports are important because they enable the sales manager to track what his or her people are actually doing out in the field. In addition, call reports provide marketing managers with timely information about marketplace activities by reporting customers' responses and objections, competitive activity in the territory, changes in the customer base, and so on.

Another important aspect of managing a sales force is providing the necessary support. This may come in the form of an automobile, secretarial help, or the sharing of intelligence reports from other parts of the company. Support also involves the use of productivity-enhancing tools such as state-of-the-art telecommunications equipment. Car phones increasingly are being issued to field salespeople to let them keep in constant contact with the home office and with clients.[39]

Another popular tool is the computer. As part of its plan to reduce sales force turnover rate from 15 percent to 5 percent, Nalco Chemical Corp, outfitted its sales force with laptop computers programmed to meet the specific needs of the field salesperson.[40] Order entry devices enable a salesperson to transmit orders over phone lines using modem hookups. Computerized routing schemes maximize customer contact time and minimize travel time. Electronic planners are replacing hard-copy day planners. Word processing capabilities and fax-sending software make follow-up correspondence more timely and less subject to delays and errors. Sophisticated expert systems enable salespeople to address challenging technical questions with only the assistance of a laptop; timeliness and accuracy become value-adding advantages. Complete cost estimates that once took weeks or days now take hours or minutes. CD-ROM units enable technical support people to access extensive documentation on products and prices without lugging around huge manuals.

Exhibit 19.6
Over 475,000 beauty consultants sell Mary Kay products to women in 25 countries. The direct selling organization offers women a business opportunity that provides unlimited earning potential, freedom and flexibility, time with family and other commitments, and company support throughout her Mary Kay career. Mary Kay is nationally recognized for its enthusiastic sales force. Annual sales meetings provide motivation, excitement and recognition more than typical stale corporate sessions. The Mary Kay motivation plan includes not just money but recognition. Mary Kay consultants are awarded cars, jewelry, office equipment and exotic trips for different levels of success.

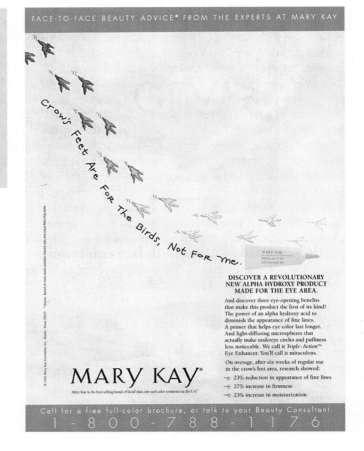

MOTIVATING SALESPEOPLE

The ideal salesperson is a motivated salesperson—that is, he or she continuously works hard to achieve goals while finding personal satisfaction with the job. Companies use a variety of techniques to motivate their sales forces. Some of these approaches emphasize tangible rewards, such as financial incentives, for good performance. Other approaches focus on fostering intangible feelings of accomplishment, stressing the psychic rewards that come from doing a good job and providing recognition for outstanding performance by senior managers. As we noted in Chapter 18, another method used by firms to motivate salespeople is sales incentives. Sales incentive programs include a wide array of rewards, such as cars, merchandise, trips, or a plaque or trophy. Programs may be run in-house or by an outside incentive provider that is hired to implement a program.[41]

EVALUATING SALESPEOPLE

Sales managers must regularly evaluate the success of their salespeople to determine whether objectives are being met. Regular performance feedback also helps individuals improve their selling effectiveness. In addition, salesperson evaluations provide data for personnel actions (raises, promotions, firing, and the like), and this makes them a motivating factor for salespeople. The evaluation can also give the firm valuable feedback as it modifies its future recruitment and training programs in light of the knowledge it accumulates about the types of people and training efforts that seem most effective at ringing up sales.

Some of the areas of performance that may be covered in salesperson evaluations are

1. Measures of behavior: number of sales calls, customer complaints, timely submission of reports and other required paperwork.
2. Measures of professionalism: attitude, appearance, self-improvement, management potential, product knowledge, time management, planning, selling skills.
3. Territory sales activities: actual sales, sales percentage improvement, meeting or exceeding sales quotas, new accounts gained, accounts lost, customer payment records.
4. Territory profitability: profit dollars and profit percentage, goods returned, expenses and cost per sales call.

Ideally, salesperson evaluation procedures include measures of *salesperson satisfaction.* Less satisfied salespersons typically exhibit lower job performance and are more likely to leave the company, so keeping these individuals happy is in everyone's best interests.

Some organizations conduct *sales audits* on a regular basis to be sure things are working as planned. A sales audit is a comprehensive evaluation of the sales organization, including planning, implementation, and control operations as well as the activities of sales management personnel. To ensure objectivity, sales audits are typically conducted by independent organizations or by company personnel outside of the sales function.

LEGAL AND ETHICAL ISSUES IN PERSONAL SELLING

The stereotype of the salesperson that we discussed at the beginning of this chapter often reflects an individual who will do anything to get a sale. Fortunately, this stereotype is not very accurate—though certainly there are notable exceptions! Both laws and a sense of social responsibility make it likely that in most cases, firms and individual sales personnel will act in a responsible manner.

Socially responsible sales behavior benefits firms in a number of ways: When salespeople act in a responsible manner, customers respond with loyalty to the salesperson and the firm. In addition, when sales force activities advance the interests of customers and when sales organizations exhibit a sense of responsibility to the communities in which they do business, government intervention is kept to a minimum. In this section we will first discuss some of the specific legal and ethical issues related to salesperson behavior toward customers and toward the company. Then we will discuss the responsibilities of the sales manager in enforcing the ethical and legal behavior of the sales force.

ETHICAL AND LEGAL ISSUES RELATED TO SALESPERSON CONDUCT TOWARD CUSTOMERS

Many firms have been forced in recent years to become increasingly concerned about the ethical and legal consequences of sales force activities. In some cases, ethical transgressions are unintentional and come about from a lack of understanding of norms and laws. In other cases, though, unethical or illegal sales practices are intentional. There are four major areas of ethical and legal concern in the behavior of salespeople toward customers: misrepresentation, bribery, high-pressure selling tactics, and discriminatory practices.

Misrepresentation

Misrepresentation means that some aspect of the company, product, or salesperson is not accurately depicted to the customer. This offense ranges from simply interpreting facts loosely to actually giving customers false data. Recent court decisions have held that a salesperson's giving false information to customers constitutes fraud. For example, a plaintiff was awarded $400,000 in a wrongful death claim because a Parke Davis salesperson did not talk about the warnings physicians should be aware of when prescribing a certain medicine.[42] In an unusually large case of fraud, agents for a major life insurance firm earned more than $4 million in commissions primarily by selling life insurance. The insurance was sold to nurses who thought they were buying retirement accounts because the salespeople substituted the word *deposits* for *premiums* when describing the policies to them.[43]

Industry leaders increasingly are concerned about sales ethics. A member of the Securities and Exchange Commission has suggested that compensation policies for stock brokers encourage quantity over quality and tempt brokers to sell more and more without regard for the suitability of the investments to the client.[44] In one case, a major brokerage firm was forced to pay an award to former brokers who lost their jobs because they refused to sell the higher-profit in-house mutual funds.[45] To avoid misrepresentation, the salesperson must study and know the product and, of course, must not exaggerate or in any way create false beliefs in order to make a sale.

Bribery

Customer *bribery* includes kickbacks from a commission or gifts to a decision maker to "encourage" selection of the firm's product over those of competitors. Company grapevines are full of stories of the salesperson who gave a customer a color TV and the one who gave a key customer a mink coat and wrote it off as entertainment at $25 a week for a year. Sometimes such bribery is initiated by an unethical sales rep, but perhaps even more often a customer gives the salesperson a not-too-subtle hint that a certain gift would mean the difference between making a large sale and leaving empty-handed. Under any circumstances, bribery is both illegal and unethical.

A particularly difficult problem occurs for firms operating in international markets where bribery of officials is an accepted way of life. As we noted in Chapter 4, in some cultures it is simply not possible to make a sale without giving the appropriate "gift" to the customer. The Foreign Corrupt Practices Act of 1977 forbids U.S. firms from engaging in bribery of foreign customers and established fines up to $1 million for each corporate violation, as well as other penalties. This legislation does not prohibit payments to lower-level figures whose assistance may be necessary to obtain the sale. Nevertheless, this law often puts U.S. firms at a serious disadvantage in competing for business in some markets.

High-Pressure Selling Tactics

Some salespeople are guilty of pushing orders on customers in order to meet quotas. The truly ethical salesperson considers the needs of the customer and sells him or her only what is genuinely needed. Door-to-door high-pressure selling was at one time so prevalent that "cooling off" laws were developed by states. These laws generally provide that for sales of $25.00 or more, customers must have three days in which to change their minds. The salesperson is also required to provide information to the customer about the provisions of this law and the means by which the buyer may contact the company to cancel his or her purchase.

Discriminatory Practices

A more subtle but equally serious ethical violation occurs when salespeople treat customers differently on the basis of their sex, skin color, or beliefs. For instance, a study by the American Bar Foundation found that black women and white women do better than black men in negotiation for a new car and that white men do the best of all groups. The study found that on the average, black men pay about $1150 more than white men for a new car, black women pay $450 more, and white women pay $200 more. Many car dealerships are actively seeking to eliminate discrimination through specially designed training programs.[46]

African-American, Asian, and Hispanic market segments have grown from niche to mainstream status in recent years. A sales force that is not effective with customers of different races and nationalities leaves its employers at a competitive disadvantage. For example, with more people immigrating to the United States, the use of international long-distance calling has increased for telephone companies such as U.S. Sprint. To meet the needs of this market, Sprint has hired bilingual salespeople and also has introduced sales training focused on being sensitive to cultural differences, avoiding stereotypes, dealing with language and accent barriers, and respecting the value systems of other cultural groups.[47]

ETHICAL CONDUCT TOWARD THE COMPANY

Unethical behavior by salespeople toward their *own companies* is an expensive problem for many firms. One common practice is the "padding" of expense accounts: Some salespeople feel no guilt when they use their company expense account to take their friends out to dinner, have a family vacation at an expensive resort, or reimburse themselves for a gift or bribe to a customer.

Sales reporting is another problem area. Salespeople who have trouble managing their time may resort to reporting sales calls that they never made. A less common but more serious problem is salesperson *moonlighting,* wherein the individual represents one or more additional companies at the same time. Because a salesperson is already calling on a particular group of customers, adding a second (or third or fourth) line can increase income dramatically—but at the expense of the primary employer, who is paying for a full-time employee and getting only part-time work. To avoid this problem, many companies require that salespeople sign contracts forbidding them to carry other product lines.

REAL PEOPLE, REAL CHOICES:

HOW IT WORKED OUT AT GENERAL ELECTRIC

Kathleen Carroll-Mullen chose Option 1—she went all out. She began by making an intensive effort to win the modest $100,000 order. She furiously collected technical information, gathered competitive data, and obsessed about the best way to communicate the proposal. Within three weeks she hand-delivered a quotation to the purchasing agent. Lo and behold, GE won the order. Her foot was in the door!

This order gave Kathleen the chance to build working relationships with the people at the plastics firm, and she didn't waste any time. She aggressively courted them, being sure to include social events such as dinners and softball games to build personal bridges with the company. Soon the company asked her to prepare a proposal on a piece of the chemical plant project, and Kathleen went into high gear. She initiated a team planning process that GE calls Managing Account Potential or MAP. The team she put together mapped all the key decision makers and the roles they would play and then plotted a strategy to win the whole project, piece by piece.

Kathleen arranged a series of meetings, some of them in Asia. She knew that these personal interactions were the only way to overcome cultural and geographic distance. She made sure that a senior vice president from GE attended one of these meetings, because she knew of the importance her Asian counterparts placed on the personal involvement of top management.

A $6 million proposal was hand-delivered to the client, and GE won the order! As time went on, the firm became impressed by GE's professionalism, customer service, and quality products. Business increased slowly but surely: an order for $50 million here, one for $18 million there. Kathleen continued to build the account through a series of orders, and working relationships blossomed. After one round of intense negotiations, drawn out over a series of 16 hour work-days, an order for a $2,450,000 purchase was hand-written just before Kathleen's plane taxied down the runway! Thanks to Kathleen's efforts, this firm became a key account, one of GE's top customers. In return, Kathleen received a bonus from GE in the form of a Customer Satisfaction Award. As a sales professional, Kathleen knew that sometimes you have to take a long shot in order to build new business—and now GE has a major new client to show for her willingness to take the chance.

General Electric Company
840 Freedom Business Center, P.O. Box 1561
King of Prussia, PA 19406-1561

September 6, 1991   *Dial Comm:*

KT Carroll
Cedar Knolls

Dear Kathleen:

It is a pleasure for me to present you with the enclosed Customer Satisfaction
Award check. This is in recognition of your having secured several power distribution orders this year from Formosa Plastics in the face of aggressive competition.
Orders have totaled about $11 million. There have been multiple proposals, packag-
ing of individual quotations, and negotiations. Two orders were secured as a result
of your trip to Taiwan earlier this year. The latest order for $4.05 million was the
packaging of proposals and a very tricky negotiation. You have achieved excellent
credibility with the product businesses and they support you in your stategy, based
on feedback that you obtained from this customer.

Congratulations and continued success.

Bill

WJ Kearney

WJK/ld

WJK0906b

ETHICAL RESPONSIBILITIES OF SALES MANAGERS

The sales manager can directly influence the ethical behavior of salespeople by how
he or she deals with individual sales force personnel. For example, managers must consider the negative results of exerting too much pressure on people to perform. If sales
quotas or goals are so high that the salesperson has little chance of reaching them, then
the salesperson may feel pressured to obtain sales in any way possible. Of course sales
managers can encourage responsible behavior by setting clear sales force policies on ethical and legal behavior. This dimension should also be assessed during evaluation to ensure
that people who violate guidelines in order to produce impressive sales don't receive
merely a slap on the wrist.

Chapter 19 Summary

Objective 1. Explain the important role of personal selling in the marketing effort.

Personal selling is person-to-person communications with customers by professional salespeople and other employees. Today's salesperson is less likely to practice transactional selling—that is,
hard-sell tactics. Rather, salespeople today often engage in relationship selling wherein they seek to
develop mutually satisfying relationships with customers. Through one-on-one selling, the salesperson can directly address customer objections, can furnish other customer services (such as installation, setup, and instruction), can provide the company with feedback on the marketing effort, and is
a source of competitive intelligence.

Objective 2. Explain the important role of personal selling in the promotion mix.

Personal selling has an interdependent relationship with the other promotion elements and is
more important with a push strategy. The importance of personal selling within the promotion mix
is related to the position and experience of the buyer and to the complexity and cost of the products. Compared to other promotion mix elements, the role of the salesperson is limited by the high

cost per customer contact and by the poor image of salespeople. Within an integrated marketing communications strategy, the personal sales function is often limited to calls aimed at prime targets.

Objective 3. Describe different types of selling jobs.

The job of the salesperson may be proactive; order getters are creative salespeople or account managers who creatively develop relationships with customers. Reactive selling means that the salesperson, such as a counter salesperson, is an order taker and facilitates transactions initiated by the customer. Sales support personnel, who include technical specialists and missionary salespeople, influence the purchase decision by providing assistance to the sales force. A sales team is often formed where creative salespeople and support personnel work together. Sales jobs also vary in the selling environment: Outside (or field) salespeople visit face-to-face with customers, whereas inside selling occurs at the selling organization's place of business. Retail selling involves selling goods and services to customers who buy for personal consumption; business-to-business salespeople sell products that are purchased for some reason other than personal consumption.

Objective 4. List and explain the steps in the personal selling process.

Prospecting, the first step in the creative selling process, involves identifying potential new customers. *Qualifying* means gathering information and determining the likelihood that a prospect will become a customer. During the *pre-approach* phase, the salesperson gathers information about the customer and develops a selling strategy for converting the qualified prospect into a customer.

Actual contact with the customer begins with the *approach,* wherein the salesperson learns more about the customer's needs and builds rapport. The *sales presentation* is the part of the process in which the salesperson seeks to persuade the customer. Effective sales presentations are enthusiastic, encourage the buyer to participate, include proof statements, and may include a demonstration of the product. Typical types of sales presentations are the canned sales presentation, the selling formula approach, the need satisfaction approach and the problem solution approach.

Effective salespeople see *objections* as an opportunity to provide more information and as a sign that the customer is interested. In the *closing* phase of the sales presentation, the salesperson asks the customer to buy the product.

Follow-up after the sale is an important final step in the selling process. It involves both immediate follow-up activities, such as arranging for delivery and payment, and later activities, such as making sure that the order was received and the customer is satisfied.

Objective 5. Explain the job of the sales manager.

Sales management entails planning, implementing, and controlling the selling function. Both general sales force objectives and individual salesperson goals direct the sales force toward what is to be accomplished. Sales managers also determine the size of the sales force and whether sales territories will be based on geographic, product, target market, or task specialization. Other sales force management activities include designing a sales force compensation package, which may include expense allowances, salary, commissions, and a variety of fringe benefits; recruiting and selecting qualified individuals for sales jobs; and sales training, supervision, and performance evaluation.

Objective 6. Discuss the legal and ethical issues that arise in the sales function.

Ethical, socially responsible sales behavior always benefits the firm. Some troubling unethical behaviors of salespeople include misrepresentation of the company, product, or salesperson; bribery of customers; high-pressure selling tactics; discriminatory practices; and the padding of expense or call reports. Sales managers encourage ethical behavior by setting realistic goals for salespeople.

Review Questions

Marketing Concepts: Testing Your Knowledge

1. What is the difference between transactional selling and relationship selling?
2. What role does personal selling play within the total marketing function?
3. How does personal selling interact with the other elements of the promotion mix?
4. What are order getters, order takers, sales support personnel, missionary salespeople, outside selling, and inside selling?
5. List the steps in the creative selling process.
6. What are the elements of the sales presentation?
7. Why should a salesperson see customer objections as an opportunity?
8. Explain how sales managers determine the best structure and size of the sales force.
9. What are the different ways in which salespeople are typically compensated?
10. Name some problem behaviors of unethical salespeople.

Marketing Concepts: Discussing Choices and Issues

1. In general, professional selling has evolved from "hard sell" to transactional selling. But does the hard sell still exist? If

so, in what types of organizations? What do you think the future holds for these organizations? Will the hard sell continue to succeed?

2. Some companies go to great effort and expense to provide a high degree of customer service. Nordstom's, for example, is known for the great lengths its "Nordies" will go to in order to please customers. But is this type of service right for all businesses? Should there be different levels of service in different types of organizations? Are there some behaviors of salespeople that should be the same across all businesses?

3. Many business-to-business firms and even some retailers have developed team selling approaches. But some people feel that the most successful salespeople, the "super-salespersons," are highly competitive and that team selling will actually make them less productive. What do you think? Will a team approach work in every situation? If not, when do you think a team approach will work best? When will it be less likely to be effective?

4. One reason cited by experts for the increase in consumer catalog shopping is the poor quality of service available at retail stores. What do you think about the quality of most retail salespeople you come in contact with? What are some ways in which retailers can improve the quality of their sales associates?

Marketing Practice: Applying What You've Learned

1. As a college senior, you think you would like to begin your career as a professional salesperson. You know there are many different sales jobs, and before you apply for a job, you want to analyze the job opportunities and develop a logical plan for your job search. Use the following list of salesperson types.

   Field sales   Relationship selling

   Inside sales   Missionary sales

   Transaction selling
   a. For each job type, list the good and bad points of the job for you personally.
   b. What are two kinds of firms that might offer each type of job?

2. Assume you have just been hired as a field salesperson by a firm that markets college textbooks. As part of your training, your sales manager has asked that you develop an outline of what you will say in a typical sales presentation to a member of a college faculty. Write that outline.

3. As a sales manager for a firm that sells heavy construction equipment, you are evaluating the current sales force compensation plan. Salespeople are paid straight commission, but you are thinking that moving to straight salary or a combination salary and commission plan might be better.

   a. With one of your classmates taking the other side, present your arguments for each option in a role-playing situation.
   b. In a similar role-playing situation, present arguments for different compensation plans that might be used in a retail clothing store.
   c. In a similar role-playing situation, present arguments for different compensation plans that might be used by a new-car sales force.

4. Assume you are a sales manager for a new company that sells electrical supplies to contractors, to industry, and to electric supply wholesalers. You are considering what type of territory structure will be most effective. You know that sales territories may be organized geographically, by product, or by customer type. Write a memo to your superior in which you outline the strengths and weaknesses of each of these territory structure types. In the memo, make and support your recommendations for the best structure.

Marketing Mini-Project: Learning by Doing

Many college students say they are "absolutely, completely lost" when it comes to knowing what type of job they want, much less how to look for the ideal job. This project gives you experience in the beginning steps in the creative selling process—but in this case your customers are potential employers, and the "product" you will be selling is yourself. (You might find the information included in Appendix A, "Careers in Marketing," helpful with this project.)

1. Working with a group of classmates your first task is to identify job characteristics that you and other members of your group might find attractive—your target market. You may consider such characteristics as geographic location, company size (local, regional, national, or international), types of business, job responsibilities, and skills required.

2. One method used by salespeople for identifying potential job prospects is networking. Therefore, with one or more members of your class, seek to talk with other people who may know of jobs that have the characteristics you have outlined for your target market.

3. Using the resources of your school or department or your college library, generate a list of potential employers that seem to match your target market.

4. Using library resources or personal contacts if available, find out as much as you can about each potential employer.

5. On the basis of the information you have gathered, classify these employers as A, B, or C leads. "A" leads warrant more of your time and effort. "C" leads warrant the least time and effort, because you have determined that their fit with your target market is not very good.

6. With your group, present your findings to your class.

Key Terms

Endnotes

1. Wilton Woods, "The Jobs Americans Hold," *Fortune* (July 12, 1993): 54–55.
2. "A User's Guide to the Sales Manager's Budget Planner," *Sales and Marketing Management* (June 28, 1993): 6–10, 62–66.
3. Marjorie J. Caballero, Roger A. Dickinson, and Dabney Townsend, "Aristotle and Personal Selling," *Journal of Personal Selling and Sales Management* (May 1984): 13–18.
4. Thomas L. Powers, Warren S. Martin, Hugh Rushing, and Scott Daniels, "Selling Before 1900: A Historical Perspective," *Journal of Personal Selling and Sales Management* (Nov. 1987): 5.
5. Martin Everett, "This Is the Ultimate in Selling," *Sales & Marketing Management* (Aug. 1989): 28.
6. Maurice G. Clabaugh, Jr. and Jessie L. Forbes, *Professional Selling: A Relationship Approach* (New York: West, 1992).
7. Stephanie Della Cagna, "The Invasion of the Nordies," *New England Business* (Jan. 1990): 24–25.
8. Quoted in Jaclyn Fierman, "The Death and Rebirth of the Salesman," *Fortune* (July 25, 1994): 38.
9. "A User's Guide to the Sales Manager's Budget Planner," *Sales and Marketing Management* (June 28, 1993): 6–10.
10. Ibid.
11. Martin Everett, "It's No Fluke," *Sales and Marketing Management* (April 1994): 66–73.
12. Nancy Arnott, "Selling Is Dying," *Sales and Marketing Management* (Aug. 1994): 82–86.
13. Dan C. Weilbaker, "The Identification of Selling Abilities Needed for Missionary Type Sales," *Journal of Personal Selling & Sales Management* (Summer 1990): 45–58.
14. W. David Gibson, "Fielding a Force of Experts," *Sales and Marketing Management* (April 1993): 88–92; Henry Canaday, "Team Selling Works!" *Personal Selling Power* (Sept. 1994): 53–58.
15. Carl Henry, "Sales: Get It Down to a Science," *Industrial Distribution* (July 1992): 33–34.
16. Aimee L. Stern, "Telemarketing Polishes Its Image," *Sales and Marketing Management* (June 1991): 107–110.
17. Wilton Woods, "The Jobs Americans Hold," *Fortune* (July 12, 1993): 54.
18. Ibid.
19. Christopher Caggiano, "Have You Been Burned by Bankruptcy?" *Inc.* (March 1993): 16.
20. Martin Everett, "This Is the Ultimate in Selling," *Sales and Marketing Management* (Aug. 1989): 28–38.
21. Jaclyn Fierman, "The Death and Rebirth of the Salesman," *Fortune* (July 25, 1994): 38.
22. "Making Employees Accountable," *Inc.* (March 1993): 34.
23. Melissa Campanelli, "Reshuffling the Deck," *Sales and Marketing Management* (June 1994): 83–90.
24. Ibid.
25. Ibid.
26. Ibid.
27. "A User's Guide to the Sales Manager's Budget Planner," *Sales and Marketing Management* (June 28, 1993): 6–10.
28. Christopher Power, Lisa Driscoll, and Earl Bohn, "Smart Selling, How Companies Are Winning Over Today's Tougher Customer," *Business Week* (Aug. 3, 1992): 46–52.
29. Ibid.
30. Andy Cohen, "Right on Target," *Sales and Marketing Management* (Dec. 1994): 59–63; "Smart Selling, How Companies Are Winning Over Today's Tougher Customer," *Business Week* (Aug. 3, 1992): 46–52.
31. Jaclyn Fierman, "The Death and Rebirth of the Salesman," *Fortune* (July 25, 1994): 38.
32. W. David Gibson, "Fielding a Force of Experts," *Sales and Marketing Management* (April 1993): 88–92.
33. Perri Capell, "Are Good Salespeople Born or Made?" *American Demographics* (July 1993): 12–13.
34. David Altany, "M. Colleen Mullens: Passionate About Diversity," *Industry Week* (March 2, 1992): 26–27.
35. Kevin Wood, "10 Ways to Lose a Sale," *Sales and Marketing Management* (Dec. 1992): 35.
36. W. David Gibson, "Fielding a Force of Experts," *Sales and Marketing Management* (April 1993): 88–92.
37. Regina Eisman, "Justifying Your Incentive Program," *Sales and Marketing Management* (April 1993): 43–48.
38. Christopher Power, Lisa Driscoll, and Earl Bohn, "Smart Selling, How Companies Are Winning Over Today's Tougher Customer," *Business Week* (Aug. 3, 1992): 46–52.
39. Phaedra Wise, "Car-Phone Pros and Cons," *Inc.* (June 1993): 49.
40. W. David Gibson, "Fielding a Force of Experts," *Sales and Marketing Management* (April 1993): 88–92.
41. Melissa Campanelli, "How to Reward All Your Sales Forces," *Sales and Marketing Management* (April 1993): 63–67.
42. Karl A. Boedecker, Fred W. Morgan, and Jeffrey J. Stoltman, "Legal Dimensions of Salespersons' Statements: A Review and Managerial Suggestions," *Journal of Marketing* (Jan. 1991): 70–80.
43. Greg Steinmetz, "Former Agents Draw a Picture of Met Life's Sales Practices," *The Wall Street Journal* (Oct. 8, 1993): B1.
44. Christi Harlan, "SEC Turns Up Heat on Brokers' Commissions," *The Wall Street Journal* (Dec. 2, 1993): C1.
45. Michael Siconolfi, "Paine Webber Is Penalized for Sales Pressure on Brokers," *The Wall Street Journal* (July 27, 1993): C1.
46. Patricia Braus, "White Men Get Cars Cheapest," *American Demographics* (June 1993): 20–21.
47. Margie Markarian, "Cultural Evolution," *Sales and Marketing Management* (May 1994): 127–129.

MARKETING IN ACTION: REAL PEOPLE AT STRYKER

Stryker Corporation is one company that has never settled for an average sales force. Whereas most firms would be quite content with 10 or 15 percent growth, Stryker demands 20 percent growth *every year*—and its sales force actually delivers on this goal. The company has had earnings growth of 20 percent or more for each of the past 17 years, and annual sales are now over $500 million.

Stryker is a medical equipment maker located in Kalamazoo, Michigan. Chairman, CEO, and president John Brown, a Tennessee native, sees to it that those goals are met by being personally involved in the sales force's efforts. If a division misses its sales goal, Brown moves in, helps to make corrections, and makes sure the same thing doesn't happen again.

Before leaving to become head of Stryker in 1977, Brown was with a subsidiary of Bristol-Myers Squibb that makes surgical instruments. At that time, Stryker's sales were pretty stagnant at $23 million. Brown had to "hit the ground running" by making a series of changes to solve the numerous problems he found at Stryker, many of which involved the sales force.

One of the biggest problems was that Stryker salespeople had been quitting in droves since the company compensation system had been changed from one based on commission to straight salary. Thus the first improvement Brown made was to bring back the commission plan. And Brown's plan imposes no "cap" for the sales rep—the sky is the limit when it comes to potential earnings. As Brown says, "The more the individual sells, the more he makes. The most ambitious and driven salespeople thrive in a commission environment."

Next, Brown broke the highly centralized company into nine different operating divisions so that each could operate like its own small company. This is especially important because Stryker carries such a vast product line—everything from hospital beds to bone saws. Brown feels that each division can and should be autonomous and "enjoy all the thrills of success and all the anxieties of failure. There's nothing like running your own business." He also feels that this entrepreneurial spirit is just what the doctor ordered to create a loyal and productive sales force. Each division now makes its own sales force decisions, even when structuring a compensation plan. These choices seem to be related to performance: The company's two most successful divisions, referred to as the surgical group, have totally eliminated salaries; salespeople are paid strictly on commission. Those same two top divisions have also freed salespeople from paperwork such as call reports. Ron Elenbaas, president of the surgical group, says that his idea is to create a salesperson's paradise. Top salespeople live and die by what they sell, they are driven to get the job done, and they absolutely *hate* paperwork.

Elenbaas also did away with company cars in his two divisions. Because the salespeople cover their own travel expenses, they can drive whatever car they want to. One benefit of this decision is that the division was able to eliminate the expense of two employees whose sole job was to maintain the fleet of company cars.

One of the major reasons why the Stryker sales force is so successful is the type of people the company hires in the first place. Stryker brings in only hyper-competitive, super self-confident, and highly ambitious people with boundless energy—the type of person who has a "burning hunger for success." The typical Stryker salesperson is on the road by 5:30 A.M. and may not get home until 10:00 P.M., so a high level of stamina is essential. "Slackers need not apply."

Stryker's top salespeople make more than $200,000 a year, but there are equally important non-monetary ways in which Stryker motivates its people. A monthly newsletter sent out by CEO Brown ranks each division by growth and includes praise, suggestions, and sometimes very sharp criticisms for the divisions. At sales meetings, the tables at awards banquets are arranged in order of performance: best region in front, poorest performing region in the back. Salespeople who make their quotas are invited to breakfast with CEO Brown, who personally hands out bonus checks. And like winners of the Superbowl, Stryker's winning salespeople receive rings with ever larger diamonds each year they make quota!

Source: Geoffrey Brewer, "20 Percent—Or Else!" *Sales & Marketing Management* (Nov. 1994): 67–72.

Things to Talk About

1. How important is the sales function to Stryker Corporation?
2. In what ways does Stryker motivate and reward its sales force?
3. What role does the compensation plan have in creating an effective sales strategy?
4. In what ways does Stryker support its salespeople?
5. What secrets of success has Stryker Corporation discovered?

MARKETING IN ACTION:
REAL CHOICES AT CUTLER HAMMER

How can expanding a sales force be like mixing oil and water? The experience of a firm called Cutler-Hammer illustrates the problems that can arise when salespeople from two competing companies are merged into one giant sales force. Sometimes corporate cultures and operating procedures just don't mix.

Cutler-Hammer, a division of the giant Eaton Corporation, has been a manufacturer of industrial control products such as circuit breakers, motor starters, and other electrical distribution equipment for over a century. Historically, its products have been sold primarily through distributors or directly to large electrical contractors. Cutler-Hammer's salespeople typically are assigned to call on several end-user accounts and distributors. Sales reps are compensated with salary plus commissions based on the performance measured against predetermined sales goals.

Cutler-Hammer has two primary markets: industrial and construction. Salespeople in the industrial market typically call on engineers. In the construction market, the customer is often the contractor of a house, an apartment complex, or a high-rise office tower. In addition, the company has a few large industrial customers, such as Ford and Mitsubishi, that demand a great deal of attention by salespeople.

Cutler-Hammer's problems began in August 1993, when its parent company purchased the $1.2 billion Distribution and Control Business Unit of Westinghouse to combine with the Cutler-Hammer subsidiary. Cutler-Hammer, with only $500 million in sales, was less than half the size of the new acquisition. Absorbing the Westinghouse unit provided some great opportunities for Cutler-Hammer, but only if the company was able to merge the two company sales forces successfully. One manager described this prospect as "solving a giant jigsaw puzzle." Merging the two sales forces meant that salespeople from both companies would have to adjust to working in a larger company, learn and adopt a new corporate culture, and, at the same time, increase sales. And it was essential that all this happen quickly in order to keep both companies' existing customers and to recoup the expenditures made by Eaton in acquiring the Westinghouse division.

For Cutler-Hammer salespeople, the purchase was both positive and negative. Having the Westinghouse products to sell would complete their line, making them more competitive with other firms such as Square D, Allen-Bradley, and General Electric. But at the same time, there was much concern about how the two sales forces would be merged and whether the people from the smaller firm would be "swallowed up" by the bigger guys. Conversely, the Westinghouse salespeople saw very few benefits to merging and were not exactly enthusiastic about the change.

Several obstacles stood in the way of a successful combination. One was the difference in customer bases. Although the two companies had been competitors within the same markets, each had different customers as its primary focus. Westinghouse salespeople had dealt almost exclusively with the construction industry, whereas Cutler-Hammer people had spent the majority of their time and energy with industrial customers. In addition, it would not be easy to adjust to working with people who just yesterday were the competition! Then there was the problem of an increase in the number of different products that the new Cutler-Hammer unit would be carrying. It was difficult enough being knowledgeable about the many products each company had sold before, but suddenly there would be nearly twice as many different items to sell. Finally, the corporate cultures in these companies were quite different. Westinghouse personnel operated under an "every man for himself" philosophy, whereas Cutler-Hammer had been developing a team-selling approach for some time. Sales managers at the newly formed Cutler-Hammer subsidiary knew they had a problem on their hands—one that made mixing oil and water almost look easy.

Source: Weld F. Royal, "Cutler-Hammer Finally Connects," *Sales & Marketing Management* (Nov. 1994): 83–86; Sonny Stuart, personal interview (Oct. 21, 1995).

Things to Think About

1. What is the problem facing Cutler-Hammer?

2. What factors are important in understanding this problem?

3. What alternatives might Cutler-Hammer consider?

4. What are your recommendations for solving the problem?

5. What are some ways to implement your recommendations?

APPENDIX A CAREERS IN MARKETING

SO YOU HAVE TO GET REAL!

Whether you are an undergraduate with no idea of what type of job you want or an older "nontraditional" student well established in an exciting job, career planning is critical to your current and future satisfaction. Just think, not only does your career provide you with that very important benefit, an income, but you will spend eight (or more) hours a day, five days a week, fifty weeks a year (about 40 percent of your waking hours), for forty or more years working in that career. Yet many people spend more time planning a weekend ski trip than they do their careers. And many undergraduate college students don't even consider a career until that last semester when they realize that their college "career" (and the free ride at Mom and Dad's expense) is about to end.

In this appendix, we will look at a career from a marketing perspective—that is, we will consider how you can use the marketing planning process to "sell" yourself to prospective employers. And whether you are a marketing major, an accounting major, an interior design major, or a theater major, it is never too early to start "getting yourself to market."

By suggesting that you use the marketing planning process for career planning, we mean that you can follow the same steps you would consider in marketing a box of laundry detergent or a new sports car. You begin by assessing your strengths and weaknesses, then you develop career objectives and strategies, and finally, you carefully implement those strategies—and keep your fingers crossed!

Assess Yourself

What does it mean to assess yourself? Well, think about how a marketer assesses a product situation. Marketers identify the strengths and weaknesses of the product and the firm. You should do the same. In a disciplined, systematic way, consider what your strengths and weaknesses are. You might want to ask (and answer) questions such as the following:

1. What are my greatest strengths? (Am I thorough, organized, a good communicator, good at quantitative skills, creative, good at getting along with others, a leader?)

2. What are my greatest weaknesses? (Am I undisciplined, a poor self-starter, or a poor writer? Do I have trouble talking with strangers, have difficulty in social situations, or hate making presentations? Do I need a lot of supervision in getting things done?)

3. What sort of things have I done well in the past—things I have been really proud of? (What things have I done for which my fellow students or teachers have given me high praise?)

4. What types of activities do I enjoy most? (Do I like to travel, enjoy outdoor activities, or like being creative? Am I a "people person"? Do I work best when challenged?)

The act of conducting a formal self assessment—and putting it in writing—helps make clear what opportunities may be best for you. For example, if you don't like talking with strangers and are not very self-disciplined, you probably would not want to consider a career in sales. On the other hand, if you're highly creative and like expressing your ideas, a job in the advertising field may be one of your best opportunities. Incidentally, it wouldn't hurt to share your assessment with a family member, a trusted friend, or a business associate to get a bit of a "reality check" on your perceptions of yourself.

Develop Your Career Objectives

The second step in your plan for marketing yourself is to develop a set of career objectives. As with product objectives, we believe these work best if they are both quantitative and qualitative in nature, clear, realistic, stated in writing, and specific for both the long term and the short term.

Of course, none of us can really predict how we will feel about our lives five or ten years in the future, but good planning means we develop goals based on our best judgment today. We can always change our goals as time goes on—and nearly all of us do. Some of the things you might want to consider in developing objectives follow.

1. What level of income will I be happy or satisfied with in a year, in five years, and in ten, fifteen, or twenty years?

2. What is really important to me? Is being financially well off the most important thing for my happiness? Am I willing to sacrifice time at home with a family and time for recreation in order to achieve job success, advancement, and a high income?

3. Would I be happier in a large firm or with a smaller company?

4. Am I willing to relocate, and if so, to what areas? Is international travel important to me?

5. What do I think will make me happy or unhappy ten or twenty years from now? Will I feel I am a failure if I don't have my ideal career, a certain income, or a certain level of power within an organization?

6. Do I want to live in a large city or a small town?

Identify Your "Target Market"

Once you have a clear, objective appraisal of your strengths and weaknesses and a set of clearly stated career objectives, it is time to consider what your target market(s) will be—what specific types of careers are likely to be best for you.

The number and variety of careers in marketing are almost limitless. In fact, about one-third of all jobs in the United States are related to marketing. And that trend is expected to increase in the future as more and more organizations recognize the value of marketing. Whereas a few years ago, marketing was primarily the domain of producers of goods, today service firms such as hospitals, law firms, and financial institutions and even not-for-profit organizations such as religious groups are recognizing the important part that marketing can play in meeting their goals. The following are just a few of the many types of careers available in marketing.

Retailing

Retailing offers more jobs and a greater variety of jobs than any other single marketing field. Recent college graduates who enter retailing can expect to be given a substantial level of responsibility far more quickly than in most other types of jobs. Although many retailers begin as sales associates, college graduates with degrees in marketing often become retail buyers or merchandisers. Buyers and merchandisers must be able to identify and understand what customers want and then purchase and merchandise products to meet those needs.

Physical Distribution/Logistics

Careers in physical distribution and logistics involve a variety of activities designed to make sure the right product gets to the right place at the right time. Often jobs in distribution include the management of incoming materials as well as outgoing products. Career opportunities in physical distribution may be found with manufacturers of both consumer and industrial goods, in wholesaling operations, and, of course, in companies such as UPS and Federal Express that are in the distribution industry.

Product/Brand Management

Product and brand management positions are very important in consumer goods companies. Typically, a brand manager is responsible for directing the entire marketing process for an individual brand—determining demand, establishing goals, working with advertising and other promotion agencies, contracting for marketing research services, and so on. Product managers have even more responsibilities; they are in charge of an entire line of related products, and the job may entail coordinating marketing efforts for a number of different brands. Both brand and product managers often deal with budgets of several million dollars. Individuals who believe they would enjoy a career path directed toward product management positions should consider entry-level jobs with consumer goods companies.

Advertising

Advertising is often perceived as the exciting and glamorous marketing career. And it is often true that people in the advertising industry are exceptionally creative and interesting. Advertising jobs can be found in advertising agencies, the media (TV stations and networks, radio, and newspapers) and with any organization that advertises. Here are some of the traditional types of jobs available in advertising:

1. Ad agency account executives act as the liaison between client and agency. Their job is to understand the needs of the client, communicate those needs to the other agency departments, and coordinate the agency services for the client.
2. Media planners and buyers develop media schedules and negotiate the purchase of media time and space.
3. Copywriters, graphic artists, and others in the creative department actually create the advertisements and other promotional materials.
4. Full-service advertising agencies often have research, sales promotion, and public relations departments as well.

As more and more firms adopt an integrated marketing communications perspective, advertising jobs will require a greater variety of communications skills and marketing expertise.

Sales Promotion

Jobs in sales promotion are usually to be found in advertising agencies or with manufacturers of consumers and business-to-business products. Sales promotion specialists are responsible for developing overall sales promotion plans and for creating the individual purchase incentives used to increase sales. In addition to planning for consumer sales promotions such as coupons or a sweepstakes, sales promotion specialists develop programs aimed at building relationships with wholesalers and retailers.

Professional Selling

Many of the entry-level positions with producers of industrial and consumer products are in professional sales. For this reason, many of the jobs available for new college graduates are in the sales field. But that does not mean that sales jobs are not important to a firm: Because sales are the only source of a company's profit, a qualified, effective sales force is essential to the health of many organizations. Most salespeople find selling jobs both personally stimulating and financially rewarding.

For qualified individuals, sales jobs are a great opportunity. Professional selling jobs demand people who are self-directed and able to manage themselves and their time effectively. Many sales jobs not only offer high levels of income but also include such added benefits as a company car, a cellular phone, home computers, internet access, and interesting travel. Some individuals see sales jobs as a training ground for other jobs. One reason is that many sales jobs provide opportunities to attend motivational and other sales seminars. Activities such as attendance at trade shows provide excellent opportunities for finding out about other jobs and for networking. Of course, many salespeople find a career in sales as an end in itself and choose to remain in sales for their entire careers.

Sales Management

For the salesperson who wants to advance with a firm, a job in sales can lead to promotion to sales management. Although many salespeople are not interested in a management job because they enjoy the freedom of working on their own out in the field, others feel that their abilities would be better used in overseeing the sales function, and some may aspire to even higher levels of management.

The activities of sales managers include recruiting, selecting, training, supervising, motivating, and evaluating members of a sales force. It is also the responsibility of the sales manager to plan the firm's territory structure and to develop objectives for the sales organization and for the individual salespeople.

Sales management jobs, like some salesperson jobs, require a lot of travel that can disrupt family life. Successful sales managers, however, are good candidates for promotion to higher levels of management.

Public Relations

Many people feel that PR involves simply being "good with people" and taking them out to lunch, but nothing could be farther from the truth. In reality, public relations specialists or PR managers are responsible for planning and implementing publicity programs to target publics. Much of this involves developing media relations and providing the mass media with written and video news releases. PR specialists may also be called on to develop corporate-image advertising campaigns, to write the company's annual report, and even to pen speeches for the CEO.

On the down side, PR jobs may require long hours and extensive travel. On the positive side, because PR people often work with the firm's top executives and may be called on to provide advice and counsel to top-level managers, they are highly visible and often become good candidates for important promotions.

Marketing Research

Careers in marketing research require expertise in the collection and analysis of data from a variety of sources. Marketing researchers must have a thorough knowledge of research methods and statistics and need considerable expertise in using statistical and data management software. In addition, they should have strong interpersonal and problem-solving skills; they need to be able to get to the root of a problem and to communicate what they have found in actionable terms to others in the firm. The activities of an individual with a job in marketing research range from supervising interviewers to conducting sophisticated statistical analyses. Although a strong foundation in research methodology and statistics is usually required for entry-level marketing research positions, much of what marketing researchers do day to day is learned on the job.

Entrepreneurship

Are you the type of person who wants to own your own business, to buy a franchise, to control your own destiny? Or maybe you have a great idea for a new product. If so, the knowledge and skills you acquire from your marketing education will put you right on track. Entrepreneurship is not for everybody. It requires people who are willing to risk losing everything (not just their business but their savings, their home—everything) in order to have a chance at being their own boss and making their dreams come true. Being an entrepreneur involves a lot of risks, but there are also no limits on what can be achieved.

Most successful entrepreneurs would agree that it is a good idea to start by getting a job: Working for someone else is a great training ground. You learn how a business operates, you see things that are done well, and you see things that you would do differently. In fact, for most of us, getting a job for a while is mandatory because starting a business requires capital—and one of the best ways to get that money is to work and save.

Purchasing

Most people think of marketing as selling something, but the same knowledge and skills can lead to an interesting and rewarding career in purchasing. Most large organizations offer careers for purchasing professionals. One of the major responsibilities of purchasing specialists is to work with all the various departments of a company and help them to identify what goods and services they need. In addition, purchasing specialists interact with the companies from which they purchase, obtaining the best prices for needed materials, negotiating the sale, and facilitating the actual purchase.

Customer Relations/Consumer Affairs

In the 1990s, almost all organizations consider the customer relations function an essential part of marketing activities. Whereas many firms have always recognized the importance of customer relations, other companies have added this important function as they have adopted total quality management programs. Although the responsibilities of customer relations vary widely across companies, the purpose is usually the same: to enhance the value of the company and its products to its customers. For the job candidate, customer relations jobs are often an excellent entry point for other jobs with the company.

Other Marketing Jobs

Where might you find other marketing jobs? Almost anywhere. For example, hospitals and health care organizations often have sophisticated marketing departments. Hospital marketing specialists may be involved in physician recruitment, advertising, and patient satisfaction activities. A variety of professionals—including physicians, law firms, accounting firms, architects, and designers—are adopting the marketing concept and hiring marketing professionals to improve their business. Marketers in banking and other areas of the financial industry develop strategies to attract new customers and to increase the utilization of services by existing customers. And the list goes on. Educational institutions from public schools to private universities, the military, not-for-profit organizations such as religious groups, the U.S. Post Office and other government agencies, private and public parks and recreation facilities, publishers—all provide exciting career opportunities for marketing professionals.

Plan Your Strategies

Once you have considered the different types of marketing careers and determined which ones seem to be best for you, it's time to develop your job-hunting strategies. Like marketing any other product, you can consider how best to plan your product, price, distribution, and promotion.

Product

In the career market, *you* are the product. It's never too late to work to improve that product. Most marketing jobs require individuals with excellent communications, computer, writing, and quantitative skills. In addition, successful marketers usually possess interpersonal skills, including the ability to work effectively with others and serve in a leadership role.

Sometimes customers are more willing to buy a product if it includes a warranty. In the career market, getting an internship or a cooperative education experience is something like giving a potential employer a warranty. Because the internship is not the same as an actual hiring, the firm can in essence "try out" the employee for a few months. If the employee works out, the firm can hire him or her permanently knowing it has made a good decision. If not, when the internship is over, both employee and employer part with no hard feelings. And that warranty goes both ways. If you don't like the job, you can walk away after completing the internship and simply chalk it up to experience. Temporary work is another excellent way to make important contacts in your field and to get references.

Price

What is your price? Or, rather, how much will you have to be paid? In applying for a job, you don't want to ask a price that is too low—and you certainly don't want to lose a job opportunity by asking for a salary that is too high. The best way to avoid making these mistakes is to find out what the average starting salary for a certain type of position is in your particular region of the country.

Salaries vary greatly in different industries and in different areas, but the average salary for marketing grads in 1993 was $24,000, somewhat above the $21,000 average for advertising majors.[1]

How much can you expect to make in a marketing job after you have been in your career for a while? For experienced people in marketing, advertising, and public relations, the overall median salary was $41,000 in 1992, and the top 10 percent of all employees in these fields earned $79,000 or more. Of course, salaries differ greatly (from under $25,000 to over $250,000) depending on education, experience, industry, and the number of employees supervised. For the same year, the median salary was $45,000 for product/brand managers, $55,000 for marketing research managers, $67,000 for regional sales managers, and $41,000 for purchasing professionals.

Place

What about distribution of the product, namely you. In marketing, "place" means getting the product to customers when and where they want it. And that is what it means for you. If the employer wants a salesperson in St. Louis and you don't want to move west of the Mississippi, you won't be "purchased." There are lots of reasons why people want or need to stay in one geographic location or another, but the best opportunities are often tied to an applicant's being willing and able to relocate. Indeed, some of the best opportunities go to people who are ready and willing to be transferred to offices in other countries where they can gain very valuable experience. (*Hint:* learning a foreign language is *never* a waste of time!) And many jobs require relocation several times during the course of a career. If you don't feel you can do this, then you must realize that you have placed constraints on your career success.

Promoting Yourself

In promoting a product, marketers have to find out how to reach their target market. Should they advertise on "Seinfeld" or on "Sixty Minutes" or on MTV? In the same way, a first step in promoting yourself is to locate good job prospects. There are a number of good ways to do this—and you should do them all.

Sources of Potential Jobs

1. Networking, or developing and nurturing professional contacts, is certainly a top activity in locating a good job. Students often do not realize that there are a lot of opportunities for them to make excellent contacts while still in school. For example, professors and student organizations often invite business professionals to speak on campus. These sorts of events give students the opportunity not only to learn about a certain business and industry but also to introduce themselves to the guest—to make a contact that may be useful a year or two later when they enter the job market.

2. Your college career placement office is a virtual treasure chest of information, and even more important, it's where you can sign up for interviews with business recruiters who visit campus. It's amazing how many students admit after graduation that they just never found the time to wander into the career placement office. Your career placement office probably offers directories of companies, information about careers, assistance with developing a résumé and a letter of application,

workshops on interviewing techniques, and "dress for success" seminars. Because the placement staff know that the perceived quality of the college may be directly related to the jobs graduates get, new programs and services are being developed every day.

3. Employment agencies can sometimes be a source of jobs. Most career counselors advise that you *never* pay to get a job. With really good jobs, the firms pay the employment agency fee.

4. Want ads not only in newspapers but also in professional publications such as *Marketing News* and *Advertising Age* are good sources of information on jobs. Jobs with large companies are often advertised in *The New York Times* or *The Wall Street Journal,* but you should also study the want ads in papers from cities or regions where you would like to be located. In addition, national or even global networks are beginning to be established on the internet, so be sure to search the World Wide Web for these new electronic classifieds!

5. Directories. Although they may get a lot of refusals, some students get jobs by sending unsolicited résumés to companies. There are many directories of firms in different industries that provide names and addresses of companies. A list of a few of these directories appears at the end of this appendix.

Developing Your Message

In promoting a product, marketers develop a wide range of messages from slick TV commercials to ads in the local high school yearbook. When you're deciding how widely to promote yourself, remember that job hunting is a numbers game. The odds of your obtaining a new position increase with every contact you make. Also, don't limit your job search to the Fortune 500 companies. That isn't where the new jobs will be.

In promoting yourself with potential employers, you are probably limited to two basic means of telling about yourself: your résumé and cover letter. A résumé is basically a summary of your education, experience, and other accomplishments. It is your "package"—often your one and only opportunity to differentiate yourself and stand out from the crowd. Thus in your résumé, it is important that you find a way to tell prospective employers how your unique background equips you to do a better job of meeting the needs of their organization. But even though it's OK to work to get a potential employer's attention, you must still be concise. Remember that the firm you are targeting may be receiving hundreds or even thousands of résumés, so don't give them a reason to throw yours out before it's even read!

Although there are dozens of different ways to develop a résumé that will "work," most experts agree on some basics.

1. Always keep your résumé to one page. If you are considered further for the job, you can always provide additional information.

2. Don't send out general résumés. Rather, be user-specific and generate different résumés for different "customers." Gear each résumé to a particular company and send it directly to an individual. "To whom it may concern" won't work in most cases.[2]

3. Don't lie on your résumé. If people tell you that companies never check on résumé information, don't believe them. Companies do check. They know that if they don't, they're exposing themselves to some expensive surprises.

4. Like it or not, looks count. Be sure to select a high-quality paper, a professional-looking type style or font, and an attractive layout—one with lots of empty space so the résumé doesn't look overly "busy."

5. Don't make errors on your résumé. If a prospective employer has a dozen (or even a hundred) résumés to look at, the one with the misspelled words, or faulty punctuation, or even irregular margins is not going to be the one he or she puts at the top of the stack.

6. Videotaped résumés are the coming wave, but keep them short and professional.

Implementation

The last (but not least) phase of your career planning is implementation—the interview. Success in this phase involves careful attention to activities before, during, and after the interview.

Before the interview, you should be sure to do your homework. You should study the company and the industry. Find out about any recent events involving the firm. If the prospective employer is a publicly held company, it would be a good idea to read the company's annual report, which may be available in your library either in hard copy or on CD/ROM. Learning about the company will not only enable you to show interviewers that you are serious about your career but will also give you hints about what questions you might be asked during the interview and suggest questions you might want to ask your interviewers.

It is always a good idea to think about the questions interviewers might ask and to practice answering them. Some of the questions typically asked in interviews are

Why are you interested in this firm?

Why are you interested in this specific job?

What are your career goals?

Why did you major in . . . ?

Tell me about your work experience.

Tell me about your college experience.

What do you feel is your greatest strength? What is your greatest weakness?

What do you think you can offer our firm?

Why do you think you are qualified for this job?

Are you willing to relocate?

How would you describe your personality?

On the day of the interview, be sure you have good directions to the interview location so you won't be late. In fact, give yourself some extra time for heavy traffic or other unplanned delays. If you arrive early, you can always sit in your car and read a newspaper until the interview time.

Dress for the interview should be conservative. If you are unsure of the dress norms for the particular company, it is always best to err on the side of conservatism. Be sure to take a pad and several pens (one is surely going to "die" on you) as well as an additional copy of your résumé. You might also want to bring your college transcript or a portfolio of work you have done while in school or at a previous job.

Nothing is quite so important as how you "perform" during the interview. In general, you should be polite and honest. You should listen carefully and answer each question. Don't allow yourself to drift off the subject because you want to tell them something they didn't ask. It's OK to pause for ten or fifteen seconds after a question is asked to think of what you want to say. And it's certainly a lot smarter than giving a quick but superficial answer.

You may also want to plan to ask some questions during the interview. Here are some examples of questions you might ask:

What is the typical career path for someone who begins in this job?

What kind of training programs do you offer your employees?

What exactly are the responsibilities of someone in this position?

To whom does someone in this position report?

What career opportunities are there with your firm?

When will you be making the decision about this position?

It is *not* a good idea to ask about such things as fringe benefits, vacation time, sick leave or the like. Asking about these things makes it seem that you are more interested in what you will get than in what you will be doing.

Finally, you should follow up every interview with a thank-you letter, even if you are not interested in the job. As the saying goes, you don't want to burn your bridges behind you. The thank-you letter should be brief and should thank the interviewer(s) for the time and information they shared with you. If, during the interview, you were asked to provide any additional material, it should be attached and noted in the letter.

What if you have not been contacted by the firm within a reasonable period of time? Certainly it is then appropriate to write or call for information. Of course, it is ill-advised to try to push an employer by saying that you have another job offer unless you actually have one.

Most of all, you should enjoy the job search. You are about to enter an exciting part of your life. You will learn more than you ever dreamed, you will meet and get to know interesting new people, and you will succeed at new challenges.

It's also important to bear in mind that once you get your first job, you don't have to like everything about it. What's important is getting experience in the work world and establishing a good work record with all the basics: good attendance, willingness to pitch in, flexibility, and some skill or knowledge in the field. Do your best always, but keep a written record of your job achievements, including special assignments and volunteer work. It will come in handy at performance appraisal time and the next time you enter the job market. Best of luck, and happy hunting!

ADDITIONAL SOURCES OF INFORMATION

Information About Different Careers

CPC Annual (available at placement office)

Peterson's Job Opportunities for Business and Liberal Arts Graduates

Occupational Outlook Handbook developed by the U.S. Department of Labor, Bureau of Labor Statistics

Directories of Companies in Different Industries

Standard Directory of Advertising Agencies

International Directory of the American Marketing Association and Marketing Services Guide

Fairchild's Financial Manual of Retail Stores

Other information on careers may be obtained from

American Marketing Association
250 S. Wacker Dr.
Chicago, IL 60606

Sales and Marketing Executives International
458 Statler Office Tower
Cleveland, OH 44115

American Advertising Federation
Education Services Department
1101 Vermont Ave., NW
Suite 500
Washington, DC 20005

American Association of Advertising Agencies
666 Third Ave.
13th Floor
New York, NY 10017

Council of Sales Promotion Agencies
750 Summer St.
Stamford CT 06901

Promotion Marketing Association of America, Inc.
322 Eighth St.
Stamford, CT 06901

Public Relations Society of America
33 Irving Place
New York, NY 10003-2376

The American Society for Health Care Marketing
  and Public Relations
American Hospital Association
840 North Lake Shore Dr.
Chicago, IL 60611

Marketing Research Association
250 Silas Deane Hwy.
Suite 5
Rocky Hill, CT

Council of American Survey Research Organizations
3 Upper Devon
Port Jefferson, NY 11777

National Retail Federation
701 Pennsylvania Ave., NW
Suite 710
Washington, DC 20004

Food Marketing Institute
800 Connecticut Ave., NW
Washington, DC 20006-2701

National Automotive Dealers Association
8400 Westpark Dr.
McLean, VA 22102

National Association of Convenience Stores
1605 King St.
Alexandria, VA 22314

1. *Jobs Outlook,* 1994–95 edition. Developed by U.S. Department of Labor, Bureau of Labor Statistics, pp. 56–59.
2. Some material in this appendix was adapted from Carol Kleiman, *100 Best Jobs for the 1990s and Beyond* (Dearborn, MI: Financial Publishing, 1992).

MARKETING PLAN FOR CHARETTE FOODS' OKLAHOMA PRIDE BARBECUE SAUCE[1]

Business Review

Company/Product History

Charette Foods was founded in 1935 as a specialty foods importer/exporter. In the 1960s the company began a program of expansion so that today, in addition to being in the import/export business, Charette produces a variety of specialty food items. Charette Foods is headquartered in Charleston, South Carolina, but its manufacturing facility is located in Emigsville, Pennsylvania. Corporate goals are to maintain the current rate of growth and to explore possibilities for future expansion.

The Charette organizational structure is relatively flat with all personnel, including vice presidents of marketing, operations, finance, and R&D, reporting directly to the president. The organization also includes three regional managers (located in Philadelphia, Chicago, and Los Angeles) who oversee a network of specialty food brokers and distributors who get the products into grocery chains and specialty food stores.

Charette acquired Oklahoma Pride Barbecue Sauce, along with other specialty foods and beverage acquisitions, in the early 1980s. The Oklahoma Pride barbecue sauce formula was created in 1933 in Nachez, Mississippi (not in Oklahoma) but remained a family secret until it was first commercially bottled and marketed in 1977. The sauce comes in six flavors (original, sweet and sour, hickory smoked, Hawaiian, Creole, and Jim Bob's Recipe) and still uses tomato paste, tomato sauce, and tomato juice with very little sugar and salt.

Oklahoma Pride is packaged in a distinctive patented bottle. The sauce's expensive foil label recounts the history of the product, and this presentation reinforces the image of an upscale product for sophisticated buyers.

Consumer Market

MRI[2] market research data show that 62.1 percent of U.S. female homemakers have used bottled barbecue or seasoning sauce during the past six months and that 50.5 percent have specifically used barbecue sauce. The number of occasions when barbecue sauce is used and the amount of sauce purchased are both growing. On the basis of their past three-months' usage of sauces, 25 percent of users were classified as light users (one or fewer bottles), 24 percent as medium users (two or three bottles), and 17 percent as heavy users (four or more bottles). These same data

also provide a demographic profile of homemakers most likely to purchase barbecue sauce:

Demographic Category	Percentage
Age: Twenty-five to thirty-four	70.6
Education: Attended college	66.3
Employed: Part-time	67.7
Type of employment: Precision/craft	76.9
Family status: Married with children	71.3
Family size: Five or more	71.6

Because Oklahoma Pride is a premium-priced specialty food product, its market is substantially different from that of the lower-priced brands. Based on Charette research, the demographic profile of the market for Oklahoma Pride is described as a homemaker aged thirty-five to sixty-four with a college education living in a household with a family income greater than $50,000. The breadwinner in the house is likely to be a professional who is employed full-time.

Sales Analysis
Total Sales Potential for Barbecue Sauces

A recent study showed that 73 percent of American households owned barbecue grills and 94 percent used barbecue sauces.[3] Nationally, sales of barbecue sauces have grown 21 percent in the past five years.

Historical Sales of Oklahoma Pride

Oklahoma Pride sales for 1991 were $2,153,300.00, which represented a 150 percent increase since 1987.[4] Total 1991 sales grew at a pace of 21.2 percent over 1990. Case sales for 1991 were 125,000, a 50 percent increase over 1987. Sales by variety of Oklahoma Pride were as follows:

Variety	Percent of Total 1991 Sales
Original	39%
Creole	24%
Hickory Smoked	21%
Sweet and sour	7%
Hawaiian	6%
Jim Bob's Recipe	4%

Oklahoma Pride has experienced tremendous growth over the past five years, but sales were only a fraction of the total barbecue sauce sales—less than a 1 percent market share—during this period.

Beginning in June 1991, Oklahoma Pride experienced a decline in sales, which may have been related to an increase in the price of the product.

Seasonality of Sales

Sales of barbecue sauces experience seasonal changes, even though more people are now barbecuing in months that traditionally did not fall into the barbecue season. The peak barbecue events are the Fourth of July, Father's Day, Labor Day, and Memorial Day.[4] Oklahoma Pride sales records show such seasonality, with sales peaking in May, probably in preparation for Memorial Day.

Sales by Geographic Territory

Nationally, barbecue sauces sell best in the South. The households that use barbecue sauce break down by region as follows:

Region	Percent of Households That Use Barbecue Sauce
Southeast	35%
Central	30%
Northeast	23%
West	12%

Of those households that use barbecue sauce, the proportion that uses Oklahoma Pride sauces also varies by region.

Region	Percent of User Households That Use Oklahoma Pride Sauce
Southeast	15%
Northeast	72%
Central	15%
West	13%

Product Awareness and Attributes

Because of limited financial resources, Oklahoma Pride barbecue sauce has never been promoted through consumer advertising. Thus product awareness has depended primarily on shelf exposure and word-of-mouth recommendations. Although consumer product awareness is low, awareness of the brand has been created among distributors and retailers through trade advertising and trade shows.

In order to obtain information on product attributes, primary marketing research was conducted. The research included a sample of two hundred barbecue sauce users. Participants in the research were first asked to answer a series of questions regarding

- The importance of various product attributes
- Barbecue sauce usage and buying habits
- Sauce trial and retrial behavior
- Brand loyalty
- Awareness of promotion activities

The research results show that 35 percent of all the research participants and 50 percent of those classified as heavy users of barbecue sauce consider themselves brand-loyal. On the other hand, 80 percent of these heavy users

try different brands from time to time. Fifty-nine percent of the sample use barbecue sauce year-round, and 93 percent buy at least one bottle of sauce per month.

The research participants were also asked to participate in a taste test of Oklahoma Pride and three competing brands (KC Masterpiece, Kraft, and Bull's-Eye) and to rank each on ten attributes (spicy, thick, zesty, rich, tangy, sweet, strong, light, hot, sour). The barbecue sauces were tested using small pieces of pork. Lemon-flavored water was provided to cleanse the palate between sauces. Each person was also asked to rank-order the ten attributes in terms of an "ideal" sauce.

The results of this research show that consumers rank attribute importance as follows: (1) spicy, (2) thick, (3) zesty, and (4) rich. In the taste tests, Oklahoma Pride received its highest rating on the following attributes (in rank order):

1. Thick
2. Spicy
3. Strong
4. Zesty

Distribution

According to a report by Package Facts, a market research firm in New York, 46 percent of all specialty food dollars are spent in supermarkets, 44 percent in the 13,000–14,000 specialty food retailers, and 10 percent in minor retail chains.

Oklahoma Pride barbecue sauces are sold through a four-tier distribution channel:

Tier 1. Regional managers: Three regional managers are located in Philadelphia, Chicago, and Los Angeles.

Tier 2. Brokers: Territorial specialty food brokers act as sales agents. Brokers do not take possession or title to the product but do earn a commission on net sales of 5 percent.

Tier 3. Distributors: Local food distributors purchase Oklahoma Pride from the brokers, warehouse the product, and sell to key accounts, primarily grocery store chains.

Tier 4. Retail outlets: Grocery store chains, specialty/gourmet food shops, and other retail outlets obtain the product from distributors and sell to the consumer.

Because Oklahoma Pride is a specialty food item, many retailers give it very limited shelf space compared to the cheaper and more popular brands such as Kraft, Heinz, and Hunt. Others tend to shelve Oklahoma Pride in their specialty food sections rather than with other barbecue sauces. However, a change in allocation and position practices is beginning to evolve as more and more grocery stores use scanner technology to track volume and determine space allocation and position for specialty products. Although mail-order food items are purchased by less than

2 percent of Americans, this segment of the market adds up to about $2 billion a year.

Pricing

The price of Oklahoma Pride is comparable to that of other "high end" barbecue sauces but is considerably higher than the price of the more popular, low-priced sauces.

Brand	Size	Price
Oklahoma Pride	17.5 oz	$2.39
K.C. Masterpiece	18 oz	1.79
Bull's-Eye	18 oz	1.75
Kraft	18 oz	.96
Woody's	13 oz	2.19

Price and Demand

Because Oklahoma Pride barbecue sauce is an "upscale" product, there is less sensitivity to changes in price—that is, increases or decreases in price have little if any affect on the quantity consumers are willing to purchase. Therefore, in 1992 Oklahoma Pride instituted an increase of $.67 per case.

Manufacturing costs per 12-count case of 17.5-oz bottles of Oklahoma Pride are approximately $10.20. The F.O.B. factory price to distributors is $15.50 per case, a mark-up of 54 percent. Broker commissions are 5% of net distributor price. Average shipping cost is $.37 per case. Retail shelf price is approximately $28.68 per case ($2.39 per bottle).

Competition

The most popular brands of barbecue sauce and their usage rates are

Brand	Percent of Total Households
Kraft	36%
Open Pit	27.1%
Bull's-Eye	15.4%
K.C. Masterpiece	12.9%

Kraft is positioned as a product liked by all ages of people and by all households. The sauce is packaged in a nondistinctive bottle that emphasizes the name Kraft. Because of high levels of product awareness and its dominant market position, Kraft is allocated abundant shelf space. Kraft sauce is marketed with high levels of trade and consumer promotions and is advertised in consumer and trade magazines, on television, in newspapers, and on the radio. Kraft comes in several flavors but has no ethnic varieties.

Bull's-Eye has a high-quality product image and is used by all households. It has been positioned as a bold sauce with better ingredients. The brand name supports this positioning. The eye-catching packaging includes the signature of the creator on the label. Bull's-Eye uses heavy trade and consumer promotions and advertises that it is the "best" brand with a money-back guarantee. Advertising media include trade publications, newspaper, radio, and television. Bull's-Eye is also a stock car racing sponsor. Bull's-Eye, like Kraft, comes in different flavors but has no ethnic alternatives.

K.C. Masterpiece sauce's image is that of a high-quality sauce used by higher-income households. It is positioned as the sauce used by better-educated, more sophisticated buyers, and the taste appeals to older purchasers. The packaging is sophisticated and includes recipes on the label. K.C. Masterpiece uses some consumer promotions but few trade promotions. The advertising message seeks to extend the use of the sauce beyond barbecuing and offers customers free recipes for using the sauce. Advertising is limited to trade and consumer magazines and newspapers. This brand also comes in different flavors but offers no ethnic varieties.

Opportunities and Threats

The business review has revealed the following opportunities and threats:

Opportunities

- The demographic and geographic profiles of the Oklahoma Pride target market differ from those of the leading market-share holders. The Oklahoma Pride target user is older and more highly educated than the average user of a national barbecue sauce.
- The barbecue market is growing.
- Barbecue is becoming a year-round activity, thus increasing the year-round use of barbecue sauces.
- Oklahoma Pride contains quality ingredients that create an excellent basting material.
- Consumers are willing to try new barbecue sauces.
- Charette has an established distributor network in place.
- Mail-order food items constituted a $1.2 billion market in 1990, and sales are expected to grow.
- Because Oklahoma Pride appeals to a more sophisticated buyer, the aging "baby boomer" market provides growth opportunities.
- Oklahoma Pride has introduced ethnic flavors, a growing market.

Threats

- Oklahoma Pride sales are strong during spring and summer; however, there are significant declines in fall and winter.
- Oklahoma Pride has never been promoted by consumer advertising and thus has not developed an advertising message.

- Oklahoma Pride is a little-known brand and has been tried by relatively few consumers.
- Oklahoma Pride sauces have very limited shelf space and poor position in grocery stores compared to other brands of barbecue sauces.
- Oklahoma Pride experienced a decline in sales after a 5 percent price increase.
- Current market share is less than 1 percent of the total barbecue sauce market.
- Oklahoma Pride is priced higher than major competitors.
- Oklahoma Pride is distributed in a limited number of grocery stores.
- Oklahoma Pride does not have financial resources for heavy promotion.
- Oklahoma Pride's media strategy has been limited to trade publications.
- Charette has limited ability to mass-market the Oklahoma Pride product.

Marketing Objectives

On the basis of this analysis, the following objectives have been developed for the marketing of Oklahoma Pride Barbecue Sauce.

1. Increase market share of Oklahoma Pride by increasing the trial to 9 percent among the target market over the next twelve months.
2. Achieve a repeat purchase of 70 percent from new users over the next twelve months.

Sales Objectives

Short-term

Increase dollar sales 16.8 percent over last year.
Increase unit sales 15.5 percent over last year.

Long-term (three-year) Sales Objectives

Increase dollar sales 21.8 percent in year 2.
Increase dollar sales 19.1 percent in year 3.
Increase unit sales 22.8 percent in year 2.
Increase unit sales 19.1 percent in year 3.

Positioning

Position Oklahoma Pride as the distinctive-tasting sauce for those who demand the best. This position will be supported with the communication theme "When the occasion demands the best, select Oklahoma Pride." Communications will also emphasize the unique recipe and quality ingredients used to make the sauces and will highlight the attributes that are important to sauce users. The Oklahoma Pride target market demands quality, and Oklahoma Pride will be positioned as the sauce that fills that need.

Target Market

In order to concentrate marketing efforts more efficiently on the portion of the population most likely to purchase the product, a target marketing strategy is recommended. The primary customer for Oklahoma Pride is substantially different from the average users of all brands of barbecue sauce. Because barbecuing is a family activity, both the head of the household and other members of the household influence the purchase.

Judging by the demographic profile outlined earlier, it is estimated that the size of the potential target market is 3,870,735 households. Because of the longer outdoor cooking season and the popularity of barbecuing, the greatest growth potential is in the Southeast region of the country.

Product Strategies

No changes in the product are advisable or needed at this time. However, there are a number of changes to be made in product packaging.

1. Because the message that the product label communicates should focus more on the needs and wants of the targeted customer, a new label that brings out more of the attributes of the sauce and more effectively communicates what is inside the bottle will be developed. The redesigned product label will send a stronger message about the Oklahoma Pride product attributes and positioning within the product market and will specifically communicate (1) thickness, (2) zesty flavor, (3) distinctive taste, and (4) the high-quality premium ingredients.
2. A Spanish-language label will also be provided to target additional consumers in geographic areas of high Hispanic population. This label will contain essentially the same information as the regular English-language label.
3. Introduce a smaller, six-ounce trial-size bottle.

Pricing Strategies

1. Set prices more in line with that of the competition throughout the country. Because competition in specialty sauces tends to be regional rather than national, pricing will be set at the regional level rather than there being one national price for all distributors.
2. Use promotional pricing twice a year: January/February and May/June. The trade allowance to distributors of $1.20 per case will be extended, the reduction in price to be passed on to the consumer.

Promotion Strategies

Personal Selling

1. Develop an aggressive sales environment that encourages regional managers and brokers to support the growth of Oklahoma Pride.
   - Identify the top fifty prospects for Oklahoma Pride.
   - Schedule a presentation for each prospect.
   - Provide financial incentives for sales managers and brokers when new distributors are added.
2. Evaluate the sales performance of brokers and regional managers monthly.
3. Support personal sales efforts with promotional materials that emphasize the advertising theme.
   - Obtain a sales ratio of 35 percent among these prospects.
   - Achieve a sales ratio of 90 percent among existing Oklahoma Pride distributors.
   - Achieve cross-sell among Charette distributors.

Sales Promotion

Expand sales promotion efforts to include consumers and retailers instead of focusing only on distributors. Sales promotions will

1. Support the theme "When the occasion demands the Best, select Oklahoma Pride" with in-store displays.
2. Utilize sampling of the product to shoppers in the store.
3. Provide potential customers in the store with coupons worth 35 cents off the purchase price.
4. Incorporate a trade allowance for retailers in order to increase shelf space and merchandising support.
5. Mount a targeted direct-mail campaign featuring 20-cents-off coupons.

Advertising

Advertising Objectives

1. Establish a 50 percent unaided awareness of Oklahoma Pride among the target market.
2. Establish an image of Oklahoma Pride as the superior alternative among barbecue sauces in 30 percent of the target market.

Creative Strategy

The theme of the advertising will be that Oklahoma Pride is the choice in barbecue sauces when the occasion demands the best and that the unique taste is a result of the quality ingredients and a special recipe.

The tone of the advertising will be sophisticated and tasteful, expressing the positive results of using Oklahoma Pride sauces.

The following copy point will be used in every ad:

"When the occasion demands the best."

Other copy points will emphasize the various flavors and product attributes.

- The various flavors: "sweet and sour, hickory smoked, creole, Hawaiian, Jim Bob's Recipe, and original"
- Product attributes: "thick, spicy, zesty"
- "Excellent basting sauce"

Media Plan

Media objectives:

1. Provide a reach of 70 to 75 percent of the target market with an average frequency of five exposures per four-week period during three time periods: May, June, and August.
2. Provide a reach of 50 percent of the target market with an average frequency of two exposures per four-week period during other times of the year.
3. Provide a media environment that is tasteful and represents a quality life-style that demands the best.

Media strategy:

1. Use thirty-second radio spots during news and programs that appeal to target consumers in different regions of the country.
2. Use quarter-page ads in metropolitan newspapers and smaller ads in local newspapers; secure advertising space in Wednesday (or other appropriate day) food sections.
3. Use a thirty-second television commerical on news program and other shows with followings that match the target market to obtain maximum impact during peak sales times in late spring and summer.

Publicity

1. Communicate all newsworthy items to newspaper business sections and food sections of selected newspapers and other media.
2. Develop feature articles on barbecuing and recipes using Oklahoma Pride barbecue sauce, and distribute them to selected newspaper and magazine food editors.

Distribution Strategies

1. Expand the distributor network to include all major marketing areas. The current distribution strategy leaves some regions of the country unserved. Increasing geographic coverage provides an easy but sure way to boost sales.

2. Use trade allowances, trade promotions, and trade advertising programs to encourage all current Charette distributors to carry Oklahoma Pride sauces.

3. Add mail order as a distribution channel. Negotiate an attractive contract with a specialty foods mail-order firm to catalog Oklahoma Pride sauces and gift baskets featuring Oklahoma Pride sauces.

4. Increase shelf space and improve position in grocery stores. By increasing consumer demand for Oklahoma Pride sauces through advertising and promotional programs, it should be possible to gain better shelf space. In-store promotions and pricing incentives for retailers will also be used to increase shelf space and improve the sauce's position in grocery stores.

Evaluation

Although disciplined marketing planning provides the best framework possible for successful marketing programs, factors both internal and external to the firm can affect the success of marketing strategies. For that reason, it is essential that the progress of the marketing programs outlined in this plan be monitored and evaluated. Such evaluations should be completed at regular intervals and should attempt to determine whether the marketing activities are achieving the stated objectives (the short-term and long-term marketing, sales, and advertising objectives) of the plan.

Should such evaluations determine that there is some question whether the objectives will be met, careful scrutiny of both the objectives and the plan should lead to adjustments in one or in both.

1. The material included in this marketing plan was adapted from class projects by the following MBA students: Cece Gardner, Jackie Reardon, Tim Whitten, and Bill Wilson. Data included are fictional to protect the confidentiality of the client–student relationship. Many of the numbers in the initial reports have been changed, because this plan is provided only for use as a teaching tool.
2. *Staples, Breakfast and Dairy Products.* Mediamark Research Incorporated, New York: 1990.
3. Laurie Levy. "Gourmet Barbecue Backyard Chef," *Fancy Foods:* (Feb. 1991).
4. Ibid.

APPENDIX C MARKETING MATH

To develop marketing strategies to meet the goals of an organization effectively and efficiently, it is essential that marketers understand and use a variety of financial analyses. This appendix provides some of these basic financial analyses, including a review of the income statement and balance sheet as well as some basic performance ratios. In addition, this appendix includes an explanation of some of the specific calculations that marketers use routinely in determining price.

INCOME STATEMENT AND BALANCE SHEET

The two most important documents used to explain the financial situation of a company are the income statement and the balance sheet. The **income statement** (which is sometimes referred to as the profit and loss statement) provides a summary of the revenues and expenses of a firm—that is, the amount of income a company received from sales or other sources, the amount of money it spent, and the resulting income or loss that the company experienced.

The major elements of the income statement are

Gross sales: the total of all income the firm receives from the sales of goods and services.

Net sales revenue: the gross sales minus the amount for returns and promotional or other allowances given to customers.

Cost of goods sold (sometimes called the *cost of sales*): the cost of inventory or goods that the firm has sold.

Gross margin (also called *gross profit*): the amount of sales revenue that is in excess of the cost of goods sold.

Operating expenses: expenses other than the cost of goods sold that are necessary for conducting business. These may include salaries, rent, depreciation on buildings and equipment, insurance, utilities, supplies, and property taxes.

Operating income (sometimes called *income from operations*): the gross margin minus the operating expenses. Sometimes accountants prepare an *operating statement,* which is similar to the income statement except that the final calculation is the operating income—that is, other revenues or expenses and taxes are not included.

Other revenue and expenses: income and/or expenses other than those required for conducting the business. These may include such items as interest income/expenses and any gain or loss experienced on the sale of property or plant assets.

Taxes: the amount of income tax the firm owes calculated as a percentage of income.

Net income (sometimes called *net earnings* or *net profit*): the excess of total revenue over total expenses.

Table C1 shows the income statement for an imaginary company, DLL Incorporated. DLL is a typical merchandising firm. Note that the income statement is for a specific year and includes income and expenses from January 1 through December 31 inclusive. The following comments explain the meaning of some of the important entries included in this statement.

■ DLL Inc. has total or gross sales during the year of $253,950. This figure was adjusted, however, by deducting the $3000 worth of goods returned and special allowances given to customers and by $2100 in special discounts. Thus the actual or net sales generated by sales is $248,850.

■ The cost of goods sold is calculated by adding the inventory of goods on January 1 to the amount purchased during the year and then subtracting the inventory of goods on December 31. In this case, DLL had $60,750 worth of inventory on hand on January 1. During the year the firm made purchases in the amount of $135,550. This amount, however, was reduced by purchase returns and allowances of $1500 and by purchase discounts of $750, so the net purchase is only $133,300.

There is also an amount on the statement labeled "Freight-In." This is the amount spent by the firm in shipping charges to get goods to its facility from suppliers. Any expenses for freight from DLL to its customers (Freight-Out) would be an operating expense. In this case, the Freight-In expense of $2450 is added to net purchase costs. Then these costs of current purchases are added to the beginning inventory to show that during the year the firm had a total of $196,500 in goods available for sale. Finally, the inventory of goods held on December 31 is subtracted from the goods available, for the total cost of goods sold of $136,200.

For a manufacturer, calculation of the cost of goods sold would be a bit more complicated and would probably include separate figures for such items as inventory of finished goods, the "work-in-process" inventory, the raw materials inventory, and the cost of goods delivered to customers during the year.

Table C1
DLL Inc. Income Statement For the Year Ended December 31, 19XX

Gross Sales		$253,950	
Less: Sales Returns and Allowances	$ 3,000		
Sales Discounts	2,100	5,100	
Net Sales Revenue			$248,850
Cost of Goods Sold			
Inventory, January 1, 19XX		$ 60,750	
Purchases	$135,550		
Less: Purchase Returns and Allowances	1,500		
Purchase Discounts	750		
Net Purchases	$133,300		
Plus: Freight-In	2,450	135,750	
Goods Available for Sale		196,500	
Less: Inventory, December 31, 19XX		60,300	
Cost of Goods Sold			$136,200
Gross Margin			112,650
Operating Expenses			
Salaries and Commissions		15,300	
Rent		12,600	
Insurance		1,500	
Depreciation		900	
Supplies		825	
Total Operating Expenses			31,125
Operating Income			81,525
Other Revenue and (Expenses)			
Interest Revenue		1,500	
Interest Expense		(2,250)	(750)
Income before Tax			80,775
Taxes (40%)			32,310
Net Income			$ 48,465

Table C2
DLL Inc. Balance Sheet: December 31, 19XX

Assets

Current Assets

Cash		$ 4,275	
Marketable Securities		12,000	
Accounts Receivable		6,900	
Inventory		60,300	
Prepaid Insurance		300	
Supplies		150	
Total Current Assets			84,525

Long-Term Assets—Property, Plant and Equipment

Furniture and Fixtures	$42,300		
Less: Accumulated Depreciation	4,500	37,800	
Land		7,500	
Total Long-Term Assets			45,300
Total Assets			$129,825

Liabilities

Current Liabilities

Accounts Payable	$70,500		
Unearned Sales Revenue	1,050		
Wages Payable	600		
Interest Payable	300		
Total Current Liabilities		72,450	

Long-Term Liabilities

Note Payable		18,900	
Total Liabilities			91,350

Stockholders' Equity

Common Stock		15,000	
Retained Earnings		23,475	
Total Stockholders' Equity			38,475
Total Liabilities and Stockholders' Equity			$129,825

- The cost of goods sold is subtracted from the net sales revenue to get a gross margin of $112,650.

- Operating expenses for DLL include the salaries and commissions paid to its employees, rent on facilities and/or equipment, insurance, depreciation of capital items, and the cost of operating supplies. DLL has a total of $31,125 in operating expenses, which is deducted from the gross margin. Thus DLL has an operating income of $81,525.

- DLL had both other income and expenses in the form of interest revenues of $1500 and interest expenses of $2250, making a total other expense of $750, which was subtracted from the operating income, leaving an income before tax of $80,775.

- Finally, the income before tax is reduced by 40 percent ($32,310) for taxes, leaving a net income of $48,465. The 40 percent is an average amount for federal and state corporate income taxes incurred by most firms.

The **balance sheet** lists the assets, liabilities, and stockholders' equity of the firm. Whereas the income statement represents what happened during an entire year, the balance sheet is like a snapshot; it shows the firm's financial situation at one point in time. For this reason, the balance sheet is sometimes called the *statement of financial position*.

Table C2 (page 737) shows DLL Inc.'s balance sheet for December 31. Assets are any economic resource that is expected to benefit the firm in the short or long term. *Current assets* are items that are normally expected to be turned into cash or used up during the next twelve months or during the firm's normal operating cycle. Current assets for DLL include cash, securities, accounts receivable (money owed to the firm and not yet paid) inventory on hand, prepaid insurance, and supplies: a total of $84,525. *Long-term assets* include all assets that are not current assets. For DLL, these are property, plant, equipment, furniture, and fixtures less an amount for depreciation, or $45,300. The *total assets* for DLL are $129,825.

A firm's *liabilities* are its economic obligations, or debts that are payable to individuals or organizations outside the firm. *Current liabilities* are debts due in the coming year or in the firm's normal operating cycle. For DLL, the current liabilities—the accounts payable, unearned sales revenue, wages payable, and interest payable—total $72,450. *Long-term liabilities* (in the case of DLL, a note in the amount of $18,900) are all liabilities that are not due during the coming cycle. *Stockholders' equity* is the value of the stock and the corporation's capital or retained earnings. DLL has $15,000 in common stock and $23,475 in retained earnings for a total stockholders' equity of $38,475. Total liabilities always equal total assets—in this case, $129,825.

IMPORTANT FINANCIAL PERFORMANCE RATIOS

How do managers and financial analysts compare the performance of a firm from one year to the next? How do investors compare the performance of one firm with that of another? Often, a number of different financial ratios provide important information for such comparisons. Such *ratios* are percentage figures comparing various income statement items to net sales. Ratios provide a better way to compare performance than simple dollar sales or cost figures for two reasons. They enable analysts to compare the performance of large and small firms, and they provide a fair way to compare performance over time, without having to take inflation and other changes into account. In this section we will explain the basic operating ratios. Other measures of performance that marketers frequently use and that are also explained here are the inventory turnover rate and return on investment (ROI).

Operating Ratios

Measures of performance calculated directly from the information in a firm's income statement (sometimes called an operating statement) are called the *operating ratios*. Each ratio compares some income statement item to net sales. The most useful of these are the *gross margin ratio, the net income ratio, the operating expense ratio,* and *the returns and allowances ratio*. These ratios vary widely by industry but tend to be important indicators of how a firm is doing within its industry. The ratios for DLL Inc. are shown in Table C3.

Table C3 (Hypothetical) Operating Ratios for DLL Inc.

Gross margin ratio	=	gross margin / net sales	= $112,650 / 248,850	= 45.3%
Net income ratio	=	net income / net sales	= $48,465 / 248,850	= 19.5%
Operating expense ratio	=	total operating expenses / net sales	= $31,125 / 248,850	= 12.5%
Returns and allowances ratio	=	returns and allowances / net sales	= $3,000 / 248,850	= 1.2%

- The **gross margin ratio** shows what percentage of sales revenues are available for operating and other expenses and for profit. With DLL, this means that 45 percent, or nearly half, of every sales dollar is available for operating costs and for profits.

- The **net income ratio** (sometimes called the *net profit ratio*) shows what percentage of sales revenues are income or profit. For DLL, the net income ratio is 19.5 percent. This means that the firm's profit before taxes is about 20 cents of every dollar.

- The **operating expense ratio** is the percentage of sales needed for operating expenses. DLL has an operating expense ratio of 12.5 percent. Tracking operating expense ratios from one year to the next or comparing them with an industry average gives a firm important information about how efficient its operations are.

- The **returns and allowances ratio** shows what percentage of all sales are being returned, probably by unhappy customers. DLL's returns and allowances ratio shows that only a little over 1 percent of sales are being returned.

Inventory Turnover Rate

The *inventory turnover rate,* also referred to as the stockturn rate, is the number of times inventory or stock is turned over (sold and replaced) during a specified time period, usually a year. Inventory turnover rates are usually calculated on the basis of inventory costs, sometimes on the basis of inventory selling prices, and sometimes by number of units.

For our example, DLL Inc., we know that for the year, the cost of goods sold was $136,200. Information on the balance sheet enables us to find the average inventory. By adding the value of the beginning inventory to the ending inventory and dividing by 2, we can compute an average inventory. In the case of DLL, this would be

$$\frac{\$60,750 + \$60,300}{2} = \$60,525$$

Thus

$$\text{Inventory turnover rate (in cost of goods sold)} = \frac{\text{cost of goods sold}}{\text{average inventory at cost}} = \frac{\$136,200}{\$60,525} = 2.25 \text{ times}$$

Return on Investment (ROI)

Firms often develop business objectives in terms of return on investment, and ROI is often used to determine how effective (and efficient) the firm's management has been. First, however, we need to define exactly what a firm means by investment. In most cases, firms define investment as the total assets of the firm. In order to calculate the ROI, we need the net income found in the income statement and the total assets (or investment), which is found in the firm's balance sheet.

Return on investment is calculated as follows:

$$\text{ROI} = \frac{\text{net income}}{\text{total investment}}$$

For DLL Inc., if the total assets are $129,825, then the ROI is

$$\frac{\$48,465}{\$129,825} = 37.3\%$$

Sometimes return on investment is calculated by using an expanded formula.

$$\text{ROI} = \frac{\text{net profit}}{\text{sales}} \times \frac{\text{sales}}{\text{investment}}$$

$$= \frac{\$48,465}{\$248,850} \times \frac{\$248,850}{\$129,825} = 37.3\%$$

This formula makes it easy to show how ROI can be increased and what might reduce ROI. For example, there are different ways to increase ROI. First, if the management focuses on cutting costs and increasing efficiency, profits may be increased while sales remain the same.

$$\text{ROI} = \frac{\text{net profit}}{\text{sales}} \times \frac{\text{sales}}{\text{investment}}$$

$$= \frac{\$53,277}{\$248,850} \times \frac{\$248,850}{\$129,825} = 41.0\%$$

But ROI can be increased just as much without improving performance simply by reducing the investment—by maintaining less inventory, for instance.

$$\text{ROI} = \frac{\text{net profit}}{\text{sales}} \times \frac{\text{sales}}{\text{investment}}$$

$$= \frac{\$48,465}{\$248,850} \times \frac{\$248,850}{\$114,825} = 42.2\%$$

Sometimes, however, differences among the total assets of firms may be related to the age of the firm or the type of industry, which makes ROI a poor indicator of performance. For this reason, some firms have replaced the traditional ROI measures with *return on assets managed* (ROAM), *return on net assets* (RONA), or *return on stockholders' equity* (ROE).

PRICE ELASTICITY

Price elasticity, discussed in Chapter 12, is a measure of the sensitivity of customers to changes in price. Price elasticity is calculated by comparing the percentage change in quantity to the percentage change in price.

$$\text{Price elasticity of demand} = \frac{\text{percentage change in quantity}}{\text{percentage change in price}}$$

$$E = \frac{(Q_2 - Q_1)/Q_1}{(P_2 - P_1)/P_1}$$

where Q = quantity and P = price.

For example, suppose the manufacturer of jeans in Chapter 13 increased its price from $30.00 a pair to $35.00. But instead of 40,000 pairs being sold, sales declined to only 38,000 pairs. The price elasticity would be calculated as follows:

$$E = \frac{(38,000 - 40,000)/40,000}{(\$35.00 - 30.00)/\$30.00} = \frac{-0.05}{0.167} = 0.30$$

Note that elasticity is usually expressed as a positive number even though the calculations create a negative value.

In this case, a relative small change in demand (5 percent) resulted from a fairly large change in price (16.7 percent), indicating that demand is inelastic. At 0.30, the elasticity is less than 1.

On the other hand, what if the same change in price resulted in a reduction in demand to 30,000 pairs of jeans? Then the elasticity would be

$$E = \frac{(30,000 - 40,000)/40,000}{(\$35.00 - 30.00)/\$30.00} = \frac{-0.25}{0.167} = 1.50$$

In this case, because the 16.7 percent change in price resulted in an even larger change in demand (25 percent), demand is elastic. The elasticity of 1.50 is greater than 1.

Note: Elasticity may also be calculated by dividing the change in quantity by the average of Q_1 and Q_2 and dividing the change in price by the average of the two prices. We, however, have chosen to include the formula that uses the initial quantity and price rather than the average.

ECONOMIC ORDER QUANTITY

The amount a firm should order at one time is called the *economic order quantity* (EOQ). Every time a firm places an order, there are additional costs. By ordering larger quantities less frequently, the firm saves on these costs. But it also costs money to maintain large inventories of needed materials. The EOQ is the order volume that provides both the lowest processing costs and the lowest inventory costs. The EOQ can be calculated as follows:

1. Determine the **order processing cost.** This is the total amount it costs a firm to place an order from beginning to end. Typically, this might include the operating expenses for the purchasing department, costs for follow-up, costs of record keeping of orders (data processing), costs for the receiving department, and costs for the processing and paying of invoices from suppliers. The simplest way to calculate this is to add up all these yearly costs and then divide by the number of orders placed during the year.

2. Next, calculate the **inventory carrying cost.** This is the total of all costs involved in carrying inventory. These costs include the costs of capital tied up in inventory, the cost of waste (merchandise that becomes obsolete or unuseable), depreciation costs, storage costs, insurance premiums, property taxes, and opportunity costs.

The formula for calculating EOQ is

$$EOQ = \sqrt{\frac{2 \times \text{units sold (or annual usage)} \times \text{ordering cost}}{\text{unit cost} \times \text{inventory carrying cost (\%)}}}$$

For example, suppose an office supply store sells 6,000 cases of pens a year at a cost of $12.00 a case. The cost to the store for each order placed is $60.00. The cost of carrying the pens in the warehouse is 24 percent per year (this is a typical inventory carrying cost in many businesses.) Thus the calculation is

$$EOQ = \sqrt{\frac{2 \times 6000 \times \$60}{\$12 \times 0.24}} = \sqrt{\frac{\$720,000}{\$2.88}} = 500$$

The firm should order pens about once a month (it sells 6000 cases a year or 500 cases a month).

CREDITS

Chapter 1

2 (Photo) Levi Strauss & Co.; 4 (Ad) Ad Courtesy of Swatch Watch; 6 (Web page) Prentice Hall; 8 (Ad) Ad Courtesy of Partnership for a Drug-Free America; (Caption) Cecelia Reed, "Partners for Life," *Advertising Age*, November 9, 1988: 122; 9 (Photo) Reebok; 12 (Ad) Hogle Zoo; 15 (Photo) Kaepa Shoes; (Caption) Elaine Underwood, "Tapping into Cheerleading," *Adweek*, 1992; 20 (Ad) Courtesy of The Document Company, Xerox; (Caption) Ray R. Gehani, "Quality Value-Chain: A Meta-Synthesis of Frontiers of Quality Movement," *Academy of Management Executive*, May 1993, 7 (7), pp. 29–42; 26 (Photo) Churchill and Klehr; (Caption) Vernon Silver, "How He Got There He Hasn't a Clue," *New York Times*, May 16, 1993, K3; 27 (Ad) Courtesy of the American Association of Advertising Agencies; 29 (Photo) Churchill and Klehr; 30 (Photo) Levi Strauss & Co.

Chapter 2

40 (Photo) Harley Davidson, Inc.; 60 (Ad) Photo by Ken Stidwell, DGM Studio; 64 (Ad) Ad courtesy of Whirlpool Corporation.

Chapter 3

74 (Photo) James Wu; 80 (Photo) Michael P. Gadomski/Photo Researchers, Inc.; 89 (Ad) Ad Courtesy of Motorola, Inc., Semiconductor Products Sector; 95 (Photo) Mercedes-Benz of North America, Inc.; (Caption) Thomas A. Sancton, "A Car, a Watch? Swatchmobile!" *Time*, March 28, 1994, pp. 56–57; 99 (Photo) Jose Caldeira/Black Star; 105 (Photo) C. O'Rear/Westlight.

Chapter 4

120 (Photo) MTV, Music Television; 131 (Ad) MTV—Music Television; 136 (Ad) Toyota Motor Corporate Services of North America, Inc.; 141 (Ad) Ad courtesy of HIGA Industries (Domino's Pizza, Japan); (Caption) Yumiko Ono, "Pizza in Japan is Adapted to Local Tastes," *Wall Street Journal*, June 4, 1993, B1.

Chapter 5

152 (Photo) Mercedes-Benz of North America, Inc.; 155 (Photo) Reproduced with permission of PepsiCo, Inc. 1996, Purchase, New York; (Caption) Debra Aho, "Pepsi Puts Callers in Touch with Ray," *Advertising Age*, November 15, 1993: 20; 163 (Photo) Frank T. Wood/SuperStock, Inc.; (Caption) Elizabeth Comte, "Thrill Seeker," *Forbes*, March 15, 1993: 116 (2 pp.); 168 (Photo) Atlanta Centennial Olympic Properties (ACOG); (Caption) Richard Sandomir, "The Atlanta Olympics Remake a Mascot, the Better to Sell the Games," *NYT*, June 23, 1993: D2; 171 (Ad) Reprinted with permission of Fruit of the Loom; 172 (Photo) Courtesy of McCann-Ericson; (Caption) Annetta Miller and Dody Tsiantar, "Psyching Out Consumers," *Newsweek*, February 27, 199: 46–47. By permission of McCann-Ericson (Research Department); 178 (Ad) Ad courtesy Ford Motor Company.

Chapter 6

188 (Photo) Sebago; 191 (Ad) Courtesy of the House of Seagram; (Caption) Michael Lev, "No Hidden Meaning Here: Survey Sees Subliminal Ads," *New York Times*, May 3, 1991: D7;

Philip M. Merikle, "Subliminal Auditory Messages: An Evaluation," *Psychology & Marketing*, 1988, 5(4): 355–372; Timothy E. Moore, "The Case Against Subliminal Manipulation," *Psychology & Marketing*, Winter 1988, 5: 297–316; Joel Saegert, "Why Marketing Should Quit Giving Subliminal Advertising the Benefit of the Doubt," *Psychology & Marketing*, Summer 1987, 4: 107–120; Dennis L. Rosen and Surendra N. Singh, "An Investigation of Subliminal Embed Effect on Multiple Measures of Advertising Effectiveness," *Psychology & Marketing* 9 (March/April 1992): 157–173; 193 (Ad) Courtesy of Benetton; 199 (Ad) Nissan; 204 (Ad) Bijan; 208 (Photo) McDonald's; (Ad) Ad source: McDonald's Corporation 1995; 211 (Ad) Courtesy of General Motors—Oldsmobile Division; 213 (Photo) Courtesy of Adbusters Quarterly. 1-800-663-1243. World Wide Web address: http://www.adbusters.org/adbusters/; 214 (Ad) Ad courtesy of Sebago Docksides.

Chapter 7

224 (Photo) UNITOG; 227 (Ad) Ad courtesy of The Document Company, Xerox; 232 (Ad) Ad courtesy of FTD, Inc.; 237 (Ad) Ad courtesy of DHL; 243 (Ad) Courtesy of MITA; (Caption) Lindley H. Clark, Jr., "Microsoft Still Expects by Year's End to Ship Chicago, Successor to Windows," *Wall Street Journal*, February 24, 1994, 223 (38), p. B7; 247 (Ad) Ad courtesy Safety-Kleen Corp.; 249 (Ad) Ad Courtesy of American Business Information, Inc.; 251 (Ad) Ad Courtesy of ARAMARK; 252 (Photo) Courtesy of UNITOG.

Chapter 8

260 (Photo) Burrell Communications; 269 (Photo) Churchill and Klehr; (Caption) Kim Foltz, "Mattel's Shift on Barbie Ads," *New York Times*, July 19, 1990: D17; Lora Sharpe, "Dolls in All the Colors of a Child's Dream," *The Boston Globe*, February 22, 1991: 42 (3 pp.); 275 (Photo) Will van Overbeek/Mercury Pictures; (Caption) Priscilla Painton, "The Great Casino Salesman," *Time*, May 3, 1993: 52 (4 pp.); 285 (Ad) Ad source: McDonald's Corporation 1995.

Chapter 9

294 (Photo) Nabisco, Inc.; 295 (Photo) Ann States/SABA Press Photos, Inc.; (Caption) Caryne Brown, "Making Money Making Toys," *Black Enterprise*, November 1993, 24: 68–77; 296 (Photo) Churchill and Klehr; (Caption) Information obtained from the Woodstream Corporation; 304 (Photo) UPI/Bettmann; 306 (Photo) Adrienne Hart-Davis/Science Photo Library/Photo Researchers, Inc.; (Caption) Lee Lescaze, "The Fastening Tale of How Flies Got Zipped," *Wall Street Journal*, June 27, 1994: N124; 318 (Photo) Nabisco, Inc.

Chapter 10

328 (Photo) Volkswagen of America, Inc.; (Photo) Volkswagen of America/FPG International; 334 (Ad) Courtesy Parker Pen Company; (Caption) Parker Pen (1993), "Parker Duofold Pearl and Black," product literature; 339 (Photo) John Sutton; (Caption) Sandy Reed, "Who Defines Usability? You Do!" *PC/Computing*, December 1992, 5 (12), pp. 220–232; 345 (Ad) Ad Courtesy of

Owens-Corning; (Caption) "How Owens-Corning Turned a Commodity Into a Brand," *Management Review,* December 1986, pp. 11–12; **348** (Ad) Courtesy of Ford Motor Company; (Caption) Neal Templin, "Ford Plans Capacity Boost for Mustang," *Wall Street Journal,* December 10, 1993, 222 pp. A3, A5; **354** (Photo) Churchill and Klehr; (Caption) Maxine S. Lans, "Temporary Victory for Private Labels," *Marketing News,* November 21, 1994, pp. 11, 16.

Chapter 11
364 (Photo) Lutheran Health System; **373** (Photo) Law Offices of Loncar & Associates; (Caption) David Margolick, "Texas Lawyers to Vote on How Far Their Ads Can Go," *NY Times,* December 17, 1993, B10; **379** (Photo) Ken Straiton/The Stock Market; (Caption) Andrew Pollack, "Japan's Radical Plan: Self-Serve Gas," *New York Times,* July 14, 1994: D1 (2); **388** (Photo) Jacky Naeqelen/Reuters/Corbis-Bettmann; (Caption) Roger Cohen, "When You Wish Upon a Deficit," *New York Times,* July 18, 1993, Sec. 2, 1 (3); Bruce Crumley and Christy Fisher, "Euro Disney Tries to End Evil Spell," *Advertising Age,* February 7, 1994, 39; Jolie Solomon, "Mickey's Trip to Trouble," *Newsweek,* February 14, 1994, 34 (5); **390** (Photo) LBJ Library Collection; (Caption) Kathleen Hall Jamieson, *Dirty Politics: Deception, Distraction, and Democracy,* New York: Oxford University Press, 1992.

Chapter 12
404 (Photo) Randall Poindexter; **411** (Photo) SuperStock, Inc.; (Caption) David Wessel, "Prices Take Off for Hot-Selling Used Cars," *Wall Street Journal,* October 18, 1993, 222, No. 76: B1, B3; **412** (Photo) John Greenleigh/Apple Computer, Inc.; (Caption) Dennis Kneale, "IBM, BellSouth Team Up to Sell 'Simon,'" *Wall Street Journal,* October 29, 1993, 222, No. 85: B1, B14. © Apple Computer, Inc. Used with permission. All rights reserved. Apple and the Apple logo are registered trademarks of Apple Computer, Inc.; **413** (Photo) Chris Brown/SABA Press Photos, Inc.; (Caption) Example courtesy of Prof. Vernon Murray (Marist College); **414** (Photo) Cliff Otto/*Los Angeles Times.* **415** (Photo) Blair Seitz/Photo Researchers, Inc.

Chapter 13
436 (Photo) MCI Center; **440** (Ad) Ad Courtesy of Florsheim Shoes; **442** (Photo) Churchill and Klehr; **443** (Photo) Sibley/Peteet Design Inc./Spoetzel Brewery; (Caption) Claire Poole, "It's All in the Image," *Forbes,* March 1, 1993: 77; **451** (Photo) Churchill and Klehr; **454** (Ad) Ad Courtesy of Sanyo; **455** (Photo) John Elk, III; **459** (Ad) Ad courtesy of the Gillette Company; (Caption) Patricia Sellers, "Brands/It's Thrive or Die," *Fortune,* August 23, 1993, 128, No. 4: 53–54.

Chapter 14
468 (Photo) Cecelia Gardner; **470** (Photo) John Elk, III; (Caption) Richard B. Woodward, "Business Is Blooming," *New York Times Magazine,* May 9, 1993: 32–37; **478** (Photo) L. Migdale/Stock Boston; **491** (Ad) Ad Courtesy of Timberland; **492** (Ad) Ad courtesy of Hallmark Cards, Inc.; **498** (Photo) SuperStock, Inc.; **499** (Photo) Larry Grant/FPG International.

Chapter 15
512 (Photo) Göran Carstedt, IKEA; **515** (Photo) Churchill and Klehr; (Caption) Isadore Barmash, "Chain by Chain, Woolworth

Reinvents Itself," *New York Times,* December 13, 1992, F5; Leah Rickard, "Woolworth Walking Down a New Path," *Advertising Age,* May 15, 1995: 4; **520** (Photo) Churchill and Klehr; (Caption) Barnaby J. Feder, "New Links: Retail and Fast Food," *New York Times,* August 16, 1993: D1 (2); Scott Hume, "Blockbuster Means More Than Video," *Ad Age;* Agis Salpukas, "Fill It Up? Send a Fax? Have a Taco?" *New York Times,* December 27, 1993: D1 (2); **522** (Photo) David Simson/Stock Boston; (Caption) Cyndee Miller, "U.S., European Shoppers Seem Pleased with their Supermarkets," *Marketing News,* June 21, 1993: 3; **524** (Photo) Caesars; (Caption) Kenneth Labich, "What It Will Take to Keep People Hanging Out at the Mall?" *Fortune,* May 29, 1995: 102 (5); **526** (Photo) Sony/Antoine Bootz; (Caption) Cyndee Miller, "Retailers Do What They Must to Ring Up Sales," *Marketing News,* May 22, 1995: 1 (3); Jennifer Pellet, "Niketown Takes Off," *DM,* October 1991: 56–57. "Brand Name, High-Profile Stores Create a Splash," *Chain Store Age Executive,* February 1994: 22 (4); **530** (Photo) The Rouse Company; (Caption) John Fondersmith, "Downtown 2040: Making Cities Fun," *Futurist,* March–April 1988, 22: 9–17; **531** (Photo) Jim Mone/AP/Wide World Photos; (Courtesy) Kate Fitzgerald, "Mega Malls," *Advertising Age,* January 27, 1992: S-1. "Country's Biggest Mall Will Offer a School," *New York Times,* January 25, 1994: A17; **540** (Photo) George Lange Photography; **543** (Photo) Göran Carstedt, IKEA.

Chapter 16
552 (Photo) Price/McNabb; **554** (Photo) Churchill and Klehr; (Caption) Stuart Elliott, "Consumer Products Dress Up to Cash in On the Christmas Spirit," *New York Times,* December 16, 1994: D18; **571** (Ad) Ad Courtesy of English Leather; **577** (Ad) Ad courtesy Vibe Online; (Caption) Keith J. Kelly, "Hip-Hopping Onto the Internet," *Advertising Age,* December 5, 1994: 20; **586** (Photo) Walt Disney/Shooting Star International Photo Agency; (Caption) Marcy Magiera, "Disney Units Energize 'Ducks,' 'Lion,'" *Advertising Age,* March 28, 1994: 13; Courtesy of Walt Disney/Shooting Star; **588** (Photo) NTN Communications; (Caption) Sidney Roslow, J.A.F. Nicholls, and Lucette B. Comer, "Measuring Place-Based Media: The Cooperation Challenge," *Marketing Research: A Magazine of Management & Applications,* Winter 1993, 5 (1): 34–39. "Chrysler Inks Deal with NTN to Advertise Neon in Bars," *Advertising Age,* May 16, 1994: 20; **589** (Ad) Ad courtesy of CKS Partners; **590** (Ad) Used with permission from The Biltmore Company; Courtesy of Price/McNabb.

Chapter 17
600 (Photo) Dentsu; **611** (Ad) Ad courtesy of Smith & Nelson; **612** (Photo) California Raisin Advisory Board; **616** (Ad) Ad courtesy of Thermoscan, Inc. **620** (Ad) © Apple Computer, Inc. Used with permission. All rights reserved. Apple ® and the Apple logo are registered trademarks of Apple Computer, Inc.; (Caption) Bradley Johnson, "The Commercial, and the Product, That Changed Advertising," *Advertising Age,* January 10, 1994, 1 (2); **623** (Ad) Ad Courtesy of Burgerville, and Sandstrom Design (Portland, OR); (Caption) Cyndee Miller, "Outdoor Advertising Weathers Repeated Attempts to Kill It," *Marketing News,* March 16, 1992: 1 (2). Lisa Marie Petersen, "Outside Chance," *Mediaweek,* June 15, 1992: 20–23; **627** (Ad) The Incredible Hulk: TM and Copyright 1996, Marvel Characters Inc. All rights reserved; **633** (Ad) Dentsu, Inc.

Chapter 18

642 (Photo) KWE-Karen Weiner Escalera Associates Inc.; **649** (Photo) Oscar Mayer Foods Corporation; (Caption) Oscar Suris, "This Year's 'Leaner' Wienermobile Has a Lot of Beef Under the Hood," *Wall Street Journal,* February 10, 1995: B1; **651** (Photo) Black/Toby; (Caption) Damon Darlin, "Shoe Biz as Show Biz," *Forbes,* June 7, 1993: 58–59; **652** (Photo) Seth Resnick/Stock Boston; (Caption) Carin I. Warner, "Applying Integrated Marketing to Brand Positioning," *Public Relations Journal,* October 1992: 15–16; **653** (Photo) Jim Beam Bourbon and Joseph D'Amore; (Caption) "The (Grand) Mother of All Contests," *Promo: The International Magazine for Promotion Marketing,* August 1994: 54; **654** (Photo) Churchill and Klehr; (Caption) *POPAI/DuPont Consumer Buying Habits Study* (Englewood NJ: Point-of-Purchase Advertising Institute, 1986). Bruce Oman, "Hey, Bubba, It's POP," *Beverage World,* August 1992: Vol. III, 72; **655** (Photo) Anderson Perlstein Ltd.; **659** (Photo) Sampling Corporation of America; (Caption) Linda Mae Carlstone, "A Lesson in Sample Arithmetic," *Advertising Age,* January 2, 1995: 22; **663** (Ad) Ad Courtesy of Ben & Jerry; (Caption) Emily DeNitto, "Ben & Jerry's Flavors CEO Search," *Advertising Age,* November 28, 1994: 42; **664** (Ad) Reproduced with permission of PepsiCo, Inc. 1996, Purchase New York; (Caption) Marcy Magiera, "Pepsi Weathers Tampering Hoaxes," *Advertising Age,* June 21, 1993: 1(2); additional information in Annetta Miller, "The Great Pepsi Panic," *Newsweek,* June 28, 1993:32; **669** (Photo) Finnish National Distillers; (Caption) Stephen Kindel, "Anatomy of a Sports Promotion," *FW,* April 13, 1993: 49–50; **670** (Photo) Boehringer Ingelheim (Canada) Ltd.; (Caption) Suzanne Lyons, "Buys & Dolls," *Sales & Marketing Manager* Canada (MII), May 1992: 10–13; **672** (Photo) Zoomi Oy/Finnish National Distillers.

Chapter 19

679 (Photo) Kathleen Carroll-Mullen; **682** (Photo) Brown Brothers; (Caption) Anusorn Singhapakdi, "Analyzing the Ethical Decision Making of Sales Professionals," *Journal of Personal Selling & Sales Management,* Fall 1991, 1: pp. 1–12. "Brady, Diamond Jim," *The Concise Columbia Encyclopedia,* Columbia University Press, Microsoft Bookshelf, Multimedia Viewer Version 1.00a.358, Microsoft Corp, 1992; **694** (Ad) Ad Courtesy of Rolm; **698** (Ad) Ad courtesy of AETNA; **708** (Photo) Mary Kate Denny/PhotoEdit; (Caption) Perri Capell, "Are Good Salespeople Born or Made," *American Demographics,* July 1993: 12–13. Gabriella Stern, "Europeans Borrow U.S. Trick: Making Car Buyer Feel Special," *Wall Street Journal,* March 7, 1995: B1. "More Women Selling Cars; Customers Like That," *Marketing News,* January 2, 1995: 39. Nancy Arnott, "Car Buyers Favor Women Sellers," *Sales & Marketing Management,* January 1995: 11. **709** (Photo) Southwestern Company; (Caption) Ginger Trumfio, "School Was Never Like This," *Sales and Marketing Management,* September 1994: 106 (6); **710** (Ad) Ad Courtesy of Mary Kay; (Caption) Pete Hoke, "Glamorous Database," *Direct Marketing,* July 1989: 54–56, 67–68. **710** (Ad) Alan Farnham, "Mary Kay's Lessons in Leadership," *Fortune,* September 20, 1993: 68–77; **712** (Ad) Ad Courtesy of Amway; **715** (Photo) General Electric.

GLOSSARY

ABC model of attitudes A behavioral theory suggesting that an attitude has three components—affect, behavior, and cognition—and emphasizing the interrelationships among knowing, feeling, and doing (p. 197).

advertising Nonpersonal communication paid for by an identified sponsor using mass media to persuade or inform (p. 601).

advertising appeal The central idea or theme of an advertising message (p. 614).

advertising campaign A coordinated, comprehensive communications plan that is tied to promotion objectives and results in a series of messages placed in different media over a specified time period (p. 608).

advocacy advertising A type of public service advertising provided by an organization that is seeking to influence public opinion on an issue because it has some stake in the outcome (p. 608).

AIDA A formula consisting of four requirements for effective advertising messages: attention, interest, desire, and action (p. 614).

approach The first step of the actual sales presentation, in which the salesperson tries to learn more about customer's needs, create a good impression, and build rapport (p. 694).

atmospherics The use of color, lighting, scents, furnishings, and other design elements to create a desired store image (p. 525).

attention The degree to which consumers focus on marketing stimuli within their range of exposure (p. 191).

attitude A learned predisposition to respond favorably or unfavorably to stimuli, based on relatively enduring evaluations of people, objects, and issues (p. 197).

augmented services The core service plus additional services provided to enhance its value (p. 378).

bait-and-switch pricing An illegal marketing practice in which an advertised price special is used as bait to get customers into the store with the intention of switching them to a higher-priced item (p. 425).

bartering The practice of exchanging a good or service for another good or service of like value (p. 405).

behavioral learning theories Theories of learning that focus on how consumer behavior is changed by external events, or stimuli (p. 195).

behavioral segmentation A way to segment consumer markets based on how they act toward, feel about, or use a good or service (p. 274).

benefit The outcome sought by a customer that motivates buying behavior; the value the customer receives from owning, using, or experiencing a product (pp. 4, 297).

benefit segmentation A way to segment consumer markets based on the different benefits they want in purchasing and using a product (p. 276).

bidding Offering a price that a business or government customer will evaluate and compare to competing offers (p. 455).

bonus pack A special container that gives the consumer more of the product than usual for the same price (p. 657).

brand A name, a term, a symbol, or any other unique element of a product that identifies one firm's products and sets them apart from those of other producers (p. 343).

brand competition A marketing situation in which firms offering similar products or services compete for consumers based on their brand's reputation or perceived benefits (p. 100).

brand equity The value of a brand related to the brand's ability to attract future customers reliably (p. 348).

brand extensions New products that are marketed with the brand name of existing products, often in a different product category (p. 349).

brand loyalty A form of repeat purchasing behavior based on a conscious decision to continue buying a product with a particular brand or trademark (p. 348).

brand manager An individual who is responsible for developing and implementing the marketing plan for a single brand (p. 335).

brand personality A distinctive image created for a brand that captures its character and the benefits it delivers (p. 282).

break-even analysis A method for determining the number of units that will have to be produced and sold at a given price to break even—that is, to neither make a profit nor suffer a loss (p. 418).

bundling A services marketing practice in which services are packaged together (sometimes with tangible goods as well) to provide added value (p. 379).

business and organizational customers Business firms and other organizations that buy goods and services for some purpose other than for personal consumption (p. 225).

business cycle The overall patterns of change in the economy—including periods of prosperity, recession, depression, and recovery—that affect consumer and business purchasing power (p. 98).

business ethics Rules of conduct for an organization that are standards against which most people in its environments judge what is right and what is wrong (p. 75).

business portfolio The group of different businesses, products, or brands owned by an organization and characterized by different income-generating and growth capabilities (p. 46).

business-to-business marketing Marketing activities that facilitate transactions involving goods and services that business and organizational customers need to produce other goods and services for resale and to support their operations (p. 225).

business-to-business selling The selling of goods and services to individuals or groups who purchase for some reason other than personal consumption (p. 691).

buy class One of three classes used by business buyers to characterize the degree of time and effort required to make a decision in a buying situation (p. 242).

buyer The member of a business buying center who has the formal authority and responsibility for executing the purchase (p. 245).

buying center The group of people in an organization who influence and participate in particular purchasing decisions (p. 244).

canned sales presentation A standard, memorized sales presentation (p. 696).

cannibalization The loss of sales of an existing product when a new item in a product line or product family is introduced (p. 331).

capacity management The process by which the offering is adjusted in an attempt to match demand (p. 385).

captive pricing A pricing tactic for two items that must be used together; one item is priced very low, and the firm makes its profit on another, high-margin item that is essential to the operation of the first item (p. 458).

causal research A type of problem-solving research that seeks to identify the cause or reason for a marketing phenomenon of interest (p. 174).

cause marketing Marketing activities in which firms seek to have their corporate identity linked to a good cause through advertising, public service, and publicity (pp. 84, 391).

centralized purchasing A business buying practice in which all organizational purchasing is performed by a central purchasing department (p. 240).

chain-markup pricing A pricing strategy that extends demand-backward pricing from the ultimate consumer all the way back through the channel of distribution to the manufacturer (p. 450).

channel leader A firm at one level of distribution that takes a leadership role, establishing operating norms and processes that reduce channel conflicts, minimize costs, and enhance delivered customer value (p. 492).

channel levels The number of distinct units that populate a channel of distribution (p. 478).

channel of distribution An organized network of firms that work together to get a product from producer to consumer or business customer (p. 470).

clustered demand Demand in which most people prefer one of a set of several product varieties (p. 264).

co-branding An agreement between two brands to work together in marketing a new product (p. 351).

cognitive learning theories Theories of learning that stress the importance of internal mental processes and that view people as problem solvers who actively use information from the world around them to master their environment (p. 196).

comparative advantage The superiority of one country in producing certain products due to its resources, technology, or some other factor that gives it an advantage over other countries (p. 121).

comparative advertising An advertising strategy wherein a message compares two or more specifically named or recognizably presented brands in terms of one or more specific attributes (p. 572).

competitive advantage An advantage over competitors that an organization gains through its superior capabilities and unique product benefits that provide a greater value in the minds of customers (p. 52).

competitive bids A business buying process in which two or more suppliers submit proposals (including price and associated data) for a proposed purchase and the firm providing the better offer is awarded the bid (p. 231).

compiled list A purchased (or rented) list that is made up of names taken from secondary sources (p. 582).

concentrated marketing strategy A marketing strategy in which a firm focuses its efforts on offering one or more products to a single segment (p. 279).

concept stores Retailers that carry only their own brands, usually in stylish or *avant garde* settings (p. 526).

consumer The ultimate user of a purchased good or service (p. 3).

consumer behavior The processes involved when individuals or groups select, purchase, use, and dispose of goods, services, ideas, or experiences to satisfy needs and desires (p. 189).

Consumer Bill of Rights The rights of consumers to be protected by the federal government, as outlined by President John F. Kennedy, including the right to safety, the right to be informed, the right to be heard, and the right to choose (p. 82).

consumer confidence An indicator of future spending patterns as measured by the extent to which people are optimistic or pessimistic about the state of the economy (p. 99).

consumer goods The good purchased by individual consumers for personal or family use (p. 7).

consumer orientation A management philosophy that focuses on ways to satisfy customers' needs and wants (p. 19).

consumerism A social movement directed toward protecting consumers from harmful business practices (p. 81).

contact management A communications strategy that seeks to provide communications exposures where and when the targeted customer is most likely to receive them (p. 587).

continuous innovation A modification of an existing product used to set one brand apart from its competitors (p. 306).

control Measuring actual performance, comparing it to planned performance, and making necessary changes in plans and implementation (p. 63).

convenience product A consumer good or service that is usually low-priced, widely available, and purchased frequently, with a minimum of comparison and effort (p. 301).

convenience stores Neighborhood retailers that carry a limited number of frequently purchased items, including basic food products, newspapers, and sundries, and cater to consumers who are willing to pay a premium for the ease of buying close to home (p. 521).

conventional marketing system A multiple-level distribution channel in which channel members work independently to perform channel functions (p. 487).

copy testing A procedure that measures whether an ad is received, comprehended, and responded to in the desired manner (p. 629).

core service The basic benefit that is obtained as a result of having a service performed (p. 378).

corporate culture The set of values, norms, beliefs, and practices held by an organization's managers (p. 93).

corporate goals Broadly defined outcomes an organization hopes to achieve within the time frame of its long-term strategic plan (p. 44).

cost per thousand (CPM) A measure used to compare the relative cost-effectiveness of different media vehicles that have different exposure rates; the cost to deliver a message to one thousand people or homes or circulated copies of a media vehicle (p. 627).

cost-plus pricing A method of setting prices in which the seller totals all the costs for the product and then adds an amount for overhead and profit (p. 447).

coupons Printed certificates redeemable for money off on a purchase (p. 656).

creative selling process The process of seeking out customers, analyzing needs, determining how product attributes might provide benefits for the customer, and then communicating that information (p. 692).

critical incident technique A method for measuring service quality in which customer complaints are used to identify *critical inci-*

dents, specific face-to-face contacts between consumers and service providers that cause problems and lead to dissatisfaction (p. 377).

cross-functional planning An approach to planning in which managers work together in developing tactical plans for each functional area in the firm, so that each plan considers the objectives of the other areas (p. 51).

cultural diversity A management practice that emphasizes people of different sexes, races, ethnic groups, and religions in activities involving an organization's employees, customers, suppliers, and distribution channel partners (p. 85).

culture The learned values and patterns of behavior that stem from the shared meanings, rituals, and traditions among the members of a society and that influence their attitudes, beliefs, preferences, and priorities toward abstract ideas, activities, and products (p. 203).

custom marketing strategy A marketing strategy in which a firm develops a separate marketing mix for each customer (p. 279).

customer Any person or organization that receives a product of value in the marketing exchange process, whether or not the person or organization will be the actual user of the product (p. 6).

customized service A service designed and delivered so that each customer receives a unique product that has been tailored to meet his or her specific needs (p. 380).

database marketing The creation of an ongoing relationship with a set of customers who have an identifiable interest in a product and whose responses to promotional efforts become part of future communications attempts (p. 553).

decider The member of a business buying center who has the authority to make the final purchase decision (p. 245).

decline stage The final stage in the product life cycle in which sales decrease as customer needs change (p. 317).

decoding The receiver's assigning of meaning to a message (p. 572).

demand Customers' desire for products coupled with the resources to obtain them; the amount of a product that customers will be willing to buy at different prices, all other things being equal (pp. 5, 409).

demand management Procedures that attempt to smooth demand by encouraging service usage during slack times and/or discouraging patronage during peak times (p. 383).

demand-backward pricing A method for setting price that starts with a customer-pleasing price and then applies cost-management strategies to produce the product at a cost that enables the firm to sell it at that price (p. 450).

demand-based pricing A method for setting price that is based on an estimate of demand at different prices (p. 449).

demographics The measurable characteristics of a population, including size, age, gender, ethnic group, income, education, occupation, and family structure (pp. 109, 266).

department stores Retailers who sell a broad range of items and a good selection within each product line (p. 523).

derived demand Demand for business or organizational products derived from demand for consumer goods or services (p. 228).

descriptive research A type of problem-solving research that seeks to describe a specific issue or problem without looking for the reason or cause of the phenomenon (p. 174).

developed country A country at the highest level of economic development, characterized by high standards of living, extensive use of modern technology, a high per-capita GDP, and a high market potential for limitless goods and services (p. 124).

developing country A country at the middle stage of economic development, characterized by rising standards of living, some use of technology, a relatively low GDP, a high market potential for many goods, and a potentially attractive labor supply (p. 122).

differential benefits Values customers obtain from using, experiencing, or possessing a firm's product that are superior to those of competing products (p. 53).

differentiated marketing strategy A marketing strategy in which a firm develops one or more products for each of several distinct customer groups (p. 279).

diffused demand Demand in which most people have very specific preferences that are not the same for everyone (p. 264).

diffusion of innovations The process by which the use of an innovation spreads throughout a society or a population (p. 308).

direct channel A channel of distribution in which there are no intermediaries or middle levels (p. 480).

direct marketing Exposing a consumer to information about a good or service through a nonpersonal medium and convincing the customer to respond with an order (p. 535).

discontinuous innovation A totally new product that creates major changes in the way we live (p. 308).

discount stores Retailers who offer a wide variety of inexpensive brand-name items in a self-service, "no-frills" setting (p. 522).

distinctive competency A superior capability of a firm in comparison to its direct competitors (p. 52).

diversification Growth strategies that emphasize both new products and new markets (p. 50).

durable goods Consumer products that provide benefits over a period of time such as cars, furniture, and appliances (p. 300).

dynamically continuous innovation A pronounced change in an existing product (p. 308).

early adopters The approximately 13.5 percent of adopters who try an innovation very early in the diffusion process but after the innovators (p. 312).

early majority The approximately 34 percent of the population whose adoption of a new product signals a general acceptance of the innovation (p. 312).

economic community A group of countries that have agreed to work together in the regulation of international trade for the good of all member nations (p. 124).

economic sanctions Government actions that prohibit or restrict trade with a particular country for political reasons (p. 127).

electronic data interchange (EDI) A method for tracking goods in transit through the use of information technology; in EDI systems, electronic scanners capture bar code information on goods, which are then tracked by computer (p. 502).

encoding The process of translating an idea into a form of communication that will convey meaning (p. 569).

entrepreneurs Individuals who assume the risks in owning, organizing, and managing their own businesses (pp. 94, 336).

environmental stewardship A position taken by an organization to protect or enhance the natural environment as it conducts its business activities (p. 83).

evaluative criteria The dimensions (or product characteristics) used to judge the merits of competing options (p. 211).

evoked set The set of alternative brands actively considered during a consumer's choice process, which includes known products and brands already stored in the person's memory, plus those that are prominent in the marketplace (p. 211).

exchange The process by which some transfer of value occurs between a buyer and a seller (p. 5).

exclusive distribution Selling a product only through a single outlet in a particular region (p. 490).

execution format The specific technique used to present an advertising message (p. 616).

experiment A research methodology in which prespecified relationships among variables are tested in a controlled environment (p. 174).

exploratory research A type of marketing research designed to investigate or explore a marketing issue or problem that is not well defined by gathering qualitative descriptive information from a small group of consumers (p. 162).

export merchants Intermediaries in international trade who negotiate sales in foreign countries on behalf of exporting firms for a fee or commission (p. 134).

exposure The degree to which a marketing stimulus is within range of the consumer's sensory receptors (p. 190).

expropriation The official seizure of foreign-owned property in a country, frequently without full-value payment to the foreign owners (p. 128).

external environment The uncontrollable elements outside of an organization that may affect its performance either positively or negatively (p. 53).

family brand A brand that is shared by a group of individual products or individual brands (p. 349).

family life cycle A means of characterizing consumers within a family structure based on different stages through which people pass as they grow older (p. 201).

feedback The reactions of the receiver to the message, which are communicated back to the source (p. 572).

fixed costs Costs of production that do not change with the number of units produced (p. 417).

focus group An exploratory research technique in which a small group of participants is recruited to join in a discussion about a product, an ad, or some other topic of interest to marketers (p. 171).

Form utility The consumer benefit provided by organizations when they change raw materials into finished products desired by consumers (p. 22).

franchising A contractual arrangement that assigns limited rights to an entire business to another in exchange for a fee or royalties on sales (p. 135).

free trade zone A designated area within a country where outside firms can warehouse and package imported goods without paying taxes or tariffs until the goods are moved from the free trade zone area to other areas of the country (p. 142).

free-standing inserts (FSIs) Preprinted advertising pages which are placed in newspapers and magazines (p. 656).

frequency The average number of times a person in a target group will be exposed to the message (p. 626).

frequency marketing A marketing strategy that reinforces regular customers by giving them prizes that accumulate in value as the customer continues to patronize the company (p. 274).

gap analysis A marketing research methodology that measures the difference between a customer's expectation of service quality and what actually occurred (p. 377).

gatekeeper The member of a business buying center who controls the flow of information to other members (p. 245).

General Agreement on Tariffs and Trade (GATT) A series of agreements that promotes international trade among participating countries by reducing taxes and restrictions (p. 128).

geodemography A way to segment consumer markets based on geography combined with demographics (p. 270).

goods Tangible products—ones that can be seen, touched, smelled, and/or tasted (p. 296).

government markets The federal, state, county, and local governments that buy goods to carry out public objectives and to support their operations (p. 238).

green marketing A marketing strategy that supports environmental stewardship by creating an environmentally founded differential benefit in the minds of consumers (p. 83).

gross margin Revenue minus the cost of goods sold, calculated as a percentage of sales; the amount a retailer makes on an item (p. 519).

gross rating points (GRPs) A measure used for comparing the effectiveness of different media vehicles; average reach times frequency (p. 626).

growth stage The second stage of the product life cycle during which the product is accepted and sales rapidly increase (p. 316).

heuristics The "rules" or mental shortcuts people use to simplify the decision-making process and make choices among alternative brands (p. 212).

homogenous demand Demand in which most people prefer the same product characteristics (p. 264).

horizontal marketing system An arrangement within a channel of distribution in which two or more firms at one channel level work together for a common purpose (p. 490).

hypermarkets Retailers with the characteristics of both warehouse stores and supermarkets; hypermarkets are several times larger than other stores and offer virtually everything from grocery items to electronics (p. 523).

implementation The stage of the strategic management process in which strategies are put into action on a day-to-day basis (p. 63).

indirect distribution Distribution of goods in which manufacturers reach end users through intermediaries—wholesalers, dealers, distributors, agents and/or retailers (p. 481).

industrial goods Goods bought by individuals or organizations for further processing or for use in doing business (p. 8).

industrial market The individuals or organizations that purchase products for use in the production of other goods and services to be resold at a profit and for their business operations (p. 235).

inertia A form of repeat purchasing behavior based on habit because this takes less effort. (p. 348)

influencer The member of a business buying center who affects the buying decision by dispensing advice or sharing expertise (p. 245).

infomercial A paid message broadcast to a TV audience in a format resembling a legitimate program (p. 558).

initiator The member of a business buying center who first recognizes that a purchase needs to be made and notifies others in the organization (p. 245).

innovations In marketing, an innovation is a product (a food, service, or idea) that is perceived to be new and different from existing products (p. 303).

innovators The first segment (roughly 2.5 percent) of a population to adopt a product (p. 311).

inside selling Selling (other than in-store selling) conducted at the organization's place of business (p. 690).

integrated marketing communications (IMC) A strategy in which an organization coordinates the different types of communication, from advertising to company letterhead, to reach customers with a message that is clear, that is consistent, and that maintains this positive relationship with them over time (p. 553).

intensive distribution Selling a product through all suitable wholesalers or retailers who are willing to stock and sell the product (p. 490).

interactive marketing A promotion practice in which customized marketing communications elicit a measurable response from individual receivers (p. 573).

internal environment The controllable elements inside an organization including its people, its facilities, and how it does things that influence the operations of the organization (p. 53).

internal marketing Marketing activities aimed at employees in an effort to inform them about the firm's offerings and their high quality (p. 375).

introduction stage The first stage of the product life cycle in which slow growth follows the introduction of a new product in the marketplace (p. 315).

inventory control A process developed to ensure that the types and quantities of goods needed to meet customers' demands are always available (p. 502).

inventory turnover The average number of times a year a retailer expects to sell its inventory (p. 519).

involvement The relative importance of the perceived consequences of the purchase to a consumer (p. 209).

joint venture A strategic equity alliance that usually results in a jointly run corporate entity (p. 137).

just-in-time (JIT) Inventory management and purchasing practices used by manufacturers and resellers that reduce inventory and stock to very low levels, but ensure that deliveries from suppliers arrive just when needed (p. 250).

laggards The roughly 16 percent of consumers who are the last to adopt an innovation (p. 312).

late majority The roughly 34 percent of adopters who are willing to try new products

only when there is little or no risk associated with the purchase, when the purchase becomes an economic necessity, or when there is social pressure to purchase (p. 312).

learning A relatively permanent change in consumer behavior that is caused by experience or acquired information (p. 195).

less-developed country A country at the lowest stage of economic development, characterized by low standards of living, little or no technology, extremely low per capita GDP, and limited market potential (p. 122).

leveling of domestic demand A market condition in which such factors as market saturation, changing tastes, and improved technology reduce domestic demand and prohibit business growth (p. 121).

licensing Agreement in which one firm sells another firm the right to use a brand name for a specific purpose and for a specific period of time (pp. 135, 350).

lifestyle The pattern of living that determines how people choose to spend their time, money, and energy and that reflects their values, tastes, and preferences (pp. 110, 203).

limit pricing A pricing strategy in which a firm sets a price low enough to discourage competition from entering the market but still high enough to make a profit (p. 453).

list price The price the end customer is expected to pay, as determined by the manufacturer (p. 458).

local content rules Government regulations on the production of goods by foreign manufacturers that control the portion of domestic components used in the manufacturing process (p. 129).

localization An international marketing perspective in which marketing mix strategies are adapted for different global markets (p. 143).

loss leader An advertised item that is offered and sold at or below cost in order to increase store traffic (p. 425).

marginal analysis A method of analysis that uses costs and demands to identify the price that will maximize profits (p. 420).

marginal cost The increase in total cost that results from producing one additional unit of a product (p. 421).

marginal revenue The increase in total revenue (income) that results from producing and selling one additional unit of a product (p. 421).

market All of the customers and potential customers who share a common need that can be satisfied by a specific product, who have the resources to exchange for it, who are willing to make the exchange, and who have the authority to make the exchange (p. 7).

market development Growth strategies that introduce existing products to new markets (p. 50).

market fragmentation A condition in society in which people are divided into many different groups with distinct needs and wants (p. 261).

market manager An individual who is responsible for developing and implementing the marketing plans for products sold to a particular customer group (p. 355).

market penetration Growth strategies designed to increase sales of existing products to current customers, nonusers, and users of competitive brands in served markets; the number of wholesalers or retailers who carry a product within a given market (pp. 49, 483).

market potential The maximum demand expected among consumers in a potential market segment for a good or service (pp. 122, 277).

market segmentation A process whereby marketers divide a large customer group into segments that share important characteristics (p. 264).

marketing The process of planning and executing the conception, pricing, promotion, and distribution of ideas, goods, and services to create exchanges that satisfy individual and organizational objectives (p. 3).

marketing budget A statement of the total amount to be spent on the marketing function and the allocation of money or the spending limit for each activity under a marketer's control (p. 63).

marketing concept A management orientation that focuses on identifying and satisfying consumer needs to ensure the organization's long-term profitability objectives (p. 3).

marketing decision support system (MDSS) A computer-based subsystem of an MIS that helps marketing managers access the MIS database and analyze data to make informed decisions (p. 153).

marketing information system (MIS) An organization's system for continuously gathering, sorting, analyzing, storing, and distributing to managers relevant and timely marketing information (p. 153).

marketing intelligence Information gathered from sources outside the firm about developments in the firm's business environment, including the activities of competitors, that affect the firm (p. 154).

marketing plan A document that identifies where the organization is now, where it wants to go, how it plans to get there, and who will be responsible for carrying out each part of the marketing strategy (p. 62).

marketing research Systematic and objective collection, analysis, and interpretation of data for use in making informed marketing decisions (p. 158).

mass customization A marketing strategy in which a firm modifies a basic good or service to meet an individual customer's needs (p. 280).

mass market All possible customers in a market, regardless of the differences in their specific needs and wants (p. 14).

mass merchandisers Retailers who offer a very large assortment of items (p. 523).

maturity stage The third and longest stage in the product life cycle in which sales peak and level off (p. 316).

media planning The process of developing media objectives, strategies, and tactics for use in an advertising campaign (p. 625).

media schedule The plan that specifies what media will be used and when the messages will be sent (p. 625).

medium A communications vehicle through which a message is transmitted to a target audience (p. 572).

merchandise assortment The range of products sold (p. 521).

merchandise breadth The number of different product lines available (p. 521).

merchandise depth The variety of choices available for each specific product (p. 521).

merchant wholesalers Intermediaries who buy goods from producers (take title to them) and sell to other producers, wholesalers, and retailers (p. 476).

message The communication in physical form that is sent from a sender to a receiver (p. 570).

mission statement A formal statement in an organization's strategic plan that describes the overall purpose of the organization and what it intends to achieve in terms of its customers, products, and resources (p. 42).

missionary salespeople Salespeople who promote the firm and try to stimulate demand for a product but do not actually complete a sale (p. 689).

modified rebuy A buying situation classification used by business buyers to categorize a previously made purchase that involves some change and that requires limited decision making (p. 243).

monopolistic competition A market structure in which many firms, each having slightly different products, compete in a market with many buyers by offering the consumer unique benefits that could allow one firm to monopolize the market (p. 101).

monopoly A market situation in which one firm, the only supplier of a particular product, is able to control the price, quality, and supply of that product (p. 101).

motivation An internal state that activates goal-directed behavior on the part of consumers in order to satisfy some need (p. 193).

multilevel marketing A pyramid type of channel of distribution in which independent contractors earn commissions on the products they sell and on the sales of others whom they recruit into the business (p. 489).

multiple sourcing The business practice of buying a particular product form several different suppliers (p. 230).

myths Stories that contain symbolic elements and express the shared emotions and ideals of a culture (p. 25).

narrowcasting The use of marketing communications in magazines or other media

tailored to the needs of small groups of people (p. 261).

national or manufacturer brands Brands that are owned by the manufacturer of the product (p. 350).

nationalization The official seizure of foreign-owned property in a country, without any payment to the foreign owners (p. 128).

need Recognition of any difference between a consumer's actual state and some ideal or desired state (p. 3).

New Era orientation A management philosophy in which marketing decision making means a devotion to excellence in designing and producing products that benefit the customer plus the firm's employees, shareholders, and fellow citizens (p. 20).

new-task buy A buying situation classification used by business buyers to categorize a new purchase that is complex or risky and that requires extensive decision making (p. 244).

niche brands Small brands that successfully compete with power brands by appealing to a narrow segment of the market (p. 350).

niche market A particularly small market segment in which a firm may often face little or no competition (p. 279).

noise Anything that interferes with effective communication (p. 572).

nondurable goods Consumer products that provide benefits for only a short time because they are consumed (such as food) or are no longer useful (such as newspapers) (p. 300).

nonprofit institutional markets The organizations with charitable, educational, community, and other public-service goals that buy goods and services to support their functions and to attract and serve their members (p. 238).

nonstore retailing Any method used to complete an exchange with a product end user that does not require a customer visit to a store (p. 534).

observational techniques Exploratory research techniques that attempt to identify people's behavior by observing their everyday activities and gathering in-depth qualitative data to understand that behavior (p. 172).

off-price retailers Retailers who buy excess merchandise from well-known manufacturers and pass the savings on to customers (p. 522).

oligopoly A market structure in which a relatively small number of sellers, each holding a substantial share of the market, compete in a market with many buyers (p. 101).

omnibus survey A research method in which a research firm asks questions on behalf of many clients in a study of a large representative sample of consumers (p. 158).

operational planning A decision process that focuses on developing detailed plans for day-to-day activities that carry out an organization's tactical plans (p. 41).

opinion leader A person who is frequently able to influence others' attitudes or behaviors by virtue of his or her active interest and expertise in one or more product categories (p. 206).

order getter A salesperson who works creatively to develop relationships with customers or to generate new sales (p. 688).

order taker A salesperson whose primary function is to facilitate transactions that are initiated by the customer (p. 689).

outside selling A form of selling in which salespeople visit face-to-face with customers away from the selling company's place of business (p. 690).

outsourcing The business buying practice of obtaining outside vendors to provide goods or services that otherwise might be supplied "in house" (p. 230).

package The covering or container for a product that protects the product, facilitates product use and storage, and supplies important marketing communication (p. 351).

parity pricing A method for setting prices in which a firm seeks to keep prices about equal to those of the key competitors, thus eliminating price as a consumer's point of comparison (p. 452).

patent Legal documentation saying that an individual or firm has exclusive rights to use a particular invention (p. 339).

penetration pricing A pricing strategy in which a new product is introduced at a very low price to encourage more customers to purchase it (p. 457).

perception The process by which people select, organize, and interpret stimuli to the five senses of sight, sound, smell, touch, and taste (p. 189).

perceptual map A research technique that constructs a graphical representation of where products or brands are "located" in relation to each other in consumers' minds (p. 283).

perfect competition A market structure in which many small sellers, all of whom offer similar products, are unable to control the quality, price, or supply of a product (p. 101).

personal selling The part of the promotion mix that involves direct contact between a company representative and a customer (p. 680).

personality The psychological characteristics that consistently influence the way a person responds to situations in his or her environment (p. 198).

place utility The consumer benefit provided when organizations make products available where customers want them (p. 22).

point of purchase (POP) An element of sales promotion that includes displays and signs for use in the retail outlet (p. 654).

point of sale (POS) systems Retail computer systems that collect sales data and are hooked directly into the store's inventory control system (p. 541).

political risk assessment A process in which international marketers weigh a foreign country's market potential against political conditions that may hinder marketing success (p. 127).

popular culture The music, movies, sports, books, celebrities, and other forms of entertainment consumed by the mass market (p. 25).

portfolio analysis A management tool for evaluating a firm's business mix and assessing the potential of an organization's strategic business units (p. 47).

positioning The marketing practice of determining and influencing how a brand is perceived by consumers relative to the competition (p. 281).

possession utility The consumer benefits provided by an organization by allowing the consumer to own, use, and/or enjoy the product (p. 22).

power brand The dominant brand in a product category (p. 349).

pre-approach A part of the selling process that includes developing information about prospective customers and planning the sales interview (p. 693).

predatory pricing Low pricing policies designed to drive competitors out of business (p. 426).

premiums Items that are offered to people who have bought a product (p. 653).

press release A description of some event that is sent to newspaper and magazine editors in the hope that it will be published as a news item (p. 669).

price The amount of outlay—that is, money, goods, services, or deeds—that is given in exchange for a product (p. 405).

price allowance A type of trade sales promotion in which a manufacturer reduces prices to retailers (p. 649).

price bundling Selling two or more goods or services as a single package for one price (p. 458).

price deal A temporary price reduction offered by a manufacturer to stimulate sales (p. 656).

price discrimination The illegal practice of offering the same product to different business customers at different prices and thus lessening competition (p. 426).

price elasticity of demand A measure of the sensitivity of customers to changes in price; the percentage change in unit sales that results from a percentage change in price (p. 412).

price fixing The collaboration of two or more firms in setting prices, usually to keep prices high (p. 426).

price leader The firm that sets price first in an industry; other major firms in the industry follow the leader by setting similar prices (p. 451).

price lining The practice of setting a limited number of different specific prices, called price points, for items in a product line (p. 424).

price subsidy Government payments made to producers that reimburse the producer who sells a product below some set price level; the subsidy can be in the form of either a cash payment or tax relief (p. 445).

price-floor pricing A method for calculating price in which, to maintain full plant operating capacity, a portion of a firm's output may be sold at a price that only covers marginal costs of production (p. 448).

primary data Data specifically collected and organized for a particular marketing information need or to solve a particular marketing problem (p. 156).

problem-solving research A type of marketing research designed to provide actionable information on a specific issue or problem by collecting measurable quantitative responses or observations of consumers who are representative of a larger consumer group (p. 163).

product A tangible good, a service, an idea, or some combination of these that, through the exchange process, satisfies consumer or business customer needs; a bundle of attributes including features, functions, benefits, and uses (pp. 7, 294).

product adoption The process by which an individual begins to use a good, service, or idea (p. 308).

product category manager An individual who is responsible for developing and implementing the marketing plan for all of the brands and products within a product category (p. 335).

product competition A marketing situation in which competitors offering very different products compete to satisfy the same consumer needs and wants (p. 100).

product development Growth strategies that focus on selling new products in served markets (p. 50).

product life cycle Concept that explains how products go through four distinct stages from birth to death: introduction, growth, maturity, and decline (p. 314).

product line A firm's total product offering designed to satisfy a single need or desire of target customers (p. 329).

product mix The total set of all products offered for sale by a firm, including all product lines sold to all customer groups (p. 331).

production orientation Management philosophy that emphasizes the most efficient ways to produce and distribute products (p. 17).

projective techniques A group of exploratory research techniques that attempt to identify people's underlying feelings by asking them to respond to an ambiguous object, picture, or other stimulus (p. 172).

promotion The coordination of efforts by a marketer to inform or persuade consumers or organizations about goods, services, or ideas (p. 553).

promotion mix The major elements of marketer-controlled communications, including advertising, sales promotions, publicity and public relations, and personal selling (p. 555).

promotion plan A document that outlines the strategies for developing, implementing, and controlling the firm's promotion activities (p. 560).

prospecting A part of the selling process that includes identifying and developing a list of potential or prospective customers (p. 692).

protectionism Government policies that erect trade barriers to protect a country's domestic industries (p. 128).

public relations Activities of organizations aimed at influencing the way consumers, stockholders, and others feel about brands, companies, politicians, celebrities, not-for-profit organizations, and governments (p. 662).

publicity Unpaid communication in the mass media regarding a company, product, or event (p. 664).

publics Groups of people—including customers, employees, shareholders, financial institutions, government, the media, and public interest groups—that have an interest in an organization (p. 95).

pull strategy A promotion strategy in which a company tries to convince consumers to want their products in anticipation that retailers will stock the items demanded (p. 563).

push strategy A promotion strategy in which a company tries to move its products through the channel by convincing channel members to offer them (p. 563).

qualify(ing) A part of the selling process that determines how likely a prospect is to become a customer (p. 693).

quality The level of performance, dependability, and cost that customers expect in products that satisfy their needs and wants (p. 87).

quantity discounts A pricing strategy of charging reduced prices for purchases of larger quantities of a product (p. 458).

quota A government trade regulation limiting the quantity of certain goods that is allowed entry into a country (p. 128).

reach The proportion of the target market that will be exposed to the media vehicle (p. 626).

rebate A short-term offer that enables the consumer to get back part of the product's original cost by mail directly from the manufacturer (p. 656).

receiver The organization or individual that intercepts and interprets the message (p. 572).

reference group A set of people that a consumer is motivated to please or imitate and that influence consumer purchasing to the extent that the purchase is conspicuous to others (p. 205).

Reilly's law of retail gravitation A theory to explain how a store's trading area is affected by its proximity to a population center (p. 532).

relationship marketing A marketing philosophy that focuses on building long-term relationships with customers to satisfy mutual needs (p. 13).

relationship selling A form of personal selling in which the salesperson seeks to develop a mutually satisfying relationship with the customer so they can work together to satisfy each others' needs (p. 682).

reliability An evaluation criterion that indicates the extent to which marketing research techniques are dependable and consistent and will give the same results time after time (p. 165).

repositioning When a brand's original "personality" is altered, often to appeal to a different market segment (p. 286).

representativeness An evaluation criterion for marketing research that indicates the extent to which data collected from respondents can be generalized to the larger customer group (p. 165).

research design The overall research plan that specifies the appropriate research techniques to be used for conducting a research study (p. 170).

reseller markets The individuals or organizations that buy finished goods for the purpose of reselling, renting, or leasing to others at a profit and for maintaining their business operations (p. 237).

response list A list of individuals or organizations that have an identifiable interest in the product and a history of responding to direct marketing promotions (p. 582).

retail life-cycle theory A theory of retailing that focuses on the various life-cycle stages from introduction to decline (p. 514).

retailing The final stop in the distribution channel by which goods and services are sold to consumers for their personal use (p. 512).

sales closing The stage of the selling process in which the salesperson actually asks the customer to buy the product (p. 699).

sales follow-up Sales activities that provide important services to customers after the sale (p. 701).

sales management The process of planning, implementing, and controlling the personal selling function of an organization (p. 701).

sales orientation A management philosophy that emphasizes aggressive sales practices and sees marketing strictly as a sales function (p. 19).

sales presentation The part of the selling process in which the salesperson seeks to persuasively communicate the product's features and the benefits it will provide (p. 695).

sales promotions Short-term programs to build interest in, or encourage purchase of, a good or service during a specified time period (p. 643).

sales support personnel Company representatives who provide support or assistance to the sales force but are not involved in actually making sales (p. 689).

sales team A group of individuals with different skills or expertise who work together in selling products to customers (p. 690).

scrambled merchandising A retail strategy in which a store carries a combination of food and nonfood items in order to increase profitability (p. 520).

screening The process of examining the prospects of a product concept achieving technical and commercial success (p. 338).

secondary data Data used by marketing, but gathered for some purpose other than a current marketing information need (p. 156).

segmentation variables Characteristics of customers that will allow the total market to be divided into fairly homogenous groups, each with different needs that can be profitably met by a firm (p. 265).

selective distribution Distribution using fewer outlets than in intensive distribution but more than in exclusive distribution (p. 492).

self-concept An individual's self-image that is composed of a mixture of beliefs, observations, and feelings about personal attributes (p. 198).

service encounter The actual interaction between the customer and the service provider (p. 373).

service system The set of interrelated procedures and facilities that work together to produce the service product (p. 381).

services Intangible products that are exchanged directly from the producer to the customer (p. 296).

shopping product A good or service for which consumers will spend considerable time and effort gathering information and comparing a number of different alternatives before making a purchase (p. 302).

single sourcing The business practice of buying a particular product from only one supplier (p. 230).

single-source data Data gathered by research services that use technologies to monitor a particular consumer group's exposure to marketing communications and to track purchases made by the group over time (p. 159).

situational cues Events and conditions—such as the shopping environment, the consumer's mood, and the time of day as well as time available—that affect how products are evaluated and chosen at the time of purchase (p. 206).

skimming price A very high, premium price that a firm charges for its new, highly desirable product (p. 457).

social class The overall rank or social standing of groups of people within a society according to the value assigned to such factors as family background, education, occupation, and income (p. 205).

social marketing The promotion of causes and ideas that are generally thought to be good for society and for people (p. 390).

social profit The benefit an organization and

society receive from its ethical practices, community service, efforts to promote cultural diversity, and concern for the natural environment (p. 75).

social responsibility A management practice in which organizations seek to engage in activities that have a positive effect on society and promote the public good (p. 82).

societal marketing concept An orientation that focuses on satisfying consumer needs while also addressing the needs of the larger society (p. 5).

source An organization or individual that sends a message (p. 569).

specialty advertising Sales promotion that employs useful or decorative items imprinted with an organization's identification, message, or logo and distributed free (p. 650).

specialty product A good or service that has unique characteristics, is very important to the buyer, and for which the buyer will devote significant effort to acquire (p. 302).

specialty stores Retailers who carry only a few product lines but offer good selection within the lines they sell (p. 522).

Standard Industrial Classification (SIC) system The numerical coding system used by the U.S. government to classify and group firms into detailed categories according to their business activities and shared characteristics (p. 234).

standardization An international marketing perspective in which the same marketing mix strategies are used in all global markets (p. 142).

standardized service A service designed and delivered in a manner in which every customer receives almost exactly the same outcome or product (p. 380).

store image The way a retailer is perceived in the marketplace relative to the competition (p. 524).

store or private-label brands Brands that are owned and sold by a certain retailer or distributor (p. 350).

straight rebuy A buying situation classification used by business buyers to categorize routine purchases that require minimal decision making (p. 243).

strategic alliance A formal partnership agreement between two firms to pool their resources in order to achieve common goals (p. 136).

strategic business units (SBUS) Individual units within the firm that operate like separate businesses, each having its own mission, business and marketing objectives, resources, managers, and competitors (p. 45).

strategic equity alliance Agreement between firms that requires an equity investment on the part of each (p. 137).

strategic planning A managerial decision process that matches an organization's resources and capabilities to its market opportunities for long-term growth and survival (p. 41).

subcontracting A contractual arrangement in which a firm purchases custom components or production services from another firm on a permanent or temporary basis (p. 135).

subculture A group within a society whose members share a distinctive set of beliefs, characteristics, or common experiences (p. 204).

supermarkets Food stores that carry a wide selection of edibles and related products (p. 521).

survey A descriptive research technique used to collect, summarize, and analyze the responses of a large number of people questioned about a research topic (p. 175).

systems buying A business buying practice in which organizations simplify the decision process by selecting a single supplier to provide everything needed for a complete production or operations system (p. 230).

tactical planning A decision process that concentrates on developing detailed plans for strategies and tactics for the short term that support an organization's long-term strategic plan (p. 41).

target market The market segment(s) on which an organization focuses its marketing plan and toward which it directs its marketing efforts (p. 15).

target market strategy A marketing strategy in which a firm seeks to serve the needs of one or more different segments (p. 262).

tariff A tax on goods entering a country that makes them more expensive than domestic goods and gives domestic industries a price advantage (p. 128).

territory The set of customers and prospects for whom a salesperson or sales team is responsible (p. 703).

time utility The consumer benefit provided by storing products until they are needed by buyers (p. 22).

total costs The total of the fixed costs and the variable costs for a set number of units produced (p. 417).

total quality management (TQM) A management philosophy that focuses on satisfying customers through empowering employees to be an active part of continuous quality improvement (p. 88).

trade advertising Product advertising directed at people and businesses who buy products related to a specific trade or industry (p. 606).

trademark The legal name for a brand name, brand mark, or trade character, trademarks may be legally registered by a government, thus obtaining protection for exclusive use in that country (p. 345).

transactional data An ongoing record of individuals or organizations who are using the firm's services or buying its product (p. 583).

transactional selling A form of personal selling that focuses on making an immediate sale with little or no attempt to develop a relationship with the customer (p. 682).

trial pricing Pricing a new product low for a limited period of time in order to lower the risk for customers (p. 457).

undifferentiated marketing strategy A marketing strategy that (1) assumes the majority of customers have similar needs and (2) attempts to appeal to a broad spectrum of people (p. 278).

unfair sales acts State laws that prohibit suppliers from selling products below costs to protect small businesses from larger competitors (p. 426).

unique selling proposition (USP) An advertising appeal that focuses on one clear reason why a particular product is superior (p. 615).

unobtrusive measures Data collection methods used in descriptive research studies that rely on evidence of people's behavior rather than responses to questions about it (p. 177).

unsought product A good or service for which a consumer has little awareness or interest until the product or a need for the product is brought to his attention (p. 302).

user The member of a business buying center who will actually use a business product after it is purchased (p. 245).

utility The usefulness or benefit received by consumers from a product (p. 22).

validity An evaluation criterion that indicates the extent to which marketing research actually measures what it was intended to measure (p. 165).

value pricing, or every day low pricing (EDLP) A pricing strategy in which a firm sets prices that provide ultimate value or price/benefit ratio to customers (p. 453).

variable costs The costs of production that are tied to and vary depending on the number of units produced; variable costs typically include raw materials, processed materials, component parts, and labor (p. 417).

vendor analysis A formal procedure for evaluating product suppliers on a variety of attributes (p. 248).

venture teams A group of people within an organization who work together focusing exclusively on the development of a new product (p. 336).

vertical marketing system (VMS) A channel of distribution in which there is cooperation among members at the manufacturing, wholesaling, and retailing levels (p. 487).

want The desire to satisfy needs in specific ways that are culturally and socially influenced (p. 4).

warehousing Storing goods in anticipation of sale or transfer to another member of the channel of distribution (p. 498).

wheel-of-retailing hypothesis A theory that explains how retail firms change, becoming more "upscale" as they go through their life cycle (p. 514).

word-of-mouth communication Product-related information informally transmitted from one consumer to another (p. 559).

World Wide Web A service that links computers all over the world and allows companies and individuals to establish "home pages" where they can visit, learn, and buy (p. 539).

INDEX

COMPANY/NAME INDEX

SUBJECT INDEX

building database for, 581–583
building relationships through, 579, 581
consumer privacy and, 583
customized services and, 380
data sources for, 582–583
in integrated marketing communications
  planning model, 586
as interactive, 578–579
measurability of, 581
by Porsche, 596–597
by Staples, 597–598
Decider in buying center, 245
Decision making, habitual, 210
Decision-making process, 209–212
  evaluation of alternatives in, 210–211
  information search in, 209–210
  postpurchase evaluation in, 212
  problem recognition in, 209
  product choice in, 212
Decline stage
  in product life cycle, *315*, 317
    managing product in, 343
    promotion and, 564
  in retail life cycle, 514
Delivery, unique, for augmented services,
  379
Demand
  in business markets, 228–229
  clustered, 264
  consumer, patterns of, determining,
    264
  cross-elasticity of, 414–415
  definition of, 5, 409
  diffused, 264
  domestic, leveling of, global expansion and,
    121
  elastic, 412, *413*
  elasticity of
    external influences on, 413–415
    substitute goods and, 413
  estimating, 411–412
  external influences on, 410–411
  homogeneous, 264
  income effect on, 410
  inelastic, 412–413
  Law of, 410
  for prestige products, 410
  price elasticity of, 412–415
  pricing and, 409–415
  pricing strategies based on, 449–450
  primary, as advertising goal, 612
  selective, as advertising goal, 612–613
  for services, management of, 383, 385
Demand curves, 409–411
Demand-backward pricing, 450
Demographics, 109–110
  changes in, future of retailing and, 539–541
  market segmentation by
    for consumers, 266–272
    for industries, 276–277
Demonstration format for advertising, 616
Dentsu, Inc., choices made by, *600, 624, 632*
Department stores, 523
Depression in business cycle, 98
Derived demand in business markets,
  228–229
Descriptive research techniques for research
  data collection, 174–177

Diebold, Inc., relationship marketing at, *61*
Differential benefits, in creating competitive
  advantage, 53
Differentiated marketing strategy, 279
Differentiation focus strategy in Porter's
  generic strategy model, 50–51
Diffused demand, 264
Direct mail marketing, 536–537
Direct selling, 537
Directories in advertising strategy, 622
Discontinuous innovations, 308
Discount stores, 522–523
Discounting, superficial, 425
Discounts
  cash, 459
  quantity, 458–459
  seasonal, 459–460
Discretionary income, competition for,
  100
Discriminatory selling practices, 713
Disintermediation, 370
Displays as consumer promotions, 655
Distinctive competency in creating competitive advantage, 52–53
Distribution, 467–509
  channels of, 470–483. *See also* Channel(s),
    distribution
  decisions on, global implications for,
    141
  ethical issues in, 494–496
  exclusive, 490, 491t
  importance of, 469–474
  innovative, at Peapod, 508–509
  intensive, 490, 491t
  legal issues in, 494–496
  physical, 496–502
    careers in, 722
    inventory control in, 502
    materials handling in, 497–498
    order processing in, 497
    transportation in, 498–501
    warehousing in, 498
  planning, 483–496
    environmental influences on, 484,
      486–487
    objectives in, 483–484
  selective, 490–491
  system for, at VF Corporation, 507–508
  unauthorized, 495
Distribution strategy in marketing mix, 61–62
Diversification in product-market growth matrix, 50
Diversity
  advertising industry and, 605
  cultural, promoting, in New Era of market-
    ing, 85–86
Dollar General Stores, location selection by,
  532
Domestic costs, pricing strategies and,
  445–446
Domestic demand, leveling of, global expan-
  sion and, 121
Drama formats for advertising, 617
Dreamer curve in product life cycle, 317
Dumping, global marketing and, 129, *446*
Durability, product quality as, 332
Durable goods, 300–301
Dynamically continuous innovations, 308

Eastern Europe, developing countries in, 123
Economic business environment in New Era
  of marketing, 98–100
Economic communities, expansion into,
  124–126
Economic order quantity, 741
Economic sanctions, 127–128
Economy
  pricing strategies and, 441–443
  subsistence, 122
edit Jack in the Box, global marketing by, 71
Ego, 194
80/20 rule, 274–275
Einstein, Peter, choices made by, *120, 126, 143*
Electronic data interchange (EDI), 502
Electronic marketplace, 538–539
Embargo, global marketing and, 128
Emergency product, 302
Emotional appeal in promotion message, 570
Empathy in positioning service, 389
Employee empowerment, quality improve-
  ment and, 90
Employment, service economy and, 365–366
Encoding in communications model,
  568–569
Endorsements, celebrity, in advertising, 615
End-use application in industrial market seg-
  mentation, 277
Entertainment marketing, 10
Entrepreneurs, 336–337
  risk taking by, 94
Entrepreneurship, careers in, 723
Environment
  distribution planning and, 484, 486–487
  external, 53–54
    scanning, 55
  internal, 53
    assessing, 54–55
  legal, global, navigating, 108
  marketing evaluating, 53–55
  regulatory, adapting to, 108
  sales, 690–691
  shopping, consumer behavior and,
    208–209
Environmental abuses, curbing, 102, 104
Environmental developments, future of retailing and, 542
Environmental factors in facility-based services, 372–373
Environmental stewardship
  in New Era of marketing, 21, 83
  by Take the Lead and Step Into a Better
    World, Inc., *13*
Eppes, Tom, choices made by, *552, 580–581,
  590–591*
Equipment, 303
  services based on, 372–373
Equity, brand, 348
Equity investment, strategic alliances with,
  137, *138*
Ethical behavior
  as good business, 26
  in marketplace, 75–78
  policing, 78
Ethical continuum, 76–77
Ethical criticisms of marketing, 26–28
Ethical issues
  in distribution, 494–496

Häagen-Dazs, global marketing at, 148–149
Harley-Davidson, Inc., 40
    choices made by, *40, 59, 65*
Hawkeye Bank, handling name change at, 678
Hedonic needs, 193
Heuristics in decision-making process, 212
Hispanic Americans as market segment,
    269–270
Historical sales in setting sales objectives, 56
Home shopping networks, 538
Home shopping party, 537
Homogenous demand, 264
Horizontal conflict in distribution channels,
    494
Horizontal marketing system, 490
    legal constraints on, 495
Horizontal price fixing, 427
Horizontal synergy between companies in for-
    eign market, 137
Hot-goods program, 231
Hughes Aircraft Co., new product develop-
    ment by, 323
Human capital in assessing internal environ-
    ment, 55
Human rights, global marketing and, 129
Humorous appeals in advertising, 615
Hypermarkets, 523
Hypotheses in casual market research, 174

Id, 194
Ideas, marketing of, 390–393
Identities, sex-role, buying decisions and, *204*
IKEA, choices made by, *512, 533, 543*
Illinois Power Company, marketing strategy
    for, 401–402
Image advantage, in developing positioning
    strategy, 284
Image enhancement objectives of pricing
    strategy, 438t, *440*
Implementation of marketing plan, 63
Impulse buying, 209
Impulse product, 302
Incentive programs in sales promotion, 646t,
    650
Income
    consumer decisions and, 200–201
    demand and, 410
    discretionary, competition for, 100
    market segmentation by, 268
    real, 98
Income statement, 735–737
Industrial goods, definition of, 8
Industrial markets, 235
    segmenting, 276–277
Industrial selling, 691
Industry, sales force specialization by, 704
Industry attractiveness index in General Elec-
    tric/McKinsey business-planning grid, 48
Inelastic demand in business markets, 229
Inertia in purchasing behavior, 348
Inflation in business cycle, 98
Influences in buying center, 245
Influentials, consumer behavior and, 206
Infomercial(s), 538
    definition of, 558
Information
    marketing, 151–186. *See also* Marketing in-
        formation system (MIS)

collecting, 156–159
monitored, 154–155
needs for, 153–156
    ongoing, 154
primary data as, 156
requested, 155–156
secondary data as, 156
    external sources of, 157–158
    internal sources of, 156–157
promotion as, 554
Information search
    in business buying decision process,
        248–250
    in decision-making process, 209–210
Information system in facilitating exchange,
    23–24
Initiator in buying center, 245
Innovation(s), 303
    continuous, 306, 308
    diffusion of, 308–310
    discontinuous, 308
    dynamically continuous, 308
    importance of, 304–305
    symbolic, 306
    techniphobia *versus,* 106
    technological, 306
    types of, 306, 308
Innovative features for augmented services,
    379
Innovativeness, marketing strategies and,
    198
Inspection buying, 231
Institutional advertising, 606–608
Insult pricing, *451*
Intangible costs, 406
Intangibles. *See also* Service(s)
    marketing expansion to include, 366–367
    marketing mix and, 393–395
    marketing success with, 367–368
Integrated communications strategy, 61
Integrated marketing communications (IMC),
    553, 584–589, 591
    advertising and, 605
    communications strategy in, 587
    consumer classification in, 586
    contact management in, 587
    customer database in, 586
    driver's perspective in, 584–585
    evaluation of, 587–588
        in integrated marketing communications
            planning model, 587–588
    marketing objectives in, 587
    personal selling and, 687
    planning model based on, 586–588
    roadblocks to, 588–589, 591
Integrated marketing communications (IMC)
    perspective, 585–586
Intel Corporation, choices made by, *326, 346,
    355*
Intellectual capital in assessing internal envi-
    ronment, 55
Intelligence, marketing, 154
Intensive distribution, 490, 491t
Intention-to-purchase measures in screening
    of new product concepts, 338
Interactive marketing, 573–577
    promotion vehicles in, 575–577
    response levels in, 574–575

Interactive media in advertising strategy,
    623–625
Interest in new product adoption, 309
Intermediaries, relationship of New Era firms
    with, 96
Internal reference prices, 422–423
International costs, pricing strategies and,
    445–446
International marketing environment,
    119–150
    direction of expansion in, 122–126
    opportunity in, 121–126
International markets, advertising adaptations
    for, 630–633
Internet as distribution channel, 500–501t,
    501
Interpretation in perceptual process, 192–193
Interviewing techniques for research data col-
    lection, 170–171
Interviews, personal, in casual market re-
    search, 176
Intrapreneur programs in New Era firms, 94
Introduction stage
    in product life cycle, 315–316
        managing product in, 341
        promotion and, 564
    in retail life cycle, 514
Inventory
    control of, in physical distribution, 502
    turnover of, retailer classification by,
        519–520
Inventory turnover rate, 739
Investment, equity, strategic alliances with,
    137, *138*
Involvement in decision-making process, 209

Joint demand in business markets, 229
Joint production and marketing agreement
    with foreign partners, 137
Joint venture, 336–337
    international, 137
Just in time (JIT) inventory management sys-
    tem, supplier selection and, 250

Kaizen, total quality improvement, 89–90
Keiretsu, Japanese, *480*
Kickbacks, drug, ethics and, *241*
Kiosks for interactive promotion, 576–577
Knockoff, 305–306
KWE Associates, choices made by, *642, 666,
    672*

Labeling regulations, 354–355
Laboratories, casual market research in, 174
Laggards in adoption process, 312
Lamborghini, pricing strategy of, 433–434
Lands' End, global catalog marketing by, *536*
Language in global marketing, 131–132
Latin America, developing countries in, 123
Law of Demand, 410
Learning
    behavioral, 195–196
    cognitive, 196
    consumer behavior and, 195–196
    observational, 196
Leasing of equipment, 237
Lecture formats for advertising, 616
Legal barriers to global markets, 128–129

Legal business environment in New Era of marketing, 106–108
Legal considerations in pricing, 425–428
Legal environment, global, navigating, 108
Legal issues
in distribution, 494–496
in personal selling, 711–715
related to conduct toward customers, 712–713
Legislation, influencing, public relations in, 667
Levi Strauss & Co., 2–3, 16, 30
choices made by, *2, 16, 30*
concern of, for exploited workers and, *130*
Licensing, 350–351
for foreign operations, 135
as marketing strategy, 196
Lieberman, Rhonda, choices made by, *74, 103–104, 110*
Life cycle
family, 268
product, 314–317
contagion curve in, 317
decline stage in, *315,* 317
dreamer curve in, 317
fad curve in, 317
growth stage in, *315,* 316
introduction stage in, 315–316
managing product over, 341–343
maturity stage in, *315,* 316
redevelopment curve in, 317
retail, 514
services, 368
Lifestyle(s)
consumer decisions and, 203
market segmentation by, 272–273
New Era of marketing and, 110–111
Lifestyle format for advertising, 617
Lighting in store layout, 527–528
Likert scale in casual market research, 175–176
Limit pricing, 453
Limited line strategy, 331–332
Line stretching, 330–331
List price, 458
Local content rules, global marketing and, 129
Localization perspective on global marketing, 143–144
Locational factors in facility-based services, 372
Longitudinal design in casual market research, 175
Loss leader pricing, 425
Loyalty, brand, 212, 274, 348
Lutheran Health Systems, choices made by, *364, 382–383, 394*
Luxuries, public *versus* private, reference groups and, 205–206

Mackesy, Rich, choices made by, *364, 382–383, 394*
Macro environment competition in, 100–101
Magazines in advertising strategy, 619t, 621–622
Mail for interactive promotion, 575
Mail order marketing, 535–537
Mail surveys in casual market research, 176

Major League Baseball International Partners, global marketing and, 150
Management
capacity, 385
demand, 383, 385
sales, 701–711. *See also* Sales management
Managers
market, 335
new product, 336
product category, 335
product line, 335
Manufacturer brands, 350
Manufacturer markets, 236
Manufacturers, introducing new products to, public relations in, 665
Manufacturer's export agent, 134
Margin, gross, retailer classification by, 519–520
Marginal analysis in pricing, 420–422
Market(s)
business/organizational, 225–234
buyer's, 19
definition of, 7
fragmentation of, 261
government, 238, 239
international, advertising adaptations for, 630–633
mass, definition of, 14
nonprofit institutional, 239–240
organizational, 238–240
penetration of, as distribution objective, 483
potential of, promotion budget allocation and, 567
segmentation of, 259–292. *See also* Segmentation; Segment(s)
segmenting, 15, 17
seller's, 17
size of, promotion budget allocation and, 567
target
definition of, 15
finding and reaching, 14–17
positioning product for, 17
selecting, 58
strategy for selecting, choosing, 17
Market development in product-market growth matrix, 50
Market differentiation, 342
Market managers, 335
Market penetration in product-market growth matrix, 49–50
Market plan, elements of, 57–62
Market potential
comparative, global expansion and, 122
determining, 277–278
Market segment(s)
definition of, 15
usable, identifying, 264–265
Market share
price and, 407
Marketers
characteristics of, 29–30
customers and, 2–3
Marketing
affinity, *207*
audit of, in control of marketing plan, 65–66

budget for, 63
business-to-business, 8–9, 225. *See also* Business market(s)
careers in, 721–727
cause, 84–85, 391
in planning public relations campaign, 669
of celebrities, 389–390
communications in, 551–598
corporate, product marketing and, 28–29
in daily lives, 25
database, 553, 577–583
advantages of, 578–581
building database for, 581–583
building relationships through, 579, 581
consumer privacy and, 583
customized services and, 380
data sources for, 582–583
as interactive, 578–579
measurability of, 581
definition of, 3
de-mass, 573–574
direct, 534–539
direct mail, 536–537
of entertainment, 10
ethical criticisms of, 26–28
ethics continuum for, 76–77
evolution of, 17–21
consumer orientation in, 19–21
milestones in, 18t
new era orientation in, 21
production orientation in, 17–19
sales orientation in, 19
exchange facilitated by, 23–25
as exchange of value, 5–6
expansion of, to include intangibles, 366–367
of experiences, 364
functional structure of, 63
global, *53. See also* Global marketing
of gray products, 495–496
green, 83–84, *449*
of ideas, 390–393
importance of, 22–28
information on. *See also* Marketing, information system (MIS)
information system (MIS), 153–160
collecting information for, 156–159
from marketing research studies, 158–159
from primary sources, 156
from secondary sources, 156–158
single-source data methodology in, 159
information needs and, 153–156
information on, 151–186
marketing decision support system in, 153
research on, 151–186
using data in, 160
of intangible products, 363–402
interactive, 573–577
promotion vehicles in, 575–577
response levels in, 574–575
internal, 375
mail order, 535–537
mass, 261–262
math for, 735–741

sociocultural, 108–111
technological, 104–106
internal business environment in, 93–97
quality in, 87–93
relationships with business partners and
publics in, 95–97
serving community in, 85–86
serving society in, 84–85
social profit audit in, 86–87
social responsibility in, 82–84
New era orientation in marketing evolution,
21
Newspapers in advertising strategy, 619t, 621
New-task buying, 244
Niche brands, 350
Niche marketing, 279
Nickelodeon, case study on, 117
Nike Corporation, trends in consumer behav-
ior and, 220
Noise in communications model, 572
Nonprofit institutional markets, 239–240
Nonprofit organizations, marketing of,
391–392
Norms, cultural, 203
North American Free Trade Agreement
(NAFTA), expansion into, 125–126
Not-for-profit marketing, 9
Nucor Corporation, customer-oriented mar-
keting at, 256

Objective-and-task method of budgeting, 63
Objectives, corporate, setting, in strategic
planning, 44–45
Objective-task method of promotion budget
setting, 566
Observability, adoption rate for new product
and, 314
Observational learning, 196
Observational techniques for research data
collection, 172–173
Off-price retailers, 522–523
Offshore outsourcing, 231
Oligopoly, 101
Omnibus survey for market research, 158
On-line services, retailing by, 539
Operant conditioning, 196
Operating expense ratio, 739
Operating ratios, 738–739
Operating variables in industrial market seg-
mentation, 276
Operational factors in facility-based services,
372
Operational planning, definition of, 41
Operations audit in assessing internal envi-
ronment, 54
Opinion leader, consumer behavior and, 206
Opportunity costs, 406
Order
getting of, in personal selling, 688
processing of, in physical distribution, 497
taking of, in personal selling, 688t, 689
Organization(s)
differences in, affecting new product adoption, 314–317
nonprofit, marketing of, 391–392
Organizational climate, business buying behavior and, 241
Organizational culture in assessing internal
environment, 55

Organizational factors, promotion budget allocation and, 567
Organizational markets, 238–240
Outdoor advertising, 619t, 622–623
Outsourcing
in business buying process, 230–231
for foreign operations, 135–136
off-shore, to meet cost limits, 450

Pacific Rim, developing countries in, 123–124
Package design, product and, 559
Packaging
of actual product, 299
for communication, 352
for containment, 351–352
decisions on, 353–354
design of, 353–354
functions of, 351–352
objectives of, 353
for protection, 351–352
for storage, 352
for use, 352
Parity pricing, 452–453
Participatory management programs, 90
Partnering by companies, 336–337
Partners, business, relationship of New Era
firms with, 95–97
Partnerships
affinity, 232
business, supporting diversity through,
85–86
cooperative, in organizational, marketing,
232, 234
Patagonia, global catalog marketing by, 536
Patent for new product, 339
Payment pricing, 456
Peapod, distribution innovations at, 508–509
Pegged pricing, 452–453
Penetration pricing, 457
People
marketing of, 9–10, 389–390
services based on, 373–374
People advantage in developing positioning
strategy, 284
People-centered corporate cultures, 94–95
in New Era of marketing, 94–95
Percentage-of-sales method
of budgeting, 63
of promotion budget setting, 565
Perception, consumer behavior and, 189–193
Perceptual filters, 190
Perceptual mapping of product/brand,
282–283
Perceptual organization, principles of,
192–193
Perceptual vigilance, 190
Perfect competition, 101
Performance goals for salespeople, 703
Personal appeals in promotion mix, 555, 556t
Personal influences on consumer decisions,
200–203
Personal interviews in casual market research,
176
Personal observation in casual market re-
search, 177
Personality
brand, 282
buying decisions and, 199–200
consumer behavior and, 198–200

Personnel, store, 528
Persuasion as goal of promotion, 555
Physical evidence of service, 385–386
Piggybacking, 499
Pipeline, product transport by, 500–501
Place(s)
in marketing mix, 12
for intangibles, 394–395
quality improvement in, 92
marketing of, 10
price and, 408
Place utility, 22
Place-based media, 588
Planning
cross-functional, 51
marketing, 14, 51–57. See also Marketing
planning
operational, definition of, 41
strategic, 39–71. See also Strategic planning
tactical, definition of, 41
Playboy Enterprises Inc., trends in consumer
behavior and, 221
Pleasure, consumer behavior and, 208
Pleasure principle, id and, 194
Poindexter, Randall, choices made by, 404,
416, 427
Point of sale (POS) systems in retailing, 541
Point-of-purchase activities in sales promo-
tion, 646t, 647t, 654–656
Point-of-purchase advertising, 566
Point-of-sale research, 174–175
Political risk assessment in global marketing,
127–128
Politicians, marketing, 389
Popular culture, marketing and, 25
Porsche Cars North America, database marketing by, 596–597
Porter's generic strategy model in portfolio
management, 50–51
Portfolio, business
business portfolio in, 45–51
management of
Boston Consulting Group matrix, 47–48
General Electric/McKinsey grid in,
48–49
Porter's generic strategy model in, 50–51
product-market growth matrix in, 49–50
in strategic planning, 45–51
Positioning
of brand as advertising goal, 613
dimensions of, 282–283
of product, 263–264
strategies for
developing and implementing, 284, 286
for services, 388–389
in target marketing, 281–286
Possession utility, 22
Postpurchase evaluation in business buying
decision process, 251
Postpurchase evaluation in decision-making
process, 212
Postum, potential revival of, advertising in,
639
Poverty, time, 206–207
Power, channel leadership and, 492–493
Power brands, 349–350
Practical advertising objectives, 613
Precision, high degree of, product quality as,
332

selecting, 707–708
trade, 689
training, 708–709
Sam & Libby Inc., marketing in action at, 35
Sampling, in-store, as consumer promotion,
647t, 654–655
Sampling buying, 231
Sampling programs in new product adoption,
310
Saturn Corp., sales strategy of, *683*
Scales in casual market research, 175–176
Scanning technology in casual market research, 177
Scrambled merchandising, *520*
Search qualities in service evaluation, 376
Seasonal discounts, 459–460
Sebago, Inc., decisions made by, *188, 202, 214*
Segment(s)
market, usable, identifying, 264–265
marketing
evaluating, 277–278
targeting one or more, 277–281
Segment profiles, developing, 265
Segmentation, market, 259–292
by age groups, 266–267
by behavior, 273–276
benefit, 276
definition of, 264
by demographics, 266–272
by ethnicity, 268–270
by family structure, 268
by geography, 270, 272
by income, 268
industrial, 276–277
by lifestyle, 272–273
by race, 268–270
by social class, 268
targeting and, 263
Selective distribution, 490–491
Self-concept, marketing strategies and, 198
Self-confidence, marketing strategies and, 198
Self-esteem advertising, 198–199
Selling
direct, 537
personal, 680–701
as adventure, 681
approach in, 694–695
business-to-business, 691
careers in, 722–723
closing sale in, 699–700
consumer *versus* industrial, 691
environment for, 690–691
evolution of, 681–684
following up after sale in, 701
functions of, 688–690
high-pressure tactics in, 713
inside, 690–691
integrated marketing communication
and, 687
legal and ethical issues in, 711–715
limitations of, 686–687
as marketing function, importance of,
684–685
order getting in, 688
order taking in, 688t, 689
outside, 690
overcoming customer objections in, 699
overview of, 680–687
pre-approach in, 693–694

process of, 691–701
in promotion mix, 555, 556t, 685–687
prospecting in, 692–693
qualifying in, 693
relationship, 682–684
retail, 691
sales presentation in, 695–698
sales support in, 688t, 689–690
transactional, 682
types of, 687–691
Selling task analysis, 703–704
Semantic differential scale in casual market research, 176
Semiotics, marketing, 192
Sensory overload for consumers, 189–190
Service(s), 296–297
augmented, developing/managing,
378–380
characteristics of, 369–370
core, developing/managing, 378–380
customized, 380
definition of, 7–8
delivery of, improving, 381, 383–385
demand management for, 383, 385
developing and managing, strategies for,
378–389
distribution channels for, 482
equipment-based, 372–373
facility-based, 372–373
failure of, sources of, 381
inseparability of, 370
intangibility of, 369–370
life cycle of, 368
marketing of, 363–402
nature of, 368–369
orientation of, 369
people-based, 373–374
perishability of, 370
physical evidence of, 385–386
positioning strategies for, 388–389
product-related, 372
quality of
evaluative dimensions for, 375–376
judging, 374–376
measuring, 376–377
relativity of, 375
result of, 369
standardized, 380
targeting strategies for, 386–389
as theater, 381–382
variability of, 370
Service advantage in developing positioning
strategy, 284
Service economy, 365–368
jobs and, 365–366
Service encounter, 373
Service markets, 236–237
Service system, 381
Sex appeal
in advertising, 615
in promotion message, *571*
Sherman Act, 426
Shopping center, locating store in, 529–531
Shopping environment, consumer behavior
and, 208–209
Shopping product, 302
Sierra Club, choices made by, *74, 103–104,*
110
Signage as consumer promotion, 655

Similarity, principle of, consumer perception
of stimuli and, 192
Single sourcing in business buying process,
230
Single-source data in market research, 159
Situation analysis for service organization,
367
Situational influences on consumer behavior,
206–209
Skimming price, 456–457
Skunk works, 336
Slice-of-life format for advertising, 617
Slotting allowances, 81
ethics of, *648*
Sociability, marketing strategies and, 198
Social attractiveness, modeling and, 196
Social class
consumer behavior and, 205
market segmentation by, 268
Social criticisms of marketing, 26–28
Social influences on consumer behavior,
203–206
Social marketing, *8,* 390–391
Social profit, 75
Social profit audit in New Era of marketing,
86–87
Social responsibility in New Era of marketing,
82–84
Societal marketing concept, 5
Society
marketing's role in, 25–28
service to, in New Era of marketing, 84–85
serving, in New Era of marketing, 84–85
Sociocultural business environment in New
Era of marketing, 108–111
Sound, type and density of, in store layout,
527
Source in communications model, 569–570
Sourcing in business buying process, 230–231
Southwest Airlines
pricing strategy of, 466
relationship marketing at, *376*
Specialty advertising programs in sales pro-
motion, 647t, 650
Specialty product, 302
Specialty stores, 522
Specification buying, 231
Sports marketing, 10
Spot TV in advertising strategy, 620
Standard Industrial Classification (SIC) sys-
tem, 234–235
in industrial market segmentation, 276
Standardization perspective on global market-
ing, 142–143
Staple product, 302
Staples, database marketing by, 597–598
Starbucks, retailing changes and, 549–550
Stimulus generalization, marketing and,
196
Storage by distribution channels, 472
Store(s)
concept, *526*
convenience, 521
department, 523
design of, 525–528
discount, 522–523
factory outlet, 522–523
image of, 524–525
layout of, 526–527